P9-EEK-481

Twentieth-Century Literary Criticism

Guide to Gale Literary Criticism Series

When you need to review criticism of literary works, these are the Gale series to use:

If the author's death date is:	You should turn to:
After Dec. 31, 1959 (or author is still living)	***CONTEMPORARY LITERARY CRITICISM*** for example: Jorge Luis Borges, Anthony Burgess, Ernest Hemingway, Iris Murdoch
1900 through 1959	***TWENTIETH-CENTURY LITERARY CRITICISM*** for example: Willa Cather, F. Scott Fitzgerald, Henry James, Mark Twain, Virginia Woolf
1800 through 1899	***NINETEENTH-CENTURY LITERATURE CRITICISM*** for example: Fyodor Dostoevsky, Nathaniel Hawthorne, George Sand, William Wordsworth
1400 through 1799	***LITERATURE CRITICISM FROM 1400 TO 1800*** *(excluding Shakespeare)* for example: Anne Bradstreet, Alexander Pope, François Rabelais, Phillis Wheatley ***SHAKESPEAREAN CRITICISM*** Shakespeare's plays and poetry
Antiquity through 1399	***CLASSICAL AND MEDIEVAL LITERATURE CRITICISM*** for example: Dante, Homer, Plato, Sophocles, Vergil

Gale also publishes related criticism series:

CHILDREN'S LITERATURE REVIEW

This series covers authors of all eras who have written for the preschool through high school audience.

SHORT STORY CRITICISM

This series covers the major short fiction writers of all nationalities and periods of literary history.

POETRY CRITICISM

This series covers poets of all nationalities, movements, and periods of literary history.

DRAMA CRITICISM

This series covers playwrights of all nationalities and periods of literary history.

BLACK LITERATURE CRITICISM

This three-volume set presents criticism of works by major black writers of the past two hundred years.

WORLD LITERATURE CRITICISM, 1500 TO THE PRESENT

This six-volume set provides excerpts from criticism on 225 authors from the Renaissance to the present.

ISSN 0276-8178

R

Volume 35

Twentieth-Century Literary Criticism

**Excerpts from Criticism of the
Works of Novelists, Poets, Playwrights,
Short Story Writers, and Other Creative Writers
Who Lived between 1900 and 1960,
from the First Published Critical
Appraisals to Current Evaluations**

**Paula Kepos
Editor**

**Marie Lazzari
Thomas Ligotti
Joann Prosyniuk
Laurie Sherman
Associate Editors**

 Gale Research Inc. • *DETROIT* • *WASHINGTON, D.C.* • *LONDON*

STAFF

Paula Kepos, *Editor*

Marie Lazzari, Thomas Ligotti, Joann Prosyniuk, Laurie Sherman, *Associate Editors*

Susan Windisch Brown, Michelle L. McClellan, Debra A. Wells,
Assistant Editors

Jeanne A. Gough, *Permissions & Production Manager*
Linda M. Pugliese, *Production Supervisor*
Jennifer E. Gale, Suzanne Powers, Maureen A. Puhl, Lee Ann Welsh, *Editorial Associates*
Donna Craft, Christine A. Galbraith, David G. Oblender, Linda M. Ross, *Editorial Assistants*

Victoria B. Cariappa, *Research Supervisor*
Karen D. Kaus, Eric Priehs, Maureen Richards, Mary D. Wise, *Editorial Associates*
H. Nelson Fields, Judy Gale, Jill M. Ohorodnik, *Editorial Assistants*

Sandra C. Davis, *Permissions Supervisor (Text)*
H. Diane Cooper, Kathy Grell, Josephine M. Keene, Kimberly F. Smilay, *Permissions Associates*
Maria L. Franklin, Lisa M. Lantz, Camille P. Robinson, Shalice Shah, Denise M. Singleton,
Permissions Assistants

Patricia A. Seefelt, *Permissions Supervisor (Pictures)*
Margaret A. Chamberlain, *Permissions Associate*
Pamela A. Hayes, Lillian Quickley, *Permissions Assistants*

Mary Beth Trimper, *Production Manager*
Shanna G. Philpott, *External Production Assistant*

Arthur Chartow, *Art Director*
C. J. Jonik, *Keyliner*

Library of Congress Catalog Card Number 76-46132
ISBN 0-8103-2417-2
ISSN 0276-8178

Printed in the United States of America

Published simultaneously in the United Kingdom
by Gale Research International Limited
(An affiliated company of Gale Research Inc.)

10 9 8 7 6 5 4 3 2

Contents

Preface

Since its inception more than ten years ago, *Twentieth-Century Literary Criticism* has been purchased and used by nearly 10,000 school, public, and college or university libraries. With this edition—volume 35 in the series—*TCLC* has covered over 500 authors, representing 58 nationalities, and more than 25,000 titles. No other reference source has surveyed the critical response to twentieth-century authors and literature as thoroughly as *TCLC*. In the words of one reviewer, "there is nothing comparable available." *TCLC* "is a goldmine of information—dates, pseudonyms, biographical information, and criticism from books and periodicals—which many libraries would have difficulty assembling on their own."

Scope of the Series

TCLC is designed to serve as an introduction for students and advanced readers to authors who died between 1900 and 1960, and to the most significant interpretations of these authors' works. The great poets, novelists, short story writers, playwrights, and philosophers of this period are frequently studied in high school and college literature courses. In organizing and excerpting the vast amount of critical material written on these authors, *TCLC* helps students develop valuable insight into literary history, promotes a better understanding of the texts, and sparks ideas for papers and assignments. Each entry in *TCLC* presents a comprehensive survey of an author's career or an individual work of literature and provides the user a multiplicity of interpretations and assessments. Such variety allows students to pursue their own interests; furthermore, it fosters an awareness that literature is dynamic and responsive to many different opinions.

TCLC is designed as a companion series to Gale's *Contemporary Literary Criticism,* which reprints commentary on current writing. Because of the different periods under consideration (*CLC* considers authors who were still living after 1959), there is no duplication of material between *CLC* and *TCLC*. For additional information about *CLC* and Gale's other criticism titles, users should consult the Guide to Gale Literary Criticism Series preceding the title page in this volume.

Coverage

Each volume of *TCLC* is carefully compiled to present:

- criticism of authors who represent a variety of genres and nationalities

- both major and lesser-known writers of the period (such as non-Western authors increasingly read by today's students)

- 14-16 authors per volume

- individual entries that survey the critical response to each author's works, including early criticism to reflect initial reactions; later criticism to represent any rise or decline in the author's reputation; and current retrospective analyses. The entries also indicate an author's importance to the period (for example, the length of each author entry reflects the amount of critical attention he or she has received from critics writing in English, and from foreign criticism in translation)

An author may appear more than once in the series because of continuing critical and academic interest, or because of a resurgence of criticism generated by such events as a centennial or anniversary, the republication or posthumous publication of a work, or the publication of a new translation. Several entries in each volume of *TCLC* are devoted to criticism of individual works that are considered among the most important in twentieth-century literature and are thus frequently read and studied in high school and college literature classes. For example, this volume includes entries devoted to Bertolt Brecht's *Mother Courage and Her Children,* James Joyce's *Dubliners,* and Thomas Mann's *Buddenbrooks.*

Organization of the Book

An author entry consists of the following elements: author heading, biographical and critical introduction, list of principal works, excerpts of criticism (each preceded by explanatory notes and followed by a bibliographic citation), and a bibliography of further reading.

- The *author heading* consists of the author's full name, followed by birth and death dates. The unbracketed portion of the name denotes the form under which the author most commonly wrote. If an author wrote consistently under a pseudonym, the pseudonym will be listed in the author heading and the real name given in parentheses on the first line of the biographical and critical introduction. Also located at the beginning of the introduction to the author entry are any name variations under which an author wrote, including transliterated forms for authors whose languages use nonroman alphabets.

- The *biographical and critical introduction* outlines the author's life and career, as well as the critical debate surrounding his or her work. References are provided to past volumes of *TCLC* and to other biographical and critical reference series published by Gale, including *Short Story Criticism, Children's Literature Review, Contemporary Authors, Dictionary of Literary Biography,* and *Something about the Author.*

- Most *TCLC* entries include *portraits* of the author. Many entries also contain reproductions of materials pertinent to an author's career, including manuscript pages, title pages, dust jackets, letters, and drawings, as well as photographs of important people, places, and events in an author's life.

- The *list of principal works* is chronological by date of first book publication and identifies the genre of each work. In the case of foreign authors with both foreign-language publications and English translations, the title and date of the first English-language edition are given in brackets. Unless otherwise indicated, dramas are dated by first performance, not first publication.

- *Criticism* is arranged chronologically in each author entry to provide a perspective on changes in critical evaluation over the years. All titles of works by the author featured in the entry are printed in boldface type to enable the user to easily locate discussion of particular works. Also for purposes of easier identification, the critic's name and the publication date of the essay are given at the beginning of each piece of criticism. Unsigned criticism is preceded by the title of the journal in which it appeared. Many of the excerpts in *TCLC* also contain translated material. Unless otherwise noted, translations in brackets are by the editors; translations in parentheses or continuous with the text are by the critic. Publication information (such as publisher names and book prices) and parenthetical numerical references (such as footnotes or page and line references to specific editions of works) have been deleted at the editors' discretion to provide smoother reading of the text.

- Critical excerpts are prefaced by *annotations* providing the reader with information about both the critic and the criticism that follows. Included are the critic's reputation, individual approach to literary criticism, and particular expertise in an author's works. Also noted are the relative importance of a work of criticism, the scope of the excerpt, and the growth of critical controversy or changes in critical trends regarding an author. In some cases, these annotations cross-reference excerpts by critics who discuss each other's commentary.

- A complete *bibliographic citation* designed to facilitate location of the original essay or book follows each piece of criticism.

- An annotated *list of further reading* appearing at the end of each author entry suggests further reading on the author. In some cases it includes essays for which the editors could not obtain reprint rights.

Cumulative Indexes

Each volume of *TCLC* includes a cumulative index listing all the authors who have appeared in *Contemporary Literary Criticism, Twentieth-Century Literary Criticism, Nineteenth-Century Litera-*

ture Criticism, Literature Criticism from 1400 to 1800, Classical and Medieval Literature Criticism, and *Short Story Criticism,* along with cross-references to the Gale series *Children's Literature Review, Authors in the News, Contemporary Authors, Contemporary Authors Autobiography Series, Dictionary of Literary Biography, Concise Dictionary of American Literary Biography, Something about the Author, Something about the Author Autobiography Series,* and *Yesterday's Authors of Books for Children.* Useful for locating an author within the various series, this index is particularly valuable for those authors who are identified with a certain period but who, because of their death dates, are placed in another, or for those authors whose careers span two periods. For example, F. Scott Fitzgerald is found in *TCLC,* yet a writer often associated with him, Ernest Hemingway, is found in *CLC.*

Each volume of *TCLC* also includes a cumulative nationality index, in which authors' names are arranged alphabetically under their respective nationalities.

Title Index

TCLC also includes an index listing the titles of all literary works discussed in the series since its inception. Foreign language titles that have been translated are followed by the titles of the translations—for example, *Voina i mir (War and Peace).* Page numbers following these translated titles refer to all pages on which any form of the titles, either foreign language or translated, appears. Titles of novels, dramas, nonfiction books, and poetry, short story, or essay collections are printed in italics, while all individual poems, short stories, and essays are printed in roman type within quotation marks.

Suggestions Are Welcome

In response to suggestions, several features have been added to *TCLC* since the series began, including annotations to excerpted criticism, a cumulative index to authors in all Gale literary criticism series, entries devoted to a single work by a major author, more extensive illustrations, and a title index listing all literary works discussed in the series since its inception.

Readers who wish to suggest authors to appear in future volumes, or who have other suggestions, are cordially invited to write the editors or call our toll-free number: 1-800-347-GALE.

Acknowledgments

The editors wish to thank the copyright holders of the excerpted criticism included in this volume, the permissions managers of many book and magazine publishing companies for assisting us in securing reprint rights, and Anthony Bogucki for assistance with copyright research. We are also grateful to the staffs of the Detroit Public Library, the Library of Congress, the University of Detroit Library, Wayne State University Purdy/Kresge Library Complex, and University of Michigan Libraries for making their resources available to us. Following is a list of the copyright holders who have granted us permission to reprint material in this volume of *TCLC*. Every effort has been made to trace copyright, but if omissions have been made, please let us know.

COPYRIGHTED EXCERPTS IN *TCLC*, VOLUME 35, WERE REPRINTED FROM THE FOLLOWING PERIODICALS:

Américas, v. 17, March, 1965. Reprinted by permission of *Américas,* a bi-monthly magazine published by the General Secretariat of the Organization of American States in English and Spanish.—*American Studies,* v. 23, 1982 for "Short Fiction Writers of the Indian Territory" by Daniel F. Littlefield, Jr. and James W. Parins. Copyright © Mid-America American Studies Association, 1982. Reprinted by permission of the publisher and the authors.—*The Antioch Review,* v. XX, Winter, 1960-61; v. XXV, Fall, 1965; v. XXVI, Winter, 1966-67. Copyright © 1961, 1965, 1967 by the Antioch Review Inc. All reprinted by permission of the Editors.—*Bulletin of Hispanic Studies,* v. XLI, April, 1964. © copyright 1964 Liverpool University Press. Reprinted by permission of the publisher.—*College English,* v. 26, March, 1965. Copyright © 1965 by the National Council of Teachers of English. Reprinted by permission of the publisher.—*Commentary,* v. 14, September, 1952 for "An Unknown Treasure of World Literature: Who Will Make Sholom Aleichem Available?" by Irving Howe. Copyright 1952, renewed 1980 by the American Jewish Committee. All rights reserved. Reprinted by permission of the publisher and the author.—*Communications from the International Brecht Society,* v. XIV, November, 1984 for "The 'Good' Woman Demystified" by Sieglinde Lug. Copyright © 1984 by the International Brecht Society, Inc. Reprinted by permission of the publisher and the author.—*The Germanic Review,* v. XLV, May, 1970 for "Thomas Mann's 'Buddenbrooks': Bourgeois Society and the Inner Life" by Larry David Nachman and Albert S. Braverman. Copyright 1970 by Helen Dwight Educational Foundation. Reprinted by permission of the author.—*Harper's Monthly Magazine,* v. CXXXI, September, 1915. Copyright 1915, renewed 1942 by *Harper's Magazine.* All rights reserved. Reprinted by special permission.—*Literature and Psychology,* v. XX, 1970. © Morton Kaplan 1970. Reprinted by permission of the publisher.—*The Massachusetts Review,* v. V, Spring, 1964. © 1964. Reprinted from *The Massachusetts Review,* The Massachusetts Review, Inc. by permission.—*Meanjin,* v. 37, April, 1978, for "Rex Ingamells and the Quest for Environmental Values" by Humphrey McQueen. Reprinted by permission of the author.—*Modern Fiction Studies,* v. 34, Winter, 1988. Copyright © 1988 by Purdue Research Foundation, West Lafayette, IN 47907. All rights reserved. Reprinted with permission.—*New York Herald Tribune Books,* March 31, 1929. Copyright 1929 I. H. T. Corporation. Renewed 1957 by New York Herald Tribune, Inc. Reprinted by permission of the publisher.—*The New York Times Book Review,* December 12, 1920; September 20, 1925; June 20, 1926; October 10, 1926; April 28, 1935; September 15, 1935. Copyright 1920, 1925, 1926, 1935 by The New York Times Company. All reprinted by permission of the publisher.—*The Old Northwest,* v. 10, Fall, 1984. Copyright © Miami University 1984. Reprinted by permission of the publisher.—*The Oxford Review,* n. 2, Trinity, 1966 for "Brecht's 'Mother Courage'" by Ronald Gray. Reprinted by permission of the author.—*Poetry,* v. LXXXIV, August, 1954. Copyright 1954, renewed 1982 by the Modern Poetry Association. Reprinted by permission of the Editor of *Poetry.*—*Prooftexts,* v. 6, January, 1986. © 1986 by The Johns Hopkins University Press. Both reprinted by permission of the publisher.—*Romance Notes,* v. III, Autumn, 1961. Reprinted by permission of the publisher.—*Russian Literature Triquarterly,* n. 9, 1974. © 1974 by Ardis Publishers. Reprinted by permission of the publisher.—*The Saturday Review of Literature,* v. XII, May 11, 1935. Copyright 1935, renewed 1962 *Saturday Review* magazine.—*Scribner's Magazine,* v. LXXXVIII, July, 1930. Copyright, 1930, renewed 1957 by Charles Scribner's Sons. Reprinted with permission of Charles Scribner's Sons, an imprint of Macmillan Publishing Company.—*Slavic Review,* v. 36, June, 1977 for "The Feminine Stereotype and Beyond: Role Conflict and Resolution in the Poetics of Marina Tsvetaeva" by Antonina Filonov Gove. Copyright © 1977 by the American Association for the Advancement of Slavic Studies, Inc. Reprinted by permission of the publisher and the author.—*The Times Literary Supplement,* n. 4066, March 6, 1981. © Times Newspapers Ltd. (London) 1981. Reproduced from *The Times Literary Supplement* by permission.—*TriQuarterly,* n. 3, Spring, 1965 for "A Poetic Epitaph: Marina Tsvetaeva's Poems to Blok" by Andrew Field. © 1965 by *TriQuarterly,* Northwestern University. Reprinted by permission of the publisher and the author.—*Twentieth Century Literature,* v. 35, Spring, 1989. Copyright 1989, Hofstra University Press. Reprinted by permission of the publisher.—*yale/theatre,* n. 2, Summer, 1968. Copyright © by *Theater,* formerly *yale/theatre* 1968. Reprinted by permission of the publisher.

PERMISSION TO REPRINT PHOTOGRAPHS AND ILLUSTRATIONS APPEARING IN *TCLC*, VOLUME 35, WAS RECEIVED FROM THE FOLLOWING SOURCES:

Ullstein Bilderdienst: **p. 1;** © PAJ Publications. Used with permission: **p. 11;** Copyright © by Willy Saeger: **p. 22;** AP/Wide World Photos: **pp. 30, 53;** By permission of The Dreiser Trust, Harold J. Dies, Trustee: **pp. 45, 70, 78;** The Estate of Carl Van Vechten by Joseph Solomon, Executor: **p. 61;** Courtesy of The University of Arkansas Press: **p. 87;** From *New Song in an Old Land,* by Rex Ingamells. Longmans, Green and Co., 1943. Courtesy of Longman Cheshire: **p. 128;** Special Collections, Morris Library, Southern Illinois University: **p. 139;** John Flower: **p. 143;** Courtesy of Elizabeth T. Layton for the Estate of William Y. Tindall: **pp. 178, 191;** Verlag Molden: **pp. 224, 257;** Hans-Otto Mayer: **p. 242;** Licinio Cappeli: **p. 340;** Culver Pictures, Inc.: **p. 419.**

Authors to Be Featured in Forthcoming Volumes

Antonin Artaud (French dramatist and critic)—Artaud is considered one of the most influential drama theorists of the twentieth century. He is best known for his writings outlining the Theater of Cruelty, which extended the possibilities of theatrical presentation by repudiating Western traditions of realistic social drama in favor of an antirationalist spectacle intended to provoke in his audience an awareness of a higher order of truth and reality.

Karel Čapek (Czechoslovakian novelist and dramatist)—Čapek is celebrated for his science fiction novels and dramas in which he warned against the dehumanizing aspects of modern civilization and satirized a wide range of social, economic, and political systems.

Benedetto Croce (Italian philosopher and critic)—Considered the most influential literary critic of the twentieth century, Croce developed aesthetic theories that became central tenets of modern arts criticism while establishing important critical approaches to the works of such authors as William Shakespeare, Johann Wolfgang von Goethe, and Pierre Corneille.

Ford Madox Ford (English novelist)—Ford was a major English novelist and a strong influence on modern trends in both poetry and prose. *TCLC* will devote an entry to *The Good Soldier,* a novel that is often considered Ford's most important.

André Gide (French novelist and critic)—Although credited with introducing the techniques of Modernism to the French novel, Gide is more highly esteemed for the autobiographical honesty and perspicacity of his work, which depicts the moral development of a modern intellectual. *TCLC* will devote an entry to *Les faux monnayeurs (The Counterfeiters),* Gide's most ambitious and stylistically sophisticated novel.

Theodor Herzl (Austro-Hungarian essayist, dramatist, and novelist)—Best known as the founder of Zionism, Herzl was also a prolific author whose essays, plays, and novels were often written in support of the Zionist cause.

Henrik Ibsen (Norwegian dramatist)—Ibsen is regarded as the father of modern drama for his introduction of realism and social concerns to the European theater of the nineteenth century. *TCLC* will devote an entry to one of his most important and best-known dramas, *A Doll's House.*

Sinclair Lewis (American novelist)—One of the foremost American novelists of the 1920s and 1930s, Lewis wrote some of the most effective satires in American literature. *TCLC* will devote an entry to his novel *Babbitt,* a scathing portrait of vulgar materialism and spiritual bankruptcy in American business.

Jack London (American fiction writer and essayist)—London was a popular writer of Naturalist fiction in which he combined high adventure with elements of socialism, mysticism, Darwinian determinism, and Nietzschean theories of race. *TCLC* will devote an entry to his most widely read work, *The Call of the Wild.*

Desmond MacCarthy (English critic)—A member of the influential Bloomsbury circle, MacCarthy was among the most prominent literary and dramatic critics of his time, praised for the great erudition and objectivity of his evaluations.

Stanisław Przybyszewski (Polish dramatist and novelist)—Enormously popular during his lifetime, Przybyszewski is remembered for his romantic, often mystical, dramas and for his frank autobiographical writings.

Algernon Swinburne (English poet)—Controversial during his lifetime for his powerfully sensual verse, Swinburne is today recognized as one of the most talented lyric poets of the late Victorian period.

John Millington Synge (Irish dramatist)—Synge is considered the greatest dramatist of the Irish Literary Renaissance of the late nineteenth and early twentieth centuries. *TCLC* will devote an entry to his drama *The Playboy of the Western World,* which is regarded as his masterpiece.

Mark Twain (American novelist)—Considered the father of modern American literature, Twain combined moral and social satire, adventure, and humor to create such perennially popular works as *The Adventures of Tom Sawyer* and *The Adventures of Huckleberry Finn. TCLC* will devote an entry to the novel *A Connecticut Yankee in King Arthur's Court,* in which Twain satirized romantic idealizations of medieval life such as those presented in Sir Thomas Malory's *Morte d'Arthur.*

Emile Zola (French novelist)—Zola was the founder and principal theorist of Naturalism, one of the most influential literary movements in modern literature. His twenty-volume series *Les Rougon-Macquart* is a monument of Naturalist fiction and served as a model for late nineteenth-century novelists seeking a more candid and accurate representation of human life.

(Eugen) Bertolt (Friedrich) Brecht

1898-1956

(Also wrote under the pseudonym Bertold Eugen) German dramatist, poet, critic, novelist, and short story writer.

The following entry presents criticism of Brecht's play *Mutter Courage und ihre Kinder: eine Chronik aus dem Dreissigjahrigen Krieg* (*Mother Courage and Her Children: A Chronicle of the Thirty Years' War*), which was first performed in 1941 and published in 1949. For a discussion of Brecht's complete career, see *TCLC,* Volumes 1 and 6; for a discussion of the play *Leben des Galilei* (*Galileo*), see *TCLC,* Volume 13.

Brecht is considered one of the most important writers of this century, and *Mother Courage and Her Children* is consistently ranked among his masterpieces. Although subtitled "A Chronicle of the Thirty Years' War," the play does not follow the story of major historical figures or battles, but rather the experiences of a poor canteen woman who loses everything in her attempts to exploit the war for profit. Antiwar and antibusiness, *Mother Courage* was designed to lead the audience to condemn the title character for her capitulation to economic and political forces and for her inability to learn from the consequences of that capitulation. However, Brecht's ambiguous portrayal of Mother Courage, which has led many critics to sympathize with her and see her as blameless, and his fatalistic depiction of the destruction of virtue in a corrupt world, have resulted in interpretations of the play as a tragedy rather than the optimistic call for societal change Brecht claimed it to be.

Because of his Marxist political beliefs, Brecht left Germany in 1933 to live in self-imposed exile in Scandinavia and later the United States. He began *Mother Courage* in Sweden in September 1939 and completed it before the end of November. Brecht hoped to make a political statement with the play, which draws parallels between the Thirty Years' War (1618-1648) and World War II. He wrote that he "imagined that the playwright's voice would be audible in the theatres of various cities, warning that if you sup with the devil, you need a long spoon." However, the premiere in Zurich in 1941 was the only production of *Mother Courage* until Brecht directed it in East Berlin in 1948. Disappointed with the sympathetic response to Mother Courage in the Zurich production—critics compared her to the tragic figure of Niobe in classical mythology—Brecht revised the play to make Mother Courage a less sympathetic character. He took extensive notes on his Berlin production and published them along with numerous photographs of rehearsals under the title *Couragemodell* as a guide for future directors of the play.

The play begins as Mother Courage, her two sons, Eilef and Swiss Cheese, and her mute daughter, Kattrin, follow troops with the hope of making a profit on their sales of food, drink, and general equipment. Although she is content to live off the war, Mother Courage fears her children will be harmed. Attempting to instill in them some of her own cynicism and determination to survive, she warns them against their particular virtues: Eilef against his boldness, Swiss Cheese against his honesty, and Kattrin against her compassion. Despite her intentions to watch them vigilantly, Mother Courage is occu-

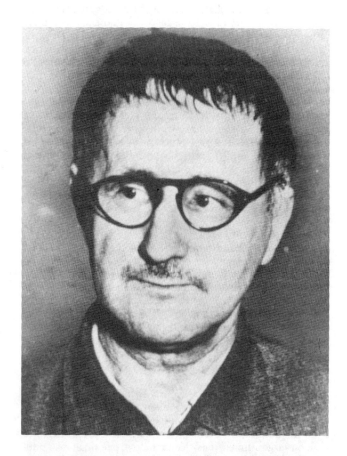

pied with trading when each child falls victim to the war. According to some critics, Brecht is suggesting that their deaths are caused partially because their virtues are a liability and partially because Mother Courage's constant bartering prevents her from protecting her children. Having learned nothing from her children's deaths, Mother Courage is seen at the end of the play pulling her wagon after the troops to continue business.

Although *Mother Courage* is frequently described as an antiwar drama, such themes as the evils of business and loss of idealism are considered equally important to a full understanding of the work. In this play Brecht condemns capitalism by having business seem to take precedence for Mother Courage over the welfare of her children. For example, she barters too long over the ransom price for her son Swiss Cheese, with the result that he is shot. Commenting more generally, Brecht speaks through Mother Courage, who identifies business, rather than conflicts over religion or politics, as the root of war. Brecht's treatment of other themes, such as the possibility or desirability of virtue in a corrupt world, is more ambiguous. Having capitulated to economic considerations in order to survive, Mother Courage urges others to emulate her abandonment of idealism and virtue. Although Brecht seems to condemn this sort of acquiescence, virtuous acts, such as Kattrin's heroic rescue of the children of Halle, lead to death, and their long-term effects seem insignificant. Brecht explained this inability to be virtuous and still survive as "a contradiction which could be resolved, but only by society itself and in long, terrible struggles."

Often cited as an excellent example of Brecht's theory of epic theater, which attempts to engage the audience's intellect rather than emotions, *Mother Courage* uses many of Brecht's "alienating" devices. For example, summaries of the action are projected onto screens at the beginning of each scene to reduce suspense, and songs comment on events rather than enhance the mood. Designed to prevent the audience from empathizing with the characters, these techniques encourage intellectual judgments, such as the one Brecht stated the spectator should make against Mother Courage. Noting, however, that Brecht's plays were rarely as doctrinaire as his own comments implied, critics have debated whether Brecht achieved, or even wanted to achieve, his stated goal of persuading the audience to see Mother Courage as a villain. Eric Bentley has maintained that Brecht undermines his harsh judgment of Mother Courage by making it seem that she could not have acted other than as she did. Excusing Mother Courage's constant bargaining as necessary for her family's survival, Bentley has attempted to show the sympathetic facets of her character and the opportunities for empathy Brecht included in the play. Bentley and others have labeled the play "fatalistic," observing that an interpretation of this work as a tragedy opposes Brecht's Marxist beliefs by denying that individuals can change society. Others, such as Roland Barthes, have contended that the play fulfills Brecht's stated goals: "If the spectator does not keep that slight distance necessary in order to see himself suffering and mystified, all is lost: the spectator must partly identify himself with Mother Courage, and espouse her blindness only to withdraw from it in time and to judge it." Robert Brustein attempts to resolve the conflict by asserting the compatibility of both views: "There is no question that Mother Courage . . . got away from the author. . . . The pathos of Courage does begin to take on larger dimensions. Nevertheless, one must also realize that Brecht *does* realize his conscious intentions with the character, and that the tragedy he unintentionally created coexists with the morality play he designed."

(See also *Contemporary Authors,* Vol. 104, and *Dictionary of Literary Biography,* Vol. 56.)

MAX SCHROEDER (essay date 1949)

[*In the following excerpt, Schroeder praises Brecht's innovative style and his effectiveness in* Mother Courage *in moving and teaching his audience.*]

On a covered wagon, pulled by two youths, two peasant-looking women roll across the bare revolving stage. A text is projected stating that the events play in the Thirty Years' War. For the audience this is no leap into the past, but a fairy-tale extension of the present. Never again will we see a covered wagon pulled by human power without recalling this scene and this song. The production [of *Mother Courage*] has, with its first scene, made an indelible mark on our knowledge, which will continue to work within us.

The economical use of props on Brecht's stage is neither aesthetic trifling nor its opposite, ascetic contempt for art. This economy helps to make the content of the writing transparent and graspable for the spectator. The romantic theatre of illusion, which reached its climax with Richard Wagner, rose to a fortissimo of colour and sound, trying to grasp and transport the spectator emotionally; Brecht, on the other hand, generally confines himself to the tones of conversation. He does not present the spectator continually with the increased emotions which are expected, but forces him actively to acquire these emotions as when reading a clearly printed book.

For the friend of the arts this may be nothing new, since every acquisition of art involves reading and digesting. In the use of his means of presentation Brecht is by no means without tradition. He has adopted stimuli from all sorts of places, ranging from the chapman's ballad to Chinese theatre. He is constantly determined that the spectator should not be lulled by illusions, that the listener should not think that he has understood something when he has actually not understood it (which is the quintessence of decadent romantic theatre—and of modern amusement art). He forces the public to learn to decipher his art, as a progressive form of society teaches its illiterates to read. He fights against the mysticism and superstition spread over the understanding of the arts by decadent bourgeois ideology. In this respect there is no contradiction in tendency between Brecht's theatre and the antique theatre or the theatres of Shakespeare and Goethe. Brecht has given himself the task of preserving, under the new historical conditions, the theatre as a factor which can move society.

Brecht perhaps takes the theatre as art—as art itself—more seriously than it has ever been taken before. He realises that it is only as a social affair that it can really be taken seriously. In antiquity, in Shakespeare's renaissance, in Goethe's time, the theatre was taken seriously in accordance with the highest level of world view achieved at the time; at the same time it was subjected to the religious and idealist philosophical limits of each epoch. Brecht is attempting to bring the theatre to the level of the most inclusive world view produced by the social reality of our times, and to use it in the struggle.

In the 1920s there were many attempts to make reforms in this direction; Brecht differs from them in that he derives his style not primarily from the fashioning of the material but from the attitude of the spectator. His style is therefore not, as is usual, developed from the work alone and from an established tradition of presentation; instead it seeks to determine and to fulfil social needs. The terms which Brecht uses, such as "epic theatre," "didactic play," etc., are not formalist dogmas, but stages of experimentation, aimed not at abolishing the "drama" but rather at producing a new encounter with the audience, a more binding encounter than that of the traditional theatre.

The discussion on this subject is by no means concluded; the production of *Mother Courage* gives us, after a long interval, finally the opportunity to re-open this discussion in Berlin on the basis of a masterpiece. It may be regarded as a fact that after a genuine Brecht production, every receptive spectator takes home the feeling with him that his eyes have been opened, as when he first deciphered the alphabet, or as if he had himself learned to try out a new art.

For Brecht himself, each production of one of his works is a serious undertaking with some resemblance to a ritual ceremony, not the ceremony of a cult entwined in the irrational and the metaphysical, but rather the propagation of culture and enlightenment necessary for the further existence of humanity. A production of *Galileo* will perhaps make this attitude completely clear; but it is also true for the production of **Mother Courage** and the many previous *Experiments* of the poet in his argument with the romanticism in his own early works.

The artistic validity of the Brechtian style is shown, for instance, by the fact that it tunes the actor to a certain gamut; but instead of restricting his creative force, this, on the contrary, develops it most excellently. Where can we see today on the Berlin stage such a moving performance as Helene Weigel as Mother Courage, presented with such harmonious unconcern? Who can forget the scene in which Angelika Hurwicz, as Dumb Kattrin, is shot down from the roof when she, as a human being, does what the backward peasantry vainly ask God to do—warns the threatened townspeople.

Paul Bildt as the cook and Werner Hinz as the army chaplain present figures of an originality and intensity derived from Jacques Callot's sketchbook, and at the same time create the impression that they had just been standing next to us in the overfilled underground train and argued about a sack of wood or less. Kahler and Teege—both of them, like Angelika Hurwicz, from the "younger generation"—condense in their acting the tragedy of the postwar young people, for whom the bourgeois world can show no honourable way out. Kühne as the recruiting officer, Bienert and Segtrop as sergeant-majors, Weber as the colonel, Grosse as the cornet present, with apparent lack of effort, their best abilities. Renate Keith plays with sharp accents and gestures the role of Yvette, the camp whore, the contrasting figure to Dumb Kattrin. The most disparate elements come together in a composition which forces even the most reluctant spectator to accept the thesis that those who plan a war like the Thirty Years' War profane the people to serve their own purposes and have no place in human society.

Brecht's stage is so very exactly arranged artistically that aesthetes attempt to construct a contradiction between this and "political theatre." But actually it reaches its artistic mastery by reason of the fact that it brings to light political truth, that it devotes all its wisdom to clearing away ruins and to building a society proof against the catastrophe politicians. The dramatist and all his co-workers deserve great thanks for this memorable production. It is time for Berlin to have its own Brecht theatre. (pp. 115-18)

> *Max Schroeder, "Brecht's Stage Style," in* Brecht: As They Knew Him, *edited by Hubert Witt, translated by John Peet, International Publishers, 1974, pp. 114-18.*

JOHN WILLETT (essay date 1949)

[*An English translator and critic, Willett has written numerous books on art and theater, as well as translating and editing several books on Brecht. In the following excerpt, he assesses the dramatic strengths and weaknesses of Brecht's East Berlin production of* Mother Courage.]

Mutter Courage, still sold out after over fifty performances, is a big success, yet without the tension between audience and stage which usually marks one. I think for most people it must be the quality of the production, not the uncompromis-

ingly unstagey play which attracts them. This quality you notice immediately the lights go down: the little orchestra in one of the boxes, the thin music, the drab dusty tattered family dragging its cart forward on the revolving stage, singing with fire and looking as if it had been rolled in dirt. The setting gives the minimum of help; the lighting is bright and straightforward irrespective of times and seasons. But at once you see these are a group of real people who have been right to the raw, miserable primitive bottom of an endless war, and at the same time that they are actors with their hearts in the play. A tremendous air of conviction.

What in the play calls out these qualities? I suppose above all, Brecht's seriousness and directness, and the ascetic simplicity which, because it is so unGerman, it takes a German to show. Item one: this is a play tackling a huge theme, the hateful implications of a war. Item two: Brecht is approaching his audience in a wholly original way, showing them one thing after another without ever appealing for their sympathy. Item three: there is neither turgid language here nor muddled thinking. And the whole sceptical, dispassionate nature of his argument—the lack of emotion and the final "take it or leave it"—is a vital corrective for the Germans, if not for others too. The play grips the actors, I would say, and the actors grip the audience. It is far from thrilling or pleasing in the orthodox way; you watch intently, but you never forget where you are. Yet there is something very strenuous and worthwhile about it which orthodox plays seem to lack. It is tough, without being difficult to understand: a highly simplified essay on profound themes.

This in itself is refreshing, and although the play is not "entertaining" it sticks in the mind as a more notable experience than most of those which are. Cutting out all the theory, that is in effect what Brecht's idea of non-Aristotelian drama boils down to. The interest of a plot, the self-identification of audience with actor, the compulsion of a strongly dramatic scene: these are the standard theatrical weapons which Brecht chooses to do without, and the play itself is as bare and unrelieved as the empty stage and whitewashed cyclorama on which, with Mother Courage's waggon and a few rags and scraps of scenery, the whole action is thrown. Concentration on the bare minimum, but a loving, scrupulous concentration which brings that minimum somehow to life.

There is so much that is prickly here that it is hard to grasp. What one has to accept however, before discussing the play's weaknesses, is that this is a justifiable way to use the theatre, and that it can create an appeal as forceful, in an entirely different manner, as the orthodox. What it loses in tension and atmosphere it gains in honesty and economy. It may be depressing, it may be tiring, but it is never cheap; at the worst it is like one of those fat stodgy books which no one wants to read, yet everyone who has read finds satisfying. Such a play is not poured into you in an effortless way, but the effort is worth making.

This is a basis from which Brecht may do great things, and sometimes, as in **The Mother** and **Fear and Misery,** he has brought it off. But **Mother Courage** has some drastic faults. First of all, Brecht has not really a great deal to say about war, and one feels that his own history has not associated him closely enough with it for him to develop any great understanding of its implications. Second, the unrelieved grey flatness of the play and the rejection of a plot are all very well, but something is needed to compensate if it is not to become an indigestible jumble of episodes and a torture for the audience as they wonder how long it is to the interval. This play lacks shape; one feels that the author has made no effort to cut or tighten up the individual scenes; there is no rise and fall apart from the one climax of Kattrin and the drum, and there is very little apparent reason why the whole pack of cards should be dealt in this particular order; you could stage the play almost equally well back to front. Whatever one's views of the plot as a help or hindrance to the development of a theme, some sort of formal unity and sequence are needed. As in music, there must be a structure if the work is to stand.

Third, Brecht compensates for his asceticism by a bunch of affectations which are extremely irritating and in no necessary connection with the core of his theory. The captions which have to be thrown on the screen between scenes: these don't belong to the theatre but to youthful memories of the silent cinema in the 1920s. The lowering of lights and a posy of old musical intruments to hover above the actors' heads every time a song is sung: what is the point of this piece of ceremonial? Is it an effort to make up for the arbitrary way in which the songs are slung willy-nilly into the text? Like the almost overdone emphasis on rags and tatters it verges on the merely quaint. And the music itself is pretty childish. The thin, acrid orchestration would be all right but for the drawing-pins which some bright chap has thought of putting into the hammers of the piano; this gives not a brittle but a tinny effect. Dessau's music has neither the nostalgia of Weill's nor the verve and conviction of Eisler's, and in trying to capture something of both it misses the simplicity of either. It is an old principle: songs must have tunes if their words are to come across. Here a lot of good poetry is flung away on a succession of desert airs.

For a German writer it is easy to wrap up such affectations in a mass of theory and present them as a justifiable part of his system. This is a type of dishonesty and inverted modishness which simply doesn't go with the bald dramatic statement at which Brecht aims. It is excellent in *Mother Courage* to see him paying more attention to his individual characters and giving them—above all to the central figure herself—a life of their own; and this humanisation of his approach will give his works immensely more weight and power. But no audience will be able to get to grips with them if he hems them in with the ugly exotic little cactus hedge of his own fads. This is his great danger, and would be good to see him overcome it. After all, he is one of the few real playwrights we have. (pp. 225-27)

John Willett, in his Brecht in Context: Comparative Approaches, *Methuen, 1984, 274 p.*

BERTOLT BRECHT   (essay date 1950-51)

[The following comments are taken from two separate essays by Brecht: "Mutter Courage in zweifacher Art dargestellt," which was written in 1951; and "Anmerkungen," which was written in 1950. Here, Brecht comments on the character of Mother Courage.*]*

In the usual manner of stage presentation, which produces a feeling of identification with the principal character, the spectator of *Mother Courage* (according to the testimony of many) comes to enjoy a peculiar pleasure: a triumph over the indestructibility of a vital person who has been visited by the tribulations and injuries of war. The active participation of Mother Courage in the war is not taken seriously; it is a

means of support, possibly the only one. Apart from this motive of participation—indeed, in spite of it—the effect is similar to that in the case of *The Good Soldier Schweik,* where—of course, in a comic sphere—the spectator triumphs with Schweik over the plans for his sacrifice by the major belligerent Powers. The similar effect in the case of Mother Courage is, however, of far less social value, because her very participation, as indirectly as it may be presented, is not deliberated. In actuality, this effect is even quite negative. Mother Courage appears principally as a mother and, like Niobe, she is unable to protect her children from the doom of war. Her trade as a dealer and the manner in which she practices it, give her at most something "realistically not ideal," without, however, taking from the war anything of its character of doom. It is, of course, here too, purely negative, but in the end she survives it, even though marred. In the face of this, Helene Weigel, employing a technique which prevented complete empathy, treated the dealer's occupation not as a merely natural, but as an historical one, that is to say, as belonging to an historical and *past* epoch, and the war as the best time for business. Here, too, trade was to be taken for granted as a means of support, but a dirty one after all, from which Mother Courage drank death. The trader-mother became a great living contradiction and it was this that defaced and deformed her, to the point of making her unrecognizable. In the scene on the battlefield, which is generally omitted in the usual manner of presentation, she was really a hyena; she brought out the shirts only because she saw the hate of her daughter and feared the use of force, and, cursing, she flung herself like a tiger upon the soldier with the cloak. After the maiming of her daughter, she damned the war with a sincerity just as deep as that with which she praised it in the scene immediately following. Thus, she gave expression to opposites in all their abruptness and irreconcilability. The rebellion of her daughter against her (at the rescue of the city of Halle) stunned her completely and taught her nothing. The tragedy of Mother Courage and of her life, deeply felt by the audience, consisted in the fact that here a terrible contradiction existed which destroyed a human being, a contradiction which could be resolved, but only by society itself and in long, terrible struggles. And the moral superiority of this type of presentation consisted in its showing man—even the most vigorous type of man—as destructible! (pp. 158-59)

In the Peasants' Wars, the greatest misfortune of German history—from a sociological standpoint—the Reformation had its canine teeth pulled. There remained: business and cynicism. Mother Courage—let this be said by way of help to the theatrical performance—together with her friends and guests and nearly everybody else, recognizes the purely mercantile character of the war: this is exactly what attracts her. She believes in the war to the end. It does not even dawn on her that you must have a large pair of shears in order to get your own cut from a war. The spectators at catastrophes expect without justification that those concerned and hardest hit are going to learn from the experience. As long as the masses are the *object* of politics, they can look upon what happens to them not as an experiment but only as a destiny; they learn as little from the catastrophe as the guinea pig in an experiment learns about biology. It is not the business of the playwright to endow Mother Courage with final insight— she does have some insight toward the middle of the play, at the end of Scene Six, and then she loses it again; his concern is, to make the spectator see. (p. 160)

Bertolt Brecht, "Observations on 'Mother Cour-

age'," translated by Herman Salinger, in The Creative Vision: Modern European Writers on Their Art, edited by Haskell M. Block and Herman Salinger, Grove Press, Inc., 1960, pp. 158-61.

GEOFFREY SKELTON (essay date 1951)

[*Skelton is a South African-born English translator, fiction writer, and critic who specializes in German theater and music. In the following excerpt, he discusses* Mother Courage *in terms of its entertainment value, its criticism of war, and its adherence to Brecht's theories of stage technique.*]

Brecht, though a passionately sincere Communist, is first and foremost an artist, and he knows how to clothe his ideas in a form that is entertaining as well as instructive: he is very insistent on the importance of the entertainment element. If his ideas often lack originality (the frequency with which he adapts the works of others is a proof of his weakness here), his character-drawing is masterly: Mother Courage herself, the servant Matti and Azdak, the people's judge in *The Caucasian Chalk Circle,* are complete human beings with nothing of the theatre about them. And the power they have to move us reconciles us, in the case of Matti, to the over-simple statement of the rich versus the poor theme, or, in the case of *The Caucasian Chalk Circle,* to the lengthy restatement of the well-known judgment of Solomon which is the backbone of the play.

Brecht is always entertaining. He is also vulgar, in the Shakespearean, not the Restoration, way, and his most vital creations are the poor, the weak and the afflicted. His gallery of these characters is magnificent. With the rich and the powerful, he, not surprisingly, fails to be convincing: his hatred of them is too great for his artistry to overcome. He can only make stock caricatures.

When his power of creating character comes into contact with a theme worthy of them, a masterpiece can emerge, and such a masterpiece is *Mutter Courage,* which Brecht wrote before the war, when he was in Scandinavia. (pp. 65-6)

Mutter Courage is the story of a camp trader during the Thirty Years' War. Mother Courage has a wagon which is drawn by her three children and from it she sells food, equipment, drink and the hundred and one things for which NAAFI [Navy, Army, and Air Force Institutes] is responsible nowadays. She lives on war and is content to do so, though she pays lip-service in the conventional way to the ideal of peace, and is deeply concerned in keeping her children out of the uglier side of war. But, as a recruiting sergeant observes, "Those that live by war must give something to it," and one by one the children fall victims to their own virtues (such is the topsy-turveydom of war that it is the virtues, not the weaknesses, that kill), leaving Mother Courage, old and bent, at the end to pull her tattered, empty wagon (for trade too has failed her) to an inevitably dismal and anonymous grave.

This most moving attack on war and mankind's tragic addiction to it is always convincing because it is never obtrusively political. The villain of the piece is not one type of human being as opposed to another, but human nature itself, which at all levels seeks its own advantage at all costs. Mother Courage is herself really an embodiment of that capitalism which Brecht abhors, though in a small and never very successful way. On this level Brecht is able to see her—a humble and misguided representative of the people—with that compas-

sion which he cannot bring to bear on richer and more powerful capitalists. There are in this play no representatives of the "upper classes": the nearest is the padre, superb realisation of a lazy man who is always able to find the best reasons for doing nothing. The real powers behind the war, the kings and generals and so on, are only spoken of, and then with a sort of resigned acceptance, as if no one were really questioning their right to play such havoc with the lives of their fellow mortals. (p. 66)

It would be possible to draw a fairly close parallel between Brecht and Sean O'Casey, not only on the political side, but also in the power of creating common people. They differ most in their language. Brecht, though in fact a poet of outstanding quality, is never poetic in his dialogue: he prefers dialect, racy, vulgar and, above all, simple: not for him the flowery Irishisms. He is also never guilty of the starry symbolism of later O'Casey. If he is symbolic at all, it is in the indirect manner of Joxer.

His stage technique is carefully thought out and exhaustively documented, and has gained for him the reputation of being an innovator. Its whole purpose is to create a critical audience. The onlookers are there, he says, not to accept but to judge: they must not be allowed to identify themselves with the persons in the play before them, but must be able to look at them objectively. To create these conditions, Brecht has written a set of maxims, in which actors are instructed not to identify themselves with their characters, but to play them critically, themselves aware of the weaknesses and strengths of the character they are portraying. The play, too, must be presented in a series of self-contained scenes, each containing a central idea which is summed up in a few words in the programme or on the screen before the scene is played, so that the audience can consider and judge the idea before the next is illustrated.

Music, too (all the plays have songs), must be used objectively, to point contrasts rather than to reinforce the mood, and scenery should not try to create an illusion of reality, but should indicate the broad background of the play's theme.

These ideas appear more novel on paper than on the stage, and really they are broadly the principles of comedy, which Brecht applies to plays of more serious content. Sometimes, in fact, he does not apply them too closely: the wagon hung with hams and leather straps and later torn and bedraggled, which dominates the scene of *Mutter Courage* from beginning to end, cannot by any stretch of imagination be considered an indication. It is as real as Mother Courage herself.

But, allowing for such exceptions, Brecht generally sticks closely and with success to his technique of alienation (*Verfremdungseffekt,* he calls it). He believes so firmly in his ideas that he will not allow his plays to be produced on lines other than those approved by him. To ensure this, he composes "models," in which the text of the play is reproduced with line-by-line instructions as to how they should be spoken and acted. These instructions must be strictly followed. A producer or an actor may suggest an alteration if he wishes, but Brecht reserves to himself the right of approval.

Well, artists have the right to be arrogant about their work if they can get away with it. Whether the public will take the work on the artist's terms is dependent finally on one thing—merit. The German public pays Brecht's price willingly, conscious that he is worth it. (pp. 66-7)

Geoffrey Skelton, "Bertolt Brecht's 'Mutter Courage'," in World Review, n.s. No. 23, January, 1951, pp. 65-7.

ROLAND BARTHES (essay date 1955)

[*Barthes was among the most influential and revolutionary writers in modern critical thought. His importance derives less from persuasive illumination of his themes or from his introduction of certain nonliterary perspectives into his writing (he has at various times employed viewpoints adopted from Marxism, psychoanalysis, and structuralism), than it does from a dominant method of critical analysis which Barthes applied to both literary and worldly subjects. This method is based on the insight that language—or any other medium of communication: painting, fashion, advertising—is a "system of signs." No given system is either natural, reflecting some necessary condition of physical reality, or transcendent, enjoying the authority of eternal spiritual laws: it is purely the artificial construction of a particular society at a particular point in history. The aim of Barthes's method is to expose the "myths" of a specific sign system, revealing their origins in custom and convention, in order to practice what Barthes views as the only valid purpose of criticism. This purpose is the observation of the inner workings and interrelationships governing a sign system, to define the symbolic elements that constitute everything from a work of literature to an advertising billboard to a striptease act. The value of Barthes's critical method, however, is not centered on the strictly intellectual pleasures of perceiving symbolic abstractions at work, but rather on the insight that what seems to be fundamental—the norms of middle-class society, the techniques of conveying "reality" in realistic fiction—are in fact accidental and artificial, supported only by the internal structure of a closed system. In the following excerpt, Barthes affirms the necessity of an emotional distance between the audience and the play in order for the spectators to escape Mother Courage's moral blindness.*]

Brecht's **Mutter Courage** is not for those who, at close range or out of earshot, get rich on war; it would be grotesque, explaining to *them* war's mercantile character! No, it is to those who suffer from wars without profiting by them that **Mutter Courage** is addressed, and that is the primary reason for its greatness: **Mutter Courage** is an entirely popular work, for it is a work whose profound intention can be understood only by the people.

This theater starts from a double vision: of the social evil, and of its remedies. In the case of **Mutter Courage,** the point is to show those who believe in the fatality of war, like Mother Courage, that war is precisely a human phenomenon, not a fatality, and that by attacking its mercantile causes its military consequences can finally be abolished. That is the idea, and this is how Brecht unites his crucial intention to a true theater, so that the proposition's evidence results not from sermon or argument but from the theatrical act itself: Brecht sets before us the whole sweep of the Thirty Years' War; caught up in this implacable duration, everything is corrupted (objects, faces, affections), is destroyed (Mother Courage's children, killed one after the next); Mother Courage, a sutler whose trade and life are the wretched fruits of the war, is so much inside the war that she does not see it (merely a glimmer at the end of the first part): she is blind, she submits without understanding; for her, the war is an indisputable fatality.

For her, but no longer for us: because we *see* Mother Courage blind, we *see* what she does not see. Mother Courage is for us a ductile substance: she sees nothing, but we see through her; we understand, in the grip of this dramatic evidence which is the most immediate kind of persuasion, that Mother

Courage blind is the victim of what she does not see, which is a remediable evil. This theater creates a decisive split within us: we are at once Mother Courage and we are those who explain her; we participate in the blinding of Mother Courage and we *see* this same blinding; we are passive actors mired in war's fatality and free spectators led to the demystification of this fatality.

For Brecht, the stage narrates, the audience judges; the stage is epic, the audience tragic. This is the very definition of a great popular theater. Take Guignol or Punch, for instance, a theater which has risen out of an ancestral mythology: here too the audience *knows* what the actor does not know; and upon seeing him act so harmfully and so stupidly, the audience is amazed, disturbed, indignant, shouts out the truth, offers the solution: one step more and the spectator will see that the suffering and ignorant actor is himself, will know that when he is plunged into one of those countless Thirty Years' Wars which every age imposes upon him in one form or another, he is in it exactly like Mother Courage, stupidly suffering and unaware of her own power to bring her miseries to an end.

It is therefore crucial that this theater never completely implicate the audience in the spectacle: if the spectator does not keep that slight distance necessary in order to see himself suffering and mystified, all is lost: the spectator must partly identify himself with Mother Courage, and espouse her blindness only to withdraw from it in time and to judge it. The whole of Brecht's dramaturgy is subject to a necessity of *distance,* and the essence of the theater is staked on the perpetuation of this distance: it is not the success of any particular dramatic style which is in question, it is the spectator's consciousness and hence his capacity to make history. Brecht pitilessly excludes as uncivic the dramatic solutions which involve the audience in the spectacle, and by heartfelt pity or knowing winks favors a shameless complicity between history's victim and his new witnesses. Brecht consequently rejects romanticism, rhetoric, naturalism, truculence, estheticism, opera, all the styles of *viscosity* or participation which would lead the spectator to identify himself completely with Mother Courage, to be lost in her, to let himself be swept into her blindness or her futility.

The problem of participation—the delight of our theater estheticians, always ecstatic when they can postulate a diffuse religiosity of the spectacle—is here altogether reconceived; nor have we seen the last of the beneficial consequences of this new principle, which is perhaps a very old principle, moreover, since it rests on the ancestral status of the civic theater, in which the stage is always the object of a tribunal which is in the audience (as it was for the Greek tragedians). We now understand why our traditional dramaturgies are radically false: they congeal the spectator, they are dramaturgies of abdication. Brecht's, on the contrary, possesses a maieutic power; it represents and brings to judgment, it is at once overwhelming and isolating: everything combines to impress without inundating us; it is a theater of solidarity, not of contagion.

Others will describe the concrete—and triumphant—efforts of this dramaturgy to achieve a revolutionary idea, which can alone justify the theater today. In conclusion, let us merely reaffirm the intensity of our response to the Berliner Ensemble's **Mutter Courage:** like every great work, Brecht's is a radical criticism of the evil which precedes it: we are therefore profoundly *edified* by **Mutter Courage.** But this edification is matched by delight: the performance proved to us that this profound criticism has created that theater without alienation which we had dreamed of and which has been discovered before our eyes in a single day, in its adult and already perfected form. (pp. 33-6)

Roland Barthes, "Mother Courage Blind," in his Critical Essays, *translated by Richard Howard, Northwestern University Press, 1972, pp. 33-6.*

HERBERT BLAU (essay date 1957)

[*Blau is an American critic, educator, and stage director. As the director of the first American production of* Mother Courage, *he relates in the following excerpt the effects of Brecht's techniques of alienation on American actors and audiences, and attempts to define the unique "dramatic rhythm" of the play.*]

The conventions of *Mother Courage* are not entirely new; others have written very intelligently about the Epic theater of Brecht, where it comes from, and what it purports to do. What it does is another thing; that is contingent on the given production, and the production on the particular audience, and both in part on the special, inescapable rhythm of the play. A distinctively European drama, *Mother Courage* has had an astonishing success abroad. It should be of value to record (conceding the limitations of director as critic and critic as director) what Americans—those who did it and those who watched it—felt and thought about the play. By doing so, not only may we learn through the theater something about the incalculable differences between Americans and Europeans, but also something about the ubiquitous art of the theater in one of its important modern forms.

In the beginning there was the idea of "alienation." For Brecht, alienation is a theory of art, a method of acting, and a type of production. The notion itself is alienating and to the unprepared sensibility—actor, director, or audience—somewhat intimidating. No wonder, then, that of all the plays done by our company, this was the first to arouse the kind of controversy which has long become foreign to the American theater, certainly the "tributary" theater: self-consciously contentious and widely variant reviews, letters of protest, public discussions and the like. We have bored audiences before; we have no doubt put some to sleep. But we have never *driven* anybody out of the theater, as we did occasionally with this play. What relationship is there between the idea of alienation, the subject of the play, and what actually occurred on stage that led to such active extremes of approval or antagonism? What are the real sources of alienation in the play and what does the reaction imply?

Brecht is a polemicist, not a strict logician. His dialectic approaches a rhetoric; Aristotle is his scapegoat. In spurning what he considers the emotional and intellectual vices of conventional western theater, he has *verbally* discarded some of its most affective qualities and he has presumed to revivify the modern drama by being undramatic: no suspense, no spurious tensions, no indulgent pathos, no chiaroscuros of mood, no continuity of plot. In reading *Mother Courage* for the first time, the company—most of whom had not been in a Brecht play before—felt that Brecht had done precisely what they had been told he would do. They were alienated; they were also bored. The play was static. Only one scene was really moving, that in which the Dumb Daughter Catherine beats her drum on the roof to warn the citizens of Halle of an at-

tack. This engaged them; this was what they wanted from the play. For the rest, it was a lot of talk.

But every play has to be discovered, and the discovery of this play was, embarrassingly, a measure of our private inadequacies and cultural prejudices. One ordinarily produces a play he knows and likes; here we were producing a play which, now, we thought we knew, and when we disliked it, disliked it for the wrong reasons. What we soon realized about the play, particularly as it went on its feet, was that its activity is manifold and unceasing: where it seemed to stand still, there were countless detailed bits of implicit business; where it appeared to be verbose, there were various stratas of relevant irony, disguised and overt. In Scene 6, for instance, Mother Courage, the Chaplain, the Regimental Clerk, and the Dumb Daughter are spending a rainy afternoon in a canteen tent, engaged in conversations on war, the two women taking inventory. The stage, which previously had been rather bare, is now full of sausages, linens, cheeses, belts, buckles, boots, tins, baskets, and shirts, all the innumerable paraphernalia of Mother Courage's enterprise. For Mother Courage, times are good. But the pre-scene projection announces that the great Commander Tilly has fallen in battle. There is funeral music. The scene opens reflectively. And though nothing "dramatic" happens until late in the long scene, the predominant impression, arising out of the talk, is one of abundance, of a steady throb of counting, checking, sorting, tallying, collecting money for drinks—the business of the actors and the business of war forming a single ritualistic image, the business of business, giving point and substance to the conscious ironies of Mother Courage and the ingenuous ones of the Chaplain.

Or take the opening scene, where Mother Courage and her children, travelling with their wagon, are stopped by a Recruiting Officer and a Sergeant, who are interested in her sons. She identifies herself and, when asked how she got her nickname, explains that she drove through the bombardment of Riga like a madwoman to save some loaves of bread she had in her cart. Her action was not heroic, as some who gave her the name thought (and as some who came to the play thought when they read the title in our advertising; one woman even called for tickets to *Mothers Courageous*). Mother Courage is a pragmatist not a martyr. But the irony is sharper and partially directed against herself. Not only does she discredit the romantic interpretation of her deed, she discredits the deed itself: what a fool, her tone implies, to risk one's life for a few moldy loaves of bread. Business comes first, *except* where it threatens survival. The same attitude prevails in the following scene when, immediately after a surprise reunion, she boxes her son's ear for having too bravely outwitted some enemy peasants. Better always to surrender than to die.

Set in the framework of great events, the mundane career of Mother Courage is alienated, then, in the various senses that Brecht intends: estranged, put at a distance, made famous (or infamous), historified. Our critical faculties are trained on that part of history which history slights. Tilly wins a battle at Lutzen; Mother Courage loses four shirts. And in the hectic little scene which juxtaposes these two important events, so much happens so quickly that one can hardly keep up with it: onstage some soldiers, taking respite from looting, are having a drink at Mother Courage's canteen. Catherine is distraught, running up and down on the periphery. Offstage, a fire is ravaging a peasant's farm. There are cries; wounded people are brought on. The Chaplain runs in, calling for linen. Mother Courage, keeping an eye on the soldiers, one of whom has already stolen a fur coat in the town, tries to protect her goods. She has given all her linen before, she says; she explains to the Chaplain that things are getting worse— taxes, duties, bribes to pay. Furious at her mother's apparent inhumanity, Catherine grabs a stick and rushes at her. Mother Courage shouts her down, but the Chaplain pulls her bodily from the wagon and takes out some shirts which he rips for bandages. There is a cry offstage—a baby is trapped by the fire. Torn between her daughter and her shirts, Mother Courage watches as Catherine dashes off to save the child. Catherine reappears with the baby. Mother Courage, relieved, stalks across the stage to chastize her and tries to take the baby away. Catherine snarls and hugs it fiercely. Meanwhile the soldier with the coat is trying to make off with a bottle of brandy. Mother Courage sees him and, instead of taking back the liquor, snatches the fur coat in exchange, even in the midst of the tumult managing to pull off a deal. The victory music, which had been playing all during the scene, mounts as Catherine joyfully raises the baby over her head.

I have recounted the activity of the scene because so much of it is missed in the reading and because—though it took us hours to work it out—all of it, and a good deal of incidental business that I have left out, happens in approximately one minute.

Thus the initial impression of alienation was mitigated for the actors by the necessity of having to *act* the play. It imposed its will and ways upon them. They could not worry about what they resented when the drama gave them so much to think about and *do*. Gradually they began to realize what Brecht means when he compares Epic theater to the painting of Brueghel. The canvas is large, diffuse, apparently undramatic. But every element has its unique energy. One looks closer and recognizes that nothing is ever still. The sensation of diversity disappears in the apprehended unity of a common vitality. Degraded and demoralized by the black marketry of war, the people of the play express their consciously rationalized submission with a remarkable vigor. What we have is the caustically robust power of ineffectuality. The stones begin to talk, as one of the projections declares, even before the mute daughter provides the climactic irony of the play with the drum that the war puts into her hands.

In structure, the idea of alienation becomes the fact of interruption. The narrative action—and *Mother Courage* is subtitled a Chronicle of the Thirty Years' War—is repeatedly intruded upon by ballads, slides, banners, insignia, dance, march music, and blackouts. The purpose of such interruptions any student of Brecht knows well: Epic theater is scientific and tactical; its aim is social criticism. Having rejected the obfuscating "magic" of the theater of illusion, it has enlisted very archaic conventions and types of entertainment to create the rational and rhetorical magic of the contemporary tribunal. Brecht pretends to be nothing but didactic; but he knows, like Shaw, that didacticism can and must be pleasurable, "from this, of course," he writes in his *A Little Organum for the Theater,* "morality can only be the gainer. . . . To demand more of the theater or to interpret its function more broadly is to put too low a value on the end proper to it."

Nevertheless, in developing "the special means of pleasure, the proper entertainment, for our own age," Brecht places his production facilities in the same relation to the theater that

the audio-visual center has to modern education, except that where the tape recorder and the camera have become devices for avoiding the issues of education, the resources of technology have become for Brecht a way of delineating and intensifying the issues of politics and society. A banner with slightly wrenched black (Germanic) letters drops from the flies announcing the place of action: Sweden, Saxony, Bavaria, Saxony, Poland. Why? Because war, like the snow settling over Joyce's Ireland, is general and undifferentiated; it looks the same everywhere. It is the source of confusion in the most classical sense of that word. You *need* to be told where you are. You also need to be reminded you are in the theater, especially when you are most engrossed in what you see. This is disturbing. But objective truth—and that is what Brecht seeks to display—*is* disturbing, more so when Brecht floods it with white, searching, surgical light. How shocked we were at our first dress rehearsal, though we should have known, that our costumes looked like costumes (and should) and how embarrassed when the minutest fault in performance or staging was exaggerated in the glare. (I must admit that, though we never put gelatins in front of our lamps, we have progressively lowered readings on our dimmers which were originally at maximum, so that now the light is naturally softer and more merciful—this a concession to our own irritated senses, as well as to the uneasiness of the audience.)

But the structure of *Mother Courage* is more than a matter of interruptions, ironies, and incongruities. What we finally realized about it none of our research on Brecht's techniques had made clear and would have been impossible to ascertain without performance. It is related to the peculiar rhythm of Brecht's dramatic perception, that rhythm which is always present and never completely manifest, and which makes of every theatrical event an important differential in the recurrent variable of the art. It is that part of a play which is unformulable and which we may know, so to speak, only through the bones. Those closest to it are the actors who, even when they are detached or alienated from their roles, become the instruments of its motion. This is what Stark Young meant, I suppose, when he spoke of the art of acting as the body of the theater, and Francis Fergusson when he describes the "histrionic sensibility" as the taproot of dramatic form. Alienation and detachment, the sundry stoppages in the action, are qualities in the special rhythm of *Mother Courage,* and the actor knows it even when he cannot speak about it, and most particularly when he is annoyed, as Brecht presumably wants him to be. The director is the instrument of provocation; in a Brecht play he is as much gadfly as counselor.

What both actors and director began to sense as rehearsals moved forward was that somehow the diffuse, omnibus, verbal, novelistic character of the play became more and more active, visual, empathic, concentrated, and dramatic toward the end. A play, like a poem, should not mean, but be; but there was meaning for us in the graduated contrast. In the beginning we had the characteristic rhythm and action of apathy and the materialistic urgency of survival by bargaining. As in a dramatist like Chekov, so apparently different from Brecht, we have continual self-justification and transference of blame by the characters through commentary on public affairs and motives in Brecht, commentary beyond their scope as people. The songs, with their discreetly sardonic music by Paul Dessau, reflect something of this tendency; even the Mother Courage ballad suggests with its insistent base the long, tedious way into the war. There is a sustained relationship with the audience; Mother Courage talks through the proscenium and there are frequent interruptions in the narrative. One desires very much to participate in the action, but Brecht makes one stand off and observe it. Later in the play, however, the characters, who have carried a heavy burden as symbols and concepts, become more strictly people, and we are made more fully aware of their human relationships with each other, which should have been obvious enough before except that we were distracted by a host of other factors.

Now we pick up events and values by reflexive reference. Back in Scene 3, Yvette, the prostitute, had sung her Song of Fraternization, prompted by memories of her unfaithful lover, Peter Piper. Much later, in Scene 8, the Cook is revealed to be the culprit. The son Eilif reappears, to be executed for a deed for which he had been previously honored. His armor is new and burnished, he dies rich. The Chaplain puts on his robe again and sings the Song of Hours, which suggests the idealistic theological student he must have been. In Scene 12, Mother Courage sings a lullaby to her dead daughter, the only song we did *ohne Verfremdung,* without alienation, although Brecht immediately cuts off the developing pathos by reintroducing the pipes and drums of a regiment on the march, as well as a choral reprise of the Mother Courage ballad. And Courage, who learns *nothing* from her suffering, makes the last "deal" of the play, paying a peasant to bury her daughter, and struggles off, bent as she is, to follow the war, which has not, according to the projected narrative, reached its end.

One realizes finally that the play of person on person has not been minimized in the earlier part of the drama, simply that it has been so forcibly brought to our attention. There was much else to say and demonstrate, and it is not until we have accepted through action, gesture, speeches, music, and all the technical elements the unrelenting presence and localized quality of the abstract war that Brecht lets us indulge in the easier and more rapid dramatic emotions. Hence the preference for the latter part of the play; most of us are still prone to recognize as dramatic mainly that which is fast-paced and violent. But drama exists at the calm peripheries of history as much as at its excited middle. In an age of speed many of us have forgotten that there is an infinite variety of dramatic action, that thought can be felt, paraphrasing Eliot, as strongly as the odor of a rose, that there is a pleasure and a tension that can only be described as dramatic in the ineluctable movement of dialectic, and that even the absolute qualities of music can acquire, in context, when one is listening and alert to analogies, the concrete force of a form which is not its own. (pp. 1-6)

We are prone to say that a play is not a play until it is staged; but this too is a qualitative matter. There are plays whose life is apparent in manuscript or at least largely discernible. But one sees very little of a Brecht play on the printed page. Despite all the anxiety that enshrouds opening nights, the sense of chance that is the peculiar delight and horror of the theater, there is something predictable about most plays. This was much less true about *Mother Courage;* however vain it might have been, we felt like Ahab's Pequod plunging into the blind Atlantic. There was no way of foretelling what to expect, because *Mother Courage,* aside from the jarring quality of its subject and the incongruity of its music, both of which made it even more threatening than *The Threepenny Opera* or *The Good Woman of Setzuan,* demanded a peculiar engagement of drama, actor, and audience that we as a com-

pany had not experienced before. The ground rules had to be written as we went along.

Now that one can read them a little better, they appear, despite the heresies of Brecht, to be the same old ones: the urgency of the special vision will be redeemed in form, and the theater will find the means of its mimicry. Unorthodox, severe, and fragmentary as it might be, the dramatic rhythm of *Mother Courage* is unavoidable because, though Brecht may not see as much of life as we would prefer, what he prefers to see he sees shrewdly and what he says he documents. And though the conventional dramatic experience is one which leads us through a series of events whose end is accompanied by emotional appeasement of some sort, a suspension of hostilities, the intention of Mother Courage *is* to alienate you. Whether you like it or not, you have been reached. (p. 10)

Herbert Blau, "Brecht's 'Mother Courage': The Rite of War and the Rhythm of Epic," in Educational Theatre Journal, *Vol. IX, No. 1, March, 1957, pp. 1-10.*

MARTIN ESSLIN   (essay date 1959)

[*Esslin, a prominent and sometimes controversial critic of contemporary theater, is perhaps best known for coining the term "theatre of the absurd." His* Theatre of the Absurd (1961) *is a major study of the avant-garde drama of the 1950s and early 1960s, including the works of Samuel Beckett, Eugene Ionesco, and Jean Genet. In the following essay, Esslin argues that Brecht's poetic instinct took precedence over his Marxist beliefs in the creation of* Mother Courage.]

Mother Courage was meant as a cautionary tale about the inevitable consequences of battening on war. Anna Fierling, called "Mother Courage," is a camp-follower who in her small way helps the prosecution of the Thirty Years' War by providing shoes, ale, and comforts for the soldiers. She was, in Brecht's conception, a negative, villainous character. Those who live by war must pay war its due. So Mother Courage loses her three children. Having sacrificed her family to her commercial instinct, she fails to learn her lesson. She continues her trade and, as the final curtain falls, she is seen dragging her cart across the stage to catch up with the advancing army.

Brecht wanted this last scene to arouse the spectator's indignation that such blindness and stupidity were possible. The public was to leave the theatre determined that something positive must be done to stop wars.

But when *Mother Courage* was first performed at the Zurich Schauspielhaus with Therese Giese, an actress of great power, in the title role, the public's response was quite different: they were moved to tears by the sufferings of a poor woman who, having lost her three children, heroically continued her brave struggle and refused to give in, an embodiment of the eternal virtues of the common people.

Brecht was furious. He re-wrote the play to emphasize the villainous side of Mother Courage's character. As he put it in a note to the text of the play in the ninth volume of *Versuche:*

> The first performance of *Mother Courage* gave the bourgeois press occasion to talk about a Niobe-tragedy and about the moving endurance of the female animal. Warned by this experience, the author

has made some alterations for the Berlin performance.

Having considerably underlined the villainy of Mother Courage, Brecht himself supervised the Berlin production, in which his own wife, Helene Weigel, also an excellent actress, but far less warm and motherly than Therese Giese and therefore more in line with Brecht's intention, played the title role. The Berlin production was a triumph. But how did the leading Communist critic, Max Schroeder, describe its impact? "Mother Courage," he wrote, "is a humanist saint from the tribe of Niobe and the *mater dolorosa,* who defends the life to which she has given birth with her bared teeth and claws. . . ." Again, hardly anyone had noticed the villainy of Mother Courage, the profiteer who battens on war. Brecht himself admitted this but tried to explain it, not by any failure on his part to make himself clear, but by the obtuseness of the spectators who remained the slaves of long-established habits of emotion:

> Numerous discussions with members of the audience and many notices in the press show that many people regard Mother Courage merely as the representative of "the little people," who are "involved" in the war and "who can't do anything about it," who are helplessly at the mercy of events, etc. A deeply ingrained habit induces the audience in the theatre to pick out the more emotional aspects of the characters and to ignore the rest. . . .

The East German authorities also noted the lack of propagandist effect. While *Mother Courage* moved people to tears about the horrors of war, if the play had any lesson at all it was that all soldiers are beasts (and the people of East Berlin automatically thought of Russian soldiers when it came to rape and rapine) and that nevertheless "life goes on" and that the little man is eternally resilient. This was not a specifically Communist message, and so it was suggested to Brecht that he might make the end of the play more explicit. Mother Courage might make a little speech drawing a more positively Communist lesson, or she might do something which showed that she had at last realized that she would have to become politically active.

If Brecht had really been as cold a rationalist and propagandist as he professed himself to be, he could easily have yielded to these demands. In fact, he did nothing of the sort. However willing he had previously been to accept advice and suggestions for alterations from practically any quarter, in this case he refused. With a great display of casuistry he argued that it was *better propaganda* to leave Mother Courage unconverted, untaught, and unteachable.

No doubt Brecht himself was convinced that he was arguing on strictly logical and rational grounds. Yet his arguments clearly are nothing but the rationalizations of instinctive responses. With the sound instinct of the creative artist Brecht knew that the suggested alterations would simply have *spoiled his play.* The suggested change did not make sense to his poetic instinct, and so he was unable to accept it. Yet the deeper needs of his personality made it impossible for Brecht to argue on any other lines than strictly rational considerations of political, or propaganda, expediency. The poet deep within him always had to hide behind the Marxist. (pp. 203-05)

> *Martin Esslin, in his* Brecht, a Choice of Evils: A Critical Study of the Man, His Work and His Opinions, *Eyre & Spottiswoode, 1959, 305 p.*

BERNARD DORT   (essay date 1960)

[In the following excerpt, Dort claims that "distanced identification" in Mother Courage *leads to growth in the audience's awareness of themselves and the tasks that need to be accomplished in society.]*

The real game of the epic theatre is played between the audience and the stage. . . . Brecht does not place between them a uniform and unchangeable distance: blindness on one side, lucidity on the other; fatality on the stage, lucidity in the audience. He never stops making them confront one another for their mutual enlightenment. Starting from an initial identification of the two areas (which almost constitute two worlds), he causes them to gradually differentiate themselves. The audience slowly adopts a definite position toward the stage. Those who see *Mother Courage* learn that Mother Courage learns nothing. They learn this because when the play began, they were at her side—they themselves were Mother Courage. A sort of two-way street is built between audience and stage resulting in a growing consciousness on the part of the former by means of the latter: a collective task. However such labor in common does not bring with it a conclusion. No order is permanently established; no universally valid truth is enunciated—either in the audience or on the stage. Their game, their labor is a function of a third term: the historical reality itself which envelops all parts of both the audience and the stage and which literally constitutes the horizon of the theatre. We can no longer speak either of the symbolic truth of dramatic action or even the infallibility or lucidity of the audience. Rather we must refer to a dialectic of stage and audience which does not close in upon itself, and which simultaneously reveals and produces its own truth: the real world in which the audience members and the actors live. In this respect, Louis Althusser speaks of a "dialectic of the wings." On stage, our erroneous and alienated way of living history is exposed. The stage reveals our behavior and ideological opinions (not a tragic or scientific truth). Hence, in the audience, through the effect of what can be called a *game of distanced identification,* a growing consciousness can slowly evolve. Through the deformed image which the stage gives back to them, the people in the audience begin to look at, question and understand themselves. In the Brechtian theatrical game, the playgoer discovers himself. More precisely, he discovers his own situation in real society and identifies those tasks which remain to be accomplished in order for him to be able to be himself. The epic theatrical production is, therefore, according to Althusser's fine definition, "the process of becoming, the production of a new consciousness in the audience—incomplete like all consciousnesses yet propelled by its very incompleteness, that acquired distance, that inexhaustible work of criticism in action; the play is indeed the making of a new play-goer, an actor who begins when the play ends, who begins only to give it a conclusion in real life." (pp. 31-2)

> *Bernard Dort, "Epic Form in Brecht's Theatre," translated by Christopher Ostergren, in* yale/theatre, *No. 2, Summer, 1968, pp. 24-33.*

ROBERT BRUSTEIN   (essay date 1964)

[Brustein is an American educator and critic whose devotion to quality in the theater has earned him widespread respect. As resident drama critic for the New Republic *during the 1950s and 1960s, he attacked what he saw as the debased standards of commercial acting, directing, and playwriting in America. A champion of innovations in the theater, Brustein put his views*

into practice when he was appointed dean of Yale University's School of Drama in 1966. In the following excerpt, Brustein discusses Brecht's antiheroic point of view in Mother Courage, *emphasizing the characters' contributions to their own downfall.*]

Mother Courage ostensibly deals with the Thirty Years' War, that seventeenth-century feast of death, fire, and pestilence. But its real subject is all wars, as seen from the perspective of one who loathes military heroism. Inspired to some extent by Grimmelshausen's picaresque novel *Simplicissimus,* this play, according to Bentley, can be partly construed as a reply to Schiller's *Wallenstein.* It is also a reply to Shakespeare's *Henry V,* Corneille's *Le Cid,* Dryden's *Conquest of Granada*—in short, to all works which glorify heroism or eulogize national ideals. Brecht has finally made the passive side of his nature the source of a positive position: that of a belligerent pacifism. He observes the exploits of war, like those of peace, from the underside, examining what Edmund Wilson has called "the self-assertive sounds" which man "utters when he is fighting and swallowing others." To achieve his satire on the morality of the military life, Brecht concentrates not on the battles but on the commonplace activities of day-to-day living, as performed by the war's orphans, truants, and subordinates. In the background of *Mother Courage* pass the victories, defeats, reversals, sieges, assaults, retreats, and advances which form the substance of history. In the foreground, the private lives of the noncombatants provide a non-heroic contrast. The external course of the conflict is narrated, like newspaper headlines, in the legends preceding each scene, but it interests Brecht only insofar as it influences local commerce: "General Tilley's victory at Leipzig," the title informs us, "costs Mother Courage four shirts."

For the real struggle is over money, food, and clothing. Brecht, still examining the relationship between Capitalism and crime, is now applying his Marxist perceptions to the

Erich Engel, Brecht, Paul Dessau, and Helene Weigel during the Berlin Ensemble production of Mother Courage.

crimes of history itself. If the businessman is identified with the gangster in *The Threepenny Opera,* then he is identified with the warmaker in *Mother Courage.* Property is not only theft, but murder, rape, and pillage; war may be the extension of diplomacy but it is also an extension of free enterprise. Locked in endless combat, the Protestant Swedes and the Catholic Germans are told they are fighting for religious ideals, but like the Swedish King Gustavus, whose zeal was so great that he not only liberated Poland from the Germans but offered to liberate Germany as well, the crusading warlords usually make "quite a profit on the deal." The Chaplain may believe that the war "is a religious war, and therefore pleasing to God," but to the Cook, it is just like any other war in "all the cheating, plunder, rape, and so forth." The God it is supposed to please is not around to help the participants; and so when it comes to a real test of the Protestant Chaplain's religious enthusiasm, he switches sides: "God bless our Catholic flag." Obviously, Brecht is again attacking Christian hypocrisy rather than Christianity itself; once again, he is measuring how far mankind falls short of its ideals. Religious piety, jingo patriotism, bourgeois respectability, all are merely synonyms for greed, acquisition, and self-advancement. And since war is "just the same as trading," the morality which justifies it must be considered an evil sanction. Brecht, in short, quarrels with Christianity because its morality has been exploited, its prophecies unfulfilled. The age of miracles is past. Man must now find his own loaves and fishes, and attend to his earthly survival.

Seen from this perspective, heroism looks like a ghastly skeleton, rattling its bones in the wind; and in *Mother Courage,* heroic actions invariably stem either from stupidity, insanity, brutality, or simple human error. The spokesman for Brecht's antiheroic point of view is Anna Fierling, the canteen woman known more familiarly as Mother Courage. Like so many of Brecht's rascally characters, this salty, cunning, self-serving woman has much in common with Falstaff; and like Falstaff, she functions as a satirical commentator and comic deflator. To her, the only quality worthy of respect is cowardice; and she commands respect herself because of her consistency—she invariably chooses the most selfish, ignominious, and profitable course. Even her nickname is ironic: her "courageous" breach of the lines during the bombardment at Riga was made to keep some loaves from going moldy. As the supreme advocate of adaptation and acquiescence, Courage is extremely cynical about the motives of others. She attributes the death of General Tilley, for example, to the fact that he got lost in a fog and strayed to the front by mistake. She is probably right; in Brecht's world, as in our own, there are no more authentic heroes. Brecht, in other words, gives us a Falstaff without a Hal or Hotspur. Courage's unhesitating assumption about the baseness of human motives belongs to the author; and it is not modified by any contrasting ideal.

Yet Brecht's all-embracing cynicism implies an ideal, for he is rebelling against a reality he despises. "The Song of the Great Capitulation"—possibly the most moving lyric in the entire Brechtian canon—reveals the history behind Brecht's cynical attitudes. For here Mother Courage, trying to discourage an indignant soldier from endangering his safety, sings of the degeneration of her own rage against injustice. Beginning as a Romantic individualist—"All or nothing. Anyway never take second best. I am the master of my fate. I'll take no orders from no one"—she eventually becomes the cautious compromiser, marching in time with the band:

"You must get in with people. If you scratch my back, I'll scratch yours. Don't stick your neck out!" It is the story of how George Garga is eventually forced to repudiate his belief in freedom. And it may very well be the story of how Brecht abandoned his early Romantic idealism under the pressure of internal passions and external constraints:

> Our plans are big, our hopes colossal.
> We hitch our wagon to a star.
> (Where there's a will, there's a way. You can't
> hold a good man down.)
> "We can lift mountains," says the apostle.
> And yet: how heavy one cigar!

Lifting that cigar has become the whole ambition of Brecht's heroine: her sole purpose is to keep herself and her family safe and alive. In the fulfillment of this difficult and ultimately fruitless task, she employs ruthlessness, charm, bribery, guile, and simple horse sense, always true to her coward's creed that discretion is the better part of valor.

Mother Courage's bitter hostility to heroism has made her, paradoxically, a heroic figure to audiences—an image of the "little people," beleaguered by forces beyond their control, yet resiliently continuing to make their way. Bentley observes that the alienation apparatus of the Berliner Ensemble must be "called into action *as a fire brigade*" to douse the natural flow of sympathy which streams toward such characters; and Esslin—noting that Brecht originally designed Courage as a "negative, villainous character"—concludes that the author was unable to control his own affection for her. There is no question that Mother Courage—like Falstaff, who was meant to be a Vice figure (Sloth and Vanity) but who somehow transcended his morality play role—got away from the author. And like the rejection of Falstaff, the pathos of Courage does begin to take on larger dimensions. Nevertheless, one must also realize that Brecht *does* realize his conscious intentions with the character, and that the tragedy he unintentially created coexists with the morality play he designed. The responses evoked by Brecht's heroine are a good deal more complicated than those evoked, say, by the pathetic Nora Clitheroe, the heroine of another antiwar play, O'Casey's *Plough and the Stars:* Courage is not just a passive sufferer, playing on the sentiment of the audience, but also an active source of suffering. She may be a victim of the war, but she is also an instrument of the war, and the embodiment of its evils. Brecht's revolt, in short, remains double. Like Macheath, Mother Courage is both the agent of the author's rebellion, and the thing rebelled against. Her determination to play it safe makes her the enemy of hypocrisy, but it also makes her cold and grasping. And though her single-minded devotion to survival is sympathetic in relation to her three children, it becomes mere aggrandizement in relation to her fourth child—the wagon. This almost human prop is a constant visual reminder that for Courage the war is "just the same as trading." Like a stockmarket investor, she builds up profits on the fluctuating fortunes of war, buying and selling on the lives of men. Thus, Mother Courage is no Niobe, all tears, but the author of her own destruction. One of those lower-class Capitalists whom Brecht was always creating, she is, as the Chaplain tells her, a "hyena of the battlefield," and those who live by the war must die by it.

Mother Courage haggles while her children die—this is the spine of the play. For while Courage is pursuing commercial advantage, her family is sacrificed, one by one, to the war. Eric Bentley has already commented on the tripartite struc-

ture of the work where, at the end of three discrete sections, another child is laid on the war's altar. The offspring of three different fathers, Finnish Eilif, Swiss Cheese, and German Kattrin are an international brigade of victims, their fates foretold in the initial scene. The episode of the black crosses, like many of the songs in the play, is prophetic. But it is not a supernatural agent which strikes the children down; it is the cruel hand of man, abetted by their own self-destroying instincts. Brecht's emphasis on the destructive power of the instincts reminds us of *The Threepenny Opera;* and indeed "The Song of the Wise and the Good" is a reprise of "The Song of Solomon," adapted, as Bentley has observed, to the instincts and "virtues" of Courage and her offspring. Caesar's bravery is identified with Eilif's heroism, Socrates's honesty with Swiss Cheese's incorruptibility, St. Martin's unselfishness with Kattrin's kindness, and Solomon's wisdom with Courage's shrewdness. The dominant qualities of both the great and the common lay them low; virtue doesn't pay: "God's Ten Commandments" have not "done us any good."

Brecht, however, cannot refrain from giving an ironic twist to his already ironic statement—for the "virtues" he describes are all, with the exception of Kattrin's kindness, highly dubious qualities. Eilif's bravery, for example, is, at best, impulsive foolishness. While the Sergeant is cunningly distracting Courage's attention by bargaining with her over a belt, Eilif is off with the Recruiting Officer, pressed into war by his lust for glory. Eilif's song, "The Fishwife and the Soldier," predicts the outcome of such rashness, for it tells how a headstrong son is killed by his own bravery, despite all his mother's cautious warnings. Impulsiveness leads to death: "The lad is swept out by the tide / He floats with the ice to the sea." The song, with its typically Brechtian water images, is obviously influenced by Synge's *Riders to the Sea;* and like Marya's Bartley, Courage's Eilif soon drifts with the tide of death because he ignored his mother's advice to drift with the tide of life. Having "played the hero in God's own war" by slaughtering a number of innocent peasants who wished only to protect their cattle (here bravery turns into sadistic brutality), Eilif repeats this heroic exploit during an interlude of peace—and is led off to be shot. Like Chaplain's Verdoux, he discovers that virtues in wartime are considered crimes in peacetime, and that law and morality shift their ground to accommodate a nation's needs.

Swiss Cheese, the "honest child," is another victim of a dubious virtue. As paymaster of a Protestant regiment, he is entrusted with the cashbox; and when he is captured by the Catholics, he refuses to surrender it up. This kind of honesty, as Courage observes, is sheer stupidity: Swiss Cheese is too simpleminded to provide for his own safety. Here, however, Courage is in a position to save her child through the exercise of her Solomon-like wisdom: "They're not wolves," she observes of his Catholic captors, "they're human and after money. God is merciful and men are bribable." Her analysis of motive is perfectly accurate, but it is precisely because of her excessive shrewdness that the device does not work. Forced to pawn her wagon to obtain sufficient bribe money, Courage is anxious to reserve enough for her own security. But the Catholics are in a hurry, and her prolonged bargaining is climaxed by the terrible realization, "I believe—I haggled too long." Swiss Cheese, the significance of his name finally clear, is carried in on a stretcher riddled by eleven bullets—to be thrown on a garbage heap because his mother is afraid to claim the body. Torn between the contradictory demands of self-survival and mother love, Courage has, in effect, killed her own child. And she suffers the consequence in terror and remorse, looking on the corpse in dumb agony, and choking back the scream which rises in her throat lest she give some sign of recognition.

Kattrin is Courage's only truly virtuous child, the soul of kindness and the most positive figure in the play. It is a characteristic of Brecht's attitude towards positive values that she is a mute; but through her expressive gestures and responses, the cruelty and horror of the war are most eloquently told. Even her dumbness is related to these terrors—"a soldier stuck something in her mouth when she was little"—and when she is attacked and mutilated by some vicious marauders, the war has killed her hopes for a home, a husband, and children, whom she especially loves. Because of her muteness, her serenity, and her love of children, Kattrin sometimes achieves allegorical stature—she is much like Aristophanes's Peace, blinded, gagged, raped, and buried by war. But Brecht's war is endless; and, unlike Aristophanes's mute figure, Kattrin is led to enjoy no hymeneal banquet at the end. Instead of being pulled out of the pit, she is hurled into one: the war buries Kattrin for all time. Courtesans like the camp follower, Yvette, may thrive on conflict, for Yvette accepts the whore's barrenness, so much like that of the war. But Kattrin is *Kinderknarr*, children-crazy, and it is her consuming love for these fruits of Peace that finally destroys her.

Once again, the death occurs because the mother is haggling. Having successfully resisted the temptation to leave Kattrin behind and find a secure berth with her lover, the Cook, Courage is, nevertheless, still looking after her profits: she has left Kattrin with the wagon while she buys stocks cheap from the frightened townspeople. While she is gone, the Catholics capture a farmhouse, preparing for an ambush of the town. The farmers, afraid for their family in the town, appeal to God to save their four grandchildren. But, to their horror, their prayers, for once, are answered. Moved by the mention of children in danger, Kattrin has climbed to the roof of the farmhouse, where she begins to beat her drum. At last, Peace has found a tongue, rhythmically commenting on its ancient, invincible enemy. To smother the sounds of this alarum, the soldiers and peasants try to create their own noises—peaceful ones, they begin to chop wood. Yet Kattrin's drumming mounts in intensity, and in desperation. When a lieutenant offers to spare her mother if she descends from the roof, Kattrin drums more heatedly; when he backs his promise with his word of honor, she drums most furiously of all. The smashing of the wagon, the knifing of a sympathetic peasant, the threat to her own life—nothing stops this desperate tattoo. She is finally shot off the roof by a hail of musketry; but the town is saved.

The episode is simple, startling, magnificent, with a mounting emotional crescendo created primarily through the use of drumbeats. But the catharsis it accomplishes, so rare in Brecht's drama, is followed almost immediately by grim, cooling irony. Kattrin's sacrifice has really been in vain. The town is saved, but the sound which signifies this is the explosion of a cannon. The war will continue for another twelve years; and after this war is finished, three hundred more years of killing will follow.

Brought on stage for the *threnos*, Courage witnesses the utter desolation of her hopes. The fault, again, has partially been hers ("If you hadn't gone off to get your cut," says an Old Peasant, "maybe it wouldn't have happened"), but she is too dazed now to know it. Thinking that Kattrin is only asleep,

she sings her a lullaby; even the lullaby concerns the need for clothing and food. Her sustaining illusion is that Eilif may still be alive. Without this illusion, only nothingness confronts her—the inconsolable blankness of life, induced by a malignant universe, inhuman men, and her own flawed nature. We are out of the world of Falstaffian comedy and into the desolate world of *King Lear;* but unlike Lear, Brecht's heroine is denied even the release of death. When the armies move by, singing her song about the certainty of the seasons and the certainty of man's mortality—the coming of the springtime of life before the winter of death—she cries to them: "Hey, take me with you"—and straps herself to the wagon. She is pulling it alone now, but it is no longer very heavy: supplies and passengers have all been destroyed. Courage and the wagon merge—both bruised and battered by war, both somehow still durable. Courage has dragged it over half of Europe, learning nothing. She will drag it a good deal further before she stops, animated only by that basic life instinct: the need to survive. The smallness and the greatness of this woman are clear at the end, as they are clear throughout this monumental work, where Brecht so angrily takes away from the human race—and gives it back so much. (pp. 268-76)

Robert Brustein, "Bertolt Brecht," in his The Theatre of Revolt: An Approach to the Modern Drama, *Little, Brown and Company, 1964, pp. 229-78.*

ERIC BENTLEY   (essay date 1965)

[*Bentley is considered one of the most erudite and innovative critics of the modern theater. He was responsible for introducing Brecht, Luigi Pirandello, and other European playwrights to America through his studies, translations, and stage adaptations of their plays. In his critical works, Bentley concentrates on the playwright and the dramatic text, rather than on the production aspects of the play. Thus, in his first important critical study,* The Playwright as Thinker *(1946), Bentley distinguishes between "art" and "commodity" in the American theater, basing his definition of commodity on the premise that most producers are more attentive to box office receipts than to the artistic quality of a play and, as a result, the dramatist is often neglected as a true artist. Some critics consider this approach an attempt to compensate for his unwillingness to accept drama as a form of popular entertainment. Bentley's most important work,* The Life of Drama *(1964), is a comprehensive study of the development of dramatic form, specifically examining aspects of melodrama, farce, comedy, tragedy, and tragicomedy. His most recent critical works include anthologies of reviews written during his years as drama critic (1952-56) for the* New Republic, *and a collection of his essays on Brecht—* The Brecht Commentaries: 1943-80 *(1981). In the following excerpt, Bentley investigates contradictions in the character of Mother Courage and their relation to the themes of the play.*]

The role of Mother Courage is hard to play and is always being miscast. Why? "Because middle-aged actresses are such ladies and lack earthiness." But who has succeeded in the role? Outstandingly, Helene Weigel. Is she very earthy, is she notably proletarian? On the contrary—there is nothing proletarian about her except her opinions. Then what is it those other ladies lack that Helene Weigel has? Among other things, I would suggest an appreciation of the role, an understanding of what is in it, and above all the ability to portray contradictions. For whenever anyone says, "Mother Courage is essentially X," it is equally reasonable for someone to retort: "Mother Courage is essentially the opposite of X."

Mother Courage is essentially courageous. That is well known, isn't it? Tennessee Williams has written of the final moment of Brecht's play as one of the inspiring moments in all theatre—inspiring because of the woman's indomitability. On she marches with her wagon after all that has happened, a symbol of the way humanity itself goes on its way after all that has happened, *if* it can find the courage. And after all we don't have to wait for the final scene to learn that we have to deal with a woman of considerable toughness and resilience. This is not the first time she has shown that she can pick up the pieces and continue. One might even find courage in the very first scene where we learn that she has not been content to cower in some corner of Bamberg but has boldly come to meet the war. A trouble shooter, we might say on first meeting the lady, but the reverse of a coward.

Yet it is impossible to continue on this tack for long without requiring an: *On the other hand.* Beginning with the reason why she is nicknamed "Courage" in the first place.

> They call me Mother Courage because I was afraid I'd be ruined, so I drove through the bombardment of Riga like a madwoman with fifty loaves of bread in my cart. They were going moldy, what else could I do?

Did those who gave her the name intend a joke against an obvious coward? Or did they think she was driven by heroic valor when in fact she was impelled by sheer necessity? Either way her act is utterly devoid of the moral quality imputed. Whether in cowardice or in down-to-earth realism, her stance is Falstaffian. What is courage? A word.

Somewhere hovering over this play is the image of a preeminently courageous mother who courageously tries to hold on to her young. More than one actress, offering herself for the role, has seen this image and nothing else. Yet valor is conspicuously absent at those times when Mother Courage (however unwittingly) seals the fate of her children. At moments when, in heroic melodrama, the protagonist would be riding to the rescue, come hell or high water, Mother Courage is in the back room concluding a little deal. For her, it is emphatically not "a time for greatness." *She is essentially cowardly.*

A basic contradiction, then, which the actress in the role must play both sides of, or the play will become the flat and simple thing which not a few journalistic commentators have declared it to be. An actress may be said to be beginning to play Mother Courage when she is putting both courage and cowardice into the role with equal conviction and equal effect. She is still only beginning to play it, though; for, as she proceeds with her interpretation, she will find that, in this play, courage and cowardice are not inherent and invariable qualities but by-products.

Of what? We can hunt for the answer by looking further into particular sequences of action. It is not really from cowardice that Mother Courage is in the back room concluding a little deal when her children are claimed by the war. It is from preoccupation with "business." Although **Mother Courage** is spoken of as a war play, it is actually a business play, in the sense that the incidents in it, one and all, are business transactions—from the deal with the belt in Scene One, through the deal with the capon in Scene Two, the deal with the wagon in Scene Three, the deals with bullets and shirts in Scene Five, through to the economical funeral arrangements of the final scene. And since these transactions (except for the last) are

what Courage supports her children by, they are "necessary." Those who condemn her have to face the question: What alternative had she? Of what use would it have been to save the life of Swiss Cheese if she lacked the wherewithal to *keep* him alive? The severe judge will answer that she could take a chance on this, provided she does save his life. But this is exactly Mother Courage's own position. She is fully prepared to take the chance if she has to. It is in determining whether she has to that her boy's life slips through her fingers: life or death is a matter of timing.

To say that Swiss Cheese is a victim of circumstances, not of Courage's character, will not, however, be of much use to the actress interpreting this character. If cowardice is *less* important here than at first appears, what is *more* important? Surely it is a failure in understanding, rather than in virtue. Let me elaborate.

Though only one of Brecht's completed plays is about anyone that a university would recognize as a philosopher, several of his plays present what one might call philosophers in disguise, such as Schweyk, the philosopher of a pub in Prague, and Azdak, the philosopher of a Georgian village. To my mind, *Mother Courage is above all a philosopher,* defining the philosopher along Socratic lines as a person who likes to talk all the time and explain everything to everybody. (A simple trait in itself, one would think, yet there have been actresses and directors who wish to have all Courage's speeches shortened into mere remarks. Your philosopher never makes remarks; he always speechifies; hence such abridgment enforces a radical misinterpretation of character.) I do not mean at all that Courage is an idle or armchair philosopher whose teachings make no contact with life. On the contrary, her ideas are nothing if not a scheme of life by which, she hopes, her family is to do pretty well in a world which is doing pretty badly.

Here one sees the danger of thinking of Mother Courage as the average person. Rather, she resembles the thoughtfully ambitious modern mother of the lower-middle or better-paid working class who wants her children to win scholarships and end up in the Labour Cabinet. (Minister of Education: Kattrin. Chancellor of the Exchequer: Swiss Cheese. Minister of War: Eilif.) Has it escaped attention that if one of her children turns out a cutthroat, this is blamed on circumstances ("Otherwise, I'd have starved, smarty"), while *the other two are outright heroes?* Anyone who considers this an average family takes a far higher view of the average than is implicit in the works of Bertolt Brecht.

What is the philosophy of this philosopher? Reduced to a single proposition, it is that if you concede defeat on the larger issue, you can achieve some nice victories in smaller ways. The larger issue is whether the world can be changed. It can't. But brandy is still drunk, and can be sold. One can survive, and one can help one's children to survive by teaching each to make appropriate use of the qualities God gave him. The proposition I have just mentioned will apply to this upbringing. A child endowed with a particular talent or virtue should not pursue it to its logical end: defeat on such projects should be conceded at the outset. The child should cunningly exploit his characteristic talent for its incidental uses along the way. In this fashion the unselfishness of a Swiss Cheese or a Kattrin can be harnessed to selfishness. The result, if the philosophy works, is that while the world may shoot itself to blazes, the little Courage family, one and all, will live out its days in moderate wealth and moderate happiness. The scheme is not utopian. Just the opposite: the hope is to make optimism rational by reducing human demands to size.

The main reason it doesn't work is that the little world which Mother Courage's wisdom tries to regulate is dependent upon the big world which she has given up as a bad job. Small business is part of the big war which is part of the big business of ownership of *all* the means of production and distribution. No more than the small businessman can live in a separate economic system from the big can the small philosopher live in a separate philosophic system from the big. *Mother Courage,* one can conclude, exposes the perennial illusions of the *petit bourgeois* scheme of things. This has of course often been done before in modern literature. But usually only the idealism has been exposed. Mother Courage, on the other hand, could claim to be a cynic. She has the theatre audience laughing most of the time on the score of this cynicism—by which *she* deflates illusions. Cynicism is nothing, after all, if not "realistic." What a cynical remark lays bare *has* to be the truth. Brecht makes the truth of his play the more poignant through the fact that the cynicism in it ultimately favors illusion. Mother Courage had gone to all lengths to trim her sails to the wind but even then the ship wouldn't move. So there is irony within irony (as, in Brecht's work, there usually is). Courage's cynicism can cut down the windy moralizing of the Chaplain easily enough, but only to be itself cut down by a world that cannot be comprehended even by this drastically skeptical kind of thinking.

What alternative did Mother Courage have? The only alternatives shown in the play are, on the one hand, the total brutalization of men like the Swedish Commander (and, for that matter, her own son Eilif) and, on the other hand, the martyrdom achieved by Swiss Cheese and Kattrin. Presumably, to the degree that the playwright criticizes her, he is pushing her toward the second alternative. Yet, not only would such a destiny be completely out of character, within the terms of the play itself it is not shown to be really preferable. Rather, the fruitlessness of both deaths is underlined. Why add a third?

Given her character, Mother Courage had no alternative to what she thought—or, for that matter, to the various "bad" things she did. In this case, can she be condemned? Logically, obviously not; but was Brecht logical? The printed editions of the play indicate that he made changes in his script to render Mother Courage less sympathetic. In other words, after having made her thoroughly sympathetic in his first version, Brecht later wanted her less so. One can see the sense of the changes in polemical terms: he did not wish to seem to condone behavior which is to be deplored. But to make this point, is it necessary to make Mother Courage a less good person? Personally I would think not, and I should like to see *Courage* played sometime in the Urtext of 1940 and without the later "improvements." But one should not minimize the complexity of the problem. Like many other playwrights, Brecht wanted to show a kind of inevitability combined with a degree of free will, and if it doesn't matter whether Courage is less good or more, because she is trapped by circumstances, then the play is fatalistic. I tend to think it *is* fatalistic as far as the movement of history is concerned, and that the element of hope in it springs only from Brecht's rendering of human character. Brecht himself is not satisfied with this and made changes in the hope of suggesting that things might have been different had Mother Courage acted otherwise.

(What would she have done? Established socialism in seventeenth-century Germany? One must not ask.)

Brecht has stressed, in his Notes, that Mother Courage never sees the light, never realizes what has happened, is incapable of learning. As usual, Brecht's opinions, as stated in outside comments, are more doctrinaire than those to be found embodied in the plays. It may be true that Mother Courage never sees that "small business" is a hopeless case, though to prove even this Brecht had to manufacture the evidence by inserting, later, the line at the end: "I must get back into business." She does see through her own philosophy of education. The "Song of Solomon" in Scene Nine concedes that the program announced in Scene One has failed. The manipulation of the virtues has not worked: "a man is better off without." The song is perhaps more symbolic, as well as more schematic, than most Brechtians wish Brecht to be, for there is a verse about each of her children under the form of famous men (Eilif is Caesar, Swiss Cheese is Socrates, Kattrin is Saint Martin), but more important is that this is the "Song of Solomon" (from *The Threepenny Opera*) and that Solomon is Courage herself:

> King Solomon was very wise
> So what's his history?
> He came to view this world with scorn
> Yes, he came to regret he ever had been born
> Declaring: all is vanity.
> King Solomon was very wise
> But long before the day was out
> The consequence was clear, alas:
> It was his wisdom brought him to this pass.
> A man is better off without.

I have heard the question asked whether this conclusion was not already reached in the "Song of the Great Capitulation" in Scene Four. Both songs are songs of defeat (Brecht's great subject) but of two different defeats. The second is defeat total and final: Courage has staked everything on wisdom, and wisdom has ruined her and her family. The first is the setback of "capitulation," that is of disenchantment. When Yvette was only seventeen she was in love, and love was heaven. Soon afterward she had learned to "fraternize behind the trees"; she had capitulated. It is perhaps hard to imagine Courage as a younger and different person from the woman we meet in the play, but in the "Song of the Great Capitulation" we are definitely invited to imagine her as a young woman who thought she could storm the heavens, whose faith seemed able to move mountains.

Scene Four is one of several in this play which one can regard as the whole play in miniature. For Brecht is not finished when he has set forth the character of Mother Courage as one who has passed from youthful idealism to cynical realism. For many a playwright, that would no doubt be that, but Courage's exchange with the angry young soldier leads to other things. We discover that Mother Courage is not a happy Machiavellian, boasting of her realism as an achievement. We find that she is deeply ashamed. And in finding this, we discover in Courage the mother of those two roaring idealists (not to say again: martyrs) Swiss Cheese and Kattrin. "Kiss my arse," says the soldier, and why? His bad language had not hitherto been directed at her. But she has been kind to him only to be cruel. If she has not broken his spirit, she has done something equally galling: she has made clear to him how easily his spirit can be broken. When you convert a man to the philosophy of You Can't Win, you can hardly expect to earn his gratitude at the same time.

In the way Courage puts matters to the soldier we see how close she came to being a truly wise woman. We also discover in this scene that, despite the confident tone of her cynical lingo, Courage is not really sure of herself and her little philosophy. She teaches the soldier that it is futile to protest, but she apparently does not know this herself until she reminds herself of it, for she has come here precisely to protest. Here we learn to recognize in Courage not only contradiction but conflict. She knows what she has thought. She is not sure what to think.

And this is communicated by Brecht in a very bold—or, if you prefer, just poetic—manner. For while Courage does not give herself to despair until the end (and not even then for those who can take at face value her: "I must get back into business"), she had correctly foreseen the end from the beginning: the despair she gives herself to had been there from the moment of capitulation. At times it would strike her between the eyes: she is very responsive and, for example, has worked out the Marxist interpretation of religion for herself. Scene Two contains a song she had taught Eilif as a boy: it accurately predicts the manner of his death. In Scene One she predicts doom for the whole family in her elaborate pantomime of fortunetelling. It could be said that everything is there from the start, for the first thing Mother Courage does is to try and sell things by announcing an early death for her prospective customers. The famous "Song of Mother Courage" is the most extraordinary parody of the kind of song any real *vivandière* might try to attract customers with. Mother Courage's Come and buy! is nothing other than: Come and die! In that respect, her fortunetelling is on the level, and her wisdom is valid.

Scene Four, I have been saying, is one of several in this play which one can regard as the whole play in miniature. The main purpose of the play, for Brecht, was, I think, to generate anger over what it shows. Yet Brecht realizes how pointless angry plays have been—and angry speeches outside the drama. It is said that Clifford Odets's *Waiting for Lefty* made millionaires angry for as long as it took them to get from their seats to where their chauffeurs tactfully waited for them at the end of the block. Such is the anger of the social drama in general.

There is the anger of a sudden fit, which boils up and over and is gone. And there is the anger which informs the work of long years of change. *Why* can't the world be changed? For Mother Courage, it is not from any inherent unchangeability in the world. It is because our wish to change it is not strong enough. Nor is this weakness innate. It is simply that our objection to the present world isn't as strong as it once was. What is outrageous does not outrage us as it once did. Today, it only arouses the "short rage" of Brecht's soldier—and of Courage herself—not the long one that is required. Because we—they—have capitulated.

Capitulation is not just an idea but a feeling, an agony in fact, and is located not just in the scene of the Great Capitulation but in the whole play of *Mother Courage.* Everything that happens is related to it, above all the things that are furthest away from it, namely, the deaths of Swiss Cheese and Kattrin. And if these children are what their mother made them, then their refusal to capitulate stems from her, is her own youth, her own original nature.

The ultimate achievement of an actress playing this role would be that she made us sense to what an extent Courage's children are truly hers. (pp. 165-71)

Eric Bentley, "Mother Courage," in his Theatre of War: Comments on 32 Occasions, The Viking Press, 1972, pp. 165-71.

RONALD GRAY (essay date 1966)

[*Gray is an English educator and critic specializing in German literature. In the following excerpt, he criticizes* Mother Courage *for its lack of ideological and artistic unity.*]

One of the most instructive things about **Mother Courage** is the note which appears at the end of the standard edition, commenting on the first performance given at Zürich in 1941, and complaining that "despite the anti-Fascist and pacifist attitude of the Zürich Theatre, mostly occupied by German emigrants . . . the bourgeois press talked of the play in terms of 'a Niobe-tragedy, and the shattering tenacity of the maternal animal'." Warned by this, Brecht says, he made a few changes, the chief of which showed Mother Courage herself in a less sympathetic light. Instead of reluctantly allowing her best shirts to be torn up for bandages, in the revised version she refuses to let a single one of them out of her hands, and by this means, quite clearly, Brecht seeks to make it less possible for a spectator to identify himself with her or to sympathize with her.

There are several puzzling features in all this. First of all, wasn't it rather naive of Brecht to suppose that by making Mother Courage ungenerous on one occasion he could undo the impression made by her on so many other occasions? After this scene of the shirts, for instance, Mother Courage refuses to abandon her dumb daughter so as to lead a comparatively comfortable life with the cook in Amsterdam, and her whole nature is, though cynical, also humorous, self-reliant, disrespectful towards officialdom, quick-witted, and devoted to her children. The impression we have of her is not going to be altered essentially by rubbing it in that she can also be stingy on occasion, and even in the rewritten scene Brecht still puts in a stage direction to show her in conflict ("torn this way and that") so that she still appears as someone with whom we can sympathize. The shirts are her livelihood, and she is a poor woman: while we know that she ought to give the shirts, for charity's sake, we don't simply condemn her for not giving them, though we would admire her for giving them.

But there is naiveté in the rest of Brecht's remark, too. In criticizing the "bourgeois" press—he had in mind the papers read by the Swiss middle-class, like the excellent *Neue Züricher Zeitung,* I suppose—he contrasts it with the "anti-Fascist and pacifist" audience, suggesting that anyone who was moved very much by Mother Courage's motherliness was likely to be pro-Fascist and a war-monger. I call this naive because attitudes towards motherliness do not depend upon political beliefs. But what Brecht may have meant to imply is that anyone who was moved at the Zürich performance by the motherliness of Mother Courage had failed to see the unscrupulous motives which nullified any such virtue in Mother Courage. This is a point to which I shall come back.

The other footnote by Brecht which I find instructive is the one which says that, although Mother Courage, like almost everybody else in the play, sees that the Thirty Years' War is purely commercial ("rein merkantil"), Brecht did not think it was his affair to make her reform herself—his concern was that the spectators should see and, presumably, draw the conclusions that Mother Courage does not draw.

Like a good many statements by dramatists about their own works, this one does not properly apply to the play Brecht offers us. For one thing, a good deal is made in the play of the fact that the Thirty Years' War was a religious war, and some anti-religious points are made which are unrelated to commercialism. Again, one of the reasons alleged for the continuance of the war is greed, and while greed may go with commerce, it can exist independently of it, too. Still, we do gain from Brecht's comments a clear view of his intentions. He wanted his spectators to see that war was essentially connected with the making of money, and, presumably, that if men ceased to make this their chief concern wars would cease.

Having said this much, I come at once upon my general impression of the play as a confusing mixture of beliefs and of puzzling scenes, coupled with a striking theatrical (that is, here, visual) effect. Especially in the production of the Berliner Ensemble, personally directed by Brecht, and with the main part played by Helene Weigel, the visual power of the play was strong. Above all, the wagon containing sausages and brandy, boots and clothing, which Mother Courage and her children pull from place to place in the wake of first the Protestant, then the Catholic army, was a strong binding force, fascinating in its shape, and striking in its rumbling movement on the turntable which Brecht expected a theatre normally to have. Just as effective were the ragged quilted jackets and Hessian cloaks which draped the characters in an unsentimental, yet aesthetically "right," shape. There was a toughness and robustness about all this which showed a capable artist at work, as almost any of the photographs of this production in the volume *Theaterarbeit* will show. In fact the whole theatrical side of the play seemed irreproachable, and a contrast of scenes from other companies' versions always leaves the Berliner Ensemble far and away ahead of the field. When, for instance, Mother Courage's daughter, Dumb Kattrin, tries on the red boots and feathered hat of the camp prostitute, she can be represented as a rather delicate creature who is all too ignorant of the harsh facts of life. She can be made to look pretty (despite Brecht's clear indications that she is not), and to pick at the side of her skirt as she launches into what could be a ruinous career. By contrast, Brecht made her pudding-faced, made her blow out her cheeks with the effort of swaggering in the approved fashion in boots that were too small for her, and generally indicated that this was a girl who was being stupid as well as unfortunate. Or again, where one producer, picking up a hint that certainly does exist, but making too much of it, showed Mother Courage holding the dead body of her son Schweizerkas as though she were the Virgin Mary in Michelangelo's Pietà, Brecht insisted on only the barest show of emotion in this scene, and certainly got more out of it that way. As a producer in the theatre Brecht, with the help of Caspar Neher and several others, had few rivals.

But this does not explain the puzzling effect of the play, or why, even after Brecht had tried to make Mother Courage more unsympathetic, audiences continued to show sympathy for her. The consequence of all these visually interesting scenes can be that audiences are actually misled about the words and actions which are meant to be the main thing in them. Take for instance the intention, clearly expressed by Brecht, that the audience should not merely see the commer-

cial nature of war, as the characters themselves do, but also take action, no doubt along Marxist lines. We would expect to find some exemplification of this point in the character of Mother Courage, and on the surface it does appear that we get it, for Mother Courage does say at the conclusion of one scene "Curse the war," only to change her mind immediately in the next, when she happens to be more prosperous, and to add, "they're not going to mess up my war for me." But this does not really illustrate Brecht's point; if we look at the occasion on which she curses war, we see that she is not perceiving the commercial nature of war at all. She curses it because her daughter has been assaulted, which might have happened in peacetime, because her daughter has been dumb since a soldier stuffed something into her mouth, which might also have happened in peace, and because both her sons have disappeared, and one of them has been killed. (She never learns of the death of the other.) All this has nothing to do with commerce, so that we must look elsewhere for evidence in favour of Brecht's assertion. We shall probably imagine we have found it in the scenes which show Mother Courage losing her children because of her exaggerated concern with money—indeed Brecht introduces this concern in the case of all three of her children. On looking closer, though, this demonstration appears forced.

In the first scene of all, Mother Courage loses her son Eilif to the recruiting-sergeant because she is persuaded to haggle over the sale of a belt-buckle while Eilif succumbs to the blandishments of the recruiter—when she looks round, her son is gone. The main point of the first scene seems to be contained in this demonstration that greed causes her misery. Yet, even if we agree that to haggle is to be too much concerned with money, it has to be conceded that anything else might have distracted Mother Courage at the crucial moment—she might have been involved in an argument or a brawl or in fending off an embrace, while Eilif was being dazzled with promises of glory, and in any case she could not be expected to tie a grown man to her apron-strings.

Similarly, the death of Kattrin, shot by soldiers for raising an alarm, is laid partly at Mother Courage's door, although she had no direct part in it. Brecht is careful to let us know that when Kattrin performs her heroic action, beating a drum to warn a beleaguered city of impending attack, her mother is in the city, buying goods cheaply from people who are fleeing from danger. He is thus enabled to put the words into the mouth of another character, after Kattrin's death, "If you hadn't gone into town to carve yourself a slice, this might not have happened." But this is a quite unjust charge—Mother Courage had left Kattrin in the care of peasants, having no one else to leave her with, and by the nature of her job she must have left her many times in pursuit of bargains. It is absurd to suggest that the desire for money implicates Mother Courage in guilt of Kattrin's death, which might equally well have happened if Mother Courage herself had been present. She would have been as powerless as the rest of them against the muskets of the soldiers. Yet the fact that Brecht introduces the same idea into the scene of the death of Mother Courage's other child suggests a consistent intention. Schweizerkas, like Kattrin, is killed by soldiers, in his case because he refuses to reveal where the regimental cashbox is. Mother Courage could save him if she were to offer the whole bribe demanded by the soldiers immediately it is asked for, but she tries to haggle and thus loses him. This, at any rate, is the superficial impression made by the scene of Schweizerkas's death. But if we look more closely we see that it is not so straightforward. In the first instance, Mother Courage does offer the whole of the bribe demanded, 200 guilders, believing that she is bound to be able to get the money back from the cash-box, which she thinks Schweizerkas has hidden. Only when she learns through her intermediary Yvette that Schweizerkas has thrown the box in the river does she offer less, 120 guilders to be precise. But this, we have to remember, is well over half the value of her wagon and all its contents at the time. Her whole livelihood is at stake, and the times are extremely hard. She may be excused for thinking that the captors of Schweizerkas will accept less, since they will get nothing at all by shooting him out of hand. What is more, when she hears that they have rejected not only 120 but the 150 which Yvette offered without her authorization, she immediately offers the whole 200; that is to say, she offers to make over every single item she possesses to save her son's life. As it turns out, she is too late, but we are never told why the soldiers executed their potentially valuable prisoner so promptly. They know that Yvette is on her way back to Mother Courage, with the chance that the ransom-money will be raised, but they shoot him out of hand. All this makes the case against Mother Courage rather weak, in fact our sympathy surely goes entirely to her in this situation. Yet, we have to ask, why did Brecht write the scene, why did he let Mother Courage say "I think I've haggled too long," and why did he suggest that the other two deaths were partly due to the same cause unless he wanted to make some case against her, suggesting greed for money? And why did he make the case so implausible?

The idea that Brecht was intent on making a case is borne out by the way in which he makes Mother Courage react to the war, and to the prospect that it may end. Mother Courage is, after all, a shrewd, hard-headed business woman. She says she got her name for driving a wagon-load of loaves out of Riga while it was under cannon-fire, so as to sell them before they went mouldy, and she shows she can make a hard bargain with the cook who wants a capon for his captain's dinner-table. Yet, the moment there is peace she is horrified: "Don't tell me peace has broken out, just when I've bought in new stock." Peace horrifies her: she will lose all her money, and she puts on funeral black at the very thought of it. But this seems scarcely likely to be a risk. A gypsy-like trader who has to find room in her wagon for herself, a man, and her daughter, as well as for supplies to sell, is not going to have a slow turnover: she will get through most of her stock in a week or two with any luck, whether there is peace or war, and the kind of goods she sells are equally salable in either event. If she were a capitalist with large stocks of munitions on her hands, and no prospects of a war breaking out somewhere else very soon, she might well talk like this with a show of reason. (Though Krupps have managed in peace and war pretty well all the same.) As things are, we can only suppose that Brecht thought of her in some way as being a capitalist, and put into her mouth words which he thought appropriate to that circumstance.

And this is not so far-fetched a notion as you might suppose. Brecht did, after all, explicitly say that the highwayman Macheath in *The Threepenny Opera* was a representative of bourgeois capitalism, and his only ground for saying that seems to have been based on Proudhon's epigram, "Property is theft" (hence, as a Shakespearean clown might argue, a capitalist is an owner of property, and an owner of property is a thief, argal a capitalist is a highwayman). Besides, it is only on the basis of some such association as this that Mother Courage can be said to see the purely commercial nature of war. Only by exaggerating her position, making her seem more concerned with matters belonging to high finance than she possibly can be, was Brecht able to suggest that he had done more than sketch a few scenes from the life of a remarkable, but historically insignificant woman. But when we come to look at his play and its pretensions, we surely must see that it scarcely gets beyond trivialities, so far as economic analysis is concerned. Richelieu, Mazarin, Gustavus Adolphus, the Emperor are scarcely thought of. We see nothing of the dreadful involvement in war of statesmen who, as C. V. Wedgwood says, did not want war, and almost without exception were dragged into it against their will and better judgement, "actuated rather by fear than by lust of conquest or passion of faith." The real issues treated in Brecht's play are not concerned with these extremely complex matters, but with something on the whole simpler.

What Brecht is really writing about here, as in *The Good Woman,* in *Galileo,* and in the *Caucasian Chalk Circle,* is the possibility and the desirability of virtue in a corrupt world. To this question he gives, as always, an ambiguous answer.

The true issue is stated where we would expect it to be stated, in the opening scene of the play. The first conversation, between the recruiting officer and his sergeant, is entirely concerned with the idea that virtues like loyalty, faith and honour, and morality in general, are associated with war, while peace, somehow, is a time of lounging about, feeding off the fat of the land, and indulging oneself. It sounds an absurd argument, it is true, when the sergeant says, "You can see there's been no war here for much too long. Where's your morality to come from, I ask you?" Or when he adds, "It's only when there's a war that you get proper lists and registers, and your shoes properly packed and your corn in sacks, and man and beast properly counted and carried off—because people know if you don't have proper order you can't have a war!" But since this argument is placed in the mouth of an unsympathetic character we need not suppose Brecht to be presenting it for our serious consideration, despite the apparently thematic role suggested by its position in the play. It is only when we find Mother Courage repeating the idea in the second scene that we begin to wonder whether we ought to be paying more attention. "Wherever you get these big virtues," she says, "it proves there's something rotten," and she goes on to demonstrate this by saying that if a general is stupid his soldiers have to be specially courageous in order to carry out his orders, and if he is lazy they have to be very cunning, and if he expects too much of them they have to show a quite remarkable degree of loyalty. This argument is as absurd as that of the recruiter, since soldiers have to be courageous whether their leaders are good or bad, and the same applies to the other virtues. In fact, Mother Courage runs into total self-contradiction when she concludes, "They're all virtues that a proper country and a good king or a good general don't need. In a good country there's no need of virtue; they can all be quite ordinary, fair to middling, and cowards too for all I care." Since this happy state of affairs is only possible where there is a "*good* country" (whatever that may be) and a "*good* king," we may well wonder what Mother Courage is driving at when she talks of there being no need for virtue, since goodness is presumably a virtue in her eyes. And we may once again pass on, thinking that we are not supposed to pay any respect to the argument on this occasion either. Yet Brecht reverts to it a third time in Scene 9, when the Dutch cook sings his song about the folly of wisdom, boldness, honesty, selflessness and Godfearingness. True, the cook has just shown a total lack of several of these virtues by suggesting to Mother Courage that she should live with him and abandon her dumb daughter, who would have to pull the heavy wagon alone in the depths of a bitter winter in a starving countryside. We may thus once again suppose that Brecht does not want us to take the argument seriously, though we may begin to wonder why he keeps repeating it, and repeating it in so unpersuasive a form. The cook sings of St. Martin, who cut his cloak in half to help a man in poverty, with the result that they both froze to death—but this is not the necessary and only consequence of charitableness. Similarly, the wisdom of Solomon is represented as that of a man who curses the hour in which he was born, which sounds more like despair than wisdom, though wisdom may not exclude such a curse. And the death of Julius Caesar is crudely attributed not to any overweening ambition, or to the envy of others, but quite simply to his boldness. There is too much sweeping generalization in all this to impress us, and we may well be left asking why Brecht continually thrusts such stuff forward for our attention.

The answer to this, if we look at the play as a whole, appears to be that to some extent, though ambiguously, Brecht did take these arguments seriously. The whole structure of the play (for it has one, despite Brecht's theoretical disavowals of structure) tends to, but does not in fact, bear out the kind of thing said by the recruiter, the cook and Mother Courage herself.

Once again returning to the first scene, we see that not only is the need for virtue questioned, it is actually presented by Mother Courage as a thing to be avoided. She warns all her children against the virtue to which they seem most inclined: Eilif is not to be too bold, Schweizerkas not to be too honest, and Kattrin not to be too kind-hearted. In the course of the play, we see how all her warnings are in vain—we see, or seem to see, how each child dies precisely because of the virtue against which he or she has been warned. And, of course, we might well conclude from this that Brecht meant us to see Mother Courage's warnings ironically—that he meant to praise virtue by showing up the true nature of those who decry it—were it not that here once again, in most cases, the argument runs badly off the rails. Eilif, for instance, is executed for a deed which, we are told, would have been accounted an act of boldness in war; his misfortune is that, whereas a few months earlier he was honoured for precisely the same thing, he happens now to have done it in peace-time and is therefore condemned. Thus he seems to be introduced into the play in order to exemplify the cook's cynical song: here is boldness, and this is where it gets you. Yet if we look at what Eilif has done, we see that it is not what soldiers are usually praised for. He is no Hector or Spitfire pilot. In wartime, he plundered some peasants of their cattle, and, when they set upon him, "cut them to pieces," as he says with relish—they being armed only with clubs whereas he had a sword. In peace-time, he has tried to burgle a peasant's cottage, and killed the man's wife. In neither case has he displayed more than a criminal low cunning, and since this is all we hear of Eilif's military activities we can only be left wondering what on earth Brecht was driving at. If he wanted to write a play about virtue, why doesn't he show us some?

We turn then to Schweizerkas, who becomes a regimental paymaster, entrusted with the custody of the regimental cash-box during a chaotic retreat. He dies, apparently, because he is too honest and loyal to betray to his captors what he has done with the box—with a little less honesty, Mother Courage might suggest, he could have got away with his life. Yet here again, though the case is very different from that of Eilif, Brecht does not provide a really satisfying contribution to the general argument. Schweizerkas is certainly honest and loyal, but he is also presented as extremely simple-minded, so that the moral issue never comes clearly into view. He believes, for instance, that the sergeant who has entrusted the box to him must have the money it contains in order to pay the soldiers who are in flight from the enemy—"if they don't get their pay they don't have to run away. They don't have to move a foot." And he has a child's dream of the fatherly sergeant patting him on the back when he does turn up with the cash: "Won't the sergeant be surprised? You have given me a pleasant disappointment, Schweizerkas, he'll say. I give you the cash-box to look after, and you bring it back again." But apart from this, Brecht spoils his own chances by making Schweizerkas throw the cash-box in the river instead of hiding it. Why Schweizerkas does this we are never told: it is a reported action which we never see, and about which we hear nothing from Schweizerkas himself. But if he were loyal, he would presumably hide the box, as in fact he intends to do, rather than throw it away, and Brecht simply does not bother to tell us why Schweizerkas behaves as he does—it may well be that fear overcomes his loyalty when he thinks he may be endangered. And having once thrown the box in the river there is nothing Schweizerkas can do. When the enemy tortures him and finally executes him, he cannot be persisting in loyalty, but only enduring helplessly without hope of escape. Thus the fact that he looks after the cash-box in the intention of restoring it to the regiment does not in itself lead to his death. He might have died in just the same way if he had kept the box to use the money for himself. And certainly no general conclusion follows about honesty being a bad policy. Yet the scene does have the superficial appearance of bearing out the prophecy made by Mother Courage in the first scene: Schweizerkas has been too honest, and, as she warned him, he suffers for it.

The case of Kattrin is different again. Here the deed of charity which she performs not only occurs at a climactic moment in the play, it is also one which is indisputably good. In beating a drum to warn the inhabitants of Magdeburg of an impending attack, Kattrin is trying to save the lives of the children in the city, about whom she has just been told, and her refusal to give up when threatened with instant death is an act of genuine heroism, so moving as to make us forget for a while all previous argument. Kattrin has a definite purpose, and she knows what she will suffer if she goes through with it. Her horror of war and of all cruelty, which makes her groan at night in her sleep and perhaps has robbed her of the power of speech, finds its true outlet and fulfilment here, and though she dies, we are glad for her and know she has acted rightly. Mother Courage may say, beforehand, that she "suffers from pity" ("leidet am Mitleid"), but this Nietzschean comment is of small account in comparison with the prolonged and exciting enactment of her bravery and compassion. (All the same, the fact that the comment is made at all is significant.)

We may, then, be inclined to say that the whole sense of the play is a refutation of the cynical and confused arguments put forward earlier, and that at its climax it asserts (in contrast, say, to *Galileo*) the value of martyrdom in a good cause. Given the position of the scene of Kattrin's death within the whole, this is an attractive view, and one which probably helps to account for a good deal of the praise which has been accorded to the play. But while I don't want to scorn that praise, I do want to say that the scene can also have the unfortunate effect of seeming to cap the arguments of the recruiter, the cook, and Mother Courage, invalid as these are. The two sons of Mother Courage have died "because they were virtuous," and now her daughter does the same, because she suffers from pity. If we do not watch out, the untruth implied in the earlier instances may obscure the truth contained in the last instance, and we shall revert to a feeling that virtue is a pointless thing after all.

Again, when we try to see the whole play in perspective, we must surely see that, for all the praise we accord to Kattrin, her action is politically without significance. She is not interested in the Catholic or the Protestant cause, she is not an early communist or even an early pacifist (since her action is meant to arouse warlike resistance, not a turning of the other cheek). She acts instinctively, to save children from harm, and while this is wholly praiseworthy, it is not linked at all to the larger issues with which the play, according to Brecht, is supposed to deal. We thought we were going to be shown the commercialism of war, to be confirmed in our anti-Fascism or persuaded towards it. Instead, we are offered a series of scenes, most of which are merely puzzling or confusing, as we try to sort out a grain of truth from a mass of paradoxes and only apparently illustrative patterns of events. The one truth that does emerge is one we readily assent to, but which did not need all this apparatus of paradox and implied political doctrine in order to make itself felt. It is right to save children, we agree, but what about the men on either side who will be killed in the battle which follows on Kattrin's warning, what about the great religious issues which were at stake, what about the responsibility of the individual in all these events? The scene of Kattrin's death only begins to raise the important issues: the others obscure them.

As the curtain falls on the last scene, with Mother Courage still pulling her wagon, alone, and imagining that Eilif at least is still, somewhere, alive, these questions remain unanswered. We return to the central character, and there seems little doubt that Brecht wanted us to feel both sympathy for her, though not too much sympathy, and condemnation of her for going on "supporting the war." But what else is she to do? The whole of Germany is involved in the conflict, her only way of keeping alive is by buying and selling to soldiers or civilians, and her case is dreadful to see. Yet no alternative offers itself, and as the play ends we are left, I think, with a sense of mere disaster. I mean by that that the earlier scenes have not really led to this end, though some of them may have appeared to do so. It is not because Mother Courage or her children believed or disbelieved in virtue of one kind or another, or because they were too eager to profit by war, that she now finds herself desolate. Nor have we been shown that powerful and general economic forces have ruined her, as we might well expect in a Marxist play. Nor again have we been shown, in the Greek fashion, an overruling Destiny at work. These things have merely happened, and the explanations or comments implicit in Brecht's presentation of them have for the greater part been misleading or spurious. There is a lack of unity and direction in the thought and structure of the play which neither the visual unity provided by the wagon nor the single moment of Kattrin's death can really compensate for.

On the whole this is not surprising, since Brecht's personal

statements, outside his plays, were never consistent; in fact they were, deliberately it seems, self-contradictory in the Hegelian tradition from end to end. At the time when he was insisting, in theory, that his audiences should think for themselves, Brecht was writing plays in which the audience was told exactly what to think, in terms which permitted no argument. (The spurious reasons advanced for killing a party comrade in *The Measures Taken* are a case in point.) On the one hand, Brecht's theory requires the "raw stuff of life," unadulterated with political views; on the other it requires that the playwright should through his plays inculcate Marxist doctrine. (Both requirements are made simultaneously, for instance, in the *Messingkauf Dialogues.*) Somehow, Brecht seems to have imagined, it was possible to combine the two, or perhaps he thought that a true representation of reality could only result in a representation of the doctrine which in his view faithfully reflected reality. But then again, throughout his life Brecht affirmed, concurrently with his belief in a political theatre, his conviction that the theatre was self-justifying, a purely artistic medium where the worker could see life unfold itself before him and enjoy it with increased enjoyment. There is never any development in him, so far as theory goes, from first to last: the contradictory statements continue to run alongside one another without either explanation or reconciliation. And this of course makes the well-known "Verfremdungseffekt," or "estrangement" or "alienation" effect, impossibly hard to realize or define. That it was meant somehow to reveal the truth of Marxist doctrine seems fairly certain. Yet Brecht's habitual illogicality in argument, whether theoretical or in the structure and writing of his plays, means that one is very seldom presented with a solidly based illustration from which to draw conclusions. Like Thomas Mann's so-called "irony," Brecht's "alienation" is not only double-edged, it operates with material that is itself ambiguous, only purporting to illustrate this point or that, while in reality it misuses concepts, takes broad similarities for identities, generalizes on too little evidence, and subtly introduces to the reader's or spectator's mind views which he may too readily accept at face-value, without due examination. Both Brecht and Mann, though poles apart in their political attitudes, belong to the same tradition of ambiguity and paradox which has undermined German literature for nearly two centuries now. It is time there was a change, and perhaps the history of Western Germany since 1945 suggests there may be at least grounds for hoping for one. But so long as the tradition goes uncriticized, as it has done for so long, we can expect the same weary list of misleading statements, pseudo-arguments, and actual falsehoods to continue. Brecht used to say that he was not claiming to be in the right, but trying to find out whether he *was* in the right. The question for his readers and spectators must be, was he trying anything like hard enough? (pp. 44-54)

Ronald Gray, "Brecht's 'Mother Courage'," in The Oxford Review, *No. 2, Trinity, 1966, pp. 44-54.*

KEITH A. DICKSON (essay date 1978)

[*In the following excerpt, Dickson analyzes Brecht's use of the Thirty Years' War as the background for* Mother Courage.]

Brecht began working on the idea for a play on the subject of the Thirty Years' War in 1939, just as C. V. Wedgwood was completing her own scholarly study of the same historical phenomenon. In her foreword to the 1949 reprint she wrote of her book: "It was written . . . under the advancing shadow of the Second World War, and it may be that the apprehension of those years can be felt vibrating from time to time in its pages." Brecht might well have said the same of his own account. Throughout the thirties he had turned out one work after another denouncing the German variant of Fascism, showing that its pernicious *Weltanschauung* leads inevitably to war. In the autumn of 1939, with Austria, Czechoslovakia, and Poland already under the Nazi yoke, it was all too clear that Hitler's foreign policy was about to plunge Europe into war on an unprecedented scale. Although theoretically the First World War might have furnished a more vivid illustration of Brecht's point, he was doubtless aware that it was still much too close to attempt an objective assessment. The Thirty Years' War, the nearest thing to a world war before 1914, facilitated a more dispassionate analysis in that spirit of "smoking observation" that Brecht sought to foster in his form of theatre.

"The Thirty Years' War," Brecht wrote in his notes on the play, "was one of the first large-scale wars that capitalism brought upon Europe." For him war belonged to that same process of economic exploitation that allegedly characterizes all class-based society, "the continuation of business by other means." This explains why, although all histories of the Thirty Years' War to date have ranked it amongst the most fanatical religious wars in history, Brecht exonerates religion from any part in the conflict of interests. In Scene 3 Mother Courage, who exploits both sides without compunction, offers her assessment of the war to the cook and the chaplain: "Wenn man die Großkopfigen reden hört, führens die Krieg nur aus Gottesfurcht und für alles, was gut und schön ist. Aber wenn man genauer hinsieht, sinds nicht so blöd, sondern führn die Krieg für Gewinn. Und anders würden die kleinen Leut wie ich auch nicht mitmachen" ["To hear the big shots talk you'd think they make war for fear of God and all things bright and beautiful. But if you take a closer look, they're not so stupid. They make war for profit. And ordinary folk like me wouldn't join in for any other reason, either"]. Mother Courage does not know the whole truth about this war, but she is certainly at this point articulating Brecht's Marxist attitude. (pp. 97-8)

Brecht's historical researches appear to have been, as usual, conscientious, and since he aimed neither at allegory nor at a tale of private woe, the seemingly arbitrary limits he has imposed on his account of the Thirty Years' War invite careful attention. A comprehensive study of the war would necessarily involve an analysis of the European situation prior to the outbreak of hostilities. The mutual antagonism of Habsburg and Bourbon, the Dutch problem, the emergent sense of national identity in Bohemia and Hungary, the rivalry of Denmark and Sweden, the formation of League and Union: all this and more is what sparked off the conflagration. Even if Brecht had begun his survey in 1618 he might reasonably have been expected to allude to the Bohemian crisis, the division into two main power blocs, the dashing of Protestant hopes at White Hill and the ensuing stalemate.

Brecht ignores all this. The first scene is set in a remote province in Sweden, where, as the recruiting-sergeant complains, there has been no war for years, and where men are in consequence happy but undisciplined. Sweden was more heavily committed than most countries after 1630 but it remained one of the few European countries the war never reached. The year too is interesting. After six years of bitter fighting 1624 was more a year of respite than of war, following Fred-

erick's enforced armistice with Ferdinand. But it was not without importance. It was the year of Mansfeld's visit to London to drum up recruits and subsidies—to the nearest month contemporary with Brecht's opening scene; it was a year of tension in Austria as anxious eyes were kept on the precarious balance of power in Bohemia; Urban VIII, newly elected, was making his anti-Habsburg policies felt, thus providing moral support for the foxy antics of Richelieu, another newcomer to the power game in 1624; John George of Saxony recognized Maxmilian's Electorate in the interest of German solidarity; it was also the year of Wallenstein's spectacular land-grab in Bohemia. Any of these incidents might have introduced Brecht's anatomy of the war, but he turns instead to peaceful Dalarne, almost as far from the nerve-centre of the war as he could have got, and ignored by all the standard histories. It is a historical fact that a three-year truce, a temporary breathing space in the protracted dynastic struggle of the Vasas, was nearing its end. This was followed by four years of intensive campaigning, during which Gustavus, obsessed with the dream of the Baltic as a "Swedish lake," secured a valuable foothold on the Continent and muzzled the Habsburg's faithful watchdog, Sigismund III. Gustavus's contemporaries saw little significance in his invasion of the Continent at the time and were obliged to look up Sweden in their atlases, while for the Emperor it was "halt a Kriegel mehr." Gustavus had in fact only been biding his time until Germany would be forced to accept his offer of intervention. All this is indisputably history, but it seems to belong to a different chapter. Few histories of the war can afford to trace so remote a connection between a recruiting-campaign in Dalarne and the war in Germany, let alone follow the fortunes of Gustavus in Poland as Brecht does in the second, third, and fourth scenes of his play.

The new perspective created by Brecht's opening gambit suggests that sooner or later war affects the whole world and directly or indirectly finds its way into the remotest valleys. Perhaps Brecht had Sweden's traditional neutrality in mind, for in such a war as this no country is truly neutral, and even if armed conflict never reaches its borders, its manpower and its economy will not be immune for long. The most important effect of Brecht's opening, however, is the implication that the familiar division into "periods," "phases," and "spheres of influence" is a mere textbook convenience which has little to do with the reality of war. S. R. Gardiner notes that 1648 marks the end simultaneously of the Thirty Years' War of Germany and the Eighty Years' War of the Netherlands, whereas "for France 1648 is hardly a date at all," since peace in one quarter for her merely meant she could devote greater energy to the continuing conflict with Spain. If at times even the historian admits that wars are blurred at the edges, for Brecht it is an axiom that affects the very structure of his play.

Towards the middle of the piece, and with no attempt at continuity, Brecht's own history of the war and that of the traditional historian momentarily overlap. We are made eyewitnesses of the sack of Magdeburg, the most sensational atrocity of the whole war, for which, Schiller said, "history has no language and poetry no brush." But Brecht's scene is in a very low key. We remain on the periphery of the event, seeing only its impact on the lives of Mother Courage and Kattrin, nor is there any indication of the criminal blundering that led to it or of the reprisals that followed. Again, we watch troops dodge the funeral of Tilly, who had been mortally wounded in a skirmish with the Swedes near Ingolstadt. It is empha-

Helene Weigel as Mother Courage.

which changed hands so many times that historians do not bother to keep the score. This insignificant Protestant victory costs only one life, but Brecht includes it in his survey of the war because it is the life of Mother Courage's last remaining child.

The last three scenes reflect faithfully the growing sense of confusion and despair, which drained the war of whatever idealism and sense of purpose it may once have had for at least some of the contestants. Mother Courage comments on the appalling results of famine and pestilence, those seasoned camp-followers of both armies, which culminated in reliably documented outbreaks of cannibalism. "The war reveals a spectacle of purposelessness and hopelessness," writes one historian of this phase, "a general fatalism and cynicism in wickedness seem to deepen as the war drags its interminable length." Brecht's army cook says simply: "Die Welt stirbt aus" ["the world is dying out"], and this is very much the impression left by the last few scenes of the play. At the end of the last scene, with Mother Courage now bereft of all her children, it still seems as though the war has a long life ahead of it, as the chaplain cynically predicted a few years earlier, and the armies march on. The final chorus prophesies that the war will last a hundred years. That the prophecy is wrong by exactly eighty-eight years is not the point, for war in Brecht's sense is continuous, an ineluctable condition of pre-revolutionary society. By choosing this particularly degrading, destructive, and protracted war as the subject of his play, and by readjusting the historical focus, Brecht has succeeded in suggesting a war that has no geographical boundaries and no clearly definable beginning and end. It bursts the artificial limits imposed on it by the historian, reaching right down to our own century and beyond. (pp. 98-102)

> *Keith A. Dickson, in his* Towards Utopia: A Study of Brecht, *Oxford at the Clarendon Press, 1978, 332 p.*

ERICH SPEIDEL   (essay date 1982)

[In the following excerpt, Speidel discusses the interaction between the individual and society in Mother Courage.*]*

The interaction between the individual and the collective reaches a more sophisticated level in *Mutter Courage und ihre Kinder* (*Mother Courage and Her Children*) [than in Brecht's earlier play *Herr Puntila und sein Knecht Matti* (*Herr Puntila and His Servant Matti*)]. As the play is set in the Thirty Years' War, the historical dimension is particularly obvious. Mutter Courage herself is, it is true, a humble person and far removed from the greatness of a Gustavus Adolphus or a Wallenstein. But she nevertheless stands out as a memorable and impressive figure because of her intelligence, alertness and immense vitality. She is indefatigable, hardworking, unflappable, and has the strength to carry on where others would have given up long ago—in short, she is the domineering figure in the play and the centre of her world. She is in many ways a likeable person, and her main concern to bring her children through the war unharmed certainly has our sympathy, so much so that some producers have found it easy to present her as a tragic figure who is noble and courageous but is destroyed by an anonymous and uncontrollable fate in the shape of war. Brecht's intentions were otherwise. In the first instance, it was Mutter Courage's decision to join the war in order to make a living, and she has therefore by her own will placed herself and her children under the laws

sized that his death will not alter the course of the war in the slightest. When Mother Courage asks the chaplain anxiously whether this means the end of the war (and thus her financial ruin) he replies cynically, and entirely in the spirit of Brecht's own attitude to heroism: "Weil der Feldhauptmann hin ist? Sein Sie nicht kindisch. Solche finden sich ein Dutzend, Helden gibts immer" ["Because the commander is gone? Don't be childish. There are dozens like him—there are always heroes"]. Similarly, we almost encroach upon the "real" scene of the war again after the Battle of Lützen, which must on any reckoning be accounted one of its major events. Even Ferdinand is said to have grieved over the death of his most formidable and chivalrous adversary, but no tears are shed for Gustavus in Brecht's play. His death causes only a temporary "outbreak of peace," as Mother Courage describes it, during which the impetuous Eilif faces a firing-squad for committing an offence that only a few scenes earlier had been rewarded as an act of heroism. After passing thus close to the centre of gravity of the war we leave it again and move into its "last phase," as the historians usually call it, with no explanation of the shift of emphasis from the Sweden-Habsburg axis to the predominantly Bourbon-Habsburg conflict, which can be dated roughly from the arrival in Brussels of the French declaration of war on Spain in May 1635. The action of the play passes on into war-torn Saxony where the Imperial Army mounts an unsuccessful attempt to storm Halle, of war. And secondly, she is bound to fail, in spite of all her personal efforts, because she cannot expect to escape in the long run from whatever misfortune will befall the collective to which she now belongs. This collective is the army. Of course, as she herself points out, what is a major setback for the army need not be the same for its individual members, and she did at one stage benefit from a defeat because she acquired a horse to pull the cart; it was taken away from her again after order had been restored. Even when she falls into the hands of the enemy, she can adapt to the new situation and continue business as usual. But the army is in the war to destroy or get destroyed, business is dangerous and leaves no room for pity, and Courage is not only the caring mother but also the "hyena of the battlefield."

The titles at the beginning of every scene remind us of the wider political and military dimensions which reflect and determine the conditions under which the army, including Courage and her children, have to live. If the destruction caused by warfare continues for a long time—the play shows us twelve of the thirty years of the war—there will be fewer material goods for everyone to share; the room for independent manoeuvre on the part of the individual will diminish. Sooner or later everyone whose spoon is not long enough to keep at a safe distance from the fighting will be affected. The disintegration of order and discipline, for example, may show itself in the rape of Courage's daughter; the general impoverishment of the collective must in turn adversely affect her business. The events on the stage show us what happens to Mutter Courage and her family, to some particular individuals; the titles inform us of what happens to the collective. As the messages of the titles get bleaker, so eventually do the lives of the individuals we see on the stage. In the end it is the development of the collective which determines the circumstances in which its members will find themselves.

The titles and the army are not the only references to a wider and more general framework we receive in this play. We are also continually reminded of the fact that expectations, attitudes or misfortunes which are expressed by or affect the figures in the play are not only experienced by these few individuals. They are also shared by a large number of people who in this war find themselves in a similar situation. These more general experiences are expressed in the songs. When Mutter Courage first enters the stage she answers the question as to who she is by one word "Geschäftsleut" ("trader") and then bursts into a song which illustrates the predicament not only of her own case but of all people doing business in war. They are dealing with customers whose numbers decrease with every battle, and who must therefore be induced to spend all their money before the fighting begins. At the beginning of the new season in the year, in the war, and in the business the dead are of no use; trade must be done with the living. The last stanza of this song with which the play ends reinforces the point that, if Courage wants to remain in business, nothing has changed except that her own children now also belong to the useless waste the war has left behind. But this dehumanizing fact does not merely apply to her alone; behind her we must see all the others to whom the same "fate" applies.

In the same way the song sung in the second scene by Eilif and completed by Courage illustrates the general contrast in the attitudes of the young, adventurous, carefree soldiers and of the women who stayed behind. The point of view of the young, which determines the first two stanzas sung by Eilif,

gives way to that of the women who have the last word and whose fears are proved to be justified by the end of the song as well as the play. And just as Eilif and his mother allow their personal attitudes to be seen in a wider context, so Yvette, the camp prostitute, shows us in the "Lied vom Fraternisieren" ("Fraternizing Song") that the misery of her own existence is suffered by innumerable girls whose love has led them into the same situation. The use of songs in this play reaches its climax in the fourth scene when Mutter Courage sings "Das Lied von der grossen Kapitulation" ("The Song of the Great Capitulation"). This is the point where she, in Brecht's view, acts most despicably, because she not only persuades herself that inaction in the face of injustice from above is the best attitude, but in doing so also discourages the young soldier from lodging a justified complaint. Mutter Courage first describes the attitude of the young who think they are special, and then the resignation of later years when one's spirit has been broken. In the refrain of the song, the individual is seen as marching in a military band and contributing his "kleinen Ton" ["little note"] to the music of the collective. Then, merely by changing the punctuation, Brecht turns the well-known saying "Der Mensch denkt, Gott lenkt" ("Man thinks but God directs") into almost its opposite: "Der Mensch denkt: Gott lenkt" ("Man thinks that God directs"), a view which is then dismissed as without substance. It is left to the spectator to conclude that if God is not in control it must be the officer commanding the band, i.e. a human being whose orders may be fallible and can be opposed. Of course there is no point in anyone acting on his own; but if the whole band decided to disobey, the officer in charge would be without power to enforce his command. The importance of the collective and of the collective action is brought out particularly strongly in this song, and so is the conclusion that if we are treated unjustly it is not the strength of authority but the weakness of those receiving and obeying orders that is to blame. The real enemy therefore is in the minds of the oppressed who capitulate because they assume far too readily that they are helpless, and the criticism of the song is directed against all who, like Mutter Courage, in similar situations persuade themselves and others that placid acceptance of orders from above is always the best option.

The play *Mutter Courage und ihre Kinder* therefore, while using one particularly strong and impressive individual and her family to illustrate the point, always carefully relates the events taking place on the stage to a far larger and wider context, constantly indicating that behind the demonstrations on the stage there are large numbers of people in the same or similar positions, with identical or at least similar motivations, interests, reactions or attitudes. The real concern of the play therefore is obviously to show the interaction between individual and collective, and to indicate that of these two aspects the collective is by far the more important factor. Thus Brecht has built up a complex framework of personal, social, economic and political forces which eventually determine the actions of individual figures. Those producers, however, who have presented Mutter Courage as a Niobe-like figure who loses her children because an inexplicable fate in the form of war has struck her have ignored the complexity of the determining factors. . . . (pp. 57-60)

Erich Speidel, "The Individual and Society," in Brecht in Perspective, *edited by Graham Bartram and Anthony Waine, Longman, 1982, pp. 45-62.*

SIEGLINDE LUG (essay date 1984)

[In the following excerpt, Lug demonstrates Brecht's demystification of motherhood in Mother Courage.]

"Alles wandelt sich" ["everything changes"], the beginning of a Brecht poem, reveals a fundamental attitude towards all being and is not necessarily limited to changes in a Marxist direction. This attitude places human systems and concepts into a historical framework, in contrast to accepting them as reflections of eternal human nature. A world that was made by man is subject to change by man—or woman, as one should add. Likewise, feminist criticism would have no basis without the conviction that present conditions are historically developed, thus changeable. Since both Brecht's writings and feminist writings are essentially re-visions, they imply a more or less hidden agenda for change.

Brecht's technique of showing the world as changeable is the *Verfremdungseffekt* ["alienation effect"] in its most general sense; it is his unexpected use of the familiar in order to stimulate fresh thinking about it and thus question it. That technique tends to deflate every sort of myth about human nature, including those about women. The idealized image of woman as man's redeemer and representative of absolute goodness and purity is just such a myth cherished in literature since medieval courtly love poetry and also in the real life of people who had the means and leisure to develop and uphold such dreams; as Simone de Beauvoir succinctly stated: "The myth of woman is a luxury." Since in Brecht's literary world adverse economic conditions play so major a role, luxurious dreams have difficulty surviving. (p. 3)

The very word "mother" in our culture seems to arouse a whole host of sentimental feelings, so much so that Brecht's increased use of mother figures in his dramas has been called indicative of a "mellowing" attitude, even though the figures themselves may contradict such feelings. Since Mutter Courage is sometimes called the archetypal mother figure, we should investigate the depiction of her maternal side systematically. The title itself, i.e., the combination of "mother" and "courage," conjures up the stereotypical image of the mother courageously fighting for or defending her children. That image is, however, immediately demystified: what people called courage—she explains matter-of-factly—was the consideration of business survival; in the process, of course, she had to endanger her children and herself. The notion that the mother image ought to be kept pure for the children is ridiculed when she admonishes the sergeant to speak decently to her in front of the children. Her "concern" is due to her literal interpretation of his use of the expression "auf den Arm nehmen," which is mild in comparison to the following description of the different fathers of all her children—which happens also in front of the children. An added irony here is that by convention motherhood is only good—even sacred—when it is legal. Only in marriage can fathers have legitimate control over their offspring and thus the future. In *Mutter Courage* such assumptions are shattered.

When Brecht puts pompous religious phrases like "unglückliche Mutter, schmerzensreiche Gebärerin" into Mutter Courage's mouth, the discrepancy between those clichéd words and her very being creates parody. The fact that the children have to draw her wagon shows clearly that her business is as much in need of the children as it is for their benefit. When the commander praises Eilif and hopes that Mutter Courage has more sons for the army, Brecht evokes the whole irony of the cultural paradox of asking mothers to love their sons with unconditional devotion, but to sacrifice them joyfully and proudly as cannon-fodder. On the rediscovery of her son after two years, the "joy" does not rob Mutter Courage of her quick business mind for even one second: she immediately sees it as an opportunity to get a fantastic price for her capon by taking advantage of the cook's position.

The third scene presents a striking parody of the daughter's initiation by the mother into love's social rites. Mixed with the clichés "Himmelsmacht" for love and the wooing of the woman described as "the man kissing the ground under her feet," she asks her if she washed her feet, and ends with the practical conclusion that after all those beautiful games, she will be the man's servant. Thus we find an effective literary clarification of the dichotomy between the ideal of the pedestal and the lack of a "chair" in reality, i.e., the idealized image as against the scarcity of practical rights throughout history. On the same page, Mutter Courage ironically refers to her son's counting on mother love for getting money, using the business term "spekulieren" ["speculate"] to express it. As long as her business is not harmed, however, she will live up to the institutional expectations of mother love. When Schweizerkas's life is in danger, she bargains for it as for a coveted item in a bazaar, just as the love for profitably completing a business deal kept her from rushing to greet Eilif after a two-year absence. Her self-control when confronted with her dead son's body confirms her overpowering urge for survival.

We understand Mutter Courage's statement that a historic moment to her is not the burial of the Commander but the injury of her daughter in the context not of a specifically maternal feeling but in that of all her disillusioned remarks about wars, the structure of power and priorities and what they do to the little people. In fact, through her remark, Brecht also questions our traditional concept of history, which stresses war, institutions, and a few prominent personalities to the exclusion of the lives of the majority of the people.

When peace comes briefly, Mutter Courage is ready to go through the motions of motherhood: she "owes" it to Schweizerkas to go to the services, including wearing a black mourning dress for the occasion. A little later, after Eilif is led to his execution in her absence, her questions about him are answered with so many hints that the mythical "true" mother would never have missed them; but she is too preoccupied with business and survival; thus the irony of the end of the play, when she thinks she still has one child, is made possible.

Even Mutter Courage's rejection of the cook's offer to join him without Kattrin is more complex than "maternal." On the one hand, Kattrin, besides being her daughter, has been her faithful companion through hard times; on the other, the cook presents an opportunity only slightly better than what she already has. She neither claims to love him nor does she have any illusions about what he or any rather poor man can offer her. Since Mutter Courage always proves to be a quick practical thinker, there is no reason to assume that she followed a vague maternal instinct rather than humane and rational considerations.

The dramatic nature of the play's final scenes is characteristic of Brecht's later dramas. He protracts the action beyond likelihood when Kattrin is shot only after she has become victorious; then we do see a glimpse of a bizarre and touching image of the mother regressing and singing a lullabye for her dead daughter. This scene destroys the critical distance of the audience as much as the eleventh scene, for which that claim is usually made. With such an ending, Brecht's anger at the audience's misinterpretations of his message is surprising. The emotions evoked by the lullaby scene are, of course, enhanced for those who are imbued with the sentimental motherhood images of our culture; it is easy then to forget the implications of the portrayals earlier in the play which instead seem to represent one great questioning or refutation of the sentimental notion of motherhood as expressed in the title.

At the end, Mutter Courage is driven on by her business or rather survival instinct, and we cannot help but see her with the wagon carrying on her petty commerce, even if she finds out the truth about her last child. Business, not the search for her missing Eilif, is the driving force in her. If Mutter Courage is an archetype of anything, she must be the archetypal businessperson or survivor. She touches us less as a mother than as one of the little people who continues living and doing business doggedly because she does not see the world as changeable. Being a mother for her is comparable to the fate of poverty-stricken mothers of all times where the home—if there is one—is not a refuge but a tough workplace. Mutter Courage does not fit into the emotional dream of the maternal, although the play's title and the lullabye scene evoke such notions; through her, the concept is demystified. (pp. 8-11)

Sieglinde Lug, "The 'Good' Woman Demystified,"
in Communications from the International Brecht
Society, *Vol. XIV, No. 1, November, 1984, pp. 3-16.*

DAVID RICHARD JONES (essay date 1986)

[*Jones is an American educator and critic specializing in drama. In the following excerpt, he uses the text of* Mother Courage *and the notes in the* Couragemodell *to demonstrate Brecht's method of presenting characters for judgment by the audience.*]

In the [*Couragemodell*], the photographs illustrating the ground arrangements of the action are followed by ten photographs of Helene Weigel in the title part. Brecht's label for these photos, "The contradictory nature of the figure," epitomizes what the scores of other photographs reveal about Weigel's Courage. Her moods were very distinct but very changeable. She was cocky, contemplative, lusty, skeptical, amused, bemused, ostentatious, self-consciously shy, and desolate. Lovers of tragedy should note that she smiled more often than she frowned. Her activities also changed rapidly, and the objects with which she interacted changed accordingly. Her facial expressions were exceptionally varied; she appears to have been a great mugger. I have received such contradictory impressions from my repeated viewings of these photographs that I sometimes doubt that any actress could blend all of these varied expressions into a single characterization. But then I recall how unBrechtian are the words "blend" and "single." Courage's dialectical existence depends upon the extremity of change in her nature.

Aside from her face, her body was difficult to see. A head scarf covered her hair in all but one scene (scene 8, when she was awakened by the bells of peace), and in that scene her hair was tied up on her head—she did not let her hair down even in sleep. Her body below the neck was draped with baggy, lumpy clothes, leaving only her hands and shoetops

visible. Her body betrayed the years of hard labor that had bent her into a graceless clench. She showed little of what is commonly defined as sexual attractiveness. Yet in her rare moments of intimacy and relaxation with the Cook or the Chaplain, Weigel hinted at another time when her body was more attractive, more liberated, and more expressive.

The woman in the photographs—Weigel's figure as much as Brecht's character—shows striking vitality. In the "contradictory nature of the figure" pages, Weigel's Courage appears to have had a basically dynamic cast: she cocked a thumb to accent a question, smartly thrust out a leg during a moment of musical exuberance, struck a match against the wagon while she sat on its steps, let her mouth utter a hearty laugh that her hand tried to smother. She seems to have been always in motion, though she was not always crossing the stage. The changing props (belts, boots, bowls, harness, coins, socks) contribute to the impression that this person was always performing a task, solving a problem, avoiding a danger, and handling the affairs of business and family. But this vitality, in Brecht's view, was itself a contradictory phenomenon. As he wrote about the characters in *The Tutor,* one should never doubt the bottomless vitality of the bourgeois: "Europe has had two hundred years in which to learn how horribly vital their class is."

Weigel's Courage was famously vital but also famously immobile, a symbol of postwar exhaustion and shock. The powerful moments of her desolation were all the more powerful because they were such a stunning change, so apparently "out of character." Naturally, these moments occurred during incidents of grief and failure, when Weigel could show Courage in pain, pessimistic, self-critical, and once or twice in a stupor so deep as to be truly terrifying. Students of Brecht's theory may be full of arguments proving that Courage is not a typical Western tragic heroine. But she certainly looks like one in these photographs. She looks like a woman in extremities.

Contradiction and change were indeed at the heart of Weigel's characterization. I no sooner call up one of her sharply focused expressions than it produces the memory of its opposite. I no sooner assert one element of her nature than I want to add "But then" or "And yet." She was a woman experiencing extreme despair and desolation, but then she always bounced back to energetic activity and a brighter countenance. And yet, as my understanding of her character grows, I realize that this resiliency was less an indication of vitality than of a failure to learn or to understand. So the viewer's reactions are turned and twisted against each other.

The photographs help us to understand Courage as a physical creature, but we need the descriptions in the modelbook's notes to penetrate her moral character. In truth this imposing character imposes less physically than morally, gains size with her words, questions, ideas, and actions. Courage is preoccupied with people and problems outside herself, with a world to which she stands in relation. She is rarely self-absorbed because in a world such as hers it pays (in several senses) to be outer-directed. And because she is intelligent, she has ideas about that world; she even likes to argue in support of them, when it is safe to do so. As with all public debaters of large questions, Courage puts herself forward as a subject for argument, which is the Brechtian ideal in character: someone about whom we need to think. And since her ideas are largely concerned with personal action, to debate her ideas is necessarily to debate her actions. Thus the play's obvious subject is her philosophic character in action.

(Is such a statement of the play's subject merely a truism, a description of the subject in all good plays? Not to the same extent as in Brecht's mature works. Perhaps the "philosophic character in action" is the subject of all of Brecht's plays? No, for we cannot judge Baal, Garga, or Galy Gay as objectively as Shen Te, Grusha, or Galileo. The early characters' makeup offers no basis for such a judgment.)

The argument over Courage's character always reduces to this vigorously roasted chestnut of moral philosophy: Is she right or wrong? The debaters' voices are varied and inconsistent, for the question has intrigued actors, producers, directors, professors, students, critics, and Brecht himself. The debate is further fueled by serious questions about Brecht's dramaturgy. Did he successfully frame the question in the drama of *Mother Courage?* Did he frame an answer? Is there a single answer? When does the audience hear or see or understand it? In what context is the assessment of her rightness or wrongness made? How are we to judge?

Brecht's dramaturgical method of judging Courage was inductive. He placed one thing after another until a final conclusion was obvious. In the opposite (and more usual) method of characterization, authors immediately reveal the general nature of their characters. In the typical melodrama of any century, characters—dirty villains, virtuous maidens, clever sidekicks, and spotless heroes—are fixed elements in a schematized moral universe and are valued precisely for their one-dimensional sturdiness of type—their consistency of personality. In most modern playscripts, the characters' general natures are described in headnotes, either at the play's beginning or on their first entrances. For example: "Lady Britomart is a woman of fifty or thereabouts, well dressed and yet careless of her dress, well bred and quite reckless of her breeding," and so on for another 125 words. "Mrs. Boyle . . . her face has now assumed that look which ultimately settles down on the faces of the women of the working-class," and so on. "Cabot . . . his face is as hard as if it were hewn out of a boulder, yet there is a weakness in it, a petty pride in its own narrow strength." Of course such explanatory notes are useful, but the authorial habit of generalizing at the beginning can condition the expectations and generalize the reactions of readers, directors, and actors who should be asking questions of the characters. Perhaps that is why Brecht never used headnotes in his plays, preferring instead to present experience, especially a character's behavior, in a moment-by-moment or linear mode, so that conclusions could be reached rather than received.

This is how he approached the character of Courage in his *Couragemodell* notes and in his directing of Helene Weigel. Avoiding headnotes or initial summaries, he began by dramatizing her experiences, her changes, and her contradictions. Only at the end of his twelve scenes did he offer a general judgment: that she was wrong for having failed to learn from her experiences.

At the beginning, in his Prologue, he offered the audience little but Courage's intention: to head someplace (the war zone, as the song makes clear) and to "shake a leg" so that she can sell to the troops. Weigel showed a great zest for business and an eagerness for experience, but this introduction was imagistic and impressionistic rather than evaluative and expository.

In scene 1, Brecht saw Courage as combining this same zestfulness with a graver tone, since she was now in contact with the war. Meeting the recruiters, she combined her lighthearted "Courage act" with another act performed for her children—a fortune-telling routine that included dire prophecies about the horrors of war. She overtly managed the early part of the scene but lost control of events when she tried to sell the Sergeant a belt buckle while trying to watch her children. By the scene's end, she had lost Eilif to the war. Weigel did not play Courage as stupid or unmindful of the threat posed by the recruiters. Her Courage wanted to keep her son, but she also needed to make her sales pitch, for that son might starve if she failed. So Weigel and Brecht made it immediately clear that her story was about the conflicting claims of business and motherhood, that her character was poised between contradictory demands ("merchant-mother," or "businesswoman-Mother Courage"), and that the inevitable consequence of certain actions in her contradictory situation would be loss.

At the conclusion of scene 1, Weigel's Courage was dismayed. At the beginning of scene 2, however, she bargained with the Cook in an artful and flirtatious manner. This change in her character carried an important lesson for the spectator: never again could one assume that her personality would be continuous between scenes. Nor could onstage characters trust her to be consistent from moment to moment. At the end of scene 2 she hugged Eilif, then immediately slapped him.

At the beginning of scene 3, the audience saw Courage from a new angle. In the model, Brecht stressed how hard she worked, her "energy and competence" and her "unflagging readiness" for work. "She is hardly ever seen not working." Even in the surprise attack, moving quickly from task to task amid confusion, she consciously attempted to save money and lives. This combination of business and family obligations absorbed her energies throughout the three extended sections of scene 3. When the captured Swiss Cheese returned and the Sergeant interrogated Courage, Weigel sat rummaging in her basket pretending to be what she usually was, "a busy businesswoman with no time for formalities." But at the end of the questioning, she lost control and ran after her son and his captors, almost revealing her motherhood. At the scene's climax, Courage's ability to manage business and family simultaneously was put to the sternest tests when she bargained for Swiss Cheese's life and again when she had to deny his corpse. Brecht brought the dramatic tension and suspense to a peak in order to provide another schematic illustration of her conflicting necessities (the wagon or the boy) and her contradictory motives (stay in business or protect the family).

A spectator might wonder what Courage will do after enduring such extraordinary suffering. Weigel changed. Brecht recommended that scene 4 ("The Song of the Great Capitulation") be played bitterly, stressing depravity rather than dejection or righteous anger. Weigel surprised the audience by changing, during the scene, from a distressed mother with a grievance to a cynical spokeswoman for capitulation to the powerful. She changed again in scene 5. Brecht wrote: "*A new Courage.* A change has taken place in Courage. She has sacrificed her son to the wagon and now she defends the wagon like a tigress. She has been hardened by the hard bargains she drives." To emphasize the cost of her change, Weigel downed several glasses of schnapps at the scene's beginning. For scene 6, which shows the Courage camp at rest during Tilly's funeral, Brecht noted: "Again Courage has changed. Increasing prosperity has made her softer and more human." The transformation is so attractive to the Chaplain (though Brecht was amusingly skeptical of his real motives) that he eventually proposes to his boss. Weigel accentuated the contrast of Courage's physical relaxation and ironic gaiety with her previous moods. When the bleeding Kattrin ran in, however, Weigel's Courage showed her distress and instantly reversed her position on the war. She had just decided to invest in its future, but now she cursed it with all the vehemence of an offended mother.

Courage again reverses her position on war in scene 7, the short scene that is mainly another rendition of the Courage song. Now she will not listen to anyone "running down the war," because the war provides. Brecht prefaced this scene with a projected title that told the audience she was at "the height of her business career," and he made her success visible by draping her in jewelry. Thus her endorsement of war was undercut by her "bribed" appearance and by the endorsement's juxtaposition with the ending to scene 6. Nevertheless, Weigel, marching at the side of the wagon, showed the prosperous Courage to be "cheerful" and in "full possession of her vitality." She showed how thoroughly agreeable riches could be to Mother Courage.

In Brecht's production of this play, scene 7 was the end of act 1, and its startling contrast with the end of scene 6 epitomized the contradictory and rapid changes that Brecht and Weigel had shown in Courage during the first act. Change, after all, is primary in Brechtian drama. Characters can change, the wagon can change, circumstances can change, the world can change. And these changes take place in his work so that the audience will see a changing world as a model for their own world, in which change is always needed and possible. Writers who dramatize unchanging characters in an unchanging world are often guilty of an unconscious pessimism. "Things long unchanged appear unchangeable," said Brecht.

The second act of *Mother Courage* (scenes 8-12) is only half as long as the first, but in it Brecht continued the dramaturgic pattern of scene-by-scene contrasts and strengthened the pattern within Courage's character of contradiction leading to loss. He filled scene 8 with images of change: Courage changes men for the first time in years; the Chaplain changes clothes and vocations; and war changes to peace, which changes to war again. In major sections of scene 8 Brecht analyzed characters from earlier scenes (the Cook, Yvette, and Eilif) and how they had changed, usually for the worse, under the impress of time and war. Brecht directed the degenerative cases strongly. He made Yvette—now "The Countess Starhemburg, my good people"—snooty, vulgar, and grotesque and portrayed Eilif as apparently prosperous but coarse, surly, and degraded by violence. Prospering in this war, the episodes argued, imperils the soul.

As she crossed the terrain of act 2, Helene Weigel showed the steadily downward curve in Courage's material conditions and humanity. She began with a lighthearted treatment of scene 8, specifically, Courage's decision to invest once more in the war's continuation. She showed Courage suffering from cold and hunger in scene 9 and behaving like a draft horse under the desperate conditions of scene 10. In the final scene, she sank further into a blank, animalistic condition. Through these scenes Weigel and Brecht simplified the character's line until little remained but the problem of whether to stay with the war and the assessment of the damages. When she discovered that the war had started again at the

end of scene 8, Weigel was "overjoyed" and "in high spirits." She packed up her wagon and her company with the certainty that both business and family matters would now improve, because "Now there's a war again, everything will work out all right" (her line was cut from the play's final edition). But the optimistic mood of this moment was crosscut by dramatic irony (the audience and the other characters knew of Eilif's execution) and by juxtaposition with her about-face in scene 9 when she was once more caught in the snares of the merchant-mother contradiction. When she understood that Kattrin could not accompany her to the Cook's inn at Utrecht, "Weigel showed plainly that Courage thought the proposition over—she thinks every proposition over," but no matter how long she calculated, she could not avoid recognizing the necessity of loss. In scene 12, Weigel created two unforgettable images of Courage—an image of grief when singing the lullaby over the dead Kattrin and an image of eternal enterprise when she marched off into the endless war zone represented by the turntable, pulling her empty wagon. She was the merchant-mother at the nadir of her life.

In the modelbook, Brecht developed each of these twelve scenes, each of Courage's many moods, and a host of details about her character and behavior. On his penultimate page, he gave a general note on the leading character of his production. Entitled "Mother Courage learns nothing," it begins, "In the last scene Weigel's Courage seemed to be eighty years old. And she understands nothing." In the scene with the peasants at the end, Weigel reacted "only to remarks connected with the war" and missed their barbed accusation about Kattrin's death. After all this loss and suffering and punishment, after all these opportunities to change her basic situation, she was no smarter than she had been at the beginning. If she had more children to lose to the war, she no doubt would. This graphic and compelling conclusion came from a playwright who had originally written his play (in the fall of 1939) as a warning against failing to learn from a war that was just beginning. In 1949-1951, with the war behind him, Brecht the director could add the pedagogical imperative: if Courage failed to learn, if it was too late for her, then an audience could (must) learn by studying her failure. And such study was easiest, this note made clear, in a theatre of alienation where the leading actress attacked the part of Courage with "a way of playing it which does not lead to audience identification with the principal character (heroine)."

With these words of judgment at the model's end, the argument over Courage's moral character can begin. (Courage could have stayed home or otherwise avoided the war, goes a familiar argument. Brecht believed that the historical character could have done so, though her modern counterpart in the age of global warfare could not.) But before the argument becomes too involved, we should note the obvious: the argument begins at the end of the model, as we leave the metaphorical theatre after having observed her changes, decisions, necessities, and failures. If we finally reject her, we must not reject her at first (in the Prologue or in scene 1), for at that point she has not yet failed to learn from the war; she has only failed to know about it, which is different. If we judge Courage too quickly, we may fail to learn, for moral condemnation frequently leads audiences to cease evaluating characters and analyzing their actions. First study, then moralize, Brecht might have said. (pp. 105-13)

David Richard Jones, "Bertolt Brecht and 'Couragemodell 1949': Meaning in Detail," in his Great Directors at Work: Stanislavsky, Brecht, Kazan,

Brook, *University of California Press, 1986, pp. 78-137.*

FURTHER READING

Bentley, Eric. "The Songs in *Mother Courage*." In *Varieties of Literary Experience: Eighteen Essays in World Literature*, edited by Stanley Burnshaw, pp. 45-74. New York: New York University Press, 1962.
   Discusses the dramatic function of the songs in *Mother Courage*, particularly their ability to universalize the action of the play.

————. *The Brecht Memoir*, pp. 37ff. New York: PAJ Publications, 1985.
   Numerous references to *Mother Courage* and to Bentley's involvement with various productions of the play.

Brecht, Bertolt. "Model for *Mother Courage and Her Children*, Scenes XI and XII." In *Directors on Directing: A Source Book of the Modern Theatre*, edited by Toby Cole and Helen Krich Chinoy, pp. 333-46. Indianapolis: Bobbs-Merrill Co., 1963.
   Notes from Brecht's *Couragemodell*, in which he expands on stage directions, provides acting advice, and offers insight into characters and themes.

Brooker, Peter. "A Choice of Critics." In his *Bertolt Brecht: Dialectics, Poetry, Politics*, pp. 179-91. London: Croom Helm, 1988.
   Includes a summary of the critical reaction to *Mother Courage* and argues that critics attempt to appropriate the play to serve their own ideologies.

Brustein, Robert. "Brecht versus Broadway." In his *Seasons of Discontent: Dramatic Opinions 1959-1965*, pp. 152-55. New York: Simon and Schuster, 1965.
   Review of a 1963 American production of *Mother Courage* that criticizes actress Anne Bancroft for creating a sympathetic Mother Courage.

————. "Thoughts from Abroad." In his *The Third Theatre*, pp. 117-22. New York: Alfred A. Knopf, 1969.
   Unfavorable review of a 1965 production of *Mother Courage* by England's National Theatre, directed by William Gaskill.

Bryant-Bertail, Sarah. "Women, Space, Ideology: *Mutter Courage und ihre Kinder*." In *Brecht: Women and Politics*. The Brecht Yearbook, edited by John Fuegi, Gisela Bahr, and John Willett, pp. 43-61, Vol. 12. Detroit: Wayne State University Press, 1983.
   Feminist critique of Brecht's work which concludes: "In analyzing the sign systems of *Mutter Courage*, I found that, in terms of space and time, all those systems could be read as part of a cyclical economy that entailed the destruction of people, animals, clothing, food, and all the other objects. The place of women in this 'mobius strip' is at the median, the intersection point where the signs meet in passing from the diegetic into the mimetic space and vice-versa. The whole movement works on the principle of a chiasmus, which we could call the signifier; its signified is the war."

Chiari, J. "Brecht." In his *Landmarks of Contemporary Drama*, pp. 161-83. London: Herbert Jenkins, 1965.
   Includes an assessment of *Mother Courage* as ineffective Marxist propaganda.

Ewen, Frederic. "Of Heroes and War: *Lucullus* and *Mother Courage*." In his *Bertolt Brecht: His Life, His Art and His Times*, pp. 349-61. New York: Citadel Press, 1967.
   Discussion of *Mother Courage* with background on Brecht's

sources in German seventeenth-century novelist Hans Jakob Christian Grimmelshausen's narratives *Simplicissimus* and *The Arch-Cozener and Vagabond Courashe*.

Fenn, Bernard. "*Mutter Courage und ihre Kinder*." In his *Characterisation of Women in the Plays of Bertolt Brecht*, pp. 162-68. Frankfurt am Main: Peter D. Lang, 1982.
   Analyzes the characters of Mother Courage and Kattrin in terms of archetypal elements such as "mother instinct" and "mother love."

Fuegi, John. "Toward a Theory of Dramatic Literature for a Technological Age." *Educational Theatre Journal* 26, No. 4 (December 1974): 433-40.
   Uses Brecht's texts of and production notes for *Galileo, The Caucasian Chalk Circle*, and *Mother Courage* to demonstrate the interdependence in drama of the literary text and the performance.

————. "Berlin: An Etching by Churchill Based on an Idea of Hitler's." In his *Bertolt Brecht: Chaos, According to Plan*, pp. 110-31. Cambridge: Cambridge University Press, 1987.
   Biographical and critical discussion of Brecht's production of *Mother Courage* in Berlin.

Gilman, Richard. "A Timid Mother Courage." In his *Common and Uncommon Masks: Writings on Theatre 1961-1970*, pp. 41-5. New York: Random House, 1971.
   Review of the 1963 Broadway production of *Mother Courage* in which Gilman maintains that the tragedy of the play "lies in the fatality with which the tough, avaricious, ingenious woman of the title is ground down and, more especially, in the inevitability with which goodness and virtue are rendered useless and brought low at the same time as they continue anguishedly to assert their claims and to thrust up their contours to our sight."

Glade, Henry. "The Death of Mother Courage." *Drama Review* 12, No. 1 (Fall 1967): 137-42.
   Records the critical reaction to productions of Brecht's plays in Moscow and emphasizes the productions' deviations from Brechtian stage theory.

Hayman, Ronald. "History of the Small Fry." In his *Brecht: A Biography*, pp. 220-32. New York: Oxford University Press, 1983.
   Covers the period in which *Mother Courage* was written.

————. "*Mother Courage and Her Children*." In his *Bertolt Brecht: The Plays*, pp. 56-63. London: Heinemann Educational Books, 1984.
   General discussion of *Mother Courage*.

Hiller, Robert L. "The Symbolism of *Gestus* in Brecht's Drama." In *Myth and Symbol: Critical Approaches and Applications*, pp. 89-100. Lincoln: University of Nebraska Press, 1963.
   Investigates the non-verbal expression of Kattrin, concluding that the "'truthful' *gestus* symbolizes a deep distrust on Brecht's part of the spoken or written word, a distrust which is not based on the inherent ambiguity of language itself which grows out of the imperfection of human nature."

Lumley, Frederick. "From Expressionism to Epic Theatre." In his *New Trends in 20th Century Drama: A Survey since Ibsen and Shaw*, pp. 80-90. New York: Oxford University Press, 1972.
   Includes a critical summary of *Mother Courage* within a general consideration of Brecht's epic theater.

Lyons, Charles R. "*Mother Courage*: Instinctive Compassion and 'The Great Capitulation'." In his *Bertolt Brecht: The Despair and the Polemic*, pp. 89-109. Carbondale: Southern Illinois University Press, 1968.
   Discusses love and motherhood as impediments to survival in Brecht's *Mother Courage*, claiming that Brecht "projects a world in which to survive is to exploit."

Mennemeier, Franz Norbert. "*Mother Courage and Her Children*."

In *Brecht: A Collection of Critical Essays,* edited by Peter Demetz, pp. 138-50. Englewood Cliffs, N. J.: Prentice-Hall, 1962.

Analyzes the themes of virtue and capitulation in *Mother Courage* and discusses methods and effects of epic theater.

Milfull, John. *"Mutter Courage und ihre Kinder."* In his *From Baal to Keuner: The "Second Optimism" of Bertolt Brecht,* pp. 128-37. Bern, Switzerland: Herbert Lang, 1974.

Argues that Brecht's view of the play's message changed from pessimistic to optimistic, but that his revisions failed to do more than imply this optimism.

Ryan, Paul Ryder. "The Performance Group in Brecht's *Mother Courage and Her Children." Drama Review* 19, No. 2 (June 1975): 78-93.

Discussion of various aspects of The Performance Group's 1975 production of *Mother Courage* in New York City.

Schoeps, Karl H. *"Mother Courage and Her Children: A Chronicle from the Thirty Years' War (1939)."* In his *Bertolt Brecht,* pp. 250-70. New York: Frederick Ungar Publishing Co., 1977.

General discussion of the play.

Speidel, E. "The Mute Person's Voice: Mutter Courage and Her Daughter." *German Life and Letters* 23, No. 4 (July 1970): 332-39.

Examines the function of mute characters in drama by focusing on Kattrin's means of expression and the relation of her actions to the dialogue of *Mother Courage.*

Tynan, Kenneth. "The German Theatre." In his *Curtains,* pp. 445-73. New York: Atheneum, 1961.

Includes a critical sketch of *Mother Courage* in which Tynan describes the play as a "dispassionate, ironic tragedy" and a "tale of endurance."

Woodland, Ronald S. "The Danger of Empathy in *Mother Courage." Modern Drama* 15, No. 2 (September 1972): 125-29.

Claims that the play's force depends upon the audience's realization of the guilt they share with Mother Courage for continuing to participate in an inhumane world.

Theodore (Herman Albert) Dreiser

1871-1945

American novelist, essayist, autobiographer, journalist, short story writer, dramatist, and poet.

For further discussion of Dreiser's career, see *TCLC,* Volumes 10 and 18.

As one of the principal American exponents of literary Naturalism at the turn of the century, Dreiser led the way for a generation of writers seeking to present a detailed and realistic portrait of American life. In such novels as *Sister Carrie* and *An American Tragedy,* he departed from traditional plots in which hard work and perseverance inevitably yield success and happiness, instead portraying the world as an arena of largely random occurrences. His works have often been criticized for their awkward prose style, inadequately conveyed philosophy, and excessive length and detail. Nevertheless, Dreiser retains critical regard for presenting powerful characterizations and strong ideological convictions in novels that are considered among the most notable achievements of twentieth-century literature.

Dreiser was born in Terre Haute, Indiana, the twelfth of thirteen children. His father, a German immigrant, had been a successful businessman, but a series of reversals left the family in poverty by the time of Dreiser's birth, and the family's members were often separated while they sought work in different cities. While Dreiser did not excel as a student, he received encouragement from a high school teacher who paid his tuition when he entered the University of Indiana in 1889. Dreiser was acutely self-conscious about differences between himself and wealthier, better-looking classmates, and he attended the university for only one year. On leaving, he worked at a variety of jobs, including a part-time position in the offices of the Chicago *Herald* which kindled in him an interest in journalism, and in April 1891 he obtained a post with the Chicago *Globe.* After several years as a reporter in Chicago, Dreiser pursued a career as a newspaper and magazine writer in St. Louis, Pittsburgh, and New York. Commentators maintain that his years as a journalist were instrumental in developing the exhaustively detailed literary style that is the hallmark of his fiction.

In New York, Dreiser supported himself—and, after 1898, his wife—with free-lance magazine writing and editing, while working on the manuscript of *Sister Carrie.* Published in 1900, the novel was not promoted by the publisher, and it sold poorly. Marital difficulties and failing health further contributed to Dreiser's suffering from severe depression. After not working for several years, he was aided by an older brother, who had become a successful music hall performer and songwriter under the name Paul Dresser. Dresser arranged for his brother to recuperate at a health resort and then helped him find work. Dreiser later credited several years of light manual labor with restoring his mental as well as physical health. In 1905 he resumed free-lance magazine writing and editing, and over the next two years rose to the editorship of three prominent women's magazines. He lost this position in 1907 because of a scandal involving his romantic pursuit of a co-worker's teenage daughter; that same

year *Sister Carrie,* which had been received favorably in England, was reissued to positive reviews and good sales in the United States. Over the next eighteen years Dreiser published a succession of novels to widely varied but rarely indifferent critical notice; the publication of *An American Tragedy* in 1925 established him as the country's foremost living novelist. Dreiser subsequently became involved in social and political affairs. He went to Russian in 1927 to observe the results of the revolution, publishing his findings in *Dreiser Looks at Russia,* and he joined investigations of labor conditions in Kentucky coal mines in 1931. At the time of his death in 1945 Dreiser was better known as a social and political activist than as a novelist.

Sister Carrie departed sharply from the gentility and timidity that characterized much realistic fiction during the nineteenth century. Dreiser uncompromisingly detailed the events that led his protagonist first into prostitution and then, as if pointedly avoiding a moral, to the attainment of success and financial security as an actress. The novel illustrates Dreiser's interpretation of complex human relationships as purely biological functions: Carrie exhibits what has been called "neo-Darwinian adaptability," surviving and prospering because she is able to adjust with equanimity to whatever advantageous situations develop. The deterioration and death of Carrie's second lover, Hurstwood, is generally agreed to be one of the most powerful and moving portraits of human defeat ever written. Critics of *Sister Carrie* have noted an apparent contradiction, which many find persists throughout Dreiser's works, between his professed determinism and his sentimentalism: although he portrayed their unhappy fates as inevitable, Dreiser evoked considerable sympathy for his defeated characters.

Dreiser's next novel was *The Financier,* the first in the Cowperwood trilogy, or Trilogy of Desire, detailing the life and career of businessman Frank Algernon Cowperwood. Both *The Financier* and *The Titan,* the second volume of the trilogy, utilize imagery based on Darwinian evolutionary theory, and offer somewhat didactic presentations of Dreiser's deterministic philosophy. In these novels Dreiser outlines his "chemicomechanistic" concept of life as little more than a series of "chemisms," or chemical reactions. Cowperwood's rise, fall, and second triumph in the world of high finance are recounted with journalistic attention to detail that some commentators contend becomes a too extensive listing of discrete facts. The third volume of the trilogy, *The Stoic,* is considered vastly inferior to its predecessors. It concludes with the death of Cowperwood and the dispersal of his fortune, ending on an incongruous note of Eastern mysticism, which was a concern of Dreiser's second wife.

Dreiser's fifth novel, *The "Genius,"* was controversial for its portrayal of the artist as a Nietzschean superman who is beyond conventional moral codes. Commentators maintain that this semi-autobiographical work is Dreiser's thinly veiled self-justification of his own behavior, and view some unflatteringly portrayed characters as Dreiser's revenge upon those who, he believed, had mistreated or misunderstood him. Sales of *The "Genius"* were initially good and early reviews largely approbatory; however, in the year following its publication *The "Genius"* came to the attention of the New York Society for the Suppression of Vice, which labeled the book immoral and sought to block its distribution. H. L. Mencken, who disapproved of the book on artistic grounds, nevertheless circulated a protest against the suppression of *The "Genius"* or any literary work. The protest was signed by hundreds of prominent American and British authors, including Robert Frost, Sinclair Lewis, Ezra Pound, and H. G. Wells. Although *The "Genius"* is considered one of Dreiser's weakest novels, Charles Shapiro has noted that it "achieved historical importance as a result of the famed fight over its suppression, a struggle that ranks with the *Ulysses* case as a pivotal victory in the fight for American literary freedom."

An American Tragedy, published in 1925, is considered Dreiser's most important work. Although critics deplored Dreiser's stylistic and grammatical flaws—what Mencken labeled his lack "of what may be called literary tact"—they considered *An American Tragedy* a powerful indictment of the gulf between American ideals of wealth and influence, and the opportunities available for their realization. The entire American system is blamed for the destruction of Clyde Griffiths, a weak-willed individual who aspires to the American dream of success. The journalistic style of Dreiser's prose, frequently assessed as a weakness of his earlier works, was found by many critics to benefit *An American Tragedy.* Grant C. Knight, for example, wrote that while it "is true that Mr. Dreiser is always at pains to spread out every fact that sometimes he even transgresses relevance, . . . in the instance of *An American Tragedy* . . . nothing short of full documentation would have been convincing."

In his final novel, *The Bulwark,* Dreiser seemingly repudiated both Naturalism and the pessimistic determinism that informs his earlier novels. In *The Bulwark* the moral scruples of a Quaker businessman, Solon Barnes, conflict with the reality of American business dealings. In a reversal for Dreiser, Barnes, who upholds traditional mores and values, is portrayed sympathetically.

Dreiser published four autobiographical works, *A Traveler at Forty, A Hoosier Holiday, A Book about Myself,* and *Dawn,* as well as volumes of poetry, short stories, sketches, and essays, many of the latter pertaining to his social and political activism. Attention to this aspect of Dreiser's life exceeded the critical attention given his literary works during the 1930s and 1940s. At the time of his death he had not published a novel in twenty years, and his career as a novelist was considered to have ended with *An American Tragedy.* Reevaluation of Dreiser's literary reputation began with the posthumous publication of *The Bulwark* and *The Stoic* in 1946 and 1947. Widely varied critical opinions still stand regarding the merit of Dreiser's individual novels, with the exception of *An American Tragedy,* which is assessed as a masterpiece of American literature. Many commentators contend that Dreiser's chief importance is one of influence. His sprawling, flawed, but powerful novels helped to establish the conventions of modern Naturalism. Jack Salzman has noted that Dreiser's "significance in the history of American letters is no longer a matter for dispute. We may continue to debate his merits as an artist, but his importance to American literature has been well established."

(See also *Contemporary Authors,* Vol. 106; *Dictionary of Literary Biography,* Vols. 9 and 12; *Dictionary of Literary Biography Documentary Series,* Vol. 1; and *Concise Dictionary of American Literary Biography, 1865-1917.*)

PRINCIPAL WORKS

Sister Carrie (novel) 1900
Jennie Gerhardt (novel) 1911
*The Financier (novel) 1912; revised edition, 1927
A Traveler at Forty (autobiography) 1913
*The Titan (novel) 1914
The "Genius" (novel) 1915
A Hoosier Holiday (autobiography) 1916
Plays of the Natural and the Supernatural [first publication] (dramas) 1916
Free, and Other Stories (short stories) 1918
The Hand of the Potter [first publication] (drama) 1918
Twelve Men (sketches) 1919
Hey Rub-A-Dub-Dub: A Book of the Mystery and Wonder and Terror of Life (essays) 1920
A Book about Myself (autobiography) 1922; also published as *Newspaper Days,* 1931
The Color of a Great City (essays) 1923
An American Tragedy (novel) 1925
Moods, Cadenced and Declaimed (poetry) 1926; enlarged edition, 1928; also published as *Moods, Philosophic and Emotional, Cadenced and Declaimed* [revised edition], 1935
Chains (short stories and novellas) 1927
Dreiser Looks at Russia (essays) 1928
The Aspirant (poetry) 1929
A Gallery of Women. 2 vols. (sketches) 1929
Dawn (autobiography) 1931
Tragic America (essays) 1931
America Is Worth Saving (essays) 1941
The Bulwark (novel) 1946
The Best Short Stories of Theodore Dreiser (short stories) 1947

The Stoic (novel) 1947

Letters of Theodore Dreiser. 3 vols. (letters) 1959

Theodore Dreiser: A Selection of Uncollected Prose (essays and journalism) 1977

American Diaries, 1902-1926 (diaries) 1982

† *An Amateur Laborer* (autobiography) 1983

Selected Magazine Articles of Theodore Dreiser: Life and Art in the American 1890s (journalism) 1985

Journalism, Volume One: Newspaper Writings, 1892-1895 (journalism) 1988

Theodore Dreiser's "Heard in the Corridors" Articles and Related Writings (journalism) 1988

*These works are collectively referred to as the Cowperwood trilogy or the Trilogy of Desire.

† This work was written in 1903.

───────────────

PAUL ELMER MORE (essay date 1927)

[*More was an American critic who, along with Irving Babbitt, formulated the doctrines of New Humanism during the early twentieth century. The New Humanists were strict moralists who adhered to traditional values in an age of scientific advances and artistic self-expression. They considered the ethical posture of a work of literature to be as important as its aesthetic qualities. More was particularly opposed to Naturalism, which he believed accentuated the animal nature of humans, and to any literary movements, such as Romanticism, that broke with established classical tradition. He is especially esteemed for the philosophical and literary erudition of his multivolume Shelburne Essays (1904-21). In the following excerpt, More discusses Dreiser's reportorial literary style, praising his Book about Myself as an important contribution to American Realism while criticizing his fiction for its lack of artistry and preoccupation with the purely sordid aspects of life.*]

As a contrast [to the aesthetes of early twentieth-century American literature], the realists who throng the left wing of the modern school come almost without exception from small towns sprinkled along the Mid-Western States from Ohio to Kansas, where for the most part they have grown up quite innocent of education in any such sense as would be recognized in Paris or London. It would not be easy to exaggerate the importance of the fact that in letters they are self-made men with no inherited background of culture. One of them, indeed, Sinclair Lewis, coming out of Sauk Center, Minnesota, has a degree from Yale University; but intellectually he is perhaps the crudest member of the group, cruder, for instance, than Theodore Dreiser who got most of his education in the streets of Chicago and from the free libraries of this and that town, or than Sherwood Anderson who apparently owes his acquaintance with the alphabet to the grace of God. Another of the group, John Dos Passos, was born in Chicago, is a graduate of Harvard, and has been influenced, one guesses, by certain French Writers and by the Spaniard Ibañez; his work is too knowing to be called crude intellectually or perhaps even artistically, but as a reflection of life it is about the lowest we have yet produced. His much-bruited novel *Manhattan Transfer,* with its unrelated scenes selected to portray the more sordid aspect of New York, and with its spattered filth, might be described in a phrase as an explosion in a cesspool.

I give these biographical facts not in a spirit of snobbishness, nor in any contempt for the Mid-West (to which indeed I my-

self belong), but because they have stamped the whole school, giving it a certain unity of character and marking it off from the contemporary realism of England, not to mention France. Of all the group Mr. Dreiser is pretty generally recognized as the most powerful and, with the possible exception of Mr. Anderson, the most typical, and it will not be out of place to look a little more closely into his career. Fortunately for our purpose Mr. Dreiser, like his compeers, is tremendously occupied with his personal importance and unimportance in the universe, to such an extent that his own character peeps in and out through all his fiction, while, again like his fellows, he has thought it necessary, or profitable, to give the world his autobiography [*A Book about Myself*]. One may smile at the conceit of an author who, at the age of fifty and with no fixed tenure on fame, spreads out the small doings of his youth and early manhood over five hundred pages octavo; and one may shrink from the immodesty—or shall we say frankness?—of a man who regrets in print that he did not seduce an innocent and trusting girl while his passion for her was strong instead of waiting to marry her after his lust had cooled down. There are some things which even a realist need not tell. But the book is a document of the highest value. (pp. 63-4)

In his twenty-second year he got a small job on a struggling newspaper, owned and controlled by a ward politician. In 1892 he moved to St. Louis, where for a while he had the advantage of reporting under "Little Mac," an editor of outstanding ability and in those days of almost incredible repute throughout the South-Western States. Here I am able to check up Mr. Dreiser's narrative in part, for he came to the city of my birth just when I was leaving it, and I can testify to his account of its streets and institutions, and to his characterization of some of its well-known citizens, as truthful and extraordinarily vivid. From St. Louis he soon drifted eastward, and ended in New York, the Mecca of all our writing men, to whom Chicago is a kind of halfway house. Lean years still lay before him; but his stories began to attract attention, and his *American Tragedy,* a novel spun out through two long volumes, has captured the heedless reading mob and has been acclaimed a masterpiece by reputable reviewers here and abroad.

For my own part I regard his autobiography, despite or possibly because of its shameless "exhibitionism," as more significant than any of his novels, as perhaps, with Sherwood Anderson's similar *Story Teller's Story,* the most significant thing that has come out of our school of realism. I may be prejudiced in its favour by the fact that the autobiography, though the events of Mr. Dreiser's life were different enough from my own, recalls so vividly the intellectual and sentimental atmosphere of the America in which my youth was passed, and which is rapidly disappearing. But, apart from such accidental reasons, it is notable that the *Book about Myself* has the telling straightforward style and method natural to a trained reporter, whereas the English of Mr. Dreiser, when, as sometimes in his novels, he tries to be literary, is of the mongrel sort to be expected from a miscegenation of the gutter and the psychological laboratory. Certainly for those interested in such matters the springs of American realism are laid bare in these autobiographical records with startling frankness. Take a boy of humble origin in a Mid-Western town some forty years ago. The only breath of immaterial things to reach him would be through religion, in the case of Mr. Dreiser a perfectly uncritical catholicism, but with most of the others a thin poverty-stricken Protestantism from which all ritual and symbolism had dropped and every appeal to the imagination had exuded. Art and letters would be about as remote from him as from the Bushmen of Africa. Intellectually and æsthetically and emotionally he is starved. Suppose then that such a lad, with no schooling to speak of or with a degree from some lonely hungry "college," is carried to the bustling conceited Chicago of those days, and, aspiring to write, gets a job on a sensation-mongering newspaper. Of knowledge of life in its larger aspects he has brought nothing, and in the new school of experience he is pretty well confined to the police courts, the morgue, scenes of crime and calamity, sodden streets where unsavoury news may be picked up, homes which scandal has made public property. We need not guess at the colours the world would assume in the eyes of such a youth, for Mr. Dreiser has described his own reactions with sufficient energy. He began his work "still sniffing about the Sermon on the Mount and the Beatitudes, expecting ordinary human flesh and blood to do and be those things"; he discovered that most of the people among whom he was now thrown "looked upon life as a fierce, grim struggle in which no quarter was either given or taken, and in which all men laid traps, lied, squandered, erred through illusion," or, more succinctly in the words of one of his admired and imitated friends, "life is a God-damned stinking, treacherous game."

Meanwhile our young aspirant to fame and wealth, being endowed with no ordinary brain, begins to read. Translations of Balzac and Zola fall into his hands, and he learns that the society of Paris, the *ville lumière,* is playing a game very much like that which he sees about him, only on a more magnificent scale and with vastly greater opportunities. And he learns, or thinks he learns, that the high art of letters is to develop the sort of realism he is acquiring as a reporter. Later he dips into the works of Huxley and Tyndall and Spencer, and finds his "gravest fears as to the unsolvable disorder and brutality of life eternally verified" by authorities who were then supposed by the uneducated or the scientifically educated to have uttered the last word on the mysteries of the universe, the last word *eternally verified.* "Up to this time," he observes rather innocently, "there had been in me a blazing and unchecked desire to get on and the feeling that in doing so we did get somewhere; now in its place was the definite conviction that spiritually one got nowhere, that there was no hereafter, that one lived and had his being because one had to, and that it was of no importance. Of one's ideals, struggles, deprivations, sorrows and joys, it could only be said that they were chemic compulsions, something which for some inexplicable but unimportant reason responded to and resulted from the hope of pleasure and the fear of pain. Man was a mechanism, undevised and uncreated, and a badly and carelessly driven one at that."

Add to this education a spark of genius, an eye to note and record the panorama of the streets, a nervous system highly sensitive to the moods of those about him, and you have the realism of which **An American Tragedy** is the most notable achievement. In his drawing of characters from the lower strata of life and from the gilded haunts of Broadway Mr. Dreiser shows an easy competence. In particular the hero of this tale, from his suppressed childhood in the home of ignorant wandering evangelists, through his career as bell-boy in a hotel, and employee in a factory, ending in trial and conviction for the murder of his mistress, is portrayed with a masterly understanding of the devious ways of a weak untutored nature. But when the author passes to the doings of conven-

tional society, even to the account of a game of tennis, he displays a ludicrous ignorance and awkwardness. The same sort of contrast is seen in other fields. At one moment the tone of comment is callous and cynical, befitting his acquired theory of life's unsolvable disorder and brutality; and then there will break through the native note of sentimentality that pervaded the atmosphere he breathed in the rural Mid-West of his childhood. Just as he himself remains, as he says, "a poetic melancholic, crossed with a vivid materialistic lust of life." In one place religion is only "religionism," a contemptible yet hated deception; and then again the spell laid on his early years reasserts itself, and at the end of the story you might suppose that his deepest sympathy was with the self-sacrificing minister of the Gospel who befriends the condemned murderer, and with the poor mother on whose face was written the "fighting faith in the wisdom and mercy of the definite overruling and watchful and merciful power" of God.

I lay down Mr. Dreiser's novel with a feeling that it is an American tragedy in a sense never intended by him when he chose that title. If only he knew the finer aspects of life as he knows its shabby underside; if only his imagination had been trained in the larger tradition of literature instead of getting its bent from the police court and the dregs of science; if only religion had appeared to him in other garb than the travesty of superstition and faded fanaticism; if only he had had a chance, he might possibly have produced that fabulous thing, the great American novel. As it is he has brought forth a *monstrum informe cui lumen ademptum.* (pp. 64-9)

Mr. Dreiser, so far at least as his creative instinct does not break through his parochial theory of art, simply reproduces the surface of life as he has seen it, with no attempt to reorganize it artistically or to interpret its larger significance. He does not create characters, he does not create anything; he merely extends the front page of the newspaper to the volume of a book, rarely venturing to go beyond the training he received as a reporter. And he reaps his reward; for he gives the great mob of readers—shop girls and tired clerks and thoughtless boys riding back and forth to business—exactly what they want and can understand, not literature which requires for its appreciation an intellectual readjustment, but a sensational dressing up of the world they know. (pp. 72-3)

Paul Elmer More, "Modern Currents in American Literature," in his The Demon of the Absolute: New Shelburne Essays, Vol. I, *Princeton University Press, 1928, pp. 53-76.*

LIONEL TRILLING   (essay date 1946)

[*Trilling was one of the twentieth century's most significant and influential American literary and social critics, and he is often called the single most important American literary critic to apply Freudian psychological theories to literature. Trilling combined sociological, psychological, and humanistic interests in essays that display a sweeping command of literature and history. John Henry Raleigh has commended Trilling's "particular blend of literary sensibility, learning, historical orientation, and a civilized, urbane, and ironical prose style." In the following excerpt, Trilling attributes the literary establishment's "long indulgence" of Dreiser to liberal intellectual enthusiasm for the cultural and political assumptions that underlie Dreiser's fiction. For an opposing view, see the excerpt by Richard Lehan dated 1984.*]

Few critics, I suppose, no matter what their political disposition, have ever been wholly blind to [Henry] James's great gifts, or even to the grandiose moral intention of these gifts. And few critics have ever been wholly blind to Dreiser's great faults. But by liberal critics James is traditionally put to the ultimate question: of what use, of what actual political use, are his gifts and their intention? Granted that James was devoted to an extraordinary moral perceptiveness, granted too that moral perceptiveness has something to do with politics and the social life, of what possible practical value in our world of impending disaster can James's work be? And James's style, his characters, his subjects, and even his own social origin and the manner of his personal life are adduced to show that his work cannot endure the question. To James no quarter is given by American criticism in its political and liberal aspect. But in the same degree that liberal criticism is moved by political considerations to treat James with severity, it treats Dreiser with the most sympathetic indulgence. Dreiser's literary faults, it gives us to understand, are essentially social and political virtues. It was Parrington who established the formula for the liberal criticism of Dreiser by calling him a "peasant": when Dreiser thinks stupidly, it is because he has the slow stubbornness of a peasant; when he writes badly, it is because he is impatient of the sterile literary gentility of the bourgeoisie. It is as if wit, and flexibility of mind, and perception, and knowledge were to be equated with aristocracy and political reaction, while dullness and stupidity must naturally suggest a virtuous democracy, as in the old plays.

The liberal judgment of Dreiser and James goes back of politics, goes back to the cultural assumptions that make politics. We are still haunted by a kind of political fear of the intellect which Tocqueville observed in us more than a century ago. American intellectuals, when they are being consciously American or political, are remarkably quick to suggest that an art which is marked by perception and knowledge, although all very well in its way, can never get us through gross dangers and difficulties. And their misgivings become the more intense when intellect works in art as it ideally should, when its processes are vivacious and interesting and brilliant. It is then that we like to confront it with the gross dangers and difficulties and to challenge it to save us at once from disaster. When intellect in art is awkward or dull we do not put it to the test of ultimate or immediate practicality. No liberal critic asks the question of Dreiser whether *his* moral preoccupations are going to be useful in confronting the disasters that threaten us. And it is a judgment on the proper nature of mind, rather than any actual political meaning that might be drawn from the works of the two men, which accounts for the unequal justice they have received from the progressive critics. If it could be conclusively demonstrated—by, say, documents in James's handwriting—that James explicitly intended his books to be understood as pleas for co-operatives, labor unions, better housing, and more equitable taxation, the American critic in his liberal and progressive character would still be worried by James because his work shows so many of the electric qualities of mind. And if something like the opposite were proved of Dreiser, it would be brushed aside—as his doctrinaire anti-Semitism has in fact been brushed aside—because his books have the awkwardness, the chaos, the heaviness which we associate with "reality." In the American metaphysic, reality is always material reality, hard, resistant, unformed, impenetrable, and unpleasant. And that mind is alone felt to be trustworthy which most resembles this reality by most nearly reproducing the sensations it affords.

In *The Rise of American Civilization,* Professor Beard uses a significant phrase when, in the course of an ironic account of James's career, he implies that we have the clue to the irrelevance of that career when we know that James was "a whole generation removed from the odors of the shop." Of a piece with this, and in itself even more significant, is the comment which Granville Hicks makes in *The Great Tradition* when he deals with James's stories about artists and remarks that such artists as James portrays, so concerned for their art and their integrity in art, do not really exist: "After all, who has ever known such artists? Where are the Hugh Verekers, the Mark Ambients, the Neil Paradays, the Overts, Limberts, Dencombes, Delavoys?" This question, as Mr. Hicks admits, had occurred to James himself, but what answer had James given to it? "If the life about us for the last thirty years refused warrant for these examples," he said in the preface to volume XII of the New York Edition, "then so much the worse for that life. . . . There are decencies that in the name of the general self-respect we must take for granted, there's a rudimentary intellectual honor to which we must, in the interest of civilization, at least pretend." And to this Mr. Hicks, shocked beyond argument, makes this reply, which would be astonishing had we not heard it before: "But this is the purest romanticism, this writing about what ought to be rather than what is!"

The "odors of the shop" are real, and to those who breathe them they guarantee a sense of vitality from which James is debarred. The idea of intellectual honor is not real, and to that chimera James was devoted. He betrayed the reality of what is in the interests of what ought to be. Dare we trust him? The question, we remember, is asked by men who themselves have elaborate transactions with what ought to be. Professor Beard spoke in the name of a growing, developing, and improving America. Mr. Hicks, when he wrote *The Great Tradition,* was in general sympathy with a nominally radical movement. But James's own transaction with what ought to be is suspect because it is carried on through what I have called the electrical qualities of mind, through a complex and rapid imagination and with a kind of authoritative immediacy. Mr. Hicks knows that Dreiser is "clumsy" and "stupid" and "bewildered" and "crude in his statement of materialistic monism"; he knows that Dreiser in his personal life—which is in point because James's personal life is always supposed to be so much in point—was not quite emancipated from "his boyhood longing for crass material success," showing "again and again a desire for the ostentatious luxury of the successful business man." But Dreiser is to be accepted and forgiven because his faults are the sad, lovable, honorable faults of reality itself, or of America itself—huge, inchoate, struggling toward expression, caught between the dream of raw power and the dream of morality.

"The liability in what Santayana called the genteel tradition was due to its being the product of mind apart from experience. Dreiser gave us the stuff of our common experience, not as it was hoped to be by any idealizing theorist, but as it actually was in its crudity." The author of this statement certainly cannot be accused of any lack of feeling for mind as Henry James represents it; nor can Mr. Matthiessen be thought of as a follower of Parrington—indeed, in the preface to *American Renaissance* he has framed one of the sharpest and most cogent criticisms of Parrington's method. Yet Mr. Matthiessen, writing in the *New York Times Book Review* about Dreiser's posthumous novel, *The Bulwark,* accepts the liberal cliché which opposes crude experience to mind and establishes Dreiser's value by implying that the mind which Dreiser's crude experience is presumed to confront and refute is the mind of gentility.

This implied amalgamation of mind with gentility is the rationale of the long indulgence of Dreiser, which is extended even to the style of his prose. Everyone is aware that Dreiser's prose style is full of roughness and ungainliness, and the critics who admire Dreiser tell us it does not matter. Of course it does not matter. No reader with a right sense of style would suppose that it does matter, and he might even find it a virtue. But it has been taken for granted that the ungainliness of Dreiser's style is the only possible objection to be made to it, and that whoever finds in it any fault at all wants a prettified genteel style (and is objecting to the ungainliness of reality itself). For instance, Edwin Berry Burgum, in a leaflet on Dreiser put out by the Book Find Club, tells us that Dreiser was one of those who used—or, as Mr. Burgum says, utilized—"the diction of the Middle West, pretty much as it was spoken, rich in colloquialism and frank in the simplicity and directness of the pioneer tradition," and that this diction took the place of "the literary English, formal and bookish, of New England provincialism that was closer to the aristocratic spirit of the mother country than to the tang of everyday life in the new West." This is mere fantasy. Hawthorne, Thoreau, and Emerson were for the most part remarkably colloquial—they wrote, that is, much as they spoke; their prose was specifically American in quality, and, except for occasional lapses, quite direct and simple. It is Dreiser who lacks the sense of colloquial diction—that of the Middle West or any other. If we are to talk of bookishness, it is Dreiser who is bookish; he is precisely literary in the bad sense; he is full of flowers of rhetoric and shines with paste gems; at hundreds of points his diction is not only genteel but fancy. It is he who speaks of "a scene more distingué than this," or of a woman "artistic in form and feature," or of a man who, although "strong, reserved, aggressive, with an air of wealth and experience, was *soi-disant* and not particularly eager to stay at home." Colloquialism held no real charm for him and his natural tendency is always toward the "fine":

> . . . Moralists come and go; religionists fulminate and declare the pronouncements of God as to this; but Aphrodite still reigns. Embowered in the festal depths of the spring, set above her altars of porphyry, chalcedony, ivory and gold, see her smile the smile that is at once the texture and essence of delight, the glory and despair of the world! Dream on, oh Buddha, asleep on your lotus leaf, of an undisturbed Nirvana! Sweat, oh Jesus, your last agonizing drops over an unregenerate world! In the forests of Pan still ring the cries of the worshippers of Aphrodite! From her altars the incense of adoration ever rises! And see, the new red grapes dripping where votive hands new-press them!

Charles Jackson, the novelist, telling us in the same leaflet that Dreiser's style does not matter, remarks on how much still comes to us when we have lost by translation the stylistic brillance of Thomas Mann or the Russians or Balzac. He is in part right. And he is right too when he says that a certain kind of conscious, supervised artistry is not appropriate to the novel of large dimensions. Yet the fact is that the great novelists have usually written very good prose, and what comes through even a bad translation is exactly the power of mind that made the well-hung sentence of the original text. In literature style is so little the mere clothing of thought—need it be insisted on at this late date?—that we may say that from

the earth of the novelist's prose spring his characters, his ideas, and even his story itself [the critic adds in a footnote that "The latest defense of Dreiser's style, that in the chapter on Dreiser in the *Literary History of the United States,* is worth noting: 'Forgetful of the integrity and power of Dreiser's whole work, many critics have been distracted into a condemnation of his style. He was, like Twain and Whitman, an organic artist; he wrote what he knew—what he was. His many colloquialisms were part of the coinage of his time, and his sentimental and romantic passages were written in the language of the educational system and the popular literature of his formative years. In his style, as in his material, he was a child of his time, of his class. Self-educated, a type or model of the artist of plebeian origin in America, his language, like his subject matter, is not marked by internal inconsistencies.' No doubt Dreiser was an organic artist in the sense that he wrote what he knew and what he was, but so, I suppose, is every artist; the question for criticism comes down to *what* he knew and *what* he was. That he was a child of his time and class is also true, but this can be said of everyone without exception; the question for criticism is how he transcended the imposed limitations of his time and class. As for the defense made on the ground of his particular class, it can only be said that liberal thought has come to a strange pass when it assumes that a plebeian origin is accountable for a writer's faults through all his intellectual life"].

To the extent that Dreiser's style is defensible, his thought is also defensible. That is, when he thinks like a novelist, he is worth following—when by means of his rough and ungainly but no doubt cumulatively effective style he creates rough, ungainly, but effective characters and events. But when he thinks like, as we say, a philosopher, he is likely to be not only foolish but vulgar. He thinks as the modern crowd thinks when it decides to think: religion and morality are nonsense, "religionists" and moralists are fakes, tradition is a fraud, what is man but matter and impulses, mysterious "chemisms," what value has life anyway? "What, cooking, eating, coition, job holding, growing, aging, losing, winning, in so changeful and passing a scene as this, important? Bunk! It is some form of titillating illusion with about as much import to the superior forces that bring it all about as the functions and gyrations of a fly. No more. And maybe less." Thus Dreiser at sixty. And yet there is for him always the vulgarly saving suspicion that maybe, when all is said and done, there is Something Behind It All. It is much to the point of his intellectual vulgarity that Dreiser's anti-Semitism was not merely a social prejudice but an idea, a way of dealing with difficulties.

No one, I suppose, has ever represented Dreiser as a masterly intellect. It is even commonplace to say that his ideas are inconsistent or inadequate. But once that admission has been made, his ideas are hustled out of sight while his "reality" and great brooding pity are spoken of. (His pity is to be questioned: pity is to be judged by kind, not amount, and Dreiser's pity—*Jennie Gerhardt* provides the only exception—is either destructive of its object or it is self-pity.) Why has no liberal critic ever brought Dreiser's ideas to the bar of political practicality, asking what use is to be made of Dreiser's dim, awkward speculation, of his self-justification, of his lust for "beauty" and "sex" and "living" and "life itself," and of the showy nihilism which always seems to him so grand a gesture in the direction of profundity? We live, understandably enough, with the sense of urgency; our clock, like Baudelaire's, has had the hands removed and bears the legend, "It is later than you think." But with us it is always a little too late for mind, yet never too late for honest stupidity; always a little too late for understanding, never too late for righteous, bewildered wrath; always too late for thought, never too late for naïve moralizing. We seem to like to condemn our finest but not our worst qualities by pitting them against the exigency of time.

But sometimes time is not quite so exigent as to justify all our own exigency, and in the case of Dreiser time has allowed his deficiencies to reach their logical, and fatal, conclusion. In *The Bulwark* Dreiser's characteristic ideas come full circle, and the simple, didactic life history of Solon Barnes, a Quaker business man, affirms a simple Christian faith, and a kind of practical mysticism, and the virtues of self-abnegation and self-restraint, and the belief in and submission to the hidden purposes of higher powers, those "superior forces that bring it all about"—once, in Dreiser's opinion, so brutally indifferent, now somehow benign. This is not the first occasion on which Dreiser has shown a tenderness toward religion and a responsiveness to mysticism. *Jennie Gerhardt* and the figure of the Reverend Duncan McMillan in *An American Tragedy* are forecasts of the avowals of *The Bulwark,* and Dreiser's lively interest in power of any sort led him to take account of the power implicit in the cruder forms of mystical performance. Yet these rifts in his nearly monolithic materialism cannot quite prepare us for the blank pietism of *The Bulwark,* not after we have remembered how salient in Dreiser's work has been the long surly rage against the "religionists" and the "moralists," the men who have presumed to believe that life can be given any law at all and who have dared to suppose that will or mind or faith can shape the savage and beautiful entity that Dreiser liked to call "life itself." Now for Dreiser the law may indeed be given, and it is wholly simple—the safe conduct of the personal life requires only that we follow the Inner Light according to the regimen of the Society of Friends, or according to some other godly rule. And now the smiling Aphrodite set above her altars of porphyry, chalcedony, ivory, and gold is quite forgotten, and we are told that the sad joy of cosmic acceptance goes hand in hand with sexual abstinence.

Dreiser's mood of "acceptance" in the last years of his life is not, as a personal experience, to be submitted to the tests of intellectual validity. It consists of a sensation of cosmic understanding, of an overarching sense of unity with the world in its apparent evil as well as in its obvious good. It is no more to be quarreled with, or reasoned with, than love itself—indeed, it is a kind of love, not so much of the world as of oneself in the world. Perhaps it is either the cessation of desire or the perfect balance of desires. It is what used often to be meant by "peace," and up through the nineteenth century a good many people understood its meaning. If it was Dreiser's own emotion at the end of his life, who would not be happy that he had achieved it? I am not even sure that our civilization would not be the better for more of us knowing and desiring this emotion of grave felicity. Yet granting the personal validity of the emotion, Dreiser's exposition of it fails, and is, moreover, offensive. Mr. Matthiessen has warned us of the attack that will be made on the doctrine of *The Bulwark* by "those who believe that any renewal of Christianity marks a new 'failure of nerve.' " But Dreiser's religious avowal is not a failure of nerve—it is a failure of mind and heart. We have only to set his book beside any work in which mind and heart are made to serve religion to know this at once. Ivan Karamazov's giving back his ticket of admission to the "harmony" of the universe suggests that *The Bulwark* is not morally ade-

quate, for we dare not, as its hero does, blandly "accept" the suffering of others; and the Book of Job tells us that it does not include enough in its exploration of the problem of evil, and is not stern enough. I have said that Dreiser's religious affirmation was offensive; the offense lies in the vulgar ease of its formulation, as well as in the comfortable untroubled way in which Dreiser moved from nihilism to pietism.

The Bulwark is the fruit of Dreiser's old age, but if we speak of it as a failure of thought and feeling, we cannot suppose that with age Dreiser weakened in mind and heart. The weakness was always there. And in a sense it is not Dreiser who failed but a whole way of dealing with ideas, a way in which we have all been in some degree involved. Our liberal, progressive culture tolerated Dreiser's vulgar materialism with its huge negation, its simple cry of "Bunk!," feeling that perhaps it was not quite intellectually adequate but certainly very *strong*, certainly very *real*. And now, almost as a natural consequence, it has been given, and is not unwilling to take, Dreiser's pietistic religion in all its inadequacy.

Dreiser, of course, was firmer than the intellectual culture that accepted him. He *meant* his ideas, at least so far as a man can mean ideas who is incapable of following them to their consequences. But we, when it came to his ideas, talked about his great brooding pity and shrugged the ideas off. We are still doing it. Robert Elias, the biographer of Dreiser, tells us that "it is part of the logic of [Dreiser's] life that he should have completed *The Bulwark* at the same time that he joined the Communists." Just what kind of logic this is we learn from Mr. Elias's further statement. "When he supported left-wing movements and finally, last year, joined the Communist Party, he did so not because he had examined the details of the party line and found them satisfactory, but because he agreed with a general program that represented a means for establishing his cherished goal of greater equality among men." Whether or not Dreiser was following the logic of his own life, he was certainly following the logic of the liberal criticism that accepted him so undiscriminatingly as one of the great, significant expressions of its spirit. This is the liberal criticism, in the direct line of Parrington, which establishes the social responsibility of the writer and then goes on to say that, apart from his duty of resembling reality as much as possible, he is not really responsible for anything, not even for his ideas. The scope of reality being what it is, ideas are held to be mere "details," and, what is more, to be details which, if attended to, have the effect of diminishing reality. But ideals are different from ideas; in the liberal criticism which descends from Parrington ideals consort happily with reality and they urge us to deal impatiently with ideas—a "cherished goal" forbids that we stop to consider how we reach it, or if we may not destroy it in trying to reach it the wrong way. (pp. 11-20)

Lionel Trilling, "Reality in America," in his The Liberal Imagination: Essays on Literature and Society, *1950. Reprint by Harcourt Brace Jovanovich, 1979, pp. 3-20.*

ALFRED KAZIN   (essay date 1955)

[*A highly respected American literary critic, Kazin is best known for his essay collections* The Inmost Leaf (1955) *and* Contemporaries (1962), *and particularly for* On Native Grounds (1942), *a study of American prose writing since the era of William Dean Howells. Having studied the works of "the critics who were the best writers—from Sainte-Beuve and Mat-*

Dreiser in his late twenties.

thew Arnold to Edmund Wilson and Van Wyck Brooks" as an aid to his own critical understanding, Kazin has found that "criticism focussed many—if by no means all—of my own urges as a writer: to show literature as a deed in human history, and to find in each writer the uniqueness of the gift, of the essential vision, through which I hoped to penetrate into the mystery and sacredness of the individual soul." In the following essay, which constitutes Kazin's introduction to The Stature of Theodore Dreiser: A Critical Survey of the Man and His Work, *edited by Kazin and Charles Shapiro, he discusses Dreiser's critical reception. Kazin refers to several of the essays included in the collection in his introduction.*]

At a time when the one quality which so many American writers have in common is their utter harmlessness, Dreiser makes painful reading. The others you can take up without being involved in the least. They are "literature"—beautiful, stylish literature. You are left free to think not of the book you are reading but of the author, and not even of the whole man behind the author, but just of his cleverness, his sensibility, his style. Dreiser gets under your skin and you can't wait to get him out again: he stupefies with reality:

> Carrie looked about her, very much disturbed and quite sure that she did not want to work here. Aside from making her uncomfortable by sidelong glances, no one paid her the least attention. She waited until the whole department was aware of her presence. Then some word was sent around, and a

foreman, in an apron and shirt sleeves, the latter rolled up to his shoulders, approached.

"Do you want to see me?" he asked.

"Do you need any help?" said Carrie, already learning directness of address.

"Do you know how to stitch caps?" he returned.

"No, sir," she replied.

"Have you had any experience at this kind of work?" he inquired.

She answered that she had not.

"Well," said the foreman, scratching his ear meditatively, "we do need a stitcher. We like experienced help, though. We've hardly got time to break people in." He paused and looked away out of the window. "We might, though, put you at finishing," he concluded reflectively.

"How much do you pay a week?" ventured Carrie, emboldened by a certain softness in the man's manner and his simplicity of address.

"Three and a half," he answered.

"Oh," she was about to exclaim, but she checked herself and allowed her thoughts to die without expression.

"We're not exactly in need of anybody," he went on vaguely, looking her over as one would a package.

• • • • •

The city had laid miles and miles of streets and sewers through regions where, perhaps, one solitary house stood out alone—a pioneer of the populous ways to be. There were regions open to the sweeping winds and rain, which were as yet lighted throughout the night with long, blinking lines of gas-lamps, fluttering in the wind. Narrow board walks extended out, passing here a house, and there a store, at far intervals, eventually ending on the open prairie.

• • • • •

"He said that if you married me you would only get ten thousand a year. That if you didn't and still lived with me you would get nothing at all. If you would leave me, or if I would leave you, you would get all of a million and a half. Don't you think you had better leave me now?"

These are isolated passages—the first two from *Sister Carrie,* the third from *Jennie Gerhardt*—and normally it would be as unkind to pick passages from Dreiser as it would be to quote for themselves those frustrated mental exchanges that Henry James's characters hold with each other. For Dreiser works in such detail that you never really feel the force of any until you see the whole structure, while James is preoccupied with an inner meditation that his own characters always seem to be interrupting. But even in these bits from Dreiser there is an overwhelming impression that puzzles and troubles us because we cannot trace it to its source. "One doesn't see how it's made," a French critic once complained about some book he was reviewing. That is the trouble we always have with Dreiser. Carrie measuring herself against the immensity of

Chicago, that wonderful night scene in which we see a generation just off the farms and out of the small towns confronting the modern city for the first time; the scene in which Hurstwood comes on Carrie sitting in the dark; Jennie Gerhardt's growing solitude even after the birth of her child; Clyde Griffiths and Roberta Alden walking around the haunted lakes when he is searching for one where he can kill her—one doesn't see the man writing this. We are too absorbed. Something is happening that tastes of fear, of the bottom loneliness of human existence, that just barely breaks into speech from the depths of our own souls; the planet itself seems to creak under our feet, and there are long lines of people bitterly walking to work in the morning dark, thinking only of how they can break through the iron circle of their frustration. Every line hurts. It hurts because you never get free enough of anything to ask what a character or a situation "really" means; it hurts because Dreiser is not trying to prove anything by it or to change what he sees; it hurts even when you are trying to tell yourself that all this happened in another time, that we are cleverer about life than Dreiser was. It hurts because it is all too much like reality to be "art."

It is because we have all identified Dreiser's work with reality that, for more than a half a century now, he has been for us not a writer like other writers, but a whole chapter of American life. From the very beginning, as one can see in reading over the reviews of *Sister Carrie,* Dreiser was accepted as a whole new class, a tendency, a disturbing movement in American life, an eruption from below. The very words he used, the dreaminess of his prose, the stilted but grim matter-of-fact of his method, which betrayed all the envy and wonder with which he looked at the great world outside—all this seemed to say that it was not art he worked with but *knowledge,* some new and secret knowledge. It was this that the reviewers instantly felt, that shocked the Doubledays so deeply, that explains the extraordinary bitterness toward Dreiser from the first—and that excited Frank Norris, the publisher's reader (Dreiser looked amazingly like the new, "primitive" types that Norris was getting into his own fiction). Dreiser was the man from outside, the man from below, who wrote with the terrible literalness of a child. It is this that is so clearly expressed in Frank Doubleday's efforts to kill the book, in the fact that most literary and general magazines in the country did not review the book at all, that even some newspapers reviewed the book a year late, and that the tone of these early reviews is plainly that of people trying to accustom themselves to an unpleasant shock.

Sister Carrie did not have a bad press; it had a frightened press, with many of the reviewers plainly impressed, but startled by the concentrated truthfulness of the book. The St. Louis *Mirror* complained that "the author writes with a startling directness. At times this directness seems to be the frankness of a vast unsophistication. . . . The scenes of the book are laid always among a sort of people that is numerous but seldom treated in a serious novel." The general reaction was that of the Newark *Sunday News,* almost a year after the book had been published. "Told with an unsparing realism and detail, it has all the interest of fact. . . . The possibility of it all is horrible: an appalling arraignment of human society. And there is here no word of preachment; there are scarcely any philosophic reflections or deductions expressed. The impression is simply one of truth, and therein lies at once the strength and the horror of it."

This was the new note of the book, the unrelieved seriousness

of it—but a seriousness so native, so unself-conscious, that Dreiser undoubtedly saw nothing odd about his vaguely "poetic" and questioning chapter titles, which were his efforts to frame his own knowledge, to fit it into a traditional system of thought, though he could not question any of his knowledge itself. Writing *Sister Carrie,* David Brion Davis comments, "was something like translating the Golden Plates." For Carrie was Dreiser's own sister, and he wrote without any desire to shock, without any knowledge that he could. Compare this with so "naturalistic" a book as Hardy's *Tess of the d'Urbervilles,* where the style is itself constantly commenting on the characters, and where the very old-fashioned turn of the prose, in all its complex urbanity, is an effort to interpret the story, to accommodate it to the author's own tradition of thought. Dreiser *could* not comment; so deeply had he identified himself with the story that there was no place left in it for him to comment *from.* And such efforts as he made to comment, in the oddly invertebrate chapter titles, were like gasps in the face of a reality from which he could not turn away. The book was exactly like a dream that Dreiser had lived through and which, in fact, after the failure of *Sister Carrie,* he was to live again, up to the very brink of Hurstwood's suicide.

It was this knowledge, this exclusive knowledge, this *kann nicht anders,* this absence of alternatives, that led people to resent Dreiser, and at the same time stunned the young writers of the period into instant recognition of his symbolic value to them. We never know how much has been missing from our lives until a true writer comes along. Everything which had been waiting for them in the gap between the generations, everything which Henry James said would belong to an "American Balzac"—that world of industrial capitalism which, James confessed, had been a "closed book" to him from his youth—everything free of "literature" and so free to become literature, now became identified with this "clumsy" and "stupid" ex-newspaperman whose book moved the new writers all the more deeply because they could not see where Dreiser's genius came from. To the young writers of the early twentieth century, Dreiser became, in Mencken's phrase, the Hindenburg of the novel—the great beast who pushed American life forward for them, who went on, blindly, unchangeably, trampling down the lies of gentility and Victorianism, of Puritanism and academicism. Dreiser was the primitive, the man from the abyss, the stranger who had grown up outside the Anglo-Saxon middle-class Protestant morality and so had no need to accept its sanctions. In Sherwood Anderson's phrase, he could be honored with "an apology for crudity"; and in fact the legend that *Sister Carrie* had been suppressed by the publisher's wife was now so dear to the hearts of the rising generation that Mrs. Doubleday became a classic character, the Carrie Nation of the American liberal epos, her ax forever lifted against "the truth of American life." So even writers like Van Wyck Brooks, who had not shared in the bitterness of Dreiser's early years, and who as socialists disapproved of his despair, now defended him as a matter of course—he cleared the way; in the phrase that was to be repeated with increasing meaninglessness through the years, he "liberated the American novel."

Dreiser now embodied the whole struggle of the new American literature. The "elderly virgins of the newspapers," as Mencken called them, never ceased to point out his deficiencies; the conservative academicians and New Humanists, the old fogeys and the young fogeys—all found in Dreiser everything new, brutal and alien they feared in American life. Gertrude Atherton was to say during the first World War that Dreiser represented the "Alpine School of Literature"— "Not a real American could be found among them with a magnifying glass"; Mary Austin was to notice that "our Baltic and Slavic stock will have another way than the English of experiencing love, and possibly a more limited way. . . . All of Theodore Dreiser's people love like the peasants in a novel by Bojer or Knut Hamsun. His women have a cowlike complaisance such as can be found only in people who have lived for generations close to the soil"; Stuart Sherman, in his famous article of 1915 on "The Barbaric Naturalism of Theodore Dreiser," made it clear that Dreiser, "coming from that 'ethnic' element of our mixed population," was thus unable to understand the higher beauty of the American spirit.

So Dreiser stood in no-man's-land, pushed ahead like a dumb ox by one camp, attacked by the other. Everything about him made him a polemical figure; his scandals, miseries, and confusions were as well-known as his books. The "liberals," the "modernists," defended books like *The "Genius"* because "it told the truth"—and how delighted they must have been when John S. Sumner tried to get the book banned in 1915 and anybody who *was* anybody (including Ezra Pound, John Reed and David Belasco) rushed to its defense. To the English novelists of the period (and *Sister Carrie* owed its sudden fame to the edition Heinemann brought out in London) he was like a powerhouse they envied amid the Georgian doldrums of literary London. How much of that fighting period comes back to you now when you discover Arnold Bennett on his feverish trips to America identifying all the raw, rich, teeming opportunities of American life with Dreiser, or listen to Ford Madox Ford—"Damn it all, it *is* fun to see that poor old language, that vehicle for conveying moderated thoughts, having the guts kicked out of it, like a deflated football, over all the fields of the boundless Middle West." While Mencken, in Dreiser's name, slew William Lyon Phelps in his thousands, the young English discovered that Dreiser was the friend of art. Each side in the controversy used Dreiser, and each, in its own way, was embarrassed. How many times did the young Turks have to swallow Dreiser's bad books, to explain away his faults, and how clear it is from reading Paul Elmer More (who was a deeper critic than his opponents and would have been almost a great one if he had not always tried to arm himself against American life) that he was always more moved by Dreiser's cosmic doubts than he could confess. More settled the problem, as he settled every writer he feared, by studying the man's "philosophy"—where he could show up Dreiser to his heart's content, and, in a prose that could not have been more removed from the actualities of the subject, prove that he had disposed forever of this intellectual upstart.

This pattern remained to the end—Dreiser was the great personifier. When he went to Russia, even the title of the book he wrote had to begin with Dreiser rather than with Russia; when Sinclair Lewis praised Dreiser in his Nobel Prize speech, he did so with all the enthusiasm of a Congressman trying for the farm vote; when Dreiser delivered himself of some remarks about Jews, the *Nation* was not so much indignant as bewildered that this son of the common people could express such illiberal sentiments; when he spoke against England at the beginning of the Second World War, there was a similar outcry that Dreiser was letting the masses down. It is typical of Dreiser's symbolic importance that a writer now so isolated as James T. Farrell has been able to find support for his own work only in Dreiser's example; that the word

plebeian has always been used either to blacken Dreiser or to favor him; that Eisenstein suffered so long to make a film of *An American Tragedy* that would be the ultimate exposure of American capitalism. When Dreiser joined the Communists, his act was greeted as everything but what it really was—the lonely and confused effort of an individual to identify himself with a group that had taken him up in his decline; when he died in 1945, in the heyday of American-Soviet friendship, one left-wing poet announced that Dreiser's faults had always been those of America anyway, that he was simply America writ large—"Much as we wish he had been surer, wiser, we cannot change the fact. The man was great in a way Americans uniquely understand who know the uneven contours of their land, its storms, its droughts, its huge and turbulent Mississippi, where his youth was spent." Even Dreiser's sad posthumous novels, *The Bulwark* and *The Stoic,* each of which centers around a dying old man, were written about with forced enthusiasm, as if the people attacking them were afraid of being called reactionary, while those who honestly liked them reported that they were *surprisingly* good. And how F. O. Matthiessen suffered all through the last year of his life to do justice to Dreiser as if that would fulfill an *obligation* to the cause of "progressivism" in America.

But soon after the war all this changed—Dreiser was now simply an embarrassment. The reaction against him was only partly literary, for much of it was founded on an understandable horror of the fraudulent "radicals" who had been exploiting Dreiser before his death. And thanks not a little to the cozy prosperity of a permanent war economy, America, it seemed, no longer required the spirit of protest with which Dreiser had been identified. The writers were now in the universities, and they all wrote about writing. No longer hoary sons of toil, a whole intelligentsia, post-Communist, post-Marxist, which could not look at Alger Hiss in the dock without shuddering at how near they had come to his fate, now tended to find their new ideology in the good old middle-class virtues. A new genteel tradition had come in. Writing in America had suddenly become very conscious that literature is made with words, and that these words should look nice on the page. It became a period when fine writing was everything, when every anonymous smoothie on *Time* could write cleaner prose about God's alliance with America than poor old Dreiser could find for anything, when even the *Senior Scholastic,* a magazine intended for high-school students, complained of Dreiser that "some of the writing would shock an English class." It is of this period, in which we live, that Saul Bellow has noted in his tribute to Dreiser [see Further Reading]:

> I think . . . that the insistence on neatness and correctness is one of the signs of a modern nervousness and irritability. When has clumsiness in composition been felt as so annoying, so enraging? The "good" writing of the *New Yorker* is such that one experiences a furious anxiety, in reading it, about errors and lapses from taste; finally what emerges is a terrible hunger for conformism and uniformity. The smoothness of the surface and its high polish must not be marred. One has a similar anxiety in reading a novelist like Hemingway and comes to feel in the end that Hemingway wants to be praised for the offenses he does not commit. He is dependable; he never names certain emotions or ideas, and he takes pride in that—it is a form of honor. In it, really, there is submissiveness, acceptance of restriction.

The most important expression of the reaction against Dreiser is Lionel Trilling's "Reality in America" [see excerpt dated 1946]. This essay expresses for a great many people in America just now their impatience with the insurgency that dominated our famously realistic fiction up to the war, and not since Paul Elmer More's essay of 1920 has anyone with so much critical insight made out so brilliant a case against Dreiser; not since William Dean Howells supported Stephen Crane's *Maggie* and not *Sister Carrie* has anyone contrasted so sharply those notorious faults of style and slovenly habits of thought which our liberal criticism has always treated as "essentially social and political virtues" with the wonderful play of mind and fertility of resource one finds in Henry James. Never has the case against the persistent identification of Dreiser with "reality" in America—coarse, heavy, external reality—been put with so much intellectual passion. For Mr. Trilling is writing against the decay of a liberal movement ruined largely by its flirtation with totalitarianism, by its disregard of human complexity and its fear of intellect. No one who has followed the extent to which our liberal critics have always acknowledged that Dreiser *is* a bad thinker—and have excused it on the grounds that the poor man at least "told the truth about American life"—can help but share Mr. Trilling's impatience with what has recently passed in this country for liberal "imagination."

But may it not be suggested that Henry James as a cultural hero serves us as badly as Dreiser once did? What happens whenever we convert a writer into a symbol is that we lose the writer himself in all his indefeasible singularity, his particular inimitable genius. A literature that modeled itself on Dreiser would be unbearable; a literature that saw all its virtues of literature in Henry James would be preposterous. If one thing is clear about our addiction to Henry James just now, it is that most of our new writing has nothing in common with James whatever. For James's essential quality is his intellectual appetite—"all life belongs to you"—his unending inner meditation, and not the air of detachment which so misleads us whenever we encounter it on the surface of the society James wrote about—the only society he knew, and one he despaired of precisely because it was never what it seemed. Just now, however, a certain genteel uninvolvement is dear to us, while Dreiser's bread lines and street-car strikes, his suffering inarticulate characters, his Chicago, his "commonness"—are that bad dream from which we have all awakened. As Dreiser's faults were once acclaimed as the virtues of the common man, so now we are ashamed of him because he brings up everything we should like to leave behind us.

There is no "common man"—though behind the stereotype (how *this* executioner waits!) stand those who may yet prepare all too common a fate for us all. Literary people, as a class, can get so far away from the experience of other classes that they tend to see them only symbolically. Dreiser as "common man" once served a purpose; now he serves another. The basic mistake of all the liberal critics was to think that he could ever see this world as something to be ameliorated. They misjudged the source of Dreiser's strength. This is the point that David Brion Davis documents so well in his study ["Dreiser and Naturalism Revisited"] of what Dreiser and the early naturalists really believed. For as Mr. Davis shows, these writers and painters were "naturalists" only in the stark sense that the world had suddenly come down to them divested of its supernatural sanctions. They were actually obsessed with the transcendental possibilities of this "real" world; like Whitman, they gloried in the beauty of the iron city. In their

contemplative acceptance of this world, in their indifference to social reform, in their awe before life itself, they were actually not in the tradition of political "liberalism" but in that deeper American strain of metaphysical wonder which leads from the early pietists through Whitman to the first painters of the modern city.

This gift of contemplativeness, of wonder, of reverence, even, is at the center of Dreiser's world—who can forget the image of the rocking chair in *Sister Carrie,* where from *this* cradle endlessly rocking man stares forever at a world he is not too weak but too bemused to change? And it is this lack of smartness, this puzzled lovingness for the substance of all our mystery, that explains why we do not know what to *do* with Dreiser today. For Dreiser is in a very old, a very difficult, a very lonely American tradition. It is no longer "transcendentalist," but always it seeks to transcend. This does not mean that Dreiser's philosophy is valuable in itself, or that his excursions into philosophy and science—fields for which he was certainly not well equipped—have to be excused. It does mean that the vision is always in Dreiser's work, and makes it possible. Just as the strength of his work is that he got into it those large rhythms of wonder, of curiosity, of amazement before the power of the universe that give such largeness to his characters and such unconscious majesty to life itself, so the weakness and instability of his work is that he could become almost too passive before the great thing he saw out there, always larger than man himself. The truth is, as Eliseo Vivas says in his essay ["Dreiser, an Inconsistent Mechanist"], that Dreiser is "not only an American novelist but a universal novelist, in the very literal sense of the word. The mystery of the universe, the puzzle of destiny, haunts him; and he, more than any other of his contemporaries, has responded to the need to relate the haunting sense of puzzlement and mystery to the human drama. No other American novelist of his generation has so persistently endeavored to look at men under the aspect of eternity. It is no . . . paradox, therefore, that . . . while Dreiser tries to demonstrate that man's efforts are vain and empty, by responding to the need to face the problem of destiny, he draws our attention to dimensions of human existence, awareness of which is not encouraged by current philosophical fashions. . . ." To understand how this gets into Dreiser's work one must look not back of it but into it for that sense of "reality" which he thirsted for—that whole reality, up to the very shores of light, that made him cry out in *Jennie Gerhardt:* "We turn our faces away from the creation of life as if that were the last thing that man should dare to interest himself in, openly."

This is what makes Dreiser so painful—in his "atheism," his cosmology; this is what dismays us in our sensible culture, just as it bothered a generation that could never understand Dreiser's special bitterness against orthodox religion, against the churches; this is what drove Dreiser to look for God in the laboratories, to write essays on "My Creator." He may have been a "naturalist," but he was certainly not a materialist. What sticks in our throats is that Dreiser is outside the agreed boundaries of our concern, that he does not accept our "society" as the whole of reality, that he may crave after its fleshpots, but does not believe that getting along is the ultimate reach of man's effort. For we live in a time when traditionalists and "progressives" and ex-progressives alike are agreed that the man not to be trusted is the man who does not fit in, who has no "position," who dares to be distracted—when this great going machine, this prig's paradise in which we live just now, is the best of all possible worlds.

Dreiser committed the one sin that a writer can commit in our society—he would not accept this society itself as wholly real. And it is here, I think, that we can get perspective on his famous awkwardness. For what counts most with a writer is that his reach should be felt as well as his grasp, that words should be his means, not his ends. It is this that Malcolm Cowley noticed when he wrote that "there are moments when Dreiser's awkwardness in handling words contributes to the force of his novels, since he seems to be groping in them for something on a deeper level than language." This is what finally disturbs us about Dreiser in a period when fine writing is like a mirror that gives back our superficiality. Dreiser hurts because he is always looking to the source; to that which broke off into the mysterious halves of man's existence; to that which is behind language and sustains it; to that which is not ourselves but gives life to our words. (pp. 3-12)

Alfred Kazin, in an introduction to The Stature of Theodore Dreiser: A Critical Survey of the Man and His Work, *edited by Alfred Kazin and Charles Shapiro, Indiana University Press, 1955, pp. 3-12.*

DONALD PIZER (essay date 1976)

[*Pizer is an American educator and critic who has written extensively on the twentieth-century American novel. In the following excerpt he offers a discussion of* Jennie Gerhardt, *focusing upon the characterization of the eponymous protagonist and of Lester Kane.*]

Jennie Gerhardt consists of two unequal narrative segments, each of which is itself made up of two parts. The first segment, twenty-three chapters of the sixty-two-chapter novel, tells of Jennie's seductions, first by Senator Brander and then by Lester Kane. The remainder of the novel deals with Jennie's life with Lester. This segment divides roughly into an upward movement culminating in the happy ménage at Hyde Park and a downward movement which includes the separation of Lester and Jennie and the deaths of Vesta and Lester.

The first portion of the novel, that devoted to the seduction of Jennie by Senator Brander, is the least successful because of its blatant theme of natural generosity and goodness misunderstood and mistreated by the rigid social and religious moralism which passes for righteousness in the world. A large, full-bodied girl with a dreamy, poetic temperament, Jennie resembles Carrie [the protagonist of Dreiser's first novel, *Sister Carrie*] in that she is a creature of emotion rather than reason. But unlike Carrie, the beauty which she finds in life and nature moves her to give rather than to take; hers is the large expansiveness of nature itself and not the necessary protective self-interest of the artist seeking to find and express the beauty in nature.

Although Dreiser anticipates this characterization in his first-chapter comments on Jennie's "innate affection" and "poetic mind," he states it most fully in the second chapter, which is cast in the form of a prose-poem. "The spirit of Jennie—who shall express it," he begins, and then makes the attempt himself by means of a series of brief vignettes and images which reveal her spirit to be essentially that of nature itself at its most beautiful and pure:

> When the soft, low call of the wood-doves, those spirits of the summer, came out of the distance, she would incline her head and listen, the whole spiritual quality of it dropping like silver bubbles into her own great heart.

> Where the sunlight was warm and the shadows flecked with its splendid radiance she delighted to wonder at the pattern of it, to walk where it was most golden, and follow with instinctive appreciation the holy corridors of the trees.

Dreiser's theme in such passages is less that of a religion of nature than of a natural religion; her spirit does not so much learn goodness from nature as find confirmed in natural beauty its own inherent goodness. But such a spirit, though it is at home in nature, is an anomaly in the world of men, a "world of flesh into which has been woven pride and greed [which] looks askance at the idealist, the dreamer." In particular, the world of men cannot understand the instinctive generosity of natural virtue, since the world of men buys and sells rather than gives. Jennie is held in contempt by society, Dreiser tells us at a later point, because she "had not sought to hold herself dear."

The novel thus begins on the edge of moral allegory. Jennie, whose warm and generous spirit reflects a natural religion, is to be judged and punished for her expression of that spirit by the narrow and prohibitive absolutes of social morality and formal religion, as personified by Dr. Ellswanger, Pastor Wendt, and old Gerhardt. And, of course, what better way to dramatize a moral allegory than by a sexual fall, one in which the reality of Jennie's innocence and virtue is poised against the illusion of wickedness imposed upon her because she has broken a commandment and violated a social law. The birth of Jennie's illegitimate child completes the allegory. Though born in what the world believes to be sin, the child is in truth a product of the beneficent "processes of the all-mother." To both Jennie and Dreiser, the birth is a confirmation of the beauty and goodness of the generative principle in life, and Jennie is not only unsullied but uplifted and strengthened by the experience.

In the context of turn-of-the-century morality and fiction, Dreiser's themes in this opening portion of *Jennie Gerhardt* have integrity and force. Like Hardy, he was drawing upon an idea present in both romantic poetry and evolutionary thought—the belief that man was part and parcel of the processes of nature—in order to raise to tragic stature a poor servant girl who was a living example of this idea. In particular, both writers sought to deal with the physical and psychological realities of sex in relation to this idea, and thus both wrote seduction stories which included much lyric prose on the heroine's affinity to nature. In Dreiser's hands, however, the story and the prose descend to the bathetic and lachrymose. His purple passages sound every cliché and hackneyed metaphor in nineteenth-century romantic poetry. And the personae and plot of Jennie's initial seduction could serve as a model for a "classic" sentimental novel: the poor but honest workingman's daughter, the upper-class family benefactor, the precipitating family crisis requiring the benefactor's aid, the pregnancy which follows his taking advantage of her gratitude, the desertion of the heroine by the lover and the resulting family and social obloquy. In short, the novel is pushed in the direction of the dead-end simplicity and sentimentality of a woman's magazine romance by Dreiser's lush initial characterization of Jennie and by her situation as a victim of her own virtue and of chance.

Dreiser saves the novel from this fate in two ways. He soon shifts its direction—initially and to a slight degree in the second seduction and then completely in the major segment dealing with Lester and Jennie after her second "fall." And he introduces even into the first portion of the novel a number of themes which relieve and indeed undermine its otherwise bathetic tone and action. For example, he endows Jennie with the same moving quality he had given Carrie—the wonder and excitement of an impressionable sensibility as it encounters for the first time the material beauty and splendors of life. The early chapters thus evoke with considerable power the emotional reality of two worlds—the Gerhardt home, with its sickness and poverty and eight people crowded into a few rooms, and the imposing elegance and plush of the Columbus House, with its warmth and light and its color and music. "How beautiful life must be for the rich," Jennie thinks at one point, and her thought has all the evocative naïveté of social innocence at its most penetrating. Jennie's response to Brander, like that of Carrie to Drouet and Hurstwood, is therefore inseparable from the dawning of her aesthetic sensibility. His room to her is a place of "wonder," and she associates it with the "heavenly" and "magical" in short, with an exultation of the spirit related to an Arabian Nights elevation of the poor beggar boy to a realm of riches and beauty. The richness of the carpet, the brightness and warmth of the room, the comfort and good taste of its furnishings—all to Jennie have the beauty of nature itself. Her response to beauty has a Keatsian depth and complexity, for the sensuous moves her spirit in whatever context she finds it. Dreiser has in this instance taken a conventional aspect of the seduction formula—the social superiority and therefore grandeur of the Lord—and transformed it into an effective and distinctively Dreiserian theme.

Dreiser also raises the seduction from its bathetic base by endowing Jennie and Brander with "human" characteristics within their stereotyped roles. Although Jennie is "beauty in distress" from her appearance in Chapter I in the hotel lobby with her mother until the birth of the dead Brander's illegitimate child in Chapter XI, the relationship between Brander and Jennie is itself complex and moving rather than superficial and formulistic. Establishing a motif which is to recur throughout the novel, Dreiser tells us that Jennie finds Brander's room a "home" for her spirit. The room is a place of gaiety and of human contact and exchange where Jennie's natural warmth has an outlet and where her qualities are appreciated. The repeated meetings of Brander and Jennie in his room thus occur within several overlapping emotional contexts. The two figures are a kind of provincial Othello and Desdemona. He is the experienced, world-weary warrior (political in this instance) who has "received his hard knocks and endured his losses" and therefore has an aura "which touched and awakened the sympathies of the imaginative." And she is the youthful innocent whose association with Brander represents her first contact with the world at large. Their propinquity, and her admiration and sympathy and his response to her natural affection and freshness, encourage the growth of love. But Brander and Jennie are also father and daughter. Their attachment therefore involves not only the affection of the protected for the protector but the more complex emotion of the provoking innocence of the daughter and the subconscious guilt of the father. When Brander announces to Jennie his generous plans for her and the Gerhardts, "reaching up impulsively, she put her arms around him. 'You're so good to me,' she said with the loving tone of a daughter."

Jennie is thus not a seduced rural maid and Brander is not a cunning upper-class villain despite the overt structuring of their relationship within this sentimental formula and despite

old Gerhardt's almost immediate belief that Jennie has suffered a fate worse than death. Brander has an intense need and desire for Jennie coupled with an almost equally powerful sense of parental responsibility for her. And his one act of sex with her occurs not as a planned seduction in which he seeks payment for his efforts as a family benefactor (though their lovemaking has this appearance), but rather has its principal source in Jennie's impulsive response to the deepest strain in her nature, her thankfulness at his generosity. (pp. 105-09)

Jennie's seduction by Lester Kane, the principal event of the second portion of the first segment of the novel, has many of the same characteristics as her seduction by Brander. The Gerhardt family has moved from Columbus to Cleveland in order to begin a new life, and Jennie finds work in the cultivated, upper-class home of the Bracebridges. Again, as with the Columbus House, her taste and awareness are improved by her contact with a new and "higher" world, but again a step upward in knowledge brings the danger of sex. Lester Kane pursues the chase with vigor and is aided by another Gerhardt family crisis, one caused by the accidental burning of old Gerhardt's hands. Jennie is again placed in the sacrificial role of appealing for aid to a man who desires her, and again his aid is followed by her acceptance of the man as a lover.

The similarity between the two seductions is in fact only superficial. They differ in most important aspects, and these differences constitute some of the most significant themes in the novel. Kane is no conscience-stricken, fatherly benefactor but an aggressively virile man of thirty-six. And Jennie now has the experience to recognize immediately Lester's sexual interest in her. The sexual basis of their response to each other is not covert and repressed, as it was throughout most of Jennie's meetings with Brander; it is a conscious and electric force in their awareness from the moment Kane sees Jennie at work at Mrs. Bracebridge's home. Moreover, Jennie's and Lester's interest in each other is not based primarily on role, as had been true for Jennie and Brander, for whom the realities of experience and innocence, father and daughter, and benefactor and beneficiary had been more vital than their distinctive qualities as individuals. Rather, the love of Jennie and Lester is to Dreiser the consequence of their essential beings. Kane is a vigorously possessive male. His "You belong to me" to Jennie echoes exactly Brander's statement, but Kane means exclusive proprietorship rather than the protection which Brander intends. Kane's powerful drive to possess and to hold is matched by Jennie's instinctive desire to be possessed and to be held. His is the masculine principle of iron, hers the feminine one of softness. In a passage heavy with sexual imagery, Dreiser describes the inevitable attraction that a Jennie will have for a Lester:

> It is a curious characteristic of the non-defensive disposition that it is like a honey-jar to flies. Nothing is brought to it and much is taken away. Around a soft, yielding, unselfish disposition men swarm naturally. They sense this generosity, this non-protective attitude from afar. A girl like Jennie is like a comfortable fire to the average masculine mind; they gravitate to it, seek its sympathy, yearn to possess it.

Each senses the basic nature of the other. "She was the kind of woman who was made for a man—one man," Lester thinks. "All her attitude toward sex was bound up with love, tenderness, service." And when Lester kisses Jennie for the first time, "She was horrified, stunned, like a bird in the grasp of a cat; but through it all something tremendously vital and insistent was speaking to her."

Dreiser was seeking to depict in the love between Jennie and Lester one kind of sexual and temperamental compatibility. Jennie and Lester are drawn to each other not only by a "magnetic" desire which might blaze and then die but by permanent needs—the need of the strong man whose strength derives in part from the act of possession, and the need of the "soft, yielding" woman whose deepest emotional life lies in the act of being possessed, in the giving of herself not only sexually but in every other way. The seduction plot is therefore now extraneous except for its efficiency in bringing together Jennie and Lester rapidly and outside of marriage. Their relationship is primarily that of mutual responsiveness, of a "natural affinity," despite its shape of an experienced benefactor taking advantage of a girl in need. When Jennie agrees to give herself to Lester, she is "sorrowful" because of the illicit circumstances of her acceptance, but her "yes" is spoken "with a strange thrill of affection."

Besides lacking the quality of betrayed innocence, the relationship between Jennie and Lester also lacks the earlier melodramatic elements of the loss of the benefactor, a pregnancy, and public exposure. Jennie and Lester begin to live together, and they soon discover more about each other and about the difficulties which their relationship entails. Put another way, Dreiser has moved the novel from the theme of Jennie as a betrayed child of nature to that of two human beings involved in the complex interaction between their love and the social reality which is the context of that love.

A major cause of this new direction in *Jennie Gerhardt* is the importance which Lester Kane now assumes in the story. In a long passage in Chapter XVII, Dreiser characterizes Lester as a New Man. Like Dreiser, Lester is a first-generation American and a lapsed Catholic whose response to the complexity, variety, and speed of communication of ideas in the modern world has been a loss both of faith and of fixed beliefs. "Life was not proved to him," Dreiser tells us. Lester is a Henry Adams who has been reading Herbert Spencer, for he has been "confused by the multiplicity of things, the vastness of the panorama of life, the glitter of its details, the unsubstantial nature of its forms, the uncertainty of their justification." His response to this confusion and loss has been to turn inward to his own interests and desires and away from all institutionalized forms of belief and behavior. Max Nordau, in his widely read and discussed *Degeneration* (1895), had dealt with this phenomenon and had stressed the personal neuroticism which he believed was one of its major characteristics. But Dreiser, though he alludes to the "insomnia, melancholia, and insanity" caused by the impact of modern life and thought upon the reflective mind, casts Kane in a different, more positive mold. Lester's doubts take the complementary forms of a desire to satisfy his "animal" nature and a desire to preserve his personal freedom. Physical need is the only certainty in an otherwise unstable universe; and freedom is necessary to escape the restrictions imposed upon life by those who believe. The two join in Lester's attitude toward women in a way which is crucial for Jennie: "He wanted the comfort of feminine companionship, but he was more and more disinclined to give up his personal liberty in order to obtain it."

The initial impression we have of Lester is therefore of a man who is strengthened rather than weakened by his realization of the multiplicity of life because his insight has led him to cultivate a primitive self-interest and an emotional integrity. But the combination of doubt and self-interest in Lester's makeup also contributes to a basic weakness in his character despite his appearance of unassailable strength. Because he is a man of reflective insight, he realizes that there are few matters in the world worth one's intense preoccupation. Most beliefs are false and most difficulties will sort themselves out in time.

> He flattered himself that he had a grasp upon a right method of living, a method which was nothing more than a quiet acceptance of social conditions as they were, tempered by a little personal judgment as to the right and wrong of individual conduct. Not to fuss and fume, not to cry out about anything, not to be mawkishly sentimental; to be vigorous and sustain your personality intact—such was his theory of life, and he was satisfied that it was a good one.

In short, Lester is an unbeliever but he is not a fighter.

Moreover, Lester is confined by the same animal self-interest which is the source of his apparent independence and strength. He is a man who desires and needs above all the "comforts" of life. Dreiser means by this term, which he uses again and again in the novel to designate that which preeminently attracts and holds Lester, a kind of sensuous ease of body and mind. This ease takes many forms, from Lester's delight in "the luxury of love" which he finds in Jennie to his pleasure in the "homey" atmosphere of his family's Cincinnati house to his satisfaction in living and working among wealthy and cultivated men and women.

Dreiser thus characterizes Lester as a man whose strength and independence seem adequate to wrench his life with Jennie out of the pattern to which its irregular origin and their different social classes have apparently destined it but whose basic inclinations are nevertheless toward an accommodation with his world rather than a struggle against it. Kane's tragic fate has two major characteristics. He is the New Man who, with some pride, believes himself free of conventional forms and institutions but who discovers that they nevertheless control him both materially and spiritually. And his belief in freedom as the one firm principle in life prevents him from securing Jennie irrevocably when he can still do so without facing a major challenge to his need for comfort. Unconsciously and subtly bound by the cords of his own temperament and ideas despite his seeming freedom and power, Kane makes his way through life increasingly puzzled by its paradoxes and ultimately dismayed by its meaninglessness.

Because Jennie's primary desire in life is to give of herself, and because in Lester she has found a satisfactory fulfillment of that need, she appears to be a static figure in the latter portion of *Jennie Gerhardt.* In fact, however, she both grows and acts, and her development and initiative contribute to the tragic irony that as the washerwoman's daughter matures intellectually and socially into a fit mate for Lester, the possibility of achieving a permanent union gradually lessens.

The matrix of Jennie's growth is now the world of men rather than of nature. From her experience at Mrs. Bracebridge's and from her early life and travels with Lester, she quickly acquires adeptness and assurance in dress, deportment, and social custom. And, more significantly, she acquires from Lester himself a knowledge of the structure of society and of life. By the time she and Lester go abroad, some ten years after their meeting in Cleveland, she is not only an appropriate and admired companion for him but can appreciate the tragic meaning of the ancient civilizations of Europe and Africa which they visit. She now shares Lester's breadth of vision. Although she clings to the ideal of marriage, she has otherwise adopted his moral relativism, particularly in matters of sex and religion.

From the opening pages of the novel, those encountering Jennie have sensed her indefinable largeness of temperament. Both Dreiser and his characters attach a constantly recurring dual motif to this quality. Jennie is not only a "good" woman but a "big" woman. At first, these characteristics are rendered primarily by her large-souled generosity. But by the close of the novel, she has also developed in perception, not only in "philosophical" matters but in her judgment of others. She continues to be generous to all whom she meets, but she now understands consciously as well as instinctively whom or what she is responding to. When old Gerhardt dies, she weeps not only because she loves him and has long since forgiven him but because she now sees his life in "perspective" and realizes its hardships and difficulties. And when she and Lester face the crisis created by Archibald Kane's will, it is Jennie who has a fuller recognition of Lester's essential character than anyone else in the novel. "He cared, in his way," she realizes. "He could not care for any one enthusiastically and demonstratively. He could care enough to seize her and take her to himself as he had, but he could not care enough to keep her if something more important appeared."

Jennie thus moves from her earlier simplicity as a symbolic equivalent of nature's generosity to a figure of some complexity. Though still cast in the pathetic role of the noble spirit hounded by the world, her actions within that role now have a hard as well as a soft edge. Her deception of Lester about Vesta, her unconscious attempts to force him into marriage by leaving him, and her later bitterness at his ready acceptance of her own suggestion of separation are the acts and emotions of a woman rather than a paragon.

At first Jennie and Lester have little difficulty, for Lester is circumspect and he and Jennie live together primarily at the Gerhardts' home in Cleveland. But when they move to Chicago their relationship becomes known—first vaguely by rumors and then fully and explicitly by Louise's accidental discovery of their flat. Lester initially believes that he can ignore the disapproval of his family and the world and live as he wishes to. But gradually he realizes that he must choose between Jennie and almost everything else he values in life—the familiar world of wealth and power in which he has flourished.

Dreiser weaves an elaborate ironic theme into his account of this long, drawn-out crisis in the lives of Jennie and Lester, a crisis which is the principal fictional event of the second half of the novel. Lester, the man of action and strength, is unable to make a decision. From his parents' discovery of his relationship with Jennie to the point ten years later when the provisions of his father's will must be faced, his characteristic response to his dilemma is to postpone a decision. It is Jennie, therefore, with her "soft, yielding" disposition, who must take the decisive step. Dreiser engages in some careful and indeed contrived plotting in order to make her aware of both the availability of Letty and the contents of the will. Jennie is thus placed in a position in which her innate self-sacrificial nature must express itself. The tragic irony in her persuasion

of Lester that they must separate is not merely that it is she rather than Lester who is the motive force in this decision but also that her generosity in this instance is victorious over her instinctive recognition of the depth and permanence of their love for each other.

Jennie's mistake is not primarily an error in judgment. It is rather a flaw inseparable from the beneficent generosity which at once elevates her above the rest of mankind and lowers her self-estimation so severely that she may actually harm others as well as herself. Any attempt, however, to describe Jennie as a traditional tragic figure would falsify both her character and the aesthetic effect of her fate. For despite her one significant error, hers is primarily a tragedy of deprivation rather than of chaos resulting from an action. She is both the "good" woman who suffers because her nature and actions are not understood by the world and the universal mother whose children have left her or died. The first is the more obvious theme because it is introduced early in the novel and because its pathetic effect is close to the surface of the work. The second, however, becomes the deeper and more compelling theme as the novel progresses. Jennie's life consists in part of a constantly narrowing focus for her love. After the breakup of the Gerhardt family, she still has old Gerhardt, Lester, and Vesta. But one by one they depart until she is reduced to the artifice of adopting orphans. And they too will soon leave her, and then will come loveless "days and days in endless reiteration."

Jennie's loss of Lester, first through his departure and then his death, must therefore be seen in the context of her other losses. There are four major deaths in the novel—Mrs. Gerhardt, old Gerhardt, Vesta, and Lester—and at each Jennie is heartbroken and weeps. The causes of these deaths or separations—old age, illness, and social convention—represent the force that makes for transience in human relationships and in life itself. Jennie, Dreiser tells us, is someone for whom "life was made up of those mystic chords of sympathy and memory which bind up the transient elements of nature into a harmonious and enduring scene." The specific "scene" which Dreiser refers to in this passage is the house at Hyde Park where Jennie, Lester, Vesta, and old Gerhardt live harmoniously and happily, thus arresting for a brief period the impermanence of life. That this scene is destroyed by the death of old Gerhardt and the separation of Lester and Jennie and eventually has its last remnant of love removed by the death of Vesta represents the fragile and temporary hold we have on our moments of joy and fulfillment. The depth of our response to Jennie's life is thus conditioned not only by her limited circumstance as a woman wronged by men within a particular social reality but by her universal circumstance as a woman "wronged" by life itself. The frequent comment that Jennie is "merely" a figure of pathos rather than of tragedy is largely irrelevant. She is a moving figure whose emotional life contains one of the great themes in all literature.

Lester's condition for several years after he and Jennie begin to live together is one of equilibrium as he successfully satisfies his desire for both freedom and "comfort." From the beginning, however, he recognizes the possible conflict between his unwillingness to "justify" his relationship with Jennie to his family and the great pleasure he derives from the order and power lent his life by his role in the family concern. "It was something," he reflects, "to be a factor in an institution so stable, so distinguished, so honestly worth while." Of these two worlds, it appears that Jennie's has the stronger hold on

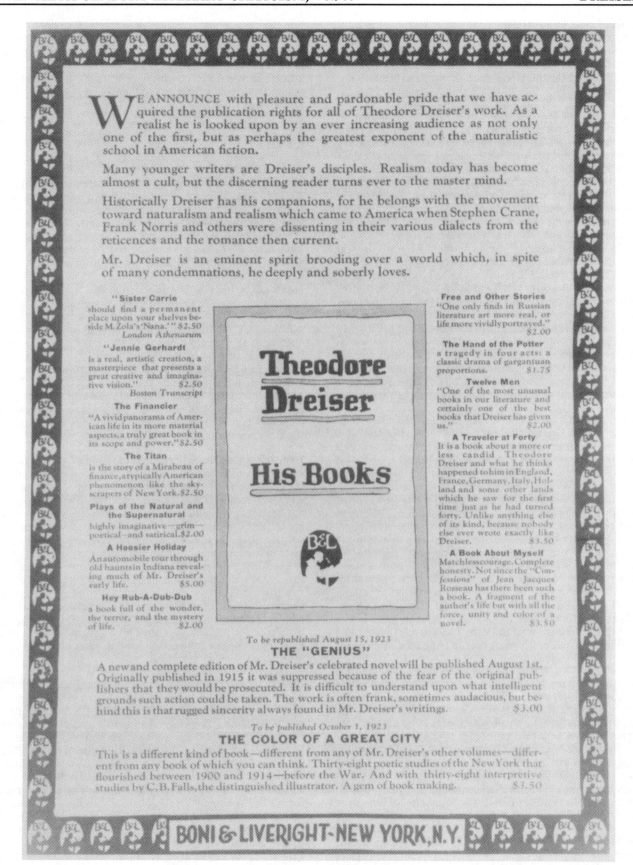

1923 advertisement by Dreiser's publisher.

Lester, for his love increases as he comes to know her fully, and he delights in her deep vein of receptive sensuality and in her love for him. And he seems as well to be fully in control of his family and to be strong enough to resist any pressure that might be brought to bear upon his personal life from any direction.

Lester does not realize at this point, however, that men are limited by their social environments and that they court danger when they violate these limits. Dreiser introduces this theme overtly in a brief chapter-opening exercise on the theory of Social Darwinism. Animals, Dreiser notes, have their circumscribed spheres of possible life and so do men, though the boundaries for men are social rather than physical. "The opinions, pleas, and judgments of society serve as boundaries which are none the less real for being intangible." Man is not necessarily doomed when he crosses such a boundary, but he cannot live "comfortably"—a key term for Lester—when he does so. Lester thus resembles Hurstwood more than he does Frank Cowperwood. Like Hurstwood, he has reached out for the forbidden pleasures of life and in so doing has cut himself off from his safe and comfortable world. He is of course superior to Hurstwood in both intellect and position, but like him he nevertheless finds that he lacks the strength to begin a new life in an alien world in middle age. Hurstwood's step was irreversible, whereas Lester can and does turn back. But for either man to choose is to choose wrongly. Not to have possessed Carrie or not to have lived with Jennie would have been torture, but to choose love is also to choose failure.

Only a superhuman Cowperwood can avoid this universal dilemma, and as Dreiser makes clear early in *Jennie Gerhardt* when he compares Lester and his brother Robert, Lester is no Cowperwood. Lester is "bigger" than Robert in the same sense that Jennie is a "big" woman. He possesses a wide-ranging, sympathetic understanding of life while Robert is cold and sanctimonious. This difference is reflected in their business principles. "Lester was for building up trade through friendly relationship, concessions, personal contact, and favors. Robert was for pulling everything tight, cutting down the cost of production, and offering such financial inducements as would throttle competition." (Lester personifies a pre-Civil War capitalist ideal, Robert the postwar reality.) In their battle for control of the company, a battle in which Lester's relationship with Jennie plays a vital role, Robert is victorious. He is "the clean, decisive man, Lester the man of doubts" who lacks the "subtlety," "guile," and "ruthlessness" necessary to succeed in great economic affairs.

An important revelation of Lester's limitations occurs in the incident involving his discovery of the existence of Jennie's illegitimate child, Vesta. On the surface, it seems that the discovery is beneficial. The last secret between Jennie and Lester is exposed, Lester soon becomes fond of the child, and his acceptance of its presence contributes to the establishment of the Hyde Park home where he and Jennie are so content for several years. But in the process of resolving Jennie's "offense" in having the child and in not revealing it, Lester reveals himself as a man powerfully conditioned by the assumptions of his class and sex despite his conception of himself as a New Man. "Jennie was before him as the criminal at the bar. He, the righteous, the moral, the pure of heart, was in the judgment seat. Now to sentence her—to make up his mind what course of action he should pursue." He decides to leave her but discovers that there is a major gap between "theorizing" about a decision and taking it in the face of the

familiar "usage" of "comforts, appetites and passions." So he determines to let matters continue as they were, with the exception that Jennie must now clearly understand that there is no possibility of marriage. Thus, by revealing his susceptibility to conventional moralism, by his indecision, and by his failure to recognize the depth of his love for Jennie and therefore his need to marry her in order to forestall his social vulnerability, Lester has anticipated the doom of their relationship at the very moment that he has apparently given it new life.

The years that follow this incident expose fully the impossibility of Lester's situation given his character and circumstances. Gradually his relationship with Jennie becomes known, initially to Chicago friends and acquaintances and then to his family—first Louise, then Robert, and finally Archibald Kane himself, who, despite his fondness for Lester, has come under Robert's control. Both Archibald's will and a Sunday supplement "feature" about Lester and Jennie cruelly distort their love as well as place Lester in an intolerable position. The will is a testament to that aspect of social morality which judges a situation rather than individuals. Lester is to receive his full share of the estate if he leaves Jennie, a small legacy if he marries her, and—after three years—nothing at all if he continues to live with her outside of marriage. The newspaper account attempts "to frame up a Romeo and Juliet story in which Lester should appear as an ardent, self-sacrificing lover, and Jennie as a poor and lovely working-girl, lifted to great financial and social heights by the devotion of her millionaire lover." The will, in brief, misunderstands because it is based upon a conventional moralism, the story upon a conventional sentimentalism.

Lester's response to the pressures stemming from the disclosure of his relationship with Jennie is a permanent indecision. He has several opportunities to give her up—most notably when she herself tries to leave him after Louise's discovery—but he cannot bring himself to do so. But neither can he bring himself to marry her in the face of the scandal and family opposition that this step would entail. A solution finally offers itself in the fortuitous reappearance of Letty, an old admirer of his, at the point when he realizes that he must make a decision within the three years permitted by the will. Now a wealthy widow, Letty appears to offer the best of both worlds: a woman of cultivation and warmth, she is also eminently eligible and a suitable social match. Beleaguered by his family, by Letty (who has always wanted him), and by Jennie herself, he permits himself to be persuaded that there must be a separation.

Although Lester successfully implements this decision by his departure and by his marriage to Letty two years afterward, it does not bring him peace. True, he now assumes a major role in business and society. And his life with Letty is placid and satisfying. But despite his successful reestablishment of himself as a man of worldly authority, Lester is troubled and unhappy. He soon realizes that whatever Letty's attractions, Jennie is by far the "bigger" woman. And he is now fully conscious of having deeply wronged Jennie both in not marrying her when it was possible to do so early in their relationship and in leaving her. His years without Jennie thus contain a growing world-weariness and pessimism and a self-indulgent Epicureanism. Dreiser's brief account of these years and of Lester's death has an allegorical simplicity. Deprived of the "spiritual" bulwark of Jennie, Lester has sunk into despair and mere animalism. Crudely put, he has an empty soul and an overactive body, both of which contribute to his early death. At his deathbed, however, with Letty conveniently absent in Europe, he and Jennie are momentarily reunited. He expresses his sorrow and guilt, she her undying love, and they are at peace. Just before his death, she tells him about her life since their separation, and "He listened comfortably, for her voice was soothing to him." So Lester again gains a measure of "comfort" in this final moment.

For many readers, however, the most memorable and significant scene in the novel is not that of Lester's death, which has mawkish overtones, but rather that of his visit to Jennie after the death of Vesta. Deeply depressed by Vesta's death and by his realization that he erred in leaving Jennie, Lester tells her that

> It isn't myself that's important in this transaction apparently; the individual doesn't count much in the situation. I don't know whether you see what I'm driving at, but all of us are more or less pawns. We're moved about like chessmen by circumstances over which we have no control.

This famous pronouncement, which has supplied several generations of literary historians with a ubiquitous image for the philosophical center of American naturalism, requires careful analysis both in its immediate context and in relation to the novel as a whole if it is to be properly understood.

Whatever the general truth of Lester's words, they represent a personal truth. His pawn image expresses both his sense of ineffectualness in the face of the central dilemma of his life and a covert supernaturalism which has characterized his thought throughout the novel despite his overt freethinking. Earlier he had attributed his difficulties merely to bad luck, as in the misadventure which allowed Louise to discover his living arrangements with Jennie. But by the time he and Jennie separate, he has elevated and generalized "fate" into a specific force which is at once social, supernatural, and (as far as he is concerned), malevolent:

> It was only when the storms set in and the winds of adversity blew and he found himself facing the armed forces of convention that he realized he might be mistaken as to the value of his personality, that his private desires and opinions were as nothing in the face of a public conviction; that he was wrong. The race spirit, or social avatar, the "Zeitgeist" as the Germans term it, manifested itself as something having a system in charge, and the organization of society began to show itself to him as something based on possibly a spiritual, or, at least, supernatural counterpart.

Lester's speculative statement that men are pawns in the control of circumstances is thus in part an explanation and a defense of his own conduct. In particular, it is a covert apology to Jennie for his failure to marry her when he could have done so. But it is also a powerful means of characterizing Lester. Throughout his life he had lived for the moment and had postponed making decisions about the direction of his life. But the decisionless flow of time contained an impetus of events which constituted an implicit and irreversible decision, and when Lester at last awoke to the fact that his life has been decided for him, he bitterly and angrily blamed fate.

Because Lester is a perceptive and on the whole an honest figure, his belief that men are pawns involves more than a rationalization of his own indecisiveness and ineffectuality. His belief also aptly characterizes social reality as that reality has

been dramatized in the novel. The pressure of circumstance on Lester in his relationship with Jennie has indeed been intense, from their initial meeting within the convention of a seduction—a convention which appears to preclude marriage—to the later opposition of Lester's personal, business, and social worlds to the continuation of the relationship. In a passage cut from Chapter XL of the final holograph, Dreiser himself, as narrator, echoed Lester's attribution of superhuman powers to social force. "The conventions in their way," he wrote, "appear to be as inexorable in their workings as the laws of gravitation and expansion. There is a drift to society as a whole which pushes us on in a certain direction, careless of the individual, concerned only with the general result."

In his final position as one deeply puzzled by the insignificance of the individual, Lester therefore reflects a persistent strain in Dreiser's thought. Before making his pawn speech to Jennie, Lester had "looked down into Dearborn Street, the world of traffic below holding his attention. The great mass of trucks and vehicles, the counter streams of hurrying pedestrians, seemed like a puzzle. So shadows march in a dream." The scene effectively images both Lester's and Dreiser's belief that life is a helter-skelter of activity without meaning either for its observers or for the "shadows" who give it motion. As a New Man, aware of the direction of modern thought, Lester is able to give this view of life an appropriate philosophical framework. In the years that pass after Vesta's death, his view of life becomes "decidedly critical":

> He could not make out what it was all about. In distant ages a queer thing had come to pass. There had started on its way in the form of evolution a minute cellular organism which had apparently reproduced itself by division, had early learned to combine itself with others, to organize itself into bodies, strange forms of fish, animals, and birds, and had finally learned to organize itself into man. Man, on his part, composed as he was of self-organizing cells, was pushing himself forward into comfort and different aspects of existence by means of union and organization with other men. Why? Heaven only knew. . . . Why should he complain, why worry, why speculate?—the world was going steadily forward of its own volition, whether he would or no. Truly it was.

It must not be assumed, however, that Lester's pessimistic response to the "puzzle" of man's role in a mechanistic world is Dreiser's principal and only philosophical theme in *Jennie Gerhardt*. For Jennie, though not Lester's equal in formal knowledge or in experience, is his equal in the "bigness" of her responsiveness to the underlying reality of life, and she discovers not only puzzlement and frustration in life but also an ineradicable beauty. Dreiser therefore follows his comments on Lester's "critical" outlook with an account of Jennie's final evaluation of life, an account which suggests, because of its strategic location, that it has a weight and significance equal to Lester's beliefs. Jennie, Dreiser writes,

> had never grasped the nature and character of specialized knowledge. History, physics, chemistry, botany, geology, and sociology were not fixed departments in her brain as they were in Lester's and Letty's. Instead there was the feeling that the world moved in some strange, unstable way. Apparently no one knew clearly what it was all about. People were born and died. Some believed that the world had been made six thousand years before; some that

it was millions of years old. Was it all blind chance or was there some guiding intelligence—a God? Almost in spite of herself she felt there must be something—a higher power which produced all the beautiful things—the flowers, the stars, the trees, the grass. Nature was so beautiful! If at times life seemed cruel, yet this beauty still persisted. The thought comforted her; she fed upon it in her hours of secret loneliness.

Jennie's and Lester's complementary views of life represent Dreiser's own permanent unresolved conception of the paradox of existence. To both figures the world "was going steadily forward of its own volition," apparently guided by some unknowable supernatural power. Individuals counted for little in this process, but individuals of different temperaments might respond to the mechanism of life in different ways. One kind of temperament might be bitter and despairing, another might affirm the beauty which was inseparable from the inexplicable mystery of life. It has frequently been noted that Dreiser himself held both views at different stages of his career—that he stressed a cruelly indifferent mechanistic universe in *Hey Rub-a-Dub-Dub* and a mechanistic world of beauty in *The Bulwark.* It has not been as fully realized that he held the two positions simultaneously as well as consecutively and that he gave each position equal weight and dramatic expression in *Jennie Gerhardt* without resolving their "discrepancy." For to Dreiser there was no true discrepancy; there was only the reality of distinctive temperaments which might find truth in each position or, as in his own case, of a temperament which might find an element of truth in both. Dreiser's infamous philosophical inconsistency is thus frequently a product of his belief that experience is a "puzzle" to which one can respond in different ways, depending on one's makeup and experience. The "philosophy" of mechanism in Dreiser's novels is secondary to the fictional role of that concept as a metaphor of life against which various temperaments can define themselves. Or, to put the matter another way, Lester's belief in one kind of mechanistic philosophy and Jennie's in another are less significant fictionally than the depiction of Jennie as a woman of feeling and of Lester as a man of speculative indecision.

As in his best novels, Dreiser concludes *Jennie Gerhardt* with a series of tableaus which sum up in dramatic form many of the central themes in the novel. Lester has died, and the first tableau depicts the Chicago home of his sister, where his body is lying before being returned to Cincinnati. "It was curious to see him lying in the parlor of this alien residence, candles at his head and feet, burning sepulchrally, a silver cross upon his breast, caressed by his waxen fingers. He would have smiled if he could have seen himself, but the Kane family was too conventional, too set in its convictions, to find anything strange in this." The image, of course, is that of Lester bound and controlled by convention even in death. If permitted consciousness, he would be amused by the incongruity between his unbelief and the trappings of belief accompanying his death, but his quizzical puzzlement would not alter the fact that the rigidity and power of his family's conventional faith have controlled him in death as in life. The second tableau is that of the funeral mass for Lester in a Chicago church. Jennie, though present, has had to secrete herself in a corner of the church and does not participate in the service. Yet in spite of her isolation, she finds something mysterious and beautiful in the very religion which Lester had sought to discard as a bondage. "The gloom, the beauty of the windows, the whiteness of the altar, the golden flames of the candles im-

pressed her. She was suffused with a sense of sorrow, loss, beauty, and mystery. Life in all its vagueness and uncertainty seemed typified by this scene." The third tableau is set in the railway station, where Lester's body is being loaded on a Cincinnati train. Again Lester is controlled by others and again Jennie observes the scene apart from Lester's relatives. But now the image projects as well a reality which silences all speculation about life—the raw finality of death as a force in the midst of life, a force which has bereft Jennie of mother, father, Vesta, and now Lester. "Hey, Jack!" one baggageman calls to another. "Give us a hand here. There's a stiff outside!" The train is drawn by a powerful black engine, "its smoke-stack throwing aloft a great black plume of smoke that fell back over the cars like a pall," yet the cars themselves are "brilliantly lighted" and contain "a dining car, set with white linen and silver, and a half dozen comfortable Pullmans." So man accommodates to death by continuing to live life at its fullest. But Jennie, alone at the station, "did not hear . . . anything . . . of the chatter and bustle around her. Before her was stretching a vista of lonely years down which she was steadily gazing."

Dreiser appended to this closing group of vignettes, which so superbly rehearse the dominant motifs in the lives of Jennie and Lester, a brief epilogue on Jennie called "In Passing." In it, he attempted, as he had in the epilogue to *Sister Carrie,* to render poetically and discursively the career and essential nature of his heroine. Heavily and lugubriously he characterized Jennie as a kind of natural object whose life could not be judged by ordinary criteria of success and failure and whose wisdom of soul transcended understanding. The passage, like its equivalent in *Sister Carrie,* is both an unnecessary apology for his heroine's errant ways and a deflating simplification of her character. Fortunately, the epilogue was set up in print as a separate concluding chapter and could easily be dropped. Belatedly heeding the advice of such critics as James G. Huneker who had attacked the epilogue in the manuscript form of the novel, Dreiser cut it from *Jennie Gerhardt* sometime after the first printing of 1911 and before Boni and Liveright reissued the novel in the early 1920s. The novel is best read in its revised form, without the epilogue. (pp. 109-24)

Donald Pizer, in his The Novels of Theodore Dreiser: A Critical Study, *University of Minnesota Press, 1976, 382 p.*

JIM PHILIP (essay date 1983)

[*Philip is an American educator and critic. In the following excerpt, he examines the conflict evident in Dreiser's works between his desire to protest the immoral and inhumane aspects of American society, in particular the pursuit of material success, and his own fascination with wealth and power.*]

"There stirs in Dreiser's books a new American quality . . . it is an authentic attempt to make something artistic out of the chaotic materials that lie around us in American life." Challenge and anxiety underlie Randolph Bourne's words [in his "The Art of Theodore Dreiser" (see Further Reading)]. We can perceive the experience of that crucial generation of American intellectuals, active in the early years of the century, who were the first to seek conscious articulation of those major transformations of the national life that had been proceeding for the previous three decades. The combined effects of industrialization and urbanization, the closing of the frontier and the increasing tide of immigration from Western and Central Europe had all played their part in creating a new society, but one whose structures and implications were still largely ignored by the "official" organs of American culture and education. As another commentator was to put it, to grow up at the turn of the century was to grow up "in a sort of orgy of lofty examples, moralized poems, national anthems and baccalaureate sermons," but to become aware at the same time of an "unbridgeable chasm between literate and illiterate America" [Van Wyck Brooks, *The Early Years* (1968)]. To open this new world to view, and to make possible fresh initiatives in literature and social criticism was the task undertaken by Bourne himself, and by other such notable figures of the period as H. L. Mencken, Van Wyck Brooks and Waldo Frank. However we cannot read far into the works of any of these without realizing that, each in their separate ways, they pay homage to one further and symptomatic figure, that of Theodore Dreiser. As these writers were the first to recognize, what made Dreiser's writing of special interest was not simply his attempt to engage the novel in the "chaotic materials" of city life, but also the fact that he was himself so obviously the product of the very forces he was describing. The son of a German immigrant, he was brought up amidst increasingly limited economic circumstances, and in the relative cultural desert of the Midwest. His formal education beyond school age consisted of one year's study at the University of Indiana. Like his elder brothers and sisters he experienced from an early age the lure of the cities, and was to undergo several years of menial labour in Chicago before obtaining the first newspaper job that was to lead eventually, and by no means directly, to his successful journalistic and literary career.

The case can readily be made, then, for the historical importance of Dreiser's fiction. Momentous changes in American life are being recorded, by a man who underwent them, and in modes that are formed by the pressure of direct experience rather than the requirements of genteel culture. More contentious, however, is the matter of Dreiser's success or failure in the mastery of his new materials, of his ability to forge them into an art that convinces both by the breadth and the depth of its approach. Few American writers have met with such a mixed critical response, and it would be fair to say that at the heart of the debates lies the problem of Dreiser's own various levels of intention. In one respect it is clear that his purpose was simply to document and describe, to give some permanence to his continuous, contrasting but at the same time fleeting impressions of city life, rather in the manner of the "Ashcan" school of painters whose achievements he so much admired. He was also, however, a persistent seeker of explanations, of general laws and principles that would give some coherence to the frantic and changeable life he saw around him. And it would be fair to say also that there are many moments in his novels in which the text moves close to personal confession, and in which we feel the immediacy of direct and participatory emotions.

Many of the predominant critical reactions can be seen to centre themselves around one or other of these issues. Perhaps the most famous attack on Dreiser's writing is that conducted by Lionel Trilling in his essay of 1946 called "Reality in America" [see excerpt dated 1946]. Complaining of the dense, descriptive, material textures of Dreiser's novels, and of those who have admired them as a kind of American truth, he claims that

his books have the awkwardness, the chaos, the heaviness which we associate with "reality." In the American metaphysic, reality is always material reality, hard, resistant, unformed, impenetrable, and unpleasant. And that mind is alone felt to be trustworthy which most resembles this reality by most nearly reproducing the sensations it affords.

Thus Dreiser's whole project is dismissed as an inadequate expression, indeed a deliberate denigration, of that liberal spirit, that humane and organizing intelligence, that Trilling locates in the contrasting figure of Henry James. Later criticism has done much to reduce the effect of these polemics by pointing to other elements in the writing. From the academy have come valiant attempts to give coherence to Dreiser's shifting philosophical positions, and to trace the effects of these on his fiction. Moreover there has been a consistent recognition, most interestingly from other creative writers, of Dreiser's open emotional presence in his own books, and of the continuity and relevance of the feelings evoked. Thus John Berryman has spoken of "the bright, vague longing or aspiration or *yearning* that every reader will probably recognize as Dreiser's central or characteristic emotion" ["Dreiser's Imagination"]. Such approaches have been useful, but it can fairly be claimed that, in their various partialities, they have somewhat distorted the actual experience of reading Dreiser's texts, of encountering his various and often contradictory presences, and the way in which these effect both the detail and the overall plotting of his works. The following account of his major novels is undertaken in the belief that the most useful task the critic can perform is that not of evading, but of revealing and exploring the elements of disjunction and struggle within them.

Dreiser told his biographer, Dorothy Dudley, that *Sister Carrie,* his first novel, was written in 1899 instinctively and without planning, as if "there was something mystic about it, as if I were being used like a medium." As the pent up thoughts and feelings are released they cast a dramatic light on even the most apparently casual moments in the book. The following is an account of "Hannah and Hogg's Adams Street place," that "gorgeous" saloon in Chicago, where Hurstwood, one of the major characters, is employed as manager.

> To one not inclined to drink, and gifted with a more serious turn of mind, such a bubbling, chattering, glittering chamber must ever seem an anomaly, a strange commentary on nature and life. Here come the moths in endless procession to bask in the light of the flame. Such conversation as one may hear would not warrant a commendation of the scene upon intellectual grounds. It seems plain that schemers would choose more sequestered quarters to arrange their plans, that politicians would not gather here in company to discuss anything save formalities where the sharp-eared may hear, and it would scarcely be justified on the score of thirst, for the majority of those who frequent these more gorgeous places have no craving for liquor. Nevertheless, the fact that here men gather, here chatter, here love to pass and rub elbows, must be explained upon some grounds. It must be that a strange bundle of passions and vague desires gives rise to such a curious social institution or it would not be.

> Drouet, for one, was lured as much by his longing for pleasure as by his desire to shine among his betters. The many friends he met here dropped in because they craved, without perhaps consciously an-

alyzing it, the company, the glow, the atmosphere, which they found. One might take it after all as an augur of the better social order, for the things which they satisfied here, though sensory, were not evil. No evil could come out of the contemplation of an expensively decorated chamber. The worst effect such a thing could have would be perhaps to stir up in the material minded an ambition to arrange their lives upon a similarly splendid basis. In the last analysis, that would scarcely be called the fault of the decorations, but rather of the innate trend of the mind. That such a scene might stir the less expensively dressed to emulate the more expensively dressed could scarcely be laid at the door of anything save the false ambition of the minds of those so affected. Remove the element so thoroughly and solely complained of, liquor, and there would not be one to gainsay the qualities of beauty and enthusiasm which would remain. The pleased eye with which our modern restaurants of fashion are looked upon is proof positive of this assertion.

Yet here is the fact of the lighted chamber: the dressy, greedy company; the small, self-interested palaver; the disorganized, aimless, wandering mental action which it represents—the love of light and show and finery which, to one outside, under the serene light of the eternal stars, must seem a strange and shiny thing. Under the stars and sweeping night winds, what a lamp-flower it must bloom—a strange, glittering night-flower, odour-yielding, insect-drawing, insect-infested rose of pleasure.

The passage well reveals those various levels of intention that have already been indicated. So far as description is concerned, Dreiser's fascination with the new spectacular settings of American city life is evident. In phrases such as "the bubbling, chattering, glittering chamber" he seeks in an original manner to convey the combined sensory bombardments of light, sound and movement. Too often his repetitions, his strings of words, his inharmonies of phrase, have been dismissed as a kind of literary *gaucherie*. What a passage like this makes clear is that part of his awkwardness should surely be recognized as a creative attempt to evoke the sensations of a dense urban world in forms appropriate to it. However, description is not the only purpose here, and it is not long before we find Dreiser presenting himself in the role of disinterested and scientific observer. He sets out to discover the truth about this "curious social institution," and the "bundle of passions and vague desires" that gives rise to it. It is this determination which produces what can only be described as a hopelessly reductive analysis. We are to imagine the saloons of Chicago populated by characters like Drouet in whom the dominant obsession has become that of associating themselves with the trappings of wealth, and the special codes of those who possess and display it. They "crave" for this experience and are drawn to its contexts with the same chemical automatism that draws the moth to light. We have evidence, then, of the way in which Dreiser's ideas, his "laws," can work against any full and complex registration of human presence.

But we must be grateful that here, as elsewhere, it is not the simplistic analyst who is in full control of the text. Despite Dreiser's attempts at distance, we cannot help noticing his closeness to the material and the way in which it works as a nexus of dynamic and contradictory emotions. We note, for instance, his eagerness to display a relaxed familiarity with the world that he describes, to present himself as one who has explored and enjoyed "the better social order." When he speaks of the "pleased eye with which our modern restaurants of fashion are looked upon" the pleasure is that of the participant, the assured insider. But if such an emotional tone is present, it is one that cannot wholly suppress the persistent and disturbed voice of the outsider. It is in fact this figure who is allowed the final comments on the scene, and we can see that his "outsideness" is registered in different ways. It is, first of all, an experience of pain and deprivation—the "rose of pleasure" invites but eludes him. But while voicing his own compulsions he also condemns the very world to which he is attracted. The ephemerality, the selfishness within the saloon are contrasted with "the serene light of the eternal stars" under which he stands. The possibility remains that in his separation he may act as the preserver of more lasting, more constructive values. The journey from outside to inside was, of course, one that Dreiser had traversed in his own life, and one that, as we shall see, remained the groundwork of his fiction. But what the present passage reveals is his remaining uncertainty as to what has been gained and what has been lost in the process. The sense of material satisfaction is countered by the reminders of a spiritual hunger that has not been satisfied. He parades his own inclusion while at the same time acknowledging the moral limitations that have accompanied it. At this fundamental level, then, the text can be read as an intense and worried autobiography, an expression of contradictions that the act of writing is intended to resolve, but patently does not.

The tensions that have been outlined here between reductive explanation and complex expression are in fact recurrent in Dreiser's fiction. An examination of the overall plotting of *Sister Carrie* will show how these affect not simply the details of his writing, but also its larger construction. At one level the book is an attempt to convince himself and his readers of the inevitability of an intensely competitive system; this is grounded in certain basic facts of human nature, in that instinctive and universal longing for wealth, status and pleasure newly stimulated by an America in the process of compounding its own riches. In the main Carrie is used as the vehicle for this argument. She comes to Chicago from a poor country background to stay in the first instance in the working-class home of her married sister. Depressed by the degrading conditions of life and work at this social level she agrees to become the mistress of Drouet, a travelling salesman she encounters on her first entry to the city. Though it contains a certain amount of affection this relationship is really based on compatible self-interests. Drouet introduces her to Hurstwood who, as a saloon manager, represents a higher level of success and assurance. By the combined effects of her attraction to him and his trickery of her, she is lured into fleeing with him to New York, after he has left his wife and stolen money from his employers. In New York his attempts to reestablish himself founder, but Carrie, forced by need into developing her latent talents as an actress, achieves increasing success on the popular stage. Eventually she rejects the declining and apathetic Hurstwood in favour of her own career. What Dreiser suggests is that Carrie's progress is essentially a self-interested one. At each important juncture of her life she is motivated primarily by a new image of herself that becomes attainable. She is led into her association with Drouet by the fine clothes, the "lace-collar," the "soft new shoes" that speak to her invitingly from the windows of the big stores. She pictures to herself the life of status and ease that she would enjoy as Hurstwood's wife. And it is the imagined pleasures and gestures of fame that spur her on in her acting career.

Yet, in tracing in characteristic detail this sequence of events, Dreiser cannot entirely exclude from his text those moments in which Carrie has thoughts and feelings of a different kind. Consider, for instance, the following:

> Her old father, in his flour-dusted miller's suit sometimes returned to her in memory-revived by a face in a window. A shoemaker pegging at his last, a blastman seen through a narrow window in some basement where iron was being melted, . . .—these took her back in fancy to the details of the mill. She felt, though she seldom expressed them, sad thoughts upon this score. Her sympathies were ever with that underworld of toil from which she had so recently sprung and which she best understood.

Here, despite her immersion in the immediate and pressing contexts of desire, Carrie reaches out for the past; despite her self-concern, she is troubled by moral denials of her family and class. But the essential point to make about this wider consciousness is that it exists in the passive and delayed forms of regret. A sympathy can be extended to the "underworld of toil," but only after this world has been escaped. Carrie has a moral awareness, then, a sense of duty, of loyalty, of wider human commitment, but it is one that is always too late, always out of time, and can never become a fully active principle.

The intensity of such moments when they occur suggests that, despite his frequent pleas for a sympathetic understanding of Carrie, Dreiser felt an underlying frustration and despair at the very character he had created. It is this frustration that breaks out in his sudden introduction, late on in the story, of a further and enigmatic figure, that of Robert Ames. A young electrical engineer from the Midwest, Ames impresses Carrie by his detachment, his intelligence and his idealism. It is not long before we find him addressing her in the following forthright terms:

> You can't become self-interested, selfish and luxurious, without having these sympathies and longings disappear, and then you will sit there and wonder what has become of them. You can't remain tender and sympathetic, and desire to serve the world, without having it show in your face and your art. If you want to do most, do good. Serve the many. Be kind and humanitarian. Then you can't help but be great.

Ames's presence in the book is really that of a voice, rather than a fully developed character, but it is clear that that voice is a totally disruptive one so far as the whole fiction, and in particular the construction of Carrie's life, are concerned. He asserts the existence of an altruistic motive and the possibilities of transforming it into action. He has a vision of an American future very different from the materialist and competitive present. We have the dramatic evidence, then, of Dreiser's inability to accept his own conclusions. Ames speaks for a part of himself that he has been unable wholly to suppress. Indeed, with this episode Carrie's story is brought to a hasty and unsatisfactory ending. She is simply abandoned as a character who has not carried the full freight of his own experience, and, because of the constraints within which she has been created, can never do so.

Repressed elements of human concern and protest are also evident in Dreiser's handling of the sub-theme of the novel,

that is to say, the fall of Hurstwood. The mere fact that he chose to include this element suggests his anxiety about the new society, about its inability to yield any position of security free of the threat of failure and exclusion. At times he argues for the acceptance of this as a further and inevitable fact of nature. Thus he states that

> a man's fortune, or material progress, is very much the same as his bodily growth. Either he is growing stronger, healthier, wiser, as the youth approaching manhood; or he is growing weaker, older, less incisive mentally, as the man approaching old age. There are no other states.

However, the actual account of Hurstwood's last months displays a direct emotional involvement in his experience of isolation and depression, his stubborn refusal to surrender the last shreds of human dignity. Implicit, though never stated, is a strong accusation against a society that can do nothing with its own casualties except ignore them. (pp. 115-23)

In *The Financier* the documentary element is precise and painstaking. It is clearly one of Dreiser's intentions to expose what he considers to be some of the worst features of the age he has lived through; the concentration of enormous power in the hands of few individuals, the penetration of the political and legal systems by financial interests. However, it must be admitted that these more constructive purposes are consistently undermined by processes of reduction and sensationalization. His awareness of the intensity of commercial struggle leads him at times into the Darwinian presentation of a social world in which nothing can be observed but the preying of the strong upon the weak. Moreover, there is the added conviction that at the heart of this world, at its centres of manipulation, there exist human individuals of a peculiarly ruthless and wilful type. It is in these terms that he presents Frank Cowperwood . . . :

> Again, it was so very evident, in so many ways, that force was the answer—great mental and physical force. Why, these giants of commerce and money could do as they pleased in this life, and did. He had already had ample local evidence of it in more than one direction. Worse—the little guardians of so-called law and morality . . . so loud in their denunciation of evil in humble places, were cowards all when it came to corruption in high ones. They did not dare to utter a feeble squeak until some giant had accidentally fallen and they could do so without danger to themselves. Then, O Heavens, the palaver! . . . It made him smile. Such hypocrisy! Such cant! Still, so the world was organized, and it was not for him to set it right. . . . The thing for him to do was to get rich and hold his own. . . . Force would do that. Quickness of wit. And he had these. "I satisfy myself," was his motto. . . .

Cowperwood, then, is a figure supremely, one might almost say absurdly, adapted to his environment. His "great mental and physical force" ensure that he is not subject to those moments of exhaustion and confusion that beset others in the competitive battle. His confident dismissal of all morality as "hypocrisy" and "cant" ensures that he can pursue without scruple his goal of self-satisfaction. His "quickness of wit" ensures that he can be faster than others to perceive both opportunities and dangers. To be sure he cannot entirely evade the accidents of chance (his temporary downfall is brought about as a consequence of the great Chicago fire), but these are to be welcomed as the unpredictable elements in the game that he plays with life. What the passage reveals is that the construction of this character has its roots not only in theory, but also in fantasy and wish-fulfilment. Cowperwood survives and prospers because of the absence within him of those elements of anxiety, self-doubt and wider questioning to which, as we have seen, Dreiser was himself so prone. To the writer troubled by the status of his own morality, his amoral hero was a source of fascination and allurement. To read the Cowperwood books, then, is to feel oneself drawn in two directions, towards two contradictory versions of American experience. One is aware first of all of a novelist concerned to open the hidden centres of power to wider view, to make them available to analysis and change; but one is aware also of a Dreiser so overawed by the atmosphere of competition that he has encountered that he can see nothing else, and do nothing else but participate vicariously in the endurance and the triumphs of his Superhero.

The Financier helped to establish Dreiser as a national figure. Perhaps, in his very ambivalence, he had exactly caught the mood of the public at large. More recent opinion, however, has often demoted the writing of this period, and sought instead to present *An American Tragedy* as the fullest achievement of his art. Here Dreiser turns away from the more lavish worlds of success to consider, as he himself was to put it, "the tribes and shoals of the incomplete, the botched, the semi-articulate—all hungry and helpless." We first encounter Clyde Griffiths, whose story this novel recounts, as he is forced to participate unwillingly in the ineffectual missionary work of his parents on the streets of Kansas City. Seeking more acceptable social status amidst the contexts of wealth he secures a job as a bell-hop in the Green-Davidson, one of the best hotels in town. When working in a Chicago club two years later he meets by accident his uncle who is a prosperous manufacturer of collars in Lycurgus, New York. Clyde solicits from him the promise of a job and moves to the town. Here he finds himself in an ambiguous social position, not fully accepted either by his relations, or by the working people of whom he is put in charge. Out of his sense of isolation he develops a relationship with Roberta Alden, a factory girl, but his attentions are later won away by a young socialite who displays an interest in him. When Roberta's pregnancy threatens his rise to respectability he turns against her. Desperation leads him into an ill-planned attempt at murder by drowning, but Roberta's actual death is the product of accident as much as deliberate purpose. Clyde is caught, tried, convicted and eventually dies in the electric chair.

Strong claims have been made for the greater realism of this book, in its handling both of the overall social environment and of particular individuals. It is certainly true that Dreiser displays a sharp eye for the detailed stratifications of an increasingly class-organized and class-conscious society. In Lycurgus Clyde comes to learn the many gradations that exist between the immigrant workers at the bottom and the families of established wealth at the top. It is true also that he does manage to present his story from a number of different viewpoints, showing how Clyde is viewed and used by others, ranging from Sondra Finchley, the vain rich girl, to Mason, the district attorney who sees his prosecution as an aid to his own political career. However, the problems of the book lie, once again, in the construction of its central figure, and it would be fair to say that in many respects Clyde is as one-dimensional a figure as was Frank Cowperwood. It is as if the writer, now more fully assured of his own success and status, can turn at last to the confession of all those experiences of

anxiety, panic and isolation that have accompanied his own long journey. Clyde, in this sense, is the expression of a nightmare, of all those things that might have been were it not for the lucky coincidence of personal effort and exterior chance. Having arrived in Lycurgus, Clyde reflects on his experience in the following terms:

> For, after all, was he not a Griffiths, a full cousin as well as a full nephew to the two very important men who lived here, and now working for them in some capacity at least? And must not that spell a future of some sort, better than any he had known as yet? For consider who the Griffiths were here, as opposed to "who" the Griffiths were in Kansas City. . . . The enormous difference! A thing to be as carefully concealed as possible. At the same time, he was immediately reduced again, for supposing the Griffiths here . . . should now investigate his parents and his past? Heavens! . . . If they should guess! If they should sense!
>
> Oh, the devil—who was he anyway? And what did he really amount to? . . .
>
> A little disgusted and depressed he turned to retrace his steps, for all at once he felt himself very much a nobody.

We note the way in which his desire to rise is thoroughly undermined by a compulsive self-denigration, a fear that the "nobody" he really is will always betray the "somebody" he aspires to be. Though he is close physically to the world of his rich relations, there is a sense that he can never become fully a part of it, that the marks of his past poverty and desperation exist upon him as a distinguishing brand. The predominant emotions, then, are those of resentment, shading to self-pity and apathy. In his actual history Clyde lives out to its bitter end the personal disintegration threatened here. He involves himself furtively with Roberta, although he knows the social dangers of doing so. When the facts of her pregnancy emerge his attempts to rescue the situation are weakened by an "everhaunting fear of inability to cope." In a schizophrenic manner he watches the rising within him of a criminal impulse that he can neither resist nor fully live out. At his trial he listens to the conflicting versions of his story, having himself abandoned any hope of personal identity or dignity. The novel retells, then, in a revealing manner Dreiser's perennial plot of the journey from outside to inside, but it does so in wholly negative terms. The fears, the horrors are all there, accurately and instinctively expressed, but Clyde has none of that determined drive of Dreiser's other characters, and none of that unsatisfied moral doubt which is, as we have seen, such an essential part of his own total response.

From what has been said it should be clear that at the heart of Dreiser's extensive fiction there lies the recurrent problem of the creation of a character adequate to embody the full and complex freight of his own past and his own social experience. That width of lived encounter emerges through the books, but it does so in incomplete, fragmentary and diverted forms. In the light of this it would seem worthwhile to recommend for fresh attention one of his more neglected books, *The "Genius."* When this novel first appeared in 1916 it met with opposition from the New York Society for the Suppression of Vice, who forced its publisher into withdrawing it from sale. A public campaign and legal action failed to alter the situation and it was not until 1923 that it was reissued. At the time the immediate notoriety of the book worked against any full critical assessment of it, and it has still not been given the respect it deserves. Like all semi-autobiographical novels it works partly to reveal and partly to disguise the author's own life. The text is used at times to provide fictional solutions to actual problems, but at others to explore those problems in considerable depth. But what is most remarkable about it is that, in the story of the artist, Eugene Witla, Dreiser comes closest to telling the whole tale, to creating a character through whom many and various currents of feeling are allowed full play. Towards the end of the book we find him in a New York hospital where his wife Angela is about to undergo a dangerous caesarian operation.

> They wheeled her out after a few moments and on to the elevator which led to the floor above. Her face was slightly covered while she was being so transferred, . . . and the nurse said that a very slight temporary opiate had been administered. . . . He walked far down the dim-lit length of the hall before him, wondering, and looked out on a space where was nothing but snow. In the distance a long lighted train was winding about a high trestle like a golden serpent. There were automobiles honking and pedestrians laboring along in the snow. What a tangle life was, he thought. What a pity. Here a little while ago, he wanted Angela to die, and now,—God Almighty, that was her voice groaning! He would be punished for his evil thoughts—yes, he would . . . What a tragedy his career was! What a failure! Hot tears welled up into his eyes, his lower lip trembled, not for himself, but for Angela. He was so sorry all at once. He shut it all back. No, by God, he wouldn't cry! . . . It was for Angela his pain was, and tears would not help her now.

Behind this moment of self-appraisal there lies a tortuous history. It is his long engagement and marriage to Angela, a farmer's daughter from the Midwest whom he met in his home town when he was 19, that have provided the element of continuity in his personal relationships. But his wider experience of city life has led to affairs with other women: with a young model during his art-school days in Chicago; with an aspiring and career-minded singer during his attempts to establish himself in New York as an artist; and, following his marriage, with a bored middle-class wife who takes him up during his period of separation and breakdown. The present crisis has been brought about by his recent infatuation with Suzanne Dale, a young New York heiress with whom his successful advertising career has brought him into contact. Out of jealousy and possessive rage Angela chooses to become pregnant despite the risks to her own life. Compulsive sexuality, extreme fantasy and a certain ruthlessness have thus all had their part to play in his relationships with women, but, as the passage makes clear, these have not gone unchallenged. As he realizes the distortions to which Angela has been driven, and his own part in them, his reaction is one of guilt, self-accusation and irrepressible sympathy. The past, with its legacy of honest commitment as well as error, cannot be excluded from the present.

Dreiser wants us to see that this unresolved personal moment takes place in the context of an unresolved social experience. In his bewilderment Eugene looks out of the window to where "a long lighted train was winding about a high trestle like a golden serpent." It is an apt image of that powerful but not unquestioned influence that the city has had upon his life. He has had his moments of success, of power, when as advertising executive and manager he has learnt what it means "to

S. S. McClure, Willa Cather, Dreiser, and Paul Robeson, 1944.

stand up firm, square to the world and make people obey." But throughout his life his wholehearted participation in this world has been undermined by other perspectives and other influences. Returning with Angela to her father's farm he has encountered the survival of an older America of craftsman labour. During his period of breakdown he has spent time in the carpentry shop of a railroad company, where the cynicism, the guardedness but also the underlying fellowship of working people becomes evident to him. Above all he has felt the need, despite external pressures, to define himself in the individual and expressive role of the artist.

Eugene's artistic ambitions in fact develop through different stages as his life evolves, but there is the consistent element of protest, of the need to assert a range of values that the surrounding culture denies. To begin with it is sensual expression that fascinates him as opposed to the repressive contexts of his childhood. In response to the city, however, his art takes on new qualities. Dreiser based this aspect of Eugene's life on the work of Everett Shinn, an acquaintance of his, and one of the "Ashcan" School. Like his real life model, Eugene paints scenes of metropolitan life that are remarkable for their attention to individual lives amidst the massive environments and the anonymous crowds. He is pleased when one reviewer of his exhibition declares that he has "the ability to indict life with its own grossness, to charge it prophetically with its own meanness and cruelty in order that mayhap it may heal itself; the ability to see wherein is beauty—even in shame and pathos and degradation." The irony is, however, that this humanitarian art becomes the fashionable plaything of a consumer class. Uncertain of how to progress, and uncertain whether there is any real role for the artist in his society, Eugene falls into his period of depression and apathy. When he "returns" as a successful businessman he mocks the poverty and marginality that he sees as the inevitable lot of the artist critic; but it is a mockery that has its roots in the undeniable and unsatisfied need to be the agent of some "noble and superhuman purpose."

In the story of Eugene's life, then, Dreiser gives us his fullest and most complex account of the journey from outside to inside. What is revealed in passages like the one above is that the resultant condition is one of continuing ambivalence and instability. Eugene is at once both insider and outsider. His drives towards immediate pleasure in fact generate an active acknowledgement of the past; his pursuit of solitary power in fact generates an awareness of other lives and a need to devote himself to some larger social project. Given these ultimate recognitions, it is not surprising to discover that Dreiser had great difficulty in finishing his book, and changed the ending several times. The conclusion as we have it is wholly mythical. Eugene returns to success as an artist, but his art is now no longer marginal, and penetrates and conditions the very centres of power. "At Washington in two of the great public buildings and in three state capitals were tall glowing panels also of his energetic dreaming." Angela has died, but has been replaced by "little Angela," for whom he cares with an unwavering loyalty. As he searches the universe it seems to him no longer "a space where was nothing but snow," but rather the scene of evolutionary advance from which "great art dreams welled up into his soul." At all levels, then, facts of disjunction have been replaced by myths of connection. In his personal life, in his social life, and in his ontological life, Eugene's divisions have been resolved in a transforming harmony. The reader may be moved to mock such evident devices, but our reaction should perhaps be different. We can allow and even respect the dreamings of a man who struggled so long and so hard to convey the full terms of his own experience, and offer it as characteristic of his generation. (pp. 124-31)

> Jim Philip, "Theodore Dreiser: Outsider/Insider,"
> in American Fiction: New Readings, *edited by*
> Richard Gray, London: Vision Press, 1983, pp. 115-
> 32.

LAWRENCE E. HUSSMAN, JR. (essay date 1983)

[*Hussman is an American educator and critic. In the following excerpt, he describes aspects of Dreiser's experiences, philosophical principles, and personal characteristics that helped shape his fiction.*]

One of Dreiser's first jobs was as a reporter, assigned to the police beat, for the Chicago *Globe* in 1892. He became a daily witness to scenes of human degradation. The cruelty of the city was a vital primer in the doctrine which he was later to know by name as the survival of the fittest. The many examples of urban man's inhumanity made a joke of the world view taught him in the parochial schools. One might half believe in the widespread application of justice and mercy in rural Indiana, but not in Chicago in the 1890s. One trip through the slums would be enough to destroy the last vestiges of such illusions. Yet his first taste of life in the metropolis satisfied him immensely as spectacle and he never lost his romantic fascination with it. He resolved to be a fit survivor by making his way in a large city as a newspaperman. During the next few years he wrote for a number of dailies, working his way toward New York, the ultimate metropolis. On the way, he read several books which were to profoundly influence his own writing.

While working for the Pittsburgh *Dispatch* in 1894, Dreiser discovered the philosophical tracts of T. H. Huxley, John Tyndall, and Herbert Spencer. Already brooding over the apparent purposelessness of his own life and the failure of his previous education to provide him with a convincing world view, Dreiser was psychologically ready for the decisive impression that these philosophers made on him. He testified to the experience in an often quoted passage from *A Book about Myself:*

> At this time I had the fortune to discover Huxley

and Tyndall and Herbert Spencer, whose introductory volume to his *Synthetic Philosophy* (*First Principles*) quite blew me, intellectually, to bits. Hitherto, until I had read Huxley, I had some lingering filaments of Catholicism trailing about me, faith in the existence of Christ, the soundness of his moral and sociological deductions, the brotherhood of man. But on reading *Science and Hebrew Tradition* and *Science and Christian Tradition,* and finding both the Old and New Testaments to be not compendiums of revealed truth but mere records of religious experience, and very erroneous ones at that, and then taking up *First Principles* and discovering that all I had deemed substantial—man's place in nature, his importance in the universe, this too, too solid earth, man's very identity save as an infinitesimal speck of energy or a "suspended equation" drawn or blown here and there by larger forces in which he moved quite unconsciously as an atom— all questioned and dissolved into other and less understandable things, I was completely thrown down in my conceptions or non-conceptions of life.

Thus Dreiser records the central event in his conversion to philosophic naturalism and the touchstone used by several generations of critics to situate his books in literary history. Through his exposure to Huxley, Tyndall, and Spencer, Dreiser formulated his declared beliefs that life is without purpose or plan, that man has no soul, that free will and original sin are myths, that human morality and motivation are based on physiological and sociological fate and that the only discernible laws are the laws of change and chance.

But to pigeonhole Dreiser's art within the naturalistic movement is to stop far short of an understanding of that art at its deepest. The way he uses the naturalistic hypothesis to explore fundamental questions about man and his institutions constitutes Dreiser's unique contribution to our literature and to our understanding of ourselves. Having accepted the belief that was to become the common inheritance of the major writers of the twentieth century, the belief that "God is dead," Dreiser was among the first to explore the question of what to make of this seemingly diminished thing called existence. One might speculate on its meaninglessness for a time, but the question of how to organize oneself for living persisted. His fiction represents an implicit attempt to answer that question. Through it he explores various paths that might lead the modern pilgrim around the Slough of Despond to personal fulfillment. Furthermore, although Dreiser's negative experiences led him to embrace the precepts of naturalism intellectually, he was never able to accept them emotionally. We need only recall that he was given to speculating that man was no more important to the universe than an expiring beetle, yet he wrote four volumes of autobiography and an autobiographical novel. The exploration of alternative ways to live life coupled with the emotional need to believe in a transcendent reality led tortuously from *Sister Carrie* to *The Bulwark.* And the passage was made possible by Dreiser's fascinated observation of an ancient problem in its modern context, man's disillusioned longing for ultimate fulfillment and the moral questions which that longing raised.

In 1898, the year before he began *Sister Carrie,* Dreiser was working as a consulting editor for *Success* magazine, a monthly which high-lighted the accomplishments of the nation's prosperous and famous by describing how they became so. He interviewed a number of rich and celebrated men for *Success,* and though most of them piously professed that spiritual peace was far more important than material well being, a remark made by Thomas Edison during Dreiser's interview of him made a far more profound impression. Edison told Dreiser that his only pleasure came from the process of working on inventions and that he lost all interest when the work was completed. This remark crystallized for Dreiser his own vague feelings of disillusionment with things he had longed for and achieved. It became, along with other of Edison's ideas expressed in the interview, a source for character and theme in *Sister Carrie* and a subject for lifelong brooding. Dreiser had always been a dreamer of large dreams and intensely ambitious for financial security, material comforts, social acceptance, and the glamour of a writer's career. His sexual appetite was enormous. When he had secured some of his wants in Chicago, however, he remained curiously restless. By the time he came to interview Edison, this aspect of human nature which makes the attainment of an object of desire disappointing had stirred Dreiser's imagination. Since he believed from his reading that existence is meaningless and since he was naturally of a melancholy turn, he was concerned less with the pleasure in the pursuit of an object than with the disillusionment that attended its acquisition. And he found his insight prefigured in the era in which he lived. With the dawning of the age of conspicuous consumption in America had come the realization that material things do not bring fulfillment. The frenzied pursuit of an illusory happiness had already struck the young writer as the most fascinating and poetic phase of American city life around the turn of the century.

Ultimate fulfillment has always been seen as beyond man's grasp in his earthly state. A religious person might take the fact in stride, perform his duties and bide his time in anticipation of the perfect bliss promised in another world. But a mechanist could find this aspect of the human predicament another persuasive demonstration of life's essential senselessness. Dreiser began brooding about disillusionment at a time when his thinking was at least tacitly mechanistic. Furthermore, if man had overpowering yearnings that could be neither resisted nor satisfied, not only must life be purposeless but also free will must indeed by a myth. Some such interpretation surely played a part in Dreiser's reading of Huxley, Tyndall, and Spencer. Because they are in the grip of inscrutable desire, Carrie Meeber, Clyde Griffiths, and even Frank Cowperwood appear to be mere pawns of blind force. Each of Dreiser's books is remarkable for its author's profound preoccupation with frustrated desire. One of his most perceptive early critics, Randolph Bourne, remarked in a review of *The "Genius"* that "the insistent theme of Mr. Dreiser's works is desire, perennial, unquenchable."

Dreiser employs a variety of terms to describe and translate desire. At times he refers to mystic longing, unreasoning passion, or chemic compulsion, but always the reference is to the fact that his characters' desires are unquenchable. They are so because the objects of these desires are not sufficient to explain the intensity of the longing. This phenomenon was hardly a discovery of Dreiser's. Plato describes the inability of the objects of our desires to satisfy us through the analogy of a perforated vessel into which water is poured. Lucretius calls desire the "thirst for life" and observes that "so long as we have not what we crave, it seems to surpass all else; afterward, when it is ours, we crave something else, and the same thirst of life besets us as ever, open-mouthed." What makes Dreiser's treatment of desire new in his time and still fresh is its twentieth-century context. The naturalistic philoso-

phers had cast doubt on the theological foundations of the western world, and the crumbling of the religious edifice would be so swift that by the twenties most of the books written by intellectuals would begin with the assumption that God was no longer an issue. Dreiser was among the first of American artists to try to make sense of a world in which science and religion seemed hopelessly split, a chasm which was to prove to be the foremost cultural fact of the first half of the twentieth century. Without a religious explanation of man's yearning for ultimate fulfillment, later writers would try to fill the void by establishing their own ersatz religions. Thus, Wallace Stevens wrote in "The Man with the Blue Guitar": "Art, surpassing music must replace empty Heaven and its hymns." James Joyce and Virginia Woolf agreed that art was the only surviving modern ideal. For D. H. Lawrence, the new faith was to be found in blood consciousness, for Ernest Hemingway, in modern stoicism, for John Steinbeck, in biological evolution. Dreiser's fiction transcribes through his characters his own relentless and vain search for a worthy reality. Carrie's aching need for material, social, and artistic success is answered with gowns, carriages, position, and career, but the end of the novel finds her still hopeful of release from "longings" and "heartaches." Frank Cowperwood, the robber baron hero of the Trilogy of Desire, acquires a succession of mansions, priceless paintings, and enchanting mistresses, but fulfillment eludes him. Eugene Witla, the artist hero of *The "Genius,"* is sustained neither by his art nor by the many liaisons that mark his frenzied pursuit of the "impossible she." Clyde Griffiths's doomed dream of money, importance, and sexual power leads inexorably to the electric chair.

Dreiser's autobiographies offer ample evidence that he was, himself, afflicted to an unusual degree with romantic desire that could never be satisfied. The absence of fulfillment intensified his brooding melancholy. For example, he writes of his youth:

> I tell you, in those days, wonderful, amazing moods were generated in the blood of me. I felt and saw things which have never come true—glories, moods, gayeties, perfections. There was a lilt in my heart and in my soul. I wanted, oh! I wanted all that Nature can breed in her wealth of stars and universes—and I found—what have I found—? [*A Hoosier Holiday*]

The insatiable desire to experience all things simultaneously which stirs his characters stirred their creator as well. He often protested gloomily against what George Santayana called "the deepest curse of existence," the need of "rejecting and destroying some things that are beautiful," for in that direction Dreiser saw accommodation, compromise, decay, and death. His brooding over the extent to which mankind's reach extends beyond its grasp penetrates his very style, through which he conveys a sense of gnawing unrest.

Although Dreiser empathized with most people who seemed fated to strive for the objects of their personal desires, he admired those few who were able to transcend desire by dedicating themselves to a higher good, as he believed his mother had. He often regretted that most were essentially self-serving and that compassion and charity were not more widespread. As a consequence, his novels before *The Bulwark* seem curiously contradictory, for they are simultaneously deterministic and humanistic. Dreiser critics have frequently identified this seeming contradiction without tracing it to its source and relating it to the novelist's ongoing quest for moral as well as spiritual moorings in a postreligious world. The apparently incompatible impulses to take what one desires for personal happiness and to give of oneself for others were the alternatives that presented themselves as a result of the new freedom that attended Dreiser's loss of religious faith with its moral imperatives. In *A Book about Myself,* he wrote two long, contiguous confessional paragraphs in which he admitted to a ravenous appetite for the world's goods as well as a profound compassion for those whose possessions were minimal. Although he sometimes seemed simply to accept these two sides of himself, he continually explored them through fictional characters and situations as alternate paths to a possible secular salvation. Could a man or woman find true happiness by storing up treasures or by succoring those who had none? It must be remembered that although Dreiser thought of himself as a determinist, he did not consistently deny free will. In *A Hoosier Holiday,* for example, he cited historical precedence in the overthrow of monarchy as evidence of the people's will. And even the characters in a determinist novel must attempt to manage their lives by making moral choices, whether or not those choices are merely illusory against the backdrop of meaninglessness. Thus, the morally uncommitted heroine of *Sister Carrie* is motivated by her "guiding principle" of self-interest in her languid quest for position and possessions, but by the end of the novel she has begun to indulge her compassionate side. Jennie Gerhardt gives totally in an utterly selfless manner. Cowperwood shamelessly indulges his will to power. Clyde Griffiths follows his tawdry dreams to their tragic terminus and begins to see in prison that responsibilities to others might be a more crucial call than desire. Thus, Dreiser's novels scrutinize characters struggling to invest their lives with meaning by pursuing self-interested goals or by curbing their personal desires to devote themselves to others. Seen in this light, they have an existential dimension that has not been previously explored.

The relationships between men and women provided Dreiser with the most illuminating case studies for his examination of the conflict between the self and the other. He was himself a notorious womanizer whose affairs of the heart and exploits in the bedroom numbered in the hundreds and spanned his entire lifetime. In the give and take of these affairs he found a useful paradigm for abstract moral considerations. He returned to such relationships again and again in his fiction. The institution of marriage was an even richer source of moral speculation for Dreiser. He met his first wife in 1893. Assigned by the St. Louis *Republic* to escort a group of school teachers on a trip to the Chicago World's Fair, he picked Sara Osborne White (also known as "Jug") from among the twenty-five teachers as the most worthy of his attentions. Soon he was lost in romance, writing highly charged, emotional letters to her and constructing a miniature shrine in his room to display her picture. Despite the warnings of friends that Sara was too old for him (at nearly twenty-five she was two years his senior) and that as a conservative churchgoer she might be too narrow for him, Dreiser decided that he must marry her. Although he went East to further his career as a reporter, he resolved to return for Sara when he had sufficient money to support her. Their five-year courtship resulted in marriage late in 1898, even though his sojourn in the East had provided him with a succession of other women and the excitement of New York. Dreiser would later recall that the marriage was prompted by his obedience to "the pale flame of duty." He soon began to find his wife too conventional and possessive and himself too driven not to crave the "artistic"

freedom to pursue younger women. His disillusionment grew incrementally, but Dreiser and Sara were not permanently separated until 1912. She refused him a divorce, preventing his remarriage until her death in 1942.

Dreiser often used marriage as a literary subject. His novels from *Sister Carrie* up to *The Bulwark* portray the institution with a mostly jaundiced eye. But it is in *The "Genius"* and in his "marriage group," a series of short stories including among others **"Married," "The Second Choice,"** and **"Free,"** that he records his most subtle analysis of the concept of lifelong commitment to one sexual partner. In these works, marriage becomes a vehicle for discussing the struggle within the individual between the desire for the world's most alluring and abundant commodity—what Dreiser called "the show of soul in some passing eye"—and the wish to know that soul intimately and fully, possible only through an emotional expenditure and commitment which disallows our knowing as intimately and fully the souls that animate the many other equally tantalizing "passing eyes." Dreiser tried to resolve the dilemma through a series of intense, mostly short-lived relationships with a legendary number of women.

By 1899, he had contributed about forty articles and poems to magazines (most to *Metropolitan* and *Cosmopolitan*), had his first short story published by *Ainslee's,* and had seen his name appear in *Who's Who in America.* He began writing his first extended work in the autumn of that year, spurred by his newspaper colleague Arthur Henry's suggestion that they both attempt a novel. Dreiser confessed that he addressed himself to the task with no idea of how to proceed. He was probably indulging in his characteristic exaggeration when he said that he wrote the title on a blank sheet of paper with no conception of the story that was to follow. After writing about one third of the book, he was forced to abandon it for several months because he could not untangle the plot complications that had developed to that point. Although he ultimately managed to realize the narrative line of the novel in impressive fashion, his admitted amateurism was responsible for several flaws in the logical underpinning of *Sister Carrie.* But he was able to successfully transform into his first major work the experiences and conflicts that were to remain among the most important sources of all of his fiction. These included the grinding poverty of his youth, which stirred his sympathy for the poor as well as his resolve not to be among them; the contrasting examples of his father's narrow outlook and his mother's rich sympathy; his struggle for survival and recognition in Chicago; his Catholic schooling and the naturalistic precepts of Huxley, Tyndall, and Spencer; a growing hatred for the bondage of marriage, along with his sexual promiscuity and a paradoxical respect for the family; a minimal education and a voracious intellectual curiosity; a love-hate relationship with the American city; and a vivid lust for life linked to an uncommon love of people. William Faulkner noted, in his Nobel Prize acceptance speech, that "the conflict of the human heart within itself alone can make good writing." By this standard, Dreiser was well-equipped for his chosen profession. His novels record his characters' attempts to resolve profound conflicts that he deeply felt himself. At their best they constitute some of the most telling fiction of the twentieth century. (pp. 9-17)

Lawrence E. Hussman, Jr., in his Dreiser and His Fiction: A Twentieth-Century Quest, *University of Pennsylvania Press, 1983, 215 p.*

RICHARD LEHAN   (essay date 1984)

[Lehan is an American educator and critic who has written extensively on the twentieth-century American novel. In the following essay, he disputes unfavorable assessments of Dreiser's works, particularly addressing the appraisal made by Lionel Trilling in his essay "Reality in America" (see excerpt dated 1946).]

Most attempts at evaluative criticism are self defeating. Reading literature is first and primarily a personal experience, and the task of convincing someone else to share our judgment and taste is at best tiresome. Yet more than most novelists', Dreiser's novels seem to encourage attack or defense. The attacks usually include discussion of both the medium and the message. The new critics attacked Dreiser's style and technique, and the neohumanists attacked his depraved view of man. No one, to my knowledge, has been foolish enough to defend the style. In my book on Dreiser [*Theodore Dreiser: His World and His Novels*], I did, however, argue that Dreiser has never been given full credit for his craft. Anyone who will take the time to study the way Dreiser's novels moved from manuscript to revision can see that Dreiser was not a stumbling craftsman—can see that he had an image of man, a world view which he was trying to realize, and which does emerge with convincing power in novels like *Sister Carrie* and *An American Tragedy.*

As I have pointed out elsewhere, reverse any one scene in *Sister Carrie* and nothing will happen. If Carrie had met Hurstwood, not Drouet, on the train from Wisconsin there would have been no story. At that moment in her life, Hurstwood would have seen nothing admirable in this little American peasant. If Carrie had not lived with her sister first, she would not have been desperate enough to become Drouet's mistress and so find an entré to a more heightened way of life, which led her in turn to Hurstwood and away from Drouet. Without his lust for Carrie, Hurstwood would crack no safe, and Carrie would not have gone to New York if Hurstwood had not tricked her, and so on. The examples could be multiplied. Behind the appearance of chance in this novel is a necessary relationship between scenes, a river running from its source to its destined end. The form of the novel—with its repetitive and syllogistic progression (to borrow Kenneth Burke's terminology)—reinforces theme. Dreiser's belief in mechanistic causality came from Herbert Spencer, from whom he also got the idea that life is a process of force and counterforce. What goes up must come down, so the river of life really runs in a circle—from birth to death, with the suggestion that all matter is alive so that death is a kind of return. The individual stories of Carrie and Hurstwood obviously find meaning in terms of this pattern—Carrie's rise of sorts, Hurstwood's fall. But what is not so obvious is the way Dreiser describes the crowds swirling past Carrie as she sits on her sister's stoop. The city itself, indeed all men, are part of this river of life, as the sea and rocking chair imagery also suggest.

If *Sister Carrie* has a consistent narrative logic so also has *An American Tragedy,* another Dreiser novel which belies the charge that he was technically sloppy. Once again Dreiser portrayed a person caught and finally destroyed by the crush of conflicting forces. Clyde is trapped between his early poverty and a world that lures him on—first the gaudy world of the Green-Davidson Hotel, then the more sedate world of the Union League Club in Chicago, and finally the prosperous world of Lycurgus, within which is not only the opulent home of his uncle but directly across the river "a miserable slum, the like of which . . . [Clyde] had not seen outside of Chicago or Kansas City." Once again Spencerian opposites come into play. Dreiser believed that there could not be bravery without cowardice, beauty without ugliness, wealth without poverty, spirit of religion without the spirit of paganism—and Clyde is indeed caught between all kinds of opposing forces as he is lured on by the mirage of wealth and success (Dreiser thought once of calling the novel "Mirage"). He is caught between his pity for Roberta and his desire for Sondra; he is caught between the ambitions of both the prosecuting and defense attorneys who are struggling between themselves for the county judgeship; he is caught between his big city upbringing and the prejudices of the small town which tries him for murder; his is caught between his desire for sexual freedom and a Puritan religious code; he is caught between the world of the impoverished father and the world of the rich uncle. Motives cancel out; Clyde's will is suspended, and he becomes a victim of his society with its own mutually exclusive values. No writer has depicted better than Dreiser the American dream as nightmare, Horatio Alger at dead end. What we have again is repetitive form. Over and over, Clyde has the same kind of experience—compare the situation when he must choose between helping his pregnant sister Esta or buying the fur coat for Hortense Briggs with his final need to help or to abandon Roberta; compare the scene in which he runs away from the hit-and-run accident in Kansas City with the scene in the boat at Big Bittern. What does change are the consequences of Clyde's actions—or more often of his lack of action, because he is one of the first passive heroes of American fiction, acted upon rather than acting. The structure of *An American Tragedy*—the counterpointing, the ironic turn of events causally ordered—all reveal Dreiser in control of his novel, working to realize a conscious view of man and of America. The criticism of the last ten years needed to rescue Dreiser from the charges that he was simply a sloppy writer. The arguments here, of course, will not make it any easier for our undergraduates to read Dreiser. I once measured the print in *An American Tragedy* and was shocked to find that the novel is a mile and a quarter long. Dreiser perhaps overdid himself here; but his method demanded and, I think, justified the long novel.

Recent criticism, I feel, has been more successful in rescuing Dreiser's technique than in rescuing his ideas. To be sure, the neohumanists are no longer a real threat. No one can take very seriously the old charges that the novels of Dreiser and Dos Passos uphold an immoral view of man—are explosions in a cesspool, to quote one famous phrase. But this kind of argument, or one that comes close to it, has been more sophisticatedly expressed by critics like Lionel Trilling in his famous essay "Reality in America" [see excerpt dated 1946]. If you recall, Trilling begins this essay with an attack on Parrington who, according to Trilling, expressed "the chronic American belief that there exists an opposition between reality and mind and that one must enlist oneself in the party of reality." Trilling is annoyed that liberal critics like Parrington are more willing to forgive Dreiser his faults than they are Henry James, because Dreiser was more obviously on the side of the poor: according to Trilling, "No liberal critic asks the question of Dreiser whether *his* moral preoccupations are going to be useful in confronting the disasters that threaten us." Trilling is also annoyed that Dreiser is more easily forgiven because the reality of his fiction seems to be more American than James's expatriated views: "Dreiser is to be accepted and forgiven because his faults are the sad, lovable, honorable faults of reality itself, or of America itself—huge, inchoate, struggling toward expression, caught between the dream of raw power and the dream of morality." The rest of Trilling's essay is given over to a discussion of how Dreiser's ideas (a word that Trilling substitutes for "reality") "are inconsistent or inadequate."

There are so many things wrong with Trilling's argument that it is difficult to know where to begin.

First, it seems to me very unfortunate Trilling should insist that we have an "either-or" choice between Henry James or Theodore Dreiser, so that if we accept one we automatically have to reject the other. Trilling's own sense of literary values, determined in great part by his work on Matthew Arnold, forced him to take needless stands. I don't think that either James or Dreiser is going to save us, as Trilling believes that literary values will either save or damn us. James and Dreiser portrayed two very different kinds of experiences, both of which are justified and are not mutually exclusive. I personally can give consent to the experiences of both an Isabel Archer and a Carrie Meeber, a Lambert Strether and a Clyde Griffiths—as vastly different as these experiences are. I don't know what is to be gained in setting up hierarchies of literary experience and trying to prove that James's reality is better than Dreiser's. To put this differently, I cannot see what benefit can come from comparing *Sister Carrie* or *An American Tragedy* with *A Portrait of a Lady,* or *Ulysses,* or *Invisible Man,* to move beyond just James. Obviously, Dreiser's novels do not have the international scope or the same kind of moral dimension as James's novels; they do not have the symbolic overlay and interior consciousness of Joyce's novels; they do not treat the topical with the comic symbolism of Ellison's *Invisible Man.* They do, however, have an inner logic of their own and need to be examined within their own terms.

Second, once this is understood, there is no need to justify Dreiser's novels on the ground that they reflect the essence of American life because they are "inchoate, and struggling toward expression." They are less inchoate than Trilling is able to see or willing to admit, and like James's novels their literary merit is an intrinsic rather than extrinsic matter.

Third, I honestly do not know what Trilling means when he condemns Dreiser's ideas as "inconsistent" and "inadequate." Inconsistent within the fiction or as ideas per se? Inadequate for what purposes? To be sure, Dreiser was an inconsistent mechanist, as Eliseo Vivas long ago pointed out. He did have strong feelings both for and against a Charles Yerkes who is the model for Frank Algernon Cowperwood. While Dreiser's own thinking is at times inchoate, his fiction is not. Dreiser's thought is muddled when he tries to project his own contradictions into a unified scientific and philosophical system. His fiction is not muddled because Dreiser does not attempt to create a system but to dramatize conflict, a conflict that is often a very personal and immediate one for him.

The individual in Dreiser's novels is at the center of this conflict, caught between two sets of determining forces—one natural, arising from man's instincts; the other social, arising from social and religious conventions. As a result, he is rarely able to satisfy both sets of demands because one set of forces will prove stronger than the other, and in this way his behavior will be determined. Although choice is thus prescribed, the individual, whether he is Hurstwood or Cowperwood, believes that he is free, and he is tantalized by the illusion of

choice, like a Clyde Griffiths who is damned and never knows it. Like Clyde, the Dreiser character believes that he has an essential self, after which he is in search. As a result, he is forever displaced, forever dissatisfied, always trying to be more than he can be. He usually rejects his origins—his family or his position in life—and struggles for more. The city attracts him because only the city is large enough to contain this heightened self. In sensitive moments, he intuits the beauty of life, but this only makes him more discontent with himself and his materialistic society. He is concerned with mutability, with bird in flight, water in motion, and crowded cities where men sweep by like rivers to the sea. (Note how these images become key in the novels.) He longs for stability but is caught in flux. He is a step behind himself, restless and yet with nowhere to go, duped by his own aspirations. He is, in short, a victim—a victim of his temperament, of time, of a society that he cannot fully accept or reject, of a world that is in constant struggle. Most of all, he is a victim of his romantic illusions: his belief in the possibility of self-fulfillment and purpose when life, in reality, is moving in a furious circle, like a raging whirlpool going nowhere. These are the ideas that Dreiser brought to his fiction where, once dramatized, they are far from inchoate, and where they are totally adequate to Dreiser's own needs as a novelist.

I have always felt that Trilling would have been much fairer to Dreiser and on more solid critical ground, if he had compared Dreiser with Howells rather than James, because Howells was treating the same material that Dreiser later used. Howells' *A Modern Instance* (1881), for example, is similar in a number of ways to *Sister Carrie.* Bartley Hubbard is an ambitious and amoral product of a small Maine town who marries the daughter of the local squire (against the squire's will) and who comes to Boston to make his fortune in journalism. Like Carrie, he struggles in the indifferent city and subordinates moral scruples to his desires for success and money. But whereas Dreiser looked at Carrie's struggles sympathetically, Howells has nothing but contempt for Bartley. When Bartley absconds to Chicago with $1,200, he has a change of heart by the time he gets to Cleveland. When he comes to buy his return ticket to Boston, however, he discovers that his wallet—with the $1,200 in it—has been stolen. At this point Howells tells us: "Now he could not return; nothing remained for him but the ruin he had chosen." Here the reader boggles, because Bartley has not chosen at all—or rather, he has chosen to return to Boston, just the opposite of what fate has allowed. The situation in Howells' novel is thus similar to Hurstwood's story in *Sister Carrie:* Bartley is driven toward a predestined end by an accident (the stolen wallet) just as Hurstwood is driven toward a predestined end by another accident (the safe slamming shut). The stolen wallet in *A Modern Instance* and the slamming of the safe door in *Sister Carrie* have the same narrative purpose.

A Modern Instance, however, is very different from *Sister Carrie,* especially the ending which is told from the point of view of the suffering Marcia. This is, of course, a major difference, because when Marcia morally triumphs and Bartley morally fails, the Christian sense of right and wrong is put in clear perspective—just as it would have been if the story of Hurstwood had been told from the point of view of Mrs. Hurstwood. By telling the story from Hurstwood's point of view, and telling it sympathetically, Dreiser created a purely amoral world and divorced his characters from Christian imperatives, something Howells was most reluctant to do.

I am a little embarrassed in insisting upon this point, because it seems to me quite obvious. Yet Lionel Trilling never considered it in his condemnation of Dreiser; and, as far as I know, no one has ever answered Trilling. Dreiser turned the novel around with *Sister Carrie.* He was the first American novelist consciously and explicitly to divorce Puritan sin from moral punishment. Not only is Hurstwood treated sympathetically, but Carrie, who is complicit in his misdeeds, is a benefactor of them. Stephen Crane never dared as much in *Maggie*, who is doomed once she gives herself to Pete, just as Mark Twain's Laura Hawkins is doomed once she gives herself to Colonel Selby. In a very tame way, to be sure, Dreiser helps free the American novel, to move it into a new realm of experience that had never before been depicted. Norman Mailer may have this in mind when he says that Dreiser came "closer to understanding the social machine than any other American writer who ever lived." He moved us beyond the genteel writers who wrote "about courtship and marriage and love and play and devotion and piety and style, a literature which had to do finally with the *excellence* of belonging to their own genteel tradition."

But it is perhaps too easy to score for Dreiser by playing him against Howells. For all its relevance, *Sister Carrie* is dated in its own way. The task of defending Dreiser becomes more burdensome when we compare a novel like *An American Tragedy* to Richard Wright's *Native Son.* I reread *Native Son* recently with such a comparison in mind. It is not a bad novel. Indeed, it has some very powerful moments and is perhaps the best sustained writing that Wright ever did, and I can see no point in disparaging Wright in order to praise Dreiser. To the contrary, Wright tells us in *Black Boy* that Dreiser was his mentor, and *Native Son* owes a considerable debt to *An American Tragedy.*

Native Son deals with the growing consciousness of Bigger Thomas after he commits two murders—one accidental, the other intentional. Combining the naturalistic elements of Dreiser with a kind of psychological gothicism, Wright introduces us to Bigger as he awakens in his rat-infested Chicago ghetto, follows him into the luxurious residence of Mr. Dalton for whom Bigger works as chauffeur, records Bigger's first impressions of Mary Dalton and Jan (her Communist friend), and analyzes the hidden motives that lead Bigger—out of both fear and hate—to murder Mary, decapitate her, and burn her body in the house furnace. When Bigger is exposed, he takes flight, and we follow him as he murders his girl friend and unsuccessfully tries to avoid the pursuing police. In the defense by a Communist attorney, Bigger's story is turned into a political argument. Bigger as we first see him is very different from Bigger as we last see him. The early Bigger has no real self-understanding. He is maddened by the fact that the welfare department has found him a job at the Daltons' and that his choice is a limited one—work or starve. While Dreiser's characters are trapped within their bodies and environment, Bigger Thomas is also trapped within his mind, a mind which begins to expand under the shock of violence. Fear and submerged hate remain with Bigger. When he finally runs away, he murders again—this time Bessie, his girl friend, whom he fears will give him away. This parallels the murder of Mary Dalton, only the same motives have now risen to the surface, and Bigger acts consciously, first forcing himself sexually upon Bessie and then brutally—fear and rage driving him on—beating in her skull with a brick. When the morning comes, Bigger looks out at a Chicago covered with snow and is conscious that in more ways than one he

is a black man in a white world—a cold, white world. He feels totally outside that world and ponders, "Why should not this cold white world rise up as a beautiful dream in which he could walk and be at home?" The question has no answer: he has murdered twice and created a new world from which he can never escape.

It is at this point that Wright should have ended his novel, as indeed Dreiser ended *An American Tragedy* with a question rather than an answer. But Wright cannot stop here, and he turns *Native Son* into a tract, Bigger's despair being absorbed by the Communist attorney's hope. Bigger's developing political consciousness is at best forced. As a result, *Native Son* is diminished in the way *An American Tragedy* is not. Not once does Dreiser proselytize; not once does he create villains. Clyde, Roberta, Sondra, the prosecuting and defense attorneys, Mrs. Griffiths, the Reverend McMillan—they all do what they have to do; their story is larger than their individual existences; their story is American and tragic in its panoramic totality. Dreiser does not point an accusing finger at Clyde's rich uncle or cousin as Wright points an accusing finger at Mr. and Mrs. Dalton. Dreiser's view of the rich was both more complex and more ambiguous than Wright's, and it was Dreiser's ambiguity that saved him as a novelist.

I should like to conclude by developing this point, at least slightly. If we take a look at American literature near the end of the 19th century, at some point we must turn to Edward Bellamy's *Looking Backward* with its optimistic belief in a utopia based upon a machine society which will bring abundance to everyone and thus end poverty and such resulting evils as crime and individual greed. Mark Twain was not convinced, and he answered *Looking Backward* with the apocalyptic ending of *A Connecticut Yankee in King Arthur's Court.* Henry Adams was even less convinced, as he tells us in the Virgin and Dynamo chapter of *The Education.* Whereas medieval man had found an imaginative unity in the Virgin, modern man had created the dynamo which fed on natural resources and which would deplete these resources as it led to social diversity too great for the mind ultimately to control.

Dreiser was aware of both traditions of thought. In the thirties he could support Howard Scott's Technocracy, based as it was on Bellamy's ideas. He tried to get Upton Sinclair, who was running for governor of California, to support Scott, until Sinclair bluntly pointed out that to create an engineer dictator was only one step away from fascism. But long before Technocracy, Dreiser was fascinated by men like Charles Yerkes, the new Prometheus who changed our very landscape with the new technology. But for all his admiration, Dreiser could not accept the new Prometheus so long as he exploited the masses, so long as the new technology benefited the individual at the expense of the many. *The Titan* ends with the defeat of Cowperwood, but even here Dreiser is in control. He doesn't hate Cowperwood; Cowperwood's defeat does not prompt editorial glee.

As a mechanist, Dreiser believed that society worked like a machine, a view that he adhered to most of his life. As a novelist, he was more interested in explaining the way the machine worked than in condemning the process. As a result, Dreiser was able to say more about the machine than a Howells, and willing to say less than a Wright. He was a realist enough to see that his own views were just one of many possible views. I have had a vision of life, he tells us, "life with its romance and cruelty, its pity and terror, its joys and anxiety, its peace and conflict. You may not like my vision . . . but it is the only one that I can give you." Dreiser was totally conscious of the antitheses of life, as this passage reveals. As a result, he had no trouble creating characters as diverse as Hurstwood and Cowperwood, Roberta Alden and Sondra Finchely, Griffiths and Solon Barnes. Lionel Trilling was totally unaware of the significance of Dreiser's use of antithesis when he spoke so condescendingly of Dreiser's sense of reality. Little did Trilling know that such dualism was the source of Dreiser's vision and his salvation as novelist. Dreiser at his best can still be read and reread. I think it is safe to say that he will survive his hostile critics, and for a novelist, this is the best kind of revenge. (pp. 307-17)

*Richard Lehan, "Dreiser and the Hostile Critics,"
in* The Old Northwest, *Vol. 10, No. 3, Fall, 1984,
pp. 307-17.*

SHELLEY FISHER FISHKIN (essay date 1985)

[*In the following excerpt, Fishkin examines the influence of Dreiser's early journalism upon his career as a novelist.*]

Journalism [was] Dreiser's primary source of income long after he had begun writing novels. Much of his writing was simply hack work done for the money. Constantly straining to balance his tight monthly budget on what he earned as a freelancer, as Thomas Riggio has noted [in *American Diaries, 1902-1926* (1982)], Dreiser would feverishly "write in the same week for magazines as diverse as *Masses, Cosmopolitan, The Seven Arts,* and *Saturday Evening Post.*" When he was truly bored he would plagiarize tedious descriptions and statistics from company catalogs or carelessly get his facts twisted; his publishers grew accustomed to receiving letters of complaint. But Dreiser was indebted to the magazines for much more than money. Amid the mindless pieces on carrier pigeons, teddy bears, the apple industry and the homes of famous people were several articles that would later be incorporated, in part or whole, into Dreiser's novels. The seeds of his finest works of fiction were gathered during the twenty years Dreiser spent trafficking in the world of fact. (p. 90)

In St. Louis Dreiser learned quickly that writing a good murder story was the swiftest way to win his editor's esteem. Of his editor at the *Republic* he wrote,

> Deaths, murders, great social or political scandals or upheavals, those things which presented the rough, raw facts of life, as well as its tenderer aspects, seemed to throw him into an ecstasy—not over the woes of others but over the fact that he was to have an interesting paper tomorrow. . . . "Ah, it was a terrible thing, was it? He killed her in cold blood you say? There was a great crowd out there, was there? Well, well, write it all up. Write it all up. It looks like a pretty good story to me—doesn't it to you? Write a good strong introduction for it, you know, all the facts in the first paragraph, and then go on and tell your story. You can have as much space for it as you want—a column, a column and a half, two—just as it runs. Let me look at it before you turn it in, though." Then he would begin whistling or singing, or would walk up and down in the city-room rubbing his hands in obvious satisfaction. . . .

"When nothing of immediate importance was to be had," Dreiser recalled in *Newspaper Days,* his editor "proceeded

to create news, studying out interesting phases of past romances or crimes which he thought might be worthwhile to work up and publish on Sunday, and handed them to me to do over." One of the earliest crimes Dreiser was sent to cover involved a St. Louis perfume dealer who freed himself of his poor and pregnant sweetheart by murdering her; it was the first of many such crimes Dreiser would encounter. As a reporter in Chicago and St. Louis Dreiser was frequently sent to cover seductions and murders; he was destined to develop, in the process of doing so, a sharp awareness of pattern and problem that his contemporaries largely ignored. It was out of this awareness that *An American Tragedy* would develop.

(Dreiser was not unaware of the cruelty and intrusiveness inherent in the reporter's exploitation of human suffering to get his story. In St. Louis, in 1893, for example, he was sent to cover a lynching in the town of Rich Hill, Missouri. The terse, five-inch story that ran in the *St. Louis Republic* under the headline "A Negro Lynched" began, "Rich Hill's first demonstration of mob violence occurred today although the town is in the fourteenth year of its existence. It resulted in the hanging of a negro rapist." Dreiser later returned to this event in his short story **"Nigger Jeff,"** in which he made a newspaper reporter the central character. The vain, self-centered, ambitious reporter shamelessly exploits the genuine suffering he encounters to get his story on the wire. In the end, however, he recognizes that "before such grief his intrusion seemed cold and unwarranted." He is moved to tears. But the newspaperman within him, as well as "the cruel instinct of the budding artist that he already was," makes him retreat from the prospect of relating to the mother of the dead man as a feeling, grieving, human being and leads him instead to "meditate on the character of the story it would make—the color, the pathos." The story concludes: " 'I'll get it all in!' he exclaimed feelingly, if triumphantly at last. 'I'll get it all in!' ") (pp. 91-2)

Artwork gave readers a more dramatic visual awareness of the broad spectrum of fortunes that made up American society, and made more concrete and more vivid what Dreiser would later refer to as the "astounding contrast between wealth and poverty" that pervaded our culture. For example, the face of a slum dweller who tried to murder his family in a feverish frenzy and the look of his dreary home and of his makeshift weapons were vividly sketched in a series of etchings that took up more space than the text of Dreiser's narrative of the event in a St. Louis paper. Again, the artist's sketch, not Dreiser's text, dominated the page when the subject was a local society ball. The artist who rendered the fair features and graceful gowns of the ladies at the ball (Gibson girls all, after the fashion of the time) enabled readers to almost hear the rustle of silk, the hushed tones of refined conversation, the gracious strains of background violins. As a journalist Dreiser constantly moved back and forth between these vastly disparate worlds. The images reflected in such illustrations—emblems of poverty and wealth, misery and contentment—allowed the paper's readers clear glimpses of those worlds as well. Dreiser would later weave such emblematic scenes of slums and society dances into the richly textured fabric of his greatest novel. (p. 93)

The bulky Sunday supplements and fat daily papers that the great spurt of advertising in the last two decades of the century helped make possible were filled with new kinds of stories and styles as well as new kinds of graphics. While European and British journals tended to cater to one or another of the clearly demarcated classes or interest groups of the "old world," a philosophy of "something for everyone" came to dominate America's mass-circulation journals. In addition to lengthy treatments of sensational news, there was new extended theater coverage, detailed interviews, "women's pages," advice columns, and fashion coverage alongside such older newspaper staples as humorous hoaxes, witty and whimsical personal commentaries, and society columns. Dreiser would try his hand at each of these forms, and each played a role in shaping his sensitivity to the ways in which a writer could cast his world into print.

But the two developments that would have the greatest effect on Dreiser's career were (1) the popularity of "color" or "feature" stories, and (2) the new emphasis on "facts." At Pulitzer's *World* posters printed with the words "The Facts—The Color—The Facts" were pasted on the walls to remind reporters of their primary charge. "Facts" had always played a role in newspaper reporting, and "features" were clearly outgrowths of the "human-interest story" Charles Dana had introduced in the *New York Sun* in the late 1860s and early 1870s, but both elements played new and distinctive roles in the world of journalism of the 1890s, and influenced Dreiser's growth as a writer in key ways.

The Sunday supplements financed by department-store advertisements were always hungry for lengthy colorful meandering pieces that vividly evoked the look and sound of a particular chapter of city life or a "human-interest" tale that would capture the reader's imagination. Chicago journalism in the 1890s, as Dreiser would recall in **Newspaper Days,** "was still in that discursive stage which loved long-winded yarns upon almost any topic. Nearly all news stories were padded to make more of them than they deserved, especially as to color and romance. . . . The city editors wanted not so much bare facts as feature stories, color, romance, and although I did not see it clearly at the time I was their man." The "discursive," "long-winded," "padded" leisurely style of 1890s journalism came easily to Dreiser. Indeed, one might argue, this early discouragement of brevity and conciseness might help explain Dreiser's tendency throughout his career (whatever his other faults and virtues may be) to write books which are, indisputably, long.

Dreiser discovered his talent for "feature" stories in the first newspaper special he ever wrote, a piece about Chicago's "vilest slum."

> Saloon lights and smells and lamps gleaming smokily from behind broken lattices and from below wooden sidewalk levels gave it a shameless and dangerous color. Accordions, harmonicas, jew's-harps, clattering tin-pan pianos and stringy violins were forever going; paintless rotting shacks always resounded with a noisy blasphemous life between twelve and four; oaths, foul phrases, a Hogarthian shamelessness and reconciliation to filth everywhere. . . .

The piece won high praise from his editor. "You may have your faults, Theodore," he had told him, "But you do know how to observe. You bring a fresh mind to bear on this stuff." (pp. 94-6)

While accuracy was highly valued in straight news stories, in the feature department, as Dreiser quickly learned, unabashed lying had its own rewards. Like Mark Twain, Dreiser was occasionally prompted to invent stories by the pauci-

Photograph of Dreiser by Carl Van Vechten.

ty of legitimate news. But unlike Twain, his invention was rarely satirical or directed at a social ill; he was more likely to lie for status and money than for a principle.

Hard-pressed to find any important personage to interview for his "Heard in the Corridors" column in the *St. Louis Globe-Democrat,* Dreiser proceeded to interview imaginary characters who proved infinitely more charming than the real ones who had previously populated his column. The free-wheeling journalism of the 1890s easily tolerated the presence of entertaining rambling in its columns, and Dreiser was urged to fill the "Corridors" with imaginary friends as often as he liked. For the *St. Louis Republic* he wrote a lengthy series of burlesques of a baseball game to be played by a fat and thin team. In New York he turned a rather dull tenement fight into a raucous fictional brawl. "I knew now," Dreiser wrote later, "that what my city editors wanted was not merely 'accuracy, accuracy, accuracy,' but a kind of flair for the ridiculous or remarkable even though it had to be invented, so that the pages of the paper and life itself might not seem so dull."

Indeed, the newspaper columnist who had sparked Dreiser's interest in journalism in the first place was a man as famous for the wit of his invention as for the wisdom of his observations, the renowned Eugene Field of the *Chicago Daily News.* "For two years or more" before he got his first job on a newspaper, Dreiser recalled, "I had been reading Eugene Field's 'Sharps and Flats,' a column he wrote daily for the *Chicago*

Daily News, and through this, the various phases of life which he suggested in a humorous though at times romantic way, I was beginning to suspect, vaguely at first, that I wanted to write, possibly something like that." Field's "Sharps and Flats" included comments in prose and verse on the world he witnessed, literature, drama, politics, and prominent personalities, as well as hoax stories, such as one about a rare imaginary animal recently donated to the local zoo, or "How Milton Dictated to a Typewriter." The varied fare he offered his readers was characterized by a light touch, a distinctively whimsical personal style, and a flair for that which might spark a reader's interest. While he often showed a fine sense of humor and a competent knowledge of history and literature, he was also prone to lapse into cliché and to indulge in sentimentality.

All of Dreiser's pure "inventions" as a journalist—both his extended burlesques and his brief imaginary "interviews" in his "Heard in the Corridors" column—are directly imitative of Field's "Sharps and Flats." But Dreiser borrowed something else from Field, a trait he kept throughout his career as a writer: an inflated, high-sounding diction which Field usually employed for mock-heroic ends, but which Dreiser often seems to have adopted straight, in strictly innocent admiration. When Field referred to a "tangent obliquity of the gifted Texan's ocular organs" his pompous diction was chosen for humorous effect. Or when he let adjectives follow nouns, when he used phrases like "glances arch" and "cunning meek," such artificial "literary" constructions were usually part of a whimsical or incongruous pose on the part of the writer. Dreiser adopted the stilted construction without the humor. He would see nothing wrong with putting such a ridiculously out-of-place phrase as "a scene more distingué than this" in *An American Tragedy.*

Critics have often berated Dreiser for his tendency to use big words where small ones would do, for his fondness for high-flown, Latinate, inappropriately complicated ways of saying things, and for writing in a manner that must have struck him as pleasingly "literary" or "erudite." Perhaps Dreiser's own lack of formal education prevented him from understanding the nuances of Field's wit. In any event, his uncritical and profuse admiration of Field, combined with his limited understanding of the columnist's games of diction, left indelible marks on his own approach to writing. Field, a journalist who mastered the art of using large words in a small genre, seems to have left one of our greatest novelists the legacy of *mis*using large words in a large genre.

While newspapers in the 1890s gave special prominence to "feature" stories, they also treated facts in a new and significant way. As press historian Michael Schudson has said, "Reporters in the 1890s saw themselves in part, as scientists uncovering the economic and political facts of industrial life more boldly, clearly and realistically than anyone before." Their shift in emphasis, he believes, might be seen as "part of the broader Progressive drive to found political reform on 'facts.'" "Accuracy—Accuracy—Accuracy," read placards on the walls of Pulitzer's *World.* Journalists like Lincoln Steffens, H. L. Mencken, and Jacob Riis all recalled, as Dreiser did, the specific directives of their first editors for factual, impersonal reporting. Dreiser learned the rewards of accuracy early in his newspaper career. The first piece to win him extravagant praise from his editors in Chicago was an exposé he wrote on the fraud practiced by mock auction shops across the city; his carefully accurate, "matter of fact" report closed

many of the shops and earned kudos for both Dreiser and the *Globe.*

When critics enumerate Dreiser's greatest virtues as a novelist, the palpable solidity of the world he creates appears near the top of the list; its sheer weight and physical density are not to be denied. Whatever his other faults, Dreiser is renowned for his ability to pile fact upon fact until the reader is dragged almost bodily into the novel's world. Dreiser's appreciation of both the importance and the power of fact is yet another legacy of his background in the journalism of the 1890s.

It was as a reporter in the 1890s that Dreiser first encountered facts that would later prove invaluable to him as a writer of fiction. The year Dreiser became a reporter in Chicago, the local papers were filled with daily investigations into the machinations of a Chicago financier named Charles T. Yerkes. They must have left their impression on young Dreiser, for it was to these same facts that he would return when he wrote his "Trilogy of Desire," *The Financier, The Titan,* and *The Stoic.* In Toledo Dreiser covered a streetcar strike, an event he would incorporate into *Sister Carrie.* It was in St. Louis that Dreiser first wrote about the sumptuous attractions of the grand hotel, and it was here that he first documented the cruel and petty tyrannies that characterized the American court of justice. All of these subjects would find their way into *An American Tragedy.*

Dreiser approached the dense world of fact with an almost pietistic sense of wonder. Indeed, it was his sense of awe before the "roaring, yelling, screaming whirlpool of life" around him that led him to enter journalism in the first place. His deep respect for fact would become a hallmark of his writing when he turned to fiction. Dreiser, known by friend and foe alike as an incorrigible liar, probably spent more time trying to get his facts straight in his novels than any fiction writer of his generation. While his autobiographies are riddled with fictions, his novels are firmly rooted in fact. They are "based upon things actually seen, heard or heard of," as his close friend H. L. Mencken has said [in his introduction to a 1946 edition of *An American Tragedy*]. "It was seldom that he departed from what he understood to be the record, and he never did so willingly." Despite his cavalier attitude toward the truth about his personal life, in his novels Dreiser devoted great pains to documenting even the most trivial fact with accuracy and precision. "He would sit down to his desk in the days when I saw him oftenest," Mencken recalled, "and bang away with pen and ink for four or five hours . . . [stopping only] to go to the library to verify a street-name, or to find out when the Pennsylvania Railroad first reached McKeesport, or to establish the precise date of the General Slocum disaster.

While Whitman may have revered the world of fact as emblematic of God and his handiwork, Dreiser stood in awe of the world of fact as emblematic of fate. The parents one had, the seemingly accidental events that crossed one's path, the time in which one lived, determined, in Dreiser's view, the life one lived. Race, moment and milieu (to borrow from Taine) were destiny; any attempt to understand life, Dreiser felt, must document contemporary realities as fully as possible. Thus Dreiser's art came to be so rooted in fact that many had trouble recognizing his novels as products of a creative imagination. His stories were often taken as literal transcripts of their times. Truth was inextricably linked with fact for Theodore Dreiser, and the freedom of the individual to see the world of fact with his own eyes would prove to be as sacred to him as that world itself. The ease with which people allowed attractive illusions to rob them of that freedom would be a major theme of Dreiser's fiction.

The facts that interested Dreiser throughout his career were the facts he had first encountered as a daily-newspaper reporter. His capacity to feel, to sympathize, to understand, was as broad and all-inclusive as the daily newspaper itself—and was molded essentially by exposure, both as reader and reporter, to the facts that medium documented. His sensibility as a novelist was closer than that of any American writer before him to the sensibility of those whose primary reading matter was the newspaper (all the real-life Carries and Hurstwoods and Clyde Griffithses). Largely self-educated, and from "the wrong side of the tracks," Dreiser shared their awe of the Broadway star, of the successful financier, of fashionable clothes and elegant homes. He shared their familiarity with poverty, deprivation, failure, jealousy, and exclusion from the American dream of success; he understood the desperation that often grew out of being poor in a land of plenty. But unlike most newspaper readers and reporters Dreiser constantly searched for meaning in the chaotic jumble of facts that surrounded him, constantly wondered where it all led, and to what end. Pages of Broadway notices; advertisements for luxury goods; sketches of breadlines; stories of strikes; statistics of unemployment, hunger, and death; all contributed to a whole for Theodore Dreiser—a whole which would first come alive in *Sister Carrie.* The triumphs of tycoons, the details of their financial machinations, the activities painted in the society pages—all this bristled with drama for Dreiser, a drama he would evoke in *The Financier.* And he would find, in repeated stories of young men's murder of their girlfriends for social and material advancement, the outlines of a recurring plot all too familiar to an ever-upwardly-mobile America; this story was the blueprint on which *An American Tragedy* was built.

Dreiser's achievement as a novelist was inextricably linked with his ability to assimilate his epoch as recorded in the daily newspaper; no other novelist of his generation was so clearly in touch with its realities and significance. In its jumbled, cacophonous montage, Dreiser found a reality that he endeavored to capture in his art.

Newspaper work forced Dreiser to focus his attention on the contemporary realities that surrounded him. Looking back in later life on his early years in journalism Dreiser readily recognized the important contribution his "newspaper days" had made to his career as a writer. It was the "kaleidoscopic character of newspaper work" which had impressed him most deeply, and "which, in its personal significance to me," he wrote, "cannot be too much emphasized."

In exposing him to a vast "kaleidoscopic" array of facts about American life, journalism also provided Dreiser with an awareness of the extraordinary contrasts that existed in our society. This theme recurs throughout *Newspaper Days.* In Chicago his work took him into the houses of the richest debutantes and those of the poorest slum-dwellers. In St. Louis, the evening he rented his first tuxedo to cover a society ball he was later assigned to cover a grim quadruple murder by a slum-dweller afflicted with brain fever. "My head full of pearls, diamonds, silks, satins, laces, a world of flowers and lights, I was now hustled out along the dark, shabby, lonely streets of South St. Louis to the humblest of cottages in the humblest of streets where, among unpainted shacks with

lean-tos at the back for kitchens, was the one which contained this story." (pp. 96-101)

The sharp contrast he saw between rich and poor was paralleled by the sharp contrast he saw between American rhetoric and American realities.

Was God to blame? Dreiser asked. Was government? Dreiser could not answer these questions. His puzzlement runs through his memoirs as a constant refrain. "I had no solution," Dreiser wrote, "and was not willing to accept any, suspecting even then that man is the victim of forces over which he has no control." These contrasts, he wrote, challenged and ultimately destroyed the vestiges of the "dogmatic and religious moral theory [he] had been compelled to listen to [all his] life," and led him to think of American lip service to democracy and equality as simple bandstand patriotism. Clearly, an "omnipotent God" would not tolerate the work of such an "industrious devil." Such contrasts would not exist, Dreiser reasoned, if there were real democracy or equality of opportunity.

Dreiser was supported in his efforts to reexamine these facts for himself by the freethinking atmosphere that pervaded the newsrooms in which he worked. He found newspapermen "nearly all mistrustful of . . . conventional principles in general." Dreiser entered journalism as a romantic dreamer, but reporting taught him to probe under, behind, and through the dream until he reached the solid, brittle fact. The city rooms of the 1890s were filled with cynics—men who admired scientists like Darwin and Spencer, who aspired to a new goal of "objectivity," and who were impatient with conventional codes, accepted systems of belief, socially sanctioned hypocrisy, and mass-produced illusions. Dreiser would emerge from his apprenticeship in journalism as one of them. Science (and pseudoscience) would loom bigger than religion as a force shaping his philosophy of life. The challenge of describing "objective reality," of capturing truth rooted in external verifiable phenomena, would preoccupy and frustrate him throughout his career as a writer. And he would continually pit himself against convention, hypocrisy, and any system of belief that resisted constant testing against experience. (pp. 101-02)

In 1895, when Dreiser undertook the job of editing *Ev'ry Month,* the "Reflections" column, which he signed "The Prophet," represented the greatest liberation thus far from the limits he had encountered as a newspaperman. Dreiser the reporter had been forced by the conventions of newspaper style to limit his accounts of the tragedies befalling the poor to objective and verifiable facts of an individual's experience. Dreiser "The Prophet," however, could place the stark newspaper account into a larger context, and often he did just that. At a time when the misery of the poor was being eloquently documented by ardent muckraking reformers like Jacob Riis in books like *How the Other Half Lives,* there was still something fresh about Dreiser's perspective on the problem. Time and time again "The Prophet" addressed himself to a dimension of the poor's problems that even someone like Riis touched only obliquely, and others completely ignored. It was a dimension which, though highly familiar to all modern readers, had no name until 1949: the problem of "relative deprivation." "The Prophet" painted, over and over again, scenes of unfortunate individuals not just starving and freezing through no fault of their own, but starving and freezing within sight of a large feast and a warm hearth.

In one piece on this theme Dreiser referred to a story in a New York paper about a woman who was very poor, sick, weak, threatened by hunger, and compelled to sort rags for fourteen hours a day to support herself and her child. One night her strength failed, and "she crept homeward—weak, fevered, blind with pain, and unable to climb the long flight of steps that led to her tenement lodging." Then Dreiser allows the camera to pan back in the closing scene of the article, to expand the context of the woman's misery:

> There she lingered, sick and helpless before her own doorstep, and there they found her, prone and dying, after a time, with a great, wealthy city lying all around her, and the roll of carriages and the laughter of the idle within an arrow's flight away.

In another piece "The Prophet" added to a brief newspaper account of a pauper's suicide in the East River the notion that

> Such a creature may have wandered about all day until that hour. . . . Carriages may have jingled past impressively, and richly garbed creatures alighted here and there, bent upon expenditures as large and reckless as they are shallow and vain. He may have glanced through gorgeous shop windows, upon wealth of endless value; may have studied the gems in the jeweler's window, the laces in the cloth fancier's, the luxury of books here, the wealth of bric-a-brac there, all barred by polished glass, and at last sadly realized that all was as distant as paradise, as impossible to him as wings. . . .

One can easily view these passages as early literary explorations of what Dreiser would call, in *An American Tragedy,* "that curious stinging sense of what it was to want and not to have."

In other magazine pieces Dreiser would often reiterate this theme. In a piece in *Tom Watson's Magazine* in 1905 on "**The Loneliness of the City,**" he would observe (somewhat clumsily),

> So exacting are the conditions under which we are compelled to work, so disturbing the show of pleasures and diversions we cannot obtain, that the normal satisfaction in normal wants is almost entirely destroyed.

And in an editorial in the *Delineator* in 1909 Dreiser would note,

> The average person, swept by unknown forces into an unknown, hardly understandable world such as this, finds himself confronted in early youth by a widening field of desire and little or no opportunity to gratify any of its various phases. . . . Only money seems to answer for most of the things which are actually worthwhile. . . . In the face of this, the average individual is born without money and with very little understanding of the subtleties which accompany the acquiring of it.

The contrasts between rich and poor; the agony of being poor not only in a land of plenty, but in a land that held out to everyone the dream of being rich; the staggering array of all that money could buy in our society (status, power, love, sex, freedom, health, and even justice); and the staggering misery that resulted from absence of money—these were some of the themes Dreiser the magazine writer explored frequently. They were themes to which Dreiser the novelist would return on numerous occasions; they were themes that would be central to *An American Tragedy.*

Another theme Dreiser first explored as a magazine journalist which would later feature prominently in his fiction was the deceptive promise of the city and the dreams it both nurtured and destroyed. The evils of the sweatshops and the tenements were already somewhat familiar to the reading public of the 1890s. Journalists had been marshaling grim statistics to support their stances of justified moral outrage for at least six years before Dreiser published a piece called "**The City**" in *Ev'ry Month* in 1896. But while most of his colleagues focused on the social and moral aspects of the problem, Dreiser alone seems to have been preoccupied by epistemological concerns as well. How do we come to know "the city," "The Prophet" seemed to ask, how might we replace our familiarity with a part of it with an awareness of the whole, what images would help us expand our limited frames of reference?

As in the piece on the suicide of the pauper, Dreiser is more interested here in people's feelings, attitudes, and perceptions about their condition than he is in the objective facts of the condition itself. . . . Unlike some of his fellow journalists, Dreiser pushes for no reform. The bleak determinism that will play a key role in his novels surfaces here in an early form. But even here, and much more so in a book like *An American Tragedy,* implicit in the writer's project is a sense of how important it is to replace misleading romantic illusions with new metaphors, images, analogies—in short, new visions—rooted not in fantasy, but in fact. Here, as in his finest fiction, Dreiser urges his reader to take a fresh view of familiar surroundings.

As a magazine writer Dreiser had occasion to interview several contemporary artists adept at discriminating the real from the counterfeit in fresh and original ways; his admiration for their freshness of vision was both candid and sincere. Writing for *Ainslee's* on Davenport's caricatures, for example, Dreiser noted that Davenport's version of the politician Hanna

> is by no means the person one meeting [Mr. Hanna] casually might imagine, or mayhap that Mr. Hanna would like to be thought; Davenport, . . . looking beyond the glad, joyous, hand-shaking surface, pretends to see the fat, collar-marked, short-term senator with whom everyone is familiar.

And in an interview with Alfred Stieglitz for *Success,* Dreiser admired the photographer's evocation of "the clear crowning reality of the thing" he photographed. Whether capturing clear and solid realities himself, exposing pretense and illusion, or admiring freshness of vision in others, Dreiser cultivated, as a journalist, a distinct taste for what he once referred to as "life as it is."

America, he felt, with its insistence on conformity and conventionality, with its intolerance of unpleasant facts and its determination to see only the good and the beautiful, has encouraged a passive acceptance of "mirage" in place of an active contemplation of actuality—an actuality more complex than his fellow Americans seemed to want to acknowledge. "The actuality of life," Dreiser once wrote in a poem,

> Is like a wraith
> That haunts.
> A shadow that eludes one—
> Escaping by a thousand ways.

Wherever he turned in America, Dreiser found people viewing the world through the blinders of romantic illusions and conventional codes, all passively accepted and rarely questioned or challenged. He felt every individual "should question the things he sees—not some things, but everything." For only then would he be able to think for himself and see the world through his own eyes. The "controlling captains of industry," Dreiser would write in a piece in *The Seven Arts,* did nothing to encourage "the freedom of the individual to think for himself." The dominant religious and commercial organizations similarly did nothing to encourage "a free mental development in individuals." College students, according to one professor Dreiser quoted at length, "do not think; they cannot, because they are bound hard and fast by the iron band of convention." Despite the fact that the platitudes they mouth and the theories they spout bear no relation to American realities, Dreiser felt, Americans accept without question lies about their past and present. "We move," Dreiser wrote, "in a mirage of illusion"; this theme would be central to *An American Tragedy,* a book whose original title, indeed, was to be *Mirage.*

Dreiser was appalled by the nation of automatons that he saw, by the lies Americans so willingly lived with, by the facts they so blindly ignored. Americans refused to see facts Dreiser himself had witnessed daily in his years as a journalist:

> the unreliability of human nature; the crass chance which strikes down and destroys our finest dreams; the fact that man in all his relations is neither good nor evil, but both. . . . With the one hand the naive American takes and executes with all the brutal insistence of Nature itself; with the other he writes glowing platitudes concerning brotherly love, virtue, purity, truth, etc., etc.

Americans, Dreiser felt, would never allow the fact that they are adept at acting as brutal as Nature itself to tarnish the roseate images of themselves which they so cherished. (pp. 104-10)

When his friend Arthur Henry prevailed upon him to start a novel in 1899, Dreiser made the key decision to place his characters (who were based on members of his family) in scenes he had witnessed and documented as a reporter. The breadlines, the railroad yards, the bustling city streets, the Broadway crowds, the factories, the luxury hotels that would appear in *Sister Carrie* were all familiar to Dreiser from direct observation. Two of his magazine articles, **"Curious Shifts of the Poor,"** which appeared in *Demorest's,* and **"Whence the Song,"** which appeared in *Harper's Weekly,* found their way into *Sister Carrie* with few revisions. Both *Sister Carrie,* and the novel that followed it in 1911, *Jennie Gerhardt* (which was similarly based on people and scenes Dreiser personally knew), forced readers to take a fresh look at some of their society's most accepted assumptions. As Swanberg has noted [in *Dreiser* (1965)], the books that were selling when those novels appeared "were the glittering and virtuous costume romances, *When Knighthood Was in Flower, Janis Meredith, Soldier of Fortune.* Lust and vice were allowable only if punished in the end—as they had been in *McTeague*—to furnish the reader a wholesome moral lesson." In Dreiser's novels, however, transgression was presented with tolerance and understanding. Dreiser required his reader to accept, in Jennie Gerhardt's case, the seeming paradox of a virtuous sinner, and in Carrie's, of a successful one. Both images challenged the moral categories implicit in the popular novels of the day.

While Dreiser's profiles of successful businessmen for *Success* and other magazines may have sparked his interest in a businessman as a fruitful subject for a novel, he would incorporate only one of his magazine articles into his next novel, *The Financier* (the piece was **"A Lesson from the Aquarium,"** published in *Tom Watson's Magazine*). Based on the life of financier Charles T. Yerkes, *The Financier* was heavily researched by Dreiser from newspaper files, books, interviews, and public documents. As Robert Penn Warren has observed [in *Homage to Theodore Dreiser* (1971)], the novel's hero, Frank Cowperwood, "is not a fictional creation based on Yerkes; he is, insofar as Dreiser could make him, the image of Yerkes." In addition to giving his reader an unprecedented inside view of the world of business and finance, Dreiser made Yerkes's life read like the epic poem of the predator-hero by allowing his grandeur and "soul-dignity" to shine through his often sleazy machinations. No conforming Babbitt, Frank Cowperwood came across as both sophisticated and (in his own way) honest. Even in prison he is, fundamentally, free. Yet while Frank Cowperwood may be, in one sense, freer than almost any character that had yet appeared in American literature, in another sense he was a peculiarly modern kind of slave. Dreiser titles the trilogy of Cowperwood books, of which *The Financier* was the first, a "Trilogy of Desire." As the title suggests, Cowperwood was enslaved by a desire which, like Carrie's, would always outstrip its attainments. In his dramatic portrayal of the amoral energy that inhered in the ever-reaching, overreaching desire of a Cowperwood, Dreiser shined a spotlight on an aspect of American life that had been largely absent from both literature and journalism despite the fact that it was the force which animated and dominated the age.

Dreiser would incorporate aspects of several of his magazine articles into *An American Tragedy.* A piece called **"Pittsburgh"** which he wrote for the *Bohemian* aptly prefigures the walks between the poor and wealthy parts of town that Clyde will take in the novel; a piece Dreiser published in 1910 on **"The Factory"** is a clear rehearsal for his fictional factory scenes; and the opening of an article called **"The Man on the Bench"** which Dreiser wrote for the *New York Call* distinctly foreshadows the opening lines of *An American Tragedy.* But Dreiser's initial interest in the subject that would form the core of the novel dates back to his days as a newspaperman in St. Louis.

"In so far as it is possible to explain the genesis of any creative idea, I shall be glad to tell you how *An American Tragedy* came to be," Dreiser wrote two years after the book was published, in response to an inquiry,

> I had long brooded upon the story, for it seemed to me not only to include every phase of our national life—politics, society, religion, business, sex—but it was a story so common to every boy reared in the smaller towns of America. It seemed so truly a story of what life does to the individual—and how impotent the individual is against such forces. My purpose was not to moralize—God forbid—but to give, if possible, a background and a psychology of reality which would somehow explain, if not condone, how such murders happen—and they have happened with surprising frequency in America as long as I can remember.

Dreiser's personal familiarity with a murder like the one Clyde Griffiths would commit dates back to his days as a reporter for the *St. Louis Globe-Democrat.*

In 1892 Dreiser covered the story of a young perfume-dealer

who murdered his pregnant sweetheart with poisoned candy. At this juncture in American history, Dreiser recalls, "Fortune-hunting became a disease," and the frequent result was what Dreiser came to view as a peculiarly American kind of crime.

> In the main, as I can show by the records, it was the murder of a young girl by an ambitious young man. But not always. There were many forms of murder for money. . . . [One variation] was that of the young ambitious lover of some poorer girl, who in the earlier state of affairs had been attractive enough to satisfy him both in the matter of love and her social station. But nearly always with the passing of time and the growth of experience on the part of the youth, a more attractive girl with money or position appeared and he quickly discovered that he could no longer care for his first love. What produced this particular type of crime about which I am talking was the fact that it was not always possible to drop the first girl. What usually stood in the way was pregnancy, plus the genuine affection of the girl herself for her love, plus also her determination to hold him. . . .

"These murders," Dreiser wrote, "based upon these facts and conditions, proved very common in my lifetime and my personal experience as a journalist." (pp. 111-14)

As early as 1906 Dreiser confided to a friend that he wanted to write a book about a murder. By 1919, he had begun two separate novels dealing, respectively, with a murder in New York City and one in Hyannis, Massachusetts. It was not until 1920, however, that Dreiser decided on the case that deserved his fullest attention: the murder of Grace Brown by Chester Gillette in Herkimer County, New York, in 1906. The first time that he and others heard of the crime, Dreiser recalled,

> was when the press in a small dispatch from Old Forge, a small town not far from Big Moose Lake, announced that a boy and girl who had come to Big Moose to spend a holiday had gone out in a boat and both had been drowned. An upturned boat, plus a floating straw hat, was found in a remote part of the lake. The lake was dragged and one body discovered and identified as that of Billy Brown. And then came news of the boy who had been seen with her. He was located as the guest of a smart camping party on one of the adjacent lakes and was none other than Chester Gillette, the nephew of a collar factory owner of Cortland. He was identified as the boy who had been with Billy Brown at the lake. Later still, because of a bundle of letters written by the girl and found in his room at Cortland, their love affair was disclosed, also the fact that she was pregnant, and was begging him to marry her. . . .

Inevitably here, as in all the other cases of this sort Dreiser encountered, the newspaper account treated the facts of the case and the trial in the conventional manner. But there was another story which intrigued Dreiser: the story of why this story kept repeating itself, of why this tragic pattern recurred so frequently, and what made it so distinctively American. (pp. 115-16)

Dreiser, working as a journalist in New York in 1906, had taken considerable interest in the stories about the Gillette case which he had read in the New York newspapers. The press devoted a great deal of space to every detail of the case, and Dreiser, like other readers, had the chance to learn many specific facts about both Gillette and his victim. The *New York World's* artists had a heyday with the story as well, often filling a full quarter of the paper's front page (even more on inside pages) with drawings of "Chester Gillette as He Appears on Trial for His Life, and the Girl with Whose Murder He Is Charged," "Chester Gillette as He Appeared in Court and His Senior Counsel," and "Chester Gillette as He Appeared on the Witness Stand Telling His Version of Grace Brown's Death." In addition, the paper gave prominent play to photos, including a "Group Photograph of Gillette Family Taken When Chester Was Fifteen Years Old," one of the "Jurors Who Will Try Chester Gillette on Charge of Murder," and a picture of the "Prisoner's Handiwork in His Cell at Jail; Corner of Gillette's Parlor-like Cell, Decorated by Himself." It is no wonder that the heavily illustrated, sensational case made an impression on a writer who had been collecting clippings on crimes of this nature for years. Dreiser did not think about basing a novel on the case, however, until four or five years after he had read the newspaper accounts.

Ten years after *An American Tragedy* was published, Dreiser reflected in print on why he had been stirred by the case. "In my examination of such data as I could find in 1924 relating to the Chester Gillette-Billy Brown case," Dreiser wrote, "I had become convinced that there was an entire misunderstanding or perhaps I had better say non-apprehension, of the conditions or circumstances surrounding the victims of that murder *before* the murder was committed."

It was this "misunderstanding, or . . . non-apprehension," on the part of Americans, of the context in which the Gillette crime took place that helped prompt Dreiser to write *An American Tragedy.* The context in which the murder must be seen, Dreiser felt, was the fascination, shared by Americans across the nation, with the dream of rising through advantageous marriage from poverty to status and wealth. Versions of this dream had filled the pages of popular magazines Dreiser had encountered in his youth. The dream thrived in the consciousness of average people across America; and it underlay all of those chillingly similar crimes Dreiser had followed since the 1890s. And, almost without exception, it was viewed uncritically by the American public. Gillette, Dreiser wrote in 1935, *"was really doing the kind of thing which Americans should and would have said was the wise and moral thing to do* (attempting to rise socially through the heart) *had he not committed a murder."* Americans were blind, Dreiser felt, to important facts about themselves, their morality, their country, and their dreams. He wrote *An American Tragedy,* in large part, to help them take a fresh look at some of those facts. (pp. 116-17)

Dreiser lets the reader see Clyde's life through Clyde's own eyes in a way which evokes both sympathy and compassion. He lets the reader witness the parched and thirsting feelings Clyde has in the poor and musty rooms of his parents' mission, stifling in their bareness. And he lets the reader share Clyde's amazement at the luxury and comfort that surround him at the Green-Davidson Hotel. The reader has trouble condemning Clyde too harshly for allowing himself to be seduced by glitter and glamor.

Clyde is not perverse. He is not driven by any desires that are considered abnormal in society. He is not given to irrational outbursts; he is not even particularly passionate. He is a typical adolescent with typical adolescent "yearnings" and fantasies. He simply puts one foot in front of the other and suddenly finds himself tumbling down a mountainside from which there is no escape.

Telling Clyde's story the way he did, Dreiser challenged his readers' most unquestioned assumptions. The crimes Americans read about in the newspapers, in the 1890s, were "supposed to represent the false state of things, merely passing indecencies, accidental errors that did not count," Dreiser wrote [in *Newspaper Days*]. In short, crimes were considered curious aberrations from an otherwise good, honest, virtuous norm; and criminals were aberrant monsters whose exploits resembled those of beasts that had escaped from the zoo. In *An American Tragedy* Dreiser explores the *normality* underlying the criminal. And his notion forced his readers to take a fresh look at aspects of American life which they had grown accustomed to distorting or ignoring. While the reader of a Horatio Alger novel is soothed by the dream that anyone (including himself) can become a millionaire, the reader of *An American Tragedy* is disturbed by the nightmare that anyone (including himself) can become a murderer.

In exploring the normality underlying the criminal, Dreiser also dared to explore the criminality underlying the normal. The thirsting after wealth and respectability that motivated Clyde is identical to that which motivates other characters in the book, from all strata of American society. What separates them from Clyde is simply a matter of degree, not kind.

Hortense Briggs lies and schemes to get Clyde to buy her a new and expensive coat that is guaranteed to raise her social standing and hence her self-worth. (Meanwhile the coat-store proprietor lies and schemes to extract from her the maximum price.) Bella Griffiths tries to manipulate her father into building a bungalow at Twelfth Lake because she craves the status that summering there involves; she longs to be part of that set of families in Lycurgus that advertises its wealth and status with flashy cars, homes, and summer cottages. When simple shopgirls and the daughters of sophisticated factory owners are seen doggedly pursuing the same ends, the universality of these goals and of the often unsavory means these characters use to pursue their ends—lying, cheating, manipulating—is clearly established. There is a distinct aspect of criminality that underlies the normal throughout the book, and Dreiser constantly emphasizes it through such parallels.

The America portrayed in this novel is a grasping, greedy, and ever-thirsting culture that rarely, if ever, questions where it is going, or why. It is a society that accepts without question the validity of the American dream—the quest for success as defined by wealth and status. If his better-educated, higher-born compatriots have little reason to doubt the validity of striving for these goals, how can we expect Clyde to do so? For Clyde, as for most of the characters in the novel, "material success" was "a type of success that was almost without flaw, as he saw it."

While the reader is made aware of the multiple blemishes inherent in lives ruled solely by the dream of material success, Dreiser points out, evenhandedly, that such quests had valid aspects as well. For money solves many if not all problems in American society. Indeed, in American society as it is portrayed in the novel, money and status, in addition to providing comforts and glittering delights, can, in fact, get one out of almost any conceivable scrape. (pp. 125-26)

In the society Dreiser documents in the novel, the pain and complexity of life's problems are constantly denied in favor of the "easy solution." Dreiser knew, however, that the easy

solutions available to the rich were usually denied the poor. Despite the lip service America paid to the notion of equality, the poor were, for all practical purposes, treated as less equal than the rich. This reality (first encountered by Dreiser as a newspaper reporter) was denied by the roseate hues that permeated the pictures of American life that appeared in literature and by the rhetoric of politicians who trumpeted that all Americans were free and equal. But Dreiser was determined to prevent his reader from ignoring realities which popular fictions and rhetoric conspired to repress. It was vital to understand what money and status bought in America if one was to understand the manic acquisitiveness that ruled the day.

When Clyde first arrives in Lycurgus he walks down streets lined with elegant mansions and then reports for work at his uncle's factory. After work he strolls down River Street past more factories, and then he

> came finally upon a miserable slum, the like of which, small as it was, he had not seen outside of Chicago or Kansas City. He was so irritated and depressed by the poverty and social angularity and crudeness of it—all spelling but one thing, social misery, to him—that he at once retraced his steps and recrossing the Mohawk by a bridge farther west soon found himself in an area which was very different indeed—a region once more of just such homes as he had been admiring before he left for the factory. . . .

Clyde continues to believe, throughout his life, that he can turn his back on poverty and deprivation as easily as he can retrace his steps out of this slum. The rich do it, after all. Why shouldn't he?

Embodying the "youth, optimism and illusion" that Dreiser felt characterized America as a whole, Clyde constantly assumes that there will be an easy way out of potential misery. His tragedy, in part, is the tragedy that stems from denying life its untidy complexity.

Clyde's catalog of problems and solutions reads almost like a parody of the advertisements that fill the magazines to which Dreiser contributed. Have you a pain? the ad would ask. Take our pill. Are you going bald? Use our cream. For Clyde, and for most of those around him, life itself seems filled with equally simple solutions. Poor? Get a job. In trouble with the law? Get a pseudonym in a new city for a fresh start. Caught in a rut? Find a rich uncle. Got a poor girl pregnant? Throw her overboard. Convicted for murder? Appeal. Appeal denied? Take Jesus. (This final "solution" brings one full circle to the hymn Clyde's family sings in chapter 1: "The love of Jesus save me whole,/The love of God my steps control.")

Each of these "solutions," however, is obviously inadequate and unsatisfactory, though Clyde has neither the mental nor the moral resources to understand why. Like millions of other Americans whose follies Dreiser often criticized, Clyde had never learned to think for himself.

Clyde comes by his inadequate mental equipment naturally, through no fault of his own. His father, we learn, "poorly knit mentally as well as physically," was the "product of an environment and a religious theory, but with no guiding or mental insight of his own." His mother accepts without question the religious maxims that hang on her mission walls despite daily challenges to their wisdom. It is not surprising that

Clyde lacks the mental and moral faculties to view his surroundings critically. He has been told all his life that he is free to choose the road to heaven or hell, and he assumes he is as free to choose success or failure, wealth or poverty, happiness or misery. He is unaware of the extent to which he is not free. Like so many other characters in the book, Clyde is bound up in a morass of illusions that impede his ability to deal effectively with the realities he encounters.

Dreiser is well aware of the inadequacy of Clyde's perspective on himself and his actions; for Dreiser knows that simplistic solutions, framed mottoes, and dreams of status and wealth fail to contain the complexities of life in the modern world. It is with stunning humility that Dreiser suggests that perhaps even a novel as long and dense and intricate as his may prove, in the end, to be equally incapable of containing those complexities.

Dreiser, willing to admit the possibility that some of the complexities which elude Clyde may elude him as well, makes the drowning of Roberta indeterminate and ambiguous, as if he were unwilling to assume authority as narrator over the truth about his characters' actions. (pp. 127-29)

The ambiguity of the evidence presented at Clyde's trial echoes the ambiguity of the events that took place in the rowboat. By a series of subtle maneuvers of syntax and diction, Dreiser manages to leave these events remarkably indeterminate. . . . (p. 130)

Clyde himself is unsure of the role he has played in Roberta's death. She sinks for the final time not after he has decided not to save her, but as he floats in his interminable indecision. "Had he [killed her]? Or, had he not?" Clyde ponders. From the moment Clyde is seen "becoming conscious that his courage . . . was leaving him," to the end of book 2, he ceases to be the subject of any active verb. Clyde's thoughts flow in sentence fragments and images. The reader sees him *in the process* of doing things (consciously or unconsciously), yet unaware of how he came to be doing them.

In a final effort to evoke the murkiness of the scene he relates, Dreiser constructs several masterfully ambiguous phrases. Dreiser shows Clyde "rising and reaching half to assist or recapture" Roberta when she falls into the water. The word "recapture" suggests that she is his captive; "assisting" (implicitly to save) and "recapturing" (implictly to be able to destroy her himself) are thus polarly charged words, and the meaning of the sentence is ambiguous. Dreiser also refers to the blow Clyde "had so accidentally and all but unconsciously administered." Clyde's action was not completely unconscious; does this mean that it was somewhat conscious? Can something be *somewhat* conscious? If an action is somewhat conscious, can it also be accidental? The answers to these questions remain as clear as the silt on the bottom of Big Bittern.

Throughout *An American Tragedy,* as we have indicated earlier, Dreiser suggests the limitations of Clyde's outlook on life. But when it comes to the death of Roberta, the reader has no reason to believe that Dreiser knows more than Clyde does. Dreiser, supremely humble as an author despite his often pompous pride as a man, prefers to remain at Clyde's side, in the dark waters of his confusion, leaving the reader to postulate an explanation of the events on his own from the ambiguous cues offered.

Few writers of fiction have elicited the amount of literal read-

er participation that Dreiser elicited in this volume. The opinions of readers as to what "really happened" in the rowboat were so strong and diverse that Boni and Liveright decided to capitalize on them by running a contest. The essay contest they ran, on the topic, "Was Clyde Griffiths Guilty of Murder in the First Degree?," drew hundreds of entries from readers across the country and was eventually won by a law professor in Virginia. Because of the special openness and ambiguity with which Dreiser narrated the death of Roberta, readers were attracted to the idea of constructing interpretations of the event on their own.

Dreiser himself, in *An American Tragedy,* seemed to be unwilling to assume authority as narrator over what really happened to Clyde because he knew the complex facts of the event were unlikely to yield to any simple explanation. He preferred to admit that even he, as narrator, could not capture the "truth" about his characters, that they, like "the actuality of life," were

> A shadow
> That eludes one—
> Escaping by a thousand ways.

And rather than end his novel with the kind of resonant finality that is the novelist's prerogative, Dreiser chose to leave *An American Tragedy* peculiarly open-ended. In his final chapter Dreiser circles back to the words with which the novel began: "Dusk, of a summer night"; he then proceeds to begin the story of Russell (the child of Clyde's sister), who is being raised by Clyde's parents, and who is likely to relive, in his own way, Clyde's story. Implicit in this strategy is Dreiser's admission of the limitations of his novel: it contains the story of Clyde—but also of Russell? His final chapter reflects his belief that even a text as panoramic and dense as this one is destined to be incomplete, that life (and the experiences, tragedies, dreams, and mysteries it entails) resists containment in the writer's forms. (pp. 132-34)

Shelley Fisher Fishkin, "Theodore Dreiser," in her From Fact to Fiction: Journalism & Imaginative Writing in America, *The Johns Hopkins University Press, 1985, pp. 85-134.*

JOSEPH GRIFFIN   (essay date 1985)

[*In the following excerpt, Griffin examines Dreiser's collected short stories.*]

In **"The Scope of Fiction,"** a brief article he wrote at the invitation of the *New Republic* for its 1922 spring literary supplement, Theodore Dreiser commented on the short story as a fictional form:

> So when all is said and done and in the face of what has but now been said the problem of scope must ever be personal and individual. It is not for academic interpretation or fixation. We know, for instance, that for Eugène Sue and his admirers five hundred thousand words and endlessly pieced together verbal canvases and tapestries are by no means sufficient to cause either himself or his followers to be excommunicated on the ground of unreasonable indulgence in scope. The man and his works are as many would have them. To those who like Richardson and his Pamela, and I confess myself one of his admirers, his epistolary flights, even unto four and five hundred thousand words are by no means too much. Because of the time in and of

which he writes perhaps, I find myself following him with interest. Since scope, in part at least, might be assumed to predicate length or brevity as well as pleasure to the reader, I would have to confess that the scope of his work is satisfactory to me. By the same token the scope of *Les Misérables* is just as acceptable, though scarcely more so, than the minute intaglio of Thaïs. And I find Sappho, Carmen and Camille as full and as satisfactorily developed scope-wise as Madame Bovary, Mlle de Maupin and *Vanity Fair*—and as interesting. In fact I accept the short story, "Without Benefit of Clergy," as full and satisfactory a picture of life as *The Brothers Karamazov, A Family of Noblemen* or *Anna Karenina* but no more so. Why? I will try to tell you.

While Dreiser seemed more concerned in this passage with the question of the length of works of art per se that with the question of genre, implicitly, at least, his statement reflected an acceptance of the short story as a form as worthy of being pursued as the novel. Indeed, Dreiser's next paragraph, the answer to the question he posed, may be taken to pertain explicitly to the comparison raised in his last set of samples:

> Each suggests in its way, though the first may require but minutes and the other days to read, that inescapable and yet somehow pitiable finiteness in the midst of infinity which, think as we will, contrives to touch and move the understanding. Each suggests, in full, a land, a people, a period, a mood. Each etches the individual against the background of enormous possibilities and enormous limitations. Each conveys with moving completeness an all embracing understanding shot through with an enfolding and comforting pity. What more, pray, is it, that we ask of scope?

Thus, Rudyard Kipling's short story, "Without Benefit of Clergy," can be compared favorably to the lengthiest of fictional works, Tolstoy's and Dostoevski's, for example.

It is useful to view Dreiser the short story writer in light of his comments in **"The Scope of Fiction."** The man who by any standard is a major novelist and whose critical and popular reputation rests mainly on eight novels, some of them of considerable length, published concurrently thirty-one short stories and produced a large number of others that never saw print. Tending naturally to the novel of broad scope, Dreiser nevertheless was consistently drawn to write short stories, although he feared the restrictiveness of the genre. "I have written about nine short stories, but it's hard work," he told an interviewer in 1912. "I need a large canvas. As I said, before I can go on I have to get a huge enthusiasm, and a short story is too small for the necessary run before the jump." Dreiser's perseverance with this intransigent genre can be explained in part by the practical advantages that derived from his persistence. Although he wrote H. L. Mencken in 1919 to the effect that his short stories were providing him with a certain amount of financial stability, material benefit was assuredly not the only reason for Dreiser's commitment to the short story.

Dreiser's *New Republic* statement, " . . . I accept the short story "Without Benefit of Clergy," as full and satisfactory a picture of life as *The Brothers Karamazov, A Family of Noblemen* or *Anna Karenina* but no more so," advances the notion that the short story has its own legitimate domain, that what can be expressed as a short story cannot be as effectively expressed as a novel, and vice versa. Most certainly Dreiser re-

turned time and time again to the short story form because he wished to create "pictures of life" that could be better expressed there than in the novel. And discouraged as he might feel about his ability to master the shorter form, he was moved to attempt it by his inner creative demands. His "I need a large canvas" statement is more the expression of a personal preference for writing novels than the dismissal of the short story form as inadequate for everything Dreiser wished to express. The evidence is the thirty-one stories themselves, many of them, the manuscripts show, gone over again and again with an obvious obsession for getting things said fully and satisfactorily. (pp. 15-17)

In a market where the major criterion of excellence was popular demand, Dreiser's stories, which more often than not questioned and even upset the moral and social status quo, met with constant opposition. And in a market that "tolerated only excellence of workmanship," and where the "emphasis pre-eminently was upon . . . technique, upon the external and striking rather than upon the internal workings of character," Dreiser, with his heavy prose and stylistic gaucheries, was hardly much in demand. The repudiation of Dreiser's short fiction by the popular magazines was on the basis of style as well as content. That whole conglomeration of effects that goes under the name of slickness was as repugnant to Dreiser as his technical awkwardness was to the editors and their increasingly sophisticated clientele.

If Dreiser's short stories evoked little positive response from the popular magazines they were even less welcome among the more prestigious publications of the day. Ever since he had perused the upper-class magazines in the 1890s—and had been so disappointed by the short stories they published—Dreiser seemed driven by the desire to get his stories placed there. Of course, he had little success. If his verism and verbal clumsiness did not please the middle-class taste, they were even greater liabilities in an exclusive market that sought to reach "an audience well above average in income and intellectual curiosity," an audience that was not likely to be drawn to his doleful tales of common life. Not only did he encounter difficulty with the *Atlantic Monthly,* he was repeatedly turned down by *Harper's* as well. His only breakthroughs into the select group were nearly twenty years apart: **"The Lost Phoebe"** appeared in the April 1916 issue of *Century,* a magazine characterized by Mott as having "the highest aesthetic and moral ideals"; *Scribner's* published **"A Start in Life"** in October 1934.

Despite the unfavorable market, Dreiser was able to place a substantial number of stories without, for the most part, compromising his vision of life. In view of the thematic direction of his stories, it is surprising that he found outlets for them at all. The fact that he did publish them is evidence of the discernment of editors such as H. L. Mencken and George Jean Nathan of *Smart Set* and *American Mercury* and William Marion Reedy of *Reedy's Mirror,* whose magazines were themselves repudiations of philistine taste. More surprisingly, occasional acceptance of Dreiser fiction came from editors of large-circulation periodicals who, although committed to the demands of advertisers and readers, risked popular or professional censure when they accepted Dreiser fiction. George Horace Lorimer of the *Saturday Evening Post,* who accepted **"Free"** on the basis of Dreiser's reputation, was deluged with "dozens of telegrams and hundreds of letters" from readers who condemned the story; Burton Kline, editor of the *New York Tribune's* fiction supplement, published

Dreiser and his wife, Helen, in 1945.

"Love"—and was fired because his boss wanted "no such advanced fiction."

The discernment and courage of editors aside, much of the credit for what success Dreiser did have with placing his stories was the result of his dogged refusal to take no for an answer. While the New York *Nation* was proclaiming that "Every [short story] sentence must have 'go' in it and stimulate the desire for the next sentence as an object in itself"; while Jack London was advising would-be short story writers "to put a snapper at the end, so if they are crowded for space they can cut off your contents anywhere, reattach the snapper and the story will still retain form"; while Frank Norris was insisting that after its publication in a magazine, a short story was "irretrievably and hopelessly dead"; Dreiser was ignoring demand, fashioning stories in terms of his own vision of truth, submitting and resubmitting them to the magazines, and revising them with a view to collection and publication in volume form. (pp. 18-19)

When Dreiser emerged as a short story writer in 1901, he had been writing professionally since 1892. His output as a journalist, as a nonfiction contributor to the magazines with which he was associated, and as a free-lance contributor to American magazines generally was voluminous. Referring to the period between November 1897 and August 1900 alone,

Ellen Moers notes that Dreiser was able to support himself as a magazine writer: "He seems to have turned out almost a piece a week, for each of which he was paid twenty-five to one hundred dollars—an excellent income for those days." But more important than guaranteeing Dreiser a profession, and at times even a lucrative one, his exhaustive production as a reporter and as a magazine writer provided him with a constant reservoir of material for his fiction and served as a kind of workshop where the power of written expression was developed. A number of Dreiser's short stories are fictionalized expansions of experiences he had encountered as a newspaperman; some are largely verbatim rewrites of nonfiction material he had written in other contexts. Stories such as **"St. Columba and the River"** and **"A Story of Stories,"** both fictionalized renderings of earlier, essentially documentary, pieces, reflect in a general way the transformation from Dreiser the reporter to Dreiser the creative artist. But . . . **"Nigger Jeff"** dramatizes that transformation, and at a time when it was being effected.

In Dreiser's 1899 version of **"Nigger Jeff,"** a young *St. Louis Republic* reporter named Davies is sent by his editor to a backwoods Missouri town to report on the assault of a young white woman by a black man and on the lynching that threatens as a result. Naïve, the holder of fixed and absolute attitudes toward good and evil, crime and punishment, Davies proceeds to the locale of his news story with all the anticipation of a boy off to see his first baseball game. For a time he remains the observer, relishing the excitement and intent on getting down all the facts for his news story. But gradually, as he begins to see his pat views contradicted by the events he observes around him, he becomes less the dispassionate documentarian and realizes that he must reckon with the emotional responses he is experiencing. As Donald Pizer has observed, the 1901 *Ainslee's* **"Nigger Jeff"** is essentially an initiation story: it "dramatizes a growth in emotional responses by the principal viewer of the action." But Davies is also a writer by trade, one who transforms his responses to reality into a communicable form; his development is not merely a personal one but is exteriorized and becomes an "aesthetic" one. When at the end of **"Nigger Jeff"** Davies exclaims, "I'll get that in. I'll get it all in," he can be seen to be speaking for his creator and alter ego, Dreiser, who only a few years before had been told by his boss on the *Chicago Globe,* "I think maybe you're cut out to be a writer after all, not just an ordinary newspaper man," and who had himself become convinced that he must "turn to letters, the art of short-story writing."

Dreiser sustained his interest in writing short stories until the very end of his life. The thirty-one stories he published were only a portion of his total production: numerous others never got beyond the manuscript stage. The evidence suggests that Dreiser was interested in turning out well-wrought stories. The process of producing a short story that was up to his own standard was often a long and arduous one, and given that standard it is not surprising that so many stories remained in manuscript form. Nor was Dreiser satisfied to produce his collected stories in their original periodical form: the large majority of them received substantial revision—and some, extensive revision—for book publication. The evidence shows, as well, that he intended that those stories he published in the magazines after his second collection, *Chains,* be collected also.

There is no doubt that Dreiser considered his short fiction an important part of his writing and that he gave it his complete attention. This short-fiction *oeuvre* deserves close study. Such a study reveals a facet of Dreiser the artist that is scarcely acknowledged to exist: his consciousness of technique. It also uncovers a substantial number of short stories that are unique artistic expressions of facets of the contemporary American scene. (pp. 21-3)

When a selection of Dreiser's short fiction appeared in 1947 under the title *The Best Short Stories of Theodore Dreiser,* none of the contents was from material that had not been collected previously. *The Best Short Stories* contained "Free," "McEwen of the Shining Slave Makers," "Nigger Jeff," and "The Lost Phoebe" from *Free, and Other Stories;* "Khat," "St. Columba and the River," "The Shadow," "The Old Neighborhood," "Phantom Gold," "Convention," "Marriage—for One," and "The Prince Who Was a Thief" from *Chains;* and two nonfiction pieces, "My Brother Paul" and "A Doer of the World," from Dreiser's book of personal sketches, *Twelve Men.* (p. 128)

One of the most intriguing aspects of *The Best Short Stories* is the selection made. One immediately questions . . . , the absolute nature of the title. Certainly some of the best stories are here: "Free," "The Old Neighborhood," "Nigger Jeff," and "The Lost Phoebe," for example; but there are some notable omissions, such as "Sanctuary" and "Typhoon." And how explain the inclusion of such colorless tales as "The Shadow" and "Phantom Gold"? The collection does present a sampling of the scope and variety of Dreiser's work in the short story. There is a broad cross section here in terms of both subject matter and form: here are Dreiser's guilt-ridden businessmen and artists, his frustrated young couples, and the creatures of his fantasies; here, as well, are his interior monologues, his experimental stories, and his conventional narratives. One feature of *The Best Short Stories* that should not go unnoticed is the inclusion of Dreiser's two Arabian fantasies. "Khat" and "The Prince Who Was a Thief" frame the volume at beginning and end respectively. Undistinguished as these two stories are artistically, they have more than passing importance in terms of Dreiser's vision of certain facets of American life. No doubt because of his boyhood reading of the *Arabian Nights* literature, Dreiser often tended to express the attractions of life, at once appealing and dangerous, in terms of the glamour, color, and exoticism of the East. Thus the pleasure of being served ice cream by a waitress in a store where he worked as a boy elicits in him the exclamation: "Oh, Aladdin! Oh, Ali Baba! What fortune!" The same pattern emerges in a far graver context in *An American Tragedy,* for example, when Clyde Griffiths, dreaming of marriage to Sondra, sees himself as "joint heir with Stewart to all the Finchley means. And with Sondra as the central or crowning jewel to so much sudden and such Aladdin-like splendor." Dreiser's Arabian short stories are important as his attempts to isolate what was a pervasive vision of his within the confines of individual works of art.

The Best Short Stories has been the only attempt to bring a general sampling of Dreiser's short fiction into print. Its several reissues, along with the reissues of *Free, and Other Stories* and *Fine Furniture,* have helped to insure for Dreiser's short fiction a lively, if not spectacular, existence despite general critical neglect. As well, the stories continue to be a staple of the collegiate anthologies, as Shapiro puts it [in *Theodore Dreiser: Our Bitter Patriot* (1962)], "[sandwiched] . . .

between the shorter efforts of Henry James and Ernest Hemingway."

Dreiser's published short stories in no way represent his entire work in the genre. Among the Dreiser papers are many completed stories and stories in various states of preparation—to mention a few: a completed manuscript about an American concert pianist whose mother dies the evening of his first appearance in the United States; the interior monologue of a man whose boss, a wealthy lawyer, has over a period of years stolen the attentions of his wife; a story entitled "The 'Mercy' of God," completely unrelated to the *Chains* story of the same name. There is also the testimony of two women who were close to Dreiser during the last few years of his life: Helen Dreiser has written that in 1941 her husband "worked on several original motion picture scripts, short stories and lectures," Marguerite Tjader that during the last year of his life Dreiser "worked along on the short stories" and in the last few months "had hoped to do a few more short stories, based on some of his Quaker material."

It is quite evident that the themes of Dreiser's short stories and of his novels frequently touch upon and traverse each other. The stories and novels are similar in their concern with such subjects as love, business, and art, and in their delineation of the manner in which their characters seek fulfillment through these means. It is interesting to note, in this context, that during the early part of the century, the American magazines, in their wholehearted concern to give their reading clientele what it wanted, consciously sought stories that dealt with love and business. Mott notes, for example [in *A History of American Magazines* (1966)], that "the dominant subject in every number [of *Cosmopolitan*] from 1912 to 1918 was sex." The same commentator, writing about the *Saturday Evening Post,* observes that "there was an emphasis on three types of subject matter—business, public affairs and romance . . . and even the romantic fiction was often based on financial deals and the pursuit of wealth." This is not to suggest that Dreiser was committing himself to certain concerns because he knew they would be marketable; it has already been established that in the fiction he submitted to the magazines he flew in the face of popular demand. Rather, what this similarity between Dreiser's subject matter and the orientation of the magazines indicates is that he was attuned, as magazine editors were, to the salience these concerns had in American life. And he was attuned to the significance these considerations had for his contemporaries not only because he shared the general American experience himself, but because the particular circumstances of his upbringing coming to bear on his intelligence and sensitivity made him especially conscious of it.

In assessing Dreiser's commitment to the American dream of success, Kenneth S. Lynn has said [in "Theodore Dreiser: The Man of Ice"] that for Dreiser "Pluck and luck meant success, and success meant wealth and women. These conclusions, arrived at in mid-adolescence, stained Dreiser's mind forever." The source of this adolescent craving was in the poverty, insecurity, and repression of Dreiser's childhood. Drawn to mature reading at an early age, he discovered a world diametrically opposed to that of his own experience. His wife, Helen, telling of his boyhood years [in *My Life with Dreiser* (1951)], wrote: "When Theodore was only twelve, he read serials in the *Family Story Paper,* the *New York Weekly, Golden Days,* and George L. Monroe's *Seaside Library* . . . showing how the poor working girl dreamed of marrying the rich scion of wealth and how, after many trials and tribulations in which he sought to betray her, true love conquered, and she became the lawful mistress of a brownstone mansion on Fifth Avenue, New York." Recalling these same years himself [in *A Hoosier Holiday*], Dreiser wrote of the appeal of the smart picture magazines, those forerunners of the twentieth-century slicks: "For my own part I preferred *Truth,* or *Life,* or *Puck,* or *Judge,* publications which had been introduced into our family by my brother Paul when we were living in Evansville." Even his reading of the English and American classics provoked in him longings that were a direct result of the unfulfilled needs in his own life: "From the public library I drew Dryden, Pope, Shakespeare, Herrick and a dozen other English and American poets. . . . I was so interested in love at this time—so inoculated with the virus of the ideal in the shape of physical beauty—that any least passage in Dryden, Herrick, Pope, Shakespeare, held me as in a vise."

But if Dreiser's mind was "stained forever" by the emphasis he placed on success, it was not spoiled by it. Although the dream of success retained permanent significance for Dreiser the man and the writer, it never, except perhaps for a short period in his life when he worked for the Butterick publications, became his sole preoccupation. What differentiated Dreiser from the mainstream of popular fiction writers, indeed what won him the animosity of the magazine establishment, was precisely this: that save for a very few stories in which he wrote to demand, the ideas of the dream of success never appeared as an unadulterated ingredient in his fiction. However intensely Dreiser protagonists seek fulfillment through love, or entrepreneurial or artistic activity, there are invariably antithetical forces at work, of which these protagonists may or may not be aware, that make fulfillment difficult or impossible. One cannot overemphasize the influence of Dreiser's childhood in the formulation of his view of reality as evidenced in his fiction. The tension existing between the harsh realities of home, family and school on the one hand, and the fantasy world evoked from such influences as his reading and the aura of his brother Paul, on the other hand, is reflected time and time again throughout his fiction.

Of the thirty-one short stories under examination, nineteen deal principally with man-woman relationships. This group of stories amounts practically to an obsession with the human heterosexual association. A wide range of relationships is examined from a number of differing perspectives. In the majority of the stories in this group there is either an actual triangle or the real threat of one of the partners establishing a relationship with a third party. With only three exceptions, these stories deal with relationships that are unsatisfactory to both the men and women concerned. Of the exceptions, one story, **"When the Old Century Was New,"** deals only superficially with the couple; another, **"Fine Furniture,"** provides a satisfactory solution to a marital conflict; the third, **"The Lost Phoebe,"** focuses on the painful aftermath of a satisfactory marriage. Generally, the best of Dreiser's stories of heterosexual love are those in which he is taken up with variations on the theme of the unsatisfactory nature of exclusive love relationships.

Four of the stories in this group follow a similar pattern. In **"Old Rogaum and His Theresa," "Typhoon," "Sanctuary,"** and **"The Second Choice"** young unmarried women become involved to a greater or lesser degree with young men of superficial attractiveness who seem to open up possibilities for happiness unknown to the women in their shoddy or restrictive lives. The beaus here are of a type: aggressive, smooth, "masculine," conscious of their own charms, and manipulative. Only one is developed to any extent beyond the type: Shirley's first choice shows some sign of thought and conscience. For each of these young men, serious and permanent involvement with the women is detrimental to success and happiness. Theresa Rogaum, Ida Zobel, Madeleine Kinsella, and Shirley are all similar to the early Carrie Meeber; they inhabit a man's world, their happiness contingent on men. Only Shirley, whose life, if colorless, is at least not utterly inhibiting, is able to achieve an accommodation to life. In these four stories there is a real dichotomy between what the women protagonists and their boyfriends conceive of as fulfilling. Arthur Bristow has a certain awareness of this dichotomy and articulates it to a degree in his expanation to Shirley that he must seek fulfillment through his vocational life. In the first three stories one is not struck so strongly by the tension of two irreconcilable opposites because focus is sharply maintained on the women protagonists. All four stories, however, contain the basic ingredient of Dreiser's better short fiction: the positing of a world in which intense suffering results from irreconcilable views as to the real source of human contentment.

A variation on this type is **"Solution,"** Dreiser's later uncollected story of young love. Here the boy and girl do not conform to types established in the other four stories: Marjorie Salter is the aggressor, seducing Harvey Stone in an effort to force marriage; Harvey is more sinned against than sinning and a far cry from the irresponsible boys who prey upon the Madeleine Kinsellas and Ida Zobels. **"Solution"** differs too in its reconciliation of the two young people in the shelter of Isaac Salter's home, although the solution is put into question by some of the more subtle effects of the story and could be interpreted as an unsatisfactory one, holding little promise for the new family's long-term contentment.

Another group of five love stories more explicitly exploits the tension deriving from divergent views about the source of satisfaction. **"Married," "Convention," "The Shadow," "Marriage—for One,"** and **"A Start in Life"** all examine young couples in their married relationships. All five marriages depicted have in common this predicament: one of the spouses is devoted to the ideal of marriage and committed to its exclusiveness; the other spouse has to a greater or lesser degree wandered from the ideal of exclusiveness to establish liaison with another person of the opposite sex, who satisfies needs not met within the marriage. In **"Married"** and **"Convention"** it is the husbands who stray. They are both men of some artistic preoccupation, a musician and a writer respectively, who cannot abide their uninspiring married relationships. Because **"Convention"** has a number of points of focus, Steele's motivation for his affair with Mrs. Davis is not explicitly documented. However, his attitude is clearly similar to Duer's, for his artistic bent seems to create demands not met in a lackluster marriage to a plain-looking woman. **"Married"** is a much more explicit and articulate delineation of a basically similar situation. In **"Married,"** the tension between the ideal of marital exclusiveness and the artist's demand for variety is not only embodied in the persons of Marjorie and Duer respectively; it is a vital recognition on Duer's part as well. In marrying Marjorie he has taken to himself a kind of ideal representation of American womanhood, and even though aware of a certain dissatisfaction with her, he still invests her with "emotional greatness."

The three other stories in this group focus on the same tension, merely rearranging the husbands and wives to suit the polarities. In **"The Shadow"** and **"Marriage—for One,"** the men are clerks with clerks' mentalities, whose views of marriage are the conventional ones of exclusiveness and permanence. The wives are dissatisfied with their husbands' conventionality and seek relief and fulfillment elsewhere: Beryl, by conducting a clandestine relationship with a novelist, Bessie Wray, by general immersion in reading and the arts, as well as in a relationship with another man. **"Marriage—for One,"** however, has somewhat of a different twist. Bessie's liberalization has come about as a result of the continued encouragement of her husband, who at the outset of their relationship has found her extremely puritanical. Bessie bears a certain resemblance to the New York Carrie Meeber: she becomes involved with a group of sophisticates, to the dismay of her husband, and eventually leaves Wray altogether. The relationship between Nelson Peterson and his wife, Ava, in **"A Start in Life,"** however, is somewhat different from that of the other two couples. In the first place, Nelson is no clerk, but an increasingly successful writer who has initially benefited from his wife's attention to the advancement of his career. And then, Ava's dejection stems less from a dissatisfaction with Nelson than from a conviction that the pursuance of the marriage will ultimately produce no good effects for either partner.

In four of the five stories under consideration, **"Married,"** **"Convention,"** **"The Shadow,"** and **"Marriage—for One,"** the straying partners seek relief from the drabness and conventionality of their married lives by association with the world of the arts and with artists. Here, musicians, novelists, and magazine sketch writers break away from the restrictions of conventional relationships and appeal in their unconventionality to their own type. (It should be emphasized that the appeal the artistic life has for certain characters does not have to do with material success per se, although it is true that there is an aura of glitter and luxury about the arts as pictured here that is part of the overall attraction they possess.) The families portrayed in these four stories seem reasonably well off; Wray, at the time his wife leaves him permanently, has become quite successful with his firm. Material success itself is not the motivation characters have for establishing extramarital liaisons. In **"A Start in Life,"** Ava's move is the reverse of those effected or threatened by the dissatisfied spouses in the other stories. She, of course, in her abandoning of Peterson is opting away from the world of art and toward a life-style, that of diplomacy, that is generally identified with conventionality. Here motivation cannot be said to be a materialistic one either, although clearly the romance she identifies with her now diplomat-husband, Rapalje, has much to do with his professional life-style.

In the final analysis, these five stories make the same point: there is no satisfactory solution to the problem posed by divergent attitudes as to the source of contentment. In **"Married,"** one senses—and the relevance of this story to Dreiser's own life and to the themes of *The "Genius"* bear this out—that although Duer is able to make some accommodation in the short run, a breaking point is not far in the future. In both **"Convention"** and **"The Shadow,"** the husband and wife, respectively, decide to resume their conventional married lives, although Beryl does so with serious misgivings and with the door at least partially open. One is not aware of Steele's deeper feelings at the discontinuation of his affair, but certainly the narrator is unequivocal in interpreting his gesture as an unsatisfactory accommodation to societal pressures. In **"Marriage—for One,"** the union is dissolved, with emphasis given to the anguish produced in the faithful, just Wray by his wife's departure. One senses in this detail of **"Marriage—for One,"** and in the other three stories as well, a slight weighing of Dreiser's sympathies in favor of the male artistic types, dissatisfied in their marriages, although there is evidently an attempt to treat women of the same sensibility with understanding. Perhaps this bias in favor of men reflects Dreiser's insistence on his own bohemian lifestyle. It is noteworthy also that, although the wives in **"Marriage—for One"** and **"The Shadow"** opt in favor of the artistic world, neither is endowed with any active creative talent, as Carrie Meeber is, for example. In **"A Start in Life"** the union is dissolved as well and Peterson suffers greatly as a result, but one senses that Dreiser's sympathy is split between the hurt male artist and the female free spirit who will not accept a mediocre relationship as a permanent state of life.

Two other Dreiser short stories again focus on the marriage relationship; **"Chains"** and **"Fulfilment"** portray marriages between older men and younger women, marriages which survive for the women because their husbands' wealth allows them to live lives of luxury with a certain independence, and for the men because they are infatuated with their young and beautiful wives. Both stories record the thoughts and feelings of the protagonists vis-à-vis their relationship to their spouses and the circumstances that have brought about what are for them unhappy marriages. The stories have in common a general theme, a narrative point of view, and a structure; beyond this, each goes its own way exploring different facets of the heterosexual relationship.

"Chains" opens up ground not heretofore seen in the Dreiser love stories, although, perhaps, there is a sense in which it extends some of the ideas suggested in such stories as **"Married,"** for it moves toward defining the tension that Duer, for example, experiences between his idealization of one woman and his desire for wider experience outside of marriage. Garrison's attraction to Idelle is more than merely a fascination with youth and an attempt to revitalize his own life. Idelle, with her promiscuous background, sensuousness, vitality, beauty, and intelligence, represents a combination of qualities that has an intense fascination for Garrison, for it embodies polarities to each of which he is drawn. Yet he is torn at the same time between the recognition of his wife as she is and the wish that she might conform to conventional forms of conduct. In effect, Garrison's frequent allusions to Idelle's surpassing beauty can be seen as attempts to transcendentalize the sexual attraction.

In **"Fulfilment,"** Ulrica, the protagonist, has seen her desire for an ideal love relationship actualized in her unmarried union with the painter, Vivian. Her relationship with Vivian has been an exclusive one, although she has been married before and the story suggests that she has also had sexual experience outside of marriage earlier in life. However, the relationship has been an unconventional one in itself and in a sense has satisfied the demand of Dreiser's artistic persons not to be restricted by convention. The ideal of beauty for Ulrica is spiritual rather than sexual. Material well-being has not been a necessary ingredient in this relationship. Vivian has articulated his attraction to Ulrica in terms of art; she is for him an embodiment of beauty of feature and line. **"Fulfilment"** is one of the few Dreiser stories in which a happy heterosexual relationship is portrayed, and significantly, the idyll has not endured. One is struck by certain resemblances between Ulrica and Carrie Meeber: both have had extramarital and marital experience with men; both have searched for an ideal of contentment. Ulrica has found hers, at least temporarily. It seems quite possible that **"Fulfilment"** is Dreiser's attempt to probe beyond the limits of *Sister Carrie* to resolve Carrie's dilemma.

Another pair of Dreiser love stories, **"Free"** and **"The Old Neighborhood,"** continue the theme of unhappy marriage. Both are interior monologues by husbands, now beyond middle age, who, as young men, have married women of their own age but who have become disenchanted with their marriages early in life. Both Haymarker and the engineer have been motivated by a desire to excel, in areas of artistic and scientific endeavor respectively; they have seen substantial material advantage accrue as a direct result of successful undertakings in their respective fields. They have looked upon their families, especially their wives, as impediments to the fulfillment of their artistic and scientific goals. They realize, ultimately, that they have deluded themselves and suffer guilt on this account. The tendency one finds in Dreiser's fiction to assert both artistic and entrepreneurial achievement as sources of male fulfillment—a tendency one sees in the similarity of the protagonists in *The "Genius"* and the Trilogy of Desire—is evident in the mutually complementary nature of these stories.

Other Dreiser stories, in which the primary interest is in matters not related to man-woman relationships, sustain their author's preoccupation with unfulfilling and unhappy love: **"The 'Mercy' of God," "The Tithe of the Lord," "Will You Walk into My Parlor?"** and **"Tabloid Tragedy"** all picture thwarted love relationships as incidental to their major themes. In each of the two discursive stories, **"The 'Mercy' of God"** and **"The Tithe of the Lord,"** the character who is the subject of the dialoguing and who acts as a kind of exemplum around which ideas are engaged, is unable to effect a lasting love relationship. Marguerite Ryan is thwarted by her physical unattractiveness; Benziger's wanderlust effectively destroys two marriages. In **"Will You Walk into My Parlor?"** Gregory, despite early protestations of loyalty to "the girl" (his wife) is relentlessly worn down by Imogene—and then disillusioned that she does not become a permanent part of his life. **"Tabloid Tragedy"** is the only story in which Dreiser focuses completely on an extramarital relationship. Here the marital dissatisfaction itself is a given, but the covert relationship is a disillusioning one for Thompson as well. And the subplot, involving the Palmeri and Del Papa families is based on a case of marital infidelity.

In Dreiser's short stories the dream of success is a pervasive preoccupation. The pattern in the stories is that the dream is sought and, if captured, found wanting. The success achieved by Dreiser protagonists is at the expense of others and with considerable liability to themselves. Success does not bring contentment. Contentment is a rare and elusive commodity, difficult in heterosexual relationships because of conflicting views among relating people as to its source. At times this conflict of views between men and women is a function of established attitudes in society about the roles of men and women, although in **"Marriage—for One"** and **"The Shadow"** the roles are reversed. Often, conflict of views results from differing sensitivities, notably between the conventional mind and the unconventional one, the latter often articulated in terms of a sensitivity to the artistic life. But if

Dreiser's sympathies tend toward the unconventional, there is no resolution in its favor, merely insoluble tension. Women long for fulfillment, a sort of composite of love and material success, and seldom achieve it. Men often achieve material success, but find exclusive love relationships inhibiting. Indeed, in the three satisfactory love relationships portrayed in the short stories, there is a notable paucity of material means; the married relationship in **"Fine Furniture"** is resolved when the young wife relents on her demands for elaborate house furnishings; the old couple in **"The Lost Phoebe"** live in near destitution, the young unmarried couple in **"Fulfilment"** are forced to separate because of material needs.

The dream of material success is the motivating force behind three other Dreiser short-story protagonists. In **"The Hand," "Phantom Gold,"** and **"The Victor"** the quest for material satisfaction occurs, for the most part, outside the context of love relationships. Mersereau, Queeder, and Osterman have devoted themselves completely to the amassing of wealth, each one, to a greater or lesser extent, involving himself in immoral activity to secure his ends. All three become victims of retributive justice: the dream of success evaporates into a living nightmare for Mersereau and Queeder; Osterman is thwarted from performing a significant altruistic service.

In a number of Dreiser's short stories the success theme is closely related to psychic phenomena and/or makes use of its vocabulary. Lynn has commented: "Evidences of Dreiser's faith in these matters occur in his fiction from beginning to end. Several of his short stories are concerned with hallucination and hypnosis and the co-relation between these phenomena and the winning of wealth and women. In *Sister Carrie* and *Jennie Gerhardt,* Dreiser dramatized sexual conquest almost completely in terms of mental magnetism and hypnotic eyepower" [Kenneth S. Lynn, *The Dream of Success* (1955)]. The presence of psychic phenomena in his fiction is a reflection of Dreiser's "faith" in them. An interesting case in point is **"A Story of Stories,"** in which the reporter, Binns, is bested in bringing in a news story by Collins, his competitor, and a man of considerably less intellectual ability. Here, the advantage of Collins resides in the magnetic effect of his stare. Binns is so distracted and pacified by the other's eyes that he lets down his competitive guard—with disastrous effects.

Examples of eyepower and magnetism recur especially in the short stories involving heterosexual attraction. As in *Sister Carrie* and *Jennie Gerhardt,* the appeal of the eyes renders its victim incapable of denial; it negates the power of the will. Madeleine Kinsella's burgeoning attraction to boys is described in terms of "the chemic harmonies in youth." Terms such as *hypnotic* and *telepathic* are used in other stories. Not only do such terms metaphorize the mystery and power of the sexual attraction; their recurrent use suggests an attempt to transcendentalize it as well.

But the use of the supernatural is not limited to the depiction of interpersonal relationships. At times it assumes more spectacular form within the dramatic texture of Dreiser's short stories. In both **"The Hand"** and **"The Old Neighborhood,"** psychic manifestations in the form of apparitions and sounds prey upon the protagonists, functioning in the former as both by-product of Mersereau's guilt and cause of his dementia, and in the latter as both evidence of the engineer-protagonist's eroding morality and foreshadowing of family tragedy.

In one way or another, or in a combination of ways, the lives of Dreiser short-story characters are controlled by forces within or outside themselves. The most persistent form of this control depicted in the stories is the false lure of material and sexual attainment. Many of the stories are miniature American tragedies in which characters, given to believe, or not disbelieve, that the American dream is capable of realization, take the lure and suffer deception. What makes Dreiser different from his popular magazine contemporaries is that he recognized the lure for what it was. What makes him unique is that in recognizing the lure as false, he acknowledged its tremendous power in American life, not only for the innocent, untutored Madeleine Kinsellas but also for the educated, sophisticated Duers and Haymakers.

At the same time it must be acknowledged that, exceptionally, Dreiser short-story characters rise above their surroundings and act as agents of refuge and inspiration for their downtrodden contemporaries. Mother St. Bertha of **"Sanctuary"** and Isaac Salter of **"Solution"** provide comfort for their charges in conventional Christian ways. **"St. Columba and the River"** introduces a less traditional kind of saint, Cavanaugh, the Irish foreman who sacrifices his life for his men and inspires McGlathery to perform his selfless act on behalf of his co-workers. The occasional presence of such exemplary figures attenuates to a degree the theme of entrapment that pervades Dreiser's short stories. But the Mother St. Berthas, Salters, and Cavanaughs are few and far between—and they themselves are in one way or another victimized: Mother St. Bertha has escaped to the House of Good Shepherd in the wake of harsh family and personal disappointments, Salter has been recently widowed, and Cavanaugh is killed by the uncontrollable forces that prey upon the builders of the Holland Tunnel.

Implicit in Dreiser's stories, as in fiction generally, is the notion of the value of art as an articulation of the human predicament. This in itself is positive: in elaborating and dramatizing man's plight, the artist has exercised control and, in a sense, salvaged man's dignity and asserted his preeminence. This, in one form or another, becomes the explicit thematic concern of Dreiser, significantly perhaps, in some of his very early stories. One sees this theme in a very general way in **"The Cruise of the 'Idlewild,'"** where men compensate for dullness by using the imagination to invent a romantic world, and in **"McEwen of the Shining Slave Makers,"** where the protagonist comes to a certain awareness of the human condition as a result of his dream experience in the ant world. In **"Nigger Jeff"** the theme is most forcefully dramatized in the transformation of a reporter into an artist. Confronted by the specter of man's brutality and nature's indifference to it, Elmer Davies, in his compulsion to "get it all in," asserts the predominance of man, the artist, over his material.

In most of his short stories, of course, Dreiser is not explicitly concerned with the role of the artist or the power of the imagination; rather these concerns are embodied in the wedding of substance and form implicit in the stories themselves. If there is any doubt about Dreiser's recognition of the principle of a suitable form to carry a specific subject matter, it can be resolved by a statement of his, quoted earlier in this study. Referring to the magazine stories he had read in 1895, he commented, after alluding to "the happy roseate way" in which they pictured life: "Most of these bits of fiction, delicately phrased, flowed so easily, with such an air of assurance, omniscience and condescension, that I was quite put out by my own lacks and defects."

The young, inexperienced Dreiser saw his "lacks and defects" as liabilities from the point of view of his dejection. In fact, they were turned into assets as he cast aside the delicate phrasing and easy flow of his contemporaries in favor of a prose that echoed his view of reality. This prose was not so much a calculated one as one that flowed directly from him, although this does not mean that he wrote without difficulty. If "as a writer Dreiser is *sui generis,*" as Michael Millgate puts it [in *American Social Fiction: James to Couzzens* (1964)], if "he continued along his own individual path, cutting out his own footholds step by step as he went," all the more reason for his attending to expression. (pp. 129-41)

A significant amount of the adverse criticism of Dreiser's short fiction centers on his alleged inability to cope with the compression demands of the short story form and on the resultant view that the stories are merely unexpanded novels. There is undoubtedly some truth in these allegations although it is well to note that at least some of the support for the position comes from the fact that Dreiser himself had seemed to verify it in his "I need a large canvas" statement to the *New York Times Book Review* interviewer Montrose J. Moses. However, the potential pitfalls of such a critical procedure as evaluating the effectiveness of works of art on the basis of the fact that their author found them difficult to write should be evident. Then too, one wonders if the tendency to see Dreiser's short stories as underdeveloped novels is not based on the fact of his established novelistic power and if, because of this, the stories have not been given too cursory a hearing. West's contention that "Almost any of Dreiser's stories might have been expanded into novels, for they are, as a rule, confined neither in space nor in time," seems exaggerated. It is true that certain of the stories lack spatial or temporal confinement; one good example is **"The Second Choice"** where one is not always sure of the length of time between events and where portions of Shirley's interior monologues are not clearly set. But this seems rather the exception than the rule. Some stories of interior consciousness such as **"Free"** and **"The Old Neighborhood"** are clearly placed in a context of time and place; other more experimental ones, **"Chains," "The Hand," "Fulfilment,"** perhaps err in the direction of an overemphasis on the delineation of time and place. The action-centered stories, especially the better ones such as **"Sanctuary," "The Lost Phoebe,"** and **"Nigger Jeff,"** have a clearly delineated setting. One wonders if West's criticism here is not directed at the fact that in Dreiser's stories of interior consciousness, and in the monological sections of his action-centered stories, there is a lack of logical direction and control in the protagonist's outpourings of thought and emotion.

In fact, it would appear that Dreiser's interior monologues, especially, are immune from the allegation that the stories "do not read as complete architectonic units within themselves, but as compressed, dehydrated novels," as Shapiro insists. Although the interior monologues depict multiple events ranging into extended portions of the past, they are essentially dramatizations set within the minds of the protagonists. **"The Old Neighborhood,"** ignored by Shapiro although it is one of the outstanding pieces in *The Best Stories* volume on which he is basing his opinion of the short-story *oeuvre,* is dependent for its effect on the fact that the interior monologue takes place over a certain two-hour period, at a certain time in the protagonist's life, and in a certain locale. It is inconceivable that **"The Old Neighborhood"** would retain its impact in a form much longer than its actual length, and to modify its structure would change its nature completely. It is true of all the interior monologues that they are depictions of intensified periods in their protagonists' lives; even the weakest of them retains this essential quality that by its nature defies expression in a form of considerably greater length.

Mencken wrote of Dreiser's novels: "The truth is . . . [they] deal fundamentally with the endless conflict between animal behaviour and the soarings of the spirit—between the destiny forced upon his characters by their environment, their groping instincts, their lack of courage and resourcefulness, and the destiny they picture for themselves in their dreams." The short stories deal with the same fundamental conflict, exploiting its numerous variations. The stories that most effectively dramatize this preoccupation of Dreiser are those in which he sees the conflict from inside the minds of his protagonists. The intensity of the interior monologues of both Haymaker and the inventor in **"The Old Neighborhood"** is a reflection of Dreiser's strong feelings about basic tension in American life. What is more, Dreiser had experienced the same kinds of tension himself: one finds in his nonfiction evidence not only of a mental tension similar to that of his characters but of a rhetoric in the face of such tension that is markedly similar as well. *A Book about Myself* offers many examples of this. In one, Dreiser records an incident concerning his relationship to a woman, Alice, with whom he has become emotionally involved but from whom he feels he must part company, pleading that he cannot afford the expense of married life. He has written her a letter to this effect and has read her reply. Here is his response to the incident as he recollected it years later:

> . . . I wavered between two horns of an ever-recurring dilemma. Sympathizing with the pain which Alice was suffering, and alive to my own loss of honor and happiness. . . .
>
> These mental stresses were always sufficient, however, to throw me into a soulful mood. . . . Indeed my heart was torn by the inextricable problems which life seemed ever to present and I fairly wrung my hands as I looked into the face of the hurrying world. . . . The few sweets which I had thus far tasted were always accompanied by such bitter repinings. No pleasure was without pain, as I had already seen, and life offered no solution. Only silence and the grave ended it all.
>
> My body was racked with a fine tremor. My brain ached.

In general, it can be said that Dreiser's effectiveness as a short-story writer is in direct proportion to the closeness of his subject matter to his own experience. A striking exception to this is **"The Lost Phoebe,"** in which Dreiser successfully projects himself into both old age and an almost primitive rural setting. But as a rule, the stories that are outside the context of American urban life, the forum where men and women are torn apart in their divergent quests for fulfillment, are not successful. Not only do Dreiser's short stories of fantasy fall within this category; an American story such as **"The Hand"** also fails, in part because of Dreiser's difficulty with an unfamiliar milieu and with dramatizing a conflict that is not so much interpersonal as psychological. Corollary to this is the observation that the effectiveness of Dreiser's short stories is directly proportional to the narrators' immersion in the events recorded. In terms of the point of view of their narra-

tion, Dreiser's best stories tend to be the interior monologues and stories of omniscient narration. Generally, the stories told by first-person narrators on the fringes of the action tend to be discursive and polemic.

It cannot be questioned that a substantial number of short stories in the Dreiser *oeuvre* are far off the standard of first-rate fiction. But there is a significant body of short fiction here that deserves the label of excellence. It is not merely the anthologists' compulsion to "represent" all major novelists that causes Dreiser's stories to be "[sandwiched] between the shorter efforts of Henry James and Ernest Hemingway." Dreiser's stories deserve to be read because they capture moods and cadences of the American experience that found such articulate expression nowhere else in the short-fiction genre. Dorothy Dudley wrote [in *Dreiser and the Land of the Free* (1946)]: "No other letter file of Dreiser's contains so many testimonials from strangers, because he has guessed their secrets, as the responses to his two volumes of short stories. 'How could you have guessed?' they keep saying. Many so-called stylists have not written with hands so supple and alive to mystery." There cannot be much more eloquent testimony than this to the success of Dreiser's short stories. (pp. 141-44)

Joseph Griffin, in his The Small Canvas: An Introduction to Dreiser's Short Stories, *Fairleigh Dickinson University Press, 1985, 172 p.*

SUSAN L. MIZRUCHI   (essay date 1988)

[*In the following excerpt, Mizruchi examines the complexity of the deterministic vision expressed in* An American Tragedy.]

Critics of *An American Tragedy* have puzzled over the title and its generic implications. "Can a tragic vision," some have asked, "govern a Deterministic universe?" The question of the novel's title is often attributed to carelessness—yet another example of the author's (or the army of editors') ineptitude. It is more revealing, however, to take this inconsistency on its own terms, to consider how the tension between a tragic and a deterministic philosophy might pervade the novel.

Most definitions of "tragedy" assert some degree of free will—that the protagonist's actions are "neither wholly predetermined nor wholly free." [The critic cites *The Princeton Encyclopedia of Poetry and Poetics* "for a discussion of 'tragedy' and 'tragic flaw'."] The genre depends upon a world where human choices have discernible consequences, and where the potential for human initiative is present. The predetermined world of Dreiser's novel seems to lack the expected components of a tragic universe. Its characters "all act out the drama of determinism," in a "God-abandoned and sanction-stripped world of natural process" [Irving Howe, in an Afterword to *An American Tragedy*]. Yet the ambiguities and contradictions of the novel, which build as it progresses—the problem of the protagonist's "character," the strain of sardonic echoes in the narrative voice, the inconsistent ideology of the American work ethic—all suggest that the determinism of *An American Tragedy* is not as self-evident as most critics have assumed. Indeed, so complex is the novel's portrayal of its deterministic vision that it can be seen in part as a meditation on that vision. Rather than simply a confused blend of deterministic philosophy and tragic pathos, the novel rises to the level of probing the social-psychological and political implications of these ideas. And the introduction of tragic concerns into a deterministic world might lead us to scrutinize the power of generic terms themselves, which serve as often to foreclose as to facilitate our access to textual meanings. [The critic adds in a footnote that "One of the novel's chief questions involves the protagonist's viability as a tragic hero. Just as Joyce's *Ulysses* redefines the possibilities for heroism in the modern age, Dreiser's novel ponders the appropriateness of tragic terms in the twentieth century. Clyde's character seems a blend of naturalist and tragic categories. Neither completely passive nor completely fixed, he is likewise alternately insensible and self-aware. And he does achieve some perspective on himself by the novel's end. Most important, the point where naturalist and tragic categories clash reveals the pervading political contradictions of the novel's society."] (pp. 242-43)

All of the significant features of the novel's society—the rags-to-riches aspirations of Clyde Griffiths, the social stratification of Lycurgus, the increasingly rationalized world of Clyde's American odyssey—are disclosed to be within the range of human agency. The novel exposes a tension between an eternal rhetoric that portrays social organization as unalterable, and more localized details that reveal the controls over social processes, and individuals' perceptions of them, to be variously accessible to society's members. This concern for the links between temporal consciousness and political power is extended to a consideration of the manipulative potential of historical narration itself.

The novel's final book depicts Clyde as caught between the partisan political squabbles of an approaching election and the moral outrage of Bridgeburg County's rural inhabitants. Compelled to narrate a version of his past that his lawyers hope will satisfy a local jury, he is dumbfounded and, as the book progresses, increasingly obsessed with his inability to achieve an articulate narration of his personal history. Clyde's public execution is a silent agony, "his eyes fixed nervously," his final look, perhaps an "appeal," perhaps a "daze," left to the bystander's interpretation. Clyde's "tragedy" is inseparable from his incapacity to achieve a clear view of his experience, his failure as a storyteller or historian of self. He is a pawn of social authorities, a test case for the intricate legalities of those more knowledgeable and powerful than he. And Clyde's speechlessness testifies to the extent to which American authors have always aligned political power with the powers of historical narration.

These links are established from the novel's beginning, where narrative authority seems to reside in the capacity to obscure historical consciousness. "Dusk—of a summer night. And the tall walls of the commercial heart of an American city of perhaps 400,000 inhabitants—such walls as in time may linger as a mere fable." We have entered upon the nervous interim between day and night—with the world in transition, marginality reigns, and crime perhaps flourishes. Despite their air of immediacy, however, these clipped sentences offer few precise historical details. The opening emphasizes the subject of time without grounding us in a specific moment of history; the setting is the amorphous "heart" of a large American city around the turn of the century. But the tacked-on final phrase, "such walls as in time may linger as a mere fable," reveals the hidden claim of this vagueness—the designation of narrative as an eternal power. Juxtaposing the substance of the city, the aggressive facade of this business landscape, and the delicate image of a "linger[ing] . . . fable," the

phrase points to a time when the reliable bluntness of America's urban world will be found in ("mere") fictions alone. Aligning narrative artistry with the power of permanence, the novel implies that the only accessible past is that which someone has chosen to transform into story.

This brief opening prepares us for a novelistic world in which anything that anyone possesses is already faded, already not sweet, because to its possessor it is so short-lived. The narrator's sense of time here presages Clyde's remark to Roberta at their love's inception: "We have so little time." Yet the novel portrays striking differences among its characters' perceptions of time—differences that reveal control over temporal perceptions to be a distinctly political power. Throughout the novel, we see characters engaging in the kinds of manipulations the narrator attempts here. Specific historical moments are cast in terms of an obscure and remote temporality as a means of rendering unchallengeable a preferred point of view. The blurring of the reader's time sense here facilitates the narrator's powerful claim that fiction may be the sole adjudicator of reality. (pp. 243-45)

The narrator of **An American Tragedy** is an exceptionally subtle voice in the Dreiser canon, less prominent and judgmental than is typical, and less given to sentimental rhetoric. The kinds of florid decrees found elsewhere in Dreiser are largely alien to this persona, who seems convinced of life's "ragged edges." In part, the narrator's greater reticence arises from the fact that this novel, more than any other by Dreiser, is recounted through indirect discourse from its protagonist's point of view. Still, the question remains as to why this technique would prevail, why the novel would tend more toward descriptive detail than philosophical judgment. Allusions to the novel's incorporation of the detached techniques of journalism as *explanations* for the deflation of its narrative voice merely beg the question. Given a novel in which the judgment of guilt or innocence is central to the plot, the significance of the narrator's judgments, whether absent or marked, cannot be overestimated.

The most obvious feature of the narrative voice is its excessive irony. What has not been noticed is how often this irony is directed at the novel's own repetitive patterns, serving as underhanded commentary on its deterministic philosophy. In addition to the larger repetitions of scenes and doublings of characters, there are smaller repetitions that reflect ironically upon such scenes or upon the characters themselves. These anachronies, which point either forward or backward in time, serve to heighten the novel's overall sense of time. [The critic adds in a footnote that "Gerard Genette uses the term 'anachrony' to 'designate all forms of discordance between two temporal orders of story and narrative'."] But they are so subtle (and so uniformly missed by critics) that they appear as the narrator's private jokes.

In the novel's first book, for example, one of Clyde's fellow bellboys, Hegglund from New Jersey, an "over-sized youth" habitually attired in a "tight" uniform, is described reclining expansively in the chop-house, looking "not unlike a large and overzealous rooster." Some three hundred pages later, in Book 2, at an elite ball in Lycurgus, the self-possessed escort of Sondra Finchley is portrayed in what seems a clear echo of the previous description. Freddie Sells in his "closely-fitting dress coat look[s] down on Clyde about as a spring rooster might look down on a sparrow." Thus, the sophisticated Princeton man appears a repetition of the ignorant bellhop Hegglund, just another product of New Jersey, though less polished. This echoing metaphor functions to reduce the upper-class youth contemplating Clyde from his great height. But it is an ironic parallel unavailable to Clyde, enjoyed by the narrator and perhaps the reader as well. Other instances of such repetitions create an impression of the narrator as a bitter, mocking figure, standing to the side of his suspenseful plot of doom, jeering subtly at the rushing pursuits of the characters and at the static complacency of the conservative caste system he describes.

Most consistently the narrator's scornful repetitions are directed at religious faith. The Griffithses' evangelism, for example, is undermined by narrative juxtaposition as well as by more overt commentary. Their "collapsible" missionary religion, it is suggested, is not only a passive creed, but may be downright dangerous. An early description of the urban marginals who find their way to the Griffithses' mission ironically, even sinisterly, foreshadows Clyde's spiritual fervor at the moment of Roberta's death. These "botched and helpless who seemed to drift" into the mission are heard continually "testifying as to how God or Christ or Divine Grace had rescued them . . . never how they had rescued anyone else." Given the dramatic emphasis on Clyde's inaction in the climactic drowning scene, this detail seems more than coincidental. Though he rejects his parents' creed, Clyde, like the derelicts at their mission, summons its self-immolating message to absolve himself of responsibility for acting in his own behalf or, as the drowning scene will bear out, in another's. Yet Clyde will find rationalization for temporizing in more powerful creeds as well.

The entire drowning scene is cast in the repetitive rhythms of biblical verse. From the first mention of Clyde's "climacteric errand" to the closing moments picturing "the peace and solemnity of this wondrous scene," the portrait of Roberta's death exudes a sacramental aura. Recalling the derelicts at the mission, Clyde's unconscious during Roberta's drowning offers a retreat from the real world of action and consequence. Though Clyde's evasion cannot be said to cause her death, it does prevent his acting to save her, an eerie echo of the mission visitors who have never saved but only been saved.

Sitting in the boat with Roberta, Clyde dissolves into a realm of "endless space where was no end of anything—no plots—no plans—no practical problems to be solved—nothing." So gripped is he by this "sacred" revery that Roberta appears no more than a "shadow or thought, really, a form of illusion more vaporous than real." Caught between his desire for Roberta's death and his abhorrence of murder, Clyde enters a different temporal domain—a static order where no action or consequence exist. Akin to the lap of religion symbolized by his parents' mission, this "still" realm signals a "quiet, unprotesting type of death." Inhabiting this mythical time, Clyde, like those at the mission, can deny responsibility for action. And his spiritual retreat from a deed that he has desperately pursued until the decisive moment absolves him, in his own mind at least, of a sense of responsibility for Roberta's death. Of interest here is the notion of religion as a kind of social welfare system whereby the lower classes may escape responsibility for past action or inaction. The way in which the charity mission allows the lower classes to evade their historical responsibilities parallels the method by which upper-class characters (such as Sondra and Belknap) *purchase* their evasions. (pp. 262-65)

The portrayal of Clyde and Roberta's first encounter on

Dreiser late in life.

water exemplifies further the elaborate irony of the narrator's repetitions. A number of critics have noted how this scene anticipates the death scene of a year later, a perverse prolepsis recognized even by the historically insensible Clyde. Yet the extent of the scene's foreshadowings has not been fully analyzed, nor has it been noticed how the characters themselves set the predetermined course of their affair. In depicting Clyde and Roberta stifling their love before its inception, the scene ultimately reveals how deterministic assumptions are invoked in order to offset fears of the new and uncontrollable. The couple's thoughts just prior to their meeting delimit and distort their responses to one another in the actual encounter.

Roberta appears in Clyde's mind's eye in two forms before he recognizes her standing on the dock, giving his perception of her the appearance of an infinite regression. First, he sees her in memory, "shapely" and "smooth," as "she worked with her swift, graceful movements at her machine." Next, she is an anonymous, "very pretty" figure, standing on the dock, alive to his immediate perception. Finally recognized, she is a "realiz[ation]" of a "dream," her lips a "wavy line of beauty." And Roberta's developing view of Clyde is similar. She is "just the least bit abashed by the reality of him," for "she had been," the narrator informs us, "thinking of him so much and wishing for him in some happy, secure, commendable way. And now here he was." Roberta's first view, like Clyde's, is a "commendable," secure vision. So pleasurable are their permissible images of one another that the actual encounter seems unwelcome.

The scene pinpoints a discrepancy between the imagination and the world it encounters, ascribing a perpetual gap between expectations and actual experience. By this logic, a fear of possessing a desired object arises from doubts that it can satisfy expectation. Yet more is at issue here. There is a fear of attaining the object of desire, precisely because it might meet and even unimaginably supersede expectations. The fear of what is not preconceived and thereby not bounded by imagination strikes most terror in this novel. Clyde and Roberta's fear of a pleasure uncircumscribed by convention inhibit and eventually destroy their bond. Each is too much the realization of a dream to the other to be deserved and fully encountered. Thus, the narrative appears to suggest that the "drama of determinism" has more to do with self-inflicted limitations than with impersonal forces. The imagination of fixity itself delimits human possibility. The idea of determinism is a construct, a socially functional and politically fused projection fantasy that incites guilt over human capacities for freedom or fulfillment. Yet some of the characters are more disposed to accept these social provisions than others.

In some instances, the narrator alludes directly, either playfully or sinisterly, to his anachronies. Most notable among these is Clyde's "accidental" view of the Alden farm at Biltz. What is striking about this second of three descriptions of Roberta's birthplace (the first is from Roberta's point of view, the last from the district attorney Mason's) is the narrator's dramatic distancing of himself from the responsibility for its "com[ing] to pass." As he intones, "Some might think, only an ironic and even malicious fate could have intended or permitted [Clyde's glimpse of the farm] to come to pass." Merely a humble recorder of predetermined events, the narrator can hardly be held responsible for an incident that might be considered pivotal in bringing about Roberta's drowning. The narrator's disavowal of responsibility here carries forth and anticipates similar evasions, which include those of the derelicts in the Kansas City mission, Clyde before the sinking Roberta, Samuel Griffiths as he contemplates the prospects for Clyde's appeal, and the authorities of the inhumane modern death house. The narrator's disavowal seems to confirm and parody this trail of denials, but there are other wry parallels here as well.

Clyde is "called to witness" a scene that is as much a depiction of his past as Roberta's, presaging ironically his forced recapitulation of his past at his trial. At this later point, however, where the memories of other witnesses prove far superior to his, he will be an impotent observer of others' versions of his experience. Here, Clyde recognizes his own past in Roberta's. "This lorn, dilapidated realm," by being connected with Roberta, is identified with "himself. . . . It even occurred to him, in a vague way for the first time, how strange it was that this girl and he, whose origin had been strikingly similar, should have been so drawn to each other in the beginning." And to further the parallel, Clyde's irresponsible dismay—"What was it about his life that made things like this happen to him! Was this what his life was to be like?"—echoes Roberta's recent hopelessness incited by the same dismal rural scene: "Life was always doing things like this to her."

For both, the oppressive scene signifies the past come back to life, a testimony to the inescapability of origins. By not liv-

ing up to her expectations, Clyde becomes Roberta's past. As symbols of "inefficiency and lack," the farm and its surroundings are the "antithesis of all to which her imagination aspired . . . [which] was identified with Clyde." Yet if Clyde did not really love her and would not take her away from all this, then "the bleakness of it all" would come upon her with additional force. Likewise, Roberta's home in all of its decline signifies Clyde's past. Clyde's view of his origins in this glimpse of the Alden farm foreshadows his imaging of Roberta while she is drowning. Unless he "disengag[ed] himself," Clyde reflects desperately, gazing upon the farm, "this other world from which he sprang might extend its gloomy, poverty-stricken arms to him and envelop him once more, just as the poverty of his family had enveloped him and almost strangled him from the first." And from the boat, looking upon Roberta drowning, Clyde sees her as "a form! It came nearer—clearer—and as it did so, he recognized Roberta struggling and waving her thin white arms out of the water and reaching toward him."

The force of the camera blow can be seen to express Clyde's anger toward his past, revealing his inarticulate rage about his lower-class origins. Yet it may be equally the case that his inability to unite desire to action in his mute confusion prior to Roberta's rising in the boat also arises from his inability to accommodate his past. The scene contains an extraordinary paradox. Clyde's past projected onto his alter ego Roberta symbolizes the barriers to his present aspirations. But his repressed past—the uneasy fusion of a commercialized romanticism and the American success ethic—thwarts his enactment of his will in critical situations like this.

The narrator's repetitive ironies often hinge on questions of human responsibility for past actions. By hinting at the social and political effects of perceiving events as predetermined, and human beings as unaccountable for their actions, the narrator seems to prod the assumptions of the novel's deterministic vision. But though this scene at Biltz reveals the narrator's partial awareness of his own and others' willed detachment from their most compromising historical entanglements, his ironic sensibility never becomes a tool of critical insight. In order to clarify what appears from the perspectives of the characters and the narrator to be a hopelessly confused vision of individual responsibility, we must examine some of the novel's deeper political implications.

An American Tragedy offers a critique of its determinist vision through the links it establishes between characters' social class positions and their abilities to manipulate temporal perceptions and historical narratives. In considering how the novel might be challenging its dominant philosophy, we can examine where individual responsibility for the past is borne and where it breaks down. Although most critics concur that rich and poor, powerful and powerless alike are at the mercy of time—pawns in the hands of predetermined circumstances—a deeper view implies otherwise, that crucial variations exist in the characters' subjections to time. Moreover, the novel suggests that the semblance of fixity functions to inhibit social change, and portrays determinism itself as a rhetorical instrument.

A recurring motif in Clyde's experiences is his incompatibility with the temporal frames of the worlds he enters into. This is not as true of the novel's early scenes, but from the moment of his arrival in Lycurgus his striving aspirations seem to jar with the town's apparently static social caste system. Walking through the streets of the town, Clyde is alarmed by the stark oppositions of its poor and wealthy sections. The slum is comparable to the worst of Chicago or Kansas City, while the palatial splendor of his relatives' neighborhood across the river is "arresting." During his first days in Lycurgus, the modest circles in which Clyde circulates convey an air of relentless immobility. The placid aspect of Walter Dillard's aunt, who turns upon Clyde at a church social to "beam . . . a fatty beam," typifies the complacency of her world.

The air of fixity is further suggested by the repetitive lives of the Griffiths factory workers. Their daily march toward their workplace, joining the "general inpour" for other factories, and nightly return, "the same throng re-forming . . . and returning as it had come," replicates the oppressive procedures of shirt collar production. The factory's workers seem hardly distinguishable from its products, which flow in "a constant stream . . . through several chutes from the floor above." The production line absorbs all human beings and objects into its utilitarian processes.

Clyde himself inadvertently exposes one of the linchpins of the Griffiths factory rule. The "hundreds" of women workers, like the collars they produce, are indistinguishable sensual baubles to Clyde, each one a mild replication of the other. Thus Ruza Nikoforitch, with her "swimming brown eyes" and "snub fat nose," seems another version of Flora Brandt with her own "swimming . . . eyes" and "snub nose." These "piece workers," Clyde's superior Ligget informs him, might be "freely take[en] on . . . and then, once the rush was over, as freely dropp[ed]." Though Ligget's terms are strictly business, his allusion to the factory's constant need for "new blood and new energy" suggests a different meaning of "rush," and facilitates Clyde's translation of his words into sensual terms. The linguistic ambiguity conveys the point: a factory ethic that dictates the exploitation of human labor underwrites sexual exploitation as well. The repetitive rounds of factory labor prove a dehumanizing temporality to its workers.

The objectifying routine of their workers' lives spurs much philosophizing by the Griffithses. As Gilbert tells Clyde, "The men and women who work for us have got to feel that they are employees first, last and all the time—and they have to carry that attitude out into the street with them." The adoption of circumspect lives, in accordance with their routinized daily labor, ensures the workers' docility, which in turn guarantees the steady production of shirt collars. The Griffithses' theory of factory management "miraculously" discovers that what is "good" for human beings—the commitment of their entire lives to their factory labor—is consonant with the interests of the factory. As the Griffithses "saw it, there had to be higher and higher social orders to which the lower classes could aspire. One had to have castes. . . . [There were] those who were destined to rise. And those who were not should be kept right where they were."

The Griffithses' inclination to be "practical rather than . . . charitable," to inveigh their workers with a feeling of "necessity and compulsion" toward their work, and to inculcate "these lower individuals to a clear realization of how difficult it was to come by money," represents their profiteering wages as morally and educationally beneficial. Serving to justify an exploitative labor system, the Griffithses' rhetoric on the nature of society transforms what is humanly interested and contrived into an image of inevitability. Their methods of labor management, the Griffithses maintain, fulfill their workers' social and spiritual destinies. But the novel's narra-

tive undermines this rhetoric to suggest that far from the effortless outcome of a world whose social facts are as constant as nature, these forms of life and labor serve the special interests of an identifiable elite in a particular historical time and place. (pp. 266-72)

The motif of Clyde and Roberta's relationship is their fear of obtrusive public eyes, standing perpetual guard on their moments of ecstasy. In pursuing, apprehensively and then exultantly, their sexual affair, moving beyond the static sources of release available to them, Clyde and Roberta's guilt is projected in the image of their vividly exposed deviance.

But the union of Clyde and Roberta is designated as deviant only because of their ignorance of the available conventions for circumventing their predicament. The couple's foiled attempts to abort Roberta's pregnancy indicate the existence of a social underground where undesired products of illicit affairs are easily disposed of. The narrator cryptically discloses that there were at least three "midwives . . . here in Lycurgus at this time" who might have been called upon to perform an abortion. Roberta's habitual detachment from the other factory girls, Clyde's own isolation, and their lack of money handicaps them. The Lycurgus barber explains concisely, "In the first place it's agin' the law. And next it takes a lotta money." As the order of summary suggests, the law can be elided if one has the essential connections and funds.

Most important, however, is the extent to which Clyde and Roberta's own self-incriminations inhibit their pursuit of likely alternatives. In a circular way, their guilt furthers their entrapment as both masochistically doubt the potential to rid themselves of their unwanted child. Though they are socially marginal, they are also deeply conventional, their sense of morality blocking the way out of their dilemma. Both feel unalterably defined by their past action, just as they feel irreversibly held by their lower class backgrounds. In fact, as Dr. Glenn's hypocritical stance in refusing them his services suggests, their act is labeled and dealt with according to their class position. Dr. Glenn's price for the suspension of morality in his mystifying blend of provincial piety, self-aggrandizement, and opportunism is beyond them for both financial and social reasons.

On first appearance Dr. Glenn epitomizes small-town reliable conservatism: all "grayness, solidity and stolidity." Informed of the true facts of Roberta's case, he refuses the request outright, declaring the immorality of abortion. But though his refusal to "rescue" Roberta gives him a feeling of superiority, his resistance is explained otherwise. He is "opposed to aiding, either by his own countenance or skill, any lapses or tangles *not heavily sponsored by others*" (emphasis added). In other words, Dr. Glenn will break the law to protect the reputations of wealthy girls, but stands his moral ground in the cases of poor ones. By his logic, it is moral to erase the "folly" of girls of "good family," but impoverished girls must endure the consequences of actions that their poverty explains. Their deeds divorced from the world of action and consequence and regarded as play, wealthy girls are aided in rewriting their pasts. Poor girls, on the contrary, reveal their low origins in every action they take, and must accept responsibility for what they are. Glenn's moral circumlocutions force Clyde and Roberta to bear the burden of their pasts, making them responsible for past actions in a way that contrasts strikingly with the novel's other main characters.

In the chapters leading up to Roberta's death, Clyde's dilemma of historical doom with her is played off against the static contentment of his trysts with Sondra. She and her friends revel in an irresponsible youth of sports and car trips that opposes Clyde and Roberta's subjection to the cause-and-effect processes of historical time. While Roberta exemplifies Clyde's "necessity," compelled to "speak out definitely and forcefully," Sondra is calm and still, "the panorama of the bright world of which [she] was the center." Sondra is once again associated with stillness at the novel's close, where Clyde holds her unsigned letter "quite still" as he contemplates her freedom. "She was free. She had beauty—wealth." Like Dr. Glenn's "girls of good family" and Clyde's lawyer Belknap, Sondra has the money and connections to erase the consequences of her actions. Her father's wealth and position ensure that her name will remain disentangled from Clyde's sordid experiences. And this is precisely how the novel defines power—as the ability to buy time and rewrite circumstance, to transcend the fixed conditions of its deterministic logic.

In the third book, others' abilities to manipulate and rearrange the facts of Clyde's past for their own uses are played off against his inability to gain any perspective on it. Book 3 opens upon a world obsessed with history's linear progress in the face of a hotly contested November election. No longer able to dream and delay with the wealthy set, Clyde must confront the localized concerns of a provincial town in early-twentieth-century America. The introductory emphasis on the immediate historical context of Clyde's indictment and trial implies that he has fallen headlong into history.

Given the importance of Clyde's sense of the past in Book 3, it is worthwhile to review his relation to the past in Books 1 and 2. Clyde's historical insensibility is established early on. One rare recollection, stirred by his sister Esta's unhappy pregnancy, evokes a memory of Esta, "sitting at his father's little street organ . . . looking so innocent and good." This momentary review arouses uncharacteristic sympathy in Clyde, an almost tearful conviction of how "strange" and "rough" life is. There are other examples of Clyde recalling the past. But it seldom brings him to an understanding or articulation of a sense of self, or place in the world.

A noteworthy exception is his first stroll through the streets of Lycurgus. Following an unhappy interview with Gilbert, Clyde's misery is mirrored in his view of a depressing slum. So struck is he by its "angularity and crudeness" that he "at once retraced his steps and recrossing the Mohawk by a bridge farther west soon found himself in a area which was very different indeed . . . very broad and well-paved and lined by such an arresting company of houses." Clyde's retracing here takes him eventually from the dismal slum neighborhood to the wealthy environs of his relatives' home. And his initially impulsive retracing and recrossing gives way to a deeper process of self-review. Coming upon the Griffithses' mansion, Clyde is struck full force by the reality of "who the Griffiths were here," as opposed to "who the Griffiths were in Kansas City." As he becomes aware of his great "difference" from the Lycurgus Griffithses and his own identity as a "nobody," Clyde's repetitive action brings him to a profound recognition of how he has been made by his past. The volitional nature of this retracing, as distinguished from later ones, provides for a moment of self-awareness.

Clyde's only retracings and returns in Book 3 are forced upon him by his lawyers, the prosecuting attorney, and the parade of court witnesses who render him powerless by unfolding a

past panorama in which he is the subject, but completely under their direction. All these recounters of Clyde's past give the impression of telling it more accurately than he, and most of them exploit it for their own uses. Clyde's past becomes a saleable commodity, a "hot" item serving others' interests. Thus, Clyde's inability to frame a believable version of his past makes him a victim of those who can. The defense lawyer Jephson's rhetorical question to Clyde under cross-examination, "After all, you didn't make yourself, did you?", seems more than a little ironic given the emphasis placed on his inability to narrate his own history.

In fact, Jephson exemplifies the questionable intentions of those who manage Clyde's past, for though commendable, his strategizing on behalf of Clyde's defense at times appears ruthless. He is described at one point, "his harebell eyes showing only cold, eager, practical," his manner "like a spider spinning a web, on his own plan." Although Jephson's professional intensity can hardly be faulted, and Clyde benefits from his personal strength at the trial, there are hints that he is so caught up in his own machinations that he objectifies and effaces Clyde as harshly as his trial foes. And some of his judgments seem actually harmful to Clyde. At least a few of Jephson's trial tactics are suspicious. We never receive an explanation for why Jephson reverses the "original plan" to have the stately and respectable Belknap cross-examine Clyde. Nor, more curiously, do we learn why Jephson suppresses a letter from the former captain of the bellboys at the Green-Davidson that would have supported Clyde's own testimony. Jephson's judgment that such a disclosure is "irrelevant" seems mysteriously misguided and arbitrary.

The boldness and rationality of others' approaches to Clyde's past provide a striking contrast to his own timorousness. Clyde's narrative befuddlement—his inability to narrate his past experiences—allows others to empower themselves through it. Clyde's role as a political pawn is replicated in his role as a literary pawn, the main character in the proliferating versions of his life. Thus, political and narrative power become one, as Clyde is shown to be a protagonist whose lack of control over his own tale proves fatal.

Repeated references to Clyde's poor plotting and scheming relate his downfall to his ineptness as a systematic narrator. Contemplating the trail of evidence left by Clyde, Mason wonders silently, "What sort of a plotter and killer would that be?" And the narrator describes Clyde at his capture, his "shrunk" form revealing the "effects of his so poorly conceived and executed scheme." The publicity pamphlets offering for a penny "an outline of 'the great plot' " provide an ironic contrast to Clyde's own plotting deficiencies. Mason quickly deduces Roberta's pregnancy from the bits of information extracted from "the broken and gloomy Titus." All the evidence, which tumbles out with astounding ease, "seemed to unescapably point to [Clyde] as the murderer of Roberta Alden." Though he is prepared to recognize some "trace of truth" in Clyde's version, Mason is more intent on seizing it in his own instinctive grasp. But while Mason's entirely intuitive detailing of Clyde and Roberta's shared life is stunningly accurate, there is an element missing in "facts" so starkly represented. Mason's seamless portrait of Clyde is a distortion not unlike his characterization of Clyde's plotting: "how shrewd and deep must be that mind that would foresee and forestall all the accidents and chances of life."

The novel's greatest irony is that despite the appearance of intentional plotting and murder, Clyde's actions ultimately recoil back upon themselves as haphazardly as unplanned chaos. Clyde's experiences present an epistemological dilemma—how to treat a situation that in every way points to a certain reality, but that fundamentally swerves away from that reality? It is not surprising that Clyde cannot convey his past coherently either to himself or to Mason. Forced to hedge about a plot he has been too ineffectual to carry out, Clyde becomes more and more implicated by Mason's whirling inquiries, trapped by fiction as well as by fact.

In its own way, the defense version of Clyde's experience is no more viable. It even seems more threatening to his sense of self in its disregard for the potential truths of Clyde's experiences due to the urgent necessity of crafting a salvational fiction. Doubting that Clyde can save himself, Belknap and Jephson shape a "straightened story," thereby entrenching his impotence. Sitting in passive contemplation as they plot his past, without any sense of participation or control in its recreation, Clyde seems to embody the idea of reification. "They talked as though he was not present or could have no opinion in the matter, a procedure which astonished but by no means moved him to object, since he was feeling so helpless." Clearly, their dismissiveness serves to alienate him the more from his own past. He repeats the greater part of his testimony mindlessly, from a page "written out for him" by Jephson and dutifully committed to memory. Dispossessed of his memories, Clyde's capacity for self-defense seems doomed. (pp. 274-80)

The superintending of Clyde's past implies that any life "artfully . . . recapitulated" and "recanvass[ed]" for its "fine points" can be made to fulfill the needs and assumptions of present viewers. Reconstructed with his "crime" in mind, the chaotic details of Clyde's experience become significant clues to his later murderous intentions and actions. Indeed, the task of narrating the past serves as the ultimate example of determinism—in the work of retrospective signification, one is invariably fixed from the start. Clyde and Roberta's affair is socially deviant because she becomes pregnant and is unable to erase its consequences. Likewise, Roberta's drowning seems to drain much of the ambiguity and ambivalence from Clyde's actions leading up to it, so that even readers doubt whether it is not murder, the outcome of careful planning and clear intent. Once it has achieved symbolic status, Clyde's life is no longer the disconnected and arbitrary events of his experience, but a rationalized and reified tale with crucial meanings for others.

Yet Clyde's own inability to articulate his past, like his inability to devise an effective plan for coping with Roberta's pregnancy, arises from an inner confusion that is in great part attributable to his unthinking incorporation of society's myths. Rather than the enactment of the doom of humanity at the hands of fate, or the requisite downfall of a character psychologically unsuited to his desired position, Clyde's life is more fully seen in terms of a social hegemony that overregulates his aspirations. The novel's narrative features a discrepancy between a social rhetoric that insists that nature (both biological and universal) is everything, the all-encompassing factor predetermining human destiny, and its own underlying political revelations, which expose how such rhetoric masks the social and political particulars governing and constricting Clyde's life. Clyde's alienation from his own actions in history, and his related inability to narrate his past, can be seen to result from his excessive belief in society's tales. The novel

reveals narrative itself to be the means by which a social determinism is entrenched.

Clyde's passive tendencies are cultivated and affirmed by those who exploit him for the purposes of their operative systems. Samuel Griffiths uses Clyde as a test case for his survival of the fittest philosophy. Sondra Finchley toys with Clyde as a test of her seductive powers. Jephson sees Clyde's case as the testing ground for his judicial powers. Repeatedly, Clyde encounters fixed systems of thought that he only mildly understands, whose operators seek to tailor him to their uses. Perhaps the ultimate example of such a systematic hegemony is the public opinion of Bridgeburg, which typecasts Clyde as an evil deviant irreverently challenging their rigorous moral code. Belknap and Jephson's treatment of Clyde's case, which turns him into an ineffectual participant in the narrative defense of his life, serves similarly to efface Clyde. In each case, Clyde's own lack of an effective governing paradigm makes him vulnerable to exploitation.

Thus, understanding how all of these relationships form a pattern that reveals Clyde's overall experience of society is as important as understanding the psychological complexities of Clyde's interactions with various other characters. Clyde's condition in the novel's third book might be seen to typify Lukács's view of the human absorption by time in the increasingly reified world of twentieth-century Western society [the critic cites Georg Lukács, *History and Class Consciousness*]. No longer possessed of a *relation* to time, Clyde *incarnates* it. Because of his inability to account for his past actions in an acceptably rational form, Clyde is given a past by various authorities. Defined by his "crime," he is stilled thereby in others' imaginations. Each view of Clyde—the prosecution's "mature" and "bearded man," the defense's "mental" and "moral coward," the Bridgeburg public's "little devil," and the "astonishingly youthly slayer" of the press and anonymous crowds—fails to see him as a specific human being in history.

The fixture of Clyde's image also allows for his incorporation into others' reified systems of thought. Thus, the lawyers see Clyde legalistically, judging his responsibility for his actions; the public sees him moralistically, insisting on the necessary repression of human instincts and passion in society; the press sees him sensationally, as a figure to incite and feed a bored public's desire for intimacy with lives seemingly more romantic than their own. Clyde comes to fulfill the rationale of each of these systems, literally "take[n] . . . up" in Sondra's phrase, his identity "incarnating" its adherents' governing concerns. The death house ideology that Clyde encounters near the novel's close proves the logical extension of all its ruling perspectives.

Following Roberta's death, Clyde's life becomes the province of the novel's death instrument, the camera. Frozen in a single moment of the past, it is pictured over and over in innumerable press and pamphlet versions for the satisfaction of public voyeurs. The inhabitants of Bridgeburg, and the nation as a whole, are gripped by this sensational case, their obsession fueled and fed by publicity on Clyde's life in newspaper stories and photographs. Their view allows sufficient distance from the unsettling though glamorous object, while it yields a feeling of intimacy. The novel's central agents of modern technology, the newspaper and the camera, provide a false illusion of familiarity with the exceptional being, guiding the community to define him or her in its own terms. Lives captured within the pages of the daily press in a written or photographic form are inevitably viewed as public property to be exploited.

Everyone associated with Clyde siphons the celebrity of his deviant act. Mason is a "true hero," his departure from the courtroom like the exit of a movie idol, "a heavy, baggy overcoat thrown over his shoulder," a "worn soft hat pulled low over his eyes," followed by his "royal train" of assistant district attorneys. Clyde's life comes to seem less and less his own as public versions of it synthesized from witnesses' testimonies overtake his already tenuous self-image. The clearer Clyde appears in the frameworks of others, the more shadowy he becomes in his own. En route to the death house, he is "astonished" by the response of crowds encountered at every train stop, all desiring to "achieve a facile intimacy with this daring and romantic, if unfortunate figure." He is "heartened" but profoundly disconcerted by the familiarity of anonymous strangers. And upon his arrival at the death house, Clyde is dismayed by the extent to which things "concerning him [were] known here."

In the face of this overwhelming public seizure of his identity and of the brutally exposed procedures of death row, Clyde turns to the spiritual preachings of his mother and Reverend McMillan in an attempt to discover a past narrative that more closely expresses his experience of his past. Yet she and McMillan are as intent as his legal advisors on fitting Clyde's history into their own schemes of judgment. Clyde's mother must know the facts of the case: "Were those things as contended by Mason true or false?" She bewails Clyde's dumbfoundedness, finding him "not positive enough." Absorbed by binomial oppositions of truth and falsehood, faith or deception, she denies Clyde the ranging exploration that might allow him to recuperate his past. Her thirst for "all the data which was the ultimate, basic truth in regard to her son," a thirst shared by Clyde's previous examiners, paradoxically sacrifices Clyde in the name of a system she believes might save.

Reverend McMillan likewise inhibits Clyde's ability to confront his past. Another representative of a rational system, his religious terms are no more adequate for accommodating ambiguity. Following Clyde's narration, McMillan's face reflects the same horrified confusion Clyde has seen in other listeners. "McMillan's face was gray and drawn . . . he had been listening, as he now felt, to a sad and terrible story—an evil and cruel self-torturing and destroying story," a story that troubles his "reason" as it moves his heart. His reason triumphs over his heart as McMillan adheres to rational judgment in refraining from supporting Clyde's appeal before the governor. Yet as the scene closes on Clyde's execution, it is implied that McMillan may forever be hounded by his heart for allowing such a victory.

The novel's final image of Clyde as storyteller is striking. "In his uniform—his hair cropped so close, Clyde sat there, trying honestly now to think how it really was (exactly) and greatly troubled by his inability to demonstrate to himself even—either his guilt or his lack of guilt." So caught up is Clyde in the persistent demands of his various audiences that his own terms have now become exclusively binomial oppositions. Incapable of reenacting or recapturing a sense of how "it" was for himself, his only framework is right or wrong, guilt or innocence. The severity of these limited frames is reflected in his close-cropped hair and sterile prison uniform.

Despairing that he will ever "get the whole thing straightened

out in his own mind," Clyde awaits his execution, absorbed in biblical texts. Compulsively "reading and re-reading the psalms," he hopes thereby to achieve "peace and strength" but never "quite catch[es] it." Like his Jewish counterpart on Death Row, who seeks absolution in ceaseless repetition of the Kol Nidre, Clyde finds that conventional narratives, religious or legal, do not serve those who have strayed beyond the boundaries of acceptable conduct. Moreover, society's terms are rational and uniform, Clyde's past is to be "taken all together and considered as a connected whole." And within this frame, the court concludes, Clyde's experiences "make such convincing proof of guilt that we are not able to escape from its force by any justifiable process of reasoning."

But the various versions of Clyde's life told in Book 3 lack the authority that characterizes a story originally told from the heart of its experiencer. The novel's plot closes on the "dazed" eyes of a protagonist who has been unable to shape a text of his life that would allow him some degree of self-expression or power. Clyde, however, does attain a certain awareness of his needs by the novel's end, paradoxically through his inability to find himself in others' versions of his past. At the opening of Book 3, Clyde's mind is caught in "fear and confusion . . . as to whether he did or did not bring about [Roberta's] untimely end." A character who has all along feared his connection to his past, Clyde doubts he "would . . . ever be able to shake [it] off." His view of the "single bundle" of clothes worn on the boat, noting "sickeningly" the "odds and ends he had worn that day," leads him to wonder at the fragmented mystery of his own past, "all he had contacted since his arrival in the east, how little he had in his youth. How little he had now, really." So severely alienated is Clyde here that he can envision himself as no more than miscellaneous threads of cloth. By the book's close, however, he has achieved some insight.

The closing description of Clyde, finally aware that he can never make his mother understand him, reveals his recognition of his inability to locate a self that can be made known to others.

> But how strange it was, that to his own mother, and even now in these closing hours, when above all things he craved sympathy—but more than sympathy, true and deep understanding—even now—and as much as she loved and sympathized with, and was seeking to aid him with all her strength in her stern and self-sacrificing way,—still he could not turn to her now and tell her, his own mother, just how it all happened. It was as though there was an unsurmountable wall or impenetrable barrier between them, built by the lack of understanding—for it was just that. She would never understand his craving for ease and luxury, for beauty, for love—his particular kind of love that went with show, pleasure, wealth, position, his eager and immutable aspirations and desires. . . . And she would and did expect him to be terribly sorry and wholly repentant, when, even now, and for all he had said to the Reverend McMillan and to her, he could not feel so—not wholly so—although great was his desire now to take refuge in God, but better yet, if it were only possible, in her own understanding and sympathetic heart.

Clyde desires recognition above all: to have his cravings and impulses corroborated by another human being. Wracked with guilt over the possible profanity and excessiveness of his desires, he needs them acknowledged as not monstrous. Yet

Clyde discovers only walls between himself and that formidable other, his mother. This "insurmountable wall or impenetrable barrier . . . built by the lack of understanding" seems an intentional edifice, erected brick-by-brick through a process of complicity that both have shared. To his mother, Clyde's desires have always been slightly monstrous.

But he has come to recognize needs that will never be rationalized out of existence, the set of fluid desires he cannot reason away. Apart from "all he had said to Reverend McMillan," despite his fears of the afterlife, Clyde seems to know that he will never completely accept the repression of desire. He can be seen to have reached this awareness through his inability to recognize others' pictures of him. Nevertheless, only coherent and very specific kinds of narratives provide for survival in Clyde's society. And the possibility that human beings are incapable of perceiving anything that falls outside the boundaries of their governing paradigms points to the subject of ideological hegemony, and the links between narrative and political power.

Many critics have recognized the extent to which the novel questions the American social system that creates, nurtures, and eventually condemns Clyde Griffiths. Irving Howe has been especially responsive to the novel's political perspective, and, in an afterword to the novel, terms it a "parable of our national experience," a portrait of "the passivity, rootlessness, and self-alienation of urban man . . . [in which] the problem of human freedom becomes critically acute through a representation of its decline [and] the problem of awareness is brought to the forefront through a portrait of its negation." But Howe's insistence on the novel's unequivocal determinism seems to belie its most complex political vision.

Rather than exemplifying the human condition in a predetermined universe, Clyde's "fractional awareness" represents the specific conditions of a lower-class youth in a society where some lives are more predetermined than others, and where the conception of a world ruled by impersonal forces might precisely serve the interests of that society's elite. *An American Tragedy* is more accurately conceived to ponder uncertainly its deterministic philosophy, in light of the social and political uses to which this philosophy is often put in the novel's world.

The use of determinism as a containment strategy that allows social authorities to deny their role in the creation and perpetuation of an oppressive social order can be seen in the discussion of the Auburn execution system. As the narrator pointedly informs us at the outset, the new death house is a place "for which no one primarily was really responsible." Erected "by degrees and without anything worthy of the name of thinking on anyone's part," it is "all that could possibly be imagined in the way of unnecessary and really unauthorized cruelty." With no one accepting responsibility for its existence, the death house, like some pure product of nature, seems to have emerged from the workings of eternal law. Yet the narrative irony here is undisguised, and the denial of any human agency or intent is immediately overriden by the allusion to "the thoughtful and condescending authorities" who have "devised" this "newer and better" death house. Alleviating the intense solitude of the previous model, this more open and "brightly lighted" death house renders its inhabitants' impending executions an excruciatingly public affair. Each inmate is now "actually if not intentionally compelled to hear if not witness the final preparations" of the soon-to-be-executed. Contrary to the opening rhetoric of botched in-

evitability, the denial of privacy in this new execution system seems remarkably consistent with the slim divide between public and private spheres in the novel's society.

The features of the new death house, in other words, are linked to an identifiable set of assumptions about the best means of social organization, reflecting a social ideology built upon the mutual policing of society's members. As the narrative implies, the links between the new death house's spotlight aura and the relentlessly public nature of self-perceptions portrayed throughout the novel—from Clyde's street-corner anguish over the shabby appearance of his family to his late embarrassment about the shearing of his hair in prison—are too precise to be accidental. For a world of selves increasingly swallowed up by their social milieu, a death house with floodlights and open cells seems entirely appropriate. As was true for the "captive bear" at Starlight Park, the lack of privacy is indeed part of the punishment.

The narrator's own stance in this passage is more difficult to assess. His waffling in first describing the new death house as "unauthorized" (however ironic), and then referring to its elaboration by "thoughtful authorities," perhaps betrays his reluctance to pin responsibility on anyone. Though he consistently unmasks others' efforts to deny responsibility for their historical actions, this does not preclude his own denials. Yet there are even more important ways in which determinism functions as a containment strategy in the novel.

Central among these is the issue of Clyde's suitability for success. The question of the primary determinants of success in the novel's society is a complex one. But an understanding of the issue is critical for assessing the interaction of psychological and sociopolitical factors in Clyde's downfall. Throughout *An American Tragedy,* allusions to the importance of education or vocation as means by which one gains entrance into the ranks of America's elite war mysteriously with references to "connections." Indeed, the obsessive repetition of this word in the novel has eluded the attention of critics.

The novel's early chapters emphasize Clyde's resentment toward his parents for their mismanagment of their children's educational and vocational training. Other mentions of Clyde's attitudes toward success, however, seem to contradict this anxiety. Seen as representative of "American youth," Clyde appears to disdain most kinds of occupational training. "True to the standard of the American youth, or the general American attitude toward life, [Clyde] felt himself above the type of labor which was purely manual. What! Run a machine, lay bricks, learn to be a carpenter, or a plasterer, or plumber, when boys no better than himself were clerks and druggists' assistants?" Clyde's perspective seems generally to deny process, to belie the work of achieving a goal. He conceives of ends without means, success without the expenditure of effort in attaining it.

But this air of impracticality or lack of initiative and commitment, the narrator assures us, is not peculiar to Clyde. Nor, more crucially, does it seem inconsistent with the American success ethic as the novel portrays it. Samuel and Gilbert repeatedly refer to Clyde's lack of training as an explanation for his low placement in the factory hierarchy, contradicting the larger social picture their rhetoric inscribes. Though the society's Horatio Alger story of business success seemingly paints the road to wealth and position as open to any American youth through hard work and self-belief, the tale's underlying message suggests otherwise. The Griffithses' continual alignment of worldly success and spiritual favor, and condonation of exploitative business practices with elevated rhetoric, implies that success cannot be pursued. Rather, success is a state or condition that one achieves naturally, by merely being a certain type of individual. Whether the outcome of predetermination or chance, success is possessed, not made.

The issue is complicated by Clyde's resentment toward Gilbert Griffiths, whose manner claims wealth and respect as his rightful due, but whose past does not justify it. While Samuel Griffiths's superiority is legendary, Gilbert effects "airs and superiorities which, but for his father's skill before him, would not have been possible." Clyde resents Gilbert's criticisms of his lack of vocation, while Gilbert's success is determined by blood alone. Of course, Clyde's own reception by Lycurgus's lower classes is based on this similarly unearned premise of high birth.

Success to the increasingly worldly Clyde of Book 2 comes to appear as a miraculous election into "a company of seemingly mentally and socially worldly elect," or a chance result of having "the right sort of contacts . . . a connection." This developing vision of success reveals its growing separation from the possibility of personal initiative. Thus, Clyde's view of success comes to accord with the prevailing deterministic ideology of the social systems he encounters. From his employment at the Green-Davidson and the Union League, Clyde begins to view success as a predestined or arbitrary phenomenon. His response to the inexplicable downpour of coins into his pocket at the Green-Davidson captures the contradictory terms of his perspective. He feels "a sense of luck and a sense of responsibility as to future luck." Clyde's inappropriate sense of "responsibility" toward his luck merely highlights the remoteness of his desires from the plane of human action.

Like the reconstruction of Clyde's past at his trial, the life becomes separated from the human actor who lives it, as choices and actions in history become mere threads in a pattern. For well-placed individuals like Samuel or Gilbert Griffiths, such an immobilized view of the world is clearly beneficent. But for Clyde it can only lead to frustration and ultimately to self-annihilation.

By the late nineteenth and early twentieth centuries, the rags-to-riches myth was beginning to seem more and more antedated, given growing perceptions of the expanding role of large institutions in American life. The absence of a relation between means and ends in success narratives might well have felt more realistic to many Americans at this time. Yet the element of futility in Dreiser's portrait, and its links to the function of American ideology, registers a far sharper critique. For Dreiser's novel is precisely interested in how the dream creates the reality, aware that the perceptions that hem human beings in cannot be separated from any actual barriers in their way. *An American Tragedy* pictures its deterministic ideology as inevitably dragging the world along in its wake. But the novel's sustained reflection on the social and political effects of its own determinism stands as a form of resistance to that vision. And that resistance reveals, above all, a faith in human powers to change the world. (pp. 281-94)

> *Susan L. Mizruchi, "The Power of Mere Fable: Reconstructing the Past in 'An American Tragedy'," in her* The Power of Historical Knowledge: Narrating the Past in Hawthorne, James, and Dreiser, *Princeton University Press, 1988, pp. 242-94.*

FURTHER READING

Bellow, Saul. "Dreiser and the Triumph of Art." *Commentary* 11 (1951): 502-03.
    Addresses criticism of Dreiser's literary style.

Bourne, Randolph. "The Art of Theodore Dreiser." In his *History of a Literary Radical, and Other Essays,* edited by Van Wyck Brooks, pp. 195-204. New York: B. W. Huebsch, 1920.
    Commends Dreiser's forceful presentation of "themes of crude power and sex and the American common life" in his fiction.

Brennan, Stephen C. "Theodore Dreiser's *An Amateur Laborer:* A Myth in the Making." *American Literary Realism, 1870-1910* 19, No. 2 (Winter 1987): 66-84.
    Examines the account that Dreiser gave in *An Amateur Laborer* of his nervous breakdown of 1902-03.

Conder, John J. "Dreiser's Trilogy and the Dilemma of Determinism: *The Financier, The Titan, The Stoic.*" In his *Naturalism in American Fiction: The Classic Phase, pp. 86-117. Lexington: University Press of Kentucky, 1984.*
    Examines Dreiser's exploration of the concept of determinism in the Cowperwood trilogy.

Dowell, Richard W. Introduction to *An Amateur Laborer,* by Theodore Dreiser, edited by Richard W. Dowell, pp. xi-xlix. Philadelphia: University of Pennsylvania Press, 1983.
    Biographical and critical sketch outlining the circumstances of Dreiser's life at the time he wrote the autobiography *An Amateur Laborer.*

Dreiser, Helen. *My Life with Dreiser.* Cleveland: World Publishing Co., 1951, 328 p.
    Biography by Dreiser's second wife.

Dudley, Dorothy. *Dreiser and the Land of the Free.* New York: Beechhurst Press, 1946, 485 p.
    Revised edition of the 1932 biography *Forgotten Frontiers: Dreiser and the Land of the Free.* Dreiser worked closely with Dudley on both the original edition and the revision.

Epstein, Joseph. "The Mystery of Theodore Dreiser." *The New Criterion* 5, No. 3 (November 1986): 33-43.
    Examines the importance of a biographical understanding of Dreiser to comprehension and appreciation of his literary accomplishment.

Fast, Howard. Introduction to *The Best Short Stories of Theodore Dreiser,* edited by Howard Fast, pp. 7-11. Cleveland: World Publishing Co., 1947.
    Commends Dreiser's achievement as a short story writer.

Gerber, Philip L. "Dreiser: The Great Sloth of the Thirties." *The Old Northwest* 11, Nos. 1-2 (Spring-Summer 1985): 7-23.
    Discusses Dreiser's activities during the 1930s, when he published little. Gerber also examines some reasons for Dreiser's lack of productivity during this period.

Griffin, Joseph. "Howard Fast, James T. Farrell, and *The Best Short Stories of Theodore Dreiser.*" *The International Fiction Review* 14, No. 2 (Summer 1987): 79-83.
    Recounts the circumstances under which the introduction by Fast was replaced with one by Farrell in the 1956 edition of *The Best Short Stories of Theodore Dreiser.* For an excerpt from Farrell's essay, see *TCLC,* Vol. 10, p. 180.

Hakutani, Yoshinobu. Introduction to *Selected Magazine Articles of Theodore Dreiser: Life and Art in the American 1890s,* by Theodore

Dreiser, edited by Yoshinobu Hakutani, pp. 15-38. Rutherford, N.J.: Fairleigh Dickinson University Press, 1985.

> Calls for critical examination of Dreiser's journalism, "which casts considerable light not only upon Dreiser the novelist, but more importantly, upon the 1890s, an exciting era in the development of American civilization."

Hovey, Richard B., and Ralph, Ruth S. "Dreiser's *The 'Genius'*: Motivation and Structure." *Hartford Studies in Literature* 2, No. 2 (1970): 169-83.

> Offers a Freudian interpretation of *The "Genius."*

Keyssar, Helene. "Theodore Dreiser's Dramas: American Folk Drama and Its Limits." *Theatre Journal* 33, No. 3 (October 1981): 365-76.

> Identifies Dreiser's published plays with the conventions of American folk drama rather than the prevailing dramatic Naturalism or Realism of his day.

Lehan, Richard. *Theodore Dreiser: His World and His Novels.* Carbondale: Southern Illinois University Press, 1969, 280 p.

> Critical study of the novels, including examination of the aspects of Dreiser's life that significantly influenced his fiction.

Lingeman, Richard. *Theodore Dreiser: At the Gates of the City, 1871-1907.* New York: G. P. Putnam's Sons, 1986, 478 p.

> Biography covering Dreiser's life through the successful second American edition of *Sister Carrie.*

Matthiessen, F. O. *Theodore Dreiser.* New York: William Sloane Associates, 1951, 267 p.

> Biography including discussion of Dreiser's principal works, with extensive delineation of the plots and themes of the major novels.

McAleer, John J. *Theodore Dreiser: An Introduction and Interpretation.* New York: Barnes & Noble, 1968, 180 p.

> Critical study of Dreiser's fiction.

Moers, Ellen. *Two Dreisers.* New York: Viking Press, 1969, 366 p.

> Biographical and critical study focusing on the impact of Dreiser's cultural background on his literary works.

Mukherjee, Arun. *The Gospel of Wealth in the American Novel: The Rhetoric of Dreiser and Some of His Contemporaries.* London: Croom Helm, 1987, 229 p.

> Examines Dreiser's fictional treatment of business practices and the businessman.

Phillips, William L. "The Imagery of Dreiser's Novels." *PMLA* 78, No. 5 (December 1963): 572-85.

> Discusses significant patterns of imagery in Dreiser's novels.

Pizer, Donald. Introduction to *Theodore Dreiser: A Selection of Uncollected Prose,* by Theodore Dreiser, edited by Donald Pizer, pp. 13-27. Detroit: Wayne State University Press, 1977.

> Biographical and critical sketch discussing the place of Dreiser's essays and journalism in his literary career.

——. "Self-Censorship and Textual Editing." In *Textual Criticism and Literary Interpretation,* edited by Jerome J. McGann, pp. 144-227. Chicago: University of Chicago Press, 1985.

> Includes discussion of the extent to which Dreiser altered the original text of *Sister Carrie* before publication, and explores possible reasons for his doing so.

——; Dowell, Richard W.; and Rusch, Frederic E., eds. *Theodore Dreiser: A Primary and Secondary Bibliography.* Boston: G. K. Hall & Co., 1975, 515 p.

> Comprehensive listing of Dreiser's works, including his newspaper writing, anonymous journalism that has been attributed to him, published letters, interviews, speeches, and library holdings. The section devoted to secondary works includes other bibliographies, criticism in journals and books, and theses and dissertations.

Riggio, Thomas P. "Theodore Dreiser: Hidden Ethnic." *Melus* 11, No. 1 (Spring 1984): 53-63.

> Examines ways that Dreiser's German-American heritage informs his works.

——. "Dreiser and Mencken: In the Literary Trenches." *The American Scholar* 54, No. 2 (Spring 1985): 227-38.

> Account of the long-standing personal and professional relationship between Dreiser and Mencken, focusing on the literary and social controversies in which the two participated.

Salzman, Jack, ed. *Theodore Dreiser: The Critical Reception.* New York: David Lewis, 1972, 741 p.

> Reprints initial reviews of twenty-four of Dreiser's works.

Schneider, Robert W. "Theodore Dreiser: The Cry of Despair." In his *Five Novelists of the Progressive Era,* pp. 153-204. New York: Columbia University Press, 1965.

> Examines Dreiser's moral beliefs as expressed in his writings.

Schwartz, Carol A. "*Jennie Gerhardt*: Fairy Tale as Social Criticism." *American Literary Realism, 1870-1910* 19, No. 2 (Winter 1987): 16-29.

> Examines Dreiser's treatment of class issues in *Jennie Gerhardt.*

Swanberg, W. A. *Dreiser.* New York: Charles Scribner's Sons, 1965, 614 p.

> Biography focusing on Dreiser's years as a successful novelist.

Ward, Joseph A. " 'The Amazing Hotel World' of James, Dreiser, and Wharton." In *Leon Edel and Literary Art,* edited by Lyall H. Powers, pp. 151-60. Ann Arbor, Mich.: UMI Research Press, 1988.

> Examines Dreiser's use of the luxury hotel as an important cultural symbol in his novels.

Warren, Robert Penn. *Homage to Theodore Dreiser, August 27, 1871–December 28, 1945: On the Centennial of His Birth.* New York: Random House, 1971, 173 p.

> Analysis of the plots and major themes of Dreiser's novels.

Whalen, Terry. "Dreiser's Tragic Sense: The Mind as 'Poor Ego'." *The Old Northwest* 11, Nos. 1-2 (Spring-Summer 1985): 61-80.

> Examines affinities between Freudian theories about the workings of the conscious mind and Dreiser's portrayal of mental processes in his fiction.

John Gould Fletcher

1886-1950

American poet, biographer, historian, autobiographer, and critic.

One of the most innovative twentieth-century poets, Fletcher contributed to the development of Imagism, a movement dedicated to replacing traditional poetics with a more concise use of language, new rhythms, and a concrete rather than discursive or symbolic treatment of subject. Although remembered primarily for his early association with this movement and with its adherents Ezra Pound, H. D., and Amy Lowell, Fletcher also wrote poetry drawing on such varied sources as French Symbolism, Oriental art and philosophy, and music. Interested in emphasizing the musical qualities of poetry, he especially devoted himself to creating new rhythmical effects in his verse. Later in his career Fletcher concentrated less on technical innovations in order to develop themes he had only touched on in his early works, including humanity's relation to nature, the isolating effects of mechanization, and the individual's search for God and salvation. During this period, he also became associated with the Fugitives, a group of American poets dedicated to renewing an agrarian way of life and traditional Southern values.

Fletcher was born in Little Rock, Arkansas, the son of a successful businessman. An isolated and lonely child, he was taught at home by his mother and by tutors until age ten, when he began his formal education at a private school. He attended a public high school and then studied a year at a preparatory school before entering Harvard University. Fletcher was not a successful student, preferring to visit art museums and read books of his own choosing rather than attend class. He began to write poetry at this time, although he did not decide to follow a literary career until several years later. When his father died in 1906, leaving him a substantial annuity, Fletcher left Harvard to independently pursue various studies in culture, history, and the arts.

In 1909 Fletcher settled in London and began to concentrate on writing poetry, publishing five collections of his poems at his own expense in 1913. At this time he became acquainted with London literary society and developed friendships with expatriate American poets Ezra Pound and Amy Lowell. Pound, who served as foreign editor for Harriet Monroe's magazine *Poetry,* supported Fletcher by selecting his work for publication; at the same time, Pound expressed negative criticism of some aspects of Fletcher's poetry, creating friction between the two writers. Their friendship deteriorated further when Pound wrote an article based on ideas Fletcher had discussed with him about the French Symbolists. Fletcher felt Pound had taken credit for his ideas and later refused to allow Pound to include his work in the anthology *Des Imagistes.* His friendship with Lowell flourished, however, and her enthusiasm for his work led her to promote his books to publishers and to incorporate his techniques in her own poetry. Fletcher's first mature work, *Irradiations—Sand and Spray,* established him as an innovative poet, a reputation which grew with the publication of *Goblins and Pagodas.* When Houghton Mifflin rejected his next poetry collection on the advice of Lowell, Fletcher felt betrayed and demoralized.

The subsequent rejection of three more collections in 1917 aggravated this emotional state, and he wrote little verse during the next few years. A concern with spiritual matters, which he had dealt with cursorily in his early verse, became a major force in his life, and he published religious verse in *Parables* and *Branches of Adam.*

In 1926 Fletcher suffered a nervous breakdown which he later said was "perhaps a result of mental overstimulation, certainly a result of the British diet to which I never became entirely reconciled or accustomed." He recovered within a few weeks and continued to write poetry, as well as producing biographies and translations. During this period, his poems focused on the spiritual poverty of contemporary life he saw as resulting from industrialization. Fletcher began to contribute to the *Fugitive,* a magazine published by a group of writers who advocated a simplified, agrarian life-style over that of modern urban life, which they found socially and psychologically detrimental. Visiting the United States on a lecture tour of the South in 1927, Fletcher met Donald Davidson, John Crowe Ransom, and Allen Tate, three members of the Fugitive group. Tate asked him to contribute to *I'll Take My Stand: The South and the Agrarian Tradition* (1930), the anthology that was to become the manifesto of this group. In 1932, another nervous breakdown kept Fletcher in a hospital for five months. Once he recovered, he left England to return permanently to Little Rock. Fletcher undertook many new projects, producing several volumes of regional poetry, an autobiography, and a history of Arkansas. His *Selected Poems* won a Pulitzer Prize in 1939. Although Fletcher remained productive, he continued to suffer from mental illness, resulting in another breakdown in 1946 and, ultimately, his suicide in 1950.

Fletcher's first five volumes of poetry were generally considered to be derivative, clumsy, and often annoyingly self-centered, although some critics, including Ezra Pound, thought they showed promise. His next volume, *Irradiations—Sand and Spray*, displays a noticeable maturity in both Fletcher's thought and technique. This volume marks the beginning of Fletcher's association with Imagism, and while it does follow the major practices of the movement, such as employing well-defined visual images and avoiding rhetoric and didacticism, its main emphasis is on the use of poetic rhythms to express emotions. In Fletcher's view: "The good poem is that in which all those effects (variations of tempo, etc.) are properly used to convey the underlying emotions of its author, and that which welds all the emotions into a work of art by the use of the dominant motif, subordinate themes, proportionate treatment, repetition, variation—what in music is called development, reversal of roles and return." He illustrated this theory in poems he called "symphonies," in which the emotional effectiveness of his musical techniques is enhanced by an emphasis on color imagery, and these works earned Fletcher a great deal of praise. Early in his career, Fletcher also experimented with "polyphonic prose," a literary form originated by Amy Lowell, that employed all the "voices" of poetry—such as rhyme, cadence, alliteration, and assonance—without the many formal restrictions of verse. Critics often cite Fletcher's "Clipper Ships" as the best example of polyphonic prose. Fletcher's experiments with Japanese verse forms were not well-received by critics, who felt that they were verbose and thus ineffective as examples of the concentrated tanka and haiku forms. Oriental art and philosophy continued to influence the themes if not the style of Fletcher's later poetry. Fletcher received more critical attention in this first period of his career than in any other, most of it focusing on his association with Imagism. Several critics claimed that his poetry lacked emotion, a charge frequently brought against the precise and unsentimental verses of the Imagists. He was also accused of being verbose and diffuse in the works that followed *Irradiations—Sand and Spray*, a problem uncommon to the verbally concise Imagists. Nevertheless, early critical response was generally favorable, praising his poetry for its vigor, its new imagery, and its variety of musical effects.

The middle period of Fletcher's career is marked by his religious verse. Although some critics see the strong religious emphasis of these poems as a new development in Fletcher's work, Fletcher explained in his autobiography that he had always been concerned with salvation, but that early in his career he felt it could be found through nature and art. As Fletcher stated: "Temporarily, I had resolved [the issue of salvation], the first of my moral dilemmas, by accepting the religion of art in its most extreme form, and by believing that beauty, unaided, could save the world." After the First World War, Fletcher left what he called his aesthetic phase behind and looked to Christianity for the answers to his moral and philosophic questions. Two major volumes from this period, *Parables* and *Branches of Adam*, deal with what

he considered "the chief tendency of humanity, . . . man's continued and ever renewed search for God." He asserted in these works an unorthodox dualism in which God is both good and evil, a view which some critics have attributed to the influence of Oriental philosophy on Fletcher's thought. Fletcher's works of this period also deal with the effects of industrialization, focusing in particular on what he viewed as the individual's loss of spirituality and sympathy with nature in the machine age.

While Fletcher continued to explore many of the same themes later in his career, particularly the evils of industrialization, he changed the subject matter of his poetry from Christianity to regional and national concerns. Although his goals were similar to those of the Fugitive movement, which sought in a simple agrarian life-style the union of intellect with intuition and humanity with nature, Fletcher's emotional poetic style never resembled the intellectual verses of the Fugitive poets, and he eventually dissociated himself from them. He nevertheless continued to write in praise of the South, and his vivid descriptions of the American landscape have led several critics to assert that Fletcher finally discovered his idiom as a regional poet.

In addition to poetry, Fletcher wrote a variety of prose works, including biographies, histories, and literary criticism. These writings are valued for what they reveal about Fletcher's philosophy and personality, as well as for their lucidity and intelligence. For the most part, however, Fletcher's prose has received little attention, and his reputation as an important figure in twentieth-century literature rests on his poetic techniques, his influence on the Imagists and other poets, and above all on his innovative, imaginative, and thought-provoking poetry.

(See also *Contemporary Authors*, Vol. 107, and *Dictionary of Literary Biography*, Vols. 4 and 45.)

PRINCIPAL WORKS

The Book of Nature   (poetry)   1913
The Dominant City   (poetry)   1913
Fire and Wine   (poetry)   1913
Fool's Gold   (poetry)   1913
Visions of the Evening   (poetry)   1913
**Irradiations—Sand and Spray*   (poetry)   1915
**Goblins and Pagodas*   (poetry)   1916
Japanese Prints   (poetry)   1918
The Tree of Life   (poetry)   1918
Breakers and Granite   (poetry)   1921
Paul Gauguin   (biography)   1921
Parables   (prose and poetry)   1925
Branches of Adam   (poetry)   1926
The Black Rock   (poetry)   1928
John Smith—Also Pocahontas   (biography)   1928
The Two Frontiers: A Study in Historical Psychology
     (history)   1930
XXIV Elegies   (poetry)   1935
Life Is My Song   (autobiography)   1937
Selected Poems   (poetry)   1938
South Star   (poetry)   1941
Arkansas   (history)   1946
The Burning Mountain   (poetry)   1946

*These works were published together as *Preludes and Symphonies* in 1922.

EDWARD THOMAS   (essay date 1913)

[*A British poet, novelist, and critic, Thomas is acclaimed for his simple, delicately rhythmic poetry which portrays life as ultimately futile. In the following excerpt, he focuses on what he considers the best of Fletcher's first five volumes of poetry,* The Dominant City.]

Mr. John Gould Fletcher has published five volumes of verse this year. Somewhere he speaks with satisfaction of not having published his "teething pains"; yet these are presumably his first books, and they do not present an achieved style or character. Since they are personal without being very individual or revealing, it might be concluded that the greater part is experiment, in which the author has not been able to extend his powers to the full. In his poem **"To the Immortal Memory of Charles Baudelaire"**—

> Baudelaire, green flower that sways
>   Over the morass of misery
> Painfully, for days on days,
>   Till it fails, without a sigh . . .

he does no more than show that he has had a common experience. Defiance, violence, ambition, seem the most natural qualities in the book. It is possible to suspect exaggeration in the defiance and violence, as when he speaks of the rain beating and wind howling round his grave:

> Like the rhymes and cries I have torn
> From my heart with desperate might.

But the ambition is unquestionable, as when he writes to unwilling editor and publisher:

> Who knows in acid-bitten bronze to scrape
> His thought, he need not fear to die unknown.

and—

> Now though I live or die, it matters not.
>   I see great cliffs of granite clothed in sun,
>   And up those cliffs I climbed apart, alone.
> It is enough. The rest of me can rot.

The nature of the ambition is not quite clear. It may be ambition pure and simple, restless and unsatiable—ambition to be a great and admired man. He says in his **"Hymn to the Sun"**:

> Not as in grey northern regions,
> Where sad, sickly men put life itself to the question,
> Would I live, but in uttermost power:
> Borne up, overwhelmed by thee!

In more than one other place the ambition seems to be a desire chiefly for conspicuous and tragic isolation, as in **"Failure"**:

> Some fail because they never choose to strive. . . .

> But I have failed,—for I reject success,—
> Because success is the only failure I know:
> Far better death or madness.

The meaning is uncertain, but the ambitious drift is not. Once he compares his sufferings favourably with those of Christ. The following is a stanza written in an inn in the St. Bernard Pass after breakfasting:

> Napoleon took his breakfast here,
>   And after rode afar:

> Napoleon conquered Italy,
>   I wage internal war.

Whatever this ambition, it has isolated, tortured the author, to the point of inspiring this utterance on Fatigue:

> Sing, O ye poets, sing on,
>   Of golden summer's gales;
> Of patented magic casements,
>   And copyright nightingales!
> 'Gainst all these harmless follies
>   I do not stir up strife,
> I am only weary of two things,
>   And these are—death and life.

Yet ambition has not been a stern taskmaster. It has admitted into print a rather large number of poor rhymes, some thin sense, some impossible constructions, and even such tame and unskilful trickling as—

> Next the cherry from which song
> Shakes the white shower all day long,
>   Ringing to stir the sluggish growth
>   Of a thousand others bursting forth
> On the glowing green hillside,
> Which becomes a mosaic pied,
>   A vast galaxy of hues
>   Whose perfume breezes catch and lose.

Yet Mr. Fletcher has a wide acquaintance with literature. His ambition is certainly directed towards literature, and in the prelude to *Fool's Gold,* he has prayed:

> Let me have strange new song, so that my soul
>   May not grow sad and cold
>   By the ashes of the old;
> Let me have strange new song to rhyme and roll.

He desires, and that violently, to be a great new poet. All his books, save *The Dominant City,* show him more or less being tortured by this ambition, and by troubles connected with it, rather than striving to gratify it. *The Dominant City* is his greatest effort. It is an effort to present visible London, together with its effect on the poet's spirit. A verse from **"The Hoardings"** will help to define its modernity:

> Poet, do not vainly dream
> Of a past forgot for long;
> Let the wonderful hoardings stream
> In their splendour through your song. . . .

Add to this a verse from **"Song of a Night"**:

> Last night I lay disgusted, sick at heart,
> Beside a sodden woman of the street;
> Who drowsed, oblivious of the dreadful mart,
> Her outraged body, and her blistered feet. . . .

But he has not read the French poets for nothing. You see "L'Eternel Luxure" in the picture of pleasure awakening at nightfall:

> Then pleasure, like a vast cat, stirs herself,
> And, yawning, stretches forth her velvet feet,
> To grasp the city in her long, curved claws.

In **"London at Night"** you get "Life and Death and Lust," and also—

> A thousand chimney-stacks and more,
> Shatter the sky-line's black brute jumble. . . .

Sometimes the chimneys are not a mere black brute jumble, but—

Blackened with grief, blistered with lust of life,
Unconquerable and unconquered. . . .

One idyll there is: **"Saturday Night: Horses Going to Pasture"**:

Hark! through the city, quiet, cool, and starred,
Longing for sleep and for repose in dreams,
Dull rattling hoofs in hundreds echo hard:
The deep reverberant groundswell upward streams.
Heavily the long cavalcade clatters and prances
Through the dazzling glare of lamps, through shad-
  ows thickly scored;
The sound in a broken rhythm quivers and dances,
As the ponderous bulks in irregular trot move for-
  ward.
Man's mighty slaves, now for a time set free,
Pass from the city that they served so well,
Churning to choppy waves its sombre sea,
Beating harsh dissonances of farewell.
Their steel-shod hoofs gleam bright as they move
  on
To green-clad, silent pastures in the sun.

If it is open to the imputation of being idyllic, it is artistically true and pleasant. But the total effect is of a sinister, multitudinous confusion, a less phantasmal "City of Dreadful Night," and of a solitary man's brave attempt to make poetry of his observation, his reading, and his ambition. He succeeds in reminding us of sublime impressions, ours and his own. (pp. 363-65)

> *Edward Thomas, in a review of "Poems," in* Poetry
> & Drama, *Vol. 1, No. 3, September, 1913, pp. 363-
> 65.*

EZRA POUND (essay date 1913)

[*Pound, an American poet and critic, is regarded as one of the most innovative and influential figures in twentieth-century Anglo-American poetry. He was instrumental in obtaining editorial and financial assistance for T. S. Eliot, Wyndham Lewis, James Joyce, and William Carlos Williams, among other poets. His own* Cantos, *published throughout his life, is among the most ambitious poetic cycles of the century, and his series of satirical poems* Hugh Selwyn Mauberly (1920) *is ranked with Eliot's* The Waste Land (1922) *as a significant attack upon the decadence of modern culture. Pound considered the United States a cultural wasteland, and for that reason, he spent most of his life in Europe. In the following excerpt, he discusses Fletcher's literary faults and virtues as they are displayed in* The Dominant City *and* Fool's Gold.]

Mr. Fletcher's "music" is more comparable to that made by a truck-load of iron rails crossing a cobbled pavement than to the wailful sound of violins. Mr. Fletcher has not the faults of the mellifluous versifier, of the great horde of publishing authors whose product reminds one more of perfumed suet than of any other nameable commodity. Mr. Fletcher has a fine crop of faults—mostly his own. He has such distinction as belongs to a man who dares to have his own faults, who prefers his own to those of anyone else.

Mr. Fletcher has apparently read a good deal of contemporary French work—and avowedly, for one volume begins with a salutation to the French Poets of To-day, and the other with a list of *Poètes Maudits,* including Corbière, de Lautréamont, Rimbaud, Laforgue and Aurier. I cannot see that his reading has harmed him or that he is guilty of what they call "servile imitation" of either one or all of his continental models. Mr. Fletcher is one of the very few men on this side of the channel who are in any sense in touch of the poetic activity on the other. And in a country where it is rank heresy to recognise any foreign discovery, whether in art or in science, there is little use in concealing the fact that Mr. Fletcher is a rank heretic. (pp. 131-32)

I do not think Mr. Fletcher is an imitator, he is influenced, if you like, as all the younger Frenchmen are influenced. If you ask south of the channel *à quoi revent les jeunes gens?* you might find that their reveries are not unlike those of Mr. Fletcher, and that a good number of them have learned to express themselves better than he does. Still, if a poem by this author were read in the café du Châtelet it would not be regarded as an antique or a grotesque, which is more than can be said for nine-tenths of his English contemporaries.

It is not my intention to subject [*The Dominant City* and *Fool's Gold*] to the measuring instruments which apply in my own school or in anybody else's. It is enough that I have read *The Dominant City* without being bored to death, without being choked on gobbets of sham Keats, and on fricasseed Francis Thompson.

To the other Thompson, the half-forgotten fellow, and to the late suicided John Davidson our author is more nearly akin.

It is a pleasure, as it is a rarity, to find an author who really cares about anything, and it is quite impossible to read Mr. Fletcher without being convinced that he cares a great deal for the truth. About beauty, I am not so sure. It is quite possible that the sense of beauty may be drawn down upon the mind of the reader by keeping it, beauty, austerely OFF the page. I am not sure that even this is Mr. Fletcher's intention. His art is an art that dares to go to the dust-bin for its subjects. There are moods and times when no other sort of art seems worth the petrol to start it.

If one were to go through [*The Dominant City* and *Fool's Gold*] with the usual sort of appraising one might note that the author has the following virtues—virtues I mean as the reviewers on the *Times* and *Spectator,* and the other echoes of the past, count virtues:

He has an abundant imagery. He gets it not out of books but from his own impulse and observation. *The Nation* would call it, at times, "bizarre."

He has an ability to build his poems into a book, he sustains "the tone" throughout.

He shows, often at his roughest, a determination to fight out his own rhythms. He declines to accept the hackneyed cadence, though he does not always escape it.

He is obviously striving "to render his own time" if not in the syntax of his own time at least in a vocabulary of his own time. He is not afraid of the unused and of the unsanctioned. This tendency will not be accounted unto him for a virtue, by any of the above mentioned worthies.

Fool's Gold lacks the unity of *The Dominant City,* yet there are within it touches of a thoroughly pleasing grimness. (p. 132)

> *Ezra Pound, "In Metre," in* The New Freewoman,
> *Vol. 7, No. 1, September 15, 1913, pp. 131-32.*

W. D. HOWELLS   (essay date 1915)

[*Howells was the chief progenitor of American realism and the most influential American literary critic during the late nineteenth century. In the following excerpt, he evaluates the success of Fletcher's* vers libre *in the volume that includes* Irradiations *and* Sand and Spray.]

If in Mr. John Gould Fletcher's *Irradiations—Sand and Spray* the reader is withheld by the preface from what may be called the illustrations of that polemic in favor of *vers libre,* we will not say it is not to his loss. Mr. Fletcher is earnestly persuaded of his opinions, and if he does not make us share his belief that in emancipation from the old forms high achievements are to follow, that is not his fault. It may be our fault, and it will certainly be our fault if we deny his *vers libre* the opportunity to prove his thesis. But we hardly know which of his rather voluntarily impassioned pieces to let bear him witness. Perhaps one will do as well as another, though as they have none of them titles, it is hard to summon them by name. But here is one as it would be in prose before it was shredded:

> It is evening, and the earth wraps her shoulders in an old blue shawl. Afar off there clink the polychrome points of the stars, indefatigable, after all these years! Here upon earth there is life and then death, dawn and then nightfall, fire and the quenching of embers: but why should I not remember that my night is dawn in another part of the world, if the idea fits my fancy? Dawns of marvelous light, wakeful, sleepy, weary, dancing dawns, you are rose petals settling through the blue of my evening: I light my pipe to salute you, and sit puffing smoke in the air and never say a word.

This is pictorial, even poetical; it is suggestive at moments if it is never very convincing. But would it be more convincing if it were printed, as Mr. Fletcher prints it in thirteen lines, long and short? The *vers libretistes* seem to think so; but suddenly here comes the question: Would *Ossian* now survive in all the original wonder and favor which hailed him if he had come from Macpherson's hand shredded into long and short fibers instead of solid blocks of prose?

> *W. D. Howells, in a review of "Irradiations—Sand and Spray," in* Harper's Monthly Magazine, *Vol. CXXXI, No. DCCLXXXIV, September, 1915, p. 637.*

H. D. [HILDA DOOLITTLE]   (essay date 1916)

[*An American poet, novelist, and playwright, H. D. is known primarily for her Imagist poems and her position as one of the founders of Imagism. Praised for the precision and clarity of her poems, H. D. avoided the unemotional tone of much Imagist poetry. Mark Van Doren wrote, "H. D. is that unique thing, an Imagist poet with passion as well as pattern." H. D. chose many of her symbols from Christianity and Greek and Egyptian mythology to express her search for spirituality. The extreme refinement of her language and her abundant use of mythology have led to her reputation as "a poet's poet." In the following excerpt, H. D. praises Fletcher's* Goblins and Pagodas.]

Readers of the *Egoist* are already familiar with certain poems in Mr. John Gould Fletcher's new volume, *Goblins and Pagodas*—particularly with the first part of the book where Mr. Fletcher presents with simplicity and directness a series of impressions—memories of a wistful, sensitive child's impressions of an old weather-beaten house and of the bleak spectres that dwelt within the shadows of the six white columns, that haunted bedroom, nursery, and attic, and crawled with the poison ivy about the roots of the old garden oaks.

In the second section of his book, Mr. Fletcher deals with a more difficult and, when successfully handled, richer form of art: not that of direct presentation, but that of suggestion. Mr. Fletcher, in the very admirable Preface to this new volume, remarks, apropos of certain current opinions concerning the so-called "new poetry," "the key-pattern on a Greek vase may be beautiful, but it is less beautiful, less satisfying, and less conclusive a test of artistic ability than the composition of satyrs and mænads struggling about the centre."

And as we come to a clearer understanding of the poet's method and his work, we are almost tempted to continue his apt metaphor; to say to the artist: the images so wrought upon the body of the vase—the mænad, poised for ever, quietly for all the swirl of draperies and of loosened head-band, or the satyr for ever lifting his vine-wreathed cup—are satisfying and indeed perfect. But how much more for the lover of beauty is the wine within the great jar beautiful—how much more than the direct image to him are the images suggested by shadow and light, the flicker of the purple wine, the glint across the yellow, the depth of the crimson and red? Who would stand gazing at a satyr and a mænad, however adroit the composition of fluttering garment and poised winecup when the wine itself within the great jar stands waiting for him?

For it is no static vision that Mr. Fletcher seeks to give us in his series of "Symphonies." He uses the direct image, it is true, but he seems to use it as a means of evoking other and vaguer images—a pebble, as it were, dropped into a quiet pool, in order to start across the silent water, wave on wave of light, of colour, of sound.

His poetry is not static, as I say—it is moving, whirling, drifting.

It is the whirling of flowers, of boats, of the seawater, of rain slanting and beating, of birds swaying and drifting, of peonies springing like rockets, of rhododendrons, of orange-blossoms dashed with rain, seeming to me to be swaying above water, where again their broken reflections swirl among scattered images of straining clouds. It is the swirling of snow, of fireflies, of forest trees. It is the drift and ripple of grass, and with it again, the flowers in the grass.

In grimmer moods, it is the swirl of guns, cannon, terror, destruction. And through it all, it is the soul or mind or inspiration of the poet, knowing within itself its problems, unanswerable; its visions, cramped and stifled; the bitterness of its own insufficiency. Knowing indeed not whence it cometh and whither it goeth, but flaunting in the face of its own ignorance, its own undaunted quest. (pp. 183-84)

> *H. D., in a review of "Goblins and Pagodas," in* The Egoist, *Vol. III, No. 12, December, 1916, pp. 183-84.*

AMY LOWELL   (essay date 1917)

[*Lowell was the leading proponent of Imagism in American poetry. Like the Symbolists before her, some of whom she examined in* Six French Poets *(1915), Lowell experimented with free verse forms. Influenced by Ezra Pound, Lowell's poetry exhibited the new style of Imagism, consisting of clear and precise*

*rhetoric, exact rendering of images, and greater metrical free-
dom. Although she was popular in her time, standard evaluations of Lowell accord her more importance as a promoter of
new artistic ideas than as a poet in her own right. In the following excerpt, she surveys Fletcher's early work, highlighting
major poems and significant discussions of methodology from
Fletcher's prefaces.]*

I think Mr. Fletcher is hardly fair to his early work in his consideration of these books. With much that was jejune, they
nevertheless contained some very interesting things. An attempt, in which he followed the French poet, Arthur Rimbaud, to render the sounds of vowels in colour, achieves, to
my mind, a more satisfactory result than Rimbaud's poem.
Still, of course, ["The Vowels"] was something of an imitation. (p. 291)

It is a purely arbitrary thing to give vowels colour values, unless the colours can be made to spring naturally from words
containing these vowels. In the piquant charm of such unexpected relations lies the whole reason for such a suggestion
in a work of art. Mr. Fletcher is a more original poet than
Arthur Rimbaud, and has a finer ear. He justifies his colours
at the very outset in

> A, flaming caravans of day advancing with stately
>   art

and holds it admirably throughout. Those vowel sounds
which are unlike the particular letter in question are so managed as either to remain subordinate:

> O, crimson clarion horn that echoes on in the bold
> Old omnipotence of power;

or else to accord so perfectly that they enhance the effect
rather than detract from it:

> U, torrid bassoons and flutes that murmur without
>   repose.

The poem is a properly rounded whole, the ends join to make
a complete conception. The vowels have a use in themselves
as building material, and as such the poet leaves them.

Undoubtedly, the initial suggestion of Mr. Fletcher's poem
came from Arthur Rimbaud's ["Voyelles"]. But poets have
ever been a light-fingered gentry in this respect, and Time,
with a complete indifference to moral considerations, invariably awards the spoils to the victor.

It is possible to trace the influence of various poets in all these
early volumes, as is natural in the work of a young man. The
fault lay, not in writing them, but in publishing them. Mr.
Fletcher is curiously unselective always. He is constantly
progressing, and has scant sympathy for the phase just left
behind. (pp. 295-96)

In a very interesting preface [to **Irradiations—Sand and
Spray**], the poet argued in favour of *vers libre,* and for the first
time in recent years, made an attempt to analyze it. He says:

> The basis of English poetry is rhythm, or, as some
> would prefer to call it, cadence. This rhythm is ob-
> tained by mingling stressed and unstressed sylla-
> bles. Stress may be produced by accent. It may—
> and often is—produced by what is known as quan-
> tity, the breath required to pronounce certain sylla-
> bles being more than is required on certain others.
> However it be produced, it is precisely this insis-
> tence upon cadence, upon the rhythm of the line
> when spoken, which sets poetry apart from prose,

and not—be it said at the outset—a certain way of
printing, with a capital letter at the beginning of
each line, or an insistence upon end-rhymes.

> Now this rhythm can be made the same in every
> line of the poem. This was the aim of Alexander
> Pope, for instance. My objection to this method is
> that it is both artificial and unmusical. In the case
> of the eighteenth century men, it gave the effect of
> a perfectly balanced pattern like a minuet or fugue.
> In the case of the modern imitator of Kipling or
> Masefield, it gives the effect of monotonous rag-
> time. In neither case does it offer full scope for emo-
> tional development.

> I maintain that poetry is capable of as many grada-
> tions in cadence as music is in time. We can have
> a rapid group of syllables—what is called a line—
> succeeded by a slow heavy one; like the swift scur-
> rying of the wave and the sullen dragging of itself
> away. Or we can gradually increase or decrease our
> tempo, creating accelerando and rallentando ef-
> fects. Or we can follow a group of rapid lines with
> a group of slow ones, or a single slow, or vice versa.
> Finally, we can have a perfectly even and unaltered
> movement throughout if we desire to be monoto-
> nous.

> The good poem is that in which all these effects are
> properly used to convey the underlying emotions of
> its author, and that which welds all these emotions
> into a work of art by the use of dominant motif,
> subordinate themes, proportionate treatment, repe-
> tition, variation,—what in music is called develop-
> ment, reversal of rôles, and return. In short, the
> good poem fixes a free emotion, or a free range of
> emotions, into an inevitable and artistic whole. The
> real secret of the greatest English poets lies not in
> their views on life,—which were, naturally, only
> those which every sane man is obliged to hold,—
> but in their profound knowledge of their craft,
> whereby they were enabled to put forth their views
> in perfect form. Each era of man has its unique and
> self-sufficing range of expression and experience,
> and therefore every poet must seek anew for him-
> self, out of the language medium at his disposal,
> rhythms which are adequate and forms which are
> expressive of his own unique personality.

This was at once an explanation and a challenge. It was taken
as both, but now that the opposition has largely died away,
we can read it quietly and perceive its excellent logic and sensible exegesis.

For the book itself, it is very difficult to classify these poems,
even to describe them. Here is imagination only, the quintessence of it. Mr. Fletcher has a fertility and vigour which is
wholly remarkable.

I can conceive of an unimaginative person saying that they
can make neither head nor tail of these poems. I say that I
can conceive of such a thing. But for me, and for many like
me, they must stand as inspiring interpretations of moods.
Possibly that is their best analysis: Mr. Fletcher's poems are
moods, expressed in the terms of nature, plus a highly fanci-
ful point of view. I admit that that confuses rather than explains, but Mr. Fletcher's poems have an organic quality
which defies explanation. They are as refreshing as an October wind, and as elusive.

That is it. Go out on a windy Autumn morning and try to
describe the wind. It will slap you and push you, it will flap

away in front of you and scurry over the sky above you. You can feel all this, you can experience the wind, so to speak, but describe it you cannot. Well, Mr. Fletcher can. Does he do so by analogy? A little. Does he name things directly? Seldom. How does he do it? I do not know. I can show you, but I cannot define. This is a description of rain. "Description" is not the right word, of course; it is really an expressing of the effect of a rainy day upon him.

VII

> Flickering of incessant rain
> On flashing pavements:
> Sudden scurry of umbrellas:
> Bending, recurved blossoms of the storm.
>
> The winds come clanging and clattering
> From long white highroads whipping in ribbons up
>   summits:
> They strew upon the city gusty wafts of apple-
>   blossom,
> And the rustling of innumerable translucent leaves.
>
> Uneven tinkling, the lazy rain
> Dripping from the eaves.

Could anything be better? We see the rain, we feel it, and we smell the earthiness which all Spring rain has. The first three lines, with the flickering rain on the pavements and the scurrying umbrellas, are exact description, of course. But the "bending, recurved blossoms of the storm" is a wild imaginative flight. And how well it makes us see those round, shining umbrella-tops! The next line is straightforward poetry—"clanging" and "clattering" are good words for the wind. But what about it coming "whipping in ribbons up summits"? That is certainly not descriptive, unless we assume that the city is built upon a series of hill-tops. No, it is another imaginative leap, and an absolutely original one, for the effect is got in a new way.

The same thing is true of the next two lines, for obviously no apple-blossoms are really blown into the city from the distant orchards, but in this way the poet has got the earthy smell into his wind. The last two lines are a marvel of exact description, with only the adjective "lazy" to unite them to the imaginative treatment of the middle of the poem.

I have said enough, I think, to show Mr. Fletcher's unusual technique. But let us make no mistake, this is more than technique; it is a manner of seeing and feeling. (pp. 298-302)

Mr. Fletcher's observation is very minute and exact. This is the more remarkable when we think how often he must have to subdue his imagination to let reality print itself upon him with the force which it does. He sees a sea-fog creeping up a river:

> In the grey skirts of the fog seamews skirl desolate-
>   ly,
> And flick like bits of paper propelled by a wind
> About the flabby sails of a departing ship
> Crawling slowly down the low reaches
> Of the river.

The poet must have watched the inconsequential flutterings of gulls about a boat very carefully to think of that simile of blown bits of paper.

In the poems I have quoted, there is a great variation of rhythms. No one is more absolute master of the rhythms of *vers libre* than is Mr. Fletcher. So much is this true, indeed,

that an Englishman has written a paper upon this side of his work alone.

The following is a most beautiful translation into a scene of that vague feeling of unrest which French eighteenth century physicians called "la maladie de l'après-midi" ["afternoon sickness"]:

I

> The spattering of the rain upon pale terraces
> Of afternoon is like the passing of a dream
> Amid the roses shuddering 'gainst the wet green
>   stalks
> Of the streaming trees—the passing of the wind
> Upon the pale lower terraces of my dream
> Is like the crinkling of the wet grey robes
> Of the hours that come to turn over the urn
> Of the day and spill its rainy dream.
> Vague movement over the puddled terraces;
> Heavy gold pennons—a pomp of solemn gardens
> Half hidden under the liquid veil of Spring:
> Far trumpets like a vague rout of faded roses
> Burst 'gainst the wet green silence of distant forests:
> A clash of cymbals—then the swift swaying foot-
>   steps
> Of the wind that undulates along the languid ter-
>   races.
> Pools of rain—the vacant terraces
> Wet, chill and glistening
> Toward the sunset beyond the broken doors of
>   today.

The slow, languorous rhythm of that poem greatly heightens its mood of futile melancholy. It is all in the choice of words, and the reader will note that Mr. Fletcher pays as much attention to his verbs as to his adjectives. The use of "spattering," in the first line, gives at the very start the note of desolation, heightened by the adjective "pale." For this matter of verbs: the wet, grey robes "crinkle," the trumpets "burst," the wind "undulates," and this last is again strengthened by an adjective, when the poet speaks of "languid" terraces. There are beautiful, still lines, like

> . . . the wet green silence of distant forests:

and this marvel of dignified gloom:

> . . . a pomp of solemn gardens
> Half hidden under the liquid veil of Spring.

Slow, stately, the movement holds to the end. (pp. 303-06)

Another fancy . . . is the following:

XV

> O, seeded grass, you army of little men
> Crawling up the long slope with quivering, quick
>   blades of steel:
> You who storm millions of graves, tiny green tenta-
>   cles of Earth,
> Interlace yourselves tightly over my heart,
> And do not let me go:
> For I would lie here forever and watch with one eye
> The pilgrimaging ants in your dull, savage jungles,
> The while with the other I see the stiff lines of the
>   slope
> Break in mid-air, a wave surprisingly arrested,
> And above them, wavering, dancing, bodiless,
>   colourless, unreal,
> The long thin lazy fingers of the heat.

It cannot be doubted by any one reading that poem that here

we have a new idiom, a new manner of seeing, a new method of interpretation. The old thoughts and attitudes are irrevocably departed. There is no ancient animus here to cause bitterness and regret. Mr. Fletcher is conscious of no necessity to be other than he is. This is strong, nervous work, untiring in its creative vision. For its technical effects, there are so many that I shall only ask the reader to notice carefully the last two lines.

Mr. Fletcher is a virtuoso of sound effects. These passages from the poems just read will prove what I mean:

> Amid the vermilion pavilions, against the jade balustrades
>
> • • • • •
>
> The clouds are their crimson howdah-canopies.

He is exceedingly fond of internal rhymes, and in his hands these effects are more than "un bijou d'un sou," ["a penny bauble"], as Verlaine called rhyme.

This is very strange, as in regular metrical verse his rhymes are often far from happy. It is as if the knowledge that he had to rhyme took away the faculty. Where it is not imperative, it is often most cunningly accomplished. But his sound effects are frequently got without the aid of rhyme, for instance:

> A clash of cymbals—then the swift swaying footsteps
> Of the wind.
>
> (pp. 307-09)

Mr. Fletcher has eminently the faults of his qualities. Such a fecundity of creation naturally leads to the production of much that is below the level of his best, and one of his marked traits is the uncritical, unselective habit of mind I have already mentioned. He has a curious desire to write in series. As we examine his work, we shall constantly observe this tendency. The method has certain advantages, but its disadvantages are peculiarly unfortunate in his case, for, when it comes to publication, he wishes to include all of any given series, good and bad together. The result is a volume in which the plums are scattered and lost in packing. I think it is largely for this reason that his work has not yet received the recognition it deserves. (p. 310)

In [*Goblins and Pagodas*], even more than in **Irradiations,** the longing for poems in sequence leads to a plethora of one sort of thing, and numbs the reader's interest by an oversameness of effect. In a long and intricate preface, Mr. Fletcher explained his method. One interesting passage will condense it for us:

> A book lies on my desk. It has a red binding and is badly printed on cheap paper. I have had this book with me for several years. Now, suppose I were to write a poem on this book, how would I treat the subject?
>
> If I were a poet following in the main the Victorian tradition, I should write my poem altogether about the contents of this book and its author. My poem would be essentially a criticism of the subject-matter of the book. I should state at length how that subject-matter had affected me. In short, what the reader would obtain from this sort of poem would be my sentimental reaction towards certain ideas and tendencies in the work of another.
>
> If I were a realist poet, I should write about the book's external appearance. I should expatiate on the red binding, the bad type, the ink stain on page sixteen. I should complain, perhaps, of my poverty at not being able to buy a better edition, and conclude with a gibe at the author for not having realized the sufferings of the poor.
>
> Neither of these ways, however, of writing about this book possesses any novelty, and neither is essentially my own way. My own way of writing about it would be as follows:—
>
> I should select out of my life the important events connected with my ownership of this book, and strive to write of them in terms of the volume itself, both as regards subject-matter and appearance. In other words, I should link up my personality and the personality of the book, and make each a part of the other. In this way I should strive to evoke a soul out of this piece of inanimate matter, a something characteristic and structural inherent in this inorganic form which is friendly to me and responds to my mood.

In this preface, also, he maps out his series of symphonies as the stages in the life of an artist. This idea is not new, and we need not pause upon it here; in fact, these poems seem rather forced into the design than written in accordance with it. The symphonies themselves are the arresting thing, each one in itself, and each built upon a dominant colour.

This is what I have called, in the preface to my own book, *Men, Women and Ghosts,* the unrelated method. As linked to the programme of the artist's life, these colour symphonies cease to be unrelated, but taken each by itself they for the most part follow it.

By the unrelated method, I mean a description which takes trees, houses, people, all the many parts of a landscape, merely as they appear to the eye or ear, or both, and with no hint of the "pathetic fallacy" intruding itself. Already, in **"London Excursion,"** Mr. Fletcher had experimented with this method. In these symphonies, it finds much fuller expression. (pp. 311-12)

Throughout these poems, no attempt is made to follow regular symphonic form, the title seems to have been given merely to indicate a certain musical, rhapsodic treatment.

These symphonies are not all of equal excellence. Each has interesting passages, but those most certainly successful are **"Blue Symphony," "Solitude in the City (Symphony in Black and Gold)," "Poppies of the Red Year (A Symphony in Scarlet),"** and the **"Green Symphony."** . . . In the less contained of these poems, the poet occasionally loses himself in vagueness, his words run into a bright mist, and cloud over the articulateness of his thought. Mannerism rides him at times to the detriment of his work, but the four poems I have named are singularly free from this fault.

I have not space to pursue the course of these symphonies at greater length. Mr. Fletcher is so rich in original conceptions and treatments that I can only indicate his work by outlines.

The anthology, *Some Imagist Poets,* 1916, contained a group of Arizona poems—they are the burgeoning of that charm which the West has for him—and a little vignette of skaters:

> **"The Skaters"**
>
> To A. D. R.
>
> Black swallows swooping or gliding

In a flurry of entangled loops and curves;
The skaters skim over the frozen river.
And the grinding click of their skates as they im-
　　pinge upon the surface,
Is like the brushing together of thin wing-tips of sil-
　　ver.

Contrast that bright little picture with this grotesque from "Ghosts of an Old House":

"An Oak"

Hoar mistletoe
Hangs in clumps
To the twisted boughs
Of this lonely tree.

Beneath its roots I often thought treasure was bur-
　　ied:
For the roots had enclosed a circle.

But when I dug beneath them,
I could only find great black ants
That attacked my hands.

When at night I have the nightmare,
I always see the eyes of ants
Swarming from a mouldering box of gold.

Or with this other, whimsical and weird, full of strange suggestion:

"The Yardstick"

Yardstick that measured out so many miles of
　　cloth,
Yardstick that covered me,
I wonder do you hop of nights
Out to that still hill-cemetery,
And up and down go measuring
A clayey grave for me?

The poet's German and Danish ancestry is interestingly in evidence in that little piece. Here is the goblin quality of Hoffmann's *Die Serapionsbrüder.* We feel a background of folklore, of gnomes and pixies, and fused with it is the allegorical seriousness of Hans Christian Andersen. This Teutonic and Scandinavian mysticism persists long. . . . [It is a] remarkable atavism in Mr. Fletcher, enduring, as it has, through nearly a hundred years of changed environment. (pp. 318-21)

Now let us turn to Mr. Fletcher's latest volume, *Japanese Prints.* . . . In the preface to this book, Mr. Fletcher analyzes the Japanese *tanka* and *hokku* forms, and sketches lightly the history of Japanese prosody, and then analyzes that chief quality of all Japanese verse—psychological suggestion. The modern poets are becoming more and more indebted to the Japanese for a realization of the value of this effect. To quote a moment from Mr. Fletcher's preface:

> Let us take an example. The most famous hokku that Basho wrote, might be literally translated thus:
>
> An old pond / And the sound of a frog leaping / Into the water.
>
> This means nothing to the Western mind. But to the Japanese it means all the beauty of such a life of retirement and contemplation as Basho practised. If we permit our minds to supply the detail Basho deliberately omitted, we see the mouldering temple enclosure, the sage himself in meditation, the ancient piece of water, and the sound of a frog's leap—passing vanity—slipping into the silence of

eternity. The poem has three meanings. First, it is a statement of fact. Second, it is an emotion deduced from that. Third, it is a sort of spiritual allegory. And all this Basho has given us in his seventeen syllables.

It is perhaps hardly necessary to state here that Japanese prosody is based upon alternate lines of five and seven syllables. The *tanka* is a poem of thirty-one syllables arranged as follows: 5, 7, 5, 7, 7. The *hokku* is a truncated *tanka* in which the last two lines are suppressed; it consists, therefore, of seventeen syllables: 5, 7, 5. Mr. Fletcher explains the peculiar adaptability of the *hokku* to suggestion in this manner:

> It must always be understood that there is an implied continuation to every Japanese hokku. The concluding hemistich, whereby the hokku becomes the tanka, is existent in the writer's mind, but never uttered.

Understanding very well the method by which the Japanese obtained these effects, he nevertheless realizes that a purely syllabic form is not well adapted to a highly accented language such as English. It should be said also that Japanese words, being capable of more than one construction, make it possible to convey more than one meaning by a single word. This leads to a sort of serious punning, and by these double meanings a poem of seventeen syllables can be made to contain many more. Mr. Fletcher says: "Good hokkus cannot be written in English. The thing we have to follow is not a form, but a spirit." Speaking of the volume itself, he adds: "As for the poems themselves, they are not Japanese at all, but all illustrate something of the charm I have found in Japanese poetry and art."

Mr. Fletcher is right in saying that these poems are not written absolutely in the Japanese idiom, but still they have a distinct perfume of Japan about them, and once again prove the poet's sensitiveness to atmosphere. This, to an occidental mind, has certainly the charm of Japan:

"The Young Daimyo"

When he first came out to meet me,
He had just been girt with the two swords;
And I found he was far more interested in the glit-
　　ter of their hilts
And did not even compare my kiss to a cherry-
　　blossom.

(pp. 336-39)

Where these poems sometimes fail is exactly in [the] matter of feeling. Mr. Fletcher loses sight of the fact that only the most simple language, the clearest image, is in keeping with the *hokku* form. The poem must be of the most limpid clarity to gain the full effect of the underlying suggestion. It is the contrast which gives the *hokku* its piquancy. So, when Mr. Fletcher writes:

"Lovers Embracing"

Force and yielding meet together
An attack is half repulsed:
Shafts of broken sunlight dissolving
Convolutions of torpid cloud.

he sacrifices the peculiar Japanese atmosphere. That poem is in Mr. Fletcher's most personal idiom, but it is not in the least in the idiom of Japan. From this point of view, the most successful poem in the book is

"Moods"

A poet's moods:
Fluttering butterflies in the rain.

That is at once Mr. Fletcher and Japan. It is brief and clear, and the suggestion never becomes statement, but floats, a nimbus, over the short, sharp lines. (pp. 340-41)

Mr. Fletcher is a virtuoso of words, and sometimes this faculty runs away with him. Some of his symphonies, some of the poems in *Irradiations,* are heaped too full of words, the changes he rings are too heavy, he confuses too many colours, too many sounds. His enormous fecundity is responsible for this. It is hard for him to curb his exuberance. Nature has given him much, and it is difficult for him to put himself to school. His books would gain by being pruned; but, as I said in the beginning, he lacks the selective instinct. It is largely for this reason that he is not yet esteemed as he should be. But, for the discerning eye, no living poet has more distinction of vision or of style. In him, indeed, we see the beginning of that new order of which I have so often spoken. To the poet, he is a real teacher, indicating new directions, opening up untrodden ways of thought. (p. 342)

> *Amy Lowell, "The Imagists: 'H. D.' and John Gould Fletcher," in her* Tendencies in Modern American Poetry, *The Macmillan Company, 1917, pp. 235-343.*

MARK VAN DOREN (essay date 1921)

[*Van Doren was one of the most prolific men of letters in twentieth-century American writing. His work includes poetry (for which he won a Pulitzer Prize in 1940), novels, short stories, drama, criticism, social commentary, and the editing of a number of popular anthologies. Van Doren's criticism is aimed at the general reader, rather than the scholar or specialist, and is noted for its lively perception and wide interest. Like his poetry and fiction, his criticism consistently examines the inner, idealistic life of the individual. In the words of Carlos Baker, Van Doren brings to his best work "warmth of epithet, a crisp precision of definition, and a luminousness of poetic insight." In the following essay, Van Doren sees in Fletcher's* Breakers and Granite *the strengths and weaknesses of Imagism.*]

[*Breakers and Granite*] is a collected edition of such old or new poems by Mr. Fletcher as lend themselves to inclusion in an imagist's panorama of America. The panorama begins with **"The Arrival,"** dated May, 1920, an impression of New York harbor after Europe and the Atlantic, and proceeds as if by rediscovery through Manhattan, New England, Chicago, the lower Mississippi, the Old South, the Far West, and the Arkansas River to a concluding "American Symphony" which itself concludes with deservedly the best known poem of Mr. Fletcher's to date, **"Lincoln."** That the rediscovery is fictitious—that many parts of the panorama were composed as far back as 1914 or 1915—does not matter if the net result is interesting, and the net result is extraordinarily interesting.

The panorama is interesting for the obvious reason that section after section of it is beautiful, but it is interesting also for the reason that it is the work of a deliberate and conscientious modern artist in words, and so is an important document in modern poetry. As clearly as any one volume of recent years it reveals the whole uncanny strength of imagism—its dauntless definiteness of phrase, its concentration, its care, its surface accuracy. The most reflective member of the imagist group who issued their manifesto in 1915, Mr. Fletcher has continued to confront a many-sided world with a sincere imagination, applying himself modestly, collectedly, and coolly to the business of registering beauty.

Yet if his book reveals imagism's strength, it reveals more clearly its weakness. If one was not convinced before, one will be convinced now that imagism not only had an inferior aim but lacked the very means of achieving it. That aim was visual truth and nothing but visual truth—about one-tenth of poetry—and the single technical problem proposed was the problem of producing effects which should not be "blurred"—a problem of which instinctive, first-rate poets have seldom if ever been so much as conscious. The aim of profound poetry now or at any time is less to see than to understand—to see, certainly, but to see with eyes unencumbered by prisms that intensify the trees and dissolve the forest. Good poetry makes us see wholes, and imagism wishes to be good poetry; but imagism so far has given us only hard, clear parts that do not blend. Sharp-sightedness has become short-sightedness, and richness has had to do for depth. Mr. Fletcher, wherever and to the extent that he has been an imagist proper, proves all the foregoing true. There is scarcely a line of his, or an image, which is not admirable, but there are many poems which fail of great effect. Applying the principles of other arts to poetry never makes it definite. Rather it makes it vague, and Mr. Fletcher, on the whole too much the painter in the present volume, is on the whole too vague. His air is often the air of one who talks abstractedly to himself before an easel; his concern is generally with the formulas of description, with the jargon of design. In no such way does a poet get power. Aloofness and fastidiousness may discover beauty, but they rarely can hold it till we come.

The error of the imagists after all was the error of supposing poetry to be a matter solely of space. If poetry is solely anything, it is solely time, and had Lessing not demonstrated the proposition in a treatise Mr. Fletcher would have convinced us of it by example. For his three best poems have more than mere extension; they have depth. They start and speed the imagination in the only direction that literature can go—backward, forward. Their magnitude is the only magnitude which poetry can assume, the magnitude of duration. The first of the three, called **"The Empty House,"** contains just one idea—the definitive wisdom of a dwelling which has served its turn—but that is enough. More ideas, more standing off, more shaping and tracing, might have left a more delicate creation, but the effect would have been to freeze the imagination. The other two pieces are great in part because they are like Whitman. In **"The Great River"** and in **"Lincoln"** Mr. Fletcher has started up out of his little "water-color ecstasy," has laid aside his "delicate fan of cool notes blending," and has plunged with Whitman into the stream of mighty time. The Mississippi becomes great for him not because it is wide or long but because it is old; his grasp, his faculties, his soul expand and roll before them masses of emotion and thought which imagism never dreamed of. Lincoln becomes great for the poet because Lincoln has character, and character, like a tree, is a product of maturing time.

> Ungainly, laboring, huge,
> The wind of the north has twisted and gnarled its
>   branches;
> Yet in the heat of mid-summer days, when thunder
>   clouds ring the horizon,
> A nation of men shall rest beneath its shade. . . .

Down to the granite of patience
These roots swept, knotted fibrous roots, prying,
   piercing, seeking,
And drew from the living rock and the living wa-
   ters about it
The red sap to carry upwards to the sun.

Imagism must soon go out. Why not on some such wave as this?

Mark Van Doren, "Poetic Space and Time," in The
Nation, *New York, Vol. CXII, No. 2910, April 13,
1921, p. 562.*

CONRAD AIKEN (essay date 1921)

[*An American man of letters best known for his poetry, Aiken
was deeply influenced by the psychological and literary theories
of Sigmund Freud, Havelock Ellis, Edgar Allan Poe, and
Henri Bergson, among others, and is considered a master of literary stream of consciousness. In reviews noted for their perceptiveness and barbed wit, Aiken exercised his theory that "criticism is really a branch of psychology." His critical position, according to Rufus A. Blanshard, "insists that the traditional notions of 'beauty' stand corrected by what we now know about
the psychology of creation and consumption. Since a work of
art is rooted in the personality, conscious and unconscious, of
its creator, criticism should deal as much with those roots as
with the finished flower." In the following excerpt, Aiken maintains that inspiration rather than craft accounts for Fletcher's
best poetry.*]

Balzac once remarked, "Without genius I am lost." One may
easily make the mistake of assuming that there could not conceivably be an artist who might not say of himself the same
thing. The remark applies with particular force to that sort
of artist whose work is "charged," who is at his best when
his pages have "flight," whose method, in other words, is in
the nature of half-deliberately guided improvisation. It hardly applies, if it applies at all, to the calmer type, the builder-
artist Trollope, for example. Nor does it particularly apply
to the mere ornamentalist, the sort of poet who learns by patience and application how to say pretty things in a pretty
way, to wreathe them into pleasantly foliate patterns. Compulsion, of a psychotic nature, is in such cases at a minimum,
and the writer is free in a sense in which the other type of artist is not. We do not expect him to give us any phoenix of art,
plumed with sheer brilliance, certainly, but we do not expect
him, either, to fall very far below the moderately good. He
is a craftsman, and his craft sustains him.

More interesting by far is the sort of artist who is more creator than craftsman. Mr. John Gould Fletcher, who continues erratically to hold one of the highest places among contemporary American poets, is as striking a case of that as we
could find. If we include his new book, *Breakers and Granite*,
Mr. Fletcher has now published ten books of verse: he is a
prolific writer. To the first five of these books Mr. Fletcher
now permits only a subterranean existence. They are not in
circulation, and presumably he considers them mere juvenilia. There was little verse in them that could be called distinguished. It was in *Irradiations* that Mr. Fletcher first found
himself—something happened to him, something to which
perhaps he alone, if he wished, could give us the clue; something more, perhaps, than a mere exposure to the influence
of pre-contemporary French poetry or the influence of Mr.
Ezra Pound. A new sort of tactilism had been given to poetry
by the French Symbolists, and Mr. Fletcher was among the

first to take this out of the general air and make it a property
of English verse. It was a sort of tactilism to which he was
born, but for which, in the American literary scene, he would
have starved. In Paris and London he found it and grew upon
it. *Irradiations* was the flower of it; *Goblins and Pagodas* and
parts of *The Tree of Life* the fruit.

It would be an error, however, to suppose that in all this Mr.
Fletcher was deliberate or orderly. He was in a sense a happy
victim: a tree pollenated by a chance air. At the outset his
self-discovery made him drunk, he committed excesses of
color, and these excesses—in *Irradiations,* in the "Symphonies," less often in *The Tree of Life*—remain perhaps his finest achievement. These poems have, for the most part, no
moral, no "meaning," no intention—they reveal no general
attitude, preach no doctrine. Those who wish poetry to embody, among other things, the concise statement of a problem, or the formulation of an answer, may pillage these
poems in vain. All they will get is a color, a fragrance. For
if it was to the new tactilism of Mallarmé and Laforgue and
Rimbaud and Verlaine that Mr. Fletcher so richly responded,
it was to the tactilism alone: to the self-analysis, half bitter,
half sentimental, with which in French poetry this tactilism
was usually alloyed, he remained unresponsive. He took the
colorism to which it was in his case the key, and omitted the
psychology, precisely as Mr. T. S. Eliot took the psychology
and omitted the colorism; the former following Rimbaud and
Mallarmé, the latter following Verlaine and Laforgue.

Mr. Fletcher's "genius" is therefore for coloristic vividness,
primarily, and it must be remarked immediately that it is the
"genius" of Balzac's comment—without it Mr. Fletcher is
undone. He is at his best when his method is that of fierce improvisation. If the initial stimulus is one happily calculated
to draw forth the poet's richest deposits of association, and
if, moreover, those deposits have not already too often or too
precisely at one point been drawn upon, then he gives us work
which has the lustre of the "inspired." But one cannot go on
for ever being inspired—the stimulus may not be always as
strong, or it may strike at exhausted rifts. Then is one fortunate if one is craftsman as well as creator, or if one knows as
well how to write with one's eyes open as with one's eyes shut,
and in full possession, perhaps, of a wide knowledge, a rich
consciousness of experience, a myriad sympathy. But Mr.
Fletcher is not, in this regard, fortunate. When improvisation
fails him, he fails altogether. Many a newspaper poet has a
better "conscious" technique in verse than he; when he attempts to write in cold blood, his verse is irregular, colorless,
and weak. The rhythmic and verbal richness, which is overwhelming in his best "inspired" work, at such moments escapes him wholly, and one would suppose the work to have
been by a different hand. One characteristic alone remains—
rhetorical speed. Great is the temptation for a poet, whom
habit rather than the compulsion of a theme urges toward
composition, to echo that part of his own manner which is
suggestible by the word "speed." But this speed, excellent
when it is the heat, the flame of the theme itself, becomes,
when superimposed upon a theme, a mere trick of rhetoric—
it is a simulation of excitement, irritating because we can find
nothing in the theme, or rather in the poet's reaction to it, out
of which the excitement might properly spring. We feel the
hollowness; we feel that the poet is goading himself, that he
is pretending to an intensity of feeling which he has on other
occasions possessed, and would like to possess again, but to
which he has lost the key.

Breakers and Granite, like *The Tree of Life,* shows Mr. Fletcher often in this predicament. There are fine things in it—notably the experiments in "polyphonic prose," such as **"Clipper Ships,"** and **"The Old South."** It is well for us to be reminded that these antedated Miss Lowell's "Can Grande's Castle." But the book as a whole does not satisfy. It is true that Mr. Fletcher's attempt to summarize America, past and present, in a series of poems in verse and prose lends a solidity and a fragmentary grandeur to this book which one cannot find in his others—one's historical sense is refreshed by it, certainly; but despite one's pleasure in this and in several poems on the Mississippi and the Mexican Quarter, and in the Lincoln poem, one comes away from the book with the feeling that Mr. Fletcher has labored heroically at a theme not designed to do him justice. Without color, to paraphrase Balzac, Mr. Fletcher is lost, for he has nothing, or little, to fall back upon. He has not the self-awareness of the good psychologist, his motives remain dark to him; and yet, on the other hand, he is too egocentric to observe widely the external world. One turns from *Breakers and Granite* to the poems by Mr. Fletcher in the recently published *Miscellany of American Poetry* with relief, for in those was not only an achievement, vivid, magical, and swift, but a promise—a hint of an earth-mysticism which might conceivably prove, for Mr. Fletcher, a new well of color. (pp. 210-13)

> Conrad Aiken, "John Gould Fletcher," in his Collected Criticism, *Oxford University Press, Inc., 1968, pp. 210-13.*

R. P. BLACKMUR   (essay date 1936)

[*Blackmur is considered one of the leading American literary critics of the twentieth century. His early essays on the poetry of such contemporaries as T. S. Eliot, W. B. Yeats, Wallace Stevens, and Ezra Pound were immediately recognized for their acute and exacting attention to diction, metaphor, and symbol. Blackmur's belief that criticism also represented an art form in its own right led him to an increasingly poetic, impressionistic style best demonstrated in his posthumously published lecture series* Anni Mirabiles 1921-25: Reason in the Madness of Letters *(1967). In the following excerpt, Blackmur criticizes the lack of depth and meaning in Fletcher's* XXIV Elegies.]

It is a hard thing to write a man of talent, sincerity, and verve down to the level where his work leaves him. Yet the easier approach of accepting his work at its face value is more disheartening in the end; instead of a small thing to keep we have an inflated thing to let go. It is the old question, with Mr. Fletcher, of how much intention can outrun ability, how much mere feeling can replace the barrier of form, how much, finally, words used conventionally can substitute for the force of idiom—and still leave a sound body of poetry. If we take Mr. Fletcher at his declared value, and try to achieve it for ourselves, we shall find, I think, that he has failed [in *XXIV Elegies*] by going too far on all three counts. Taken solemnly, his poems are inflations of his private experience: you feel what he feels, not what the object felt like. Taken seriously, for what there is in them, what stays in the mind, we have again and again to recognize, strikingly deployed, the elements of poetry presided over by a genuinely poetic figure. There is hardly more in many than a greater reputation; and it makes an amount, with a value, large enough to keep if not great enough to incorporate; there is always the possibility, the suggestion, the fragment—if never the achieved composition.

The causes of his substantial failure lie partly in his mode of using language and partly in the personal relation between his language and his themes. Mr. Fletcher's language is rhetorical, loose, and unsyntactical. It would never stand up as prose; without rhythm and line structure it would seem only a vocabulary. At his worst he takes words by their colored covers and opens and shuts them loudly. At his best he does not put much meaning into his words, only colors them with his moods; hence it takes a great many words piling up, clattering, singing, to collect a semblance of the meaning that was in him. Never concerned with what words force into each other from their insides, his words change little and are a good deal alike in their different appearances. He takes—and this is his rhetoric—the nearest statement, image, or phrase to be the ultimate. Master his vocabulary and you have mastered his rhetoric. When it succeeds, his rhetoric is fresh because it is right with the usual poetic rightness; but it is not right because it is fresh, or organic, or inexhaustibly alive. The words clatter, they do not clash.

As with the words so with the larger units of expression. There is nothing to burrow in to find and feel the meaning out. There is more meaning immediately, at first glance, than can ever be found on subsequent intimacy; that is because the general intent, not the specific datum, is viable. You do not anywhere weigh these poems; you run through them. If you run through a lot of them you will get quite a lot of Mr. Fletcher himself, a generous, brilliant, prodigal lot; and you will come to know what obsessed him, drove him—in love and death, machinery and the sea, cities and landscapes—to write verse.

His poems are not objects but media. Within themselves the parts do not modify and compose, do not share and discover and brim with an inner light; they make a light-shot procession, almost a mob, that cannot be added up. You get the breathlessness but not the breath of experience. Take as good a line as any: "God is the thunderbolt that falls, when the heart otherwise would be broken." It is best in its breathless immediacy. Look for the breath, its ultimate quake and savor, and it will have been stopped; it was never there, in the poem.

As Mr. Fletcher is to his language so his language is to his themes. The relation is personal and immediate, and there is no barrier of form. Or his form is of that looseness that it exists only in the degree that it cannot help itself. Mr. Fletcher is a personal poet in that it is the prevalent sense of his personality that animates his poems and alone gives them form. As the poems are never made objects, so they never become their own subjects but remain in both respects fragments preserved of their author. The striking result—always to be observed of this mode of language—that his subjects fit into words as given; the subjects neither add to the life of the language nor stretch its scope, nor does the language absorb the subjects and become idiom. Thus the poems are versions, not discoveries. (pp. 344-47)

> R. P. Blackmur, "Versions of Fletcher," in Poetry, *Vol. XLVII, No. VI, March, 1936, pp. 344-47.*

EUGENE HAUN   (essay date 1951)

[*In the following excerpt, Haun provides a general consideration of Fletcher's poetry.*]

I am trying to scrape together enough poems to

make another volume—about the fourteenth I have published in my lifetime! I suppose I have written more poetry than all the Fugitives put together (but I can't say that my work is better—because so far as sales or reputation goes, I haven't any). I want to keep on, though.

So wrote John Gould Fletcher, in a letter dated April 29, 1930, from London, to Donald Davidson. His supposition was very nearly correct, for by the time of his death twenty years later, he had published some eighteen volumes of poetry, to say nothing of those poems which appeared in magazines and were never collected, or of those which were never published at all. Nor does this reckoning take into account the large body of his critical writings, social as well as artistic. In addition, his letters would have to be enumerated literally by thousands.

To have brought forth so much, a man must have labored day in and day out. One must admire the effort, but the effort of so much production is plethoric. Confronted with eighteen volumes of the careful poetry of John Crowe Ransom (a condition which might come to pass if Mr. Ransom should live two hundred years longer), one might feel the same consternation; but, even in reading single poems of Fletcher, one is likely to feel that they are too long, that they could have done with revision and pruning. Good lines are undergrown with cliché; a trope which has a promising growth to begin with will become entangled in its own rhetoric; dull stanzas close with an image like a Turner sunset, an image which shows them up without illuminating them. His publication is an uncritical wilderness.

This failure adequately to judge his own work was a prime fault, but to discuss the causes of it is rather the business of the biographer than of the critic. One may not assume, however, that Fletcher was arrogantly assured of greatness, nor that he was immodest in any way. He simply was not able to estimate the comparative values of his several efforts until after a long time had elapsed; meanwhile, he would have published the work if he could. It is a natural failing among artists in any medium, but it seems to have prevailed over Fletcher's discretion to an unhappy degree. He wrote under the stress of honest emotion, but his craftsmanship was not always adequate to the demands of his vision.

Art may be, finally considered, a process, not a thing in itself. (These are merely pragmatic theses, introduced for purposes of discussion here, and by no means intended to stand as conclusive.) Art is not static; it is kinetic, or empathic. A definition of art may include the ideas of the communication and the recreation of an individual (though not necessarily esoteric) synthesis of human experience, a process to be carried on by integrating a group of symbols within a given artistic medium.

The activity involved in choosing and integrating these symbols is craft. The aesthetic success of the artist will be largely dependent upon his success as a craftsman, but craft is essentially a means and not an end. To be valid, a symbol must be a last desperate means of communication, a final effort to explicate a thought or a feeling or a complex of both, too subtle for forthright exposition; yet it should appear to evolve spontaneously from its substance. The symbol must *stand for* some aspect of the significance inherent in human experience. It is not enough for the art object merely to be beautiful. The repetition of any sensual experience, however beautiful, will

become monotonous and irritating, as the treble sing-song of a child might, if it does not signify.

The task of the artist lies then not alone nor even primarily in an attempt to perfect his craft. Perfect his craft he must, to whatever extent he may, but his fundamental effort lies in effecting his own synthesis of human experience. The artist is great in proportion to the validity of his synthesis; he is effective as an artist, after that, in proportion to the excellence of his craft. The task of the artist, as craftsman, then becomes that of finding out and integrating the symbols which will most efficiently convey his synthesis. The artist achieves his style, first by gaining an insight into human experience, then by telling, within the privilege of his medium, the truth about what he sees, as exactly and as simply as possible, unequivocally subordinating virtuosity to honesty.

The synthesis effected by Fletcher was not unworthy of a great poet. Let it be said—respectfully, and to his credit both as a man and as a poet—that Fletcher was not a minor poet who succeeded; he was a major poet who was not able successfully to carry out a major poetic effort. His view of life was consistent and profound, and the line of its development may clearly be followed from the juvenilia through his latest work. In the climacteric poem of the volume which marked the climax of his career, *The Black Rock,* he wrote:

> Have mercy upon us, O God, because the end is
>   darkness,
> Because faithless, hopeless, loveless, we yet cry out
>   to You,
> Who have deafened Your ears for eternity and will
>   never make us an answer;
> Because we have nothing left but to cry out and to
>   pass on in the darkness,
>   • • • • •
> But for one little instant, because we cry out without cause,
> Without reason, without excuse, merely because we
>   dare cry out,
> Have mercy now upon us!

Here is a key statement in the synthesis of John Gould Fletcher. Its tonic is romantic, its dominant rebellious, and its general tone tragic.

This is romanticism in the great tradition of Byron and Melville: The feeling that life is essentially tragic, that man is foredoomed, that "the end is darkness," that—though God may not be importuned—a man is yet a man: It is his glory to be able to recognize his doom, and it is his ineluctable right to protest it, to call the Creator to account, even to struggle against Him, as an angry child might struggle in the arms of his dispassionate father, knowing that his father will conquer and will furthermore restrain him from undue violence.

> With your (*sic*) outlaws, O God, let me stand up at
>   the judgment;
> With those that blasphemed You, because they
>   sought You always;
> With those who denied You because You denied
>   Yourself to them;
> With those who were broken on the great terrible
>   wheel of this earth.

This disposition towards rebellion always qualified Fletcher's pessimism, and pessimistic he was throughout his career as a poet. But it was not the pagan pessimism of Housman, nor the agnostic pessimism of Hardy, nor the pessimism of the renegade Catholic, Baudelaire. "I have never felt *comfortable* in pessimism, as has Jeffers, for instance," Fletcher once re-marked, for his was that peculiarly Protestant pessimism which causes more torment than all other kinds put together. A pagan or an agnostic pessimist may face life with an atti-tude of dignity, or an attitude which may be consciously iron-ical, or even humorous, for he is at the disposal of forces which are, as he believes, entirely impersonal. Mercy he does not ask, because he thinks there is nothing which might grant it. For the Protestant pessimist, however, the conflict is in-tensely personal, involving, as it does, not a loss of faith in the existence of an anthropomorphic god, but a loss of faith in the possibility of mediation between that Divine Personali-ty—which is omniscient, omnipresent,—and his own. His as-sumption is that God could have precluded evil; He did not; evil thrives; and God ignores its consequences to live in a state of misery which He could alleviate: The misery must be borne; there is no changing that; but it need not be borne without protest.

This note of protest sounds the pedal point in Christian trage-dy, but the protest does no good; it is simply to be made for the record, "because we dare cry out." As Fletcher visualized it, Christ Himself protested this unnecessary suffering:

> There was darkness over the earth till the ninth
> hour,
> And then those watching heard a far-off cry:
> "Eli! Eli!" it said, and it had power
> That seemed to split the solitude of sky.

Even the cry of Christ brought no relief:

> It brought the darkness nearer.

The truth was, according to Fletcher, that man's condition is hopeless, and he was not going to degrade himself by at-tempting to compromise truth.

> Humbling themselves and their immortal pride,
> Men chose the barren stone where Peter's courage
> died.

This pessimism and the rebellion consequent upon it charac-terize the whole range of his utterance, from the time when he closed **"The White Symphony"**:

> Dark graves never changing,
> White dream drifting, never changing above them:
> O that the white scroll of heaven might be rolled
> up,
> And the naked red lightning thrust at the smoul-
> dering earth!

and when he referred to the house where he was born:

> All over the house there is a sense of futility;
> Of minutes dragging slowly
> And repeating
> Some worn-out story of broken effort and desire.

It pervaded the writings of his middle years, showing up con-stantly in such poems as those previously quoted, from *The Black Rock.* In his last volume, *Burning Mountain* (1946)—which he had originally intended to call *Walking Shadow*—he was still to write:

> We hear nothing
> But a cry that mankind is betrayed; that the children must
> scatter in panic;
> The famine is moving on fast behind the fury
> Whereby the legions were battered. We have nothing;
> Nothing but a shattered hope and a stubborn

> Will to resist, and to add horror to horror.

It is not an attitude which leads to resignation. It is too per-sonal to allow detachment, without which, of course, humor is impossible. In all the poetry of Fletcher, it is very difficult to find any humor. As a poet, he took himself with great seri-ousness.

Pressed by the conflicts inherent in this attitude, however, poets have written greatly, and they might conceivably yet, for this inner struggle affords no minor theme, and men still contend so within themselves. Indeed, the problem of theodi-cy has been central in Renaissance thought, and the failure to resolve it may be one reason why our society is by now Christian in hardly any more than name. To expound the rea-sons for Fletcher's failure to deal with this theme is, again, the task of his biographer. To Fletcher, during his Imagist pe-riod, might be applied the criticism applied to Monet by Cé-zanne: He was "only an eye. But good God, what an eye!" Later, when he began to attempt to generalize upon what he saw, his craftsmanship failed him. Until the last phase of his career, he was hard put to master the essentials of conven-tional verse. He did not frequently—until that time—achieve a style unequivocally his own, nor was he often able to sustain the production of verse of consistently good quality through-out a work of any length, with the possible exceptions of *Irra-diations* and the "Symphonies," if they are to be considered unified works. Even such a consideration would be open to ready challenge, for it was in the achievement of form that Fletcher suffered his most serious lapse as a craftsman.

Other lapses there were, but they might almost be passed over as personal foibles: The inversions, the archaisms, the naive use of cliché. But the failure to achieve form one may not overlook. Not to be protested here is the lack of pattern in the verse itself; but there is not in these poems that precise integration of verse-movement, image, and idea which char-acterizes great poetry. Without it, aesthetic communication is ineffectual. With his usual vigor, Fletcher himself, in the **"Preface to Preludes and Symphonies,"** defended his poetry against the charge of metrical formlessness. Sometime later (1945), he wrote, in affirmation of a comment by a critic:

> In stating that the idea of the Symphonic structure
> came to me by accident, in **"Blue Symphony"** you
> are quite correct. But later on, I developed it delib-
> erately into a structure of four contrasting move-
> ments. Thus for instance, the poem **"Lincoln"** writ-
> ten April 19, 1916 has this sort of structure. So too
> has **"Manhattan"** in *Breakers and Granite.* Other
> poems in this book, all written before 1920, are like
> a suite, rather than a symphony; for instance, the
> "Down the Mississippi," the "Arizona Poems"—
> which deal loosely with the whole Southwest, rath-
> er than Arizona. These poems are less subjective,
> less allusive, than the Symphonies. But the musical
> research (balancing of theme with opposing theme)
> went on, in my case—and can be found in the
> *XXIV Elegies,* if not in *South Star.* J. G. F.

But this statement, too, bears the same marks of *ex post facto* rationalization noted by Amy Lowell and Edward Garnett when they examined Fletcher's prefatory claim that he had written the "Symphonies" according to a preconceived pro-gram. Are there really any formal resemblances to be noted among the poems mentioned here, as, for instance, between **"Lincoln"** and **"Manhattan"**? If there are, they are only of the most tenuous nature. The "themes" have not really the musical exactitude which he holds to be inherent in them.

Fletcher during his association with Imagism.

And how do they oppose each other? or in what manner do they contrast? Can one achieve anything like sonata-form poetry? There comes the uneasy feeling that, in such pronouncements as the one foregoing, Mr. Fletcher was really elaborating figures of speech. Only by making the most careless generalization could one say that he never achieved form in his poetry, but it is not often to be found, even in his better efforts.

If he did not often achieve form, he frequently achieved mood and manner, throughout his career, but most notably during the period of his association with the Imagists, which began when he became acquainted with Amy Lowell, and which had ended by the time of the publication of *Breakers and Granite* in 1921. It need not be assumed that his achievements at that time were the results of his association with them. By the restrictions of their craft, the Imagists were cut off from any expression of idea as such and were left dependent upon image, usually pictorial. With pictures, they said whatever they could, but that, of course, was not much. One picture is not really worth ten thousand words; it usually takes about ten thousand words adequately to explicate one picture. Fortunately for Fletcher, he was then interested in working within the strict limits of Imagism; by means of images he would evoke general sensations and emotions.

Some years after their composition, he wrote of *Irradiations* and the "Symphonies":

The value, then, of this book resides rather in its display of lyric temperament than in any ideas it may contain. It does not belong to that main branch of poetry, the branch that is pure folk-song. . . . Neither can it be classed with the kind of poetry that presupposes a steadily-held philosophic background. . . . But perhaps there is still a third category of poetry, the kind of poetry that has nothing to justify it except its own eagerness for beauty. . . . To that kind this book belongs.

He may have misjudged his own intentions somewhat. Certainly the poems belong in the category to which he assigns them; but mere eagerness for beauty would not justify poetry. On the contrary, these poems do presuppose a philosophic background, held with firm steadiness, that one already discussed in this consideration. The beautiful imagery in the "Symphonies" dilutes that bitter pessimism; however, the imagery exists, not apart from the pessimism, but because of it. It may not be the hopeless gloom which pervades much of his later work, but it is of the same stuff, and it does provide a constant philosophic background.

These poems, informed as they are by deeply felt emotion arising from profound pessimism, give to Fletcher his purchase on immortality. They may well stand as the largest single achievement of the Imagist Movement, as its most representative if not its most characteristic production; for, of those who really qualify as Imagists (Mr. Ezra Pound and D. H. Lawrence did not.), Fletcher is the only one with the approach of a major poet. The Imagist Movement never became any more than what Miss Lowell would have called a "tendency," perhaps not because of any differences among the poets concerning details of craftsmanship, but because of a failure to make a common approach to the problem of life, a failure to effect any synthesis of experience which might have had its greatest components in common. But Fletcher had already made his own synthesis: It is almost completely recorded in the five volumes of the juvenilia, published simultaneously in May, 1913, before he had become acquainted with any of the Imagists; so that, although the discipline of the Imagist manner precluded direct expression of idea, his ideas come through in such force that they make the work of certain more thorough-going Imagists seem puny and ineffectual by comparison.

The major technical device at his command during this time was a development on metaphor which he had worked out, following the examples of certain French poets, principally that of Verhaeren. Amy Lowell referred to it as the "unrelated method," and Garnett called it the "allusive method," an appellation which Fletcher came to accept. The allusive method was employed in verses which were, to use Fletcher's term, orchestrated. Orchestration was at once an extension and an amalgamation of conventional metrics and phonetic ornaments to a condition the full richness of which may be appreciated by reading his most successful attempt at what he called "polyphonic prose," **"Clipper Ships."** One of the most subtle efforts to combine these two techniques—the allusive method and orchestration—is **"The White Symphony."** Of its themes, he wrote, in his autobiography, *Life Is My Song:*

I had intended the **"White Symphony"** to symbolize only my restless and ever-dissatisfied search for perfection; but it seemed to me, in the end, rather to restate still more clearly the themes of loneliness and frustration.

It is very difficult, as a matter of fact, to ascertain just what were the themes of this poem. There is no direct statement, and there are no clues beyond a few scattered guide-words, usually adjectives. The images used in this poem he acquired through contemplation of a bowl of peonies, the view of London from the Crystal Palace, and some Hiroshige snow-scenes. Once the sources of the imagery are known, the images can be related to them with difficulty, but what they symbolize beyond that remains an intriguing mystery. The trope is transacted, not within the poem, but between the poem and the poet; if the reader is to know what the poem intends, he must align his mood with that of the poet. What the allusive method finally becomes is a process of communication and recreation, by means of decorative symbols, of the mood set up in the poet's mind by an emotion or an idea, the symbols being drawn from reality but re-ordered by the poet.

The allusive method might just as well have been called the illusive or the elusive method, for it is all somewhat indefinite. This indefinite quality is at once the fault and the fascination of the "Symphonies." When despair is presented in terms of a stoker on board ship, the danger and the delight of the allusive method—indeed, of symbolism in general—are apparent. The danger, of course, is that of incomplete communication or actual misunderstanding; the delight is that of personal participation, on the part of the reader, in creation.

Because of his intense desire to express directly what he felt,—a desire so strongly satisfied in his talk and in his letters,—such guarded communication as might result from a symbological approach did not content him for long. On June 28, 1916, he wrote to Amy Lowell:

> As regards my own work, I recognize in myself a change in the direction of greater breadth, simplicity of means, and also a stronger impersonal note—I am going out for "high seriousness" as you say, and I feel more sure that I am on the right track than I did six months ago, when I was in the transition stage. It seems to me that I was, in *Goblins and Pagodas,* too preoccupied with style, that is to say, with the way in which to say things, rather than in the thing said. Now I am all the other way about.

The reversal was not perhaps quite so complete as he had intended. Try as he might to "wither into the truth," he could not make the act of withering proceed in a uniform fashion; the result was a long period of stylistic confusion. He was left with a dilemma which may have been in part responsible both for his failure to achieve significant form and for his failure therefrom to deal greatly with the subject-matter inherent in his synthesis: How could he resolve his habit of producing a poetry of symbolism with his urge towards a poetry of statement? Confusion resulting from that dilemma is apparent through *Branches of Adam, The Black Rock,* and many of the *XXIV Elegies.* It was not until after the publication of *The Black Rock* in 1928, when his thoughts began to turn homewards, that he achieved a style which to some degree resolved his problem. This was the style which he used throughout *South Star* and *The Burning Mountain.* Its simple success is evident in such a poem as his **"Requiem for a Twentieth-Century Outlaw: In Memoriam Charles, 'Pretty Boy', Floyd."**

Who knows what dreams assailed the alley cat

Whose forbears had been lions? Does the hand
Of time too hurriedly altered, alter that
Which chimes like music through a bygone land?

Yet so it was that none might heed his dream;
Eating the gall of lead for all his pride,
Harried from town to town, past field and stream,
He turned and fled and turned and fled—then died.

The dark earth took him back to her wide breast,
Unreckoning of all things but the star-sown sky.
Having already rocked to perfect rest
Wilder and bolder sons, in years gone by.

Those two latter volumes attest his love for his native region. In them he speaks finally with his own voice, because it is the voice of his own. The speech is not polished, but it is moving, and it is never false. He made an authentic summation of his own place as it stood when he knew it. Regionalism has now to a degree gone out of fashion; but it is a worthy thing to have committed to literary memory, in a way oftentimes not merely fine but final, a place which is changing and a generation who are gone.

For to recount the career of John Gould Fletcher would be to tell of a great return. He went off to a foreign country as a young man, leaving behind not only his people and his place, but also his culture, his religion and politics, all that would have been his by custom if he had stayed at home, taking with him only the ethics of his group. After a time of this exile, moral and physical, he began to assay what he had given up, and it seemed to him too much. He tried hard to make his peace with estrangement: by immersing himself in the culture of the place in which he was living, by attempting to align his thought with culture patterns older and more general than any ones which were contemporaneous; and finally by attempting to resolve his isolation in mysticism. Unable to complete himself as a personality by any or all of the three efforts, he began almost desperately to try to get home. After long struggle, at the end of twenty-five years, he returned to Arkansas and lived there until he died.

> It is a land
> Of waste where nature sprawls, setting at naught
> The ruined plans of man. A land unknown,
> Blazing in summer with the sumach blooms,
> And glossy leaves of oaks, as raindrops slide
> Into the shy stream, and beneath the boughs
> Only the darkness stirs; where year on year
> The hawk hangs to the withered branch to tell
> Whatever it is that moves amid cloud-shadowed hollows.

(pp. 4-15)

Eugene Haun, "Of Broken Effort and Desire: A General Consideration of the Poetry of John Gould Fletcher," in Shenandoah, *Vol. II, No. 1, Spring, 1951, pp. 3-16.*

STANLEY K. COFFMAN, JR.   (essay date 1951)

[*In the following excerpt, Coffman explores Fletcher's association with Ezra Pound's Imagistes and Amy Lowell's Imagists (also referred to here as "Amygists").*]

Fletcher understood the principles upon which doctrinaire Imagism had originally been based. In *The Little Review,* he cited four cardinal beliefs as the basis for the movement, the first being to "present the subject as an image," so that the reader may re-enact for himself the "emotional complex" the poet is trying to convey. He warned against confusing Imagist aims with those of the nineteenth-century Symbolists, and drew a further, equally just, distinction between Imagism and *vers libre:* "Imagism is an attitude of mind that can appear just as easily in rime."

Fletcher had refused to contribute to *Des Imagistes.* When the *Poetry* manifesto was published in 1913, he stated to Harriet Monroe his disapproval of the school, as such, rather than of the principles for which the school stood.

> With Mr. Pound's "school" of "Imagisme," I am in even greater disagreement. "Imagisme" is an attitude towards technique, pure and simple. I am unable, and I wish everyone else were unable, to impose upon myself the pedantic yoke of any particular technique. . . . I have informed Mr. Pound that I do not intend to hamper myself with his technique and his "don'ts."
>
> (pp. 175-76)

Fletcher's attitude towards Pound was not, at the moment, friendly; but their relationship soon grew more cordial, and he wrote for Pound what he considered an Imagist poem. Still, he would not make the public declaration which appearance in *Des Imagistes* would have implied. Amy Lowell, on the other hand, completely won his confidence. He accepted the invitation to join her group, but the association was an uneasy one.

Fletcher's major effort during the years to 1917 was a series of "Symphonies," which were to present important phases in the intellectual and emotional development of an artist. Each phase was to be symbolized by a color, each color evoking in the poet's mind certain pictures which were to impress the desired emotional and imaginative effect upon the reader.

> I have tried to state each phase in the terms of a certain color, or combination of colors which is emotionally akin to that phase. This color, and the imaginative phantasmagoria of landscape which it evokes, thereby creates, in a definite and tangible form, the dominant mood of each poem.

The **"Blue Symphony"** deals with the young artist's search for beauty; confused at first by his own immaturity and by the influence of other men, he finally attains self-assurance through recognition that the vision which he pursues will always elude him. The color *blue* was suggested to Fletcher by the emotions accompanying perception of mystery, depth, distance—emotions which he thought appropriate to the theme; at the same time, it evoked in his mind the specific images of mist, smoke, death-mountains, which would stimulate these emotions in the reader. To heighten the effect of unreality, Fletcher introduced his imagery in the logically unrelated pattern characteristic of certain poems by Rimbaud.

The **"White Symphony"** follows a pattern that resembles the Rimbaud technique even more closely. The title of the poem recalls Gautier's *Symphonie en blanc majeur"*; its "symphonic" progression (by sections or movements, each developing a mood through its color symbolism) also derives, in some measure, from the possibilities suggested by the title of the French poem. However, its theme, the struggle for the inaccessible, the eternal, is neither Parnassian nor Imagist, and its use of *white* to symbolize this absolute repeats a Symbolist device. Its images, products of the hallucinatory imagination, directed by the subconscious, resemble the phantasmagoria of *Les Illuminations.* In the opening passage, for example,

white petals of peonies thrust out to embrace the onlooker, thrust out until they lose their identity and are transformed first into flakes of snow, then the dazzling white of clouds; the transition from one image to the next is handled in such a way as to recreate the "impossible" behavior of images in dreams.

Fletcher, in fact, develops his imagery from the correspondences for *E* (white—mists, lancelike glaciers, etc.) and for *O* (blue—Omega, silences of the heavens) indicated by Rimbaud in his "Vowels" sonnet—**"White Symphony"** moving from the radiance of the ecstasy in section I to the blue of the eternal in section II and back to white in section III, now the pallor of death as the human dream fails. In the "Symphonies," Fletcher tries to state each mood, through his color imagery, in terms the reader can see or feel, and the poems have little meaning in the conventional sense: to this extent they are Imagistic (as are the Japanese poems which interested Fletcher and Amy Lowell, as well as Pound). Yet they make assumptions which Imagism, at least implicitly, denies; they deal with the imprecise—no matter how precisely—and go beyond the Imagist's tendency to make language more scientific and precise, its almost naturalistic tendency to confine expression within the limits of the solid, physical sensation or feeling.

Fletcher used this technique in poetry that was to be Imagistic. **"Blue Symphony,"** again with its *long-O* words to establish the correspondences suggested by Rimbaud, was written as an Imagist poem; **"London Excursion,"** which employs the same "unrelated" method of progression, was also published in the anthology of 1915. Its attempt to communicate a reaction to the modern city is not inconsistent with Imagism, because the poet sees no transcendental significance in his object. Its method, however, is not to bring the reader closer to the object that he may react to it or see it more clearly as it is, but to interpose the poet's quite subjective impressions of the scene. The images are wholly impressionistic, and their final effect derives from the strangeness and individuality of the poet's view; being one significant step removed from reality, they lose the hardness and objectivity of Imagism: domes of bowler hats vibrate in the heat, the city seems to throw its streets after those who flee from it.

Certain descriptive poems that Fletcher contributed to the anthologies demonstrate other characteristics not inconsistent with Imagism. For example, they reveal his ability to depict color vividly:

> Shadows of blue hands passing
> Over a curtain of flame.
>
> Grey rain curtains wave afar off,
> Wisps of vapor curl and vanish.
> The sun throws soft shades of golden light
> Over rose-buttressed palisades.
>
> Now the clouds are a lazy procession,
> Blue balloons bobbing solemnly
> Over black-dappled walls.

On occasion, he could create an image like that advocated by Hulme. He wrote of **"The Unquiet Street"**:

> On rainy nights
> It dully gleams
> Like the cold tarnished scales of a snake;
> And over it hang arc-lamps,
> Blue-white death lilies on black stems.

Or

And the grinding click of their skates as they im-
    pinge on the surface
Is like the brushing together of their wing-tips of
    silver.

Such imagery, however, is so rare as to pass unnoticed in his predominantly Symbolist technique, and would not seem to justify his inclusion in Imagist volumes. Privately, to Amy Lowell, Fletcher admitted the anomaly of his association with the three anthologies.

> I do not believe that a poem should present an "image," I believe it should present an emotion. I do not believe in "clear, hard, and definite presentation." I believe in a complete, that is to say, shifting and fluid presentation. I do not believe in "absolute freedom in choice of subject."—I believe that the very word "choice" means lack of freedom. If one chooses, one has certain standards whereby one chooses. I do not believe that the "exact word" is possible. I do not believe in cadence, but in rhythm (a different thing altogether). I do not believe altogether in "externality." Therefore I do not accept Imagism. I am a Rhythmist or a Symbolist, but not an Imagist.

It is little wonder that the prefaces [to the Imagist anthologies], accepted as the official statement of doctrinaire Imagism, consist of broad and disappointingly unrevolutionary principles. How otherwise could they present a program upon which there was a reasonable semblance of agreement among poets of such diverse techniques; how otherwise could they reconcile the assumptions of Imagist and Symbolist? Of course, they incline toward the beliefs of those who wrote them, toward the ideas of Aldington and Amy Lowell; but they had, nevertheless, in some measure to cover the practice of a poet like Fletcher, who refused to join Pound's group and who even repudiated (though in private) the generalities of "Amygism." (pp. 176-81)

> *Stanley K. Coffman, Jr., " 'Amygism'," in his* Imagism: A Chapter for the History of Modern Poetry, *University of Oklahoma Press, 1951, pp. 163-86.*

BEN KIMPEL   (essay date 1954)

[*Kimpel is an American educator and critic. In the following excerpt, he surveys Fletcher's works and discusses his association with various literary groups.*]

The fact that [Fletcher] consistently refused to follow a road built by someone else may be as responsible as anything for his comparative obscurity—comparative, that is, to his originality and importance. Also, he has been unlucky in anthologies. Mr. Untermeyer, for example, in whose anthology the beginner generally makes his first samplings of all but the biggest names of modern poetry, has left out most of Fletcher's best work and has included several trivial second-rate poems. More important, superficial critics have been able to brush Fletcher off as one member of the Imagist group—a group with which, as has been pointed out several times, his connection was brief and largely fortuitous.

Still more important, Fletcher had a knack for saying things at the wrong time. He knew most of the important poets and critics of his day personally, and his knowledge of what his contemporaries were writing and thinking was thorough. This knowledge is hardly apparent in his poetry. Fashions meant nothing to him, even when, briefly, he found himself fashionable. His independence was the kind you would expect in a provincial whose acquaintance with movements at the center is vague and late. When he returned to Arkansas, he was no more cut off from the main line of modern poetry than he had been in London. As Ezra Pound said at the beginning of his career [see excerpt dated 1913]:

> Mr. Fletcher has a fine crop of faults—mostly his own. He has such distinction as belongs to a man who dares to have his own faults, who prefers his own to those of anyone else.

This independence saved him from facility, but it made his job hard. It gives a special value to his successes, and it goes far to explain his numerous failures.

One of the standard things to say about Fletcher is that he lacked humor. This is, I suppose, true, but does not mean very much. There is no reason why every writer should have humor, or any other given quality, when there are so many possible kinds of excellence. In *Life Is My Song* he takes himself very seriously. He was a serious problem to himself, and he could no more assume a modest, deprecatory tone than he could write an article treating H. L. Mencken as a leader of modern thought when his and his first wife's livelihood seemed to depend on his being able to do so.

Still, Fletcher did not overestimate his value. His work is full of expressions of a modesty which is real, deep-seated, and miserable. In the **"Preface to *Preludes and Symphonies*"** he is certainly sincere when he regrets not having written poems in the main stream of "folk" poetry or poems with a steadily-held philosophic background, when he hopes that his early work falls into a possible third class with "nothing to justify it except its own eagerness for beauty." When he wrote this, Fletcher did not regard such poetry highly.

Even such poetry did not come easily to him. He was twenty-seven when he began *Irradiations*, the poem in which he forged his first individual idiom. Two things at least can be said about *Irradiations* and about the best of the color symphonies which followed it—they are lovely, and they are Fletcher's. No one else had done quite this sort of poetry. At least not in English—it was French symbolist poetry and post-impressionist painting which set them off. Not only the unusual images and gorgeous diction, by which these poems are often characterized, make his early manner. These things are part of it, but he can do without them, as we learn from the **"White Symphony,"** perhaps the most nearly perfect of his early poems:

> Downwards through the blue abyss it slides,
> The white snow-water of my dreams,
> Downwards crashing from slippery rock
> Into the boiling chasm:
> In which no eye dare look, for it is the chasm of
>   death.
>
> Upwards from the blue abyss it rises,
> The chill water-mist of my dreams;
> Upwards to greyish weeping pines,
>
> And to skies of autumn ever about my heart,
> It is blue at the beginning,
> And blue-white against the grey-greenness;
> It wavers in the upper air,
> Catching unconscious sparkles, a rainbow-glint of
>   sunlight,
> And fading in the sad depths of the sky.

There is an inevitability of phrasing here which Fletcher often missed in his more ambitious work, and there is a special flavor as of some made dish, in which unlikely ingredients combine surprisingly in a new taste.

It is certainly not Imagism. Fletcher himself said that he was never as interested in reproducing an image as an emotion, and the result was rather Symbolist than Imagist. Precision, that favorite word of the Imagists, does not describe much of his poetry. There are, of course, comparisons which the Imagists could accept—the often-praised lines on the

> Sudden scurry of umbrellas:
> Bending, recurved blossoms of the storm.

The appropriateness of this grotesquerie escapes me, but I bow to general opinion and assume that it is good Imagism. At any rate it is not typical Fletcher. *Irradiations* and the symphonies are beautiful when they succeed in reproducing a mood, a complex set of emotions, the flavor of which lies in its imprecision. Most of the images do not exist in their own right; they are not seen; they suggest. And it is the triumph of these poems that they do often suggest the mood which Fletcher wants to suggest.

One technical device from which Fletcher does not get much help even here is rhythm. In the Preface to *Irradiations—Sand and Spray* he speaks of the basis of English poetry as cadence. The length of the lines must be varied to vary the cadence, and that length "depends altogether upon the apparatus which Nature has given us" (that is, each line should be a breath). When, in his later poetry, he abandons this untenable theory and uses enjambment, the result is only to make the line-divisions meaningless. Evidently he thought in breath groups, and this gives his verse at times a choppy, gasping motion. M. René Taupin has noted that Fletcher's "free verse" is rather *l'ancien vers métrique décomposé* ["old metric verse broken up"], which indicates a real weakness in the early poems when they are short of entire perfection. But Fletcher's later metrical poetry is even weaker in rhythm, and his blank verse especially is almost unendurably stiff and broken-winded. Nor when he tried regular end rime were his rimes distinguished; but he is unusually skillful in handling alliteration, in varying internal rimes and sound echoes, and in sonorously repeating or contrasting his vowel sounds. Perhaps his technical equipment was really better suited to the abortive experiment of polyphonic prose.

After coming as close to fame as he was ever to come, Fletcher evidently felt that he had done what he could do in this manner. He speaks in his autobiography of the "Gateway" poems of the *Black Rock* volume as "coming" miraculously after a long struggle to make his poetry "more stark and realistic." And it is in the "Gateway" poems that he suddenly finds a new idiom.

After the symphonies he tried several new tacks. A few of the epigrams of *Japanese Prints* are truly Imagist and are among the best products of Imagism. (pp. 285-89)

The American descriptions of *Goblins and Pagodas* and *Breakers and Granite* were a more conscious effort to do something different, to prune his style and get back down to earth. Critics have found in "Ghosts of an Old House" a genuine native air which is a relief to many after the hothouse atmosphere of the symphonies. Fletcher, it is said, has found his roots again, and of course a poet can write best about his roots. However that may be, his American trip of 1915 showed him two of the four landscapes which stirred him the rest of his life—the deep south and the desert; the prairie and, most important of all, the Ozarks, appear later. These first poems about places are written in that deliberately bare style which he always used when describing America. This style is evidently the product of a theory—it did not "come to" him. Many of the descriptions are very pleasant, and **"Mexican Quarter"** especially can probably be enjoyed by more people than can any other of Fletcher's poems.

Later he tried another type of ready-made subject, reproducing a historical epoch, and in his elegies on Napoleon and on the Russian Revolution he does something with words that no other American poet, so far as I know, has tried. The historical poems are written in a special diction, with a sweeping forward movement which appears rarely in his work. The place descriptions are less rare and less individual, but the best of them compare with the best of any one's descriptive poetry.

Fletcher, however, was no longer interested in what he calls the "poetry of objects." He tells in his autobiography of his conscious and long-drawn-out effort to turn to a "poetry of human beings." It was, like every effort he made, a sincere and vigorous effort—but it was a failure. There are no people in Fletcher's poems—not even in the often admired **"Lincoln."** (pp. 289-90)

Fletcher could feel sympathy for the "average man" in the mass, but only at a distance. Individuals failed to live up to his delicate ideal either in manners or in morals, and they were hostile to his ideas and to his art. His inability to savor the individuality of real men was not due to hardness. It was the natural result of his attitude towards the "bourgeoisie," and most Americans are bourgeois. Later Fletcher managed to sympathize with many Americans of the past and with his picture of the Ozark farmer of the present, who was, however, largely an imaginary being, rather an anti-bourgeois than a person in his own right.

Not surprisingly, Fletcher decided "that what was, after all, interesting about humanity was less the accidents of any individual life than the tendencies inherent in humanity as a whole." The prose and later poetry show a natural trend towards abstraction, towards jumping from, and at times over, the individual to the general.

This point brings up the most difficult of Fletcher's poems to discuss, the philosophical poems of the Twenties in which he set out to examine the "tendencies inherent in humanity as a whole," *Parables* and *Branches of Adam.* They are poems (or, for part of *Parables,* prose sketches) about the "eternal" problems of good and evil and man's search for God. *Branches of Adam* is Fletcher's most ambitious work, an epic on the Creation, the Fall of Man, and the Flood. As he himself says, it is a prime example of his untimeliness—no one in the Twenties was interested. The fact that he did not include it or any of the *Parables* in his *Selected Poems,* together with the brief and hesitant remarks he makes about them in *Life Is My Song,* may indicate that he felt more lacking here than timeliness.

In *Branches of Adam* Fletcher comes close to creating the grand style he needs. He builds on the Bible and on Blake, whose influence almost overwhelms him, but there are long passages, especially of description, which are not derivative in tone. His love of hugeness and violence, which threatens at times to split some of the symphonies as it does some of the later elegies, is here in place. The poem blazes and throbs. The figures are superhuman, and the might of their passions is conveyed in a series of elemental nature images rolled along on a long line which can both thunder and flash. For a poem which had to make its own technique unlike anything other poets at the time were interested in making, **Branches of Adam** is an amazing achievement, and it deserves to be known as one of the few impressive long poems of the century.

If Fletcher recognized a partial failure, it was probably due to his basic plan. He set out to make a myth. There is no evidence that myths have ever been "made" in this way—a myth which is recognized by its maker as a myth is merely a symbol. And the symbol in this demonic, reversed version of Genesis only partly covers the abstract message, so that the concrete and abstract do not fuse but merely exist side by side. In Cain, at least, Fletcher finds a symbol of one side of man's nature which is perhaps his most striking single creation.

He is not, of course, to blame for not having a more positive message than the misery of man in his search for God. The lack of God and the longing for Him Fletcher strongly felt, and, of course, they have made poetry before. Perhaps the contrast between the terrific framework of the poem and its inability to affirm anything seems somewhat incongruous.

In **The Black Rock** Fletcher found another way of dealing with the same problem, and such little-known lyrics as **"The Last Frontier," "The Future," "Isle Iranim"** and **"Brahma"** solve temporarily his difficulty of finding an individual poetic idiom for philosophic poetry. That there are so few of these lyrics may be a sign that Fletcher had said what he had to say. The title poem of the volume is only less striking because it suffers from one of Fletcher's commonest faults, not knowing when to stop. In **The Black Rock** Fletcher gets his second wind and writes the second group of poems that is indisputably his, poems he regarded as dealing with more important themes. Unfortunately he never reached a third period of such sureness of style.

Other poems in the volume are, like the descriptive poems, essays on set subjects—Whitman, Columbus, Nietzsche. They seem, like the earlier **"Lincoln,"** a little wilful, as if Fletcher had sat down and decided to write a poem on Whitman or whatever. This wilfulness is even more apparent in **XXIV Elegies.** The **"Jade Elegy"** is lovely and the **"Elegy on the Last Judgment"** is fitfully impressive and the **"Elegy on the Russian Revolution"** is a survey of Russian history which is realized completely in the poetic imagination and applies Fletcher's earlier coloring to a larger canvas. Most of the elegies are commentaries which, in spite of a large bag of poetic tricks, never quite struggle out of prose.

Fletcher was determined to write intellectual poetry, and he was an intellectual, who had many ideas worth conveying. He had already proved his ability to convey them in prose. His biography of Gauguin, written in a lucid, restrained prose so perfect that the reader need not notice it, is full of discerning comment on art. **John Smith—Also Pocahontas** proves again how sharply and effectively he could apply his intelligence to a given problem. Fletcher would have made a first rate historian. **The Two Frontiers,** his comparison of America and Russia, in epigrammatic prose which recalls the Senecan style of the Renaissance, is slightly marred by over-ingeniousness and a tendency to let pat contrasts run away

with him, but it is full of unexpected insights, and its neglect today, when its subject has finally become timely, is inexcusable. Except for **Life Is My Song,** which has curious lapses into banality and awkwardness, all of Fletcher's prose is excellent in form.

In the poems on contemporary life this comment is simplified and boils down to one attitude—hatred of the machine and of its users, the bourgeoisie. Fletcher never made poetry out of this attitude—he could do the same thing better in prose—and the attitude itself wore him out. The people who might profit by it will not be reading **XXIV Elegies,** and I question what the people who do read it will be able to do with a disgust for modern American life that amounts at times to physical sickness. But I say this tentatively, and with admiration for the man who could preserve his disgust so consistently and uncompromisingly in his loneliest years.

Perhaps dissatisfaction with this attitude as a final solution finally led Fletcher back to Arkansas. He must have needed something to admire, and he found it finally in the Ozarks. Primitivism had always appealed to him, as he shows in the Gauguin book. The primitive for him was finally embodied in the figure of the Ozark farmer, which he created rather than portrayed and which, however little it had to do with the real Ozark farmer, proved a useful vehicle for presenting his own ideal of simple, proud endurance.

Fletcher's association with the agrarian group, like his earlier association with the Imagists, was fortuitous. His poetry never resembled their poetry, which he says "proceeded from a process of intellectual ratiocination, rather than from any emotional identification with the subjects which they handled."

His regionalism produced some very good descriptive poetry, in the best of which description is made to convey an attitude towards life; and it filled his last years with new interests. Fletcher was almost the first strong intellectual force to which Arkansas had been exposed, and the state owes him a considerable debt. Unfortunately regionalism also produced his very worst poetry. When he tried to write the simple poetry which he seems to have felt suited his subject he often fell into flat, oratorical prose broken up into functionless lines and tagged with stale rimes. His efforts to reproduce folk songs are spiritless and lack the all-important quality of rhythm. His historical poems fail to realize imaginatively the Old South, as he had realized Russian history, and drop to Fourth-of-July orations.

"The Story of Arkansas" in the **South Star** volume (it was published separately earlier for the state's centennial) is Fletcher at his worst. He did exactly the same thing later in prose, in his book **Arkansas,** and succeeded fully—it is another of Fletcher's misfortunes that few people will probably want to read a book about Arkansas, and this masterpiece (considering the type, the word is not too strong) will never be known as it deserves.

There are poems here like **"In Mount Holly"** and **"Thunderstorm in the Ozarks"**—weather and especially clouds always stimulated Fletcher to write his best—which would be a credit to most poets. In **"Hillbilly Philosophy"** he presents his new Ozark ideal effectively because he presents it in his own style, not in the imagined style of the hillbilly. Perfect, simple little poems like **"The Christmas Tree"** and **"Dogwood"** are in the same manner as such earlier poems as **"Advent"** and **"I Had Scarcely Fallen Asleep"** (the only poem I know which recalls Emily Dickinson), or the love poems **"The Gifts Demanded"** and **"The Vow."**

In his last volume, *The Burning Mountain,* Fletcher has no really weak poetry, and he has some poems like **"Journey Day," "Salem Campground,"** and **"The Land Is Cleared"** that evoke the Ozarks as no one else has. It is curious that the mountains of Arkansas always call forth Fletcher's best, whereas the cotton section often leaves him bogged in platitudes. It would seem to be another example of his dependence on a stimulus, whether from within or from outside.

I have insisted on what seem to me to be Fletcher's failures and comparative failures because I believe that what his reputation mainly needs is discrimination. If his poetry is disappointing, it is only a comparative disappointment. Partly he never succeeded in finding a sure, personal style, like the style of *Irradiations,* to treat the problems which, in his middle years, he was determined to treat. He has written enough good poems, like **"Mexican Quarter"** and the Ozark lyrics, to make anyone a respectable reputation, but they are not what he mainly wanted to do. At least twice, in his early poems and in *The Black Rock,* something more "came to" him; but when he tried deliberately to say what he believed to be important, he never quite managed to say it. His own dissatisfaction is apparent in *Life Is My Song* and in his last volumes of poetry.

The disappointment is also that the man remained bigger than the poet. He never put more than a small part of himself into words. His selflessness, his intense devotion even when he had no cause to devote himself to, his willingness to sacrifice, found no object to fasten onto. (pp. 290-95)

Ben Kimpel, "John Gould Fletcher in Retrospect," in Poetry, *Vol. LXXXIV, No. 5, August, 1954, pp. 284-96.*

HOXIE NEALE FAIRCHILD　(essay date 1962)

[*An American educator, Fairchild is the author of numerous essays and books on literary and religious subjects. His major works include* The Noble Savage: A Study in Romantic Naturalism *(1928), which is a lengthy discussion of the depiction of the unspoiled primitive life in literature and its relationship to romantic naturalism, and a six-volume study,* Religious Trends in English Poetry *(1939-68), which traces religious thought and feeling in English poetry from the eighteenth to the twentieth century. In the following excerpt, Fairchild explores Fletcher's religious philosophy as expressed in his poetry.*]

In May, 1913 . . . Fletcher had published simultaneously, chiefly at his own expense, no less than five little volumes of early poems classified according to their moods and themes. He longed to see his verses in print, but apparently he also hoped to shake off his immaturity by externalizing it and thus cleaning his slate for a fresh start. I have not read these volumes; they are said to be interesting only to students of the diseases of childhood. By the time they appeared, however, Fletcher had already

> begun a series of new poems, written without respect to fixed metrical standards, which were to be exact transcriptions not of thought, but of mood, and which, in their combinations of vowel and consonant sounds, were designed to produce the effect of modern music. These poems, conceived under

the triple influence of Mallarmé, Gauguin, and Debussy, I decided to call "Irradiations."

In 1915 Amy Lowell got them published by Houghton Mifflin under the full title, *Irradiations—Sand and Spray.*

The typical "irradiation"—there are unimportant divergencies from the norm—responds to the emotional suggestiveness of a natural scene in somewhere between five and fifteen free-verse lines, unrhymed, strongly cadenced, and usually rather long. It has no "point," but it conveys a blurry mood with some success. The images, though meant to be French, are more like those of Shelley or Swinburne in their excessive abundance and lack of precision: for Fletcher, to be poetic was to be indefinite and musical. "The triple influence of Mallarmé, Gauguin, and Debussy" can be discerned if we are willing to think of symbolism as vague impressionism, of painting as color without line, and of music as sound without structure. Conrad Aiken's criticism [in his *Scepticisms*] of Fletcher's writing cannot be bettered:

> In a sense it is like the symbolism of such poets as Mallarmé, but with the difference that here the symbols have no meaning. It is a sort of absolute poetry, a poetry of detached waver and brilliance, a beautiful flowering of language alone, a parthenogenesis, as if language were fertilized by itself rather than by thought or feeling.

Although Aiken's words, published in 1919, were not intended to apply solely to *Irradiations,* the style of that volume remains, on the whole, the predominant style of Fletcher's poetry up to the terminus of our period and even beyond it. He tells us that he always "tried to be full, clangorous, unrealistic, and confusedly rhetorical," and he paid the inevitable penalty of his preferences. In 1937 he confesses: "As a poet, I realize that I have been, and must remain, for my lifetime, an anchronism."

It would, however, be an exaggeration to say that his work manifests no changes whatever. As a married man responsible for two stepchildren he was not called upon to serve in the American forces, but the war made him think harder and with a stronger sense of the artist's social responsibilities. His early admiration for Whitman returned in the guise of patriotic enthusiasm. A visit to America bore fruit in regional descriptive poems considerably more realistic than *Irradiations.* Increasingly he communicates with the reader through traditional verse patterns in which conceptual statements are primary and images secondary. Sometimes he tries to deal not merely with moods but with ideas, and many of those ideas bear more or less directly upon religion.

The subject appears rather frequently in his memoirs. His mother was a "somewhat narrow and censorious" Low Church Episcopalian. His father, though nominally of the same persuasion, was at heart "a tolerant agnostic; . . . in his latter years his favorite reading was Darwin and Huxley." In childhood Fletcher was horrified by the Old Testament; as for the New, he was "too secure economically and physically, to be moved by . . . that gospel of the poor par excellence." Soon after he entered Harvard in 1913 his indifference to Christianity changed into hostility under the influence of a Nietzschean classmate who convinced him that "It was easier to have no religion at all than to believe in such an absurd one." Yet, as he says, "Men must believe in something," and so he adopted the art of poetry as his religion. At Rome, in 1908, his discovery of "the supreme importance of the Catholic faith as the basis for all European culture" almost led him to become a convert. But being at this time a sentimental liberal with leanings toward Guild Socialism, he shrank from an institution so obscurantist and reactionary. During his early years in London, however, he "retained respect for the formal ritual, the magical unity and communion of spirit that prevailed in the high Anglican, the Orthodox Greek, and the Roman Catholic Churches." Amy, we know, scolded him for his notion "that what art had to offer was exactly, in another form, the same unique value that was offered by religion"—the value of symbolic thaumaturgy: "I had attempted to build up in my art a spell of which I felt these churches held the secret. . . . I had tried to hold, with Morris and Dostoevsky, that it was not through morals or dogma, but through beauty, that man could come to perfection and the world be saved." This is the unspoken but clearly implicit faith behind *Irradiations.*

But the cult of beauty-magic was shaken by the war, by his marital troubles, and by his sense of personal and professional inadequacy. Feeling that "the earth was entering a new dark age, and the Renaissance was at an end," he cultivated "a stoic paganism" in which man subjected himself to natural forces that were neither friendly nor hostile to his desires. The influence of Hardy, whose grim fortitude Fletcher now envied, is probably at work in **"The Future."** Ten thousand centuries hence, man,

> since he has no further heights to scale,
> And gods care not to witness that he came this way,
> On the wind-bitten ice-cap, shaken by the gale,
> Will watch the sunset fading of the world's last day.
>
> And blazing stars will burst upon him there,
> Dumb, as if heedless of his hope or pain,
> Speeding no answer back to his last prayer,
> And, if akin to him, akin in vain.

Even Hardy, however, could not steadily believe in absolute cosmic indifference; and Fletcher, at heart a very unstoical man, was still less capable of doing so. The universe must say either Yes or No; that it should say nothing at all was inconceivable. Hence we need not be surprised to find him floundering in a welter of affirmations and negations. The ideas which I am about to illustrate from poems later than 1915 and earlier than 1921 exhibit no definable trend: hope and despair run side by side, each canceling out the other.

There is plenty of hope in the poem entitled **"Faith,"** and the hope appears to be genuinely religious. Fletcher cannot believe that death means annihilation:

> My heart beats fully and steadily, faith is reborn
> with each breath;
> Faith in that part of me which was not mine, which
> was given to me to use,
> Which shall live on though all the suns fall dead
> into the night;
> Faith in a love which rules all things: for though I
> fall and lose,
> I shall live on forever, for I have held with the light.

Elsewhere he seems willing to recognize Christ as the most potent symbol of the "love which rules all things." In **"Spring,"** the death and renewal of nature are associated, somewhat in the manner of a liberal preacher's Easter sermon, with the Crucifixion and the Resurrection. "Have you forgotten your graves?" Lincoln's voice challenges the still neutral Americans of 1916:

> Listen long to their unstirred lips. From your hostages to silence
> Learn there is no life without death, no dawn without sun-setting,
> No victory but to him who has given all.

The poem ends with the suggestion that the most appropriate flower to strew over Lincoln's own grave is the passionflower,

> With the nails that pierced, the cross that he bore
> and the circlet,
> And beside it there lay also one lonely snow-white
> magnolia,
> Bitter for remembrance of the healing which has
> passed.

The magnolia, of course, is the tribute of the South. As for the passionflower, Lincoln is indeed one of the few men whose human nature is even faintly comparable with that of Jesus of Nazareth. One feels, however, the implication that Christ is not so much a person as a symbolic name for the spirit of sacrificial love which the Emancipator embodied in *real* life.

In **"The Well in the Desert,"** the first of the group of "Arizona Poems," the spiritual focus is blurred still further: Christ becomes a name for any shepherd. Falling asleep by the well, the poet dreams that he sees a Navajo Indian:

> Sheep were feeding about him.
> And I said to him, "Where do you come from?"
> And he replied,
> "From Nazareth, beyond the desert,
> In Galilee."

The association seems a trifle forced. If this poem is merely silly, **"Advent"** is a puzzle. Despite the title, the symbolism is drawn from the Epiphany. Fletcher can offer the Babe no gold—"I spent it all on foolish songs." All his incense has been "burned / To the great idols of the world."

> Myrrh I lost
> In that darker sepulchre
> Where another Christ
> Died for man in vain.
>
> I can only give myself,
> I have nothing left but this.
> Naked I wait, naked I fall
> Into Your Hands, Your Hands.

We could take this as a highly sophisticated version of Christina Rossetti's familiar Nativity carol were it not for the perplexing "myrrh" stanza. What can *another* Christ mean? If He is the Crucified, to whom is the poem addressed? The likeliest answer, however absurd it may appear to Christians, is that there are two Christs because there are two ways of thinking about Him: as the Infant in the manger, and as the suffering Man on the Cross. Fletcher has renounced the latter to give himself to the former. If, as seems possible, the poem is really about the birth of the poet's own child, "Christ" may stand not only for springtime, for Abraham Lincoln, and for a Navajo shepherd, but also for any baby. The most effective way of stifling the thought that Jesus ever actually existed anywhere is to assert that He exists everywhere as a value symbol.

Fletcher believes also in a historical Christ, but He was a mere man who "died for man in vain." He functions more frequently as a vehicle for the poet's despair than for his hope. **"An Unbeliever to the Church"** interprets "Eli, Eli" as the universal human cry to a nonexistent or indifferent God. The Church has shrunk from this bitter truth:

> The hopelessness of that eternal Cross
> Was far too great for human hearts to bear:
> We must have easy balm for our despair,
> Some soothing hope; not horror and sheer loss.
> Humbling themselves and their immortal pride,
> Men chose the barren stone where Peter's courage
>   died.

Less cowardly than Peter, Fletcher announces in his autobiography the fresh and startling discovery that "the path to 'the kingdom of heaven' lay in man himself, and not in the dogmas of the churches." But since Fletcher believes in no such path and no such kingdom, this thought cannot have been very sustaining to him. His usual view of unaided human nature is in fact so deeply pessimistic that he is compelled to reinvent God as a scapegoat. He envisages the **"Last Judgment"**:

> Now out of every graveyard on the earth
> There suddenly writhed in flame and stood up new
>   as man
> A being whose girth no human eye could span;
> Two heads it had—one like a babe at birth,
>
> The other like a skull. It hollowly spoke,
> • • • • •
> "Now ended is God's high and pitiless joke."

Again we think of Hardy.

Fletcher derives some consolation from associating his own spiritual emptiness with that of his contemporaries. **"Song of the Moderns"** strikingly describes what Joseph Wood Krutch was later to call "the modern temper":

> We more than others have the right to cast away
> Thought like a withered leaf, since it has served its
>   day;
>
> Since for this transient joy which not for long can
>   burn
> Within our hearts, we gave up in return
>
> Ten thousand years of holy magic power
> Drawn from the darkness to transcend death's
>   hour.
> • • • • •
> And there shall be no more the spirits of the deep,
> Nor holy satyrs slumbering upon the steep,
>
> Nor angels at a manger or a cross.
> Life shall go on; to ugly gain or loss;
>
> Yet vaster and more tragic, till at last
> The present too shall make part of the past:—
>
> Till all the joy and the tragedy that man knows
> To-day, become stiff gravestones in long rows;
>
> Till none dare look on the mountains ranked afar,
> And think, "These are the cast-off leavings of some
>   star."

Usually, however, Fletcher conceives of the modern predicament in personal terms. In **"The Silence,"** the concluding section of the "Down the Mississippi" series, the silent river pushes its way through the "Deep, matted green silence of my South" toward extinction in the completer silence of the sea. The symbolic analogy is made explicit:

> There is a silence I carry about with me always;

> A silence perpetual, for it is self-created;
> • • • • •
> There is a silence I have achieved: I have walked
>   beyond its threshold;
> I know it is without horizons, boundless, fathom-
>   less, perfect.
> And some day maybe, far away
> I will curl up in it at last and sleep an endless sleep.

Endless sleep, curled up at last in the womb of Mother Death. Possibly that is what he had always wanted more than anything else. (pp. 487-93)

> *Hoxie Neale Fairchild, "Overtly Romantic Modernists," in his* Religious Trends in English Poetry: Gods of a Changing Poetry, 1880-1920, Vol. V, *Columbia University Press, 1962, pp. 486-536.*

EDNA B. STEPHENS (essay date 1967)

[*In the following excerpt, Stephens studies Fletcher's regional period, focusing on* South Star *and its blending of agrarianism and Eastern philosophy.*]

According to Fletcher's own classification, the first phase of his literary career was esthetic; the second, religious. The third is frequently classified as his regional period. As early as 1922, Fletcher had become interested in the Agrarians. At that time, he lectured to a group at Oxford University upon American poetry; a member of the audience expressed shock that Fletcher made no mention of John Crowe Ransom and the Fugitives. Fletcher at once proceeded to repair the gap in his knowledge of contemporary American poetry by subscribing to the Fugitive magazine, by reading it, and by contributing to it. Despite his alliance with Amy Lowell, Fletcher considered himself a Southern poet, and he was eager to find others of the same background and to determine what the essential characteristics of American poetry might be.

For all these reasons, when Fletcher was invited during his lecture tour of the South in the spring of 1927 to speak before the Centennial Club of Nashville, he eagerly accepted. He expected to be challenged by the Fugitives in his audience on his theory that future American poetry would be epic rather than analytical. For, although Fletcher felt at one with the Fugitives in their love of the old South and its traditions, he did not share their interest in purely intellectual poetry. Instead, he continued to believe that the poet must be emotionally identified with whatever he writes about. It was hard for him to see how the Fugitives could reconcile their love of tradition and their purely analytical approach to poetry. He was not challenged, however; instead he met both Ransom and Donald Davidson and was given Tate's address. Accordingly, he looked up Tate as soon as he arrived in New York.

Even though Fletcher did not accept Tate's defeatist attitude that the last hope for America had died in 1860, the meeting had an important consequence: in 1929, Tate invited Fletcher to contribute to a Fugitive symposium. Fletcher instantly agreed to do so; but he did not accept the Fugitives' idea that poetry should be entirely intellectual. He felt, however, at one with them in their advocacy of the culture of the old South and in their criticism of Northern industrialism. Fletcher considered the Fugitive movement an answer to the prayer he had cherished since he went abroad in 1908 to the effect that some section of America might be stirred to revolt against the civilization of the machine.

In 1931, Fletcher made a further commitment to the cause of Agrarianism by taking part in a round-table conference on regionalism at the University of Virginia. Representing the Agrarian group, Fletcher argued against a mechanized, highly industrial civilization. He believed the future of regionalism to be connected with a deliberate agrarianism that would be opposed to centralization of industry and to the culture of the big city. "Moreover, perhaps now the time was ripe for America to take moral stock, to see that behind all this talk of economic planning . . . lay another question . . . of what were the best elements upon which man *could* plan, and which would be the most conducive to the good and full life."

Thus, by writing the essay and by taking part in the conference on regionalism, Fletcher confirmed his faith in America: a faith that led him, in 1933, to return to America and to his native Little Rock. For the rest of his life, he devoted many of his best efforts to the cause of regionalism. Not only did he give great energy to the cause of bringing the best of music, art, and literature to his native state: he fully expected to see the South assume the intellectual leadership of the country.

Of the two volumes of poetry, *South Star* and *The Burning Mountain,* which Fletcher wrote during his regional phase, *South Star* is the earlier one. A large segment of the book, **"The Story of Arkansas,"** had appeared on June 15, 1936, in the State Centennial Supplement of the *Arkansas Gazette.* The other sections of the book are "Echoes of Arkansas," "Upper South," "Deep South," and "Epilogue"; and they consist of short lyric poems about Arkansas with Southern subjects and imagery. Underlying the poems are an attitude of anti-industrialism and a philosophy compounded of primitivism, the Confucian doctrine of the superior man, and the mystical quietism of Taoism.

Fletcher's abiding primitivism, earlier shown in *Gauguin* and *John Smith—Also Pocahontas,* manifests itself largely in the subject of the Arkansas pioneers and their simple lives in such poems as **"The Pioneers," "Lost Corner,"** and Book III of **"The Story of Arkansas":**

> In simple faith
> They drove their plows and purposes home to
>   earth,
> And heaped above the grave rough stones and slabs
> To mark them theirs; poor was their life and plain,
> But full of patience and the things of might:
> Might of birth, sorrow, death.

As early as 1926, in his introduction to his translation of Rousseau's *Reveries of a Solitaire,* Fletcher had advanced the doctrine of the superior man as the answer to modern social problems: "What we need now . . . is 'Superior men' in the sense that Confucius used the word." And in his contribution to the regional symposium, *I'll Take My Stand,* Fletcher had tested the educational principles of the South against the principles advanced by Confucius of the superior man. Balance and harmony, he quotes the Chinese sage as saying, are the basis of the world and its permanent law. "We employ our minds in order to . . . become the balanced personalities, the 'superior' men of Confucius' text, the 'gentlemen' of the old South."

In *South Star,* Fletcher set about, therefore, to re-create the tradition of a past culture as a solution to the problem of the modern social chaos, with emphasis on the Confucian superior man. The idealized Golden Age is the early period of Arkansas. Of the four parts of **"The Story of Arkansas,"** three of them idealize the state's traditions, as represented by the Spanish conquistadores, the French explorers, and the pioneers. The earliest superior man making his appearance in the book is De Soto, "An armoured man—a knight of ancient Spain." The poem traces the tragedy of De Soto through his three retreats, his illness, and his death. De Soto seems to exemplify the readiness of the superior man to die for the good way; furthermore, he had courage and faith in the great dream of conquest for which he was at last to die. Fletcher reinforces the tradition by creating the myth of De Soto's ghost riding in the Gulf storm: "Over the cotton, over the high-plumed grain, / De Soto rides again, seeking his dream of Spain."

Book II, "France Founds Arkansas," begins with the introduction of the French tradition, symbolized by Marquette and Joliet's canoes, and the French lilies:

> Paddle to paddle spoke;
> Into the heart of the South;
> Trailing the lilies past,
> Gold lilies of green France.

In the French tradition of Arkansas, the superior man was La Salle. According to Confucius, the superior man is the opposite of the petty man, the mean man. La Salle was a dreamer of dreams: "A marvelous vision cheered La Salle's stern heart." Like De Soto, he was courageous: "You stood your outpost watch, La Salle, / Lionlike, looking across the portages." Though he knew failure, he had great endurance: "Hard was your fate, La Salle; / Failure on failure heaped, yet you went on." After La Salle, other French explorers continued the Gallic tradition:

> They spread their songs afar:
> Their quick and savage wit, their lithe fierce fire;
> The lilt of fiddle under the evening star:
> *"J'ai cueilli la belle rose"*—such their desire
> To keep the sun-bronzed speech of vineyards that
> Knew their forefathers.

And so the French tradition became a part of the people of Arkansas.

To symbolize the pioneers and their moral strength, Fletcher begins Book III with a description of granite:

> Gray rock of the South,
> Granite amid the green oaks loosely twining
> Their scallop-work of leaves; the forest hides
> Your sleepy strength; but he who sees, believes
> How many waves of life have beat on you,
> Gray brow uplifted to the sky, unstained.

In the rock symbol is a suggestion of Confucius' superior man: "Imperturbable, resolute, tree-like . . . such a one is near goodness." The pioneers met the requirements of the superior man in several ways. Confucius said, "The superior man thinks of virtue; the small man thinks of comfort." Lovers of freedom, the pioneers disdained comfort:

> Their sparse settlements went up the river, till at
>   last the forests knew
> The sound of their long keen rifles, the glimmer
>   that their campfires cast;
> The bear crawled into green thickets, the Indian
>   withdrew,
> And the broadax hacked at the logs, till the cabin
>   stood fast.

Confucius said, "The wise find pleasure in water, the virtuous find pleasure in hills." And again he said, "It is virtuous manners that constitute the excellence of a neighborhood." The Arkansas pioneers lived and died near the hills and the water; in their simple way, they established the rituals of civilization:

> But in the backwoods deep,
> Where the people grew up with the canebreaks
>   along the green sluggish streams,
> And were lonely and shy like the deer or the dog-
>   wood, shaking its blossoms at the April sky,
> There was infare and wedding and birth as there al-
>   ways will be,
> And the slow oxen dragging the rude pine coffin up
>   to the top of the hill,
> Lonely and still,
> Solemn and free.
> Life here was simple and crude,
> But still it was good;
> "An Arkansas fandango with trimmings of Mis-
>   souri etiquette."

Book IV has as its theme the destruction wrought upon the state by the Civil War and Reconstruction. Perhaps Fletcher had in mind Confucius' words, "A people that no longer trusts its rulers is lost indeed," when he wrote:

> Weep, weep for the South,
> Let it never be forgot
> That the freedom which both sides sought
> And fought for, was stolen by knaves.

Fletcher continues in his task of creating deliberate tradition: the death of young David O. Dodd is an example of the superior man cleaving to virtue in time of danger:

> Let us remember the example of David O. Dodd,
> Caught and hanged as a spy at seventeen years of
>   age;
> Refusing to betray his own countrymen. As he
>   mounted to the scaffold at last,
> He turned to the executioner and said: "You will
>   find a handkerchief there in my pocket,"
> Willing that his eyes be blinded since he held to his
>   own inner light.

"The Story of Arkansas" ends with the suggestion of pioneer tradition:

> Cease your fiddling and your scraping,
> Draw up the latchstring, let the guests go home;
> Tread out the smoldering fires,
> Snuff up the guttering candles;
> Tomorrow we shall ride beyond the hills
> To seek our star.

Throughout the rest of the book, too, are Confucian ideals of tradition and the superior man. In **"Magnolia"** the three traditions—Spanish, French, and pioneer—are all included; they are fused by the symbol of the magnolia tree:

> De Soto stood under your branches
> Whetting his sword;
> Marquette tied his boat where you stood overshad-
>   ing some bayou,
> Knelt there and prayed;
> La Salle planted beside you the golden lilies of
>   France
> Proud and alone.
>   • • • • •
> Calico-clad settlers tied your blooms to the bonnets
>   of their wagons.

Besides the Confucianism of the book, *South Star* contains a number of poems based on the Taoist-Zen "recognition that something characteristic and structural in every organic and inorganic form is friendly to man, and responds gladly to the changing moods and powers of his spirit." In the poem **"Mount Holly,"** the sweet gum, the red haw, and the acorn mirror the poet's mood of meditation and reflection and dream:

> Here beyond hope, beyond dreams,
> Under this soft and lazy sky dreaming, in depth of
>   midwinter,
> Where the sweetgum casts to the earth its brown
>   prickly balls, where the holly
> Flashes its scarlet clusters, where the feather pine
>   sways its long needles,
> Where the redhaw blazes with berries threaded
>   bright on thin outspraying stems,
>   • • • • •
> Here was I fashioned and made.

In **"Arkansas Red Haw,"** nature mirrors something of the despair and sadness of the Old South and its lost cause:

> Darkened the thicket now,
> Snow drops its first faint wreath far down the west-
>   ern sky;
> Twilight is lowered
> Over the hill where so many men found the dignity
>   to die;
> And the slow, smoldering winter
> Turns over its burning heap of leaves and brown,
>   dried grasses again;
> Night runs over the furrow
> To the tune of the slow splash of rain.
>
> "Lost, rutted roads that ran to the South
>   • • • • •
> Here is hard living,
> Since so many hopes, sprung from the past, lay long
>   forgotten and dead."

Besides the Confucianism and the Zen Buddhism, *South Star* contains something of the quietism and mysticism of Lao-tzu, the founder of Taoism, and of Taoism's basic book, the *Tao Teh Ching*, especially in the poem **"Hillbilly Philosophy."** The following lines of the *Tao Teh Ching* concern the Tao, the Cosmic Mystery:

> The Tao that can be told of is not the absolute Tao;
>   the names that can be given are not Absolute
>   Names.
> The Nameless is the origin of Heaven and Earth,
>   the Named is the Mother of All Things.
> Therefore: Oftentimes one strips one's self of pas-
>   sion in order to see the Secret of Life;
> Often, one regards life with passion in order to see
>   its manifest forms.
> These two (the Secret and its manifestations) are (in
>   their nature) the same;
> They are given different names when they become
>   manifest.
> They may both be called the Cosmic Mystery:
> Reaching from the Mystery into the Deeper Mys-
>   tery is the Gate to the Secret of all Life.

As in other mystic apprehensions of the Absolute, the Tao "cannot be named, told, nor discussed in any great detail." Now let us see how Fletcher has translated the mystery, the elusiveness, the unnamable qualities of the Tao into the idiom of Arkansas hills and clear streams:

You will not wish to follow me
Across the twisted hills;
Along the milkwhite streams,
Adown green limestone sills;
Where challenging whippoorwills
Cry through the sky at dawn:
For into empty space
You'll find that I am gone.

Here is the Taoist (and Zen) love of mountain and water, the one suggesting "vastness and solitude, the other pliability, endurance, and continuous movement" [Huston Smith, *The Religions of Man*]. And here is the importance of empty space, the nonexistent; as the *Tao Teh Ching* puts it:

> 3. Forever and aye Reason remains unnamable, and again and again it returns home to non-existence.
> 4. This is called the form of the formless, the image of the imageless. This is called the transcendentally abstruse.

Fletcher's poem continues its Taoist ideas of the mystery of the unnamable, sung in a pronounced rhythm which may be meant to suggest the rhythm of the universe that is the Tao itself:

> For I have watched the snakes
> That glide—how swift—away;
> Like these, I learned to coil the rock,
> Like these, to melt in gray.
> You will not quickly find
> Nor love, the snake's dark house;
> Far less, the place where, vast and blind,
> The hills' great echoes rouse.

The *Tao Teh Ching* praises the mysterious in these words: "We look at Reason [Tao] and do not see it; its name is Colorless. We listen to Reason and do not hear it; its name is Soundless. We grope for Reason and do not grasp it; its name is Bodiless." Fletcher's song of the Deeper Mystery, too, stresses the difficulty of its access:

> You will not find me out;
> No man may easily find
> Where, behind laughter of the rocks,
> I hide my mind.
> Ungainly, gaunt and blind,
> It moves away from men,
> Threading, through age on age,
> The woodland's dark refrain.

In summation, **South Star**, for all its Ozark imagery and local color, is a blend of the Confucian ideals of deliberate tradition and the superior man, the Taoist-Zen idea of the moods of nature as an analogy to the moods of man, and the Taoist belief in the mystery and elusiveness of Tao. In the strange, alien path of Taoism, Fletcher is continuing his passionate search for the Absolute. As he quotes St. Augustine in his own biography, "We are lonely and dissatisfied, and our hearts are ever restless till they rest in Thee."

In quality, the poetry of the volume ranges from the direct statement of **"The Story of Arkansas"** to the power, the inevitability, and the sheer radiance that suddenly blaze out of the last two lines of **"The House to the Man"**:

> Therefore I say it is better to let me go,
> Better to break me down,
> Shear the wall off, topple the trees, with their burden,
> Trek for the North, and be gone;

Than to sit here still, listlessly brooding on quiet,
Still aimless and wan,
While over the Southern fields swings the immitigable
Gold hawk of the great Sun.

(pp. 128-37)

Edna B. Stephens, in her John Gould Fletcher, *Twayne Publishers, Inc., 1967, 160 p.*

EDMUND S. DE CHASCA   (essay date 1978)

[*In the following excerpt, de Chasca explains the similarities and differences between Fletcher's poetic theories and those of the Imagists.*]

Fletcher agreed with Pound, Aldington, and H. D. that English poetry needed a stylistic cleanup. In his reviews of the period, he repeatedly denounced rhetoric, inversions, archaic diction, and clichés. In a 1918 review of Thomas Hardy's *Moments of Vision,* for instance, he writes: "But we are all of us weary of the old poetic diction, which is utterly inapplicable to modern conditions and ideas. And that Hardy eschews rhetoric is perhaps the greatest thing to his credit." Two years later, in an article for the *Freeman,* he condemns the Georgian poet Robert Nichols for his "Tortured inversions, clever Elizabethan conceits, pedantic archaisms, overstrained rhetoric." Fletcher was not as concerned with the abuse of adjectives as were Pound and Aldington, but abstractions and stilted word order aroused his sarcasm. Particularly amusing are two reviews of war poetry that he wrote for the *Egoist* in 1914. In noticing an anthology of *Poems of the Great War,* for example, he observes that two separate poets use the line "God defend the right," and comments: "The mystery deepens. Which was the first to think of that immensely original line?" Two weeks later he mercilessly quotes the following quatrain from Stephen Phillips's *Songs and Sonnets of England in War-time:*

> There is a hush before the thunder-jar
>   When white the steeples against purple stand;
> There is a hush when night with star on star
>   Goes ashen on the summer like a brand.

Fletcher quips: "Mr. Phillips is evidently a foreigner who is trying desperately to write English, and not succeeding." He asks of a similar passage, "Is this Greek or Hebrew?" In his aversion to rhetoric and scorn of stilted, unnatural word order and speech, Fletcher was thoroughly a critical imagist.

He also shared the group's general attitudes toward subject matter. We might presume that Fletcher would readily assent to the principle of "absolute freedom in the choice of subject," as stated in the 1915 preface [to *Some Imagist Poets*], since not only the imagists but all of the "new" poets took for granted their freedom to write about whatever area of life engaged their interest. More exclusively imagistic was his advocacy of "definite treatment." He believed that the poet should write not merely from a general awareness but from some specific and exact vision. In his **"On Subject Matter and War Poetry,"** which appeared in the *Egoist,* for example, Fletcher maintains that the imagist is free to choose as his subject something either as trivial as a leaf on a windowsill or as large as a city or a period of history (an unlikely subject for an imagist), "so long as the subject is definitely something and not a mere indefinite abstraction." And in his evaluation of Amy Lowell in the "Special Imagist Number" of the *Egoist,* he lists among her special qualities the ability to "visualize," saying that "She sees her image before she sets it down. She has a horror of vagueness, of the cliché, of the abstract. Here she shows her Imagist tendencies. She is not ashamed to make pictures of anything that impresses her imagination, because she knows she can make good pictures." Fletcher and his colleagues had a "horror of vagueness" and the abstract because they associated these qualities with the kind of poetry that incorporated lines such as "God defend the right." Fletcher tellingly remarks near the end of **"On Subject Matter and War Poetry"** that it is reserved for some imagist to put "the reader face to face with the imaged reality" of the war. The implication is that if an imagist wrote about the war he would not shirk the truth with rhetoric but would confront it by making pictures of what he saw; he would make an "imaged reality" of the war as opposed to an abstract unreality. "Seeing your image before setting it down," therefore, was not only a technical formula but also implied a shared view of life.

Indeed, the chief point that Fletcher had in common with the rest of the imagists was his attitude toward life. Both Pound's early imagists and Amy Lowell's group thought that the current verse-writing tradition reflected a dishonest posture before life and sought to replace it with a steady, honest gaze toward experience. Fletcher felt comfortable as a member of the imagist group because he could make the following sort of statement with conviction:

> The very thing that distinguished a modern poet from a poet of the seventy years preceding today is precisely this: that a modern poet accepts experience at its face value, without wishing to warp it by some preconceived ethical judgment, or sentimental reaction, or aesthetic sensation. In other words, a modern poet writes about his feelings and experiences without preaching about them, as Tennyson did; or gushing over them, as Rossetti did; or insisting that they were beautiful, as Swinburne, Wilde, or Rupert Brooke did.

Fletcher frequently uses the word *imagism* as though it simply means "Don't preach." He judges a group of his own unpublished poems, for instance, to be "didactic and nonimagistic" and describes his verse **"Lincoln"** as "the first I had written in which the technique of Imagism was complemented by stanzas expressive of nothing but plain, unabashed, didactic purpose." Judging from these remarks, Fletcher believed the "technique of imagism" to be purely a matter of writing concretely and keeping one's opinions in the background.

In place of bluff and artifice, Fletcher and his co-imagists claimed to offer the qualities of honesty, directness, and restraint. They believed that they were replacing rhetoric with a straightforward, unpretentious approach to life, characterized by adherence to the simple, unembellished truth. It is quite instructive that in his judgments of his colleagues Fletcher looked more for these qualities than for traits that specifically exemplified imagistic theory. He was capable of writing an entire review of Aldington, for instance, without once mentioning the word *imagism,* instead citing the poet's "simplicity and restraint," his ability to write only "to satisfy . . . his own artistic conscience," and his veridical attitude ("Mr. Aldington is a poet who speaks the truth"). Nor is this review an isolated example. Talk about imagist doctrine is conspicuously absent from most of Fletcher's articles on the other members of the group. In the second part of the **"Three Imagist Poets,"** for example, he makes no effort to apply the principles explicated in the first part of the article

to the poems of H. D., Flint, and Aldington but treats the individual characteristics of their verse. References to imagism consist only of general, defensive statements such as, "It is time people understood that an Imagist is free to deal with whatever he chooses, so long as he is sincere and honest about it." Similarly, in a 1916 review of Mary Aldis, whom Fletcher at one time recommended for possible inclusion in the 1916 anthology, he praises her for being able "to face the uncomfortable facts of existence, and to write about them sincerely," with a "hard simplicity of statement." One must conclude from these and other examples that, along with free verse, imagism meant most importantly for Fletcher "sincerity" in art. He saw the movement as an attempt to restore this quality. Fletcher had written Miss Monroe, "I agree with schools only in the French sense, that a 'school' represents a certain attitude towards *life* held in common by a certain group." Both his actions and critical writings during the period 1914-1917 bear out this belief.

A final major point of agreement between Fletcher and the imagists—and the most important in the eyes of the public—concerned free verse. Of all the group members, Fletcher was one of the staunchest defenders of vers libre: in his prefaces to **Irradiations** and **Goblins,** he attacked rhyme and meter and argued for free forms; he had a strong hand in the anthology preambles, particularly in the 1916 preface, with its elaborate defense of cadence; and he favorably reviewed vers librists in numerous articles. Fletcher's discussions in support of free rhythms need not detain us at length since they consist for the most part of the usual imagist rhetoric. In the **Irradiations** preface, for instance, he criticizes the "fatiguing monotony" of "rag-time" iambic pentameter and declares "It is time to strip poetry of meaningless tatters of form, and to clothe her in new, suitable garments." A year later, in the preface to **Goblins and Pagodas,** he maintains that "the mere craftsman-ability to write in regular lines and metres no more makes a man a poet than the ability to stencil wall-papers makes him a painter." His best statement of the "form-should-follow-substance" idea, a staple item of the period, occurs in **"Three Imagist Poets,"** where he writes: "The rhythmical form of the poem . . . should follow, as far as possible, the ebb and flow of the emotion throughout the poem. It should be an integral part of the poem itself, as indissoluble from it as the substance of the words themselves. Therefore the Imagists hold that the theory and practice of vers libre is necessary." This notion was expressed many times between 1913 and 1917. The concluding sentence of the paragraph, however, is an interpretation purely of Fletcher's making: "In their desire to create a full emotional range of rhythmical nuances, inclusive of rhyme and metre as well as freer rhythmical figures, the Imagists derive direct from the first great romantic poets of England—Blake and Coleridge." Aside, possibly, from Miss Lowell, none of the other imagists believed that they derived from the "first great romantic poets of England." Furthermore, the phrase "freer rhythmical figures" hints at polyphonic prose, a form endorsed only by Fletcher and Miss Lowell. The sentence it belongs to may have been a slap at the short, staccato kind of vers libre practiced by Pound, Aldington, and H. D.—Fletcher preferred a longer-lined, more highly rhythmed free verse with a pronounced "swing." So we see that in his otherwise predictable defense of free form, Fletcher managed to work in some of his own aesthetic preferences. These were minor differences between him and the London imagists, however, and did not interfere with their basic agreement that verse should be unhindered by prescribed meters and stanza patterns. (pp. 162-67)

Fletcher agreed with the "technical hygiene" aspect of imagism; he shared his colleagues' aversion to preaching and rhetoric; he agitated vigorously for free verse. At this point, however, their poetics diverge.

First of all, he aimed at a different kind of poetic quality than the early imagists. Fletcher was interested in the musical possibilities of verse from his early years onward. In 1900-1901 he "swallowed all of Poe's theories wholesale" and later, during his poetic apprenticeship (1909-1912), he admired, among others, Shelley, Swinburne, and the lesser French symbolists, all poets for whom the musical value was an important consideration. The five early volumes he published in 1913 show the influence of these poets. At the time Fletcher met Pound and his circle, therefore, he had already taken his poetic mold from a group of sources entirely different from those drawn upon by "Les Imagistes." Pound was attracted by Anglo-Saxon and Provençal verse and the Aldingtons were enraptured with the poetry, spirit, and values of ancient Greece. Fletcher, on the other hand, was enthusiastic about poets who exploited "sound effects," and in his own verse made full use of assonance, consonance, alliteration, and other musical devices. The "best tradition" of Sappho, Catullus, and Villon referred to in the *Poetry* manifesto was alien to him. No wonder that Pound criticized the assonances in *Irradiations* or that Fletcher bridled at his remarks; they were working from antithetical points of view.

Fletcher exposes his preference for a rich-sounding verse most conspicuously in the *Irradiations* preface, dated January 1915. Like a true imagist, he attacks rhyme and defends free verse, but his argument against rhyme reveals distinctly nonimagistic tendencies:

> Poetry is an art which demands—though not invariably—the utmost richness and fulness of musical effect. When rhyme is considered as an additional instrument of what may be called the poetic orchestra, it both loses and gains in importance. It loses because it becomes of no greater import than assonance, consonance, alliteration, and a host of similar devices. It gains because it is used intelligently as a device for adding richness of effect.

Fletcher is cutting off his nose to spite his face here, for as the ever-alert Conrad Aiken points out: "What on earth, Mr. Fletcher, one is moved to ask, is richness so achieved if not decorative, and the very negation of your platform?" Aiken is right; Fletcher's statement does negate the imagist platform. A strict imagist would shun "richness and fulness of musical effect" for fear of blurring the outlines of his subject. Sumptuous sounds made for the "muzziness" that Pound, Aldington, and H. D. were trying to avoid. By arguing in favor of sound effects, Fletcher was unwittingly placing himself in another camp.

Fletcher's fondness for the musical in verse accounts for certain of his critical judgments that might otherwise be puzzling. It explains, for example, why he judged the work of H. D. to be "too purely visual—not . . . a combination of visual imagery and auditory echo." It also explains his attraction to the poetry of Conrad Aiken, one of imagism's peskiest opponents. Aiken's forte was word-music, the ability to invest his psychological narratives with a sensuous mist of sound. Fletcher praised his tone poems for their "haunting melody" and for being "cunningly constructed for the eye and ear," in a July 1916 review for *Poetry Journal,* much to Amy Lowell's exasperation. Finally, Fletcher's love of sound explains his great enthusiasm for polyphonic prose. With its surfeit of assonances, internal rhymes, and flamboyant working-up of emotion, that clanging, banging monstrosity was a suitable vehicle for every kind of musical device. Its effects, of course, were the very opposite of the spare, dry, hardness favored by the early imagists. As Pound told Harriet Monroe, "An imitation . . . of Paul Fort, can't be imagisme." Fletcher's zeal for this form reveals the extent to which his artistic orientation differed from that of Pound, H. D., and Aldington. Ironically, the period of his greatest enthusiasm for polyphonic prose, the first half of 1915, coincided with the period of his greatest involvement with Miss Lowell and the imagist movement.

A second area in which Fletcher differed from the early imagists was in his advocacy of a "soft" method of approaching poetic material. He seems to have taken his attitude toward subject matter from Oriental art. He relates in a letter to R. N. Linscott that in 1914 the Boston Museum of Fine Arts made a deep impression on him and set him to studying the art histories of Ernest Fenellosa, Laurence Binyon, and Ralph Adams Cram. He then went through the volumes of *The Select Relics of Japanese Art* by S. Yajima and capped off his efforts with a thirty-two-hundred-word article for the January 1917 *Dial* entitled **"The Secret of Far Eastern Painting."** Fletcher may be guilty of overstatement when he says in his memoirs that by 1915 he had "already been aware of the power of oriental art, in all its phases, to furnish subjects and to govern their treatment, for all my poems, without exception, since my writing of *Irradiations*," but Edna B. Stephens is not exaggerating when she writes that "one of the most important influences upon Fletcher's poetry was Far Eastern painting."

The *Dial* article contains the gist of Fletcher's thinking about the Oriental approach to subject matter. The secret of their method, he declares, rests on the belief that "everything in nature has, not only its outer form, but its inner state of feeling, with which the artist must be in sympathy before he can properly paint it." While the Western artist merely parrots or copies nature, the Oriental artist makes plain the "underlying emotions and feelings" in a figure or landscape. He continues: "If one proceeds by the Oriental method, one does not necessarily seek to put down any of the statistics of the reality. One selects from the whole object or series of objects before one a few features which contain all the emotional import of that object, and strives to render these in such a way as to suggest all the rest." In other words, the objects on a Japanese screen or roll picture suggest an entire emotional atmosphere. If the perspective in a Far Eastern painting is distorted, as when a flower on a distant mountain appears magnified to ten times its size, then it is because the artist is showing the true significance of that object. "A thing may be true to fact without being true in art," Fletcher affirms, adding that "the real perspective is the mental perspective, not the ocular." In sum, the Oriental artist renders, interprets, and even distorts nature in order to reveal the inner meaning he perceives in it.

Fletcher transfers this idea to poetry in the preface to *Goblins and Pagodas.* Using the unfortunate example of a book lying on his desk—Amy Lowell might write a poem about a book lying on her desk, but Fletcher never would—he explains how the various schools, Victorian and realist, would treat it as subject matter, saying that, as for himself, he would "strive to evoke a soul out of this piece of inanimate matter, a something characteristic and structural inherent in this inorganic form which is friendly to me and responds to my mood." He goes on to explain that this method has not often been used in Western countries but has been employed by Chinese and Japanese artists for centuries.

Perhaps Fletcher's best statement of his use of this method is in a 7 December 1915 letter to Harriet Monroe concerning the "Arizona" poems:

> What I have tried—and tried very seriously to do, was not to give an exact rendering of the Canyon, nor of any single feature of Arizona. . . . My poems are not guidebooks, neither are they impressions. They are for those who have never seen the Southwest—they are an evocation in my memory and imagination of its essence.
>
> Hence if I make my people and elements and scenery behave queerly at times, it is because I am not a realist . . . ; an Imagist (if the term means anything) strives to give at one and the same time, a reconstruction of the essence of the place, an interfusion of life and landscape, which interpret, explain, and illuminate each other.

The source of these ideas is anything but imagist doctrine which, as Fletcher's parenthetical remark suggests, he interpreted very broadly. His statement that the "Arizona Poems" are an "evocation in memory and imagination" brings to mind the anecdote he relates in his study of Paul Gauguin about the Chinese painter who was sent by his emperor to paint some landscape views, only to return empty-handed. When asked where his pictures were, he replied: "I have them here," and pointed to his forehead. Like the Chinese painter, Fletcher believed that the artist's duty was to transform his material into its imaginative substance. His remarks about the "Arizona" poems correspond to the Oriental approach to art.

Unlike the "hard" qualities that Pound, H. D., and Aldington strove for, Fletcher dealt with qualities of scene and his efforts to "heighten" reality made for imprecise, "soft" effects. The strict Imagist believed in treating even intangibles in a precise, tangible manner, as in H. D.'s "Heat," but Fletcher frequently rendered even solid objects intangibly. His aim was to capture emotional nuance, and while "Les Imagistes" did not preclude nuance, they did emphasize a severity of outline and tone, a starkness, even harshness of imagery, which was quite different from the delicate gradations of mood and subtle distinctions of color and tone favored by Fletcher. In short, he preferred the "larger, organic conception" to the briefer, more firm, classical realizations of Pound, Aldington, and H. D. As a result, they were far apart in belief and practice. Both in his attitude toward the function of individual words and in his method of handling subject matter, Fletcher was a "soft" poet. (pp. 167-72)

[A] survey of Fletcher's poetry from 1913 to 1916 reveals that very little of his large and varied output was, strictly speaking, imagistic. Certainly the "Symphonies," **"London Excursion,"** polyphonic prose pieces, "Mississippi" and "Arizona" poems, and most of *The Tree of Life,* in their length, frequent abstraction, and courting of the infinite, do not even remotely approach imagist ideals. As for the many short, objective, free-verse poems that Fletcher composed—*Irradiations,*

"The Ghosts of an Old House," *Japanese Prints,* "The Skaters," and other 1916 and 1917 anthology pieces—these have often passed for being imagistic, but they do not consistently possess the qualities of precision and "hardness" so crucial to the imagist aesthetic; nor do they aim at the sudden, intense release of energy that Pound associated with his image. At no time did Fletcher wholeheartedly adopt or try to realize imagist goals, i.e., to write poetry of a plastic nature or to "present an Image." Indeed, that he could produce the glaringly nonimagistic love poems that comprise *The Tree of Life* throughout the period of his association with the movement indicates that he was indifferent to some of the central tenets of imagism.

Fletcher's own beliefs in regard to the function of poetry as compared to those of the early imagists may be summarized as follows. He did not favor a maximum of visual content but felt that poetic style should be an attempt to develop the musical quality of literature. As a result, his poems cultivate not a sharpness of outline, but a richness of sound. Furthermore, while the early imagists focused on concrete objects and small pieces of reality, Fletcher tried to bring out the underlying essence of a scene. His most common way of doing this was through his "symphonic" method, which led to the quiet prolongation of effect rather than to the forceful "hit" or impact Pound tried to attain in his "image." It also resulted in the writing of many long poems, something the imagists were not known for. Lastly, Fletcher's manner of composition was different from that of the early imagists. They prided themselves on paring down their utterances to the fewest words possible and strove, through careful pruning, to give their compositions a finished, "made" quality. Fletcher customarily dashed off his poems in improvisational bursts and left them essentially unrevised. His work, characteristically, is not restrained and severe in tone, but has an exuberant and overflowing quality.

In spite of these differences, Fletcher was a bona fide participant in the movement, strongly involved in its intrigues, active in helping to write its prefaces, and a vocal defender of some of its tenets. How do we account for this paradox? The explanation is that Fletcher and his fellow imagists had a very broad concept of what constituted a literary school. Imagism, like the French "-isms" from which it took its cue, did not demand from its members rigid adherence to a specific doctrine, but only required that they agree to follow loose guidelines in writing poetry and share a common attitude toward life. It was this undefinable but real "attitude toward life" that Fletcher held in common with his imagist colleagues. Much more important than the flexible principles in the various manifestoes was their belief that they could rely on each other to write directly and "sincerely" about whatever moved them. Something was in the air, a new attitude toward experience which the principles of the manifestoes could only intimate, but which was, above all, their reason for banding together. Fletcher, by expressing his distaste for the mannerisms of recent poetry and by committing himself to metric freedom and definite treatment of a subject—indeed, by his whole artistic demeanor—showed that he shared this attitude toward experience and as a result could unhesitatingly be accepted as a peer.

John Gould Fletcher, imagist, fought many battles for Amy Lowell and the movement, but he was much more than one of her troopers: he was a gifted poet and intelligent man of letters whose work deserves a better fate than it has received.

Now that the story of Fletcher's role in the imagist movement has been told, let us hope attention may shift to his verse. (pp. 220-22)

> *Edmund S. de Chasca, in his* John Gould Fletcher and Imagism, *University of Missouri Press, 1978, 242 p.*

FURTHER READING

Aiken, Conrad. "Possessor and Possessed: John Gould Fletcher." In his *Scepticisms,* pp. 105-14. New York: Alfred A. Knopf, 1919.
    Discusses Fletcher's poetic intuition, maintaining that his "striking feature has always been his habit of surrendering himself, almost completely, to the power of these automatically unravelling verbal reflexes."

Baltzly, Alexander. "*The Two Frontiers.*" *Current History* 32, No. 3 (June 1930): 604-05.
    Criticizes Fletcher's historical study as factually inaccurate and diffuse, but praises Fletcher's insights as a cultural historian.

Behrens, Ralph. "John Gould Fletcher and Rimbaud's 'Alchimie du verbe'." *Comparative Literature* 8, No. 1 (Winter 1956): 46-62.
    Proposes "some specific comparisons between Rimbaud's 'Alchimie du verbe' and Fletcher's poetic theories."

Cappon, Alexander. "An Alien among the Imagists: John Gould Fletcher." *University Review* 4, No. 3 (Spring 1938): 165-72.
    Asserts the fundamental difference between Fletcher's poetry and that of the Imagists.

Cowley, Malcolm. "These Things Are Banal." *The Dial* 70 (June 1921): 700-04.
    Review of *Breakers and Granite* in which Cowley approves of certain individual poems but finds little merit in the volume as a whole. Cowley also discusses the literary influence Fletcher and Conrad Aiken had on each other.

Crowder, Richard. "John Gould Fletcher as Cassandra." *The South Atlantic Quarterly* 52, No. 1 (January 1953): 88-92.
    Describes the evolution of Fletcher's anti-industrial attitudes as they are presented in his poems about America.

Davidson, Donald. "In Memory of John Gould Fletcher." In his *Still Rebels, Still Yankees, and Other Essays,* pp. 31-40. Baton Rouge: Louisiana State University Press, 1957.
    Obituary tribute which provides a sketch of Fletcher's life and work.

Dembo, L. S. "Imagism and Aesthetic Mysticism." In his *Conceptions of Reality in Modern American Poetry,* pp. 10-47. Berkeley and Los Angeles: University of California Press, 1966.
    Sees in Fletcher's poetry an "impulse to escape from the self into the object in a mystical-aesthetic moment." Dembo also draws parallels between Fletcher's poetic philosophy and that of Hart Crane.

Fulkerson, Baucum. "John Gould Fletcher." *The Sewanee Review* 46, No. 3 (July-September 1938): 275-88.
    Review of *Life Is My Song* and *Selected Poems.* Fulkerson discusses Fletcher's life, his works, and his involvement in the Imagist movement.

Harmer, J. B. "Poems and Poets." In his *Victory in Limbo,* pp. 45-104. London: Secker and Warburg, 1975.
    Discusses Fletcher's Imagist period, concluding that "Fletcher is interesting as a lesser poet of his period who moved from romanticism in its nineteenth-century form to an updated method based on free verse and personal impressionism."

Hughes, Glenn. "John Gould Fletcher: Pictorialist and Mystic." In his *Imagism and the Imagists,* pp. 125-52. New York: The Humanities Press, 1960.
    Biographical sketch and critical survey of Fletcher's work to 1929.

Lund, Mary Graham. "John Gould Fletcher: Geographer of the Uncharted Province of Beauty." *The Sewanee Review* 56, No. 1 (Winter 1968): 76-89.
    Survey of Fletcher's poetry.

———. "John Gould Fletcher: An Anachronism." *Southwest Review* 51, No. 1 (Winter 1966): 37-45.
    Discusses Fletcher's search for a poetic theory, focusing on the role others played in his literary development.

Monroe, Harriet. "John Gould Fletcher." In her *Poets and Their Art,* pp. 87-91. New York: Macmillan Co., 1932.
    Survey of Fletcher's early volumes of poetry.

Pender, R. Herdman. "John Gould Fletcher." *The Egoist* 3, No. 11 (November 1916): 173-74.
    Asserts Fletcher's status as a poetic innovator, praising his use of rhythm and imagery in expressing emotion.

Perkins, David. "Imagism." In his *A History of Modern Poetry,* pp. 329-48. Cambridge, Mass.: The Belknap Press, 1976.
    Contains a biographical and critical sketch focusing on Fletcher's Imagist period.

Pound, Ezra. "Peals of Iron." *Poetry* 3, No. 3 (December 1913): 111-13.
    Review of *Fire and Wine* and *The Dominant City* in which Pound states that Fletcher "can at his best be concrete and grim and specific. . . . I have here come upon a work that moves me, although my own canons suffer violence."

Squires, J. Radcliffe. Review of *The Burning Mountain,* by John Gould Fletcher. *The Chicago Review* 1, No. 3 (Summer 1946): 172-73.
    Negative review in which Squires claims that "Mr. Fletcher's technique is simple. First he says, 'Look-what-beauty-I-see.' Then he defines, redefines; but beauty, like a joke, becomes tedious with explanation."

Review of *Irradiations—Sand and Spray,* by John Gould Fletcher. *The Times Literary Supplement,* No. 705 (22 January 1915): 247.
    Unfavorable review which states that Fletcher's "vein of inspiration is thin."

Untermeyer, Louis. "The Imagists." In his *American Poetry since 1900,* pp. 305-22. New York: Henry Holt and Company, 1923.
    Criticizes Fletcher's early poetry for its wordiness and occasional incoherence, but claims that the poems in *Breakers and Granite* "mark the advent of a new poet, one who has grown through 'schools' and rococo innovations to a passionate mysticism."

Warren, Austin. Review of *Preludes and Symphonies,* by John Gould Fletcher. *The Bookman* 72, No. 1 (September 1930): 89.
    Praises the "fragile beauty" of these poems and the "sure self-criticism" in the preface.

Webster, Harvey Curtis. "Music vs. Eloquence." *Poetry* 69, No. 6 (March 1947): 353-56.
    Praises the musical qualities of the verses in *The Burning Mountain,* but criticizes their diffusion of meaning.

Zabel, Morton Dauwen. Review of *XXIV Elegies,* by John Gould Fletcher. *New Republic* 85, No. 1101 (8 January 1936): 263-64.
    Asserts that Fletcher's intelligence and cultural consciousness save these poems from the self-indulgence of Imagism.

Rex Ingamells

1913-1955

(Born Reginald Charles Ingamells) Australian poet, critic, and novelist.

Ingamells is best known as the founder and leader of the Jindyworobaks, a group of Australian poets of the 1930s and 1940s who sought to develop a unique national culture and literature based on the Australian environment. Their prose and poetry, which featured vivid descriptions of the Australian landscape as well as Aboriginal terms and imagery, has been recognized as an important influence on the development of Australian literature and culture.

The son of a country minister, Ingamells was born in Orroroo, a small town in South Australia. After attending Prince Albert College, he studied history at Adelaide University. While a student, Ingamells began writing poetry and became interested in Aboriginal culture. He was strongly influenced by W. B. Spencer and F. J. Gillen's *The Arunta* (1927), an anthropological work that examines the Alchera (the "Dreamtime" or "Dreaming"), the creation myth that is the basis for every aspect of Aboriginal culture. The subjects and themes Ingamells explored during this period remained central to his work throughout his life. Following his graduation from Adelaide University, he held a series of jobs, working as a free-lance journalist, teacher, and publisher's representative, and traveled extensively throughout South Australia and Victoria. His first book of poetry, *Gumtops,* was published in 1935. This work, like many that followed, featured memorable descriptions of the Australian landscape. During the late 1930s, Ingamells developed the social and artistic ideas that resulted in the formation of the Jindyworobak movement. Outlining the purpose and tenets of the movement in his 1938 essay *Conditional Culture,* Ingamells concluded that a distinctly Australian literature did not exist and could not develop until Australian writers based their works on the Australian environment and Aboriginal culture, rejecting English terminology that was not appropriate to Australian life and incorporating Aboriginal language and symbols, especially the imagery of the Alchera. Ingamells and other Jindyworobak poets, including Ian Mundie and Roland Robertson, were immediately characterized as misguided and overzealous by critics who argued that English-language literature had nothing to learn from such an "uncivilized" people as the Aborigines. Ingamells was further criticized for his involvement in Australia First, a controversial nationalist group, and his attempts to express political and social opinions through his poetry were deprecated as lacking artistic merit. He died in an automobile accident in 1955.

Ingamells's Jindyworobak philosophy is reflected in both his prose and his poetry. *Aranda Boy,* a children's story, describes the experiences of an Aboriginal child, while his novel *Of Us Now Living: A Novel of Australia* is a complex narrative that recounts the history and settlement of a fictional Australian township. Much of Ingamells's poetry focuses on various aspects of the Australian continent: many of his poems feature description of the landscape, while others, such as the epic *The Great South Land,* describe the process of European discovery and settlement. Whereas many contemporary critics derided Ingamells's frequent use of Aboriginal terms in his poems as superfluous and artificial, others applauded this innovation. Later commentators have noted that, contrary to what some critics asserted at the time, the Jindyworobaks did not strive to imitate Aboriginal poetry, but rather incorporated Aboriginal elements into traditional European poetic forms. Commentators generally maintain that Ingamells's shorter poems best exhibit his skillful description and evocative imagery. By contrast, *The Great South Land,* which has been praised as containing some of Ingamells's best writing, has for the most part been described as overly long and pretentious. In his *History of Australian Literature,* H. M. Green concludes that Ingamells's poetic talent was "genuine and not without individuality, but not great." Ingamells was most important in Australian literature for encouraging the development and expression of an Australian consciousness.

PRINCIPAL WORKS

Gumtops (poetry) 1935
Forgotten People (poetry) 1936
Conditional Culture (essay) 1938
Sun-Freedom (poetry) 1938
Memory of Hills (poetry) 1940
News of the Sun (poetry) 1942
Content Are the Quiet Ranges (poetry) 1943
The Unknown Land (poetry) 1943
Yera (poetry) 1945
Come Walkabout (poetry) 1948
The Great South Land (poetry) 1951
Of Us Now Living: A Novel of Australia (novel) 1952
Aranda Boy (novella) 1954

REX INGAMELLS (essay date 1938)

[*In the following excerpt from his essay* Conditional Culture, *Ingamells explains the purpose of the Jindyworobaks and asserts the importance of developing a genuinely Australian culture.*]

"Jindyworobak" is an Aboriginal word meaning "to annex, to join," and I propose to coin it for a particular use. The Jindyworobaks, I say, are those individuals who are endeavouring to free Australian art from whatever alien influences trammel it, that is, to bring it into proper contact with its material. They are the few who seriously realize that an Australian culture depends on the fulfilment and sublimation of certain definite conditions, namely:

1. A clear recognition of environmental values.
2. The debunking of much nonsense.
3. An understanding of Australia's history and traditions, primaeval, colonial, and modern.

The most important of these is the first. Pseudo-Europeanism clogs the minds of most Australians, preventing a free appreciation of nature. Their speech and thought idioms are European; they have little direct thought-contact with nature. Although emotionally and spiritually they should be, and, I believe, are more attuned to the distinctive bush, hill and coastal places they visit than to the European parks and gardens around the cities, their thought-idiom belongs to the latter not the former. Give them a suitable thought-idiom for the former and they will be grateful. Their more important emotional and spiritual potentialities will be given the conditions for growth. The inhibited individuality of the race will be released. Australian culture will exist.

The natural distinctiveness of the Australian continent from other lands of the world is too fundamental to vanish in the period of human history. The massive gum trees along the banks of the Murray, the gums and the mallee and the tea-tree that straggle about this vast continent; the empty spaces of our deserts; and the atonal music of the magpie and the good-natured mockery of the kookaburra—these are things that must remain. They belong to the indestructible spirit of the place about which D. H. Lawrence has written in a superb piece of natural description at the beginning of *Kangaroo*. But D. H. Lawrence realized that spirit, however intensely, only in a small part: he did not feel at home in the bush, although its power gripped him. There are thousands of Australians today who, if they have not found eloquent tongue, feel, nevertheless, with childlike devotion, the familiar beauty and utter loveliness of the outback environment in many of its moods.

Our pioneers, or the majority of them, were Englishmen who brought to this country the English manners and customs of the moment of their migration. As long as they lived they were strangers in a strange land. Many of them may have become more or less used to their new environment, but they never could become one with it. The background of their minds was made up of other associations. Yet they were isolated from the current movements of fashion and culture in the old country: in this sense they slipped behind the times. The English manners and customs which they inculcated into their children were bound to be considerably out of date by the time those children reached maturity. Thus the word "colonial" was justified, in so far as it signified rawness and lack of sophistication.

Although fresh influences were continually coming in, these were neither sufficient nor strong enough to compete with the isolation and environmental resistance, and could work only superficially. Hence any genuine culture that might develop in Australia, however it might be refreshed and inspired by English influences, would have to represent the birth of a new soul. A fundamental break, that is, with the spirit of English culture, is the prerequisite for the development of an Australian culture. Without the fact of ultimate individuality, separate identity, any general sense of culture in any country must be misty and anaemic. However strong and innumerable, however desirable and inevitable, however traditional our cultural ties with Europe may be, it is not in these ties that we must as a people seek our individuality. Its quintessence must lie in the realization of whatever things are distinctive in our environment and their sublimation in art and idea, in culture.

Australian culture is at present in a nebulous stage, because our writers have not come clearly to any such realization. I do not wish to be misunderstood. Some of the greatest Aus-

tralian literature yet to be may have no local colour at all. Its settings may be in China or Mars. Our best poetry must deal with universal themes; and whether or not the Australian environment forms a background is a matter for individual poets. But all this does not affect the essence of my argument. The real test of a people's culture is the way in which they can express themselves in relation to their environment, and the loftiness and universality of their artistic conceptions raised on that basis. When, for example, someone begins a novel and sets the scene in Australia, he cannot hope to produce great art unless he has a true conception of environmental values. When our writers understand these, they will look at most of what they have written to date and say, "That is the way not to write about Australia."

The biggest curse and handicap upon our literature is the incongruous use of metaphors, similes, and adjectives. It is usual to find Australian writers describing the bush with much the same terminology as English writers apply to a countryside of oaks and elms and yews and weeping willows, and of skylarks, cuckoos, and nightingales. We find that dewdrops are spoken of as jewels sparkling on the foliage of gum trees. Jewels? Not amid the stark, contorted, shaggy informality of the Australian bushland. Nothing could be more incongruous. Jewels? I see the pageantry of the Old World, and of the march of history from the time when the Norman ladies came to England to the present day, when glittering cosmopolitan crowds mingle in the casinos of Monte Carlo and the ornate ballrooms of Venice; I see the royal courts of England, and those of France and Spain now forgotten; and I see, if you like, a vice-regal gathering or a theatrical party in Adelaide—but I do not, cannot, see jewels metaphored off on gum trees, which are so far removed from all the things with which jewels are traditionally associated. I cannot deplore too vehemently the dangerous habit of using figures of speech with regard to essentially Australian things which call up such a flood of Old World associations as to gloze over all distinctiveness. It has been a piteous custom to write of Australian things with the English idiom, an idiom which can achieve exactness in England but not here.

We look to poetry for the keenest perception and expression of aesthetic values; so that, if we want to find how the Australian natural environment has been appreciated by the British stock which has become acclimatized here, we cannot do better than to study the appropriate section of its poetry. It soon becomes obvious that the very achievements of English poetry have been the fetters of Australian. When will our poets realize that by writing variations upon Australian themes in the wide and established range of verse vocabulary which tradition has built up in England, they are dodging the issue and compromising their intelligence? Individuality can only discover itself where there is an independent spirit; and the individuality of nearly every Australian poet so far has been subservient—subservient to the spirit and idiom of English poetry.

Here are the first two stanzas of George Essex Evans's poem, "On the Plains," which is dealing with an Australian scene; but there is not a hint of Australian individuality in the whole fourteen lines, because they are simply webbed about by the spider of northern verse idiom:

> Half-lost in film of faintest lawn,
>   A single star in armour white
> Upon the dreamy heights of dawn
>   Guards the dim frontier of the night,

Till plumed ray
And golden spray
Have washed its trembling light away.

The sun has peeped above the blue;
    His level lances as they pass
Have shot the dew-drops thro' and thro',
    And dashed with rubies all the grass,
And silver sound
Of horse-bells round
Floats softly o'er the jewelled ground.

"Armour white," "frontier of the night," and "jewelled ground" are inexcusable.

An English poet, A. E. Housman, writes very beautifully and appropriately:

. . . when the light in lances
Across the mead was laid,

but "lances" cannot be associated with the Australian landscape, which is primitive, and has no European mediaeval associations. "Spears" is obviously the right word. Metrically, of course, it would require the revision of the whole line, and it would not even occur to a writer whose mind is still subservient to the language of the English countryside.

All our poets show this fault. Gordon writes:

Hark! the bells of distant cattle
    Waft across the range,
Through the golden-tufted wattle,
    Music low and strange;
Like the marriage peal of fairies
Comes the tinkling sound . . .

It is all very well for Australian children to be told Old World fairy tales—which demand more make-believe from them than they do from English children—but our poets are creating false associations when they try to fit fairies of the *Midsummer Night's Dream* tradition into the mood of the bush. Picaninnies and Gumnut Babies are at least more appropriate.

When will our writers achieve a sense of the fitness of things? Kendall wrote:

On the tops of the hills, on the turreted cones,
    Chief temples of thunder,
The gale like a ghost in the middle watch moans,
    Gliding over and under . . .

That is false to the very roots of its inspiration, and therefore not poetry, but plain doggerel. The Australian hills were in Kendall's mind, but they might as well have been the Alps surrounded on all sides by civilizations centuries old. The atmosphere of the bush, the brooding solitude of ages of time passing over the sombre, stark beauty of twisted trees was intrinsically lost on him. Kendall is practically valueless as an Australian poet.

It is so easy, considering the dearth of good Australian writing, for a person who has any knowledge of the literature of England to think of the bushland grass and trees as "jewelled" on a summer dawn; and it is easy, in the same way, to think of the hills as appearing like the turrets of Norman castles or being "crowned" with stars. This last image spoils these otherwise perfect lines from Evans's "Australian Symphony":

The grey gums by the lonely creek,

The star-crowned height,
The wind-swept plain, the dim blue peak,
    The cold white light.

Such imagery does not convey one atom of the individuality of the Australian landscape. People of other countries can gain no real conception of this land by reading such trash.

If we cannot apply typically Old World imagery to the Australian landscape, what can we substitute? Obviously, only such imagery as is truly Australian. This limits the field! Any writer's field at any time should be defined and limited by his subject.

Here is a modern instance, taken from Roderick Quinn, of the type of inaccuracy against which culture in this country must fight:

Out in the dark where the night-winds hurry
And dead leaves carpet the silent bush . . .

The word "carpet" makes the bush seem like a drawing-room or, at best, like Epping Forest or Sherwood. Inexpressibly beautiful as these forests may be, it is an insult both to their own individuality and to that of our bush to write in that way.

How much more vivid is it to read such lines as these from Evans's "On the Plains," from which I quoted earlier! Although even here we note unsuitable exoticisms in such expressions as "motley," "vanguard," "monarch," and "satrapies," the fundamental impression is one of inspired observation, in which the spirit of the place lives:

Afar I mark the emu's run;
    The bustard slow, in motley clad;
And, basking in his bath of sun,
    The brown snake on the cattle-pad;
And the reddish-black
Of a dingo's back,
As he loit'ring slinks on my horse's track.

And now I watch, with slackened rein,
    The scattered cattle, hundreds strong,
As, slowly feeding home again,
    The lazy vanguard feeds along
To the waters cool
Of the tree-fringed pool
In the distant creek when the moon is full.

Slip girth and let the old horse graze;
    The noon grows heavy on the air;
Kindle the tiny campfire's blaze,
    And, 'neath the shade, as monarch there,
Take thou thine ease:
For hours like these
A king had bartered satrapies.

The last stanza, of course, which begins with three splendid lines, degenerates into a welter of incongruity. Evans and Gordon were equally unaware of any essential distinction between the poetical language of Australian landscape and that of England. Their best writing, like their worst, was spontaneous; accompanying their spontaneity, they had no such adequate sense of self-criticism as must be the condition of sustained merit.

P. R. Stephensen has very broadly delineated the development of Australian poetry in the following terms:

"From Gordon, the Englishman, writing about Australia in an English way, to Kendall, the Australian, writing about Australia in an English way; thence to Lawson and Paterson, the Australians, writing about Australia in an Australian way. . . ." Stephensen should have said: " . . . to Lawson and Paterson, the Australians, writing about Australia in a larrikin Australian way; and what we now want is Australians writing about Australia in a literary Australian way."

Even in Lawson and Paterson we find certain English tricks of thought and expression, incongruous in poetry of the Australian countryside. Thus Lawson writes:

> The cattle-tracks between the trees
> Were like long dusky aisles,

which simile robs the cattle tracks of any vigorous reality or faithful idealism. But such infidelities are exceedingly rare in Lawson and Paterson. We find many whole poems which contain not one unsuitable exoticism. Australians should be prouder of these two writers than they apparently are. They are not great writers; they are very limited in their powers, and too often sing-song and jingoistic, melodramatic and sentimental; but, in their own way, they are faithful to the spirit of the place. Such poems as "Outback" and "Clancy of the Overflow" have a significance. Their significance lies in the purity and forcefulness of the vision in them, however circumscribed this may be.

Significant as was the lesson taught by Lawson and Paterson, it has borne very little fruit in those that followed after. Dorothea Mackellar's poem, "My Country," marks an advance; but we must conclude that luck played a part, because elsewhere Dorothea Mackellar falls into the old, happy feeling, deplorably uncritical flow of so-called inspiration. The happy flow of emotion without a keen sense of values and unwavering honesty of criticism is quite incapable of maintaining consistently such a standard of worth as Mackellar's one poem.

Doctor Johnson wrote: "What we wish to do with ease we must first learn to do with diligence."

And there is a lesson in that for all Australian writers.

One of A. A. Bayldon's short poems, "The Swamp," has caught as well as anything else I know something of the grotesque side of the Australian place spirit:

> Huddled round leering pools, the haggard trees
> Await their doom, the black ooze to their knees.
> Sighing together, when, with elfin spite,
> A small breeze whispers of a world of light,
> They strain crooked limbs toward that bright blue plain
> The dank sweat drips—a stifling hush again.
> In goblin gloom maimed weaklings moaning fall
> Into the pools ahunger for them all.

This poem would be perfect were it not for the two epithets, "elfin" and "goblin." The words "cunning" and "reeking" are the first substitutes that occur to me. The poet at the time of writing, with a little extra critical attention, might have thought of better. I may be thought to be quibbling here, to be running a theory to death. Poetry, it is said, is among the materials of poetry. But I maintain that poetic idiom with a Hans Andersen flavour, while it may be suitable to Europe, is not suitable for an Australian outback scene. Integrity! Integrity!

I trust that it is now plain what I mean by environmental values: the distinctive qualities of an environment which cannot be satisfactorily expressed in the conventional terms that suit other environments, scrupulous care being necessary for the indication of their primal essence.

The whole of the English vocabulary is ours for appropriate use, but we must discriminate. D. H. Lawrence came to Australia from the centres of northern culture, but his description of the bush is appropriate. He was a great writer and instinctively avoided incongruities. The huge electric moon he saw above the bushland scene was the same he knew the world over, symbolical of the old lesson that Art is international, universal, but its expressions specialized and individual.

The reason why Australian culture is not yet something unmistakably defined is that its individuality, its permeating essence, has been smothered with exoticisms, which, unless most carefully handled—and they have not been—are absolutely impossible of permeation. Australian writers have too often imitated English writers, instead of assimilating lessons from their styles and working out styles of their own on the basis of inspiration of their own.

Good writers in Australia have been very few, and great examples of indigenous literature are rare.

Australian literary criticism has been of little help.

H. M. Green's *Outline of Australian Literature* is disappointing—little more than a catalogue. "Australia," says Mr Green, "belongs, by race, politics and language to a great civilization that reaches back for thousands of years, and it is constantly receiving an inflow, ideal as well as human, from the centre of that civilization." Again, he says, "When we add that Australia has her own peculiar characteristics and problems, we shall realize that her literature, a reflection of her civilization, is likely to diverge in some, perhaps in important respects, from the course taken by the parent literature."

In these two quotations we have distinctly shown to us the two forces which must be synthesized into an Australian culture, the temperament of the land and that of the people, in so far as it has its roots elsewhere, but the indication of the necessary distinctiveness which must result from this synthesis is too cautious, ridiculously cautious. Australian literature *must*, to develop, diverge in *important* respects from the course taken by the parent literature.

There has been too much of this pro-English pandering. Not that anyone—especially Mr. Green—means to pander. But it has been in our bones too long and it comes out where we might least expect it. *The Outline* is useful as a catalogue of (for the most part) feeble Australian writers, but there its value ends. There is no spark in the middle of it. Mr. Green speaks of the need for criticism in Australian literature, yet the shaft of his criticism is so mild as to be of little use. It dodges the issue. The question is: What is wrong with our Australian literature? The answer is: Our writers have not looked at Australia with any honest perception of its values. They have taken the easy course, followed the line of least resistance; they have simply appropriated English methods of expression without attempting to hammer out a really suitable idiom of their own. A scientific attack seems necessary for the first stage in view of the facts; spontaneity can then be of the right sort.

Every civilized culture (the two terms are not synonymous) and every literature contains within itself countless exotic elements which have been assimilated and permeated and coloured by the individuality of the particular culture. But that individuality is the all-important thing. It is the distinctiveness, the essence, the *sine qua non* of the culture.

Yet, in a valiant editorial which, however, misses most points, Mr. P. R. Stephensen says:

> We admire the English, we love them frequently, we never fail to respect them, we are astonished by their spectacle of culture, and by their castles, churches, and ruins. . . . But . . . unless we can use imported English culture here as one element (concede it to be the most important element) in building up our indigenous culture, it is a meaningless nothing to us.

I cannot concede, as Mr. Stephensen does, that imported English culture is the most important element in Australian culture, even if it does at present, unfortunately, occupy the front of the scene. The most important thing in any *man,* surely, is that spark of individualism which is the man himself and distinguishes him from other men. He has a body like other men, but it is the individuality of the man which transcends the body and gives his presence significance. The same with a nation. The same with a nation's culture. However indispensable imported elements of culture may be to a people, before there can be said to be an indigenous culture among them there must be self-awareness, a form of egoism, perhaps, but certainly a genuine feeling of the nation's individuality.

Ours is a country of endless contrasts, of beauty and terror, of fertile lands and empty deserts. It is a country of moods, of ever-changing, incalculable moods. But always the land's individuality, the spirit of the place (which Stephensen learnt vaguely without analyzing), is there, speaking through the medium of the mood, for those who have eyes to see and ears to hear.

The growth of spiritual affinity of the people with the country has been slow and difficult and, up to the present, very imperfect. But the time has come when . . . the roots have gone down deep into the soil; and when the imperfections must be obvious to anyone who makes the effort to think intelligently—and can be remedied. (pp. 249-59)

> Rex Ingamells, *"Conditional Culture,"* in The Writer in Australia: A Collection of Literary Documents, 1856 to 1964, *edited by John Barnes, Oxford University Press, Melbourne, 1969, pp. 245-65.*

C. R. JURY (essay date 1940)

[*In the following excerpt, Jury criticizes the extreme nationalism of the Jindyworobak movement.*]

With Australian poets who aspire to treat the universal subjects of literature in a manner consistent with Australian conditions I am wholly in sympathy, so long as the consistency they demand is not rigid or specific. Parochialism is bad; so is distortion of facts. I do not like this harping on the oppressiveness of the European tradition. We Australians are most of us Europeans, whether we like it or not; and for us the difference in value, whether aesthetic or practical, between the European tradition and any that can with accuracy be called purely Australian is enormously large in favour of Europe. Besides, even if it were desirable, we cannot turn into aborigines; and if we could and did, we should inevitably go the way they have already gone. To do Jindyworobak justice, it does not advocate quite so drastic a step as this, at least not in such crude terms; but it does seem to lay stress on the throwing off rather than the adjustment to ourselves of what we have

derived from Europe, and this is not conducive to the balance of the mind. . . . I have ventured to make some small verses of my own in this connection, as follows.

Kangaroo My Totem.

As I stand here on the hill-top in the very early morning
The shadows of the gum trees
Shape themselves like kangaroos:
Magic of the Land!
Kangaroo my totem, kangaroo,
Keep from the Land
Not only the gods and the traditions of Europe,
Asia, North and South America and Africa,
But also their inhabitants! Protect me, totem!
I prefer to be purely, simply Australian.
Kangaroo my totem, kangaroo,
Change me first to an aborigine
With lubra, with humpy
In a great silence;
Then make me truly
A kangaroo.
When shall I feel in my hams
An inclination to hop?

(pp. 35-6)

> *C. R. Jury, "Phoenix, 1939," in* Southerly, *Vol. 1, No. 2, April, 1940, pp. 33-6.*

THELMA HERRING (essay date 1940)

[*In the following excerpt, Herring reviews* Memory of Hills.]

Whereas most of our local writers have of late protested against the gum-tree tradition, the Jindyworobak Club, of which Rex Ingamells is a member, is fostering a new movement towards nationalism in Australian literature. Much may be said for both points of view, and if the one side can point to Brennan, the other can cite Lawson to support its case. To be sure, the poetaster self-consciously parading as a patriot is a distressing spectacle; but in his collection of poems entitled **Memory of Hills,** Mr. Ingamells writes with unmistakable sincerity. His purpose is stated in the opening piece:

> I have hard faith to keep in midst of sham
> because suburban tritenesses would damn
> the human spirit, and defeatist breath
> fails under load of bitter pang
> in cramped backyards of memory-death
> where moon-pale mists of washing hang.

Bush and desert provide the setting for most of his poems, some of which are slight, but none commonplace. He several times contrasts city and country, to the advantage, of course, of the latter; thus in **"Cross-Section"** the triviality of the city-dwellers' pursuits is emphasised by contrast with the black duck and the crows, symbols of "nature's unconcern." The aborigines provide the subjects of other poems: in **"Maiden Form,"** for instance, he gives us a graceful picture of a little native girl, and in **"From a Dying People"** he speaks with dignity and restrained defiance for an unfortunate race.

Notwithstanding his rejection of European traditions, Mr. Ingamells is no bush-balladist, but a careful craftsman with a fine command of cadence, not scorning to use conventional metres where they suit his purpose, but able to handle more irregular and flexible rhythms as well. He has, too, a gift for picturesque description, as of the hills with

their reflex of moonlight, their kind
wrinkled acknowledgment of the moon's clarity.

The opening stanza of **"From a Dying People"** provides another example:

> The sun shall wound with flickering fang
> night-weary ridge and shadowy plain
> and send the blood of evening down
> the western gorges time again.

(pp. 30-1)

*Thelma Herring, in a review of "Memory of Hills,"
in* Southerly, *Vol. 1, No. 4, November, 1940, pp.
30-3.*

MAX HARRIS   (essay date 1943)

[*In the following excerpt, Harris condemns the Jindyworobaks
in general and Ingamells in particular for lack of poetic qualities in their work.*]

All that the critic can do is to examine the poetry that is produced according to the highest aesthetic judgment and sensitivity that he can develop within himself. But how little competent poetic analysis, discussion of rhythm, texture, poetic integrity has gone on in this country since the Jindyworobaks and others started screeching about National Resurgence and What Poetry Should Be About, and the Important National Values Poetry Should Set Up. Have they judged according to poetic standards where the best work is coming from in this country, how the medium is being used, the verbal success of the vision?

The sole issue of any importance so far as the literature of this country goes is the poetic quality of the poetry. I will take the poetry of Rex Ingamells as the example, simply for the reason that he is perhaps the most representative of the plague of national poets. In this series it will not be the nationalist nor the universalist that I will examine, but the poet.

Mr. Ingamells's work has developed quite peculiarly along with his thought. His first book, *Gumtops,* published in 1935, contains a certain sincerity and quiet feeling that hints at poetry. At this unsophisticated stage he is most certainly undergoing sensitive feelings towards the world about him. The prevailing atmosphere is of mood and rather vague romanticism. Nostalgia does not offer a very profound poetic experience in association with certain perspectives (contrast Rainer Maria Rilke) but at times the young Ingamells gets it across through a pleasing feeling for word-texture, for hard and soft.

> I have seen a flaming peak at dawn
> Across a sea of sand. Alone it stood,
> And bare of all but colour.

But often the spasms of genuine feeling and poetry are thwarted by an uncertainty of idiom, a degeneration of the simple and genuine feeling imposed by an inability to express it. Not being at home in poetry he falls constantly into the trap of "poeticism."

> There was nought else in that vast lonely place
> To breathe of Beauty; and I gazed in awe,
> To think that even there she held her sway;
> To think that, her staunch slave, with such fierce grace
> That peak at dawn blazed centuries before,
> And so blazed now, and so should blaze for aye.

Here the verse has ceased to be the peculiar and integral vi-

sion of the poet, and is becoming an echo of the way Wordsworth, and possibly Keats, experienced.

As he developed Ingamells's vision became literary-political; it entered the field of attitude rather than feeling. All his later poetry has this atmosphere of attitude towards what he sees, rather than reaction to what he sees.

His technical capacity, his idiom becomes slicker, but there is a thinning out of the tension of experience underlying it. The strengthening of attitude impoverished the poetry. Being aware of this lack of poetic force behind their attitude-poetry, almost all of the Jindyworobaks fell behind a developing sort of jargon. This jargon has become just as much a form of "poetic diction" as that Wordsworth and Coleridge disposed of. On sincerely studying the poetry I cannot help coming to the conclusion that it is the product of a sense of artistic deficiency.

Here are some examples:

> Spirits shall haunt this land. O we
> Shall roam a dim Alcheringa,
> Our gods shall show us mystery
> And you not know it, Waruntha.
>
> Far in moorawathimeering,
> Safe from wallan darenderong,
> Tallabilla waitjurk, wander
> Silently the whole day long.

The jargon consists in "Aboriginalizing" language. All Australian poets must be European to the extent of using the English language. If only for the sake of the audience and the fact that poets do feel and articulate in a language, the working off of liberal doses of foreign language should be avoided. If I were to use a Hindu or Arabic word per line I doubt very much whether I could expect it to be accepted as a serious attempt to communicate poetic experience. The subject is not the question—let it be Alcheringa if you like—but it is the inadequacy of the expression which has to involve the "exoticism" of foreign verbiage. If the subject were intensely felt it would articulate cleanly either in Aboriginal dialect or English.

Fundamentally, a serious "Jabberwocky" might be made to mean as much in poetic terms as this parochial "poetic diction."

I suppose it was inevitable that Australia should give rise to a Jindyworobak movement, and a school of young poets whose chief concern would be with what they experience rather than the way they experience. It is to be expected that such an approach would be fatal to genuine poetry, but popularly successful. The theory behind it is this. Australian poetry must not be servile imitation of European artistic forms and artistic values. If Australian writers function genuinely, they will express in their poetry the real world of their immediate experience . . . the actual material of life that will impact their consciousness. In this case poets will find, in a similar fashion to poets in other places in the world, their field of experience, and consequently of poetic expression, conditioned by the environment in which they find themselves.

This is what Mr. Ingamells describes as "conditional culture." The broad striking rural environment of Australia, its peculiar archaic aspects, are the things which will play a large part in the poet's life, they are things and the mysteries of his immediate life with which his faculties would be most intimately concerned. Poetry in this country would then be expressive of its landscape, the emotional associations of its pioneering life. Mr. Ingamells's own poetry for instance concerns itself with expressing two things so far—one, the disgusting and repulsive life of the city, Big Business and Small Emotions; and two, a nostalgic self-identification with the Aborigine and the spiritual values of his life (!)

Beneath the popular appeal of this unfortunately parochial theory the simple error is easily spotted. To correct the error of the Jindyworobaks may seem to indicate indulgence in stating truisms, but the simple evidence is necessary, as some critics have honoured the cause of Mr. Ingamells with sophisticated repudiations which have led the issue astray.

Poetry is not concerned ultimately with visual sensation, although all poetry uses to some measure visual sensation. But poetry primarily emerges as the expression of attitude or emotion towards the facts of experience. It concerns itself with that which is peculiar and individual in the artist's vision of his surroundings. His fundamental environment is himself. The depiction of environment and landscape in poetry only exists for the purpose of the artist saying something about it. When he speaks in verbal terms he must consequently express himself in that language which is his own, that with which he thinks and that with which he articulates his feeling, and definitely not with that which will correlate most closely with the evidence of his eyes. If the poet finds that language with which he articulates his feelings and attitudes is inadequate, then it argues either a mistaken sense of what poetry is and does, or it argues a complete poverty in artistic equipment.

I have unfortunately had to come to the conclusion that it is more the latter with Mr. Ingamells and members of his school. It reveals a disintegrating instinct for poetic expression that he has come more and more to use Aboriginal dialect for its own sake in his work. It exemplifies a pitiful lack in his own make-up that he has to capture the associative values of his environment through the use of a language which is foreign to him. His capacity at this point of decline consists in conveying a sense of place, but saying nothing about it. The need for poetry at all has gone, for the emotional content of his living has ceased to be important. More generously, we may say it has been swamped. (pp. 259-62)

> *Max Harris, "Dance Little Wombat," in* The Jindy-
> worobaks, *edited by Brian Elliott, University of
> Queensland Press, 1979, pp. 259-63.*

KELVIN LANCASTER   (essay date 1952)

[*In the following excerpt, Lancaster examines the themes, structure, and style of Ingamells's poem* The Great South Land.]

Poems, when considered not for their intrinsic being, but for their relationship to the poet himself, may be divided into two broad classifications, peripheral and central. Peripheral poems are those which express some mood or facet of the writer's thought and feeling, without plunging to the heart of his beliefs. In the case of a poet with a strongly unified personality, his peripheral poetry will always be strongly oriented, pointing towards those central beliefs which are not explicit in the poems themselves. A poet lacking an inner focus of ideas or feelings will always write peripheral poetry, and a central poem is not possible from his pen, for such a poem

is one that tackles the poet's heart's desire, the force behind his attitudes.

To choose an almost perfect example of a central poem of this kind, we need go no further than FitzGerald's *Essay on Memory,* and, as such, we shall not find its peer in the range of Australian poetry. Indeed, few Australian poets have faced the problems and difficulties of such a poem; Slessor, for example, has, ever since the *Cuckooz Contrey* volume, deliberately avoided even the attempt.

In Ingamells' **The Great South Land** we have this poet's attempt to gather himself into one poetic focus, for **The Great South Land** aims to be a true central poem. That FitzGerald could achieve the cosmic scope of the *Essay on Memory* in 347 lines, while Ingamells achieves less in 9,000, is indicative of the fundamental differences between the two poets. Ingamells has never attained conciseness of style, whereas FitzGerald is one of the most genuinely concise poets writing in English. . . . Nevertheless, the length of Ingamells' poem is not solely due to his natural verbosity; it is mainly the result of his structural approach to the problem of a central poem.

Ingamells' concluding lines to **The Great South Land** are:

> Keep with this Land our Timeless Covenant.
> Still cleaving close to cosmic origins
> through all vicissitude, and planning
> the vast symphonic continental theme
> of Youth-with-Age and Age-with-Youth, the Land
> calls mind to mystery and heart to knowledge.

These express the fact that to Ingamells, Australia, "The Great South Land," is much more than just a country, as his poem is much more than a historical narrative. In fact, the dominant theme of **The Great South Land,** as it is of the *Essay on Memory,* is continuity, and this theme is stated explicitly many times:

> I see myself a potential before the World was born,
> a dream of fulfilment.
> ("Overture," lines 77-78)

> Man's history is good and evil both.
> Good and Evil have woven through centuries
> varied contrasting threads, not simply warp
> and woof; variously disposed; assigned
> criss-cross and parallel, tangled, askew.
> ("Overture," lines 183-187)

> The Wind controls beating
> the hands of the Present from me,
> beating them back, till I rise easily
> in deathless imagination of Time's
> illimitable flight, the wind outside
> breathing all Yesterday and all Tomorrow,
> in Yesterday's pregnant Dreaming.
> (Book I, lines 10-16)

> We are our ancestors and all they knew:
> their thoughts and deeds are active in our blood;
> and we are wrought to pulse of millenia,
> perceiving the promise of our Destiny,
> and daring it with hearts of love and fear.
> ("The Timeless Covenant," lines 76-80)

These passages have been chosen more or less at random from many similar ones: their resemblance to FitzGerald's poetry in content, and sometimes in image and symbol, is remarkable. Perhaps one does not have to assume any direct influence of FitzGerald on Ingamells here, for the whole fabric of thought in contemporary Australian poetry is impregnated with these ideas, deriving originally from Norman Lindsay and reaching their fullest and finest expression in FitzGerald's work. It is not too much to say that the cosmology of the *Essay on Memory* has become the basis of an identifiably Australian mode of thought in contemporary poetry.

FitzGerald's brain is mathematical, and he can present his ideas with a remorseless poetic logic: Ingamells' brain is of a different cast; he does not prove his point with logic, but illustrates it with history. History is a verbose science and Ingamells' approach to the problem of his own central poem necessarily leads to a work of great proportions.

Ingamells expresses best, in his own words, the methodology by which he attempts to solve his poetic problem:

> Here must I tell at first of Time Primeval,
> then draw much History before the eyes,
> till, shining within the vast periphery
> of such reports, and making their very centre,
> stands, clear and beautiful, the Great South Land.

or again:

> this task of ardour, which is to present
> account of Man's approach to the Great South Land:
> one glorious goal of many glorious goals . . .

The centre of the poem, Books Three to Ten, shows Australia emerging slowly from the dreams of men, and solidifying into a physical entity. Ingamells, adhering firmly to the FitzGerald doctrine of the infinite inter-dependence of events, shows how the final discovery of Australia was the result of an enormous complex of events of all kinds. Men inspired by all possible motives, attempting many different things, making many errors; these men, Portuguese, Dutch, Spanish, French, English, each added something to the blank map of the South Seas. Stroke by stroke, the outlines of the southern continent are made to appear.

This main body of the poem, the historical picture, is fitted to a double frame. The inner frame, Books One, Two and Eleven, presents Australia the reality rather than the myth; the former book as it actually was while man searched for it, the latter book as it became when the white man discovered it. The outer frame, "Overture" and "The Timeless Covenant," is the philosophic summary of the poem. Between these inner and outer frames there fits Book Twelve, a section in that tone of conventional patriotism which Ingamells, thankfully, avoids elsewhere.

Having analysed the poem structurally, we can criticize it so, determining the success or failure of each part of the poem relative to the function it is required to perform in the whole work.

The central portion of the poem is, in general, successful in its aim of portraying the gradual coming into historical existence of the Australian continent. But the picture is too carefully drawn, the reader can scarcely see the unity of the canvas for the multiplicity of the parts, and he gains much the impression he would from standing close up to a large mural. He does not even obtain the satisfaction of seeing a complete picture in each part, for Ingamells is so intent in adducing a huge number of witnesses in his favour that he fails to cross-examine them fully. I should think that Books Three, Four, and Five could have been condensed into a single book with a great gain in power, and that similar benefit would derive from a selection and expansion of those events in the latter

voyages most relevant to the matter in hand (as it is, Ingamells seems to include snippets from the voyages chosen almost at random). There is something dry and abstracted about these descriptions of the explorers; they do not ever burst into life like Slessor's Captain Cook or FitzGerald's Tasman. One suspects Ingamells of holding his nose too close to the history book to breathe in the necessary atmosphere of life.

Ingamells has always, or at least since he took to social poetry in the 'forties, suffered from two major defects: an inadequacy of style and technique which he seems to have been either unaware of or uninterested in overcoming, and a certain pettiness of tone which crept into some of his social criticism. In *The Great South Land,* some trace of both these faults is still evident: there are still ridiculous phrases, such as

> Coo-ee-ing my way down the stony years
> to the city . . .

and many passages where the attempt at a loftiness of tone falls quite flat.

Nevertheless, I feel that Mrs. Vassilieff does a gross injustice to Ingamells in what purports to be a review of *The Great South Land* [see Further Reading]. The truth is that the poem contains by far the finest of Ingamells poetry to date, particularly in thought. Ingamells seems to have, at last, almost outgrown the rather immature patriotism of his earlier verse, and to have caught sight of a vision with the breadth of O'Dowd's.

The "Overture," in particular, is a fine piece of poetry, both in thought and expression: Ingamells, with some direct help, I think, from FitzGerald's work, has come somewhere near an adequate expression of himself. Many passages throughout the work could stand as poems in their own right, and the central body of the work, even with its uneven quality, performs its designated function well.

The Great South Land is, I think, Ingamells' entrance card into that group of really important (I will not necessarily say great) Australian poets, a group of which Ingamells has been hitherto denied membership, in spite of some twenty years of poetic output. In fact, were I Ingamells, publishing a selection of my poetic output over the years, I would discard nine-tenths of my poetry from *Forgotten People* to *Come Walkabout,* and substitute fragments of *The Great South Land.*

(pp. 101-04)

Kelvin Lancaster, "On the Slopes of Parnassus," in Southerly, *Vol. 13, No. 2, 1952, pp. 101-04.*

S. E. LEE (essay date 1954)

[*In the following excerpt, Lee praises the formal innovations of Ingamells's novel* Of Us Now Living *but suggests that Ingamells was too ambitious in defining the scope of the work.*]

A character in Rex Ingamells's latest work, *Of Us Now Living: A Novel of Australia,* expressed the modest hope, "I am thinking of Charley as the chronicler of Quongdong." Charley you must know is the autobiographical narrator who tells the story of an imaginary South Australian township (Quongdong) settled about 1880. The speaker is Miss Singwood, Quongdong's pioneer teacher who has inspired Charley's literary and historical ambitions and carefully nurtured an "intense" love for his birthplace. Miss Singwood has helped Charley further by making available, in the form of posthumously revealed diaries, most of Quongdong's history as she has discovered it by personal interview with the pioneers. There are, however, several mysterious gaps in the information Miss Singwood has collected. Charley's task is to fill in the gaps, and this he does by modern historical research. When the story is complete, it is found that Quongdong has a link with practically the whole of Australia's one hundred and seventy-five years of recorded history in a geographical setting extending from South Australia through Victoria to New South Wales. This Australia-wide relevance for the novel, justifying its slightly pretentious sub-title *A Novel of Australia,* has been forced by relating incidents from the lives of Quongdong's pioneers, and their descendants and ancestors, to such important historical phenomena as the convict system, the gold rushes of the fifties, the squatting era, the troubles of the nineties, the Boer and the two World Wars.

It will be obvious that the novel has a very wide scope; and Ingamells is to be congratulated for the skill with which he has arranged and presented an enormous mass of raw material. Three strands, each unified about a dominant character, are cleverly inter-related to illustrate the central theme, "How inevitably involved with the Past are the lives of us now living." The first, having as its unifying figure the convict girl, Hannah Raffin, deals with the years preceding Quongdong's settlement (1800-1880 approximately). The second, dominated through her diaries by the tiny figure of Effie Singwood, is the full story of Quongdong from its settlement (1880-1950 approximately). The third strand is an account of contemporary Quongdong interpreted (in terms of the past) by Charley, the narrator. All stories are carefully integrated. The Hannah Raffin story links naturally with the second in that her own son is a pioneer of Quongdong. Coming in the middle, Effie's story naturally leads into Charley's: her researches take her back to Hannah Raffin, while her influence lives on through Charley. The most difficult link is that of Hannah and Charley. This is achieved, rather fortuitously, by the circumstance that enabled John Bellamy (Charley's remote ancestor) to help Hannah in a moment of crisis. But more important is the intimacy that Charley feels for Hannah, mainly through a portrait painted by her husband about 1840. The portrait survives as a kind of Forsterian symbol and, as its cluster of associations grows, assumes more and more significance in the pattern Charley is revealing. The pattern is completed only when he discovers the portrait (lost for some time) with its melodramatically concealed message. As Miles Franklin has observed, a measure of the effectiveness of Ingamells's symbol is the sense of personal loss the reader feels when the picture is destroyed and Charley concludes his work with the words, "I can still see the flame consuming the picture, burning up from the Past into the lives of us now living."

The novel is interesting for the difficult and challenging technical discipline its author has accepted. The story is told from a single "centre," that of the autobiographical narrator, Charley Bellamy. Ingamells has faithfully authenticated every snippet of information that Charley conveys and carefully avoided the prescience of an editorial intruder. Further he has attempted to suggest a feeling of immediacy by linking Charley's personal life very closely with that of the recorded history; to his end he tells us exactly how Charley unearthed each piece of information and gives the details (often in their raw form of letter, diary entry, newspaper cutting, etc.) as

they are discovered. Thus there is the constant juxtaposition of past and present which has the additional point of emphasizing Charley's philosophy, "to me, the past is alive in the present, which is its ripe fruit, holding its rich juices and bearing its blemishes." However, certain difficulties arise. One is that much of the authentication is static in that it holds up the movement of the narrative. Ingamells accentuates this fault by drawing undue attention to his machinery, by his conscientious but misguided attempts to help the reader and explain exactly what he is trying to do and how he is doing it. If a convention is worth using, surely its understanding can be left to the critical intelligence of the reader. Since the omniscience is denied, the method is at its best in the leisurely exposition of a comparatively narrow range of material. Quite obviously the wide scope and rapid movement of Ingamells's story provide difficulties, and towards the end, he must have sighed for the freedom of a less restrictive form. As it is he asks the reader to accept the staggering sequence of coincidence by which, through Charley's researches alone, the whole intricate pattern is pieced together.

There are certain pitfalls inherent in the method that Ingamells has not entirely avoided. It is rather embarrassing, for example, to hear Charley Bellamy Ingamells discussing the literary merits of Effie Singwood Ingamells's much quoted diaries: "The most naive charm of her earlier writings has become transmuted into a rich, a wise, maturity, which has not lost, but has sublimated, the impulsive expressiveness of youth." Particularly when on the evidence provided one cannot altogether agree with the criticism! Also, the inclusion of "source" material pre-supposes an ability on the author's part to write in many styles. As it is the diaries of a school mistress, the letters of a rouseabout or convict, the anecdotes of a pioneer all smack of the slightly pedantic style of the narrator. Listen, for example, to George Saunderson (the pioneer who misquotes Herrick):

> It was early summer when we reached our destination . . . and depastured(!) our stock . . . where, although yellowing and sere, there was an abundance of grass.

Or note again the colloquial ease of this man whose "ingenuousness and simplicity . . . were superb and full of charm," as he delivers a Jindyworobak manifesto:

> Contrary to most people, I say that the blacks in the bush, livin' their own lives and followin' their own intricate beliefs, are really more civilized in spirit— or, at least, more richly endowed with experience of what life means to the heart and mind of a human being—than hordes of white savages in cities.

The last pronouncement suggests a further serious criticism. Ingamells makes lavish use of dialogue, but has no ear for the rhythms of colloquial speech. Here is how the suspicions of a troubled woman who has received a letter from her husband's mistress are allayed:

> "No," lied John, "she tried to win your husband's affections, as she tried to win mine, but she made no headway. Abe confided in me at the time, but didn't wish you to know. The girl was a good worker. He put her in her place very firmly, and was most anxious to spare you knowledge of the distasteful situation. It would be kinder to Abe if you didn't let him know you received this letter."

John Bellamy was determined to preserve the peace

between Abe and his wife. Mrs. Sencrieux, reassured, gave him the promise. . . .

The irritating redundant comment of the last sentence is a direct insult to the reader's intelligence, while the mechanical motivation of action is almost as bad as some of the later glib psychological analyses of character which in a work of art, surely are the function of the reader not the author.

At times, too, the action strains the reader's credibility. The report "Stan Nebley died at Dernancourt, and was posthumously awarded the V.C. for taking the bayonet thrust meant for his captain" is most unusual in the democratic Australian context. Further, the tactics that win a convict brawl are dubious to say the least.

The book is rich in character material but, with one notable exception, the people are flat, undeveloped "types." The exception, of course, is Charley, who has the complexity and mixture of motives of a real human being. His feeling for his birthplace, his enthusiasm for Australian history, the sincerity of his admiration and respect for Miss Singwood, the honesty and integrity of his literary purpose are conveyed with convincing insight. On the other hand there is the cruelty of the humiliation of Aunt Agatha (a harmless old dear), the vindictiveness of his comments on Prim (the rejected lover), the smugness of his introspections on the possibility of a love affair with Biddy ("the darling of the forces") and so on. On the whole Charley is a likeable, because human, character. Hannah Raffin is an interesting and complex person but is hardly seen from the inside. The rest are far too arbitrarily drawn in blacks and whites. Effie Singwood, for example, has two dark spots ("a slip in her youth" and her consequent attitudes towards it) carefully sketched in and then washed out to a very dim grey. The villains (rarely native Australians!) could have stepped straight from a Victorian melodrama and the minor characters are little more than caricatures (like Nigger) or shadowy ghosts (like Chadby). The already discussed defects in dialogue do not help the characterization.

Ingamells has considerable stylistic resources and gives some really fine writing, especially in the spare, accurate narration of the broad historical sweeps or the detailed, often poetic, impression of places and people. However, there is far too much looseness, particularly in the static pieces where Charley gets on his philosophic or literary hobby-horse. Certain words are badly overused; one has the impression that *intense, vivid, unique, intrigue, individual,* etc. recur so frequently not because they are the best, but because they are the first words that come to mind. Some sundry illustrations of the use of *intense* (there are many more also of *intensely* and *intensity*) will make my point: Charley has an "attack of intense blues"; describes "a curiously intense desire"; "intense relief"; "intense interest"; and "intense nausea"; and has his mind "tantalized by sympathetic efforts to appreciate in imagination the intense pathos of that noble and forlorn character, Ah Lee. . . ."

In conclusion, Ingamells's book is an interesting, even an exciting, experiment in the novel form. It fails to achieve the highest rank not from any deficiency in subject matter or technique, but rather from a self-conscious surfeit of both. Ingamells has the knowledge and sensitivity to do for Quongdong what Faulkner has done for Yoknapatawpha County. But he needs to reflect that Faulkner's twelve Yoknapatawpha stories in no wise attempt to fill in a complete pattern, that each is an artistic treatment of some feature of the pat-

tern, each is complete in itself suggesting more than it states because the pattern is implicit not explicit. Further, Faulkner has transmuted his material into an artistic form and given it a life and shape in its own right. He would not attempt (as Dos Passos), "a novel of America." The lesson for Ingamells is that in attempting too much he has achieved too little. (pp. 188-91)

> *S. E. Lee, "Chronicler of Quongdong," in* Southerly, *Vol. 15, No. 3, 1954, pp. 188-91.*

H. M. GREEN (essay date 1961)

[*In the following excerpt, Green assesses the Jindyworobak philosophy and outlines the strengths and weaknesses of Ingamells's poetry.*]

In favour of the Jindyworobaks it may be said that they occasioned more controversy than any other body of writers in Australian literature. Their fundamental principle, that Australian culture must be based upon the Australian environment, would be accepted by most Australian critics; but this is by no means a new principle, and many of its applications as well as many of the Jindyworobaks' assumptions are unacceptable even to some of their strongest admirers. "Jindyworobak" is an aboriginal word, meaning to annex, to join, and the school and its anthology were founded in 1938, with the object of bringing Australian writers, and in particular Australian poets, into intimate contact with their environment. The founder, Rex (Reginald Charles) Ingamells, a graduate of the University of Adelaide, worked and wandered over a considerable part of South Australia and Victoria, and was a tutor for the Workers' Educational Association and a high school teacher in South Australia. Justifiably provoked by the wet-blanketing of Australian literature in an ill-advised article by an English-born Melbourne professor and stimulated by P. R. Stephensen's *Foundations of Culture in Australia,* by a holiday in Central Australia and an acquaintance with the anthropologist T. G. H. Strehlow, Ingamells decided, apparently without a very wide reading of either Australian or modern English literature, that Australian writers had not been Australian enough; that Paterson and Lawson had written larrikin verses, sometimes in incongruous English idiom, and that because of his misleading associations Kendall was "practically valueless as an Australian poet." And in a pamphlet, ***Conditional Culture,*** from which these assertions are taken, he urged that Australian culture depended not merely upon a clear recognition of environmental values, but upon the use of only such imagery as was "truly Australian," and upon an understanding of Australian history and traditions, including those of the aborigines, from whose art and song "we must learn much of our new technique." It is true that he added that some of the best Australian literature must deal with universal themes and might have no local colour at all; but this has the air of having been an afterthought, a saving proviso ignored in practice; in the early numbers of his anthology Ingamells deliberately and admittedly rejected "poetically better non-Australian verse in favour of mediocre Australian." It is clear that Ingamells could not have known his bush balladists very well, or understood Kendall in relation to his surroundings, and he ignores O'Dowd's "The Bush," Lawson's short stories, and Furphy's *Such Is Life,* and all the other founders or precursors of Australianism in Australian literature; moreover, many of the idioms and images that Ingamells grouped as English were in fact worn-out tag-ends of Victorian romanticism, of which few traces were left by that time in English or for that matter Australian poets of standing. He was therefore flogging a dead horse, or, as he would probably have preferred to say, shooting a dead kangaroo; he was also using a weapon that must recoil on the wielder, since though a writer is foolish to use worn-out or inappropriate images, he must be free to write what he likes. And finally Ingamells ignored the fact that the culture of the aborigines is farther from us, more alien than any European culture could be. Yet, with all this, Jindyworobakism was valuable in several respects: it helped to keep the current cosmopolitan tendency, itself in part a revulsion from the parochialism of the Australian nineties, from going to extremes; it encouraged young poets to try to give expression in their own ways to their own feelings, their own moods, in surroundings with which they were familiar; and it emphasized a very important fact, that, in the words of a Jindyworobak supporter, "we have to let the sunshine of this land into our souls." Ingamells' own verse may be judged from his *Selected Poems,* in which his love for the Australian outback and his admiration for the aborigine and his legends find expression by means of a poetic talent that is genuine and not without individuality, but not great. He can give bright little glimpses, in rhyme or free verse, of birds and beasts and moods and incidents of the bush, and he can tell an adventurous story; but except where, as in such cases, his material is given him, he fails. In his longer poems especially there is little substance; his ideas are neither new nor profound and he is unable to develop them in poetry; with an exception to be mentioned, he is at his best in his glimpses and in a few episodes from early Australian history, in which atmosphere as well as subject is provided, as in **"Ship from Thames"** and **"Macquarie Harbour."** But he has a fine line or phrase here and there, as

> . . . in the Bright
> rollers will bring the stars ashore at night;

and

> The sun, with shattering bird-bright shout,
> tears star-dusk's glittering gloom,
> and all day long goes walkabout
> from Botany to Broome.

And there is one outstanding exception to what has been said about Ingamells' longer poems; in **"Memory of Hills,"** of which here are a couple of verses, he surpassed himself:

> There are rock-rooted ranges to dominate
> the ways of man with peace, enforced but healing;
> there are crows settling on the boundary gate,
> or poised in the sky, or wheeling.
>
> Slowly the sun moves over the red land, slowly
> over the dust-puff silence that never changes
> except for crow caws that suddenly, wholly
> envelope those random ranges. . . .
>
> The old hills are obstinate in my mind,
> and I thank them now for the long familiarity.
> Merely I shut my eyes to find
> their reflex of moonlight, their kind
> wrinkled acknowledgment of the moon's clarity.

(pp. 984-86)

H. M. Green, "Verse: Lyrical and Lyrically Descriptive Poets Continued," in his A History of Australian Literature: Pure and Applied, Vol. II, 1923-1950, Angus and Robertson, 1961, pp. 965-92.

HUMPHREY McQUEEN (essay date 1978)

[In the following excerpt, McQueen discusses the ways in which Ingamells's interest in Aboriginal culture and his political views shaped his Jindyworobak philosophy and poetry.]

Jindyworobak is probably the most misunderstood and misrepresented aspect of Australia's cultural past. To some extent this is its founder's fault, since Rex Ingamells was given to public overstatement. It is necessary to disentangle the substance of Jindyworobak from its allegedly slick Aboriginality, so that the relationship of both to the crisis mentality of the 1930s can be explored.

Some of the Jindyworobaks' problems have to be traced to Ingamells' temperament, and to his limited talents. Indeed he chose the name "Jindyworobak" partly because of its shock value, while his 1941 reply to Douglas Stewart's mild criticisms on the *Bulletin*'s "Red Page" showed how readily he could take offence. When he felt at ease, as he did with Hart-Smith for a time, Ingamells recognised that he was a "cock-eyed coot" whose efforts "to be both truthful and reasonable . . . probably succeeded in being exasperating." Much later, after a public quarrel between Ingamells and H. M. Green, Hart-Smith told Green that:

> I've kept the peace with Rex all these years because I've never really told him what I think, about his poetry and his criticism. . . . He belongs to that category of creative individuals which pursue a single idea with fanatical devotion, an almost wilful lack of self-criticism, in order to make the idea effective. I sometimes suspect that Rex himself has more than inkling of this because more than once in a conversation with him I've found an astonishingly liberal appreciation of the other fellow's point of view. . . . Much of this quarrelling with others may be Rex arguing with himself.

This opinion is confirmed by Ingamells' letters to other friends whose grasp of Jindyworobak he thought inadequate. In these private discussions, he was usually subtle and receptive. The public inflexibility was partly a product of the parsonage upbringing which helped to drive his brother, John, to mental collapse. Moreover, it was the "vice" which gave him the determination to persist with a poetry anthology for sixteen years: an essential ingredient in his battle against seemingly insurmountable hostility and indifference.

Ingamells' poetic talents were decidedly minor, and were surest, as H. M. Green said, when dealing with material provided directly by nature or from history; Alec Hope rightly thought that Ingamells was "unequal to the task he has set himself." Jindyworobak, as an idea, suffered because its founder was so rarely able to achieve his stated aims in his own writings.

Another of Ingamells' difficulties was that, when he launched Jindyworobak, he had only a slight acquaintance with previous Australian writing; in this sense, he was a primitive. Almost everything about Australian literature came as a great surprise to him. And yet, that was at the heart of his argument. Australian culture needed to be promoted precisely because it remained unknown to people like him. Henry Handel Richardson was virtually unheard of here before 1929; Furphy's *Such Is Life* won a tiny group of readers, but only through the devoted efforts of the Palmers and Kate Baker; many booksellers and librarians declined to stock Australian works, and the public generally refused to buy or borrow

NEW SONG IN AN OLD LAND

AUSTRALIAN VERSE

CHOSEN BY

REX INGAMELLS

"we drink
an older culture, old as Alcheringa,
through every pore from bush-fed,
dust-fed, wattle-and-gum-fed, air."

Ian Mudie, *Echo of Alcheringa.*

JINDYWOROBAK
PUBLICATION

LONGMANS, GREEN AND CO.

LONDON - NEW YORK - TORONTO

Title page of New Song in an Old Land.

them when they were available. When Ingamells started Jindyworobak, Australian literature was largely ignored in the universities, and unwanted or unavailable in the community. Writers often found it difficult to get each other's works: Ingamells did not see the complete version of Stephensen's *The Foundations of Culture in Australia* until 1941, five years after it was published. If all this helps to explain some of Ingamells' wrong-headedness, it also accounts for some of his outraged sense of urgency to establish "environmental values."

A broad notion of "environmental values" existed in all those who, in the years after 1788, drew their material from local sources: from early diarists like Watkin Tench to painters like Frederick McCubbin a century later. The decorative possibilities of Australian plants and creatures were developed from the 1880s onwards, for a while as gum-nut *art nouveau.* Far more substantially, Margaret Preston published the first of many articles on Aboriginal art in 1924, and went on to fulfill her discoveries in paintings. There was growing opposition to populating Australian painting and poetry with nymphs and satyrs in the style of Syd Long and Hugh McCrae. About the same time, Aboriginal studies were becoming more scholarly; the publications of Basedow (1925), Radcliffe-Brown and Porteous (1931), were followed by the foundation of *Oceania,* a Sydney University-based anthropological journal, in 1930, while A. P. Elkin took up the chair of anthropology at Syd-

ney three years later. Aboriginals were also the subject of several important Royal Commissions and Inquiries after the Dala (W. A.) massacre of 1927, from Bleakley in 1929 to Thomson in 1938. Aboriginals, or rather what were called "half-castes," became protagonists of two of Australia's finest novels: *Coonardoo* (1929) and *Capricornia* (1938).

As Ingamells readily acknowledged, the idea of borrowing or learning from Aboriginal culture did not begin with Jindyworobak in 1936, and the widening interest in Aboriginals helped to provide an atmosphere through which Ingamells could perceive the validity of Aboriginal culture in the broadest sense. Yet the changes did not represent a qualitative transformation in informed opinion. Claims that Aboriginals were intelligent still met with public disbelief and editorial wonder. "Half-caste" novels were unpopular. The tremendous success of Namitjira's imitative watercolours is the best indication of what was expected from blackfellas. Ingamells' ideas were scorned partly because of the racial prejudices held by literary Australians: the very notion that British civilisation had to learn from the dying race was proof that Ingamells could not be taken seriously. [As he stated in his *The Flesh and the Spirit*] Douglas Stewart believed that it would be "fantastic . . . to bother about defending civilised art against the primitive" if it were not for the tendency of white civilisation to abdicate its superiority. "The simple African negro," Stewart argued, "had at least the wit to perceive that never during the centuries of his 'culture' had he been able to devise a work of art so elegant as the top-hat." Against this kind of conventional wisdom, it is surprising that Ingamells won as much support as he did. Stewart was right to explain at least some of the interest in Aboriginal culture as a result of the "fraying out and decaying" of European civilisation.

Ingamells' own interest in Aboriginal culture had been aroused in 1930-31 when, aged about seventeen, he travelled in Central Australia, where T. G. Strehlow drew his attention to the legends of the Aranda and to the meaning of Alchera, the dreamtime. While these experiences laid a groundwork, they had almost no impact on Ingamells' first book of poems, *Gumtops* (1935), which limped after the advice which L. F. Giblin gave in the "Foreword": "Australian poets . . . must forget all they have learned of the poetry of other lands; shut their ears to all the familiar, captivating echoes, and try to give us their first-hand, direct reaction to nature and man as they find them in Australia." Giblin recognised that Ingamells had not "always completely succeeded. This devil of the second-hand is not cast out save with prayer and fasting." *Gumtops* included a long poem **"Sea-Things,"** full of love of foreign places and travel, and another about a lion. Worst of all for someone wanting to get the words and images right, there was the line "I see you agèd royal gum."

The breakthrough came in the eighteen months between late 1935, shortly after which Ingamells read P. R. Stephensen's essay, "The Foundations of Culture in Australia," and early 1937, when he wrote his own essay, **"On Environmental Values."** Stephensen's essay encouraged Ingamells to read D. H. Lawrence's *Kangaroo,* from which he "gained a strong sense of the primaeval in Australian nature. . . . But . . . rejected Lawrence's view of strangeness in the Spirit of the Place: my own first hand experience of outback life made it familiar for me." More significant was Ingamells' reading of James Devaney's *The Vanished Tribes,* of which he wrote in 1948 [in *Jindyworobak Review;* see Further Reading]: "I have seldom felt more excitement than upon my first reading of these beautifully told stories. From the glossary I took the name 'Jindy-worobak' (Jindy-Worobak) because of its Aboriginality, its meaning, *and its outlandishness to fashionable literary taste*" [emphasis added by critic].

Ingamells first used "Jindyworobak" in a preface to a set of poems in the 1936 edition of *Chapbook,* explaining that it meant "to annex, to join":

> It should appropriately indicate what I have tried to do in the poems published here: namely, express something of the Australian place *spirit which* baffles expression in English words, so often strongly coloured by European associations. The native words I have chosen seem to me to have in them much of the striking quality of Australian primevalism.

The first poem after this declaration reads like a satire on Jindyworobak:

> Goomblegubbon in the scrub
> Does not fear the boondee club.
> Billadurra at erragoden
> Need not haste on plunging in . . .

Ingamells never again indulged in such exoticisms. Henceforth, he sought Australian words and images, rather than an Aboriginal vocabulary. Nonetheless, Jindyworobak is still dismissed as nothing more than "grafting on Aboriginal words in an attempt to achieve a quick 'authenticity' " [T. Shapcott in *The Literature of Australia,* ed. G. Dutton].

Earlier critics, like Douglas Stewart, rightly argued that " 'movements' in poetry are judged not by their theories, but by their fruits." When this rule is applied to Ingamells' poetry, it is clear that Aboriginalities played almost no part at all. *Gumtops* (1935) contained only words in general usage—wurlies, lubras and corroborees; one poem in *Forgotten People* (1936) used a few Aboriginal words and legends; *Sun-Freedom* (1938) reprinted the three poems from the 1936 *Chapbook,* but otherwise had only two Aboriginal words in poems, plus two others as titles; two poems in *Memory of Hills* (1940) had two Aboriginal words each, but they in no way interrupted the flow of meaning; *At the Boundary* (1941) contained none at all; *News of the Sun* (1942) only "Boolee"; *Content are the Quiet Ranges* (1943) had three in one poem—Mirabooka, Alcheringa and pinaroo; *The Unknown Land* (1943) had a dozen—including the familiar ones—Alcheringa, Arandas, nardoo and euro. By the time of *Selected Poems* (1944), Ingamells had banished two of the worst offenders from the *Chapbook;* his glossary had thirty-four words, of which twenty-nine were unusual, but these appeared on only fifteen of the volume's 106 pages, and were largely concentrated in nine short poems from 1935 or 1942. The yearly *Jindyworobak Anthologies* had even fewer Aboriginal words and never contained a glossary, and perhaps needed one only for a brief poem by Ingamells in 1941.

If Jindyworobak usage of Aboriginal words was so infrequent, how did the movement acquire a reputation for primitivism? Undoubtedly its very name—Jindyworobak—can still blind those who are too lazy to investigate further. The name made it easier for deliberately malicious critics to misrepresent the movement. Jindyworobak was certainly easy to satirise. From Adelaide, a lecturer in English, C. R. Jury [see excerpt dated 1940], wrote:

> Kangaroo my totem, kangaroo,
> Change me first to an aborigine
> With lubra, with humpy
> In a great silence;
> Then make me truly
> A kangaroo.
> When shall I feel in my hams
> An inclination to hop?

In addition, it is probable that some Aboriginal-style writings by non-Jindyworobaks were blurred in the minds of the movement's opponents. Mary Gilmore's twelve line "Aboriginal" appeared in *Southerly* with about 500 words of explanation: Shakespearean pedagogues and the devotees of T. S. Eliot were shocked when Aboriginal-inspired poems needed explanatory notes.

Just as Ingamells' poems very rarely employed Aboriginal words, so they played little or no part in his general statements of aim. His 1937 lecture, **"Concerning Environmental Values,"** does not mention them. On the contrary, he argued that "The Whole of the English vocabulary is ours for appropriate use, but we must discriminate." He wanted "lances" replaced by "spears," not by "Jiggi." His attacks were directed against "[t]he biggest curse and handicap upon our literature . . . [namely] the incongruous use of metaphors, similes and adjectives." Thus, he criticised Lawson for writing:

> The cattle-tracks between the trees
> Were like long dusky aisles . . .

and Roderic Quinn for the line,

> And dead leaves carpet the silent bush

because Quinn "makes the bush seem like a drawing room." "I cannot deplore too vehemently," Ingamells wrote, "the dangerous habit of using figures of speech with regard to essentially Australian things which call up such a flood of Old World associations as to glaze over all distinctiveness." All of this lecture was incorporated into a 1938 pamphlet, *Conditional Culture,* to which Ingamells tacked on a section "The Culture of the Aboriginals" which, he said, "must be of primary importance to the proper evolution of our culture." Ingamells does not mention language in his context. The contribution of Aboriginal culture was its "spirit," by which he meant those close bonds with the environment which had let Aborigines effortlessly express their own experiences. White Australians had to learn to be just as much at ease with their environment. Then came the suggestion that "From Aboriginal art and song we must learn much of our new technique. . . ." This remark is neither elaborated nor explained, and appears as an afterthought, as a throwaway idea: it was hardly taken up by Ingamells in practice.

Although Ingamells sometimes strayed into byways of Aboriginality, these were no more than the enthusiasms and stumblings which are part of every artist's career. The real thrust of his endeavours was in a different direction. It was not the wisdom of hindsight which led Ingamells to explain, in 1948, that:

> We identify ourselves with Australia, which is our Mother-land, and English, which is our Mother Tongue. Our aim is synthesis, adjustment of the two, and our use of Aboriginal words is a legitimate contribution. We are the first to acknowledge that only such of our usages as both have significance in

themselves, and suit the genius of the English language can survive.

There is a direct line from Ingamells' 1939 assertion that "Australian vowels *are* different from English vowels" to his 1948 claim that "the prime point of the Jindyworobak argument . . . concerns the accurate use of language."

Although language had been Jindyworobak's prime literary concern, language was the product of, and never the motive force behind, Ingamells' search for environmental values. This search was determined by the social forces threatening Australia from within and without, forces which gave a special urgency to his quest for "environmental values." Ingamells was concerned more with culture in the broad, anthropological sense of how people live—how they organise their society and how they reproduce their material needs—much more than with those things normally associated with culture in its narrower sense of the arts.

Since what Ingamells wanted was for Australian poetry to be about Australia—and not about England, Greece or fairyland—Jindyworobak did not close his mind to the rest of the world. Early in 1940, he boasted that the following books had "strongly influenced" his thinking in the past year: J. W. N. Sullivan's *Outline of the Universe;* Herbert Read's *Collected Essays in Literary Criticism*; J. S. Mill's *On Liberty*; Arthur Weigall's *Akhenaton; Modern Poetry* by Louis Macniece; *Essays in Popular Science* by Julian Huxley; *Social Life in the Insect World* by J. H. C. Fabre; and an explanation of Surrealism by Hugh Sykes Davies. Three years later in **"Tribute"** to a friend killed in the war, Ingamells wrote that

> Within the compass of our friendship walk
> Akhenaton and Zoroaster, Christ and Buddha,
> Mahomet and shrewd Confucius, Lao Tse;
> Dante and Milton; Shakespeare and Keats and Shelley;

He praised *Such Is Life* because its "classicism inhered *in character* and not *in scene*" and because Furphy saw "Australia *between* his classical figures and not . . . through them. . . ."

When Ingamells turned inwards on Australia's outback, it was not because he knew nothing about what was happening overseas; rather, he knew only too well. Like Alec Hope, Ingamells turned away from the chatter of cultured apes in the expectation that Australia's deserts would comfort him; and while Hope meant deserts of the mind, Ingamells believed that the outback provided environmental values with which people could survive the crisis that was destroying European civilisation: the triple abyss of wars, economic collapse, and fascism versus Bolshevism. These forces were active inside Australia; and not just active, but the dominant concerns. "Modernism" in the arts moved from being an outside challenge in the early 1930s to centre stage by the end of the decade; a founding member of Jindyworobak, Max Harris, became the leading advocate of apocalypticism, a champion of Surrealism, and editor of *Angry Penguins*. To appreciate the casual links between the European crisis and Jindyworobak it is necessary to investigate Ingamells' politics, his attachment to Australia First and his proclaimed communism.

In 1934, when he was looking for a publisher for **Gumtops,** Ingamells had the briefest of commercial dealings with P. R. Stephensen, who launched the magazine *Publicist* in July 1936, and the Australia First Movement in October 1941. In 1936 Ingamells read the first short version of Stephensen's "Foundations of Culture in Australia," which he criticised for claiming "that imported English is the most important element in Australian culture. . . ." Their next contact was through Ian Mudie, an organiser for Stephensen's Australia First Movement. Ingamells met Mudie for the first time on 8 September 1940. Thereafter they corresponded regularly and warmly, but Mudie kept aside from Jindyworobak for a time so as not to harm it with Australia First associations. Despite this intermediary, or perhaps because of it, Stephensen and Ingamells did not write to each other until July 1941. Ingamells was so impressed by Stephensen's practical advice that he dedicated an unpublished book, "The Truth About Australia" to him. In turn, Stephensen told Ingamells "now you are in my Tribe as securely as such an initiation ceremony can place you there; and I am in yours." Late in 1941, Ingamells joined the Australia First Movement and received a copy of *The Protocols of Zion* from Stephensen, who was arrested and interned on 10 March 1942 on suspicion of being a Japanese agent. Ingamells always, and rightly, thought that Stephensen was "innocent of the ridiculous charge of treason. He showed intolerance because he had suffered it in excess. . . . Considering the dangerous pass Australia was in during the war, it must be said that he asked for victimisation and got it." While Stephensen was still interned in 1943, Ingamells gladly accepted money, secretly, from Stephensen's Australia First associates in Sydney to finance a poetry competition in memory of one of the movement's founders, W. J. Miles.

To understand Ingamells' attachment to Australia First we have to recall briefly some of the attitudes which encouraged it. As well as its pro-fascist anti-semitism, which Ingamells rejected, Australia First was based on the appeal to put Australian interests above those of Britain. In 1939-41, this meant keeping troops here. Most Australians had reason to remember the slaughter of 60,000 of their fellows some twenty years before. Stephensen recalled that of his five near relatives in the Great European war, two were killed and two died later of wounds. Australia First could also mean, as it certainly did for Stephensen, a recognition that the Pacific conflict was an inter-Imperialist rivalry between Japan, Britain and the U.S.A., although he characterised the latter two as the "Pom-Jew-Coms-Usas."

Overlaying these political aspects was the growing demand for a distinctive Australian culture, in which Stephensen played a leading part, and of which Jindyworobak was merely the most aggressive manifestation. Although the Australia First Movement and Stephensen had their vilely repulsive aspects, these should not blind us to the attraction which the demand to put Australia first held for people like Ingamells and Xavier Herbert, who were neither fascists nor antisemitic. In an editorial for the "War Issue" of *Venture,* Ingamells supported the war for "freedom and liberal culture," while arguing for "a stay-at-home attitude among our creative artists."

To some extent, Ingamells was drawn to the Australia First Movement because of the Communist Party's decidedly Russia-first outlook, which has since been criticised by a leading official from those days as "entirely wrong" since it meant that local communists "were caught in situations quite unreal for Australians. We appeared to be a Russian party and an instrument of Soviet foreign policy" [E. F. Hill, *Class Struggles within the Communist Parties*].

As William Hart-Smith moved towards the Communist Party throughout 1943, Ingamells reminded him that,

> Jindy must be Australian. Australia is its life. Communist? A.F.P.? While one soap-box orator reminds me of the bush, the rivers, the mountains, the abos, while the other doesn't, I have more in my heart for the one that does. . . . When the Communists are as vital to Australian culture as the A.F.P., which *has* done more than any other political body for it, then the Communists will be down to earth in Australia and will . . . put the kybosh on A.F.P.. . . . You make the Coms Aussies and Communism will win in Australia. . . .

The self-acknowledged "perversities" of Ingamells' politics were more apparent than real. Although he claimed that his politics were "Communism and . . . Australia First," they were, as he constantly reminded people, best expressed in his poem, **"The Gangrened People."**

The Australia First aspect of **"The Gangrened People"** is unmistakable, although it is expressed in mythopoetics. The Communism is harder to see because it is not there. Instead, there is petty-bourgeois reformism. For Ingamells, the enemy was not capitalism but "excessive rents," "cunning" money-makers and "advertising"; he defended "honest commerce" against "Commercialism." His reform program was limited to increased spending on education, encouragement for the arts and for clear thinking programs. He called himself a Communist, partly to maintain the support of people like Hart-Smith, and partly because the word did describe his ideal society in which communal proprietorship would be restored to the position it had held with the Aboriginals. For him, "communism" was a way of avoiding the conflicts of capitalism; it was never something to be achieved through their violent resolution.

Above all, **"The Gangrened People"** expressed Ingamells' politics in its title. He looked on Australians as corrupt, diseased, or as he said, "gangrened": "Australia is a land that has no people," neither the destroyed Aboriginals nor the transplanted Europeans, those gangrened people against whom he had a

> . . . hard faith to keep in midst of sham
> because suburban triteness would damn
> the human spirit . . .

This rejection by and of the Australian people had not been present in Ingamells' earliest poems. In *Gumtops* (1935) he found the landscape hateful while working people were men of "dauntless hearts." In the first *Jindyworobak Anthology* (1938) he noted "that most of the best work printed here is pessimistic" but believed "that, as Australian writers progress in sympathetic understanding of their environment, we will achieve a proportion of happier poetry of equal merit."

Yet this happier verse would not be about human joys. Instead, in the same year, Ingamells realised that

> . . . more than another thing in life
> I wished to plunge again
> in a quiet where the world was bare
> of all but the bush and rain.

In **"Memorandum,"** also from 1938, he went even further and reasoned that since

> . . . men are out to keep and get,
> plotting for self with twisted truths . . .

he would listen henceforth only to the wind, to the reeds and to the frogs which all cry

> . . . the simplest things are best,
> Nature suckles Truth upon her breast.

His contribution to the 1939 anthology, **"Memory of Hills,"** was as pessimistic as those he had complained of twelve months before. In 1941, he pictured himself plodding "through the ineffectual days" when "To live gloriously is my right"; the harsh reception handed out to Jindyworobak was turning him ever more away from ordinary people, and in this mood he wrote **"The Gangrened People"** as a political credo. His 1943 volume proclaimed his despair of ordinary people in poems such as **"Mankind," "War after War"** and **"Voice of the Crow."** After he had largely rejected the false usage of Aboriginalities in his poetic language, Ingamells accepted a profounder primitivism when he sought refuge in an Alcheringa as a spiritual homeland, safe from the troubles of Europe.

Ingamells' growing rejection of European Australians did not lead him towards the Aboriginals as living people. From the first, he saw them as forgotten and dying; those who remained were "a degenerate, puppet people, mere parodies of what their race once was." (Naturally, he wanted a more considerate welfare policy, especially for "half castes," to ease the pillow of the dying race.) Part of the attractiveness of Aboriginal culture lay in his supposing that it was cut off from its living roots in human experience, and was thus available for appropriation by European Australians who could cannibalise it. In retreat from decadence, Ingamells devoured death. Like so many other petty-bourgeois intellectuals, he turned away from the lives of working people to seek comfort in the landscape. The "environmental values" of appropriate language became Ingamells' primary artistic concern. When opponents complained that he ignored the way European Australians lived, they missed the point. Ingamells was turning away from the life and work of ordinary people to communicate with pristine nature. Magical and exact words guarded these rites of purification. (pp. 29-38)

Humphrey McQueen, "Rex Ingamells and the Quest for Environmental Values," in Meanjin, Vol. 37, No. 1, April, 1978, pp. 29-38.

BRIAN ELLIOTT (essay date 1979)

[*Elliott is an Australian critic, biographer, and novelist who has written extensively on Australian literature. In the following excerpt, he examines the social and political background of the Jindyworobak movement, analyzes the artistic and ideological tenets presented in Ingamells's* Conditional Culture, *and traces the development of Jindyworobak qualities in Ingamells's poems.*]

[The] Jindyworobak movement was a generation of Australian poets at school. The nation in the decade 1930-1940, which saw their rise to articulation, was still emotionally and intellectually a colony in adolescence, awaiting cultural maturity. It must come. But when? The need of change was the more urgent because the times were gloomy and a great cloud of ugliness and terror was descending upon the older European vision. Spain, Italy, Germany, Russia smouldering: and then upon all these, industrial depression relieved only by a feverish anxiety to build up weapons of destruction. The older world suffered from disastrous forms of heart disease.

The young Australians wished, if they could, to assert their youth and difference, to relish the natural freedom of the human spirit, and they wished to look for it, since other resources had clearly failed, only in their own country. There was a sense that poetry—the loftiest, if not the only focus of spiritual values—in particular had failed, and it had failed because it no longer represented fundamental experiences of living. It had become a decorative frill. The impulse of the young Australians was to say, We must find it again; and we must find it here.

So they set themselves to learn how. First to find out, and then to teach others.

They were inexperienced and earnest; in a word, novices. They may be thought of as the class of '38, because it was in that year they graduated—matriculated, rather—and produced their first magazine and manifesto, the 1938 *Jindyworobak Anthology;* also Ingamells's declaration of war against the provincial philistines, the pamphlet *Conditional Culture* [see excerpt dated 1938]. It is of course true that spade-work had been done long before then, but this was the definitive move. The *Anthologies* were produced annually from 1938 to 1953. By then the class was ready to disperse, but it had done its work.

Reginald Charles, known as Rex Ingamells, was clearly the founding father of Jindyworobakism. He attacked the idea with a fiery devotion and a fanatical enthusiasm, which were catching and attracted in time a number of followers and disciples. The first of his active supporters, however, Wilfred Flexmore Hudson, who was at one with him for poetry as the national desideratum, was never a thorough-going convert to the Jindyworobak theory of it. Nevertheless his reservations did not prevent him from contributing all he could. After him came Ian Mayelston Mudie, who brought energy to the movement, some of it at times a little strident. These three, with the backing of a large number of loyal lesser voices, made up the first phase. All three were Australian born; in point of fact, all South Australians and natives of the same city, Adelaide. Though a state capital it was still then a provincial city, but perhaps for that very reason closer than the larger, more sophisticated Melbourne or Sydney to the mood of the hinterland. At any rate, between them these three produced a wild, bright, fresh music.

The two principal figures of the phase which followed, William Hart-Smith and Roland Edward Robinson, were both born abroad. Hart-Smith was English, Robinson Irish. It may be a question whether being Australian only by adoption, even when quite young, may have an important bearing upon a nascent Jindyworobak. Be that as it may, Jindyworobaks they became; Hart-Smith for a season though not for ever, and Robinson with final commitment. But the main difference between the phases was that the second was for art and poetry mainly and for Jindyworobak theory only as the way to reach them; for the first three, the theory itself was primary and obsessive.

It is not yet possible to claim that any one of the five principal Jindyworobaks stands out in isolated distinction. Time may modify this view; for the present at least, they cohere as a group. It will in the end be necessary to judge Hart-Smith and Robinson by tougher, more traditional standards than the others; they will have to stand by their achievements alone, whereas for the first three, idealism and good intentions will also enter into consideration. It is they more particularly who

seem the novices; it is they who appear more eagerly full of novelty and promise. They occupy the desks at the front, with a lively *esprit-de-corps* coming up from behind. But on the whole their sanguine hopes outshone their achievements. The poets might have done better to apply their minds with greater concentration; the results have inclined somewhat towards distraction and slipshod conclusions. A misguided idealism has led too often to impractical solutions. At the very worst, ignorant and obstinate. But by and large a good group, working well together, and genuinely concerned for the spiritual welfare of the nation. (pp. xvii-xix)

There were always two more or less clearly defined streams of poetical development in Australia; probably in all colonial poetry. The settlers in America set the pattern. They had two aims: first to re-enter the lost paradise (which the discovery of new worlds out of Europe seemed to promise), and second, to exploit it. In the early years of Australia practical hardships (coupled with the awareness that the place was a convict settlement anyway) tended to stress material progress, though never to the utter exclusion of hopes and visions. Among writers many were motivated strongly by the settlers' struggles for mastery over farm and station land, but for others landscape and vista were what mattered. By 1900 there was a conventional dichotomy which divided "Sydney" from "the bush"; this could signify the division between sophisticated and natural art; or, more narrowly, between cabinet or drawing-room literary conventionalism, album lyricism and the like, and the vigorous outdoor traditionalism of the bush yarn and the balladry of action and heroism. Victor Daley, Sydney Jephcott, James Hebblethwaite with innumerable others, including a host of literary ladies, represented the one; writers like Lawson, Paterson, Ogilvie, Brady and the balladists generally the other. All found a home in the *Bulletin,* which, for all its active (and successful) campaigning for a national literature in line with its motto, "Australia for the Australians," saw no inhibiting incompatibility between the genres. A result was that even in that enterprising paper (which one of its detractors once disparaged as the *Bul-let-in*) a high degree of favour was bestowed upon the best of both kinds. The "action" strain led to poems about horses and heroism; the "cabinet" persuasion developed into paeans to "Beauty." By the time the first Jindyworobak had managed to mature a year or two beyond callow puberty he was ready to rebel against the complacent colonial acceptance of both. He found it all weary, stale, flat and unprofitable; and worse, boringly *unrelated* to the experiences of wonder that were daily before his eyes: the sights and sounds of the landscape he knew, the response of his own blood and muscle to the physical environment about him. Above all, there was no spirituality, nothing of a true bond between the man and his natural world, in what the poets appeared to feel. He was conscious, as were his friends and contemporaries, of something not yet adequately expressed yet very real in what his generation more than earlier ones sensed of that vital bond. Not that it had never been noticed before; emphasis had been placed upon the *strangeness* of Australian nature and the *uniqueness* of the sensations which it induced. A poem like Charles Harpur's "Midsummer Noon in the Australian Forest" is not hard to interpret as a child's—a young boy's—recollection of delicious moments of communion with the natural bush environment as direct, unliterary emotion: a fully and articulately *related* experience. This appeared to him genuine; of the "opal-hearted country, a wilful, lavish land" about which Dorothea Mackellar had rhapsodized, he was not so sure. But there really was a dreamland of Australia into which the young could enter; they were all aware of it, now more than ever before. As the vision of the old world lost its appeal (who could long for Europe now?), the vision of the new one, the immediate experience, grew more compelling. How to grasp it was the problem; convention did not yet sanction these values. But the time was ripe for change, and a key was provided. The old dream*land* became the new Dream*time*. This shift enabled Ingamells and the others to put a name to the quality of Australian uniqueness they had so piquantly experienced but not been able to express. It was *Aboriginal.*

It was this new fact they went to school to learn; it was this they became missionaries to teach. It cannot be stated too early, or asserted too positively, that the Aboriginal element in the Jindyworobak programme, whatever may be the common impression, was not part of any impulse to write Aboriginal history or to propound Aboriginal law or morality, or even to describe Aboriginal culture. They were not archaeologists and anthropologists, and if they were missionaries—as I have unhesitatingly called them—their mission was directed not to the blacks, but to the whites, to the civilization which now exists and is in control. They cannot be faulted by pointing out that their ethnological information was often faulty; they were never scientists, and their use of the material was always directed to literary ends. They were poets—for the most part lyrical poets. Even that makes them un-Aboriginal, as will appear.

But the Aboriginal linkage calls for explanation. The Jindyworobaks were not even the first to posit it; they had predecessors whom it is proper to place in the picture. When, earlier, I specified which were the two prevailing poetical *genres* of turn-of-the-century Australian writing, I might well also have listed a third, almost as prevalent: the didactic. There was enough of the preaching strain in Australian verse already for the Jindyworobaks themselves to inherit a rather uncomfortable infusion of it. I would rather not think of this preaching as characteristic of them—though, unfortunately, it too often was. The style was already present in Adam Lindsay Gordon but its high priest was Bernard O'Dowd, who learnt his art from listening to Moody and Sankey hymns and to Salvation Army preachers on street corners. But he was earnest and sincere, not less so than the Jindyworobaks when they carried on in the same strain; and it was Bernard O'Dowd who first rationalized the Dreamtime for white Australian consumption.

O'Dowd's imagination (if that was what it really was) ranged over political-philosophical and ideal themes, and expressed itself with all the glamour of a university extension lecture on some industriously knowledgeable topic; but he had read a notable book and referred to it. This was Spencer and Gillen, *The Native Tribes of Central Australia,* 1899. Significant allusions to it occur in his long and not always wholly unattractive poem, *The Bush,* 1912. Spencer's was not the first study of the native culture to be published, but it was by far the most systematic yet to appear, and it was followed by others; not only that, but scholars abroad took notice of it. Among Australian poets, however, O'Dowd was the only one of distinction to refer to it, and no doubt his interest in it was at the time attributed to the same kind of overworked eccentricity which applied to his other obscurities. The public as a whole was not yet ready to pay attention to the Aborigines; interest so far had not advanced beyond mere curiosity. Nor was the reference to Spencer the only aspect of *The Bush* which might be expected to capture the attention of an Ingamells. O'Dowd's national-political idealism was harmo-

nious with Ingamells's, and so was his disposition to see the real Australia in terms of physical experiences. I think particularly of the lines,

> When, now, they say "The Bush!", I see the top
> Delicate amber leaflings of the gum
> Flutter, or flocks of screaming green leeks drop
> Silent . . .

He was aware of O'Dowd's theme of destiny and waiting:

> For Great Australia is not yet: She waits
> (Where o'er the Bush prophetic auras play) . . .

Never mind what she waits for; for Ingamells it was not the same. O'Dowd also saw the Australian *mystery* and declared

> She is the scroll on which we are to write
> Mythologies our own . . .

He insists constantly on the indwelling *spirits* of the bush, though in a way perhaps to have more meaning for Irish Robinson than for Ingamells of Orroroo: "And you have Children of the Dreaming Star. . . ." Above all this, the poem has two references to Alcheringa: in one O'Dowd says he has "In Alcheringa found the Golden Age" (which is not ridiculous, allowing for a measure of poetic licence), and the other is a direct tribute to Spencer:

> And Spencer sails from Alcheringa bringing
> Intaglios, totems and Books of the Dead.

More poetic licence; these "intaglios," and possibly the "Books of the Dead," otherwise meaningless, may be tjurungas (churingas) . . . but what does it matter? The book had been read.

Though this precedent might be relevant, one cannot see Ingamells or any other Jindyworobak simply following it. *The Bush* is a poem still too much encrusted with fustian and old-fashioned poeticisms of the Victorian-romantic kind (what O'Dowd himself referred to as "the cheap parterres of Europe"—another idea Ingamells would have accepted, though not its wording) to be of any value as a model. But it exhibits the Aboriginal vision, at least in the form of a faint glimmer, and the next example provides more. If few Australians had read *The Native Tribes of Central Australia,* readers elsewhere valued it and a new edition of the same work was called for and brought out under the title *The Arunta* in 1927. By then the public was more ready to receive it and this was the edition which the young Jindyworobaks read. Ingamells was only fourteen in 1927 but it cannot have been long before he discovered it. . . . But what was so attractive about Spencer's Alcheringa to allure the poets at all? The answer, so far as it touches Ingamells, may appear in the circumstances of his early life.

Rex Ingamells . . . was born at Orroroo in South Australia, a location of some symbolic importance since it was a town on the edge of the salt-bush plain, on the railway line to Broken Hill: a last-outpost meeting-place of the civilized and the savage. This meant actually that he was born at one of the far limits of the Arunta tribe, the Central Australian people of whom Spencer wrote. This fact does not imply close proximity, especially in 1913, but occasionally, on journeys, he may as a child have seen a little of some Aboriginal encampments. It was experience of which, likely enough, the detail could be forgotten but the effect carried long in his memory. He left Orroroo at a young age to go to school in Adelaide, afterwards to the university where he studied history. He was in fact to become for a time a teacher, but abandoned that eventually to be a publisher's agent. His historical reading did not, as far as I am aware, concern itself intimately with Australian documentation but it was no doubt at the university that it led him to his discovery of *The Arunta.*

Neither of us read the book with scholarly attention; we read it impatiently. The work is large and detailed; I am sure Ingamells read it more carefully, and more often, than I did. It crystallized for him a number of ideas and attitudes. Above all it presented him with the concept of the Dreamtime. "Dreamtime," however, is only an anglicization (and an often abused and sentimentalized one) of the Arunta terms used by Spencer. Properly the word should be Alchera in Arunta; the form Alcheringa is an adjective formed from it (but the distinction is pedantic). It should be added that the same mythical concept (or one very like it) is common to all Australian Aboriginal tribes, though different languages have different words for it.

This is no place to attempt a scientific explanation of the Alchera; nor is it necessary to an understanding of the Jindyworobak use of it. One does not need an anthropological explanation of Hades to understand *Orpheus in the Underworld,* of the *Nibelungenlied* to follow *Das Rheingold.* The Jindyworobaks used the Alchera symbolism with as much or as little detail as they required; and it was not usually complicated. In effect it is a myth of a time outside the limits of history in which whatever exists has the reality of myth, not of fact; it exists in eternal terms as "then" or "now" or "in the future" or "always"; it is the time to which all other time goes back, in which the first things were done, the first creatures came to life, the creation-time. The first men and the first animals and plants came together then and were, not physically but totemistically, identified and (as the legends relate) interchangeable. It is a vision of the world which is so like a dream that it is also called the "Dreaming" (a more accurate expression than "Dreamtime"). All men of today belong to their proper totems and are reincarnations of the creatures (animals, human heroes, spirits, wanderers) of the original creation-time. Taken in conjunction with aspects of Aboriginal ritual and law, social structure and moral and religious institutions, it is easy to see how O'Dowd could find the "Golden Age" in Alcheringa. We do not, however, need to see the phenomena in terms of such ideal perfectionism to realize that their "dreaming" aspect, which means one thing to an Aboriginal and another to a youthful white poet, has a sufficiently elastic validity to work on a number of levels and with satisfaction to the user on many of them.

An important question is whether such an image can be as useful to a reader as it obviously has been to a group of writers. For Aboriginal minds it is not merely a plausible image, the philosophical-intellectual-religious-ethical medium in which all their myths, legends, ceremonies, institutions and even their very thoughts cohere, it is the very basis of their faith; it is at the root of their concept of reality. It is of no use to pretend that white Australians, even Jindyworobak poets, can give that kind of sacred belief to it. So for them it is a figurative image, a symbol, a large metaphor. And as such it either does or does not work. Flexmore Hudson, as we are aware, found it hard to swallow. Ian Mudie could take it or leave it; for him it was an instrument, to be used or left alone. Hart-Smith accepted it as a device of the mind: he tended to stand off and use it imaginatively, but always preserving his own perspective. Robinson let it work like a yeast in his mind,

an intoxicant, much as the poets of Ireland used the Red Branch. Only for Ingamells, really, was it in any closely resembling sense an article of faith; and it was a white Dreamtime, really, that sustained that faith most of the time. The Aboriginal Dreamtime excited him. But it was the Australian one—the Great Australian Uniqueness—that he most deeply believed in.

If the edges of this explanation seem fuzzy, they must be left so; I think no permanent good can come of an attempt to reduce the concept of the Australian Dreamtime to precise definition. Some of it must certainly be left to be taken on trust. Yet the curious thing—for really it is an astonishing concept, quite a wild kind of fantasy and not one it might have seemed likely a nation as pragmatic as the Australian would easily accept—is that it has, upon the whole, been favourably taken. Among the poets, the Jindyworobaks themselves apart, few have been ready to accept it unqualified; but it has gone somehow into the background of their thinking. Some even who have been openly critical, even derisive, towards the Jindyworobaks, have been influenced by it, sometimes to an extent they hardly realize. What one can say, is that a myth may exist and be recognized even if nobody accepts it at face value; the Jindyworobaks' Dreamtime is such a myth and can well function in that way. Even for Ingamells it was a part of literature and not, like the Arunta Alchera, part of life as a whole. That is where, for us now, its real value lies and must lie. It is not the Real Presence; it is a tjurunga (churinga), a totemic symbol, a stone elaborately carved or painted with a sacred design, the serious representation of its contained truth, not the fact itself.

Put to the political application that O'Dowd made, the Golden Age of the Alchera was a pastoral simplification not equalled by the prettiest fancies of a Theocritus or a Virgil: for both those poets knew well enough that a farmer is at bottom a farmer. It is true, though, that, seen wholly under a colour of idealism, the tribal life of the Aborigines, politically ordered by a rule of democratic custom and mutual consent, and spiritually controlled by the mythological authority of the Alchera, seemed to constitute the kind of perfect human community which nothing in the inherited white civilization could equal. This thought, however unreal (and I imagine nobody was actually deceived) had a genuinely imaginative appeal for a group of young poets who, in the bad times of the 1930s, all felt trapped within a national and political "environment" which appeared hopelessly and inescapably evil, and threatened to close in on them and destroy them and Australia utterly.

Ingamells was already writing short poems and lyrics with a Jindyworobak drift in 1930. Two modest volumes appeared, in both cases with the friendly encouragement of Edgar Preece, an Adelaide bookseller who published **Gumtops** in 1935 and **Forgotten People** in 1936. There were some amiable verses here, but from the Jindyworobak point of view they were still tentative. In 1936, however, there was also a tentative use of the magic word: "Jindyworobak." It appeared in *Chapbook,* the second (and final) issue of a small magazine, also issued by Preece, along with some other experimental writings which included the poem **"Moorawathimeering"** to be discussed presently. Ingamells brooded over these innovations for two years, preparing for the Jindyworobak *annus mirabilis,* 1938. In that year three significant works appeared—slender pamphlets, but with a strong impact. These were his third volume of poems, **Sun-Freedom;** the prose manifesto, **Conditional Culture,** and an even more vital challenge, the first *Jindyworobak Anthology.*

In **Conditional Culture** he wrote:

> "Jindyworobak" is an aboriginal word meaning "to annex, to join," and I propose to coin it for a particular use. The Jindyworobaks, I say, are those individuals who are endeavouring to free Australian art from whatever alien influences trammel it, that is, bring it into proper contact with its material. They are the few who seriously realize that an Australian culture depends on the fulfilment and sublimation of certain definite conditions, namely:
>
> 1. A clear recognition of environmental values.
> 2. The debunking of much nonsense.
> 3. An understanding of Australia's history and traditions, primaeval, colonial and modern.

As he saw it, the need was to "annex" or "join" the white to the black, or the black to the white—it is not clear how, except that the process would involve some "debunking," and require some revaluation of "Australia's history and traditions." As a manifesto it might have been more precise and lucid, but that does not mean nothing can be made of it. In the light of what followed it can be interpreted. "Environmental values" means what it says: the relationship, subjective or objective, between a man and the world about him. In poetry this mostly comes to mean the relationship between personal or individual sensibility and the physical or social landscape. With the Jindyworobaks if often comes to a way of looking at the "primaeval" landscape, whether that implies that Aboriginal, mythical and original Australia or something rather closer to mere geology. It is epitomized in a man-landscape equation. As for the second "condition," it is obvious enough what Ingamells had in mind; it mainly refers to proprieties of local diction, and was a complaint with more urgency to it when he wrote than it has now. Especially in the poetry of Kendall, but also in the drawing-room lyrics and album and magazine verse of the half-century which followed, there was an excessive abundance of what Ingamells regarded as inappropriate "English" poeticisms—mostly mere words, but also conventional concepts and allusions—O'Dowd's "cheap parterres":

> I know she is fair as the angels are fair,
> For have I not caught a faint glimpse of her there,
> A glimpse of her face and her glittering hair,
> And a hand with the Harp of Australia?
>   Kendall, "The Muse of Australia"

Ian Mudie considered that this Jindyworobak objection was justified well enough, and effectively made; but it is odd that Ingamells should choose to use an American colloquialism ("debunking") to make the point. Others, of course, felt similarly and the Jindyworobaks may not claim the whole credit for reforming the "parterres," but their vehemence was a natural ingredient in the programme. The third "condition," especially as it includes the term "primaeval," is more important and original. "Primaeval" implies more than merely "old" and its powerful message had not been heard in Australia alone—at least there may be a tone here that echoes Longfellow's American "forest primeval." Whether or not, it is the Aboriginal association that Ingamells had most specifically in mind, and this implied the other terms. "Australia's history" did not begin in 1788; it began thousands of years before that (the archaeologists now say something like fifty thousand, but in 1938 the figures advanced were less). Ingamells's

point is to promote a recognition of *total* Australian identity; a range of history in which the Aborigines have much the largest part, but which requires to be seen in the three aspects mentioned, Aboriginal, colonial-pioneering and modern-contemporary. *All three* are component parts of Ingamells's "Dreamtime." "Alchera" or "Alcheringa" is the specifically Aboriginal Dreamtime, but the Jindyworobak Dreamtime is "Australia's history" as a whole, or whatever part of it he chooses to emphasize. That is, it is the national identity viewed *sub specie aeternitatis.*

It should be clear enough from these principles that (although they were accused of it) the Jindyworobaks never set out to write Aboriginal poetry in English words. Their desire to "annex and join" was not a desire to invade and conquer. Nor did they design to be conquered: they always retained their white character, shown in the most unmistakable way in their continuation in the European tradition of lyrical styles. Possibly there is an assertion concealed here which calls for amplification. If we go to what seem to be the purest, the least contaminated and therefore the most fundamental conceptions of Aboriginal poetry accessible to us, the Arunta or Aranda epics which are the subject of T. G. H. Strehlow's elaborate study, *The Songs of Central Australia,* it is plain that the earliest and most primitive kind of poetry—and poetry it certainly is, in spite of certain dissimilarities to what we are accustomed to—is impersonal and cannot be lyrical. The Aranda *Songs* are ceremonial and ritual epics, sacred texts, never ascribed even inferentially to any single personal author, and handed down through the generations without (conscious) modification. The conventions of language and diction, which are complex, but need not concern us, are in themselves preservative even though the literature is, historically, entirely an oral tradition. As the Jindyworobaks paid no visible attention to the actual "literature" of the songs there is little point in attempting to examine technicalities. Even though Ingamells was acquainted with Strehlow and discussed his ideas and received some encouragement from him, I doubt very much that his acquaintance with the songs was extensive; in any case, most of Strehlow's published studies came later. (He published "Ankotarinja, an Aranda Myth" in *Oceania* IV, 1933, but I have seen no evidence that Ingamells used it.) It is, in fact, an unprofitable exercise to try to establish any connection between Aboriginal and Jindyworobak poetry, and even the striking forms and designs of Aboriginal visual art seem to have made only a picturesque impact. Most people, including the poets, who were acquainted with Aboriginal artifacts in the 1930s regarded them as quaint, decorative, but impenetrably symbolic and made no attempt to understand them more than very superficially. The white writers could not write with anything resembling the commanding impersonality of the Aboriginal epics, whether or not they knew them.

That impersonality is a mark of the extremely early primitive state of Aranda poetry. It is difficult to be positive, but as far as I am able to tell from a comparison with the northern (Arnhem Land) poetry of which careful and admirable translations are available by Ronald Berndt . . . , it remains my impression that the completer isolation of the Central Australians has preserved more closely intact the primitive function of poetry with them than was the case elsewhere. In the north some degree of contact with visitors from beyond the sea (or some other cause) had introduced at least a minor degree of quasi-literary sophistication into their styles. According to the impression conveyed by Strehlow, at least, there appear to be few Central Australian verses which do not derive from the epics, even those that serve as charms and incantations; and above all, nothing that could be called lyrical in a European sense. It is impossible for an inherited, ritualistic poetical system whose origins are lost in the remote past (are, in fact, accepted as being part of the creation itself, the heroes who are the subject of the poetry being themselves regarded as the creators of the verses) to retain personal accents, and therefore to function, even when fragmented, as European lyrics do. The essence of European lyric is that it expresses a personal emotion; the *passion* in the verse is an outflow of the poet's own heart ("the spontaneous overflow of powerful feelings," said Wordsworth). There are passages, certainly, in the epics which arouse strong, even excited emotion (and this comes through impressively in translation, though we may not understand them exactly as a primitive Aborigine would). But the Jindyworobaks never aimed at poetry of that tribal and ritual kind; they were lyrical poets, lyrists in the classical, European and even (deny it as they might) the English tradition; and they were never anything else. They were romantics still, whether they liked to think so or not; and their romanticism persisted even when they stood ranting and preaching on the hustings, uttering what was perhaps barely even poetry at all.

What one will claim for the Jindyworobaks, especially for the first three and Ingamells above all, is that they had *some* of this impersonal detachment. They caught it in the first place from their own prophetic seriousness: teachers and propagandists, it was not for them to dwell, or to dwell exclusively, on emotions they did not share freely with others. Second, it appears to be something absorbed from the landscape, the "environment" or "spirit of the place," and in this respect a response of their own to something which had great importance in the Aboriginal mind. It must be interpreted for the Jindyworobaks, principally as a broad, pervading influence, an atmosphere, but as the Aborigines understood it, it came down to specific detail. Every location, every feature of the visible landscape was inhabited with mystical, mythical and totemistic presences—places where mythical events had occurred, where the wandering ancestors had rested, and (of vivid importance to individuals) spots where the quickening had occurred which first identified them as the living unborn and assigned them to their totems. Naturally in these circumstances there was a profound suggestiveness in all places, ritually important to the natives, imaginatively so (in a more or less Wordsworthian sense) to the poets; a mystical experience, in fact, which may be designated for both the white and the black, though with different implications, as Australian site-magic.

For Ingamells the mystical sensations of site-magic were the key to his imaginative expression. His inspirations, and also his limitations, were for the most part visual; at any rate, sense-impressions. And as they were impressionistic, so were they, for the most part, brief. A single image or image-vista may constitute the whole content, the whole essential content, of his poem. Always he writes best about what he can touch or see: rocks, most often; or effects of light; the open landscape, people who animate it. His **"Black Mary"** is human but is equally a living sculpture: she "walks wonderfully." He is vividly responsive to moods of dawn or dusk, the splash of light on a cliff face. He also has another and a particular responsiveness, to language—that is, to words heard in a romantic ear. In "Jindyworobak" there is a striking instance; in fact he uses the word out of context and perversely,

but it still serves his creative purpose and retains the magic which it had first for him when he discovered it. Undoubtedly the sound of the words Alchera and Alcheringa enchanted him before he had fully digested their meaning. This enchantment found in words is a European characteristic; to the Aborigines, though they might be sacred, those words were not exotic. But it is now convenient to turn to a poem which raises and perhaps may answer a few queries of the kind which has just come into context, touching both language and the vision of Alchera; and at the same time to refute the accusation that Ingamells attempted to compete with Aboriginal poetry by writing lines of his own in imitation of it. It will be apparent at once that this last charge is nonsense. (pp. xix-xxxi)

[The poem **"Moorawathimeering"**] may be guaranteed to have an instant effect, but whether sympathetic or hostile may be unpredictable. Here at any rate is at first sight an array of impenetrable Aboriginal words: yet . . . they can all be interpreted painlessly:

> Into moorawathimeering, where atninga dare not tread,
> Leaving wurly for a wilban, tallabilla, you have fled . . .

This was a "debunking" of English artificiality in diction with a vengeance. Was the effect merely an exchange of nonsense for nonsense, or was there new magic in it? Obviously the attempt was experimental, and even if successful in the way of novelty, not likely to be very freely repeatable. But in this one poem, if not so clearly in the others (a few only) which accompanied it, it does seem to me that he captured the magic he sought. It makes little difference to point out that here again there has been some minor verbal confusion. When the poem first appeared (obviously it was one of the very early products of his Jindyworobak awakening) he spelt the word "moonawathimeering," and that was the spelling used in the first reprint in **Sun-Freedom**, 1938. But at this stage he must have glanced back at its source in *The Vanished Tribes* and realized he had miscopied it. All later printings (and it remained a favourite poem) replace "moon—" with "moor—." Captivated as he was by native words (which he never troubled to relate with any system to their proper original languages and dialects), he could also be careless with them and in one instance, may I be forgiven for suggesting, amusingly reckless—as when, in another of his early experiments he wrote,

> Flat upon her mooloona
> Innerah eats the kombora . . .

Yet against the bathos of this set the line

> fine as late allinga light.

These are trifles: **"Moorawathimeering"** is perhaps rather more. Clearly it has an Aboriginal subject. It is not an Aboriginal poem. It makes vivid use of Aboriginal and Dreamtime ideas; it respects the decorum of site-magic and time-magic equally. But it never loses touch with the European lyrical tradition. (pp. xxi-xxxii)

The more I reflect about the Jindyworobak achievement, the more I am inclined to believe that the vigour was [Ingamells's] and that he at his best epitomized it—but when I say so, it is the occasional brilliant, light-flooded image that comes to my mind, not his reasoning about the experience. He was the first, the most passionate and perhaps in the high moments of his success the most effective of the Jindyworobak "joiners": but I will not assert that he always knew with complete precision what were the elements he was joining. It is important to see him feeling his way: often enough in the dark.

There is a love of light and warmth, but not much that is specifically Jindyworobak, in his early experimental pieces. One of the earliest to survive (dated 1930; but as we have it, a later revision) is his fragmentary **"Luis de Torres,"** in which there is a plentiful romanticism but nothing Aboriginal. Ingamells did not, at any rate consciously, begin with an Aboriginalized vision. It was only that the Dreamtime, when it came, captured for him with astonishing vividness the sense of Australia's magical uniqueness which was his first conscious poetical preoccupation. It was something imbibed in childhood and **"Luis de Torres"** symbolized it: the mythical experience of history, the glamour of the "Great South Land." All Australian school children were told about that at the age of perhaps nine or ten. We were the heirs of that marvellous late discovery, the last and best to be made in an expanding world of golden, mysterious wonder. The heritage was not for him only: we all shared it. Especially it was the sea-voyagers who captivated us: theirs was the irresistible appeal. If I remember rightly a second wonder hung about the stories were told in junior classes about the enviable lives of Little Aborigines, who lived in wurlies, on lizards and snakes and kangaroos, and ran free and naked in a world of sunshine and kindness.

It is possible to be ironical about this childish mythology but for many it was a formative force; it was for Ingamells. I do not think it too extravagant to suggest that when he formulated his Jindyworobak theories, these myths were a potent ingredient. Ultimately they entered into the Jindyworobak impulse; what was to be joined and mutually annexed was surely not two histories but two mythologies.

When he was first aware of poetical sensibility he produced verse like **"By the Fire,"** which is characterless:

I am sitting by the fire,
Watching the warm raying of its light,
And treasuring remembered conversations . . .
(1931)

But in **"The Old Telegraph Station, Strangways"** (also 1931) he has already caught a little of the passionate, though as yet unformulated, Jindy colour:

It is the most unhappy place these eyes
Have seen: forlorn old ruins . . .

From here we go to "heartless cries of crows," a plangent Jindy emblem. If the way to Alcheringa lay first through the evocation of old and nostalgic times (and it almost certainly did)—with "drear floods" and "affrays with blacks" in lonely country, "small campfires in dark wastes," this was well on the track. We come closer still with **"The Afghans,"** . . . but the first convincing Aboriginal landmark is **"Boomerang"** (1932). Ingamells never considered it good enough to reprint. Perhaps the best of this early trial-and-error poetry was **"The Bullocky,"** which has perception, feeling and some poetical substance. The bullocky comes at noon in a cloud of dust and pauses outside a bush school to hear the children singing:

the smoke
From his old black pipe curled up;
Then, when the singing ceased, he called
To his blowing team—"Gerrup!"
(1932)

"Forlorn Beauty" (1933) shows some regression: half the po-

etical energies of the late colonial lyrical impulse exhausted themselves in singing the praises of Beauty (more often than not capitalized and personified). And yet in this (on the whole jejune) poem occurs one of Ingamells's most splendid Jindyworobak images . . . glimpses, rather:

O I have seen one flaming peak at dawn
Across a sea of sand . . .

The true Jindyworobak fusion is attained with a group of short bird-pieces in 1935: **"Garchooka the Cockatoo," "Garrakeen"** (the parakeet), and one or two other associated fragments. **"Garchooka"** in seven lines is his first unimpeachable lyric in the Jindyworobak mode. A flight of cockatoos passes, screeching, along a reach of some river—I fancy the Murray is meant—and the noise of the birds, the flash of their colour, the mood of evening, the gold light and the rippled water, all cohere in a brilliantly native Aboriginal impressionism. Its Dreamtime significations could easily escape notice, so may be pointed out. For Ingamells there is, to begin with, the magic of the bird's name, a response which never failed in him; but it is reinforced with tribal echoes, since it is natural to assume the birds are totemic tribal spirits as well as physical creatures. Of course this requires a contribution from the informed imagination, but it is not at all difficult to supply.

Perhaps these bird poems were lucky successes: he was by no means so happy with frogs.

I hear, ere sleep, the medleyed notes
Escape the wet, moon-gleaming throats.

There's one old bull-frog's bass . . .

. . . giant reed-growths in a marsh
Where starlight streamed insipid on
The slime of Labyrinthodon.
(1935)

Imageless and banal; nothing of Alchera here. . . . [This piece] is full of faults which break the poet's own canons: weakly artificial diction, lumbering rhyme. The "one old bullfrog" has a personality—but as a rule Ingamells is happier with light than with sound. These fragments come near to his true landscape:

Look at the rocky range . . .
The black crows are calling, forlornly crying out . . .
"Evening in the MacDonnells" 1933

There are rock-rooted ranges . . .
There are crows settling on the boundary gate
or poised in the sky . . .
"Memory of Hills" 1939

Black boulder,
gust-chilled,
dew-filmed for starlight . . .
I know you are
a raging-red coal of the sun
earth-flung
to set this mountain on fire . . .
"Black Boulder" 1940

Sound may support vision, but vision is first. If he wholly forsakes the visual his talent may fall limp:

How can a stranger hope to understand?

(Dorothea Mackellar said that: "All you who have not loved here, You will not understand.")—But if that individual line was abysmal, its companion was not:

Dark ghosts go with me all about the land.
"Forgotten People" 1936

In **"The Gangrened People"** 1941, where he preaches grossly, there are not even dark ghosts to save him:

We, the Gangrened People,
swollen up with fabricated virtue,
virus of hypocrisy,
call ourselves the champions of Justice
and Liberty and O Democracy . . .

Jindyworobak indignation of this quasi-political kind was pious and well-intentioned but in effect nothing to the poetical point. The Jindyworobak imagination could never (even in Ian Mudie, a somewhat more robust political personality) be made with any grace to work like a horse on the hustings. Yet they were both tempted to mount the noble hobby. Ingamells in particular was an ineffective satirist—in the romantic, rhapsodical, lyrical and visionary vein he could be memorable, but as a Jindyworobak Jeremiah, performing concertos for the political didgeridoo, he is almost always flat and tedious. The truth is, he lives by his insights and they tend to be of a brief, almost flashing duration: he does not well sustain a large design. His attempt at a narrative of some length, **"The Bloodwood Tree"** 1936, meant to be harsh, grim and heroic, is merely gothically uninspired. He did not so much lack imaginative passion as humour; often it was simply this that failed his design. And perhaps if he had possessed a more lively sense of proportion he would never have embarked upon that poetical old-man-of-the-sea, *The Great South Land* (1951). This work, which he boasted ill-advisedly was longer than *Paradise Lost,* has passages of a certain not unadmirable rhetorical eloquence. His earnestness shines right through it. But it never rises above the grandeur of a nobly planned compilation. It is the childhood history lesson conscientiously expanded; it is a young man's homework laboriously performed. All that it contains of the real Jindyworobak spirit returns to those happy nursery days before he had yet heard of Alcheringa. But it celebrates the great Australian uniqueness; the mystery, not the consummation. (pp. xxxvii-xli)

There are signs of a restlessness in some few of Rex Ingamells's later lyrics which might lead us to suppose he was moving towards a more balanced and mature complex of poetic values than had carried him forward—joyously and brilliantly at his very best—so far. Unfortunately in December 1955 he was killed in a motor accident. The poem **"The Pensioner"** . . . is one which could suggest a change in his style and outlook. But it was not to be. (pp. xli-xlii)

Brian Elliott, in an introduction to The Jindyworobaks, *edited by Brian Elliott, University of Queensland Press, 1979, pp. xvii-lxvi.*

FURTHER READING

Ashworth, A. W. Review of *Aranda Boy,* by Rex Ingamells. *Southerly* 15, No. 2 (1954): 129-32.
  Favorable evaluation of Ingamells's book for children.

Elliott, Brian. "Jindyworobaks and Aborigines." *Australian Literary Studies* 8, No. 1 (May 1977): 29-50.
  Examines Jindyworobak use of Aboriginal language and poetry, asserting that critics have over-emphasized the importance of Aboriginal culture in the Jindyworobak philosophy. Elliott suggests that Ingamells did not clearly articulate the artistic and ideological values of the Jindyworobaks and thereby contributed to the critics' misinterpretation.

Hagney, M. "Some Australian Poets and War." *Southerly* 5, No. 1 (1944): 51-2.
  Negative review of seven volumes of war poetry published by Jindyworobaks, including Ingamells's *Content Are the Quiet Ranges* and *Unknown Land.* Hagney maintains that "Australian war poetry of any significance will not be found" in these collections.

Hope, A. D. "Culture Corroboree." *Southerly* 2, No. 3 (November 1941): 28-31.
  Review of several Jindyworobak volumes published in 1941. Hope disagrees with the Jindyworobak perspective on the nature of Australian culture and calls Ingamells's poem "The Gangrened People" "a long piece of versified journalese."

Ingamells, Rex, et al., eds. *Jindyworobak Review, 1938-1948.* Melbourne: Jindyworobak Publications, 1948, 128 p.
  Collection of essays about the Jindyworobak movement. The volume contains an introduction by Ingamells outlining the development of the movement and its place in Australian literature.

O'Brien, C. J. H. "Anthology and Mythology." *Southerly* 2, No. 1 (April 1941): 28-30.
  Positive review of *Jindyworobak Anthology 1940,* which was edited by Ingamells.

Vassilieff, Elizabeth. Review of *The Great South Land,* by Rex Ingamells. *Meanjin* 10, No. 47 (Summer 1951): 403-06.
  Contends that Ingamells's epic work is overly long and displays a "dearth of poetry."

James (Augustine Aloysius) Joyce

1882-1941

Irish novelist, short story writer, poet, dramatist, and critic.

The following entry presents criticism of Joyce's short story collection *Dubliners* (1914). For discussion of Joyce's complete career see *TCLC*, Volumes 3 and 8; an entry devoted to *A Portrait of the Artist as a Young Man* is included in *TCLC*, Volume 16; an entry devoted to "*Ulysses* and the Process of Textual Reconstruction" is included in *TCLC*, Volume 26.

Joyce is the most prominent writer of English prose in the first half of the twentieth century. Many critics maintain that his verbal facility equals that of William Shakespeare or John Milton, and his virtuoso experiments in prose redefined both the limits of language and the form of the modern novel. *Dubliners*, Joyce's only short story collection, is considered a master achievement in that genre as well as a revealing indicator of his preeminence as a prose stylist.

Joyce was born in a suburb of Dublin to middle-class parents. Due to adverse financial circumstances, the family relocated several times into progressively poorer neighborhoods around Dublin, a situation that afforded Joyce a great familiarity with the city during his childhood and youth. He was educated at Jesuit schools, his instruction financed largely by scholarships, and showed outstanding aptitude for essay writing, religious studies, languages, and music. However, he experienced much the same emotional hardship throughout his school years as he later attributed to Stephen Dedalus, the hero of his first published novel, *A Portrait of the Artist as a Young Man*. The influence of the Jesuit priests on Joyce was great, and although he eventually rejected Catholicism, his notion of the artist as a secular priest may be seen as a result of his education. After graduating from University College in Dublin in 1902, Joyce left Ireland and established himself in Paris, in order to abandon the milieu that *Dubliners* depicts in harsh detail. In 1903 he returned to Ireland when his mother developed a serious illness. Following her death in 1904 Joyce moved permanently to the Continent with his future wife, Nora Barnacle. Though so disgusted by what he considered the narrowness and provincialism of Ireland that he spent most of his life in self-imposed exile, Joyce nevertheless made Ireland and the Irish the subject of all his fiction. In Trieste, where the couple's two children were born, Joyce supported himself and his family by working as a language instructor while struggling to find a publisher for his short stories.

By the end of 1904 three of Joyce's *Dubliners* stories—"The Sisters," "Eveline," and "After the Race"—had been published in the journal *Irish Homestead*. He completed eleven further stories and revised and expanded the *Irish Homestead* stories for book publication, an event that seemed imminent in 1906 when English publisher Grant Richards accepted the collection. However, after a series of setbacks, including censure by Richards's printer, who refused to print the work because he judged some of the stories indecent, the project was abandoned. In explaining to Richards why he would not allow bowdlerization of his stories, Joyce underscored his

aim in writing *Dubliners:* "My intention was to write a chapter of the moral history of my country and I chose Dublin for the scene because that city seemed to me the centre of paralysis. . . . I have written it for the most part in a style of scrupulous meanness and with the conviction that he is a very bold man who dares to alter in the presentment, still more to deform, whatever he has seen and heard." In 1912 an Irish publisher, Maunsel and Company, printed the collection—to which a fifteenth story, "The Dead," had been added—but destroyed all copies of the volume before they could be distributed, due to concern that libel actions would result from Joyce's use of the names of well-known people, places, and businesses in Dublin. Ultimately, Richards published the volume in 1914. While contemporary reviews praised Joyce's realistic presentation of Dublin life in the stories, notice of the volume was soon eclipsed by interest in *A Portrait of the Artist as a Young Man,* which was then appearing serially in an English periodical.

Reflecting what Joyce viewed as the intellectual and spiritual torpor of Ireland, *Dubliners* is the first literary product of Joyce's enduring preoccupation with Dublin life. The *Dubliners* stories are also important individually as examples of Joyce's aesthetic theory of epiphany in fiction: each is concerned with a sudden revelation of truth about life inspired by a seemingly trivial incident. To clarify Joyce's use of the term *epiphany* and his understanding of the role of the literary artist, critics often refer to a statement defining the aesthetic theory of the eponymous protagonist of Joyce's unfinished novel, *Stephen Hero:* "By an epiphany he meant a sudden spiritual manifestation, whether in the vulgarity of speech or of gesture or in a memorable phase of the mind itself. He believed that it was for the man of letters to record these epiphanies with extreme care, seeing that they themselves are the most delicate and evanescent of moments." Each story in *Dubliners* contains an epiphanic moment toward which the controlled yet seemingly plotless narrative moves; among the best-known epiphanies are those occurring in "Araby," in which a young boy recognizes the vanity and falsity of his ideal of romantic love, and in "The Dead," in which a husband realizes that his understanding of his wife and the nature of their relationship has been to a significant extent illusory.

Joyce's Dubliners are invariably middle-class Catholics, but from that social group he extracted a wide range of characters—from pre-adolescent schoolboys to decaying priests and from idealized adolescent beauties to aged spinster music teachers—and the structure of the book shows progressively their entrapment in Dublin society. Joyce arranged the stories to present a portrait of the physical, moral, and social paralysis in Irish life in four distinct stages: Childhood, in three stories related by narrators who become aware of the stifling, corrupt milieu surrounding them; Adolescence, in four tales describing young adults facing decisions about their futures; Maturity, in four stories detailing moments in the lives of protagonists who must learn to live with the constraining choices they have made; and Public Life, in three stories viewing typically Irish concerns—politics, music, and the Church—from a social perspective. "The Dead," the longest and last story in the volume, is often regarded by critics as an epilogue or coda to the collection, resolving and complementing prominent issues, themes, motifs, and symbols developed throughout the book.

The stories of childhood—"The Sisters," "An Encounter," and "Araby"—describe their narrators' first recognition of the repressive quality of Dublin life. The first story introduces important themes and symbols explored by Joyce throughout the collection and in some cases throughout his career. For example, the theme of moral paralysis—especially in relation to the Roman Catholic church in Ireland—is introduced in the character of Father Flynn, a retired priest suffering from hemiplegia. The young narrator of "The Sisters" professes in the opening paragraphs his fascination with the words *paralysis, simony* (the buying or selling of church offices or ecclesiastical favors), and *gnomon* (the portion of a parallelogram remaining after a similar parallelogram containing one of its corners has been removed), all of which in Bernard Benstock's words "have thematic reverberations throughout the ensuing stories" in Joyce's concern with repression, personal and public corruption, and absence or incompleteness in his characters' lives. The remaining two childhood stories depict the frustrated expectations that Joyce associated with Dublin life: in "An Encounter" the plans of a truant schoolboy to visit a seaside landmark, which for him symbolizes the mystique of seafaring life, are abandoned when he encounters a threatening stranger who describes his fondness for beating little boys; in "Araby," the romantic ideals of a young boy are shattered when he arrives at the alluringly named benefit bazaar "Araby" to purchase a token of love for a schoolgirl,

only to discover cheap, inappropriate merchandise and witness the vulgar flirting of an English salesgirl.

The stories of adolescence—"Eveline," "After the Race," "Two Gallants," and "The Boarding House"—depict young protagonists who lose the chance to escape their constricted lives. Two of the stories present young people facing decisions about marriage because of a momentary indiscretion or simply their own moral inertia. In "Eveline," nineteen-year-old Eveline Hill deserts her fiance as he boards the ship on which they are to sail to their new life in Buenos Aires, remaining in Dublin to keep house for her abusive father and younger siblings. In "The Boarding House," a talented clerk employed in a respectable wine merchant's firm is seduced by and subsequently trapped into marrying the socially inferior daughter of a boardinghouse keeper in order to avoid a scandal, which would hinder his career more than an improvident marriage.

The stories of maturity include "A Little Cloud," "Counterparts," "Clay," and "A Painful Case." Of these, "A Little Cloud" and "Counterparts" depict married office clerks whose prosaic lives exemplify the confinement of Dublin, while "Clay" and "A Painful Case" each focus on unmarried celibates. The latter stories are highly regarded for neatly depicting Joyce's intentions for this section, which details the consequences of such choices as those faced by the protagonists in the earlier stories of adolescence. "Clay" follows an unmarried, middle-aged laundry worker as she visits the home of young family friends on Halloween and unwittingly chooses clay, symbolizing death, in a divination game. The story's central character, Maria, has undergone critical scrutiny unmatched by other *Dubliners* protagonists. In the 1950s Marvin Magalaner presented a symbolic reading of the story, in which he attributed to Maria three levels of significance: her literal character, a Virgin Mary figure, and a Halloween witch. Debate on this matter has been considerable but inconclusive; to at least one critic she constitutes a mature counterpart to Eveline Hill, who must come to terms with her decision not to marry. "A Painful Case" concerns James Duffy, whose ascetic, withdrawn life-style is called into question by his brief association with an understanding and sympathetic woman, who some time after his rejection of her intimacy is struck by a train while drunkenly attempting to cross the tracks.

Each of the stories of public life—"Ivy Day in the Committee Room," "A Mother," and "Grace"—highlights the stagnation and degeneration of a facet of Irish society. "Ivy Day in the Committee Room" relates the conversation of self-inflated and ineffective political canvassers drinking in a campaign office on the anniversary of the death of Irish nationalist leader Charles Stewart Parnell. "A Mother" depicts the lamentable state of Irish culture through a glimpse behind the scenes of a series of musical concerts held at Dublin's Antient Concert Rooms. In the story, a mother destroys the career of her daughter through her own greed when she refuses to allow her to accompany the singers on the program until payment for her services has been tendered in full. "Grace" offers Joyce's views on the contemporary Church in Ireland while ostensibly presenting the redemption story of Tom Kernan, who, while recuperating from a drunken fall down the basement stairs of a pub, is convinced by his friends to attend a Jesuit retreat for businessmen. Recalling the simony theme traceable throughout the collection, salvation is equated at the retreat with a simple accounting of spiritual debits and credits. Critics have generally accepted Joyce's brother Stanislaus's assertion that this story, originally the culmination of the collection, is an ironic rendering of Dante's *Divine Comedy,* connecting the three scenes of "Grace"—the basement lavatory of the pub, the sickroom in which Kernan receives his friends, and St. George's Church (the scene of the retreat)—with the *Inferno, Purgatorio,* and *Paradiso* sections of Dante's epic poem.

In his correspondence of September 1906 Joyce professed to Stanislaus a desire to soften the condemnation of the Irish in *Dubliners,* declaring that he had not been altogether fair in his presentation of Irish life and conveying his decision to add a story that would reflect the Irish gift for hospitality. The story that he added, "The Dead," is considered Joyce's greatest achievement in the short story genre; according to David Daiches, it is "done with a subtlety and a virtuosity that makes it one of the most remarkable short stories of the present century." The story recounts a holiday party at the home of three spinster music teachers, hosted by their nephew Gabriel Conroy, who is a teacher and literary reviewer with a love of Continental culture. At the close of the evening, after a tenor at the party sings an Irish air that Gabriel's wife, Gretta, associates with a long-dead suitor, Gabriel learns that he is not the only man who has ever loved his wife. The title of the story points to its underlying subject, but critics have argued exactly which "dead" are to be emphasized in explication, and even which characters comprise the "dead." To some, "The Dead" refers only to those mentioned in the story as dead, most notably Michael Furey, Gretta's adolescent beau, who died after leaving his sickbed on a rainy night to keep a vigil outside her window on the eve of her leaving Galway for Dublin. To others, "The Dead" signifies everyone at the party but Gabriel, and through association, everyone in Ireland. Also widely debated is the ambiguity surrounding Gabriel's epiphany at the conclusion of the story, which closes with his assertion that it is time to begin his journey westward and a vision of the snow falling over all Ireland. The meaning of the journey westward is sometimes associated with death, but a more prevalent recent view is that Gabriel's journey westward signifies a rejuvenated view of life; similarly the meaning of the snow, which in some readings signifies the pall—or even shroud—of death covering Ireland, in others represents universal cleansing, bringing expanded consciousness and renewed life to all upon whom it falls. Florence L. Walzl has asserted that ambivalence and ambiguity were purposefully written into the narrative by Joyce to reflect his changing attitude toward Ireland at the time he wrote the story.

For several decades *Dubliners* was considered little more than a slight volume of naturalist fiction evoking the repressive social milieu of turn-of-the-century Dublin. Its very accessibility to nonspecialist readers rendered it less interesting to critics, who largely overlooked it in their race to explicate Joyce's later works, *A Portrait of the Artist as a Young Man, Ulysses,* and *Finnegans Wake.* "First Flight to Ithaca," a landmark analysis by Richard Levin and Charles Shattuck which examined the thematic and structural resemblances of *Dubliners* to Homer's *Odyssey,* was published in 1944 and introduced an era of extensive critical debate. While many critics disagreed with the thesis developed by Levin and Shattuck, most recognized that *Dubliners* held greater significance than had previously been attributed to it, and subsequent studies examined the symbolic significance, structural unity, and autobiographical basis of the stories. Critical inter-

est in *Dubliners* has remained intense in recent decades as each story has been closely examined within the context of the collection and as an individual narrative. The resultant explications have demonstrated that in *Dubliners* Joyce experimented with the subjects and themes that would become the focus of his career and refined the multidimensional narrative method that would revolutionize modern literature. These processes, critics agree, are of considerable importance both to Joyce's development as a literary artist and to the enrichment of short story writing in the twentieth century.

(See also *Short Story Criticism,* Vol. 3; *Contemporary Authors,* Vols. 104 and 126; and *Dictionary of Literary Biography,* Vols. 10, 19, and 36.)

JAMES JOYCE   (letter date 1906)

[*In April 1906 Joyce submitted the last story of the* Dubliners *collection to his publisher, Grant Richards, and in a series of ensuing letters, Joyce and Richards negotiated publication of the volume. However, Richards's printer judged several passages in the collection indecent and refused to print "Two Gallants" and "Counterparts" as they were; further, Richards himself asked Joyce to substitute a gentler word for "bloody" in the story "Grace." Responding in late April, Joyce insisted that nothing be altered. On 1 May, Richards reiterated that changes should be effected if for no other reason than that the printer's views were probably indicative of the opinion of an "inconveniently large section of the general public." The following excerpt is taken from Joyce's reply to Richards written 5 May 1906. In it, Joyce defends his work and describes his intentions in* Dubliners.]

[I] am sorry you do not tell me why the printer, who seems to be the barometer of English opinion, refuses to print **"Two Gallants"** and makes marks in the margin of **"Counterparts."** Is it the small gold coin in the former story or the code of honour which the two gallants live by which shock him? I see nothing which should shock him in either of these things. His idea of gallantry has grown up in him (probably) during the reading of the novels of the elder Dumas and during the performance of romantic plays which presented to him cavaliers and ladies in full dress. But I am sure he is willing to modify his fantastic views. (pp. 132-33)

He has marked three passages in **"Counterparts"**:

> a man with two establishments to keep up, of course he couldn't. . . .
>
> Farrington said he wouldn't mind having the far one and began to smile at her. . . .
>
> She continued to cast bold glances at him and changed the position of her legs often; and when she was going out she brushed against his chair and said "Pardon!" in a Cockney accent.

His marking of the first passage makes me think that there is priestly blood in him: the scent for immoral allusions is certainly very keen here. To me this passage seems as childlike as the reports of divorce cases in *The Standard.* Or is it possible that this same printer (or maybe some near relative of his) will read (nay more, actually collaborate in) that solemn journal which tells its readers not merely that Mrs. So and So misconducted herself with Captain So and So but even how often she misconducted herself with him! The word "establishment" is surely as inoffensive as the word "misconducted."

It is easier to understand why he has marked the second passage, and evident why he has marked the third. But I would refer him again to that respectable organ the reporters of which are allowed to speak of such intimate things as even I, a poor artist, have but dared to suggest. O one-eyed printer! Why has he descended with his blue pencil, full of the Holy Ghost, upon these passages and allowed his companions to set up in type reports of divorce cases, and ragging cases and cases of criminal assault—reports, moreover, which are to be read by an "inconveniently large section of the general public."

There remains his final objection to the word "bloody." I cannot know, of course, from what he derives the word or whether, in his plain blunt way, he accepts it as it stands. In the latter case his objection is absurd and in the former case (if he follows the only derivation I have heard for it) it is strange that he should object more strongly to a profane use of the Virgin than to a profane use of the name of God. Where is his English Protestantism? I myself can bear witness that I have seen in modern English print such expressions as "by God" and "damn." Some cunning Jesuit must have tempted our stout Protestant from the path of righteousness that he defends the honour of the Virgin with such virgin ardour.

As for my part and share in the book I have already told all I have to tell. My intention was to write a chapter of the moral history of my country and I chose Dublin for the scene because that city seemed to me the centre of paralysis. I have tried to present it to the indifferent public under four of its aspects: childhood, adolescence, maturity and public life. The stories are arranged in this order. I have written it for the most part in a style of scrupulous meanness and with the conviction that he is a very bold man who dares to alter in the presentment, still more to deform, whatever he has seen and heard. I cannot do any more than this. I cannot alter what I have written. All these objections of which the printer is now the mouthpiece arose in my mind when I was writing the book, both as to the themes of the stories and their manner of treatment. Had I listened to them I would not have written the book. I have come to the conclusion that I cannot write without offending people. The printer denounces **"Two Gallants"** and **"Counterparts."** A Dubliner would denounce **"Ivy Day in the Committee Room."** The more subtle inquisitor will denounce **"An Encounter,"** the enormity of which the printer cannot see because he is, as I said, a plain blunt man. The Irish priest will denounce **"The Sisters."** The Irish boarding-house keeper will denounce **"The Boarding-House."** Do not let the printer imagine, for goodness' sake, that he is going to have all the barking to himself.

I can see plainly that there are two sides to the matter but unfortunately I can occupy only one of them. I will not fall into the error of suggesting to you which side you should occupy but it seems to me that you credit the printer with too infallible a knowledge of the future. I know very little of the state of English literature at present nor do I know whether it deserves or not the eminence which it occupies as the laughing-stock of Europe. But I suspect that it will follow the other countries of Europe as it did in Chaucer's time. You have opportunities to observe the phenomenon at close range. Do you think that *The Second Mrs. Tanqueray* would not have been denounced by a manager of the middle Victorian period, or that a publisher of that period would not have rejected a

book by George Moore or Thomas Hardy? And if a change is to take place I do not see why it should not begin now.

You tell me in conclusion that I am endangering my future and your reputation. I have shown you earlier in the letter the frivolity of the printer's objections and I do not see how the publication of *Dubliners* as it now stands in manuscript could possibly be considered an outrage on public morality. I am willing to believe that when you advise me not to persist in the publication of stories such as those you have returned to me you do so with a kind intention towards me: and I am sure you will think me wrong-headed in persisting. But if the art were any other, if I were a painter and my book were a picture you would be less ready to condemn me for wrong-headedness if I refused to alter certain details. These details may now seem to you unimportant but if I took them away *Dubliners* would seem to me like an egg without salt. In fact, I am somewhat curious to know what, if these and similar points have been condemned, has been admired in the book at all.

I see now that my letter is becoming nearly as long as my book. I have touched on every point you raise in order to give you reason for the faith that is in me. I have not, however, said what a disappointment it would be to me if you were unable to share my views. I do not speak so much of a material as of a moral disappointment. But I think I could more easily reconcile myself to such a disappointment than to the thousand little regrets and self-reproaches which would certainly make me their prey afterwards. (pp. 133-35)

> *James Joyce, in a letter to Grant Richards on May 5, 1906, in* Letters of James Joyce, Vol. II, *edited by Richard Ellmann, Faber & Faber, 1966, pp. 132-35.*

EZRA POUND (essay date 1914)

[*Pound, an American poet and critic, is regarded as one of the most innovative and influential figures in twentieth-century Anglo-American poetry. He was instrumental in obtaining editorial and financial assistance for T. S. Eliot, Wyndham Lewis, James Joyce, and William Carlos Williams, among others. His own* Cantos, *published throughout his life, is among the most ambitious poetic cycles of the century, and his series of satirical poems* Hugh Selwyn Mauberly (1920) *is ranked with Eliot's* The Waste Land (1922) *as a significant attack on the decadence of modern culture. In the following excerpt, Pound offers a favorable review of* Dubliners, *praising Joyce's artistry, universality, and selection of details.*]

Freedom from sloppiness is so rare in contemporary English prose that one might well say simply, [*Dubliners*] "is prose free from sloppiness," and leave the intelligent reader ready to run from his study immediately to spend three and sixpence on the volume.

Unfortunately one's credit as a critic is insufficient to produce this result. . . .

Mr. Joyce's merit, I will not say his chief merit but his most engaging merit, is that he carefully avoids telling you a lot that you don't want to know. He presents his people swiftly and vividly, he does not sentimentalise over them, he does not weave convolutions. He is a realist. He does not believe "life" would be all right if we stopped vivisection or if we instituted a new sort of "economics." He gives the thing as it is. He is not bound by the tiresome convention that any part of life,

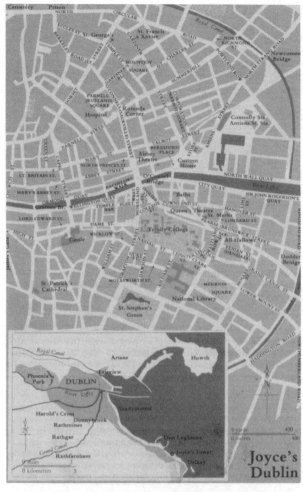

A map showing the locations of Dublin streets and landmarks made famous in Dubliners *and Joyce's later works.*

to be interesting, must be shaped into the conventional form of a "story." Since de Maupassant we have had so many people trying to write "stories" and so few people presenting life. Life for the most part does not happen in neat little diagrams and nothing is more tiresome than the continual pretence that it does.

Mr. Joyce's **"Araby,"** for instance, is much better than a "story," it is a vivid waiting.

It is surprising that Mr. Joyce is Irish. One is so tired of the Irish or "Celtic" imagination (or "phantasy" as I think they now call it) flopping about. Mr. Joyce does not flop about. He defines. He is not an institution for the promotion of Irish peasant industries. He accepts an international standard of prose writing and lives up to it.

He gives us Dublin as it presumably is. He does not descend to farce. He does not rely upon Dickensian caricature. He gives us things as they are, not only for Dublin, but for every city. Erase the local names and a few specifically local allusions, and a few historic events of the past, and substitute a few different local names, allusions and events, and these stories could be retold of any town.

That is to say, the author is quite capable of dealing with

things about him, and dealing directly, yet these details do not engross him, he is capable of getting at the universal element beneath them.

The main situations of *Madame Bovary* or of *Doña Perfecta* do not depend on local colour or upon local detail, that is their strength. Good writing, good presentation can be specifically local, but it must not depend on locality. Mr. Joyce does not present "types" but individuals. I mean he deals with common emotions which run through all races. He does not bank on "Irish character." Roughly speaking, Irish literature has gone through three phases in our time, the shamrock period, the dove-grey period, and the Kiltartan period. I think there is a new phase in the works of Mr. Joyce. He writes as a contemporary of continental writers. I do not mean that he writes as a faddist, mad for the last note, he does not imitate Strindberg, for instance, or Bang. He is not ploughing the underworld for horror. He is not presenting a macabre subjectivity. He is classic in that he deals with normal things and with normal people. A committee room, Little Chandler, a nonentity, a boarding house full of clerks— these are his subjects and he treats them all in such a manner that they are worthy subjects of art. . . .

I think that he excels most of the impressionist writers because of his more rigorous selection, because of his exclusion of all unnecessary detail.

There is a very clear demarcation between unnecessary detail and irrelevant detail. An impressionist friend of mine talks to me a good deal about "preparing effects," and on that score he justifies much unnecessary detail, which is not "irrelevant," but which ends by being wearisome and by putting one out of conceit with his narrative.

Mr. Joyce's more rigorous selection of the presented detail marks him, I think, as belonging to my own generation, that is, to the "nineteen-tens," not to the decade between "the 'nineties'" and to-day.

At any rate these stories and [*A Portrait of the Artist as a Young Man*] are such as to win for Mr. Joyce a very definite place among English contemporary prose writers, not merely a place in the "Novels of the Week" column, and our writers of good clear prose are so few that we cannot afford to confuse or to overlook them.

Ezra Pound, "'Dubliners' and Mr. James Joyce," in The Egoist, *Vol. I, No. 14, July 15, 1914, p. 267.*

PADRAIC COLUM   (essay date 1926)

[*An Irish poet, dramatist, editor, and critic, Colum was one of the major writers of the Irish Literary Renaissance. He was most noted for his efforts to make better-known the varied heritage of Irish literature through his writings and public lectures, but he is perhaps most important as a historical dramatist who established many precedents for the Irish national theater. Colum's poetry incorporated his knowledge of dramatic technique; in addition, his poems are admired because they avoid the nationalistic didacticism so prevalent in the poetry of his contemporaries. Because of his close and genuine links with the people and culture of Ireland, he is considered one of that country's few authentic national poets. In the following excerpt, Colum offers an appreciative overview of* Dubliners *and discusses the narrative detachment with which the stories are related.*]

Dubliners followed the publication of Joyce's single book of verse, *Chamber Music.* It was followed by the publication of the novel *Portrait of the Artist as a Young Man,* after which came the play *Exiles,* and then the epical satire *Ulysses. Dubliners* is related to all of them. The first three stories in the collection, obviously out of personal memory, might be incidents that were pared away from a draft of *Portrait of the Artist;* the boy in **"Araby"** who, walking through flaring streets, jostled by drunken men and bargaining women, thinks of himself as bearing "my chalice safely through a crowd of foes," is surely the Stephen Dedalus of the novel. Gabriel Conroy, in the last story, **"The Dead,"** by the way he makes a problem out of another man's influence over his wife, is like the hero of *Exiles.* When we take these four stories out what remains of *Dubliners* is distinctly related to *Ulysses.* Many of the characters who figure in *Ulysses* have their first appearance in *Dubliners*—Martin Cunningham, "Hoppy" Holohan, Lineham, Mr. O'Madden Burke. It is not surprising that *Dubliners* has this relation to a book written so long afterwards, for Mr. Bloom's day was planned originally for a story in the collection.

Joyce as a young man knew Dubliners very well on two characteristic sides: he knew them on their bar-hunting side and he knew them on their political side; he knew them too on a side that is not very characteristic: on the musical side. His father was a well-known Dublin personage, and his father's sociability gave a basis for Joyce's wide and miscellaneous acquaintanceship. (pp. viii-ix)

"Ivy Day in the Committee Room" is characteristic of the largest group of stories in *Dubliners.* Certain men meet more or less casually in a bleak committee-room; they talk more or less absurdly, one of them is prevailed upon to recite a poem that he had written some years before, "The Death of Parnell, 6th. October 1891." It is an amateurish and conventional piece of rhetoric, and yet, amazingly enough, a real grief and a real loyalty break through the hand-me-down verse. A few words are said to the maker of the poem, a gesture is made, and the story ends. We get a feeling of complete detachment. But it is borne in on us too that the whole happening has been understood by the author in all its implications and that it has been completely rendered for us. He must have entered into Hynes's mind before he could recreate the verses that have just the exact heat, just the exact flourishes that a passionate and semi-literate man would give to his subject writing according to the literary convention which he knew. " 'What do you think of that, Crofton?' cried Mr. Henchy, 'Isn't that fine? What?' Mr. Crofton said it was a very fine piece of writing." And that line ends the story. Had Joyce given Mr. Crofton's words, his barest words of appreciation, he would have wronged that gentleman's fine reserve. For Mr. Crofton, former canvasser for the Conservative faction, must have felt that there was a taint of treason in the verses he had listened to. Still he was a man of the world, and it would not have been becoming in him to be anything but tolerant upon the occasion. "Mr. Crofton said it was a very fine piece of writing." His aloofness is felt.

In the stories of which **"Ivy Day in the Committee Room"** is the type, James Joyce is letting us look at a happening through his eyes while making no comment. Hence the feeling of detachment that is in these stories. It would seem that he had decided to illustrate the life of Dublin through a series of reports, taking this and that incident and being as clear and as unconcerned in the reporting of it as a scientific historian might be. **"The Dead,"** however, is not written in this way.

"The Sisters," "An Encounter," and **"Araby,"** are, as I have suggested, out of personal memory, and have not this unconcern, this detachment. But the main group of stories have detachment. There is something more to be said about the stories in this main group: In three of them there is a woman for central character—**"Eveline," "Clay," "A Mother."** The story that has the title **"A Mother"** is told as the stories about the men are told, without concern. But there is concern in the other two: Joyce, one feels, has been touched by the fate of Eveline in the story that bears her name, and by the personality of Maria in **"Clay."** Each girl is single-minded, conventual, and devoted.

The characters in these stories are very lonely, very unrelated people. Most of them live in little terraces and face the world with a certain gentility. Some are articulate, some are inarticulate. And those whose stories are the most memorable have been stirred by a look they have taken into the darkness. The book closes with **"The Dead,"** but the dead are in the first story; the boy of **"The Sisters"** has been confronted with the death of his neighbour, the old priest; as he lies dead the old man becomes to the childish man a living enigma. Eveline is haunted by the memory of her dead mother. The omen that is concealed from Maria is the omen of her death. In **"A Painful Case,"** the news of the death of a woman he had rejected haunts and makes lonelier the life of a lonely man. In **"Ivy Day in the Committee Room"** the story shapes itself around a dead man, Parnell. And in **"The Dead"** a man whom he had never known and of whom he might never have heard, recalled from the dead by a song, makes a husband realize that there is a portion of his wife's life in which he has no part. Yes, the stories in *Dubliners* that are the most memorable are about people who have been touched by death. And the words that close the last story in the book have the music of a requiem.—

> A few light taps upon the pane made him turn to the window. It had begun to snow again. He watched sleepily the flakes, silver and dark, falling obliquely against the lamplight. The time had come for him to set out on his journey westward. Yes, the newspapers were right: snow was general all over Ireland. It was falling on every part of the dark central plain, on the treeless hills, falling softly upon the Bog of Allen and, further westward, softly falling into the dark mutinous Shannon waves. It was falling, too, upon every part of the lonely churchyard on the hill where Michael Furey lay buried. It lay thickly drifted on the crooked crosses and headstones, on the spears of the little gate, on the barren thorns. His soul swooned slowly as he heard the snow falling faintly through the universe and faintly falling, like the descent of their last end, upon all the living and the dead.

(pp. x-xiii)

Padraic Colum, in an introduction to Dubliners *by James Joyce, The Modern Library, 1926, pp. v-xiii.*

RICHARD LEVIN AND CHARLES SHATTUCK (essay date 1944)

[*In the following excerpt, Levin and Shattuck examine the thematic and structural resemblances of* Dubliners *to Homer's* Odyssey.]

For three decades now *Dubliners,* though caviar to the discerning, has been for most readers merely one of Joyce's "easier" books, a pleasant readable minor effusion, a collection of discrete sketches. No one has publicly recognized, nor did Joyce ever reveal, that **Dubliners** has an architectural unity in a secret technique—that like **Ulysses**, only far more obviously and demonstrably, as is our purpose here to make plain, **Dubliners** is based upon Homer's *Odyssey*. (p. 76)

The reading we here propose need not be altogether surprising, for clues exist which might lead one to suspect that this was Joyce's method. Gorman records a number of manifestations of Joyce's life-long interest in the *Odyssey*, extending even to a schoolboy essay in praise of Ulysses as "My Favorite Hero." Clues occur in his correspondence with his prospective publishers: in his insistence upon printing certain "objectionable" stories, or if they be omitted, upon stating in a preface that the "book in this form is incomplete"; in his insistence that the stories be printed in an exactly specified order—an order which, incidentally, does not always correspond to the ages of the central characters. In these insistences, which were urgent, we may read a sign that Joyce was operating under some structural compulsion more exacting than any he chose to reveal. More tantalizingly suggestive than any of these clues, however, is the remark Joyce once made to one of his language students: "When I wrote **Dubliners**," he said, "I was tempted to give it the title of *Ulysses at Dublin* but I changed my mind." The temptation could hardly have been idle whim: the title would imply a pervasive Homeric reference in the book, and so scrupulous an artist as Joyce would never aim to impose such unity by the title alone; the Homeric unity must be there if the title was to be entertained.

Why Joyce decided not to call the book *Ulysses at Dublin*, why he never mentioned his concealed technique in the long years of correspondence with his publishers, why he always kept it so tight-lipped a secret, are questions that can be answered only conjecturally after intimate study of the book. Some probable factors in the decision are these. It will be noted that the original twelve stories gave coverage to little more than the first half of the *Odyssey*—hence Joyce may have been reluctant to call attention to a structure that was markedly incomplete. It is possible that Joyce undertook the analogizing process without any particular intention of recreating the *Odyssey* as an artistic whole, but simply using the old tales without respect to their order to help him write new ones as a lame man uses a cane—hence even though the book grew into a unity he was not content that its unity was perfect enough to be advertised. Again, it will be noted that in two of the stories of latest composition (**"Two Gallants," "A Little Cloud"**) Joyce's technique appears to be developing in the direction of symbolic imagery—hence it may be that already he envisioned that richer exploitation of the material to be realized in **Ulysses**, and wished therefore to conceal his hand. Certainly this was true by the time **Dubliners** was actually published, for even then the first sketches of **Ulysses** were getting on paper. (pp. 77-8)

The first movement of **Dubliners**, three stories of childhood, is to be equated with Homer's Telemachia—the first four books and part of the fifteenth book of the *Odyssey*. The central figure of all three is a Telemachus-type, a fatherless boy. The hostile and repressive environment of Telemachus—the wooers—is represented in the boy's guardians, playmates, and teachers. Telemachus' motivations—the desire for father, happiness, and beauty—are the boy's motivations. Homeric action is adumbrated in its general pattern: one should

observe that in the first story the boy does little but brood over the lost father and listen to others' talk about him, that in the following stories he goes on two quests—just as Telemachus in Book I but passively attends the council of the wooers, and in the following books makes trips to Pylos and to Sparta. Within this general framework many details of action are reproduced, sometimes sequentially, but it should be recognized that on the whole the analogizing process operates here more thematically and less exactly than in the eight stories which make up the second and third movements. (p. 79)

1. **"The Sisters"**: Telemachus at Ithaca.
   Odyssey, I.
   Ulysses, I, "Telemachus."

The boy of Joyce's story, like Homer's Telemachus, is a fatherless youth, living in a house ruled by strangers (his aunt and uncle), longing for his father (his father transubstantial, Father Flynn), and unwilling to believe that his father is dead. In the first action of the story, the boy takes food in the presence of an enemy, Mr. Cotter, just as Telemachus is first shown at a feast of the wooers. Mr. Cotter, like the wooers in general and Antinous in particular, is an habitual visitor in the house, is used to taking food there, has very bad manners ("spat rudely into the grate"), is spitefully disrespectful to the boy, and not only asserts that Father Flynn is dead but reflects hostilely upon his character and influence. The boy, like Telemachus, hates Cotter ("Tiresome old fool!"), keeps as far from him as possible, knows he is being watched by him, broods in silence, and restrains his anger with difficulty.

In the second and third actions, the boy is visited by visions of Father Flynn, first in a nightmare, next in vivid daydreams as he wanders the streets the following morning; Telemachus was vividly assured of the living reality of Odysseus through supernal apparition—the visitation of Pallas Athene.

The final action, in which the boy and his aunt visit the dead man's house and talk with his sisters, has no Homeric model as a whole, but contains many details of present interest. Thus, the dead man is survived by two females who have kept his house for him and now mourn for him: Eliza resembles Penelope in her dignity and command and tearfulness; and Nanny, subservient to Eliza and all "wore out" with menial tasks, suggests Eurycleia. The boy's visit to the dead-room, which is upstairs and is lighted by two candles, and to which he is escorted by Nanny, is reminiscent of Telemachus' ascent to his bed-chamber, led by Eurycleia bearing torches.

The main interest in this last section is the talk about Father Flynn and the ingenious reading Joyce here delivers of the Odysseus-role. Odysseus is, of course, languishing in exile because of the crime he has committed upon the body of the son of a god—putting out the eye of Poseidon's son, Polyphemus; his exile will soon be ended, for Zeus is well-disposed towards him and Poseidon is absent from the Olympic council, but for many years he has suffered woes, wandering the deep, and now, as the prisoner of Calypso, he alternates between a longing for home and a desire to die. Father Flynn's crime against the son of god was the breaking of a sacrificial chalice. His exile was, first, mental ("he began to mope by himself, talking to no one and wandering about by himself"); second, spiritual (as a simoniac and as a mental case he has had to retire from active priesthood). "His life was . . . crossed." His longing for home is doubly expressed in his desire for the state of grace and (a typically playful detail) in his desire to "go out for a drive one fine day just to see the old house again where we were all born down in Irishtown." He knew he was about to die and "was quite resigned."

Like Odysseus, too, he was a travelled man, and was eager to impart the fruits of his experience to his "son." Something of Odysseus' wiliness is suggested in his pastime of "putting difficult questions" to the boy. He is remembered by the boy in connection with a physical object, his snuff-box, as Odysseus is typically recalled with a spear.

The main theme of the story—the boy's father-hunger and his Telemachan hope that the father is not dead—is marked everywhere. He passes the priest's house nightly to reassure himself, he refuses to acknowledge Cotter's announcement of the death, he extends the priest's life by the vividness of his dream, he fancies the dead man smiling in his coffin, his final image is of the priest "wide-awake and laughing-like to himself."

2. **"An Encounter"**: Telemachus at Pylos.
Odyssey, II, III.
Ulysses, II, "Nestor."

The unhappy youth, repressed and frustrated by his daily surroundings, goes on a journey with a companion to find his happiness elsewhere; is disappointed. The story opens with a summary account of the boy's relations with his playmates in Wild West games, mirroring the situation of Telemachus among the wooers. The boy does not like the games because Joe Dillon (Antinous) "played too fiercely for us who were younger and more timid," and always won; yet he is forced to participate, being, like Telemachus, admittedly weak and fearful. In the first action, a school scene, the boy is shamed by his teacher for his addiction to penny-dreadfuls, and this weakens his realization that real adventures are not to be found in fiction or in play but "must be sought abroad": he determines to run away. This action corresponds to the formal council of Homer's second book, in which Telemachus and his few loyal supporters are accused of folly and double-dealing by the tyrannical wooers. Father Butler's speech to Leo Dillon closely resembles Eurymachus' to Halitherses. Halitherses' deed was the interpreting of a marvellous omen; Leo is caught with a copy of "The Halfpenny Marvel." Eurymachus accuses Halitherses of prating idly in order to get a gift from Telemachus, and threatens him with violence; Father Butler denounces Leo's book as "rubbish," supposes the author of it "writes these things for a drink," and threatens Leo with violence if he doesn't get at his work. It may be noted that the first sentence of the history lesson, "Hardly had the day dawned," is a Homeric tag.

The preparation for the trip involves several Homeric echoes. Telemachus had two friends, Mentor and Halitherses, who, as Leocritus suggested, might go with him, but only Mentor (really Athene) went; the boy planned his trip with Mahony and Leo Dillon, but only Mahony went. The boy collects sixpences as Telemachus collects provisions. The fear of being caught by Father Butler parallels Eurycleia's fear that Telemachus will be harmed by the wooers. Telemachus' trip is by sea; the boy's takes him to the waterfront where he ambles along the quays studying sailors and ships, and he crosses the Liffey by ferry.

Both journeys end in wide open fields giving onto the water (the sea-shore at Pylos; the field at Ringsend along the Dodder), where the hero is engaged in embarrassing and somehow disappointing conversation with an old man: Nestor, whom Telemachus is afraid to speak to, is garrulous enough

about the scandalous affairs of the house of Atreus, but knows nothing of Odysseus; the gray moustached stranger frightens and revolts the boy by his perverted talk and behavior. The stranger's unaccountable shift from amiability to severity perhaps reflects Athene's abrupt transformation from Mentor to an eagle.

The Telemachan lost-father motif is not explicit here as in **"The Sisters,"** yet it is subtly suggested in the boy's confused feelings of attraction to and revulsion from the elderly stranger.

3. **"Araby"**: Telemachus at Sparta.
Odyssey, III, IV, XV
Ulysses, III, "Proteus."

This story takes the boy on another quest for happiness which ends ashily. Since the point of departure is again the fatherless home, the motifs of repression and father-hunger are repeated. The house had once been occupied by a priest now dead (the father-image of **"The Sisters"**). The boy's trip is hindered, though not prevented, by the perversity of his uncle; the boy again, as in **"An Encounter,"** suffers dangers of the playground ("we ran the gauntlet of the rough tribes from the cottages"), and, because of his preoccupation with plans for the trip, danger of discipline at school.

Structurally Telemachus' Spartan expedition is only an extension of his search for his father, but its essence is romance of another kind: Homer introduces us to the living presence of Menelaus' Helen, and there renews the old irony that woman's beauty is dust and illusion. Menelaus' story of Helen's treacherous attempt to reveal the Argives hidden in the wooden horse—delivered as a rebuke to Helen when she over-protests her joy in the Greek victory—is not lost upon Telemachus, who changes the subject of discourse, nor upon Joyce, who informs his story with this theme of disillusionment in beauty.

Helen is represented first by Mangan's sister, whom the boy has never exchanged words with but devoutly worships, just as Telemachus addresses Helen but once, and then to promise her "worship, even as to a god." A few physical details confirm the identity, but the idealization and the intensity are the main thing ("her name was like a summons to all my foolish blood"). When at last one day the ice is broken and she asks if he is going to "Araby," a bazaar in a distant part of town, and he promises her that if he does go he will bring her a gift, from this moment the symbolic equation shifts, and "Araby" itself becomes the ideal. The Homeric action proceeds to a typically Joycean frustration. After painful delays and hindrances the trip begins. It is accomplished by train, as Telemachus' trip to Sparta was by chariot, with one stop on the way. Like Telemachus the boy arrives at his destination late in the evening, is allowed entrance by a wearily indifferent doorkeeper, finds himself in a brilliantly decorated hall. The main events of the day's festivities are over, however: most of the patrons of "Araby," like the guests at Menelaus' daughter's wedding, have departed. Telemachus finds one minstrel still performing; the boy notices a deserted booth labelled Café Chantant. Telemachus can get no certain news of his father; the boy cannot buy a gift. Telemachus is wryly reminded of Helen's falseness; the boy finds the bazaar a delusion and vanity. The bitterness of the discovery and its symbolic value is intensified by the salesmen's jocularly accusing one of the saleswomen of falsehood.

This story, like its original, is heavy-laden with oriental imagery. The tales of Troy-town and of Egypt, the luxurious furnishings of Menelaus' house, the drugged wine—all these are remembered by Joyce in the bazaar labeled "Araby," in the uncle's song "The Arab's Farewell to His Steed," in the "great jars that stood like eastern guards," and other such phrases. (pp. 80-2)

[The second] movement follows the adventures of Odysseus from Ogygia through Phaeacia (Books V to XIII), scrupulously omitting all the contents of his recapitulation (Books IX to XII), which will furnish the contents of the third movement. The final story of the third movement, **"A Painful Case,"** it should be noted, will sound a last variation on the theme of Odysseus in Phaeacia. In all stories of this group except **"The Boarding House,"** which is modelled on a Homeric digression (and even here indirectly), Odysseus is represented. He is shown, as in the original, as a man of the world, free of family ties, looking forward to a return home, and dominant in his relations with women. (p. 83)

4. **"Eveline"**: Odysseus at Ogygia.
Odyssey, V.
Ulysses, IV, "Calypso."

Homer's tale of Odysseus and Calypso is here rendered from Calypso's point of view. Later, in **"A Painful Case,"** Joyce will treat the story again, with Odysseus at center.

The equations of the few characters are obvious. Calypso, the woman who loves a sailor and who allows him to return without her to his home in a city far across the sea, becomes Eveline Hill. Odysseus, the sailor, is Frank. Zeus, who forbids Calypso to keep Odysseus, is Eveline's father. Calypso's sister-goddesses, who suffered like meddling from the tyrant-god, are Eveline's brothers and sometime playmates who used to fear her father's blackthorn stick.

The settings are similar. Both women dwell on islands (Ireland, Ogygia), and the homes of both lovers are in far-off cities (Ithaca, Buenos Aires) to which they wish to return. The women's houses, at which the deliberative portion of both stories occurs, resemble each other in many details: both are dark; both have interesting odors—the "odour of dusty cretonne" which Eveline breathes, Calypso's fragrance of burning cedar and sandalwood and of flowering trees; both have music about them—street organs, singing nymphs (incidentally, both sailor-lovers are fond of music); both are carefully tended by their mistresses. The brief active portion of both stories—the parting—occurs at the sea's edge, with the lover's vessel moving out to sea.

Eveline is drawn to Frank, as Calypso to Odysseus, because he is a traveller, a man-of-the-world, and can entertain her with tales of his adventures (tales, for instance, of the "terrible Patagonians"—a curiously Homeric phrase); and because of his personal ease and strength, he being like Odysseus "kind, manly, open-hearted"—"his hair tumbled forward over a face of bronze."

Both women very much desire the marriage (Eveline "would be married . . . people would treat her with respect then"; Calypso is ever "longing to have him as her lord"); and they forgo marriage for like reasons. Both are forbidden by the father (Eveline's father "found out the affair and had forbidden her to have anything to say to him"; Zeus ordered Calypso to "send him hence with what speed thou mayest"). The father's ostensible reason is the lover's unworthiness (Eveline's father says, "I know these sailor chaps"; Zeus "grudges goddesses openly to mate with men") but the immediate reason is more immediate and personal (Eveline's father has a quarrel with Frank; Zeus acts because of Athene's plea). Both women rebel against the order (Eveline continues to "meet her lover secretly . . . she had a right to happiness"; Calypso complains that "hard are ye gods and jealous exceeding"). But both submit, for three reasons: first, out of fear of the father (Eveline "felt herself in danger of her father's violence"; Calypso is warned that Zeus would "be angered and bear hard on" her); second, because of an oath to the dead (Eveline has promised her dying mother to keep the home together; Calypso swears by the "falling water of the Styx, the greatest oath and the most terrible" not to hinder Odysseus' leaving); third, because of their own domesticity and timidity (Eveline, who characteristically is dusting furniture, does not find her homelife "wholly undesirable," and she fears drowning at sea; Calypso, who characteristically "fared to and fro before the loom, and wove," urges Odysseus to "abide with me and keep this house," and warns him of the perils of his voyage).

Once the decision is made to let the lover sail alone, the women accept their lot submissively. Calypso actually assists Odysseus to build and stock his raft and cheerfully speeds his departure. Eveline's resignation is pathetically incomplete, but in the last instant she watches Frank go without "sign of love or farewell or recognition." (pp. 83-4)

6. **"Two Gallants"**: Odysseus in Phaeacia, Nausicaa.
Odyssey, VI, VII, VIII, XIII.
Ulysses, XIII, "Nausicaa."

This story and **"After the Race"** are printed in reverse order of their Homeric antecedents—the only violation of Homeric order in the book. The reason for the inversion probably lies in the relative ages of their respective Odysseuses, Jimmy Doyle of **"After the Race"** being the younger. For convenience we follow the Homeric order here.

"Two Gallants" is an ironic reading of Odysseus' friendship with Alcinous, his "romance" with Nausicaa, and his departure from Phaeacia. This was one of the last of the stories to be written, and its technique of allusion is more than usually free, rich, and witty. The heightened style is evident in the gaily mock-heroic translation of characters. Odysseus is given to us as the active gallant, Corley, a burly fellow with oily hair (Odysseus' heroic strength, his frequent anointing himself after bathing—compare Bloom's hair-oil in ***Ulysses***), who constantly talks about himself and his amours (Odysseus' epic recapitulation of his adventures, including the amorous), who is at present "about town" (Odysseus' role as wanderer), who is often seen walking with policemen in plain clothes and knows the inner side of all affairs (Odysseus' intimate acquaintance with Athene, who often appears in human guise, and who keeps him informed). Nausicaa becomes Corley's slavey: Nausicaa is the daughter of a sailor king—the slavey wears blue and white (sailor colors) and a "white sailor hat"; Nausicaa is beautiful—the slavey is coarse-featured but sexually attractive; Nausicaa is eager for marriage and half in love with Odysseus—the slavey is "a bit gone on" Corley and uses all her little tricks on him; Nausicaa gives Odysseus garments and guides him to her father's house where he will be honored with princely gifts—the slavey gives Corley smokes and tramfare to their rendezvous, and guides him to her employer's house where she gives him a gold coin which she either takes from her savings or steals from her employer.

Alcinous is the leechgallant Lenehan. Joyce has relieved him of the responsibility of fatherhood, but endowed him with the rest of Alcinous' qualities. The sailor-motif is expressed in his yachting cap, his water-proof, his white rubber shoes, and the "waves" of expression that pass over his face; like Alcinous he is interested in sports, especially racing; his appetite for food, drink, and company is insatiable; he is a collector of anecdotes; he responds actively to music, shuffling his feet and drumming with his fingers; and he spends much time listening to Corley's talk, as Alcinous with Odysseus, flattering him and leading him on with questions. One curious background figure is worth noting: the Homeric blind harpist Demodocus is represented by a weary-eyed street-harpist. . . . (pp. 84-5)

Many details of action ring the changes of Homer's. Odysseus first meets Nausicaa near a temple of the sea-god—Corley first met his tart under Waterhouse's clock (compare Bloom, Gerty, and the Abbey of Howth: Joyce telescoped the geography of Phaeacia). Odysseus sallies toward Nausicaa like a lion, speaks to her straightway, asks for succour—Corley saunters toward the slavey like a conqueror, begins talking at once, his purpose being to get, among other favors, money for food. Odysseus conceals his name from Nausicaa ("Odysseus of many wiles"), but she recognizes his nobility—Corley has kept his from the slavey ("I was too hairy for that"), but she thinks him "a bit of class." Nausicaa has had other suitors—the slavey has had previous lovers, including a dairyman. Odysseus recounts to Alcinous his past love-affairs, including that with the possessive Calypso at Ogygia (an omphalos)—Corley so favors Lenehan, dwelling especially on the girls "off the South Circular," who took all, gave nothing. Odysseus at the end of his story-telling is almost rudely eager to be on his way—at the end of Joyce's story Corley is hurrying away from Lenehan, will not deign to answer Lenehan's questions. The gold coin is of course the Phaeacians' gift to Odysseus. (p. 85)

5. **"After the Race"**: Odysseus in Phaeacia, feasts and games.
Odyssey, VIII, XIII.

The narrative action of Odysseus' entertainment at Alcinous' court and his leave-taking is a plotless round of athletic events, banquets, song, dance, story-telling, gift-giving, and so on. Joyce follows this episodic structure with clearly traceable if not slavish care.

First, some of the equations of characters. Odysseus, an Ithacan among Phaeacians, is represented by Jimmy Doyle, an Irishman among foreigners. Odysseus is the guest of Alcinous, a wealthy ship owner who is to provide him with gifts and passage home; Jimmy is the guest of the rich Ségouin, who owns a thriving automobile factory and who is to allow Jimmy an interest in it. Ségouin is of course Alcinous, with obvious parallels in his great wealth and in his roles as transportation expert, host, and benefactor. Laodamus, Alcinous' son, a dancer, is Rivière, Ségouin's cousin, who dances with Farley (Farley is therefore Halius). Euryalus, who quarrels with Odysseus about athletic prowess, is the Englishman Routh, who quarrels with Jimmy about politics. The harpist Demodocus, a servant, who is honored and fed by Odysseus, is Jimmy's friend Villona, a poor hanger-on of this company, always hungry, who plays and sings throughout the festivities and is an authority on ancient musical instruments.

Joyce takes up the action at the point of the Homeric foot-

race, paralleling it with an auto race, and borrowing hints for metaphor to describe it: Clytoneus won "by the length of the *furrow* that mules cleave in a *fallow* field"; Joyce likens the Naas Road to a "groove," and the track between the sightseers as a "channel" of "poverty and inaction." Just after the race Joyce describes all his characters and their relationships, as Homer had done just before.

After a transitional passage Joyce describes Ségouin's dinner-party, which corresponds to Odysseus' participation in the weight-throwing contest. Rivière encourages Jimmy to invest in the French factory by boasting of "the triumph of French mechanicians," as Laodamas urges Odysseus to join the games by discoursing on the value of athletic prowess. Jimmy quarrels lengthily with Routh, as Odysseus with Euryalus, until a truce is imposed by the host. Homer's next item, Demodocus' song, which Joyce will use in **"The Boarding House,"** is here passed over, marked only by the carousers' singing in the street enroute to the yacht.

Joyce's yacht party (the yacht reflects the Phaeacians' interest in ships) parallels Alcinous' further entertainment of the first day. First a dance is executed by two men and it ends in a great din with all present participating and the Odysseus-character expressly enjoying it. Food is spread. Peace is made between erstwhile antagonists—Euryalus giving Odysseus a present, Jimmy and Routh and all drowning their political differences in a series of toasts to the nations. Jimmy makes a long speech, eagerly applauded at the pauses and the end—here in a sentence Joyce reflects and passes Odysseus' much applauded four-book recapitulation, to be treated later.

A cardgame develops (Homer's thirteenth book, the festivities of the last day), with Villona, like Demodocus, providing musical background. Jimmy loses rather heavily—a playful reversal of the Phaeacians' gift to Odysseus. A toast to the Queen of Hearts recalls Odysseus' last chivalrous speech to Arete. Jimmy's head aches and he wishes the party were over, as Odysseus longs to be on his way. As the Phaeacian sun sets and the Irish sun rises, the revellers disperse.

7. **"The Boarding House"**: Odysseus in Phaeacia, Demodocus' song.
Odyssey, VIII.

Here, in an Irish boarding house, Joyce sets Demodocus' song, the comic tale of the love of Ares and Aphrodite. Except by the way of a secondary recall of the Cyclops-blinding, Odysseus is not represented in this story.

Pretty grey-eyed Polly Mooney of the "light soft hair"—a "little perverse madonna"—is Aphrodite "of the fair crown." Her lover, Bob Doran, is, like Ares, red-bearded. The representative of Hephaestus, the outraged party, is Polly's mother—this shift of sex and relationship being perhaps an acknowledgment of the passing of cuckoldry from the canon of modern comedy. Mr. Leonard, who employs Bob and will fire him if he hears of any scandal, is Apollo god of vengeance, or Zeus the father, whose wrath Ares would fear. Polly's brother Jack, a horse race addict, who dislikes Bob, is Aphrodite's uncle Poseidon, patron of horse races, who hates Ares for the slaying of his son Halirrhothius. The little blonde music hall artiste who slurred Polly's morals is Hermes, patron of music, who makes a bawdy joke about Aphrodite (compare Weathers in **"Counterparts"**).

The parallels in action are obvious and may be reduced to a general summary. In both stories an illicit love affair gives offense to a near relative of the female lover. The affair is consummated in the home of the outraged relative, who discovering what is going on keeps silent and arranges a trap. The relative is activated more by profit motive than moral consideration—to get a daughter married off or to exact a fine. In both stories the springing of the trap may involve public exposure, though Joyce reduces this to mere threat.

When the trap is sprung the male lover's predicament is complicated by fear of two men who may do him harm—Mr. Leonard and Jack Mooney, Zeus and Poseidon. A joking reference to the female's morals occasions angry outburst from one of her near relatives—Jack, Poseidon. The female is pretty well content with the outcome. Both stories end with a washing-motif—Aphrodite bathing at Paphos, Polly washing away tear-stains with a towel. (pp. 85-7)

[An] echo of the Cyclops-blinding is heard. Bob, as Odysseus, incurs the wrath and vengeance of a parent, Mrs. Mooney-Poseidon, for injury done the parent's child, Polly-Polyphemus. The rashness of Bob's act, as much out of character for him as Odysseus' foolhardy revelation of his name; the phonic coincidence of Polly-Polyphemus; and the implicit bawdy recall of "fiery-pointed brand" are all signs confirmatory that Joyce deliberately intended the parallel.

The third movement derives mainly from the tales of Odysseus' wanderings as he tells them to Alcinous (Books IX to XII). Joyce was later to work this section of the *Odyssey* exhaustively, deriving ten episodes of *Ulysses* from its eleven tales (omitting only the Cicones); but at the time of *Dubliners* he had but begun to plumb its possibilities. He does not use Book IX at all, except by indirect use of the Cyclops story in **"Counterparts"** and in earlier stories as noted above. Three of the stories of this movement cover the four Homeric tales of Books X and XI. The fourth, **"A Painful Case,"** pays but passing heed to three of the four tales of Book XII, and mainly returns to the Phaeacian and Ogygian adventures which have been otherwise developed in the second movement. (p. 87)

8. **"A Little Cloud"**: Odysseus at the Isle Aeolian.
   Odyssey, X.
   Ulysses, VII, "Aeolus."

This story, like **"Two Gallants,"** was of late composition, being added to the book three months after the original group of twelve stories was sent to the publisher. As in the Aeolus episode of *Ulysses,* Joyce here renders Odysseus' encounter with the wind-king in terms of the "windiness" of the modern press. (p. 87)

Aeolus the wind-king is Gallaher, sometime a Dubliner, now of the London Press (compare Myles Crawford in *Ulysses*). Gallaher is loud-voiced, hail-fellow, backslapping, gusty, domineering—all implicitly Aeolian qualities. He is notably capricious, as a "wind-king" ought to be—especially in such self-contradictions as, "It's not so beautiful, you know. Of course, it is beautiful. . . ." He has extremely hard-headed and unethical views on marriage ("I mean to marry money"; "I don't fancy tying myself up to one woman"); Aeolus solved the problem of disposing of his daughters by the practical, if shocking, device of marrying them to his sons. He drinks much, as Aeolus is always at the feast.

Odysseus, suppliant to Aeolus, is Chandler seeking literary assistance from Gallaher (compare Bloom.) Both are timid and embarrassed in the situation, and soft-voiced in their be-

seechings. Just as Odysseus is impressed by the abnormal sex-life of the Aeolian household, so Chandler is naively curious about the immorality of Gallaher's world and muses on the "voluptuous longing" of "rich Jewesses." Chandler is of course the "little cloud" of the title, blown about by Gallaher's whim, and the title is thus a clue to the theme of the story and to its Aeolian symbolism.

The scene of the story, Corless' restaurant, is a particularly interesting rendition of Homeric locale—more generous in types of detail than the corresponding newspaper office in *Ulysses.* Like Aeolus' palace it is a famous place ("he knew the value of the name"), and splendidly furnished. Much feasting goes on there, and the fare is exotic ("oysters and liqueurs" renders "dainties innumerable"). It is crowded with "richly-dressed ladies," whom Chandler regards with the awed wonderment that Odysseus showed for the daughters of Aeolus. Above all (as in *Ulysses*) the scene is noisy: the "light and noise of the bar," the women's "noisy" dresses, the clink of glasses, Gallaher's loud jargonistic speech and vulgar manner all provide a running aural imagery for the scene. Two minor Aeolian features, not mentioned by Homer but implicit in Joyce's acceptance of the theory that the Isle Aeolian is the volcano of Stromboli, are smoke and fire, rendered here symbolically in Gallaher's cigar-smoke and the running imagery of redness (blushes, wine-glasses, sunset.)

The action is faithful to Homeric pattern, though Joyce expands the time-elements proportionally and puts two units of the action into the past. Odysseus' friendship with Aeolus is of a month's length; Chandler's with Gallaher was for many years. Odysseus is separated from Aeolus for something beyond ten days; Chandler from Gallaher for eight years. Odysseus revisits Aeolus for a few minutes; Chandler sees Gallaher for an evening.

During the interim of separation, Chandler's fortunes like Odysseus' have declined. He knows that this is his own fault ("His unfortunate timidity"), and feels that it is also caused by his wife, as Odysseus blames himself for falling asleep and blames his "evil company." He looks forward to this second meeting in eager expectation of help from his old friend, who has the power. Like Odysseus, he approaches the meeting place sometime after lunch. He gets off his course because he "pursued his reverie so ardently" and has to "turn back," as Odysseus' turning back was caused by "sweet slumber." At the entrance he "halted before the door in indecision," as Odysseus "sat by the pillars of the door on the threshold." He thinks that the people in the room are "observing him curiously," as the family of Aeolus "marvelled" to see Odysseus. He is abruptly hailed by his friend.

The conference is very brief in Homer and nine pages in Joyce, but its course and result are the same, a timid beseeching frustrated by denial. Poor Chandler is so abashed by his inferiority to Gallaher, so fearfully eager to meet Gallaher on equal terms, that he never dares ask for what he came to ask, substituting instead the request that Gallaher visit him at home, which is denied. And he returns to his life of dull, unhappy domesticity quite as depressed, ashamed, and hopeless as Odysseus resumed his unhappy wandering "making heavy moan" and "stricken at heart." (pp. 88-9)

9. **"Counterparts"**: Odysseus at Lamos and
   Aeaea.
   Odyssey, X; also IX.
   Ulysses, XIII, "Laestrygonians"; XV,
   "Circe."

Here is the story "in counterparts" of Odysseus' adventures with the Laestrygonians and with Circe. The story in brief, Homeric or Joycean, presents its hero in a transition from a state of humiliating defeat to one of power. The details in parallel are so numerous that brief analysis is hopeless to account for them.

In the first seven pages, Farrington at the land office is Odysseus at Lamos, with reminiscences too (as there are in Homer) of Odysseus in Cyclops-land. Like Odysseus of "stalwart neck and mighty strength," Farrington is "tall and of great bulk," with a reputation as a strong man, and is wont to boast of his strength and accomplishments. He is unhappy in his employment here in the domain of his enemy and superior, Mr. Alleyne, and is eager to be elsewhere. Alleyne, an implacable tyrant over his employees, is Antiphates: Antiphates being a non-Ithacan, Alleyne is represented as an Ulsterman; Antiphates "raised the war-cry," and Alleyne in "a furious voice called out" and always seems to be shouting; both are startlingly abrupt of decision and hostile in action; Antiphates is described as a giant, and Alleyne with effectively ironic reversal as "a manikin" and "a dwarf."

The action opens with Miss Parker at the tube, sending Farrington to Alleyne's office; she corresponds to Antiphates' daughter at the well, sending Odysseus' men to her father's house. Farrington climbs up a stairs, as Odysseus "went up a craggy hill." In his second visit to Alleyne's office, he finds Miss Delacour, who is Antiphates' wife: Alleyne was "said to be sweet on her"; she is Jewish (non-Ithacan); she is "stout," as Antiphates' wife was "huge of bulk"; she occasions Alleyne's most violent attack on Farrington. Alleyne threatens to fire Farrington, as Antiphates to destroy Odysseus; and Farrington apologizes, as Odysseus withdraws. Alleyne had already "hounded little Peake out of the office," as Antiphates had eaten "one of my company," so that Farrington knows what will happen if he does not knuckle under. Both our "heroes" leave the scene sorely depressed but glad to escape without worse loss—life or job. The other officeworkers, hostile to Farrington, and subservient to Alleyne, are the host of Laestrygonians who hurl rocks at the fleeing Ithacans.

The quarrel between hero and enemy is heightened and expanded with hints from the earlier Odysseus-and-giant-herdsman story, the Cyclops episode. Thus, the quarrel develops in three encounters, corresponding to Odysseus' three "conversations" with Polyphemus. The hero in his anger commits a verbal error, so that something has to be redone: Farrington "was so enraged that he wrote Bernard Bernard instead of Bernard Bodley and had to begin again on a clean sheet"; after Odysseus' ill-timed taunt, the giant hurled a rock at the ship, and the wash of it forced the ship back to shore, whence it had to be rowed again. Farrington's catastrophe is precipitated by a non-characteristically foolhardy remark—"everyone was astounded (the author of the witticism no less than his neighbor)"—just as Odysseus' taunts, boasts, and curses, are out of character for this "man of many wiles." Alleyne, like Polyphemus, is last heard threatening the hero with ills to come.

The next six pages, the hero's transition to power, represent Odysseus' early adventures at Aeaea. Farrington is concerned to get money to stand treats, as Odysseus goes out to get food for his men. Suddenly it occurs to him to pawn his watch ("That was the dart!" he exclaims), as suddenly Odysseus sees before him a stag, and slays it with his spear. He

leaves his watch in the pawn shop in exchange for six shillings, which he carries away neatly "in a little cylinder"; so Odysseus leaves his "brazen shaft" on the ground ("and let it lie") and carries home the stag with its feet neatly bound together. Farrington proceeds joyfully to his friends in Davy Byrne's, stands them drinks, and enters upon an evening of doing the bars; Odysseus feeds his joyful men at the ship and feasts with them all day long.

Farrington's company leaves Byrne's and splits into two groups, one of which disappears; Odysseus' men divide into two groups, one of which goes off to Circe's palace to become swine. Farrington's group goes to the Scotch House, where they "pushed past the whining match-sellers at the door"; the one group of Odysseus' men enters Circe's palace by passing through beasts that "ramped about them and fawned on them, wagging their long tails." Farrington meets Weathers, an English (i.e., deity) acrobat and a sponge, who will later identify the femme fatale of the story; Odysseus will presently meet Hermes, god of gymnastics and of fraud, who will describe Circe.

At Mulligan's bar, Farrington beholds his Circe-in-Dublin, who is, like her prototype, English (i.e., deity), a singer, and of seductive manner. . . . Farrington is prevented from approaching her because Weathers has drunk up his funds; Odysseus is fortified against Circe because Hermes has given him the moly. Odysseus' struggle for mastery over Circe is obviated in Joyce by the artiste's departure, but is replaced by a contest of strength between Farrington and Weathers, which, ironically, Farrington loses.

The last two pages, with the hero dominant, takes place at Farrington's home, as the corresponding Homeric incident occurs at Odysseus' ship. Both heroes are longing to be back where they have just come from. In both stories the hero is offended by a subordinate who is a near relative—son Tom or Eurylochus "very near of kin"—and prepares to beat the offender with a long, thin weapon—cane or sword. The offender prays (Tom), or is prayed for (Eurylochus), and according to Homer the hero's wrath is stayed; but Joyce for once, and with especially bitter irony, converts the threat into act—"the boy uttered a squeal of pain as the stick cut his thigh."

> 10. **"Clay"**: Odysseus at Aeaea and his descent
>   into Hell.
>   *Odyssey*, X, XI.
>   *Ulysses*, VI, "Hades."

The hero, in amiable exile far from home, makes a long journey by special permission to visit dear relatives, with them recalls the old days, and is granted by mantic process a clouded glimpse into the future. Thus, in a mood of gentle melancholy, with little of the graveyard reek of the Hades episode of *Ulysses*, Joyce reads the theme of Homer's eleventh book. Only in the occasion—Hallow Eve, in the title, and in the cryptic reference of the prophecy are the darker potentialities of the theme suggested.

Odysseus for once is figured in a woman, Maria Donnelly. Like him, she has long been separated from her loved ones, especially from brother Joe and his family. Her exile, like his, is among strangers, in a laundry run by Protestants, but they are "very nice people." She wants to visit Joe but is fearful that he may be drunk, just as Odysseus fears the perils of his journey to hell. The matron of the laundry, like Circe, is encouraging and helpful in planning for the excursion. The main elements of Odysseus' journey are faithfully reproduced. Odysseus left Aeaea weeping; Maria departs in rain. Maria rides the train sitting on a stool at one end facing all the people, like Odysseus on his ship. Both journeys are made in two parts, Odysseus' by sea and by land, Maria's on two trains. Both travellers take food-offerings with them. Both arrive at their destination in rain.

Odysseus' colloquy with the departed is freely rendered, some of the matter being used during Maria's tram-ride: the young men who would not notice Maria to give her a seat are the host of spirits who could not speak until Odysseus fed them; the stout, talkative old gentlemen who has taken a drop and who makes off with the plumcake is Teiresias. Joe's house is Hades proper—his wife, who marshalls the children's games, being Persephone, and the girl children the host of young women Odysseus interviewed. Joe himself, the only adult male present, does multiple symbolic duty—like Agamemnon he is stern with women, like Minos authoritarian, like Achilles the father of a son and a good fighter, like Ajax tenacious of old grudges, like Tantalus forever reaching for another bottle of stout.

Parallels of action are numerous. Both heroes are greeted by cries of thanks and recognition when they present the food-offering. Both have failed to do something important—Maria to bring the plumcake, Odysseus to bury Elpenor. Both talk with their relatives about old times. Both receive somewhat cloudy information about the future—Odysseus through Teiresias' mystic, secretive prophecy which omits all reference to Penelope and the wooers, Maria through the saucer game with its ambiguous and frightening results: her hand first falls upon the saucer of clay, which portends death, and the other players, embarrassed at the fact, conceal the truth from her and make her play again until she touches the prayerbook, which means only that she will take the veil. The last incident, Maria's song, though without prototype, is a most ingenious Odyssean recall: the words of "I dreamt that I dwelt in marble halls—with vassals and serfs at my side," express very prettily the mood and situation of Odysseus at the end of his visit with the dead.

> 11. **"A Painful Case"**: Odysseus in love.
> *Odyssey,* V-VIII, XI, XII, XIII.
> *Ulysses,* IV, "Calypso," IX, "Scylla and
>   Charybdis," XI, "Sirens," XIII, "Nausicaa,"
>   XIV, "Oxen of the Sun."

The next Homeric adventures at hand are those of the Sirens, Charybdis and Scylla, and the Oxen of the Sun, but these, which with the Wandering Rocks were to furnish four episodes of Ulysses, Joyce now but lightly acknowledges as he passes beyond them to stories already worked but still rich in ore. When we behold our hero, James Duffy—solitary, middle-aged—entering by way of an affaire de coeur the household of a sea captain with a wife and daughter, we are inescapably minded of the lone Odysseus' entry into the household of Alcinous. In this analogue, Captain Sinico is Alcinous, the sailor-king who would welcome Odysseus as a son-in-law; Mrs. Sinico is Arete; the daughter is Nausicaa. Joyce's interest now centers in the wife-mother, whom he has hitherto not noticed, and he transfers to her qualities and actions from the others. Thus in Homer the daughter makes the initial advances—in Joyce the wife-mother; in Homer the husband is addicted to drink—in Joyce the wife-mother becomes so; Homer but hints an illicit affection in the wife-mother—Joyce develops this theme abundantly, informing

the lady with the passion of Calypso. It is in the latter half of the story that the action is most notably pendant to that of the Phaeacian story. Odysseus' curiously final farewell to Arete becomes Mr. Duffy's breaking off with Mrs. Sinico. The death of Mrs. Sinico under the wheels of a train, the coroner's investigation, Mr. Sinico's testimony, the railway company's safety measures correspond to the catastrophic events which befall the Phaeacians, all of which occur after Odysseus' departure: the fettering of their ship, the council of the gods, Alcinous' harangue, the rites of appeasement. Mr. Duffy's grief and loneliness are the feelings of Odysseus alone on what he takes to be a strange shore.

The minor Homeric episodes affect only the first half of the story. The music of the Sirens provides a background to the lover's first meeting—at the opera, where the house, like Odysseus' boat, is thinly peopled and silent, and the performers sing to empty benches. Music continues to unite the lovers as the years go on, and after the break Mr. Duffy keeps away from concerts. Odysseus' painful choice between Scylla and Charybdis is suggested only in Mr. Duffy's initial choice between mother and daughter. Helios, the absentee landlord of Thrinacia, lends to Captain Sinico his habit of being so often from home and his aspect as a source of danger to the hero; thus Sinico's non-Irish name is doubly motivated: as Alcinous he is non-Ithacan and as Helios he is a god. (The name is, incidentally, that of an Italian music-master under whom Joyce studied.)

Calypso's story, fused here with Arete's, is worth more. If Mrs. Sinico is like Arete in her domestic relations and in her amiable regard for the stranger-hero, she is far more like Calypso in her desperate intentness to get and hold her man. Like Calypso she is the aggressor in the love-affair: it is she who speaks first at the opera, she at whose house they meet, who leaves the lamp out as darkness falls, who catches his hand passionately and presses it to her cheek, who is heart-broken at the sundering of their relationship. Thus it is here, as not in **"Eveline,"** the earlier rendition of Calypso's tale, that Joyce creates the special pathos of "unwilling lover by a willing lady."

The three stories of the fourth movement, which originally concluded *Dubliners* ("The Dead" was written later) carry the tour de force to a dwindling, imperfect close. Half the *Odyssey* lay yet before Joyce, and these three stories do it technically scant justice. The first, **"Ivy Day,"** renders thematically three or four Homeric books; the second, **"A Mother,"** may be pendant to a brief section of another book but is quite as much a reversion to an earlier tale; **"Grace"** is again thematic in relevance and reuses some books covered by **"Ivy Day."** (pp. 89-92)

The distinguishing mark of these three stories is that indicated in Joyce's label for them, their common concern with Public Life. The eleven stories that precede them are preeminently studies in the psychology of individuals—Joyce himself and persons he has known. Now he launches a set of stories thematically centric in the civilization of contemporary Ireland, turns in earnest to his intention of writing "a chapter of the moral history of my country." **"Ivy Day"** is Irish politics; **"A Mother"** is Irish art; **"Grace"** is Irish religion. . . .

The list ends, rather abruptly, probably because there was nowhere else for it to go: the topical subject-matter was in all important respects exhausted. (pp. 92-3)

> 12. **"Ivy Day in the Committee Room"**: Odysseus

A Painful ~~HHHHHHHHH~~ Case

Mr James Duffy lived in Chapelizod because he wished to be as far as possible from the city of which he was a citizen and because he found all the other suburbs of Dublin mean, modern and pretentious. He lived in an old gaunt house and from his window he could look into the disused distillery or upwards along the shallow river on which Dublin is built. The lofty walls of his uncarpeted room were free from pictures. He had himself bought every article of furniture in the room; a black iron bedstead, an iron washstand, ~~too~~ three cane chairs, a clothes rack, a coal-scuttle a fender and irons and a square table on which lay a double desk. A bookcase had been made in an alcove by means of shelves of white wood. The bed was clothed with white bedclothes and a black and scarlet rug covered the foot. A little handmirror hung above the washstand and during the day, a white-shaded lamp stood as the sole ornament of the mantelpiece. The books on the white wooden shelves were arranged from below upwards according

The first page of a draft of "A Painful Case."

at Eumaeus' hut.
Odyssey, XIII-XVI.
Ulysses, XVI, "Eumaeus."

It is theme and situation—the nation sick with longing for the return of its lost leader—that interests Joyce in the first books of Odysseus' return to Ithaca. The bitter truth of history precludes Joyce's use of Homeric action, for the story Homer tells of Odysseus' homecoming and covert preparations to destroy the enemies of his state is for Ireland only an idiot's dream: Parnell is dead. So Joyce can only sketch plotlessly the bewilderment, chicanery, and loneliness of the political men who follow in Parnell's place.

The scene of the story, the Nationalist Party Committee Room, is Eumaeus' hut, the caretaker Old Jack being Eumaeus and most of the other characters rather dank representatives of Eumaeus' helpers and the other servants of Odysseus' house. The weather, as in Homer, is dismal and cold, so that fires must be kept going. The distinctive date, Parnell's birthday, is reminiscent of the round-number twentieth year since Odysseus' departure. The occasion is the imminence of a political election, adumbrating the struggle for power in Ithaca between the wooers and Telemachus. The stronger candidate, Tricky Dicky Tierney, a machine politician, in cahoots with moneyed interests, employing many canvassers whom he rewards grudgingly and capriciously, stands for the wooers; Telemachus is one Colgan, who stands for labor, is right and honest, but being without influence fights a losing battle alone. The servants in Homer were caught in an unhappy dilemma: devoted to the memory of Odysseus, they "knew" he would never return; loyal to Telemachus, they labored perforce to fill the bellies of the wooers. And that is the situation of the party workers in the Committee Room—Old Jack, Henchy, Crofton, Lyons, O'Connor: they yearn for the dead hero but spend their strength in half-willing service to Tierney. Joyce dourly denies them, though, the redeeming feature of "loyalty to Telemachus"; blind to the right they fail to recognize Colgan as Parnell's true moral heir, and they despise him as a mere brick-layer, a tinker. Only one of the lot, Joe Hynes, has his eyes open. He defends Colgan, belittles Tricky Dicky, is the first to remind the company of Parnell, and climaxes the sketch with his spell-binding verses on Parnell's death. In his curious detachment from the others, in his higher vision, in his power to create in the minds of the others the living presence of Parnell, Hynes' function is that of the disguised Odysseus and the goddess Athene.

A couple of minor correspondences are worth noting. Eumaeus has a thrall, Mesaulius, who prepares meals and clears away; he is the prototype of the boy who brings the beer, in whom Old Jack takes a sudden paternalistic interest. In this section of the epic appears a mysterious soothsayer, Theoclymenus . . .; a mystery man turns up here too, bent on some dark political mission—he looks like a clergyman or an actor and is called Father Keon, but no one knows whether he is a priest or not. (pp. 93-4)

The Parnell-Odysseus equation is enhanced with some striking details, as for instance the recollection of Parnell's irregular love-life. But the most compelling way to feel the analogy at work is to read Eumaeus' speeches in Book XIV of the epic, at each mention of Odysseus saying to oneself "Parnell", and for each reference to those who long for his return saying "Ireland."

13. **"A Mother"**: Penelope and the wooers, Demodocus' song.
    Odyssey, XVIII; VIII.

For a time in the last half of the epic the initiative passes from Odysseus to Penelope or Athene, the women in the case, and probably Joyce here takes the cue for **"A Mother,"** his satiric backstage report on Irish Revivalist art. Thus, Happy Holohan, who limps up and down Dublin talking about his series of concerts, resembles at the beginning of the story Odysseus, who though he does not limp, has a strong scar on his leg, who is planning an "entertainment" for the wooers, and who talks more than he acts. And Mrs. Kearney, who in the end arranges everything, and her daughter Kathleen, the pianist, represent in a sliding relationship Athene and Penelope. In her Athene-role, Mrs. Kearney advises Holohan how to arrange a program, dresses her daughter becomingly, is backed up by the Zeus-like, indefinite, secure strength of Mr. Kearney; in her Penelope-role, she refuses to deliver the promised musical goods without payment in advance, as Penelope demands gifts from the wooers before she will give herself to any of them.

This may be—and many minor correspondences might be added in support of the analogue, but the major development of the action—the male resumption of initiative and control through violent quarrel with the woman—is not motivated here in Homer at all. For this portion of the story, one must look to the Hephaestus-Aphrodite tale of Book VIII, Demodocus' song. Here, in Hephaestus, is a hero who is literally lame, who arranges an entertainment for an audience, whose quarrel is with a woman, who claims rebate of a bargain price (the return of his wedding gifts), who refers his claim to higher authorities (the gods, the Committee), who wins the quarrel; a heroine who prostitutes herself (Joyce would apply the word to any contribution to the Revivalist program), who is caught in cunning bonds, who is backed up by a personally impressive male (Poseidon, Mr. Kearney), who goes off defeated, the laughing stock of a crowd of male observers.

It is not unlike Joyce to re-use Homeric materials (as Ogygia, Phaeacia), nor to combine two or more Homeric tales into one, though in all other instances (even **"A Painful Case"**) the combined materials are contiguous in the action of the epic. Hence it is best to rest this analysis on the broad probabilities sketched above, and recognize in the story the beginning of the end of Joyce's faithfulness to his tour de force plan.

14. **"Grace"**: Odysseus' homecoming.
    Odyssey, XIII-XVIII.
    Ulysses, XVII, "Ithaca."

This story, a study of rotarianism in Irish religion, is difficult to assign specific analogue for, though its relevance to the situation and theme of Odysseus' return to his country and his house, and of his relations with Penelope and the wooers, is plain.

Tom Kernan is the Odysseus, the wanderer. Not only is he tagged "a commercial traveller of the old school," but he is vagrant in a higher sense: for twenty years, like Odysseus, he had been away from "home"—i.e., outside the pale of the Church; and for about that long he has been indifferent to (hence, "away from") his wife. He is activated by none of Odysseus' heroic determination—not even consciously by urgent wish—to return to home and wife, and must be prodded by others around him. The urge lives mainly in Mrs. Kernan, the Penelope; she, who has all these years "kept house shrewdly for her husband," dwells sentimentally in memories of their earlier happiness, and longs earnestly to see her husband reformed into a "good Catholic" and a sober man. The role of Telemachus is in the first pages filled by Jack Power (though later Power appears to join the rank of the wooers). Power is young, tall, and fair; he respects Kernan and is fond of him; he is the first to recognize Kernan in the bar-room (as Telemachus was the first to recognize Odysseus in Eumaeus' hut); he takes over responsibility for Kernan from his subordinate the constable (as Telemachus takes over Odysseus from his servant Eumaeus); he guides Kernan to his house; he is eager to restore Kernan to sobriety, the Church, and the good graces of his wife.

Analogues of action in the early part include Kernan's fall downstairs and the dirtying of his clothes, which recall Athene's sudden transformation of Odysseus into a filthy-garbed beggar; his bitten tongue and hazy memory and the disappearance of his drinking companions, which recall Odysseus' being left alone on the shore and his need to fabricate tales about his past; the recognition by Power; the journey to his house.

In the bulk of the story, Kernan, like Odysseus, is in his own house surrounded by men who are conspiring against him. The villainous plot of the Homeric wooers Joyce converts into the relatively harmless plot of Kernan's friends to trick Kernan into attending a retreat with them. Ostensibly their purpose is benevolent, but inherent is a feeling that Kernan, like Odysseus, is alone among enemies: he resents them, suspects them, resists them (at least mildly), restrains his impulses to sharp retort, and rather unwillingly submits. And Joyce is telling us (though poor stupid Kernan pathetically cannot see it) that the "home" the friends seek for themselves and would lead Kernan to is not a home where he can truly rest, any more than Odysseus could rest in Ithaca if Penelope fell to the wooers: the retreat as Kernan's friends use it, is no source of spiritual light to lost souls who need light but a business men's club organized to secure God's approval upon business men's expediency. (pp. 94-5)

As first submitted to the publisher, **Dubliners** ended with "**Grace**," thematically at zenith, but in terms of the secret technique dangling and incomplete. Joyce the artist had yet to be satisfied. . . . Somewhere—perhaps from his wife, who like the Gretta of the story came from Galway—he heard the sad tale of Michael Furey, and by reviewing with it his own experience as an embarrassed intellectual among Dublin medical students and berlitzing business men on the Continent, he achieved the elements of this magnificent finale. "**The Dead**" is so rich in thematic implications that it not only can fitly follow, but easily transcends, those stories that make up the "moral history" of Ireland. (pp. 95-6)

> 15. "**The Dead**": Odysseus' destruction of the wooers and reunion with Penelope.
> *Odyssey,* XX to XXIII.
> *Ulysses,* XVII, "Ithaca"; XVIII, "Penelope."

In the climactic forty-first day of the epic Odysseus attends his enemies' last revels, watches and engages in the contest of the bow, converts the banquet-hall into a shambles for his enemies, and at last is alone with his wife, to whom he relates stories of his past. So too Gabriel Conroy attends his Aunt Morkan's Christmas party (possibly their last) with people he dislikes, listens to several verbal contests and is even drawn

into one, carves the goose at supper and makes a speech aimed to discomfit his enemies, and at last is alone with his wife, who relates to him a story of her past. So faithfully does Joyce follow these main lines of Homeric action that he twice sets asterisks to mark Homeric book-divisions.

The parties, in both books, begin with maid-servants engaged in preparations—Lily receiving wraps, Eurycleia directing the activities of the underservants. The hosts—the aunts, Telemachus—question the maid-servant about the hero—Gabriel, Odysseus—and subsequently are much emboldened by the hero's presence and rely on him for help. Both parties are customs of long standing ("For years and years it had gone off in splendid style," Joyce writes, "as long as anyone could remember").

Both heroes, when they enter, converse first with servants—Lily; Eumaeus, Melanthius, Philoetius—and midway in each conversation the servant utters a sharp rebuke which the hero broods over in silence (Gabriel "was still discomposed by the girl's bitter and sudden retort. It had cast a gloom over him"; Odysseus "in silence . . . shook his head, brooding evil in the deep of his heart"). Both heroes linger at the outskirts of the revelling company at first—Gabriel "outside the drawing-room door," Odysseus at a little table "by the threshold"—a post of vantage.

Gabriel, like Odysseus, is much concerned about his relations with the other guests: he is aware of his own superiority (his "superior education," Odysseus' ability to string the bow); he senses that if he does not conceal his superiority and use it with the right strategy he may suffer injury from them (he feared "he would only make himself ridiculous by quoting poetry to them which they could not understand"); and he therefore revises his speech. Just so, Odysseus deliberately conceals his power (accepting insults in silence), and all day long revises and improvises his plan of action to suit the circumstances.

Like Odysseus, too, Gabriel is a cosmopolitan traveller, and out of this rises some question of his proper status here in his own land. In this first section we find that he makes Gretta wear galoshes because "everyone wears them on the Continent," and Gretta resists the innovation. More is made of this later in his quarrel with Miss Ivors over the Nationalist movement: he can't join her excursion to the Aran Isles, he tells her, because "every year" he goes on "a cycling tour with some fellows . . . to France or Belgium or perhaps Germany"; for this and other reasons, Ivors denies him his Irish nationality and labels him "West Briton." Thus are reflected Odysseus' past and future wanderings and the wooers' efforts to prevent his repatriation.

Both parties are infested by rude men who offend the ladies—the Homeric wooers, "haling the handmaidens in foul wise through the fair house"; Joyce's Mr. Browne, who is too attentive to the ladies and shocks them with vulgar anecdotes, and Freddy Malins, who ignores the ladies, is drunk, tells dirty stories to the men, and wanders about with his fly open. Odysseus' only direct contact with the wooers in Book XX is with Ctesippus, a "ribald fellow" (Butler's translation), who hurls an ox's foot at him; Gabriel's only contact in this section is with Freddy, who offends him with a piece of smut. Both heroes accept the offence in silence and inward burning (Odysseus "smiled right grimly in his heart," Gabriel's "brows were dark"); and the host—Telemachus, Aunt Kate—condemns the offender. Of all the wooers' company, incidently, the only one to be spared from slaughter as "blameless" was Phemius, "the minstrel . . . who sang among the wooers of necessity"; Joyce parallels him with Bartell D'Arcy, the tenor—the most gentlemanly of the guests, guilty of minor bursts of temper but always excused by circumstances—who in spite of his bad cold is forced by popular insistence to sing one song.

Homer concludes Book XX with a scene in which Athene stirs the wooers to "laughter unquenchable," and drives "their wits wandering . . . and their eyes were filled with tears"; and Theoclymenus tries in vain to scold them into sobriety. Joyce concludes the first section with Browne trying to sober Freddy with a glass of lemonade, but falling into laughter himself as Freddy "exploded . . . in a kind of high-pitched bronchitic laughter and . . . began to rub the knuckles of his left fist backwards and forwards into his left eye, repeating words of his last phrase as well as his fit of laughter would allow him." (Asterisks, end of Book XX.)

Homer opens Book XXI with Penelope's visit to the treasure room "with her handmaidens" to fetch the unbendable bow; Joyce renders this as Mary Jane ("and Aunt Kate standing at her elbow to turn the page") playing an extremely difficult and baffling piece of music. The description of the treasure-room is answered with a description of the Morkan's drawing-room. The history of the bow and the story of the hostility between Heracles and Iphitus are paralleled by Gabriel's memories of his mother and her hostility to Gretta.

The Homeric contest of the bow is paralleled by the progress of a dance aptly called "lancers"; by Gabriel's quarrel with Miss Ivors over Irish Nationalism; and a little later, after Aunt Julia's song, by a series of quarrel-sequences: Browne and Freddy clash lightly in rival efforts to praise Julia; Aunt Kate lashes out at the pope for banning women from the choir; Miss Ivors offends the company by leaving before supper; and Mary Jane remarks that "we are all very quarrelsome." When the wooers set the contest aside, Penelope speaks after long silence to defend Odysseus' right to try the bow; she is rebuked (by her son), and "in amaze" she retires. So too, after the "lancers," Gretta appears for the first time in this section; she is interested in Gabriel's quarrel with Ivors, is answered "coldly" by Gabriel, and retires in surprise. Where Odysseus prepares himself for the slaughter by "handling the bow, turning it every way about, and proving it on this side and that," Gabriel retires to a window niche and "ran over the headings of his speech," revising it once more in the light of his quarrel with Ivors.

In Book XXII Homer converts feast into slaughter, and Odysseus achieves his climax of heroic action; but Joyce must let the feast quietly proceed, for his hero is a painfully ordinary man. The feast opens with a striking Homeric reference. When called to the table by Aunt Kate, Gabriel starts out of his mood of abstraction and "with sudden animation" cries, "Here I am, Aunt Kate . . . ready to carve a flock of geese, if necessary." Not only is the suddenness of gesture exactly that of Odysseus as he leaped to action, but the witticism perfectly recalls the auspicious bird-imagery of the epic—especially in Penelope's dream of the crooked beaked eagle and the twenty geese. One should note too, how Joyce describes the dishes on the table, marshalling them like opposing military forces: the goose and the ham are "rival ends"; between them run "parallel lines" of dishes; the decanters are "sentries" to the fruit-stand; the pudding "lay in waiting";

"three squads" of bottles are "drawn up according to the colours of their uniforms."

Throughout the banquet, with typical subtlety, Joycean arrows whisper through the air. As in the "Ithaca" section of *Ulysses,* arrows become words. Mary Jane and Aunt Kate have quarreled about applesauce for the goose; Aunt Kate and Aunt Julia keep bumping into each other and "giving each other unheeded orders"; disagreements arise over the contralto of D'Arcy's company, a negro tenor, the race problem, the relative merits of contemporary singers and those of the past, the pudding. Browne quibbles over the customs of the monks of Mount Melleray. D'Arcy refuses to take wine, then submits. Gabriel fancies himself, by cutting allusions in his speech, disposing of the whole bluestocking host of Ivorses who sponsor the Revival. The final jubilation of Odysseus' faithful servants is echoed in the song "For they are jolly gay fellows." (Asterisks, end of Book XXII.)

Joyce uses Homer's Book XXIII, the reunion of Odysseus and Penelope, freely, but at relevant points with keen irony. The noisy departure of the Morkans' guests, which occupies the first half of the story, is without Homeric antecedent, unless it be construed as an elaboration of Telemachus' merry-making to impress the neighbors. It may be noted that Gretta's descent of the stairs—a grand entry—resembles Penelope's in some details; and Gabriel's eagerness to be alone with his wife and to draw her out of her seeming coldness is like Odysseus'. But it is in the second half, the scene of the hotel, that we are brought back to Homer. Through seemingly trivial revelations—the secret of the bed-post, the loan of a pound to Freddy Malins—the woman is brought to yield; Penelope "fell aweeping, and ran straight toward him and cast her hands about his neck, and kissed his head"; Gretta stands before Gabriel, "then, suddenly raising herself on tiptoe and resting her hands lightly on his shoulders, she kissed him." For the Homeric lovers the reunion is complete; they withdraw to the bed and "take their fill of sweet love," and all night he delights her with tales of his adventures in the west, including even, but tactfully, the story of Calypso. But not so for Gabriel. It is not he, but Gretta, who tells a tale of a lover in the west, the sweet-voiced, delicate boy named Michael Furey, who used to sing "The Lass of Aughrim" to her, and who died for love of her when she came out of Galway. Her grief in the memory is inconsolable, and she goes to bed alone, weeping. Gabriel lies awake beside her, a hero troubled, shamed, and deflated, and somehow cleansed by the baffling of his desire—brooding upon the imminence of death ("His soul had approached that region where dwell the vast hosts of the dead"; Odysseus' descent into hell), contemplating his own death ("The time had come for . . . his own journey westward"; Odysseus' thoughts of his further journeys and death prophesied by Teiresias), and hearing the "snow falling faintly through the universe and faintly falling, like the descent of their last end, upon all the living and the dead." (pp. 96-9)

Richard Levin and Charles Shattuck, "First Flight to Ithaca: A New Reading of Joyce's 'Dubliners'," in Accent, *Vol. 4, No. 2, Winter, 1944, pp. 75-99.*

JULIAN B. KAYE (essay date 1958)

[*In the following excerpt, Kaye explicates "An Encounter" and "The Dead," introducing to Joyce criticism the idea of "The Dead" as an "epiphany" story.*]

Recent textual studies of *Ulysses* and *Finnegans Wake* have tended to make *Dubliners* look thin, simply because it has not been "read" with the same critical attention. Moreover, Hugh Kenner's founding of a "Stephen-hating" school of Joyce criticism has led inevitably to the depreciation of *Dubliners.* The critics who hold that Joyce portrays the Stephen Dedalus of *Ulysses* as a hopeless failure must, willingly or unwillingly, give the impression that the stories Stephen is writing are inferior Joyce. Consequently, there has been a tendency to make two Joyces—one for *Dubliners* and *A Portrait,* the other for *Ulysses* and *Finnegans Wake*—and to see the first Joyce as a mere literary apprentice.

I believe this view of Joyce's career to be both unfortunate and—more important—untrue. Although Joyce's prose in *Dubliners* is conventional in syntax and vocabulary, it often has the richness of texture of that of *Ulysses* and *Finnegans Wake.* By giving it the same kind of attention, I hope to demonstrate that even so uncomplicated a story as "An Encounter"—one of the first stories Joyce wrote (1903)—is *echt* Joyce and that by the time Joyce wrote "The Dead" (1906) he was already at the height of his powers.

The only explication of "An Encounter"—that of Marvin Magalaner in *Joyce: The Man, the Work, the Reputation*—treats the excursion of two truant schoolboys as an attempt to escape from the paralysis of Dublin life by visiting the Pigeonhouse Fort, which is interpreted as a religious and paternal symbol. "The Pigeonhouse, then, is identified in Joyce's mind with the 'father' of Christ and with fathers in general." The pervert whom the boys encounter after they have abandoned their attempt to reach their destination is, according to this interpretation, both a perverted God and a perverted father.

This excellent reading is solidly based not only on the story itself but on Joyce's treatment of Stephen Dedalus's search for a father and for religious faith in *A Portrait* and *Ulysses.* Nevertheless, I feel that a detailed re-examination of the text is necessary if we are to appreciate the rich ambiguity of Joyce's symbolism and the dramatic intensity of the story.

"An Encounter" is a story of escape. The boys who play hooky are weary of the routine of school life; and we are prepared for their adventures by three pages (one quarter of the story) about their previous attempts to vary the monotonous routine of their days, all of which were unsatisfactory because, in the words of the boy narrator, ". . . I wanted real adventures to happen to myself. But real adventures, I reflected, do not happen to people who remain at home: they must be sought abroad."

Therefore, it is not surprising that the boys plan to "go along the Wharf Road until we came to the ships, and then to cross in the ferryboat and walk out to see the Pigeon House." When they reach the ships they feel an impulse to run away to sea. Instead they cross the Liffey in a ferryboat and the narrator looks about for a foreign sailor with green eyes, "for I had some confused notions . . . [author's ellipsis]." The narrator breaks off and does not tell us what his confused notion was, perhaps because he cannot verbalize it. At any rate, his expectations are not fulfilled: the only sailor with green eyes whom he sees does not seem to be foreign and the boy does not reach the Pigeonhouse because "it was too late and we were too tired . . .".

For a long time I did not understand why a visit to the Pigeonhouse should be the climax of a day spent in seeing for-

eign ships; I then learned that in the late eighteenth and early nineteenth century the Pigeonhouse was the Irish terminus of the Irish-English packet service. Certainly some one so well informed about Dublin local history as Joyce must have known the history of the landmark that so strongly stimulated his imagination. The fact that the packet service had been established at Kingstown and the North Wall before Joyce's birth is not significant. For one thing, children distinguish past from present much less exactly than adults. The boy narrator of "An Encounter" may very well have read an old story which mentions the landing of a packet at the Pigeonhouse—e.g., *The Absentee* of Maria Edgeworth—and may have assumed the Pigeonhouse was still used as a terminus.

More important, it seems to me, is the theme of belatedness that pervades all the fictional representations of Joyce as child and adolescent. In "The Sisters" we see the boy narrator with the dead Father Flynn and his two aged and decrepit sisters. He seems bound to them and to the dead and dying past which they represent. In "Araby" he arrives at a bazaar—the object of another enthusiastic expedition—just before closing time on the last day; and he sees only the winding up of things in the almost deserted and half-darkened hall. Stephen Dedalus, his *alter ego,* is wounded to think that his ". . . monkish learning . . . was held no higher by the age he lived in than the subtle and curious jargon of heraldry and falconry" (*Portrait*).

Thus, much of the pathetic futility of the boys' attempt to escape lies in the fact that they try a path that had been closed before they were born. (pp. 31-3)

The boys, although they are unable to attain their goal, do have an adventure. We may say that, unable to escape, they are confronted with Ireland itself. Instead of the green-eyed sailor, who represents the romance of the exotic, they encounter the green-eyed pervert (green for Ireland).

The perversion of love into cruelty is one of the most common themes in *Dubliners.* To Joyce it is one of the characteristics of Dublin life. The working out of this theme is explicit in "Counterparts" and is implicit in such stories as "The Boarding House," "Two Gallants," and "A Little Cloud." In Irish political life the bitterness and personal animosity of the battle that followed the Bishops' condemnation of Parnell, described so powerfully in *A Portrait,* is an analogous example of disappointed love delighting in the infliction of pain.

The sterile autoeroticism and sadism of the pervert is an excellent symbol of Joyce's view of political Ireland after Parnell—the Ireland of "Ivy Day in the Committee Room." It may be significant that the narrator insists that he and his friend give the pervert the false names of Smith and Murphy if he should ask their identity. Beyond psychological realism and the primitive superstition that plays an important role in the Lohengrin legend and in the Cyclops episode of the *Odyssey,* there is Joyce's fear of Ireland's hatred of its artists—a fear which he often voices.

There is yet another level—in my opinion, the most important one—on which the symbols of the story function. Stanislaus Joyce has pointed out that the first three stories of *Dubliners* are about early adolescence. Of all three "An Encounter" deals most explicitly with sex. One may say that the three principal characters—the boy narrator (Joyce), his friend Mahony, and the pervert—are defined by their attitude towards sex. The restlessness and desire for adventure and escape that motivate the day's "miching" are principally puberty. The narrator is fascinated by the "unkempt fierce and beautiful girls" of American detective stories. At about the same age (Stanislaus Joyce, in his "Background to *Dubliners*"), says that his brother was about fourteen at the time of the incident recorded in **"An Encounter"**) Stephen Dedalus is impelled to restless wandering and romantic fantasy: "He returned to Mercedes and, as he brooded upon her image, a strange unrest crept into his blood. Sometimes a fever gathered within him and led him to rove alone in the evening. . . . He wanted to meet in the real world the unsubstantial image which his soul so constantly beheld. . . . They would be alone, surrounded by darkness and silence: and in that moment of supreme tenderness he would be transfigured. . . . Weakness and inexperience would fall from him in that magic moment."

Joyce quite explicitly connects Stephen's fantasy with the desire to escape to foreign lands which is stimulated by roaming around the docks of Dublin:

> He [Stephen] passed unchallenged among the docks and along the quays. . . . The vastness and strangeness of the life suggested to him by the bales of merchandise stocked along the walls or swung aloft out of the holds of steamers wakened again in him the unrest which had sent him wandering in the evening from garden to garden in search of Mercedes. . . . A vague dissatisfaction grew up within him as he looked on the quays and on the river and on the lowering skies and yet he continued to wander up and down day after day as if he really sought someone that eluded him.

Thus the itinerary of the boys' trip may be viewed as an attempt to find an object that will assuage their restlessness. Experience itself—i.e., the foreign, the exotic—seems to be an abstraction of that object.

Marvin Magalaner has observed that the Pigeonhouse may function as a phallic image of fatherhood as well as a religious symbol of God as father and as paraclete. W. Y. Tindall has pointed out that some of the historic functions of the Pigeonhouse ("successively a fort, a lighthouse, and a power station") may be interpreted symbolically (*James Joyce*, 1950). All these themes are part of the meaning of the Pigeonhouse to the narrator. Since he lives with his aunt and uncle, he is presumably an orphan; and he seems anxious to find a father. Significantly, Stephen Dedalus thought of himself as an orphan when he was the narrator's age.

We know from *A Portrait* that Stephen's adolescence was extremely painful because of his family's decline from affluence to scarcely genteel shabbiness and that he held his father responsible for the family misfortune; and we may guess that Stephen's diffidence about sex was partially due to the feeling of insecurity caused by his family's loss of wealth and his father's loss of status.

In **"An Encounter"** the insecure and diffident narrator is contrasted with the aggressive and self-confident Mahony, who accompanies him on the outing. Mahony does not care about reaching the Pigeonhouse; instead, he wants to have some fun with his catapult. "While we were waiting he brought out the catapult which bulged from his inner pocket and explained some improvements which he had made in it." He intends "to have some gas with the birds," from which one may surmise that Mahony and the narrator have widely differing conceptions of the Pigeonhouse. We do not, however, hear anything

about Mahony shooting birds; instead, "he chased a crowd of ragged girls, brandishing his unloaded catapult . . .". The next independent action he performs is to chase a cat. When the boys decide that they will have to give up the expedition to the Pigeonhouse, Mahony seems concerned only because he has not been able to use his catapult. During the boys' conversation with the pervert, Mahony answers the pervert's questions about their sweethearts by saying that he has "three totties," while the narrator answers that he has none. Later Mahony goes off to chase a cat and leaves the narrator alone with the pervert.

The reiteration of the images of brandished catapult and pursued cats, the pursuit of birds and girls, the bold assertion that he has three sweethearts, the insouciant indifference to the pervert—this is essentially all we are told about Mahony, and it is all we need to know. His character, for this story, is his aggressive sexuality, which is conceived primarily as a contrast to the confusion and tortured uncertainty of the boy narrator. Mahony does not seem to need the support of a father—earthly, heavenly, or national—to confirm his manhood. Living for instinctual satisfactions, he remains unperturbed by the paralysis of family, church, and state that is the theme of *Dubliners.* He is the first of a series of males whom Joyce contrasts with his fictional surrogates: Cranly in *A Portrait* and Buck Mulligan in *Ulysses* with Stephen Dedalus; and Shaun the Post with Shem the Penman in *Finnegans Wake.*

Unlike the happy-go-lucky Mahony, the boy narrator *is* disappointed by his failure to reach the Pigeonhouse and to find the green-eyed foreign sailor. It is therefore significant that the pervert is dressed in greenish-black (like another symbol of unsuccessful paternity, Father Flynn of **"The Sisters"**) and has green eyes. When he begins talking about "Sir Walter Scott and Lord Lytton," the boy narrator, who is of course literary, attempts to impress his interlocutor by pretending that he has read every book the former mentions. He is therefore presumably pleased when the pervert says of Mahony: "Now . . . he is different; he goes in for games." When Mahony asks a question which the narrator thinks is stupid, he is both ashamed of his friend and afraid "the man would think I was as stupid as Mahony."

The pervert then changes the subject to girls, and the narrator, detecting the lack of conviction in the pervert's praise of normal sexuality, begins to feel vaguely uneasy about his new friend. Then the pervert walks across the field away from the boys and performs the unnamed act which the boy narrator—unlike Mahony, who observes the pervert's exhibitionism with scientific curiosity—"I say . . . He's a queer old josser!"—refuses to acknowledge that he has seen. He immediately, however, insists that they give the pervert false names; and we can infer, from the horror and guilt that Stephen Dedalus feels about his autoeroticism when he is about the same age, the painfulness of the narrator's observation, in the man with whom he momentarily hoped to identify himself, of a perverse form of the behavior he detests in himself.

The pervert returns to the boys and Mahony runs off in pursuit of a cat, leaving the boy narrator and the man together. The pervert again begins talking about sex, but this time he says what he believes—sex is cruelty. Here he speaks not only as a priest instructing a catechumen—as, for example, Father Flynn in **"The Sisters"** instructing the same boy narrator—but also as a father telling his son about life: "He described to me how he would whip such a boy as if he were unfolding some elaborate mystery. He would love that, he said, better than anything in this world; and his voice, as he led me monotonously through the mystery, grew almost affectionate and seemed to plead with me that I should understand him."

The *mystery*—and the word is applicable to sex as well as religion—disgusts the boy narrator, who is now anxious only to escape the father whom he has been seeking and by whom he has been welcomed. He calls for the recently disavowed Mahony. When the latter responds immediately to his summons, he feels ashamed of himself. "And I was penitent; for in my heart I had always despised him a little."

The words of penitence with which the narrator concludes the story measure his loss of hope, of which the story is the record. The narrator hoped for escape, hoped for a father who would give him the counsel and companionship he needs; instead he encounters the epitome of all he detests. He is obliged to ask for help not from the superior being for whom he is searching but from Mahony, whom he has thought his inferior. He is reduced to accepting the friendship of a commonplace contemporary for the fostering love and wisdom of a father.

Thus **"An Encounter"** is a symbolic history of the boy narrator's rejection of the authority of father, church, and state as perverted and degenerate and his despairing substitution of the friendship of a contemporary who, although mediocre, can assuage his loneliness.

"The Dead" is the acknowledged masterpiece of *Dubliners.* Even those critics who have poohpoohed many of Joyce's stories as mere sketches have expressed admiration for it; and it has probably received as much critical attention as all the other stories put together. It is therefore surprising that students of Joyce have left so many questions unanswered. They have not even been able to agree on what happens to Gabriel Conroy: some think he suffers spiritual death; others believe that he is reborn.

Several critics have pointed out that **"The Dead"** contains the ultimate epiphany of *Dubliners;* but no one has observed that the story takes place on Epiphany. The Misses Morkan's annual dance takes place at the end of the Christmas season. Aunt Kate says of Mr. Browne that "He has been laid on here like the gas . . . all during the Christmas." She also comments on the fact that Freddy Malins has come drunk to her party: " 'Now, isn't he a terrible fellow!' she said. 'And his poor mother made him take the pledge on New Year's Eve'." In Europe the end of the Christmas season is not New Year's Day—which is, moreover, ruled out by the absence of New Year's greetings at the party—but Epiphany or Twelfth Night, traditionally associated with Christmas festivities.

The most convincing reason for reading **"The Dead"** as an Epiphany story, however, is that it works. Mr. Brewster Ghiselin has pointed out [in "The Unity of *Dubliners*," excerpted in TCLC, Vol. 3, pp. 266-67] that in Ireland every one must accept material substitutes for spiritual values and that the feast in **"The Dead"** is a material substitute for spiritual communion. In my opinion, the principal incidents of **"The Dead"** are a bitter parody of the events celebrated by the Roman Catholic Church in its Epiphany Offices: the marriage at Cana, the visit of the Magi, and the Baptism of Christ. In Joyce's Ireland, these revelations are mocked.

The marriage at Cana is represented in **"The Dead"** by the encounter of Gabriel with Lily, the caretaker's daughter. Gabriel gaily suggests that "we'll be going to your wedding one of these fine days with your young man, eh?"

> The girl glanced back at him over her shoulder and said with great bitterness:
>
> "The men that is now is only all palaver and what they can get out of you."

Girls who cannot afford enough wine for the wedding do not usually get married at all in Joyce's Dublin. And Gabriel is reduced to consoling Lily for the loss of love by giving her a gold coin—a poor substitute for the turning of water into wine.

The visit of the Magi to the Christ child and their showering of gifts upon Him becomes the Misses Morkan's annual dance. Gabriel refers to the three hostesses as "the Three Graces of the Dublin musical world" and praises them for their hospitality. But although they are genuinely kindly and hospitable, they are certainly not searching for a new revelation. Their name—Morkan—suggests that they are mawkins or spectres. They are the "three potatoes"—probably cold—which Lily reserves for Gabriel.

Mary Jane, the niece, saves the best slices of goose for her pupils. Her artistic gift to the party is an elaborate academy piece which no one enjoys and which is performed principally to exhibit her technical virtuosity and to advertise her merits as a teacher. Aunt Julia—who, like one of the Three Kings, is rather hard of hearing—sings "Arrayed for the Bridal" "with great spirit," but Gabriel sees her arrayed for the bridal of death. Her voice is alive, but she is not. Aunt Kate, although she gives piano lessons, has very little knowledge of music. She does not realize that the singer Bartell D'Arcy is hoarse, but she stoutly maintains that a tenor of her youth named Parkinson—which is also the name of a disease symptomatized by progressive paralysis—is the greatest of all singers. One must admit that, despite their loyalty and lovableness, Aunt Julia and Aunt Kate are, in Gabriel's words, "only two ignorant old women"—mawkins rather than Magi.

Their world suffers, like the rest of Joyce's Dublin, from Parkinson's disease. The possibility of rebirth, of regeneration—the revelation commemorated in the Epiphany service as the Baptism of Christ—is very small indeed. Brother Pat (Patrick for Ireland, perhaps) has long been dead, and his daughter Mary Jane is a middle-aged spinster.

Their sister Ellen seemingly attempted to escape from the sterility of Ireland. At any rate, she married T. J. Conroy of the *Port and Docks.* Describes as "the brain carrier of the Morkan family" and as "serious" and "matronly," she "had chosen the names of her sons for she was very sensible of the dignity of family life." Unable to make a pilgrimage to the Holy Land to see the Infant Jesus, like the Magi, or to discover the Cross, like her prototype St. Helena, Ellen instead devotes her son Constantine to the Church. St. Helena went to the East; her son Constantine made the city of Constantinople his capital, primarily to facilitate the establishment of Christianity as the state religion of the Roman Empire against the opposition of the conservative, pagan Roman aristocracy. Ellen also seems instinctively to have recognized the East as a source of life. Constantine is part of the Roman Catholic Church, which is of course international and centered on the Continent.

Her other son, Gabriel, with his university education—for which, we are told, his mother is largely responsible—attempts to remain in touch with contemporary Europe. He spends his vacations on the Continent to keep up his languages, and he tells Miss Ivors, who wants him to vacation in the Aran Isles instead, that Irish is not his language. He makes a pitiful attempt to be European, for Europe is life to him too. But he lives in Monkstown, and his wife Gretta, whom his mother had disliked as "country cute," comes from Nuns' Island in Galway. His children Tom and Eva, at home with their nurse Bessie (a variant of Eliza), belong to the transatlantic world of *Uncle Tom's Cabin,* and his very name, as Gerhard Friedrich has noted, belongs to the hero of Bret Harte's *Gabriel Conroy,* which begins by describing a group of pioneers trapped by a blizzard in the Far West. His cousin and aunts, who live on Usher's Island—a place doubly significant because it suggests not only the decadent house of Usher but the transatlantic origin of Poe—have also "gone west."

In the climactic scene of the story, Gabriel hopes to win his wife to a new life with him—in a sense, to escape with her from Ireland: " . . . he felt that they had *escaped* from their lives and duties, *escaped* from home and friends and *run away together* with wild and radiant hearts to a new adventure" (my italics). He had been thinking of their honeymoon abroad—an escape from Ireland—and he felt that they could escape again. But the attempt is doomed to failure. Gretta belongs completely to the west. Even the word *goloshes,* which to Gabriel represents the progressiveness of European life, reminds her of the west—that is, "of Christy Minstrels." Moreover, she has been deeply moved by Bartell D'Arcy's singing of a song in "the old Irish tonality," "The Lass of Aughrim."

At the hotel Gabriel hopes to begin a new life—i.e., to be baptized, as Jesus was by John on Epiphany. But the other Epiphany revelations have been parodied rather than celebrated, and Gabriel's failure to fulfill his scriptural role as consoler is repeated. All the omens foretell disaster. The electricity in the hotel has failed, and Gabriel rejects the candle which the porter offers him. The light from the street—which Joyce describes as ghastly—will be enough for them, he says. The natural symbolism of the rejection of light is strongly reinforced by the symbolism of the lighted candle in the Epiphany ritual of the Primitive Church, in which lighted candles were carried in procession to "symbolize the spiritual illumination of Baptism."

In the "ghastly" light he learns that not only are he and Gretta not to escape again, but also that they never had escaped; that Gretta has always loved Michael Furey, her girlhood sweetheart from the West of Ireland, who, she believes, died for her. The dead had been with them from the very beginning.

The final revelation of **"The Dead"** is of the dead Michael Furey, Gretta's dead saviour—not the risen Christ. And the change in Gabriel—interpreted by some critics as the birth of a new and better man from the death of an outworn self—is his final acquiescence in death. He can afford to weep "generous tears" because he accepts the fact that he belongs among the dead. "It hardly pained him now to think how poor a part he, her husband, had played in her life. He watched her while she slept, as though he and she had never lived together as man and wife." Later he confesses to himself that he has never loved. "He had never felt like that himself towards any woman, but he knew that such a feeling must be love." Then

"His soul had approached that region where dwell the vast hosts of the dead. . . . The time had come for him to set out on his journey westward."

Michael, the Archangel of snow, has conquered Gabriel, the Archangel of fire. When Gabriel goes west (i.e., dies), the world is left to Michael, and Joyce's ultimate epiphany is of Ireland covered by snow. It is the domain of a dead man, not of the leader of the Messiah's Hosts at the Armageddon which precedes the Day of Judgment. Although surrounded by the emblems of the Passion—crosses, spears, thorns—Michael's grave is filled, not empty. His cross is covered with snow (frozen water), not dipped in flowing water, as it is in the Greek Church's commemoration of the Baptism on Epiphany. Gabriel sees the snow "falling, like the descent of their last end, upon all the living and the dead." The Day of Judgment has come, but Michael is dead. The epiphany of **"The Dead"** is a revelation of death. (pp. 33-41)

Julian B. Kaye, "The Wings of Daedalus: Two Stories in 'Dubliners'," in Modern Fiction Studies, *Vol. 4, No. 1, Spring, 1958, pp. 31-41.*

HARRY LEVIN   (essay date 1960)

[*Levin is an American educator and critic whose works reveal his wide range of interests and expertise, from Renaissance culture to the contemporary novel. He has long been an influential advocate of comparative literature studies, and he has written seminal works on the literature of several nations. Among his best-known critical works are* James Joyce: A Critical Introduction *(1941), a work partly inspired by Joyce's comment that Levin had written the best review of* Finnegans Wake; The Power of Blackness: Hawthorne, Poe, Melville *(1958); and* The Gates of Horn: A Study of Five French Realists *(1962). Levin has noted that his "focal points have been the connection between literature and society" and that his "ultimate hope is for a kind of criticism which, while analyzing the formal and esthetic qualities of a work of art, will fit them into the cultural and social pattern to which it belongs." In the following excerpt from the revised and enlarged edition of* James Joyce: A Critical Introduction, *Levin presents an overview of the literary techniques, subjects, and themes of* Dubliners.]

The reader of Joyce is continually reminded of the analogy between the role of the artist and the priestly office. The focal situation of **Dubliners** is that described in **"Araby,"** where we walk through the streets of the city, glimpsing places "hostile to romance" through the eyes of a child: "These noises converged in a single sensation of life for me: I imagined that I bore my chalice safely through a throng of foes." The same symbol is given a darker purport in the first story of the book, **"The Sisters,"** when it is recalled that the dying priest had disgraced himself by breaking a chalice. The broken chalice is an emblem, not only of Joyce's interrupted communion, but of the parched life of the metropolitan *Waste Land.* This early story is also glimpsed from the point of view of a small boy. The very first sentence consists entirely of monosyllables, and the paragraph proceeds toward a childish fascination with the word "paralysis."

Joyce's intention, he told his publisher, "was to write a chapter of the moral history of my country and I chose Dublin for the scene because that city seemed to me the centre of paralysis" [see excerpt dated 1906]. In every one of these fifteen case histories, we seem to be reading in the annals of frustration—a boy is disappointed, a priest suffers disgrace, the elopement of **"Eveline"** fails to materialize. Things almost happen. The characters are arrested in mid-air; the author deliberately avoids anything like an event. In **"The Boarding House"**—when there is some hope of a wedding—the aggressive landlady, the compromised daughter, and the abashed young man are presented in turn, and an actual interview becomes unnecessary. Joyce's slow-motion narrative is timed to his paralyzed subject. Both are synchronized with his strangely apocalyptic doctrine, which assigns to both author and characters a passive part. The author merely watches, the characters are merely revealed, and the emphasis is on the technique of exposure.

Realism had already established the artist as an observer; naturalism made him an outsider. In contrast to the promiscuous documentation of earlier novelists, the *tranche de vie* ["slice of life"] was sliced thin. A writer like Balzac, claiming to be only the secretary of society, could take a rather officious view of his position. The modern writer stands apart, waiting for a chance encounter or a snatch of conversation to give his story away. Strictly speaking, he has no story, but an oblique insight into a broader subject. Things happen just as they always do—the things you read about in the papers. There is business as usual, but it is none of his business. He is not concerned with romantic adventure or dramatic incident. He is concerned with the routines of every-day life, the mechanisms of human behavior, and he is anxious to discover the most economical way of exposing the most considerable amount of that material.

This is simply an attempt to define what is so often referred to as the *nuance*. The epiphany, in effect, is the same device. Though grounded in theology, it has now become a matter of literary technique. It has become Joyce's contribution to that series of developments which convert narrative into short-story, supplant plot with style, and turn the *raconteur* into a candid-camera expert. The measure of success, in so attenuated a form, is naturally the degree of concentration. The achievements of Chekhov and Katherine Mansfield, or Hemingway and Katherine Anne Porter, can almost be computed in terms of specific gravity. And Joyce, with **"Two Gallants,"** can say as much in fifteen pages as James T. Farrell has been able to tell us in volume after volume. It is hard to appreciate the originality of Joyce's technique, twenty-five years after the appearance of **Dubliners,** because it has been standardized into an industry. This industry is particularly well equipped to deal with the incongruities and derelictions of metropolitan life. Its typical products are the shrewd Parisian waifs of *Les hommes de bonne volonté* and the well-meaning nonentities who blunder through the pen and pencil sketches of the *New Yorker*.

In their own way, the tangential sketches of **Dubliners** came as close to Joyce's theme—the estrangement of the artist from the city—as does the systematic cross-section of **Ulysses.** They look more sympathetically into the estranged lives of others. They discriminate subtly between original sin and needless cruelty. **"Counterparts,"** in its concatenation of petty miseries, suggests the restrained pathos of Chekhov's "Enemies": it begins with an employer rebuking a clerk, and ends—after several drunken rounds—with the clerk beating his little son. Joyce's point of view, like Dickens', is most intimately associated with the children of his stories. He arranged his book under four aspects—childhood, adolescence, maturity, and public life. As the stories detach themselves, they assume what Joyce called "a style of scrupulous meanness." But "the special odour of corruption," in which he

took pride, was by no means peculiar to Dublin. It was also endemic in middlewestern villages like Sherwood Anderson's *Winesburg, Ohio.* (pp. 29-32)

If the vices of Dublin are those of any modern city, the virtues of "the seventh city of Christendom" are unique. An unconscionable amount of talking and singing and drinking goes on in **Dubliners.** This promotes style and poetry and fantasy—all peculiarly Irish qualities, and talents of Joyce. "The imagination of the people and the language they use is rich and living," Synge was discovering. The richness of Irish conversation mitigates the sordid realities of Joyce's book. He was always ready to take full advantage of the common speech of his fellow townsmen—the most expressive English he could have encountered anywhere. He could always portray life most vividly when he was writing by ear. What seems an aimless political discussion, in **"Ivy Day in the Committee Room,"** is really tight dramatic exposition. In the end the dead figure of Parnell dominates the campaign headquarters. It is his birthday, and an amateur poet is persuaded to recite a maudlin and mediocre eulogy. The finishing touch is the comment of the hostile Conservative, when pressed for his opinion: "Mr. Crofton said that it was a very fine piece of writing."

Notice the irony, so frequent with Swift, in the use of indirect discourse. In Joyce's attitude, however, there is an underlying ambiguity: he eats his cake and has it. We, too, are moved by the poem, in spite of—or perhaps because of—its cheapness. We are asked to share both the emotion and the revulsion. In **"Clay,"** with a different situation, we are subjected to the same treatment. The epiphany is no more than the moment when an old laundress stands up and sings "I dreamt that I dwelt in marble halls." She is made to boast of wealth, rank, beauty, and love—none of which she has ever possessed—"in a tiny quavering voice." A listener, affected by this pathetic incongruity, explains his tears by remarking that there is "no music for him like poor old Balfe." Here, as so often in Joyce, the music is doing duty for the feeling. The feeling is deliberately couched in a cheap phrase or a sentimental song, so that we experience a critical reaction, and finally a sense of intellectual detachment. Emotionally sated, we shy away from emotion.

Such passages have the striking and uncertain effect of romantic irony. Jean Paul's formula—"hot baths of sentiment followed by cold showers of irony"—still describes them. They show Joyce, in his isolation from society, confronted by the usual romantic dichotomy between the emotional and the intellectual. At his hands, the problem becomes a characteristically verbal one, which allows him to dwell upon the contrast between the rich connotations and the disillusioning denotations of words. Since the days of *Don Quixote* this has been a major premise for fiction. The point of **"Araby"** is the glamor of the name, and the undeception of the small boy when he learns that it stands for a prosaic church bazaar. Yet no disillusionment would seem cruel enough to justify the last sentence, which should be contrasted with the objective description of Mr. Crofton's comment: "Gazing up into the darkness I saw myself as a creature driven and derided by vanity; and my eyes burned with anguish and anger."

Another point is scored by the same method in **"Grace,"** where the distance measured lies between the benign effulgence of religious doctrine and the hangover which brings a group of businessmen back to church. The distinction between words and things, in **"Ivy Day in the Committee**

Room" and in **"Grace,"** is ground for political and religious satire. Church and state should enrich the lives of the citizens and impose a pattern on the city, but for Joyce they are tarnished symbols, broken chalices. Meanwhile, the Dubliners go their own ways. Martin Cunningham, the prominent layman, goes to church in **"Grace"** and appears at the funeral in *Ulysses.* Bartell D'Arcy, the tenor, sings a few hoarse notes in **"The Dead"** and figures in Mrs. Bloom's reminiscences. Mr. O'Madden Burke goes on writing for his paper, and Lenehan goes from bar to bar and book to book.

Joyce puts himself into his early book, not directly this time, but as he might have been if he had remained a Dubliner. Mr. Duffy, the timid socialist clerk in **"A Painful Case,"** is translating *Michael Kramer.* He meets a lady whose husband does not understand her, and who for some reason bears the name of Joyce's Italian music-master, Sinico. Though he considers falling in love with her, he continues to brood on "the soul's incurable loneliness." One day he reads in the newspaper that she has been killed in an accident of her own seeking—again the title is an echo. Again, in *Ulysses,* we hear of her funeral. Death is one of the few things that happen in *Dubliners;* it is the subject of the first and last stories in the volume. The last and longest story, **"The Dead,"** concerns the brother of a priest we meet in *Ulysses.* Gabriel Conroy is a Stephen Dedalus who stayed on to teach school and write occasional reviews, and who is already beginning to show symptoms of middle age. He is a pompous master of ceremonies at the Christmas party of his musical maiden aunts—incidentally Joyce's, and godmothers of Stephen Dedalus. Among others, he meets there a girl he knew, a Gaelic student who earnestly upbraids him for having taken his holidays abroad.

But he is a less significant character than his wife, Gretta, and she is not so significant as a memory awakened in her by a snatch of song at the end of the evening. It is the memory of a boy named Michael Furey, who had once loved her and who had died. Gabriel, who had not known of him before, feels a pang of the soul's incurable loneliness. He can never participate in this buried experience, even though it has become a part of the person he has known most intimately; he suddenly recognizes that he and Gretta are strangers. And, as he tries to imagine the dead boy, he realizes that his own identity is no more palpable to others than Michael Furey's is to him. In the light of this epiphany, the solid world seems to dissolve and dwindle, until nothing is left except the relics of the dead and the hosts of the dying. "One by one, they were all becoming shades." The final paragraph, in slow, spectral sentences, cadenced with alliteration and repetition, takes a receding view of the book itself. It sets up, like most departures, a disturbing tension between the warm and familiar and the cold and remote. In one direction lies the Class of Elements at Clongowes Wood, in the other the Universe:

> A few light taps upon the pane made him turn to the window. It had begun to snow again. He watched sleepily the flakes, silver and dark, falling obliquely against the lamplight. The time had come for him to set out on his journey westward. Yes, the newspapers were right: snow was general all over Ireland. It was falling on every part of the dark central plain, on the treeless hills, falling softly upon the Bog of Allen and, farther westward, softly falling into the dark mutinous Shannon waves. It was falling, too, upon every part of the lonely churchyard on the hill where Michael Furey lay buried. It lay thickly drifted on the crooked crosses and headstones, on the spears of the little gate, on the

> barren thorns. His soul swooned slowly as he heard the snow falling faintly through the universe and faintly falling, like the descent of their last end, upon all the living and the dead.

>   (pp. 33-7)

> *Harry Levin, in his* James Joyce: A Critical Introduction, *revised edition, New Directions, 1960, 256 p.*

ROBERT S. RYF (essay date 1962)

[*In the following excerpt from his study* A New Approach to Joyce: The "Portrait of the Artist" as a Guidebook, *Ryf discusses the motivations of characters in* Dubliners *and interprets the collection through major themes of* A Portrait of the Artist as a Young Man *(1916).*]

Dubliners has been described and studied in various ways by Joyce scholars. Some see the stories as epiphanies revealing the frustrations and defeats of modern life. Others emphasize the theme of paralysis running through the stories. Some have, with perhaps excessive ingenuity, probed the stories for Homeric parallels.

We need not quarrel with these interpretations; we are interested here in another matter: the relationship of *Dubliners* to the *Portrait* and, more particularly, the interpretation of *Dubliners* through the *Portrait.* Thus we shall be concerned primarily with those aspects of the stories which most clearly reveal their relationship to the *Portrait.*

The image or idea that organically connects the short stories to the novel is, it seems to me, that of the three nets. Stephen in the *Portrait,* it will be remembered, identifies these nets: "When the soul of a man is born in this country there are nets flung at it to hold it back from flight. You talk to me of nationality, language, religion. I shall try to fly by those nets." The image of the nets inevitably suggests related or consequent ideas. One of these is paralysis, which as Joyce and Joyce scholars have pointed out, is one of the key themes of *Dubliners.* But there is another related idea which I think is even more important—captivity. The two are not quite the same, and the difference, though apparently slight, is essential. Captivity presupposes an active restraining force, and here may be directly equated with the three nets Stephen fears and seeks to elude. Language, nationality, and religion are captors—agents of confinement, restraint, frustration. Captivity *results* in paralysis. Thus the relationship between the two ideas is one of cause and effect.

If the *Portrait* tells the story of Stephen's battle with the three nets and his attempted escape from them, *Dubliners* tells of those who did not escape. Further, among those captives may be found various projections of Stephen and his condition if he had not fled the nets.

We are introduced to captivity, paralysis, and the nets early in **"The Sisters,"** the opening story of *Dubliners.* This story concerns the death of the eccentric priest Father Flynn and its impact on the boy he had befriended and to whom he had acted as a substitute father. At the outset we see the boy gazing up at the window of the room in which Father Flynn lies dying after his third stroke:

> Every night as I gazed up at the window I said softly to myself the word paralysis. It had always sounded strangely in my ears, like the word gnomon in the Euclid and the word simony in the Cate-

chism. But now it sounded to me like the name of some malificent and sinful being. It filled me with fear, and yet I longed to be nearer to it and to look upon its deadly work.

This paralyzed priest with his stained vestments that have a "green faded look" and the oblique reference to simony clearly connote the net of religion; perhaps the connotation may be broadened to include nationality. . . . [The] "green faded look" seems to suggest not only decay but decayed Ireland. The theme of nationality is further implied in the insensitive, conformist, and anti-intellectual remarks of Mr. Cotter and the boy's uncle, as is the matriarchal state of the nation by the roles of the boy's aunt and the sisters.

Also in **"The Sisters"** we find the first projection of Stephen if he had remained in Dublin all his life. Clearly, there are analogies between Father Flynn and Stephen as we know him. The boy reads the card announcing the death of the priest:

July 1st, 1895
The Rev. James Flynn (formerly of S. Catherine's
Church, Meath Street), aged sixty-five years.
R.I.P.

We are reminded here of the passage in the *Portrait* wherein Stephen contemplates a priestly vocation. We may also be quite confident that Father Flynn's first name was not idly chosen.

There are other indications that this priest is a projection of Stephen. We learn that the priest was "too scrupulous always," that the "duties of the priesthood was too much for him," that "his life was, you might say, crossed," and that he was "a disappointed man." After he breaks the chalice, he begins to "mope by himself, talking to no one and wandering about by himself." He is finally found alone in the dark in his confession box, "Wide-awake and laughing-like softly to himself." This final vision of dementia serves as a horrifying projection of Stephen's possible condition if he had remained in Ireland and accepted the vocation to which he was by his nature unsuited.

In **"The Sisters"** the idea of captivity is strongly suggested by narrative and imagery. The priest is a captive of the Church; the Church is the captive of, or is paralyzed by, decay and corruption. "Paralysis" and "simony" are linked in the boy's mind. Ireland is a captive of the matriarchy. The sisters, performing religiously significant rituals, such as serving wine and biscuits, have usurped the function of the priesthood. And the fatherless boy is a captive not only of his aunt and uncle but of the dead priest, as he was of the living priest. Mr. Cotter's warning that a young boy should "run about and play with lads of his own age" indicates that the boy has spent a great deal of time with the priest. He cannot rid himself of the presence of the paralytic, even in the sanctuary of his own room: "But the grey face still followed me. It murmured; and I understood that it desired to confess something. I felt my soul receding into some pleasant and vicious region; and there again I found it waiting for me." The boy finds himself arrested and frustrated by the card announcing the death of the priest. "The reading of the card persuaded me that he was dead and I was disturbed to find myself at check."

The dominant images of **"The Sisters"** are invariably those of confinement. The "lighted square of window" behind which the paralyzed priest is dying, the boy's room in which

the vision of the priest pursues him, the priest's coffin, the "little room downstairs" in which the boy and the women gather for a kind of communion after the priest's death—all suggest restraint or captivity. And these images prepare us for the final image of ultimate captivity, the confession box in which the priest had been discovered laughing softly to himself in the dark.

"An Encounter," essentially a story of initiation, represents the first attempt at escape from the nets. The word "escape" appears several times in this study of an excursion of two young truants which, significantly enough, is frustrated short of its goal.

At the waterfront the two boys see a Norwegian ship and a sailor with green eyes. The "green" motif here seems to suggest creativity and imagination, as the ship from Norway suggests Ibsen, for whom Joyce, through Stephen, has expressed great admiration. But creative green changes to sinister green as the boys later encounter the perverted stranger who has a pair of "bottle-green eyes." In this felicitous phrase we have the suggestion not only of decaying Ireland but of imbibing Ireland, and the stranger, with his talk of whipping, reminds us of the pandybat episode of the *Portrait,* and thus of perverted authority, an aspect of the net of nationality. The man terrifies the boy, who at the end of the story, shouts for his comrade: "How my heart beat as he came running across the field to me! He ran as if to bring me aid. And I was penitent; for in my heart I had always despised him a little." The boy shrinks back before the vision of the stranger, and returns to the fold defeated. Escape changes to retreat.

The nature of the stranger suggests that the story is one of initiation. The two boys have attempted an escape toward a realm of fantasy fulfillment, in which motifs of the "Wild West" and the Norwegian sailing ship represent a romantic pseudo-reality. But actuality confronts them in the disturbing presence of the green-eyed man. Suggesting reality, disorder, and evil, this perverted stranger, with the "great gaps in his mouth between his yellow teeth," stands as a potential captor. That he himself is captive of his own condition is clear when we learn that "his mind was circling round and round in the same orbit." We are later to be confronted with this same image of circular captivity in the delineation of Gabriel Conroy's situation in **"The Dead."**

"Araby," another story of initiation, also represents an attempted but frustrated escape in the form of a defeated quest. Infatuated with a neighbor girl, the boy journeys to a bazaar named Araby to bring back a gift for her. But he is delayed by the thoughtlessness of his uncle, and arrives at the bazaar too late to purchase anything of value. The story ends as he gazes into the darkness, seeing himself a creature "driven and derided by vanity," his eyes burning "with anguish and anger." This moment of self-realization climaxes an exceptionally rich story in which all three nets are indicated. The name **"Araby"** suggests an escape from the Church: the boy's aunt hopes that it is not "some Freemason affair." And the name casts an "Eastern enchantment" over the boy, and in this aspect seems to stand for romance and imagination. The boy's uncle, with his unfeeling sententiousness, suggests, as in **"The Sisters,"** Ireland. Characteristically, having forgotten that the boy had planned a trip to the bazaar, he arrives home so late that the project is almost abandoned.

The net of language is treated specifically for the first time in **"Araby."** There seem to be two categories to this net. One implies a close association with nationality: we recall Stephen's sporadic attendance at, and disgust with, the Gaelic League. The other category involves *use* of language and Stephen's dedication to its creative use. The contrast between the boy's language and the language that surrounds him is graphically depicted in **"Araby"**:

> We walked through the flaring streets, jostled by drunken men and bargaining women, amid the curses of labourers, the shrill litanies of shop-boys who stood on guard by the barrels of pigs' cheeks, the nasal chanting of street-singers, who sang a *come-all-you* about O'Donovan Rossa, or a ballad about the troubles in our native land. These noises converged in a single sensation of life for me: I imagined that I bore my chalice safely through a throng of foes.

This "throng of foes," then, functions as the net of language, which the boy seeks to evade by bearing his chalice safely through. It is interesting to note here that he is attempting to do what the paralyzed priest who broke the chalice in **"The Sisters"** could not do. Readers of Joyce are well aware of the more determined and frontal assaults he made on this net of language in *Ulysses* and *Finnegans Wake.*

The patterns of **"Araby"** and **"The Encounter"** are similar. In each story the young boy pursues his romantic dream but is confronted with reality—a reality with which he is unable to cope and from which he retreats into captivity. In **"Araby"** we also find various images of confinement that reinforce the meaning of the narrative. The "blind street" on which the boy lives, the "back drawing-room" in which the priest has died, the air itself, "musty from having been long enclosed"—all these images serve to establish the condition of captivity. Significantly, the boy journeys alone to the bazaar in the third-class carriage of a deserted train. The ultimate image—the deserted bazaar hall with its empty stalls—suggests a penitentiary.

In **"Eveline"** the perspective changes but the theme remains constant. The central character is now a girl, but she too is trapped. In this story the idea of captivity receives one of its most overt statements. During most of the tale she sits looking out her window. As a picture of an unknown priest—a kind of captor—broods over her, she reviews her life. We learn that she is on the verge of eloping to Buenos Aires. Thoughts of her insular father and "the pitiful vision of her mother's life" lay powerful hands on her, goading her toward escape. But at the quay, her lover beckoning her toward the ship, she draws back, suddenly terrified at the thought of freedom. The net is too strong for her to break through: "She set her white face to him, passive, like a helpless animal. Her eyes gave him no sign of love or farewell or recognition." She shrinks back into the captivity of family, country, tradition, and past.

Weaker than the other stories, **"After the Race"** hints at, but does not clearly convey, definite meaning. The son of a *nouveau riche* Irish butcher mingles with wealthy Frenchmen and an American. He loses heavily in a game of cards. It is not clear whether this loss will prevent him from going into business with one of the Frenchmen, as his father wants him to do. Perhaps the story is intended to portray the attractiveness but impossibility of escape to a fuller life.

The meaning of **"Two Gallants"** is clearer. Corley and Lenehan, the two central characters of this ironically titled story, are representative young Dubliners. The plot, such as it is, concerns Corley's attempt to get money from a serving girl to whom he has granted his favor. At the end, he produces a coin triumphantly. The surroundings and the outlooks of the two youths are sordid, and the outlines of the net of nationality are clear. The two men are of contrasting types: Corley is the egotistical and successful lover. Lenehan seems to be another projection of Stephen. His yachting cap and rubber shoes are familiar trappings to us. His eyes twinkle occasionally with "cunning enjoyment," but in repose his face bears a "ravaged look." His conversation is tedious. In short, he is a bore, and he is plainly weary of his lot:

> His tongue was tired for he had been talking all the afternoon in a public house in Dorset Street. Most people considered Lenehan a leech but, in spite of this reputation, his adroitness and eloquence had always prevented his friends from forming any general policy against him. He had a brave manner of coming up to a party of them in a bar and of holding himself nimbly at the borders of the company until he was included in a round. He was a sporting vagrant armed with a vast stock of stories, limericks and riddles.

Parasite, talker, Lenehan is also a voyeur. Corley's purpose with the servant girl is plain, but Lenehan only wants to "get a good look" at her. Both Corley's and Lenehan's lives are sordid and empty, but Lenehan's is sterile as well.

Again, the theme of captivity or capture is implicit throughout the story. The dominant image is that of a coin—itself a symbol of ransom—which Corley exacts from the captive serving girl. Yet, as in several of the other stories, the captor is also captive. Corley, like the stranger in **"An Encounter,"** is enmeshed in his own net—that of nationality.

Perhaps the most significant passage in **"Two Gallants"** is that in which Lenehan, an obvious captive of his lot, orders and eats a plate of peas while awaiting Corley's return from the assignation. This isolated incident is not particularly significant in itself, but in context with the *Portrait* it becomes richly meaningful. At the end of the *Portrait,* Stephen, about to depart, meets Emma Clery for the last time: "Talked rapidly of myself and my plans. In the midst of it unluckily I made a sudden gesture of a revolutionary nature. I must have looked like a fellow throwing a handful of peas up into the air." These two lots of peas now suggest pottage and birthrights. Stephen, leaving Ireland, pays his ransom by rejecting the symbol of bondage, and reclaims the birthright that Lenehan, remaining behind, trapped, sells daily. This motif recurs in *Finnegans Wake,* where Shem, acting out the Jacob-Esau pattern, ". . . even ran away with himself and became a far-soonerite, saying he would far sooner muddle through the hash of lentils in Europe than meddle with Irrland's split little pea."

In **"The Boarding House,"** the boarder Mr. Doran seduces Mrs. Mooney's daughter Polly (although apparently the seduction is mutual), and is bulldozed into marrying her by Mrs. Mooney, who is of course aided by social and religious mores and pressures. Mr. Doran seems to be another projection of a settled-down Stephen. We learn that he had sown his share of wild oats as a young man, had boasted of being a freethinker, denying the existence of God to his companions in pubs. "But all that was passed and done with . . . nearly." He is now a respectable and hard-working employee of a wine merchant. (We recall that a clerkship in the brewery was once recommended for Joyce.) Doran resents Polly's bad grammar and her mother's vulgarity, but in the end he takes the only course open to him within the nets. The theme again is entrapment, the rooming house is an image of captivity, and the mother, suggesting Ireland, is the captor.

Little Chandler, the frustrated poet of **"A Little Cloud,"** is another trapped Stephen. Clerk, husband, and father, he conjures up in his mind favorable reviews for books he will never write, and realizes that one "could do nothing in Dublin." The return of Gallaher, a successful journalist, serves to crystallize Chandler's vague discontent and melancholy. He resents Gallaher's vulgarity and success while envying his experience and reputation. Convinced that he could do better if he "had a chance," he returns home and is confronted with the inartistic realities of wife, furniture, and crying baby. Unable to soothe the child, he is shouldered out of the way by his wife and, submitting to matriarchal authority, he steps back into the shadows while she deals expertly with the child. Shame and remorse visit him, and we are left to guess whether the shame is at his inadequacy or at his entrapment.

In **"Counterparts"** we meet a different version of the trapped family man. Where Little Chandler is meek, Farrington is choleric. Buffeted by a day of defeats, he pawns his watch and seeks his habitual alcoholic solace, reliving his one minor triumph of the day: an impertinent answer to his superior. But he is defeated even in his desire to get drunk—his money runs out. The vision of a plump feminine arm in a pub, together with the defeat of his own in a hand-wrestling contest, goads him into a son-beating rage upon his arrival home. This prisoner revolves in his orbit around places of confinement— office, pub, home. Our sympathies are not so directly involved with Farrington as with Little Chandler, yet we see them both as enmeshed Dubliners.

"Clay" concerns a middle-aged spinster named Maria, a cheerful but unfulfilled woman who cooks in a laundry. By name, description, and function she seems to suggest aspects of both nationality and religion. There is a certain witchlike quality about her: when she laughs, her nose and chin almost meet. She is known as a peacemaker, but she cannot establish peace between Joe, whose family she visits on Hallow Eve, and Athy, Joe's estranged brother. She brings a present to the family, but leaves it by mistake on the tram. As Joe often has said of her, "Mamma is mamma but Maria is my true mother." This "true mother" is pressed into a traditional choosing game at Joe's. Blindfolded, her hands touch clay first. But this grim reminder of death, the ultimate captor, is quickly removed and Maria, oblivious, now chooses the prayer book. She is prevailed upon to sing "I Dreamt That I Dwelt," but she omits the verse about marriage. Joyce closes with an ironic commentary: "But no one tried to show her her mistake, and when she had ended her song, Joe was very much moved. He said that there was no time like the long ago and no music for him like poor old Balfe, whatever other people might say; and his eyes filled up so much with tears that he could not find what he was looking for and in the end he had to ask his wife to tell him where the corkscrew was." If Maria is trapped, she shows no sign of awareness or rebellion, but in her very condition, into which are skillfully blended suggestions of unfulfillment, country, Church, and death, we see the outlines of the nets. And we see also the emergence of a motif to be elaborated on in **"The Dead"**—the idea of death itself, here symbolized by clay and Maria's living death, as ultimate captivity.

In **"A Painful Case"** Stephen's surrogate reappears, this time in the form of Mr. James Duffy, a middle-aged celibate whose pride and emotional impoverishment result in self-imposed isolation. In this poignant story he makes friends with a Mrs. Sinico, but when she reveals the extent of her emotional involvement he quickly draws back and they "mutually" agree to break off the alliance. He resumes his solitary ways and, four years later, learns of her degeneration and death. His initial reaction is one of self-justification, but this gives way to a feeling of guilt at having denied or rejected her love. Guilt in turn yields to despair at his own situation, and his final realization is one of his complete aloneness. His is a case history of emotional starvation. We need read only the description of his small, bare, ascetic room to realize that he is a prisoner, barred from the warm richness of the emotional life, one of the living dead, living in a cell.

In **"Ivy Day in the Committee Room"** the net of nationality is clearly manifest. This colloquy among a group of Irish ward heelers is played against the backdrop of the brooding spirit of the dead Parnell. The sordid realities of vote canvassing and of priests in politics dramatize the gulf between Parnell's ideals and practicality. The story is climaxed by the reading of a mawkish poem about the dead hero, a poem punctuated with popping corks and applauded with beery sentiment.

"A Mother" reintroduces the idea of Irish matriarchy. Mrs. Kearney, who married out of spite and who had been educated in "a high-class convent, where she had learned French and music," brings up her daughter Kathleen in like fashion and then starts promoting and managing the girl's musical career. Joyce here pokes fun at the Irish Revival: "When the Irish Revival began to be appreciable Mrs. Kearney determined to take advantage of her daughter's name and brought an Irish teacher to the house. Kathleen and her sister sent Irish picture postcards to their friends and these friends sent back other Irish postcards." Soon Kathleen is in the thick of social life with musicians and Nationalist friends who are adept enough in the old language to say "goodbye to one another in Irish." Kathleen is offered a job as an accompanist at a series of concerts, and Mrs. Kearney takes over. The concert series is poorly attended, and Mrs. Kearney further disrupts it by staging a sit-down strike, with her daughter as sitter. Using the Revival and the second-rate concert, Joyce jibes at Dublin's cultural pretensions in this story, but the central image is that of the dominating mother—one of the nets. Like the mother in **"The Boarding House,"** she seems to embody Ireland, and functions as a captor imprisoning the spirit of her daughter Kathleen.

If **"Ivy Day in the Committee Room"** exhibits the net of nationality, **"Grace"** is its religious counterpart. The story, in the nature of a parody on the *Divine Comedy,* opens with the fall of boozy Tom Kernan down some stairs into a latrine. This fall from grace gives the well-meaning and stanch supporters of the Church Messrs. Power, Cunningham, and McCoy the opportunity to attempt the regeneration of Kernan, who has not attended church for twenty years and who is "fond, moreover, of giving side-thrusts at Catholicism." Kernan's wife is willing that the attempt be made, but skeptical of its outcome: "Religion for her was a habit, and she suspected that a man of her husband's age would not change greatly before death. . . . Her beliefs were not extravagant. She believed steadily in the Sacred Heart as the most generally useful of all Catholic devotions and approved of the sacraments. Her faith was bounded by her kitchen, but, if she was put to it, she could believe also in the banshee and in the Holy Ghost." Conversing on papal infallibility in an atmosphere of genial self-righteousness and liquid cheer in Kernan's bedroom, the salvationists mention a forthcoming Jesuit retreat, to be presided over by Father Purdon. ("Fine jolly fellow! He's a man of the world like ourselves.") They all plan to attend—to "wash the pot together," as Mr. Cunningham puts it. Mr. Kernan, invited with studied casualness, is noncommittal, but when his wife enters the bedroom she is presented with a *fait accompli*. They inform her that they are all going to attend the retreat, her husband included. Mr. Kernan essays a nervous smile and says he does not really mind. A would-be rebel, he thus joins the long list of the trapped in *Dubliners.*

At the retreat Father Purdon climaxes the story as he speaks to a full house of businessmen "in a businesslike way." He proclaims himself their "spiritual accountant," and he asks everyone to "open his books, the books of his spiritual life, and see if they tallied accurately with conscience." The most important thing, he continues, is to be "straight and manly" with God. If their accounts tally, they are to say: "Well, I have verified my accounts. I find all well." But if there are discrepancies, they are to admit it like a man: "Well, I have looked into my accounts, I find this wrong and this wrong. But, with God's grace, I will rectify this and this. I will set right my accounts." Perhaps Joyce in this epiphany—this cosily unspiritual discourse—is, in addition to delineating the net of religion, here exposing the real fall from grace, the real trap.

The final story in the collection—**"The Dead"**—defies brief analysis. This remarkable work, rated by T. S. Eliot as one of the finest short stories in the English language, reinforces many of the themes of the other stories of *Dubliners.* **"The Dead"** concerns a Christmas dance given by the Misses Kate and Julia Morkan and attended by their nephew Gabriel Conroy and his wife Gretta among others. After the party Gabriel's desire for his wife is aroused, but she, because of a song she has heard at the party, is grief-stricken at the memory of young Michael Furey, who died for love of her in Galway years earlier. Gabriel's mood changes from frustrated desire and injured pride to acceptance, impersonal understanding, and union with the universal twilight of the soul.

There is at least a shadowy correspondence among **"The Dead," "An Encounter,"** and **"Araby."** In one sense, **"The Dead"** is also a story of initiation. Gabriel, like his younger counterpart in the earlier stories, learns something new about his world, and is deflated and defeated by this knowledge. The fundamental patterns of the three stories are thus roughly analogous. But the analogy ceases when Joyce, in his later and much more considerable story, carries Gabriel beyond the point of deflation and defeat to acceptance and understanding.

In one sense, the fundamental action of **"The Dead"** is a succession of deflations of Gabriel by three women. His expansive hopes for an early marriage for Lily, the serving girl, are met with her bitter retort, "The men that is now is only all palaver and what they can get out of you." Later he is deflated by Miss Ivors, a fervid Nationalist, who calls him a "West Briton." And Gretta's tale of Michael Furey is of course the final deflation.

But to ascribe so limited a theme to this story is to impoverish

it. From the title, the ending of the story, and much of what lies between, it seems clear that the over-all theme is death—more particularly, living death. The ambiguity of the snow and the Christmas season, both suggesting life and death as well, hint at the union of life and death which is the essence of the story. And the idea of decay and death is reinforced by frequent references to the superiority of the past, notably in Gabriel's speech at the dinner table. This motif is also present in such stories as **"Ivy Day in the Committee Room"** and **"Clay,"** and Gabriel's speech in the final story functions as a kind of reprise.

The relationship of **"The Dead"** to the *Portrait* is clear. First, there is in Gabriel Conroy the most nearly complete projection of Stephen to be found anywhere in *Dubliners.* By description and in attitudes he tallies closely with Stephen as he might have developed had he remained in Dublin. Essentially an unfulfilled man of letters, Gabriel feels superior to his surroundings and writes book reviews mainly so that he can fondle books. In telling and acting out the story of the mill horse who walks interminably in a circle, he is speaking more autobiographically than he knows. His manner is stiff, his conversation is stilted, and his speech on Irish hospitality is stuffy. Near the end of the story, deflated by the tale of Michael Furey, humiliated by the realization that Gretta for years "had been comparing him in her mind with another," Gabriel experiences a bitter moment of self-revelation:

> A shameful consciousness of his own person assailed him. He saw himself as a ludicrous figure, acting as a pennyboy for his aunts, a nervous, well-meaning sentimentalist, orating to vulgarians and idealising his own clownish lusts, the pitiable fatuous fellow he had caught a glimpse of in the mirror. Instinctively he turned his back more to the light lest she see the shame that burned on his forehead.

The other implication of the story which connects it with the *Portrait* is that of the nets. More completely than the other stories, **"The Dead"** shows life in the nets and, further, shows that this life is a living death.

Every person in the story is a captive. The Misses Morkan are ensnared by the past, Miss Ivors by the net of nationality; the snow, suggesting the ultimate captor—death—broods over and confines all. But with the three principals of the story—Gabriel, Gretta, and Michael Furey—the situation is more complex. I include Michael Furey as a principal character because, although dead, he governs a substantial part of the story. These three characters are mutually involved in two series of highly significant relationships.

The first of these involves captor-captive relationships. Gabriel, in some respects a total image of captivity, is the captive not only of his heritage and emotional poverty but of Gretta. Gretta is at once captor and captive. Gabriel and Michael are her captives, yet she cannot escape from Gabriel; she is also the captive of Michael, and cannot escape from the bonds of her past emotional involvement with him. And Michael is the captive of Gretta and death. He died for love of her, and his coffin represents ultimate confinement.

The second relationship is that between life and death. Death in **"The Dead"** represents figurative as well as physical lack of life. Gabriel, although physically alive, is emotionally dead. Gretta, once emotionally alive in her relationship with Michael Furey, is now emotionally dead although physically alive. And Michael, once emotionally alive, is now physically dead. Thus Joyce, relating the emotional life to the physical, suggests a vital correspondence between the two. Emotional death becomes living death.

At the end of the story Gabriel achieves a deeper vision and greater awareness of this union of life and death. In one of Joyce's most evocative and memorable passages, which begins with the tap of snow on the window and thus is reminiscent of the gravel Michael Furey used to throw at Gretta's window, Gabriel accepts this union and, moving from the specific to the general, identifies himself and all living with the universal dead. The uniting agent is the snow:

> A few light taps upon the pane made him turn to the window. It had begun to snow again. He watched sleepily the flakes, silver and dark, falling obliquely against the lamplight. The time had come for him to set out on his journey westward. Yes, the newspapers were right: snow was general all over Ireland. It was falling on every part of the dark central plain, on the treeless hills, falling softly upon the Bog of Allen and, farther westward, softly falling into the dark mutinous Shannon waves. It was falling, too, upon every part of the lonely churchyard on the hill where Michael Furey lay buried. It lay thickly drifted on the crooked crosses and headstones, on the spears of the little gate, on the barren thorns. His soul swooned slowly as he heard the snow falling faintly through the universe and faintly falling, like the descent of their last end, upon all the living and the dead.

Thus Joyce in *Dubliners* cocks a penetrating, understanding, yet ironic eye at the life he has rejected. He views the lives of those who have stayed behind, and delineates the paralysis, decay, and defeats of those lives. He imagines himself still in Dublin, and sketches in the frustrations that would have been in store for him. And over all the glimpses he affords us, we see one superimposed, central, and dominant yet always implicit image—the nets.

Perceiving the ubiquity of the nets in *Dubliners* will illuminate what has been a problem for some Joyce scholars—the motivations of the characters. If we keep the *Portrait* in mind, these motivations are painfully clear—they are the motivations of the trapped. Rebellion against the nets, resignation to them, unthinking acceptance of them, rationalization of them—these make up the motivations. And within the frame of reference that involves not only *Dubliners* but the *Portrait,* they are only too logical.

Although the stories of *Dubliners* are independently meaningful, they are, then, considerably enriched when viewed and interpreted through the *Portrait.* And *Dubliners* in turn gives meaningful background to the *Portrait.* We see in considerably more detail what Stephen is fleeing and why. The two works are mutually and organically concomitant. (pp. 59-76)

> *Robert S. Ryf, in his* A New Approach to Joyce: The "Portrait of the Artist" as a Guidebook, *University of California Press, 1962, 211 p.*

GERHARD FRIEDRICH   (essay date 1965)

[*In the following excerpt, Friedrich discusses the narrative perspective of Joyce's* Dubliners, *focusing on the collection's first and last stories—"The Sisters" and "The Dead."*]

"I am writing a series of epicleti—ten—for a paper," James Joyce confided to Constantine Curran sometime in 1904. "I have written one. I call the series *Dubliners* to betray the soul of that hemiplegia or paralysis which many consider a city." The paper to which Joyce referred was *The Irish Homestead,* and the first of the *Dubliners* stories published in its pages was **"The Sisters."** Only two other Joyce stories, **"Eveline"** and **"After the Race,"** were also printed in that journal. But the idea of a *Dubliners* sequence soon developed into a book of fifteen "epicleti," and **"The Sisters"** proved of special importance, retaining its position as the opening story, in considerably revised form. The most noteworthy revision occurred in the opening paragraph of **"The Sisters,"** which came to assume the function of a thematic prologue or overture for the entire collection, just as the concluding paragraph of the last story, **"The Dead,"** serves as a general coda. Indeed, only in the course of revising **"The Sisters"** did the key term "paralysis" enter into the book itself, though Joyce—beside using it in his letter to Curran—stressed its crucial appropriateness by explaining to his publisher [see excerpt dated 1906]: "My intention was to write a chapter of the moral history of my country and I chose Dublin for the scene because that city seemed to me the centre of paralysis."

The central consciousness of **"The Sisters"** (at least in its revised version) is that of a perceptive schoolboy, apparently orphaned, whose disturbing involvement in the life and death of a priest is narrated from hindsight in adult language. The decline of the priest is referred to as "one of those . . . peculiar cases," and the narrator remarks in the opening paragraph: "the word paralysis . . . filled me with fear, and yet I longed to be nearer to it and to look upon its deadly work." This statement, which may be autobiographical of Joyce, has much in common with Hawthorne's comment in *The Scarlet Letter:* "A strange case! . . . I must needs look deeper into it. A strange sympathy betwixt soul and body! Were it only for the art's sake, I must search this matter to the bottom!" The boy is drawn to, and seeks to look in upon and to comprehend, the destruction of the Rev. James Flynn, his supposed friend, yet he is at the same time puzzled by feeling "as if I had been freed from something by his death." Since the paralytic condition with which Joyce was concerned is symbolic and pervasive, he could not through the minds and mouths of children—big or little—give more than hints toward a diagnosis of the real disease. The unfinished sentences of the story reflect an incomplete understanding, not only on the part of the boy, but also on the part of the priest's sisters, Nannie and Eliza, and of the boy's foster parents and the visiting, garrulous Old Cotter. Yet, though the story ends vaguely and with ellipsis points, concluding only that "there was something gone wrong with him . . . ," the reader may complete the analysis by contemplating a number of clues, such as the faded and snuff-stained priestly garments and the priest's massive, truculent face, or the observation: "It was that chalice he broke. . . . That was the beginning of it."

Father Flynn is presented as a figure of unspiritual decadence, dead of a stroke in 1895 (when Joyce himself was thirteen years old), but stricken long before that by the paralyzing sin of simony. He had, however queerly, cause to be "sitting up by himself in the dark in his confession-box, wide-awake and laughing-like softly to himself." While he is pointedly associated with empty and idle and broken chalices, the high mystery of the mass had come for him to be replaced by snuff-packets of High Toast. As to his learning, impressive like that of Gabriel Conroy in the last story in *Dubliners,* the most that could be said was that "education is all very fine and large," for it did not clarify or strengthen a spiritual awareness and commitment, but produced instead an eroding skepticism. And like Gabriel Conroy also, Father Flynn had apparently no roots of loyalty in his own land, having moved from his native Irishtown to Great Britain Street. All normal human relationships—those of family, country, and religious communion—have in **"The Sisters"** suffered serious and bewildering dislocation; thought, feeling, and will are afflicted. It is a momentous fact that the light of life has been extinguished in the window of the priest's room, that the warming glow has died in his fireplace, and Joyce aims in story after paralytic story to sensitize the reader to the overwhelming, cumulative darkness.

Not only the disastrous condition to be probed, but also the method to be employed, are indicated by Joyce in his curious revision of the opening paragraph of the book. As a nimble linguist he became later notorious for his verbal chain reactions and short circuits. Here he insisted on linking the word "paralysis" with the words "gnomon" as used by Euclid and "simony" as used in the Catechism, by its supposedly similar sound, adding that it sounded also "like the name of some maleficent and sinful being." Since Euclid defined a gnomon as a parallelogram from a corner of which a parallel portion has been taken, and since paralysis and parallelogram share the characteristic of being loosened or disabled at the side, the following word-chain is suggested: paralysis-parallelogram—gnomon (implying no-man)-Simon-demon. None of these linked phenomena is solid, upright, and foursquare: they share a major lack. If paralysis may be regarded as the physical counterpart to the benumbed spiritual state of simony, then the gnomon may be viewed as perhaps the aptest geometric or structural equivalent of such a pathetically partial existence. The actual value of the gnomon lies, however, in its use as the index of a sundial, indicating the time of day by casting a shadow-line on a sun-brightened background. The world of the Dubliners Joyce chose to portray is, by contrast, a benighted world, so that Joyce had to invert the gnomonic technique, indicating Ireland's predicament by throwing a shaft of illumination into the obscure of wrongnesses with which he was preoccupied. Thus the adoption of the term "epiphany" for the enlarged perspective of those "instantaneous intensities" in which, to quote Melville, "every revelation partook more of significant darkness than of explanatory light."

It should be noted that the term "epicleti" mentioned above is at least as important to the understanding of Joyce's story-telling art, and in particular of **"The Sisters,"** as his explanation of the literary-spiritual technique of "epiphany" in *Stephen Hero*. "Epiclesis" refers to the invocation of the Holy Spirit for the purpose of consecrating the eucharistic elements of bread and wine, at the point where these are to become the body and blood of Christ the Redeemer. The paralyzing guilt of chalice-breaking lies in that spiritual and physical corruption which prevents sacramental fulfillment. It is a comprehensive ailment, of which all of Joyce's stories are symptomatic, and his "epiphanies" are therefore not so much manifestations of the spirit of redemption in mundane and trivial situations as they are occasions for a momentary acknowledgment of the very pathos of mundaneness and triviality. No new and better priest provides a happy ending to **"The Sisters."** Furthermore, the narrator's second memorable episode, **"An Encounter,"** merely accentuates a bewildered anxiety, while puff-faced Leo Dillon, who "had a voca-

tion for the priesthood," proves confused and unreliable. And the parent-less boy in **"Araby,"** bearing the empty chalice of his romantic notions to an alluringly named temple of money-changers, knows at last only the grueling sensation of utter disillusionment. Beginning with a reference to an uninhabited house at the blind end of a street in which a priest had died, the terminology and the context of **"Araby"** become appropriately and inescapably religious or quasi-religious.

If the boy's three oppressive recollections from his own childhood experience have thus distinctly a priestly reference point, the subsequent third-person stories enlarge the sense of pathos by an assortment of gnomonic men and women no less grotesque than the troubled citizens of Sherwood Anderson's *Winesburg, Ohio.* Joyce's instances of Old World hemiplegia are, however, conditioned by the decline of an ancient city civilization, and they are much more subtly drawn than Anderson's small-town Americans. The sterile spinsterhood of **"Eveline"** as of **"Clay,"** the failure of playboyish excitement in **"After the Race,"** the sordid satisfactions of pseudo-master and disciple in **"Two Gallants,"** the calculated entanglement of an eligible male in **"The Boarding House,"** the ineffectual outbursts of domesticated clerks in **"A Little Cloud"** and **"Counterparts,"** and the old-maidish obtuseness of Mr. Duffy in **"A Painful Case"**—these are all seen against a decadent Dublin, exhausted and exhausting. To highlight these debilitating influences, Joyce follows up with three stories in which patriotism has become a politician's memorial game (**"Ivy Day in the Committee Room"**), interest in art is vain and mercenary (**"A Mother"**), and the Church has withdrawn into innocuous retreat (**"Grace"**). Such, in brief, is the diagnosis of "dear dirty Dublin," as Joyce later called it in *Ulysses.* The full import of these stories, and of many of their nuances, depends however upon seeing their progressive interrelationship, and their absolute culmination in the subtlety and sweep of **"The Dead."** (pp. 421-23)

The title-term, **"The Dead,"** stands like a headstone above a buried world and applies to anything and everything in it—certainly to every one of the many characters introduced or only alluded to. With varying shades of meaning, it becomes the collective verdict with which Joyce concludes: "all the living and the dead."

The story opens with a young girl appropriately named Lily for whom the possibility of pure love has died in disillusionment, and ends with oblique reference to crucifixions in a doomed universe ("crooked crosses . . . spears . . . barren thorns.") Along the way we encounter hospitable monks who, silently, remind us of our physical and spiritual "last end" by sleeping in their coffins. The pointed explanation "that the monks were trying to make up for the sins committed by all the sinners in the outside world" and the uncomprehending question whether "a comfortable spring bed [wouldn't] do them as well as a coffin," help to generalize and domesticate the existential problem of imperfect being and imperfect communion, of life in death and death in life. The central character, Gabriel Conroy, and his nominal wife Gretta also live in Monkstown, however unaware of Joyce's implication.

The range of comic touches in **"The Dead"** is masterful, including a superb parody of after-dinner speeches, but the paralyzing effect of human limitations must essentially be a matter for serious and solemn assessment. The individuals engulfed by the cosmic snow register the physical and metaphysical winter in psychological and ethical terms. The displaced existences of **"The Dead"** belong thus with Eliot's later "The Hollow Men" and "The Love Song of J. Alfred Prufrock" as well as with Arnold's earlier "The Buried Life" and "Dover Beach" and with Hawthorne's "The Haunted Mind." They suffer from the paralysis of cowardly incompetence as much as from paralyzed vision. Their blindness being habitual, they have accumulated apparently meaningless, still-born experiences, and the tomb-womb of memories will not yield anything except in startling moments of sudden rebirth.

The paragraphs of this sophisticated story aimed at self-discovery are shot through with cumulative hints and ironic multiple *entendres*. Words and sentences echo through the pages so that the entire narrative, told in retrospect with third-person onmiscience, becomes a haunting, thought-tormenting, distant music which crescendoes into shocks of recognition. When we are told at the beginning of the Misses Morkan's annual dance that "never once had it fallen flat . . . as long as anyone could remember," we may suspect but do not know yet that not merely the party but a whole world will cave in, once somebody really remembers. When the aunts remark upon Gretta's arrival that "she must be perished alive" and ask whether "Gabriel [was] with her," and when Gabriel—"as right as the mail"—calls from the dark: "Go on up. I'll follow," the innocuous conversation is charged with all the tragic truth as the chain of events will reveal them. If what the spinster sisters Kate and Julia Morkan seem to believe in is eating well, the pathetic substitute is common enough, but Joyce proceeds to suggest the cause by directing attention to the balcony scene in *Romeo and Juliet* and Shakespeare's two murdered princes in the Tower which Aunt Julia (!) has rendered in needlework. And when Gabriel speaks of "absent faces that we miss here tonight" and admonishes his captive audience to "cherish in our hearts the memory of those dead and gone great ones whose fame the world will not willingly let die," the ghost of Michael Furey is evoked before he is ever mentioned. Joyce employs this technique of the flash-forward as freely as Shakespeare did oracles and omens; his literary determinism is worked to the point of obvious diagnosis, as when the nationalistic Miss Ivors criticizes Gabriel Conroy for not "visiting your own land . . . that you know nothing of, your own people, your own country." As storyteller, Joyce is simultaneously realistic and symbolic, notably in the following passage:

> He stood still in the gloom of the hall, trying to catch the air that the voice was singing and gazing up at his wife. There was grace and mystery in her attitude as if she were a symbol of something. He asked himself what is a woman standing on the stairs in the shadow, listening to distant music, a symbol of. If he were a painter he would paint her in that attitude. Her blue felt hat would show off the bronze of her hair against the darkness and the dark panels of her skirt would show off the light ones. *Distant Music* he would call the picture if he were a painter.

Parallel to Gabriel's perpetual failures and annoyances, half-guesses and evasions, and to his unshared passionate recollections, there runs the portentous undercurrent of Gretta's unfulfilled attraction for the boy Michael Furey, who was apparently consumed by love ("I think he died for me"). Gretta has not been able to acknowledge and accommodate the vitality of her idealized past, but in this miraculous Christmas and

New Year's season of her soul the mention of a place name (Galway) and the singing of a song ("The Lass of Aughrim") associated with the person of Michael Furey coincide to give to memories an unusual vividness and urgent voice, and to their confession an extraordinary illuminating power. While she, exhausted from the ordeal, is submerged in sleep, it is Gabriel who sees Gretta and himself honestly at last, amid the transitoriness of all earthly things. The supreme irony lies of course in the paradoxical fact that Gabriel's ultimate insights are so unnerving as to disable him: the snow melts and yet does not melt within the confines of the story. So there is need for Easter in Joyce's snowbound Christmas, the one implying the other. While the spirit of Michael Furey has risen from the grave to walk overpoweringly among the survivors, the living dead remain to be resurrected.

Since **"The Dead"** is a story of such penetrating self-realization, windows and mirrors are important to it—in contrast with closed doors and with Gabriel's "glimmering gilt-rimmed eyeglasses." Even more important is the breaking-in of unaccustomed light into the recesses of obscured privacies, ironically just when illumination is least desired. "We don't want any light. We have light enough from the street," says Gabriel jovially to the hotel porter. Yet, away from home and rid of electric light and candle, the Conroys take in quick succession these Joycean steps toward revelation:

> A ghastly light from the street lamp lay in a long shaft from one window to the door. Gabriel . . . crossed the room towards the window. He looked down into the street in order that his emotion might calm a little. Then he turned . . . his back to the light. She . . . was standing before a large swinging mirror . . . She turned away from the mirror slowly and walked along the shaft of light towards him . . . She went on to the window and stood there, looking out; . . . he did not hear her come from the window. . . . As he passed in the way of the cheval-glass he caught sight of himself in full length. . . . She looked away from him along the shaft of light towards the window in silence.

We are told incidentally: "No, it was not the moment yet," the moment of epiphany unlocking a heart heavy with memories, the gnomonic instant measuring precisely the nighttime of two who have lived beside one another in ignorance, and unfolding their convenient lies. That moment is the predetermined goal, and all sorts of "moments" (the term is used prominently in **"The Dead"**) lead up to it. When it is reached, Joyce projects the conclusion of an earlier story, **"Araby,"** to the adult level: "He saw himself as a ludicrous figure. . . ." Moreover, he converts the dubious financial generosity of Gabriel Conroy, of which several examples have been given, into genuine humaneness: "a strange friendly pity for her entered his soul. . . . Generous tears filled Gabriel's eyes."

That Gabriel Conroy, a college teacher, is particularly given to the complexities of Browning's dramatic monologues is then not surprising, but symptomatic. The experience to which he is driven may be analogous to Rabbi Ben Ezra's, but is more aptly summarized in Thoreau's lines:

> I hearing get, who had but ears,
> And sight, who had but eyes before;
> I moments live, who lived but years,
> And truth discern, who knew but learning's lore. ("Inspiration")

The perspective opened up to Gabriel and to the reader is certainly universal and religious. As to the universality, there are in this final *Dubliners* story references to Belgium, England, France, Germany, Scotland, and America, to Glasgow, London, Milan, Paris, and Symrna, and more significantly to the Aran Isles out in the Atlantic as opposed to the continent, and to such figures as Lucrezia Borgia and Mignon as well as to Shakespeare's tragedies of love and social corruption and to Browning's psychological verse portraits. As to the religious import of **"The Dead,"** the story is a parable of love versus lust, personified primarily in Michael and Gabriel, and also an allegory in which these influences modeled after the two highest archangels contend for Gretta, to whom grace is first attributed and then denied.

Since the incomplete existences of the sisters Kate and Julia Morkan, who are the party-givers among **"The Dead,"** may be regarded as crucial to the story, like their counterparts Nannie and Eliza Flynn in the first story of the *Dubliners* sequence, and since in that first story the death of the priest is in fact the main event, the titles of **"The Sisters"** and **"The Dead"** could conceivably be interchanged. This possibility suggests that the first and the last stories overlap significantly, and that the *Dubliners* sequence moves as a spiral, widening inward and outward, toward awareness and purgation. The paralysis and death of the priestly role which fascinates the boy in the first story indicates the cause of all the derangements that follow, for wherever vision is troubled and decadent, there the harmonies of spirit and flesh give way to naturalistic case studies. (pp. 423-26)

Gerhard Friedrich, "The Perspective of Joyce's 'Dubliners'," in College English, *Vol. 26, No. 6, March, 1965, pp. 421-26.*

HARRY STONE (essay date 1965)

[*In the following excerpt, Stone presents an explication of the symbolism in "Araby." For an opposing reading, see Robert P. apRoberts excerpt dated 1966.*]

"We walk through ourselves," says Stephen Dedalus in *Ulysses.* Stephen is trying to show how Shakespeare, or for that matter how any artist (creator of "Dane or Dubliner"), forever turns to the themes which agitate him, endlessly bodying forth the few crucial events of his life. "Every life is many days, day after day," says Stephen. "We walk through ourselves, meeting robbers, ghosts, giants, old men, young men, wives, widows, brothers-in-love. But always meeting ourselves." Stephen's theory may be an ingenious *jeu d'esprit*—though Joyce himself was heavily committed to such views. But whether or not Stephen's words are appropriate to Shakespeare, they are exactly appropriate to Joyce. In his writings, Joyce was always meeting himself—in ways which must at times have been beyond his conscious ordinance—and the pages of **"Araby"** are witness to that fact.

For **"Araby"** preserves a central episode in Joyce's life, an episode he will endlessly recapitulate. The boy in **"Araby,"** like the youthful Joyce himself, must begin to free himself from the nets and trammels of society. That beginning involves painful farewells and disturbing dislocations. The boy must dream "no more of enchanted days." He must forego the shimmering mirage of childhood, begin to see things as they really are. But to see things as they really are is only a prelude. Far in the distance lies his appointed (but as yet unimagined) task: to encounter the reality of experience and forge

the uncreated conscience of his race. The whole of that struggle, of course, is set forth in *A Portrait of the Artist as a Young Man.* **"Araby"** is the identical struggle at an earlier stage; **"Araby"** is a portrait of the artist as a young boy.

The autobiographical nexus of **"Araby"** is not confined to the struggle raging in the boy's mind, though that conflict—an epitome of Joyce's first painful effort to see—is central and controls all else. Many of the details of the story are also rooted in Joyce's life. The narrator of **"Araby"**—the narrator is the boy of the story now grown up—lived, like Joyce, on North Richmond Street. North Richmond Street is blind, with a detached two-story house at the blind end, and down the street, as the opening paragraph informs us, the Christian Brothers' school. Like Joyce, the boy attended this school, and again like Joyce he found it dull and stultifying. Furthermore, the boy's surrogate parents, his aunt and uncle, are a version of Joyce's parents: the aunt, with her forbearance and her unexamined piety, is like his mother; the uncle, with his irregular hours, his irresponsibility, his love of recitation, and his drunkenness, is like his father.

The title and the central action of the story are also autobiographical. From May fourteenth to nineteenth, 1894, while the Joyce family was living on North Richmond Street and Joyce was twelve, Araby came to Dublin. Araby was a bazaar, and the program of the bazaar, advertising the fair as a "Grand Oriental Fête," featured the name "Araby" in huge exotic letters, while the design as well as the detail of the program conveyed an ill-assorted blend of pseudo-Eastern romanticism and blatant commercialism. For one shilling, as the program put it, one could visit "Araby in Dublin" and at the same time aid the Jervis Street Hospital.

But the art of **"Araby"** goes beyond its autobiographical matrix. The autobiographical strands soon entwine themselves about more literary patterns and enter the fiction in dozens of unsuspected ways. For instance, embedded in **"Araby"** is a story, "Our Lady of the Hills," from a book that Joyce knew well, *The Celtic Twilight* (1893) by William Butler Yeats. "Our Lady of the Hills" tells how a pretty young Protestant girl walking through the mountains near Lough Gill was taken for the Virgin Mary by a group of Irish Catholic children. The children refused to accept her denials of divinity; to them she was "the great Queen of Heaven come to walk upon the mountain and be kind to them." After they had parted and she had walked on for half a mile, one of the children, a boy, jumped down into her path and said that he would believe she were mortal if she had a petticoat under her dress like other ladies. The girl showed the boy her two skirts, and the boy's dream of a saintly epiphany vanished into the mountain air. In his anguish, he cried out angrily, "Dad's a divil, mum's a divil, and I'm a divil, and you are only an ordinary lady." Then he "ran away sobbing."

Probably reverberating in **"Araby"** also are chords from one of Thomas De Quincey's most famous works, "Levana and Our Ladies of Sorrow." In "Levana," Our Lady of Tears (she bears the additional title, "Madonna") speaks about the child who is destined to suffer and to see, a type of the inchoate artist:

> Lo! here is he whom in childhood I dedicated to my altars. This is he that once I made my darling. Him I led astray, him I beguiled, and from heaven I stole away his young heart to mine. Through me did he become idolatrous; and through me it was, by languishing desires, that he worshipped the worm, and

prayed to the wormy grave. Holy was the grave to
him; lovely was its darkness; saintly its corruption.
Him, this young idolater, I have seasoned for thee,
dear gentle Sister of Sighs!

He who is chosen by the Ladies of Sorrow will suffer and be
cursed; he will "see the things that ought *not* to be seen, sights
that are abominable, and secrets that are unutterable," but
he will also be able to read the great truths of the universe,
and he will "rise again *before* he dies." In this manner, says
Our Lady of Tears, we accomplish the commission we had
from God: "to plague [the chosen one's] heart until we had
unfolded the capacities of his spirit."

The ideas and images of "Levana" (witness the parody in
Ulysses) had sunk deep into Joyce's imagination. His imagination had always sought out, always vibrated to, the
Levanaesque constellation—a constellation that fuses religion, sexuality, idolatry, darkness, ascension, and art.
"Araby," both in its central idea and its characteristic imagery—in the image of Mangan's sister, in the boy's blind idolatry, and in the boy's ultimate insight and dawning ascension—is cognate with "Levana."

Other literary prototypes also contribute to "Araby." In
"Araby" as in Joyce's life, Mangan is an important name. In
life Mangan was one of Joyce's favorite Romantic poets, a little-known Irish poet who pretended that many of his poems
were translations from the Arabic although he was totally ignorant of that language. Joyce championed him in a paper delivered as a Pateresque twenty-year-old before the Literary
and Historical Society of University College, Dublin, and
championed him again five years later, in a lecture at the Universita Popolare in Trieste, as "the most significant poet of
the modern Celtic world, and one of the most inspired singers
that ever used the lyric form in any country." In "Araby"
Mangan is the boy's friend, but, what is more important,
Mangan's sister is the adored girl. In each lecture Joyce discussed Mangan's poetry in words which could serve as an epigraph for the boy's mute, chivalric love for Mangan's sister
and for his subsequent disillusionment and self-disdain. In
the latter lecture, Joyce described the female persona that
Mangan is constantly adoring:

> This figure which he adores recalls the spiritual
> yearnings and the imaginary loves of the Middle
> Ages, and Mangan has placed his lady in a world
> full of melody, of lights and perfumes, a world that
> grows fatally to frame every face that the eyes of a
> poet have gazed on with love. There is only one
> chivalrous idea, only one male devotion, that lights
> up the faces of Vittoria Colonna, Laura, and Be-
> atrice, just as the bitter disillusion and the self-
> disdain that end the chapter are one and the same.

And one of Joyce's favorite poems by Mangan—a poem
whose influence recurs in *A Portrait of the Artist as a Young
Man, Ulysses,* and *Finnegans Wake*—is "Dark Rosaleen,"
a love paean to a girl who represents Ireland (Dark Rosaleen
is a poetic name for Ireland), physical love, and romantic adoration. In "Araby" Joyce took Mangan's idealized girl as an
embodiment of the artist's, especially the Irish artist's, relationship to his beloved, and then, combining the image of the
girl with other resonating literary associations, wrote his own
story of dawning, worshipful love.

It is easy to follow the external events of the story. A young
boy becomes fascinated with his boyfriend's sister, begins to
dwell on her soft presence, and eventually adores her with an
ecstasy of secret love. One day the girl speaks to him—it is
one of the few times they have ever exchanged a word—and
asks him if he is going to Araby. She herself cannot go, she
tells him, for she must participate in a retreat. The boy says
if he goes he will bring her a gift. When he finally visits the
bazaar he is disillusioned by its tawdriness and by a banal
conversation he overhears, and he buys no gift. Instead he
feels "driven and derided by vanity" and his eyes burn with
"anguish and anger."

"Driven and derided," "anguish and anger"—these reactions
seem far too strong. Indeed they seem pretentious when compared to the trivial disillusionment which caused them. And
they are pretentious, certainly they are inappropriate, if related only to their immediate external causes. But the boy is reacting to much more than a banal fair and a broken promise.
He is reacting to sudden and deeply disturbing insights.
These insights are shared by the attentive reader, for by the
end of "Araby" the reader has been presented with all that
he needs in order to resolve the story's intricate harmony into
its component motifs.

Most of those motifs, both personal and public, are sounded
at once. The former tenant of the boy's house, a house stale
with the smell of mustiness and decay, had been a priest who
had died in the back drawing room. In a litter of old papers
in a waste room behind the kitchen the boy has found a few
damp-stained volumes: "*The Abbot,* by Walter Scott, *The Devout Communicant,* and *The Memoirs of Vidocq.*" The only
additional information Joyce gives us about these books is
that the boy liked the last volume best because "its leaves
were yellow." The musty books and the boy's response to
them are doubly and trebly meaningful. Joyce chose works
that would objectify the themes of "Araby," works that
would exemplify in the most blatant (yet unexpressed) manner the very confusions, veilings, and failures he was depicting in the priest and the boy. The books and their lurking incongruities help us arraign the priest and understand the boy.
That the priest should leave a romance by Scott with a religious title that obscures the fact that it is the secular celebration of a worldly queen, Mary Queen of Scots, a queen enshrined in history as saint and harlot; a book of rules, meditations, anthems, and prayers for Holy Week by a Protestant
clergyman named Abednego Seller, a clergyman who had
written tracts against "Popish Priests," engaged in published
controversy with a Jesuit divine, and was eventually relieved
of his office; and a volume of lurid and often sexually suggestive memoirs by a notorious imposter, master of disguise,
archcriminal, and police official—all this is a commentary on
the priest and the religion he is supposed to represent. At the
same time this literary debris objectifies the boy's confusions.

That Scott's unblemished romantic heroine, an idolized
Catholic queen by the name of Mary, should also be (though
not to Scott) a "harlot queen," a passionate thrice-married
woman who was regarded by many of her contemporaries as
the "Whore of Babylon," as a murderess who murdered to
satisfy her lust—this strange dissonance, muted and obscured
by Scott's presentation, is a version of the boy's strikingly
similar and equally muted dissonances. That the dead priest's
book of devotions is a Protestant manual by a man bearing
the significant name, Abednego Seller—a name which combines in equal parts ancient religious associations (in particular associations of refusing to worship a golden image and of
a faith strong enough to withstand a fiery furnace) with an
ironically incongruous modern surname that has to do with

selling and commercialism—this juxtaposition, position, also, is appropriate to the boy: it typifies one of his fundamental confusions.

That Vidocq should escape from a prison hospital disguised in the stolen habit of a nun, a veil over his face; that he should then assist a good-natured curé in celebrating mass, pretending to make the signs and genuflections prescribed for a nun—this is a version of what the boy will do. That *The Memoirs* should also contain the history of a beauty "who seemed to have been created as a model for the divine Madonnas which sprang from the imagination of Raphael," whose eyes "gave expression to all the gentleness of her soul," and who had a "heavenly forehead" and an "ethereal elegance"—but who, from the age of fourteen, had been a debauched prostitute who was ultimately caught by the police because, in the midst of committing a robbery, she and her accomplice became utterly engrossed in fornicating with one another—this, also, is a version, a grotesque extension, of the boy's confusions. The boy does not know, can not face, what he is. He gazes upon the things that attract or repel him, but they are blurred and veiled by clouds of romantic obfuscation: he likes *The Memoirs of Vidocq* best not because of what it is, a volume of exciting quasi-blasphemous criminal and sexual adventures, but because he finds its outward appearance, its yellowing leaves, romantically appealing. The boy, like the priest, or Vidocq's characters, or disguise-mad Vidocq himself, is, in effect, an imposter—only the boy is unaware of why he feels and acts as he does; the boy is an imposter through self-deception.

Joyce, in accordance with his practice throughout *Dubliners* (and for that matter, in accordance with his method throughout his writings) included these books so that we would make such generalizations about the priest and the boy. This is clear, not merely from his habitual usage in such matters or from the ironic significance of the books themselves, but from the highly directive import of the sentences which immediately follow these details. These sentences tell us that behind the boy's house was a "wild garden" containing a "central apple-tree"—images which strongly suggest a ruined Eden and Eden's forbidden central apple tree, a tree which has to do with man's downfall and his knowledge of good and evil: fundamental themes in **"Araby."** The last of the sentences is artfully inconclusive. "He had," concludes the narrator, "been a very charitable priest; in his will he had left all his money to institutions and the furniture of his house to his sister." Joyce's ambiguity suggests that the priest's charity may have been as double-edged as other details in the opening paragraphs. Yet the possibility of an incongruity here never occurs to the boy. As usual he fails to examine beneath the veneer of outward appearances; he fails to allow for the possibility of a less public, more cynical interpretation of the priest's charity. If this worldly priest had been so "very charitable" why, at his death, was he able to donate "all his money" to institutions? His charity, so far as we know about it, began at his death.

These and other ambiguously worded ironies had already been sounded by the three opening sentences of **"Araby."** Joyce begins by telling us that North Richmond Street is blind. That North Richmond Street is a dead end is a simple statement of fact; but that the street is blind, especially since this feature is given significant emphasis in the opening phrases of the story, suggests that blindness plays a role thematically. It suggests, as we later come to understand, that

the boy also is blind, that he has reached a dead end in his life. Finally, we are told that the houses of North Richmond Street "conscious of decent lives within them, gazed at one another with brown imperturbable faces." These words, too, are ironic. For the boy will shortly discover that his own consciousness of a decent life within has been a mirage; the imperturbable surface of North Richmond Street (and of the boy's life) will soon be perturbed.

In these opening paragraphs Joyce touches all the themes he will later develop: self-deluding blindness, self-inflating romanticism, decayed religion, mammonism, the coming into man's inheritance, and the gulf between appearance and reality. But these paragraphs do more: they link what could have been the idiosyncratic story of the boy, his problems and distortions, to the problems and distortions of Catholicism and of Ireland as a whole. In other words, the opening paragraphs (and one or two other sections) prevent us from believing that the fault is solely in the boy and not, to some extent at least, in the world that surrounds him, and still more fundamentally, in the nature of man himself.

The boy, of course, contributes intricately to his own deception. His growing fascination for Mangan's sister is made to convey his blindness and his warring consciousness. Joyce suggests these confusions by the most artful images, symbolisms, and parallelisms. The picture of Mangan's sister which first sinks unforgettably into the boy's receptive mind is of the girl calling and waiting at her doorstep in the dusk, "her figure defined by the light from the half-opened door," while he plays in the twilight and then stands "by the railings looking at her." "Her dress," he remembered, "swung as she moved her body and the soft rope of her hair tossed from side to side."

This highly evocative, carefully staged, and carefully lit scene—it will recur throughout the story with slight but significant variations—gathers meaning as its many details take on definition and thematic importance. That importance was central to Joyce, and versions of the scene occur often in his writings. As his Mangan essay (1902) indicates, he had early chosen the adored female as an emblem of man's vanity, an emblem of false vision and self-delusion followed by insight and self-disdain. The female who appears in **"Araby"** (she appears again and again in his other writings) is such an emblem. The prototypical situation in all these appearances is of a male gazing at a female in a dim, veiled light. There are other features: the male usually looks up at the female; he often finds her standing half obscured near the top of some stairs and by a railing; he frequently notices her hair, her skirts, and her underclothes. But though the scene varies from appearance to appearance, the consequences are always the same. The male superimposes his own idealized vision upon this shadowy figure, only to have disillusioning reality (which has been there unregarded all the time) assert itself and devastate him. Joyce found this scene—with its shifting aureola of religious adoration, sexual beckoning, and blurred vision—infinitely suggestive, and he utilized it for major effects. (pp. 375-83)

"Araby" is a version—perhaps the most primordial version in Joyce—of this obsessively repeated scene. For in **"Araby"** the image of the worshipped girl is coterminous with, is a metaphor of, the entire story. The boy in **"Araby,"** like [Gabriel Conroy in **"The Dead"**], will soon see that the portrait he has created—a romantic portrait that one might call *Young Adoration*—is a mockery, and his life will never again be the same. In **"Araby"** that portrait is of a girl in the dusk at her doorstep calling and waiting at her half-opened door, her figure defined by the light behind her. The picture is also of a boy standing by the railings looking up at her worshipfully. The suggestions evoked by the scene are of two utterly opposed sorts. On the one hand the image calls up associations of religious worship and spiritual adoration—the boy at the altar railing venerating a softly lit statue of the Virgin Mary—associations which will soon be powerfully underlined and elaborated. On the other hand, the image also suggests a seductive girl, even a harlot, calling and waiting at her half-opened door—the boy stares at her outlined figure, her swaying dress, her moving body, and her softly swinging hair—and these suggestions, too, will soon be underlined and elaborated. Lastly the image suggests Ireland, a country traditionally personified in Irish literature as a beautiful girl who is worshipped with mystical fervor. The two most famous literary embodiments of this personification are Cathleen ni Houlihan and Dark Rosaleen, the latter given its definitive popular form in "Dark Rosaleen," the poem by Mangan that Joyce knew so well. In **"Araby"** Mangan's sister is adored and worshipped as Dark Rosaleen is in Mangan's poem, a parallel which many Irish readers would note at once, and a parallel which helps suggest that Mangan's sister is an embodiment of Ireland, is a new and more equivocal Dark Rosaleen. In **"Araby"** the girl is known only as Mangan's sister, an awkward and unaccountable substitute for a name (Mangan, the boy, is of no importance in the story) until one realizes that the circumlocution is designed to catch the reader's attention and direct his associations. Once the Mangan-"Dark Rosaleen" associations are called up, the parallels become charged with meaning. For Mangan's poem contains the same blend of physical love and religious adoration that Joyce makes the boy show for Mangan's sister. Dark Rosaleen has "holy, delicate white hands," is "my virgin flower, my flower of flowers," and can make the lover "kneel all night in prayer." Dark Rosaleen's name is like "lightning in my blood"; Mangan's sister's name is "like a summons to all my foolish blood." The poem exactly depicts the boy's unrest, his obsessive focus on the girl, his fusion of queen and saint, and his strange holy ardor:

> All day long, in unrest,
>   To and fro, do I move.
> The very soul within my breast
>   Is wasted for you, love!
> The heart in my bosom faints
>   To think of you, my Queen,
> My life of life, my saint of saints,
>   My Dark Rosaleen!
>   My own Rosaleen!
> To hear your sweet and sad complaints,
> My life, my love, my saint of saints,
>   My Dark Rosaleen!

Joyce begins, then, with a subtly evocative blend of spirituality, sexuality, and nationality; he immediately goes on to develop each motif in concert with the others. The boy remembers Mangan's sister as a "brown figure," and every morning, in an unvarying ritual, he actually prostrates himself before her image, lying on the floor in the front parlor and waiting for her to emerge so that he can follow her. This ritualistic abasement and prostration is appropriate to the boy's rapidly developing obsession. Like De Quincey's young boy, he has had his heart stolen away; he, too, has become idolatrous; through this girl, "by languishing desires," he has, all un-

known to himself, "worshipped the worm, and prayed to the wormy grave."

For the boy has begun to worship Mangan's dark sister as all that is spiritual and holy and romantic; he has begun to utilize her idolatrously as an interceding saint, as a charm against the commercialism and materialism of the market place. When on Saturday evenings the boy accompanies his aunt in her marketing, the "image" of Mangan's sister is always with him. The language of the passage suggests that unconsciously, from the boy's point of view, two warring services are being conducted in the market place: the world's materialistic service in worship of mammon, and the boy's holy service in worship of his mild madonna. The "flaring streets" are filled with their proper votaries: drunken men, bargaining women, and cursing laborers; they are also filled with an appropriate liturgical music: the "shrill litanies" of shopboys, the "nasal chanting" of street singers. In this materialistic world, so hostile to all that the boy imagines he believes in, he keeps himself inviolate by invoking his own secret service of worship. That service transmutes the stubborn commonplaces of everyday life into holy artifacts, holy strivings, and holy deeds of chivalry. The image of Mangan's sister becomes his sacred chalice; he guards it as he makes his way through the alien market place. "I imagined," he says, as he walks one Saturday evening through the market place, his mind fixed on the holy "image" of Mangan's sister, "that I bore my chalice safely through a throng of foes." This religious imagery continues to clothe and veil his impulses. He soon finds himself venerating his lady in "strange prayers and praises." His eyes often fill with tears, emotion floods from his heart; he wonders how he could ever tell her of his "confused adoration."

One evening, while in this excited state of sensual religiosity, the boy enters the back drawing room in which the priest had died. Thus begins the first of two vigils the boy will keep for Mangan's sister. The boy is about to lose himself in an ecstasy of devotion, and Joyce wants us to see that the boy is tenanting the same rooms and worshipping at the same shrines as the dead priest; that is, that the boy, like the priest, has begun to mix devotion with profanation, spirituality with materialism. The evening is dark and rainy. Through a broken pane the boy hears "the rain impinge upon the earth, the fine incessant needles of water playing in the sodden beds." The collocation of images is part of a cluster that Joyce used throughout his writings to suggest earthiness and bodily appetites (just before Mangan's sister's first appearance Joyce associated the boy with "dark dripping gardens where odours arose from the ashpits, [and] the dark odorous stables") and now, watching the rain and the earth and the sodden beds through his broken window, the boy again begins his confused adorations. Below him gleams "some distant lamp or lighted window"—Joyce continues to light his special scenes in ways equally suggestive of a sanctuary or a brothel—and then the blind boy, living on his blind street, looking through his broken window, says with deepest irony: "I was thankful that I could see so little."

In a moment the boy will be invoking love incarnate; senses veiled, swooning in self-delusion, palms pressed together in devotion, he will murmur his fervent prayers. Joyce conveys this tremulous sublimation—how the boy veils his sensual responses in the garment of religious ritual—by the most artfully directive language. "All my senses," says the boy, "seemed to desire to veil themselves and, feeling that I was about to slip from them, I pressed the palms of my hands together until they trembled, murmuring: '*O love! O love!*' many times." Every phrase is loaded with ironic meaning. The boy does not realize how truly his senses are veiling themselves (or for that matter, in what manner they are being veiled), nor does he understand, in the context, the religious connotations of the word "veil," or the physical connotations of the word "desire"; and slipping from his senses is what he emphatically is not doing as he tremblingly invokes Love.

The next sentence in the story, one which begins a new paragraph, is short and disconcerting: "At last she spoke to me." The abrupt transitionless juxtaposition of the boy's swooning invocation of Love, palms pressed prayerfully together, and the girl's sudden apparition is purposely ambiguous. Without saying so—without, that is, introducing the supernatural by having the girl materialize before him upon his prayerful invocation (for the remainder of the passage makes it clear that the girl did not speak to him that night), Joyce suggests, at least he gains the effect, that a visitation, an epiphany, has indeed occurred as a result of the boy's invocation. But whom has the boy invoked? Love? The Virgin? His Lady? Ireland? Levana? A harlot? He is too confused to know. The girl's first words to him—"Are you going to Araby?"—confound him. It will be a "splendid bazaar," she tells him; she would "love" to go, but she must attend a retreat in her convent. The boy is "so confused" he does "not know what to answer." His confusion is understandable. For here in epitome are correlatives of the very things that have confused and will continue to confuse him: materialism (the splendid bazaar), sensuality (love), and spirituality (the convent retreat).

As Mangan's sister speaks to him, she turns a "silver bracelet round and round her wrist." The boy stands "alone at the railings," gazing at this Madonna of the Silver Bracelet. "She held one of the spikes, bowing her head towards me. The light from the lamp opposite our door caught the white curve of her neck, lit up her hair that rested there and, falling, lit up the hand upon the railing. It fell over one side of her dress and caught the white border of a petticoat, just visible as she stood at ease." (pp. 386-90)

This second evocation of Mangan's sister is . . . filled with strange harmonies. On the one hand the passage calls up Mary Magdalene and the Blessed Virgin Mary (both were present at the crucifixion) and soft overtones of a tender and dolorous *pietà*; one easily extracts and then extrapolates the appropriate images—the patient hand on the cruel spike, the gentle head bowed submissively, the mild neck arched in grief. But a coequal and co-ordinate pattern in the scene is the harlotry associations of Mary Magdalene, who, in Catholic liturgy, is specifically associated with exotic Near Eastern imagery, bracelets, and crossing the city in search of her love—all strong elements in **"Araby"**; while on the more personal level the name "Mary" is also the name of the girl Joyce regarded as his original "temptress" and "betrayer"—Mary Sheehy; and perhaps, at the same time, this "shady Mary" pattern is connected with the harlotry associations of still another Mary, the "harlot queen," Mary Queen of Scots, the heroine of the dead priest's book, *The Abbot,* who was executed in her petticoat. In any case, the negative pattern incorporated in the shadowy image of Mangan's sister combines hints of commercialism and sensuality with connotations of sexuality and betrayal—the turning and turning of the silver bracelet, the head bowing toward the boy, the white curve of the bare neck, the soft hair glowing in the light, the side of

the dress accentuated by the dim glow, the white border of the petticoat just visible beneath the dress (one recalls the dream-shattering petticoat of the false Protestant madonna in "Our Lady of the Hills"), and the whole figure standing at ease in the dusk.

The boy now makes his pledge. "If I go," he says, "I will bring you something." The consequences of his pledge are immediately apparent. "What innumerable follies," writes the narrator in the very next sentence, "laid waste my waking and sleeping thoughts after that evening!" The shadowy "image" of Mangan's sister constantly comes between him and everything he undertakes; his schoolmaster, puzzled and then exasperated, hopes that he is "not beginning to idle"—a phrase which again, now punningly, underlines that the boy, like De Quincey's young boy, has indeed begun to worship false idols, that he is well on his way to Araby.

Araby—the very word connotes the nature of the boy's confusion. It is a word redolent of the lush East, of distant lands, Levantine riches, romantic entertainments, mysterious magic, "Grand Oriental Fêtes." The boy immerses himself in this incense-filled dream world. He tells us that "the syllables of the word *Araby* were called to me through the silence in which my soul luxuriated and cast an Eastern enchantment over me." That enchantment, or to put it another way, Near Eastern imagery (usually in conjunction with female opulence or romantic wish fulfillment), always excited Joyce. It reappears strongly in *Ulysses* in a highly intricate counterpoint, which is sometimes serious (Molly's Moorish attributes) and sometimes mocking (Bloom's dream of a Messianic Near Eastern oasis). But the boy in **"Araby"** always interprets these associations, no matter how disparate or how ambiguous they are, in one way: as correlatives of a baroquely beatific way of living. Yet the real, brick-and-mortar Araby in the boy's life is a bazaar, a market, a place where money and goods are exchanged. The boy is blind to this reality lurking beneath his enchanted dream. To the boy, his lady's silver bracelet is only part of her Eastern finery; his journey to a bazaar to buy her an offering is part of a romantic quest. But from this point on in the story the masquerading pretenses of the boy—and of his church, his land, his rulers, and his love—are rapidly underlined and brought into a conjunction which will pierce his perfervid dream world and put an end to "enchanted days."

The boy has arranged with his aunt and uncle that he will go to the bazaar on Saturday evening, that is, on the evening of the day specially set aside for veneration of the Virgin Mary. Saturday evening arrives but the boy's uncle is late from work and the boy wanders at loose ends through the empty upper reaches of his house. In the "high cold empty gloomy rooms" he begins his second vigil. Off by himself he feels liberated. He goes from room to room singing. Hidden, he watches his companions play and listens to their weakened, indistinct cries. Then he leans his forehead against a cool window pane and looks over at the "dark house" where Mangan's sister lives. "I may have stood there for an hour, seeing nothing but the brown-clad figure cast by my imagination, touched discreetly by the lamplight at the curved neck, at the hand upon the railings and at the border below the dress."

When he goes downstairs again he is brought back from the isolated world of his imagination to the ordinary world of his everyday life. He finds Mrs. Mercer sitting at the fire. "She was an old garrulous woman, a pawnbroker's widow, who collected used stamps for some pious purpose." The sentence is packed with ironic meaning. The old lady's name—Mercer, that is, merchandise, wares, a small-ware dealer—links her to the commercial focus of the story. That her husband was a pawnbroker sharpens this focus, introducing as it does commercialism in its most abhorrent form from the church's point of view—commercialism as usury. But that the church accepts, even lives on, this same commercialism is also made clear: for garrulous old Mrs. Mercer (another embodiment of Ireland) is a pious woman with pious purposes; ironically, she expresses her piety in good works that depend upon empty mechanical acquisitiveness: she collects used stamps. (One recalls, in this connection, the "pious purpose" of the actual Araby bazaar—to collect money for a hospital; and one also recalls that the "Wonderful" or "Perfumed" bazaar in *Ulysses*—the bazaar that allowed Bloom to gaze worshipfully under Gerty's skirts while a choir celebrated the Host and hymned the Virgin Mary—was an attempt to collect money for another "pious purpose," for a hospital named "Mercer's.") Joyce is saying, in effect, that everyday religion and piety in Ireland are based upon self-deluding and mindless materialism. When Mrs. Mercer's unexamined commercial religion is remembered in conjunction with the boy's and then the dead priest's (one recalls that the priest's book of heretical devotions was by a man named "Seller")—we get some idea of how insidiously mammonistic is Ireland's religious bankruptcy.

The boy will soon have some insight into this and other bankruptcies, but at the moment he is taut with frustrated anticipation. "I am afraid," says his aunt, when his uncle still fails to appear, "you may put off your bazaar for this night of Our Lord"—counterpointing "bazaar" and "Our Lord," money and religion. Then, at nine o'clock, the uncle finally returns, tipsy and talking to himself. He has forgotten the bazaar, and he tries to put the boy off, but the aunt insists that he give the boy money for the bazaar, and he finally agrees, after the boy tells him twice that he is going to Araby. The word "Araby" sets the uncle's mind working. He asks the boy if he knows "The Arab's Farewell to His Steed," and as the boy leaves the room, the uncle is about to recite the opening lines of the poem to his wife. Those lines never appear in the story, but they are fraught with thematic significance:

> My beautiful, my beautiful! that standeth meekly by,
> With thy proudly-arched and glossy neck, and dark and
>   fiery eye!
> Fret not to roam the desert now with all thy wingèd speed;
> I may not mount on thee again!—thou'rt sold, my Arab
>   steed!

The notion of betrayal, of something loved and beautiful being sold for money, of something cherished and depended upon being lost forever, is central to what has already happened in **"Araby"** and what is about to take place. But the poem goes on with even greater cogency:

> The stranger hath thy bridle-rein, thy master hath his
>   gold;—
> Fleet-limbed and beautiful, farewell!—thou'rt sold, my
>   steed, thou'rt sold!

This cogency—turning the bridle reins over to a foreign master for money, saying farewell to a beautiful part of the past—has another and even more startling appropriateness. For the poem is by Caroline Norton, a great beauty and a member of a famous Irish family (her grandfather was Richard Brinsley Sheridan), who was sued for divorce by her husband, the Hon. George Chapple Norton, on the grounds that she had

committed adultery with Lord Melbourne, then Home Secretary but at the time of the suit in 1836 prime minister of Great Britain. As Home Secretary, Lord Melbourne had been the minister responsible for Ireland, and in 1833, while still Home Secretary, he had supported the Coercion Bill, a bill of great severity aimed at Irish nationalists. The trial which ensued—one of the most notorious in the nineteenth century—was used by Dickens in the breach-of-promise suit in *Pickwick,* by Thackeray in the Lord Steyne-Becky Sharp relationship in *Vanity Fair,* and by Meredith in some of the climactic scenes of *Diana of the Crossways.* The jury found for the defendants, but chiefly on grounds other than Caroline Norton's constancy. The defendants won after conclusive testimony was introduced showing that Norton had been the chief advocate of his wife's liaison with Lord Melbourne, that he had initiated and perpetuated the liaison as a means of advancing himself, and that he had brought suit only after he had suffered reverses in that advancement.

That an Irish woman as beautiful as Caroline Norton should have been sold by her husband for English preferments; that she should have been sold to the man who, in effect, was the English ruler of Ireland; that she, in turn, should have been party to such a sale; that this very woman, writing desperately for money, should compose a sentimental poem celebrating the traitorous sale of a beautiful and supposedly loved creature; and that this poem should later be cherished by the Irish (the uncle's recitation is in character, the poem was a popular recitation piece, it appears in almost every anthology of Irish poetry)—all this is patently and ironically appropriate to what Joyce is saying.

So also is the next scene in **"Araby."** The boy leaves his house on the way to Araby with a florin, a piece of silver money, clutched tightly in his hand. That Joyce, out of all the coins and combinations of coins available to him, chose to have the boy clutch a florin is doubly meaningful. The original florin, the prototype of all future coins bearing that name, was a gold coin, famed for its purity, minted in Florence in 1252. It received its name, "florin," that is "flower," because, like many of its progeny, it bore a lily, the flower of Florence and of the Virgin Mary, on one side. On the other side it bore the figure of Saint John the Baptist in religious regalia, a man who gave his life rather than betray his religion. The florin the boy clutches, however, is a silver coin minted by the English with a head of Queen Victoria on one side and the Queen's coat of arms (including the conquered harp of Ireland) on the other. Owing to the fact that the customary "Dei Gratia, F.D." ("by the grace of God, defender of the faith") was omitted from the coin when originally issued in 1847, it became infamous as the "Godless and Graceless Florin" and aroused such a popular outcry that it had to be called in before the year was out. As a result, the Master of the Mint, a Roman Catholic, was dismissed, and a few years later a new but almost identical florin was issued with the usual motto. The malodorous genesis of the English coin, its association with a Catholic scapegoat, and the restitution of a motto which, from an Irish Catholic point of view, made the coin as idolatrous and offensive as the Godless version—all this is ideally suited to Joyce's purpose.

For the duped boy is now acting out his betrayal in the most emblematic way. We recall the intricate liturgy of his self-delusion. Despising the market place, he had summoned and protected the image of Mangan's sister as a holy chalice antithetical to all such worldly commerce; mistaking his impulses, he had transformed his sexual desires into prayers and praises for the Virgin, into worshipful Catholic devotions. That the boy who immersed himself in such ceremonious self-deception should be hastening to buy at a bazaar (where, incidentally, he will meet his English masters) and that he should be clutching an English florin, an alien and notorious silver coin sans Virgin's lily and sans Catholic saint but bearing instead symbols of his and Ireland's servitude and betrayal, is, of course, supremely ironic.

That irony continues and expands in what follows. It is Saturday night. The boy tells us that "the sight of streets thronged with buyers and glaring with gas recalled to me the purpose of my journey." The flaring streets "thronged with buyers" and the clutched silver coin call to the reader's mind a purpose far different from that which the boy thinks he is pursuing. The sights, the words, the Saturday evening, the silver florin, also recall that the last time the boy went into the flaring streets shopping through throngs of buyers on a Saturday night, he had said, speaking particularly of those buyers, "I imagined that I bore my chalice safely through a throng of foes." They recall also that Saturday is the day most particularly devoted to veneration of the Blessed Virgin Mary. We now see clearly what the boy bears through a throng of foes, what his chalice is: it is not the image of a mild spiritual madonna, it is money, the alien florin of betrayal—betrayal of his religion, his nation, his dream of supernal love; he, like his country, has betrayed himself for the symbolic piece of alien silver he clutches in his hand as he hurries on to Araby. We also begin to get a better notion of who the shadowy madonna is that he worships with such febrile spirituality. We recall that he is rushing headlong to a bazaar to buy his lady a token (he, too, is one of the throng of buyers), and then we recall how his madonna—could she be a false, sensual, materialistic madonna, a projection of his own complicated self-betrayal?—"turned a silver bracelet round and round her wrist."

The boy at last arrives at the large building which displays "the magical name" of *Araby.* In his haste to get into the closing bazaar, he passes through a shilling rather than a sixpenny entrance, handing the gatekeeper his silver coin as he goes through the turnstile. The interior of the building is like a church. The great central hall, circled at half its height by a gallery, contains dark stalls, dim lights, and curtained, jar-flanked sanctuaries. Joyce wants us to regard this temple of commerce as a place of worship. "I recognised a silence," says the boy as he stands in the middle of the hall, "like that which pervades a church after a service." The service is, of course, the worship of mammon, and Joyce, by his use of religious imagery here and throughout the story, lets us see both that the money-changers are in the temple (if one looks at the bazaar as a correlative of the church), and that the really devout worship which goes on in Ireland now, goes on in the market place: the streets thronged with buyers, the shrill litanies of shopboys, the silver-braceleted madonnas, the church-like bazaars. Even he who imagined that he bore his chalice safely through a throng of foes finds himself in the temple of the money-changers ready to buy. Shocked, and with growing awareness, the boy begins to realize where he is and what he is doing. In the half-dark hall, as the bazaar closes and the remaining lights begin to go out, he watches as two men work before a curtain lit overhead by a series of colored lamps upon which a commercial inscription is emblazoned. The two men "were counting money on a salver. I listened to the fall of the coins." The boy also has fallen. We recall the "wild garden"

with its "central apple-tree," that the words "falling" and "fell" are crucial to the description of Mangan's sister during her epiphany before the boy, and that the word "fall" again recurs—again in connection with money—when the boy, in his penultimate action, an action reminiscent of how Judas let the silver of betrayal fall upon the ground after his contrition, allows "two pennies to fall against the sixpence" in his pocket as he finally turns to leave the bazaar. But right now the fallen boy is witnessing the counting of the collection before the sanctuary of this church of mammon (the curtain, the salver, the lamps, the inscription all suggest simultaneously the sanctuary of a Catholic church); he is listening to the music of this service of mammon, the clink of falling coins. The boy is so stupified that he can remember only "with difficulty why [he] had come."

His shock and his disillusionment are not yet over. He sees a young saleslady standing at the door of one of the dark stalls. The reader, like the boy, instantly feels that he has viewed this scene before: the girl standing in the doorway, the dim lighting, the churchlike atmosphere. Then, suddenly, the reader realizes that the scene enforces a crucial juxtaposition; the waiting salesgirl is a parody of the boy's obsessive image of female felicity, she is a counterpart (an everyday, commercial counterpart) of Mangan's tenebrous sister. The boy looks steadily at this vulgar avatar of his longings; and then his other vision—his vision of a comely waiting presence, of a heavenly dolorous lady—dissolves and finally evaporates. The boy, at last, glimpses reality unadorned; he no longer deceives himself with his usual romanticizing. For the moment, at least, he truly sees. There before him stands a dull, drab, vacuous salesgirl; she is no mild Irish madonna, no pensive *pietà,* no mutely beckoning angel. He listens as she talks and laughs with two young gentlemen; the three of them have English accents:

> "O, I never said such a thing!"
>
> "O, but you did!"
>
> "O, but I didn't!"
>
> "Didn't she say that?"
>
> "Yes, I heard her."
>
> "O, there's a . . . fib!"

This snippet of banal conversation is Joyce's, the boy's, and now the reader's epiphany—the word "epiphany" used here in Joyce's special literary sense of "a sudden spiritual manifestation, whether in the vulgarity of speech or of gesture or in a memorable phase of the mind itself "—and the conversation the boy overhears bears an unmistakable resemblance to a well-defined type of epiphany which Joyce recorded (bald exchanges of fatuous, almost incoherent conversation), several examples of which have survived. But what we have here is the epiphany surrounded by all that is needed to give it significance; the private *quidditas* has been transformed into a public showing forth; the artist, the priest of the eternal imagination, has transmuted (to paraphrase another of Joyce's religious metaphors) the daily bread of experience into the radiant body of everliving art.

For what the boy now sees, and what we now know he sees, is that his worshipped madonna is only a girl, like the ordinary girl who stands before him, that his interest in his madonna is akin to the gentlemen's interest in the young lady before them, and that their pedestrian conversation about fibbing—the very word is a euphemism for "lying"—is only a banal version of his own intricate euphemisms, his own gorgeous lying to himself. Like the Catholic boy in Yeats' "Our Lady of the Hills," who sobs in anguish because his vision of a palpable madonna must give way to the reality of an ordinary Protestant girl, the boy in **"Araby"** can now also cry out angrily, "I'm a divil, and you are only an ordinary lady."

That this ordinary lady is an English lady is another shattering part of the boy's painful epiphany. The English accents are the accents of the ruling race, the foreign conquerors—Joyce makes much of this notion in **A Portrait** and more in **Ulysses**—and now the boy begins to understand that England, this nation which rules over him, is quintessentially vulgar, the servant par excellence of mammon. England is one with Ireland and Ireland's church, and the boy is one with all of these. He has felt the first stirrings of desire and converted them into masquerading religiosity; he has wanted to go shopping at a bazaar and has told himself that he is making an enchanted journey to fetch a chivalric token; he has been exposed to the debased vulgarities of *The Memoirs of Vidocq* and has admitted only that he liked its yellow pages. Yet he is no worse than the rest of Ireland—its dead priests (part of a dying church), its Mrs. Mercers, its faithless drunken surrogate fathers—and for that matter, no worse than Ireland's rulers. Ireland and Ireland's church, once appropriately imaged as a romantic lady or a sorrowful madonna, has now become cuckquean and harlot—she is sold and sells for silver. (pp. 393-401)

Other elements in **"Araby"** are also connected to patterns that transcend the immediate action. The two most crucial events in the story, the two vigils, harmonize with specific occasions in the Roman Catholic liturgy. The first vigil—the one in which Mangan's sister appears after the boy's invocation, *"O love! O love!"*—suggests the Vigil of the Epiphany. The most striking passage in that Vigil tells how "in those childish days of ours we toiled away at the schoolroom tasks which the world gave us, till the appointed time came"—a passage which is exactly appropriate to how the boy, after his first visitation or epiphany (that is, after Mangan's sister has appeared to him and directed him to Araby—just as in the original Epiphany an angel appeared to Joseph directing him to go from Egypt to Israel) feels about the schoolroom tasks ("child's play, ugly monotonous child's play") while he waits for the time of his journey to Araby. But the "appointed time" spoken of in the Vigil is the time of the journey to Israel and of the coming of the spirit of Jesus, not of a trip to Araby; it is the time when the spirit of Jesus cries out to a child, "Abba, Father," and he becomes no longer a child, a slave, but a son of God, entitled to "the son's right of inheritance." For the boy in **"Araby"** that cry and that inheritance turn out to be far different from what he believed them to be—he comes into a majority, but it is the disillusioning majority of the flesh, of all the sons of Adam, not of the spirit; he makes his journey, but it is a journey to Egypt, to Araby, to the market place, not back to the Holy Land.

These reverberating liturgical harmonies are continued in the boy's second vigil—the one he keeps during his long evening wait, and then during his journey to and sojourn in Araby. The connections here are with Holy Week (especially the Passion) and with Holy Saturday (the night before Easter Sunday). In **"Araby"** the trip to the bazaar takes place on a Saturday night; the boy's aunt refers to the Saturday night in question as "this night of Our Lord," an expression which can be applied to any Saturday (or Sabbath) night, but which calls up most particularly the pre-eminent Saturday "night of Our Lord," that is, Holy Saturday. The service appointed for this occasion is the Mass of Holy Saturday. This Mass, owing to its great beauty, and especially to the rich symbolism of the Tenebrae, haunted Joyce. (The whole of Book IV of **Finnegans Wake,** for example, takes place in the instant between Holy Saturday and Easter Sunday.) The Mass of Holy Saturday was the only Mass Joyce regularly tried to witness later in life, always leaving, however, before communion. Central to this Mass is the imagery of light and darkness, the extinguishing of the old lights and then the rekindling of new lights from new fire. On the other hand, prominent in the Passion is the notion of betrayal: Peter's lying threefold denial of Jesus, and Judas' selling of Jesus for thirty pieces of silver. The idea of profound betrayal, then the adumbration of awakening and rising, all combined with imagery of light and dark, and the whole counterpointed with liturgical overtones, informs the conclusion of **"Araby."**

The boy, for instance, comes to Araby with silver in his hand (with the idolatrous successor to the Godless Florin, it will be remembered); and he watches as the money of betrayal (his and his nation's) falls clinking on the salver. Like Peter's lying threefold denial of Jesus, the banal conversation about lying that the boy overhears also involves a threefold denial (the girl denies three times that she said what she is accused of saying). The foreign English accents continue the parallel, for Peter, like the English, is a foreigner, and his denials involve his accent. "Even thy speech betrays thee," he is told. When Peter recognized his betrayal (at the crowing of the cock) he "wept bitterly"; when the boy recognized his (at the call that the light was out) his "eyes burned with anguish and anger." In the service for Holy Saturday the lights are extinguished and then relit; in the service the boy witnesses there is no rekindling, the boy merely gazes "up into the darkness." And yet, of course, here too a new light is lit; for though an old faith is extinguished, we witness a dawning.

These liturgical and religious parallels and disparities (one could list other much more subterranean ones: the story of Abednego is told *in extenso* in the Holy Saturday Mass, and Abednego Seller's heretical *Devout Communicant* is a manual for Holy Week), these parallels lie unobtrusively in the background. They are not meant to be strictly or allegorically interpreted; they are meant to suggest, to hint, perhaps to condition. Unconsciously they tinge our associations and responses; they also harmonize with the more explicit motifs of the story.

The boy standing in front of the young lady's shadowy booth, listening to her bantering inanities, perceives all these significances only dimly. He is shocked, hurt, angered; but he intuitively feels, and will later understand, what the reader already comprehends. Yet even in his dim awareness he is ready to make one decision. While still at the "dark entrance" of the young lady's stall, he tells her he is no longer interested in "her wares." He lets the two pennies fall against the sixpence in his pocket; he has come to buy, but he has not bought. Someone calls that the light is out. The light is indeed out. Like De Quincey's young boy, the boy in **"Araby"** has been excluded from light, has worshipped the "lovely darkness" of the grave; he has (in the words of **Chamber Music,** XXX) been a "grave lover." But again like De Quincey's young boy, at last he has seen. He has risen again *before* he has died; he has begun to unfold "the capacities of his spirit."

As *Chamber Music,* XXX, has it, he welcomes now "the ways that [he] shall go upon." For the boy has caught a glimpse of himself as he really is—a huddled, warring, confused paradox of romantic dreams, mistaken adorations, and mute fleshly cravings—and one portion of his life, his innocent, self-deluding childhood, is now behind him. In his pride and arrogance, and, yes, in his purity and innocence too, he had imagined that he bore his chalice safely through a throng of foes; instead, he had rushed headlong toward that which he thought he most despised. In a land of betrayers, he had betrayed himself. But now he understands some of this; and now, raising his eyes up into the blackness, but totally blind no more—the Christlike fusion here of ascent, of sight, and of agony is all-important—he can say, "Gazing up into the darkness I saw myself as a creature driven and derided by vanity; and my eyes burned with anguish and anger."

Joyce has succeeded, here, in taking the raw, rather humdrum, unpromising facts of his own life and transforming them into abiding patterns of beauty and illumination. He has taken a universal experience—a more or less ordinary experience of insight, disillusionment, and growth—and given it an extraordinary application and import. The experience becomes a criticism of a nation, a religion, a civilization, a way of existing; it becomes a grappling hook with which we can scale our own well-guarded citadels of self-delusion. Joyce does all this in six or seven pages. He manages this feat by endowing the simple phrases and actions of **"Araby"** with multiple meanings that deepen and enlarge what he is saying.

The image of Mangan's sister is a case in point. Joyce takes this shadowy image, this dark scene which fascinated and obsessed him and which he returned to again and again, and shapes it to his purposes. He projects this image so carefully, touches it so delicately and skillfully with directive associations and connotations, that it conveys simultaneously, in one simple seamless whole, all the warring meanings he wishes it to hold—all the warring meanings it held for him. The pose of the harlot is also the pose of the Virgin; the revered Lady of Romance (kin to Vittoria Colonna, Laura, Beatrice, Levana, Dark Rosaleen, and the beloved of any artist) is also Ireland and at the same time a vulgar English shopgirl. One need not belabor the point. These meanings are conveyed not merely by the juxtapositions and evocations of the chief images—of Mangan's dark sister and the English shopgirl, for example—but by the reiterated patterns, allusions, and actions which bind the whole work together: the dead priest's charitableness, Mrs. Mercer's used stamps, the fall of money on the salver; Araby, Eastern enchantment, the knightly quest for a chivalric token; the swaying dress, the veiled senses, the prayerful murmur, *"O love! O love!"* Scarcely a line, an evocation, an object—the central apple tree, the heretical book of devotions by Abednego Seller, "The Arab's Farewell to His Steed," the blind street—but adds its harmony to the whole and extends and clarifies the story's meaning. (pp. 402-05)

Joyce's art in **"Araby,"** and in many of his other writings, may be likened to a palimpsest. Perhaps more than any artist of his era he was willing, for the sake of his over-all design, to obscure, even to wipe out rich nuances and powerful ironies. But at the same time, and again perhaps more than any contemporary artist, he was careful to lacquer his images and actions with layer after layer of translucent, incremental meaning. The finished palimpsest is rich with shimmering depths, strange blendings, and tantalizing hints: here something has been rubbed out, there a few faint lines coalesce meaningfully and then dwindle away, while in the center a figure, distinct, yet merging with myriads of dim underforms, swims slowly into focus and then turns and dissolves and reforms before our gaze. Abednego Seller drops out of view, only the misleading, enigmatic *Devout Communicant* remains; England's silver florin gleams brightly in the boy's tight grasp, the ancient golden lily and golden saint glimmer darkly in the shaded depths; Saturday evening shopping trips and "this night of Our Lord" stand boldly in the foreground, the liturgical engrams of which they are a part loom faintly in the distance. Mangan's shadowy sister—a version of the darkling siren Joyce drew so often—is limned and limned again. Harlot and virgin, temptress and saint, queen and shopgirl, Ireland and England—she is a miracle of blendings, mergings, and montages. While a multitude of harmonizing designs, some clear, some dim, some just faintly discernible—Mary Queen of Scots, "Our Lady of the Hills," Dark Rosaleen, a criminal dressed as a nun, Levana, Eastern bazaars, Caroline Norton, and idolatrous vigils—complete the deceptive palimpsest.

In **Dubliners** we sometimes become fascinated by the more legible figures in the palimpsest. But the more obscure figures are there too, and Joyce, by his reticences, encourages us to seek them. We know at the end of **"Araby"** that something devastating has occurred, and we would like to know exactly what it is. Ultimately, the full radiance of sight, of meaning, is ours, not the boy's. He has caught a glimpse of reality, of himself as he really is; he can reject the old encumbering vision, he can decide to dream "no more of enchanted days," but he can not yet fashion a new life. As the story has it, the light is out; the boy must grapple in the dark. But like blind Oedipus, in the dark the boy finally sees: his moment of illumination is given to him as he gazes "up into the darkness." That moment of blinding sight is also the moment of artistic vision, of the unfolding of "the capacities of [the] spirit"; not merely because the moment is later seen and reseen with the clarity, the penetration, the rich ramification of the artist's eye, but because the moment itself is a *sine qua non* for the artist's eye. The boy's end is his beginning; he has walked through and met himself. (pp. 408-10)

> Harry Stone, " 'Araby' and the Writings of James Joyce," in The Antioch Review, *Vol. XXV, No. 3, Fall, 1965, pp. 375-410.*

ROBERT P. APROBERTS (essay date 1966)

[*In the following excerpt, apRoberts refutes Harry Stone's explication of "Araby" (see excerpt dated 1965).*]

Let me declare at the outset that I do not understand what Mr. Stone's thesis is. Nowhere can I find an exact statement of it. But, clearly, whatever that thesis may be, one of its elements is the concept that in **"Araby"** are to be found, for the first time, ideas and themes which recur in Joyce's later work. Despite Professor Stone's curious claim that "in his writings Joyce was always meeting himself—in ways which must at times have been beyond his conscious ordinance," surely the appearance of an idea in a later work of Joyce's is not proof of its existence in **"Araby."** The Joyce that wrote *Ulysses* and *Finnegans Wake* is the Joyce that had written **"Araby,"** but the Joyce that wrote **"Araby"** is not the Joyce who had written the later works. Just as clearly, before we can accept the claim that an idea in **"Araby"** recurs in a later work or is re-

North Richmond Street, the home of the narrator of "Araby," where the houses "gazed at one another with brown imperturbable faces."

lated somehow to its appearance in the work of another author, we must be convinced of its existence in **"Araby."**

We may, then, dismiss from consideration Mr. Stone's contention that Yeats's story "Our Lady of the Hills" is "embedded in **"Araby'** " (whatever that means) or his suggestion that chords from "Levanna and Our Ladies of Sorrow" reverberate in it. In the absence of evidence external to **"Araby"**— evidence of the kind that would be provided by a statement of Joyce's that such linkages exist—both connections are dependent on the validity of Mr. Stone's reading of **"Araby."** (pp. 471-72)

Just as the precise thesis of Mr. Stone's article is not clear, neither is his precise interpretation of **"Araby."** But it is clear that Mr. Stone believes that we are to see beneath the surface of the story certain themes, and that without such penetration we cannot understand the story. To an ordinary glance the final sentence of the story might seem the perfectly straightforward informing idea: "Gazing up into the darkness I saw myself as a creature driven and derided by vanity; and my eyes burned with anguish and anger." But Professor Stone counters any such idea at the very beginning of his discussion of the story:

"Driven and derided," "anguish and anger"—

these reactions seem far too strong. Indeed they seem pretentious when compared to the trivial disillusionment which caused them. And they are pretentious, certainly they are inappropriate, if related only to their immediate external causes. But the boy is reacting to much more than a banal fair and a broken promise. He is reacting to sudden and deeply disturbing insights. These insights are shared by the attentive reader, for by the end of **"Araby"** the reader has been presented with all that he needs in order to resolve the story's intricate harmony into its component motifs.

Professor Stone does not claim that the meanings he finds in the story are merely ancillary to, or concomitant with, the surface narrative. They are for him necessary to an understanding of the story. And, indeed, it must be so, for were these meanings merely underlying, then the attentive reader of Professor Stone's article might see no need to plunge into such murky depths when all seemed clear without arcane explanation. Professor Stone must and does claim that **"Araby"** can be fully understood only through the symbolic meanings he finds in it.

But though Professor Stone does not make his view of **"Araby"** clear, he does make clear his belief that a chief revelation of the story is that Irish Catholicism is decayed and corrupted, principally by mammonism. This indictment is first made by the details given about the dead priest, details which, according to Mr. Stone, were intended by Joyce to arraign the priest.

The case against the priest rests on two points. The first is the books he left behind. *The Abbot* has for its heroine that notoriously evil woman, Mary Queen of Scots. *The Memoirs of Vidocq* is "a volume of exciting quasi-blasphemous criminal and sexual adventures." *The Devout Communicant* is a devotional manual written, according to Mr. Stone, by a heretic and anti-Catholic, Abednego Seller, whose first name is that of one who would not worship the golden image and whose last suggests commercialism. The second point is the "highly directive import" Professor Stone finds in the "artfully inconclusive" final sentence about the priest.

> "He had," concludes the narrator, "been a very charitable priest; in his will he had left all his money to institutions and the furniture of his house to his sister." Joyce's ambiguity suggests that the priest's charity may have been . . . double edged. . . . If this worldly priest had been so "very charitable" why, at his death, was he able to donate "all his money" to institutions? His charity, so far as we know about it, began at his death.

From these two pieces of evidence Professor Stone deduces that the priest is an imposter, a finding of the greatest importance, for on it Professor Stone rears the superstructure of his article. He speaks of the first two paragraphs of the story in which the evidence appears as involving the themes of "decayed religion" and "mammonism" and as linking the story "to the problems and distortions of Catholicism and of Ireland as a whole," and he returns to these themes over and over, often referring to their relation to the priest and his defection from true religion. But their primary importance, of course, lies in their relation to the boy, for, as Mr. Stone tells us later, in worshipping the girl "the boy, like the priest, has begun to mix devotion with profanation, spirituality with materialism." And a principal revelation to the boy at the end of the story is that this worship is corrupt.

How well does the case against the priest stand examination? The attentive reader that Mr. Stone posits for **"Araby"** might naturally, in reading his article, wonder why, if it is so important for us to know that the author of *The Devout Communicant* was Abednego Seller, Joyce does not tell us. He does tell us that *The Abbott*—surely a somewhat more famous book—was by Walter Scott. Certainly Professor Stone attaches great importance not only to the paradox of the author's name but also to his having been a heretic and an anti-Catholic:

> When Mrs. Mercer's unexamined commercial religion is remembered in connection with the boy's and then the dead priest's (one recalls that the priest's book of heretical devotions was by a man named "Seller")—we get some idea of how insidiously mammonistic is Ireland's religious bankruptcy.
>
> . . . the story of Abednego is told *in extenso* in the Holy Saturday Mass, and Abednego Seller's heretical *Devout Communicant* is a manual for Holy Week. . . .
>
> Scarcely a line, an evocation, an object—the central apple tree, the heretical book of devotions by Abednego Seller . . .—but adds its harmony to the

whole and extends and clarifies the story's meaning.

Abednego Seller is the first piece of evidence Professor Stone adduces for the mammonism of the priest and hence of Ireland, and, if the arraignment of the priest is the foundation of Mr. Stone's article, Abednego Seller is its cornerstone.

Such emphasis might well lead the attentive reader to be curious about this author whose concealed name is of such paramount importance, a curiosity that would be further whetted by the discovery that no word-index or concordance to any work of Joyce's lists "Abednego Seller." If he were to satisfy this curiosity, he would find that Seller lived from about 1646 to 1705, that *The Devout Communicant* was first published in 1686, and that, after the sixth edition in 1695, there is no record of its having been reprinted under that title.

This information would raise for the attentive reader the question, "Could there be another religious manual with the same title of Roman Catholic provenance and published in Ireland?" Such an enquiry pursued would lead to the discovery that Pacificus Baker, a prominent English Franciscan, wrote such a manual in the eighteenth century. This *Devout Communicant* was first published in London and underwent a number of editions and reprintings—second edition (apparently the earliest extant) 1765, sixth edition 1798; reprintings in 1813, 1823 (Manchester), 1826, 1827, and 1828 (Liverpool). An edition without the author's name, revised and enlarged by William Gahan, an Augustinian, was printed in Cork in 1794 and a copy of this edition is the only copy of any work with the title *The Devout Communicant* in the National Library of Ireland. (There are also indications that the work was reprinted in Dublin at least twice during the nineteenth century.)

At this point the attentive reader would ask what proof Professor Stone can offer that Joyce knew of the existence of Abednego Seller's work? (The enquiries I have made have failed to locate a copy in Ireland, though these enquiries have been by no means exhaustive.) Even if Professor Stone can prove that Joyce knew of the seventeenth-century manual, how would he persuade the reader of the likelihood that the reference in **"Araby"** is to this work and not to the popular and often reprinted Roman Catholic work? In view of the realism of the Dublin setting with North Richmond Street and the Christian Brothers School, why should the attentive reader, supposing he knew of the two *Devout Communicants,* feel that Joyce refers to Abednego Seller's heretical manual rather than to Pacificus Baker's orthodox one? If the title *The Abbot* were given alone without the name of the author, the reader might well assume that, because the book had belonged to a priest, it was a religious book. Any reader exerting the proper scholarly and critical attention that the attentive reader should exert would feel that he could not accept Mr. Stone's ascription of *The Devout Communicant* unless Mr. Stone could prove, first, that Joyce knew of Seller's work and, second, that Joyce was referring to this work and not to the Roman Catholic one. (We may note, in passing, that Professor Marvin Magalaner in his study *Time of Apprenticeship: The Fiction of Young James Joyce* ascribes the work to Pacificus Baker.)

The Devout Communicant is, then, not a piece of evidence which can be used to arraign the priest. What of the other books? The very most that can be said against a priest who reads works of the sort of *The Abbot* and *The Memoirs of Vi-*

docq is that he is guilty of venial sin, for they are vanities that stand in marked contrast to works entirely suitable for a priest to read, works such as *The Devout Communicant.*

Mr. Stone's other piece of evidence, which concerns the priest's charity, is easily disposed of. "If this worldly priest had been so 'very charitable' why, at his death, was he able to donate 'all his money' to institutions? His charity, so far as we know about it, began at his death." If Mr. Stone had only realized that his question is not a rhetorical one, he might have answered it himself. First, a secular priest is permitted to own property. Second, the priest may have given away vast sums during his life and still have left "all his money" to institutions. Finally, Mr. Stone's statement that the priest's charity, as far as we know, began at his death is an argument *ex silentio.* We might just as well say that the priest was unchaste on the grounds that we are told nothing at all about his chastity.

Once we think of this last point, we can see that Professor Stone missed a good opportunity to indict the priest for lust. Spiritually a priest might be regarded as both male and female, and for this the abandoned bicycle pump is a magnificent symbol. Its rustiness points to the waste of the priest's fertility. But underneath this obvious symbolism there is the more important idea of masturbation for which a pump is an unmistakable correlative, a symbolism reinforced when we recall Bloom's masturbation at the moment of the elevation of the Host—to which Mr. Stone refers in his article—a false priest elevating himself at the altar of lust. So too in **"Araby"** the priest is a false priest guilty of mammonism and fruitless lust just as we are to find the boy guilty of mammonism and fruitless lust. But there is still another layer of the palimpsest to be revealed. Such an article as a bicycle pump is clearly of British manufacture, for the Irish were not allowed to develop industry. It is then a symbol of the British commercial materialism which has corrupted Irish Catholicism—a symbol of Mammon, the strange god after whom the priest has gone a-whoring. This exegesis is not merely facetious; it illustrates a serious issue. A critic of Professor Stone's persuasion should find every detail in a story symbolic, for, if he admits that any detail is present for verisimilitude alone, he raises the question of how to distinguish such a detail from one which is symbolic.

But it is time to deliver a final verdict on the priest. And that verdict is not even "Not proven"; it is "Not guilty." And the other contentions dependent on the case topple with it like a file of upright dominoes falling with the first—the corruption of Irish religion, the other subliminal hints of this in the opening paragraphs, its parallel in the boy's worship of the girl, and the revelation to the boy at the end of the story that his worship is corrupt. The case has not provided a sound foundation for the interpretation of **"Araby"** let alone an Archimedean base from which to shift the understanding of the entire canon of twentieth-century allusive writers.

It would be simply tedious to expose the complete lack of substance of other and far less important readings by Professor Stone of the palimpsest of **"Araby."** Two of these baseless interpretations, however, are worth examining, for they illustrate beautifully the pitfalls that await the thesis-monger who grinds the axe of symbolic interpretation: false association and the creation of non-existent facts.

Among those symbols of betrayal Mr. Stone finds everywhere in the story is the florin, the coin which the uncle gives the

boy for the bazaar. "That Joyce, out of all the coins and combinations of coins available to him, chose to have the boy clutch a florin is doubly meaningful." The original florin of 1252, a gold coin noted for its purity, bore emblems of the Virgin and of John the Baptist. The boy's coin is silver and bears the emblems of Ireland's foreign masters. The first issue in England, coined in 1847, was known as the "Godless and Graceless Florin" because the title "Dei Gratia, F.D.," customary on coins, had been omitted by the Roman Catholic Master of the Mint, who was subsequently discharged for the offense. As Mr. Stone believes that the boy in his visit to the fair is "acting out his betrayal in the most emblematic way," he finds it "supremely ironic" that the boy "should be clutching an English florin, an alien and notorious silver coin sans Virgin's lily and sans Catholic saint but bearing instead symbols of his and Ireland's servitude and betrayal."

The reason why the seven stars are no more than seven is a pretty reason, and the reason why Joyce chose to have the boy clutch the florin is that he did not choose to have him clutch something else. What reader, no matter how attentive, would call to mind the history of the florin, even if he knew it, on the strength of its single mention in this sentence: "I held a florin tightly in my hand as I strode down Buckingham Street towards the station"? How many readers, well-read, cultivated, or attentive, know that history? Did Mr. Stone know it when he first read **"Araby"**? A florin is almost as common a coin for an Irishman or an Englishman as a fifty-cent piece is for an American (I say "almost" simply because the florin shares its equivalence to the fifty-cent piece with the half-crown), and no Irish or English reader would give a second thought to the single and simple mention of a florin any more than an American would to such a mention in a story of a fifty-cent piece, a coin which has associations as rich as those of the florin. (pp. 472-78)

Since Mr. Stone gives the history of the florin because he is searching the palimpsest of **"Araby"** for symbols of betrayal, we may remark here on his curious failure to note a word in the sentence containing "florin" much richer as such a symbol, a failure which illustrates how endless are the associations anyone can establish once he gives his fancy up unrestrainedly to symbol hunting. For the name of the street down which the boy hastens is Buckingham, a name rich in overtones of betrayal. I have no intention of exhausting these associations. Consider only those involved in the Buckingham who figures in *Richard III*—Richard's "second-self" in the practice of treachery and a traitor to Richard. How much more would this one association—an association within the knowledge of any cultivated reader—add to the irony Mr. Stone finds in the boy going to the bazaar bearing a coin symbolic of "his and Ireland's servitude and betrayal" by providing the further irony that to reach the bazaar the boy passes down a street with a name redolent of betrayal!

But our main point is that the significance Professor Stone sees in the word "florin" is an example of what I have called "false association." It is true that the florin has a history of association with the Virgin Mary and with the idea of godlessness and gracelessness, but it is false to assume that these associations would be aroused in the reader by the bare mention of the name of an everyday coin.

The second misinterpretation involves the creation of a nonexistent fact to establish a false association. Mr. Stone says that when the boy "allows 'two pennies to fall against the sixpence' in his pocket," his action is "reminiscent of how Judas let the silver of betrayal fall upon the ground after his contrition." The context of this statement makes it quite clear that what establishes for Mr. Stone the association between Judas' act and the boy's is the action of "letting fall":

> The two men "were counting money on a salver. I listened to the fall of the coins." The boy also has fallen. We recall the "wild garden" with its "central apple-tree," that the words "falling" and "fell" are crucial to the description of Mangan's sister during her epiphany before the boy, and that the word "fall" again recurs—again in connection with money—when the boy, in his penultimate action, an action reminiscent of how Judas let the silver of betrayal fall upon the ground after his contrition, allows "two pennies to fall against the sixpence" in his pocket as he finally turns to leave the bazaar.

Judas did not let the silver of betrayal fall—he threw it down, he cast it down, he hurled it, he flung it, but he did not let it fall. In Matthew 27:5, we are told that, after the betrayal of Jesus, Judas repented and attempted to return the thirty pieces of silver to the chief priests and elders in the temple. When they refused to take them back, Judas threw them away and went off and hanged himself. The words used to describe the action of throwing the money away are in the Greek original "rhipsas ta argyria en tō naō," in the Vulgate "projectis argenteis in templo," in the Challoner-Rheims revised "he flung the pieces of silver into the temple," in the King James "he cast down the pieces of silver in the temple," and in the Revised Standard "throwing down the pieces of silver in the temple." Nowhere in the original or in any standard translation is it said that Judas let the silver fall in the temple. Professor Stone finds an association which does not exist between the boy's act of letting his money fall and Judas' act of throwing away the money of betrayal.

"Gazing up into the darkness I saw myself as a creature driven and derided by vanity; and my eyes burned with anguish and anger." Professor Stone, as we have seen, finds this final state of the narrator unconvincing in terms of what we might call the surface meaning of the story. It is with this judgment, from which Mr. Stone begins his examination of **"Araby,"** that the attentive reader of the article must take issue. For the final sentence records the reaction which the reader has been awaiting since the boy's entrance to the bazaar and which has been prepared for by all the details given after his entrance. Mr. Stone finds the reaction inappropriate to the triviality of the disillusionment, but what is important is not the triviality of the disillusionment but the strength of the illusion which led up to it. The occasion of the disillusionment is unimportant just as is the cause of the illusion. The important thing is the revelation to the boy of the triviality of what he had attached so much significance to. That revelation is universal and its truth is none the less keen for all its reputation over the centuries:

> Now I have seen the face of death and am sore afraid. One day too I shall be like Enkidu.

> Therefore I hated life; because the work that is wrought under the sun is grievous unto me: for all *is* vanity and vexation of spirit.

> her bifeoh læne,   her bifrēond læne,
> her bimon læne,   her bimaeg læne;
> eal pis eoran gesteal   idel weorpe!

> And thinketh al this world nis but a faire
> That passeth soone as floures faire.

The boast of heraldry, the pomp of power,
And all that beauty, all that wealth e'er gave,
Awaits alike the inevitable hour.
The paths of glory lead but to the grave.

The Worldly Hope men set their Hearts upon
Turns Ashes—or it prospers; and anon,
Like Snow upon the Desert's dusty Face,
Lighting a little hour or two—is gone.

Man is in love and loves what vanishes
What more is there to say?

The "anguish and anger" are the reactions of a young boy feeling this truth for the first time, and the self-centeredness and self-dramatization are quite in keeping with his age and with the earlier creation by the boy of an inner world of love and hope at odds with reality. Our awareness that the story is told by a narrator who sees the boy's reaction in this way cuts against any tendency to find the reactions too strong, pretentious, or inappropriate—they are the reactions of a boy, and they are none the less important nor is the insight less true because in later life he will react differently.

Viewing the story in the light of its final revelation, we can see how beautifully every stroke prepares us for this revelation with the delicacy and simplicity of high art. The setting of a lower-middle-class district, though not of great importance, has a double appropriateness: it is a drab, respectable neighborhood whose inhabitants might well dream of a more beautiful environment; second, such a neighborhood does not crush the spirit out of its inhabitants as a working-class neighborhood might nor satisfy their longing for beauty as an upper-class neighborhood might. The more immediate and more important setting is not, however, the respectable bourgeois world of North Richmond Street but the world of boys which is described in much greater detail. The narrator has known a world occupied in school-time and play-time entirely by boys. In such a world women, old or young, have being only as they relate to the members of this world—"John's mother wants him! Bill's aunt is calling him!" "Mangan's sister" is the girl's natural appellation here and not "an awkward and unaccountable substitute for a name . . . designed to catch the reader's attention and direct his associations" to James Mangan and Dark Rosaleen. (Granted the fame of James Clarence Mangan, why should the phrase direct an Irish reader to him when Mangan is such a common Irish name? Even if it did, why should "sister," which certainly has no connotations of romantic love, bring to mind Dark Rosaleen? The use of the last name rather than the first is the common practice in an English or Irish boy's school.)

The boy is at an age where his emotional fancies are strong and where he is experiencing a first awakening of a generalized impulse toward sexual love. Twelve years of age would fit very nicely and would accord with the biographical experience which the story no doubt reflects—Joyce was twelve in 1894 when his family lived in North Richmond Street. At this point in the boy's life a girl captures his attention. He has no idea of the mechanics of sex or that what he feels is the beginning of a period of strong sexual drive. What he notices are the precise details that such a boy would notice: the things that mark a girl as different externally from a boy—the dress with a petticoat showing at times below the hem, the long braid, the way she bends her head to one side, the way she holds the top of one of the iron uprights of the railing (no doubt swinging back and forth) and the common simple first piece of jewelry for a girl, a silver bracelet. Nothing could be more suggestive of girlhood and less suggestive of the "desecrating lust" and the "hints of commercialism and sensuality with connotations of sexuality and betrayal" which Mr. Stone finds in these details. And no one could be a less likely prototype of Gerty MacDowell or Molly Bloom or less suggestive of the harlot.

So too, nothing could be less suggestive of a response to sensuality and lust than the response the boy makes. His reaction is that of one who has been stirred by chivalric love in the tradition of the Arthurian romances. His love kept secret from the world becomes a treasure which he sees himself guarding safely from all harm, as a knight errant would guard the precious object of a quest (the most precious object in the Arthurian story is, of course, a chalice, the Holy Grail). His confused and generalized emotion is engendered as much by the exciting idea of being in love as it is by the object which calls forth such romantic intensity, a diffuseness which is shown when, in an ecstasy of feeling, he prays to the lord of terrible aspect with the intensity of a young Dante.

While he is in this feverish state, the girl speaks to him of Araby, and immediately her desire to go transfers to him with an intensity made greater because she cannot go and because he promises to bring her something from the fair—the knight now has a quest to undertake for his lady.

From this moment on suspense builds. The intervening days drag interminably until at last the appointed Saturday arrives. Knowing his uncle's habit of lingering late in a snug on a Saturday night, he reminds his uncle that he is going to the fair that night. The curt reply shows the irritation of a man acknowledging a request he does not want to carry out and it gives the boy a sense of foreboding. Arrived home, he waits feverishly for dinner and his uncle's return, cooling his forehead against the window which faces the house where the girl lives. When he comes downstairs he finds a Mrs. Mercer there for supper. To Professor Stone, Mrs. Mercer's name, her dead husband's occupation of pawnbroking, her collecting of stamps for a pious purpose all mean that "Joyce is saying, in effect, that everyday religion and piety in Ireland are based upon self-deluding and mindless materialism." But the function of every detail about Mrs. Mercer can be accounted for much more simply. What can be more infuriating when one is in a fever of doubt and expectation than to have to go through the formality of being polite to an outsider? How much more so when the outsider is a tedious person? How beautifully Joyce makes us feel this for the boy! The more trivial Mrs. Mercer, the greater our sense of the boy's anguish. She is the garrulous widow of a pawnbroker (pawnbroking is not the most glamorous of occupations) with nothing better to do than collect stamps for some "pious purpose" (the alliteration almost makes us hear the boy spitting out the words contemptuously). We feel the boy's relief when, after she takes her garrulous leave, he is able to walk up and down the room physically venting his anxiety.

Hope when the uncle at last appears is offset by the precautionary wait enforced by a drunkenness that may turn to nastiness before it is partially tempered by food. But at last, late though it is, the boy is off with money in his hand. At the same time that the complete emptiness of the train, the slowness of its journey, and the late hour of the arrival make us anticipate the disappointment to come, they heighten our sense of the boy's desperate anxiety not to miss the bazaar. Joyce could not have got him to Araby in a more feverishly anxious state.

And Joyce could not have got him there at a time when the contrast between his expectations of something wonderful and the reality of the bazaar would be greater—no bright lights but a half darkened fair, no gay noisy crowds but a nearly empty building about to close up, no busy booths with shouting hucksters but nearly all closed stalls and attendants counting their receipts before those still open. The one stall the boy stops before is hopelessly expensive for someone with eightpence in his pocket (four of which he would need for the train home). What price a present for his lady now? At this stall he overhears the most banal flirtatious talk, talk that bears as much relationship to a romantic love as his own exchange with the girl.

I do not see how Joyce could have achieved a greater build-up or a greater let-down. Not all boys would dream of romantic love in such bookish terms as the narrator, though surely the young Joyce would, but what boy has not experienced dreams of romantic love focussed on some girl, dreams which grow and flourish in a secrecy guarded by shyness? What person has not felt the disillusionment that comes when an expected delight proves disappointing? What more than a fair or a circus promises a glamor it does not have—a fair is the very symbol of vanity; witness Bunyan's representation of the world as Vanity Fair. Then too, the boy's love for the girl is made to run parallel to his anticipation of the bazaar. Exciting enough in itself, the visit to the fair is made doubly exciting because it is a quest undertaken for his lady who longs to go and cannot, a quest from which he will bring back for her some wondrous object. Suspense mounts with the agonizing wait for the uncle and the intolerable slowness of the eleventh hour journey. The bazaar could never have lived up to the boy's expectations—no bazaar could have—but at no time could it have come less up to them than at the time of the boy's arrival.

At the end of the story we can see the true conflict and how details in the story reinforce our sense of its universality. The main conflict is between the desire of mankind for a perfection of beauty in life and the impossibility of realizing this desire. At first the boy feels a conflict between his "love" for the girl and his environment; he keeps his "love" to himself and protects it from the unworthy, hostile world—"I imagined that I bore my chalice safely through a throng of foes." This same conflict is involved in the case of the boy and the uncle—the uncle is indifferent to the intensity of the boy's desire to go to the bazaar. But at the end the boy realizes that the true conflict is not between himself and his environment, or at least not so much so, as it is between the enormous power of his fancy and the impossibility of reality ever corresponding to his fancy. "Vanity of Vanities, saith the preacher, all is vanity"—what the story is concerned with is the moment of first realization, the moment when its truth is most deeply felt. (pp. 479-85)

The whole of "Araby" is finally symbolic of the way in which men are driven and mocked by illusions. Some details in the story take on a symbolic cast and some do not, though this dichotomy is overly simple. It is more accurate to say that the details give verisimilitude and that, at the same time, some may take on symbolic significance in the light of the central idea of the story. Joyce suggests to us, at several points, that though men universally realize the truth the boy comes to experience, they never lose their vain desires. Of all men, a priest should be most keenly aware of the vanity of things, and yet the books the priest leaves behind are a mixture of a devout treatise and two highly romantic works. Even those whose lives are informed by an awareness of the contrast between the corruptible and the incorruptible are subject to the vanity of human wishes. The garden of the house is, as all gardens are, an attempt to achieve beauty, but its decayed condition shows a failure to achieve it or to maintain it even if it is momentarily achieved. This wild garden with its central apple tree may symbolize the vain aspiration of man to create beauty here where it cannot keep its lustrous eyes and may even, if some reader wishes, be taken as a symbolic allusion to the Garden of Eden, which man dreams of but can never achieve in his fallen condition. Again, the uncle, unresponsive though he is to the wild longing of the boy, is stirred by the name **"Araby"** to recite what, from the title alone, the reader recognizes would be a highly romantic poem. The ordered neighborhood with its "decent lives," the world of business and routine where adult men and women are preoccupied with making a living, checks and subdues the fancy but it never completely conquers it. Man still remains discontent with his condition—like the uncle, many men seek the public house "to see the world as the world's not" or they may become puritanical, as many Irish are, and seek to repress their vain desires, a reaction suggested when the boy feels anger at being driven and derided by vanity. Finally, there is the implication that one of the bases of religion, at least of Christianity, is the vanity of human wishes for which religion offers a consolation—the girl cannot go to the bazaar because her school is going to have a "retreat," a period devoted to a consideration of the difference between things eternal and things *sub species aeternitatis* ["under the aspect of eternity"].

Symbolic significances which supplement the central idea of a story, expand it, provide overtones for it, reinforce it, or in any way arise naturally from it are not to be objected to even if such significances might not occur to all readers. But symbolisms which run counter to the central idea, are discordant with it, are unrelated to it, or are claimed to be concurrent with it but to be perceived only by an understanding of an arcane network of unstated details obliquely connected with it are to be rejected unless evidence is adduced from outside the story to show that the author saw such symbolisms in the story. On this basis we must reject Mr. Stone's view that the girl with her silver bracelet holding one of the spikes of the area railing, head bowed and petticoat showing, is at once a symbol of the Virgin Mary as she appears in *pietás* (in what *pietá* does she appear standing and holding one of the nails?) and of Mary Magdalene and hence, by the name "Mary" called up through this symbolism, to be associated with Mary Sheehy and Mary Queen of Scots. We reject the harlot symbolism, not merely because the associations reek of the lamp and would never occur to any reader however attentive, but rather because the idea of the girl as a harlot and of the boy's love for her as lust jars with the idea of a young boy's first romantic illusion of love. Our rejection of the Virgin symbolism would be based on Ockham's principle—the details beautifully bespeak young girlhood and need no further explanation. Or, again, we can reject the idea that the opening lines of "The Arab's Farewell to His Steed" "are fraught with thematic significance" and that the story of Caroline Norton, the author of the poem, "is patently and ironically appropriate to what Joyce is saying." The story is self-contained and does not depend for its effect upon whether the reader knows these matters or not—the details that Joyce gives are the details the reader needs.

The flaw which stands at the very heart of Professor Stone's

article is his basic assumption that **"Araby"** is not self-contained. He seeks to give substance to this belief by the idea that in this early story Joyce employs the allusive method of his later works. For Mr. Stone **"Araby"** cannot be understood by itself, and he proceeds to rewrite the story as Editor X unconsciously realized when he felt that, in reading Mr. Stone's article, he "was being told the story in considerably more detail than Joyce gave." Apparently neither Editor X or Mr. Stone conceived that, if Joyce had wanted to tell the story in more detail, he would have told it in more detail and that, if he had not done so, he would have written an imperfect story. If Joyce wanted the reader to arraign the priest, he would have made it clear that the priest was to be arraigned—if the arraignment were to depend upon the anomaly of Abednego Seller's name then Joyce would have made it clear that *The Devout Communicant* referred to was the one by Seller and not by any other.

The palimpsest Professor Stone sees in **"Araby"** is not in the story but in Professor Stone's mind, and what he takes for depths shimmering with rich, half-obscured images is a mirror wherein the figures of his own perfervid fancy glimmer and shift. Mr. Stone uses **"Araby"** as a sort of Rorschach test, a starting point for a long free association fantasy that might be of general human interest insofar as *humani nihil a me alienum,* ["nothing pertaining to humanity is alien to me"]. However, it is quite alien to any academic discipline. For it is free association; there is no control whatsoever except the limit of what happens to be Mr. Stone's awareness.

Intellectually, Mr. Stone's approach to **"Araby"** is not different from Baconianism. It is only a jump—no, not even that— to move from the idea that the **"Araby"** Joyce wrote is not the **"Araby"** of the common reader but the **"Araby"** Mr. Stone reads beneath the surface, to the idea that it was written not by Joyce at all but by someone else as part of the Great Cryptogram. And the effect of such neo-Alexandrianism upon students, not to mention editors of reputable journals, may be a double disaster. It may either turn them into little apostles who see all works of art as double-acrostics and who are led to those displays of vanity against which Helen Gardner so sensibly warns us:

> The critic's task is to assist his readers to read for themselves, not to read for them. . . . He is not writing to display his own ingenuity, subtlety, learning or sensitiveness; but to display the work in a manner which will enable it to exert its own power.

Or it may drive them away from literature as something whose esoteric incomprehensibility repels the reason and destroys the humanistic illumination of art. (pp. 485-88)

> *Robert P. apRoberts, " 'Araby' and the Palimpsest of Criticism; or, Through a Glass Eye Darkly," in* The Antioch Review, *Vol. XXVI, No. 4, Winter, 1966-67, pp. 469-89.*

WILLIAM J. HANDY (essay date 1971)

[*In the following excerpt, Handy offers a formalist reading of "The Dead," focusing his discussion on such themes as spiritual death and rebirth and spiritual freedom.*]

"The Dead" is certainly one of the masterpieces in the Joyce canon. Its themes, recognizably present in the later works, are embodied in a much more direct manner of presentation:

the theme of spiritual death, of spiritual rebirth, and the theme of the freedom of the human spirit as a necessary condition for living and loving. It would be folly for the critic of whatever persuasion not to grant that a sound reading of **"The Dead"** is an obvious prerequisite to the reading of Joyce's later works. I would like to examine some scenes and episodes from the first half of the story which is intended to suggest the way Joyce has built his meanings to a climactic embodiment in the second half.

When we examine the opening episode, in the light of the work itself taken as one large presentation, one major contrast with subsequent episodes immediately emerges: the opening episode is an *objective* presentation of the world of the action. That is, here is the way the world actually is before Gabriel enters. Once Gabriel is present, the objective view diminishes, sometimes clouded by his responses, sometimes altogether distorted by its presentation through his viewpoint. The tone of the opening scene of the three-scene episode is quite different from the tone after Gabriel enters the action:

> Lily, the caretaker's daughter, was literally run off her feet. Hardly had she brought one gentleman into the little pantry behind the office on the ground floor and helped him off with his overcoat than the wheezy halldoor bell clanged again and she had to scamper along the bare hallway to let in another guest.

For the simple tastes of Lily, scurrying about her duties of greeting the guests, and for Miss Kate and Miss Julia, who "were there, gossiping and laughing and fussing," the party to come had no quality of spiritual sterility about it. Although the party was long since a ritual, "always a great affair, the Misses Morkan's annual dance," it did not occur to these sensibilities that at the same time it had become a spiritually sterile ritual. Although not evident in the opening episode, later episodes will present the gathering as the very expression of spiritual sterility. The conversation at the table just prior to Gabriel's speech is a good instance:

> The subject of talk was the opera company which was then at the Theatre Royal. Mr. Bartell D'Arcy, the tenor, a dark-complexioned young man with a smart moustache, praised very highly the leading contralto of the company but Miss Furlong thought she had a rather vulgar style of production. Freddy Malins said there was a negro chieftain singing in the second part of the Gaiety pantomime who had one of the finest voices he had ever heard.

An understanding of the scene turns on the realization that Bartell D'Arcy is not one of the spiritually dead. In contrast to Gabriel, he is presented as one who feels no compulsion to put himself forward, as Gabriel does in, for example, his annual speech, or as Mr. Browne does in his insistence on telling stories, or as Miss Furlong and Freddy Malins do in their contrary responses in this scene. They are, of course, "the dead" of the story. The point here is that with "the dead," all qualities of the real world are dissipated by subjective responses. In this scene the possibility of communication vanishes, as each participant except Bartell D'Arcy responds. (Mary Jane may also be an exception. But Mary Jane is also a victim, but of another kind. She is reminiscent of Maria in **"Clay."**) The conversation, about opera singers and judgments about them, becomes less a subject for conversation as the scene develops than a vehicle for the expression of judgments directed to call attention to the speaker. Mr. Browne's lengthy account of the history of the opera companies who

used to come to Dublin concludes with a judgment which is also something of a challenge to the group. The responses of the participants in the conversation embody one central theme of the work: the inability to celebrate the world of objective reality is synonymous with the inability to be alive. Mr. Browne concludes: "Why did they never play the grand old operas now, he asked. *Dinorah, Lucrezia Borgia*? Because they could not get the voices to sing them: that was why." Then the objective response: " 'O, well,' said Mr. Bartell D'Arcy, 'I presume there are as good singers today as there were then'." Now the subjective defense: " 'Where are they?' asked Mr. Browne defiantly." And the answer is recognizable as objectively real: " 'In London, Paris, Milan,' said Mr. Bartell D'Arcy warmly. 'I suppose Caruso, for example, is quite as good, if not better than any of the men you have mentioned'." But again what is real about the subject disappears in the defensive response: " 'Maybe so,' said Mr. Browne. 'But *I* may tell you I doubt it strongly'." And then one who in her mindlessness is not really a part of the conversation: " 'O, I'd give anything to hear Caruso sing,' said Mary Jane." Now the real is once more obscured in the response of sentimentality:

> "For me," said Aunt Kate, who had been picking a bone, "there was only one tenor. To please me, I mean. But I suppose none of you have ever heard of him."

> "Who was he, Miss Morkan?" asked Mr. Bartell D'Arcy politely.

> "His name," said Aunt Kate, "was Parkinson. I heard him when he was in his prime and I think he had then the purest tenor voice that was ever put into a man's throat."

There is no rejection in the response of Bartell D'Arcy, simply an impulse to be objective: " 'Strange, I never even heard of him'." But Mr. Browne seizes the opportunity to put down D'Arcy: " 'Yes, yes, Miss Morkan is right,' said Mr. Browne. 'I remember hearing of old Parkinson but he is too far back for me'." In the final utterance the last vestige of what could have been human communication is submerged in sentimentality: " 'A beautiful, pure, sweet, mellow English tenor,' said Aunt Kate with enthusiasm." These, then, are "the dead," as fully realized and as expressionistically valid as that other famous objectification of drawing-room sterility: "In the room the women come and go / Talking of Michaelangelo."

The theme of spiritual death dominates the entire first section of the work, which, considered from the standpoint of its ontological structure, is divided into two large presentations: the first is the party, which embodies the subject matter of "the dead"; the second is the marriage relationship between Gabriel and Gretta, which comprises the rebirth of Gabriel.

Although it is those episodes of the first section which focus specifically on Gabriel that are dominant, one other episode, focusing on Mr. Browne and Freddy Malins, also presents variations of the theme of death-in-life. When Mr. Browne arrives at the affair, he moves at once to be the center of attention. He leads the three young ladies, who have been instructed to present him to the assembled guests, into the back room where he performs dramatically as he pours himself a drink. When his performance becomes of questionable taste and is rejected by the ladies, he "turned promptly to the two young men who were more appreciative." That is, like Freddy Malins and like Gabriel, Mr. Browne's interest is not in people, but in getting people to attend to him. Here in Joyce's presentation of Freddy Malin's entrance:

> He was laughing heartily in a high key at a story which he had been telling Gabriel on the stairs and at the same time rubbing the knuckles of his left fist backwards and forwards into his left eye.
>
> "Good evening, Freddy," said Aunt Julia.

Presently he catches sight of Mr. Browne and seizes the meeting as an opportunity for further dramatic action:

> Mr. Browne, whose face was once more wrinkling with mirth, poured out for himself a glass of whisky while Freddy Malins exploded, before he had well reached the climax of his story, in a kind of high-pitched bronchitic laughter and, setting down his untasted and overflowing glass, began to rub the knuckles of his left fist backwards and forwards into his left eye, repeating words of his last phrase as well as his fit of laughter would allow him.

The point is, of course, that Mr. Browne's face that is "once more wrinkling with mirth" is like Freddy Malins's uncontrollable mirth and Gabriel's after-dinner speech: each carefully prepared and artfully timed.

The central focus of the long opening section which constitutes the first half of the work is on Gabriel, who throughout is presented as one quite incapable of attending to any reality, apart from his own subjective relationship to it. That is, Gabriel is presented as one who seldom sees or listens to any quality of the world external to himself, except as that quality is in some way enmeshed with his own self-interest in it. The impulse in Gabriel is presented as overwhelming the entire range and scope of his relationships with his fellow-man.

His first encounter with another is that with Lily, the maid, which occurs when he enters the house. His first communication with her, following the greeting, is the recognizable informal exchange characteristic of the acceptable mode of the occasion for two people with little in common. But the ritual which maintains distance with civility, with a minimum degree of engagement, is broken by Gabriel with his overly familiar questions. We see that he doesn't really mean his questions to Lily, that he has, however unaware of his action, adopted an air of condescension toward her and thus asserted his own superiority. He is annoyed and mildly shocked when her response is something more than an anticipated cliché. That is, it is clear that he has no real interest in Lily in spite of his questions and no wish to have his attention to her engaged in any but the most superficial manner.

> "Tell me, Lily," he said in a friendly tone, "do you still go to school?"
>
> "O no, sir," she answered. "I'm done schooling this year and more."
>
> "O, then," said Gabriel gaily, "I suppose we'll be going to your wedding one of these fine days with your young man, eh?"
>
> The girl glanced back at him over her shoulder and said with great bitterness:
>
> "The men that is now is only all palaver and what they can get out of you."
>
> Gabriel coloured, as if he felt he had made a mistake and, without looking at her, kicked off his ga-

loshes and flicked actively with his muffler at his patent-leather shoes.

And then presently: "When he had flicked lustre into his shoes, he stood up and pulled his waistcoat down more tightly on his plump body. Then he took a coin rapidly from his pocket."

The coin, of course, is not a gift; it is a gesture which at once redefines the relationship which he intends. That is, for Gabriel, Lily is not Lily; she is the servant girl. We see that in his initial presentation of Gabriel, Joyce has worked painstakingly to establish at once that Gabriel's concern is always centered in Gabriel.

The encounter with Miss Ivors is another failure in human intercourse. Miss Ivors, who is also a teacher, is obviously impressed by Gabriel's book reviews, and attempts to engage his attention by a kind of simulated hostility. There should be no question that her seeming aggressiveness is intended irony. Joyce presents her at the outset as open, not deceptive, "a frank-mannered talkative young lady, with a freckled face and prominent brown eyes." Her charge when they take their places as dancing partners is quite obviously made in the spirit of the occasion, and her tone is unquestionably more of lighthearted banter than hostility:

> When they had taken their places she said abruptly: "I have a crow to pluck with you."
>
> "With me?" said Gabriel.
>
> She nodded her head gravely.
>
> "What is it?" asked Gabriel, smiling at her solemn manner.
>
> "Who is G. C.?" answered Miss Ivors, turning her eyes upon him.
>
> Gabriel coloured and was about to knit his brows, as if he did not understand, when she said bluntly:
>
> "O, innocent Amy! I have found out that you write for *The Daily Express.* Now, aren't you ashamed of yourself?"
>
> "Why should I be ashamed of myself?" asked Gabriel, blinking his eyes and trying to smile.
>
> "Well, I'm ashamed of you," said Miss Ivors frankly. "To say you'd write for a paper like that. I didn't think you were a West Briton."

That Miss Ivors's intention was not to rebuke Gabriel is obvious at the point at which she realizes that he has taken her literally:

> He continued blinking his eyes and trying to smile and murmured lamely that he saw nothing political in writing reviews of books.
>
> When their turn to cross had come he was still perplexed and inattentive. Miss Ivors promptly took his hand in a warm grasp and said in a soft friendly tone:
>
> "Of course, I was only joking. Come, we cross now."

Gabriel's misunderstanding is much more than just that; it is, in reality, a rejection; and more than a rejection of Miss Ivors, who presently will leave the affair before the dinner is served, it is a rejection of *what is* in the world apart from Gabriel's distortion of it.

We see finally that Gabriel's speech, the climax of the Misses Morkan's annual party, has no validity as an expression of anything but Gabriel's calculations about what will impress his listeners and Gabriel's defensive hostility, which was inadvertently engaged by Miss Ivors's playful attempts at drawing-room irony. In one final attempt at reconciliation, Miss Ivors somewhat pathetically reveals her regret at having annoyed him:

> Gabriel tried to cover his agitation by taking part in the dance with great energy. He avoided her eyes for he had seen a sour expression on her face. But when they met in the long chain he was surprised to feel his hand firmly pressed. She looked at him from under her brows for a moment quizzically until he smiled. Then, just as the chain was about to start again, she stood on tiptoe and whispered into his ear:
>
> "West Briton!"

And we see that Miss Ivors is not attacking Gabriel. She is more nearly flirting with him. It is clear that her intention throughout was to have a conversation with him. In her overzealous approach, she has inadvertently offended him, because Gabriel is constitutionally unable to attend to anyone except in relation to his own concerns. Further, her quizzical look also suggests her dismay at not finding what she had a right to expect from another human: a living, not a deadening response. In the following scene, Gretta enters, but Gabriel's attitude toward her is somewhat distant, and his response to her enthusiastic proposal that they act on the suggestion of a trip to the west of Ireland is abrupt:

> His wife clasped her hands excitedly and gave a little jump.
>
> "O, do go, Gabriel," she cried. "I'd love to see Galway again."
>
> "You can go if you like," said Gabriel coldly.

What we see emphasized in the scene is one instance in which Gabriel's relationship with his wife is distorted because he is incapable of attending to her as she is. Like a child he is still caught up in his hostile feelings for Miss Ivors. The scene, however minor, makes its contribution to that climactic scene at the hotel room when Gabriel at the outset is once again dead to any objectively real relationship with his wife and for similar reasons.

Gabriel's misconception of Miss Ivors's remarks has another significant ramification in its effect on the subject matter of Gabriel's speech, one which further contributes to the character of the speech itself. He contrives a theme which has its basis in his desire to vent his hostility. The validity of what he would say was of little concern; what he would say involved using Aunt Kate and Aunt Julia for his carefully calculated purposes:

> He would say, alluding to Aunt Kate and Aunt Julia: "Ladies and Gentlemen, the generation which is now on the wane among us may have had its faults but for my part I think it had certain qualities of hospitality, of humour, of humanity, which the new and very serious and hypereducated generation that is growing up around us seems to me to lack." Very good: that was one for Miss Ivors.

> What did he care that his aunts were only two ignorant old women?

And we see that Gabriel's characteristic defensiveness and hostility function finally in the same way that his annual practice of using the Misses Morkan's party as a vehicle to project himself as the center of attention functions: each celebrates the self at the expense of the qualitative existence of the real world. In Joyce's presentation of the Misses Morkan's drawing-room world, it is just such a rejection of the real that is the chief characteristic of "the dead."

One moment of awakening does occur both for Gabriel and for the participants at the party: the excellent performance by Aunt Julia. The little incident establishes the latent potential for living that does still exist in the gathering and especially in Gabriel. Joyce is precise in the embodied theme of the presentation:

> Gabriel recognized the prelude. It was that of an old song of Aunt Julia's—"Arrayed for the Bridal." Her voice, strong and clear in tone, attacked with great spirit the runs which embellish the air and though she sang very rapidly she did not miss even the smallest of the grace notes. To follow the voice, without looking at the singer's face, was to feel and share the excitement of swift and secure flight. Gabriel applauded loudly with all the others at the close of the song and loud applause was borne in from the invisible supper table. It sounded so genuine that a little colour struggled into Aunt Julia's face.

This celebration of an objectively real quality of the world external to the self is, however, short-lived. Freddy Malins seizes the moment for his own interests, and the dead once more obliterate the living:

> Freddy Malins, who had listened with his head perched sideways to hear her better, was still applauding when everyone else had ceased and talking animatedly to his mother who nodded her head gravely and slowly in acquiescence. At last, when he could clap no more, he stood up suddenly and hurried across the room to Aunt Julia whose hand he seized and held in both his hands, shaking it when words failed him or the catch in his voice proved too much for him.

But presently Freddy Malins is thrust aside by that other master of attention-getting:

> Mr. Browne extended his open hand towards her and said to those who were near him in the manner of a showman introducing a prodigy to an audience:
>
> "Miss Julia Morkan, my latest discovery."

As readers we readily discern the nature of the difference between the performances of Aunt Julia and presently Bartell D'Arcy on the one hand and the performances of Freddy Malins, Mr. Browne, and Gabriel in his speech on the other. It is, of course, a necessary discernment for the reading of the work.

Near the close of the long first part, two significant episodes underscore Gabriel's inability to be present to the real world around him, which in Joyce quite clearly means to be alive to it: the first is Gabriel's total failure to comprehend why Miss Ivors is leaving the party.

On the landing outside the drawing room Gabriel found his wife and Mary Jane trying to persuade Miss Ivors to stay for supper. But Miss Ivors, who had put on her hat and was buttoning her cloak, would not stay. She did not feel in the least hungry and she had already overstayed her time.

Mary Jane reveals a vague awareness of Miss Ivors's reason for leaving the party: " 'I am afraid you didn't enjoy yourself at all,' said Mary Jane hopelessly." But Gabriel's response reveals that he is completely insensitive to Miss Ivor's feelings and completely oblivious to his own part in her withdrawal: " 'If you will allow me, Miss Ivors, I'll see you home if you are really obliged to go'." And, again, after her dismay, which is followed by her "abrupt departure," Gabriel's reflections reveal his inability to participate in the objective reality of any human situation. We see him virtually imprisoned within a world created by his own distorted vision: "Gabriel asked himself was he the cause of her abrupt departure. But she did not seem to be in ill humour: she had gone away laughing. He stared blankly down the staircase." Viewed externally, Gabriel seems to be alive to his world: a scholar who "had taken his degree in the Royal University," and now a writer of reviews for the *Daily Express* and a teacher in the college. But with our insight into his internal world we see that he is quite dead to what is most real in his intercourse with other humans. His specific failure is presented as his characteristic inability to be present to the present. The second episode of the long first section is Gabriel's false speech to the assemblage, which comes to a climax in his praise of the Misses Morkan as "the Three Graces of the Dublin musical world." What makes the speech false from beginning to end is centered in the realization that it is not an honest assertion of an individual self, but the projection of a masked self: "As long as this one roof shelters the good ladies aforesaid—and I wish from my heart it may do so for many and many a long year to come" . . . etc. We remember that what hangs over his pronouncements is an earlier one spoken to himself: "What did he care that his aunts were only two ignorant old women."

It is in the light of our understanding of the presentations of the first part of the work that our reading of the second, the climax of the rebirth epiphany, can best be read. It begins with Gabriel's rapt attention on Gretta who is standing at the top of the stair: "She was leaning on the bannisters, listening to something. Gabriel was surprised at her stillness and strained his ear to listen also." Here is his first celebration of a present reality after the Aunt Julia playing scene: "If he were a painter, he would paint her in that attitude." Presently what is Gretta becomes lost again, this time in his seeing her as the object of his sexual interest and gratification: "He could have flung his arms about her hips and held her still, for his arms were trembling with desire to seize her and only the stress of his nails against the palms of his hands held the wild impulse of his body in check."

It is this anticipation of the forthcoming sexual encounter that blinds him once again to what is real about his wife's mood. The conversation which he directs to her at this point becomes as false as his earlier after-dinner speech. He introduces the story of Freddy Malins's returning money which Gabriel had loaned him and compliments Freddy, which is quite the opposite of his real being at the moment: "Gabriel strove to restrain himself from breaking out into brutal language about the sottish Malins and his pound." The marriage relationship, which is the chief subject matter of the story's

second part, is now distorted by his confused attempt to communicate with her: ostensibly concerning Freddy Malins (and that falsely) but really concerning his sexual desires. The point is that Gabriel is presented as needing to calculate his responses, with the result that he masks his real feelings, and there is no real communication. There is a fine irony in Gretta's response: "Then, suddenly raising herself on tiptoe and resting her hands lightly on his shoulders, she kissed him. 'You are a very generous person, Gabriel,' she said." That is, she praises him for his caring about Freddy Malins because she has taken what he says as real. And the distortion of their communion in their spiritual marriage is as complete as the distortion and confusion of their physical relationship.

> Gabriel, trembling with delight at her sudden kiss and at the quaintness of her phrase, put his hands on her hair and began smoothing it back, scarcely touching it with his fingers. The washing had made it fine and brilliant. His heart was brimming over with happiness. Just when he was wishing it she had come to him of her own accord. Perhaps her thoughts had been running with his. Perhaps she had felt the impetuous desire that was in him, and then the yielding mood had come upon her. Now that she had fallen to him so easily, he wondered why he had been so diffident.

And we see that for Gabriel, Gretta is not Gretta, she is his conquest. In this respect the order of his relationship to Gretta is closer to that of his relationship with Miss Ivors and earlier with Lily than it is to a marriage relationship.

The climax in the presentation of the distortion occurs when he asks, "Gretta, dear, what are you thinking about?"— expecting, of course, just one answer. Her answer that she is thinking about the song, "The Lass of Aughrim," is the first shock in the process of his return to the realm of the living. Joyce's device of the mirror image of Gabriel is one of the most effective presentations in the story. The mirror functions as the first step in the whole process of Gabriel's rebirth; it is the self confronting the self in a revelation which had heretofore never been consummated: "Gabriel stood stock-still for a moment in astonishment and then followed her. As he passed in the way of the cheval-glass he caught sight of himself in full length, his broad, well-filled shirt front, the face whose expression always puzzled him when he saw it in a mirror."

Her answer when he presses to know her concern merely intensifies his anger, and his masked feelings begin to show: " 'Someone you were in love with?' he asked ironically." The irony reflects his complete inability to see her and the way she feels. Joyce's subject matter, we realize, has been the complex relationship between living and loving. Gabriel here is still one of the dead in his inability to grant the independent being of another. But consistent with her character as one who is nowhere indirect, Gretta misses the irony of his question. Her answer is a candid revelation of herself: " 'It was a young boy I used to know,' she answered, 'named Michael Furey'." Gabriel's response on the other hand intensifies the embodiment of Joyce's theme. His is at once the calculated response: "Gabriel was silent. He did not wish her to think that he was interested in this delicate boy." For Gabriel, in his present being as one of the spiritually dead, there is no possibility of accepting what is her real concern. " 'What was he?' asked Gabriel still ironically. 'He was in the gasworks,' she said."

In the light of the final scene in which Gabriel is shocked into his first real undistorted view of himself as not merely one of the assembled dead but one who played a leading role in carrying out their ritual, each scene and episode that constituted the party is singularly unambiguous in meaning. We see that it is not merely the banality of their concerns and preoccupations which define what it means to be a participant in the rituals of the dead. And even their characteristic inability to comprehend the real existence of the world apart from the self does not finally differentiate those whom Joyce presents as the dead. We see that they are unfree to respond in any but their own narrow pattern of response. Each is an imprisoned victim, alternately asserting and defending a self which he seems to have no contact with or awareness of. The result is a kind of spiritual hell from which only Gabriel, precisely because of his sudden consciousness of himself as a total failure, becomes free. And Gabriel's failure, which finally he himself realizes, has been a failure in his humanity. It is at this point that Gabriel is shocked into the objectivity that characterizes the world of the living.

> Gabriel felt humiliated by the failure of his irony and by the evocation of this figure from the dead, a boy in the gasworks. While he had been full of memories of their secret life together, full of tenderness and joy and desire, she had been comparing him in her mind with another. A shameful consciousness of his own person assailed him. He saw himself as a ludicrous figure, acting as a pennyboy for his aunts, a nervous, well-meaning sentimentalist, orating to vulgarians and idealising his clownish lusts, the pitiable fatuous fellow he had caught a glimpse of in the mirror. Instinctively he turned his back more to the light lest she might see the shame that burned upon his forehead.

It is from this new condition of his being that Gabriel can attend to his wife. And when she reveals herself, he for the first time can hear her speak. The scene marks the first real moment in the evolution of their reborn marriage: "He did not question her again, for he felt that she would tell him of herself. Her hand was warm and moist: it did not respond to his touch, but he continued to caress it just as he had caressed her first letter to him that spring morning."

There is no rejection of his humanity in the dénouement following his awakening. The final episode presents a rapid series of Gabriel's new responses; they are a direct contrast to the responses of "the dead." When he attends to Gretta, it is Gretta that is his concern: "She stopped, choking with sobs, and, overcome by emotion, flung herself face downward on the bed, sobbing in the quilt. Gabriel held her hand for a moment longer, irresolutely, and then, shy of intruding on her grief, let it fall gently and walked quietly to the window." In this first response which follows Gabriel's new vision of the world, the formal presentations now all embody a new thematic meaning: they present what it means to belong to the world of the living. When Gabriel sees that Gretta had, in the midst of his comforting, fallen asleep, his response is in direct contrast to his earlier self-concern:

> Gabriel, leaning on his elbow, looked for a few moments unresentfully on her tangled hair and half-open mouth, listening to her deep-drawn breath. So she had had that romance in her life: a man had died for her sake. It hardly pained him now to think how poor a part he, her husband, had played in her life. He watched her while she slept, as though he and she had never lived together as man and wife.

It is here that we realize that Gabriel's relationship to his wife has undergone a radical change. It is here that we realize that for Joyce one meaning of being able to love is being able to attend to the object with the kind of attention that wishes to know it as fully as possible: "His curious eyes rested long upon her face and on her hair: and, as he thought of what she must have been then, in that time of her first girlish beauty, a strange, friendly pity for her entered his soul." Throughout the scene Gabriel's love for his wife is presented as more realistic than romantic, given to matter-of-factness rather than to sentimentality: "He did not like to say even to himself that her face was no longer beautiful, but he knew that it was no longer the face for which Michael Furey had braved death."

It is clear that the singular result of Gabriel's new ability to live resides in his being able to love. But it is not merely Gabriel's love for his wife that marks his new state of being; his new-found capacity extends to those of his immediate world. As his reflection turns to the party, to what he now sees as "his own foolish speech," suddenly into his consciousness comes a new image of his aunts:

> Poor Aunt Julia! She too would soon be a shade with the shade of Patrick Morkan and his horse. He had caught that haggard look upon her face for a moment when she was singing "Arrayed for the Bridal." Soon, perhaps, he would be sitting in that same drawing room, dressed in black, his silk hat on his knees. The blinds would be drawn down and Aunt Kate would be sitting beside him, crying and blowing her nose and telling him how Julia had died. He would cast about in his mind for some words that might console her, and he would find only lame and useless ones. Yes, yes: that would happen very soon.

Joyce, that "consummate master of form," brings together in this scene thematic presentations which have been expressed earlier but with different connotative meaning: Aunt Julia's singing had been a moment of living in the world of the dead. For Gabriel it was his one moment of attending: "To follow the voice, without looking at the singer's face, was to feel and share the excitement of swift and secure flight. Gabriel applauded loudly with all the others." But now it is clear that in his one instance of being present to another, Gabriel had indeed been "looking at the singer's face": "He had caught that haggard look upon her face for a moment when she was singing 'Arrayed for the Bridal'." The point is that in the earlier instance, the single presentation of *the living* in the midst of *the dead,* Joyce had presented Gabriel as merely responding to Aunt Julia's singing with applause. Not only had no significance been attached to his vision of "that haggard look," the vision itself had not even risen to consciousness. The contrast marks by stylistic omission the experienced difference between the thematic embodiment of "the dead" and that of "the living." Again the associations accompanying that earlier explosive utterance, "What did he care that his aunts were only two ignorant old women?" reverberate ironically in this passage. That is, it is in his new state of being capable of *caring* that makes possible Gabriel's vision of Aunt Julia arrayed, not for "the bridal" but for the burial. A further irony is evident in Gabriel's present inarticulateness in contrast to his earlier facility to rise to any occasion.

But the central irony resides in the way Joyce works with the theme of death. In an earlier presentation of the ritual of the dead, Mr. Browne and Mary Jane inadvertently come to an expression in their facile drawing-room conversation of the work's central theme. When Mr. Browne, who is "of the other persuasion," questions the practice of the monks in sleeping in their coffins rather than in "a comfortable spring bed," Mary Jane dutifully, however unconsciously, provides an explanation: " 'The coffin,' said Mary Jane, 'is to remind them of their last end'."

Further, one of the central themes which Gabriel has chosen for his speech, and again in the context of presentation of the dead, is the theme of death. Here, of course, the assertion of the fact of death as a reality in the history of the community is ironic in the light of Gabriel's ultimate realization of death. In his speech his intention is focused solely on directing the emotions of his hearers. He does not have to "cast about in his mind" for words. His images are clichés and his rhetoric empty. The passage, however, conditions the climax of the work:

> "[Let us] still cherish in our hearts the memory of those dead and gone great ones whose fame the world will not willingly let die."
>
> "Hear, hear!" said Mr. Browne loudly.
>
> "But yet," continued Gabriel, his voice falling into a softer inflection, "there are always in gatherings such as this sadder thoughts that will recur to our minds: thoughts of the past, of youth, of changes, of absent faces that we miss here tonight. Our path through life is strewn with many such sad memories; and were we to brood upon them always we could not find the heart to go on bravely with our work among the living."

As it is presented in Gabriel's speech, the realization of death is a cliché of the drawing room. The contrast with Gabriel's final realization of death and the meaning of death completes the essential contrast that gives the work its thematic structure, its meaning through its form. In the final scene Gabriel's mind goes back to the party, but now with an objective vision, one freed of the imprisonment which had blocked and distorted his being able to live. It is at this point that **"The Dead"** becomes another kind of symbol, at first a realistic symbol of what is universally true about human existence: "The air of the room chilled his shoulders. He stretched himself cautiously along under the sheets and lay down beside his wife. One by one they were all becoming shades." But presently Gabriel's experience of death becomes associated with his reflections on the meaning of living: "Better pass boldly into that other world, in the full glory of some passion, than fade and wither dismally with age." The utterance is presented not so much as a reasoned conclusion but as a sudden response—a response that establishes Gabriel's real, because experienced, relationship to death. It is an affirmation of living as its own justification for human existence.

Then in the same pattern of the sudden juxtaposition of continuing awarenesses, Gabriel's thoughts turn to his wife and her relationship to her dead lover:

> He thought of how she who lay beside him had locked in her heart for so many years that image of her lover's eyes when he had told her that he did not wish to live.
>
> Generous tears filled Gabriel's eyes. He had never felt like that himself towards any woman, but he knew that such a feeling must be love.

The point is, of course, not Gabriel's judgment on the validity of his wife's lover's protestations but on Gabriel's concern with Gretta's state of mind in living with her secret. Whatever the lover's feeling may be, it is quite obvious that it is Gabriel's feelings that "must be love."

Joyce's dénouement continues this theme; namely the caring for and recognition of the dead becomes the final step in the actualization of human love. In his rebirth Gabriel is presented as not merely responding to the universe of man; Gabriel's response here expands to a celebration of a larger universe:

> His soul had approached that region where dwell the vast hosts of the dead. He was conscious of, but could not apprehend, their wayward and flickering existence. His own identity was fading out into a grey impalpable world: the solid world itself, which these dead had one time reared and lived in, was dissolving and dwindling.

The snow, which had been merely a realistic detail in the opening episode, becomes during the unpleasantness attending Miss Ivors's imagined attack a symbol for a place of refuge for Gabriel's withdrawal from that unpleasantness. Then in the final scene the snow image again reflects the developing theme of the work: here the snow is a symbol expressing the broader scope of Gabriel's new-found capacity for conscious awareness of man's world. In Gabriel's story, the capacity for awareness has been a prerequisite for seeing and caring for that world which is apart from his own inner concern. Now for Gabriel the snow falls through this new world—one quite different from the world of the dead which he had formerly inhabited:

> snow was general all over Ireland. It was falling on every part of the dark central plain, on the treeless hills, falling softly upon the Bog of Allen and, farther westward, softly falling into the dark mutinous Shannon waves. It was falling, too, upon every part of the lonely churchyard on the hill where Michael Furey lay buried. It lay thickly drifted on the crooked crosses and headstones, on the spears of the little gate, on the barren thorns. His soul swooned slowly as he heard the snow falling faintly through the universe and faintly falling, like the descent of their last end, upon all the living and the dead.

(pp. 40-61)

William J. Handy, "Joyce's 'The Dead'," in his Modern Fiction: A Formalist Approach, *Southern Illinois University Press, 1971, pp. 29-61.*

BERNARD BENSTOCK   (essay date 1988)

[*Benstock is an American educator and critic who has written and edited several works devoted to James Joyce. In the following excerpt, he examines Joyce's use of gnomonics in* Dubliners.]

In Tom Stoppard's *Rosencrantz and Guildenstern Are Dead* Rosencrantz's last line as he is about to disappear is "Now you see me, now you. . . ." The reader knows from Shakespeare's text that he is now a ghost through death; the auditor from Stoppard's play that he is a ghost through absence. The pregnant ellipsis is itself a ghost through absence, suspended aloft and rattling its chains, unspoken but nonetheless "heard" by the process of subliminal anticipation as we instinctively complete the line by availing ourselves of a preexisting text. The gnomon of Euclid resurfaces thousands of years later in the opening paragraph of **"The Sisters,"** trailing after itself clouds of meaning probably only dimly perceivable to the young dilettante of words who is the central intelligence of the story and variously apprehended by the variety of readers of **Dubliners.** Gnomon coexists in the boy's mind in an unholy trinity with paralysis and simony: he incarnates paralysis, the *new* word, as "some maleficent and sinful being." Paralysis is the recent apparition come to claim Father Flynn; by extension simony, actually derived from a personified Simon Magus, is one who sometimes appears but should be kept away; and gnomon is a nonappearance suggesting a presence made palpable only by the concept of its absence.

The ghosts who haunt **Dubliners** outnumber those conjured up by either Henrik Ibsen or Charles Dickens, beginning with Father Flynn himself, and followed by green-eyed sailors, Father Butler, O'Donovan Rossa, Mrs. Farrington, Alphy Donnelly, Mrs. Sinico, Charles Stewart Parnell, Richard J. Tierney, Johannes Josef Ignaz von Döllinger, Father Constantine Conroy, and hosts of others, including the Holy Ghost.

Frequent attention has been given to the priestly presence and absence in **Dubliners,** a volume that begins with the death of Father Flynn. He is dead before the boy is aware that he has died, although he had been anticipating the death and attempting to read the signs of that death in the candle-lit window. Apprised of the news by Old Cotter, the boy feigns indifference rather than give the adults the satisfaction of seeing his reaction: later he finds that the pretense of indifference has evolved into a sustained absence of emotional reaction ("I found it strange that neither I nor the day seemed in a mourning mood"). The signs that eluded him at night in the priest's window he belatedly encounters by day on the shop door, the formal notice that inadvertently discloses that Father Flynn before his death was already a ghost through absence ("formerly of S. Catherine's Church, Meath Street"). Even before his official verification of the death, the boy is afraid of being haunted: "In the dark of my room I imagined that I saw again the heavy grey face of the paralytic. I drew the blankets over my head and tried to think of Christmas." The ghost of course materializes in his dream, strangely smiling, the smile reflected in the boy's responsive smile until roles are interchanged and the child absolves the priest ("I felt that I too was smiling as if to absolve the simoniac of his sin"). The smile recurs when the boy does see the dead body (and the candles *are* lit), but it is only the ghost of a smile:

> The fancy came to me that the old priest was smiling as he lay there in his coffin.

> But no. When we rose and went up to the head of the bed I saw that he was not smiling.

Each of the three childhood stories has its obligatory Catholic cleric, but whereas Father Flynn is so recently deceased, the priest that haunts **"Araby"** is remote, anonymous, unrelated to the boy who now tenants his transferred house. His domain is the "waste room behind the kitchen . . . littered with old useless papers"; his legacy is a suspicious trio of abandoned books reflecting either his interests (ostensible or covert) or rejection, books he purposely has discarded—in either case they transfer to the accidental recipient who prefers the one with yellow pages. Bracketed by dead priests, Father Butler of **"An Encounter"** is very much alive, but his pres-

ence is confined to his school so that the truants in absenting themselves from classes for the day manage to disengage themselves from his living presence. Nonetheless, the spectre of Father Butler threatens to hover over them as they plan their disengagement: "Leo Dillon was afraid that we might meet Father Butler or someone out of the college." It is a fear that no rational disclaimer can dispel, for Leo proves a ghost through absence, preferring to face the priest in the flesh than risk the priest in spirit at the Pigeon House, and becomes truant to the planned truancy. Mahony's contrasting insensitivity is nonetheless "sensible" to the protagonist ("Mahony asked, very sensibly, what would Father Butler be doing out at the Pigeon House"). Lulled by this logic, the boys risk ghostly encounters on the day's adventures, but they manage to procrastinate sufficiently in their journey toward their destination never actually to arrive at the Pigeon House—it too an unrealized goal that may portend more than it promises.

The notable absence of priests becomes endemic throughout the adult stories of **Dubliners;** absence and anonymity, established in **"Araby,"** return in **"Eveline,"** once again associated with yellowing:

> And yet during all those years she had never found out the name of the priest whose yellowing photograph hung on the wall above the broken harmonium beside the coloured print of the promises made to Blessed Margaret Mary Alacoque. He had been a school friend of her father. Whenever he showed the photograph to a visitor her father used to pass it with a casual word:

> —He is in Melbourne now.

The tone of indirection, the degree of insignificance, the remoteness of the location in Australia, the indifference in Eveline's idle curiosity—all these relegate the departed cleric to obscurity. And there is no one until **"Ivy Day in the Committee Room"** to represent the Dublin clergy in **Dubliners.**

As a prelude to the mysterious appearance of Father Keon, we have the mention of "Father Burke's name" conscripted into service by candidate Tierney's canvassers as one of the nominators of their man, a name with ironic reverberations once we hear about the revered Father Tom Burke eulogized in **"Grace,"** although at the other end of the spectrum there is Daniel Burke, the Dublin publican in whose premises Mr. Duffy has his lunch (Tierney too is a publican). It is Keon of course who excites the interests of the canvassers, an apparition out of nowhere, bundled up so that his clerical collar is concealed, hovering in the doorway of the darkened committee room, seeking someone who is not there. (His face has "the appearance of yellow cheese"!) First designated as "A person resembling a poor clergyman or a poor actor," Father Keon is classified in terms of a false façade (a clergyman dissembling? an actor impersonating?), and Henchy voices an immediate disbelief apparently in his actual existence: "O, Father Keon! . . . Is that you?" Failing to find the object of his visit, Father Keon quickly and inconspicuously disappears, leaving behind enthralled speculation:

> What is he exactly? . . .

> Is he a priest at all? . . .

> And how does he knock it out? . . .

> Is he attached to any chapel or church or institution or—."

The lapsed question, although answered in the negative, re-surfaces immediately in a new context emphasizing once again that which is missing from the committee room and that which their employer could logically and easily have provided: "Is there any chance of a drink itself?" And de-spite the temporary fascination with the "black sheep" pas-tor, he is summarily allowed to fade into inconsequence.

Father Keon has the almost unique distinction of being a ghost through *change of manners*, although he may have an analogue in the famous Father Purdon of **"Grace,"** the one story in **Dubliners** in which the clergy are of pronounced im-portance. The centrality of religion does not guarantee the sanctity of ecclesiastical stature: as the comforters gather around the Kernan sickbed (at which Fogarty intrudes as an uninvited, unexpected guest), the talk is of popes who do not behave like popes ("there were some bad lots," Cunningham concedes), but write poems on photography; cardinals who either change their beliefs or leave the Church; priesthoods that are "unworthy of the name"; the Jesuit Order that "never fell away," although in reality it had been suspended on several occasions; and a sermon that is "not exactly a ser-mon, you know. It's just a friendly kind of talk, you know." Mrs. Kernan's contribution to Catholic orthodoxy intro-duces the banshee as part of a quadrilateral Trinity, parallel-ing Fogarty's presence as a Fourth Comforter. When Father Purdon does make his appearance, he justifies his reputation as "a man of the world like ourselves" (Kernan had never heard of him) and lectures the businessmen on double-entry spiritual accountancy. It is a resuscitated Kernan who at-tends the retreat, apparently unmindful that no spiritual comforter from the Church has been present at his bedside, only well-meaning but ill-informed laity involved in luring him to the Gardiner Street church through duplicity. No spiritual emanation attends the Christmastime festivities at the Morkans' in **"The Dead"** either, although the reigning pope is taken to task for eliminating women from the choirs, and monks at Mount Melleray are lauded for sleeping in their coffins, although not yet dead. Particularly conspicuous for his absence is Gabriel's brother, Father Constantine Conroy, senior curate at Balbriggan; no one mentions him at all dur-ing the evening, and it is only in a photograph that Constan-tine is present, not as a priest but as a child "dressed in a man-o'-war suit."

When Gabriel Conroy posits a general paralytic condition of snow falling generally throughout Ireland, he envisions the Oughterard graveyard as a paradigm of Ireland, "snow falling . . . upon all the living and the dead." These two dis-crete categories had undergone a series of fusions in **"The Dead,"** a process anticipated by almost every story in **Dublin-ers.** Deaths occur only in two of the stories, **"The Sisters"** and **"A Painful Case,"** but the margin separating life and death is often depleted: Eveline Hill is not yet twenty, yet has lost her mother and a brother; even a childhood playmate, Tizzie Dunn, is already dead. She herself has undergone a change from childhood into a prematurely responsibility-ridden young adult, for whom the efficacy of escape is justi-fied by the changes in the world around her ("Everything changes"). When she assumes that "Now she was going to go away like the others," does she mean like the Waters, who "had gone back to England," or like Tizzie Dunn? The pho-tograph of the forgotten priest returns her own image should she leave; she may not be able to imagine the prospective house in Buenos Aires, but she can visualize herself as *absent* from her own home, a fading, yellowing, discarded memory,

Sidney Parade, the scene of Mrs. Sinico's demise in "A Painful Case."

a vacuum that only the dust fills. It is the fear of nonexistence that eventually paralyzes Eveline into remaining a ghost in her own home.

Negative haunting—the absence of an expected ghost—is a motif introduced in the first story as the child realizes the lack of emotional response to the news of the priest's anticipated death. **"A Painful Case"** further develops the concept: by maintaining no real contact with other living beings, Duffy has insulated himself from their ghostly visitations after death ("He lived his spiritual life without any communion with others, visiting his relatives at Christmas and escorting them to the cemetery when they died"); by living "at a little distance from his body, regarding his own acts with doubtful side-glances," he has established himself as his own ghost, a comfortable ghost he knows and has accommodated himself to. Although the official verdict records that "No blame at-tached to anyone," Duffy suspects that he has compromised himself into qualifying as Mrs. Sinico's intended victim by temporarily conducting his inadvisable relationship with her (Captain Sinico, a ghost through absence, had created a vacu-um into which Duffy allowed himself to be drawn). As long as Duffy can convince himself that Mrs. Sinico is to blame, he can remain free of her haunting; as soon as he implicates himself as responsible for her neglect (he too a ghost through absence), the danger of her ghost accosting him becomes im-minent: "She seemed to be near him in the darkness. At mo-ments he seemed to feel her voice touch his ear, her hand touch his. He stood still to listen. Why had he withheld life from her? Why had he sentenced her to death? He felt his moral nature falling to pieces." A third turn of the screw, however, eliminates any possibility of ectoplasmic contact from the dead Mrs. Sinico; instead, it is the *absence* of any such emanation that haunts Duffy:

> He could not feel her near him in the darkness nor her voice touch his ear. He waited for some minutes listening. He could hear nothing: the night was perfectly silent. He listened again: perfectly silent. He felt that he was alone.

The ease with which the dead evaporate from memory, a subject of concern to Leopold Bloom ("People talk about you a bit: forget you. . . . Even Parnell. Ivy day dying out" [*Ulysses*]), as if he had witnessed the events a year or so earlier in the Tierney committee room. Parnell's ghost, wanly evoked by Joe Hynes, fails to generate fire or warmth among the jejune political canvassers; nor does the ethereal presence of Christ fare much better in the hothouse atmosphere of the Morkans' Christmas party, where no bursting forth of an epiphany illumines the twelfth night of the Yule season. Father Flynn's corpse is as devoid of spirit as his dropped chalice was of sacramental wine; Eveline Hill's mother is recalled for her dying gibberish; and the missing mother of the Donnelly brothers in **"Clay"** has long been supplanted by Maria (even while alive the mother had been relegated to a back bench—"Mamma is mamma but Maria is my proper mother"—and then displaced completely, her death presumably responsible for the "break-up at home"). And the dead of **"The Dead"** outnumber the living, literally as well as metamorphically. The presence of Gabriel, the two aunts, and niece Mary Jane is overbalanced by the absence of the third sister Ellen, Gabriel's mother; of the brother Pat, Mary Jane's father; of Gabriel's father, T. J. Conroy; of grandfather Patrick Morkan; of Mary Jane's mother—by implication, although she is never mentioned. (While the grandfather is "late lamented," his horse commands even greater immortality as "The never-to-be-forgotten Johnny"). All the adults in the family enclave of **"The Dead"** are parentless, an epidemic situation in *Dubliners,* where even young adults seem devoid of parents (except for the fathers of Jimmy Doyle and John Corley, and the disunited parents of Polly Mooney). The genesis of this condition is apparent in the boyhood stories where the protagonist of **"The Sisters"** and **"Araby"** lives with an aunt and uncle instead, and not even surrogate parents are as much as mentioned in **"An Encounter."**

The extent to which the boy's parents have been refined out of existence is all the more poignant by the negative evidence, particularly in **"The Sisters,"** where death is the immediate subject matter. There is ample time even in this brief narrative for the death of Father Flynn to invoke recollections by the boy of the death of his own parents (should he have been aware of the instances of their dying) or the condition of their being dead (should he have been too young when it actually happened). Instead, there is a vacuum, as if those deaths were too remote for his conscious comparison, or were a blocked passage of thought that will not allow the boy's mind to consider the traumas of the past. The psychological gnomon of **"The Sisters"** has two faces: that which shows itself in the first half of the story, as the protagonist actively investigates his reactions to the death of the priest, and that which hides itself in the second half, as he abdicates his function as active reactor and allows the events in the priest's death room to unfold themselves "objectively," ghost writing on the *tabula rasa* of his mind, to which he adds no marginal notations. By failing to comment on the conversation between his aunt and Eliza Flynn, by refusing to allow himself to think critically of the tenor of their talk, the boy not only succumbs to a form of mental paralysis, but also "disappears" from the scene (like Nannie in her deafness and fatigue), abstracted from the parallelogram.

Joyce's stage direction for the gnomon is particularly specific, "the word *gnomon* in the Euclid"—some of his indicators are left vague, some self-explanatory, some pointedly marked. The parallel image of the three words of **"The Sisters"** can be found in the opening portion of **"Araby"** in the three books (books are repositories of words), where the author of *The Abbot* is specified, the author of *The Memoirs of Vidocq* implicit, and the author of *The Devout Communicant* a ghost through absence. Yet even the Euclidian gnomon is self-reflexive, and the gnomonics of *Dubliners* are of parallel possibilities: "the remainder of a parallelogram after the removal of a similar parallelogram containing one of its corners" suggests both presence and absence, that which has been taken away and that which remains. Both conditions are operative in *Dubliners* and both germane to the technic of the book. The presumably orphaned boy of the book's "Telemachiad" is the remaining factor in a construction that has lost its initial construct; and in the two social situations he is an uncomfortable fourth corner (uncommunicative when his aunt, uncle, and Old Cotter discuss the death of the priest, and when his aunt, Eliza, and Nannie conduct a dismal wake at his bier). Whereas in the first instance he comments silently to himself, in the second he has given up even that degree of participation so that, totally abstracted, he silently observes a parallelogram consisting of his aunt, the Flynn sisters, and the dead man. In the "Nostos" of *Dubliners,* **"The Dead,"** some of the living return home, constantly casting their shadows over those dead that have been removed from the box stage of the Morkans' residence (itself a corner transplanted from the original house in Stony Batter), and in turn are shadows themselves of those who haunt the corners of the rooms.

The "Odyssey" proper of *Dubliners,* stories four through fourteen, contains numerous instances of spiritual legerdemain, inexact substitutions, substances that cast no shadows, and frames that enclose no solid constructs. Eveline's rooms are mysteriously invaded by dust despite her weekly effort to eliminate the dust (just as "the evening invade[s] the avenue" as she watches from her window). She has chosen to replace the dusty air of Dublin with the clean air of Buenos Aires, removing herself from an area in which she cannot prevent invasions. "Down far in the avenue she could hear a street organ playing," a further uninvited invasion of her thoughts, and the familiar "air" conjures up an involuntary memory of her promise to her dying mother. The dead mother has been replaced by the blessed Margaret Mary Alacoque (temporarily, Eveline assumes, but by the end of the story it proves to be a permanent replacement). Eveline had become of late a substitute for her absent brothers (Ernest now dead, Harry "in the church decorating business . . . nearly always down somewhere in the country" as the recipient of her father's wrath. Should she escape, she would undoubtedly be replaced in the victim's position by the young siblings that she promised her mother she would protect—as a surrogate mother. "Ernest had been her favourite," but he was no longer in the equation, his place miraculously taken by a sailor named Frank, "kind, manly, open-hearted," assuredly earnest. Eveline mentally deconstructs the substance of her Dublin dwelling ("Home! She looked round the room, reviewing all its familiar objects which she had dusted once a week for so many years, wondering where on earth all the dust came from. Perhaps she would never see again those familiar objects from which she had never dreamed of being divided") and reconstructs it in her imagination at the other end of the world ("But in her new home, in a distant, unknown country, it would not be like that. Then she would be married, she—Eveline"). The assumption that "she would not be treated as her mother had been" is a chancey one, predicated on a false syllogism—after all, her mother had been married too and nonetheless had been treated badly. The ghost of the "melancholy air of Italy" returns to project her memories back to her mother: the projection forward to her new life is censored in her thoughts but was obviously instrumental in preventing her from boarding the ship. Adept at handling the Dublin market crowds on terra cognita ("holding her black leather purse tightly in her hand as she elbowed her way through the crowd and returning home late under her load of provisions"), she rebels against the "swaying crowd in the station at the North Wall" and refuses to be pushed along toward that "distant, unknown country," preferring The Devil That You Know. (pp. 519-26)

Eveline's successful maneuvers through her neighborhood market suggest one of the few instances in which she holds her own against a sea of troubles. Her youthful counterpart in **"Araby"** has also attempted to buck the tide of a similar environment, concentrating on the phantasm of Mangan's sister rather than the necessity of doing the shopping:

> Her image accompanied me even in places the most hostile to romance. On Saturday evenings when my aunt went marketing I had to go to carry some of the parcels. We walked through the flaring streets, jostled by drunken men and bargaining women, amid the curses of labourers, the shrill litanies of shop-boys who stood guard by the barrels of pigs' cheeks, the nasal chanting of street-singers who sang a *come-all-you* about O'Donovan Rossa, or a ballad about the troubles in our native land. These noises converged in a single sensation of life for me: I imagined that I bore my chalice safely through a throng of foes.

The boy assumes himself above the battle; Eveline persists as a vital part of it. She has temporarily escaped the hostility of her home, where she had fought her father for the money with which to shop, and engaged herself in the pursuit of her provisions; the boy has been wrenched away from his romantic isolation to carry the aunt's purchases. Eveline's mundane black leather purse is mirrored in his ethereal chalice, and although he envisions himself as a romantic knight templar, the shouts of the shop-boys are to them their own plebian "litanies."

Like Eveline Hill, Jimmy Doyle also has only a single extant male parent, but no mention is made of the significance—if any—of the missing mother. In his own life the father had undergone a major transformation, from merely a "butcher in Kingstown" to an entrepreneur "rich enough to be alluded to in the Dublin newspapers as a merchant prince." But in doing so, Mr. Doyle has had to remove a part of himself that would no longer fit the new pattern: having "begun life as an advanced Nationalist," he "had modified his views early." The transformation that Jimmy himself undergoes during the one-day duration of **"After the Race"** is an ironic reverse image of his father's rise to wealth, especially ironic because Jimmy "had a respect for his father's shrewdness in business matters." As much as he would like to emulate his father's success by investing his patrimony in the automobile enterprise of his continental acquaintances, he loses it instead in

a reckless evening of card-playing. The flaw in his procedure becomes apparent when he drunkenly and angrily adopts the role that his father had so prudently abandoned: the presence of the Englishman Routh goads him into "advanced Nationalist views": "Jimmy, under generous influences, felt the buried zeal of his father wake to life within him: he roused the torpid Routh at last." Here in Kingstown Harbour, within a stone's throw of the location of his father's first butcher shop, the son brings the family fortune full circle. The card game results in Routh's victory and Doyle's defeat. And looming behind the action is the prudent Hungarian Villona, the calm and cautious musician whom Jimmy should have emulated, abstaining from the card game and refusing to risk financial loss. The parallel position is obvious: as we know from the Arthur Griffith pamphlet mentioned in *Ulysses* (and probably ghost-written by Leopold Bloom), Hungary stands in mediate relation to Austria as Ireland to England. Doyle, in his zeal, had failed to notice the significant shadow cast by Villona, his ideal other self, until it is too late:

> The cabin door opened and he saw the Hungarian standing in a shaft of grey light:
>
> —Daybreak, gentlemen!

Whereas the geometric pattern formed by the time of the discourse in **"After the Race,"** from Doyle *père*'s origins to Doyle *fil*'s rude awakening, executes a full circle, the shape of the narrative, from the Naas Road into Dublin and out again to Kingstown Harbour, arcs like a campaniform crested in the center of Dublin where Mr. Doyle made his money and the Doyles now live. The specifics are vague (Jimmy's house is somewhere just north of the Bank of Ireland), but the general line is carefully circumscribed. In **"Two Gallants"** the details are so precise as to graph the route taken by the protagonists, especially Lenehan's lone stroll elliptically through central Dublin. His peregrinations mark three distinct orbits of increasing greater circumference with each excursion, and although he often retraces his steps along one side of a previous route, each of the three swaths that he cuts through Dublin topography creates a separate parallelogram contiguous with one of the others. Entry into the Dublin maze is effected in the company of Corley, a man of straight and direct approaches—they saunter "down the hill of Rutland Square" (itself a parallelogram) down into the center of the city, cut west on Nassau Street, south on Kildare, west again on the north of the Green, until Corley makes contact with his slavey a short block south on the Hume Street corner. Lenehan then follows them till they board their tram and begins his solitary meanderings through the streets. North on Merrion Street and the west side of Merrion Square and east on Clare and Leinster Streets bring him back to the corner of Kildare and Nassau, completing the first circumambulation of a small parallelogram. Even before reaching Kildare Street and the spot where he saw the harpist playing "Silent, O Moyle," Lenehan finds himself responding to the sweetness of that "unheard music," an echo vestigal within him of the harpist's song, an auditory gnomon; but as he passes the place itself in front of the Kildare Club where the harpist stood, there is no mention of either the harpist still being there or of Lenehan aware of the significance of the location. The narrative concerns itself with Lenehan's absorption of and with the music: "The air which the harpist had played began to control his movements. His softly padded feet played the melody while his fingers swept a scale of variations idly along the railings after each group of notes." The railings in question are along the Duke's Lawn, which means that Lenehan has not yet reached the point of origin, yet the next sentence finds him already heading west on St. Stephen's Green South, a mental ellipsis parallel to Stephen Dedalus' gnomonic visit to the Gouldings in "Proteus"—yet even Lenehan's obtruding thoughts are as silent as the Moyle.

By heading north on Grafton Street, Lenehan approaches the corner of Nassau Street and completes his second parallelogram, larger than the first but also containing a portion of his previous walk with Corley. Only the third and most far-reaching of the parallelograms is constructed of four sides of isolated and individualized walking by Lenehan, its first long side completed when he returns to the point at Rutland Square where some time before he and Corley were coming down the hill ("*If Judas go forth tonight it is to Judas his steps will tend,*" Stephen mused in Scylla and Charybdis; "We walk through ourselves, meeting robbers, ghosts, giants, old men, young men, widows, brothers-in-love. But always meeting ourselves" [*Ulysses*]). As if hoping to avoid such a confrontation, Lenehan turns sharply left at the Square, along a street that is never named in the text but where he finds a "poor-looking shop" and has his meager meal. In a story in which so many street names are catalogued, every one of them proven to have strong associations with the British hegemony in Ireland, the silent but ghostly significance of that "dark quiet street" with its "sombre look" is a gnomonic omission: Lenehan has found himself on Great Britain Street, where Father Flynn had died.

Once inside the shop he finds himself a fourth corner in what had previously been an equilateral triangle. Seating himself opposite "two work-girls and a mechanic," Lenehan is palpably out of place, but "to appear natural he pushed his cap back on his head and planted his elbows on the table. The mechanic and the two work-girls examined him point by point before resuming their conversation in a subdued voice." The uneasy alliance of the four designates Lenehan as the odd man out, but in his thoughts he divorces himself from the parallelogram to conjure up an avatar, a married self seated at his hearth with a wife who finances his new incarnation. His next real encounter (he has since turned south on Capel Street and east on Dame Street) is with two friends with whom he stops to talk; they in turn speculate on a fourth, a mysterious Mac whom one of them had seen on Westmoreland Street (the fourth side of the present geographic square beginning with Great Britain, Capel, and Dame), and Lenehan had seen the night before. The shadowy Mac, his name only a hint of his full appellation, is here, there, everywhere, seen "an hour before" in one place and "the night before" in another, and he might have won some money at billiards, which would make his present whereabouts important.

When Lenehan arrives at Grafton Street, he has completed his third rhomboidal diagrammatic wandering, and a glance at the College of Surgeons clock tells him that time too has run out—he rushes forward to his reunion with Corley. Now the basic quest for the gnomon begins: what has been lurking behind the Corley-Lenehan conspiracy has been kept from the reader, for the overheard part of their conversation remained ambiguous and no clear statement of intention is disclosed in Lenehan's thoughts. The elusiveness of the quest is accentuated as Lenehan's anxieties mount; he focuses on an anticipated entity that does not exist ("kept his gaze fixed on the part from which he expected to see Corley and the young woman return"). What he sees is emptiness ("His eyes

searched the street: there was no sign of them"), but he persists ("He strained his eyes as each tram stopped") until he concludes that they have eluded him ("They must have gone home by another way"), and despairs of success ("He knew Corley would fail"). When they do materialize, a significant eclipse blocks his view: Corley's "broad figure hid hers from view for a few seconds and then she reappeared running up the steps." And now with success in sight Lenehan finds Corley strangely evasive; Lenehan presses on and is vouchsafed a glimpse of the missing element, the yearned-for grail for which the knight had quested: "He extended a hand towards the light and, smiling, opened it slowly to the gaze of his disciple. A small coin shone in the palm."

The overall gnomonic presence in **"The Boarding House"** persists in a familial parallelogram in the Mooney family: when Mr. Mooney has been abstracted from the pattern, a vacuum was created into which Bob Doran unconsciously drifts against his will and better judgment. Changes have been rampant: the daughter of a butcher and the wife of a butcher, Mrs. Mooney has become a boarding-house keeper; her daughter, once a typist, has been withdrawn from her job and is resident in the boarding house; her son has been transformed into "a hard case"; and her discarded husband is now a bailiff's man, but mostly he sits "all day long . . . in the bailiff's room, waiting to be put on a job." From Spring Garden the remaining three Mooneys have transplanted to Hardwicke Street, where the missing Mooney received "neither money nor food nor house-room." The remaining trio could have held its own had the father not imposed himself on his daughter where she worked: once she has been removed from the corn-factor's office, her only option is marriage, and into the gap ventures timid Bob Doran like a mouse. When the trap snaps shut, he has only one way out—by going over the wall—but he visualizes himself removed from his job after "thirteen years in a great Catholic wine-merchant's office," and, rather than risk that, he capitulates. One ironic aspect of the pattern remains for a future glimpse of Bob Doran in **Ulysses,** where, as a perennial drunk married to Polly Mooney, he has come full circle, replacing her drunken father in the family quadrilateral equation and probably as out of a job as his father-in-law.

The next three stories of **Dubliners** track the three protagonists as they venture forth to encounter reality, not only for the millionth time, as the Stephen of **A Portrait** intends, but also for the first time, walking through themselves, "meeting robbers, ghosts, giants," and so forth. Of the three, Chandler of **"A Little Cloud"** is the most optimistic that this evening will be eventful: he expects to meet a gnomon of himself, what he might have been had he too broken out of his environment and traveled abroad like Gallaher, and he comes armed with a new image of himself, "T. Malone Chandler," poet "of the Celtic school." His ammunition is illusory, however; his armorplating, threadbare: crossing the Liffey he has a moment of inspiration in which the houses look like tramps, and he wonders whether this ability to perceive the essential substance beneath a shadowy façade could be translated into original poetry, further speculating whether "Gallaher might be able to get it into some London paper for him." Before long Chandler has already glimpsed the English reviews of his volume of poems, almost unaware what an important solid entity has evaporated: the poems themselves. In meeting Gallaher (the robber—"he got mixed up in some shady affair, some money transaction"; the ghost through absence in London for eight years; a giant in Chandler's estimation—

"Ignatius Gallaher on the London Press!"), he seems to realize that this avatar of himself is someone he could never have become, nor would want to have become, yet is unsure whether he is relieved or all the more despondent at his pronounced inability to evolve into anything other than his insignificant self. His attempt to set himself on a new path, the reading of Byron presumably in preparation eventually to become a Celtic Byron, proves shortlived: the reading of the first poem in the volume is interrupted, the poem truncated in the middle of the sixth line, another ellipsis disclosing the missing section of the structure.

In **"Counterparts"** (a title that reverberates with gnomonic import), Farrington Sober goes forth to encounter Farrington Drunk, yet the desired drunkenness by night proves as elusive as sober efficiency by day. Hitherto he had been able to cover his tracks by several sleights-of-hand: providing himself with glasses of porter during working hours; augmenting a half-hour lunch period into an hour and half; keeping a cap in his pocket for the walk to the pub, while its surrogate remained on the hatrack; adding a caraway seed to disguise his breath. Eventually he will pawn his watch when money is unavailable, even to the extent of extracting six shillings in lieu of the five offered by the pawnbroker. But on this decisive day the missing segments in his presumably ordered life in the offices of Crosbie and Alleyne have been consistently uncovered: letters are missing from the Delacour file; the Bodley and Kirwan contract cannot be copied out in time; the washroom ploy has been exposed by Mr. Shelley; *Bernard Bernard* has intruded on *Bernard Bodley,* the second Bernard a shadow of the first, the Bodley deleted entirely from the construct; the cashier cannot be relied on for an advance. When thoughts of riotous drinking subsume him at his desk, he finds that "his imagination had so abstracted him that his name was called twice [like *Bernard Bernard*] before he answered." And he had already been threatened with a report by the omnipresent Mr. Alleyne to the mysteriously abstracted Mr. Crosbie, a titular figure lurking somewhere in the wings.

The failure of the evening is caused by Farrington not being the man he claims to be. With six shillings and a good retort to repeat in the bars, Farrington should have been able to get drunk enough to satisfy his desire for a "spell of riot," but instead he finds himself standing more drinks than he receives, outclassed even in the telling of his own story by Higgins (surrogate raconteur from his office), losing his title as strong man to Weathers, and failing to win the "woman in the big hat" because he had run out of money. The homecoming is also replete with portentous absences, "the kitchen empty and the kitchen fire nearly out." His wife has retreated to the chapel; and the wrong son (in the dark he thinks Tom is Charlie) apprehended; no dinner readily available; and when our hero (himself a Norman with no given name) is on the verge of revenging himself against Tom, the boy offers to say a *"Hail Mary,"* in lieu of the probably more appropriate *"Our Father."* But failure was always in the offing for Farrington because of his own lacunae in retelling the incident with Mr. Alleyne: instead of faithfully repeating his comment, "I don't think, sir, that that's a fair question to put to me," self-interest causes him to omit the word *sir.*

Maria's journey in **"Clay"** has all the earmarks of a familiar one, almost a ritualistic Halloween excursion on which she anticipates few if any surprises—although she stresses her preference that she encounter Joe Donnelly sober rather than

Joe Donnelly drunk: "He was so different when he took any drink." The implication has an ironic reverberation when Maria approves of a total stranger, the "colonel-looking gentleman" on the tram, insisting that it was easy "to know a gentleman even when he has a drop taken"—Joe is apparently a poor imitation of a gentleman. Maria is easily deceived by appearances, partly because she lives in a world in which "barmbracks seemed uncut; but if you went closer you would see that they had been cut into long even thick slices" (Maria "saw that every woman got her four slices"). Equilateral squares removed from a seemingly whole rhomboid imply both a completeness and unity that are misleading: Maria *never* gets the ring baked into one of the slices, although Lizzie Fleming *always* assures her that she will. When Maria laughs, "the tip of her nose *nearly* met the tip of her chin"; she sits in the tram (the only seat available is the stool at the end; on the second tram the only seat is the one offered by the only gentleman), "her toes *barely* touching the floor" (emphasis added). Credited with being a peacemaker at the laundry, Maria is a failure in attempting to make peace between Joe and his brother Alphy, for whom she was the "proper mother." At the Donnelly's, brother Alphy has a stand-in, his nephew Alphy, obviously named for him.

That there are vast lacunae in Maria's life is obvious as the story develops, and they are mirrored in almost comic fashion in the minutia of missing items: by giving away "one or two slips" from her plants, Maria is creating gnomonic patterns, but these are expected to grow back and recomplete the pattern; by serving tea she disappoints Ginger Mooney, who would prefer "a sup of porter"; she changes cake shops because "Downes's plumcake had not enough almond icing on top," and then of course she manages to lose the plumcake on the tram; offered stout or port she wants neither, but Joe insists and she has to accept; Joe first cannot find the nutcracker and then cannot see the corkscrew (a missing corkscrew will temporarily inhibit the festivities in the Committee Room); mischievously offered the clay in the divination game, she has it mysteriously withdrawn from her, replaced by a prayerbook—but still no ring. And finally, when singing "I Dreamt That I Dwelt," Maria fails to sing the second verse but repeats the first one instead. Readers have scoured the missing verse for excessive elements of romanticism that Maria might have unconsciously repressed, although it hardly seems any more romantic than the first. Apparently Maria has become *fixed* on the elements of the verse she sang. She is a case of arrested development: her body is still tiny ("In spite of its years she found it a nice tidy little body"); she still blushes like a schoolgirl; her immaturity makes her the butt of both condescension and mockery (there is no wedding cake in the offing for her and no ring). And even the assumption that a lack of maturation means only a stasis that is permanent is unrealistic; "Coming events cast their shadows before," as Leopold Bloom muses (*Ulysses*), and Maria's holds on her position at the laundry and on life are tenuous.

No one maintains as tight a control on the status quo as Maria's successor, the James Duffy of **"A Painful Case."** By a monkish ordering of his life he allows for no surprises, no vulnerable gaps in a solid façade, no expectations that can lead to disappointment. The route that he has carefully circumscribed for himself takes him from his room in Chapelizod to his bank on Baggot Street; lunch at Dan Burke's and dinner in "an eatinghouse in George's Street" make his day fixed and predictable. Evenings are somewhat less structured, and when he found himself an inappropriate bourgeois intellectual among hardheaded workmen at meetings of the Irish Socialist Party, he abstracted himself from a situation in which he did not properly fit. Concerts were certainly more consistent with his position in life until he chanced to meet Mrs. Sinico, a woman for whom a vacuum had been created because her husband, a ship's captain, "was often away." Introducing himself into the Sinico household, Duffy finds himself sailing under false colors: "Captain Sinico encouraged his visits, thinking that his daughter's hand was in question. He had dismissed his wife so sincerely from his gallery of pleasures that he did not suspect that anyone else would take an interest in her." At least two interesting gnomons emerge from the Duffy/Mrs. Sinico/Captain Sinico/Mary Sinico parallelogram.

As a construct, Joyce's **"A Painful Case"** is a narrative that contains as its centerpiece a newspaper item titled "A Painful Case," the second title serving as an indicator pointing toward Mrs. Sinico, but the overall title eventually directing toward Mr. Duffy. The one case impinges on the other: what was relevant for Mrs. Sinico was relevant for Mr. Duffy. He was quick to read certain signs that disturbed him and that led to his rupture with her ("she had shown every signal of unusual excitement"); she in turn failed to heed the signs which warned her of danger ("The company had always taken every precaution to prevent people crossing the lines except by the bridges, both by placing notices in every station and by the use of patent spring gates at level crossings"). In the interim between dismissing her from his life and the end of her life, several discrete sections from Mr. Duffy's ordered existence were deleted: "He kept away from concerts. . . . His father died; the junior partner of the bank retired." On the night in which she died all other members of her family were absent from her life: Captain Sinico "was not in Dublin at the time of the accident," and Mary "was not at home until an hour after the accident." That "No blame attached to anyone" is as equally applicable to the exonerated engine driver as to the victim herself, and by extension to the innocent bank cashier who once "allowed himself to think that in certain circumstances he would rob his bank, but as these circumstances never arose, his life rolled on evenly—an adventureless tale."

The public life stories of **Dubliners** extend the structures and thicken the textures of the increasingly complex narratives that lead to **"The Dead."** Each of the last four narratives takes on the proportions of a parallelepiped, prismatic as well as parallelogrammatic, from which solid segments are deftly deleted as we watch forms take shape and in which empty sections are enigmatically filled. In Tierney's election headquarters in **"Ivy Day in the Committee Room,"** the man himself never turns up, although he is a mere shadow of the Parnell politician to whose coattails he nominally adheres. Parnell himself is a shade of a shade, present primarily in a poem praised for its fine writing but containing various qualities, like sincere appreciation, yet totally devoid of fine writing. That Tierney is so unlike Parnell has allowed Wilkins, the Conservative candidate, to withdraw from the race (he is too exactly duplicated by Tierney), and imposes his canvasser Crofton on the Nationalists, despite his discomfort among them. Clear lines of demarcation are blurred, and the linear succession of parent and child rarely results in an exact duplication: the caretaker Jack complains of the ingratitude and dissoluteness of his son; Joe Hynes is declared as not being "nineteen carat," although his father Larry is lionized ("Many a good turn he did in his day"); and Tierney is re-

duced to a "mean little tinker" and "mean little shoe-boy of hell," although in denigrating his origins Mr. Henchy unintentionally sets up the opposite equation: Tierney's father had a second-hand clothes shop and kept a bottle on hand for Sunday morning cronies, whereas his son has become a publican selling drinks on a large scale. Nor is the parallel between King Edward VII and his mother devoid of irony: his profligate life is excused by Henchy, who welcomes his visit to Ireland, all the more because Queen Victoria never deigned to make the voyage—whereas in actuality she did more than once. Disproportion in **"Ivy Day"** is often caused by the myopic sighting through the wrong end of the telescope, although reversals are possible under the right circumstances. For the assembled canvassers, who are in the process of talking about their achievements but are not out canvassing at the moment, the missing items are payment and promised drinks from Tierney's pub. As long as neither is forthcoming their attitudes are jaundiced. As soon as the dozen bottles of stout make their belated appearance (even without the necessary corkscrew), the missing money goes unmentioned and Henchy, who had suspected Joe Hynes of being a spy for the opposition, now praises him as a loyal Parnellite, having been significantly altered by the intrusion of a bottle of stout.

Over generous dollops of whiskey, Hoppy Holohan and Mrs. Kearney in **"A Mother"** sign a contract for the musical services of her daughter at a series of concerts sponsored by the *Eire Abu* Society. Although these are the constants apparent in the foreground, two variables lurk in the shadows: Mr. Kearney, "sober, thrifty and pious," whose "conversation, which was serious, took place at intervals in his great brown beard"; and Mr. Fitzgerald, the secretary of the Society (Holohan is after all only the "assistant secretary"), with a "vacant smile" that Mrs. Kearney immediately finds irritating. Holohan himself is progressively eliminated from the configuration: even at the beginning he is eclipsed by Mrs. Kearney ("it was Mrs. Kearney who arranged everything"), and once he is challenged by her, Holohan effaces himself, deferring to his superior ("You'd better speak to Mr. Fitzgerald, said Mr. Holohan distantly"). And when confronted by her, Mr. Fitzgerald invokes an even vaster and more mysterious entity: "Mr. Fitzgerald, who did not catch the point at issue very quickly, seemed unable to resolve the difficulty and said that he would bring the matter before the committee." Mrs. Kearney, however, is dubious but withholds her sarcastic question, "And who is the *Cometty*, pray?"—although later she does give vent to her annoyance, insisting, "I haven't seen any Committee."

"A Mother" is replete with several four-sided figures that are constantly losing their fourth sides. Initially there were to have been four concerts, but as the projected attendances failed to materialize, one of the performances was cancelled. Kathleen Kearney was to have been paid eight guineas for the four concerts, but with one missing, Mrs. Kearney suspects that she won't receive her entire contracted fee. When she comes to a confrontation with Mr. Fitzgerald, he gives her half the fee now and promises the other half to be paid later, yet even the half offered is a shade off (pounds in lieu of guineas, so that for each of the pounds a shilling is missing). The mathematics of the story parallels its geometrics as the equation reduces itself down to almost nothing. Mrs. Kearney has counted on the formidable presence of her husband, marshalled for the showdown on the final night. She had married him when the romantic young men did not manage to get beyond her "ivory manners." In effect she is playing her trump against Mr. Fitzgerald's high card, the *Cometty;* "She respected her husband in the same way as she respected the General Post Office, as something large, secure and fixed; and though she knew the small number of his talents she appreciated his abstract value as a male." But Mr. Kearney hardly proves effective, having long since had his masculinity abstracted from him by the ivory manners of his dominant wife, and in conflict with so abstract a quantity as the Committee, he is powerless. Opposing forces line up as two pockets of people form:

> In one corner were Mr. Holohan, Mr. Fitzgerald, Miss Beirne, two of the stewards, the baritone, the bass, and Mr. O'Madden Burke. . . .

> In another corner of the room were Mrs. Kearney and her husband, Mr. Bell, Miss Healy and the young lady who had recited the patriotic piece.

The proportions are already unequal, and one of the minority party at least is uncomfortable on Mrs. Kearney's side: "Miss Healy wanted to join the other group but . . .". When Mrs. Kearney mocks Hoppy Holohan as "a great fellow fol-the-diddle-I-do," he in turn reduces her stature ("I thought you were a lady"). "After that Mrs. Kearney's conduct was condemned on all hands" and the disbalance of power is complete. The parallelogram takes on its complete form, rejecting the gnomonic Kearney contingent, who retreat from the fray. Mrs. Kearney refuses to be removed from the pattern ("I'm not done with you yet, she said"), but Hoppy Holohan makes the removal complete: "But I'm done with you, said Mr. Holohan."

Many of the gnomons of these stories are comic effects: abandoned plumcakes, misplaced nutcrackers and corkscrews, anticipated bottles of stout, fires that give no light or heat, priests who look like actors, narrow gaps between nose and chin, toes and floor, solid males who prove abstract, audiences composed of "paper," and unknown sopranos from London in "faded" dresses over "meagre" bodies (Madame Glynn has the distinction of personifying both aspects of the gnomon, that which is hidden and that which is prominently exposed: "The shadow took her faded dress into shelter but fell revengefully into the little cup behind her collar-bone"). Yet nowhere are the gnomons more comic than in "Grace": Mr. Kernan has a piece of his tongue missing; Mrs. Kernan adds an Irish fourth to the Holy Trinity; three comforters find themselves augmented into a quadrumvirate; Pope Leo XIII is credited with extolling photography in verse (a photograph is a gnomonic presence after the subject is already absent); two so-called gentlemen accompanied Kernan on his drinking bout but disappeared when he fell down the stairs; Mr. McCoy has changed professional identities at least six times; Mr. Harford is denounced as an "Irish Jew" but shows up at the Catholic retreat, where Father Purdon sounds more like a businessman than a priest, delivering a non-sermon on an ambiguous text given in a translation that would rarely be acknowledged as accurate. And to complete the pattern, the party of five who turn up in the church reconstitute themselves strategically in the only way five can make up a quadrilateral shape, "the party had settled down in the form of a quincunx." Mr. McCoy of course is the odd man out (he "had tried unsuccessfully to find a place in the bench with the others"), yet he becomes the central point in the quincunx by being seated alone in the middle, with two before and two behind.

The gnomons that abound in *Dubliners*—or would abound

if they were not so blatantly missing—reflect the narrative strategies of the stories: absence of climactic instances, deleted resolutions of plot, inconclusive closures, inexact overlays of perception on the part of the characters, insufficient information about them: so that Maria has no family name and Farrington no given name, and the boy in the first three stories no names at all (although we know that the boy in "An Encounter" *cannot* be named Smith because that is the alias he designates for himself), and so trivial a character as the railway company representative in "A Painful Case" is fully equipped with a handle like "Mr. H. B. Patterson Finlay." Nominations are gnomonic ("Sounds are impostures," Stephen Dedalus contends, "like names. . . . What's in a name?" [*Ulysses*]), and Farrington is often referred to in the text as "the man," yet in losing his wrestling match with Weathers he is unmanned, becoming a Noman. Many another male in *Dubliners* is deprived of his full masculinity: Bob Doran at the hands of the Mooney women; Mr. Kearney in the hands of a determined wife with ivory manners; Gabriel Conroy, a self-styled Romantic Man, deflated by the intrusion into his life of the ghostly Michael Furey, a stripling long-dead who had long outdistanced him as a lover. And Little Chandler, already in trouble with his wife for having forgotten to bring home "the parcel of coffee from Bewley's," is further demeaned when she returns to find their baby wailing. Turning her back on her husband ("Giving no heed to him"), she concentrates her attention exclusively on the child, calling the infant "My little man! My little mannie!"

The word gnomon comes from the Greek, meaning "interpreter, discerner, pointer on a sundial, a carpenter's square." The most pointed indicators as such in *Dubliners* are the story titles, the first indications in each instance. The book title designates an entire population and by internal reference a place of residence, yet the parts that stand for the whole are the handful of Dubliners actually delineated in the fifteen stories. Of the story titles, some pinpoint characters ("The Sisters," "Eveline," "Two Gallants," "A Mother"); others a place ("Araby," "The Boarding House," "Ivy Day in the Committee Room"); one a time-frame ("After the Race"); one an event ("An Encounter"); and several a condition ("A Painful Case," "Grace," "The Dead"). The directness of most of them is deceptive, but a handful are highly elliptical and ambiguous. Irony informs "Two Gallants," where gallantry is decidedly unobservable; that it is Ivy Day during the course of the political tale arranges for ironic contrast with the diluted Parnellism of the canvassers. "Grace" as well is intentional overstatement, for few would consider either Mr. Kernan or any of the others in a state of grace despite their presence in the Gardiner Street Church, although Kernan may in fact be in a state of animated suspension, during a period of grace. "Clay" offers various possibilities in the literal substance brought forth and withdrawn during the game: its applicability to the malleable character of the unfortunate Maria and its symbolic import as a designator of the condition of death, prefigured as such in the Byron poem that Chandler attempted to read. "Counterparts" is itself a counter of various parts, contrasting Farrington with each of his adversaries throughout, from Mr. Alleyne to Weathers to his son Tom, and extending outward to counterpartite applicability to the Chandler of the preceding story, where "A Little Cloud" both parallels the person of Little Chandler and a condition that marks him and affects him. That "The Sisters" deflects attention away from the dead priest to his surviving sisters indicates the Joycean method of narrative counterpoint, as also in the case of "The Dead," a story in which two sisters figure prominently. The possibility for interexchange of the titles of the first and last story offers a circular construct for **Dubliners,** a cycle that Joyce artistically quadratures in his gnomonic parallel structures, squaring the circle, encircling the numerous squares. (pp. 527-39)

Bernard Benstock, "The Gnomonics of 'Dubliners'," in Modern Fiction Studies, Vol. 34, No. 4, Winter, 1988, pp. 519-39.

JAMES P. DEGNAN (essay date 1989)

[*Degnan is an American educator, critic, and short story writer. In the following excerpt, he offers a Freudian reading of "An Encounter."*]

Just as Ernest Jones used ancient and Renaissance works like *Oedipus* and *Hamlet* to validate the twentieth-century insights of Sigmund Freud, so also might Jones have used James Joyce's brilliant little short story, **"An Encounter."** For **"An Encounter,"** although it was written before Joyce read Freud, is, in its subtlest images, gestures, and speeches, perhaps Joyce's most thoroughly Freudian work.

The story of two ostensibly ordinary young boys playing hooky from grade school, **"An Encounter"** ends with its young narrator-protagonist rather surprisingly confessing that he has always "despised . . . a little" his hooky-playing pal, Mahony. Answering the question why the narrator so despises Mahony becomes the key critical task to understanding the story and to appreciating its Freudian essence.

That a reasonably sensitive, intelligent, and imaginative person such as the narrator would naturally "despise . . . a little" the rather callous, crude, and cruel Mahony—who bullies smaller children, is cruel to animals, and is rude to older people—is certainly part of the answer. However, Joyce's story suggests a considerably more complex and universal answer: that the narrator's despising Mahony a "little" is an unconscious, symbolic confession of the age-old antipathy (an antipathy deriving from a mixture of repulsion and attraction, of contempt and envy) that the man of thought feels for the man of action; the man of imagination for the man of "common sense"; the man of conscience for the man of instinct; the civilized man for the primitive man. Thus, in **"An Encounter,"** the major conflict is between the values represented by the narrator and those represented by Mahony, and, at its essence, the story is a dramatization of the complex struggle in human nature between superego and id.

Although there are a few hints of an overt conflict between the two boys—the narrator's mild protest against Mahony's bullying the smaller children, for instance—essentially the struggle mentioned above takes place in the consciousness of the narrator-protagonist. Within the person of the narrator, the reader sees, throughout the story, a struggle the narrator himself is never clearly aware of: the struggle between the narrator's values (those of the superego) and Mahony's (those of the id).

A beautifully subtle Joycean metaphor for dramatizing this struggle occurs early in the story when the narrator thinks of himself as a "reluctant Indian," thereby describing his attitude toward the "Wild West" games played at a friend's house, games the narrator calls "remote from my nature." Mahony, though, slightly later at the beginning of the story's hooky-playing adventure, is described as enthusiastically

adopting the role of "the Indian"; that is, as *instinctively* becoming the natural, amoral, associal man, the primitive, the savage. Instinctively, for example, Mahony pockets Leo Dillon's sixpense, intimidates the smaller children, looks for birds to shoot with his slingshot, chases the cat, calls Father Butler—symbol of church, school, tradition (superego)—"Old Bunser," and is rude to the old pervert. None of this bothers Mahony's "conscience"; none of this causes him a moment's "reflection"; he simply behaves this way naturally and effortlessly.

On the other hand, the narrator, the "reluctant Indian," cannot instinctively and naturally enjoy the hooky-playing adventure: he is too intelligent and too imaginative. Notice how often he "reflects," "imagines," "pretends"; notice also that he regards the hooky session as a "plot," as something usually associated with the imaginary world of literature. The narrator cannot think or behave like Mahony because the narrator is too sensitive to other people's rights and feelings; he is too conscientious, too civilized, too bound to the demands of the superego. The narrator wonders, for example, why Mahony brings along the slingshot, a symbol of the aggressiveness Mahony possesses and the narrator lacks. The narrator is conscientiously "puzzled" about the "right thing" to do with Leo's money; he finds Mahony's "free" use of slang worthy of commenting on; he conscientiously reminds Mahony that it is not fair to bully the smaller children; and, finally, he worries about hurting the feelings of the old pervert.

What Joyce is brilliantly articulating with this metaphor, the "Indian" metaphor, is not only the narrator's central problem and the major problem of the story, but, certainly according to Freud, the central problem of civilized man. In order to be civilized, man must check, must repress, his natural impulses, his appetites, his instincts and aggressive tendencies, his selfish "Indian" nature. And, in so doing, in trying, for example, to live by conscience, by codes and laws and ideals, by conventions and traditions and institutions and commandments, by the decrees of the superego, civilized man, like the narrator-protagonist, is frustrated and runs the risk of neurosis, emotional paralysis (the inability to function caused by perfectionism and scrupulosity) and of perverting his nature.

The conflict between what Mahony represents and what the narrator represents, the conflict between id and superego, resolves itself in the final scene of the story, the major recognition scene in the story. Here the narrator, explicitly for the first time, confesses his real feeling for Mahony—that is, his dependence on the strengths Mahony represents. In this scene Mahony brings "aid" to the narrator, and the narrator, in his characteristically conscientious way, feels "penitent" or guilty for having "always despised him (Mahony) a little." The "aid" Mahony brings, of course, is the aid the "enthusiastic Indian" can bring to the "reluctant Indian," that the man of action can bring to the man of thought, the man of instinct to the man of conscience, the id to the superego—the aid to act, the aid to escape the spell of the pervert, a spell ironically made possible by the narrator's "superior" humanity, by his superior intellect and imagination and sense of decency.

On one level, the narrator's inability to break away easily from the pervert may be attributed to the narrator's sensitivity, to his good manners, to his unwillingness to hurt the old man's feelings by rudely taking leave. However, on a more significant level, the narrator's inability to break away may be attributed to his fascination with the pervert. The pervert, as suggested above, has *captured* the narrator's imagination. Whereas the old man with his literary pretensions and compulsive monologues simply bores Mahony—who commonsensically dismisses him as a "queer old josser" and then runs off in his characteristically natural way to chase a cat—the old man appeals strongly to the narrator's intellectual curiosity, something of which Mahony has little.

Besides being interested in and sympathetic toward the pervert, the narrator, Joyce suggests, actually identifies with the pervert. Both the narrator and the pervert, for example, are described as "bookworms" in contrast to Mahony, who the pervert says is "different; he goes in for games." (Here again Joyce suggests the mind-body, superego-id conflict that informs the story.) From the narrator's point of view, the pervert is "well spoken" and "well read," though the pervert's taste in literature, in keeping with his character, is apparently for a kind of decadent romanticism; and the narrator immediately hopes that the old man will think well of him, that the old man will not think him as "stupid as Mahony."

Perversion, according to Freud, is a sickness of civilization, a sickness caused by over-civilization, by the development of the mind, imagination, and conscience at the expense of the "natural," the instinctive life. The pervert in **"An Encounter"** functions as a symbol of this over-civilization—as a symbol of decadence. That the narrator-protagonist "encounters" the pervert, momentarily finds himself in league with the pervert—he and the pervert become men of breeding and intelligence pitted against the "stupid" barbarian, the primitive Mahony—and, ultimately, needs Mahony's "aid" to escape the spell of the pervert, is Joyce's method of dramatizing through symbolic action the central conflict in the narrator's mind and the central and universal problem of civilized man.

If we ask ourselves what "happens" in **"An Encounter,"** at least on this level of the story's action, we can answer that as a result of the encounter, the boy becomes to some extent conscious of the irony that his virtues—sensitivity, intelligence, conscientiousness, and imagination—have in them the seeds of the vices the old man embodies; that, in short, he (the narrator) could become what the old man is. The narrator's reluctant acknowledgment of his "need" for Mahony thus becomes, symbolically, Joyce's way of dramatizing the truth that if the narrator (and all civilized men) is to achieve genuine maturity, reality, identity, he must master the art of balancing the conflicting demands of his nature, the demands of the superego and the id.

In terms of symbolic action it is interesting to note that during his dialogue (his encounter) with the pervert, the narrator assumes a "false identity," a false name. He has been, once again, "imaginative and intelligent" enough to lie to the old man that he is "Smith" and Mahony is "Murphy." Thus the "aid" that Mahony brings the narrator is the aid that restores the narrator to reality, to his real name (his identity) and self, the aid that saves the narrator from his false name and from the unreality of the pervert. Once again Joyce dramatizes the psychic risks the civilized man runs: because he is intelligent and imaginative, civilized man has the capacity to lie, to falsify, to pervert reality; thus civilized man's virtues, ironically, can function as vices to destroy him, to pervert his nature. (pp. 89-93)

James P. Degnan, "The Encounter in Joyce's 'An

Encounter'," in Twentieth Century Literature, *Vol. 35, No. 1, Spring, 1989, pp. 89-93.*

FURTHER READING

Baker, James R., and Staley, Thomas F., eds. *James Joyce's "Dubliners": A Critical Handbook*. Belmont, Calif.: Wadsworth Publishing Co., 1969, 188 p.

  Includes discussion of Joyce's aesthetic theories and the short story genre, examination of the structure and unity of *Dubliners*, critical analyses of the stories, and a comprehensive bibliography of criticism on *Dubliners*.

Beck, Warren. *Joyce's "Dubliners": Substance, Vision, and Art*. Durham, N.C.: Duke University Press, 1969, 375 p.

  Discusses Joyce's biography, the publication history of *Dubliners*, prominent critical approaches, and stylistic elements as they pertain to individual stories and the collection as a whole.

Benstock, Bernard. " 'The Sisters' and the Critics." *James Joyce Quarterly* 4, No. 1 (Fall 1966): 32-5.

  Challenges the literal interpretation submitted by Thomas E. Connolly in his essay "Joyce's 'The Sisters': A Pennyworth of Snuff " (cited below).

———, ed. *The Seventh of Joyce*. Bloomington: Indiana University Press, 1979, 266 p.

  Collection of essays that includes Florence L. Walzl's "A Book of Signs and Symbols: The Protagonist," Mary T. Reynolds's "The Dantean Design of Joyce's *Dubliners*," and Phillip Herring's "Structure and Meaning in Joyce's 'The Sisters'."

Blotner, Joseph L. " 'Ivy Day in the Committee Room': Death without Resurrection." *Perspective* 9, No. 4 (Summer 1957): 210-17.

  Analyzes Joyce's treatment of Irish politics after the death of Parnell in "Ivy Day in the Committee Room" by drawing parallels between the story and "the events of Christ's death and resurrection as reported in the Gospel according to St. Luke and St. John and in the Acts of the Apostles."

Boyd, John D., and Boyd, Ruth A. "The Love Triangle in Joyce's 'The Dead'." *University of Toronto Quarterly* 42, No. 3 (Spring 1973): 202-17.

  Suggests that a central theme of the story is illustrated by the relationship between Gabriel and Michael, "a theme which is partly obscured if one stresses only their opposition. That is the theme of the continuity among all men, living and dead, linked by the feelings, aspirations, and sufferings universal to human experience (and symbolized by the falling snow)."

Boyle, Robert, S. J. " 'Two Gallants' and 'Ivy Day in the Committee Room'." *James Joyce Quarterly* 1, No. 1 (Fall 1963): 3-9.

  Considers the harp the central image of "Two Gallants," and outlines a double movement crucial to the structure of the story: 1) as Corley moves toward the slavey's money, he moves away from the romantic ideal of gallantry; and 2) his movement away from gallantry is "symbolized in the story . . . by the gradual fading of the faint romantic moon, its complete disappearance behind the rain-clouds, and its replacement by the shining gold coin."

Burgess, Anthony. "A Paralysed City." In his *Re Joyce*, pp. 35-47. New York: W. W. Norton & Co., 1965.

  Discusses Joyce's understanding of his artistic function in *Dubliners*, paying particular attention to his notion of aesthetic epiphany and his themes of paralysis and frustration.

Burke, Kenneth. "Three Definitions." *The Kenyon Review* 13, No. 2 (Spring 1951): 186-92.

Defines three stages in the narrative of "The Dead," all amplifying the theme of death: 1) the preparations for the party, during which the "keynote is expectancy"; 2) the party scenes, comprising "a catalogue of superficial socialities, each in its way slightly false or misfit"; and 3) the post-party events during which "the cycle of realistic expectations and eventualities" draws to a close.

Carpenter, Richard, and Leary, Daniel. "The Witch Maria." *James Joyce Review* 3, Nos. 1-2 (1959): 3-7.

Analyzes the character Maria in "Clay," concluding that Joyce "intended for us to see Maria as an unintentional spirit of discord who pathetically and ironically does not even realize her own agency."

Carrier, Warren. "Joyce's Dantean Vision." *Renascence* 17, No. 4 (Summer 1965): 211-15.

Considers Dante's *Divine Comedy* the model for *Dubliners*.

Collins, Ben L. "Joyce's Use of Yeats and of Irish History: A Reading of 'A Mother'." *Eire-Ireland: A Journal of Irish Studies* 5, No. 1 (Spring 1970): 45-66.

Traces allusions and references to Irish history and William Butler Yeats's drama *Cathleen ni Houlihan* (1902) in "A Mother." In Collin's view, Mrs. Kearney's relationship with her daughter in the story represents that of the Catholic church with Ireland.

Connolly, Thomas E. "Joyce's 'The Sisters': A Pennyworth of Snuff." *College English* 27, No. 3 (December 1965): 189-95.

Offers a literal reading of "The Sisters," disputing elements of symbolic readings by Marvin Magalaner and Richard Kain, Julian B. Kaye, William Bysshe Stein, and others. Connolly concludes that "the hulk of Father Flynn spiritually and physically paralyzes the society which he dominates. He has become an example of paralysis to which society continues to pay respect, even if it is the respect only of pious clichés uttered by ignorant old women and vaguely felt by one small boy." For an opposing view, see Bernard Benstock, " 'The Sisters' and the Critics" (cited above).

———. "Marriage Divination in Joyce's 'Clay'." *Studies in Short Fiction* 3, No. 3 (Spring 1966): 293-99.

Describes three traditional divination tools in "Clay"— barmbrack cake, nutcracking, and the three saucers—and connects "Eveline" and "Clay" by asserting that Maria represents a middle-aged Eveline, triumphing over her dull situation.

Cooke, M. G. "From Comedy to Terror: On *Dubliners* and the Development of Tone and Structure in the Modern Short Story." *Massachusetts Review* 9, No. 2 (Spring 1968): 331-43.

Maintains that in *Dubliners* "Joyce developed a singularly modern articulation of the possibilities of the short story form." Cooke particularly praises the stories "An Encounter," "Araby," "Two Gallants," "Clay," and "The Dead."

Corrington, John William. "Isolation as Motif in 'A Painful Case'." *James Joyce Quarterly* 3, No. 3 (Spring 1966): 182-91.

Discusses "A Painful Case," focusing on the central character, Mr. Duffy, and his response to Mrs. Sinico and the news of her death.

Daiches, David. "*Dubliners*." In his *The Novel and the Modern World*, pp. 63-82. Rev. ed. Chicago and London: University of Chicago Press, 1960.

Offers an appreciative overview of Joyce's achievement in the short story form, concluding that the selection and arrangement of detail in "The Dead" make it "one of the most remarkable short stories of the present century."

Davis, Joseph K. "The City as Radical Order: James Joyce's *Dubliners*." *Studies in the Literary Imagination* 3, No. 2 (October 1970): 79-96.

Examines Joyce's rendering in *Dubliners* of the city of Dublin as a prototypal modern city.

Deming, Robert H., ed. *James Joyce: The Critical Heritage, Volume One, 1902-1927*. London: Routledge & Kegan Paul, 1970, 385 p.

Excerpts early assessments of *Dubliners* by Irish, English, and French critics.

Dilworth, Thomas. "The Numina of Joyce's 'Eveline'." *Studies in Short Fiction* 15, No. 4 (Fall 1978): 456-58.

Draws parallels between Joyce's characterization of Eveline and Homer's portrait of Helen.

Easson, Angus. "Parody as Comment in James Joyce's 'Clay'." *James Joyce Quarterly* 7, No. 2 (Winter 1970): 75-81.

Analyzes Joyce's use of parody to comment on the character Maria in "Clay."

Ellmann, Richard. "The Backgrounds of 'The Dead'." *The Kenyon Review* 20, No. 4 (Autumn 1958): 507-28.

Traces autobiographical elements in "The Dead."

———. *James Joyce*. Rev. ed. New York: Oxford University Press, 1982, 928 p.

Comprehensive biography of Joyce which has become the standard work on his life.

Engel, Monroe. "*Dubliners* and Erotic Expectation." *Twentieth-Century Literature in Retrospect*, edited by Reuben A. Brower, pp. 3-26. Cambridge: Harvard University Press, 1971.

Suggests that "The Sisters," "An Encounter," and "Araby" depict "the thwarting of the eroticized life expectations" of their respective narrators.

Foster, John Wilson. "Passage through 'The Dead'." *Criticism* 15, No. 2 (Spring 1973): 91-108.

Reading of "The Dead" in which Foster interprets Gabriel Conroy as the only character truly alive among a funereal gathering of Dublin dead.

Freimarck, John. " 'Araby': A Quest for Meaning." *James Joyce Quarterly* 7, No. 4 (Summer 1970): 366-68.

Cites the quest as the underlying narrative pattern in "Araby." According to Freimarck: "The myth element enriches the story, but we are never really on the quest for the grail—we are in Dublin all the time with the psychologically accurate story of the growth of a romantic boy awakening to his sexuality, idealizing Mangan's sister and encountering frustration in the process."

Gifford, Don. "Notes for *Dubliners*." In his *Notes for Joyce: "Dubliners" and "A Portrait of the Artist as a Young Man*," pp. 29-84. New York: E. P. Dutton & Co., 1967.

Textual notes explaining Joyce's references to such subjects as geography, Irish history, and Catholic teachings, as well as his use of Dublin vernacular in *Dubliners*.

Gould, Gerald. Review of *Dubliners*. *New Statesman* 3, No. 64 (27 June 1914): 374-75.

Praises "Araby" and "The Dead" as "the best things in the book" and declares Joyce a genius with "an original outlook, a special method, [and] a complete reliance on his own powers of delineation and presentment."

Hardy, Barbara. "James Joyce." In her *Tellers and Listeners: The Narrative Imagination*, pp. 206-76. London: The Athlone Press, 1975.

Examines the function of narrative imagination in *Dubliners*.

Hart, Clive, ed. *James Joyce's "Dubliners": Critical Essays*. New York: Viking Press, 1969, 183 p.

Contains fifteen original essays, one on each of the stories in *Dubliners*. Among the contributing critics are Bernard Benstock [see excerpt in *TCLC,* Vol. 8], Robert Boyle, S. J., Adaline Glasheen, Clive Hart, Richard M. Kain, Robert Scholes, and Fritz Senn.

Jackson, Robert Sumner. "A Parabolic Reading of James Joyce's 'Grace'." *Modern Language Notes* 76, No. 8 (December 1961): 719-24.

    Connects "Grace" with the scriptural parable of the unjust steward (Luke 16) and relates this parable to St. Paul's teaching that grace is a gift from God.

Jones, William Powell. "*Dubliners:* or the Moral History of Ireland." In his *James Joyce and the Common Reader,* pp. 9-23. Norman: University of Oklahoma Press, 1955.

    Analyzes the progressive arrangement of the stories from childhood to public life with regard to Joyce's plan for presenting a moral history of Ireland in his short story collection.

Joyce, Stanislaus. "The Background to *Dubliners.*" *The Listener* 51, No. 1,308 (25 March 1954): 526-27.

    Recalls the biographical inspirations for several *Dubliners* stories.

Kelleher, John V. "Irish History and Mythology in James Joyce's 'The Dead'." *Review of Politics* 27, No. 3 (July 1965): 414-33.

    Traces three levels of meaning in "The Dead": 1) Irish myth based on the Old Irish saga "Togail Bruidhne Dá Derga" ("The Destruction of Da Derga's Hostel"); 2) a level of reference to early nineteenth-century Catholic Dublin history; and 3) "a symbolistic level on which Death is personified in Mr. Browne."

Kenner, Hugh. "*Dubliners.*" In his *Dublin's Joyce,* pp. 48-68. New York: Columbia University Press, 1956.

    Examines the narrative techniques through which Joyce aimed to expose the societal paralysis of turn-of-the-century Dublin in his short stories.

Lachtman, Howard. "The Magic-Lantern Business: James Joyce's Ecclesiastical Satire in *Dubliners.*" *James Joyce Quarterly* 7, No. 2 (Winter 1970): 82-92.

    Examines Joyce's satiric treatment of clerics in *Dubliners.* According to Lachtman: "In *Dubliners,* the Church becomes an object of Joyce's wit, ridicule, sarcasm, and contempt. . . . [His priests] do not inspire faith; on the contrary, they encourage considerable doubt, if not open skepticism. Taken together, they comprise what is surely one of the least inspiring congregations of clerics in modern short fiction."

Leatherwood, A. M. "Joyce's Mythic Method: Structure and Unity in 'An Encounter'." *Studies in Short Fiction* 13, No. 1 (Winter 1976): 71-8.

    Studies archetypal conventions of the knight's quest and the warrior's initiation in "An Encounter." According to Leatherwood: "In controlling the plot with archetypes, Joyce creates a parallel between the contemporary and mythic worlds, a type of parallel used extensively by Joyce in his later work and hailed by T. S. Eliot as 'the most important expression which the present age has found'."

Macy, John. "James Joyce." In his *The Critical Game,* pp. 317-22. New York: Boni and Liveright, 1922.

    Praises narrative subtlety and irony in *Dubliners.*

Magalaner, Marvin. "The Other Side of James Joyce." *Arizona Quarterly* 9, No. 1 (Spring 1953): 5-16.

    Includes the famous reading of "Clay" in which Magalaner suggests that in addition to her literal character, Maria is symbolically equated with the Virgin Mary and a witch.

———. "The Evolution of *Dubliners.*" In his *Time of Apprenticeship: The Fiction of Young James Joyce,* pp. 72-96. London: Abelard-Schuman, 1959.

    Examines the revision of "The Sisters" and "A Painful Case" through three successive versions.

———, and Kain, Richard M. "The Work: *Dubliners.*" In their *Joyce: The Man, the Work, the Reputation,* pp. 65-111. New York: Collier Books, 1956.

    Detailed explication of symbolism in *Dubliners,* focusing on "The Sisters," "An Encounter," "Araby," "Ivy Day in the Committee Room," "Clay," and "The Dead."

Mandel, Jerome. "The Structure of 'Araby'." *Modern Language Studies* 15, No. 4 (Fall 1985): 48-54.

    Examines conventions of medieval romance in "Araby."

Montgomery, Judith. "The Artist as Silent Dubliner." *James Joyce Quarterly* 6, No. 4 (Summer 1969): 306-20.

    Examines silence in the opening stories of *Dubliners*: "The Sisters," "An Encounter," and "Araby." According to Montgomery: "The trilogy marks the progressive withdrawal of a boy—or, several parallel boys—into silence as both defense and liberation for the future artist."

Morse, Donald E. " 'Sing Three Songs of Araby': Theme and Allusion in Joyce's 'Araby'." *College Literature* 5, No. 2 (Spring 1978): 124-32.

    Concludes that " 'Araby' succeeds in eliciting our sympathy for the boy's plight while amusing us with his excesses—a double vision which appears remarkably similar to the one most adults adopt towards their own first encounter with romantic love."

Moynihan, William T., ed. *Joyce's "The Dead."* Boston: Allyn and Bacon, Inc., 1965, 134 p.

    Collection of essays examining "The Dead" in the context of Joyce's life, of Ibsen's influence, of *Dubliners,* and of Joyce's aesthetic theories, as well as critical perspectives on the story by Kenneth Burke, George Knox, C. C. Loomis, Jr., and others.

Munich, Adrienne Auslander. "Form and Subtext in Joyce's 'The Dead'." *Modern Philology* 82, No. 2 (November 1984): 173-84.

    Maintains that in their form and subtext the sections of the story "describe Joyce's emotional strife in evolving his modernist style," and that "the ending . . . is mock-epic but comic in its broadest implications—a celebration of and reconcilement to the human condition."

Murphy, M. W. "Darkness in *Dubliners.*" *Modern Fiction Studies* 15, No. 1 (Spring 1969): 97-104.

    Examines the pervasive darkness in *Dubliners.*

Nebeker, H. E. "James Joyce's 'Clay': The Well-Wrought Urn." *Renascence* 28, No. 3 (Spring 1976): 123-38.

    Discusses the complex point of view, ambiguous tone, and characterization in "Clay," as well as the significance of Maria's song.

Newman, F. X. "Joyce's 'Grace' and the Book of Job." *Studies in Short Fiction* 4, No. 1 (Fall 1966): 70-9.

    Interprets "Grace" as a parody of the Book of Job.

Niemeyer, Carl. " 'Grace' and Joyce's Method of Parody." *College English* 27, No. 3 (December 1965): 196-201.

    Discusses Dante's *Divine Comedy* as the literary model on which Joyce drew to parody Dublin life in "Grace." According to Niemeyer: "Here as in *Ulysses* [Joyce] takes a great book and by deliberately echoing it, by applying it to squalid situations, of which we get no suggestion in the book itself, makes fun not of the original but of an age of civilization so debased that, measured by the great classics, it is ridiculous."

Norris, Margot. "Narration under a Blindfold: Reading Joyce's 'Clay'." *PMLA* 102, No. 2 (March 1987): 206-15.

    Asserts that "Joyce displays a surprising technical maturity in this early work, whose object is . . . to dramatize the powerful workings of desire in human discourse and human lives."

O'Connor, Frank. "Joyce and Dissociated Metaphor." In his *The

Mirror in the Roadway: A Study of the Modern Novel, pp. 295-312. New York: Alfred A. Knopf, 1956.

Outlines the metaphorical structure of "Ivy Day in the Committee Room," "Grace," and "The Dead."

O'Hehir, Brendan P. "Structural Symbol in Joyce's 'The Dead'." *Twentieth Century Literature* 3, No. 1 (April 1957): 3-13.

Explication of "The Dead," focusing on symbols, dramatic action, and characterization.

O'Neill, Michael J. "Joyce's Use of Memory in 'A Mother'." *Modern Language Notes* 74, No. 3 (March 1959): 226-30.

Details the autobiographical basis—Joyce's performance as a vocalist in a program held in Dublin's Antient Concert Rooms, Saturday, 27 August 1904—of the events portrayed in "A Mother."

Ostroff, Anthony. "The Moral Vision in *Dubliners.*" *Western Speech* 20, No. 4 (Fall 1956): 196-209.

Traces the importance and value of *Dubliners* for its "remarkable accomplishment in rendering dramatic a variety of lives and a moral vision of consequence, and needless to say, accomplishing this with the greatest artistry."

Rosenberg, Bruce A. "The Crucifixion in 'The Boarding House'." *Studies in Short Fiction* 5, No. 1 (Fall 1967): 44-53.

Maintains that Bob Doran in "The Boarding House" may be seen as a diminished Christ figure and that the " 'facts' of Bob Doran's life and of his sad affair with Polly loosely parallel, yet are an inversion of, the life of Christ."

San Juan, Epifanio, Jr. *James Joyce and the Craft of Fiction: An Interpretation of "Dubliners."* Rutherford, N.J.: Fairleigh Dickinson University Press, 1972, 260 p.

Discusses Dubliners in the context of Joyce's aesthetic theories.

Smith, Paul. "Crossing the Lines in 'A Painful Case'." *Southern Humanities Review* 17, No. 3 (Summer 1983): 203-08.

Considers the significance of Nietzschean misogyny in "A Painful Case," suggesting that Mrs. Sinico's demise occurs as a result of her attempt to "cross the lines" of Mr. Duffy's fixed, patriarchal order.

Smith, Thomas F. "Color and Light in 'The Dead'." *James Joyce Quarterly* 2, No. 4 (Summer 1965): 304-09.

Sees the complementing and reconciling of light and dark as important to the symbolic structure of "The Dead."

Somerville, Jane. "Money in *Dubliners.*" *Studies in Short Fiction* 12, No. 2 (Spring 1975): 109-16.

Concludes that Joyce used money in *Dubliners* to portray economic impotence and the corruption in Dublin of such traditional values as work, politics, religion, family, masculinity, and adulthood.

Staley, Thomas F. "Moral Responsibility in Joyce's 'Clay'." *Renascence* 18, No. 3 (Spring 1966): 124-28.

Disputes Marvin Magalaner's theory that Maria dually symbolizes a witch and the Blessed Virgin in "Clay." According to Staley, at the beginning of the story she represents "the adult product of the paralysis that is Dublin—unaware of the disintegration of community, never cognizant of the meaning of her existence," but through the events of the story she reaches an "understanding of herself and is for the first time confronted with the terrible emptiness of her life."

Stein, William Bysshe. "Joyce's 'Araby': Paradise Lost." *Perspective* 12, No. 4 (Spring 1962): 215-22.

Explicates Catholic terms and symbols in "Araby," concluding that Araby represents paradise lost.

———. "The Effects of Eden in Joyce's 'Eveline'." *Renascence* 15, No. 3 (Spring 1963): 124-26.

Interprets the character Eveline as a "little Eve," struggling in

a corrupt environment and seeking salvation through Frank, a false redeemer.

Stern, Frederick, C. " 'Parnell is Dead': 'Ivy Day in the Committee Room'." *James Joyce Quarterly* 10, No. 2 (Winter 1973): 228-39.

Offers a political reading of "Ivy Day in the Committee Room," noting the prominent imagery and symbolism related to clergy, fire, betrayal, father-son relationships, and the dominant figure of Charles Stuart Parnell.

Tate, Allen. "Three Commentaries: Poe, James, and Joyce." *Sewanee Review* 58, No. 1 (January-March 1950): 1-15.

Praises "The Dead" as an example of Joyce's success in attributing symbolic value to naturalistic detail.

Review of *Dubliners. Times Literary Supplement,* No. 648 (18 June 1914): 298.

Defines the scope of Joyce's collection and praises his delineation of mood in *Dubliners.*

Torchiana, Donald T. *Backgrounds for Joyce's Dubliners.* Boston: Allen & Unwin, 1986, 283 p.

Examines Joyce's literary method—"a laying on of national, mythic, religious, and legendary details, often ironically"—in *Dubliners.* Torchiana writes: "*Dubliners* strikes me . . . as a series of representative pictures—or mirror-images, if you will. That is, they catch a permanence in Irish life that has a timeless quality as though each detail in any story had about it a built-in significance that no educated native Irishman could really miss and no outsider, armed with a guide to Ireland and a bit of imagination, could fail to detect."

Walzl, Florence L. "The Liturgy of the Epiphany Season and the Epiphanies of Joyce." *PMLA* 80, No. 4 (September 1965): 436-50.

Discusses Joyce's concept of literary epiphany and its function in *Dubliners,* and explicates the stories in terms of Catholic liturgy and theology.

———. "Gabriel and Michael: The Conclusion of 'The Dead'." *James Joyce Quarterly* 4, No. 1 (Fall 1966): 17-31.

Discusses ambiguity in "The Dead," maintaining that the story's ambivalent conclusion resulted from Joyce's own altered outlook on Ireland by the time he wrote the story and added it to his unpublished short story collection in 1907.

———. "*Dubliners:* Women in Irish Society." In *Women in Joyce,* edited by Suzette Henke and Elaine Unkeless, pp. 31-56. Urbana: University of Illinois Press, 1982.

Determines the accuracy of Joyce's depictions of "Irish family mores and of social and economic conditions as they affected women in Dublin at the turn of the century."

West, Michael, and Hendricks, William. "The Genesis and Significance of Joyce's Irony in 'A Painful Case'." *ELH* 44, No. 4 (Winter 1977): 701-27.

Maintains that "though frequently read as a kind of tragedy *manqué,* ["A Painful Case"] is one of the more purely comic [stories] in *Dubliners.* Enmeshed in a web of authorial irony, the automaton Duffy scarcely becomes human, even in his final anguish and remorse."

Wiggington, B. Eliot. "*Dubliners* in Order." *James Joyce Quarterly* 7, No. 4 (Summer 1970): 297-314.

Examines several hypotheses concerning Joyce's use of color imagery, the gradual progression of the protagonists' ages from youth to old age, the failure of meaningful interpersonal relationships between characters, the presence of death, and the important role of clergymen in *Dubliners.*

Wilson, Edmund. "James Joyce." In his *Axel's Castle: A Study in the Imaginative Literature of 1870-1930,* pp. 191-236. New York: Charles Scribner's Sons, 1948.

Calls *Dubliners* "French in its objectivity, its sobriety and its irony, at the same time that its paragraphs ran with a music and a grace quite distinct from the taut metallic quality of Maupassant and Flaubert.''

Thomas Mann

1875-1955

German novelist, short story writer, essayist, and critic.

The following entry presents criticism of Mann's novel *Buddenbrooks.* For a discussion of Mann's complete career, see *TCLC,* Volumes 2 and 8; for a discussion of the novella *Der Tod in Venedig (Death in Venice),* see *TCLC,* Volume 14; for a discussion of the novel *Der Zauberberg (The Magic Mountain),* see *TCLC,* Volume 21.

Buddenbrooks, Mann's first novel, is regarded as one of the classic works of modern literature. Written in the tradition of the genealogical novel and subtitled "The Decline of a Family," it chronicles the lives of the Buddenbrooks, a wealthy Hanseatic family whose bourgeois robustness evolves gradually over four generations into an artistic sensibility unsuited for survival in the practical world. According to Erich Heller, *Buddenbrooks* contains "almost all the elements of vision and thought of which [Mann's] later works are made." In particular, the central theme of the book, the relationship between the artist and bourgeois society, concerned Mann all his life. *Buddenbrooks* has also been read as autobiography, with many commentators remarking on similarities between the Buddenbrooks and the Manns, and as sociology, with some analysts arguing that the decline of the Buddenbrooks symbolizes the end of an entire age and culture. The most popular and accessible of Mann's novels, *Buddenbrooks* is also considered by some critics to be his greatest achievement.

Mann began work on *Buddenbrooks* while living in Italy with his brother Heinrich in the late 1890s. During this period, Thomas Mann was heavily influenced by Scandinavian, French, and Russian literature, and after reading the Goncourt brothers' *Renée Mauperin,* in which he admired the use of characters to represent historical developments, he planned to work with Heinrich on a similar novel. The collaboration was not successful, and Thomas then labored alone on *Buddenbrooks,* which assumed massive proportions. He had originally intended to focus the novel on Thomas Buddenbrook and his son Hanno but found that a full portrayal of these characters required an account of earlier generations of Buddenbrooks. When Mann completed the manuscript of *Buddenbrooks,* his publisher thought it was too long and urged Mann to reduce it by half. Believing that the length and scope were essential features of the novel, Mann refused. Initially published in 1901 as an expensive two-volume set, *Buddenbrooks* sold slowly, but with laudatory reviews and a less expensive one-volume edition, sales increased and the young author was established as one of the leading figures in modern German literature. Critical response to the book has been positive throughout the twentieth century, and the novel was an important factor in Mann's winning the Nobel Prize in literature in 1929.

In *Buddenbrooks,* as in other genealogical novels, the family rather than an individual serves as the focus of the narrative. Mann's decision to begin the novel when the Buddenbrooks' fortunes are at their highest point has been praised by critics for providing a comprehensive view of the family and their

ultimate fate. The earlier generations of the Buddenbrooks are successful because of their vigor and unquestioning belief in their way of life. The family declines not because of scandal or commercial ruin but as the result of increasing susceptibility to personal and philosophical doubt, a diminishing physical vitality, and the emergence of an artistic sensibility which Mann associates with social and psychological decadence. Much of the story focuses on the third and fourth generations: the siblings Thomas, Antonie (Tony), and Christian, and Thomas's son Hanno. While Thomas takes over the family business and suppresses any personal desires that might conflict with the best interests of the firm, his sister Tony is pressured to marry a man she detests to increase the family fortune; at the same time, Christian, a neurotic hedonist, rejects the business world for a life of unproductive self-indulgence and is scorned by the rest of the family. Hanno, the only male heir, is a sickly child who prefers music to business and whose death from typhus as a teenager marks the end of the dynasty. Remarking on Mann's characterizations, which have been widely praised, Sol Liptzin has commented, "With astounding virtuosity and psychological subtlety, Mann projects four generations of Buddenbrooks before us, each individual carefully differentiated from his neighbors and kin and yet each retaining the main characteristics of his class and forebears."

In addition to the plot, technical and stylistic elements of the work were shaped by Mann's reading of other genealogical novels, particularly *Renée Mauperin*. Mann was influenced by the short chapters of *Renée Mauperin* and by the realistic and detailed attention given to matters of everyday life and societal conventions in that novel. Henry Hatfield has remarked that *Buddenbrooks,* though "far from naturalistic in spirit, demonstrates [Mann's] mastery of the techniques of naturalism and impressionism: elaborate accounts of dinners, the bank balances, and the ailments of the Buddenbrooks alternate with swift evocations of mood." The novel's universality and its status as a masterpiece of German and world literature have been partly attributed to Mann's successful recreation of an entire age in his portrayal of the patrician class of northern Germany from the middle to late nineteenth century. This documentary quality of the work has led to critical debate as to whether there is any historical or sociological significance in the fate of the Buddenbrooks. Georg Lukács, a Marxist critic, has asserted that because Mann was personally concerned with such larger questions, the Buddenbrook saga is also "the story of what happens to Germany's cultural traditions in the nineteenth century." Other critics, however, including Erich Heller, assert that while it is possible to read the book as a sociological novel, *Buddenbrooks* was not intended as such.

The relationship between art and decadence is a frequent theme in Mann's work and one that is central to *Buddenbrooks.* As the fortunes of the Buddenbrooks decline, each generation exhibits increasing sensitivity, introspection, and refinement—qualities which Mann associates with both the artist and the decadent. Liptzin has explained, "Mann speaks of himself as the chronicler and interpreter of decadence, as a lover of the pathological and of death, as an aesthete with a tendency toward the abyss. In his eyes, art is a kind of sickness, a form of degeneracy. The artist must ever be a lonely individual, a person apart, a creature branded and outlawed." The difficult relationships among some of the characters, especially that of Thomas with his brother Christian and his son Hanno, are implied by Mann to be the result of the differences in values and temperament between the burgher and the decadent. As R. J. Hollingdale has suggested, "Expressed in terms of the Buddenbrook code, decadence is the inability to subordinate one's natural inclinations and desires to the interests of the family and firm."

In exploring Mann's treatment of the subject of decadence, many critics have examined *Buddenbrooks* as an autobiographical work, asserting that many similarities exist between the Buddenbrooks and the Manns. Like the Buddenbrooks, the Manns had a family grain business that was more than one hundred years old when it was liquidated at the death of Mann's father. Mann often emphasized the disparate elements of his own background: while his father was a German burgher, his mother was born and spent the early years of her life in Brazil and was an accomplished musician. Mann ascribed a similar heritage to Hanno, whose musically gifted mother Gerda represents an artistic consciousness in contrast to the Buddenbrook bourgeois ethos. While the Buddenbrooks were obviously modeled on Mann's family, exactly how the novel reflects his own experiences and feelings is not clear. The ironic treatment of the characters may result from an ambivalent Mann felt because the material was so personal. Critics disagree regarding which character was most like him; most commentators believe Hanno represents Mann, and many agree with the following assessment by

T.E. Apter: "In *Buddenbrooks* Mann showed artistic sensibility to cut one off from life, and his sympathies were on the side of artistic sensibility."

Mann's ideas on decadence and the ways in which these ideas emerge in *Buddenbrooks* were influenced by three principal figures: the philosophers Friedrich Nietzsche and Arthur Schopenhauer, and the composer Richard Wagner. Mann regarded Nietzsche as the greatest analyst of decadence and incorporated into his own philosophy and writings Nietzsche's idea that bourgeois decay is caused by a lack of will and energy. Schopenhauer confirmed Mann's pessimistic view of life and sympathy with death. Mann claimed he had ascribed to Thomas Buddenbrook his own sense of having experienced a revelation while reading Schopenhauer. Though he does not understand it completely, Thomas Buddenbrook finds in Schopenhauer's philosophy a spiritual relief; he feels prepared for death and dies soon afterward. Some critics argue that Mann did not completely understand Schopenhauer either, and they disagree on the extent to which the philosophical underpinning of *Buddenbrooks* is derived from his writings. Wagner's music inspired Mann to use the leitmotif as a literary device. Each character in the novel has a "descriptive tag" with which he or she is identified; for example, Christian rubs his left side, and Grünlich always sports gold-colored whiskers. From Wagner Mann also learned the importance of music as an escape from reality; believing that music was the most decadent of all the arts, Mann thought that Wagner's music in particular is a force that accelerates the process of decay. Liptzin has elaborated, "Increased devotion to art on the part of the third generation of Buddenbrooks is described as a major symptom of decline, and when Hanno Buddenbrook, the last heir of the venerable family and the representative of the fourth generation, surrenders completely to his artistic instincts and revels in music instead of in business ledgers, then all hope of averting financial, social, and even physical extinction must be abandoned."

The enduring popularity of *Buddenbrooks,* the most often read of Mann's works, has been attributed to the novel's engaging narrative. According to Henry Hatfield, "One need know nothing of Wagner and Schopenhauer, of the theory of decadence or the metaphysical allure of death to find the novel absorbing, and this is all to the good. Nor need one have heard of the leitmotif to 'get' the effect of Mann's repetitions." Nonetheless, the lasting significance of the novel lies in its thematic and technical complexity. In *Buddenbrooks* Mann succeeded in creating a work that combines philosophy, realism, symbolism, social commentary, insightful characterizations, and effective narrative techniques.

(See also *Contemporary Authors,* Vol. 104 and *Dictionary of Literary Biography,* Vol. 66.)

LEVIN LUDWIG SCHÜCKING (essay date 1909)

[*In the following excerpt, Schücking praises the powers of observation and descriptive abilities displayed in* Buddenbrooks.]

Thomas Mann belongs to a nation which prides itself on understanding what the "reality of life" means, a nation which smiles at the idea of its forefathers having the weakness to feel flattered at being called by a famous English novelist the "nation of poets and thinkers." Many are the characteristics which show this author to belong to a time which posterity perhaps will call the "Bismarckian period" of Germany. The very leading feature of **Buddenbrooks,** the endeavour to show the gradual decadence of a great Lübeck trading firm in three generations is an *aristocratic* idea, for it presupposes the reader's sympathy with the "old family." But present Germany, or at least present Prussia, *is* aristocratic. The little word "von" before your name has not had as much importance as it has now, for the last hundred years. Large parts of the inner service are being reserved for the aristocracy, the conservative party having got hold of it and considering it indisputably its domain. Democracy is struggling hard. The country *is* interested in everything aristocratic and it *has* sympathies with an old family like the Buddenbrooks, slowly losing to the rising plebeians their powerful influence in the old free-town republic. Neither is it to be disputed that the "jujet" has some artistic attraction in itself. It is a pity only, that Thomas Mann should be so wordy and diffuse. He certainly uses a tub full of paint to colour a pencil. That requires a certain amount of patience on the part of the reader, but he will be rewarded by getting to know from the book the most minute details of present-day German life. There never was a shrewder observer than Thomas Mann. To be sure there is in his work much of that "unimaginative realism" that Mr. Swinburne detests so heartily. You notice the influence of Zola with him. But it always will have a certain charm to see everyday life reflected in the mirror of a really clever and sometimes satirical writer's spirit. Such books grow upon the time. If their artistic qualities are strong enough to stand the test of years they become more interesting still to later generations as being living monuments of bygone periods. When Fielding wrote his *Amelia* the realism of the book appeared awkward to the great majority of English readers, who were accustomed to devouring Richardson's descriptions of an imaginary world, created in Salisbury Court, Fleet Street. But a book like *Amelia* was written for the reader of a hundred years later, who would read it also with the historian's eye. I do not think, however, that Thomas Mann's books will enjoy a life as long as that. Yet his descriptions are undoubtedly valuable. He pictures you the quaint manners of old Lübeck, he shows you how the men are simply products of the distinct "milieu" of a place, where there is a form ready and prepared for each utterance of life which may come to the surface with respectable people; he demonstrates to you the difference between the light-hearted, jovial, unconventional South German and the solemn, reserved, aristocratic North German, to whom life ever remains a very serious thing and who feels himself always responsible for something; and if for no other reason, Mann's work deserves special notice for his observations of the half-unconscious. Passages like the following bear testimony to the psychological side of his art: "He spoke with naïve and kindhearted indignation, he tried some gesticulations, but noticing them to be ungainly he left off again." Or, talking of the "Bohémien" son coming home after many years' absence: "He went up the prodigious staircase, he leaned his hand upon the white-varnished open stair rail, lifting it up at every step and letting it fall again upon it quite smoothly at the next, as though he were trying if it were possible to take up the former intimacy with the old solid banister again." Subtle impressions of this sort are cultivated in German literature nowadays. Refinement of artistic feeling is the great aim of the day. (pp. 167-69)

Levin Ludwig Schücking, "Some Notes on Present-
Day German Literature," in The English Review, *Vol. II, April, 1909, pp. 165-71.*

HUNTER STAGG (essay date 1924)

[In the following excerpt, Stagg examines Mann's development of his themes throughout the narrative of Buddenbrooks.]

[Thomas Mann] was born in 1875, the son of a North German merchant and a lady of South German descent, which fact, I judge after reading **Buddenbrooks,** is of some significance. These two sections of Germany, the North and the South, represent, broadly speaking, materialism and spiritualism, and the two conflicting elements are apparent in the work of Thomas Mann. In his own life it would appear that the spiritual element won out, since when hardly more than a youth he rebelled against the wishes of his father, deserted commerce and proceeded to make himself editor of a magazine called *Simplicissimus.* He is now one of the most distinguished among the living German novelists.

Considering this, it is rather interesting to observe that the spiritual element certainly does not win out in the life that Thomas Mann depicts in **Buddenbrooks,** the greatest of his novels. The book is the chronicle of a family through four generations. In the first we find one who, building on a foundation laid by his father, has lifted his family to what is called the class of Merchant Nobility in Germany, and upper middle class in England. This old Johann Buddenbrook, respected head of a prosperous family, is a truly impressive figure, drawn in, as is the atmosphere and quaint paraphernalia of the period—the 1830's—with consummate skill. In the next generation, with Consul Buddenbrook, his son, all the appearance of prosperity and continued success are still there. The Buddenbrooks remain the most important people in the town, and (with the aid of wise and careful marriages) leaders of the social life—always, of course, below the actual blood nobility, who have the "von" before their names, and are looked upon with awe, even by proud Buddenbrooks. Nevertheless, Consul Buddenbrook is not, one sees, the man his father was. He is just as strong, just as forceful; but his judgment is not so clear, and his action not so incisive.

Then, in the third generation, of Thomas and Christian Buddenbrook, a decided decline is noticeable. The firm is just perceptibly sinking, and not even the civic honour of Thomas' election as senator can conceal that the family is on the downward grade. And if it is seen that Thomas is something that neither his father nor his grandfather was—a man of culture and some artistic perception, it is also seen that the source from which these qualities spring is also the source of his weakness—some indefinable inner decay. Even on the social side the Buddenbrooks have lost something, for their usual acumen in the selection of husbands for their daughters and sisters has failed in the case of Antonie, pretty, volatile Antonie, whose first husband, chosen for her, proved an impostor and fell afterwards into financial disgrace. Her second husband, chosen by herself, proved equally unsatisfactory on other grounds, so that Antonie returned again to the home of her fathers . . . and in those days and in that place divorce was looked at askance. And then, as if all this were not enough, there was Christian—poor futile, amusing, reckless Christian—a disgrace to any family. Yet, in spite of these blows, and smirches on the name, Thomas Buddenbrook himself managed to stand secure, for he had married a wife whose very presence lent an air of aristocracy to her surroundings. Really this Gerda might have been of the nobility, and as long as she was there, beautiful and aloof, the Buddenbrooks could feel that all was not lost, that they still had one link with distinction.

But Gerda was strange. The gods of the Buddenbrooks were not hers. She was musical, and no Buddenbrook had ever been musical. She was, moreover, spiritual, and save for the vague and destructive dawning of this quality in Thomas, no Buddenbrook had ever been spiritual. What chance then had the son of Gerda and Thomas—little Hanno? This helpless heir to a great commercial tradition proved a dreamer, musical too, like his mother, but, unlike either mother or father, weak, ineffectual, neurotic. So long as the Buddenbrooks remained true to the instincts and the traditions upon which their greatness was founded all went well with them. But their downfall was certain as soon as they began to develop new faculties, and were touched by modern influences fundamentally at variance with their own traditions. In Hanno is symbolized the extinction of a proud, strong strain through over-refinement. Thus, though after all it may be said that the spiritual element conquered the material in the Buddenbrook blood, it was only as decay conquers the firm tough fibre of the oak.

In weaving the extraordinarily complicated pattern of the daily middle class round which *Buddenbrooks* is, apart from the clear thread of its narrative, Thomas Mann has successfully avoided any appearance of monotony or repetition. Technically his treatment of his theme, the evolution of the family, refining itself as it becomes less objective, more introspective and sophisticated, is perfect. And his methods are equally adapted to suggesting and reflecting the whole life of the community in which the Buddenbrooks lived and its development through various periods, each of which gave birth to new orders in thought and science. One notices too an interesting alteration in the author's style and methods as his history progresses. The scenes, events and people in the early part of the book are painted with broad bold strokes. But as the Buddenbrooks slowly alter, grow thoughtful, slip into the slough of neurotic introspection, the author's style grows more subtle, his characterizations more monite, his narrative more detailed, his canvas smaller. From a painter Thomas Mann develops, according to the need of his material into an etcher, and each figure in the books, even the least important, is extraordinarily alive and liable to crop up in the reader's memory at odd moments for a long while after the details of the story have become blurred. The figure of Thomas Buddenbrook particularly stands out, with something in his character reminding one insistently of the third Napoleon. (pp. 237-40)

Hunter Stagg, "Decay and Dissolution," in The Reviewer, Vol. IV, No. 3, April, 1924, pp. 236-47.

ROBERT MORSS LOVETT (essay date 1931)

[*An American literary critic, educator, and statesman, Lovett served on the editorial staff of the* New Republic *during the 1920s and 1930s, where his book reviews and editorial policy reflected his leftist social and political thought. In the following excerpt, he praises various elements of Mann's artistry in* Buddenbrooks, *particularly his ability to blend realism and symbolism and his skillful use of irony.*]

Buddenbrooks itself covers little more than fifty years, but it brings into prominence four generations of the family whose name supplies its title. It focuses particular attention on the third of these four generations: Tom, Tony, and Christian, of whom Tom is the most important since in him the story of the Buddenbrooks is recapitulated. But Tom is a mere episode in that larger narrative which concerns the gradual dissolution of the family and the dissipation of the wealth acquired by its progenitors.

To describe a novel as a story of decay is to suggest an emphasis on the morbid and unpleasant which is quite apart from the actual tone of Mann's book. The tragedy of dissolution is foreshadowed even in the heyday of Buddenbrook prosperity, but the process is effected in a manner which brings out the beauty inherent in decay, and reminds one that the term decadence implies an increase in refinement and sensibility as well as a decrease in vitality. The very style, even in translation, carries that suggestion of beauty in death which is called elegiac. It is a suggestion always, for in this, his first novel of importance, published in 1901, Thomas Mann established himself as a craftsman who accomplished his effects by means so subtle as to seem only a happy accident. He also established himself as perhaps the foremost contemporary writer of German prose, a position recognized by the award of the Nobel Prize in 1929.

A novel covering so many years and dealing with so many characters demands an unusually convincing background. This Mann has supplied in terms of the physical, the social, and the historical. Most of the action takes place in the little Hanseatic city of Lübeck, and before the book is finished the reader is comfortably familiar with its geography. One becomes acquainted with its climate as with its topography—its rain, its snow, its mist, the occasional burst of sun and heat, are an integrated part of the lives and deaths of the people who move through its pages. These include not only Buddenbrooks, but also the numerous families who compose the social stratification of Lübeck: the aristocratic Krögers, with whom the Buddenbrooks are intermarried, the upstart Hagenstroms and Köppens who are *nouveaux riches* and so inferior to the Langhals and Möllendorpfs. All this human background is unobtrusive, but it supplies that social third dimension which adds solidity to *Vanity Fair,* and even more strikingly to Proust's *A La Recherche du Temps Perdu.* The same unobtrusive presence of detail achieves the same sense of solidity with regard to the routine of daily life. One knows how the family mansion is furnished, what the characters wear, what they eat. This matter of menus is apt to be prominent in genealogical novels, since the dinner table is a natural gathering place of the family. The *Forsyte Saga* includes a surprising number of meals; and a comparison of the two novels would bear out the statement that perhaps no other typical scene is so helpful in suggesting the atmosphere and *mores* of a group.

The historical events which occur during the course of *Buddenbrooks* creep in as casually but as correctly as the gradual changes in fashion and manners. The Napoleonic epoch is still a lively memory to old Consul Buddenbrook and his contemporaries. The Revolution of '48 furnishes to his son an opportunity for displaying his solid bourgeois courage. To Tony it vouchsafes the slogans of liberalism which she employs long after the event is as remote as the lover who preached them is to her. The Austro-Prussian War brings to Lübeck the benefits of having sided with the winner, but strikes at the Buddenbrooks through their financial interests in Frankfort. The Danish and Franco-German conflicts, however, reach the town chiefly as an echo of distant marching and a painless flare of patriotism. War is thus a significant element in the background of the century.

Against this firm, though lightly indicated background, the more immediate drama of the Buddenbrooks is enacted. The structure of the novel depends on a series of family scenes, beginning with the joyous housewarming at the mansion on Mengstrasse—"Such plenty, such elegance! I must say you know how to do things!" Thus the ill-bred wine merchant, Köppen, proud to be admitted to the gathering, sounds the keynote of the occasion. Years later, the celebration of the family centenary furnishes a companion piece to this introductory group picture. Again the atmosphere is one of prosperity. The family has reached the pinnacle of its worldly position. But Tom, now acting patriarch, already feels within him the symptoms of decay; and during the festivities he is called out to receive a telegram announcing his disastrous failure in a wheat speculation. One feels that his ancestors, who had amassed the fortune which he inherited, would not have speculated; but if they had, they would have won. So the family scenes progress, each marking a step in the rise and fall of the collective hero's career; until at the final gathering, after the death of the last male Buddenbrook, his mother announces her decision to return to her girlhood home in Holland. She is the first member by marriage to resist the assimilative power of the clan; and its members are left, convicted and convinced of ruin, to seek in some mystical assurance the compensation for worldly decline.

Birth and death of necessity bulk large in the chronicles of a family. But it is significant that the death scenes are far more elaborated than the births; and that the one birth which is dwelt upon—that of little Hanno, last of the line—is in itself the threat of a death temporarily averted. Because he comes into the world ill equipped to cope with the life his lusty ancestors had relished, his birth is really a signal to prepare for the funeral. (pp. 83-7)

The death scenes throughout *Buddenbrooks* bear witness to Mann's consummate blending of realism and symbolism, and this is true whether they are taken singly or considered as a progression. For the earlier ones are easily passed over, while with the growing decadence of the family the demise of its members assumes an ever more tragic aspect. It is as if the author placed himself on the very line where the two types of writing merge, so that this book in itself demonstrates how realism may develop into symbolism, how the choice of significant naturalistic detail inevitably suggests a meaning beyond its concrete limits. He has not spared unpleasant physical trivia—the minute odors and sensations which can be made to endow a scene with reality. But neither has he overlooked symbolical values. Part of the horror of Tom's death rises from the fact that he who had been so immaculate in life was borne home to his death-bed coated with mud and slush, his white kid gloves streaked with filth. And when his son Hanno comes to die, we are made to feel that he has succumbed, not to the power of death, but to the weakness of his own grasp on life.

This blend of realism and symbolism makes itself felt in the constant use of physical detail, and of objects that serve almost as stage properties: the Buddenbrook hand, "too short but finely modeled," modified to an almost unearthly delicacy and whiteness in Tom, but still recognizable in Hanno; the leather-bound volume wherein are inscribed the family births, marriages, deaths, and important events as they occur.

A reverent perusal of this record impresses upon Tony Buddenbrook the duty to family which must come before her individual happiness; and her submission is registered by inscribing in her own hand, wet with the tears she is weeping, her betrothal to the despised Grünlich. Little Hanno also peruses the book years later, and is moved to rule in, after his own name, the double line which signifies in book-keeping that an account is closed. When rebuked by his father, he stammers: "I thought—I thought—there was nothing else coming." Contrary to Mann's custom, the symbolism here is patent. And it is doubly significant, indicating the end of the family, and also, the commercial element which is inseparable from Buddenbrook history. (pp. 87-9)

Buddenbrooks is . . . explicit about the size of the family fortune, the various losses it suffers through marriage settlements and bad speculations. Because this is a commercial family, the state of its fortune serves as an index to its general state. When its possessions decline, its morale and its very hold on existence likewise deteriorate. Even the crimes which affect its standing are commercial crimes, the bankruptcy of Tony's husband, the embezzlement of her son-in-law.

In portraying his characters Mann has, for the most part, been content with classical methods. There is no attempt to limit the point of view, which shifts easily from one to another, though it is always given to some member of the family. Nor is there much stress on that exploring of the unconscious which recent psychological developments have brought so strongly to the fore, and which plays so large a part in *The Magic Mountain.*

The restraint which makes Mann's literary devices almost imperceptible is admirably illustrated in the case of Tom Buddenbrook, who is revealed as much through behavioristic as through analytical detail. His "Buddenbrook hand," and his death have been mentioned as examples of realism and symbolism. The modification of the hand may be taken to indicate the suppressed artistic impulses hinted at in his choice of a wife and openly expressed in his son. The strange deterioration which takes place within him so that he feels himself eaten away by a species of spiritual dry rot, is revealed through his growing obsession with details of wardrobe and toilet. As the inner man melts away he strengthens his armor of spotless elegance, till in the end he is but the exquisite shell of a man. Here Mann achieves a realistic and far more effective treatment of the theme which Henry James played upon more crudely and more fantastically in *The Private Life.*

The character of Tom is effective, just as the general technique of *Buddenbrooks* is effective, because it hovers on the border line between two types, and benefits by both. Apparently normal, he yet suffers from conflicts and suppressions which play a large part in abnormal psychology. One feels that he is straining against the bars which hold him to stolid decorum, and this sense of stress increases the poignancy of his characterization. The distance he has traveled between self-confident young manhood and his final state, is well brought out by two scenes which also illustrate Mann's masterful economy: the first, Tom's interview with his mistress, the little florist's assistant, when moved, but very much master of himself, he bids her a final good-by; the second, his suffering as he sits alone in his office listening to his wife and the handsome lieutenant making music in a room above—a prey to suspicions of a spiritual betrayal far more torturing than those based on physical infidelity.

Tom's evolution from assured and almost callous conservatism to anguished sensitivity is counter-balanced by that of Tony, who changes from an impetuous young girl into the spirit of conventionality and the personification of the family point of view. Her very conversation grows to be a compote of *clichés* in which the jargon of the Forty-eighters, sole vestige of her youthful revolt, clashes oddly with the bromides of the seventies and eighties, by which she shapes her life.

The family deterioration, recapitulated in Tom's character, takes final form in Hanno's physical weakness and artistic temperament. His tooth troubles, described with extreme realism, also serve as a symbol of general debility; and that his weakness stems directly from his father is emphasized by the fact that it is a decayed tooth which precipitates Tom's death. In addition, the teeth offer opportunity for implied comment on the rôle of dentistry in modern life, and the essential impotence of dentists, doctors, and all the agents of science to exercise that helpful control which is supposed to be their function. As for the aesthetic leanings suppressed in Tom and evident in Hanno, they too become symbols of decadence since they are wholly at odds with the sturdy commercialism which is the essence of the Buddenbrooks. The genius of the family has been the sort that could be reflected through rooms shining with comfort and cleanliness, opulent fur coats, and superabundance of good things to eat. When it descends to such a vessel as a frail, tearful boy with bad teeth, a weak digestion, and a burning love for music, it has declined indeed!

Because the point of view is limited to the family which is the group hero, the real touch of caricature is reserved for outsiders, such as Tony's second husband, Herr Permaneder from Munich, who is sketched with something of the good natured satire turned upon those beyond the pale. The Buddenbrooks are always sympathetically portrayed. Yet irony is never far from the surface, though so suavely insinuated that the reader feels it his own, developed from a strictly realistic representation of the material. Herein lies Mann's triumph. *Buddenbrooks* seems to take seriously the family and the family ideals; it almost does so. Nevertheless, by methods more veiled than innuendo, it does imply a satirical comment on pride of family, on provincial, and even national pride. One suspects, even though it is not hinted, that Tom's later preoccupation with clothes is a sly dig at the last Kaiser.

The irony strikes deeper, however, down to the very roots of human aspiration, both worldly and otherworldly. Its full force is for an instant released during Tom's one moment of vision, which gives the most eloquent passage in the book, and which by implication adds to the painfulness of his death when at last it comes. Dipping into a stray treatise on philosophy he seems to find an inkling of the strength he needs, and an assurance of some deeper portent in life itself. The assurance grows as he thinks it over during the night:

> "I shall live!" said Thomas Buddenbrook, almost aloud, and felt his breast shaken with inward sobs. "This is the revelation; that I shall live." . . . He wept, he pressed his face into the pillows and wept, shaken through and through, lifted up in transports by a joy without compare. . . .
>
> . . . He never succeeded in looking again into the precious volume—to say nothing of buying its other parts. His days were consumed by nervous pedantry: harassed by a thousand details, all of them unimportant, he was too weak-willed to ar-

rive at a reasonable and fruitful arrangement of his time. Nearly two weeks after that memorable afternoon he gave it up—and ordered the maid-servant to fetch the book from the drawer in the garden table and replace it in the bookcase.

This might be, as it purports to be, merely an account of what happens. Yet it carries overtones of comment on Tom and his species as well as on the value of mystical assurances concerning the life everlasting. A similar chord is struck in the very last scene. The Buddenbrook women on the eve of the family's final disintegration, meet in a pathetic conclave that recalls by contrast the buoyant group with which the novel began. There are quiet tears but there is also courage; and Tony in a moment of exaltation asks whether there can be an after life in which may occur a joyous reunion of Buddenbrooks. Her kinswomen are silent—this is not their field. But Sesemi Weichbrodt, Tony's old teacher and the family's staunch friend, undertakes to answer:

> "*It is so!*" she said, with her whole strength; and looked at them all with a challenge in her eyes.
>
> She stood there, a victor in the good fight which all her life she had waged against the assaults of Reason: humpbacked, tiny, quivering with the strength of her convictions, a little prophetess, admonishing and inspired.

Does Thomas Mann see Sesemi as sublime or ridiculous, or a little of both? The essence of his art lies in leaving the question open. (pp. 90-6)

Robert Morss Lovett, " 'Buddenbrooks'," in his Preface to Fiction: A Discussion of Great Modern Novels, *Thomas S. Rockwell Company, 1931, pp. 81-96.*

JAMES CLEUGH   (essay date 1933)

[*In the following excerpt, Cleugh traces the development of the theme of decadence in* Buddenbrooks *and examines the ways in which philosophy and music influence the themes, structure, and style of the book.*]

Three of [Mann's] stories, **"Little Herr Friedemann," "Der Bajazzo"** and **"Tobias Mindernickel"** may reasonably be regarded as preliminary exercises to the great masterpiece which appeared in 1901. The physical weakness of the central figures, the courage of Friedemann, the gaudiness of Bajazzo, the shy, hypersensitiveness of Mindernickel were to re-appear in three of the principal characters of **Buddenbrooks,** actually in three of the members of that ancient and honourable house. Ideas such as that of the raw, blunt cruelty of life, the unsuitability of the volatile artistic temperament for the solid business of practical living and the self-torture that results from the attempt to conquer the feeling of being a square peg in a round hole, the whole notion of decadence as a frailty, a declension from sanity, and yet mysteriously seductive in its appeal to pity and the sense of wonder, enter into the first long novel by Thomas Mann.

His readers knew more or less what to expect and they found it. But they found it in a richly varied and vast, an epic atmosphere, one too, since it was entirely commercial, that the rather exclusively "bohemian" setting of most of the preceding stories would seem to have forbidden to the author. There was as much astonishment as admiration in the first wave of enthusiasm for **Buddenbrooks.**

The novel opens in the year 1835. Johann Buddenbrook, head of the wealthy firm of grain merchants founded by his ancestor in 1768, is a genial old materialist, an admirer of Voltaire and Napoleon, a sceptical, cool, hard-headed business man through and through. His friends and contemporaries are the humorous, worldly *abbé,* Pastor Wunderlich, and the rococo, typically eighteenth-century poet Hoffstede, who writes a charming trifle to celebrate the house-warming party given by the Buddenbrook family and brilliantly described in the first thirty pages of the book. The three generations which are to exemplify the idea of decadence implicit in the subtitle of the novel, "Decline of a Family," are already present on this occasion. Johann, son of old Buddenbrook, is a mature benedict, serious-minded and inclined to piety, though still not far inferior to his father as a business man. His ideal, at which old Johann good-humouredly scoffs, is the age's notion of progress as incarnated in the contemporary king of France, Louis Philippe. The younger Johann's three small children, Thomas, Antonie and Christian, already show certain further divergences from the family type. In the first two generations the contrast between the gay and somewhat cynical, Frenchified elders, old Johann and his friends, and the more solemn and sentimental epoch which was succeeding Goethe and the romantics is very noticeable to a reader who may have been accustomed in his youth to adolescent scepticism and parental austerity. Of the children it is the seven-year-old Christian, with his nervous excitability, who is, at the moment, chiefly significant. Or perhaps a better word would be, ominous.

From this point until the sudden death in 1855 of the younger Johann Buddenbrook, who is still only on the threshold of old age—his father predeceases him by many years—the reader feels himself to be in a world definitely of the past. The characters, the settings, the conversational idioms, the clothes, the history itself of the period, including the revolutionary tumults of 1848, are amazingly vivid and delineated with the accuracy and consistency which are conspicuous features of all Thomas Mann's work. He had his own family archives to draw upon. The Buddenbrooks, who resemble very closely the ancestors of Mann himself, had theirs too. But the historical imagination, as he was to show again and again in future years, is a peculiar gift in his versatile psychology.

With the accession of the young Thomas Buddenbrook to the headship of the firm the Wagnerian overture, containing the fundamental *motifs* of what is to follow, concludes. The development of the main theme of decadence now gathers force and complexity. Thomas Buddenbrook, though he occupies considerably less space in the novel as a whole than his enchanting sister Toni, sustains the most serious burden of commentary. Like Johann Friedemann [in **"Little Herr Friedemann"**] and Paolo Hofmann [in **"The Will to Happiness"**] he is a true tragic hero in the German sense of a strong man whose strength is nevertheless not equal to his fate. He is efficient in commerce, but he is the first Buddenbrook for whom to be efficient in commerce is to make an effort. His mind takes account of other things besides buying cheap and selling dear. Like Mann's own father he has certain literary, even, just before his death, philosophical, interests. And he marries, as Johann Mann did, a mysterious beauty whose soul is in her music. He is the first "individual" in the firm, but he pays heavily for setting his personality against the mass-consciousness of his time. Physically he is not strong. For the last few years, especially, of his comparatively brief life he sufers from nerves, not improved by the eternal cigarettes which are a characteristic resource of the age. *Il faut toujours avoir une cigarette* ["one should always have a cigarette"], maintains a famous French decadent only a few years later than this period, at the beginning of one of his best known satirical tales. Thomas Buddenbrook is also a victim of high blood-pressure and the life-weariness which Mann had already noted in his *Novellen* as one of the definitive symptoms of decadence.

A celebrated passage at the end of a chapter preluding this hero's end marks the final stage of the elegant and efficient merchant's conflict with his fate. He is standing, with his sister Toni, on a desolate seashore.

> "Great waves," said Thomas Buddenbrook. "How they come on and break, come on and break, one after another, endlessly, idly, empty and vast! And yet, like all the simple, inevitable things, they soothe, they console, after all. I have learned to love the sea more and more. Once, I think, I cared more for the mountains, because they lay farther off. Now I do not long for them. They would only frighten and abash me. They are too capricious, too manifold, too anomalous. I know I should feel myself vanquished in their presence. What sort of men prefer the monotony of the sea? Those, I think, who have looked so long and deeply into the complexities of the spirit, that they ask of outward things merely that they should possess one quality above all: simplicity. It is true that in the mountains one clambers briskly about, while beside the sea one sits quietly on the shore. This is a difference, but a superficial one. The real difference is in the look with which one pays homage to the one and to the other. It is a strong, challenging gaze, full of enterprise, that can soar from peak to peak: but the eyes that rest on the wide ocean and are soothed by the sight of its waves rolling on for ever, mystically, relentlessly, are those that are already wearied by looking too deep into the solemn perplexities of life. Health and illness, that is the difference. The man whose strength is unexhausted climbs boldly up into the lofty multiplicity of the mountain heights. But it is when one is worn out by turning one's eyes inward upon the bewildering complexity of the human heart that one finds peace in resting them upon the wideness of the sea."

In the next chapter Thomas Buddenbrook is to die. For business worries, ill-health, troubles with Toni, who makes two unlucky marriages, and with the delinquent brother Christian, who is another "Bajazzo," bring the strong man down at last. After the painful extraction of a tooth he collapses in the street. The second movement of the symphony is over.

Hanno, his little son, is delicate, hypersensitive and on the way to becoming a musical prodigy. It is clear that the commercial strain in the Buddenbrooks has given out. The boy himself is made to signalise this dissolution of the greatness of his family in a remarkable way.

> He had practised for a long time on the piano and now was idling about in the living-room. He half lay, half sat on the *chaise-longue,* tying and untying his sailor's knot, and his eyes, roving aimlessly about, caught sight of an open portfolio on his mother's nut-wood writing-table. It was the leather case with the family papers. He rested his elbow on the sofa cushion and his chin in his hand and looked at the things for a while from a distance.

Papa must have had them out after second breakfast and left them there because he was not finished
with them. Some of the papers were sticking in the
portfolio, some loose sheets lying outside were
weighted with a metal ruler and the large gilt-edged
note-book with the motley paper lay there open.

Hanno slipped idly down from the sofa and went
to the writing-table. The book was open at the Buddenbrook family tree, set forth in the hands of his
various forbears, including his father, complete
with rubrics, parentheses and plainly marked dates.
Kneeling with one knee on the desk chair, leaning
his head with its soft waves of brown hair on the
palm of his hand Hanno looked at the manuscript
sideways, carelessly critical, a little contemptuous
and supremely indifferent, letting his free hand toy
with Mama's gold and ebony pen. His eyes roved
all over these names, masculine and feminine, some
of them in queer old-fashioned writing with great
flourishes, written in faded yellow or thick black
ink to which little grains of sand were sticking. At
the very bottom, in Papa's small, neat handwriting,
that ran so fast over the page, he read his own name
under that of his parents, Justus Johann Kaspar,
born April 15, 1861. He liked looking at it. He
straightened up a little and took the ruler and pen,
still rather idly, let his eye travel once more over the
whole genealogical host, then with absent care, me-
chanically and dreamily, he made with the gold pen
a beautiful, clean, double line diagonally across the
entire page, the upper one heavier than the lower,
just as he had been taught to embellish the page of
his arithmetic book. He looked at his work with his
head on one side and then moved away.

After dinner the Senator called him up and surveyed him with his eyebrows drawn together.

"What is this? Where did it come from? Did you
do it?"

Hanno had to think a minute whether he really had
done it. Then he answered:

"Yes."

"What for? What is the matter with you? Answer
me! What possessed you to do such a mischievous
thing?" cried the Senator, and struck Hanno's
cheek lightly with the rolled up notebook.

And little Johann stammered, retreating with his
hands to his cheek:

"I thought—I thought—there was nothing else
coming."

Soon after Thomas Buddenbrook's fatal stroke his child dies
of typhus. For life is will, according to Schopenhauer, and
Hanno has not inherited his father's strength of character.
The old house is bought by a rising Jewish family, the Buddenbrooks are dispersed. Only the invincible Toni survives.
The resolution of the theme, the third movement of the symphony, ends in a fugal lament for the cruel war of destruction
waged by life.

This novel is epic in scale, conception and treatment. It grew
to its extensive, but not excessive, proportions out of Mann's
own experience in early youth, which led him to account for
the financial misfortunes of his own family by a reference to
the gradual outcropping of noncommercial instincts, becoming definitely of an artistic type in himself, his brother and

Heinrich and Thomas Mann in 1900.

younger sister. Hence arose the idea of an artist as a decadent,
one who refuses to accept the normal life of a specifically
commercial age and who is therefore an outcast, a useless declension from type. Christian Buddenbrook with his sensitiveness amounting in the eyes of the sober citizen to mania,
his restive recusancy of a decent, stable existence, his mimetic
talent blocked by his extreme nervousness, his utter lack of
reserve, is the first clear example in the house of Buddenbrook, as perhaps Heinrich Mann had been in the author's
own, of the indubitably artistic temperament. The portrait is
a bitter caricature which fails to be cruel only because of the
typical sympathetic irony which informs it. The reader ends
by pitying as much as he despises Christian the mountebank,
the charlatan, the weak debauchee and hypochondriac.
Thomas Buddenbrook's thunderous scorn in the great scene
between the brothers after their mother's death is almost
counterbalanced by the shrill Strindbergian protest of the culprit.

"Don't you realise, you fool," cried Thomas Buddenbrook in a passion, "that all these horrors are
the consequence and effect of your vices, your idleness and your self-tormenting? Go to work! Stop
petting your condition and talking about it!" . . .
"Work! Suppose I can't work? My God! I can't do
the same thing long at a time! It kills me. If you
have been able to and are able to, thank God for it,
but don't sit in judgment on others, for it isn't a virtue. God gives strength to one and not to another.
But that is the way you are made, Thomas. You are
self-righteous. Oh, wait, that is not what I am going
to say, nor what I accuse you of. I don't know

where to begin and however much I can say is only a millionth part of the feeling I have in my heart against you. You have made a position for yourself in life and there you stand and push everything away which might possibly disturb your equilibrium for a moment—for your equilibrium is the most precious thing in the world to you. But it isn't the most precious thing in life, Thomas—no, before God it is not. You are an egoist, that is what you are. I am still fond of you, even when you are angry and tread on me and thunder me down. But when you get silent, when somebody says something and you are suddenly dumb and withdraw yourself, quite elegant and remote, and repulse people like a wall and leave the other fellow to his shame without any chance of justifying himself—! Yes, you are without pity, without love, without humility. Oh," he cried, and stretched both arms in front of him, palms outward, as though pushing everything away from him, "Oh, how sick I am of all this tact and propriety, this poise and refinement—sick to death of it!"

The outburst was so genuine, so heartfelt, it sounded so full of loathing and satiety that it was actually crushing. Thomas shrank a little and looked down in front of him, weary and without a word.

Each voice is that of Thomas Mann. And their conflict is the storm that ploughed the virgin fields of his youth and made them bear the first harvest, in *Buddenbrooks,* of his greatness.

The young writer had discovered at school that his originally vague notions of the ruinous antithesis between burgher and artist, between the robust business man and the delicate intellectual, had been anticipated by Friedrich Nietzsche. That philosopher's sweeping and vindictive analysis of decadence had cleared his conceptions. But Thomas Mann had a level head. He suspended judgment, merely chronicled, with a greater elaboration and a cooler insight, the workings of the struggle. The end of *Buddenbrooks* is no vindication of either side. It leaves the reader with a sense as much of the admirable vitality of the unimaginative merchant as of his ruthlessness, with a sense as much of the marvellous intuition of the aesthetic temper as of its futile cowardice.

This drawn battle is waged with every resource of epic genius. Its movement is in the depths of thought and feeling, its picture is the vivid and accurate reflection of the world in the soul of a single personality, its technique is as polished, as ingenious and as effective as that of Homer. Thomas Mann, in the nursery, had preferred Hector and Achilles to Hawkeye and Leatherstocking. The *Leitmotiv,* the device invented by the author of the Iliad and patented by Wagner, is a prominent feature of the style of *Buddenbrooks.* The autocrat of Bayreuth had early become an influence scarcely inferior to that of his friend and subsequent enemy Nietzsche in the life of the young amateur, for whom music was so much more than a pendant to literature. The contrivance was not new to letters. Besides Homer the modern Europeans Goethe, Zola and Dickens, to name only three of many writers, had used it. But Mann was a musician and his repetitive notes have a value not only intellectual but emotional. Thomas Buddenbrook's trick of raising one eyebrow draws attention, when it is referred to, as much to the significant mood of a passage as to its logical importance in the development of the plot. When poor Toni unconsciously quotes, as she does at intervals throughout her long life, the phrases used by the revolutionary young doctor, who was the object of her early, unhap-

py and only love, the deft and unobtrusive hint thus introduced into the narrative deepens almost intolerably the tragedy of her life and through her tragedy the tragedy of her house. Not Wagner himself equals Thomas Mann's dexterous mastery of such effects, which can be, as they not infrequently are in the composer, deprived of value by over-emphasis, incongruous appearance and excessive repetition, tending to become mechanical and at last empty.

Wagner's works have been called the artistic interpretation of the philosophy of Schopenhauer, whose view of and deep interest in music explains so much of his general theory. It is true that the pages in the operatic scores devoted to the fateful figures of Wotan and Tristan seem to support this contention. But, however, this may be, it is clear that of the spiritual sponsors of *Buddenbrooks* the third great intellect, apart from Nietzsche, in whose work, too, music looms large, and Wagner, is the apologist of pessimism. He is only mentioned explicitly when Thomas Buddenbrook is near his end. The outwardly imperturbable, inwardly stricken and weary head of the ancient house finds an incomplete copy of *The World as Will and Idea* in a summer pavilion of the new and elegant mansion for which, since his marriage, he has deserted—another symptom of decadence—the venerable pile occupied by his forefathers.

He was filled with a great, surpassing satisfaction. It soothed him to see how a master mind could lay hold on the strong, cruel, mocking thing called life, dominate it and condemn it. His was the gratification of the sufferer who has always had a bad conscience about his sufferings and conceals them from the gaze of a harsh, unsympathetic world until suddenly, from the hand of an authority, he receives, as it were, justification and licence for his suffering, justification before the world, this best of all possible worlds, which the master-mind scornfully demonstrates to be the worst of all possible ones.

Schopenhauer, with his peculiar doctrine of personal immortality, prepares Thomas Buddenbrook for death. But, with Nietzsche, the earlier philosopher is behind the whole conception of the idea of decadence in the novel. At the third stage, where the focus of the treatment is the little Hanno, Wagner takes over. For Hanno, to understand *Tristan and Isolde* is to die. His improvisation on the piano in the last chapter but two of *Buddenbrooks,* just before he is taken ill with typhus, is Wagnerian. It is the composition of a child. But throughout the brilliant description of it, which occupies three full pages in the book, the tragic pathos of the life of a man is marvellously conveyed.

The fanatical worship of this worthless trifle, this scrap of melody, this brief, childish harmonic invention, only a bar and a half in length, had about it something stupid and gross and at the same time something ascetic and religious, something that contained the essence of faith and renunciation. There was a quality of the perverse in the insatiability with which it was produced and revelled in: there was a sort of cynical despair, there was a longing for joy, a yielding to desire, in the way the last drop of sweetness was, as it were, extracted from the melody till exhaustion, disgust and satiety supervened. Then at last, at last, in the weariness after excess a long, soft arpeggio in the minor trickled through, mounted a tone, resolved itself in the major and died in mournful lingering away.

Hanno sat still a moment, his chin on his breast, his

hands in his lap. Then he got up and closed the instrument. He was very pale, there was no strength
in his knees and his eyes were burning. He went
into the next room, stretched himself on the *chaiselongue* and remained for a long time motionless.

The main presentation of the idea of decadence in ***Buddenbrooks,*** the gradually darkening picture of the decline of a
great trading family through increasing sensibility, is enhanced by a hundred subordinate touches throwing the variants of character and atmosphere into a relief that not only
prevents the tragedy from becoming intolerable but lifts it
into the air of the highest comedy.

It is Toni Buddenbrook, that Madame Bovary seen through
German spectacles, an eight-year-old child on the first page
of the book, a woman of fifty with the face and the nature of
a child on its last, who softens the stark outlines, warms the
sharp air of this narrative of inexorable destiny. All Germany
and, as time went on, most of Europe, fell in love with her.
Her quaint docility, her instant and intense, if brief, reactions
to pleasures and pains, her absurd and fascinating dignity,
her dauntless vitality, revive a complex feminine charm that,
in its entirety, has vanished with the "emancipation" of the
sex.

An episode very typical of life in the forties of the last century
establishes Toni, at eighteen or so, once for all as a tragic figure in the book. Her character appears to remain unchanged.
But it is this very fact which increases the emotional tension.
Toni does not need any more to draw in her chin and raise
her shoulders, in that delightful way of hers, at important
moments, though she continues to do so. She has henceforth
in the reader's mind the melancholy majesty of a princess of
Sophocles beneath her lively, infantile envelope, however in-
contestably a part of herself that envelope persists. It is significant that her most dramatic gesture, to pass her tongue over
her upper lip, is a prelude sometimes to laughter and sometimes to tears.

Herr Bendix Grünlich was a pretty young gentleman with a
rosy face, long golden whiskers and a feebly criminal mentality. He imposed on the upright and industrious man of business, Johann Buddenbrook the Second, but not on the innocent Toni, who hated him at sight. Her father took the traditional view. The *partie,* he considered, was an advantageous
one. His daughter was too young to know her own mind. She
must go to the seaside to think it over. Toni went, and met
Morten Schwarzkopf, the medical student who was anticipating the theories of Garibaldi. The idyll by the northern sea,
which Mann knew and loved so intimately, has an ethereal
sweetness and poignancy. But it is crowned only by a single
kiss. Grünlich appears, Morten's father intervenes, Toni returns, family feeling crushes natural instinct. The first of the
ominous marriages of convenience takes place, with the inevitable result. Johann had to fetch his daughter home and the
union was dissolved.

In spite of this affair and the equally disastrous second marriage with a grossly festive and unbalanced, not to say unbut-
toned, Bavarian—a further variety of decadent—Toni continues to provide quite half the humour in a novel singularly
rich in that quality. Her very agonies, as so often happens in
life, exhibit the comic strain. The telegram in which she announces her second matrimonial failure is an admirably ironic epitome of her nature, with its contrasting touches of impe-
riousness and self-dramatisation.

"Don't be frightened. Am coming at once with Erica. All is
over. Your unhappy Antonie."

Again, at Thomas Buddenbrook's death-bed, in the presence
of the whole grief-stricken family, Toni began to sing a hymn
in a loud voice, but found she could only remember the first
three lines "and had to make up for her abrupt ending by the
increased dignity of her manner."

Buddenbrooks, perhaps more than any other European novel
published before 1900, certainly more than any other German novel, conveys convincingly the sense of what Rabelais
called life itself, *"ceste insigne fable et tragicque comédie."*

The secondary ideas and influences at work in the book were
not often new to those who had read **"Little Herr Friedemann"** carefully. They were in general consistent with the literary personality with which the earlier production had already invested Thomas Mann. It is the epic note, the sway
of Tolstoy, and the consequent elaboration of the thought,
which chiefly differentiate ***Buddenbrooks*** from the *Novellen.*
Music had taught Mann to compose, like Homer and Milton,
a logical texture woven of different themes and this method
incalculably enriched his style and form. He was not by any
means exclusively devoted to Wagnerism, which has certain
decadent aspects only appropriate when the main theme of
the novel is in full play. Bach, and more particularly Chopin,
preside in many passages. The fastidious elegance, however,
of the writing, throughout the book, never otherwise than fit
for an aristocratic *salon,* has always the sureness and the continuous charm of the Polish composer, his extreme intelligence and avoidance of the commonplace, his extraordinary
faculty for translating the most tragic and profound desires
of the soul into polite language. So, too, the exact framework,
the use of counterpoint, climax and, in the more crowded
scenes, of chorus, recall the idiom of Bach, as do the rhythmic rise and fall of mood, the storms and the breezes of the
style, the touches of humour, the symbolic phrases, the more
or less elusive hints and suggestions. Like a musician, again,
Mann respects his material, knows the souls of words, understands their potential melody, their dynamic power.

The texture of the prose, in fact, as that of a good symphony
should be, is so closely studied, the intellectual analysis so
concentrated, all facile thought, feeling and expression so rig-
orously pruned, that it is easy to remember how ***Buddenbrooks*** was written. It was composed as in a laboratory, behind the closed doors of the flat in Rome, shut in the narrow
rooms at Munich, while an alien life streamed by unmarked,
without significance for the slowly growing pile of manuscript.

Lübeck only was near, and the grey Baltic, whose air swept
through the Scandinavian romances read in the Via Torre
Argentina. Such dream-images were clearer in the author's
mind than those of the two southern cities where his novel
was conceived and executed. They make the pictures in ***Buddenbrooks,*** the interiors, the streets, the land and sea-scapes,
the West Prussian bodies and minds. They make the thought
acute and tender, the style pure and flexible, of a masterpiece
that stands alone in German literature. (pp. 78-96)

James Cleugh, in his Thomas Mann: A Study, *Martin Secker, 1933, 208 p.*

HENRY HATFIELD (essay date 1951)

[*An American educator and critic, Hatfield is the author of numerous books on German literature and has served as editor of* The Germanic Review. *In the following excerpt from* Thomas Mann: A Collection of Critical Essays, *of which he is the editor, Hatfield discusses the technical innovations of* Buddenbrooks, *such as Mann's use of the leitmotif, and studies Mann's treatment of the themes of decadence and death.*]

T. S. Eliot once remarked on the "usefulness" of a type of poetry "which could cut across all the present stratifications of public taste," and cited the plays of Shakspere, with their "several layers of significance" as examples of works of the desired universality of appeal. Eliot was writing only of poetry, but his *aperçu* illuminates the enormous success of *Buddenbrooks.* Essentially a rather complicated and deeply pessimistic book, it has an abundance of sheer narration, of humor, of easily grasped character and local color, which make its vast popularity natural enough; and also a certain sympathetic warmth in dealing with character which is more agreeable to most readers than the cool temperature of the early novellas. One need know nothing of Wagner or Schopenhauer, of the theory of decadence or the metaphysical allure of death to find the novel absorbing, and this is all to the good. Nor need one have heard of the leitmotif to "get" the effect of Mann's repetitions; indeed it would be difficult to miss most of them. To say this is not, of course, to disparage the less obvious attractions of the book: its tendency and meaning, its overtones and associations. The comparison with Galsworthy's *Forsyte Saga,* sometimes facilely and misleadingly made, can be enlightening. *Buddenbrooks,* besides its "popular" elements, has precisely what the *Saga* does not: the broad range of "layers of significance," unexpected finesses, and a technique which, if at times obviously used, points ahead from the straightforward historical arrangement of nineteenth-century narration to the musical complexities of the novel of the twentieth century. Mann's own reference to Wagner's *Ring* furnishes a needed clue.

Despite his doubts about the bulk and nature of the book, Mann completed *Buddenbrooks* in about two and a half years; it was published late in 1900. The actual writing was begun in Italy, where he spent a year with his brother Heinrich. Yet there is no trace of the South in the novel. This was no "Italian journey" in Goethe's sense; it had nothing to do with the traditional attempt of the German writer to experience the Mediterranean and classic world; it was rather a period of deliberate self-isolation, which afforded no doubt perspective and concentration on his work. Mann tells us that his mood at the time was made up of "indolence, a bad conscience as a bourgeois, and the secure sense of latent talents." For the "bad conscience" there were presumably two reasons: his rejection of any sort of middle-class career, and his choice of the decay of his own family as a subject. At times, Mann must have felt that he was committing an indiscretion if not a downright betrayal. Thomas Buddenbrook is closely modeled after Mann's own father, and his exotic wife Gerda would seem, to a lesser extent, reminiscent of Mann's mother, Julia Da Silva-Bruhns. Psychologically, the novel may be said to represent a sort of reckoning with the father image by a young man who has broken with family tradition and gone off to carry on a "questionable" existence in Munich and Italy. He has rejected the ancestral firm, business, the whole world of Lübeck; his revolt has been successful and, outwardly, not very difficult, but a sense of guilt and remorse remains.

The reckoning is unusually gentle, as such things go; the rejection reluctant. Sympathy and admiration for the father's world persist, and with them the chronic bad conscience of the Mannian hero. Without this ambivalence towards the burgher, so different from the harsh singlemindedness of Heinrich Mann, Mann's view of the world would be clearer and sharper, but his books cooler and less "felt." As he states in *Tonio Kröger,* the problematic love for the bourgeois world represented by his father (and arbitrarily called the "normal") was one of the strongest forces impelling him to write. The same emotion must have produced the psychological tension, the "charge," which saves *Buddenbrooks* from being only another family novel. (pp. 31-3)

To deal with the fortunes of four generations of Buddenbrooks, Mann found that he needed over seven hundred pages, divided among a host of chapters which are organized into eleven parts. For all its bulk, the novel has structure: the prestige and power of the family rise, reach a sort of plateau, and then imperceptibly slip into a decline which gradually gathers a terrifying momentum. It is Thomas, the central figure of the third generation, on whom the welfare of the family comes essentially to depend, so that the crisis of his life is also the crisis of the novel. The failures of his brother and sister, both obvious by the center of the work, isolate him increasingly, and the slow erosion of his strength makes inevitable the fall of the whole group.

This group does not exist in a vacuum; Mann shows its life against the background of the city-state of Lübeck, in whose oligarchic government the Buddenbrooks play a considerable role. Farther in the background, we are aware of the evolution of Germany from 1835 to about 1878: the emergence of German unity, prosperity, and material power as reflected in the customs union among the German states, the victorious Prussian wars with Denmark, Austria, and France, and the sharp rise of commerce and trade. The broader developments are briefly mentioned without didactic digressions; the focus is always upon the Buddenbrooks as a particular group of very special individuals. Mann did not intend to write a symbolic novel of the German middle class, which was rising to new heights of prosperity during the period he describes, but rather to represent the decline of cultivated patricians, pushed to the wall by the new bourgeoisie. The testimony of his brother Viktor shows how Mann "stylized" the history of his family to heighten the impression of decadence. Yet the European reaction to *Buddenbrooks* suggests that his interpretation was by no means a merely arbitrary one but illuminated a very real social process.

Buddenbrooks is a novel of tradition as well as of decadence; the one implies the other. For the tradition of the patrician burgher, quite different from that of the "ordinary" middle class, Mann has profound respect. It stands for activity, energy, a degree of cultivation, and certain not too rigorous ethical standards, for "life" in a good sense. Despite ironic indications—fewer than one would expect—that the burgher's devotion to money is extreme, Mann is clearly on his side. There is no implication that the Buddenbrooks have amassed an undue amount of wealth; on the contrary, when the family bank balance sinks, we feel that the world is out of joint. Before their decline begins, the Buddenbrooks accept the business world in a robust, unquestioning way. Only in the third generation, with Thomas, do they become too delicate for the ethics of competition; only the sick Buddenbrook questions a *laissez-faire* capitalism. (Thomas, after a business reversal, perceives that his "best friends" react not with sympathy but with frigid distrust; he is weary and sensitive enough to consider this a personal injury.) Before that point, the Darwinian struggle for survival is taken as a matter of course. Not that the Buddenbrooks are Nietzschean buccaneers. "My son, engage joyfully in business during the day, but make only such deals that we can sleep well at night" is their motto—a very bourgeois code, but still a code. Without hypocrisy, one must be deeply concerned in preserving the appearance of solidity and respectability. Bankruptcy is the unforgivable sin. Thomas' feckless brother, Christian, can be excused for his failures, his sexual divagations, even his idleness; but when he remarks that every businessman is "really a swindler," no pardon is possible; his brother, a person by no means given to melodramatic gestures, is driven to pronounce a downright curse on him. The ideal Buddenbrook is a non-religious churchgoer whose ethic might have served as an instance of the inner bond between Protestantism and capitalism argued by Max Weber and Tawney. Religious fervor is suspect—it is not "solid"—music is still more so, and Thomas' taste for French novels and habit of citing Heine are clearly indications of danger.

Occasionally, Mann does treat his worthy patricians ironically, as in the repeated accounts of their fabulous meals, but his identification with them is too close to allow him to depart often from the tone of respect. His most ironic pages deal with the liberal bourgeoisie and the hopelessly docile working class. Thus the young student, Morten Schwarzkopf, believes ardently in the ideals of the ill-fated German liberal revolt of 1848—abolition of class distinctions, academic freedom, freedom of the press, and all the rest. He is a charming fellow, but clearly naive; we cannot take him seriously. When the "revolution" breaks out in Lübeck, the novel enters the realm of farce. The "people" break a few windows, demonstrate aimlessly for some hours, and then are sent home in good humor after some friendly words of paternal advice by the younger Johann Buddenbrook. Undoubtedly this account has a good deal of historical validity. One is reminded of Trotzky's remark that the German workers would not seize a railway station unless they had bought tickets first. In any case Mann's personal sympathies are clearly with the conservative side, where they remained until after the defeat of 1918.

Yet despite this affectionate respect for the patrician tradition, the theme of decadence clearly predominates. Decay is considered as an inevitable spiritual and biological process, not as an occasion of moral reproach. It is most strikingly shown in the succession of four male Buddenbrooks, three of whom are heads of the ancestral firm. Johann Buddenbrook, Sr. is a type of the eighteenth century as popularly conceived—rationalistic, optimistic, skeptical, and of uncomplicated, single-minded energy. His son, the younger Johann, is an excellent businessman and devoted to money; but his sentimental religiosity causes a split in his nature which leads to unconscious hypocrisy and "practical ideals." The Buddenbrooks are on the way to becoming problematic. With Thomas Buddenbrook they have become so. Thomas is the most appealing and impressive of the line. Cultivated, able, and enormously conscientious, he guides the family to its greatest successes, but he has no real belief in the value of his enterprises; his energies are eaten away.

Despite all his efforts, he cannot overcome the somehow innate tendency to dissolution which has overtaken the family like a sort of fate. At one point he violates the traditional ethics of the firm in a desperate effort to recoup its fortunes, but the manoeuvre fails. After long and bitter struggles, he is utterly defeated. Yet his prolonged endeavor gives him stature: he has much of that "heroism of weakness" which Mann so greatly admires, and which he was to represent later in the more impressive figures of Schiller, in *A Weary Hour,* and of Gustave von Aschenbach. In Aristotelian terms, Thomas' flaw may be said to lie in his externality, evident in his sacrifice of human values to the welfare of the firm, and in his supreme concern for maintaining appearances. As his vitality decreases, he is forced more and more to mask his actual condition. Only Hanno, the most sensitive of the family, fully perceives this.

Shortly before his death, Thomas has an experience which could have saved him, spiritually speaking, but he lacks the force and courage to hold it in his grasp. More or less by chance he comes upon a volume of Schopenhauer and finds in it a source of metaphysical ecstasy. His cares suddenly appear unspeakably petty and indeed irrelevant; his own individuality and even that of his son seem unimportant.

> Have I hoped to live on in my son? In a personality yet more feeble, flickering, and timorous than my own? Blind, childish folly! What can my son do for me—what need have I of a son?
>
> Where shall I be when I am dead? Ah, it is so brilliantly clear, so overwhelmingly simple! I shall be in all those who have ever, do ever, or ever shall say "I"—*especially, however, in all those who say it most fully, potently, and gladly!*

Schopenhauer—or better, Schopenhauer modified by Nietzsche—could then have freed him from the tortures inflicted by the will. But he lacks the intellectual energy to maintain himself on these philosophical heights. He never opens the book again. One feels that this failure, like the others, is due less to any tangible defect in Thomas than to that inner weariness which, Mann implies, must be taken as given and lies beyond explanation.

Mann has made no secret of the fact that he has attributed to his not very intellectual hero a metaphysical experience of his own. One admires all the more the tact and skill which make the episode credible, and the control which keeps ideology in its place. *Buddenbrooks,* in this regard, is more of a work of art than most of the later novels.

While Thomas, in his way, is a tragic figure, his son Hanno is pathetic. He is possessed of some musical talent but lacks the strength for any sort of career, let alone that of restoring the shaken fortunes of the family. He is phenomenally sickly, and dies while still a schoolboy, physically of sickness but essentially of decadence. With him the family comes to an end. The theme of successive and cumulative decline is repeated in a number of lesser figures.

What happens to the Buddenbrooks is a decline only from the point of view of normality. As always, Mann shows the opposite aspect: in terms of "the spirit" the process is one of ascent to greater awareness and intellectuality, to art, and to—death. Life and the spirit are irreconcilable foes; there is no hope, in Mann's early thought, of a possible synthesis, and the suggestion of a possible *juste milieu* would have been rejected as childishly optimistic. Mann clearly implies in *Buddenbrooks* that the game of the spirit is not worth the candle. (pp. 37-43)

Decadence then is inevitable and has a potentially creative aspect, but it is greatly to be feared. Mann devotes all his powers of naturalistic description and all his psychological subtlety to develop the theme. It is with the sentimental religiosity of the younger Johann Buddenbrook that feelings "other than the normal, every-day sentiments proper to good citizens" enter the family tradition and begin to alienate it from life. From this point, early in the novel, until the horrible death of the adolescent Hanno, the process takes its inexorable course. (At times Mann implies a dubious biology: decay would seem to be in the blood.) Largely it is seen as a physical development: all the later Buddenbrooks are labile, they tend to migraines, carious teeth, premature aging, and "bluish shadows below the eyes." The terms "nervous" and "exhausted" occur again and again. But primarily the evolution is psychological: with greater self-consciousness come extreme subjectivity and introversion. Energy, and finally the will to live itself, fall away; it is Hanno's lack of *élan vital* that makes him succumb to typhus. In him, as earlier in Christian, the "death wish" becomes dominant. Loyalty to the family and the firm gradually becomes a problem, and then an insoluble one. Artistic, and above all musical endowment is not merely a symptom of the decline; it is a causal factor. Christian, the artist *manqué,* is merely grotesque, but Gerda and her son Hanno are mortally threatened. In Gerda's affair with Lieutenant von Throta, music is linked, as so often in Mann, to illicit love; for Hanno, it is his chief solace, but also his greatest danger. The cumulative effect of the workings of the forces of decay is such that one welcomes Hanno's death as a release too long withheld.

Looking back on the novel, we realize with what careful persistence Mann has developed the theme of death as a force possessed of an uncanny fascination. This note is first sounded briefly, without apparent emphasis, during the last illness of the wife of the elder Johann Buddenbrook. "Something new, alien, extraordinary seemed to have entered the house, a secret which they read in each other's eyes; the thought of death had gained admission and ruled silently . . ." It is struck again and again, with increasing frequency and force. Schopenhauer makes death seem a boon to Thomas in his worst days; and Hanno's boyhood is so filled with funerals that it is almost an education for dying. The smell of death, "the alien and yet so familiar odor," repels and yet attracts him, as it was later to attract Hans Castorp.

That death should play a part of central importance in a story of decline is hardly surprising, but Mann elaborates on the theme in a way which goes far beyond what the inherent logic of the situation or the tenets of naturalism could demand. It becomes increasingly obvious that he found death (or what the Germans curiously call the "problem" of death) more important, more interesting, more germane to his talents than life. It is here above all that he appears as the heir of German romanticism. Not that he indulges in any facile raptures; he is far too much the conscientious observer for that. One needs to recall only the famous chapter on typhus, or the picture of Thomas Buddenbrook after his collapse on the street:

> Since the street sloped sharply downwards, the upper part of his body was quite a bit lower than his feet. He had fallen on his face, from under which a pool of blood at once began to spread out. His hat rolled down a way on the road. His fur coat was spattered with filth and melting snow. His hands, in their white kid gloves, lay outstretched in a puddle.

As the novel of the eighteenth century tended to end in a marriage or series of marriages, *Buddenbrooks* draws to its close in a succession of deaths. At the beginning of the last section, four minor characters are dispatched on a single page. The development of the theme reaches its climax in the chapter which recounts Hanno's death of typhus. This follows immediately, with all the shock of suddenness, upon an ironic, in part almost comic account of Hanno's day at the gymnasium. "A case of typhus takes the following course." Picturing the disease as a general force strengthens its impact by making its power more impersonal, greater, and more ghastly. Mann withholds no clinical detail, but he has given these pages an eloquence and rhythm of their own. Hanno's illness is transformed into a drama; the crisis is dramatic as well as medical; and it is a psychological force, not the illness as such, that prevails.

The account of the onset of typhus is one of the high points of German naturalism, and it is only one of many passages in *Buddenbrooks* which demonstrate that Mann had little more to learn about exact observation and description. Whether or not the story that Mann once scrutinized a departing friend through opera glasses is true, it is highly credible; when one reads that Grünlich had put "a little powder on the wart on the left side of his nose" on the day of his wedding with Toni Buddenbrook, one thinks of Zeiss glasses and telescopic lenses. Permaneder, who succeeds him in Toni's affections, is described with equal accuracy but less malice. One notes also, especially in the first part, the careful documentation to give historical flavor. Mann's method is phonographic as well as photographic, employing Bavarian dialect as well as *Plattdeutsch,* and reproducing even the curiously modified vowels of Sesemi Weichbrodt's dialect.

But there is much more here than naturalistic reproduction. As so often, Mann displays his flair for giving the effect of a musical work; above all in his account of Hanno's composition.

> Soft and clear as a bell sounded the E-minor chord, tremolo pianissimo, amid the purling, flowing notes of the violin. It swelled, it broadened, it slowly, slowly rose: suddenly, in the forte, he introduced the discord C-sharp, which led back to the original key, and the Stradivarius ornamented it with its welling and singing. He dwelt on the dissonance until it became fortissimo. But he denied himself and his audience the resolution; he kept it back. What would it be, this resolution, this enchanting, satisfying absorption into the B-major chord? A joy beyond compare, a gratification of overpowering sweetness! Peace! Bliss! The kingdom of Heaven: only not yet—not yet! A moment more of striving, hesitation, suspense, that must become well-nigh intolerable in order to heighten the ultimate moment of joy.

His use of light and his feeling for subtle gradations of color as well as for brilliance, relate him closely to the impressionist school. Thus, in description of a warm January day:

> The pavement was wet and dirty, and snow was dripping from the gray gables. But above them the sky stretched delicate blue and unmarred, and billions of atoms of light seemed to glitter like crystals in the azure and to dance.

The scene around the Buddenbrooks' Christmas tree is a Manet in words: the whole picture is constructed of a multitude of lights—the countless flames of little candles, the larger lights, the reflections. Mann is equally successful with softer tones, as in this sentence describing an interior just before a storm.

> The colors in the room, the tones of the landscapes on the walls, the yellow of the furniture and the curtains had faded, one could no longer see the play of nuances in Toni's dress or the brightness in people's eyes.

The leitmotif is employed prodigally in *Buddenbrooks,* and put to a variety of uses, from the rather trivial to the broadly symbolic. It can emphasize a purely physical characteristic, like Toni's "somewhat prominent upper lip" or Gerda's dark-red hair. More importantly, it can pick out a physical trait which has psychological significance: Tom's nervousness, either explicitly stated or implied by repeated mention of his Russian cigarettes; or the bluish shadows below Gerda's eyes. The extension of such a motif from one character to another of course establishes a bond between the two: thus Toni later shares in Tom's nervousness, and Hanno "inherits" his mother's bluish shadows. (That he possesses this sign of weariness at the age of four weeks would seem to be an instance of the triumph of theory over artistic judgment.)

A repeated word or phrase can of course characterize the speaker: thus the insuperably childish Toni never outgrows the word *vornehm* (upper-class; "Ritzy"); or a motif can be used with humorous intent or for a dozen other purposes. It is most successfully employed, however, as a device of reminiscence; this sort of leitmotif can call up a whole cluster of associations and psychological subtleties. To have its full, "musical" value, the associations evoked must be emotionally charged; the motif with purely descriptive or ironic intent, like "who associated with the best families," has a far less powerful appeal, and its repeated use tends more easily to tire the reader. Broadly speaking, the motifs of *Buddenbrooks* do not have as much emotional content, so to speak, as those of later works, notably *Tonio Kröger* and *The Magic Mountain.* There is one very striking exception: the phrase "to sit on the stones," ultraprosaic though it seems, is used both subtly and movingly. Toni's first lover had been obliged to sit on a pile of stones while she chatted with upper-class friends; then the phrase came to mean, to the two of them, "to be neglected and lonely"; after giving up her lover, Toni uses the phrase again and again, in all sorts of contexts, sometimes without herself remembering, apparently, the whole richness of association. But the alert reader does remember, and the five words revivify a whole series of recollections, causing the story of Toni to "be all there in a given moment."

This economy of means, which makes the leitmotif a sort of shorthand for the emotions, is perhaps its chief merit. When used too often, as it occasionally is towards the end of *Buddenbrooks,* the device can very easily become as boring as an old family joke.

The manipulation of a variety of other techniques shows how far from the novel of naturalism *Buddenbrooks* really is. For example, the use of contrast: after telling of a particularly depressing incident in the life of Thomas Buddenbrook, Mann shifts quickly to the music of Bach; it is no accident that the discussion centers on counterpoint. A similar contrapuntal effect is produced by the introduction of the Christmas festival as a pleasant interlude within the sordid story of Herr Weinschenk's troubles with the law. Musical also is the effect of acceleration gained at the end through the rapidly repeated blows of death and disaster and the accumulation of the evi-

dences of decay. Probably Mann gives us too much of a good thing—that the Buddenbrooks' dentist, for instance, is decadent too would seem to be a clear case of piling Ossa on Pelion; it may be that the influence of Wagner has something to do with this tendency towards excess. Possibly Mann's later device, so notable in *Joseph,* of repeating a whole incident, or introducing, under another name, a character who is "archetypically" the same as one who has preceded him, is foreshadowed in his first novel. Thus Toni's first husband, Grünlich, turns out to be a swindler, and the marriage ends in divorce; her daughter Erika goes through fundamentally the same experience with Hugo Weinschenk.

Buddenbrooks is an end and a beginning. After writing incomparably the best of German "family novels" Mann abandoned the genre, and never again was he to come so close to the pure epic. *Buddenbrooks* is obviously the least problematic and complex of his major works, but it is not without its paradoxes: realistic in manner, it is romantic in spirit; abundant in Dickensian *Gemütlichkeit,* its essence is the mood of "the cross, death, and the grave"; apparently unilinear in its treatment of time, it uses the leitmotif on occasion to give the effect of emotional simultaneity. From the perspective of half a century, one can see how the technical innovations of the novel point forward to more experimental works to come. (pp. 43-50)

> *Henry Hatfield, in his* Thomas Mann, *New Directions Books, 1951, 179 p.*

R. HINTON THOMAS (essay date 1956)

[*Thomas is an English scholar and critic who has written extensively on German literature and culture. In the following excerpt from his* Thomas Mann: The Mediation of Art, *a critical study focusing on Mann's major works, Thomas examines narrative techniques in* Buddenbrooks, *exploring in particular Mann's use of the leitmotif, the treatment of time, use of foreshadowing, and the way in which the structure of the novel precludes the need for an intrusive author.*]

Mann described [*Buddenbrooks*] as a work "without pathos . . . and unsentimental," "pessimistic, humorous, fatalistic and genuine in its melancholy submissiveness as a study of decay." The fact that he was conscious in himself of "formalistic as well as spiritual elements no longer belonging to this epoch but to another" is mirrored in the attraction for him of the Goncourts' *Renée Mauperin.* The sophisticated precision of this novel was, he confessed, the immediate stimulus for the writing of *Buddenbrooks.* (p. 35)

Mann's remark that the Goncourts' novel "set his work in motion" indicates . . . the limits of the relationship, though parallels in unimportant respects are hardly fortuitous. The quick succession of short sentences in the dialogue of *Renée Mauperin* is matched in the early sections of *Buddenbrooks,* as a comparison of the opening conversations in the two novels reveals, and in both cases the narrative style is adopted after a page or two in which the characters have been thus introduced. Like *Renée Mauperin,* Mann's novel is characterized by an accumulation of short chapters—ninety-seven in all, divided into eleven "parts" and distributed originally over two volumes. In the case of *Buddenbrooks* this feature corresponds to the way every situation grows out of a preceding situation and contains within itself the seeds of a future in which each member is "like a link in a chain." The chronological sequence is underlined by the recurrent emphasis on time passing, most obviously in the frequent statements of the date and year and also in the many references to the changing ages of the characters. A similar effect is obtained through Pastor Pringheim's recurring visits at crucial stages in the family history, at births and deaths. These features become less conspicuous in the second half, where there is less concern with external events and more with the psychological qualities of inwardness and sensitivity. In the latter half of the book, where correspondingly more space is occupied by the reflections of the characters, the longest description is the account of a day in the life of Thomas Buddenbrook's musical and decadent son Hanno. But the emphasis is entirely on the inward situation and so the account becomes a portrayal in musical and symbolical terms of the ultimate disintegration of the family.

In this representation of the passage of time special significance attaches to the family diary. It is first introduced when Johann Buddenbrook on 14 April 1838 records in it the birth of Klara to his wife Elisabeth. It becomes the symbol of the family, of its pride in the past and of the attachment of individual members to its tradition. The first intimation of Tony's decision to marry Grünlich is when she opens the diary and against an earlier entry about herself adds: "Became engaged on 22nd September 1845 to Mr. Bendix Grünlich, merchant in Hamburg," and in due course she is careful to note there the fact of her divorce. The chapter in which she records her betrothal illustrates these aspects:

> She turned the pages to the end of the large volume where on a rough folio sheet the whole genealogy of the Buddenbrooks . . . had been summarized in the Consul's hand: from the marriage of the earliest head of the family to the clergyman's daughter, Brigitta Schuren, up to the marriage of the Consul Johann Buddenbrook to Elisabeth Kröger in 1825. From this union, it was stated, had sprung four children . . . at which point their christian names were set forth one under the other together with the year and date of birth; behind the name of the elder son, however, was already noted that at Easter 1842 he had entered his father's business as an apprentice.

There is irony in the fact that it is after thus recapitulating an earlier, vigorous, and developing stage in the family history that she notes her engagement, for its primary purpose is to provide capital for the now declining business. The irony is heightened by her thoughts when she first opened the diary a few moments before: "She picked it up, turned the pages, began to read and buried herself in it. What she read was mostly simple things familiar to her; but each of those who had written in it had taken over from his predecessor a style simple and without exaggeration, a chronicle style from which spoke the discreet and for that reason all the more dignified respect of a family for itself, for tradition and history." The phrase "simple but without exaggeration" has a significance beyond the diary itself. It suggests the contrast with the more complicated existence of the later Buddenbrooks and the unbalance due to the extravagances of sensibility. Tony is careful to preserve that earlier style of writing, just as in all other respects she is a conscientious exponent of the family tradition in circumstances conspiring to make mockery of it.

The episode exemplifies the ironization of time in its quality as "the highest and most valuable gift, related in its essence to and even identical with all that is creative and active, all desire and effort, all perfection, all progress towards what is

higher and better." The consistent chronology reinforces the fatalistic element in the story through the way in which the final tragedy is seen to grow out of the hopeful beginnings. In his struggle to correct inner weakness by redoubled effort and resolution, Thomas Buddenbrook's father already reveals features destined in his son to develop into decadence. Tony's observations in the chapter describing his death convey this aspect of the Consul:

> "The way father behaves is enough to make one weep," Tony said, choosing strong words, as was her wont. "Can he ever be ready at a fixed time? He sits at his desk and sits . . . and sits . . . this, that and the other *must* be settled . . . ; God in Heaven, perhaps it really is necessary, I couldn't tell . . . although I do not think that we would really have to declare ourselves bankrupt if he had put down his pen a quarter of an hour earlier. Alright . . . when he is ten minutes late, he remembers his promise and dashes up the stairs two steps at a time, though he knows that he gets breathlessness and palpitations. . . . It is like this every time we expect company, every time we go out. Cannot he leave himself time? Cannot he set out at the right time and go slowly?"

The weather, symbolically adapted to the situation, releases its charged tension just before the maid brings the news of the Consul's sudden collapse:

> And this mysterious pressure, this tension, this growing physical oppression would have become unbearable if it had lasted a fraction of a moment longer, if, its climax having been reached, there had not ensued a relaxation, a diversion of the tension . . . a small, saving break . . . if, in the same moment, almost without being preceded by a single drop, the rain had not suddenly poured down, so that the water foamed in the gutter and danced on the pavement.

This description of the setting of the Consul's death subtly anticipates the struggle and ultimate collapse of his son. The reference in the last sentence of the quotation has its deeper associations in the light of the actual circumstances of Thomas Buddenbrook's later collapse: "He turned half round and fell head first with outstretched arms on to the wet pavement." The paragraph immediately following the account of the storm opens with a reference to Thomas's nerves, the symptom of his own decadence. But this aspect has been suggested in the early stages of the novel when the firm was outwardly flourishing. In the chapter dealing with Thomas's entrance into the firm there is reference to his "rather poor teeth," and it is after the extraction of a tooth that he dies. By the time of Johann Buddenbrook's death we are familiar with Thomas's habit as a young man of smoking numerous Russian cigarettes, and this passion assumes increasing significance as a manifestation of the nervous strain under which he labours. Shortly after the grandfather's death the Consul writes to Thomas in Amsterdam: "But it pains me that your health is not quite of the best. What you wrote to me about your nerves reminded me of my own youth." In the same way Christian's love of the theatre, manifesting his rejection of bourgeois values, is revealed while still a schoolboy. "The symptoms are there," his father had lamented, hearing of his young son's visit to an actress's dressing room.

The decline of the firm in the period of Thomas's control is adumbrated in the earlier phases. The first of its significant material setbacks had been the losses incurred through Johann Buddenbrook's death. In the meantime no real progress had been made, as the Consul observes. By the time of the Consul's death there are already indications in plenty of declining business. The times, he remarks, are "bad for the merchant." The leadership of the firm has grown unsure of itself, lets opportunities slip, is caught out even on its own ground. The Consul presses Tony to marry Grünlich because, as an expert in business, he regards it as a good proposition. But he has been deceived by Grünlich's skill in faking accounts which he himself had carefully scrutinized. The opening of the novel foreshadows decline through remarks which acquire ironic significance in the context of later developments. During the party to celebrate the move into the Buddenbrook's new house there is discussion about the firm which built it. "With Ratenkamp and Co.," observes Thomas's father, "things were at that time beginning to go splendidly. Sad, this sinking of the firm in the last twenty years." Then: "A general break in conversation occurred and lasted half a minute. People looked at their plates and thought of this once so brilliant family, which had built and occupied the house and which had gone away, impoverished and in reduced circumstances." In due course Thomas and his family move in their turn to a new house and the reference to the Ratenkamps is echoed in the conversation between Thomas and Tony. "Yes," says Thomas, reflecting sadly on leaving the old home,

> . . . that's what they must have thought when they had to leave the house when grandfather bought it. They had lost their money and had to go away and were ruined and died. Everything has its day. Let us rejoice and thank God that things have not gone so far with us as once with the Ratenkamps and that we can take our leave in happier circumstances than they.

"Everything has its day"—despite Thomas's hopeful remark at the end of the passage, we may sense that the doom of the Buddenbrooks is to come.

Under Schopenhauer's influence fatalism and irony together constitute an essential feature of the novel. "As soon as the Will had objectivized itself," Mann wrote later about Schopenhauer, "and . . . had entered the sphere of individuation, nothing remained of freedom nor for the same reason of guilt or deserts. Man acted as he had to act, being what he was and under the influence of definite motives. . . . Every being was not only the bearer of existence in general but also of the existence peculiar to himself—of his individuality—and in everything that happened or could happen to him justice was done." Schopenhauer's influence, however, is felt in more ways than this. The "political indifference" of his philosophy, Mann said, "finds its explanation in its *objectivism,* in the power of salvation which it attributes exclusively to objective contemplation. For Schopenhauer genius is nothing other than objectivity, i.e. the ability to exist in a purely contemplative state, merely as a percipient subject, as the "clear eye of the world." Art and philosophy, he added, "are thus quietistic (for pure objectivism is quietism). They want above all not to change anything, but only to contemplate." This helps to explain why the author of *Buddenbrooks* never intrudes into his narrative in the first person. Persons and situations are characterized above all through the experiences or reflections of the individuals concerned. We read of Thomas Buddenbrook's new house: "There was no more attractive subject of conversation in the town! It was called tip-top. It was called the finest house far and wide. Was there anything in Ham-

burg finer?" The oblique style of narrative here hides the author, as does the vocabulary itself; tip-top was the jargon of such circles, not Mann's language.

A few years after writing *Buddenbrooks* Mann discussed the claim that the drama is distinguished from the novel by its "technical distinction, higher obligations of composition." He disputed this, stressing the "purposeful selection and differentiation, that tautness, concentration and ideal terseness" of the novel. . . . The supremacy of the novel as a genre lay for Mann at this stage in its "ironic non-committal," and with equal "objectivism" he "contemplates" both the sorrows of the Buddenbrooks and the jeering of the Möllendorfs, the Kistenmakers, the Langhals, and the Overdiecks. When he worked on *Buddenbrooks* in Rome, "my home town had not much reality for me. . . . I was not very convinced of its existence. With its inhabitants it was not essentially more than a dream, at once scurrilous and venerable, dreamt long ago, dreamt by me and in the most peculiar way my own." As a man, Mann remarked, "you may be kind, patient, affectionate, positive, you may have a quite uncritical inclination to describe all phenomena as good, but as an artist your daemon compels you to 'observe,' with a flash and with painful maliciousness to take cognisance of every detail which in the literary sense is characteristic . . . ruthlessly to make note of it as if you had no human relationship to what you have seen." This is the source of the extensive use in this novel of the naturalistic "leit-motiv," fixing in a single, often mocking, phrase, some external aspect of the characters. In no other major work was Mann more directly involved emotionally in his theme, yet none can match, for example, the coldness of the apparently scientific account, of aspects of Hanno's final illness ("Typhus has the following characteristics . . ."). Schopenhauer's "objectivism" is here jointly involved with Nietzsche's doctrine of the Apolline task of art, Mann's process of self-emancipation from the "Bürger" world of Lübeck with his struggle against the temptations of art, against his heritage of romanticism. He cultivates an "objectivity" in which "perception is torn from the slavish service of Will and the attention is no longer troubled by any motive of desire." All objectivity, Mann said, "has reference only to the element of the picturesque, the mask, the gesture, that which is external and which presents itself as a characteristic, as a sensuous symbol. . . . All the rest—and the rest is almost everything—is subjective, is intuition and lyric, belonging to the . . . soul of the artist."

Thus, in *Buddenbrooks,* order, achieved through the "aesthetic phenomenon" of form, is interposed between the author and the disorder of the characters and their situation. Hence those qualities in the book fittingly described as "Apolline and objective" (*apollinisch-objektivistisch*). The opening sections of the book illustrate the meticulous care with which all is organized and arranged. In the first chapter the three generations of the Buddenbrooks are presented together in a neatly contrived relationship. Old Johann Buddenbrook, his son and the latter's wife are here brought together and there are the first and as yet seemingly casual references to Thomas and Christian. We notice the features later to be brought to our attention as the decadent symptoms in Johann's son: "The Consul bent over his chair with a rather nervous movement"; "He had the slightly deep, blue, and attentive eyes of his father, even though their expression was perhaps a little more dreamy." An apparently chance remark ironically foreshadows Tony's later history: "You are very kind," said the Consul's wife, "Tony will strive to become a wise and capable wife." The chapter ends with a reference to Thomas and Christian returning from school and the second chapter concerns largely the different characteristics of the two brothers. The essence of their later development is summed up in a sentence spoken by the poetaster Hofstede: "Thomas, he is a solid and serious mind; he must become a merchant, there's no doubt about that. But Christian, on the other hand, seems to me to be rather a gay spark, how shall I say? a bit incredible." Christian's propensity to mimicry is already in evidence in his attitude to his teachers, and the observation that Thomas did not share this gift has a deeper significance than the reader can yet realize. The apparently trifling matter of Thomas's teeth ("His teeth were not particularly beautiful, but small and rather yellow") will likewise acquire its fuller meaning as the story unfolds. The third chapter brings out the social pride of the Buddenbrooks, anticipating later talk of their "aristocratic" qualities and their "representative" position. The careful reader will return again and again to the beginnings of the novel, discovering hardly a remark or an incident not arranged in relation to a highly contrived pattern. Hofstede's festal poem, for instance, which he reads at the dinner party at the new house, fulfils a highly ironical function. It is at this dinner too that Christian overeats and feels—foreshadowing his later morbid preoccupation with his health—"bloody awful."

Dr. Grabow is called to his assistance: "Young as he was, he had held in his own the hand of many a worthy citizen who had consumed his last leg of beef and his last stuffed turkey and, whether suddenly and unexpectedly in his office chair or after some suffering in his solid old bed, commended himself to God. People mentioned a stroke, paralysis, a sudden and unexpected death. . . ." The sudden death years later of Thomas Buddenbrook sets the observation in its fuller context. This aspect of the novel explains the length of its exposition, which extends to the end of Part Two. The opening of Part Three introduces Grünlich and thus starts the action proper.

Through this manipulation of events and situations the story itself makes the points that would otherwise have to be made by the devices of the intrusive author. The design, in other words, is itself an instrument of "objective" contemplation. At the same time, in respects which require our further attention, it subserves the irony. (pp. 36-45)

The Buddenbrooks live . . . in a world narrowly bounded by the refinements of their class and situation. It can be regarded as a limitation of realism that the element of accident and chance is virtually eliminated from the narrative. At the same time Mann is consistent with the demands of realism in limiting the range of his novel to the experience of his characters. We hear extraordinarily little about the broader world. Any connexion between the events concerning this particular family and the objective social and economic developments are, except incidentally, ignored or disregarded. In the period of **Buddenbrooks** Mann's attitude was one "which regards life and intellect, art and politics, as totally separate worlds," which views "political and social matters as non-essentials that might as well be entrusted to politicians."

The scenes, for example, relating to the events of 1848 are portrayed only in the provincial way in which they affected the secure small world of the patrician middle class of Lübeck. The episode when Johann Buddenbrook addresses the crowd and persuades the people to go home quietly has mainly a psychological relevance, pointing the contrast between

the father's boldness of decision and the declining power of his son to impose his will on the world around him. The Danish war is merely a passing incident in the background against which the story of Hanno's weakness is unfolded. Christian's trouble with his leg is the symptom of his particular form of decadence. Thomas "dies of a tooth," but his death comes in reality as the climax to a gathering process of inner disintegration. "For precisely because the attraction which disease exercised on me was of a spiritual kind," Mann said, "I was instinctively concerned with spiritualising it, knowing full well that it is only naïve naturalism that pursues the cult of the pathological for its own sake and that the pathological can only enter the sphere of poetry for spiritual, poetical, symbolical purposes." A doctor treating a case of typhus, we learn, does not know whether what he calls typhus is merely the material result of an accidental infection "which perhaps could have been avoided and countered with the resources of science—or whether quite simply it is a form of dissolution, the cloak of death itself, which could equally well appear in a different mask and against which nothing whatever can be done." The symptoms—"a malaise of the soul rapidly deepening and disintegrating into despair," "a physical weariness," "a strong craving for sleep"—turn out to be also those associated with Thomas's decay, while the "blue shadows" that develop under Hanno's eyes relate his situation further to the decadent musicality of his mother.

Thus, as he himself said, Mann's concern in **Buddenbrooks** was the inner world of the soul; the sociological and political elements entered his work at this stage largely unconsciously and, as he observed, caused him little concern. If the crisis of the German middle class appeared to Mann's brother Heinrich mainly in the form of its "hardening" in the age of imperialism, his own particular experience was rather of the "decay of this old and genuine 'Bürgerlichkeit' in the direction of the subjective and the artistic. It was an experience and a problem not of hardening but of hyperrefinement and debilitation. . . . What I expressed and experienced . . . was also a development and modernization of the 'Bürger,' not his development into the bourgeois, but his development into the artist." In the case of the Buddenbrook family it is Hanno who embodies the culmination of this process. This is the significance of the fact that his nature, in which sensibility is heightened to a degree incompatible with the demands of practical existence, finds its inmost expression in music. The account of one day of his life, the theme of the second chapter of the final section of the novel, concludes with the wonderful description, deep in the debt of Schopenhauer, of the fantasia of his own invention played by himself on the piano, a piece which in its yearning chromaticism unmistakably recalls in its portrayal the music of Wagner's Tristan. It is music "of wild and irresistible longing," of a voluptuous yearning for death. Its essence is contained already in its opening motif, constantly returning in one form or another and constituting, so to speak, "one single process of dissolution (Auflösung), a yearning and painful sinking (Hinsinken) from one key into the next" and in such a way as to lend it "a mysterious and significant value." The piece finished, "Hanno remained at his seat for a moment, his chin resting upon his chest, his hands on his lap. Then he got up and shut the piano. He was very pale, there was no strength left in his knees and his eyes burnt. He went into the next room, lay down on the chaiselongue and remained there for a long time without moving." The connexion between the account of his improvisation on the piano and his physical state at the close, described in its last stages of disintegration in the following chapter, is obvious enough without necessitating the author's intervention to underline its symbolism. His father now dead, Hanno has, in effect, played the dying song of the Buddenbrooks, a venerable and once successful family thus transfigured, as in the words of Mann's own *Tristan,* at the culmination of its decline in the inwardness of music. (pp. 49-51)

R. Hinton Thomas, in his Thomas Mann: The Mediation of Art, 1956. Reprint by Oxford at the Clarendon Press, 1963, 188 p.

FRITZ KAUFMANN (essay date 1957)

[*In the following excerpt, Kaufmann defines* Buddenbrooks *as Mann's account of the artist's existence and examines the characterizations of Thomas and Hanno in light of Schopenhauer's philosophy.*]

It is the artist's privilege to realize the typical in the particular, the essential types and universal laws of being in the single instance. No one has ever been more tireless than Thomas Mann in observing the minutest features of outer life, or more astute in reporting and representing them. The almost unbelievable wealth of human content in **Buddenbrooks** earned for its young author the emphatic "recognition" of a world which in this account recognized its own rise and decay. This account was so full and perfect a rendition of life that the cup of bitterness was presented and could be enjoyed as the pure wine of art. A melancholy rejection of the world is suspended in the medium of irony. And the few shrill dissonances, such as the unseemly death of dignified Thomas Buddenbrook, serve only to enhance the awareness of the *sotto voce* style in which this slowly developing *danse macabre* is set. The miracle of the artistic transubstantiation of heavy suffering into composed language is in moving contrast with the wild eruptions in **Doctor Faustus,** the work in which the writer returns to the old German town and its musical climate, while flinging away the comfort of temperate, well-measured form.

As a sum total of personal experience, **Buddenbrooks** does not leave out any trait that may contribute to the meaning and actual presentation of the past. But, here as elsewhere, Thomas Mann is far from the chimerical aim of objective completeness. He registers what found a positive or negative response in his own existence and thus took on validity as a symbol of, or as a contrast to, his own inner being. Conversely, only because he felt his own development to be of universal significance does that development emerge both as subject matter in his single works and in the way they complement one another. What takes place here, under the guise of telling a story about a Lübeck family, is a bringing forth, through a selection of autobiographical material, of the conditions of the artist's existence. This impulse marks the scope of artistic representation and determines its limits. **Buddenbrooks** is no mere bourgeois novel. Significantly enough, it had its germ-cell in the story of little Hanno. It tells the growth of the citizen into an artist and is developed, therefore, from the point where Thomas Mann's poetic ethos is still in contact with the quondam Protestant ethos of work and its everyday hero, working "at the brink of exhaustion." "I have never depicted it"—this modern bourgeois type—"as a political-economic phenomenon. For that I had neither the sympathy nor the knowledge. But the truly poetical—this I have always considered to be the symbolical."

However real and palpable they may appear, the four generations of Buddenbrooks are essentially symbols, representing stages of existence. In each successive stage, more and more breaks and fissures appear on the placid surface of sound bourgeois life. There is the old "radical" Buddenbrook, who can afford to be Voltairian. Born a representative of his class and his city, he does not need to be elected as such. Then there is Consul John Buddenbrook, representative of the Restoration era, who already needs religious justification for his business transactions and feels under obligation to the firm— and God—to make a dignified showing. This dignity is in jeopardy in the following generation. John's chubby daughter Toni is still full of bourgeois instincts and ambitions, but they miscarry one after the other in an ominous way. Of John's sons, Thomas and Christian, the latter disgraces not only his family but his very name. With him, Christian self-concern degenerates into the shameless exhibition of petty grievances, and genuine life into a disreputable show. But even with highly responsible Senator Thomas Buddenbrook the almost heroic struggle against fate assumes the nature of a spectacle. Social stage-acting becomes to him at once an aesthetic need, an idiosyncrasy, and a stratagem. He must "worthily represent" what he no longer really is; he "represents" in order to keep up the façade, without any real belief in what he officially stands for.

At the same time Thomas longs to be released from this wretched, painfully limited kind of representation, to escape the boundaries of his individuality and attain a universal representation, the power of selfsameness with the whole of life. Through a reading of Schopenhauer he is eventually assured of just such a blessed state of boundless life which corrects the blunder of this individual existence. "The walls of his native city, in which he had consciously and willfully shut himself up, were thrown open to him and to his gaze disclosed the world, the whole world, of which he had seen this or that little piece in his younger days, but which death promised to bestow upon him whole and entire."—as one perennial present.

This whole experience—the beatific, yet fleeting vision of a single night—is reported almost literally in the words of Schopenhauer. But it is Schopenhauer's doctrine without Schopenhauer's asceticism; it is Schopenhauer in a Nietzschean interpretation, asserting a "fuller, stronger, happier" existence. While a family's will to life may be drowned in the lust for death, for instance, in the drunkenness of musical excesses, life as such, immortal life, will march on triumphantly through the various forms, the strong self-assertions of the creative will.

It may well be that Thomas Buddenbrook does not fully decipher the meaning of the Indian gospel—the "That art thou" (*tat tvam asi*) and "I am Brahman" (*aham Brahma asmi*)—in Schopenhauer's interpretation. The substance of his experience must be distilled from the rather cloudy form in which he is able to grasp it. But the ecstasy of his "That is me," "I am he as well as I" is the first recognition of Thomas Mann's lasting credo that the boundaries between ego and non-ego are fluid, that man reaches beyond his individual self into other, greater existences and they into his. It is the metaphysical version of the ambiguous mythical formula—the "I am it"—out of which Thomas Mann's Joseph is to make so much capital in his profoundly knowing play.

Thomas Buddenbrook's is the mystic unification wherein "the deceptive forms of knowledge, such as space, time, and consequently history" break down, and the *nunc stans,* "enduring eternity," is certain. As Indian mysticism thus filters into German Critical Idealism—a trend initiated by Schopenhauer—time and space are existentially annihilated, and history loses its character as ultimately real. This is what occurs in *Buddenbrooks:* "Nothing ever began and nothing ever ceased. There was only one endless reality." And for the last so-called representative of the family, Hanno Buddenbrook, as well as, later on, for the young Hans Castorp, human salvation lies in an escape from the "flatland" of busy, everyday life with its social responsibilities. It lies in a trancelike state of metaphysical absorption. Only on his descent from the magic mountain did the poet achieve the consecration of life in all its temporality. (pp. 88-91)

Historical feeling is bound up with the sense of individuality. Inasmuch as he is painfully aware of the bounds of individuation, Thomas Mann's attitude in *Buddenbrooks* cannot be described as unhistorical; rather it is *counter*-historical, not only in principle, as an offspring of Schopenhauerian metaphysics, but also as a revolt against the torn conditions and idleness of the historical life of his time. Somehow it expresses his (and Nietzsche's) aversion to the glitter of the Wilhelmine era and his early apprehension of the imminent catastrophe of the whole historical system. Throughout the decades, from *Buddenbrooks* and *Death in Venice* to *Joseph in Egypt* and *Doctor Faustus,* there is the nightmarish feeling that chaos will come again, that it lurks within the bulwarks of our civilization and threatens the whole defense mechanism, the rigid self-discipline we set up against it. Thomas Buddenbrook is weighted down with "anxiety for maintaining the prestige of the past," and filled with dread "of some eventual historical dissolution and decomposition."

The hope of finding "in nothingness the Whole" soon dies in Senator Thomas Buddenbrook himself, but it gains tenuous realization in his son Hanno, who has inherited from his mother a musical gift not present in the Buddenbrook strain. The "metamorphosis of the *bourgeois* into an artist" is the descent from the world of convention into the realm of origins, but also (to speak with Goethe) into the realm of mere shadows in which actual being is prefigured in an eternal process of "formation and transformation." Thus the sick little artist moves toward translating being into pure, creative representation, the redemption of life through its pure expression, "a unique dissolution . . . a melancholy modulation from one key to another." A tiny motif of one and one-half beats, "a nothing," grows in the course of its development into an expression of the Absolute. "It brings resolution, dissolution, fulfillment, perfect satisfaction." This is a renewal of Thomas Buddenbrook's Schopenhauerian experience on an incipient creative level, as though "curtains were torn apart, doors sprang open, thorn hedges opened up, and walls of fire sank down."

The unbounded "will to ecstasy and decline"—the merging and submerging of the one in the whole, the Tristan motif—here reaches its appointed end in the death and transfiguration of a series of generations. The life of the Buddenbrooks negates itself at last in the fever that consumes Hanno's delicate, boyish frame. The play of life thus ends in the (qualitatively) eternal life of play. With a gesture, whose symbolic meaning he did not fully realize, of course, but which was not wholly foreign to him even so, the little Johann had already drawn the final stroke under his name in the family album. "I thought . . . I thought . . . nothing would come after that," he replies to his father's reproof. (pp. 91-3)

Art is a divine gift, giving what the artist needs. It composes

his inner chaos. Poor Hanno, however, is not vouchsafed this grace of the sons of God. He is not permitted to stand "underneath God's thunderstorm" and "grasp the Father's shaft" without being burned by it. His life does not find redemption in art. Rather does art redeem him from life. Art leads him out of life, by catering to his will to boundless nothingness. On the other hand, it would be wrong to assert with Schopenhauer that herein a power, enhanced by knowledge of the world's essence, "at last tires of playing and takes a serious turn." Hanno perishes not by reason of his power, not by the tension between life's lust and art's law; he knows only the lust of death; and his music (an offshoot of Wagner's) is but a discharge of this lust. He perishes of weakness, due to the disproportion of spirit and life in his own personal make-up. He lacks the vital energies for real work. Only with the strength of life can art grow beyond it.

In *Buddenbrooks* Hanno's end is still interpreted in Schopenhauerian terms, namely, as the spirit's withdrawal from life's summons, from "this bright, cheerful, slightly derisive warning to turn and come back," which "may reach the spirit on his fevered, alien path, that leads into the cool shades, the peace" of Nirvana. (p. 94)

Fritz Kaufmann, in his Thomas Mann: The World as Will and Representation, *Beacon Press, 1957, 322 p.*

ERICH HELLER   (essay date 1958)

[*A Czechoslovakian-born American educator, Heller is a literary critic who has also written on intellectual and cultural history. He is the author of* The Ironic German: A Study of Thomas Mann. *In the following excerpt from that work, Heller analyzes the influence of Schopenhauer's theories on the themes, plot, and characterizations of* Buddenbrooks.]

"An unforgettable initiation of the soul," "a metaphysical intoxication"—this is how Thomas Mann described the effect upon him, at twenty, of Schopenhauer's philosophy. Small wonder then that *Buddenbrooks,* his early masterpiece, derives its intellectual plot from Schopenhauer; and so completely had philosophy become assimilated into the *imaginative* order of the writer's mind that, despite this philosophical spell, he succeeded, almost for the only time in his long career, in writing a novel without once alarming the susceptibilities of those readers who want "life" and not "ideas." On the plane of literary history, then, it is a consistently realist or, for what the term is worth, naturalist novel, unthinkable without the example of the great masters of the genre, but more directly inspired by minor Scandinavians and above all by *Renée Mauperin* of the Goncourts; and in so far as this "naturalist novel"—"for Germany perhaps the first and only one," as its author once said—is also a humorous novel, its literary manner owes something to Dickens and the Low German writer Fritz Reuter. In fact, the accumulated European experience in the art of composing a novel is brought to bear upon a domestic German story—a marriage between the cosmopolitan and the narrowly national which is announced on the first page in the first words of old Buddenbrook (*"Je den Düwel ook, c'est la question, ma très chère demoiselle"*) raising at once, with this mixture of Low German and French, the problem of translation, a difficulty which was to increase with every successive work, made the rendering of Thomas Mann in another language an almost heroic literary venture, and its relative success a triumph of devoted labour as well as of sheer substance over the inevitable injuries done to its organic form.

A French critic, reviewing *Buddenbrooks* in the *Mercure de France* of 1908, was convinced that it was untranslatable, with the translator's work bedevilled not only by the use of dialect (particularly important in the juxtaposition of North German and South German mentalities) and other linguistic perplexities, but also by the very "structure" of the book; and this structure is an organization of ideas which, giving the lie to a conventional prejudice, enhance, rather than reduce, the life of the story. These ideas, having been enveloped by the living organism of the work and rendered as invisible as the anatomical sketch behind the body on the painter's canvas, form the intellectual plot of the novel and, to a large extent, determine its status. It is this *intellectual* plot which makes the reader *feel* that, in following the lives of these Lübeck burghers in their provincial seclusion, he yet comes face to face with a comprehensive view of the world.

The intellectual consistency of its plot endows the story with a kind of relentless logic which is rare in modern literature. *Buddenbrooks* is an old-fashioned book in the sense that its characters are in the undisturbed possession of their fates. Their stories *belong* to them in a manner which Thomas Mann later emphasized in the foreword to *The Magic Mountain,* saying that the extraordinary story of the simple-minded hero, although told for its, not his, sake, is yet *his* story, "and not every story happens to everybody." This is only worth remarking because modern novels are full of dispossessed persons: characters deprived of "fate," and either at the mercy of "crass casualty," as Thomas Hardy called it, or, as with Proust, Joyce, or Kafka, in search of their "lost time," their "mythological pattern," their "unattainable reality," or else, as with Gide and the existentialists, violently appropriating an unauthorized destiny through an *acte gratuit* or an existential choice. In *Buddenbrooks* no time is lost, no reality is in suspense, and no act is gratuitous. Indeed, the Buddenbrooks in their decline come to doubt all certainties, but their author envisages all their doubts against no uncertain background: a firm order of reality within which the human person occupies a definable place. Hence the fate of the individual, what he does and what happens to him, is only the dramatic unfolding of what he is meant to be. Fate and character, therefore, are indissolubly one. Thus the novel, in all its unsparing pessimism and sceptical irony, conveys a sense of meaningful order existing not only in and through the aesthetic organization of the written work but in the world itself. For, beginning with *Buddenbrooks,* Thomas Mann's artistic practice was a struggle against the temptation of that aesthetic purism which has determined the nature and shape of so much in literature and poetry ever since Flaubert sought relief from the strain of a senseless reality in the purity of prose, yearning to write a book that was uncontaminated by "life," a "book about nothing at all which, free of any external connection, would support itself entirely by the internal force of style." What Thomas Mann, rather naïvely, was in the habit of calling his own *"Bürgerlichkeit,"* his sense of having roots in a definite social order at odds with the free play of the imagination and the adventurousness of art, was only a way of voicing his moral protest against an aesthetic passion paradoxically inspired and sustained by the void of "real" meaning.

Buddenbrooks is a story without surprises. What is surprising is the subtle art with which the young writer manages the gradual illumination of inevitability through an organically continuous sequence of shocks of recognition. Of course there are lapses, passages where the author is carried away by the persuasiveness of his plot, indulging in melodramatic allegorizing. Thomas, the third in the line of Buddenbrooks (and he is to be the last to honour their tradition of business and citizenship), has married Gerda. It is an unconventional choice. Gerda, extravagantly refined, detached, musical, is bound to remain a stranger among the Buddenbrooks; and how improbable it is that she will produce sons to fall in with the Buddenbrook ways! Indeed, her child, young Hanno, is to suffer from nightmares, will be lonely among his school-fellows, show no interest whatever in the concerns of the firm, soon be enslaved by music, and die before his time. Here we meet Gerda for the first time as Thomas's wife:

> The door opened, and there stood before them in the twilight, in a pleated piqué house-frock, white as snow, a slender figure. The heavy dark-red hair framed her white face, and blue shadows lay about her close-set brown eyes. It was Gerda, mother of future Buddenbrooks.

Similarly, there is a scene which yields its meaning with a keenness as unrestrained as this allegory of nightfall and sweet-scented decay. Hanno, the child who is so strikingly lacking in the virtues of a future burgher and businessman, finds himself one day alone in his father's study. Thomas, his father and by now Senator of his city, has been occupying himself with the family papers, and the last page, showing the family tree, lies on top of the pile. Hanno reads it and then, in dreamy half-consciousness, takes pen and ruler and draws a double line underneath and across the whole page. When Thomas discovers the misdeed:

> "What does this mean? What is the matter with you? Answer me! Why do such a mischievous thing?" cried the Senator, and struck Hanno's cheek lightly with the rolled-up paper.
>
> And little Johann stammered, retreating, with his hand to his cheek, "I thought—I thought—there wouldn't be any more."

But such lapses into the obvious are surprisingly rare, considering the youth of the author and the enthusiasm of logicality with which the plot of the novel must have filled him. On the whole he safely relies upon the inner logic of his characters for evolving their fates, and on the unity of fate and character for establishing the coherence of the world he has created; and so closely-knit is this coherence that, in retrospect, the suspense in which the reader is held appears almost like the mere appeal to solve a mathematical equation, with the unknown quantity withheld and yet intrinsically given. The casual affliction of a toothache: if its victim is Thomas Buddenbrook at a certain point in his life, it 'contains' his death. Once the perfect correspondence between the inner and the outer story of a character is established, the writer can afford to pass on to the reader a piece of information apparently detached from the narrative, inviting him, as it were, to put it in the place where it is needed for the completion of the picture. This is what Thomas Mann actually does in the case of Hanno Buddenbrook's death; and a comparison of the logic of death in *Buddenbrooks* with, for instance, E. M. Forster's calculated casualness in allowing his characters to die, would support what has been said about the solid order of Thomas Mann's world in contrast to the disordered universe of some of his contemporaries. When Hanno Buddenbrook's end comes, it is not only he who dies: the whole tradition of the Buddenbrooks has played itself out. His death is a logical necessity.

This point calls for critical caution. Tidy and representative deaths are, of course, not in themselves an artistic merit. On the contrary, such is the character of the age and the intellectual temper of its literature that any obvious "scheme" is more likely to be the contrivance of a second-rate mind. Sophistication and refinement of sensibility, on the other hand, excel in the subtle aesthetic organization of chaos, and in salvaging the last semblance and memory of order through a hard-won victory of form over all but form-proof matter. And it is precisely this new kind of artistic excellence of which the young artist Hanno Buddenbrook is the embodied promise—a fact which proves the imaginative richness and intellectual authenticity of the idea of order underlying the composition of the novel. It is an idea of order which comprehends, as it were, the *creative* aspect of negation. For Hanno is not merely the last of the Buddenbrooks, but also the first precocious practitioner of an art which only after their death, and after the death of the artistic convention within which their story is told, can come into its own. It is an art which, conscious of originating in destruction, anxiously cherishes the hope of a new freedom, even if before long Thomas Mann himself was to write, in ***Doctor Faustus,*** the tragic story of how that hope was shattered and that freedom renounced. ***Buddenbrooks,*** however, does not simply tell of the end of a family, or mark the end of the literary tradition to which as a realist novel it strictly adheres. It also points, by virtue of the logic of its intellectual plot, to those creative forces which are released by the collapse of the old order. It is because of this that the logical tidiness of the novel is far from being antiquated. By gathering into its own conventional organization the very idea of an art which is bound to overthrow the convention, ***Buddenbrooks*** ironically refutes the charge of conventionality.

We have come to know Hanno, the sad, hypersensitive, excessively musical child and only heir to the house of Buddenbrook, have seen how he suffers at the hands of his teachers and schoolmates, and now watch him at home, playing the piano and losing himself in a musical fantasy of pain, yearning, and a relief so shattering that life itself seems to yield to its finality; and the next chapter opens with the sentence: "Typhoid fever takes the following course," and continues to describe the symptoms of the disease with the objectivity of a medical textbook. The reader, with a shock, obeys the implied order, putting the piece of detached information into the place where it is needed to bring a story to its logical conclusion. This transformation of matter into organic life depends for its success upon the unity of concrete story and intellectual plot, upon a logical order of ideas binding together both the fates and the characters of the figures in the novel. Thus the "first and only naturalist novel" in German literature is also a philosophical novel. And as the philosophy derives from Schopenhauer, so the two cosmic antagonists in Schopenhauer's thought—the World-as-Will and the World as the human mind which, forming the true idea of this Will-World, comes to deny it—appear in the guise of life and spirit. Yet the novel also exploits, on two decisive occasions and each time with splendid aesthetic ruthlessness, the logical break in the philosopher's system; and the tactics of these moves are suggested first by Nietzsche, and then by Wagner.

Buddenbrooks is the story of a Hanseatic burgher family,

The house in Lübeck on which Mann modeled the Buddenbrook family home.

grain merchants who play an important part in the social life of their city. It is a story of four generations: Johann Buddenbrook senior, Consul Johann Buddenbrook junior and his stepbrother Gotthold, the first black sheep of the clan, then the Consul's three children, Thomas, Christian, and Antonia, called Tony, and finally Thomas's only son Johann, called Hanno. The action is concentrated in forty years, from 1835 to 1875. It is a time of great political and social change in Europe. Within the lifetime of the Buddenbrooks fall the dramatic events of 1848, 1866, and 1871, with their repercussions making themselves felt even in the Baltic remoteness of Lübeck, the unnamed but obvious residence of the family.

"The Decline of a Family"—this is the subtitle of the novel, and clearly their decline represents the dissolution of a whole social order, of a European era politically and culturally dominated by the burgher, the pre-industrial bourgeois. There are interpreters of ***Buddenbrooks*** who call on Karl Marx rather than the family doctor to diagnose the true nature of Thomas Buddenbrook's toothache and Hanno's typhoid fever; and indeed, the novel itself suggests the fatal role which class-consciousness itself plays in the undoing of a doomed class. There might have been a few more healthy generations of Buddenbrooks if Thomas had married his first mistress, the girl from the flower-shop who later becomes Frau Iwersen, the strong mother of numerous children, and who, at the time of Thomas's death, is "as usual, expecting." Instead, their parting comes as a matter of course, because, as Thomas says, "one is carried along—you see. If I live, I shall take over the business, and make a good match." Or if his sister Tony had taken as husband Morten Schwarzkopf, the son of the Master-Pilot of Travemünde, student and social reformer, athletic, charming, sincere, and hopelessly beneath her station, instead of obeying, at once and without a struggle, her father's letter: "My child, we are not born for our little personal happiness. We are not free, separate, independent individuals, but like links in a chain . . ." Of course, she marries the man the family has chosen, the disastrous Bendix Grünlich, and a few of Morten Schwarzkopf's rebellious phrases about the aristocracy and the reactionary local newspaper, so disarmingly out of place in her mouth, are all that will remain of Tony Buddenbrook's first and only love.

It is easy, therefore, to regard *Buddenbrooks* as a sociological novel, although Thomas Mann himself would not have it so. He even claimed that he remained long unaware of one of the most important social facts of the age: the emergence of the capitalist bourgeois. In discussing his "old-fashioned" allegiance to the tradition of the burgher, he once wrote: "True, I must have been almost asleep while the German burgher changed into the bourgeois." Yet the Marxist critic George Lukács is right when he objects that "with this remark Thomas Mann underrates his own production." For the novel does show clearly enough how the most reckless type of bourgeois moves in where the burgher leaves off; it is the Hagenströms, unscrupulous parvenus of the new financial hierarchy, brigands of the stock exchange, who take over the house and firm of Buddenbrook, carried into their position on the current of "historical necessity." Yet the determinism at work in the novel cannot be defined after the fashion of "historical laws", it is of a different order. No *historical* necessity can be abstracted from the destinies of its characters lest violence be done to the nature of the work. As Thomas Mann has created them, they partake, in pity, pathos, and humour, of the paradoxical distinction of man: to feel that he is the free agent of his fate even when his mind persuades him of its ineluctability. "We are like links in a chain," writes Consul Buddenbrook to his daughter in order to remind her of her *moral* duty to part with Morten Schwarzkopf; and "one is carried along," says Thomas Buddenbrook to his mistress when he feels he has to make the *decision* to break with her. Indeed, it is in Thomas Buddenbrook that this very paradox turns into tragedy: he is consumed by the conflict within himself between the sense of being "carried along" to his doom and the sense of being free to avert it.

In Schopenhauer's cosmic drama the crisis of the Will occurs as soon as man emerges from unreflective Nature, bringing into the world the fatal gifts of reflection and introspection. In *Buddenbrooks* this drama is, as it were, re-enacted, on the human level itself, through the gradual refinements of consciousness. Thomas is to the Buddenbrooks what, in Schopenhauer's philosophy, Man is to Nature. For through Man, as Schopenhauer puts it, "the Will comes to know itself and, astonished at its own activities, begins to enquire into its own character." Its perplexity is the greater as now, for the first time consciously, it faces death and is overwhelmed by the thought of its finite existence, the vanity of all its labours, and the illusoriness of its freedom. In Thomas the will of the Buddenbrooks suffers a similar embarrassment. Yet Thomas, ever more convinced by his reflective consciousness that the sense of futility which has taken possession of him is but the

voice of inescapable catastrophe, seeks to employ all his moral resources in support of the Will, the will to be a Buddenbrook. On one occasion he even tests his moral courage and tries to assert his freedom with all the perverse logic of doom by entering, for the good of the firm, into a dubious business contract from which his moral character shrinks. Of course, he is defeated. For no wilful blindness can obscure a sight once seen by the reflective eye, and no manœuvre of perversity heal the damaged integrity of the will. But before the spirit of reflection reaches such momentum in Thomas, it has first to rehearse its strength in his father, Consul Johann Buddenbrook.

The novel begins with little skirmishes between "Will" and "Idea" taking place in the drawing-room of the Buddenbrooks. Old Buddenbrook, the Consul's father, represents the Will in its perfect integrity. His mind is precisely what Schopenhauer says it is in its simple and harmonious adjustment to the needs of the Will, "a lantern illuminating the way of the Will"; and very far from being the luminous power to which Schopenhauer likens the mind of genius: "the sun revealing the world." On the contrary, no ray of light is to be wasted on regions better left in the dark lest the Will be deflected from its straight path. Not even in children will old Buddenbrook tolerate useless exercises of the imagination. His grand-daughter, little Tony, has just discovered a new theory about the respective activities of lightning and thunder: "If the lightning sets something on fire, then it's the lightning that strikes. If it doesn't, why, then it's the thunder." The family circle is amused; not so the grandfather. With Voltairean rational jealousy he wishes to know who puts such nonsense into the child's head. His son defends the autonomous right of a child's imagination, but he: "*Excusez, mon cher! Mais c'est une folie!* I don't like children's minds getting muddled like this."

With Johann Buddenbrook junior the "lantern" begins to be unsteady and light is allowed to fall on "useless" parts of the land. His religion is pietistic, his sense of business not immune from morbid scruples, his politics idealistic, and his relationship to nature romantically nostalgic. All these inclinations of the son's are utterly alien to the father and ridiculed by him as so much extravagance. Later that evening, at the dinner given to celebrate the completion of the magnificent new family house, the *leit-motif* of decline and doom is sounded for the first time. The conversation turns on the bankruptcy of the local firm Ratenkamp and Co. Someone suggests that it was all due to Ratenkamp's choice of an unreliable partner. Johann junior is not content with so simple an interpretation. With his face assuming a gloomy expression, he suggests that Ratenkamp acted as if hypnotized by a sense of catastrophe. So, someone asks, things would have turned out just the same if there had been no new partner? Perhaps not, the Consul replies, but still, Ratenkamp chose the partner "inevitably," driven by something "inexorable," and in order to "fulfil his destiny." Not surprisingly, the party is embarrassed by this portentous note, and old Buddenbrook intervenes to change the subject: "*Assez,* Jean, that's just one of your *idées.*" *Idées* are not to the old man's liking, nor is any other sort of "nonsense" and sentimentality. One of the guests mentions the garden the Buddenbrooks own just outside the gates of the town. It's a mere nuisance, old Buddenbrook protests, deteriorated as it has into a wilderness, a jungle. One should tidy it up, cut the grass, trim the bushes, shape them into cones and cubes. His son protests. It would spoil everything if nature were to be deprived of all her freedom. "What the deuce," cries old Buddenbrook, "if the 'freedom of nature' belongs to me, haven't I the right to do with it what I please?" For the Will dislikes all wills not its own.

His will is wonderfully intact, and unassailable by his son's romantic fancies; he is, in so far as this state of innocence is attainable at all within the human species, that "perfect objectivation of the Will" and its "perfect enjoyment of itself" which Schopenhauer discerns in Nature. But in Buddenbrook junior the Will, to adapt Schopenhauer's description of the human mind emerging from the mindless state of the world, acquires the power and compulsion to "reflect upon itself. At this point, however, it is bound to be struck by the dubiousness of its own existence, and cannot escape the question of what is the origin and purpose of it all." And although the younger Buddenbrook's will is still far from losing itself in this perplexity, it is yet baffled already, on decisive occasions, by the demands of "ideas" interfering with its business—the Buddenbrook business. Consul Buddenbrook's character is, in Thomas Mann's rendering, a superb study of the subtle hypocrisy contrived by the spirit in its self-righteous subservience to the Will.

Late at night, after the departure of the guests, the embarrassing affair of Gotthold is discussed between father and son. Gotthold, old Buddenbrook's son by his first wife, has fallen foul of the family: he married against his father's will, started business on his own, and disgraced the name of Buddenbrook by opening a shop. A quarrel ensues over his future inheritance. Johann junior is to be the sole heir of the new house. Gotthold demands a considerable compensation. His letters hint at "certain influences" working against him. This is aimed at his stepbrother Johann, himself divided between his self-interest, his sound business sense, objecting to a substantial weakening of the firm's resources, and his Christian conscience. On the day of the dinner-party yet another letter from Gotthold has arrived. Consul Buddenbrook has withheld it from his father until now. At last the old man reads it and asks for his son's opinion: "Father, surely you understand my dilemma. For the sake of family harmony I ought to suggest—but . . ." The conversation goes on for some time, with many a "but" and "however" from Johann junior, with many an angry resolution, on the part of his father, to refuse Gotthold's demands. Then:

> "Father," said the Consul softly, "this affair with Gotthold causes me much anxiety."
>
> "Nonsense, Jean! Why anxiety?"
>
> "It has been a very happy day for all of us. We celebrated our new house. We felt proud and glad at what we have accomplished . . . But this bitter feud with my brother, your eldest son—it's like a crack in the house we have built. A family should be united, Father. It must keep together. 'A house divided against itself will fall.' "
>
> "Fiddlesticks, Jean! He is an insolent fellow, that's what he is."
>
> There was a pause. The last candle in the room burned lower and lower.
>
> "What are you doing, Jean? I can hardly see you."
>
> And the Consul said drily: "I'm calculating."

And in the sobering light of commercial arithmetic—one of the most reliable weapons the Will can hope to find in the ar-

senal of the intellect—his sense of business recovers from the attacks of conscience:

> "I must advise you not to give in."
>
> "Thank goodness! *Fini. N'en parlons plus! En avant!* Let's get to bed."

Johann Buddenbrook is the first Buddenbrook to suffer the pains of self-awareness, and the last whose will is still strong enough to force its way through the gathering crowd of ideas. It is a costly victory. He spends what is all but the last resources of the will in a manœuvre to disentangle it from a delicate situation demanding a far subtler strategy than the case of Gotthold. By dutiful persuasion he has caused his daughter Tony to marry the exquisitely repulsive rascal Bendix Grünlich, who struck him as a man of good manners, sincere feelings, and commercial promise. But, of course, he is an impostor. After a few years, the inevitable occurs: a bankruptcy of disquieting dimensions. Johann Buddenbrook could still save him, as he had, unconsciously, saved him once before by giving him Tony, her dowry; and the credit invested in the name of Buddenbrook. To save him now would mean a very considerable drain on the firm's capital. His "will" says no, but what about his conscience, his "ideas"? He knows Tony did not love Grünlich when she married him. But meanwhile a child has been born; and may she not have come to love Grünlich in the years of their marriage? And the marriage itself? Johann Buddenbrook is a sincere Christian, believing in the sanctity of the institution. True, the law provides the possibility of divorce in such a case. But is he not himself responsible for this marriage, and is it not, therefore, his duty to make its continuance possible? He must see his daughter. She shall decide.

Thomas Mann has succeeded in involving, as it were, three *dramatis personae* in the scene between Johann Buddenbrook and his daughter: Tony, Johann Buddenbrook's true will, and Johann Buddenbrook's moral idea.

> "Listen, my dear child," said the Consul, stroking her hair. "I want to ask you something very serious. Tell me: you love your husband with your whole heart, don't you?"
>
> "Of course, Papa," said Tony with a face of innocent hypocrisy—precisely the face of the child Tony when she was asked: "You won't tease that old woman again?" The Consul was silent for a while. Then he asked again: "You love him so much that you could not live without him, under any circumstances, even if by God's will his situation should change and he could no longer provide you with all these things?" And his hand described a quick movement over the furniture and portières, over the gilt clock on the étagère, and finally over her own frock.
>
> "Certainly, Papa," repeated Tony, in the soothing tone she nearly always used when any one spoke seriously to her.

And then he reveals to her Grünlich's circumstances. The word "bankruptcy" rings in her ears more fearful than death. It means tumult, shame, misery, and despair.

> "I am asking you," he said gently, "if you are ready to follow your husband into poverty?" He realized at once that he had instinctively used the hard word to frighten her, and added: "Of course, he may recover."

"Certainly, Papa," she answered. But it did not prevent her from bursting into tears. . . .

"You mean it?" he asked . . .

"I must, mustn't I?" she sobbed. "Don't I have to—?"

"Certainly not," he said. But, from a sense of guilt, corrected himself:

"I should not necessarily force you, my dear Tony. Assuming, of course, that your feelings do not bind you indissolubly to your husband. . . ."

Tony wants to know whether Grünlich is to blame for his misfortune. Very probably, he says, but again corrects himself: "That is—no, I don't know, my child. I have not yet discussed things with him or his banker." And then he asks again whether she loves her husband.

"Oh, what a question to ask, Papa! Of course, I have never loved him—he has always been repulsive to me. Surely you must have known that?"

It would have been hard to say what Johann Buddenbrook's face expressed. His eyes looked shocked and sad, and yet he pressed his lips hard together so that great wrinkles appeared at the corners of his mouth and on his cheeks, as used to happen when he had brought a piece of business to a profitable conclusion.

Although it is not so very hard to say what Johann Buddenbrook's facial expression meant, this is yet admirably done: his eyes reflecting the moral idea, and his mouth the deep satisfaction of the will at having its way. For the day is all but won. Before long Tony will be not only ready but determined to leave Grünlich and return with her child to the parental home. And what tactics on the part of Buddenbrook! The crucial question has been withheld until now when the field is already cleared of serious opposition: can Grünlich's downfall be avoided? Of course, Johann Buddenbrook could pay his debts:

"How much is it?" she asked.

"What does it matter, my child? A very large sum." And Consul Buddenbrook nodded several times, as though the weight of the very thought of such a sum pushed his head up and down. "Also, I should not conceal from you," he went on, "that the firm has suffered losses already, quite apart from this affair, and that the surrender of a sum like this would be a blow from which it would not easily, by no means easily, recover. However, I do not say that in order to—"

He did not finish. Tony had leapt to her feet, had even taken a few steps backward, and with the wet handkerchief still in her hand, she cried: "Enough! Never!" She looked almost heroic.

At this moment she seems to be a reincarnation of her grandfather's forceful will, repeating almost the very words with which he once concluded a similar conversation: "*Fini. N'en parlons plus! En avant!*" Among her generation of Buddenbrooks she is alone in having preserved the naïveté of the will. But in her the will is only saved from defeat because the combat does not take place: spirit has withdrawn from the fight. It is not that she has no ideas. On the contrary, she has quite a number of them, but all mercifully miss their Schopen-

hauerian target: the Will. They are almost exclusively engaged in the activity which, according to Schopenhauer, produces the comic: the registration of a phenomenon in an incongruous category. Had she no ideas at all about what is happening to her and her family, she would be pathetic. She is comic—and one of Thomas Mann's most successful comic creations—because she has hopelessly incongruous ideas. If the Great Flood were upon her, she would find complete relief in being angry about the inadequacy of the weather forecast. She enacts the "tragedy of her marriage" with immense gusto and a ceaseless flow of conversational reflections on the meaning of matrimony and the dignity of suffering— "dignity" is the idea by which she lives. Then she marries again: Herr Permaneder from Munich, a hop merchant, exceedingly Bavarian and "very jolly." But soon the Buddenbrooks in their northern abode receive a telegram from the south: "Don't be frightened. Am coming at once. All is over. Your unhappy Antonia."

Her second marriage has come to an end in the manner of a farce. Yet she puts the farcical phenomenon in the category of the tragic. One night Permaneder is late in coming home from an alcoholic party. In the hall he meets Babette, the maid. Tony is roused from her sleep by the noise of flirtatious aggression, steps out of her bedroom—and sees. It might be by Wilhelm Busch, but Tony reacts tragically. "Carried away by a frenzy of desperation, she heaped upon his head her disgust, her abhorrence, her profound contempt and loathing for him and all his ways." And leaves him, never to return, never—for he shouts a word at her, an unrepeatable word, which "shall never pass my lips." It seems to be capable of shattering the very idea of "dignity" and blotting out the light of her world. This magic curse is, as the reader is told much later, a Bavarian commonplace of masculine annoyance: "*Geh zum Deifi, Saulud'r dreckats!*"—as untranslatable as are all the more urgent requests, conveyed in popular parlance, that someone should go to Hell. It must indeed put an end to the second marriage of Antonia Buddenbrook, who exists by what is dignified alone, safely wedded to the tradition of her family, and blissfully at rest in the embrace of a vigorous illusion. In her the "will" of the Buddenbrooks attains once more to a firmly defined form—it is a comic one. Her father, the Consul, would pore for hours on end over the family records, filled as he is with vague misgivings of instability, and in need of the comfort of history, some soothing token of continuance. "Compare yourself! Discover what you are!" These words from Goethe's *Torquato Tasso*—the appeal to a despairing man to recover his strength in the contemplation of his eternal type—would not be lost on Johann Buddenbrook (and were, by the way, to serve as the motto of Thomas Mann's *Meditations of a Non-political Man*). Yet Tony is all present. She does not grow or change. True, after the first divorce she takes to saying "I am only an old, ugly woman," but in her mouth it sounds like the part a child has learned for a school play. For she is the parody of a final principle superior to time or change, in fact, the comic incarnation of Schopenhauer's "idea of the species" within which the individual partakes of a kind of "immortality in time," and the power of which is such that "at every moment we may be serenely sure that, despite time, death and putrefaction, we shall all be here, always."

Tony Buddenbrook is like a comic version of the "unfathomable mystery," which Schopenhauer perceives in animals: "Just look at the first you see. Look at your dog: how unafraid it is, how calm! Millions of dogs had to die ere it was its turn to live. But the perdition of those millions has not affected the idea 'dog,' it has not been dimmed in the very least by all that dying. This is why the dog stands before you in all its vivacity and vigour, as if this very day were its first, and none could be its last, and its eyes are alight with the radiance of an indestructible principle. . . ." Tony's indestructible principle is the idea of a species called Buddenbrooks, and not even the demonstrable end of this species can shake her certainty. It is by virtue of this principle, so blissfully incommensurable with the actual state of affairs, that, in her touching silliness, she is immune from time and many a death. Dignified amidst indignities, unharmed by bankruptcies, divorces, or even Bavarian insults, she outfools the tragedy, just as her brother Christian is the melancholy fool of the piece, the natural outcast of the species.

If Tony, then, is a parody of "life," a "willing" self operating in a void and unreachable by the questioning insinuations of the spirit, Christian, who owes his name most certainly to Nietzsche, is Thomas Mann's first essay in caricaturing the spirit which has broken away from the business of seriously living and willing. Moreover, the memory of Christian was destined to become an essential element in Thomas Mann's vision of the artist, so much so that the true nature of the moral scruples with which Thomas Mann surrounds the artistic vocation can hardly be grasped without the help of Christian Buddenbrook. When the reader first meets him, a boy coming home from school on the evening of the dinner-party, accompanied by one of the guests, the town poet Jean Jacques Hoffstede, whom he had met in the street, he is introduced by Hoffstede as "a devil of a fellow, a little *incroyable,* eh? I will not conceal my *engouement.* He must study, I think—he is witty and brilliant." And he is all this, and something of an actor too, mimicking his teachers with a genuine gift of caricature. Old Buddenbrook is, of course, suspicious of his talents: "*n' Aap is hei!,*" he says in Low German, and adds mockingly: "Why not say at once that he should become a poet, Hoffstede?" Indeed, what should he become? A merchant? An actor? A writer? Like all Buddenbrooks he tries to become a merchant, but fails miserably. Nor do his histrionic talents lead to anything, save the part of *raconteur* of the gentlemen's club, and connoisseur of actresses. With increasing age he surrenders more and more to neurotic introspection, describing his numerous ailments with such dramatic force that his listeners are hypnotized into almost suffering the same symptoms: the "vague agony" down the left leg where "all the nerves are too short," the sudden inability to swallow, the irresistible urge to jump out of the window.

All in all, he is the creature of the species Buddenbrook at the lowest point of its vitality, and becomes the victim of that "hypochondria and spleen" which Schopenhauer describes as the invariable psychological result of the natural will sagging without the succour and sanction of moral resolution; and because Christian is such a victim, he is also the caricature of the *décadent* who in Nietzsche's diagnosis would ultimately usurp, enfeeble, and destroy the cultural tradition of Europe. Christian has the makings, if not the format and nervous energy, of Nietzsche's aesthetic nihilist who, having lost the taste of reality and the power of vital feeling, exhausts himself in the pursuit of sensations, self-destructive and recaptured only by means of ever stronger stimulation. This type abounds when a tradition loses its vital coherence and its will to survive. For eccentrics become the norm when the centre no longer holds; and when the limits of a pattern are reached, what else can there be but border-line cases? Where

there is no order, the extraordinary becomes trivial, uniqueness common, the freak typical, the outsider the rule, and in the general confusion any raucous sounds of anger may easily be mistaken for a calling to higher things.

It is at such a time that the artistic impulse itself is laid open to suspicion due to the inflationary abundance of cheap talent—and nothing is more conducive to the rash breeding of talent than the dissolution of solid substance. Who can be quite sure then that the apparent artistic impulse is really a creative urge so powerful that no less creative manner of activity could satisfy it? That it is not merely a restless groping for aesthetic satisfaction to compensate for the loss of any meaningful social routine? Or, still worse, the aspiration of wounded pride, the desire of the unemployable to prove his productive worth? Or are the motives inextricably mixed and, alas, reflected in the fumbling uncertainty or coarse triviality of the works then produced? Thomas Mann never ceases to ask such questions. They issue from the questionable shape of Christian Buddenbrook, the *bourgeois déraciné,* the man of the vague agony, deserter of life, and travesty of the spirit.

In an argument with Thomas Buddenbrook, Christian tries to explain his ways to his angry brother. Yes, he was wasting his time on trifles, on the theatre, on flirting. But had Thomas, before he was married and head of the firm, never indulged in such pleasures? "Yet this is the difference between us," he continues, "you have always known how to combine it with the serious business of living. But I don't know how to do it. You see, I am quite exhausted and used up by the other things, the trifles. There is nothing left over for the serious stuff. . . ." And Thomas flies into a rage: "For heaven's sake, have you no pride? How can you go on living in a way which you don't even dare defend? But that's just like you: all that matters to you is to see a thing, understand it, describe it . . ." So much of the image of Christian entered later into Thomas Mann's interpretation of the artist that in his first portrayal of a writer, in **Tonio Kröger,** Tonio describes artists like himself in all but identical words: "This is the *credo* of the artist: once a thing is made articulate, it is finished. If the whole world is expressed, it is finished, redeemed, done with." And adds his moral protest: "But I am not a nihilist." (pp. 30-50)

[The] peculiar understanding of life which is embodied in a work of literature—and it is this *understanding* which determines also the *formal* aspects of the work: its organization and its style—may have crystallized in the contact between the writer and a philosopher, between an imagination and a thought. In such a case the philosophy will be as relevant to the nature and quality of the writing as is its vocabulary, rhythm, or syntax. Indeed, every major literary work has a *syntax of ideas* upon which it may ultimately depend for its rank and status. If, moreover, the philosophy in question is not so much a systematic essay in the solution of problems as, like Schopenhauer's, an attempt to gain absolution from them, an act of liberation from the stresses and distresses of the mind; if, in fact, it is "no philosophy at all," as many of our contemporary philosophers would misguidedly be ready to protest, then its assimilation in a piece of literature may proceed as naturally and spontaneously as that of a scene of nature in a romantic poem. The quality of a writer's feeling for ideas will then decide the quality of his writing as much as, in another case, a writer's feeling for the sea or a landscape. However, it may be objected that "nature" differs from "ideas" in that she possesses an attribute which we also expect from imaginative literature: concreteness. It is a fallacious expectation: the kind of concreteness we expect is not that of nature; what strikes us, metaphorically speaking, as "concrete" is the artist's idea of nature. Besides, is love—to choose another example from the common subject-matters of literature—concrete? Only in so far as it moves human beings to act out their destinies. And it is possible for an idea to move a man passionately, and possible for a man to fall in love with an idea. This is precisely what, in **Buddenbrooks,** one day happens to Thomas. There is hardly another way of describing his state of mind when, having chanced upon the book, he reads the chapter "On Death" from the second volume of Schopenhauer's *The World as Will and Idea;* and it is by no means, as we have seen, an arbitrary literary contrivance that the scene which marks the climax in the story of Thomas Buddenbrook, and may be regarded as the climax of the novel, is linked to this philosopher (who, incidentally, remains unnamed). It is an inevitable consummation, demanded by the syntax of ideas inherent in this most "concrete" narrative.

Senator Thomas Buddenbrook, forty-eight and maintaining, with ever-increasing effort, the appearance of success in the face of the undeniable decline of his business and his vitality; incongruously opposing the sense of decay with the meticulous elegance of his attire and an addiction to *eau-de-Cologne;* anxiously watching his only child Hanno, who is so ill-equipped by nature for the future task of conducting the increasingly difficult affairs of the firm; and filled with a vague but intense fear, which he wishes he could call jealousy, of "the mysterious little scandal above his head," over his office, where, in the drawing-room, his wife Gerda, looking astonishingly young and as if preserved by her own coolness, is joined ever more frequently in duets by a young lieutenant with a passion for music—Thomas Buddenbrook, then, is possessed by a restlessness which often drives him from his desk into the garden, where he aimlessly wanders about, or sits lethargically in the pavilion. It is here that he casually opens the second volume of a "metaphysical system," and, although unskilled in this kind of reading, is immediately engrossed in it. Thomas Mann describes the effect upon Thomas Buddenbrook in a manner reminiscent of the words he used, in the autobiographical sketch already quoted, of his own initiation into Schopenhauer's philosophy. Thomas Buddenbrook's mind and soul, oppressed as they were by the premonition of death, now feel "immeasurably expanded" and as if "intoxicated with the alluring promise of an unheard-of enchantment." And during the night that follows he suddenly wakes, gazing out of his darkness into an "unfathomably deep prospect of light," and hears his own voice saying: "I shall live!" "End and dissolution? Pitiable words, and thrice pitiable he whom they fill with terror! What would end and dissolve? Why, this my body and individuality, this clumsy, obstinate, hateful incumbrance, *preventing me from being something other and better.*" The italics are of the interior monologue itself, which is Schopenhauerian word for word; or almost word for word—for Schopenhauer knows no "other and better" unless it be the condition of saintliness. But for the time being Schopenhauer dominates the nocturnal vision until this point is reached: "Do I hope to live on in my son? In a creature yet weaker and more timid and insecure than myself? Blind and childish folly! What is a son to me? I need no son! Where shall I be when I am dead? Wherever there will be an 'I'! Ah, it is so radiantly clear, so overwhelmingly simple: I shall be in all those who for ever and ever will say 'I'."

This again is Schopenhauer, almost verbatim, and comes from the very chapter which Thomas Buddenbrook read that afternoon. But although those are the words of Schopenhauer, the jubilant emphasis belongs entirely to Thomas Buddenbrook or Thomas Mann. Schopenhauer, it is true, does in that chapter deal with death and immortality, but an immortality without grace or comfort: an immortality which rests in the assured survival of the species. For the species, Schopenhauer believes, is the only level of life at which a measure of individuation is safeguarded by the arrangements of the cosmic Will. The individual itself is produced, and killed again, in careless profusion, as wasteful as the exquisite craftsmanship spent on countless shells that litter the beaches of the sea. It is the species that alone matters to the Will, the species and its procreation, excessively guaranteed by a superfluity of sex-craving entities. Therefore, it is in sex that Schopenhauer, anticipating Freud, discovers "the focus of the Will" and thus the source of the individual's greatest raptures and distresses. For sex is the point at which the individual is exposed, in powerful immediacy, to a force vastly transcending himself: the will of the species, the promise of life everlasting. But what an eternity is this? An eternity stretching, according to Schopenhauer, into the dismal immensity of time without hope of salvation, an eternity into which the individual has to be tricked by the delirium of sex, "a fever, longing still / For that which longer nurseth the disease." By virtue of Schopenhauer's passionately lucid prose, mockery turns to sublimity in sentence after sentence devoted to the grand fool and slave of the Will: man in love, deceived by the mirage of self-fulfilment into subservience to a master so cruelly indifferent to the individual's selfhood.

Yet it is in this vision of a bleak Schopenhauerian eternity, strung together on the endless thread of generations, that Thomas Buddenbrook conquers the fear of death: "I shall be in all those who for ever and ever will say 'I'." What can such survival mean to him? Has he himself found happiness in saying "I"? Is it not exactly here whence issues Schopenhauer's plea to renounce for good all "I-saying" and seek that state of purest contemplation where the willing self is at last abandoned in saintly "nothingness"? Clearly, Thomas Buddenbrook has—and how significantly!—misunderstood *The World as Will and Idea,* and may indeed have read yet other books, although we are not told.

For his soliloquy continues thus: ". . . but above all in those who say it in the full vigour of joy. Somewhere in the world a child is growing up, endowed with great gifts, free to use them, well-built and untroubled, innocent, ruthless, and serene, one of those whose sight makes joy more joyous and despair more desperate. This is my son! *This is myself,* soon, soon, as soon as death frees me from the wretched delusion that I am not he as much as I am myself. . . ." This, of course, is no longer Schopenhauer. It is a romantic distillation from Nietzsche, the blondest version of the Superman. And the following words, still under the spell of Nietzsche, also anticipate Tonio Kröger: "Have I ever hated life, life in its innocence, cruelty, and strength? What foolish confusion! Myself I have hated because I could not bear it! But I love you. . . !" (pp. 56-60)

Thomas Buddenbrook's vision and monologue is perhaps the only passage in the book that gives the attentive reader a clue to the author's age, which, for the rest, is so extraordinarily, indeed uniquely, concealed behind such epic composure and ironical detachment as is usually held to be the literary temper of maturity. At this point, however, youthful emotion is in control of scene and style. Moreover, it is one of only two scenes in the novel which are dominated by the vocabulary of the passion of love; and as happens to be the case in the other scene too, its passion is also the rapture of death. And for the writer of *Buddenbrooks,* the spiritual status of love and death, these twin enchantments of the romantic imagination, is—and largely remains throughout his later works—determined by his experience of Schopenhauer, Nietzsche, and . . . Richard Wagner. Although Thomas Mann himself once said that only Schopenhauer and Wagner influenced *Buddenbrooks,* while Nietzsche had to wait until *Tonio Kröger,* it is yet true that the peculiar irony of his first novel is the attitude of a mind hovering in creative indecision between the extremes of Schopenhauer and Nietzsche. If there could be any doubt about this, it would be dispelled by Thomas Buddenbrook's vision.

The impetuosity and spontaneity with which Thomas Buddenbrook passes the dramatic crossing of the Schopenhauerian and Nietzschean ways without, as it were, noticing the signposts, is as impressive as it is revealing. What it reveals is an inclination of the modern mind shared not only by the national heirs of the two philosophies. It is clear that Thomas Buddenbrook, if he followed Schopenhauer, should resolutely turn from that never-ending vista of life, that desolate continuity of the Will, which he glimpses in the eyes of all those who "for ever and ever will say 'I'," and seek the dominion of "nothingness" where all "I-saying" ends in the absolute negation of our Will-ruled existence. But in no time whatever, and before the sentence is finished, he is in a place where it is no longer the World-as-Will which gives offence, but we ourselves in our imperfection, with our wills enfeebled by sensibility and doubt; in a place where, with Nietzschean psychological daring, he sees through the Schopenhauerian denial of Will and self, recognizing its dubious motives, such as weakness, fear, maladjustment, impotence, and the wounded love of life proclaiming in self-defence the superiority of the spirit. At one moment Schopenhauer is accepted: the world is Will, and the spirit is its enemy. At the next moment Schopenhauer is ousted by Nietzsche: the Will is good, and the enmity to it is wicked. However, Thomas Buddenbrook does not put the alternatives quite so radically; indeed, he feverishly runs them into one. And what is it that has enchanted the bleak world of Schopenhauer and, at the same time, breathed the warmth of romance into Zarathustra's glacial landscape? Has God returned to the creation, or else some other meaning, majestic and unanswerable? A god, perhaps, but his name is Eros. And Eros does not ask if life is worth living. He bestows that worth through the irrefutability of desire. Is life, then, desirable? Eros does not care: the desire of love is worth living. It is by this dubious route that Thomas Buddenbrook reaches the point at which the dejected spirit turns for consolation to the life-force and to beauty, pessimism to vitalism and aestheticism—and he passes this turning-point so smoothly because he has moved with the logic of a European movement.

It is indeed amazing how far and fast Thomas Buddenbrook out-dreams the book that causes him to dream. Yet it is the book that is as much to blame as the dreamer. For Schopenhauer's *World as Will and Idea,* being the most inspired statement of European pessimism, advances, with all its fineness of thought and beauty of reasoning, a simple belief: what is real, is worthless; what is valuable, lacks reality. And where reality and value are thus seen and felt to be mutually exclu-

sive, there *all* values, indeed truth itself, must in the end lose any *real* significance. Then the transition is speedy, and so smooth it is hardly perceptible, from one metaphysical illusion to another: from redemption through the denial of the Will to redemption through the Will's increase, from art as salvation to art as damnation (and Thomas Mann's damned composer Faustus-Leverkühn descends in a straight line from the Buddenbrooks) or from Eros as a saviour to Eros as a curse (and with the saving grace of Thomas Buddenbrook's new love for life we draw close to that death which lurks for Gustav Aschenbach in Venice).

"I love you!" exclaims Thomas Buddenbrook, with Nietzsche now prompting a text which was begun by Schopenhauer. Love—whom? His neighbour? It depends; if he is young, well-built, strong, and handsome. Clearly, it is Eros who speaks, a divinity common enough, and calling, it would seem, for no strenuous exercise of philosophical reason. Nevertheless, the situation is questionable in the extreme. For here the erotic delight is uttered with the accents of a quasi-religious expectation. Also, it is conceived in no friendly spirit. Its ecstasy is not the love of life enhanced by passion. On the contrary, it rises from the depths of despair, intoxicating with "the alluring promise of an unheard-of enchantment" a mind lost in the dejected contemplation of a world which, right to its core, seems the denial of all love. Thus it is a profoundly impossible love, a love in a world without love.

Perhaps there are, after all, only two themes which are new in modern literature, distinguishing the nineteenth and twentieth centuries from any previous literary epochs: this kind of love and the tedium of the frustrated spirit. They are all but identical themes and Thomas Mann is master of both. (pp. 61-3)

> *Erich Heller, in his* The Ironic German: A Study of Thomas Mann, *Little, Brown and Company, 1958, 298 p.*

BERNARD N. SCHILLING   (essay date 1965)

[*In the following excerpt, Schilling studies the comic elements in* Buddenbrooks.]

[The] prosperous world of Thomas Mann's *Buddenbrooks* . . . [begins amid] the ease and gayety of success. With comic exuberance, playfulness, and delicate mockery of a number of human weaknesses Mann leads us gradually toward failure and decline, the defeat of all attempts at improvement, while our responses change with the fate of those commanding our sympathy. The comic elements cease to amuse us when they begin to undermine individual happiness as with the gloomy preachers and Tony's dreadful husbands, or to lead us into the family's decline as with Grünlich at first, and finally into the sad ineptitude of little Hanno.

Once, in answer to a question, Thomas Mann made the conventional distinction between humor and irony: humor shows a less intellectual and objective laughter than irony, "*das herzaufquellende Lachen*" ["laughter springing from the heart"] is warmer and more humane. Mann is happy when readers find him more of a humorist than an ironist; indeed he is growing bored by constant reference to the irony that dominates his work.

By now his vast achievement has been studied and interpreted in thousands of books and articles, and recently the undiminished power of his later career has offered problems of great complexity to criticism. While **Buddenbrooks,** *"ein Buch pessimistischen Humors"* ["a book of pessimistic humor"] in Mann's own phrase, remains the most popular and accessible of the great novels, it has seemed to demand less recent attention than the output of fifty years later.

To be followed by **Der Zauberberg,** the Joseph tetralogy, and the all-but-incredible **Dr. Faustus,** to mention only the summits, would make any novel seem a minor work, and its comic aspect, however delightful at times, must seem lost amid the sombre tones not only of Mann's highest achievements in the later works, but in the tragic decline of the Buddenbrook family itself. Mann is praised for being the poet of death, of our common sorrow, of loss and bereavement; the reader of those unforgettable pages that tell of the death of Joachim Ziemessen, or the sacrifice of Rachel in giving life to Benjamin, will acquiesce. In **Buddenbrooks** itself the death of Tom displays a fearful power from which there can be no recovery.

But death is not the only mark of decline and fall in this masterpiece of a youthful writer, barely twenty-five. If we recall the dreadful tension as Tony's father examines the financial records of the bankrupt Grünlich; the well-nigh unbearable quarrel scene between Tom and Christian after their mother's death, while Tony in agonies of grief and shame constantly reminds them of the dead body in the very next room; the final tableau with its Euripidean lamentation of the eight women clothed all in black—recalling these and other moments of comparable grandeur, we might well pass over the comic element, content with our riches.

And yet as one begins the account of little Tony's lesson in catechism and moves into the family life, a certain tone as of amused detachment, a way of looking at things and people and presenting their lives, seems to emerge with a subtly comic effect. In a kind of Dickensian exuberance or excess, a love of seemingly irrelevant but vivid detail, an eye for the various forms of affectation or pretense, of hypocrisy, of ignorance, professional pomp and vanity, of the clash between what is professed and what is done, between the pretended and the real—in all these classical forms wherein comic discernment has declared itself, we find **Buddenbrooks** rich and full to our delighted astonishment.

But the exact nature of Mann's humorous posture undergoes so many and complex changes, and moves with such subtlety back into the sombre outlines of the work as a whole, that we shall find him elusive, as he wishes. We shall meet a blending of several attitudes as the forms of our common human weakness pass before his eye: affectionate sympathy, scornful antagonism, or more likely tender pity—all somehow related to amused indifference, as of one keeping himself at a distance from the object, ever above his creation so as to see it as it really is and only rarely becoming one with it when the movement toward decline and fall must have its way.

The book opens with genial gäyety and the harmlessly mocking laughter of a sweet old man, Johann Buddenbrook, who is amused by the catechism lesson of his grandchild, Tony. A playful amusement is joined by his wife and daughter-in-law, as we find ourselves drawn into the life of the family, with its assured prosperity and serenity in the year 1835. Dealing as it does in people and their daily relationships, the novel is bound to contain studies of character and behavior in typical human situations wherein so much of the comic

shows itself—those clashes and incongruities that make up the endless variations of human absurdity.

And like all novels of family life, **Buddenbrooks** contains a great many meals; the family table with its activity becomes a principal means of portraying character, the family atmosphere and its habits, the tone of succeeding generations. Like Dickens, Mann invests these occasions with a kind of excitement and fascination until we read with avidity every detail of what was consumed and the manner of serving it. In fact, the richness of what Orwell sees as irrelevant but interesting detail in Dickens is soon obvious as we become involved in Mann's similarly inexhaustible creative invention—an energy of imagination that continues throughout his career and is marked in **Dr. Faustus** as well.

Here in **Buddenbrooks** it delights us constantly from Herr Stuht, the tailor, whose belly was clothed in a wool shirt and fell with astonishing roundness over his breeches, to the speck of powder to be seen on the wart on the left nostril of the bridegroom, Bendix Grünlich; and the thin nose of the old retainer Grobleben, from which at all seasons there hung a long drop of something that never actually fell off.

At the great dinner in celebration of a magnificent new family mansion, we read with mounting excitement of the colossal, brickred ham, the shallot gravy, the masses of vegetables on such a scale that one might have satisfied his appetite from a single dish. The solemn function of carving, *das Tranchieren* is taken over by Lebrecht Kröger with uplifted elbows and index fingers stretched out precisely on the back of knife and fork, he cuts with deliberation the juicy slices one by one. The masterpiece of Konsulin Buddenbrook, *der Russische Topf,* is then passed and we savor a rich and pungent mixture of fruit conserves, meanwhile seated on heavy chairs, using heavy silverware, and drinking heavy wine. We share the obvious satisfaction of Herr Hoffstede, as he shoves into his mouth, his brows elevated, a single fork on which are accumulated ham, brussels sprouts, and potato. We see the general astonishment at the capacity of Klothilde, a poor relation and the butt of family jokes throughout. She is emaciated, tough, patient, and hungry, consuming two enormous helpings of every course, with heaps of supplementary ingredients.

All is in vain, for Klothilde is destined to grow ever more gaunt and attenuated, unlike Herr Köppen who, after the vast *Plettenpudding* is served—a mixture of layers of macaroons, raspberries, biscuits, and custard—is obliged to resist the strong need to loosen some buttons of his vest. The gayety is finally suspended by nothing more solemn than the stomach ache of a small boy, Christian, who lies groaning in agony from an excess of flaming plum pudding especially prepared for the children, while the adults are heavily faced by the last course of butter, cheese, and fruit, to be followed still by coffee, cigars, and liqueur. Christian's affliction is diagnosed as a slight indigestion, and the family physician, Dr. Grabow, prescribes some children's powder, camomile tea, and a strong diet of pigeon and French roll—the same and only remedy, alas, that the old man suggests for all afflictions throughout, trivial or mortal.

At the regular Christmas dinner nearly forty years later, we observe the same vast amounts of food and drink narrated in occasional repetitions of the same language used at the outset; but the tone of exuberant comic excess no longer moves us to burst out laughing as when being tickled, for the sombre movement of the family's life must have its way.

Christian's stomach ache has given cause for both amusement and alarm, with the development of his character showing him as much the object as the source of ridicule. He is early distinguished from the more solid and promising Tom, destined to become *Konsul* and head of the family grain business. Christian is a gifted mimic, but moody and capricious, given to a variety of silly jokes, at times delighting and dismaying the family by his escapades. Once he terrifies the company at table by seeming to strangle on a peach stone; they are relieved when Christian recovers quickly, saying that he was only supposing what would happen if he swallowed the stone.

His performance in school is generally deplorable, and he early reveals his strong bent toward the theatre when he is smitten with love for a young actress and spends money on a bouquet of flowers for her. His imitations are full of *unwiderstehlicher Komik,* irresistible to the family as when he imitates the extravagant movement and gestures of an impassioned piano virtuoso; his long anecdotes and stories are wildly entertaining, and at his club he soon becomes a great favorite with his imitations and pointless tales. Yet it is not long before the prevailing laughter seems in danger of being at, rather than with Christian and, where the family is concerned, his lazy indifference to business threatens a hard-won stability and unity. His account of a typical day in his life as a businessman is a burlesque of his brother's serious dedication, and Christian seems never to lose a chance to make fun of business, or indeed work of any kind.

This gradually alienates his brother until what began as a form of harmless and exuberant horseplay becomes a source of estrangement between the brothers, a cause of decline and fall. Thus Christian jokes his life away, and the business is well rid of him when he departs for Hamburg in May 1857. His good-for-nothing cronies come to the station to see him off, amid much reminiscent laughter, presents of flowers and cigars, and a final joke at Christian's own expense. This was the gift of an emblem to decorate his coat lapel, celebrating his exploits in a local brothel. In later years, Christian is still able to entertain the family with wildly extravagant performances, by imitations in numerous languages and dialects, but suddenly breaking off and lapsing into gloomy silence, as if knowing deep within that his play has played out.

The movement of Tony's life from a normally mischievous childhood to a maturity marred by sorrow begins with delightful sympathy and tenderness. Mann's understanding of the children's world, and the aloofness, the detachment of his role as their creator, are joined to form an amusing incongruity between the insignificant smallness of their actions and the children's own belief in their importance. As a little girl Tony becomes the friend and rival of Julchen Hagenström with whom she engages in splendid contests of boasting on the way to school. Julchen's brother Hermann is occasionally pleased to join them, and Tony is soon fascinated by the possible taste of a special kind of roll which Hermann carries in his lunch box. This creation is soft and oval in shape, citrus flavored, and containing currants as well, over which Hermann is pleased to lay slices of tongue or goose-breast.

When Tony longed to have a taste of this exotic combination Hermann of course demanded a price, a kiss in fact, which he then impetuously dared to collect. The ensuing struggle was interrupted by Julchen, who burst forth from behind a tree, tore off Tony's hat, and scratched her cheeks most lamentably. We are told simply that after this event, there was virtually an end to the *Kameradschaft.*

Tony's further behavior leaves much to be desired, given her bold and inquisitive nature, a certain proud and impudent assurance that involves her in various escapades. She goes about the town like a little queen, friendly or cruel, according to her taste or mood. On returning from a sojourn with her mother's family, the Krögers, Tony seems ever more unruly and vain. She is caught reading *Mimili,* a questionable book, and she has been seen out walking alone with a school friend of her brothers'. When this is forbidden, she carries on a secret correspondence in a hollow tree, so that finally at the age of fifteen Tony is placed under close supervision in the boarding school of Fräulein Sesemi Weichbrodt.

So far we are touched and amused as Tony's mischievous young life unfolds, the narration offered in a tone the most delicately comic, as we join in the kindly smile of Tony's creator.

The years wander past, and Tony's generally happy youth remains untroubled, until one lovely afternoon in early summer. As the family sit reading and talking in the garden after their coffee, the servant Anton appears with a calling card on the tea tray, announcing the arrival of one Grünlich, agent. There now appears the first in the series of men in Tony's life who seem at first glance preposterous in manner or behavior yet who in the end make of her life a scene of unhappy waste and loss. Grünlich is a man of medium height in his early thirties with thin, light blond hair and a rosy, smiling face somewhat disfigured by a striking wart on one side of his nose. Although his chin and upperlip are shaven, he wears a set of mutton-chop whiskers or *Favoris,* yellow gold in color.

We should think here of Lucian's suspicion of all conspicuous gravity, especially if it wears a beard; but now we are interested in making Grünlich's acquaintance as he comes forward with an air of submissive amiability. As his character develops we get a sense of one presenting a carefully planned façade, of one serious in business, constantly engaged in energetic activity, the *rastlose Tätigkeit* which he never ceases to emphasize. After professing his industrious zeal in a flourishing business, he expresses admiration for the conspicuous virtues of the Buddenbrook family, for the goodness, Christian virtue, and spirit that constitute his own ideal.

A note of pious intimacy with divine providence now creeps into Grünlich's discourse, and we long to cry out to Tony's unsuspecting parents to beware: to the eye of comic discernment, an explicit religious profession on the surface of any character must imply the opposite deep within. To his piety Grünlich adds the love of flowers, admiration for the beauties of nature, and constant praise of everyone and everything. He makes ingratiating inquiry after each one present and praises Christian's name so as to mention the implied holiness of his own—for Bendix is of course derived from Benedict, a name charged with blessedness and monastic austerity, a name borne by his ancestors of the pastoral calling.

He now inquires after Christian's studies, is delighted to hear that he is reading Cicero, praises the Latin classics and adds a bit of quotation to show his learning—this with a slight cough or clearing of the throat which gives a further impression of carefully rehearsed performance. He finds himself in complete agreement with everything said by Tony's parents, and then in a convenient lull he turns to her as next in line for praise and declares himself carried away by the beauty of her hair in the afternoon sunlight. With elaborate politeness and considerate apprehension lest he be intruding, Grünlich is called again by his *Tätigkeit* to take his departure, but is struck dumb with gratitude on receiving an invitation to take pot-luck with the Buddenbrooks during his stay in the city. The final note of one studying to give a certain impression of himself and his status is carried by a casual reference to the *paar Zimmer* he occupies at his hotel—not just one room but a suite of two as befits his place in the world.

After the stiff formality of his departure, Tony shows her direct insight into Grünlich's mixture of absurdity and selfish calculation. Christian imitates him with devastating effect, since Grünlich is so plainly an abstracted play-actor. But the *Konsul* dismisses their young realism, and draws together the impression that Grünlich had striven so hard to achieve, into a series of four adjectives: Grünlich is a Christian, able, industrious, and cultivated young man, the order and pomp of the German epithets having just the right air of pretentious formality to suit Grünlich's determined hypocrisy.

Despite the studied insult of Tony's reply to him on a chance meeting in the street, he appears for Sunday dinner, rosy and smiling with carefully groomed *Favoris*. He falls upon a magnificently ample six course dinner with enthusiastic praise for every item, being unable in the end to resist asking for a second helping of the pudding. His conversation maintains the ingratiating deference to all and sundry of his first appearance, and he seems undismayed by Tony's studied indifference, her sarcastic response to his advances. He works steadily away at the portrait of himself as an ideal union of Christian goodness, business success, and worldly cultivation. When Tony hears from her father eight days later that Grünlich has asked for her hand in marriage, his image rises before her still in all of its pretentious absurdity, and she declares a scornful refusal.

Grünlich's behavior is studied, careful, calculated; if one is looking for them, the stigmata of Fielding's theory of hypocritical affectation soon emerge. But Grünlich quickly passes beyond any comic tolerance despite the ludicrous effect of his appearance. Still in the impassioned discourse which he delivers to Tony when they are alone, amid its fearful implications for her there intrudes an incongruous note. Her name, he cries, with indelible letters is written on his heart, *"geschrieben."* No, he suddenly corrects himself and says rather *"gegraben,"* that is dug or engraved forgetting that, while this has a more serious meaning on the surface, it suggests burial as well. So the insincerity of a speech which has been clearly memorized and rehearsed for the occasion is exposed.

Tony now finds herself looking closely at his features, as he takes her hands and stares into her eyes: the red face, the wart on his nose, the blue eyes—blue as those of a goose. The very features that on first sight were laughable take on a sinister aspect before Tony's painful aversion. She is left in tearful exhaustion, but Grünlich is not to be denied. When he chooses to interpret Tony's response as a form of encouragement he sends her a ring, with a letter referring to himself in the third person as *"Endesunterfertigter,"* a kind of Micawberesque use of the undersigned in a tone of legal detachment. But when he learns of Tony's affair with young Morten Schwarzkopf, Grünlich hastens to the scene to declare his rights. On first seeing him Morten, like almost everyone else, can barely

keep a straight face before the red, gold-yellow, and blue now so familiar to us.

But there is nothing laughable about the product of Grünlich's appearance, unless it is the autocratic finality of Morten's father, the sudden, pompous, and humorless word with which he puts a lifelong end to Tony's only chance for happiness: it is all a futile childsplay, *"und damit Punktum!"* Later on we cannot help a rueful smile at the engagement itself which lacks the fire and intensity of the proposal; Grünlich is content to seal the engagement with a discreet kiss upon Tony's brow in the company of her parents. A few reserved advances in private complete the courtship, and on his wedding day Grünlich appears with an air of calm possession—his face red, the whiskers groomed, and that little excess of powder visible on the wart of his left nostril. The ceremony proceeds by order and usage, but Grünlich has to clear his throat before saying *ja* to the final question; after this there is a massive consumption of good food, and Tony is doomed.

Her life is unrelieved until the unspeakable villainy of her husband comes to light, and she returns home once more. When their only child is born, a slight dispute as to her name is settled in favor of Grünlich's choice, Erika—a half-comic revelation of the man's pompous autocracy, as if there were any chance of an opinion other than his own prevailing.

Tony's first marriage ends in failure, she returns home with Erika, and assumes her place in the family circle once more. After the death of Uncle Gotthold we read of a family gathering on the traditional Thursday, and of the presence of the three unmarried daughters of Gotthold who are not slow to remark with accustomed sharpness upon any sign of weakness or failure in other members of the family. We become aware of the great distance between harmless comic enjoyment and the cruel mockery of deliberate malice in these bitter creatures who see matter to condemn in everyone down to the innocent little Erika whose growth is held to be retarded and who displays an alarming resemblance to her father, the perfidious Grünlich.

But as the years go on Tony finds life at home monotonous, particularly as the religious obsession of her mother intensifies with age and the daily devotions at home grow ever more fierce and prolonged. Tony endures the exercises as best she can, but one morning a particularly odious hymn, sung with words of embarrassing crudity and unconscious metaphorical absurdity, is too much for her, and she throws the hymn book away out of inner contrition—*"Zerknirschung,"* a delightfully ambiguous word.

Still Tony was compelled to attend the *Jerusalemabend,* a pious exercise established by her mother for the benefit of missionary work abroad. Some twenty ladies, of an age when one is inclined to look about for a secure place in heaven, would gather once a week for the reading of holy hymns and treatises, during which useful handwork would be done, the whole accompanied by delicious helpings of food and drink. The concern for heaven seems to have deepened as the ladies neared the time of entering it, but the enjoyment of good things here and now was not forgotten in the zealous pursuit of salvation and the doing of good works. Mann's ridicule of the entire superstition is here, as if anything could be more absurd than to suppose that heaven was a local habitation containing specific places, like reserved seats in a railroad compartment, the whole indicating the intellectual level of the ladies who were capable of believing it.

This concern for heaven is the more ludicrous in being fairly recent, something not pressing while the ladies were young or unlikely to die, but coming on only now that old age is near, an inconsistency that they were too stupid to see or were afraid to admit.

The commentary on these Jerusalem evenings keeps a tone of amused detachment and delicate mockery, as Mann stays far above his subject and so affords a tolerant smile.

He describes the membership with relish, including a wrinkled little creature named Himmelsbürger, rich in the favor of God and crochet patterns who, being the last of her family, described herself as indeed the last citizen of heaven. We meet as well the two eccentric old maids, the Gerhardt twins with their remarkable union of spiritual knowledge and insight, pious quotations, predictions, and good works. Of these the deaf one, Lea Gerhardt, is official reader to the circle, but to hear herself she must read in a fearful voice, sounding like the wind in a stovepipe to long-suffering ears. Tony's response to Lea's fear lest Satan should devour her is a most earthly question: will she ever become as ugly as these scarecrows?

In time this heavily laden piety is burdensome to the house and family, especially when a great series of pastors and missionaries, in long hair and black clothes, pass through for the collection of money and the consumption of vast quantities of expensive food.

On one occasion Tony could not help playing a joke on one conspicuous consumer to whom she served an uneatable stew. She grumbled audibly at people who eat widows out of house and home, and began to hate these black-clothed gentlemen bitterly. As comic types, these are among the hills of flesh with the massive, tubercular appetites of the pious, recalling Mr. Stiggins of Pickwickian fame and the holy ones of *Bleak House.* As in Tony's first suspicions of Grünlich, the sight of long black garments, solemn faces, and uplifted eyes made her question the virtue within, and inspired the malice of her sarcastic reply to the missionary Jonathan—a man with large, reproachful eyes and sad, low-hanging jowls—who desired to know whether the careful grooming of her forelocks might be consistent with true Christian modesty. Jonathan forgot that in his own Micawberesque baldness he was vulnerable to Tony's rapier question, whether she might beg the pastor to concern himself with his own ringlets?

Her sufferings among the holy guests of her mother allow Mann to display his masterly economy, an infallible deftness of stroke, letting the portrait of a single human being emerge in a few lines, as in Dickens. The triumph of this compression is Pastor Tränen-Trieschke from Berlin, a creation worthy of Boccaccio, Fielding, or Dickens, who appears to us in one supremely vivid paragraph. His nickname comes of a fervent religious emotion causing him to burst into tears in the midst of his sermon every Sunday.

Now he stays with the Buddenbrooks eight or ten days, vies with Klothilde in absorbing enormous meals, conducts pious devotions for the family and, despite the existence of a wife and many children in Berlin, falls in love with the countenance and still blooming figure of Tony. Again, carried away by emotion, the pastor does not weep, but writes a letter that mingles Biblical quotation and remarkably ingratiating tenderness, causing the same to be delivered by Anton to Tony's bedroom.

Rarely must we regret that something is missing from the text in a work by Thomas Mann, the most thorough of writers, concerned to exhaust the whole of every experience before he has done with it. But we now long for a copy of this letter in full, shown quickly to her mother by the indignant Tony. Disillusioned again before the realities of masculine hypocrisy, Tony utters the first of a series of half-comic outcries in which, with the force of a trumpet blast, her bitterness is summarized in the names of the men, mostly swindlers, who have betrayed her. Thus far, only one name compels remembrance, declaring all that she has learned of perfidy and pious hypocrisy is in "Grünlich."

Tony's vigilance against an erring clergy at times leaves us uncertain of her own provocation, as when in her letter from Munich she reports that a high episcopal figure driving by in a coach made eyes at her with the boldness of a young lieutenant. But Tony is not alone in remarking the comic aspect of a minister whose outer performance cannot conceal a falsity within. The one who presides over the christening of little Hanno Buddenbrook is seen through the veiled mockery of Gerda's mysterious eyes, the child's mother. He belongs with the ministerial portraits, among the *schwarze Herrn* of Tony's exposure, presenting one more clash between his ideal and the mechanical manner of his performance.

Mann's touch is infallible when describing a given company assembled for an occasion like the christening of Hanno. With his expert, sure strokes he portrays them as a whole and as individuals, each one singled out from the rest, his character and appearance isolated, the author at once creating and observing in a masterly command of imaginative resources. The concealment of weakness or some unlovely inner reality is impossible before an eye so penetrating and relentless, an intelligence so cool and aloof, a reading of human nature so charged with confident mockery. Now we meet and quickly see to the core, the man Andreas Pringsheim, *pastor marianus.* Although he bears the family name of the author's wife, the name as it comes forth in this company grows ever more telling as Pringsheim's own nature is deftly exposed: it comes to suggest his worldly, unctuous character, that is all things to all men, his ingratiating yet solemnly pious manner, all balance and calculation, the dexterous Capuchin perhaps of Gibbon's phrase.

Meanwhile, however, a new man has come into Tony's life in the person of one Alois Permaneder, at first sight the most Dickensian of the great portrayals in *Buddenbrooks,* an unconsciously headlong character bent only on being himself. Absurd in speech, figure, and action, he is never so wicked as Grünlich, but ends much as he begins—essentially formless, good-natured, and harmless, with a face somewhat like a sea-lion's.

On his first visit from Munich he introduces himself to Tony's mother after apologizing for having no personal card. His voice is loud, his accent crude, the dialect so thick as to be barely comprehensible. His gestures are uninhibited, as of one not used to the reserve and self-possession of formal society. Having a number of nervous tics, he rubs his knees, sighs loudly, and makes wide circular gestures in the air. He seems a kind of preposterous social mistake, something that has been attempted but abandoned before completion as not having quite succeeded. Thus his voice, speech, and behavior are exactly those suggested by his somewhat formless and undisciplined appearance. He is clearly a man who has become what he is absent-mindedly, without thinking about it—his face, figure, voice, and manner all the result of forgetfulness by one who never had realized that there was anything to think about in such matters, to be curbed or adjusted by an outside standard.

When Tony comes in, Permaneder seems unable to stop moving, in contrast to his later *unverdrossenen Seszhaftigkeit,* indefatigable capacity to sit. Now he becomes a violent windmill of motion, gesticulation, and excited comment. When he is invited to stay for refreshments he accepts almost before the invitation is complete, as if expecting it; he is so fat that he must sit some distance from the table, but he finds himself very comfortable and soon takes out a huge pipe of fearful steam power that rapidly fills the room with smoke. His manner, almost incomprehensible speech, a certain formlessness of behavior, and a depressing amiability continue to astonish.

At last, after three hours, he begins to take his departure. The measure of his vulgarity is seen again in the spontaneous acceptance of a polite invitation to stay with the family rather than at his modest hotel; he will have his baggage sent 'round directly and will himself return when his business is transacted. It is now clear that the house and family are to be spared nothing; shaking his head and muttering grotesquely phrased compliments to Tony, Permaneder finally takes his clumsy departure.

When he moves into the house the already conspicuous qualities of this loud, shapeless, and incomprehensible provincial become fixed and obvious in everyone's view. To his unwearied stationariness he adds a habit of seeming to groan, not out of dismay but from an intensely deepening comfort and sense of smug well-being. Like some of the ecclesiastical visitors, he stays on in the house long after his business seems to be completed. He is clearly alien to the world of this patrician merchant family, yet he seems harmless, with none of the hypocritical knavery of his predecessor in Tony's life.

Events take their course and, after her second marriage, Tony goes to live with Permaneder in Munich. He soon discloses a variety of personal weaknesses that are not unanticipated and though he is still no villainous Grünlich, he shows a tendency to grumble and, on the other side of his *Formlosigkeit* and undisciplined amiability, an obstinate wilfulness, becoming an irresponsible self-indulgence. His evenings pass in the *Hofbräuhaus* drinking and playing cards with his cronies. He abandons all pretense of regular employment, deciding to live on Tony's dowry and his own property. Permaneder thus makes an undignified surrender and loses all sense of obligation to Tony and her family.

She now faces a life of hopeless monotony, of a depressing emptiness and dullness as her husband goes his own way, leaving her as much a stranger in his world as he was in hers. The crude lack of style might have been endurable, if Tony's last hope had not died with the loss of her new child, a girl that barely survives her birth.

Not surprisingly, considering the generally good-natured, but dull-witted fatalism with which Permaneder accepts the loss of his child, he returns after two or three days to his established way of life and his regular three pints at the *Wirtshaus* of an evening, showing the amiable, but thin, unsubstantial quality of his nature. Beyond this, however, he is guilty of a degree of infidelity revealed late one night when Tony is awakened by some unmistakable sounds on the stairway near her bedroom. A certain rustling, creaking, hoarse giggling, and scuffling place the matter beyond doubt, and Tony suddenly bursts upon Herr Permaneder attempting to kiss and embrace Babette, the cook, she meanwhile resisting his advances with something less than entire success.

Despite the painful implications of the scene in Tony's life, her agonized account of it seems irresistibly comic. The pomp and abstractness of the language make the events related appear trivial. A highly formal mode of discourse recounts something of little consequence, establishing the incongruity on which so much of the comic experience depends. Permaneder's antics become absurd when told so pompously by the narrator and received so violently and tragically by Tony.

At the moment of discovery, Babette profanely brings forth something like *"Jessas, Maria und Joseph,"* while Permaneder can do nothing but repeat the same after her in his consternation, *"Jessas, Maria und Joseph,"* as she disappears. This cry for succor to the holy family is at once an exclamation of fear, surprise, and dismay together with an anguished appeal for help from heavenly powers, all earthly assistance being now clearly in vain, even if at hand.

We must, to be sure, sympathize with Tony's fearful anguish and the bitter end to her last hope for personal happiness, yet the sudden intrusion of *"Jessas, Maria und Joseph"* is absurdly comic. Permaneder's first speech to the family had contained this peculiar dialect spelling, *Jessas,* and as now employed the change from "Jesus" suggests either another person than the revered Jesus of Christian tradition, his family sanctified by goodness that would never stoop to such behavior as that now exposed—or it implies a different version of Jesus, a person with a name spelled a little differently, to identify one called on for aid by evil-doers in their moments of crisis or exposure. Reeking now of alcohol after a long celebration of a friend's name day, Permaneder offers lame excuses to Tony sobbing on her bed, his halting dialect even more than ever preposterous under these conditions as a form of speech to convey meaning.

Now Tony's whole revulsion of feeling against her husband gets the better of her; things are said on both sides from which there can be no retreat or recovery, which no apology or contrition can hope to absolve. In another of the long dialogs between Tony and her brother Tom which carry so much of importance in the work as a whole, he pleads with her to take a dispassionate view of the affair. Yet Grünlich marries Tony to pay his debts, Permaneder to avoid work: both marry for money and neither loves her. Everything about them seems at first ridiculous, but they end as serious elements in the decline of the family.

But Tom, while willing to concede the impropriety, summarizes the harmless nature of Permaneder's offense: an excusable or at least understandable weakness to be forgiven. Charging that Tony does not take the matter comically enough, he tries to restore Permaneder to the comic tone and condition once more, wherein as throughout these readings so far, his weaknesses are seen for what they are but are accepted with a silent, kindly smile. Thus if Tony will be rather amused than indignant, she may even draw closer to her husband after all. He has made himself ridiculous, but if Tony will see this with the eye of comic tolerance rather than retributive justice, she will find her position happier than ever.

But she is adamant, insisting on divorce, and so the failure of her comic sense, of growing to maturity as Tom sees it, insures the failure of her life. This is a bagatelle and she ought to be relieved that it is nothing worse, yet she responds with bitter tears instead of shouting in relieved laughter. Her final outburst of enraged sensibility is not to be answered; her feelings pour out in a torrent of language before which the forms of dispassionate reason, of detached irony, are helpless. This too must then run its course, and at almost the exact half point of the book Tom is left alone to sustain the family's honor.

Alas, poor Tony, the narrator cries, as her life like the great book that contains her moves from a beginning in happy laughter to a scene of tearful mourning. Yet she remains half comic in her incongruous ideas, as Erich Heller says, something of a child without the knowledge of life she constantly professes to have learned. Her refrain of sorrow over what life has done to her, and what this has taught her of the earnestness of existence, has an air of self-conscious pride and satisfaction. She is naively deceived as to her own nature and survives all that fate can do against her, being in fact a little too stupid to realize the meaning of it.

Does she really believe all her outcries, assertions of betrayal and suffering? It seems not, and so despite bravery and pride, she remains, in A. F. B. Clark's view, a muddle-headed failure. She sees nothing laughable in her lists of the odious men who have offended her—lists that begin with Grünlich alone and steadily increase in length as the number of *Filous* grows. Like the blasts of a trumpet, the litany of ecclesiastical hypocrites and worldly knaves sounds forth, the identity of her two husbands given as before, during and after marriage simply in their last names: *"Tränen-Trieschke . . . Grünlich! Permaneder! Tiburtius! Weinschenk! Hagenströms! . . . Was für Filous, Thomas."*

A parcel of rogues in varying degrees perhaps, yet all beginning laughably, they come each to play his role in the sombre movement of the story and become one with its sorrow. One after another the comic elements move toward the doom that closes in upon the novel from all sides—symbolized in the mysterious, blue-tinted shadows about the eyes of Gerda and her only son. As Grünlich and Permaneder are lost in the sad failure of Tony's life, so we shall find the absurd schoolteachers, their efforts at formal education, and all that is done in the name of health and well-being, to lose itself, obscurely and uselessly in the pathetic end of Hanno Buddenbrook. (pp. 194-216)

Bernard N. Schilling, " 'Tränen-Trieschke . . . Grünlich . . . Permaneder'," in his The Comic Spirit: Boccaccio to Thomas Mann, Wayne State University Press, 1965, pp. 194-216.

RONALD GRAY (essay date 1965)

[*Gray is an English educator and critic specializing in German literature. In the following excerpt, he discusses Mann's use of irony, examining in particular the narrator's tone toward the characters and their actions, and contends that Mann constructed aspects of the plot to support the theories of Schopenhauer and Nietzsche.*]

[*Buddenbrooks*] is, as the sub-title indicates, the story of the "decline of a family," and its structure seems, accordingly, to outline an increasing debility. At the beginning there is the robust generation represented by the elder Johann Buddenbrook, untroubled by scruples, unreflecting, committed to what has been called "blind living," and standing no doubt for what Professor Heller calls, in the Schopenhauerian sense, "the Will in its perfect integrity" [see excerpt dated

1958]. With each successive generation, reflectiveness becomes greater: the younger Johann, his son Thomas and his grandson Hanno become increasingly self-conscious, increasingly hampered by doubts and conscientious objections to the harsh methods of the business-world. The blind, irresistible urge which, according to Schopenhauer, the Will is—self-seeking, power-grasping and brutal—is increasingly questioned and criticized, and with this comes an increasing inability to conduct the affairs of the family business with the calm efficiency of its earlier heads. Together with moral scruples goes a leaning towards art: Thomas marries the musically inclined Gerda, and at length the line dies out with the most artistically gifted of them all, the boy Hanno.

The structure of decline looks obvious enough. Yet, if we look more closely, we may hesitate to place the elder Johann at the upper end of a descending scale. We are told, quite early on, that his face is "incapable of expressing malice," and there is indeed some idealization of his character. Yet, as the story unfolds, we perceive that the Buddenbrook ideal is nakedly egocentric: it is to "exploit the situation without shame," to jib at nothing that will maintain the family's position in society. The development is very largely the story of the successive marriages of convenience through which, to the complete disregard of individual happiness, this is attempted. And thus, if there is a decline, it is a decline from a materialistic bonhomie, a conscienceless devotion to money-making, towards a moral awareness such as Thomas and Hanno have. From a different point of view it might be called an ascent, for the male line does end, even though disastrously, in the person of a boy who is perhaps a musical genius.

With all this in mind, it is tempting to regard the sub-title as itself a piece of irony. We are surely not meant, it may be argued, to regard the elder Johann as the summit from which the rest of the family declines. To make this assumption is, however, to . . . assume a morality which the novel contradicts, and to ignore the signs that Mann invites such a reading only to "transcend" it, that he registers awareness of immorality only as a preliminary to "affirming" it.

That this is so—or, to be more accurate, that Mann wrote almost the whole of the novel in terms of such "transcending"—may be partly seen from the very fact of the elder Johann's being idealized. We see him at the beginning of the story as a figure of Pickwickian geniality: "His round, rosy, benevolent face, which could express no malice, no matter how hard he tried, was set in a frame of snow-white powdered hair, and the suggestion of a pigtail fell over the broad collar of his mouse-coloured coat." The affectionately drawn picture is evidently meant to establish him in our minds as a benevolent old gentleman who will stand as a contrast, throughout the work, with the devious and increasingly self-torturing figures of his descendants. "His mind," as Professor Heller says, "is precisely what Schopenhauer says it [the will] is in its simple and harmonious adjustment to the needs of the Will . . . his will is wonderfully intact . . . he is, in so far as this state of innocence is attainable at all within the human species, that 'perfect objectivation of the Will' and its 'perfect enjoyment of itself' which Schopenhauer discerns in Nature." In other words, he is the Will in its perfectly unreflective state, a man unconcerned with his own motives or with anything else but the here and now: "he stood with both feet firmly planted in the present." However, Professor Heller's phrase, "in so far as this state of innocence is attainable at all within the human species," betrays some awareness of what

I have referred to as an idealization. We are, in fact, asked to believe that such a state of unreflecting innocence is a possibility for a business man of seventy in the year 1835, that the elder Johann can conduct his business without the least trace of scruple and yet somehow still remain an honest citizen. And even if this possibility be granted, we find, when we look at the passages which treat of Johann, nothing at all about his business methods. We are left as much in ignorance of them as we are of the life of Christian Buddenbrook's wife—the assumption is made that all was well with them, but we never learn the details. (Indeed, what we do see of the elder Johann could contradict even the statement that his face is incapable of expressing malice, for the first expression we see on it is a snigger—"sein helles, verkniffenes Kichern"—at his granddaughter's recital of the catechism.) This absence of information, in view of the course taken by the rest of the novel, is a clear indication of Mann's intention. We are meant to accept the elder Johann as a paragon, and the slurring over of those difficulties which would present themselves if we looked more closely is a mark of Mann's sympathy with the ideal.

The consequences of the idealization are seen in the passage, much later on, when Johann's grandson Thomas is confronted with the problem of whether or not to buy the Pöppenrade harvest "in the blade." This is presented as a moral issue for Thomas: on first hearing of the deal he declares that only a cut-throat would take it up, and it is not until he realizes the perilous financial position of his own business that he begins to regard it as a serious possibility. Thereupon, the issue becomes for him a matter of proving himself a man unhampered by moral scruples, which he can only do, as it turns out, by buying the harvest at a bargain price, ruthlessly profiting from its owner's misfortune. "Was he, Thomas Buddenbrook, a businessman, a man of untrammelled action, or was he a contemplative, riddled with scruples? . . . Did Thomas Buddenbrook, like his forefathers, stand firmly with his two feet in face of this hard practicality of life?" The last phrase recalls that used of the elder Johann, "with both feet firmly planted in the present," and suggests that the grandfather at least would not have been troubled as Thomas is: that he would have regarded the infliction of harsh conditions as a matter of course, "not as harshness, but as something to be taken for granted." And as the inner argument develops, Thomas seems to come to that conclusion: "Would his father, his grandfather, his greatgrandfather have bought the Pöppenrade harvest in the blade? . . . No matter! . . . No matter! . . . The thing was that they were practical men, more naturally, more vigorously, more impeccably practical than himself, that was the point!"

Now it is true that Thomas was convinced, on first hearing of the deal, that nothing of the kind had ever been accepted by the Buddenbrooks for a hundred years. On the other hand, the firm has never been in the financial difficulties it faces now. What would in fact have been the decision in the present circumstances of the elder Johann? The answer given here— "No matter!"—evades this point, yet the issue remains. Would he have rejected the deal, and if he had done so, would he not have needed to reflect, to take a moral decision? Or would he have regarded the harshness as a matter of course, as somehow natural, in which case the genial picture of him presented in the opening pages was evidently misleading? We have nothing to go by. The earlier generations were, in some unexplained way, untroubled by such problems, and this is all we may know. The episode itself, however, is evidently

constructed so as to suggest that it is precisely because Thomas has scruples that he finally accepts the deal. He accepts it in order to prove to himself that he is a ruthless businessman, and thus makes his action not only harsh but self-conscious and shabby.

If we bear in mind the way in which Weinschenk's deliberate fraud is defended, and his loss of self-esteem deplored, it must appear that the "harvest" episode is included as an illustration of the evil of hesitant self-consciousness, an illustration somewhat weakened, it is true, by the evasiveness about the elder Johann. This interpretation, one affecting the whole structure and tendency of the novel, is borne out by reference to the climactic episode, that in which Thomas is momentarily caught up in a new vision of the world, as a result of his reading a philosophical work generally assumed to be the principal work of Schopenhauer (the book is never named). It is a matter of dispute whether this passage reflects Mann's own view or not. Although Mann did, by his own account, read Schopenhauer while writing the novel, and was overwhelmed by him in much the same way as his namesake Thomas, it is contended by Professor Pascal, in company with Georg Lukács, that the account in the novel is presented ironically. (Henry Hatfield, on the other hand, takes it straightforwardly [see excerpt dated 1951].) "Schopenhauer," writes Pascal, "does not appear here as the philosophy of the novel; it is only the outlook of this particular man in his particular situation." Now this is true enough, in that what Thomas derives from Schopenhauer is not at all like the thought of the philosopher. It is *not* true, in that Thomas's ideas fit very closely into the framework of the novel thus far hinted at: the framework within which unreflecting self-assertion is preferred to self-doubting.

First, it is not the case that Thomas "gratefully accepts" the doctrine "that life is suffering and that it is impossible to conquer life's difficulties except by withdrawing from the struggle into contemplation." His ideas have a much more Nietzschean ring; they are Schopenhauerian only in the sense of that "affirmation of the Will" which Schopenhauer defined but rejected.

> Wo ich sein werde, wenn ich tot bin? Aber es ist so klar, so leuchtend klar, so überwältigend einfach! In allen Denen werde ich sein, die je und je Ich gesagt haben, sagen und sagen werden: *besonders aber in Denen, die es voller, kräftiger, fröhlicher sagen.* . . .
>
> Irgendwo in der Welt wächst ein Knabe auf, gut ausgerüstet und wohlgelungen, begabt, seine Fähigkeiten zu entwickeln, gerade gewachsen und ungetrübt, rein, grausam und munter, einer von diesen Menschen, deren Anblick das Glück der Glücklichen erhöht und die Unglücklichen zur Verzweiflung treibt:—Das ist mein Sohn. *Das bin ich,* bald . . .bald . . . sobald der Tod mich von dem armseligen Wahne befreit, ich sei nicht sowohl er wie ich. . . .
>
> (Where shall I be when I am dead? Ah, it is so brilliantly clear, so overwhelmingly simple! I shall be in all those who have ever, do ever, or ever shall say 'I'—*especially, however, in all those who say it most fully, potently, and gladly!*
>
> Somewhere in the world a child is growing up, strong, well-grown, adequate, able to develop its powers, gifted, untroubled, pure, cruel and joyous, one of those beings whose glance heightens the joy

of the joyous and drives the unhappy to despair. He
is my son. *He is I, myself,* soon, soon; as soon as
Death frees me from the wretched delusion that I
am not he as well as myself.)

This is, taken straightforwardly, a reversion of Thomas's attitude to that of the ruthless businessmen he admires, although
on a different plane. They stand, so to speak, at the beginning
of the cycle, unreflective in their harshness, "ungetrübt" as
the boy is in this vision. But while they are unaware of the
possibility of moral criticism, Thomas is aware of it and passes on to an affirmation of selfhood which includes it. Nor does
he merely imagine this as the thought of a state "after death,"
as Professor Pascal claims; he enjoys this state now:

> Und während er es nun begreifen und erkennen
> durfte—nicht in Worten und aufeinander folgen-
> den Gedanken, sondern in plötzlichen, beseligen-
> den Erhellungen seines Inneren—*war er schon frei,*
> *war er ganz eigentlich schon erlöst* und aller natür-
> lichen wie künstlichen Schranken und Bande
> entledigt.

> (And in that he could now understand and recog-
> nize—not in words and consecutive thoughts, but
> in sudden rapturous illuminations of his inmost
> being—he was already free, actually released and
> free of all natural as well as artificial limitations.)

His release into self-identification with those who affirm their
egos, the healthy and cruel (the standard translation modifies
"grausam" into "relentless"), the happy few who drive the
unhappy to despair—is realized here and now, within his lifetime. (The definiteness of this is scarcely qualified at all by
the slightly odd construction with "während." At the same
time, it is a self-identification with the ideal represented by
his grandfather Johann, for while Johann stood "with both
feet in the present," Thomas now realizes that there exists
"nur eine unendliche Gegenwart," an endless present in
which he himself is now able to participate. The wheel has
come round full circle. What began, in Schopenhauerian
terms, as the Will in its perfect integrity, has now become
aware of itself in its own reflection, or "Vorstellung": it has
recognized its own creativity, vitality, cruelty and harshness,
and has resolved not to take the self-annihilating course advocated by Schopenhauer but the self-affirming one advocated
by Nietzsche. Thomas, could he remain at this level of vision,
could become as resolute and as unhampered by scruples as
his grandfather was. The sole difference between them is that
the grandson is aware, and reflects the Will perfectly in his
"Vorstellung," while the grandfather is unaware and simply
is the Will, undivided and unconscious, having no "Vorstellung" as yet. For a moment, the novel reaches a point where,
if we could concede its assumptions, the decline might be
halted.

Thomas, however, does not live up to his insight. Next day,
he is already in doubt whether it was valid; his "bürgerlich"
(that is, here, his convention-regarding) instincts rebel, and
he fears to appear ridiculous. Routine business takes his attention, and he never finishes the book to which the insight
was owed. Should we, then, regard the episode as ironically
narrated? Does Mann stand outside it, as Pascal suggests he
does? "When we read that [Thomas] relapses into his old
bourgeois habits, after 'his hands had reached out towards exalted and ultimate truths,' we do not take these last words as
an objective assessment of Schopenhauer, but ironically as
the illusion of this worn-out man." Is that the case?

If it were, we should expect some indication from Mann that
he means to be so read, but there is none. On the contrary,
we learn that Thomas "sinks back" from the "exalted" truths
into belief in those Christian concepts and images in which
he had been brought up. These, for their part, are quite decidedly satirized:

> Er ging umher und erinnerte sich des einigen und
> persönlichen Gottes, des Vaters der Mensch-
> enkinder, der einen persönlichen Teil seines Selbst
> auf die Erde entsandt hatte, damit er für uns leide
> und blute, der am jüngsten Tage Gericht halten
> würde, und zu dessen Füßen die Gerechten im
> Laufe der dann ihren Anfang nehmenden Ewigkeit
> für die Kümmernisse dieses Jammertales ent-
> schädigt werden würden. . . . Dieser ganzen, ein
> wenig unklaren und ein wenig absurden Geschi-
> chte, die aber kein Verständnis, sondern nur ge-
> horsamen Glauben beanspruchte, und die in
> feststehenden und kindlichen Worten zur Hand
> sein würde, wenn die letzten Ängste kamen. . . .
> Wirklich?

> (He went about recalling that One, personal God,
> the Father of all human beings, who had sent a per-
> sonal part of Himself upon earth to suffer and bleed
> for our sins, and who, on the final day, would come
> to judge the quick and the dead; at whose feet the
> justified, in the course of the eternity then begin-
> ning, would be recompensed for the sorrows they
> had borne in this vale of tears. Yes, he strove to sub-
> scribe to the whole somewhat confused absurd
> story, which required no intelligence, only obedient
> credulity; and which, when the last anguish
> came, would sustain one in a firm and childlike
> faith. . . . Really?)

The mocking note is unmistakable here and even overdone:
the mere thought of Christianity releases it. But if we look
for this mockery in the passage of Thomas's vision we shall
find not a word or a construction hinting at irony. It is rather,
perhaps, our own sense of the absurdity of these ideas in a
man like Thomas Buddenbrook which makes us hesitate to
believe that they can be seriously meant. If, in fact, Mann is
ironically detached, from what viewpoint does he view that
episode? It cannot be from a Christian one, so much is evident. It can scarcely be from a Nietzschean one, and there is
no sign of irony here from a Schopenhauerian one. The biting
attack implicit in our second passage is simply not conveyed
by the first at all. Thus once again, the supposition that Mann
somehow stands on both sides will not really help. The novel
can only be interpreted in terms of traditional or Christian
concepts of morality by refusing to take any sentence or episode in it as meaning what it appears to mean, and supposing
that the opposite is intended. But, taking it as a whole or in
its parts, the novel lends no support to such a reading.

There can be no doubt that Mann's own enthusiastic reception of Schopenhauer is reflected in his namesake Thomas's
words, or that it is presented as a solution by which the character in the novel fails to profit. Everything points to this: the
personal experience, the italicizing of the important words
(used similarly in *Der Zauberberg*), the unambiguous delight
with which the revelation is narrated, whether in Thomas's
own words or the narrator's. Indeed Thomas is, in Mann's
own words, his "Doppelgänger" and a "man after my own
heart." And yet there is still a forced solemnity, suggesting
not irony but rather a certain self-consciousness, a desire to
draw attention to the impressiveness of the revelation, rather

than to let it impress by its own quality. The scene opens with Thomas reclining on his back and gazing into darkness, and at once the vision begins:

> Und siehe da: plötzlich war es, wie wenn die Finsternis vor seinen Augen zerrisse, wie wenn die sammtne Wand der Nacht sich klaffend teilte und eine unermeßlich tiefe, eine ewige Fernsicht von Licht enthüllte.
>
> (And behold, suddenly it was as though the darkness were rent from before his eyes, as if the velvet wall of night parted wide and disclosed an immeasurable boundless prospect of light.)

The first words, "And behold," strain after an effect; they lend a magisterial note which, far from being ironical, seeks to induce a reverent attentiveness and yet, by being an archaism, fails to do so. This quasi-biblical note is heard again in the course of this section:

> Ende und Auflösung? Dreimal erbarmungswürdig Jeder, der diese nichtigen Begriffe als Schrecknisse empfand!
>
> (End, dissolution? Thrice pitiable he who felt such vanities as terrors!)

The high-flown expression, so strange in the mouth of Thomas Buddenbrook, reveals the spurious element of self-conscious pathos in him at this moment, which recurs from time to time:

> In meinem Sohne habe ich fortzuleben gehofft? In einer noch ängstlicheren, schwächeren, schwankenderen Persönlichkeit? Kindische, irregeführte Torheit!
>
> (Have I hoped to live on in my son? In a personality yet more feeble, flickering and timorous than my own? Childish, deluded folly!)
>
> Habe ich je das Leben gehaßt, dies reine, grausame und starke Leben? Torheit und Mißverständnis!
>
> (Have I ever hated life? pure, cruel, stark life? Folly and misunderstanding!)

These exalted linguistic gestures of refusal, thrusting away the offending thought as it were with a grand sweep of the hand and arm, have something theatrical about them: they belong to the melodrama of Schiller's stage, rather than to the world of either Thomas Buddenbrook or religious enlightenment. Yet our attention is not drawn to them, and when the narrator himself takes up the thread we have the impression that all this is approved. That is, if we can define at all closely when the thoughts are meant to be Thomas's and when the narrator's: the passage moves frequently from the first person to indirect speech and then back to a present tense which can sometimes seem to be a general statement by either Thomas.

Perhaps, however, the theatrical gestures are themselves an indication of Mann's ironical standpoint? We may do him wrong to impute to him unawareness of what we perceive ourselves, and should rather suppose that he is at least as aware of such things as we claim to be? There is some weight to this argument, but not enough to counterbalance the impression formed by the passage as a whole. For the "philosophical" outlook expressed in it (the "Weltanschauung," rather) is highly paradoxical, not to say contradictory. On the one hand, Thomas Buddenbrook welcomes death, declares that every man is "a mistake and a blunder," that death is

"the correction of a lamentable error"—namely the error of ever having been born at all. On the other hand, he rejoices at the thought "I shall live," and affirms that he has never hated life, but rather hated himself for not being able to endure it. The transformation he envisages after death is not a transformation into a superhuman, angelic, or saintlike state, but into the form of all those who are glad to be themselves in this present life, and he quickly moves from this thought to the thought that he himself can welcome this present, mortal life, as it is, without change, in a mood akin to Nietzsche's in his teaching of the "Eternal Recurrence." Yet Thomas has no sooner realized his *present* freedom from "all natural as well as artificial limitations," when he speaks of the liberation from such bonds which *death* promises to bring. All this may be the paradoxical kind of utterance which goes with most forms of religious belief: it would take us too far afield to examine the pros and cons of that. Yet it is at least as true to say of it that it is "a little unclear" and "a little absurd," and that it does not demand "understanding," as it is to use these words of the version of Christian belief presented by Mann immediately after Thomas's vision. The point is, the words are not used, nor anything like them. The rational criteria advanced against Thomas's adherence to Christianity, and the condescending, even sneering, tone in which these are presented, are not used against Thomas's vision. We must surely conclude, then, that the vision is sincerely and straightforwardly intended to occupy the place in the structure of the novel we have assigned to it.

These are the terms with which the novel operates: an unreflectiveness, which involves harshness and brutality as well as tolerance, but is unaware of itself; reflectiveness, which rejects all forms of harshness but thereby makes itself incapable of living; or a kind of second innocence, the "miracle of innocence regained" as it is called in *Der Tod in Venedig,* which passes through reflectiveness, through the moral world of "Vorstellung," to a paradoxically conscious acceptance of the first attitude. No other moral terms are taken into account: there is no reference, for instance, to the parallel Christian concept of not letting the right hand know what the left hand is doing, which teaches a similar unawareness without forsaking the distinction between good and evil, or to the possibility of discrimination, rejecting certain actions in the name of morality without becoming thereby unfit to live. The concepts of the novel are extreme, and each development takes place within the confines of a rigid duality.

To say this, however, is not to exhaust the implications of the novel. Mann operates with these concepts; they have the consequences and the implications we have seen, and yet he does stand, in a special sense, outside them, and is in a certain way their seismograph. Nothing shows this so well as the episodes concerned with the youthful Hanno at the end of the novel. In Hanno, the male line of the Buddenbrooks dies out. His moral opposition to the harshness of business life is represented as part of his life-denying frame of mind, leaving him defenceless against the typhus which kills him. Before he dies, however, Hanno spends an afternoon at the piano, playing an improvisation which is in fact a rehearsal of all the themes of the novel, as though he were aware of the essential meaning of all that has gone on earlier, before his birth. To read the account of this improvisation is thus both to see the novel as it were in microcosmic form, and to realize the extent of Mann's self-distancing from it.

The playing begins with a fragment of a mere bar and a half, a motif which is soon repeated in the bass as though meant to be orchestrated for trombones, then again in the treble, mysteriously and yearningly, and then develops into a series of rapid passages "torn by shrieks like a soul in unrest and tormented by some knowledge it possesses and cannot conceal"; this section ends with victory over the expressed disquiet in the form of a "contrite, childishly imploring chorale"—"a sort of ecclesiastical cadence."

It soon becomes clear that the disquiet is a reflection of Hanno's experience of the world, which he attempts to assuage with music in the style of Bach. (Later, he turns to Wagnerian music, reminding us of the discussion of the "new morality" of Wagner earlier in the novel.) What, then, is the motif itself? It is first described as "*ein Nichts* [a trifle], das Bruchstück einer *nicht vorhandenen* Melodie [a fragment of a non-existent melody]"; when it is repeated in the bass, however, it is "as the *source* and fount of all that was to come, as though it were to be announced in imperious unison by a burst of trombones." We are surely invited, then, to see it as a representation in music of the Will, in a Schopenhauerian sense, that Will which was for Schopenhauer precisely "ein Nichts" and at the same time the origin of all things. It is also, in terms of the novel, the beginning, the symbol of the perfect integrity of the Will seen in the elder Johann. At the same time, it is the Will in its inevitable decline: in the treble it "proved to consist essentially of a yearning and painful *sinking* from one key into another"—it has all the ambivalence of self-assertion and decline which we have seen running through the novel. The first section ends with an attempt at quelling the expressed emotions by traditional, Christian music: with a chorale.

After a pause, however, the first motif reasserts itself: "a paltry invention, a figure either stupid or mysterious," as it is now described. Why "dumm"; why "stupid" as an alternative to "mysterious"? Surely because the Will is ultimately to come full circle. It begins as unreflective living, as the vitality of, amongst others, a Weinschenk, and returns to affirm that vitality. Mann is as aware as Tonio Kröger will be in his later story, of "life in all its seductive banality," yet his solution never looks beyond this banality, always comes back to asserting its value. The motif, then, is stupid in so far as it stands for banal, unreflective, untransfigured life, and yet may be mysterious in so far as the secret key to living is to "affirm" that life, still untransfigured. The banality remains banality and yet is accepted.

The difficulties inherent in such an attitude, if they are not already obvious enough, are brought out by the passage in which Hanno attempts a new theme, "a bold improvisation, a sort of lively, stormy hunting-song." With this he seeks to ignore the banality, to rejoice unfeignedly—"but there was no joy in it; its note was one of defiant despair. Signals sounded through it; yet they were not only signals but cries of fear . . ."—his moral consciousness will not let him proceed. Yet he is determined to triumph, and with this determination the Wagnerian music first makes its appearance: the notes begin to suggest the killing of dragons, the striding of Siegfried through the flames surrounding Brünnhilde. From here onwards, although the Christian music makes an ineffective attempt to reassert itself, there is a struggle to accept ambiguity. The first motif is heard again, its earlier dual aspect now pushed to extremes, if not developed out of all recognition: it appears now as "a yelling laugh," or as "an ineffably sweet promise," as though it were capable of being at one and the

same time a source of hellish mockery and of heavenly bliss, like the music of Adrian Leverkühn in *Doktor Faustus,* or like the eyes of Goethe in *Lotte in Weimar.* The meaning here is surely that the motif, the Will, both mocks at human inadequacy and promises bliss as the reward for accepting it joyfully, and yet that the bliss is inseparable from the mockery, that the two must go together. We have heard something like the "yelling laugh"—or at any rate a sneer—in the tone of Mann's description of Christian Buddenbrook and of the personal appearance of Weinschenk, and have seen that we must attribute this tone to the author rather than to the upholders of conventional morality. We have also seen how he welcomes people like Christian's wife, and Weinschenk as he was before prison crushed his spirit as well as his own self: in the acceptance of these lies the bliss—in fact for Tonio Kröger such acceptance of the "Bürger" will be akin to Christian love at its highest. For Hanno, however, this dual mood is still hard to accept, as it still was for Thomas Buddenbrook before his vision.

Not until the end of the improvisation does the acceptance come, and when it does so, it is with all the marks of a solution and a resolution of Hanno's disquiet. "The resolution, the redemption, the complete fulfilment—a chorus of jubilation burst forth"—yet hardly has it announced itself in harmonious tones than it slips into another harmony—"it was the motif, the first motif that sounded out!" Here, surely, is not only the discovery of Brünnhilde by Siegfried (we are told that it is as though walls of flame were sinking down), but also the moment of Thomas's vision, reflected in music. Just as Thomas returned momentarily to the spirit of his grandfather Johann, to the unreflective integrity of the Will at a stage where it has passed through self-knowledge, so in the music the moment of solution is the moment of return to the first motif. The motif has, it is true, been present throughout, with a kind of symbolical omnipresence, and yet the triumph consists in the return of the motif in an even more marked form.

In the final "untrammelled orgy" of sound, however, the duality still continues: it is not transcended in some higher unity, if that were possible.

> Es lag etwas Brutales und Stumpfsinniges, und zugleich etwas asketisch Religiöses, etwas wie Glaube und Selbstaufgabe in dem fanatischen Cultus dieses Nichts, dieses Stücks Melodie, dieser kurzen, kindischen, harmonischen Erfindung von anderthalb Takten . . . etwas Lasterhaftes in der Maßlosigkeit und Unersättlichkeit, mit der sie genossen und ausgebeutet wurde, und etwas cynisch Verzweifeltes, etwas wie Wille zu Wonne und Untergang in der Gier, mit der die letzte Süßigkeit aus ihr gesogen wurde, bis zur Erschöpfung, bis zum Ekel und Überdruß, bis endlich, endlich in Ermattung nach allen Ausschweifungen ein langes, leises Arpeggio in *moll* hinrieselte, um einen Ton emporstieg, sich in *dur* auflöste und mit einem wehmütigen Zögern erstarb.

> (The fanatical worship of this worthless trifle, this scrap of melody, this brief, childish harmonic invention only a bar and a half in length, had about it something brutal and stupid, and at the same time something ascetic and religious—something much resembling faith and renunciation. There was a quality of the perverse in the insatiability with which it was produced and revelled in: there was a sort of cynical despair; there was something like a longing for joy, a yielding to desire, in the way the

last drop of sweetness was, as it were, extracted from the melody, till exhaustion, disgust, and satiety supervened. Then, at last; at last, in the weariness after excess, a long, soft arpeggio in the minor trickled through, mounted a tone, resolved itself in the major, and died in mournful lingering away.)

The contrasted opposites, brutality and asceticism, faith and despair, stand side by side. If this is truly meant for a resolution, as it is said to be—and there is in all this as little evidence of irony as there is in the account of Thomas's vision—we are struck by the dichotomies rather than by their fusion. Yet the sexual overtones which this last passage certainly carries give us some reason to wonder just what Mann was really about. He can scarcely have been unaware of them. In fact, the scrap of dialogue between Hanno and his school-friend Kai shortly before the improvisation passage seems designed to prepare our minds for these overtones. Hanno has just confessed that he will probably "play" this afternoon, and the word is given a special sense since he adds that he ought really to practise his *études* and sonatas and then stop—the playing of these is not what he means. Kai's reply can clearly still refer to the improvisation, and yet may be ambiguous:

> "I know what you mean," said Kai after a bit, and then neither of the lads spoke again.

> They were both at the same difficult age. Kai's face burned, and he cast down his eyes, though without lowering his head. Hanno looked pale and terribly serious; his eyes had clouded over and he kept giving sideways glances.

The shamefacedness is oddly inapposite if only the improvisation is meant, and seems to be linked with Hanno's secretiveness before he seats himself at the piano: he suddenly steps to the French windows and roughly draws the curtains, leaving the room in a yellow half-light. All this lends a suggestive note, so that the music becomes representative not only of a "Weltanschauung" and of the course of the novel, but also of a perverse sexuality. The "first motif" becomes phallic, and phrases such as "source and fount of all that was to come," "this short, childish, harmonious invention," "this stupid or mysterious figure," "under Hanno's labouring fingers," "a swelling, a long, irresistible mounting," "And it came; it could no longer be kept back," "it came as though curtains were rent apart," "complete fulfilment burst forth," "with all the bursting, foaming, dripping magnificence," "the last drop of sweetness," "exhaustion, disgust and satiety," "weariness after excess," "died away with a melancholy hesitation" take on a sexual sense which need not, however, conflict with the interpretation of the motif as Will.

The improvisation remains a piece of piano-playing. Yet its total effect, whether or not the sexual overtones come into the reader's consciousness, is one of sly and secret self-gratification, and it is incredible that Mann, highly self-conscious writer that he was, can have been unaware of this; equally incredible, that he should not have been aware that he was writing a résumé of his own novel. (To complete the story, the lapse into decadence of Thomas Buddenbrook, and perhaps the death of Hanno, are mirrored in the final bars.) We must, then, ascribe to him as a writer the kind of destructive cynicism which he often puts forward in his characters for our awe. It is impossible, however, to ascribe to him also the praiseworthy features which he always links with the abominations, at least so far as these passages are concerned: impossible to see "something ascetic and religious," "some-

thing like faith and renunciation" ("etwas wie Glaube und Selbstaufgabe": the standard translation wrongly translates this as "something that contained the essence of faith and renunciation"). We are told, in so many words, that there are these qualities, but we have no actions to go by. Rather, Mann presents us with a novel whose structure is already questionable—in the idealization of the elder Johann, for example, on whom so much of the "argument" depends—only to recognize its nature and reject it. The rejection is not total, for Mann continues to operate with the same basic concepts throughout his life. It is, rather, ambiguously meant: both a rejection and an affirmation. He holds by his novel, does not, apparently, regard it merely as an experiment within a given framework of thought, but at the same time sees more clearly into its nature than his readers are likely to do. This is the strangest aspect of his ambiguity.

For Mann does after all stand outside **Buddenbrooks.** The résumé in the final pages is not his own, it is Hanno's, the onanistic artist's, the improvisation of a boy who cannot face life and has not the strength to combat the typhus fever which kills him. Mann, for his part, is the artist who is able not merely to set down the suffering he sees, the attempt at triumph, and the failure to realize the triumph, but also to live on and narrate the whole story of these defeats. He sees what he himself has done, sees through it, and still goes on to record his failure and affirm it. But this can never, in the nature of things, be a wholehearted affirmation; it must always be a "yes" and a "no" in rapid alternation. Not only this, Mann can also withdraw more or less completely from the whole system of ideas within which he works—less in **Buddenbrooks,** more in **Der Zauberberg** and in **Doktor Faustus.** . . . He put it on record himself that he felt his own personal life to be quite distinct from his role as a writer: that in the one he might feel tolerantly and benevolently disposed, while in the other he was impelled to deploy every cynicism at his command, and this "personal" quality does frequently make its appearance within his fictional work (just as the "writer's" quality appears in some of his political and social utterances—the distinction is never so complete as Mann would like to make it). The benevolence and tolerance are certainly the source of the humour which has helped to make him popular; we owe to it such figures as Permaneder and such scenes as his cursing of Tony Buddenbrook. It may also be responsible for the epilogue in the Buddenbrook household after the death of Hanno, a scene which seems, in mood, to be at odds with the mood we have just been exploring.

The death of Hanno is described in an impersonal way: it is an almost textbook-like account of the symptoms of typhus, never referring to Hanno personally at all, so that the suffering is brought home to the reader through the very dryness of the narration, and is the more telling since he only gradually realizes that this is the suffering of Hanno. The passage ends with the comment that the invalid who cannot bring himself to return with the feeling of "a bond existing still between him and that mocking, colourful, brutal business of living which he thought he had left so far behind him" can only succumb: ". . . No, it is quite clear, he will die." The tone here is as ambiguous as ever. These last words can be spoken either in sympathy or in supercilious indifference. They are followed at once, however, after the interval of a section heading, by the words "it is not right, it is not right, Gerda!" spoken by the aged Sesemi Weichbrodt, and since these words are unexplained for several sentences to come, they seem a comment on what has just gone before. In fact, as

Manuscript page of Buddenbrooks.

Da aber kam Sesemi Weichbrodt am Tische in die Höhe, so hoch sie nur irgend konnte. Sie stellte sich auf den Zehenspitzen, reckte den Hals, pochte auf die Platte, und die Haube zitterte auf ihrem Kopfe.

"Es ist so!" sagte sie mit ihrer ganzen Kraft und blickte Alle herausfordernd an.

Sie stand da, eine Siegerin in dem guten Streite, den sie während der Zeit ihres Lebens gegen die Anfechtungen vonseiten ihrer Lehrerinnenvernunft geführt hatte, bucklig, winzig und bebend vor Überzeugung, eine kleine, strafende, begeisterte Prophetin.

(But now Sesemi Weichbrodt stood up, as tall as ever she could. She stood on tip-toe, rapped on the table; the cap shook on her old head.

"It *is so!*" she said, with her whole strength; and looked at them all with a challenge in her eyes.

She stood there, a victor in the good fight which all her life she had waged against the assaults of her schoolmarm's Reason: hump-backed, tiny, quivering with the strength of her convictions, a little prophetess, admonishing and inspired.)

Mann's brother Viktor believed that this ending displayed the "true" Mann, seeming to imply that the affirmation of Christian belief was more in his true nature than the ideas derived from Schopenhauer, Wagner and Nietzsche. This is more than can properly be said, at any rate from reading the novel. Sesemi's puny fury is portrayed with a sympathetic humour, but the ironical withdrawal from her is evident also. Yet these are the final words, and final words have an importance of their own in a novel. In this case, they hark back to the opening of the first chapter in which the elder Johann heard Tony's recital of the catechism, so that the whole is contained within these two affirmations of belief. At the beginning as at the end, the affirmations are mocked, though more gently than is Hanno's improvisation through the undercurrent of suggestiveness. The fact that they are placed where they are, however, is at least a reminder, like the "ecclesiastical cadence" which interrupts Hanno's playing, of a different scale of values. Probably one cannot say more than that. This is after all a novel, not a personal confession or a work of philosophy or theology, for all its philosophical themes. Perhaps, though, we might interpret more and say that in a detached way Mann does still keep one part of his mind, however ironically, in a vaguely Christian atmosphere. We . . . see him doing so repeatedly in later works, in *Tonio Kröger, Der Zauberberg,* the Joseph novels, and *Doktor Faustus,* as also in *Der Erwählte,* and in most of these there is less justification than in *Buddenbrooks,* in so far as in them the vaguely Christian affirmations are made by the narrator, and apparently without irony. Unironical affirmation, where it occurs in these other works, makes a clean break with the ideas which are their main theme, and becomes a sudden, incoherent reversal. In *Buddenbrooks,* however, a better unity is preserved. That at least can be said.

The total impression is thus of a novel in which the author is sufficiently committed to Schopenhauerian and Nietzschean ideas to construct a slightly disingenuous plot in support of them, and to omit occasionally, again in a slightly disingenuous way, information which might tell against the points he is making; a novel which also is so destructively cynical at its own expense that we are compelled to see a perversity in its main intention, and yet also a novel in which the

shortly appears, they refer to the coming departure of Hanno's mother Gerda, the widow of Thomas, but the delayed explanation allows the impression to grow, that the injustice spoken of is the death of the boy towards whom all feel such attachment. The remainder of this, the concluding section of the novel, continues as it were under the aegis of Fräulein Weichbrodt, with whose protest it begins and with whose protest it ends. The survivors are assembled, all of them women: Sesemi herself, Gerda, Tony Buddenbrook-Permaneder, her daughter Erika, her cousin Klothilde, and the three daughters of Gotthold Buddenbrook. In Tony alone does the real Buddenbrook tradition continue: she carries her head high, and remembers her grandfather Johann "who used to drive a four-in-hand." Tony's presence is, in terms of the structure of the novel, a reassertion, even though in humorous style, of the ideas central to the whole. Yet the last word does not remain with her, but with Sesemi Weichbrodt. The talk turns to the recent deaths, to a lament for Hanno, Thomas, his father and his grandfather, at which one of the Gotthold daughters announces flatly and smugly that "There will be a reunion." Tony would like to believe it; she speaks of the times when she has lost all faith in divine justice and goodness, notions which have hitherto played no part in the novel. ". . . A reunion. . . . If that were so—." And at this, Sesemi rises in wrath, to speak the concluding words:

author detaches himself at least to some extent, as though rejecting the basis both of its assertions and its denials. Mann seems to feel that he can afford to make any self-exposure, allow his characters any form of self-gratifying fulfilment (which is what he means by feeling love for them) while at the same time, and as it were unwittingly, he sweepingly condemns himself and them out of hand. The one attitude is the complement and justification of the other, so to speak. Hanno's onanism is permissible, even to be gloried in, for it is after all an epitome of the whole novel, yet also to be punished ruthlessly with the "inevitable" death which follows on Hanno's Narcissistic refusal to face Life. Knowing this also—not being purely and simply a reveller in boyish fantasies, Mann stands outside the moods of enjoyment and self-laceration, seeming at times to hold by neither. Whether he was aware of his disingenuities is doubtful: he does not either explicitly or implicitly draw our attention to them, but this is no proof. Nevertheless, the extent of his self-awareness is astonishing, so great in fact that one would hardly expect him to continue in the same vein—it is almost unbelievable that an author who had seen so clearly the Narcissistic basis of his work would go on building on the same foundations. Yet the fascination of the pattern of ideas set out in *Buddenbrooks* was evidently powerful enough to hold Mann as a novelist for the rest of his life. He had, perhaps, found the ideal key to permanent self-enjoyment. (pp. 116-36)

> *Ronald Gray, " 'Buddenbrooks' (2)," in his* The German Tradition in Literature: 1871-1945, *Cambridge at the University Press, 1965, pp. 116-36.*

LARRY DAVID NACHMAN AND ALBERT S. BRAVERMAN
(essay date 1970)

[*In the following excerpt, the critics offer an analysis of the evolution of the personalities and cultural environments of successive generations of Buddenbrooks and examine what* Buddenbrooks *reveals about Mann's intellectual development.*]

In his essay on Schopenhauer, written in 1933, Thomas Mann, describing his early and momentous encounter with the philosopher, remarks:

> one can think in the *sense* of a philosopher without in the least thinking according to his sense; I mean that one can avail oneself of his thoughts and thus can think as he would by no means have thought.

He thus suggests that his youthful relation to this beloved and admired system was, like his attitude to his middle-class background, equivocal and complex.

Equivocal and complex, indeed, is the whole body of Mann's early work and weighty with implications for the unique and extraordinary achievements of his later years. It is, nevertheless, our contention that the early works of Thomas Mann are entirely intelligible, provided only that one grasps two points. First, from the very beginning of his career, his relation to the presumed antipodes of his thought—bourgeois society and the late German Romanticism of Schopenhauer, Nietzsche, and Wagner—was critical and dialectical and never involved merely an unconscious influence or naive acceptance. Secondly, Mann's art was a direct and conscious encounter with the specific structure and problems of his own age and place.

Erich Heller's approach is of interest in this context [see excerpt dated 1958]. After considering briefly the possibility that *Buddenbrooks* might be regarded as a "sociological

novel," Heller rejects the idea and then goes on to analyze Buddenbrooks entirely in terms of abstract categories drawn from Schopenhauer's metaphysics. We believe that *Buddenbrooks* is unintelligible in such terms. The problem involved in Heller's analysis, and, as we shall see, in other important critics, is a failure to understand the fundamental ground that underlies the whole opus of the young Thomas Mann. For this deep and hidden entity, this metaphysical substratum, is not the will, not Nirvana, not the realm of the Dionysian and Appolonian, nor even the overwhelming power of Wagner's music.

What Mann begins with, what he is sundered from, what he longs for, and what he continually returns to, is the world of an active and effective life, amidst other men, and in intimate contact with them. The note of joy, rare for Mann's works in this period, in *Royal Highness* is, after all, based upon the fact that its hero, though *like* an artist, is, at least potentially, a ruler of men. Mann's relation to bourgeois society was certainly equivocal because, as *Buddenbrooks* demonstrates, its specific character had the effect of alienating one's humanity. But the world, society in its most general sense, remained Mann's deepest love and deepest need.

At the time he wrote *Buddenbrooks,* Mann was certainly apolitical in the sense that he believed that society, as he knew it, was immutable. German upper middle class life, or middle class life in general, was, for him, the world itself. Therefore, if bourgeois society was insufferable, his only conclusion was that somehow the world must be abandoned. The source of the poignancy of Mann's early period was that he could neither abandon his deep commitment to the human community nor live as a member of the only community he knew.

It has often been noted that society was for Mann a problem and that the antithesis between the artist and the burgher was the dominant theme of his early works. But for this child of the city and scion of an old and powerful merchant family, society was more than a problem: it was the sphere of action of his fathers. What we see, then, in Mann's early works is, first of all, a serious effort to depict that reality, bourgeois society, in precise and concrete terms.

Buddenbrooks provides us with the strongest possible evidence for this assertion. For, after all, the graphic detail of Mann's description of the specific social structure is a far more striking and pervasive feature of the work than those direct allusions to Schopenhauer's philosophy which have received so much critical attention. The social structure portrayed in *Buddenbrooks* has, in general, not been taken seriously, as if to do so were to belittle the book. But the condition of life at a certain moment in time, in a certain place and in a certain class, is at least as much Mann's concern in *Buddenbrooks* as is Schopenhauer's system.

We hope to show that the ultimate reality of *Buddenbrooks* is a human society; that the development of the book is a demonstration of the exact manner in which this specific human society destroyed self-conscious human personality or alienated it from the world; and, finally that the function of Schopenhauer's philosophy in *Buddenbrooks* is to provide a key to the psychology of this alienated soul.

A word about the method which will be employed in this study. Because we are concerned with demonstrating the concreteness with which Mann describes his society, it will be necessary to consider his novel in considerable detail. Moreover, a novel in the tradition of realism insists that we accept a whole unseen world by implication. Above all, we cannot get beyond its characters; they may never have had flesh, but if we think of them only as characterizations we are lost. Whatever Thomas Mann had to say must emerge from a serious and thorough consideration of the personalities of his characters. And we will consider them from any point of view that seems helpful, including psychoanalysis.

Buddenbrooks is concerned with the history of a family. To speak of the history of a family implies a certain peculiar status for that family, as distinct from the usual, almost biological connotation of the term. A family which, in any real sense, has a history, is one whose forbears wrested significant reserves of power and property from the world. It is a family thereby freed from that necessity which reduces the great majority of men to laboring for the simplest needs of life. The history of such a family is the way in which it used its freedom.

We encounter the earliest Buddenbrook of the book, Johann the elder, in the midst of a vigorous and productive old age. Here, at the beginning of the novel, is a successful and, at times, ruthless businessman who is, nevertheless, cultured, liberal, receptive to new ideas, and, in contrast to his son, a free thinker and mocker of piety. Johann's breadth and complexity is most concretely revealed by the varied society that appears at his housewarming: nouveau riche, patrician bourgeoisie, clergyman, physician and poet. Probably never before, and certainly never again, will a Buddenbrook move at ease in such a company and be at home in so many worlds.

What is noteworthy about Johann is not so much a concern with culture (as a retired merchant might take up art), but a free and natural intercourse with ideas. There is no strain or tension in his culture because it had never been severed from his life. Both his worldly activities and his culture were expressions of his strikingly independent personality.

At this point we might consider Erich Heller's view of old Johann as somehow a manifestation of will unsullied by the idea. He bases his position on the old man's strength of character, self-confidence and "naivete." It is this last attribute which suggests the problems with Heller's position. For Johann is hardly naive. He seems to have been a fairly sophisticated man of the enlightenment. His breadth of culture, insistence on arranging his garden in a civilized manner, his objections to "practical education" and generally explicit rationalism are hardly comprehensible in terms of pure and brutal will to live.

Heller's analysis seems to us to be posited on a fundamental over-extension of Schopenhauer's categories. They are appropriate to an age and a human type which embody an ineluctable contradiction between thought and action. Now Johann Buddenbrook was not forced to suppress his self-consciousness—the spontaneous and refined activities of his mind—in order to play an effective role in the world. Moreover, this was not merely his good fortune; his confidence was a reflection of an age in which the new mercantile elite rejoiced to find its deepest values articulated in the thought of a Voltaire and a Diderot. Of this age he was a very late representative—perhaps the last.

Mann clearly recognized that this extraordinary form of human fulfillment was associated with a specific historical moment. He grasped the fragile and perishable nature of such integration and his portrayal of Johann can be understood as a nostalgia for the classical.

What emerges directly from the novel, then, is a sense of association between spontaneous, healthy personality, fulfilled in the world, rationality, and culture. By implication, Johann Buddenbrook represents the claim of bourgeois society that it alone provides a completely fulfilled and materially self-sufficient life. *Buddenbrooks,* from this point on, can be considered an examination and criticism of the ultimate validity of this claim.

Johann Buddenbrook was in a position to be the source of an enlargement of freedom. Instead, because of his peculiar emotional relation to his sons, in the context of the nature of the family business, freedom was ultimately stifled. For after all, there was a sense in which Johann was naive; he expected his son to be naturally disposed to obey him. He could not handle his elder son's independence, but dealt with Gotthold with Spartan severity for marrying out of his class. But this reaction was related to the old man's arbitrary dislike for his elder son, whose birth had caused the death of his first and beloved wife. The unreasonable actions which arose from these passions was, perhaps, a result of a certain bogus rationality, which led to clumsy dealing with the inner life. This self-certainty, unconscious rage posing as reason, is the perversion of enlightenment.

Thus, Johann was ultimately left with an obedient son, Jean, who had the most profound respect for his father's ethical and commercial principles and practices. But what was the real content of this respect? Johann Buddenbrook, the elder, determined his world: the patterns of his active and contemplative lives emerged from an interplay between his personality and experience. For him, self-consciousness did not involve conflict with the world, because his life was an expression of his individuality. His son, Consul Buddenbrook, resolved such potential conflicts, not through active integration, but by passive acceptance of his role in the world.

In an early encounter we find Consul Buddenbrook alone writing long prayers into his diary and reverently reviewing the family history (his father, he notes, was far too "rooted in the present" to be very much concerned with the historical past). He is, in fact, the very embodiment of traditionalism and piety, in rather curious contrast to his enlightened father. There is, of course, little psychological ground for expecting close affinities between sons and fathers. In this case, however, the basis of the difference is not merely personal or reactive, but has, in fact, the broadest social implications. The elements of Jean's character are figured in the whole aftermath of the European enlightenment. (pp. 201-05)

In the scenes in which the older and the younger Buddenbrooks appear together, the differences in their epochs, their personalities, and their styles of life are thoroughly developed. The tone of their conversation is itself revealing. It is the old man who, even when speaking from deep conviction, adopts a light and jocular tone; the form of his speech suggests a tolerance, not merely of opposing positions, but of the men who express them. Johann's tolerance of diverse ideas was based on a philosophical detachment. There is, however, another form of detachment which makes a later appearance in the Buddenbrook family.

The moral earnestness of Jean is contrasted with his father's cool and subtle comments on Napoleon. The old man unashamedly admired the strength and brilliance of the conqueror of his native city and the plunderer of his house. He is clearly edified by the heroism and historic grandeur of the

Great Man's actions, and the completeness with which his personality impressed itself on the world.

Jean, however, is evidently far more sensitive to Napoleon's crimes than his father, and it is in attacking them that we first observe the enthusiasm which draws "mocking smiles" from his father and Pastor Wunderlich. Before our eyes, enlightenment confronts Romantic sentimentality. The Consul's sentiments are certainly unexceptionable, as is his praise of Louis Philippe and "practical idealism." But as is often the case in unregulated and personal arguments (particularly between relatives) the reply Jean receives from his father appears, as we shall see, at best, obliquely related to what he says.

The second form of detachment from principle may be described as the practical. It is the attitude of the plain businessman for whom ideas are mere games—trifling play of the mind—and the supreme reality is that necessity by which he lives. The practical detachment from thought is thus the detachment of contempt.

Now it is, curiously enough, this philistinism that old Johann discerns in his son's humane arguments and refusal to appreciate great and free personality. The old man's spontaneous association to the mention of practical ideas is the following:

> "Practical ideals—well, ye-s—" The elder Buddenbrook gave his jaws a moment's rest and played with his gold snuff-box. "Practical ideals—well—h'm—they don't appeal to me in the least." He dropped into dialect, out of sheer vexation. "We have trade schools and technical schools and commercial schools springing up on every corner; the high schools and the classical education suddenly turn out to be all foolishness, and the whole world thinks of nothing but mines and factories and making money . . . That's all very fine, of course. But in the long run, pretty stupid, isn't it? . . . I don't know why, but it irritates me like the deuce."

The sanctification of necessity is somehow unbearable for the old man, and ideals seemed to him to have quite adequate substance and life without being justified by practicality.

It is not long before we have a clear demonstration of what old Johann objected to in his son. In their passionate discussion about whether to satisfy Gotthold's demand for a larger share of the family fortune, the Consul's personal attitude toward the problem has a striking peculiarity—it is quite indefinable. Initially, he manifests sincere anxiety about being held responsible by his brother for his father's hostility and he is concerned with division in the family. He then undergoes a rather abrupt change of heart, when his horror at discord is replaced by fear of possible damage to the firm from a large expenditure. His personal attitude to his brother and his plight is never expressed. His doubts seem entirely lost in his concern with such objective institutions as the family and the firm.

The firm was, to a large degree, the creation of the old Johann. It was the extension of his personality, the instrument of his power. For his son, the firm and family were venerable and immutable institutions to which he and his were to be ultimately subordinated. The different positions of father and son were made most explicit as the Consul reverently examined the family records and heard his father's voice in the next room.

> What a pity he had so little taste for those old records! He stood with both feet planted firmly in the

present, and concerned himself seldom with the past of the family. Yet, in times gone by he too had made a few entries in the gilt-edged book. The Consul turned to those pages, written in a florid hand on rather coarse paper that was already yellowing with age. They were chiefly about his first marriage. Ah, Johann Buddenbrook must have adored his first wife, the daughter of a Bremen merchant! The one brief year it had been granted him to live with her was the happiest of his life—"*l'année la plus heureuse de ma vie,*" The words were underlined with a wavy line, for all the world, even Marie Antoinette to see.

For Consul Buddenbrook, the book was a memorial of the family tradition, a repository of the history of an institution. But his father clearly regarded it as something else—a personal diary. And he came to it, not to record the objective details of his own history, but to satisfy his need to express his passionate and joyful love for his wife. He needed no *Sturm und Drang* Romanticism to realize and sanctify his personality, and found no inconsistency between this sanctification and rationality. In his son we see the mutation of enlightened rationality into submission of the personal to the practical and institutional. The most intimate human relationships, such as those between members of a family, take on rigid and externalized forms and become part of a social order with needs and demands of its own over and against the desires and claims of its individual members. The world, then, the objective order in which men live and act has become intractable and unresponsive; it is no longer a domain in which personality can realize itself because there is no place for the free play of spirit. The human personality has become an outcast from the world and can find a place for itself only in worldless inwardness, i.e., in pure subjectivity.

If the center of Jean's worldly life, the family and the firm, were institutions which stood above and beyond his personality, in what did he find his real self-expression? The answer lies in his worldless religiosity. Consider again the attitude for which his father reproached him—the idealization of the practical. The danger here is not that the practical is elevated but that the ideal is degraded: the social is exhausted in the economic and every human relationship must be understood in economic terms and controlled by economic imperatives. Without an autonomous idea of the social and the human, the cultural values to which the old man alluded in his attack on practical ideals are simply inexplicable.

We must not think of Jean as a money-grubber or brutal man of affairs. It is his negativity which is striking. He is given over to the economic because he has deprived himself of any alternative. Now the Romantic movement, in all its stages, has taught us this lesson: if the social is identified with the economic, if human reality is reduced to mechanism, the personal, nevertheless, will insist on its self-expression. It will assert its own reality against all odds, but the assertion may be strained, sickly, and worldless. This, then, is the explanation of Jean's Christian humility. Jean, of course, was no Romantic, but a pietist,—that is, a representative of another historical alternative to this reduction of human personality. The time spent in such devotional exercises as entering long prayers in his diary was time stolen from his worldly obligations. His Christianity was a manifestation of an urgent personal need to abandon the world—the inevitable consequence of a lifeless practicality.

The real dangers of Jean's position are revealed by the part he played in his daughter's marriage. That he should have desired, or actually forced, his daughter to marry a man of wealth and good prospects was hardly surprising and quite consistent with his position in the world. Toni herself, despite her dislike for Grünlich, was in some sense in sympathy with her father's view, insofar as her feeling for social and financial status was, at least, as strong as his.

Jean had no apparent difficulty in grasping the general implications of his bourgeois position; the disaster that ensued lay in the rigid and unintelligent manner in which he applied his principles to a specific situation. With the most limited sensitivity (and Jean was by no means a coarse man), he might have seen what his family saw so quickly: that Grünlich, his daughter's suitor, was a shameless toady and manifestly her inferior. With his perfectly adequate business abilities, he might well have investigated more searchingly the recommendations of those who could have had a personal stake in Grünlich's making a rich marriage. He might even have discovered that this exemplary young merchant was close to bankruptcy.

Jean's devotion to practical ideals seems to have been related to a curious inability to act intelligently on a human level. Like many conservatives, he did not know that the worthiest and most time-honored principles must be applied to reality with some imagination. The very desperation with which he insisted on Toni's marriage suggests that his ideals were not general rules to guide him in his active life, but blindly accepted imperatives upon which he was utterly dependent. The irony of his apparent worldliness and practicality lay in the fact that the marriage of interest these tendencies inflexibly ordained proved, in the end, to be a major financial disaster, while, incidentally, destroying his daughter's life.

If Consul Buddenbrook represented a certain stagnation of middle-class life, Thomas, his eldest son, appeared to be the instrument of revitalization for the principles of that life and of his family's position in the world. For he was not merely a competent and industrious young businessman; he was an individual of unusual refinement, sensitivity and demonstrably superior talents. He was, furthermore, ambitious and energetic. And if his principles and way of life were similar to his father's, one, nevertheless, had the feeling that he accepted them less blindly.

In the first decade or so after Jean's death, we see the effects of his son's talents. Business advanced, the family was enriched, a new and greater house was built and, as a crown to his success, Thomas became a Senator of the municipality. Yet, unexpectedly and with apparent abruptness, Thomas lost his nerve and with it, his capacity to act. This loss was followed by worldly failure, an early death and the total dissolution of the Buddenbrook firm and family. To understand the real nature of Thomas' collapse is of overwhelming importance. For not merely does this event constitute the central action of the novel, it is also the epitome of those problems which were the primary concern of the young Thomas Mann.

There are three types of critical approach to the decline of Thomas Buddenbrook. The simplest is embodied in statements such as these [by Henry Hatfield (see excerpt dated 1951)]:

> One feels that this failure . . . is due less to any tangible defect in Thomas than to that inner weariness

which, Mann implies, must be taken as given and lies beyond explanation.

> Decay [in *Buddenbrooks*] is considered an inevitable spiritual and biological process.

The problem with such a view is its lack of content. It is difficult to entertain seriously so naive and antiquated an idea as "biological decay" as an explanatory principle for the events of human life. It recalls the naive concept of atavism in late 19th century psychiatry. It is our contention that Mann makes Thomas' life completely and extensively intelligible in *Buddenbrooks.* Thomas can be understood, but only through that combination of refined psychology and social awareness which was uniquely Thomas Mann's.

Erich Heller comes more closely to grips with the text and presents the two other ways of elucidating the problem of *Buddenbrooks.* He notes the significance of the Hagenstroms as a new type of decidedly non-patrician bourgeoisie with which Thomas could not compete. This is true as far as it goes, but we must not confuse Toni's view of the Hagenstroms with Mann's. They did not represent a merely new and crude class (their crudeness is questionable in the context of the novel). The fact is that the Hagenstrom's worldly position rested on the same basis as the Buddenbrook's: successful economic enterprise. The ostensible superiority of the Buddenbrooks was based only on the fact that they got there first.

Heller's second approach involves working out the events of the novel in terms of Schopenhauer's philosophy. Reference to Schopenhauer is never irrelevant when one is discussing Mann. However there are various ways in which one can use a tool. Heller suggests that Thomas' decline was based on an increasing reflectiveness which must, inevitably, enervate the will and weaken the character. The idea of the necessary conflict between *Geist* and *Leben* is pervasive in Mann and surely related to Schopenhauer's metaphysics. Unfortunately, the bare concept has not much more content than "biological decay." It was Mann's enterprise in *Buddenbrooks* to elucidate the origins and substance of this very significant conflict. It is through his exploration of the interaction of consciousness and the world that the phenomenon of decadence is to be understood; to see it as the product of entirely autonomous psychological, biological or social phenomena is to ignore the substance of the novel and the reality it represents.

To understand the tragedy of Thomas Buddenbrook it is necessary to examine the lives of his two oldest siblings, Toni and Christian. They shared with him a common experience and their lives were ultimately as frustrated as his. But if we consider them in their youth, we find no real mental or physical evidence of that "biological and spiritual decay" which is supposed to account for their ultimate tragedies. It was only as they were confronted with the established patterns of Buddenbrook life that they found, long before Thomas, that conformity was impossible without the annihilation of their personalities.

The rigid, and rigidly enforced, patterns of the bourgeois life of Jean were for his haughty, vivacious, and attractive daughter, Toni, fairy tales set off against an ever more painful reality. The attack on her personality was most direct and devastating; she was forced to marry a man she loathed. Her submission to this requirement was based not only on the strength of the demand, but on her naive conviction that this type of marriage was, after all, the right kind. For her, too, the family's position came first. Only in the short period of revolt prior to her marriage did she develop the one relationship that was suitable to her in human and personal terms. She might have actually attempted to marry the medical student whose character she was strong enough to appreciate despite the "social gap" between them. But she did not. This infatuation was the last expression of her individuality. For, when her marriage failed in its own terms and her husband was bankrupt, she was no longer capable of insight or action. She had become totally committed to the principles which were the source of her suffering and humiliation. She became, more than any member of the family, the most rigidly devoted to the Buddenbrook name and the Buddenbrook position. Her pride became more and more pathetic as the family dissolved, but she remained to the end without knowledge.

Christian was the black sheep of the third generation of the Buddenbrooks. He was undignified, irresponsible, lazy, and dissipated. He was the living contradiction of every quality necessary for success in bourgeois life. Throughout his life he remained a constant source of humiliation and exasperation to his family.

But we, as critics, would repeat the injustice done to Christian by his own, if we judge him solely by bourgeois standards. For after all, he had his good points; he was affable, clever, and genuinely sympathetic. And, in his demand to marry the humble woman he had loved so long, he showed that he was quite capable of recognizing certain responsibilities in the world.

What, then, was the basis of Christian's failure? What transformed him into a clown, a hypochondriac, and, ultimately, a madman, disdained and abandoned by his family? Christian, when all is said, had only one great defect—he could not work. He was not an economic man. He was hardly stupid or untalented and, perhaps, if he had not borne the burden of the Buddenbrook name he might have been a successful impresario. We would not deny that Christian's ability either to accommodate himself to or reject the world in which he was raised was limited; he was no Tonio Kröger. But the spontaneous development of his natural talents was suppressed in a very substantial way. And for what? Christian was destroyed in the name of an ethos which denies the status of human being to a man who does not work and produce in the most basic and economic sense of those terms. His name was, perhaps, not without significance.

> Consider the lillies of the field, how they grow; they toil not, neither do they spin. And yet I say unto you that even Solomon in all his glory was not arrayed like one of these [St. Matthew 6:28].

Christian embodied those qualities of man which cannot fulfill themselves in work. But such attributes—the aesthetic and the moral—may be more specifically and uniquely human than those which do find their fulfillment in work.

What, then, was Christian? He stands for free, simple and unreflective self-consciousness; he was personality which loves itself, seeks to realize itself and is thereby ever sympathetic to other human beings. Yet Thomas disliked his brother:

> Christian busies himself too much with himself, with what goes on in his own insides. Sometimes he has a regular mania for bringing out the deepest and the pettiest of these experiences—things a reasonable man does not trouble himself about, for the simple reason that he would not like to tell them to

anyone else. There is such a lack of modesty in so much communicativeness.

Yet the willingness and capacity to talk about one's feelings is, in the first place, a recognition of their importance and, in the second place, the assertion that these feelings are universally experienced and thus can evoke that common sympathy which is a basis for morality. Thomas' reserve, on the other hand, was a wall erected around the personality and limited human communication to the purely necessary and practical. The exclusion of the private, the personal, and the intimate from one's consciousness stands for both lack of sympathy with mankind and for a certain callousness towards oneself.

Toni and Christian Buddenbrook were certainly failures in bourgeois terms. They had not been productive nor had they lived up to the demands of their station. We have argued that there was nothing about their characters which made their frustration inevitable and that they were weak only in the context of their environment. Nevertheless, it is in this context that they must be judged and somehow their personalities had to do with their inability to function. One may dismiss them with a shrug of the shoulders as two unfortunates who just did not have what it takes to succeed in the world. But it is impossible to attempt to explain the sudden and awful deterioration of Thomas Buddenbrook in terms of such arbitrary factors of personality. For at the time of his crisis, Thomas was not merely a successful man but one of the most substantial and influential citizens of his city. He had utterly mastered the world in which Toni and Christian floundered throughout their lives.

As we return to the question of Thomas' decline, we are alerted to the possibility that the ultimate explanation for it may well lie at least as much in a problem in the social structure in which he lived as in any weakness in his character. Now the work of Thomas' grandfather was the spontaneous expression of his personality; Jean, on the other hand, submerged his personality in his work. Thomas, however, implicitly asserted that his much wider ranging activities were, like his grandfather's, the result of free and enthusiastic personal commitment. His devotion and enthusiasm indicated that he desired to fulfill himself in his work, rather than merely to do his duty as his father had done.

Yet the very "violence" with which he performed his tasks and his peculiar inability to relax hardly suggest a state of mind comparable to Johann's. Thomas had a problem and by no means a simple one. The almost desperate intensity of his work was a clear indication that he had something to repress and forget which lay as deep as his nervous system. In this sense, the problem resembles the weakening of the will which Heller describes but its nature can be stated more precisely.

It is characteristic of the burgher to take his work and position seriously and Thomas was, indeed, a serious man. Yet it is clear that the consummation of his worldly ambitions did not fulfill his personality. His accomplishments were, to borrow a phrase, ego alien. But did the problem lie in his personality or in the nature of his ambition? From the beginning Thomas was aware that there were elements of his personality which would have to be suppressed in order for him to be able to function. He told his sister that,

> I have thought a great deal about this curious and useless self-preoccupation, because I once had an inclination to it myself. But I observed that it made me unsteady, hare-brained, and incapable—and

control, equilibrium, is, at least for me, the important thing. There will always be men who are justified in this interest in themselves, this detailed observation of their own emotions; poets, who can express with clarity and beauty their privileged inner life, and thereby enrich the emotional world of other people. But the likes of us are simple merchants, my child; our self-observations are decidedly inconsiderable. We can sometimes go so far as to say that the sound of orchestra instruments gives us unspeakable pleasure, and that we sometimes do not dare try to swallow—but it would be much better, deuce take it, if we sat down and accomplished something as our fathers did before us.

If Thomas' chosen mode of life was to become in some sense unsatisfactory, he was lost indeed. For so completely had he devoted himself to the pursuit of public and business achievement that he entirely lacked any escape or possible source of rejuvenation. It was part of Thomas' tragedy that he saw some of the richest elements in his personality as sources of moral weakness.

> Was he, Thomas Buddenbrook, a man of action, a business man,—or was he a finicking dreamer . . . Ah, how many times had he asked himself that question? And how many times had he answered it: in strong, purposeful hours with one answer, in weak and discouraged ones with another! But he was too shrewd and honest not to admit, after all, that he was a mixture of both.

Thomas Buddenbrook would have agreed with Heller that any intrusion of self-consciousness is destructive to the will. But for Mann, this is not a metaphysical truth but a peculiar psychological and social phenomenon which must be understood. Thomas had so determined his life that there was for him no way out. But Mann, in one of the most remarkable transitions in the book, makes poignantly clear what might have been. He evokes this unrealized possibility in the person of the living representative of Thomas' unbusinesslike impulses—his wife.

During the celebration of the firm's centennial, Thomas received news of the failure of his inept and disgraceful attempt to revive the firm's fortunes—the usurious loan on a crop which was destroyed by hail. At this moment of overwhelming despair, as he saw his inner dissolution reflected as never before in his worldly activities, he was tormented by the cacophony of a third-rate band hired to celebrate the glory of the firm.

With a description of this music the chapter ends. But the next chapter opens with another music—the subtle, cultivated and deeply committed music-making and music-talk of Gerda Buddenbrook and Edmund Pfühl, the organist and learned musicologist of the local church. Here is the evocation of culture and, as such, the concrete symbol, the matchlessly eloquent expression of all that Thomas had long ago irretrievably lost.

Amidst Toni's vacuous and pathetic family pride, and Christian's increasing derangement, amidst Thomas' rapidly increasing deterioration and pitiful concentration on the forms of that life which he had ceased really to live, Gerda's quite unworldly culture—the expression of her deepest personal need—stood forth as the only healthy, the only real and vital activity in the Buddenbrook house. Thomas could never share in this culture. His wife knew this and reproached him for the banality of his musical tastes for she had no doubt that

he was capable of better things. She knew in fact, what was obvious from the beginning, that Thomas was not merely a more complex man than his father, but was a man of distinctly superior and (up to a point) developed personal gifts. *His* sacrifice did not merely mean the self-discipline necessary to play an active role in the world. It meant a total rejection of self-consciousness for life. But in this very act, for such a man as he, lay a contradiction. Too sensitive and able a man to live by predetermined forms, in order to suppress his "dreaming" he had vitiated what were precisely the well-springs of his life—creative personality and originality. In the end, he destroyed his ability to deal effectively with a changing and recalcitrant world. His self-consciousness did not weaken his will merely by its presence. It was rather that his denial and terror of his own impulses and aspirations poisoned his life and made willing futile.

The actual substance of Thomas' decline was a sudden loss of the ability to act effectively in commercial and public life. He became a failure.

> It is as though something had begun to slip—as though I hadn't the firm grip I had on events.— What is success? It is an inner, and indescribable force, resourcefulness, power of vision; a consciousness that I am, by mere existence, exerting pressure on the movement of life about me. It is my belief in the adaptability of life to my own ends. Fortune and success lie with ourselves. We must hold firmly—deep within us. For as soon as something begins to slip, to relax, to tire, *within us,* then everything without us will rebel and struggle to withdraw from our influence. One thing follows another, blow after blow—and the man is finished.

Clearly, Thomas' grip was weakened by the awareness of the nature of striving and willing.

Fritz Kaufmann, one of Mann's most perceptive critics, argued that, "At the bottom of his heart man cannot rest content with a "calling" which no longer presses on toward any ultimate goal, but ensnares him in a network of means." Kaufmann confronted Mann and the bourgeois society which was his subject-matter from the perspective of a religious thinker. Kaufmann took the position that work had been sanctified by the Protestant ethic which looked to worldly success as the outward manifestation of inward grace. Kaufmann believed that only with such a sanctification was it proper for the human being to devote his energy and vitality to the pursuit of economic goals. Now, with the religious sanction gone, work descended again to the purely natural activity of providing for oneself the wherewithal to live. Kaufmann's position was that not only a bourgeois but any naturalistic ethics is inadequate. We need not follow Kaufmann in this broader attack on naturalism to appreciate the real contribution he has made in elucidating the limitations of the bourgeois imperatives of ceaseless work and unlimited striving.

At the time we first encounter the Buddenbrook family, it had amassed sufficient wealth to liberate itself from work for at least several generations. We can understand why Johann continued to work into his old age: he enjoyed it. But it becomes more difficult to understand why his descendants felt it incumbent upon themselves to increase and enlarge the family fortune. Jean did not question or analyze this obligation and, consequently, his life as a burgher was exemplary. But his children, each in his own way, did question this way of life and did seek to understand its justification. However, the problem is that it cannot stand questioning and it cannot be justified. Mann had learned from Schopenhauer that the fundamental metaphysical principle of reality was futile striving. Mann then applied this metaphysical conception to the world he knew most intimately, the commercial society of his fathers. When Thomas says, "What is success? It is an inner, and indescribable force, resourcefulness, power of vision; a consciousness that I am, by my mere existence, exerting pressure on the movement of life around me," he has completely cast aside the traditional values of the Buddenbrook family. For it is characteristic of bourgeois society that it does establish outward and visible standards of "fortune and success" and has absolutely no means for asserting that "fortune and success lie within ourselves."

Thomas Buddenbrook, who found in mid-career that he was dissatisfied with his life, discovered that he had an autonomous personality whose needs could not be met by the achievement of every goal to which he aspired. It is for this reason that the moment of greatest "outward and visible success" is often the moment of decline. For it is only when the consequences of a set of values have been actualized, that their implications for the self can really be understood.

> Often, in an hour of desperation, Thomas Buddenbrook asked himself what he was, or what there was about him to make him think even a little better of himself than he did of his honest, limited provincial fellow-burghers. The imaginative grasp, the brave idealism of his youth was gone. To work at his play, to play at his work, to bend an ambition that was half-earnest, half-whimsical, toward the accomplishment of aims that even to himself possessed but a symbolic value—for such blithe skepticism and such an enlightened spirit of compromise, a great deal of vitality is necessary, as well as a sense of humor. And Thomas Buddenbrook felt inexpressibly weary and disgusted. What there was in life for him to reach, he had reached. He was well aware that the high-water mark of his life—if that were a possible way to speak of such a commonplace, humdrum sort of existence—had long since passed.

It is important to emphasize the particular type of personality to which this experience of disillusionment is vouchsafed. Thomas Buddenbrook was consciously and strongly committed to the specific kind of life and system of values which he was eventually to reject. Without this initial commitment, and the superior individuality required to make it, the question of disappointment with success does not arise. Furthermore, the need for personal fulfillment in action arises in the historical context of bourgeois life. Only in this context can personality understand itself as thwarted.

Returning to the context of Thomas' life, we see the "symbolic" character of his aims exhibited in his subordination to economic imperatives, that is, to the problems associated with man's natural need to survive. But since the issue of survival, in practical terms, could never have been a problem to Thomas, and since he clearly had a developed sense of uniqueness, the futility of his life is clear on the most superficial level.

Mann, at the beginning of his career as a writer, was extremely sensitive to the bourgeois predilection for purposeless striving. This insight was not, at this stage in his career, explicit social criticism. Mann understood the mores of the middle

class as being identical with life itself—with active and productive life. At the same time, he saw the immense and sombre human significance of such pure action:

> He (Thomas) recalled the catastrophe of the year 1866, and the inexpressibly painful emotions which had then overwhelmed him. He had lost a large sum of money in the affair—but that had not been the unbearable thing about it. For the first time in his career he had fully and personally experienced the ruthless brutality of business life and seen how all better, gentler, and kindlier sentiments creep away and hide themselves before the one, raw, naked dominating instinct of self-preservation. He had seen that when one suffers a misfortune in business, one is met by one's friends—and one's best friends—not with sympathy, not with compassion, but with suspicion—cold, cruel, hostile suspicion. But he had known all this before; why should he be surprised at it? And in stronger and hardier hours he had blushed for his own weakness, for his own distress and sleepless nights, for his revulsion and disgust at the hateful and shameless harshness of life.

Thomas was, therefore, right to fear the consummation of his ambitions; for this fulfillment gave him a clear insight into the real nature of his values and those of the world around him. The banality and destructiveness of bourgeois life were ruthlessly exposed.

What Thomas discovered, what was expressed in the meditations quoted above, was the impact of the values of commercial life on human personality. In an agonizing moment, Thomas grasped the psychology of bourgeois man and he drew back in horror at what he had seen. For the bourgeois man,

> the Felicity of this life, consisteth not in the repose of a mind satisfied. For there is no such *Finis ultimus,* (utmost ayme,) nor *Summum Bonum,* (greatest Good,) as is spoken of in the Books of the old Morall Philosophers. Nor can a man any more live, whose Desires are at an end, than he, whose Senses and Imaginations are at a stand. Felicity is a continuall progresse of the desire, from one object to another; the attaining of the former, being still but the way to the later . . . I put for a generall inclination of all mankind, a perpetuall and restlesse desire of Power after power, that ceaseth onely in Death.

Thomas Hobbes here gives us a positive expression of the approach to that life which was so repellent to Thomas Buddenbrook. C. B. MacPherson has demonstrated that Hobbes' idea of human psychology is peculiarly appropriate to life in a possessive market society. Thomas Buddenbrook, the once committed bourgeois, has implicitly rejected this philosophy. To what mode of thought, to what reality does he finally appeal for consolation? With exquisite irony, Mann has him read Schopenhauer.

Schopenhauer's metaphysics of the will has, as its final significant content, the exploration of the realm of the unconscious. As such, it points to the future and to a whole new realm of intelligibility. This aspect of the philosophy had no meaning for Thomas Buddenbrook. But the world which produced Schopenhauer's idea of the will as ultimate and total reality was Hobbes': it was that bourgeois society which crushed Thomas. The consolation Thomas finds in Schopenhauer is in the form of resignation. He recognizes this intolerable world as being related to the very essence of reality, in fact, as being inevitable. Thus, he is caught in the toils of a system which is derived from the very source of his own torment.

Of course, Schopenhauer's assertion of the will as ultimate reality—as thing-in-itself—was pessimistic. Thomas' relation to Schopenhauer's thought was, therefore, indirect. For it was Nietzsche, Schopenhauer's devoted pupil and opponent, who first extolled the will and made it the basis of his ideal of spontaneous, strong personality. He was, in fact, the most radical critic of the stultifying and destructive nature of 19th century middle class life. This assertion of personality moved Thomas, in a way which no aspect of society had power to any longer.

At this point, it is proper to raise the question what are the differences between the Hobbesian man who restlessly seeks "power after power" and the Nietzschean man who asserts his own impulses in freedom from the contamination of morality. Hannah Arendt has provided us with a very useful insight into the consequences of Hobbes' psychological doctrines. She has reminded us that the inevitable result of an endless striving for power is the complete and absolute surrender of the individual to organized society which alone can preserve him from the risks of such a perilous quest.

> He [Hobbes] foresaw the necessary idolatry of power itself by this new human type, that he would be flattered at being called a power-thirsty animal, although actually society would force him to surrender all his natural forces, his virtues and his vices, and would make him the poor meek little fellow, who has not even the right to rise against tyranny, and who, far from striving for power, submits to any existing government and does not even stir even when his best friend falls an innocent victim to an incomprehensible raison d'état.

What makes this development not only possible but necessary is that, for Hobbes, the way in which men satisfy their desires is through domination of others. The Hobbesian man is quickly confronted by his fellowman whom he must use or be used by. Competition is carried on for its own sake and, in the end, a man considers power, which is instrumental, more important than satisfaction of desires, which began as a goal.

It was against this inversion of human activity that Nietzsche protested when he demanded that men return to their own desires as the source of their action. Nietzsche was not repelled by the brutality of bourgeois society, but by its vulgarity. He opposed to the Hobbesian drive for power the autonomy of the inner life and made the aristocratic assertion that only a few had an inner life worth developing—artists and heroes, in particular. But behind this assertion lay the Romantic principles that only the individual *qua* individual is aristocratic and that only if uncorrupted by society and its morals can man develop a suitable humanity. Nietzsche thus asserted the human as over and against society, as against all civilization, in fact. But we can appreciate the motivation for this most radical attack on bourgeois society when we see its effects on the lives of the Buddenbrooks. Thomas was annihilated by his deliberate submission to the middle class pattern of life. Yet we suspect that the child Thomas envisaged, who was to be completely at one with his will, would resemble his great-grandfather, Johann, far more than he would Zarathustra.

Mann was exceedingly clever and in his hands Nietzsche's

thought underwent a fascinating transmutation. Mann accepted Nietzsche's glorification of aristocratic individuality but rejected the idea that that individuality could ever be the achievement of the free-willing "blond beast." Mann knew the "blond beast" too well to have any illusions about his real identity: he was—irony of ironies—none other than the simple burgher, voracious for life and perpetually hostile to the whole realm of spirit. Mann, until much later in his career, identified 19th-century bourgeois society with life itself and saw no other worldly alternative. But because he, like Nietzsche, saw that in this world there was no opportunity for the higher, the aristocratic aspects of personality to develop, he became concerned with possible alternatives, such as the life of the artist. For as long as Mann could not conceive of the possibility of a reform or reconstruction of society, his writings would not be precisely social criticism and his solutions—if there were any—would have to lie in the direction of the development of pure "inwardness" in isolation from society.

Thomas Buddenbrook was even farther removed than his creator from critical social consciousness. The horror he experienced at the brutality of the life around him only convinced him of his own weakness and of his excessive sensibility. His reading of Schopenhauer served, as Mann himself later remarked, "to ripen him for death."

> The human being stares hopelessly through the barred window of his personality at the high walls of outward circumstance, till Death comes and calls him home to freedom! Individuality?—All, all that one is, can, and has, seems poor, grey, inadequate, wearisome.

Here Thomas *is* referring to Schopenhauer; in particular, to the philosopher's sense of the vanity of human life. Schopenhauer regarded the human being's sense of his own uniqueness and importance as a delusion. The world was, for him, absolutely inimical to human consciousness. The world, the only reality, was blind, brutal, purposeless will. We have seen, in *Buddenbrooks,* that the highly developed late 19th-century bourgeois society exhibited itself as just such a world. It was this truth, concealed behind the glories of an increasingly complex and powerful civilization, that horrified the thinkers of a whole epoch. Schopenhauer's system, when utilized as moral philosophy, or even a theology, is merely the statement of the absolute frustration of a sensitive individual who attempted to engage himself in this particular society.

We have the suspicion that Thomas Buddenbrook's life would have been much more successful, had he early been given the opportunity to develop his personal gifts. He himself complained of his lack of schooling and the opportunities he lost thereby. At the very least, liberal education might have given him the resources with which to refresh himself at the time of his depression, when his personality no longer seemed equal to his responsibilities.

This deprivation seems, however, to have been more or less inevitable. Consul Buddenbrook was not the man to consider something as original as educating his son for an unfamiliar role. That Thomas took the identical course with *his* son seems much less inevitable. In fact, Thomas' relationship with his son in general seems forced, cruel, and somehow inappropriate or obsolete. Thomas was far less completely and naively committed to the mercantile life than his father. Indeed, at the time of his greatest influence on Hanno's development, he was hardly committed to that life at all. In the end, all he was able to give his son was a set of somewhat hollow standards without the self-confidence required for their realization.

Thomas' very considerable appreciation of those aspects of life which are not purely commercial did not enable him to sympathize with or encourage their manifestations in his son. He thwarted and discouraged Hanno's spontaneous cultural interests and thought of nothing better for him than the mercantile course at school. The result of this education in Hanno intensified his already committed worldlessness. His love of music, the most spontaneous expression of his personality, together with every humane impulse, existed as over and against almost any type of action or vitality.

In this context, we may refer again to Johann's indictment of practical education. What we must understand here is that Johann's comment has no relevance to contemporary questions such as the value of vocational schools. What he was talking about were the institutions which would train the sons of those who already held responsible positions in society. A commercial curriculum in this context implied an attitude on the part of both the school and the parents that the children must be educated to fulfill a precise, predetermined, and narrow role in society.

The classical education whose passing he lamented assumed a certain community of human concerns: an identity between culture and the world. The very nature of this kind of education was to identify, for the child, the wide range of human potentials and responsibilities which would be his as a man. The practical curriculum meant the subordination of the cultural, the personal, and the human needs of the student to the external demands of commercial society. Johann's allusion was apt; the school was turned into a factory. And in his great-grandson Hanno's school experiences we see the operation of an institution whose mindless regimentation was a sign of its subjection to necessity. It was in this institution, above all, that Hanno's rich and vital personality was ruthlessly attacked and forced to turn ever more inward.

In Hanno, the last of the Buddenbrooks, uncompromising and unashamed personality appeared for the first time, and with tragic irony, for its vehicle was a child. Sensitive, imaginative, and refined, Hanno led, with his aristocratic friend, Kai, a rich and satisfying private life. He expressed his humanity by a complete rejection of the cruel and competitive standards of necessity he encountered at school. There was, therefore, a sense in which Hanno's short life was a triumph: a triumph of personal self-assertion, of free and rich imagination, unknown to his fathers. But this achievement, the work, after all, of a child, was as terribly fragile as his life. It involved an absolute retreat into his own childhood state and a rejection, not merely of the Buddenbrooks' world and its ethos, but all action. Hanno was neither a successful student nor a potentially competent pianist. He was not, in fact, capable of functioning at all. In order to meet the needs of his own personality, he had sacrificed the hope of all power to control the world and impress himself upon it.

The loss of power did not merely involve potential lack of success in the bourgeois world. It meant, in fact, impotence, deformity, and, ironically, the destruction of the personality. This weakness opened the way to destruction of a refined human soul by just those trifling and brutal forces which it had rejected so completely and had rejoiced to stand so far

above. The saintly decision to retreat became, in the end, enforced seclusion and imprisonment in the self.

We are describing here what seems to have been Thomas Mann's earliest and deepest fear. Before beginning *Buddenbrooks,* he had already published **"Little Herr Friedemann,"** a story about a hunchback who, through immersion in culture and refined society, reconciled himself to a celibate and constricted life. He continually congratulated himself on the triumph of his most human parts over uncontrollable physical circumstances. But he fell in love and was at last driven to declare himself to the woman. She rejected him with scorn and he drowned himself. This deep and pathetic contradiction in the flesh is the metaphor, the physical symbol, for Hanno's tragic position. The irony of Hanno's life lay in this: that in seeking to free and develop his personality, he had, without the assistance of a bodily deformity, become a little Herr Friedemann.

Mann's almost somatic horror of the fate in store for such a character is illustrated in Hanno's early and gruesome death. We must view this event from two perspectives to grasp its significance. On the one hand, Hanno's death was the result of his weakness. He succumbed to his disease as he would, inevitably, have succumbed to any attack life might have made upon him. But from another point of view, this adolescent boy's dying was the strongest possible expression of Mann's terror at the condition of worldlessness. The death of one so young is especially painful because he has never lived—because he has never moved out into the world and developed a context for his life. There is simply no way of remembering what may have been a very gifted and attractive human being. But Hanno might well have become no more than this had he lived to maturity. The point of having Hanno die so young was perhaps to suggest that the years ahead were unlikely to have made much difference to him. He had only the horrible prospect of remaining pure potentiality. Such a man, who has retreated into himself and severed all vital connections with the world, has already made a pact with death. Decadence and self-absorption are most completely at the mercy of death.

Thus *Buddenbrooks* closes with unrelieved pathos: a totally unresolved conflict between personality and the world. It is appropriate that the last character is a child, who never reaches adult life. The necessarily sequestered and limited position of a child in the world suggests the burden of the latter part of the book—the extraordinarily limited opportunities for development that an ostensibly rich environment can provide for a human being.

The issue is, thus, clearly stated. Once self-consciousness, sensitive and gifted personality, makes its appearance as the not uncommon result of generations of worldly success and freedom from necessity, a problem exists. The personality may choose to submerge its unique gifts and consciousness in purely worldly activities, in which case it runs the risk of finding itself ultimately unfulfilled and lost. Or, on the other hand, it may, like Hanno, reject the world and action entirely, and concentrate on its own pure and uncorrupted enjoyment. In this fundamentally decadent state, personality must, eventually, find itself crushed by the world. At about the time he wrote *Buddenbrooks,* Mann wrote a short story, **"The Dilettante,"** which eloquently depicted the excruciating nature of such a state.

It comes to the same thing: if you take care not to

be a man of action, if you seek peace in solitude, you will find that life's vicissitudes fall upon you from within and it is upon that stage you must prove yourself a hero or a fool.

The setting of the story and the background of its hero are almost identical with that of *Buddenbrooks,* again indicating Mann's almost obsessive concern with the dangers of rejecting bourgeois life.

Yet it is clear, in *Buddenbrooks* and in later works, that Mann himself could not accept that life. Let us here reiterate that for Mann life is defined essentially as the commercial life of the bourgeoisie. What Mann had not grasped at this stage of his intellectual development was that this equation of the economy with the totality of social life was not a general and inevitable human condition but the historically conditioned result of the development of capitalism with its characteristic view of society as fundamentally an organization for the production and distribution of economic goods. Mann saw that, if society, life, and the commercial world were looked upon as completely congruent terms, the needs of the personality which could not be satisfied by a commercial career would appear to be somehow dissevered from life and the world, and would seem to represent an illegitimate and irresponsible desire to fly from reality. But Mann did not yet understand that such a conception and such a society were not the only ones possible. He had not yet arrived at the idea of society, which he would later term civilization, as the domain in which man, in all the richness and complexity of his life and personality, can find his fulfillment. And so, in this early period, he was faced with mutually exclusive alternatives neither of which he could bring himself to choose. He would not forsake the world and sacrifice vitality for the sake of an aesthete's dream paradise. On the other hand, he could not accept the world as it was. He could not substitute his sensibility, his refinement, and his critical self-consciousness for the grossness and hard-headedness of the typical man of affairs. Thus, the problem posed was how was the personality to find its unique development in a fundamentally inimical environment.

The initial solution, which Mann examined in his writings up to the First World War, was escape into the purely private and personal, yet active and creative, life of the artist. But the ultimate answer that Mann made to this problem of his youth was quite different. It involved a critique of that supposedly given and immutable society and the actual construction of alternatives. (pp. 206-25)

Larry David Nachman and Albert S. Braverman, "Thomas Mann's 'Buddenbrooks': Bourgeois Society and the Inner Life," in The Germanic Review, Vol. XLV, No. 3, May, 1970, pp. 201-25.

R. J. HOLLINGDALE (essay date 1971)

[*An English journalist and critic, Hollingdale is the author of several books on philosophy and economic issues and has translated works by Nietzsche, Schopenhauer, and Goethe. In the following excerpt from his* Thomas Mann: A Critical Study, *a thematically organized examination of Mann's works, Hollingdale evaluates* Buddenbrooks *as social criticism, focusing on the family's moral code, and discusses the theme of decadence.*]

Buddenbrooks is probably Mann's most widely-read novel; it is certainly the easiest to read. Its plot is usually summarized as the description of a family like his own and of its de-

cline through four generations as business acumen gives place to artistic sensibility. This theme is, of course, present and very prominent; it is one of the novel's most important themes, as we shall later see; but there is another equally important: the decline of the Buddenbrooks coincides with the rise of the Hagenströms. If the Buddenbrook family is old Europe—and it is pretty clear that that is what the Buddenbrooks do represent—then the Hagenström family is that which displaced and succeeded old Europe, namely new Europe, the Europe of the twentieth century. But the Hagenströms represent nothing but primitive acquisitiveness. That they have no culture worth speaking of, that by comparison with the Buddenbrooks they are very vulgar and commonplace, is perhaps no more than colouring, something laid on to render them as unattractive as possible: the vital distinction, that which would remain if all the accidental or surface distinctions were removed (and will remain when, through the agency of wealth, security and position, they *are* removed) is the absence of *morality.* That which made the Buddenbrooks something more than brigands, the moral element, is lacking in the Hagenströms.

The non-moral Hagenströms defeat the moral Buddenbrooks, and do so easily and quickly. How quickly is obscured by the habit of thinking of the novel as covering four generations, although its time-span is not nearly so great as that description suggests. Tony Buddenbrook is present on the first page as a girl of eight and on the last as an elderly lady: the decline of the family takes, in fact, just one lifetime. And the reason this family is so vulnerable is precisely the most obvious fact about it: that it is the model bourgeois family and its morality that transitional form which constitutes an unstable halfway stage between morality founded on belief in the known will of God and the disappearance of all morality with the disappearance of this belief. The future belongs to the Hagenströms because they already embody that morality of the future which is no morality at all.

The *instability* of bourgeois morality—the difficulty it experiences in standing upright and its consequent disposition to fall over when pushed—is insisted on again and again in *Buddenbrooks.* The central point of this morality—at once its symbol and the actual point at which moral behaviour is of the greatest practical necessity—is honest dealing over money. Dishonesty over money is, in the Buddenbrooks' world, dishonesty *per se.* What does the author tell us about the attitude of this world towards such dishonesty? A certain Weinschenk has been detected in what the law insists on regarding as a financial swindle, and has gone to prison; but "this man had in all probability done no more than his business colleagues did every day and thought nothing of; if he had not been caught he would have gone his way with head erect and conscience clear . . . His testimony before the court had been given with the most sincere conviction; and people who understood the technicalities of the case supported his contention that he had merely executed a bold manœuvre for the credit of his firm and himself—a manœuvre known in the business world as usance." A little later the "people who understood the technicalities of the case" discuss a similar case and reveal the moral uncertainty concealed behind such a term as "usance": "They began to talk about the latest town scandal—about P. Philipp Kassbaum, who had been falsifying bills of exchange and now sat behind locks and bars. No one felt outraged over the dishonesty: they spoke of it as an act of folly, laughed a bit, and shrugged their shoulders."

It might be thought that these people—the Weinschenks and Kassbaums and the people who talk about them and share their outlook—are of the Hagenström persuasion and provide no evidence that the moral convictions of the genuine old-style bourgeois were in any way shaky or unsound. That this is not necessarily the case is evidenced by the fact that the Buddenbrooks, the model bourgeois, are themselves infected with a tendency to dishonesty over money.

The case is made, gradually but at last unmistakably, that the acquisition and preservation of money is for the Buddenbrooks the ultimate purpose of existence, that the family's tradition of "loyalty to the firm" means in practice setting aside everything that hinders the acquisition and preservation of money, and that this "everything" includes, if need be, that bourgeois morality whose central point is honesty over money. The fact is crucial for an understanding of this family and, indeed, for an understanding of the whole book and of Thomas Mann's attitude towards bourgeois morality. The ideology of "loyalty to the firm" is so inimical to the true happiness of the Buddenbrooks that, although it seems to the most upright and strong-willed of them the very backbone of the family tradition, it is on the contrary and in reality a kind of ancestral curse which helps to ruin the lives and decompose the souls of the entire tribe: the lives and souls of those members of it who adhere to that ideology and of those who do not.

The effects of this curse are perceptible throughout the book. Jean, the father of Thomas, Christian and Tony, sacrifices his daughter's happiness to the acquisition of money by morally compelling her to marry Grünlich. That Grünlich turns out to be a swindler is not only the first grand instance of an honest exterior concealing corruption within and a hint that bourgeois rectitude may in general be none too certain (a hint more than borne out by the affair of Weinschenk), but also a poetic punishment of both Jean and Tony, in as much as Tony preeminently shares her father's ideology of "loyalty to the firm." Tony goes on to a succession of unfortunate marriages, all of them a direct consequence of this loyalty and of that original betrayal of life for the sake of the Buddenbrook fortune which she perpetrated when she abandoned Morton Schwarzkopf, with whom she was in love, in order to marry Grünlich, whom she disliked. It may be noted that the memory of this original act of betrayal, and of the possibilities of natural happiness which its commission annihilated, lingers on in her subconscious mind throughout her life: its presence is revealed by her uttering, on the most diverse occasions, Schwarzkopf's unorthodox opinions in the very words in which he had long ago uttered them to her. Thomas, the central figure of the book and the embodiment of the Buddenbrook ideology, naturally falls most heavily under the curse, and we shall later see it working upon him in other connexions; here it will suffice to say that the scene in which he has his only serious quarrel with his mother is the book's most unambiguous declaration of the deleterious effect of that ideology. "What was going on? Something amazing, something dreadful, something at which the very actors in the scene themselves stood aghast and incredulous. A quarrel, an embittered disagreement between mother and son!" What is this unprecedented quarrel about? "One hundred and twenty-seven thousand five hundred marks current" which the Frau Consul has given away to the fortune-hunting pastor Tiburtius.

As for those who find they cannot share the family ideology,

it is enough to point out that their lives are made difficult and they are on occasion virtually persecuted precisely because they cannot share it: Christian and Uncle Gotthold, for example, are regarded by the others almost as criminals, and despised as drop-outs, solely because they are by temperament incapable of subordinating everything in their lives to "loyalty to the firm."

But this is not the worst: that obsession with acquiring and preserving money—the curse of the Buddenbrooks—is precisely the agency through which the instability of that bourgeois morality which the Buddenbrooks represent is first made palpably evident. If the morality in which they believe happens to stand in the way of acquiring or preserving money, then the Buddenbrooks are capable of shutting their minds to it and acting dishonestly: and in that they are capable of doing so they reveal themselves as being *potentially* what the Hagenströms are *actually*—and reveal too why the latter experience so little difficulty in displacing them: they stand to the Buddenbrooks in the relation of actual to potential. The scene in which the speck of decay is first disclosed in the Buddenbrooks' moral core is worth reproducing in detail: it shows the skill and subtlety with which Mann goes to work on this theme.

Jean is discussing with Grünlich the amount of Tony's dowry:

> "I entirely agree with you, my good friend. This important matter must be settled. In short, then: the usual dowry of a young girl of our family is seventy thousand marks." Herr Grünlich cast at his future father-in-law a shrewd, calculating glance—the glance of the genuine man of business. [At this "genuine man of business" we should remember that Grünlich is a conscious and calculating swindler.] "You know, my honoured father," he began again, "the deep respect I have for traditions and principles. Only—in the present case is not this consideration for the tradition a little exaggerated? A business increases—a family prospers—in short, conditions change and improve." "My good friend," said the Consul, "you see in me a fair-dealing merchant. You have not let me finish, or you would have heard that I am ready and willing to meet you in the circumstances, and add ten thousand marks to the seventy thousand without more ado." "Eighty thousand, then," said Herr Grünlich, making motions with his mouth, as though to say: "Not *too* much; but it will do." Thus they came to an affectionate settlement; the Consul jingled his keys like a man satisfied as he got up. And, in fact, his satisfaction was justified; for it was only with the eighty thousand marks that they had arrived at the dowry traditional in the family.

Thus the "fair-dealing merchant." A little thing in itself, perhaps, but big in implication: Jean's morality is such that it permits him to start what is supposed to be a lifelong relationship with Grünlich by lying to him about and swindling him over money.

Although the Hagenströms and their kind are certainly "bourgeois" in the accepted meaning of the word, they cannot be bourgeois in the sense in which Mann uses it in the title of his essay *Goethe as Representative of the Bourgeois Age.* The "bourgeois age" is the age of the defeated Buddenbrooks and therefore lies in the past. The new age, bourgeois in name but something else in spirit, is the property of the victorious Hagenströms, the representatives of a new barbarism characterized by the absence of any moral imperative. That, in its aspect as social criticism, is the conclusion of **Buddenbrooks.** (pp. 24-8)

[Neither] Schopenhauer nor Nietzsche has anything to say against the artist as such, though both distinguish between good and bad artists. But how, then, can Thomas Mann have derived his conception of the artist as *decadent* from them? The answer is that he followed Schopenhauer and not Nietzsche in accounting for the origin of art in an abnegation of the will, but then followed Nietzsche and not Schopenhauer in viewing abnegation of the will as a mark of decadence. "Wherever the will to power declines in any form there is every time also . . . a *décadence*," Nietzsche maintains, and it is in any case true quite generally throughout his philosophy that "strength of will" is good, "weakness of will" bad, that "power" is good, its absence bad. "What is good?" he asks, and answers: "All that heightens the feeling of power, the will to power, power itself in man. What is bad? All that proceeds from weakness. What is happiness? The feeling that power *increases*—that a resistance is overcome." It was a fusion of this idea with the idea that the artist is "will-less" that produced Mann's conception of the artist as weak, as incapable of a happy existence, as decadent. It must be admitted at once that this fusion is highly illegitimate and "unphilosophical": Schopenhauer's "will" and Nietzsche's "will to power" are conceptions so different in nature that their combination in the manner just described is like mating an eagle and an oak-tree. But . . . Mann was no logician and was capable of philosophical blunders of the most thumping description: he was an artist, who used, indeed needed, philosophical concepts in order to set to work, and the mating of an eagle and an oak-tree, impossible in the mundane world, is quite possible in art. As his mother's son, Mann needed to approve of art, as his father's he needed to disapprove of it: Schopenhauer came to the aid of the mother, Nietzsche to the aid of the father. What matter if the union was *philosophically* illegitimate? *Artistically* it was fruitful and that was the main thing. And so the artistic mother's son became an artist and devoted his life to the production of works of art; but the bourgeois father's son got his revenge by making the artist employ his artistry to demonstrate the *decadence* of art.

Or—for what is more devious, more full of hidden twists and turns, than the mind of Mann?—or did he *really* get his revenge? Did the mother's son perhaps let him think he had, only to deprive him of it in a way in which he, being merely healthy and philistine, would be incapable of detecting? The first grand instance of artistic sensibility as an expression of decadence is Hanno Buddenbrook, the last of the Buddenbrooks and a mother's son with a vengeance. What an awful, what an appalling child! how incapable of life and how unworthy of it! how sickly, how timid, how *weary*! What does he want, this little Hanno, even before he is out of school? He wants to die: he has had enough of living before he has really begun to live. Life is too much for him, his spirit is too weak to endure it; he needs stimulants even to endure it to the extent he does: better by far if he had not been born. He is everything one means by the word "decadent," and his artistic giftedness, the one positive quality he possesses, depends upon and derives from his decadence. The artist as decadent: a victory for the father, no doubt about that. Or—*is it* a victory? Did little Hanno appear out of the air? Did he create himself? Was he, even, the son of his mother *alone*? No, of course not, he was a Buddenbrook. He was the son of Thomas, the grandson of Jean, the great-grandson of Johann. Were the Buddenbrooks themselves decadent? Is little Hanno only the unhappy inheritor and *final stage* of a decadence present all along in the Buddenbrook line? Does the artist, by making his artist so extremely exhausted and life-weary a creature—a procedure the bourgeois must, in his blindness, approve of—not also make it certain that this exhaustion must be inheritance, must have been bequeathed to him by his *bourgeois* forefathers?—so that decadence would be precisely that which the artist had in common with them, and his artistic giftedness a form of *strength,* an attempt to surmount his inheritance? Later on the artist will present in one and the same book a serious and a comic confrontation of bourgeois and artist in which each is genuinely the dialectical opposite of the other; but he will not do this until, in **Buddenbrooks,** he has shown how close a relation the artist, the *decadent* artist, is of the healthy bourgeois.

Expressed in terms of the Buddenbrook code, decadence is the inability to subordinate one's natural inclinations and desires to the interests of the family and firm, and that is in the first instance identified with marrying into an inferior class. Bad uncle Gotthold marries a shopgirl, worse brother Christian marries a prostitute; but good son Thomas gives up *his* shopgirl, and good daughter Tony gives up her Morton Schwarzkopf. The short chapter in which Tom says farewell to his girl is our first extended view of him: the contrast with Uncle Gotthold is obvious, as is the fact that, contrary to the clearly expressed opinions of the rest of the Buddenbrooks, the author prefers Gotthold to Thomas. This chapter is, moreover, essentially a preparation for Thomas's self-approving monologue over his uncle's dead body—a speech in which Mann makes his namesake appear utterly odious:

> He came just in time to see the last convulsive motions of the old gentleman. Then he stood a long time in the death-chamber and looked at the short figure under the covers, at the dead face with the mild features and white whiskers. "You haven't had a very good time, Uncle Gotthold," he thought. "You learned too late to make concessions and show consideration. But that is what one has to do. If I had been like you, I should have married a shopgirl years ago. But for the sake of appearance—! I wonder if you really wanted anything different? You were proud, and probably felt that your pride was something idealistic; but your spirit had little power to rise. To cherish the vision of an abstract good; to carry in your heart, like a hidden love, only far sweeter, the dream of preserving an ancient name, an old family, an old business, of carrying it on, and adding to it more and more honour and lustre—ah, that takes imagination, Uncle Gotthold, and imagination you didn't have . . . And you had no ambition, Uncle Gotthold. The old name is only a burgher name, it is true, and one cherishes it by making the grain business flourish, and oneself beloved and powerful in a little corner of the earth. Did you think: 'I will marry her whom I love, and pay no attention to practical considerations, for they are petty and provincial'? Oh, we are travelled and educated enough to realize that the limits set to our ambition are small and petty enough, looked at from the outside and above. But everything in this world is comparative, Uncle Gotthold. Did you know one can be a great man even in a small place; a Caesar even in a little commercial town on the Baltic? . . ." Thomas Buddenbrook turned away . . . He had his hands behind his back and a smile on his intelligent face.

The insolent repetition of "Uncle Gotthold" sets the tone: young Thomas thinks he has a right to despise his uncle. But the ground upon which he proceeds to establish this right is, although he does not know it, morally rotten: his instincts have strayed so far from what is naturally desirable and healthy that he can regard giving up the woman you love in order to become a petty-bourgeois Caesar as *good*. One must also add that his conviction that Uncle Gotthold has led an *unhappy* life finds no support anywhere in the novel.

Now just as Tony's aberrant instincts lead her continually to marry the *wrong man,* so Thomas's lead him to marry the *wrong woman.* Gerda Arnoldsen, the daughter of a "great merchant and almost greater violin artist," is herself a musician, and in fact an altogether typical Mann artist: "The corridor door opened, and there stood before them in the twilight . . . a slender figure. The heavy dark-red hair framed her white face, and blue shadows lay about her close-set brown eyes", there is a suggestion of sickliness and nocturnal living about her from the first: "Thomas Buddenbrook took a solitary breakfast . . . His wife usually left her room late, as she was subject to headaches and vapours in the morning . . . [He] met Gerda only at dinner, at four in the afternoon"; when she is compelled to rise early her skin looks "whiter and more even-toned than ever, and the bluish shadows deeper and darker in the corners of her close-set brown eyes," and we are now told explicitly that "she lived in the twilight of her curtained living-rooms, and dreaded the sun, the dust, the crowds of townsfolk in their holiday clothes, the smell of coffee, beer, and tobacco." This is "Gerda, mother of future Buddenbrooks": would that Thomas had married his shopgirl instead—but his instinct for what is good and healthy has decayed too far, he must needs choose and prefer that which he ought most resolutely to have shunned.

Thomas's decadence is pre-enacted very vividly—so vividly as almost to amount to a pre-enactment of Hanno's—in his brother Christian, who inherits the "bad" tendencies of Uncle Gotthold but, coming a generation later, i.e. a generation further into decadence, has a bad conscience about them and consequently allows them to lead him into neurosis. In accordance with the novel's dialectical scheme he is presented as being artistic. As a boy he reads Cicero while Tom discusses business with their father; as a man he has a passion for the theatre and is a first-rate raconteur: "he would have held a large audience spell-bound. He narrated like one inspired; he possessed the gift of tongues." He is clearly an actor *manqué,* and it is natural that he and Gerda should "get on quite well together." But as he grows older he becomes more and more subject to nervous disorders and he ends as a mental patient and a grotesque.

In him Thomas comes to recognize his own features. During the course of their inevitable final quarrel he tells him: "I have become what I am because I did not want to become what you are. If I have inwardly shrunk from you, it has been because I needed to guard myself—your being, and your existence, are a danger to me—that is the truth." This is a very frank admission and in fact nothing less than the moral zenith of Thomas's existence: nothing he has said before or will say again until the very end reveals so great a degree of self-awareness or, rightly considered, of charity towards his brother. But it reveals too that Thomas's strength is the opposite of natural strength: it is more like a terrified reaction or, in terms of the philosophical scheme of another novel, "fear in the face of pessimism and flight from it," a "means of self-

defence against—the truth." But the truth will not, in the case of Thomas Buddenbrook at any rate, be for ever put down: at length it gets the upper hand and gives Thomas his quietus. In one of the most famous passages of the novel Thomas, grown prematurely old and tired, gains spiritual enlightenment from a certain book:

> He sat . . . one day . . . and read for four hours, with growing absorption, in a book which had, partly by chance, come into his hands . . . It was a large volume . . . the second part, only, of a famous philosophical system . . . He was filled with a great, surpassing satisfaction. It soothed him to see how a master-mind could lay hold on this strong, cruel, mocking thing called life and enforce and condemn it . . . he struck on a comprehensive chapter and read it from beginning to end . . . with a concentration which had long been strange to him, completely withdrawn from the life about him. The chapter was called "On Death, and its Relation to our Personal Immortality" . . . He felt that his whole being had unaccountably expanded, and at the same time there clung about his senses a profound intoxication, a strange, sweet, vague allurement which somehow resembled the feelings of early love and longing.

That night he has an ecstatic revelation founded on the sentiments aroused by this chapter on death and immortality.

What Thomas has accidentally got hold of is the second volume of Schopenhauer's *The World as Will and Idea,* and he was not the only man of his generation to be suddenly enlightened by it. Briefly enough—for the next day Thomas finds it impossible to recapture the mood of the previous night—the philosopher of pessimism has illumined the depths of the official representative of the bourgeois world: the values by which he has tried to live are false; his speech over his dead uncle was vanity and falsehood; his life has been—no, life itself is—a mistake, a long straying in error; and he is exhausted and wants to sink into the voluptuous arms of death. A longing for death which is like the love-longing of youth—the formula of the *Wagnerian pathos,* the Tristan-and-Isolde cult of night- and death-worship—is what from then on alone occupies the soul of Thomas Buddenbrook and is the cause of his sudden and otherwise unaccounted-for expiry. Thomas dies because he desires to die.

The accumulated decadence of the family is at last heaped upon the shoulders of Hanno, who is unable to bear it. He is *altogether* an artist, and is "artistic-looking" in the most obvious and banal sense; and it is taken for a fact that his artistic giftedness unfits him for the business world into which he has been born. But it is made plain that the traits he bears are merely exaggerations of traits borne by the Buddenbrook line for as long as we have known them. As a concept, an "idea," Hanno is simply the act of self-abnegation of the will: that which was in the father a sudden and transient vision of salvation from a painful existence is in the son flesh and actuality; that which was for the father a fleeting intuition is for the son a normal state of being. The reader has to deduce for himself that Thomas died because he no longer wished to live, but the novel tells him explicitly that Hanno wants to die:

> Cases of typhus take the following course: When the fever is at its height life calls to the patient . . . and summons him in no uncertain voice . . . And there may well up in him something like a feeling of shame for a neglected duty; a sense of renewed

energy, courage and hope; he may recognize a bond existing still between him and that stirring, colourful, callous existence which he thought he had left so far behind. Then, however far he may have wandered on his distant path, he will turn back—and live. But if he shudders when he hears life's voice, if the memory of that vanished scene and the sound of that lusty summons make him shake his head, make him put out his hand to ward off as he flies forward in the way of escape that has opened to him—then it is clear that the patient will die.

And Hanno does die: the decadent artist, unfit for life, voluntarily passes out of it. But by that act he also extinguishes the Buddenbrook line—and thereby executes the secret wish and will of a race whose instincts had long before turned awry and led it into courses along which life could be only an error. (pp. 55-62)

We shall examine, again, the decline of the Buddenbrooks. "Decadence," artistic sensibility and physical indisposition go together, they form a syndrome. Christian is artistic and neurotic in equal measure, and these symptoms of degeneration are attended by physical symptoms: "It isn't a pain, you know," he says, "it is a misery, a continuous, indefinite ache. Dr Drogemüller in Hamburg tells me that my nerves on this side are all too short. Imagine, on my whole left side, my nerves aren't long enough! . . . I never go to sleep properly. My heart doesn't beat, and I start up suddenly." He suffers from rheumatism, "difficulty in breathing and swallowing . . . and a tendency to paralysis—or at least to a fear of it. He did not look like a man at the end of his thirties. His head was entirely bald except for vestiges of reddish hair at the back of the neck and the temples." Thomas tells him in an outburst of anger: "You are a growth, a fester, on the body of our family"—a rather unkind remark, but its imagery is suggestive and sticks in the mind. The author is delineating, not some vague "spiritual decline," but a decline into sickness.

In Christian Buddenbrook physical morbidity is accompanied by moral uncertainty. When he leaves for Hamburg his departure is "a heavy loss to the club, the theatre, the Tivoli, and the liberal livers of the town. All the 'good fellows' . . . took leave of him at the station . . . And Lawyer Gieseke, amidst general applause, fastened to Christian's overcoat a great favour made out of gold paper. This favour came from a sort of inn in the neighbourhood of the port, a place of free and easy resort where a red lantern burned above the door at night, and it was always very lively. The favour was awarded to the departing Chris Buddenbrook for his distinguished services." The irony is laboured, but that is an effect of the year 1900: the point is that, by the standards of the Buddenbrooks, Christian is immoral and a debauchee; and this characteristic is bestowed upon a man who, it is perpetually insisted, is ill.

The association of physical decline with moral decline is repeated in the case of Thomas. At the high point of his career, Thomas declares that "just now I feel older than I am," and delivers himself of the opinion that "the outward and visible material signs and symbols of happiness and success only show themselves when the process of decline has already set in." At 43 he is "an old, worn-out man": the muscles of his mouth and cheeks are flabby, his face betrays "an anguished weariness," his eyes are tired, red and watery, and his mind is filled with "dull, confused, rambling thoughts." It is precisely while he is in this condition that he decides to under-

take a transaction which he has earlier denounced as unethical but which would be profitable to the firm, thus confirming Christian's remark of many years before that every businessman is a rascal.

Hanno's decadence is associated so closely with sickliness as to be virtually identified with it, so that his artistic sensibility seems to be as directly a product of his physiology as does that of little Herr Friedemann. Hanno almost dies at birth and as an infant he is constantly unwell: "soon after the christening a three-day attack of cholera-infantum was almost enough to still for ever the little heart set pumping, in the first place, with such difficulty." He has convulsions while teething. He suffers from *"pavor nocturnus"*—night fears and visions. He weeps excessively. His second teeth cause him even more suffering than his first; the extractions required leave him exhausted and are followed by attacks of gastric fever, fitful heart action, giddiness. He is plagued by bad teeth for the whole of his brief life. His skin is very pale and his bodily strength inadequate, the reason being his failure to manufacture a sufficiency of red corpuscles. The medicines he has to take are all horrible except one: arsenic pills, which he is given once and which do him "a world of good . . . But however much he asked to have the dose repeated—for he felt almost a yearning for these sweet, soothing little pills—Dr Langhals never prescribed them again": he is, in fact, in physical need of narcotics, and he starts smoking very young. Cuts and bruises take a very long time to heal. He has deep blue shadows about his eyes. Blue shadows about the eyes are in Mann an unfailing sign of artistic sensibility, and bad teeth are an unfailing sign of general physical decay: and since Hanno's mother has the blue shadows and his father the bad teeth, Hanno, as inheritor of both, ought to have counted himself lucky to have survived as long as he did. Enough: Hanno Buddenbrook is loaded with sufficient ailments to kill a family—which, of course, is what they eventually do succeed in doing when they kill *him*.

Buddenbrooks, then, presents us with a vast *programme* of decline: of decline as loss of wealth, of decline as loss of status, of decline as loss of moral certainty and fibre, of decline as "artistic decadence": but underpinning them all is decline as physiological decay. The Buddenbrook family becomes *sick*—the rest follows. (pp. 149-51)

> *R. J. Hollingdale, in his* Thomas Mann: A Critical Study, *Bucknell University Press, 1971, 203 p.*

T. J. REED (essay date 1974)

[*In the following excerpt, Reed discusses the relationships among theme, subject, and literary technique in* Buddenbrooks.]

Buddenbrooks, Thomas Mann's only conventional novel, belongs very obviously to the traditions of nineteenth-century realism and draws on its predecessors for inspiration and in details of technique. It is also governed, beneath the realistic surface, by ideas derived from a nineteenth-century speculative tradition; the nature and degree of realism the novel achieves can only be understood when the role these ideas play is clear. In addition, this first novel is related to Mann's heritage of tradition because it is an amazingly complete and sudden solution of the problems which were created for him by his literary and intellectual background, as sketched in the last chapter.

Drawing of Mann by Rudolf Grossman, 1929.

The solution is not a permanent one, but it does become a permanent point of reference in Mann's later work and all his thinking about his art. It lies in the way a balance was for the first time struck between the young writer's stylistic means and a substantial subject to extend them. This balance can in turn be explained by the nature of the realistic approach in general and by the particular possibilities for applying it which were open to Thomas Mann.

Buddenbrooks comes closest of all Mann's works to fulfilling the basic realist aim of rendering a recognizable reality. Its techniques are "receptive and reproductive" to an extent unknown in the preceding stories. In place of the caricaturally sharp observation of detail, ungoverned by any commitment to a consistent large picture and hence essentially piecemeal in effect, there is now a sustained attempt to grasp the totality of a place, a historical span, a group of people, and an ethos. The precondition for this, as for all true realism, was a full and embracing knowledge of the particular reality to be rendered. From at least the time of the Goncourt brothers and Flaubert onwards, writers had met this demand by preliminary study and documentation. The only alternative was for the writer to write only about worlds he already knew intimately, which is clearly a severe limitation. One may write, say, an *Education sentimentale* without laboriously accumulating materials, but not a *Salammbô.*

Yet the documenting process has its own limitations and leaves problems to be solved. For the purposes of literary cre-

ation, there are different qualities of knowledge. Intensive study and extensive documentation may not produce the same result as intimate familiarity. Such a distinction, between "two kinds of knowing," has been suggestively drawn apropos Tolstoy. In *War and Peace,* it has been argued, "things are as he says they are, not because he has found out about them, but because he has drawn instinctively upon his matured awareness, that vast and privileged awareness which his family and position, as well as his own being, had conferred upon him. Knowing in *Resurrection* is by contrast a process of accretion. . . ." The distinction is relevant to Thomas Mann because so much of his later work rests on just such a process of accretion, by which the novelist attempts to make himself into an initiate, "zum Eingeweihten der liebend ergriffenen Welt." These words are spoken by Goethe in *Lotte in Weimar* in a passage which, between the lines, tries to suggest the legitimacy of Mann's own montage technique by assimilating it to Goethe's artistic processes.

In writing **Buddenbrooks,** on the other hand, Thomas Mann was able to combine both possible means to realism, the more mechanical supplementing the more intuitive. If he had an intimate familiarity with the Lübeck in which he had grown up—with its topography and even more important its ethos—he also took full advantage of a direct access to the city's past, from its most general character and mood right down to its most minute detail, through the older members of his family. (pp. 37-8)

It is evident in the novel how useful such informed accounts were. They served to give the writer a firm grasp on the detail of his subject, to back up his feeling for the organism of Lübeck life. (pp. 39-40)

The first preparatory notes for the novel are preserved in a notebook of 1897 and very early 1898. Within the first few pages, major structural members of the novel are present—Christian on page 1, "der kleine Johann" ["little Johann"] on the reverse, a sketch for the description of Old Johann on the third (the second preserved) leaf. In embryo, the "gesamte Vorgeschichte" ["entire previous history"]. Leaf 6 verso carries the novel's opening "Was ist das," page 19 a sketch of its close, the gathering of female characters "nach dem Tode des kleinen Johann" ["after the death of little Johann"].

That Hanno's death is the already planned ending, taken jointly with the generation scheme which has so quickly sprung into being, is important. It confirms that the full history of decline was there practically from the first, and also that it was all along seen, teleologically, from the viewpoint of that ending: of Hanno's inadequacy to face life and the compensating value of his accompanying sensitivity. The novel's central theme is set by the hero of a short study which was compelled by circumstances to strike longer roots. And this theme, although by no means the only one, is the governing factor in the novel.

Equally significant are two other points about the preparatory sketches. The very first name to occur, with motifs to be worked out, was Christian. Paul Scherrer thought this important because Christian is the most decadent member (*das geistig brüchigste Glied*) of the family, and thus proves the original interest in decline. But this, given Hanno as the starting-point, does not need extra proof. What is more important, against the background of Mann's early methods, is the immediate recourse to the one more or less major character in the novel who invited a caricatural treatment of the sort

Mann was by now practised at. That is to say, the author's first move is into country where he feels stylistically at home. One might see this as a slight dragging of the foot before he is drawn on, despite himself, to do something new.

This last is also a process we can document. In some other relatively early sketches, Tony Buddenbrook begins to monopolize attention—to such an extent that she almost seems to be becoming the central figure of the novel. This impression remains true of the early sections of the book as finally executed, for not only do we begin with Tony, we have the full treatment of her love for Morten Schwarzkopf and her marriage to Grünlich before ever Christian and Thomas—thematically more important characters—have become of any note. What does this suggest? That once the materials of a family history are taken in hand, some parts may begin to attract undue attention in their own right whatever their relevance to any preordained pattern. Tony Buddenbrook is an example, almost a symbol of the tension in *Buddenbrooks* between chosen theme and material—a tension which proved in the end entirely beneficial.

The pull of a theme; the pull of an old method; the pull of new material: these three factors are at work in *Buddenbrooks.* The upshot is that the seriousness of the theme (and arguably also its intimate importance to the writer, who was exploring his own prehistory as well as Hanno's), together with the volume and dignity of the materials, stimulate new methods and put the old all-too-playful irony in its place; but also that the rich materials, conceived of originally as a medium in which to work out a theme, assert their independent interest to such an extent that, far from being subordinate to that theme, they achieve equal standing and a kind of counterpoint with it. They also bring with them at least one new theme of some importance, which was unavoidably part of a business family's history: the effect of commercial motives on human living. This is interwoven with the theme of inner decline and strengthens it—which it needs.

For the idea of "decadence," of a decline in vitality linked necessarily with the rise of intellectuality (or artistic gifts or "spiritual" differentiation), is shaky by itself. The particular form of heredity theory which ultimately underlies *Buddenbrooks* is not a scientific one, and was not so even in Thomas Mann's own day. That is, it was not a Naturalist theory, respectable then, superseded now. Nietzsche is its origin, and it is a mystical assumption, on Nietzsche's authority. If, as Mann said, *Buddenbrooks* set out to present "die Psychologie ermüdenden Lebens, die seelischen Verfeinerungen und ästhetischen Verklärungen, welche den biologischen Niedergang begleiten" ("the psychology of waning vitality, the spiritual refinements and aesthetic transfigurations which accompany biological decline"), then it was Nietzsche who provided that psychology: "Der junge Verfasser von *Buddenbrooks* hatte die Psychologie des Verfalls von Nietzsche gelernt." It is Nietzsche's ideas, so limited in their basis of experience and personal in their angle of vision, that Mann was guided by: general ones in the first instance, like the idea that it is impossible to be an artist without being profoundly sick, or that the artist is the final result of the accumulated work of generations. These are ideas which Mann was to carry with him for life, but they are never more than assumptions for which a certain selection of artists provide some support. (Hence Mann's considerable difficulties over digesting the phenomenon of Goethe.) *Buddenbrooks* comes no nearer to demonstrating such a thesis than **"Der Bajazzo"** had. That "general

explanation" which Mann had accepted in the early stories as a commonplace of his day becomes *artistically* fruitful when extended back into the past in a family history; it becomes no more *intellectually* conclusive. Symptoms of decadence simply have to be scattered, with increasing frequency, over successive generations. The scattering is itself the novel's theme, "thesis" even, a deliberate dosing with decadence. The experiment had to fit the known result.

Thus the crucial and most complex figure in the Buddenbrook decline, Thomas, is no less mystified than the Bajazzo was by the malaise he experiences. Like the Bajazzo, he passionately envies and yearns to emulate the unreflectingly happy and successful children of life; like him again, he had the illusion once that he was one of those to whom success comes easily, as a kind of innate gift; and he finally has to recognize, once more like the Bajazzo, that he is not of that type and that he can do nothing about the type he is. It is the complexity of the transition which Thomas represents, from predominant normality to predominant non-normality, that makes him the key figure of the novel. Despite the initial interest in Hanno, it is Thomas to whom Mann later referred in terms suggesting the most intimate involvement: "der mir mystisch dreifach verwandten Gestalt, dem Vater, Sprössling und Doppelgänger." "Father" because Thomas was based on his father, Senator Mann; "offspring" because he was his literary creation; "double" because his mixture of bourgeois qualities and "spirit" was closer to Thomas Mann than Hanno's more extreme state.

There is of course more of the "offspring" and the "double" in Thomas Buddenbrook than of the "father." He belongs to Mann's scheme of ideas rather than to the reality he was reconstructing. His real-life counterpart, if the testimony of the one unliterary son is to be believed, was neither a tired snob nor in any way "decadent"—unless refinement and intellect, which he did have, are to be equated *a priori* with decadence. Senator Mann represented the high point of the family's period as *haute bourgeoisie* and his early death ended that phase without any slow process of decline.

But however questionable and "period" the ideas on which *Buddenbrooks* was based, their elaboration is managed with supreme delicacy and literary tact. If the theme of decline had not had such undue attention from critics, it would be possible to ignore the mystical biology it rests on. Nothing, certainly, should be done to bring this yet more into the foreground. But since it has been so much discussed, it is worth making clear that in its detail as well as in the general guiding ideas, Nietzsche was the great provider. If we leave aside the unhealthy Buddenbrook teeth, the shadows under Buddenbrook eyes, and the veins which show through at Buddenbrook temples, and pass direct to psychological detail, we find in Konsul Jean not just religiosity (doubtless what is referred to when he is said to have had the first ever "unalltägliche, unbürgerliche und differenzierte Gefühle" in the family, but something more important: a reflective consciousness in the form of interest in the family's history. His father Old Johann never had this: "Er stand mit beiden Beinen in der Gegenwart und beschäftigte sich nicht viel mit der Vergangenheit der Familie" ("he stood with both feet in the present and concerned himself very little with the family's past"). Reflection in the form of historical consciousness is pure Nietzsche, the sign of "angeborene Grauhaarigkeit." As Nietzsche presents it, it is a symptom of a more general psychological condition, a hampering self-consciousness: activity is undermined by thought, whatever is too much reflected on cannot be performed. So we find that Christian, taking up a post in the family business, expatiates embarrassingly on the joys of the merchant life, but after two weeks cannot stick the work. Thomas too, when weary and defeated, recognizes that his early successes were the product of "Reflexion." Reflection was the only basis for his conscious pursuit of aims he knew were trivial in a world he knew was small; only reflection and a "sense of poetry" could give these things a (purely symbolic) meaning, summed up in repeated allusions to Goethe's famous lines from the end of *Faust*. This slim reflective defence against reflection finally breaks down.

It is not hard to find other examples of the "psychology of decadence" woven deftly into the intrinsic interest of episodes. Yet no amount of philosophical source-tracing can demonstrate literary quality. If these details were as obtrusive in the novel as they have become in discussions of it—by Thomas Mann as well as by his critics—it would be a much less fine work than it is. Its salvation from being a mere *roman à thèse* lies in the touch with which ideas and psychological insight were embedded in real character and action—and, once again, in the sheer substantiality of the material subject. For all the skill, *Buddenbrooks* is in a sense a triumph of matter over mind.

The relationship between theme and substance is epitomized by the balance between title and subtitle. One need only imagine them in the reverse order—"Verfall einer Familie, Geschichte der Buddenbrooks"—to feel the effect which the actual order produces. Moreover, the main title, plain *Buddenbrooks,* has effects of its own, and of a subtlety out of proportion to its terseness. The family name without definite article (contrast Fontane's *Die Poggenpuhls*) is the normal way of referring in German to a family known to one, a part of one's own society. It thus renders the Buddenbrooks immediately real, evoking a community within which the name is one to conjure with. By thus speaking as if with the voice of that community, it is an economic creation of viewpoint. Beyond this, the single word perhaps suggests the omnipresence of the family, its power to fill and dominate the narrative scene, even its existence as a plentiful substance which can absorb attention. The simplicity of the one-word title is, finally, at the furthest possible remove from the rhetorical effects which are sought by a play with grammatical and syntactical forms in the earlier short stories. Some of those stories, it is true, have themselves single-word titles, but they are of very different content. From *Gefallen*, "Gerächt," and "Enttäuschung" to *Buddenbrooks* is the distance from melodramatic suggestiveness to realistic sobriety.

All this substantiates Mann's later claim that his novel is not a negative book. Contemporaries, arguing perhaps from a general assumption about his literary character rather than from the novel itself, judged it *zersetzend* ("undermining, subversive"). Mann replied that *Buddenbrooks* was too "positiv-künstlerisch," too "behaglich-plastisch" for that. Every good book written against life, he went on, is itself an inducement to live. If we stress the word "good" in that statement, it exactly catches the counterpoint between the theme of decline and decadence ("against life") and the material substance in which it is worked out. This is not to deny the general—indeed, increasing—pessimism the story-line of the novel imposes, but only to stress the positive effect which is achieved by the *artistic* fusion of this outlook with a demandingly complex reality.

It is thus not certain that "against life" is a fair description of the final effect of *Buddenbrooks,* as Mann appears by 1906 to have realized. But it does seem to describe the spirit in which he set out to write it, if we can judge by the epigraph he chose for the whole work. It is taken from Platen's poem "Vision" and has that characteristic Platen note of slightly self-conscious pessimism which the young Thomas Mann seems to have found in tune with his own outlook. The passage reads:

> So ward ich ruhiger und kalt zuletzt,
> Und gerne möcht ich jetzt
> Die Welt, wie ausser ihr, von ferne schaun:
> Erlitten hat das bange Herz
> Begier und Furcht und Graun,
> Erlitten hat es seinen Teil von Schmerz,
> Und in das Leben setzt es kein Vertraun:
> Ihm werde die gewaltige Natur
> Zum Mittel nur,
> Aus eigner Kraft sich eine Welt zu baun.

("And so in the end I grew calmer and cold, and now I should like to view the world, as if outside it, from afar. My timorous heart has suffered desire and fear and horror, suffered its share of pain, and it has no confidence in life. Let it now make mighty nature a mere means of building a world for itself, from its own strength.")

Perhaps the most significant thing about the epigraph is that Mann finally chose to delete it.

Not only Thomas Mann himself, but a number of early critics of *Buddenbrooks* used the term *plastisch* or *Plastik,* especially of the character-depiction. The word suggests a three-dimensional, almost tangible reality as of sculptured figures, but not a statuesque lifelessness. On the contrary, it implies intensely live creations, the work of a true *Dichter,* and is high praise. It was indeed a form of praise Mann was to set great store by later, when critics of his "intellectual" art denied it him. (pp. 46-53)

[In *Buddenbrooks,*] against a background of predominantly pictorial narrative, the techniques of greater penetration find their function. The book opens with a scenic fragment, the exchange between Tony and her grandfather, before ever the narrator's voice begins to fill in the social picture. Scenic method goes from strength to strength—Tony's scenes with Grünlich, the 1848 rising, Thomas's confrontations with Christian, Permaneder's arrival and first conversation with the Konsulin, Tony offering Thomas the Pöppenrade harvest deal, Thomas reproaching his mother for giving the dead Clara's inheritance to her husband—the list could be more than doubled. Scenic method goes with whatever is of such vivid interest and plain meaning that the commenting narrator is redundant. Whereas slender anecdote, treated pictorially, left plenty of slack in the virtuoso narrator's hand and resulted in excessive verbal play, the kind of substance which the Buddenbrook subject offered takes the slack up fully and demands the scene.

Even where scenic method is interrupted (and in the scenes listed above it works in phases, not exclusively) the intervening narrative in pictorial form is not playful but fully occupied with the matter in hand, often pictorial in the literal sense of rendering material surroundings, sated with detail. The decision not to use scenic method in places where it seems ideally suitable can itself be subtle policy—e.g. in the Jubilee of the family firm, with Thomas's house brim-full of congratulating Lübeckers, noise, and bustle. Here the more distant pictorial method not only gives a sovereign survey of the whole scene without getting involved anywhere, it also matches Thomas's weariness and distaste for the whole thing. It culminates in two pages which describe the crowd at its thickest, the noise at its noisiest, faces and figures on every side, even the city theatre band playing in the hall—all described in the present tense, as if to ask: will it never end?

Scenic method is half-way to intimacy in that it gives us the character direct, rendering what is spoken and leaving the inner life to be inferred. With someone as spontaneous and heart-on-sleeve as Tony, this is entirely sufficient. What would a closer inspection of her inner life add? Only a confirmation that there is virtually no further substance beneath her familiar mannerisms, her repeated and usually derivative phrases. Hence *erlebte Rede* is not necessary for her, and hardly occurs. The techniques of *erlebte Rede* and narrative from the viewpoint of the character set in with Thomas and grow more intensive with Hanno. The Senator's self-doubts, for example, and his son's sufferings at school are experienced from within. The reason is plain: these later Buddenbrooks are so much more complex than their predecessors that they require deeper probing. Moreover, their complexity is part of the writer's developing theme and also the basis of his sense of solidarity and sympathy with them. And yet these techniques are notably not used for the equally "late" and complex Christian . . .

At this point, one suddenly realizes how precise is the correspondence between technique and inner meaning in *Buddenbrooks,* how careful Thomas Mann's manipulation of viewpoint was, and how indispensable it is to understand it if we are to grasp the characters, their place in the novel, and the novel's structure. For, looking back, one can see a progression in the handling of character which exactly matches the development of the theme.

Old Johann needed only to be seen from without. Our angle of vision in his case is effectively set by Tony's child's-eye view of him on the opening page. His inner life has the inaccessibility, incomprehensibility even, of another age. His being cannot be refuted, but it cannot be penetrated. If the simple exterior conceals depths, they are not of a kind that lends itself to copious verbal analysis. In his last days and dying moment, he summarizes his experience in the one word "Kurios!"

Konsul Jean, similarly, is viewed from without, although his more extended role in the action helps to fill out our understanding (an external, not a particularly sympathetic understanding) of him, and other ways are found to make clear such complexities of motive and feeling as he does have.

Tony has already been placed, in the technical sense. In Thomas, the process of decline and spiritual or intellectual complication reaches its crucial, transitional stage, and accordingly he is treated from within. We eavesdrop increasingly on his thoughts and feelings (which is made even more necessary because of his meticulous keeping up of appearances, "die Dehors wahren") and the process culminates in the rendering of his Schopenhauer experience. But from Christian, by contrast, we are kept separated by a barrier of reserve in the narrator which matches the distaste which Thomas feels for his brother. Thomas compares Christian's embarrassing *Mitteilerei* to the self-analysis and self-expression of poets but rejects it because its content in Christian's case is trivially

pathological and sordid. The narrator's technique implies a similar judgement, for although he describes Christian's grotesque performances and records his words, he never takes us any deeper into the character. And we would surely have to go deeper in order to understand him fully and sympathetically—unlike the case of Tony's simple character, which is all surface and can be fully rendered by pictorial and scenic technique. Thus Christian inspires for the most part only an unpleasant fascination. He is marked out as an aberration even within the process of decline.

Finally, in the treatment of Hanno—the character and the thematic end towards which the novel moves and out of which it grew—there is expressed the total sympathy which his degree of sensitivity and suffering deserve, and which their link with artistic talent is bound to evoke from a narrator who has accepted unreservedly the Nietzschean doctrine about the nature and origin of artists. By the standards of this novel, which remains basically conservative in its use of the pictorial perspective, involvement with Hanno is, in a discreet way, of the maximum intensity. We see through his eyes deeply enough and long enough to be fully aware of the alternatives to Buddenbrook vitality.

It should be clear from this technical progression that the term *plastisch* for the characters in *Buddenbrooks* (and indeed in any other literary work which achieves this degree of life) is misleading in so far as the analogy with visual art suggests that the effect is managed by external description. It is not. The great figures of modern literature come alive for us because their experience is rendered, not their appearance. Is there a set-piece description of Natasha in the whole length of *War and Peace?* True, there are physical details of the major characters in *Buddenbrooks* to which our attention is drawn time and again: Thomas's raised eyebrow, Tony's haughty attitude with head back and chin in. But these are identifying marks, not descriptions, and the concentration on them—besides making for a sense of continuity—is true to the way we see those we know well most vividly in their mannerisms. Admittedly, too, there *are* set-piece descriptions of people in *Buddenbrooks,* but they tend to be of minor figures, and the effect is often on the edge of caricature, like the descriptions in the early stories. Certainly that is the result if a corresponding inner life is in no way added to complement the externals. Description alone can only give us the human being as an object, his human substance needs other approaches. (pp. 55-8)

Even where such identification does not occur, there is still a dampening down, if not a putting by, of irony. Satire and the grotesque do still have a place—the Konsulin's religious gatherings ("Jerusalemsabende"), the ugly daughters of Uncle Gotthold who are reminiscent in detail of little Herr Friedemann's sisters, Christian's more extreme oddities, the death of the diabetic James Möllendorpf from furtive cake-eating in a hired room in a poor quarter, and the almost Dickensian masters at Hanno's school. But their effect is diluted by the broad context in which they occur, in much the same way as the narrator's sharp observations of detail are often marginal to some absorbing scene: the semi-educated bourgeoisie mispronounce foreign words ("Kongflick," "Infamje") but this is only a tiny stroke in the depiction of a Buddenbrook dinner-party or a political upheaval. Moritz Heimann, the chief reader of the Fischer Verlag, thought that the satirical and grotesque elements supported rather than disturbed the large epic form. Rilke, in a remarkable review of *Budden-*

brooks, praised the objective epic presentation within which even the crueller details came to appear necessary and in place [see *TCLC,* Vol. 8, pp. 252-53].

This has brought us back to our central theme, the absorption of irony in the rescuing format of the full-length novel. It is most marked in the treatment of the major characters, who are too large and too real for the ultimately precarious irony of the early stories to find a hold. In general there is little verbal over-elaboration in *Buddenbrooks.* Where it does occur, it is a means of characterizing the pompous Grünlich, who speaks and writes a comic *Papierdeutsch.* Even Tony's foibles are only gently made fun of, not exposed to elaborate verbal ridicule. They are evoked with the affectionate tolerance of one who has learned to make allowances. Tony's character, with its real-life core in the character of Elisabeth Haag-Mann, was aesthetically rich though psychologically not complex. It offered creative scope—or, put the other way round, demanded scenic presentation. Thus, if the question "who was who" has less fascination for us than it had for contemporary Lübeckers, who read the book again and again until they "had them all," the fact remains relevant that there were real-life models. It was a factor in the making of the novel, and of the novelist.

If excess irony has largely disappeared, something akin to it—a maturer and more acceptable form of irony—remains, both in the detailed treatment and the larger structures of the novel. At the level of detail, it is fastidiousness, self-discipline, "eine Art geistiger Zucht, Disziplin, '*Haltung,*' artistischer Würde." It is what, in *Buddenbrooks,* prevents too complete an involvement of the author with particular characters, or his too complete absorption in the recreated material world of Lübeck. Sympathy with certain characters could have become sentimentality, absorption could have become descriptive wallowing. They do not do this firstly because an over-all narrator-perspective is regularly asserted, the techniques for creating immediacy and intimacy are given strict limits within the setting of a more conservative pictorial convention. But in addition new ways were devised to keep sympathy in check where it was strongest. The indirect account of Hanno's death through the montage of bare fact about the course of typhus is a celebrated and brilliantly successful instance. It does not return to the callousness of the early tales, but it avoids a tear-jerking climax. Equally good, if less obvious, is the conclusion of Hanno's piano recital before the family. After the abrupt ending of his composition (*abbrach*), the sympathetic involvement with the playing might have modulated into a moving account of the family's incomprehension, of Hanno's total isolation. But the scene is dissolved in humour—the humour of Tony's love for the boy and the incongruous form her enthusiasm takes: " 'Gerda, Tom, er wird ein Mozart, ein Meyerbeer, ein . . .' und in Ermangelung eines dritten Namens von ähnlicher Bedeutung, der ihr nicht sogleich einfiel, beschränkte sie sich darauf, ihren Neffen, der, die Hände im Schosse, noch ganz ermattet und mit abwesenden Augen dasass, mit Küssen zu bedecken." (" 'Gerda, Tom, he will be a Mozart, a Meyerbeer, a . . .' and in the absence of a third name of equal significance, which did not at once come to mind, she confined herself to covering her nephew with kisses as he sat there with his hands in his lap, still quite exhausted and his eyes far away.") Mozart and Meyerbeer—and a name of "equal" significance! The chapter closes with Thomas's reply; Gerda's reaction to the pairing we are left to imagine. Hanno is left with his far-away look, but the reader is back in the ordinary world.

Similarly with Thomas. Against the sympathy inspired by his—thematically important—divided inner self must be set the impartial account of the effect it has on his relations with his family: his harsh and clumsy alienation of Hanno, his self-righteousness towards Christian. The brothers' row after the death of the Konsulin shows this balance well: Christian's accusations make a strong case against Thomas, which he accepts. But what he is accused of—coldness, self-righteousness, egoism—sprang all along from the fear of becoming like Christian, for which he felt the potentiality within him. This admission is at the thematic heart of the novel, but the result in human terms is presented wholly objectively.

The devices which Thomas Mann uses to avoid overabsorption in the material richness of the setting can also be pinpointed, though they are even more unobtrusive, often tiny details: the brevity of the vignettes in the prolonged scenic opening of the novel, where we are taken from one area to another of the social gathering without being allowed to get involved too deeply in any; the delicate fade-out into ' . . .' with which six of the ten chapters covering this grand party end, distancing the numerous characters and their conversations by something like a *Verfremdungseffekt;* the reflections on rich men's eating and sudden dying which are induced in Doctor Grabow by the young Christian Buddenbrook's eating himself sick; or the seemingly simple descriptive sentence: "Man sass auf hochlehnigen, schweren Stühlen, speiste mit schwerem Silbergerät schwere, gute Sachen, trank schwere, gute Weine dazu und sagte seine Meinung" ("they sat on high-backed, heavy chairs, ate heavy, good food with heavy silver implements, drank heavy good wines with it, and spoke their minds"), which recreates and yet simultaneously makes the things recreated recede into the distant past, so that we see them as through a kind of historical telescope. (The effect is achieved not just by the repeated *schwer,* but by the word *man,* which both generalizes about all those present and suggests that this is the way "people" lived once.)

Such discipline on the author's part creates, in comparison with the early stories, the effect of a neutral rather than a sharply hostile narrator. No more is needed, because the larger novel-form has techniques which make it unnecessary to use those fiercer forms of immediate verbal irony. Compressed, pointed effects yield place; the narrator's point can be made more subtly over a longer span. Any criticism or undermining of the characters and the values they hold can be carried out gradually without the narrator's declaring his hand so crassly. This is the second form which irony takes on. The tactics of ironic formulation give way to the strategy of ironic structures. The aim is still to undermine critically, with the difference that now there is a real target and a recognizable moral alternative to what is criticized.

Firstly there is the religious sentiment of the Konsul, almost always juxtaposed, without comment, with thoughts of financial gain for the firm and the family. His high-minded scruples first appear in his role of unwilling mediator between old Johann and the estranged son of his first marriage, Gotthold. After all the younger Johann's expatiation on family feeling, on the need to retain God's blessing by family unity, after his concern to act justly in a situation which gives him every chance to influence his father against Gotthold, all of this culminating in the father-son discussion after the dinner-party which opens the novel: after all this build-up, and some final moral-religious reflections, there is a pause. Old Johann can scarcely see his son in the dying candle-light, he asks what he is doing. Calculating, the Konsul answers drily. His calculations make it plain that the settlement Gotthold wants would do undue harm to the firm. The Konsul's conclusion is energetic, not morally reflective: " 'Nein, Papa!' beschloss er mit einer energischen Handbewegung und richtete sich noch höher auf. 'Ich muss Ihnen abraten, nachzugeben.' " (" 'No, father!' he concluded with an energetic gesture of the hand and drew himself up still further. 'I must counsel you not to yield'.") In neutral narrative language and direct reported speech, the decisiveness of the business motivation is established.

Later we hear of the extreme diligence of the Konsul, "der mit zusammengebissenen Zähnen arbeitete und manches Gebet um Beistand in sein Tagebuch schrieb; denn es galt, die bedeutenden Mittel wieder einzubringen, die beim Tode des Alten der 'Firma,' diesem vergötterten Begriff, verlorengegangen waren" ("who worked with clenched teeth and wrote many a prayer for support in his diary; for it was imperative to regain the considerable sums which the 'firm,' that deified concept, had lost at the old man's death"). The stylistic pointers—denn ("for") and vergöttert ("deified")—are not obtrusive, certainly not heavily ironic. What is done is done by juxtaposition, and by the echoes it awakens of the previous incident.

When the Konsul puts pressure on Tony to marry Bendix Grünlich, we are well prepared to understand his motivation. Much is made of the idea of duty—to the family, and religious duty—to the point where the local pastor is put up to preaching fiercely on the text that a woman shall leave her father and mother and follow her husband. The hard fact is that Grünlich is thought a good match, with his "lively business." Little else matters. Even when the Konsul seems most understanding towards his daughter, as when, on first broaching the subject, he urges that things be proceeded with slowly—"Das alles kann mit Ruhe erwogen werden, muss mit Ruhe erwogen werden [. . .] Es gibt da viele Dinge zu überlegen . . ."—what he really means is that time is needed to make inquiries into the solidity of Grünlich's firm, inquiries which those in Hamburg, deeply engaged themselves by Grünlich's debts, will answer with lying reassurances.

The Grünlich episode is a second, and related, ironic structure, a tour de force even within the uniformly high performance of **Buddenbrooks.** As in a good detective story, all the clues are given, but not forced on the attention of the reader. Every action of Grünlich's has a plausible motive (which the Buddenbrooks believe) and is also compatible with the hidden one: the need to marry a daughter of some major firm to save his shaky enterprises. It is the kind of episode most enjoyed on second reading, where the double motivation, appearance and reality, can be savoured in detail: Grünlich's proprietorial air towards Tony after their engagement ("er betrachtete sie lediglich mit einer heiteren Besitzermiene,"), the immediate decrease in his attentiveness after the marriage, the increasing demands of his "lively business," the way Tony is kept from contact with local people, stranded without a coach of her own in an out-of-town villa, not taken into society, not encouraged to talk to people—can Grünlich be jealous? Visiting parents are so monopolized by Grünlich that they have no chance to call on their relatives locally. And finally Kesselmeyer, the banker who is always in and out of the Grünlich house, has a habit of patting Tony's cheek and saying what a blessing from above it was for Grünlich when he acquired her. All the clues become apparent as such on the day of reckoning, but are unforced in themselves and

give the episode a perfectly managed double nature. It is managed with most virtuosity in the two scenes in which Grünlich makes appeals to Tony—first to marry him, then not to leave him. This is the culmination of the "proposal" scene:

> "Tony . . . ," wiederholte er, "sehen Sie mich hier . . . Dahin haben Sie es gebracht . . . Haben Sie ein Herz, ein fühlendes Herz? . . . Hören Sie mich an . . . Sie sehen einen Mann vor sich, der vernichtet, zugrunde gerichtet ist, wenn . . . ja, der vor Kummer sterben wird," unterbrach er sich mit einer gewissen Hast, "wenn Sie seine Liebe verschmähen! Hier liege ich . . . bringen Sie es über das Herz, mir zu sagen: ich verabscheue Sie—?"
>
> "Nein, nein!" sagte Tony plötzlich in tröstendem Ton. [. . .]
>
> "Nein, nein," wiederholte sie, indem sie sich ganz ergriffen über ihn beugte, "ich verabscheue Sie nicht, Herr Grünlich, wie können Sie dergleichen sagen! . . . Aber nun stehen Sie auf . . . bitte. . . . "
>
> ("Tony," he repeated, "see me here . . . This is what you have brought me to . . . Have you a heart, a feeling heart? . . . Listen to me . . . You see before you a man who is destroyed, ruined, if . . . nay, who will die of a broken heart," he interrupted himself with a certain haste, "if you spurn his love! Here I kneel . . . can you find it in your heart to say to me: I abhor you—?")
>
> "No, no!" said Tony suddenly, in a consoling tone. [. . .]
>
> "No, no," she repeated, bending over him quite moved, "I do not abhor you, Herr Grünlich, how can you say such a thing! . . . But now do stand up . . . please . . ."

And in the second scene, we find this:

> "Antonie . . . !" sagte er. "Sieh mich hier . . . Hast du ein Herz, ein fühlendes Herz? . . . Höre mich an . . . du siehst einen Mann vor dir, der vernichtet, zugrunde gerichtet ist, wenn . . . ja, der vor Kummer sterben wird, wenn du seine Liebe verschmähst! Hier liege ich . . . bringst du es über das Herz, mir zu sagen: Ich verabscheue dich—? ich verlasse dich—?"
>
> Tony weinte. Es war genau wie damals im Landschaftszimmer. [. . .]
>
> "Steh auf, Grünlich," sagte sie schluchzend. "Bitte, steh doch auf!" Und sie versuchte, ihn an den Schultern emporzuheben. "Ich verabscheue dich nicht! Wie kannst du dergleichen sagen! . . ."
>
> ("Antonie . . . !" he said. "See me here . . . Have you a heart, a feeling heart?" . . . Listen to me . . . you see before you a man who is destroyed, ruined, if . . . nay, who will die of a broken heart if you spurn his love! Here I kneel . . . can you find it in your heart to say: I abhor you—? I am leaving you—?"
>
> Tony wept. It was exactly like that other occasion in the Landscape Room.[. . .]
>
> "Stand up, Grünlich," she said, sobbing. "Please, do stand up!" And she tried to raise him up by the shoulders. "I don't abhor you! How can you say such a thing! . . .")

The words "It was exactly like that other occasion . . ." mean precisely what they say. Not only are the situations similar, but the words the characters speak are virtually identical, and so are their gestures, which the author accordingly describes in exactly the same terms. "It was exactly like that other occasion . . ." is the author's commentary on his own device, as well as being a rendering of Tony's thoughts in the form of *erlebte Rede*.

The point of the device is not to show, in a Naturalist-deterministic spirit, that people's reactions to similar situations are identical, but to bring out the consistency of Grünlich's motives, which are commercial. Any difference between the two scenes is inessential, a matter of merely superficial changes like marriage. In both cases, Grünlich is really pleading for financial rescue, which only the Buddenbrook credit can secure. His words, "destroyed, ruined," have the ambiguity inherent in the whole episode. Technically, the repetition of these identical formulas completes a structure, linking two scenes which lie over a hundred pages apart, at the beginning and end of Grünlich's confidence trick. Morally, it reminds us that Tony the person meant nothing to him at any stage, and was torn away from Morten Schwarzkopf merely to keep Grünlich solvent.

Yet although these points are made by use of a verbal repetition, the effect is not like that of the ironic formulas in the early tales. It is only the last touch to a portrayal which depends on accumulation and connection, and which has had to be conducted with restraint: too pointed a verbal irony at any stage would have weakened the final effect. An ironic structure of this kind would be impossible in a short work. The very gentleness and unobtrusiveness of the clue-scattering requires, among other things, the intervention of other unrelated episodes to act as a distraction.

But the discussion of technique has now led us to a surprising conclusion. Once given the vicissitudes of real figures within a major subject, the "immoralist" Thomas Mann turns out to be a moralist. In the analysis of Konsul Johann Buddenbrook's guilty feelings towards his daughter, and in the description of the action which follows (the final negotiations with Kesselmeyer and Grünlich) the catastrophe of Tony's first marriage is rounded off with full moral restitution. The lesson that people's lives ought not to be sacrificed to the "deified concept of the firm" emerges clearly—at least as clearly as any moral issue in Fontane, if not as explicitly as those in George Eliot.

As such, it is part of a theme which the novel persistently returns to, that of the conflict between commercial interest and human feeling. It can be heard, unobtrusively, in small details like the report of old Madame Kröger's death, where the narrator's phrasing renders the way of thinking, perhaps even the words, normal in Buddenbrook society: "Man musste den Verlust der alten Dame mit Fassung ertragen. Sie war steinalt geworden und hatte zuletzt ganz einsam gelebt. Sie ging zu Gott, und Buddenbrooks bekamen eine Menge Geld, volle runde hunderttausend Taler Kurant, die das Betriebskapital der Firma in wünschenswertester Weise verstärkten." ("The loss of the old lady had to be borne with composure. She had reached a ripe old age and at the end had lived quite alone. She was taken by the Lord, and the Buddenbrooks got a great deal of money, every bit of a hundred thousand thalers, which reinforced the firm's working capital in the most eminently acceptable way.") It becomes explicit in Thomas Buddenbrook's reflections on the brutal cruelty of business life and

is scenically demonstrated in his furious reproaches to his mother for giving up the dead Clara's inheritance to her husband, in the course of which he states as his justification what is surely itself the indictment of business mentality: "meine Eigenschaft als Sohn [wird] zu Null, sobald ich dir in Sachen der Firma und der Familie als männliches Oberhaupt und an der Stelle des Vaters gegenüberstehe" ("my capacity as your son becomes null and void as soon as I stand before you in matters which concern the firm and the family, as its male head and in father's stead").

These criticisms culminate in the ironic coincidence whereby Thomas's most ruthless act as a businessman, the Pöppenrade deal, ends in disaster on the very day of the firm's hundred-year jubilee: the day on which the Konsulin has once again thanked God for his support, and the other members of the family have presented Thomas with a plaque bearing the founder's exhortation to do only such business by day as will allow easy sleep o' nights. Yet where, given the brutality of business life, can a line be drawn? As in the case of Hugo Weinschenk's insurance practices, where a swindle is an almost imperceptible extension of accepted *Usancen,* the judgement on Thomas's action seems a creeping indictment of business life as such.

The rich seam which this critique of commercialism offered is yet another illustration of how the material subject saved **Buddenbrooks** from being a schematic *roman à thèse.* For the author, the relationship between his "decline" theme and the theme of commercialism was that between two different levels of reality. As we saw, he shows piety and high principle to be a superstructure, in the Marxian sense, underlying which are economic interests and an unquestioning acceptance of the existing social order. The Konsulin prays for the poor, and can start on the first course of her Christmas dinner, carp in butter sauce and old Rhenish wine, with a good conscience. But this ironic revelation of the reality beneath the religious superstructure is for him only a first stage: socioeconomic reality is itself in turn a superstructure, beneath which forces yet more "real" are at work.

These forces are briefly brought to our attention in the opening pages of the novel when the sad falling off of the Ratenkamp firm and family (it is the Ratenkamps from whom the Buddenbrooks have just bought their new house in the Mengstrasse) is discussed at the celebration dinner, a kind of skeleton at the feast. Konsul Jean states his view that the dishonest partner Geelmaack who completed the Ratenkamps' ruin was less a cause than an effect. Ratenkamp was subconsciously looking for someone to bear part of the responsibility for his ruin, because he could feel the irresistible force of decline. "Diese Firma hatte abgewirtschaftet, diese alte Familie war passée" ("the firm had had its day, the family was *passé*"). Fate is thus not the sum of human actions, but a higher force affecting them. For the purposes of the social occasion being portrayed, this theory is dismissed by Old Johann Buddenbrook's remark that it is just a bee in his son's bonnet—"so eine von deinen idées"; but for the purposes of the novel, it sets a tone and creates a sense of epic premonition. The point is made that economic causes are only the realization of others less tangible. In **Buddenbrooks,** the action of Fate, in the particular "period" form of decline, merely takes on the outward dress of commercial occasion. The criticism of mercantile morality then lay near to hand as a reaction to the material subject. Moral criticism operates on the substance of episodes, it is not what determines their function in the thematic development. Thus, even so commercial a thing as Thomas's ruthlessness over the Pöppenrade affair has its thematic importance as an attempt to prove to himself that he is a hard man of action, and not an overscrupulous dreamer; it springs directly from the self-doubts which are his heritage in the process of decline. The decline itself, determined by forces to which morality is irrelevant, must not be seen as a moral judgement or nemesis on the family.

But however clear this relationship between levels of reality for the author, the final effect on the reader is less clear-cut. At the very least, commercialism becomes a theme in its own right. It interweaves with the theme of decline, as when Thomas takes Gerda to wife for reasons which include business considerations and thus contributes to the decay in Buddenbrook vitality. She, presented with such deft dramatic irony as "die Mutter zukünftiger Buddenbrooks," will bear only Hanno. And the two themes are joined in a symbolic tableau at the Jubilee celebrations when the family present Thomas with the inscribed plaque. It is to be handed over by Tony and Hanno—Tony, the victim of family and firm in her failed marriages, Hanno the victim of the very different forces of biological decline: "Tony trug die Tafel beinahe allein, da Hannos Arme nicht viel vermochten, und bot in ihrer begeisterten Überanstrengung das Bild einer entzückten Märtyrerin" ("Tony bore the plaque almost alone, since Hanno's arms could do little, and presented in her enthusiastic overexertion the tableau of a rapt female martyr"). A martyr to the interests of the family, and a decadent scion it has thrown up, both borne down by the emblem of its hundred years' activity: here the two themes meet on an equal footing. (pp. 58-69)

What are the facts about the philosophers and *Buddenbrooks*? Thomas Buddenbrook's reading of Schopenhauer occurs in part 10 of the novel, more than four-fifths of the way through it. This accords with Thomas Mann's two accounts of his own reading of Schopenhauer and of the way he at once transferred his experience to the book. He stresses that the composition of *Buddenbrooks* was already well advanced, that it was time to prepare Thomas Buddenbrook for death, that the young writer was delighted to have an opportunity to use this intense experience straight away in his nearly completed fictional work.

Besides the main Schopenhauer episode, there are unmistakably elements of Schopenhauer's thought in two passages concerning music, the description of Hanno's performance before the family and a conversation between Gerda and Thomas on musical taste. Both use the concept of a transitory and illusory moment of happiness towards which the Will strives. To these might be added the description of the organist Edmund Pfühl, whose gaze, when playing, "die Dinge träumerisch zu durchschauen und jenseits ihrer Erscheinung zu rühen schien" ("seemed dreamily to see through things and to rest somewhere beyond their appearance")— conceivably a reference to Schopenhauer's view that music is a direct expression of the ultimate reality of the Will and not, like the other arts, a mere response to the phenomena (*Erscheinung*) in which the Will is objectified. All three passages are likewise relatively late in the novel and hence fit well enough what Mann said about Schopenhauer, for that need not be taken to mean that Thomas Buddenbrook's death was the very next thing to be taken in hand.

Nothing else in the novel requires us to invoke Schopenhauer in order to clarify or deepen our understanding.

What Erich Heller [see excerpt dated 1958] says about the genesis of *Buddenbrooks*—that it "derives its intellectual plot from Schopenhauer," that it is a "philosophical novel in the sense that the imagination which conceived it bears the imprint of Schopenhauer's thought"—is wholly disposed of by Mann's own accounts. Hence Heller's whole interpretation of *Buddenbrooks* by reference to Schopenhauer's general thesis of the intellect, with its products, art and saintliness, rebelling against the life-force which has gradually evolved it— this whole interpretation, stimulating though it is, rests on an oversight.

Of course the correspondence between the line of development in *Buddenbrooks* and the general pattern of Schopenhauer's thought is not in every sense a coincidence. Mann's ideas were derived from the theory of decadence current in the period and in particular from Nietzsche. The young author of *Buddenbrooks* "learned the psychology of decline from Nietzsche," as he said. This explains perfectly well why the development in *Buddenbrooks* could appear Schopenhauerian: the similarity between Nietzsche's system and Schopenhauer's, from which it derives its general shape, means that any derivative of the one will be bound to resemble the other. Where the two philosophers diverge is in their valuation of "vitality" (*Leben*) and "intellect." Mann's own valuation of these things is no clue to where his direct allegiance and indebtedness lay. It depended clearly enough on his own experience as a *fin de siècle* artist and it is in any case an ambivalent valuation. (pp. 81-2)

The Schopenhauer case has further ramifications. The unrepresentativeness of that chapter of *Die Welt als Wille und Vorstellung* which is the core of Thomas Buddenbrook's reading ("Über den Tod und sein Verhältnis zur Unzerstörbarkeit unsers Wesens an sich"), its tendency if taken in isolation to run counter to Schopenhauer's general argument, leads Thomas Buddenbrook—as it had perhaps led Thomas Mann—to misunderstand that argument. It inspires in him a hope of mystical union after death with all the more harmonious, powerful embodiments of life. Perhaps a shade embarrassed by the misreading he had lent his character and called the "essential" in Schopenhauer ("das eigentlich Wichtige"), Mann later tried to make it plausible by suggesting that a striving for erotic union is what Schopenhauer is more profoundly and "really" about than the negation of the life-force he so lucidly and repeatedly preaches. As an alternative explanation, Mann took over the discovery by critics of a Nietzschean admixture to Thomas Buddenbrook's (and perhaps his own) reading of Schopenhauer. "Hier dachte freilich einer, der ausser Schopenhauer auch schon Nietzsche gelesen hatte." The misreading makes it quite plain that there was no intention of making that episode a "consummation" for a Schopenhauerian "syntax of ideas" in *Buddenbrooks,* since an untypical chapter and a misunderstanding of an argument are an inept consummation of that argument's effect; while Mann's later adjustments illustrate the dilemmas of a writer caught in the meshes of *Geistesgeschichte* by the simple fact of having used an experience which happened to be the excitement of reading Schopenhauer.

It would be tedious to follow all this out in detail. I have had to say this much to unpick some of the strands of "tradition" plaited by Thomas Mann and his critics. This has meant wandering from the central concerns of a reader of *Buddenbrooks.* He must be recommended to keep a sense of proportion; to take seriously the ideas which were current at the time Mann wrote the novel, especially where there is clear internal and external evidence that particular ideas were important; and not to read the Schopenhauer episode as part of an intellectual plot except in the sense that it is itself the finely conceived culmination of Thomas Buddenbrook's history as a divided burgher. The reader can safely take *Buddenbrooks,* whatever may later be true of the complex weave of *Der Zauberberg* and *Doktor Faustus,* as a novel in the nineteenth-century manner, concerned with story, character, psychology, and moral criticism, all of which give substance to a general thesis. The Thomas Mann of *Buddenbrooks* is not yet predominantly a novelist of ideas. His ideas are buried in that rich substance, fused with it successfully if involuntarily. We separate them out and stress them only to the detriment of the novel.

Only by taking *Buddenbrooks* on these terms as a successful, if highly sophisticated and late essay in nineteenth-century realism do we grasp the novel's significance in Thomas Mann's career, in his thinking about his art, in his ambitions for future works. In retrospect, the novel and his composition of the novel came to appear transfigured, ideal. It represented for him a standard of achievement and a solution to problems of technique and balance which was exemplary. Substance, so problematic in his later works, was there in this first masterpiece in plenty, enough to extend the writer technically, and apt to express his ideas not allegorically but in full fictional fusion. (pp. 83-4)

T. J. Reed, in his Thomas Mann: The Uses of Tradition, *Oxford at the Clarendon Press, 1974, 433 p.*

T. E. APTER   (essay date 1978)

[*Apter is the author of the critical study* Thomas Mann: The Devil's Advocate, *which contends that Mann believed "an investigation of evil's force and fascination would result in refreshing disgust with evil." In the following excerpt from that work, Apter explores the emotional lives of the Buddenbrooks.*]

The dramatic structure of [*Buddenbrooks*] is based upon the tension between artistic sensibility and life-orientation, but the "life" which Mann posits in opposition to imagination is comically depleted life. Life is the collection of physical objects as symbols of wealth and business success. It is social position and family tradition—tradition as public display. The comedy of manners is a tremendous success, and in itself places the novel among Mann's best. Indeed, the characters have a vividness which is uncommon in his later works, and this vividness redeems them as characters, despite their empty lives and ambitions. The scene in which Tony's parents try to persuade her to marry Grünlich because they believe, very mistakenly, he will be an asset to the family and to the firm, is one among many examples of the characters' shallowness, selfishness and confusion drawn lightly and pointedly, with their complacency balanced by the ruthless social forces that are outstripping their simple burgher mentality:

> "How nice to find you still here, for once, Papa," [Tony] said as she held her egg in her napkin and opened it with her spoon.
>
> "But today I was waiting for our slug-a-bed," said the Consul. He was smoking a cigar and tapping on the table with his folded newspaper. His wife finished her breakfast with her slow, graceful motions, and leaned back in the sofa.

> "Tilda is already busy in the kitchen," continued the Consul, "and I should have been long since at work myself, if your mother and I had not been discussing a serious matter that concerns our little daughter."

> Tony, her mouth full of bread and butter, looked first at her father and then at her mother, with a mixture of fear and curiosity.

> "Eat your breakfast, my child," said the Frau Consul. But Tony laid down her knife and cried, "Out with it quickly, Papa—please." Her father only answered, without for one moment ceasing to play with his newspaper, "Eat your breakfast first."

> So Tony drank her coffee and ate her egg and bread and green cheese silently, her appetite quite gone. She began to guess. The fresh morning bloom disappeared from her cheek, and she even grew a little pale. She said "Thank you" for the honey, and soon after announced in a subdued voice that she had finished.

> "My dear child," said the Consul, after a further moment's silence, "the matter we desire to talk over with you is contained in this letter." He was now tapping the table with a big blue envelope instead of the newspaper. "To be brief: Bendix Grünlich, whom we have learned to regard as a good and charming man, writes to me that during his stay here he has conceived a strong inclination for our daughter and he here makes a formal request for her hand. What does my child say?"

> [. . .] "I don't know him the least little bit," Tony said in a dejected tone, wiping her eyes on the little white batiste serviette, stained with egg. "All I know is, he has golden-yellow side whiskers, and a flourishing business. . . ." Her upper lip, trembling as she wept, had an expression indescribably touching.

> With a movement of sudden tenderness the Consul jerked his chair nearer hers and stroked her hair, smiling.

> "My little Tony, what could you possibly know about him? [. . .] You are a child, with no eyes yet for the world, and you must trust other people who mean well by you [. . .] Meanwhile I shall write an answer to Herr Grünlich's letter, without either consenting or refusing. There is much to be considered.—Well, is that agreed? What do you say?—And now Papa can go back to his work. Adieu, Betsy."

> "Auf Wiederschen, my dear Jean."

> "Do take more honey, Tony," said the Frau Consul, who sat in her place motionless, with her head bent. "One must eat enough."

The scope of the Buddenbrooks' emotional life is fully covered by Tony's slight bout of paleness, by the indescribably touching trembling of her upper lip, by her father's sudden tenderness that contains no understanding, and by the mother's belief that more honey will compensate Tony for her unappealing husband. The parents' knowledge of Grünlich as a good and charming man is based upon forged business records and references granted by creditors who have been promised payment upon receipt of the Buddenbrook dowry. The Buddenbrooks' assessment of the world as a straightforward place which can be governed by hard work and good sense is overtaken by Grünlich's schemes.

All the old burgher families of the Buddenbrook type decline while the new, unscrupulous merchants thrive. The latter are untroubled by sentiment and aesthetic sensibility. Their children, Hanno Buddenbrook's schoolmates, are interested only in physical bravado, crude jokes and the glory of the fatherland. These boys, with their arrogance and conceit, clearly belong to the generation that will encourage Nazism. These boys despise the arts, and Mann has not, at this point, drawn any connection between aesthetic and political interests. The aristocratic class, which declined while the burgher class was still strong and which has now accepted its failure in the practical world, has emerged as a new type, as the artistic class, while the burghers flounder amid the mingling of their practical ambitions and their aesthetic natures.

Like Nietzsche, Mann did not believe that the surviving specimen was the best possible specimen of man. A practical, shallow consciousness had the strength of the herd behind it and could therefore defeat the fragile but more valuable imagination; but unlike Nietzsche—and this is characteristic of Mann's portrayal of the artist—he did not see the man who undermined the values of the herd as a strong man. Nietzsche believed that eventually the higher man's resentment at the denial of his imagination would prove creative; in the decay of the old order, the higher man would create new values with his abundance of life and strength. For Nietzsche life and strength were allied to creativeness. Mann, however, lacked a thoroughly positive evaluation either of life or creativeness. His comedy of manners does not simply register the stupidities and confusions of the patrician class; it provides a definition of life which offers a poor alternative to imagination.

Nonetheless, in the first seven parts of the novel, artistic sensitivity is no more robust or valuable than the burghers' impoverished "life." The first deviant from a purely practical way of life is Gotthold Buddenbrook, Johann Senior's child by his first wife, whom he married out of love rather than prudence. Gotthold, is in turn, married for love and disgraced the family by his marriage, and his half-brother Johann Junior, reveals an imaginative strain in his sentimental love for the family record book and his pietism. Christian Buddenbrook's imagination, the most pronounced of his generation, is totally morbid, debilitating, melancholic. It is not until Hanno, the last male Buddenbrook, that, vaguely, the imagination reaches towards something of real value.

The tension between art and life, then, is presented primarily as that between the bland, dull-witted and insensitive on the one hand, and the morbid, nervous and idle on the other. The problem is presented as an emotional battle, a battle between conflicting impulses, rather than a Nietzschean battle of values. The poverty of the alternatives, therefore, is less important in this novel than the struggle itself.

Tom Buddenbrook is the focus for the destructive work of the imagination upon ordinary, healthy life. He believes he can use his imagination to serve the family's reputation, but his admiration of elegance is at odds with the solid, substantial, tasteless regard for wealth that had served the previous generation so well. The new light and airy house he builds in Fischer Lane wastes the family's capital on mere appearance. He designs it according to aesthetic principles and thus it lacks the spirit upon which the family's survival depends. He is unable to keep pace with current business methods because

he seeks inspiration from some ideal, rather than from reality. He is indecisive and bewildered when faced with the need to make practical decisions, for there is no meeting point between his imagination and the world.

Soon after the death of Consul Johann, Tom's father, Mann mentions that Tom's hands are different from the typically broad Buddenbrook hand, that they have well-groomed, oval fingernails and make little gestures of shrinking sensitivity and painful reserve. His physical constitution, too, is weak; the blue veins show clearly at his narrow temples, and he has a tendency to chills. At forty-eight he looks and feels like an old man; yet, like an artist, he believes in the power of appearance, and hopes to restore his energy by preserving an immaculate exterior. Aware of his inward dissolution, his life becomes that of an actor. Every hour he has to withdraw to groom himself again; and, since his essence has become his appearance, he must always have the spotlight upon himself; to have his appearance ignored is, for the actor, annihilation.

Imagination wills the destruction of practical life, and Tom is helpless in face of this will. He believes that sense and sensibility can be combined, but, in Mann's view, imagination will not rest until it is supreme. Only when imagination is self-sufficient, only when the significance of reality—other than as fodder to the imagination—is denied, can the imaginative person thrive, as Felix Krull thrives. In the case of an imaginative person who values a practical life, the conflict results in inward dissolution; there is a total split between what he finds attractive and what he values. This impasse creates a sympathy with death; for in death the conflict is resolved; in death one is freed from practical striving and one merges with the eternal force, the eternal longing which in all Mann's works is allied to the imagination.

When Tom sees his traditional values—the continuation of the family line and the progress of the business—as a dead end, when his only son proves to be totally unsuited to business affairs, when even his wife deserts him for music, he finds a volume of metaphysical philosophy inside a drawer of a garden table. For the most part, this volume reads like the third book of Schopenhauer's *The World as Will and Idea,* in which the reality of death is denied. In Schopenhauer's view, generation and death are equal manifestations of the Will; and wherever Will exists, life exists, for the Will is life. When the individual dies, the Will is freed from the deception and limitation of individuality; it wakes again in its eternal, primal aspect.

Tom Buddenbrook feels a tremendous release as he confronts this metaphysical view. For a few hours he is able to see the unreality of the merchants' ambitions and the pettiness of his failures. Since his release is the same sort of negation of 'life' that music, as the strongest representative of the imagination, provides, it is not surprising that the language in which Tom's metaphysical ecstasy is described, is similar to the language Mann uses to describe other musical experiences. Tom feels a strange, pressing but sweet intoxication that renders him incapable of consecutive thought, yet which seems to flood his mind with light. He is welcoming the power of the imagination, which destroys him, as it will destroy Hanno and Aschenbach and Mario.

The joyful expansion, the life-assertion Tom sees in his volume of metaphysics, is not actually found in Schopenhauer. Indeed, the philosopher lamented the fact that individual death was not actual death. He recommended complete suppression of one's will, so that one's individual death might more plausibly be an end to that carefully starved will. For only in annihilation of one's will is there rest from pain, deprivation, yearning on the one hand, and ennui and despair on the other. In the volume Tom Buddenbrook finds, however, the Will's passion and indestructibility are embraced with Nietzschean energy. He reflects that he has been mistaken in worrying about the survival of the family name and of the family firm. He had been accustomed to supposing that only the survival of these would ensure his own immortality, but this metaphysical argument convinces him that he will live on in all those who discover the elemental, eternal Will in their own selves; he will live on in all those who say "I"—especially in those who say "I" potently, fully, gladly. In death, as he merges with the Will, he will realise the fundamental and valuable part of his self. It is a vision based not as much upon a metaphysical supposition of the world's constitution, as upon a way of life. Tom sees his capacity for vitality and life-confidence as the measure of his true worth. He sees the possibility of kinship with other people who share this power and conviction. He does not discover a new metaphysics as much as a new morality—a morality in light of which his commercial ambitions seem unreal, unreal in the sense of being shallow and unimportant. He discovers his share in a humanity and joy that will never be destroyed as long as any life remains, and this participation satisfies him as an image of his own immortality.

Tom, however, cannot sustain this vision. In the morning he feels ashamed of the previous night's extravagance, and he never returns to the volume. The cruel failure of his hold upon this positive image of death can be seen in Tom's actual death. Mann shows the seedy-looking Senator leaving the assembly early, continually flexing his mouth as though to swallow an unpleasant liquid. In a grotesquely comic scene the dentist tries to extract the tooth that has been bothering Tom, but the crown of the tooth breaks, which means that the four roots will have to be extracted separately. On his way home, Tom collapses in the street. Mann's emphasis on the ugliness of his death—his mud-spattered clothes, the pool of blood lying beside his mouth, the abrasions on his face—confines it to the petty world of respectable appearances and business dealings in which Tom has failed. Nor is there any personal connection that might redeem this sordid picture. His wife Gerda turns her face away in disgust as he is carried upstairs. His sister Tony tries to uplift the wake with a hymn, but in mid-phrase she forgets the words, and the sentimental effect becomes an excruciating embarrassment.

In *Buddenbrooks* life is defined as business and social concerns. Tom's single redemption was a denial of the importance of life, and though this denial carried an atmosphere of vitality, it was allied to death. In Schopenhauer's metaphysics, the vision of the personal will as a part of one Will, the vision which for a few hours entranced Tom, is a starting point of morality; for in acknowledging the ultimate reality as a single Will, the conflict of desires is seen to be absurd and one sees oneself as the subject of all suffering—therefore one seeks to mitigate suffering. For Tom, however, the sympathy is more selective; he identifies only with those who say "I" potently and gladly. More importantly, the sympathy he discovers through this identification has no relevance to his attitude towards the people around him. The metaphysics offers a release from concern for those people rather than a deepening of his sympathy with them. Any happiness of a value greater than complacency, it seems, can only be found apart

from immediate life. There can be no resolution between practical, active life and reflection or imagination because the practical and immediate world is shallow, whereas imagination seeks vision and meaning. Mann presents the two in utter opposition, one destructive of the other.

Human emotion and the need for human connection might provide an area of possible resolution between the appeal of the imagination and the limiting bonds of life. If one made the highly plausible assumption that people have certain emotional needs, that at least part of human meaning is realised in close personal relations, and that emotions are in some way tied to the imagination, that the kind of stimulus either passion or family affection provides is akin to the expansion and intensity promised by the imagination, then we have a starting point for resolution. The imagination is a vagrant; it cares nothing for actual commitment but only for that which will present the most satisfying image. Personal ties demand responsibility and commitment; people, generally, want to be connected to others, and this connection limits other possibilities and gives the actual emotional situation a meaning which compensates for the loss of freedom. If emotion is understood to be real and valuable, then imagination's need for meaning, intensity and communion would have some fulfilment in life. Imagination's values would have some possible realisation in the actual, immediate world, though to achieve this realisation imagination's vagrancy would have to be controlled by a limiting reality.

In most of Mann's writing, however, the need for human connection is ignored and the value of emotion is denied. The bridging of the gap between life and imagination is not seen as something which our own emotional needs render necessary but rather as something which is prudent for social survival. The gap is so great, in short, because there is no convincing reason to bridge the gap, so long as one prefers the profundity of image as opposed to the shallowness of life. Love is, *prima facie,* on the side of imagination; it is not an emotion which the sturdy strain of Buddenbrook values, and the first sign of 'bad blood' in the family—of character, that is, not totally committed to practical issues—is Gotthold, who is the product of a love match (Johann Senior was married to Gotthold's charming mother for one year, but in Mann, love and health do not go together, and she died in giving birth) and who, in turn, disgraces the family in his choice of a love-mate. In subsequent works Mann presents passion as a feverish aggravation of the imagination, as an emotion which isolates one from the world rather than as one which binds one to it; his notion of passion is not desire for contact or connection with another person but rather a longing to be steeped in one's own longing and to be destroyed by it. In *Buddenbrooks* love works against practical success, but it is too weak to be anything more than a nuisance. Emotional compulsion in the family line is incipient and frail; it emerges as little more than stupidity. Gotthold's clandestine love-marriage is never presented directly, but the grotesque offspring indicate that the marriage does not provide fulfilment. When Christian is finally able, after the deaths of his mother and brother, to marry the woman he loves, the woman who, he believes, will give him the affection and respect his family deny him, she commits him to an institution and appropriates all his money. Even young Tony, who is so thoroughly committed to being a Buddenbrook that she fails miserably whenever she tries to join another family, is tempted by love to deviate from purely practical considerations; and in this case, too, love turns out to be pathetic and illusory. Morten blurts out his request that Tony wait for him until he takes his medical degree; she gives her promise and they seal the agreement with a kiss: "Then they stared in different directions into the sand, and both felt the utmost shame."

It is plausible that in this situation the initial spark of love did die and leave nothing but shame. However, Mann is seldom able to present a more robust view of love. (Even Aschenbach, despite the fervour of his feelings, is afraid to speak to Tadzio lest he be disillusioned.) When Pierre proposes to Hélène in *War and Peace,* Pierre's shame indicates the emotional hollowness of this particular situation; but Mann's portrayal of the nervousness and distaste in emotional expression is a comment not on one particular situation, but on emotion itself. The obvious irony of these love situations (for Morten becomes a successful doctor and therefore would have been, both in social and financial terms, a better match for Tony and the Buddenbrook family than was Grünlich, for whom she forsakes Morten; and Christian's love-marriage, which he believes will shield him from the loneliness he suffers within his own family, results in total isolation) is not an example of Mann's notorious irony of ambiguity. He does not, in *Buddenbrooks,* present love as an emotion which appears to be utterly satisfying but which actually is destructive, or which destroys even as it satisfies; he simply shows love to be shallow. Imagination, even as it undermines practical life, seems to realise some human need; but in this novel love is a mere mistake. The irony in these love situations does not emerge from a balance of good and evil or from a sense of good within evil; it is the comic irony which emerges as the characters move towards their own downfall while they see themselves as cleverly avoiding it.

This reductive portrayal of love is one aspect of Mann's slender understanding of any interpersonal emotion. When a marriage is successful as a financial and social arrangement, Mann seems to believe that only social and financial issues are relevant to a description of the marriage. Johann Junior married Elizabeth Kröger when his father tapped him on the shoulder and pointed to the daughter of the wealthy aristocrat. From that moment, Mann says, Johann Junior honoured his wife as the mate entrusted him by God. These remarks constitute the total emotional story. And when Johann Senior's wife dies, Mann says, "She had never given him either a great joy or a great sorrow; but she had with good breeding played her part beside him for many long years— and now, likewise, her life was ebbing away."

It is not the lack of love between married people that is implausible but the lack of any feeling whatsoever. It is difficult to believe that Tony does not even hate Grünlich after living with him and bearing his child and being cheated and ignored by him. Her revulsion is not developed beyond the initial distaste; it is simply part of the comedy. Consistently Mann refuses to give his characters an emotional dimension.

Sometimes Mann's failure to focus personal relationships results not only in an incomplete presentation of character but also in an inconsistent one. Mann says of Tom and his wife Gerda that there was not much love in their feelings for one another, though there was a correct, respectful politeness due not to estrangement but to a peculiar, silent, profound mutual knowledge. This assertion, however, cannot be accepted in light of his other descriptions of the couple. It is possible that Gerda, with her cool, reserved sensibility has some deep, silent knowledge of Tom, though there is no indication that she has any respect for his business concerns nor that she has any

understanding of his confused battle with imagination. It is inconceivable, however, that Tom has a deep knowledge of her. Mann, in fact, emphasises Tom's bewilderment in face of his wife's absorption in music. He feels threatened and utterly at a loss when she shares that interest with another man because he knows he cannot understand her. The couple exhibit a marked lack of mutual respect in their conflicting attitudes towards their son's musical inclinations and lack of business acumen; and there is no sign of regard for her husband in the way Gerda turns her face away in disgust as Tom's body is carried into the house.

Nonetheless, it would be misleading to call Mann an insensitive writer. His awareness of feeling comes alive in the tension his characters suffer between life and imagination. His portrayals of isolation, despair, ecstasy, alienation and fear of death, are unrivalled. In such cases the characters are not reduced to social and financial considerations. Their physical defects become unimportant, and however ironic the situation, sympathy is not undermined—as it is in his love situations—by the sense that their emotions are ridiculous. Frau Consul Buddenbrook, Tom's mother, has been presented as her husband's proper but insignificant partner, as a well-meaning but ineffective mother—in short, she is nothing more, emotionally speaking, than a moderately competent Buddenbrook, until she becomes ill; and alone, outside the family structure, she struggles with death. Then, brilliantly, her personality is given a new dimension. She is no longer the character in the comedy of manners, defined by the solid expensive objects in her house, she is a force battling bravely against terror and decay. This new dimension is not inconsistent with Mann's earlier presentation of her character, but brings out the value in what had previously seemed mere shallowness. The Frau Consul's fight against death is one aspect of her commonplace healthiness. Her consciousness had once been bound by practical interests (with the exception of an excessively religious sentimentality which was probably responsible for the unhealthy, imaginative traits in her children) but now the respect for survival emerges as a positive force. She has a naïve, robust hatred of illness, and therefore her soul will not give in to disease. The disease, therefore, has to break her down both physically and spiritually. Her symptoms are described in cold, ugly detail; but the blood-impregnated mucus she brings up with her cough, the failing digestion, the bed sores that grow worse and will not heal, her sunken, roving eyes, her delirium, are not here—as are similar symptoms in *The Magic Mountain*—subjects of fascination. Rather, they show the battle between life and death, a battle whose cruelty is far more vivid than in the Berghof Sanatorium, where dissolution is always welcome. When Frau Consul's healthy spirit is destroyed she struggles towards death, but not because she has become corrupt in the way Hans Castorp or Aschenbach are corrupt. Her desire for death is not a Romantic yearning but a desire to escape useless pain.

Certainly this breakdown of the healthy spirit into a craving for death is a model of the Buddenbrook family itself, with the once healthy, naïve practical consciousness passing through a variety of painful spiritual diseases until, in Hanno, death is the only possible resolution; but Frau Consul's death gives some dignity and significance to the will to survive which so often in the novel is presented as petty and shallow. Frau Consul faces death and fights it, whereas imagination faces it and is hypnotised by it.

Mann is similarly sensitive to the sufferings of Tom and Hanno, but always the emotions he sympathetically explores are those which define a character's isolation and his rejection of the ordinary world. In subsequent works Mann treats the longing to escape with careful irony. The sweetness of release is set against the necessity of self-control and commonplace existence, but in *Buddenbrooks,* escape from the merchants' practical life—though the only escape is death—is welcomed with only very slender modification. Tom's metaphysical ecstasy which denies the reality of his business worries and which puts him in contact with all those who say "I" potently and gladly, is based upon a vision of death, and his joyful sense of release from boundaries and barriers is the sense that is he approaching death. Music, too, the vehicle of his son Hanno's release, is a path to death.

Schopenhauer believed that music was the highest art form because it was the most direct expression of the Will that could appear in the phenomenal world. Music itself, as sound, is of course phenomenal, but it does not depend upon concepts as do other art forms. Music is a first-hand representation of the Will, for it expresses longing, strife, desire, and despair without reference to particular manifestations of these emotions. Other art forms generally refer to the world in its phenomenal aspect; for the painter, sculptor and poet, the world he represents is the phenomenal world, the world of individual things—trees, bodies, people, subjects and objects of desire and need. Therefore, art forms other than music are representations of representations of the Will, and are therefore less immediate and powerful than music.

Though Mann shares Schopenhauer's assessment of music's power and believes that the power depends upon its special access to the deepest energies of the psyche, he does not use Schopenhauer's metaphysical argument. After all, Schopenhauer concludes from the argument with which he supports music's claim to superiority, that opera, in which individual people and situations are represented, is the lowest form of music. For Mann, however, this musical form was particularly compelling; it is the meeting-place of the Will's prime representative and the actor, the man who values illusion more than reality.

The imaginative strain in the Buddenbrook line—which appears in Consul Johann Junior's love for the family record book, Tom's admirations for elegance and his compulsion to keep up his appearance as a successful merchant, Christian's hypochondria and passion for the theatre—has its final development in Hanno's love for music, especially for Wagner. The doors to life are now closed tightly, and imagination finds so perfect a satisfaction that it can never again turn to practical existence. (pp. 15-26)

In *Buddenbrooks* Mann did not offer any resolution to the opposition between imagination and life. He merely stated the opposition and left it at an impasse. The only fulfilment imagination could have was in death. The chapter that follows the detailed account of Hanno's love for Wagner constitutes nothing more than a description of the course of typhoid fever. The despondency, lethargy and delirium which characterise the disease are a counterpart of his response to music. The longing Hanno hears in Wagner's *Lohengrin* and which he suffers as his own, stifles him; but the life alternatives presented in this novel are so impoverished that this passive acceptance of death commands not only sympathy but also approval. It is against this obviously limited vision which Mann's humanistic principles subsequently struggle. (p. 30)

T. E. Apter, in his Thomas Mann: The Devil's Advocate, *Macmillan Press Ltd., 1978, 165 p.*

HUGH RIDLEY   (essay date 1987)

[*Ridley is the author of* Thomas Mann: 'Buddenbrooks,' *a study of Mann's first novel which includes information about Mann's life and description of the historical context of the novel as well as literary analysis. In the following excerpt from that work, Ridley discusses the ways in which elements of* Buddenbrooks *and its place in German and world literature illustrate the complex evolution of the genre of the novel.*]

In its narrative technique, its analytical approach to social reality, its reliance on observation and documentation and its pragmatic commitment to reality *Buddenbrooks* meets the expectations of the realist movement in European fiction and brings them to artistic fruition.

Within the context of German literature *Buddenbrooks* occupies the place of a landmark, and its achievement is to have brought the German novel into line with the great tradition of European fiction. One novel cannot create an intellectual revolution on its own, but it can demonstrate the possibilities of the moment, and the work of Thomas Mann (and to an important extent that of his brother Heinrich also) brought new standards into German fiction. The break with provincialism was achieved while—as Eberhard Lämmert has shown—bringing together European styles and traditional German forms, notably the novel of education ("Bildungsroman"), integrating the new and progressive with positive elements of the national tradition. The notorious lack of continuity of German cultural life in this century, broken repeatedly by wars and revolutions, by Hitler's Reich and by division, has made this achievement less fruitful than it might have been, but even such discontinuity cannot diminish its stature.

The literary achievement of one generation cannot simply be copied by the next. However much they are admired, the forms and genres that are valid for one age cannot be adopted by the next without modification, and the more radical the breaks between generations, the greater these modifications will be. As a recent critic has observed, literary forms and genres are "historically conditioned forms of communication and mediation": it is their appropriateness to the quality of personal and social experience that causes them to rise and fall with the succeeding generations. . . . [Mann's search for genre as he worked on *Buddenbrooks*] was anything but a shopping-trip to a treasure store of externally valid forms of the novel, rather an attempt to find forms appropriate to the themes and attitudes his historical situation had given him.

Many aspects of the modern movement can be seen as an approach to Mann's central problem in *Buddenbrooks:* to portray individual characters within a society whose values increasingly contradict theirs. As society has become less personal and less stable than the world of the Buddenbrooks, so the techniques of the novelist have had to change. The individual techniques and attitudes which the nineteenth-century realist writers used in their art (for instance, documentary, reported speech, interest in history) have not lost their validity; what seems unattainable is the ensemble of formal techniques and attitudes, in short the genre itself. Mann's situation in twentieth-century literature and the reception of *Buddenbrooks* are, therefore, inseparable from what is loosely called the "crisis of the novel." Indeed we may argue that the passage of time has eroded precisely those elements in the work which we can now recognise as having constituted the genre of the nineteenth-century realist novel. We may list these variously as: a vision of totality, confidence in narrative detachment, and the commensurateness of private and public history.

It is one of the hallmarks of the realist novel that, like a genie emerging from the lamp, or like that process by which a zoom lens turns close-up into long-shot, a picture of totality was created out of the portrayal of individuals enmeshed in personal and social relations, a totality which transcended individual experience. In his famous remarks on art at the end of the classical period, Hegel had argued that the novel could not assume that each individual was the complete expression of his age and society—this had been the feature of the epic which gave it such luminous pre-eminence in the history of human culture. In an age of alienation and the division of labour Hegel had suggested that the novel, as the successor to the epic, had the task of portraying a different type of historical experience, in which the individual appears "not as the independent, complete and at the same time individually living representative of this society itself, but only as a limited member of it." The novel must reconstruct in the telling of its plot the lost totality of the ancient epic and is concerned not with the natural unfolding of character in the plot, but the conscious search and struggle for self-realisation in the world. It was the achievement of realism, perhaps its purpose too, to give artistic form to this search for meaning, to demonstrate that it is possible to be a St. Teresa in Middlemarch, a Caesar by the Baltic; to prove through the writing of fiction that "Yvetot is worth Constantinople" (Flaubert), or that (in Fontane's example) a single drop of pond water is as intensely full of the totality of life as an heroic event such as Columbus discovering America. In this way the realists expressed their confidence in being able to enfold within their stories the totality of life which idealist philosophy had shown to be under threat. *Buddenbrooks* participates in this confidence, in part in the skill with which it sees ideas clothed in events. J. P. Stern refers to Thomas's death, for instance, as the "consummation of its [the novel's] events and ideas alike" ["The Theme of Consciousness: Thomas Mann," in *Modernism 1890/1930,* eds. Malcolm Bradbury and James McFarlane]: the identity of idea and event being the novelist's achievement. Clear too is Mann's faith in the novel to create that lesser totality, between the individual character and the historical movement. It was, after all, the skill in using individual characters to represent distinct periods of historical development that had first attracted Mann to *Renée Mauperin.* This is a lesser form of totality, for it may be that what history gives to a character is precisely fragmentation and lack of rounded totality. So, for instance, Henri Mauperin was described as being marked by "this important feature of the second half of the nineteenth century"; yet this was a description of an unnatural combination of characteristics, namely that of youth and coldness. Even such portrayals, however, presupposed the ability of the novel to summarise historical totality within individual characters, a confidence which we [see] also in *Buddenbrooks.*

Such linking of subject and world, the creation of totality, is the achievement of the novel's narrator. If "history," as Hegel argued, "by itself" no longer created individuals who in themselves enshrined either the full totality of man's being or even the limited totality of the historical moment, then the novelist must create these for himself. Since the intention of realism is to restore totality as a feature of reality, rather than

to present it as a personal vision of the artist's, the realist novel seldom personalises the act of narration. This is not to diminish the personal nature of the narrative achievement, for, as Adorno remarked in an important commentary on "The Position of the Narrator in the Contemporary Novel" (1954), "the subjectivity of the narrator is preserved in the power with which the illusion of reality is produced." . . . [This] accurately denotes the techniques used in the narration of *Buddenbrooks.* Mann shares with realism the reluctance to locate sense only within subjective experience. His personal narrative stance achieves objectivity by being multipersonal, providing a shifting series of viewpoints, establishing sense and meaning in different places and in ways different from those suspected by the characters. Its mixture of identification and distance, empathy and analysis, consensus and outsider status is characteristic of the traditional realist novel.

It is a truism of literary history that these, the constitutive elements of Mann's novel, are precisely those features which the so-called "crisis of the novel" has made problematic. Totality seems inaccessible to most novelists, and it is to make excessive demands on the novel that its knowledge should make sense of the world. Modernist writing, "the one art that responds to the scenario of our chaos" as Malcolm Bradbury and James McFarlane described it in [*Modernism 1890/1930*], has no longer any confidence that it can achieve a totality which the world does not yield, and it sees no chance to create within itself a meaning which is more than private, which might reach out and signify the meaningfulness of the world. In an age of anonymous trusts and cartels, of mass-killing and of institutionalised inhumanity, the modern novelist seems unwilling to commit his work to public statement or to bring together private and public world as his nineteenth-century predecessors had done. His own function being so radically changed, the narrator figure takes on the task of questioning the narrative which in the traditional novel it was his subjective achievement to have created. As Adorno pointed out, the modern novel is characterised by the writer's "committed stance against the lie of the presentation [of reality], in fact against the narrator himself." Hence the proliferation of prose forms in which the narrative stance is either parodied or constantly reflected upon, or the fiction is created (in documentary writing) that narration is negated altogether.

It is understandable that these sweeping changes in the form and presuppositions of the novel should have had a considerable influence on the reception of a novel which, like *Buddenbrooks,* had brought the traditional skills of the genre to a late flowering. Whether one sees these changes as blight or blessing, whether they represent a shift of taste or a change in the superstructure responding to change in the economic base, they have created a situation in which the literary form of *Buddenbrooks* is unlikely to provide a model for those writers who, like Mann himself at the turn of the century, endeavour to find the forms most appropriate to their historical situation.

In Germany, although Mann remained at the forefront of literary life for some fifty years after the appearance of his first novel, his own works showed that it was not sufficient to rest on the formal achievements of *Buddenbrooks.* His second major novel, *The Magic Mountain,* takes its place with Alfred Döblin's *Berlin Alexanderplatz* and Robert Musil's *The Man Without Qualities* as one of the seminal works of formal innovation, while *Doctor Faustus* is a magnificent exploitation, for the purpose of the historical interpretation of Germany's situation in this century, of the breaks in narrative certainty. The achievements of *Buddenbrooks* were not forgotten by critics, and still less by Mann's enormous popular following, but they were not emulated. When writers in western Germany tried to reconstruct a literature from the ruins of the Third Reich, they naturally turned to the models offered by writers and genres disapproved of by the National Socialists (for instance, the form of novel created by Döblin). It was less likely that they would orientate themselves towards the nineteenth-century realism of *Buddenbrooks.* Traditional German forms, such as the "Bildungsroman," tend after 1945 to exhibit elements of parody. The major writers have not, for instance, generally used the traditional form of the family chronicle to tell the story of German history in this century, and one of the few major works written in this form—the late Heinrich Böll's *Billiards at half-past Nine* (1959)—departs radically from Mann's style, although Böll's admiration for *Buddenbrooks* was clear from his Frankfurt lectures of 1966.

Buddenbrooks' reception . . . soon reached more widely than Germany and increasingly, in recent years, it has been widely appreciated in the English-speaking world and enjoyed that kind of popular success which has accompanied its literary reputation in Germany. This has not always meant, however, that Mann's novel had received either so positive a response from critics or the tribute of imitation by his fellow-writers. Lawrence's dismissive attitude towards Mann, then taken over by the Leavis school, did not make it easy for *Buddenbrooks* to be assimilated into English culture as, for instance, Ibsen had been. Even in the 1960s D. J. Enright could suggest that on the basis of "a nervous perusal of the opening pages of *Buddenbrooks*" English readers might find Mann "wordy, philosophical, humourless, highly abstract and crammed with details." Such insular judgements are fortunately less common now, so too is the tendency to see Mann as a pendant to Galsworthy. In France the continuance of the tradition of family chronicle novels gave Mann's work a stronger place in the critical debate, although it was in France that the consequences of Mann's political aberration in 1914 had the sharpest repercussions. In America, where Mann spent the years of the Second World War and wrote some illuminating commentaries on his own works, . . . it might still be difficult to trace much direct influence of this novel. Saul Bellow's obvious debt in *Herzog* to *The Magic Mountain*—an exciting transfer of Mann's central concerns to the American situation—only emphasises that the predominant influence on the early Bellow was not *Buddenbrooks* but the work of Franz Kafka.

Here we return to the pairing of names so significant for the reception of Mann in the last years. The work of Georg Lukács . . . is remarkable also for its apodictic attempt to set up evaluative models for literature in the post-modern period, categorising the possibilities of literature according to the models indicated in the title of the essay "Franz Kafka or Thomas Mann?" (1954). We need not exaggerate the importance of this essay with its authoritarian alternative prescriptions, nor suggest that Mann is plausible as a socialist realist. Lukács was, nevertheless, recognising a need to harness the tradition of bourgeois realism to the task of the twentieth-century writer, trying to show that the "crisis" of the novel and the experience of *Angst* and alienation so typical of our age do not have to mean the abandonment of the narrative techniques of realism. As a result, the essay neatly summa-

rises a dilemma that is implicit in the literary historical situation of *Buddenbrooks.*

The choice Lukács sees for the contemporary novelist is between realism, even in the "God-forsaken world" of the present age, and the avant-garde. Is fiction to provide, through the techniques of realism, a reflection of a distorted and alienated reality, Lukács asks; or should it abandon realism and the picture of totality which the realists communicated (the school-master's tone is typical of this piece), and provide instead a "distorted reflection" of reality, bringing into its own narrative techniques the absence of totality, and showing the disjointed and broken nature of modern man's experience of life? That reality is alienated is accepted. The dehumanised world of the modern—whether or not one shares Lukács' understanding of this condition as a symptom of the highest form of capitalism—is certainly seen by the realist Thomas Mann. In Thomas Buddenbrook he gives a picture of the *Angst* which is the "dominant existential condition" of the avant-garde. As a realist, Lukács argues, Mann understands this *Angst,* places it socially and psychologically, and uses his narrative to demystify it. Kafka on the other hand (we are told), as a representative of the avant-garde, lacks such a perspective. He identifies the essentially subjective, "distorted" experience of *Angst* with reality itself, and discloses nothing of the objective world outside individual, subjective experience. So Kafka provides a distorted portrayal of reality, rather than a realistic portrayal of distortion. The realistic details scattered in his work do not provide, as they do for realist writers, "the nodal points of individual or social life" but they are instead "cryptic symbols of an unfathomable transcendence."

Lukács' presentation of choice had limited validity. Only within the orthodox canon of socialist realism (and even there only for a limited time) did his dogmatic tone achieve a reorientation of literary models. In practice it has been the opposition to Lukács' argument by Brecht, Bloch, Anna Seghers and Adorno which has been the more influential. Certainly Lukács' essay is not the best way to make Thomas Mann's work attractive, for not only does that essay underrate the social-critical element in modernism; it judges realism far too narrowly, seeing the reader's role in an altogether too passive way, and underplays Mann's modernism of style as well as theme, "the increase in consciousness portrayed and a corresponding increase in the consciousness of the portrayal" [J. P. Stern, "The Theme of Consciousness: Thomas Mann"]. Nevertheless, Lukács' essay does underline, usefully, the "perennial" mode of Mann's realism. It pin-points Mann's determination, even when tackling themes of great abstraction—as in *Doctor Faustus*—to create a framework of reference to the real. To situate, to place, to analyse—this endeavour which characterised Mann's approach to the subject of his own early life in *Buddenbrooks* remained central to his subsequent work. What we [suggest is] a particular achievement at a particular historical moment—the portrayal of the escape by Thomas Buddenbrook out of the conceptual world of business, and into the world of contemplation and art, a portrayal which shows both the attraction and the limitations of the means of escape and situates it socially and psychologically in its exact position in the society of his day—that achievement reflected the perennial concern of all Mann's works. His first novel is remarkable not merely for bringing the German novel into the twentieth century, or for representing á highpoint in the art of the realist novel; not merely for fusing national and European traditions of fiction, but for achieving at so early an age a maturity and authenticity of personal style which would reach through a life's work of great novels, of which, as Mann wryly remarked in later years, ***Buddenbrooks*** was "probably" the best. (pp. 104-12)

Hugh Ridley, in his Thomas Mann: Buddenbrooks, *Cambridge University Press, 1987, 117 p.*

FURTHER READING

Berendsohn, Walter E. *"Buddenbrooks."* In his *Thomas Mann: Artist and Partisan in Troubled Times,* pp. 23-29. University, Ala.: The University of Alabama Press, 1973.
    Briefly discusses various aspects of the novel, including theme, characterizations, point of view, and humor.

Brennan, Joseph Gerard. "Disease, Art, and Life." In his *Thomas Mann's World,* pp. 37-75. 1942. Reprint. New York: Russell and Russell, 1962.
    Discusses Mann's treatment of disease and death in *Buddenbrooks.*

Burkhard, Arthur. "The Genealogical Novel in Scandinavia." *PMLA* 44, No. 1 (March 1929): 310-13.
    Criticizes Zucker (see entry dated 1928 below) for his assertion that *Buddenbrooks* was inspired by the works of Emile Zola—a claim which Mann himself denied—and for neglecting to mention the influence of Scandinavian authors on Mann's novel.

Clark, A. F. B. "The Dialectical Humanism of Thomas Mann." *University of Toronto Quarterly* 8, No. 1 (October 1938): 85-105.
    Discusses Mann's humanistic philosophy. Clark asserts that while *Buddenbrooks* deserves high praise as art and as "an embodiment in fiction of the Nietzschean theory of *bourgeois* decadence," the novel represents only a "tentative first stage" in the development of Mann's dialectical humanism.

Feuerlicht, Ignace. "The Decline and Fall of a Family." In his *Thomas Mann,* pp. 13-21. New York: Twayne Publishers, 1968.
    General discussion of *Buddenbrooks,* briefly examining plot, theme, characterizations, narrative technique, and style.

Ireland, Kenneth R. "Epics of Decline: The Institution of the Family in Thomas Mann's *Buddenbrooks* and Junichiro Tanizaki's *The Makioka Sisters.*" *Arcadia* 18, No. 1 (1983): 39-49.
    Comparative study which focuses on the two novels' "common thematic attention to the function and role of the family in specific social backgrounds." Ireland maintains that despite differences in cultural and literary origins, the books "share important features of epic scale, narrative attitude, and structural articulation."

Kolb, Jocelyne. "Thomas Mann's Translation of Wagner into *Buddenbrooks.*" *The Germanic Review* 61, No. 4 (Fall 1986): 146-53.
    Examines Wagner's music as a model for *Buddenbrooks,* influencing Mann's use of the leitmotif and his treatment of the theme of decadence. Kolb suggests that the novel's structure, featuring a combination of literal and figurative meanings which allow for different levels of interpretation, reflects the subtlety and complexity of Wagner's influence on Mann.

Liptzin, Sol. "The Apocalyptic Novel." In his *Historical Survey of German Literature,* pp. 215-30. New York: Prentice-Hall, 1936.
    Compares characters, plots, and themes of selected works by Mann and by Jakob Wasserman.

Lukács, Georg. "In Search of the Bourgeois." In *The Stature of Thomas Mann,* edited by Charles Neider, pp. 469-73. New York: New Directions, 1947.
    Maintains that Mann "is an extreme example of that type of author whose greatness it is to be a 'mirror of the world' " and describes him as "the symbol of what is best in the German middle class." Lukács claims that Mann is unique for having fused his philosophical convictions with his artistic work; offering as illustration Thomas Buddenbrook's reading of Schopenhauer, Lukács explains that "the erroneous elements in his theoretical writings . . . in his narrative work are so easily confuted by the artistic autonomy of his characters, his plots and his situations." (Excerpts from this essay appear in *TCLC,* Volume 2.)

McWilliams, James R. *"Buddenbrooks."* In his *Brother Artist: A Psychological Study of Thomas Mann's Fiction,* pp. 15-49. Lanham, Md.: University Press of America, 1983.
    Asserts that "in *Buddenbrooks* Mann deals with a major eruption of material from the subconscious that embraced in a unified sequence the basic experiences, reactions, and judgments of his childhood. The result is a singularly great work." McWilliams traces the genesis of the work to explore its autobiographical aspects and contends that Mann's intimate relationship to his material caused some incongruities in his perspective and required him to develop the theme of decline in the novel to distract the reader from the "embarrassing personal secrets" uncovered in the work.

Nicholls, R. A. "Beginnings: The Early Novellen and *Buddenbrooks.*" In his *Nietzsche in the Early Work of Thomas Mann,* pp. 7-19. Berkeley and Los Angeles: The University of California Press, 1955.
    Asserts that the influence of Nietzsche "may be seen in the consistency of values that helps to give [*Buddenbrooks*] its unity."

Schroeter, James. *"Buddenbrooks* and *The Sound and the Fury."* *Etudes de lettres* 4, No. 1 (Janvier-Mars 1983): 43-54.
    Comparison of the two novels which indicates that Faulkner was influenced by Mann and by European realism. Schroeter states that the most important similarity between the two works is their portrayal of the life of a family and the placement of that family in a particular time and place.

Swales, Martin. "The Artist and Historical Change." In his *Thomas Mann: A Study,* pp. 15-28. London: Heinemann, 1980.
    Examines characterizations and the theme of decline and analyzes Mann's use of philosophy and history in *Buddenbrooks.*

Winston, Richard. *Thomas Mann: The Making of an Artist, 1875-1911.* New York: Alfred A. Knopf, 1982, 325 p.
    Biographical account of Mann's early years. The section on the period of *Buddenbrooks* covers influences on the work, Mann's research for the book, and the process Mann used to construct the novel.

Wolf, Ernest M. "Hagenströms: The Rival Family in *Buddenbrooks.*" *German Studies Review* 5, No. 1 (February 1982): 35-55.
    Compares the structure, characteristics, and behavior of the Hagenström and Buddenbrook families. Wolf asserts that "the ascent of this rival family constitutes one of the most important subsidiary themes of the story. The fortunes of the Hagenströms serve as ironic and dialectic counterpoint to those of the Buddenbrooks."

Zucker, A. E. "The Genealogical Novel: A New Genre." *PMLA* 43, No. 2 (June 1928): 551-60.
    Discusses the development of the genre of the genealogical novel, describing several examples. Zucker calls *Buddenbrooks* "the finest example so far produced in this genre."

———. "The Genealogical Novel Again." *PMLA* 44, No. 3 (September 1929): 925-27.
    Responds to Burkhard's accusations (see Burkhard above) and maintains that since the process of literary influence is complex, it is "highly probable that Thomas Mann, known to have been

a great admirer of French contemporary fiction, derived the
idea for the plan of [*Buddenbrooks*] from Zola."

John M(ilton) Oskison

1874-1947

American novelist, short story writer, biographer, and journalist.

Oskison is best known for novels and short stories in which he depicted life in the Cherokee Indian Territory of the American West during the late nineteenth and early twentieth centuries. At the time these works were published, the Cherokee heritage of their author was unknown, and only in recent years have they been examined as native American literature. In addition to his fiction, Oskison wrote two biographies and earned a national reputation for his work as a journalist.

Of Cherokee and white descent, Oskison was born in Vinita, in that part of the Indian Territory which became Oklahoma when that state was admitted to the Union in 1907. After attending college in Vinita, he entered Stanford University and began publishing short stories in popular magazines. One of these stories, "Only the Master Shall Praise," was awarded *Century* magazine's prize for student writers in 1898. Set in the Indian Territory during the late 1880s, this story of a white ranch hand and his companion, a cowboy of Cherokee and white descent, has been praised for its authentic characterizations and its accurate portrayal of regional dialect and manners. After receiving a degree from Stanford in 1899, Oskison did graduate work in literature at Harvard University and later moved to New York City to pursue a career in journalism. Working as a special writer and editor for the *New York Post* and *Collier's* magazine, he wrote extensively about frontier life in nonfiction articles and short stories. During this time he also published biographies of American general and Texas statesman Sam Houston and Shawnee chief Tecumseh. Oskison's first novel, *Wild Harvest,* was published in 1925, and over the next two decades he continued to write about the history of his native region. He was working on an autobiography at the time of his death in 1947.

Critics who study Oskison's fiction note differences between his short stories, many of which date from the turn of the century, and his novels, written during the 1920s and 1930s. Like "Only the Master Shall Praise," most of his short stories are set in the Indian Territory and depict the landscape, dialect, manners, and customs of the region. These works portray the reactions of native Americans to political events of the last decades of the nineteenth century, as the United States government gradually reduced the amount of land the native Americans were allowed to live on, causing disruption in tribal authority and customs. "Tookh Steh's Mistake" (1897), for example, is the story of a Cherokee who cannot adjust to the changes that result when the tribal government is disbanded. While Oskison's novels are also set in the Indian Territory, native American characters and themes figure only slightly in these works. Generally adhering to the conventions of frontier romances, such novels as *Wild Harvest* and *Black Jack Davy* follow the fortunes of white settlers in the Indian Territory and have been criticized for a rambling style, contrived action, and stilted characterizations. According to Charles R. Larson, the native American characters Oskison included in his novels merely "provide a kind of backdrop authenticity, as part of the Indian Territory setting." *Brothers Three,* Oskison's last novel, is considered superior to his earlier novels because of its more polished style, skillful characterization, and fuller thematic development. In this work, based in part on Oskison's life, the three sons of a white father and Cherokee mother return to their family farm in the Indian Territory after finding other pursuits unprofitable or unsatisfying. The theme of spiritual renewal through closeness to the land demonstrated in *Brothers Three* is regarded as one of the few native American elements in Oskison's longer fiction. While some critics have expressed regret that Oskison focused only occasionally on the significant native American issues of the period, his writings are nevertheless considered an important rendering of an often-neglected period in American history.

PRINCIPAL WORKS

Wild Harvest   (novel)   1925
Black Jack Davy   (novel)   1926
A Texas Titan: The Story of Sam Houston   (biography)   1929
Brothers Three   (novel)   1935
Tecumseh and His Times: The Story of a Great Indian   (biography)   1938

THE NEW YORK TIMES BOOK REVIEW   (essay date 1925)

[*In the following review of* Wild Harvest, *the critic considers the nature and value of the work as a social document of the American West and as a frontier tale.*]

This novel of transition days in Oklahoma is a striking instance of what can happen when an author tries to tell two stories at once. **Wild Harvest** collapses somewhere between the rip-snorting, two-gun, ride-'em-cowboy staple of Western fiction and the sweetly solemn, mock-cosmic surge attempted by Emerson Hough in *The Covered Wagon* and *North of 36.*

The action takes place in an Oklahoma that was still Indian Territory, owned and administered by tribes with rather more economic and political acumen than had been shown by the average Plains Indian. White squatters were creeping in, and as they learned that the noble red man could not here be easily dislodged they asked themselves: "Why can't we all be friends?" a thought which "was echoed by most of the invading whites; she stood on the edge of a new experiment on the last of the great West's frontiers and felt its thrill."

"She" was Nan Forest, heroine of this tale of love among the cow ponies, and the experiment from which arose modern half-breed Oklahoma is rather crudely drawn by following the course of her romantic vacillation between Tom Winger, Texas cowboy, who is captor of her heart, and Harvey Stokes, a rich and devoted hay baler. This experiment is the institution on Indian Territory of a Winter feeding ground on the great cattle trail from Texas to Kansas City.

The "cosmic" nature of this transition is suggested by Nan's remark, "I'll bet a King somewhere in Europe will eat the meat that is cut from the steer that eats the hay that I raked." A similar importance is suggested, in rather more portentous terms, by such paragraphs as this annotation on the first Spring round-up in the new territory:

> It was a sweeping spectacular gesture by the cattle-men, emphatic advertisement of the new era that had come upon a verdant, dreaming land of easy-living full bloods, mixed bloods and contented "squawmen." In arranging it Indians and white cattlemen had come together in amity, and in carrying it out Indian, mixed-blood and white Texas cowboys rode together. Esau had spoken with Jacob, not to barter his birthright but to share it on equable [sic] terms.

Another transition with which the book deals is the taming of the wilderness of the wild West. As Nan's aunt observed, ". . . Us women can't always see the joke in the shootin' an' hellin' around our menfolks do." So the old days of dances at which bootleg whisky flowed freely as the fiddlers called the numbers, "Chase that rabbit an' chase that squirrel, chase that pretty girl around the world," yielded place to the soda fountain of Mr. Mencken's Baptist desert of prayer-meetings and fraternal organizations ("Every man ought to have the support and comfort of a noble fraternal order"). Nan's neighbors, the wild Jack Hayes, the dull Harvey Stokes, the hot-blooded Ruby Engel, are suddenly divided into the two cosmic fraternal orders, the sheep and the goats.

> Against the Hayes family and what Ruby Engel represented stood the forces of order and decency. . . . Here were Tom, Bill Ridge, Cox and Wes Madden instantly and willingly taking up the defense of Harvey, the defense of law and order that must be established if life was to become secure.

Sic transit Oklahoma. Nan marries her Tom, after Harvey kills himself in a fit of jealousy. The bootlegger, the outlaw and the gay lady are driven away. Schools and churches and banks spring up. Indians and whites pursue the dollar where once they chased the bison, and the frontier, that restless, unregenerate force which had molded American institutions for nearly three centuries, came to an inglorious end in a welter of hay bales, cattle pens, homesteads and cradles.

Wild Harvest might have ranked as a very good tenth-rate stock Western story if the author had not been ambitious to introduce some intelligence into the substance and background of his yarn. As a result, although it makes interesting reading throughout, the novel will fail to attract that large audience which stampedes at the sight of an idea. At the same time the book does not do the idea itself sufficient justice to permit it to rank with any of the more serious novels of the frontier. (pp. 22, 24)

> "Out Oklahoma Way," in The New York Times Book Review, *September 20, 1925, pp. 22, 24.*

THE NEW YORK TIMES BOOK REVIEW   (essay date 1926)

[*In the following review, the critic praises* Black Jack Davy *as a significant rendering of frontier life.*]

The Indian Territory, before Oklahoma was, is the scene of John M. Oskison's tale of high-stepping, determined youth, heart-thrilling hopes and grim struggle between the forces of lawlessness and those of orderly, upright living. [*Black Jack Davy*] opens with the migration thither of a couple from Arkansas, Jim Dawes and his crippled wife, Mirabelle, with their nineteen-year-old adopted son, David. Middle age and years of crippledom have not cooled the ardor of Mirabelle's fiercely romantic heart, and as they enter their new home she scents with the joy of the war-horse the possibilities of thrilling times to come. She has given to her beloved adopted son the sobriquet of "Black Jack," because of the grim old ballad about "Black Jack Davy," and because she fondly hoped that some day he would go adventuring. It is not long until things begin to happen, for outlawed men by the hundreds were finding refuge in the Territory and the times were sizzling with the menace of evil deeds and sinister conditions they were brewing. The Dawes family are pitched by events into the middle of it, and finally "Hell broke loose on Horsepen Creek," with a beleagured cabin and a girl slipping out and riding miles upon miles through the night to enlist help. It is a fine, juicy, suspense-holding yarn, and Mr. Oskison has built up its developments with a skillful hand. But it is more than merely a tale about riotous frontier conditions, for the way the author has handled his material makes it also a bit of vivid light upon the dramatic and sensational of all the circle of our States. Behind his narrative always is a colorful but restrained imagination that lifts it above the level of the ordinary frontier tale and gives it more of significance, interest, individuality. (pp. 10-11)

> "In Indian Territory," in The New York Times Book Review, *October 10, 1926, pp. 10-11.*

MARGARET CHENEY DAWSON   (essay date 1929)

[*In the following review, Dawson discusses the strengths and weaknesses of Oskison's portrayal of Sam Houston in* A Texas Titan.]

Unpretentious of scholarship, Mr. Oskison presents his story of Sam Houston as "fictionized biography," but he need hardly have taken the precaution of so doing. Though there are perhaps a few inaccuracies and certainly many embroideries, he has scarcely taken more liberty with the facts than is considered permissible by the interpretive school of biographers. Perhaps the most serious discount should be made on the score of the author's thoroughgoing partiality for Houston. Always Sam's enemies are made to seem unspeakably and improbably mean, stupid and treacherous; and Sam's faults—his instinct for a rather inferior type of showmanship, his mighty drunkeness, his uncertain response to bad fortune—are tucked into the crevices of his vast character. Quite pardonably, though, for the figure of Houston is big and glamorous, deserving of romanticism and best drawn by a frank hero-worshipper. Not ranking, for all his brilliance and bravery, in the first line of American statesmen and soldiers, he is most important as a symbol of all that Americans cherish so warmly when they think of the pioneering days. That there are any bony facts, historically, back of his prodigious shadow is a marvel, since everything he did was of the nature that gives rise to myth and fable. His long, intimate visits to the Cherokee Indians, his powerful stride back to power and prominence after what had seemed a dismal ending to his career, his generalship in leading 700 ragged Texans to victory against Santa Ana's 1,400 well drilled troops—these things, combined with a number of grand, chivalrous gestures (never without a certain hickory shrewness) give Houston's story endless dramatic appeal.

Mr. Oskison has made the most of the obvious crises in Houston's career, recounting with particular zest those occasions when he triumphed over an enemy. One of these incidents is especially amusing: When Mirabeau Bounaparte Lamar took Houston's place as head of the Texas forces he mustered the troops, paraded before them and asked for a vote of confidence. "Those who approve my appointment march south, those against it march north!" he shouted. There were 1,800 men in the ranks; 100 marched south! The army was without a head—and Texas roared at the joke.

In dealing with less boldly outlined passages in Houston's life, *A Texas Titan* is not so satisfactory. Sam's adolescence, about which there are probably few authentic facts, is rather mawkishly treated, so that the opening chapters are disappointing. His relationship with the Cherokees, which must have been mysterious and subtle, is made quite conventional, and the Indians themselves are crudely drawn. Where imagination was most needed Mr. Oskison uses a bare, stilted style, and he does not really hit the pace until he reaches more solid ground. Since the book makes no effort to enrich history by the presentation of new data, or to offer a startlingly new interpretation of Houston, awkwardness in straight story telling is a serious defect. Nevertheless, it is forgotten in the color and speed of the later chapters.

Margaret Cheney Dawson, "Lone Star," in New York Herald Tribune Books, *March 31, 1929, p. 19.*

LOUIS KRONENBERGER (essay date 1935)

[*A drama critic for* Time *from 1938 to 1961, Kronenberger was a distinguished historian, literary critic, and author. In the following excerpt, he asserts that Oskison failed to make* Brothers Three *an interesting and engaging novel.*]

[*Brothers Three*] is concerned with the fortunes of three brothers brought up on a farm. Their father, Francis Odell, had come to the old Indian Territory as a pioneer in the 1870s and married a woman with Indian blood in her veins. He took to farming and prospered, his pioneer vigor reinforced by wisdom about life and understanding of the land. But not one of his three sons felt their father's interest in farming—each aimed at doing something else. Bud, the eldest, wanted to be a mechanic and store-keeper; Bunny, the second son, was a born cattleman; and Mister, the youngest, landed in New York as a writer.

Yet Mr. Oskison has contrived to show how all three men felt more and more, as time went on, the pull of the old farm, and recognized in it not only the spirit that had belonged to their father's generation but also the one thing that united them and could be looked upon as home. In the end, when they have made and lost fortunes as cattle-dealers and store-keepers and market speculators, they come to see how much the farm means; they come to wish they could have worked it as their father did. Bunny dies; but the two other brothers, late in middle age and surrounded by a large family, agree that they must go back to farming as a source of livelihood and a means of preserving a home that is all but lost.

That is the theme of *Brothers Three*; as a narrative, however, it simply rambles along in the usual fashion of a family chron-icle, recording in much detail the births, marriages and deaths of a large tribe, the numerous love affairs and business projects of the three brothers, the family reunions and get-togethers, the customs of the country, and the changing state of the Odell finances. It is a long while since I have read a novel in which dollars and cents come in so often for mention as here, where we know, season by season, the exact amount of money that the Odells are worth. Their economic ventures are highly representative of American life during the past two generations, and consequently valuable; but I cannot feel that Mr. Oskison has made them very interesting.

Indeed, everything considered, he has not made his novel very interesting. In spite of the fact that it develops a clearly plotted theme and makes use of a dozen important characters, it never seems to find its stride. One thing happens, and then another, but everything is pitched in the same key and told in the same prosaic detail. There is an absence of drama and to my mind—though the author has obviously striven to impart it—an absence of warmth. The two "heroic" characters—Odell, the founder of the family, and his daughter-in-law May, who shares his passion for the farm—are people we are told about rather than made to see. The pioneer richness and sinew that we remember of characters in other farm novels never communicate themselves in Odell and May. Even the feeling about the farm becomes a matter of reiteration on Odell tongues rather than of affirmation from Odell hearts. And the farm might be any farm; we never become aware of its sights and smells, we never know it as something peculiarly alive, or even as something in Oklahoma rather than in Ohio.

Mr. Oskison quite lacks the power to stir our emotions and sympathies; he equally lacks the power of creating a richly physical world. All he has done is to tell a story whose simple, prosaic, familiar facts we can believe in, and whose intended significance we can perceive, but not profit by. This must have been a better book at half its present length, because we should not have been wearied by too many dry and repetitious episodes; but it could scarcely, on any terms, have been a good book. The juice of life is somehow not in it.

Louis Kronenberger, " 'Brothers Three' and Some Other Recent Works of Fiction," in The New York Times Book Review, *September 15, 1935, p. 6.*

CHARLES R. LARSON (essay date 1978)

[*Larson is an American critic, novelist, and editor, and is considered a leading scholar of Third World and minority literature. He is the author of* American Indian Fiction, *the first book-length study of novels by native Americans. In the following excerpt from that work, he analyzes the presentation of native American subjects, themes, and characters in Oskison's three novels.*]

John M. Oskison's early novels—*Wild Harvest* (1925) and *Black Jack Davy* (1926)—might best be described as romances of frontier life. The setting for both is the Cherokee Indian Territory which became part of Oklahoma when the area became a state in 1907, and the action takes place some years before that date, around the turn of the century. . . .

The locale for both stories is in and around a growing frontier town called Big Grove; and Oskison carries several of the characters in *Wild Harvest* over to *Black Jack Davy*. Both novels describe the hustle and bustle of activity on the frontier (especially the influx of white settlers) shortly before statehood. Unfortunately, they have little to do with Native Americans.

In *Wild Harvest,* the author is concerned about getting fifteen-year-old Nan Forest married to Tom Winger, a handsome cowboy and foreman. This should be an easy matter, since their suitability for each other is established early in the story, but Oskison constructs barriers that postpone the event. First, there is Nan's father, Chester Forest, described as "a fumbler" and not very successful rancher. Oskison dispatches Forest by having him shoot a cattle rustler and then spend most of the story in jail while he awaits trial; eventually he is freed. The obstacles that produce a temporary estrangement between Nan and Tom are Ruby Engle (a seventeen-year-old frontier seductress) and Harvey Stokes (Tom's rival for Nan's hand). While all of these characters are interacting, Nan lives with her aunt and uncle Dines (Forest's older sister and her husband). The plot, for the most part, is unconvincing—needlessly extended so that Oskison can create a narrative long enough for a book. (His previous fiction had been limited to short stories, published in magazines.)

In an attempt to create a sense of life in the Indian Territory, Oskison introduces a number of minor frontier character types and digresses into self-contained substories involving them. There are accounts of cowpunching, cattle rustling, and making money from cattle raising. There are descriptions of roundups, and "neighborhood literaries" designed to bring a little culture to the area, of cutting hay, of cattle stampeding, and like events which Oskison no doubt felt would give a sense of local color for his eastern readers. Other digressions from the main story tell of several murders, a bank robbery, and various events contrived to hold the reader's interest. (The chapter titles also attempt to do this: "Nan Counts Her Chickens," "The Amateur Detective," "The Game of 'I Spy.'") Mostly, however, these authorial machinations fail, and I think it can safely be said that artistically, at least, *Wild Harvest* is the very nadir of Native American fiction.

Generally speaking, the few Indian characters in *Wild Harvest* are there to provide a kind of backdrop of authenticity, as part of the Indian Territory setting. One of these, named Joe Tiger, moves in and out of the story, usually drunk. Another one, Hank Rosebud, Big Grove's half-blood police officer, periodically helps restore peace and quiet. The few statements about Indians in the book tend to be spoken by the white characters. In the most important of these, occurring at the end of the novel, Nan and Tom foresee the inevitability of allotment, and argue that Indians are ready for assimilation.

> "One of these days, the Indians'll be argued into allottin' all these miles an' miles of prairie, like them Kansas politicians are tryin' to make 'em do now. Then there'll be land for sale, an' the Indians'll have to buckle down to farmin' an' cattle raisin' to keep even with us white folks. Good thing for 'em, too."

> "Yes," Nan agreed, "Uncle Billy says Indians like Chief Littlespring, Ross Murray, and 'Sofkey' Horseford are already showing the way to the others. Uncle Billy likes these Indians; he says they're as smart as anybody—no reason why they shouldn't move ahead with the rest of us."

> "An' they sure will," Tom asserted. "At the bank in Big Grove they're already beginnin' to open ac-

counts, make loans an' carry on like regular fellows."

Two significant events in the narrative involve Native Americans. Curiously, it is an Indian who discovers the missing gun that belonged to the man Chester Forest shot; its discovery saves Forest's life, since it frees him from being convicted of shooting a man in cold blood. More important, however, is the wedding ceremony that unites Nan Forest and Tom Winger—presided over by an Indian preacher ("The Indian preacher wore a collarless blue shirt, a short black coat, yellow trousers and weather-stained moccasins; he was completely at ease, smiling, exchanging friendly comment with his Indian neighbors who had come to the wedding.") When his wedding speech is translated into English, we are again aware of the assimilation theme of the novel:

> "He says he is glad to ask God's blessing on this man an' this woman because he loves them both. . . . He says times has changed since he was a young man like him an' his old woman was a girl like her an' they got married out in the woods, but he ain't sorry old ways are goin', because we got to have new ways an' good men an' women from the outside to help build up this Eenyan country. . . . He says the same Great Father loves this girl Nancy an' this man Tom that loves his old woman an' him. . . . He says he gives his blessing on this marriage. Amen."

The novel ends with a particularly revealing comment by Tom Winger: "We're elected now to help make this long grass country one of the greatest states in the Union, you an' me an' the folks we know an' them that's comin' after us." Although it was written after the fact, *Wild Harvest* was propaganda for Oklahoma's statehood.

Black Jack Davy also has a romantic focus—the marriage of Davy Dawes, the main character, to Mary Keene—but the main thrust of the story is to establish peace for the white settler families at Six Bulls River and Horsepen Creek, near Big Grove, in the Indian Territory. Shortly after Jim and Mirabelle Dawes and their foster son, Davy, arrive at Horsepen Creek, Jerry Boyd declares open warfare on the new arrivals. Boyd, who is married to a part-Cherokee woman, and therefore able to own property in her name, decides that if the Daweses and the Keenes (Mirabelle's brother, his wife, and their daughter) can be driven out of the Territory, it will be a simple matter to annex their property. The Daweses and the Keenes both lease land from Ned Warrior, a full-blood Cherokee, and his wife, Rose; so Ned Warrior must also be eliminated before the land-grab will be successful.

The novel concludes with Boyd and his henchmen laying siege to the Keenes and the Daweses, who manage to hold out against the attackers until a posse, led by Tom Winger (and several other characters who appeared in *Wild Harvest*), comes to their rescue. In a sense, Tom Winger becomes the deus ex machina, saving the Daweses and the Keenes from the evil embodied by Jerry Boyd. Ned Warrior enters the final shoot-out also, wounding Boyd and killing his good-for-nothing son, Cale. In the final few pages, Jim Dawes insists that Davy and Mary Keene be married before he dies of gun wounds incurred in the fighting; yet since that is not quite a happy ending, Oskison brings in Davy's real mother (who has appeared earlier in the story) and she stakes Davy and Mary for cattle ranching. (Davy's last name is surely an ironic reference to the Dawes Allotment Act of 1887, which—perhaps more than anything else—led to the break-up of Indian tribal lands.)

The West is wilder in *Black Jack Davy* than it is in *Wild Harvest.* There is a prostitute (who reveals to Davy that Boyd is out to get them), a gambling and drinking house, an excessive amount of shooting, and one violent murder. The general lawlessness of the Indian Territory is contrasted to the superior stock of the settler blood represented by the Daweses and the Keenes. Oskison states of Jim and Davy Dawes: "In their blood was the strain of pioneers who had fought similar battles while waiting for the establishment of organized society: men like Boone, Crockett, Houston and Kit Carson." (Oskison also makes some attempt to romanticize Davy's origins by having Mirabelle connect him to a character in a folk ballad, from whom he derives his name, "Black Jack Davy.")

From this summary of the story, it should be apparent that the Indian characters in *Black Jack Davy* are more important than the ones in *Wild Harvest.* Ned Warrior is the most significant. He is initially pictured as a rather sleazy individual, but by the end of the novel he reforms and not only helps control the lawlessness of the land but settles down and marries Rose in the requisite Christian wedding ceremony. (Shades of Pocahontas?) Ned's reformation is revealed in one of Oskison's final comments about him:

> Ned understood better than ever before why old Running Rabbit and his fellow full-bloods of the hill country met in secret councils and planned to drive out the aliens and close the borders to them. If they only could! Of course, there were many honest whites, good friends of the Indians and good neighbors. . . . But they appeared, sometimes, to be a helpless minority. . . .

> Ned himself was no tabby cat. He had walked his own path in defiance of tribal law, had carried Rose Lamedeer off without the formality of marriage, had crippled the deputy Burke in resisting arrest for boot-legging, had all but given up his life in that battle against Cap. Black and his men, has served time in prison. But he was a shining saint compared with these whites.

Rose, Ned's half-blood wife, for a time lures Davy away from Mary Keene, but she is also reformed by the end of the story. As in *Wild Harvest,* Oskison does not make much use of the Indian setting of the story, except for an occasional aside on Indian "progress." One of these comments, spoken by Ross Murray, a "half-blood tribal chief, prosperous cattleman and graduate of the University of Missouri," returns to the subject of allotment and the Indians' eventual assimilation into the mainstream of American life:

> "It is said that the history of a nation is the history of its wars, but in our case it is rather the history of forced cessions of land. That process is now ended, we can cede no more, and the course of our history must change. We must become builders. Put the money you get into the development of good farms."

Regrettably, *Wild Harvest* and *Black Jack Davy* are unconvincing both in plot and character. Events in both novels border on the ludicrous, the unbelievable, the cliché, and I suspect that few readers today would have the patience to struggle through either work. Oskison's characters, whether major or minor, never become anything more than types. His older women are particularly unconvincing. I have a feeling that

Oskison recognized this last limitation, since he tended either to kill older women off early in the story (Nan's mother) or relegate them to wheelchairs (Mirabelle), a device he also uses in his next novel, *Brothers Three.* (Usually there is a kind of Old Testament justice for past transgressions. Mirabelle ran off with Jim Dawes against the wishes of her parents. The night of their elopement, she fell from a horse and was henceforth confined to a wheelchair.)

A statement made by Judge Pease early in *Black Jack Davy* conveniently summarizes the subject matter of both these novels: "It seems that bad men from the whole United States are flocking into the Indian country." Unfortunately, Oskison chose to focus both novels upon the incoming whites rather than on the Indians who were already in the Territory. The result was predictable: potboilers typical of mass-market fiction set in the West, with background characters potentially far more interesting than those in the foreground.

Oskison's *Brothers Three* (1935), which appeared nine years after *Black Jack Davy,* is in every way a more rewarding novel, although it still has little to do with the Native American experience. It is altogether the work of a more mature artist (Oskison was approaching sixty when he wrote it). Though there is still little introspection, the characters are mellower and more believable than in his earlier works; the pace is more relaxed; the story is convincing and reflective. This does not mean that *Brothers Three* is without flaws: it is too long (the longest novel written by a Native American); at times overly sentimental; and in spite of the author's attempts at writing a kind of regional epic, read today the story is dated if not simply boring in places. It is clear that Oskison wanted to write a chronicle of the events of his own family dynasty—a story of the land and its development from Indian Territory to statehood, a little like Edna Ferber's much later novel, *Giant* (1952), though Oskison is writing once again about Oklahoma.

Brothers Three is divided into three sections. In the first of these, called "Timmy," Francis Odell arrives at Redbud Creek in the Indian Territory with his part-Cherokee wife, Janet, and their five-month-old son, Timothy. The year is 1873. The early narrative concentrates on Odell's establishing his ranch and Timmy's later growth into manhood as a leading businessman of the community. Two other sons are born, Roger and Henry ("Mister"), and Janet dies six years after the latter's birth (after being confined to a wheelchair for all six years). Timmy marries May Akers, and the other sons also marry in turn. As the first section ends (immediately after World War I), Francis Odell dies, leaving a large estate which has prospered because of his careful working of the land.

Part Two, "The Herdsmen," shifts to Roger, the second son, the subject turning from farming to money and how to make it. Francis Odell's empire begins to crumble because of the poor management of his sons. Roger makes money in cattle raising, but quickly loses it when the bottom falls out of the market. When he tries to recoup his losses through mining investments, he is swindled out of $130,000 of the family money. In his frustration, Roger begins drinking heavily and eventually becomes paralyzed from an automobile accident that occurs when he is intoxicated. Throughout this section of the novel, May (Timmy's wife) stands for the voice of reason and moderation.

The last part of the novel ("Mister") concentrates on the

third Odell son, Henry, whose turn it now becomes to try to salvage the family estate. Living in New York City as a free-lance writer, he is for a time successful in rebuilding the lost fortune by playing the stock market. Eventually, he builds up the estate to nearly a million dollars, but when the market collapses in 1929, almost everything is lost. The novel concludes with May persuading the remaining members of the family to return to the farm, to work the land and pay off the bankrupt mortgage on their property.

Brothers Three is a long novel, influenced by the regional economic novels of Frank Norris and Theodore Dreiser, though Oskison does not share their naturalistic thesis. The theme is simpler than that: the three Odell sons fail because they leave the land, because they want more than their rightful share. Roger's greed leads to his attempts to make a quick profit in cattle raising; he should never have become involved in mining because he knew nothing about it. Mister should have stopped playing the stock market once he recouped the family losses; his error was deciding to stay in and double or triple their money. Only Timmy achieves a margin of success in his business ventures because they are modest transactions. If all three sons had remained farmers, working the land, the farm would have continued to prosper as it did during their father's time.

The attitude expressed toward the land in *Brothers Three* is the only truly Indian aspect of the novel. . . . If the land is respected, not exploited by agribusiness or destroyed by mining, it will supply all of a man's needs—and more. The land is boundless and plentiful if man lives in harmony with it and does not try to conquer it. Oskison's feelings toward farming are consistent with Cherokee beliefs. Before their removal from Georgia in 1838 and relocation in the Indian Territory, the Cherokee Indians were farmers, living off the land, with individual plots designated for specific families. They were not nomads or hunters, as were Indians of many other tribes.

As in Chief Pokagon's *Queen of the Woods* [1899], there is an ironic contrast in *Brothers Three* between the implicit and explicit threads of the narrative. The three Odell sons (Cherokee "blood citizens . . . entitled to land on account of their inheritance from their mother"), have forgotten their Indian heritage and decided instead to pursue the American Dream. For all practical purposes they have been assimilated into the white economic structure of the country, and for a time they are successful. Oskison, however, makes his position clear. The reader is always aware that it is only a matter of time before the family fortune will be reversed. The mortgaged farm at the end of the story symbolizes this opposition, yet the land remains waiting for their return. As Mister states at the conclusion of the novel,

> "The Farm's a living organism. It's on starvation rations just now, but we've got to do better by it. It's nourished by the lives that are fed into it. If they're clean and sane and competent, like Pa's and Ma's were, the Farm will flourish . . . it's real and solid still—beautiful!"

Other than this attitude toward the land (and the fact that the three Odell sons are one-sixteenth Cherokee), Oskison makes few references in *Brothers Three* to his Indian heritage. As in his two earlier novels, there are a number of allusions to "the invaders of this Indian land, turning it from Indian serenity to white man turbulence." These whites, Oskison tells us,

were contemptuous of the Indians, and promised to hasten the movement for making the Indian Territory into a "white man's state." They carried on, in grotesque caricature, the tradition that the "savage red man" must, because of his incompetence, give way to the white. Their dirtiest tow-headed moron child of fifteen was taught to feel superior to such boys as Timmy—to any child however slightly "tainted" by Indian blood.

Occasional remarks such as this one suggest that by the time Oskison wrote *Brothers Three* he thought of his Indian heritage as something far back in his past—perhaps almost too painful to write about. It is hard to know how to interpret these asides in light of the three Indian characters he included in the novel: a seventeen-year-old girl, Es-Teece Bellflower, with whom Timmy has a lengthy affair (Timmy thinks "It must be the Indian in her that makes her [so loose]"); Mrs. Elphy Otter, a con artist who helps swindle Roger out of his mining investments; and an unnamed bank robber—a seedy lot, to be sure.

One final aspect of *Brothers Three* deserves mention. Oskison's picture of Henry ("Mister") is highly autobiographical. Like Oskison, Mister went to Stanford and became a writer who lived in New York City, eventually writing two novels set in the Indian Territory: *Prairie Dust* and *Bee Creek Neighbors*. There is an element of self-parody in *Brothers Three* whenever Oskison speaks of Mister's career. Of *Prairie Dust*, he says, "It was the brain storm of a victim of the romantic-historic fiction craze that flourished when I was in college," an apt description of *Wild Harvest* or *Black Jack Davy*. Once he becomes involved in the stock market, Mister suffers from writer's block, yet the novel he is unable to write (called *The Book of Timothy the Second*) is clearly the novel that *Brothers Three* in time became. How ironic that *Brothers Three* not only became Oskison's most successful novel (the only one to go through more than one printing) but also concluded his career as a writer of fiction. (pp. 46-55)

> Charles R. Larson, "Assimilation: Estrangement
> from the Land," in his American Indian Fiction,
> University of New Mexico Press, 1978, pp. 34-65.

DANIEL F. LITTLEFIELD, JR. AND JAMES W. PARINS (essay date 1982)

[*Littlefield and Parins are American critics who have collaborated on several extensive studies of native American writings. In the following excerpt, they provide an overview of Oskison's short fiction, discussing literary influences on his work and examining such elements as characterization, dialect, plot, and theme.*]

Oskison chose the twilight years of the Territory as the historical backdrop for most of his stories. Although he set stories in various parts of the Indian Territory, his favorite geographical setting was the northeastern part of the Cherokee Nation, particularly Vinita, the rolling prairies to the west of the town, and the rugged, timbered hills to the east and south. Oskison's fiction was a response to the historic changes that were occurring in his native land. Since the Civil War, the Cherokee Nation had been beset by internal factionalism and external pressure from railroad companies, bureaucrats, politicians and others with vested interests in dissolving the tribal government and opening the territory to non-Indians. Although the Cherokees resisted, the non-Indians came anyway. The Cherokee Nation was overrun by intruders, mainly whites, who came to the Indian Territory to make their fortunes, take up "free" land or hide from the law. Federal law and bureaucratic sloth made it practically impossible for the Indians to have such people removed. Violence was common because the Indians had no jurisdiction over the intruders. With the appointment of the Dawes Commission in 1893, Congress took the first step toward taking the decision regarding tribal status out of the Indians' hands. As it became apparent that the tribal title ultimately would be dissolved and the lands would be allotted in severalty, the Indians reacted variously. Some prepared themselves for inevitable American citizenship, while others, like the Cherokee full bloods, resisted by refusing to enroll for allotments or to accept allotment certificates or by attempting to emigrate to Mexico. Oskison had observed all of the types of participants in these historic events. Most of the social, economic and racial classes of the region are represented in his work. There one finds the full-blood and the mixed-blood Indians and the white "do-gooders," adventurers, cowboys, desperadoes and true friends of the Indians.

"Tookh Steh's Mistake" (1897), for example, is the story of a full blood who cannot adapt to social changes that will come with the imminent dissolution of the tribal government; he decides, like many of his historical counterparts did, to emigrate to Mexico but, ill-equipped to make such a trip, starves to death en route. On the other hand, **"The Problem of Old Harjo"** (1907) is about a Creek full blood who adjusts to social change and wants to join the church but is refused because he has two wives. The main character in **"When the Grass Grew Long"** (1901) is Billy Wilson, a lower-class white cowboy who has come to the Territory to make his fortune; he is saved from a prairie fire by the full-blood Jinnie Jake, who perishes with her father when the fire destroys their homestead. **"The Schoolmaster's Dissipation"** (1897) is about a white school teacher who anticipates his post in the Territory with an altruistic missionary enthusiasm, but soon finds himself in a grubby, mundane and unheroic position, becomes addicted to morphine, and is cured by a woman doctor who is in the Territory to study diseases of Indian children. **"The Quality of Mercy"** (1904) is about Venita Churchfield, a young mixed-blood Cherokee who returns to the Territory from finishing school and convinces a local white editor to stop using his columns to try the case of a young man who, unknown to her, has committed a robbery to obtain money with which he hopes to impress her.

Oskison knew these types of people, and he carefully recorded their language. Abbreviated statements, mixtures of English and Cherokee, the expletive "maybe so" and the use of appositives after pronouns are common in the English dialect of the full bloods. For instance, Tookh Steh says, "We no more hunt deer, no shoot turkey. Land all gone. I go to Mexico where Great Father no take my land. I tell you, goodbye." And when Billy Wilson ropes an errant calf for Jinnie Jake, she says, "Much welcome. Awful nice rope. Bad little *oyah.*" When she carries Billy from the fire, she says to herself, "Maybe so, save him, little fellow!" No peculiarities of dialect mark the speech of the educated Venita Churchfield or the editor. But the dialect of the uneducated cowboy is carefully represented in **"When the Grass Grew Long," "Only the Master Shall Praise,"** and **"The Fall of King Chris"** (1903).

In 1898 Oskison was awarded *Century Magazine*'s prize for college graduates for **"Only the Master Shall Praise,"** which clearly demonstrates his achievement of verisimilitude in such matters as topography, manners, occupations and dialect. Set near Vinita in the late 1880s, the story concerns the relationship between Hanner the Runt and Bill Seymour. Hanner is a half-blood Cherokee cowboy, physically deformed, dressed in old clothes, floppy hat and mismatched spurs, and mounted on a "knotty and scrubby" pony named Pignuts, after a species of scrubby timber that grew in the region. In Sancho Panza fashion, he is the constant companion of Seymour, a handsome, hard-drinking white ranch hand, who rides a fine horse and dresses in the latest cowboy fashions. Oskison adds to the contrast by allowing Hanner to misuse more pronouns, drop more word endings and double more negatives than Seymour. Hanner says, for instance, "Bill, ye ain't a-goin' to git drunk to-day, are ye? They say they's goin' to be a lot of extra marshals 'at ain't lettin' any drunk walk the streets to-day." And Bill replies, "Oh, go to the devil, you old woman! Who said I was goin' to get drunk? Somethin' I never do. Come on; let's ride up."

Unfriended, Hanner is utterly loyal to Seymour, who has cruelly mistreated him at times—in fact, it was Seymour who caused Hanner to have the "caved in" ribs—but who finds it "convenient" to have Hanner wait on him. Together they attend the Fourth of July celebration at Vinita, where Hanner rides a wild mule to demonstrate his bravery to Seymour, who despite his promise, gets drunk. Hanner, afraid that his idol will be arrested, entices him away from the celebration by pretending to be ill. When Seymour learns the truth, he feels deprived of his fun. In his drunken state, he decides to rob the mail stage as a joke, despite Hanner's appeals to the contrary, disguising himself in Hanner's floppy hat and bandana. The joke goes wrong, and a guard is killed. They go into hiding, but Hanner decides to save his friend by explaining to the posse that the robbery was intended as a joke. Because of his hat, they mistake him for the killer, and he decides to remain silent. He is hanged, sacrificing himself for his friend. The reader is prepared for the act by Oskison's gently probing the psychology of the attachment to and loyalty of the weak for the strong. Too, Hanner has proved his courage by riding the wild mule. A final, ironic twist comes at the end; when Seymour is told of Hanner's fate, he looks the teller full in the face and says, "The poor little fool, to do a thing like that!"

Even Oskison's early writing shows a surprising maturity, and there is much in his work to suggest his closeness to literary models. The idyllic flavor of some stories is reminiscent of Bret Harte's work. Hanner's loyalty, too, is as deep and lasting as Tennessee's Partner's, and the reader is struck by the similarity of Oskison's plot to Harte's. **"The Schoolmaster's Dissipation"** is also reminiscent of Harte's "The Idyll of Red Gulch" (1879), in which Mary the teacher cures Sandy of his drinking, and he trades the addiction to alcohol for an addiction to love for her. In Oskison's story it is the teacher who is saved and who trades his addiction to morphine for addiction to love for Dr. Pless. Oskison, like Harte, also had a penchant for physically grotesque characters. Hanner had one shoulder "knocked down a quarter of a foot lower than the other," two caved in ribs, and a scar on his face. Billy Wilson had a dislocated hip and walked with a side-swing of one leg. Finally, names like Runt, Convict, Smear and JIC-Bert remind the reader of the nameless people, such as Tennessee's Partner and the Duchess, who populate Harte's West. These parallels suggest, if not close reading of Harte, a mutual recognition of the possibilities for plots and characters in the raw western setting.

There is evidence to suggest that Oskison was also attuned to the spirit of short fiction of the 1890s. His works contain sociological themes, usually less blatantly stated than those in Garland's stories such as "Up the Coulé" (1891) and often less subtly than those in Crane's stories such as "The Bride Comes to Yellow Sky" (1898). The poverty and poor health conditions of the Cherokees are apparent in **"The Schoolmaster's Dissipation"** as is the plight of the conservative full bloods in **"Tookh Steh's Mistake," "When the Grass Grew Long"** and **"The Problem of Old Harjo."** The rough and rowdy demeanor of the cowboys, their willingness to fight and their cruel jokes reflect the violence that was inherent in and often erupted without warning in western society. But their genuine sense of humor and their enjoyment of such pastimes as the rodeo are reflected in stories such as **"The Fall of King Chris."** The themes are not editorial but are made an integral part of the setting, character or plot of the stories. In **"Only the Master Shall Praise,"** for instance, Hanner's mixed blood is central to the story's fabric. Oskison uses the pejorative term "half-breed" to describe the misshapen cowboy. From his Indian mother, Hanner gets an "innocent trust" in humanity that causes him to remain loyal to Seymour and a stoicism that allows him to face death in silence. From his white father, he inherits a "physical energy and mental weakness" that constantly gets him into trouble and makes him a social outcast. With his blood polluted, the Indian has cast his lot with the white man, who dominates him. The "half-breed" misfit is ultimately sacrificed, and the white man gets off free. (pp. 32-5)

Daniel F. Littlefield, Jr. and James W. Parins, "Short Fiction Writers of the Indian Territory," in American Studies, *Vol. 23, No. 1, Spring, 1982, pp. 23-38.*

FURTHER READING

Sherman, Caroline B. "A Vigorous Tale of a Stalwart Family." *New York Herald Tribune Books* 12, No. 2 (15 September 1935): 6.
> Positive review of *Brothers Three* in which the critic praises Oskison's skill in telling a "straightforward, vigorous story with a noteworthy restraint."

Skinner, Constance Lindsay. "Redman against Paleface." *New York Herald Tribune Books* 15, No. 8 (23 October 1938): 22.
> Favorable review in which Oskison's *Tecumseh and His Times* is compared with two other works published contemporaneously: Albert Britt's *Great Indian Chiefs* and Frank C. Lockwood's *The Apache Indians.*

Wiget, Andrew O. "Native American Literature: A Bibliographic Survey of American Indian Literary Traditions." *Choice* 23, No. 10 (June 1986): 1503-512.
> Mentions Oskison's *Black Jack Davy* as part of a resurgence of native American literature after World War I. According to Wiget, *Black Jack Davy* is the only one of Oskison's novels that "can be said to really turn on Indian themes or issues."

José Eustasio Rivera

1889-1928

Colombian novelist, essayist, and poet.

Rivera is best known as the author of *La vorágine* (*The Vortex*), one of the first novels to realistically portray the South American jungle and its inhabitants. Esteemed for its evocative, lyrical prose style and the fidelity of its descriptions, *The Vortex* has also been applauded for its frank disclosure of the social injustices inflicted on Colombian peasants. Rivera's novel exerted a marked influence on South American literature, helping to inspire the trend toward the use of native themes and settings that has culminated in the internationally recognized achievements of such authors as Gabriel García Márquez and Mario Vargas Llosa.

Rivera was born into a family of modest means in the southern Colombian town of Neiva. Graduating from a teachers' college in Bogotá at the age of twenty, he received a law degree from the National University eight years later. Rivera subsequently established himself both as a lawyer and as a member of Bogatá's intellectual community, publishing a collection of sonnets, *Tierra de promisión,* in 1921. The following year he traveled to the Colombian jungle as secretary of a congressional committee investigating a border dispute between his country and Venezuela, an experience that provided the inspiration for *The Vortex.* In particular, Rivera was impressed by the majestic beauty and destructive power of the jungle, and his sympathies were aroused by the abominable conditions to which Colombians working for the nascent rubber industry were subjected. While in the jungle, Rivera contracted beriberi, and it was during his convalescence that he wrote *The Vortex.* The novel was an immediate success, bringing Rivera international acclaim. However, his health remained poor due to the lingering effects of his disease, and in 1928 he died of pneumonia while on a speaking tour in the United States.

Displaying Rivera's literary talents as well as his keen powers of perception, *The Vortex* has been described by L. H. Titterton as an admirable combination of "stark realism and lyrical romanticism." In the novel, Rivera sought to portray the dramatic conflict between human beings and the South American jungle, which is described by Rivera's protagonist, Arturo Cova, as a "green hell." Some critics have therefore argued that Rivera viewed the jungle as a hostile environment which inflicts physical and mental pain on its human inhabitants and evokes savage behavior. Arturo Torres-Ríoseco has written that, in *The Vortex,* Rivera "shows how [the] forest dominates the human beings who drag themselves through its depths; how it attacks their minds and bodies, incubating fevers and insanity; how with its thousand tentacles it seizes men and transforms them into wild beasts." However, some oppose this view of *The Vortex,* most notably Richard Callan, who asserts that Rivera depicted the jungle as a testing ground where an individual might yield to baser impulses but might also display heroic endurance.

The Vortex purports to be the memoirs of Cova, a young Colombian intellectual. At the beginning of the novel, he elopes with his girlfriend, Alicia, leaving Bogotá to settle among the lawless cattle herders of the Colombian plains. When Alicia is subsequently abducted and taken to the jungle, Cova follows. There he meets Don Clemente Silva and Ramiro Estévañez, whose accounts of Colombian history and its impact upon life in the jungle combine with Cova's story to form the sweeping narrative of *The Vortex.* The story ends when Cova, having found Alicia and killed her abductor, disappears with her into the jungle. While *The Vortex* has generally been applauded for its exciting plot, lyrical prose, and colorful descriptive passages, the narrative has also been criticized for what many view as a lack of coherence between Cova's accounts of his adventures and the historical accounts related by Silva, Estévañez, and other minor characters. Eduardo Neale-Silva has speculated that Rivera wrote the purely fictional passages separately from the sections based on Colombian history and later attempted to fuse them. However, Seymour Menton disagrees with the widely held view that the narrative lacks coherence and suggests that *The Vortex* is a carefully constructed allegory. In his view, the novel should be regarded as "a complex Christian vision of man's fall from paradise and his punishment and ultimate death in the concentric circles of Hell."

The Vortex has long been appreciated as both a richly descriptive regional novel and a compelling, romantic adventure story. In addition, recent analyses have emphasized the psychological complexity and technical sophistication of Rivera's narrative, as well as the author's skillful allusions to classical and modern literature. Highly esteemed in Spanish-speaking countries, Rivera is also one of the few Colombian writers to have achieved international recognition.

PRINCIPAL WORKS

Tierra de promisión   (poetry)   1921
La vorágine   (novel)   1924
   [*The Vortex*, 1935]
Obras completas   (novel, essays, and poetry)   1963

L. H. TITTERTON   (essay date 1935)

[*Titterton was an American critic, editor, and language scholar. In the following excerpt, he commends the realism and narrative power of* The Vortex.]

"Death closes all the exits of the jungle," wrote Señor Rivera. Death spared him to write this single novel [*The Vortex*] a complex book of exceptional distinction. It is a tale of the cruelty of nature and of man, of love and of lust, of heroism and disease, of foulness and misery, and great beauty; it is the tale of rubber in the raw. In a translator's foreword Mr. [E. K.] James states that Rivera suffered many of the tribulations which Arturo Cova experiences in the book—"trudging through leech-infested swamps barefooted, half-starved, crazed by mosquitos and fevers"—for he served on the commission which traced the definite boundary between Colombia and Venezuela; that his characters are not inventions, but studies from life, some even appearing in the book under the names which made them infamous. No man who had not been moved to his very depths by what he underwent and what he saw and heard could have written **The Vortex.**

The facts of the atrocities perpetrated on the Putumayo were reported to an incredulous world more than twenty years ago by Sir Roger Casement. W. H. Hudson looked on the beauties of the jungle and wrote a romantic masterpiece [*Green Mansions*]. It has remained for Rivera, with his Spanish heritage, to combine stark realism with lyrical romanticism. Man may be infinitely cruel to man and join with tropical nature in torturing and enslaving him. But man has also ideals which will keep him in a living hell because he cannot leave without finding and removing from that land of terror the bones of his dead son.

A woman such as the amazing Madona Zoraida Ayram, gross, lascivious and hardened by trade, plays her accordion at night, telling through her music of redemption to come when some hand has aroused the people of the world against the horrors of the jungle. And Cova himself, one of the truly great characters of modern fiction, poet and lover, spurred by revenge, tender and ferocious, sure of his mission and doubting all things, counting on the aid of consuls, and sure they will find that the matter is outside their jurisdiction.

Mr. James feels that the Anglo-Saxon reader may find **The Vortex** perplexing. He does less than justice to his magnificent translation. The receptive reader will find that Señor Rivera's mingling of introspection and objectivity, poetry and passionate exaltation has resulted in a book of marvelous strength and unity. (pp. 8, 17)

> L. H. Titterton, "In South America's Rubber Jungles," in The New York Times Book Review, April 28, 1935, pp. 8, 17.

THE SATURDAY REVIEW OF LITERATURE (essay date 1935)

[*In the following review of* The Vortex, *the critic finds little to recommend the novel.*]

Whatever it may be in Spanish and read in more or less the air in which it was written, in our air and in American, [*The Vortex*] is curiously un-nourishing. There are bits of vivid and undoubtedly authentic description of South American jungle life; characters here and there—"La Madona," for instance, the fat old harpy whom the hero meets in the heart of the rubber country—which ring true. But in general, the story is very wild, very queer, and it's difficult to make head or tail of it.

The narrator is a tempestuous Colombian, half contemporary man, half something out of the cloak-and-sword theatre, who runs away with his mistress from Bogotá to the rubber country. The girl disappears with another man and a vague sort of pursuit begins. The rubber country and the horrible life led by the rubber tappers is not seen realistically and through the patient following of an actual rubber tapper's day-to-day life, as it was recently in Ferreira De Castro's *Jungle,* but rhetorically and through the reports of others. There is much violence of one sort and another, blood and sudden death, and

in the end, according to the brief epilogue, the narrator just disappears, swallowed by the jungle.

> G. S., in a review of "The Vortex," in The Saturday Review of Literature, *Vol. XII, No. 2, May 11, 1935, p. 25.*

ARTURO TORRES-RÍOSECO (essay date 1942)

[*Torres-Ríoseco was a Chilean-born American scholar of Spanish-American literature. In the following excerpt, he praises* The Vortex *as the best example of South-American jungle fiction, discussing the power of Rivera's descriptions and his exposition of the plight of the rubber workers.*]

[The] phrase "novel of the land" suggests the observation that the land itself is the chief actor in a good many Spanish American novels. In itself, this does not of course guarantee any great originality. For example, the Chilean short-story writer, Mariano Latorre (1886-) has painstakingly studied and written about the rural regions of his native land—only to produce works that resemble those of the Spanish novelist Pereda. But where South American writers have chosen to do books on the uncivilized parts of the continent, like the still-unexplored forests of the Amazon basin, the results have been remarkable.

The novel of the *selva,* to take a striking case, has been cultivated in many countries from Bolivia to Brazil. The greatest book of all this jungle fiction, and the one which will best serve as a prototype for the rest, is that extraordinary novel **The Vortex,** by José Eustasio Rivera, a gifted Colombian poet and novelist who, by a strange whim of fate, died prematurely of pneumonia in New York, the greatest city in the world. The "vortex" in his novel is of course the tropical forest itself, which Rivera, during his brief life as poet, lawyer, and civic figure, had the occasion of visiting as a member of the Venezuela-Colombia Boundary Commission. His journey took him across the valleys of the Casanare, the Meta, the San Martín, and the Vaupés; he travelled along the Orinoco, the Río Negro, the Casiquiare; he lived among the river Indians, and he was lost for a while in the *selva,* where he suffered the torments of thirst and mosquitoes and ants and fever; and while he was convalescing from beri-beri, at his journey's end, he wrote his masterpiece, **The Vortex.**

In this novel, the vast tropical forest comes to life, all its horrors transmuted by Rivera's poetical imagination: He describes dark cities of trees, which no human being has ever entered; trees covered with living nets of parasitic plants, and these in turn covered with millions of insects and larvae; trees that talk and move as if endowed with magic life. And this *selva* has its myriad inhabitants: howling tribes of monkeys; swarms of ants that descend unexpectedly over all living beings, devouring them in a few seconds; blind alligators in their stagnant waters. Even more important, the entire forest is never static for a moment; it is frightfully alive, in all its monstrosity of gestation, decay, violence, and death—with no room for romantic visions:

> Here there are no amorous nightingales, no Versailles-like gardens, no sentimental panoramas! Here are the croakings of hydropic toads . . . the trickle of putrefied springs. Here, the aphrodisiac parasite that covers the ground with dead bees; the multitudes of flowers, contracting themselves with sensual palpitations and sticky sweat, that intoxicate one like a drug; the malignant liana whose fuzz

blinds animals; the *pringamosa* that inflames the skin, the seed of the *duruju* that looks like a prismatic globe and contains only caustic ashes. . . .

Here, at night, unfamiliar voices. . . . The sound of the ripe fruit falling . . . the dropping of a leaf. . . . And when the dawn sheds its tragic glory over the forests . . . the constant noise of the shrieking wildfowl, the snorts of the wild boar, the laughter of the ridiculous monkey. . . .

Here, indeed, is a magnificent background for fiction—and it is this savage setting itself that governs the story of Rivera's novel. For he shows how this forest dominates the human beings who drag themselves through its depths; how it attacks their minds and bodies, incubating fevers and insanity; how with its thousand tentacles it seizes men and transforms them into wild beasts.

Thus, Rivera has painted the tragedy of rubber exploitation in the midst of this tropical *selva,* the plight of Indians and half-breeds, enslaved by European adventurers and hurled by the thousands into this green hell to toil and to die. Sometimes they try to flee, and perish in the forest; sometimes they commit suicide by drinking the thick liquid of the rubber trees. Rivera has written a terrible exposé of these conditions, describing the horrors of the *caucheros* in all their brutal intensity, with a violence and passion that may be judged by the following excerpts:

I have three hundred trees to take care of, and it takes me nine days to lacerate them; I have cleaned them of creepers and lianas; I have opened a path towards each of them. On trudging through this army of giants, to fell the ones that don't shed latex, I often find tappers stealing my rubber. We tear each other with fists and machetes; and the disputed latex is splashed with red. But what does it matter if our veins increase the supply of sap? The overseer demands ten liters a day, and the lash is a usurer that never forgives.

And what if my neighbor dies of fever? I see him stretched out on the leafy mold, shaking himself, trying to rid himself of flies that will not let him die in peace. Tomorrow I shall move away, driven elsewhere by the stench. But I shall steal the latex he gathered. My work will be so much lighter. They'll do the same with me when I die. . . .

As I gash the dripping trunk, as I channel it so that its tears may flow into the tin cup, clouds of mosquitoes that protect it suck my blood, and the miasmas of the forest dim my eyes. Thus both the tree and I are suffering, are tearful in the face of death; and both of us struggle until we succumb.

(pp. 178-81)

Arturo Torres-Ríoseco, "The Spanish American Novel," in his The Epic of Latin American Literature, *Oxford University Press, 1942, pp. 168-208.*

JEFFERSON REA SPELL (essay date 1944)

[*In the following excerpt, Spell finds that despite structural flaws,* The Vortex *is a great novel, notable in particular for its dramatic narrative and impressive presentation of the struggle between human beings and nature.*]

Unquestionably of unusual merit and interest, *La vorágine* is marked by certain characteristics—its epic-like nature, the

vast territory it covers, and its time element—which do not make for unity or a well integrated plot. Interest is largely centered on one character, Cova, and his wanderings through an almost impenetrable region. His own story, which constitutes the main plot, covers only some seven months of the year 1920, but the relations of Don Clemente Silva and Ramiro Estévañez carry the novel back in point of time to the early years of the century. Such details and other circumstances that affect the action of the main plot are entirely out of proportion. One feels, too, that those details were the principal concern of the author and not the story of Alicia and Cova, which seems to have been invented merely as an excuse to lure the reader into the forest regions and to reveal to him the appalling conditions that exist there. The main story is probably fictional, but its setting, as Mr. Eduardo Neale-Silva has clearly demonstrated [in his essay "The Factual Bases of *La vorágine*"], is based to a very large degree on fact. The geography of the two regions is presented with great fidelity; Cova's journey through them can be accurately plotted; the life of the people that is portrayed, whether of the plains or the forest, comes first-hand; the mistreatment of the workers in the rubber-producing districts, of which Don Clemente told in great detail, is substantiated by reliable documents; and many of the characters—Julio César Araña, the rubber baron of the Putamayo; Colonel Funes, who massacred the inhabitants of San Fernando del Atabapo in 1913; and others less notorious—existed in actual life.

While through these and many other realistic details in the setting a sense of actuality is attained, and while the treatment of certain aspects of nature contributes greatly to its artistry, the main charm of *La vorágine* is enhanced by a certain dramatic presentation of the narrative itself. For the story unfolds largely through a series of scenes, of a nature so dramatic and vivid that one feels in reading them that he is witnessing an animated play; and, too, as at a play, he judges the characters by what they say and do. The scenes in the first third of the book are particularly effective. Almost in the very opening pages, Cova and Alicia disclose in a quarrel not only the relation that exists between them but also their very natures. And so it is with all the other characters that are introduced in this part: the crafty and thieving Pipa; Don Rufo, the wise old peddler; the mulattress Sebastiana and her son Correa; Barrera, wily and oily-tongued; Franco, faithful and upright; Zubieta, the wary old rancher; and the corrupt judge of Orocué, whom Cova, when he found him lost on the plains, sent in the opposite direction to that of his destination.

In the second third of the book, that dealing with the experiences of Cova and his comrades in the jungle, the narrative moves forward through a series of vivid pictures rather than dramatic scenes. Cova describes graphically the effects of the tropical fever which attacked him and the manners and customs of an Indian tribe on the Meta River. Later, Helí Mesa pictures to him and his friends the horrors of the enslavement of the Colombian laborers that Barrera had lured away with rosy promises. Then in a series of lurid pictures Don Clemente recounts his sufferings in the jungles for sixteen years. The dramatic scene is, however, by no means entirely absent in this section. There is dialogue between Cova and his men, between them and Helí Mesa and Don Clemente; and the latter often drifts from pure narrative into a dramatic scene in order to present more vividly some ghastly situation in his past.

After the conclusion of the stories told by Don Clemente and Ramiro Estévañez, the interest in the third section again centers on the difficulties of Cova and his comrades. Here again, as in the first part, the story moves swiftly forward through a series of scenes, in which Cova, La Madona, Váquiro, Griselda, and many others take part. Here there are two very memorable examples of pictorial skill: the description of the half-starved beings around the huts of Guaracú, and of the hand-to-hand conflict in which Cova disposed of Barrera on the banks of the Yaguanarí. With his destruction—the denouement of this human drama—justice triumphs, at least temporarily, in its struggle against wrong and oppression, for the impulsive Cova, with his many faults, was ever a "friend of the weak."

But the struggle between human beings is not the only one that is enacted; it is paralleled by another, that between man and nature, which brings with it a poetic and lyric tone. Nature, as it impresses Cova, is, if not actually terrifying, always astounding: whether sunrise, sudden storms, or torrential downpours on the limitless plains or that most awe-inspiring aspect of nature—the *selva* itself, its foliage so dense as to shut out the sun, its insects so poisonous and destructive, its sounds so appalling! Always the forest is hostile to man, and Cova feels its menace as he apostrophizes it:

> Oh forest, forest, spouse of silence, mother of solitude and of shadows! What evil spirit left me a captive in thy green prison? Like a great vault, the canopy of thy huge branches stretches always above my head, between me and the bright heavens for which I long, of which I catch a glimpse only at the sad hour of twilight when the trembling tops of thy trees move like billows. Where is the beloved star that frequents the hill? And those hues of gold and purple with which the west adorns itself, why do they not shimmer in thy canopy? How many times—as I looked over in the direction of my land, with its unforgettable plains and its snow-capped peaks on whose summits I have stood at a height equal to the cordillera itself—have I not sighed, O forest, imagining across thy labyrinth the reflection of the moon coloring with its purple shadows the distances! Where does that heavenly body now shed its placid and silvery light? Thou, forest, hast robbed me of those pleasant fancies I had when I beheld the horizon; for my eyes now there is only the monotony of thy zenith, over which passes a pale light which never penetrates the dense foliage of thy damp recesses.

> Thou art the sanctuary of sorrow, where unknown gods speak in a whisper, in a murmuring language, promising long years to the imposing trees, which are as old as heaven itself, which were already venerable when the first tribes appeared, and which await impassively the passing of the centuries to come. Thy vegetation forms upon the earth a powerful family, among whom there are no traitors. The embrace that thy huge branches do not give to one another, is received by the winding vines and lianas. Thou art as one, even in the grief of the leaf that falls. Thy numberless voices blend, on weeping for the dead trunk of a tree that gives way and falls, in a single echo; but in each breach thus made new germs speed their gestation. Thou hast the gravity of cosmic force, and in thee is embodied the mystery of the creation of the world. My spirit, nevertheless, borne down by the weight of thy immortality, yearns for the transitory; and it has come to love, not the tough oak, but the languid orchid; because, like man, its life is of short duration and it passes away like a dream. Let me flee, O forest,

from thy sickly gloom, formed by the dying breath of all the beings that yielded up their lives within thy desolate realm. A vast cemetery thou seemest in which there is everlasting decay and rebirth. Let me return to the realm where the unknown frightens none, where bondage is unknown, where the view is clear, and bright light surrounds the spirit. Let me return to the land whence I came on this pilgrimage of blood and tears, when, through the caprice of a woman, I pressed on through woods and desert realms, in search of vengeance, an implacable goddess, who smiles only upon tombs.

And finally, when the forest—like a dread monster—devours the group, it is Nature, after all, that has conquered man.

Rich in information about strange and little-known regions, abounding in emotion that is deeply felt, endowed with a high and noble purpose, *La vorágine* is, in spite of its shortcomings, a great book. In it the forest and the jungle have been masterfully interpreted. Here is a Colombia unknown before in the annals of literature. (pp. 186-90)

Jefferson Rea Spell, "The Secrets of the 'Selvas' of Colombia Unfolded by José Eustacio Rivera," in his Contemporary Spanish-American Fiction, *The University of North Carolina Press, 1944, pp. 179-90.*

WILLIAM E. BULL   (essay date 1948)

[*Bull was an American scholar and critic. In the following excerpt, he examines the emotional instability of the three principal narrators of* The Vortex, *arguing that their accounts fail to accurately interpret reality and so present no coherent statement of Rivera's own attitudes.*]

The "Green Hell" which dominates Rivera's single masterpiece is ostensibly, according to the literary pretense of the prologue, not his own creation but a factual account of reality by three informants: Arturo Cova (the fictitious author and poet-hero of the novel), Clemente Silva, and Ramiro Estévanez. To these three first-person narrators, his literary emissaries, Rivera entrusts his social thesis and the detailed description of the tropical rain-forest environment which, as the title suggests, is essentially the main protagonist of *La vorágine.*

Perhaps no author as high-minded and serious as Rivera has ever presented an extensive study of nature through the eyes and emotions of characters so incapable of describing nature in an objective fashion. It seems that Rivera has unconsciously injected a most puzzling dilemma into the literary complex of characters, nature description, and social aims. If, on the one hand, he is identified psychologically and philosophically with his main narrator, Arturo Cova—if it is believed that Rivera subscribed to the attitudes toward life exhibited by his main characters and agreed with their interpretation of nature—then there can be but little doubt that *La vorágine* is one of the most astonishing public revelations of an author's "inner soul" in literary history, comparable only, perhaps, to that of Swift. If, on the other hand, it is presumed that Rivera's intention was to create a purely imaginative work in which the characters, their philosophy, and their vision of natural reality was to be independently their own (in consonance with what Rivera believed to be most in accord with their psychological attributes), then it must be assumed that the author saw no significant objection to entrusting his story and his obvious social thesis to a first-person narrator whose competence as an accurate and trustworthy reporter is rendered questionable by the personality Rivera chose to give him.

Whichever alternative is accepted for the moment, the psychology, the philosophy of life, and the behavior of Arturo Cova become the portal through which the nature presented in *La vorágine* must be observed.

Arturo Cova is, on the surface, the stereotyped hero of an adventure novel, but on closer observation he emerges as a character who seems to have been drawn directly from some textbook of abnormal psychology. Cova is, by any standard, inadequate to deal with his problems and highly unstable emotionally. During the seven months of his life presented in *La vorágine* he frequently weeps over his misfortunes and frustrations. Cova's self-confidence is so weak that his ego and vanity are easily hurt and he must rationalize his own defeats. He is so extremely jealous that he contemplates murder. He goes to great lengths to establish his reputation for manliness, he turns misanthropic and hates his friends because they pity him and are kind to him, and he feels the need of ego-building, self-praise.

Cova has great difficulty controlling his temper and becomes angry very easily. He is often extremely quarrelsome and quick to fight; he has frequent urges to kill people, and finally does commit homicide. He drinks excessively without being able to get drunk and when in a drunken rage strikes his hostess, insults his mistress, and threatens to kill anyone who comes near him. He alternates between moods of despondency, elation, and rage, suffers from insomnia, nightmares, hysterical laughter, and exhibits, during emotional crises, physical disorders which have no organic cause. He worries about whether he is sane or insane, is incapable of controlling himself and gouges his head with his fingernails until it bleeds during one nervous crisis and breaks his fingernails on a table during another.

In spite of all his bravado and apparent daring Arturo Cova is not a man who can face the world of reality and the consequences of his own actions. After he has seduced Alicia, an interest of a passing moment, he flees with her from Bogotá in order to escape social criticism and the possibility of a jail sentence, but when the full consequences of his actions are clearly laid out before him he secretly hopes that they will be captured so he will be freed of the responsibility of Alicia. His inclination to run away from difficulties, however, has a still more serious side. He is also haunted by the urge to commit suicide. He threatens to do so once and actually prepares to shoot himself on another occasion, but he lies in his hammock with his jaw against the muzzle of his carbine without being able to bring himself to pull the trigger. Having failed in this attempt to escape his difficulties, he kills himself symbolically in a fit of hysteria during which he imagines himself suddenly paralyzed, dying, being pronounced dead, and being buried.

The abnormalities of the man to whom the greater part of the nature description of *La vorágine* is entrusted do not, however, stop with these. Cova is tormented by illusions and hallucinations: a house whirls through the air before his eyes; he thinks he is an eagle and tries to fly; the ground moves in the opposite direction when he attempts to walk. The forest, in Clemente Silva's opinion, bewitches him. The trees take on fantastic shapes, his head seems excessively heavy, and he walks sideways with his head cocked over his shoulder while a spirit voice encourages him in this idiosyncrasy, and he finally runs frantically in all directions howling with fear.

This inability to distinguish between reality and non-reality naturally leads Cova into many flights of day-dreaming in which mild delusions of grandeur are not uncommon. Although he is almost penniless, a refugee from the law, and without occupation or any concrete possibilities of making a living, he imagines that he has suddenly become rich in the cattle trade. He returns to Bogotá an envied hero, brags of his exploits, overcomes all social opposition to his escapades, becomes a literary light, takes a degree, and is adored by his former women friends; or he becomes the embattled hero of the *selva,* sets in action governmental machinery to free the rubber gatherers from their slavery, personally kills their worst enemy in the presence of Alicia and the slaves, and hears his companions exclaim: "El implacable Cova nos vengó a todos y se internó por este desierto!" His exploits in the world of fantasy are sometimes so real to him that after having dreamt them he behaves as though they were true.

It should be obvious at this point, especially if it is kept in mind that the novel deals with only a few months of Cova's life, that the vortex, the symbol of the whole novel, is as much in the tortured and unstable mind of Cova as it is in the realities with which he comes in contact, and that, as a result,

Letter by Rivera.

Cova is hardly capable of seeing the objective world of nature in a realistic fashion.

This air of unreality, and the enigma about Rivera's aims and intentions, are intensified by Cova's thoroughly romantic attitude toward life. Arturo Cova, in addition to the psychological abnormalities which have already been catalogued, exhibits many of the abnormal attitudes which are particularly common among romantics. He is a Childe Harold pretending to be a bored Don Juan, while inside, his heart is filled with aching loneliness. He is proud of an individuality and nonconformity which are the result of neurotic compulsions and pleased, in spite of his miserable experiences, over the daring and spectacular nature of his exploits.

Since Cova is incapable of controlling either his emotions or, as a natural consequence, his own destiny, he feels that he is plunging through life haunted by an inexorable fate:

> . . . Los que un tiempo creyeron que mi inteligencia irradiaría extraordinariamente, cual una aureola de mi juventud; los que se olvidaron de mí apenas mi planta descendió al infortunio; los que al recordarme alguna vez piensen en mi fracaso y se pregunten por qué no fuí lo que pude haber sido, sepan que el destino implacable me desarraigó de la prosperidad incipiente y me lanzó a las pampas, para que ambulara, vagabundo, como los vientos, y me extinguiera como ellos sin dejar más que ruido y desolación.

Death, his heart tells him, is his destiny and he plunges onward blindly, unaware that other alternatives might exist. . . . (pp. 307-10)

Cova, in typical romantic fashion, is forever searching for some mysterious, ideal, and ineffable happiness and, with doom upon him and the air of the martyr, he weeps, like Rubén Darío, "por mis aspiraciones engañadas, por mis ensueños desvanecidos, por lo que no fuí, por lo que ya no seré jamás." His dream solutions of life's problems are illusory and romantic. He will settle down with Alicia on the plains in a "casa risueña" built with his own hands. (p. 310)

His treatment of love and marriage is, in the modern concept of the sociologist, romantic and infantile. He feels that he can be unjust and violent with Alicia and, after insulting and abandoning her, expect her to come to him and beg his pardon, and he believes that all his love problems can be solved only by some day finding "la mujer ideal y pura, cuyos brazos brinden serenidad para los vicios y las pasiones."

The romantic philosophy which characterizes Arturo Cova is not an attitude restricted primarily to the poet-hero of *La vorágine*. Rivera has cast a heavy shadow of romanticism over the entire novel. He seems to have selected his supporting characters, historically real as they are in many instances, with the feelings of a romantic. Aside from the inevitable group which the idealist must fight (the hostile elements of society), the more important characters fall into two categories: the exotic type, the mysterious *madona,* Zoraida Ayram; *El Cayeno,* who has escaped by superhuman efforts from the prisons of Devil's Island; Pipa, the renegade bandit-outlaw, who lives with the Indians and possesses diabolic knowledge; and the second group who, significantly, relate most of the novel in the first person and who are stereotyped by Rivera according to the principal standards of romanticism. They are outcast by and fighting against society, on the one hand, and all the world of nature, on the other. There is Cova him-

self, the main protagonist, romantic to the core, and Griselda, who kills a man to save her honor, and Franco who for love of her deserts from the army and gallantly assumes responsibility for the murder. Both flee from society in a desperate attempt to build a new life in the *llanuras.* There is Clemente Silva, whose daughter is seduced, whose reputation is besmirched and who, forsaken in this crisis by his friends, goes with strange compulsions to spend sixteen years searching for his son's bones in order to fulfill a promise made over the dead body of his bereaved wife. And, lastly, there is half-blind Ramiro Estévanez, frustrated in his one great love of a woman by the rules of social stratification, who plunges into the forest to forget and be forgotten.

Rivera seems to have placed no great significance on the fact that his major characters are all suffering from especially tense emotional stresses and that the compulsions which drive them into the *selva,* the vortex, are contained largely within themselves or are the direct products of their own behavior. He prefers, rather, to picture his characters as driven by fate, chance, and a hostile society into the forest. Since they are at once confronted with an entirely new environment which they are inadequately prepared to meet, either psychologically or practically, they are naturally beset by constant fears and a strong sense of foreboding which are not an accurate reflection of the objective character of the environment. This fact is extremely significant in setting the major tones for the treatment of nature in *La vorágine.* The narrating characters disregard their own frailties and place the causes for their fears entirely outside of themselves, that is, they project them upon the environment. Rivera accepts this rationalization and, as a result, the new environment must of necessity be depicted as actually being as horrible as his characters' reaction to it. The interpretation of nature which is to emerge from the novel will be, consequently, distorted in direct proportion to the characters' inability to dominate their emotions and to establish a proper cause and effect explanation of their own fears.

Cova, very early in the novel, establishes this pattern by comparing himself and Alicia to a seed swept aimlessly before the wind, afraid of the land that is awaiting them. This is the normal fear of the unknown, but it is soon converted, because of Cova's excessive lack of emotional security, into an exaggerated foreboding of evil and doom by a horrible nightmare in which he sees Alicia going across a "sabana lúgubre, hacia un lugar siniestro." He is watching her and trying to protect her against the advances of Barrera, but every time he points his gun it becomes a "serpiente helada y rígida," and, meanwhile, Don Rufo shouts at him: "Véngase! Eso ya no tiene remedio!"

The dream goes on in an even more macabre tone and, although clearly evidence of Cova's abnormalities and subconscious fears of the future, it is apparently aimed by the author at creating an unfavorable emotional reaction in the reader to the whole new and "horrible" world into which Cova and Alicia are about to plunge. (pp. 310-11)

Cova's neurotic fears and compulsions serve Rivera as a useful device to build up this atmosphere of doom and destruction with which nature must be in consonance, and in a fashion strongly reminiscent of Isaac's *María,* the novel is liberally sprinkled with prognostications of death and destruction which Cova reports in retrospect. (p. 312)

It would be amazing indeed to discover that Rivera's treatment of nature in *La vorágine* did not reflect the peculiar emotions and distorted attitudes of his characters and the general romantic tone which pervades all other aspects of the novel. Rivera does not, as Earle K. James felt, blast "Arcadian conceptions of idyllic nature" with "furious realism." He is forced, rather, by the exigencies of his story and thesis, to describe unpleasant things—maggots in open sores, man-eating fish, armies of carnivorous ants, filth and slime—but his method, the technique which creates the nature atmosphere of the novel, can hardly be classified as that of the realist.

Arturo Cova, in one of his dreamy flights of fancy, expresses, almost as a literary pronouncement, the basic attitude from which Rivera's description of nature springs:

> Quizá mi fuente de poesía estaba en el secreto de los bosques intactos, en la caricia de las auras, en el idioma desconocido de las cosas; en cantar lo que dice el peñon a la onda que se despide, el arrebol a la ciénaga, la estrella a las inmensidades que guardan el silencio de Dios.

Cova, the pretended author, in keeping with his character, is hardly capable of looking upon the external world of nature with the eyes of a realist. He must poetize nature, idealize it, project upon it his moods, feelings, and emotional reactions. By his hypostatizations he makes it, in short, anthropomorphic. Since there is a whirling vortex in his own mind there must also be a vortex of equal violence in nature, and, as a result, nature is endowed with human attributes and made to harmonize with the states of mind of the characters observing it. Rivera generalizes this attitude to all his characters and nature is made as horrible as their moods.

When Cova recalls the moment he left the savanna and plunged into the *selva*, the scene before his eyes is, in contrast with his miserable life in the tropical forest, most delightful, and the plains, in memory's eye, are lost in a "nébula dulce" and he thinks of colors of rose and opal, "crepúsculos cariñosos," and a "cielo amigo." When he can no longer endure with emotional equilibrium the realities of the selva and is tormented by thoughts of insanity, by terrifying illusions and dreadful hallucinations, he turns against his own and romantic idealism in general and, in an agony of emotional desperation, cries out:

> Cuál es aquí la poesía de los retiros? Dónde están las mariposas que parecen flores traslúcidas, los pájaros mágicos, el arroyo cantor? Pobre fantasía de los poetas que sólo conocen las soledades domesticadas!
>
> Nada de ruiseñores enamorados! Nada de jardín versallesco! Nada de panoramas sentimentales! Aquí los responsos de sapos hidrópicos, las malezas de cerros misántropos, los rebalsos de caños podridos.

The "affectionate twilights" and "friendly skies" have disappeared with Cova's changing mood and are replaced by a fantasmagoric and misanthropic nature, the "selva inhumana."

As Cova's psychological insecurity mounts he generalizes his emotional reactions to apply to everything about him and carefully selects, as a rationalization of his own inadequacy, everything he finds horrible for description: "árboles deformes," "reptiles ciegos," "hormigas devastadoras," "flores inmundas," "la liana maligna," etc. The Amazon forest, whose many natural beauties have been delightfully and objectively described by both laymen and scientists, becomes a seething, writhing, tortured mass of disgusting life struggling in a kind of botanical warfare and tainted by "el hálito del fermento, los vapores calientes de la penumbra, el sopor de la muerte, el marasmo de la procreación."

It has been customary to take this passage seriously as an exact description of the stark reality of the background against which the story of the novel takes place. Serious doubt, however, may be cast upon Rivera's intentions by two very contradictory descriptions of the same forest. In another paragraph of this same passage, Rivera has Cova say:

> Por primera vez, en todo su horror, se ensanchó ante mí la selva inhumana. Arboles deformes sufren el cautiverio de las enredaderas advenedizas, que a grandes trechos los ayuntan con las palmeras y se descuelgan en curva elástica, semejantes a redes mal extendidas, que a fuerza de almacenar en años enteros hojarascas, chamizas, frutas, se desfondan como un saco de podredumbre, vaciando en la yerba reptiles ciegos, salamandras mohosas, arañas peludas.
>
> Por doquiera el bejuco de matapalo—rastrero pulpo de las florestas—pega sus tentáculos a los troncos, acogotándolos y retorciéndolos, para injertárselos y trasfundírselos en metempsícosis dolorosas.

At first glance this appears to be description motivated only by a desire to be objective with only slight weighting on the side of the unpleasant, but when Cova is in a different mood the same vegetation which appears here struggling in a "fratricidal" war is described locked in amorous solidarity. Notice especially how the terrible "enredaderas" and "bejucos" of the above paragraph become the bearers of a friendly embrace:

> Tus [the selva's] vegetales forman sobre la tierra la poderosa familia que no se traiciona nunca. El abrazo que no pueden darse tus romanzones (sic: Ramazones?) lo llevan las enredaderas y los bejucos, y eres solidaria hasta en el dolor de la hoja que cae.

The most acceptable artistic significance of the first description would seem to lie not in its being an accurate word-picture of the selva, "furious realism," but a very precise description of Cova's frantic reaction to it. In this sense it may well be considered entirely realistic and valid artistically. Much of what Cova sees is true, but he cannot free himself of his anthropomorphic attitude toward nature and is incapable of seeing his situation objectively and realistically. He does not properly evaluate his own emotional instability and so places the causes of his fears upon the forest which, after all, is totally incapable of reacting to him in the fashion his fancy presumes. His rationalization, however, endows it with peculiarly human psychology:

> Esta selva sádica y virgen procura al ánimo la alucinación del peligro próximo. El vegetal es un ser sensible cuya psicología desconocemos. En estas soledades, cuando nos habla, sólo entiende su idioma el presentimiento. Bajo su poder, los nervios del hombre se convierten en haz de cuerdas, distendidas hacia el asalto, hacia la traición, hacia la asechanza. Los sentidos humanos equivocan sus facultades: el ojo siente, la espalda ve, la nariz explora, las piernas calculan y la sangre clama: Huyamos, huyamos!

Cova cannot recognize a simple case of hysteria, and Rivera lets the attitude pass as though Cova's explanation were completely acceptable. This is not poetic description or mere romantic exaggeration; it is the stark account of a man so frightened that he is on the verge of psychological collapse.

This vagueness of perception of the real problem is not a special characteristic of Cova as a created character. It is, rather, an attitude toward the forest which Rivera shares with all of his main characters. Clemente Silva also tries, in a manner very similar to Cova's, to explain a like situation:

> —Nadie ha sabido cuál es la causa del misterio que nos trastorna cuando vagamos en la selva. Sin embargo, creo acertar en la explicación: culquiera de estos árboles se amansaría, tornándose amistoso y hasta risueño, en un parque, en un camino, en una llanura, donde nadie lo sangrara ni lo persiguiera; mas aquí todos son perversos, o agresivos, o hipnotizantes. En estos silencios, bajo estas sombras, tienen su manera de combatirnos: algo nos asusta, algo nos crispa, algo nos oprime, y viene el mareo de las espesuras, y queremos huir y nos extraviamos, y por esta razón miles de caucheros no volvieron a salir nunca.

Silva, like Cova, describes a typical case of hysteria, yet he feels that somehow the forest must be to blame.

Ramiro Estévanez, the third important first-person narrator of *La vorágine,* is also depicted by Rivera as believing in the strange powers of the *selva*. Since he cannot face his own life problems and therefore subconsciously does not wish to leave the forest, he rationalizes his behavior and subscribes to the belief that the forest has the power to hold men as though in some enchantment:

> Un sino de fracaso y maldición persigue a cuantos explotan la mina verde. La selva los aniquila; la selva los retiene: la selva los llama para tragárselos. Los que escapan, aunque se refugien en las ciudades, llevan ya el maleficio en cuerpo y en alma. Mustios, envejecidos, decepcionados, no tienen más que una aspiración: volver, volver, a sabiendas de que si vuelven perecerán.

It should by now begin to be more than evident that Rivera was somewhat confused about his task as a novelist. On the one hand, he creates characters who, either because of personality distortions or great emotional strain, are particularly incapable of describing nature in an objective fashion, and, on the other hand, he builds his novel on the assumption that what they report will be accepted as actual reality by his readers. Rivera seems not to have been able to distinguish sharply between what his characters might legitimately do and feel as characters and what was permitted to him as an author with a thesis to be developed.

It is obvious, of course, that a character in a novel may believe whatever he likes: that trees have souls and hate people, that it is wise to offer propitiatory prayers to a vengeful nature, that forests have evil powers of enchantment, and that his rationalizations produce scientific facts, but the author must clearly rise above the ignorance and superstitions of his characters and maintain a sharp distinction between the "reality" his characters observe and the objective reality which his characters misinterpret and distort. That Rivera did not seem to grasp the importance of such a distinction is more sharply outlined by the artistic devices he employs in his description of nature.

Rivera demonstrates, in *Tierra de promisión,* that as a poet he is a member of that school of writers which uses anthropomorphic metaphors as a means of embellishing style and as a device for evoking easy emotional responses. However, when he turns to the novel and creates his poet-hero-narrator, Arturo Cova, he does not seem to comprehend clearly that what may be put down as merely pretty writing in a perfectly normal poet can hardly be interpreted in the same fashion when presented by a character whose profound psychological disturbances naturally cause him to project human characteristics upon nature. The resulting figures may look alike, but in the first case both the poet and the reader are aware of the metaphorical pretense. In the second instance, the character actually feels that nature possesses human characteristics: trees can "hate," hills can be "misanthropic," and the *selva* can "conspire" against man. There is no longer any pretense. Critical judgment has been overwhelmed by emotion and metaphor and fact are assumed to be identical.

There are, consequently, two kinds of anthropomorphism in *La vorágine:* that of the poet who pretends, and that of the man who cannot see clearly. Both are in constant artistic conflict with each other.

In the first part of the novel, where Rivera is simply describing nature prettily, Cova talks of the "garzas meditabundas," a "brisa discreta," stars that "se adormecieron," and a "constelación taciturna." The palm trees are especially endowed with human characteristics. At times they bow down their heads "humillándose hacia el oriente"; they "greet" the returning bronco-busters with "tremulantes cabeceos," and after a storm they straighten themselves up "con miedo." They "groan" before the "insolent power" of the wind, and they are "heroic" before the storm and die in it without "humiliating themselves."

However one judges this type of writing, whether one accepts it as a serious and legitimate attempt at poetic description or condemns it, with John Ruskin, as the pathetic fallacy and merely bad poetics, the fact remains that Rivera places himself in a serious artistic dilemma by using such devices. Throughout *La vorágine* he builds up the character of his fictitious author as a man incapable of distinguishing between illusion and reality, between his own hypostatizations and objective nature; yet in the first part of the novel Rivera has Cova so clear in his perception of nature that he can dally with these literary metaphors simply for stylistic effects and, in the second part, he has him honestly believing that the nature created by such figures in his imagination is objective reality. At the same time, Rivera, as the real author, seems to expect these devices to recreate artistically the true realities of the *selva*.

When the reader is introduced to the *selva* he meets it as a personification: "Oh, selva, esposa del silencio, madre de la soledad y de la neblina." From this point on, in the windows of the characters' tortured emotions, it is the "selva inhumana," and its inhabitants, plants, and geographical features are humanized and leagued against man. Its rivers and streams are "sinister," "invidious," "perfidious," "savage," and "sobbing." Its days are "vicious," its islands "barbaric," its hills "misanthropic," its rains "impertinent," and its branches "rebellious." The trees are "perverse, aggressive, hypnotical"; they make signs and gestures. The *selva* "hates" the people who gather rubber; it must be treated properly or it will be "provoked"; it is the people's "enemy." The forest is "aggressive" and "defends itself" against its attackers, but, worst of all, it possesses a horrible power which drives men mad, perverts them, and holds them as though in some mad enchantment.

Whatever the realities of the selva may be, these figures convert it into a hobgoblin forest out of an evil fairy tale.

One might suppose, granted Cova's emotional state, that this type of description was a legitimate product of his psychological disturbances and personality distortions. However, as has already been pointed out, every character whom Rivera has describe the forest sees it the same way. Clemente Silva, when lost during an attempt to escape, looks up at the high trees and wonders: "Por qué los árboles silenciosos han de negarse a decirle al hombre lo que debe hacer para no morir?" And, then, with a mixture of paganism and Christianity, he begins, in the desperation of fear, to "rezarle a la selva una plegaria de desagravio."

Another description of Silva's plight during the same episode sharpens his attitude toward the forest. Cova presents the passage in indirect discourse. Silva is talking to his companions:

> Para qué se pusieron a pensar en el extravío? No los había instruído una y otra vez en la urgencia de desechar esa tentación, que la espesura infunde en el hombre para trastornarlo? Él les aconsejó no mirar los árboles, porque hacen señas, ni escuchar los murmurios, porque dicen cosas, ni pronunciar palabras, porque los ramajes remedan la voz. Lejos de acatar esas instrucciones, entraron en chanzas con la floresta y les vino el embrujamiento, que se transmite por contagio; y él también, aunque iba adelante, comenzó a sentir el influjo de los malos espíritus, porque la selva principió a movérsele, los árboles le bailaban ante los ojos, los bejuqueros no le dejaban abrir la trocha, las ramas se le escondían bajo el cuchillo y repetidas veces quisieron quitárselo.

Silva, after sixteen years in the *selva,* can see it no more objectively than Cova or Ramiro Estévanez.

It is extremely important in an analysis of Rivera's art that the three persons in *La vorágine* who give any significant description of nature all are presented as romantic types, that all three are endowed with emotionally unstable characters, that Arturo Cova, the main narrator, is psychotic, that all three, in practically every description they give, make nature anthropomorphic, and that, finally, it is through the weird emotional reactions of these three people that the anthropomorphic monster of a *selva* is created which Rivera, as the real author in the epilogue, accepts without any hesitation. The horrid brain-child of his characters' overwrought imaginations comes to have a real existence in his mind also and Rivera is satisfied to end his novel on this note with a final anthropomorphic metaphor: "Los devoró la selva!"

This ending raises the paradox inherent in *La vorágine* to its peak. If Rivera's thesis, the exposé of "la desolada historia de los caucheros," is to be taken seriously, then it must be assumed that his own identification with his characters was so complete that their interpretation of the realities of the forest and his own were identical. Such an assumption implies a startling consequence which is drawn with great caution, namely, that Rivera did not comprehend that the vortex was, in a large measure, in the minds of his characters, that his

novel, instead of being the tale of the rubber gatherers, is essentially the strange story of emotionally distraught, idealistic romantics suffering the agonizing process of defeat and disillusionment on contact with a grim reality which they were neither philosophically nor psychologically prepared to meet.

Such a conclusion, perforce, implies that Rivera did not consider his characters to be abnormal and this, presumably, could have been possible only if his identity with them was complete. The positive answer to this question must be provided by Rivera's biographers. (pp. 312-18)

> *William E. Bull, "Nature and Anthropomorphism in 'La Vorágine',"* in The Romanic Review, *Vol. XXXIX, No. 4, December, 1948, pp. 307-18.*

RICHARD J. CALLAN   (essay date 1961)

[*Callan is an American scholar who specializes in the study of Spanish-American language and literature. In the following essay, he argues that in* The Vortex *the jungle is portrayed not as a destructive force which reduces human beings to savagery, but as a testing-ground which evokes the best or worst in people.*]

La vorágine is sometimes thought to be the first in a series of Spanish-American novels in which the destructive power of untrammeled nature engenders violence in the men who inhabit it and reduces them to the state of savagery. Inhuman acts of cruelty are habitually committed in the jungle, seemingly, for vicious or puerile reasons, or for no reason at all. To the main characters of the novel, however, these occurrences are but background material—albeit a background that presses close around, like the seething vegetation that besets them. On closer reading it becomes clear that, in spite of the passionate tone of his narrator, Rivera does not expound the theory that in attempting to conquer nature, man is himself conquered by it and transformed into a wild beast. We shall consider the principal characters, Arturo Cova and Clemente Silva, and some others, and see whether the humanized, malignant forest brutalized them or was the origin of their violence.

Silva went into this "vortex" with the relatively unselfish motive of finding his son, and during sixteen years he persisted in this resolution. Singleness of mind and inbred nobility kept him from degradation; beaten, tortured, treated like an animal, he did not lower himself to retaliation. His sense of personal dignity and his compassion for other victims of brute force were his identifying characteristics. According to Arana his very face proclaimed him to be honorable. To cite but one case: in the *tambochas* episode the six men whom he is guiding, crazed by fear, attack him; later Silva thinks of them and their anguish, lost in the rain forest, and feels so deep a compassion that he resolves to console them, at least temporarily, by a lie. Nights later, after they have abandoned him, he hears their shouts but does not answer for fear that in their madness they will kill him. Then he weeps with remorse for his lack of pity. Yet with all his virtues Silva is not a superman; he is as weak as any other in the jungle and prey to its terrors. To him, as to the other feverish rubber tappers, the trees speak and gesticulate threateningly. He too has been half crazed with hunger, sickness, despair, and the hostility of nature. But his mind is always able eventually to surmount brute matter and regain control. The horrors of his jungle experience, far from having transformed him into a monster, have ennobled him. As he leaves Cova and the reader forever, he counsels, nay, beseeches the young lover to forgive Alicia, just as he, the offended father whose family name was stained, would now forgive the daughter who dishonored him: " Pero perdone a la pobre Alicia! Hágalo por mí! Como si fuera María Gertrudis". Over the years and through the afflictions he had borne in the jungle, he had learned to rise above the norm of human justice contained in the Spanish honor system to the heights of superhuman forgiveness. The savage forest, like any other decisive trial in life, can break weak minds only. The strong are strengthened.

The change that Arturo Cova undergoes during his journey through this region confirms this idea in another way. The young poet's character is portrayed with originality and skill. A first-person narrator, he reveals his qualities and defects with convincing unwariness. He shows himself to be a vain exhibitionist, prone to dreams of grandeur, and at the same time he has a charm that can provoke friendship and devotion in other men. A weak and unbalanced nature, he is pervious to the nobility of Don Clemente and somewhat stabilized by association with him. But the unbridled life of the wild is too much for such a disposition; Cova falls prey to increasing violence during his jungle trip. In fact, that is what he foretells of himself in the first sentence of the tale: " . . . jugué mi corazón al azar y me lo ganó la Violencia." Shortly after his party enters the hot and rainy region, Cova succumbs to fevers from which he never fully recovers. He contemplates suicide, then toys with the idea of quietly killing his companions; he entertains wild visions of revenge against Alicia and in a mood of exhilaration he exults over what he considers the beautiful drowning of two friends. The faithful Franco, exasperated by this display of inhumanity, calls Cova detestable, unbalanced, theatrical. The poet continues on his violent way and in his final triumph over his enemy, Barrera, he attacks him barehandedly like a wild man, bites the scoundrel's facewounds to bring blood, and pushes his head into the river for flesh-eating *caribes* to devour as he watches.

But if Cova grows more violent as the book progresses, with fevers, hallucinations, and beri-beri to ravage his mind and body, the fact is that from the very beginning of his story he was inclined that way. Only a few miles out of Bogotá we see him pounding a man in the face with the heel of Alicia's shoe; a week later in Casanare he planned to shoot Barrera on a mere suspicion. Before Cova ever thought of going into the *selva* he had mistreated Alicia, punched Griselda in the nose, knocked down Millán, and had a fist-fight with Barrera over a dice game. Obviously in his case it was not the jungle that engendered his violence—it merely nurtured it and provided occasions that released it.

Some of the minor characters support the idea that the jungle is not the cause of human depravity, but that it tends to aggravate defects which already exist. Ramiro Estévanez, who left Bogotá merely to forget a girl, had seen and suffered many horrors in the green hell, but he manifested no traits of savagery. Balbino Jácomo, the cripple, had devised a means of helping the rubber slaves at El Encanto, while seeming to work closely with the bosses. Nor were Cova's companions, Franco, Correa, Mesa, brutalized. Franco's motive in accompanying Cova, to vindicate his honor in connection with Griselda's flight, closely parallels the poet's. Although he too is caught up in this nightmare he continues an essentially unchanged personality; he suffers trials as challenging as Cova's but remains steady, patient, dependable. On the

other hand, the brutal Petardo Lesmes, who sold his friends into slavery, had come to this natural labyrinth to hide from justice. For the escaped convict, El Cayeno, the dense forest was an ideal location in which to exercise his ruthless greed with impunity. We do not know what first brought Barrera, Funes and other tyrants there, but Silva gives some of the reasons men have for coming to that region: " . . . algunos solicitan enganche sólo para robarse lo que reciben, o salir a la selva para matar a algún enemigo o sonsacar a sus compañeros para venderlos en otras barracas." Accordingly, many of the rubber workers brought violence into the jungle with them.

Spanish American writers who, inspired by *La vorágine,* have taken a pessimistic view of man faced with the untamed nature of this vast continent, "ese sentimiento trágico de la Naturaleza," have not followed Rivera's interpretation of the problem according to his book. The conclusion to be drawn from *La vorágine* is that for each individual who ventures into it the jungle is a supreme test, bringing out the best or the worst in him. If he is a man of character and ideals, as was Clemente Silva, he will grow morally stronger in his struggle against the forces of nature. If he is not, he is likely to degenerate to the level of the primitive savagery that surrounds him. (pp. 13-16)

> *Richard J. Callan, " 'La Vorágine': A Touchstone of Character," in* Romance Notes, *Vol. III, No. 1, Autumn, 1961, pp. 13-16.*

JEAN FRANCO (essay date 1964)

[*Franco is an English critic and editor who has written numerous studies of Latin-American literature. In the following excerpt, he identifies elements of Romanticism in* The Vortex.]

Eustasio Rivera's novel, *La vorágine,* is usually considered to be the prototype of the novel of the jungle. The closing sentence, "Los devoró la selva," indeed seems to epitomize the theme of the "telluric" novel in which natural forces triumph over the human protagonist. Critical attention, therefore, has tended to be concerned with the truth of Rivera's picture of the *selva* and with establishing the novel's faithfulness as an account of events in Rivera's life and as an account of historical events whilst the literary background has tended to be ignored. Nevertheless, whilst the limitless plain, the river which was a "camino oscuro," the narrowing walls of the jungle, the "vórtice de la nada" all had their basis in Rivera's experience, students of poetry will recognize them as landmarks in a familiar myth.

Rivera absorbed many of his attitudes to life and art from the Romantic poets. His biographer [Eduardo Neale-Silva] relates that in childhood he enjoyed reading and reciting poems by Zorrilla, Espronceda and Spanish-American Romantic poets. One of his first projects was to write a patriotic ode in imitation of Olmedo's *La victoria de Junín.* His literary mentors were Antonio Gómez Restrepo, who for many years was working on a translation of Leopardi's Cantos, and Miguel Antonio Caro, a poet and a translator of European Romantic poetry and of classical verse. Sonnets from Rivera's own collection *Tierra de promisión* are full, as his biographer states, of "resonancias románticas." There is nothing surprising in the fact that the real experiences that form the basis of *La vorágine* should be fitted into a framework of images which have their precedents in Romantic poetry.

One has only to read Shelley's *Alastor* to realize how closely the theme of *La vorágine* is related to Romantic myth. In *Alastor,* the poet, in search of "Vision and Love" sails along a river in which he is almost sucked to his death by a vortex. The river takes him between the narrowing walls of a forest where he "sought in Nature's dearest haunt, some bank / Her cradle and his sepulchre." The landscape of *La vorágine* is strikingly similar and Cova's journey like Alastor's is motiveless on a realistic plane but makes sense in terms of myth. Thus the initial flight from Bogotá would be absurd on the realistic plane since Cova and Alicia do not love one another; on the plane of myth, however, Cova is a victim of ineluctable fate. The preface to *La vorágine* makes this clear: "el destino implacable me desarraigó de la prosperidad incipiente y me lanzó a las pampas, para que ambulara vagabundo, como los vientos, y me extinguiera como ellos sin dejar más que ruido y desolación." There are thus two levels in the novel—one of reality and of action and a deeper level of myth in which the characters are the playthings of fate. Alicia is described as "como la semilla en el viento." Don Rafo's wandering life is attributed to the fact that "el destino le marcó ruta imprevista." Verbs such as "me lanzó," "me arrojaba" emphasize Cova's helplessness; even when an apparently free decision is taken at the beginning of the second part in which Cova after determining to go back to Bogotá changes his mind and throws in his lot with Franco, this decision does not seem to be a genuine choice. The journey through the jungle is still ascribed to fate; the canoe, Cova says, would take them "a donde un fátum implacable nos expatriaba, sin otro delito que el de ser rebeldes, sin otra mengua que la de ser infortunados."

Rivera conceived of Cova's character in terms of the Romantic hero who rejects all inner control over his emotions, who is receptive to fleeting changes of mood and glories in sensation. Thus Cova admits, "Frecuentemente las impresiones logran su máximum de potencia en mi excitabilidad, pero una impresión suele degenerar en la contraria a los pocos minutos de recibida" or again, "En el fondo de mi ánimo acontece lo que en las bahías; las mareas suben y bajan con intermitencia." He seeks sensation, sometimes by drinking "para conocer la sensación tiránica que bestializa a los bebedores" or by forcing himself to stare at a mutilated dead body, by gambling, cock-fighting or deliberately inducing in himself tormenting fantasies.

The Romantic preoccupation with man's dual nature, the contrast between his infinite desires and the limitations of his human state, is expressed both in Cova's character and in the structure of the novel. Rivera's images are here drawn directly from Romantic poetry; soaring wings, the image of man's infinite desires and aspirations, enter into one of Cova's fantasies where he dreams of snatching up Alicia and flying to Heaven with her: "Subía tan alto que contra el cielo aleteaba, el sol me ardía el cabello y yo aspiraba el ígneo resplandor." The frustration which man's soaring spirit inevitably meets was often represented in Romantic poetry by the wingless bird or the bird with broken wings. Rivera had already used the image, or rather his own version of it, in a sonnet of *Tierra de promisión* where the eagle is described as: "enamorada ilusa de un sol que no se alcanza / . . . sabe que todo vuelo sólo encuentra el vacío. . . ." The same image occurs in a lyrical outburst in the third part of *La vorágine:* "Quién estableció el desequilibrio entre la realidad y el alma incolmable? Para qué nos dieron alas en el vacío?"

"El desequilibrio entre la realidad y el alma incolmable" is a commonplace of Romantic poetry. In *La vorágine* the "desequilibrio" is expressed in the structure of the novel, especially in the first part where, instead of a continuous narration, there are disconnected scenes in which brief, violent action is preceded by Cova's dreams. Thus, at the beginning of the novel, immediately following a lyrical meditation in which Cova "en espíritu penetraba una sensación de infinito," Alicia is set upon by a drunkard whom Cova attacks "a golpes de tacón sobre el rostro." When the drunkard has been silenced, the pair escape into the "llanuras intérminas." Cova's dream projections inevitably end in an abrupt manner, often in violence. Gambling, knife fights, a stampede, a brutal goring, an immense fire break in on lyrical fantasies.

What are these dreams of which Cova is so proud and which he feels are part of his poetic vocation? Generally they are nothing more than the most puerile self-projections, or dreams that compensate for his feeling of inferiority. Thus, when his friend Franco makes him a business proposition, Cova immediately converts this into a grandiose fantasy in which he returns to Bogotá a millionaire, marries Alicia and becomes a literary success. In the euphoria that follows this dream of glory he forgets that the first step in his rise to power has yet to be made and treats Franco as if he were a mayordomo reporting on the administration of the Cova estates. His dreams thus affect his attitude to people. Another of his dreams concerns his physical prowess. The *llaneros* do not take Cova's *machismo* very seriously and do not invite him to join him on the round-ups. The niña Griselda also considers him inferior as a male to his rival Barrera. Cova, therefore, begins to weave a fantasy in which he is the *hombre macho.* He imagines himself returning from the round-up, "el rostro ensombrecido de barba, aparentando el porte de un macho almizcloso y trabajador." The scene would be comic if the consequences were not so disastrous, for Cova acts on this dream. He goes on the round-up against Franco's advice and, in disobeying his friend, leaves the way clear for his rival Barrera to carry away Griselda and Alicia.

Not all of Cova's fantasies are puerile, for Rivera clearly associates the *llanura* with the spirit's attempt to free itself from earthly limitations, so that in the plains Cova feels "una sensación del infinito." This association of great spaces with spiritual freedom has many precedents. The transition from unbounded space to infinite time is easy to make so that the plains and the sea are often associated with both infinity and eternity. Leopardi, for instance, in *L'Infinito* surveys a huge valley from the top of a hill and beyond the horizon imagines "interminati / spazi di là da quella, e sovrumani / Silenzi. . . . " The poem ends with an almost mystical union between the poet and the "immensity." In a sonnet of *Tierra de promisión* which bears some resemblance to Leopardi's poem, Rivera associates the infinite with the unbounded plains: "abriendo al infinito su clámide argentina / La inspiración se tiende sobre la luz del llano." In *La vorágine,* the *pampa libérrima* clearly represents more than picturesque background. Cova's first night in the Casanare is spent under the "cielos ilímites" in "un silencio infinito" where "en espíritu penetraba una sensación de infinito que fluía de las constelaciones cercanas." The plains are described as the place where "se encumbra el espíritu en la luz libre." Cova's dreams are most intense in the *llanura;* and absurd as they often seem, they are attempts to transcend reality and to escape a brutal, violent and unjust society in which qualities of poetic imagination are of little value. Once Cova leaves the plains, these spiritual flights become increasingly rare; in the jungle freedom is no longer possible.

The transition from plain to jungle is marked by a tremendous fire. Earth and air had predominated in the first part of the novel; the journey through the jungle is partly by water. It is fitting therefore that fire, the destructive and purifying element, should destroy all traces of Cova's old life. Again the scene is more than more picturesque background. The flame is described as "aliado luceferino" and Cova watches the blaze laughing "como Satanás." The fire "ávida de abarcar los límites de la tierra" attains universal proportions with the flames driving animals and snakes across the plains now "ennegrecidos." The fire destroys more than Cova's illusions; from this point onwards, his freedom of imagination goes too; in the grip of a torturing obsession, he is "thrown" into jungle "por el incendio que extendía su ceniza sobre mis pasos."

That the parallel with the Satanic fall in the fire scene is not accidental is born out by the anecdote of the jungle spirit, Mapiripana; which Helí Mesa relates in the second part of the novel. The anecdote seems at first sight to be a picturesque regional legend; the Mapiripana takes a missionary noted for his libidinous nature to her cavern in the jungle where she holds him captive and where she at length gives birth to an owl and a vampire who haunt her victim until he dies. The cavern and the vampire are both images in Rafael Pombo's poem, *La hora de tinieblas,* in which the human soul is described as a dove which escapes into the beauty of the pampa only to fall into a trap. Man's anguished state, when his early hopes are thwarted, is described as "Caverna odiosa, y al centro / Un ojo para mirarla / Luz que en vez de iluminarle / Permita que se entrevean / Vámpiros mil que aletean. . . ." Cova like Pombo feels that having lost all illusion, existence is a prison from which there is no escape. This is illustrated by the Mapiripana story whose moral is given as: "Quién puede librar al hombre de sus propios remordimientos?"

Cova's inability to escape the relentless drift towards death and disaster is expressed in images of the vortex and the river. Again both images have literary precedents in Romantic poetry. *El estudiante de Salamanca*'s death dance imitated the ever-decreasing circles of a whirlpool: "Mientras la ronda frénetica / en raudo giro se agita / más cada vez precipita / su vértigo sin ceder." In Spanish-American poetry the sight of a huge cataract, the Niagara or the Falls of Tequendama, almost always tempted and horrified the poet. To Heredia, the Niagara was like "el destino irresistible y ciego" and Montes del Valle peered into the "horrible vórtice" below the Falls of Tequendama and saw the destruction of hope and illusion. In Arboleda's Byronic poem, *Gonzalo de Oyón,* the hero on the verge of suicide, "Contempla ufano el vórtice profundo." In *La vorágine,* the vortex like the plain and the fire is both part of the actual experience and also a symbol of Cova's state of mind. On the plane of experience, the travellers come upon rapids and whirlpools in the river in which several of their Indian companions are drowned "y antes que pudiéramos lanzar un grito, el embudo trágico los sorbió a todos." On the plane of symbol, the river is described with conscious or unconscious recollections of Lethe, as the "camino oscuro que se moviera hacia el vórtice de la nada."

The change of tone between the scenes set in the plains and the scenes in the jungle can best be described by the word *contraction.* This is, in fact, a common pattern of Romantic poetry and drama where the energetic, expansive rebellion of the hero at the beginning of a work is followed by the conscious-

ness that he is, after all, in a trap. Thus Don Álvaro suddenly discovers that the world is a "calabozo profundo," Zorrilla's Don Juan, after breaking all conventions, finds himself enclosed in a tomb, and Espronceda in his *Canto a Teresa* instead of mounting to Heaven on wings of love contemplates "la funesta losa, / donde vil polvo tu beldad reposa." The jungle, in *La vorágine,* represents this prison in which the disillusioned Romantic finds himself, though this is only a part of its significance, for the jungle is a very complex image. In contrast to the unbounded plain whose wide horizons offer man hope of eternal life, the jungle hems Cova in and continually reminds him of his limitations. The trees form a barrier between himself and the sky; they are like labyrinths from which there is no escape. Cova describes the river as running between "márgenes paralelas, de sombría vegetación y de plagas hostiles." The boat is "un ataúd flotante" or "un féretro" and Cova describes himself as feeling like "un condenado a muerte" when he has to take leave of the plains and enter into the jungle.

The jungle/prison theme takes on an even more powerful and universal significance in the third part of the novel, where not only Cova but thousands of rubber workers are imprisoned in the jungle, and where the hopelessness of attempts to escape is emphasized again and again:

> Esclavo no te quejes de las fatigas; preso, no te duelas de tu prisión; ignoráis la tortura de vagar sueltos en una cárcel como la selva, cuyas bóvedas verdes tienen por muros ríos inmensos. No sabéis del suplicio de las penumbras, viendo al Sol que ilumina la playa opuesta, a donde nunca lograremos ir! La cadena que os muerde los tobillos es más piadosa que las sanguijuelas de estos pantanos; el carcelero que os atormenta no es tan adusto como estos árboles, que nos vigilan sin hablar!

The prison analogy recurs over and over again. Clemente Silva finds himself trapped with other escaped rubber workers and wanders in circles in the jungle without being able to find the way out. On another occasion, Cova, maddened by fever, rushes away from his companions in an effort to escape: "eché a correr hacia cualquier parte, ululando empavorecido, lejos de los perros, que me perseguían. No supe más. De entre una malla de trepadoras mis camaradas me desenredaron."

But what does this jungle prison signify? In an often-quoted passage, Rivera describes the jungle as an implacable cycle of life and death, an eternal treadmill, "the electric chain," as Byron says, "wherewith we are darkly bound." Again Rivera is restating an attitude found among certain Romantic poets. Hugo in *La légende des siècles* declares: "les arbres sont autant de mâchoires qui rongent / Les éléments" or again, "Tout leur est bon, la nuit, la mort; la pourriture / Voit la rose et lui va porter sa nourriture; . . . A toute heure, on entend le craquement confus / Des choses sous la dent des plantes." In his poem *A la naturaleza,* a Colombian admirer of Hugo also dwelt on the destructiveness of Nature with her "leyes de muerte y exterminio"; "Entre tus garras toscas / Destruyes, nervio a nervio, los miembros infelices / Nos tragas en la tumba." Rivera's picture of the "selva inhumana" is more violent than Hugo's but the attitude is essentially the same:

> Óyese el golpe de la fruta, que al abatirse hace la promesa de su semilla; el caer de la hoja, que llena el monte con vago suspiro, ofreciéndose como abono para las raíces del árbol paterno; el chasqui-

do de la mandíbula, que devora con temor de ser devorada.

Leopardi is another poet who dwells on the cruelty of Nature. "Madre temuta e pianta / Dal nascer già dell'animal famiglia, / Natura, illaudabil maraviglia / Che per uccider partorisci e nutri. . . ." Nature's law, the "immutata legge," is one of death. Rivera too protests against the "immutata legge"; in one of the most powerful descriptions in the novel, he compares the "árboles imponentes, contemporáneos del paraíso" with ephemeral man; and he dwells on the relationship between procreation and death:

> al pie del coloso que se derrumba, el germen que brota, en medio de los miasmas, el polen que vuela; y por todas partes el hálito del fermento, los vapores calientes de la penumbra, el sopor de la muerte, el marasma de la procreación.

The prison of the jungle is now seen to encompass the conditions of man's earthly life. When Cova clamours to escape, he is, like Leopardi, clamouring against the very conditions of earthly existence, against Nature's "immutata legge":

> Déjame huir, oh selva, de tus enfermizas penumbras, formadas con el hálito de los seres que agonizaron en el abandono de tu majestad. Tú misma pareces un cementerio enorme donde te pudres y resucitas.

In the first part of **La vorágine,** Cova has been allowed his dreams and illusions, and occasionally his spirit was able to escape from the limitations of reality; there had sometimes been intuitions of eternity. Nature had reminded him of spiritual qualities; the sky had been "amigo," the palm tree had wept in sympathy or waved goodbye and during a storm had shown the courage and pride of a human being. Even where Nature had appeared threatening as when a snake appeared at the water-hole or a bull had gored a peon, man had at least seemed to be on equal terms. But in the jungle all spiritual aspirations disappear, and with them, man's superiority. Cova is in the grip of a powerful material force which blocks out his spiritual horizons, and limits his dreams until he is almost completely obsessed with the idea of vengeance and death. Not only do the trees physically hem him in but the jungle determines his thoughts and sensations, and even changes his personality. He has hallucinations in which the earth and trees suffer like human beings. He has no control over his feelings; at one time he wishes to kill himself, at another he wants to kill his companions. He falls into a cataleptic state, during which he thinks that he is dead and hears his own grave being dug. The jungle plays on his senses in the same way that narcotics affected Baudelaire's senses but with the significant difference that, whereas Baudelaire's hashish marvellously enlarges his range of sense impressions, the jungle afflicts Cova with an obsessive craving for death.

There are several passages, however, in which even Nature rebels against this law of death. In Pipa's drug-induced dream, the trees are captive giants trying to escape from the grip of the earth: "condenado a retoñar, a florecer, a gemir, a perpetuar, sin fecundarse, su especie formidable, incomprendida." The jungle is thus caught in this eternal treadmill as much as man and there are dreams of a Satanic rebellion:

> Aquí no siento tristeza sino desesperación! Quisiera tener con quién conspirar! Quisiera librar la batalla de las especies, morir en los cataclismos, ver invertidas las fuerzas cósmicas! Si Satán dirigiera esta rebelión!

Man and Nature then protest vainly against the law which turns them one against the other in a battle for life and which also turns man against man. For a whole society inhabits the jungle and obeys only jungle law—the society of the rubber-workers and their exploiters who are engaged in a war of two fronts against the jungle and against one another. These "journalistic" episodes in which Rivera reported on the Funes massacre and on the exploitation of the rubber-workers have not lost their interest with the passage of time (as mere social documents would have done) because they fit into the whole pattern of the novel. Man's life in the jungle is a ferocious imitation of the *selva inhumana,* where plants and insects devour each other.

In the second and third parts of **La vorágine** Rivera frequently uses the word *trayectoria.* The image again suggests man's inability to control his fate; thus, Cova tells his companions: "Déjame solo, que mi destino desarrollará su trayectoria." When told of the convict, Cayeno, he reflects: "nuestros destinos describirían la misma trayectoria de crueldad." Again in a lyrical outburst, "Yo he sido cauchero, yo soy cauchero" which occurs during Clemente Silva's account of his life but seems to be more an expression of Cova's sentiments, the speaker attributes his misfortunes to "incógnita fuerza" which "disparóme más allá de la realidad. Pasé por encima de la ventura como flecha que marra su blanco, sin poder corregir el fatal impulso y sin otro destino que caer! Y a esto lo llamaban *mi porvenir!*" Man's failure to fulfill his aims is here attributed not to nature's implacable law but to social forces which thwart man and the trees of the jungle are compared to the exploiters: "el que intentó elevarse, cayó vencido, ante los magnates indiferentes, tan impasibles como estos árboles que nos miran languidecer de fiebres y de hambre entre sanguijuelas y hormigas!" The jungle here parallels the forces which limit man's aspirations; the victim is the dreamer, the one who tries to transcend limitations and escape from reality. "Ved en lo que ha parado este soñador; en herir al árbol inerme para enriquecer a los que no sueñan." Thus we return to one of the recurrent themes. Man is punished for his illusions, but what helps to defeat him is his own nature, his animal instinct. The ending of the novel is a violent illustration of this. Cova and Barrera at last meet and fight and the fight is a repetition of the struggle that is going on all around them. Their bodies are intertwined like snakes. Cova wounds Barrera by biting him and then pushes his head under the water as if he were a pigeon. The *caribes* then tear the flesh from Barrera's bones in an "hervor dantesco" leaving only the white skeleton trembling among the reeds. At this moment Alicia's premature baby is born. Cova, Barrera and Alicia are all caught in the same implacable struggle for life as the jungle itself. The appeal to Cova of a plague-stricken mob who wish him to be their *redentor* goes unheeded; he is now only concerned for the safety of his child. Rather than help his fellow-men he trusts himself to the jungle and disappears into it.

Plains, river, vortex, jungle are thus both real landscape and aspects of human experience. Freedom, aspirations, indulgence in the senses brings disillusion and awareness of limitations and of the inevitable march towards death which is both feared and desired. Rivera perhaps identified himself too strongly with Cova's point of view to modify this vision; but there are signs in the characters of Clemente Silva, Franco and Ramiro Estévenez of attempts to offset Cova's view of life. Franco's practical skill and his humanity form a contrast to Cova's egoistical day-dreaming. Clemente Silva's journey into the jungle parallels Cova's search but his experiences are different. Silva has sacrificed everything to look for his son. He is subjected to the worst humiliations, witnesses scenes of barbaric cruelty, but unlike Cova he never succumbs to jungle law. On the contrary, he alone of the characters breaks out of the bounds of his own egoistical drives and helps others. He has the courage to protest against the exploitation of the rubber-workers, and to try and remedy their situation. He alone of the escaped rubber-workers is able to find his way out of the jungle because he uses his knowledge of the trees. He it is who searches for Cova at the end of the book. Silva is a man who acts on behalf of others and has forgotten self but this is also because he carries a talisman, the bones of his dead son, which represent the loss of all hope and illusion and the acceptance of death.

Less successful, as a contrast to Cova, is the philosopher Ramiro Estévenez. By philosopher, Rivera evidently understood Platonist. Cova describes Estévenez thus: "Él optimista, yo desolado. Él virtuoso y platónico; yo, mundano y sensual." The philosopher is, however, even more helpless than Cova. He seeks the jungle to escape the grief of a Platonic love for a married woman, goes blind after witnessing the Funes massacre, and lies helpless and ill in a hammock unable either to act effectively like Silva or like Cova to seek death.

Neale-Silva points out in his biography of Rivera that the novelist tried to justify *La vorágine* to his critics on the grounds that it was a social document. This view of the novel diminishes its importance; a report on the conditions of the rubber-workers would have carried more weight than Cova's outbursts. The justification of the novel must be on the grounds of the total vision of human experience that it presents, and in Rivera's powerful revival of certain images. The plain and the jungle indeed seem to objectify what Hugo in the preface to *Cromwell* calls the "deux êtres, l'un périssable, l'autre immortel, l'un charnel, l'autre éthéré, l'un enchaîné par les appétits, les besoins et les passions, l'autre emporté sur les ailes de l'enthousiasme et de la rêverie. . . . " Cova's journey from the freedom of the plains to the prison of the jungle, and his disappearance into the *vórtice de la nada,* is thus a familiar pattern though the insubstantial Romantic landscape has been replaced by a powerful and unfamiliar setting. Despite the implicit criticism of Romantic attitudes in the ending of the novel, in the character of Clemente Silva, in the suggestions of remorse and guilt, Rivera's novel is an interesting illustration of the way a writer fits his experience into existing forms even where, as in *La vorágine,* that experience is alien and new. (pp. 101-10)

> Jean Franco, "Image and Experience in 'La Vorágine'," in Bulletin of Hispanic Studies, Vol. XLI, No. 2, April, 1964, pp. 101-10.

EDMUND S. URBANSKI (essay date 1965)

[*Urbanski is a Polish-born critic whose writings include studies of Spanish-American and Polish literature. In the following excerpt, he compares and contrasts W. H. Hudson's novel* Green Mansions *(1904) and* The Vortex.]

For some strange reason the novels of the Amazon receive little attention in our academic midst. Their sporadic publication is perhaps responsible for creating spontaneous but temporary rather than permanent impressions among us. And yet, as a literary genre, these tropical novels play a significant role in Hispano-American fiction. This is very true of J. E. Rivera's *La vorágine* (*The Vortex*) and W. H. Hudson's *Green Mansions.* Depending on their classification by literary historians, they are considered regional novels by some, novels of nature or of the land by others, and realistic novels or those with indigenous accent by still others. Rivera's and Hudson's jungle narratives combine, of course, many of these qualities, and in addition have certain biographical characteristics.

Judging from the copious number of editions and translations, Rivera's and Hudson's jungle narratives have become popular and classic works of their kind. This is undoubtedly due to their unusual qualities, such as a high degree of sensitivity, love of nature and adventure, concentration of folklore, and an almost incredible degree of imagination. Both authors are native sons of South America, even though one wrote in Spanish and the other in English.

La vorágine and *Green Mansions* are almost unmatched by anything produced elsewhere, although there are some writers, for example Conrad and Kipling, who achieved similar reputations through their descriptions of virgin forests in other exotic countries. Without underestimating the literary worth of any one, perhaps one trait should be pointed out in which many tropical authors differ in their approach to their fascinating jungle milieu. A European writer who is deprived of tropical environment reacts spiritually in a different way from a Latin American novelist who is more closely associated with it because of ecological conditions. The intimacy of the latter with nature's mysteries explains the Latin American intensity of feeling, which is frequently manifested by unbridled spontaneity and an almost mystic sense of aesthetic perception. There are, however, various degrees of emotional intensity as well as imagination that, along with the artistic qualities of their work, appear in different writers.

Departing from this premise, Rivera's and Hudson's novels distinguish themselves in many ways from other South American tropical narratives, even if topical similarities exist in the fine works of Gallegos, Quiroga, Uribe Piedrahita, Aguilera Malta, Adalberto Ortíz, Pavletich, Rendón, to mention only a few of the best known. It is true that these writers have chosen a similar background, but it is frequently too much overshadowed by the intriguing plots their protagonists play out and does not leave enough space to the strange relationship or dependence of the human upon nature, so forcefully presented by Rivera's and Hudson's pens. They have done this under the pretext of no less intriguing adventures, handling their subjects in a unique way, in which nature and temperament sometimes mingle in divine unity and sometimes are unavoidably polarized. These varied and combined forces produce a literary effect similar to the turbulent overflow of tributary rivers of the grandiose Amazon, the region that constitutes the background for our novels. The incredible jungle mystery attracts while at the same time the jungle dangers frighten the protagonists of Rivera's and Hudson's novels.

The tropical wilderness is a source of life and death, of supreme bliss for some and incredible suffering for others. The presentation of this mysterious dualism of the jungle is treated by each author in a very different and individualistic way. So also are the adventures, which are based on moving love stories, and are closely interwoven with this Amazonian virgin forest background. In Rivera's novel they constitute only lively episodes to justify a more ponderous account of the misfortunes of the Colombian *caucheros* (rubber gatherers) in the Orinoco region. In contrast, Hudson's description of the romance between a city dweller lost in the Venezuelan jungle and an enchanting Indian forest girl almost fills the whole melodramatic narrative. But the jungle presence is felt in each step of these protagonists, for better or worse. (pp. 33-5)

La vorágine and *Green Mansions* offer an excellent chance for comparison and contrast, especially in their artistic treatment of the jungle.

To Rivera, in accordance with his individual perception of Amazonia's grandeur and the violent adventures of his protagonists, the tropical wilderness is presented as an ominous green jail. Nature is horrifying and devastating, in the midst of which a human being is powerless and reduced to innumerable sufferings that consume his physical strength. Each plant, each animal and each insect struggles for its own survival. And yet, in spite of infusing this tragic Dantesque feeling, the jungle is magnificent in its frightful splendor and mystery. It does not leave much chance to weaker species, nor to the inexperienced intruder who falls victim to exhaustion, insanity or destruction.

This may be the result of the author's projection of his disappointed idealism, victim of the turbulent vicissitudes in Colombian politics, in which he took an active part. Rivera presents the jungle with extraordinary verbal plasticity. Frequent mood changes from epic pathos to lyrical atmosphere, always unbridled in spontaneity, passion, and vigor, cover some structural deficiencies in his novel. Neale-Silva in his recent critico-biographical study [*Horizonte humano vida de José Eustasio Rivera*] points out that "a background of humanism and quixotism are in perfect accord with the temperament of Rivera" and that *"La vorágine,* written in prose, has the cadences of a poem." Horacio Quiroga, the great Uruguayan tropical writer, admired Rivera's masterpiece as "an immense poem of the jungle that vibrates with an epic pulse never before attained in New World literature." There is hardly anything to be added to this penetrating evaluation except the fact that the jungle is the real protagonist in Rivera's novel, while the various adventurers play only secondary roles.

In his fantastic tale Hudson assumes a view of the jungle contrary to Rivera's. For him it is an enchanting paradise where fauna and flora live in almost romantic harmony. As a naturalist, Hudson is extremely sensitive to nature's beauty, which he wants to keep preserved in its primitive splendor, along with the animals. Therefore he scorns the Indian hunters and white sportsmen who devastate game and even birds. He considers it some kind of desecration of the tropical forest. The wanton killing of birds was one of the reasons he left Argentina, which he loved so much. In his idealism he is a champion of the weak, whether animal or human. Galsworthy, who after the death of Tolstoy considered Hudson the most valuable writer of the twentieth century, said: "*Green Mansions* immortalizes as passionate a love of all beautiful things as ever was in the heart of man. Hudson's fancy is akin to the flight of the birds that are his special loves." Torres-Ríoseco expresses admiration in the following way: "Hudson is the supreme word artificer for whom the jungle is a kind of lyre from which the poet pulls out delightful sounds."

Hudson finds in the jungle happiness and peace, in contrast to the nervousness and gloominess he found in the urban-technological civilization. Perhaps *Green Mansions* was his protest against the city, for while he was living in his London flat he felt like a bird in a cage. A follower of animism, he believed that all natural objects had souls. He also adhered to the doctrine of metempsychosis or transmigration of souls, even at the expense of procreation. This seems rather paradoxical since Hudson admired the plenitude of the equatorial wilderness which, we believe, is the result of a biological process and not of a theoretical speculation.

Another interesting aspect in *La vorágine* and *Green Mansions* is the problem of love. Rivera's protagonist, Arturo Cova, is impulsively in love with Alicia, who reciprocates without calculating the risk. She sacrifices her future for an unknown fate and shares with him the uncomfortable life in the wilderness. Alicia is exposed to violent changes of feeling by her lover, whose whims and unpredictability are almost like the mysterious idiosyncrasies of the jungle. It attracts and horrifies both of them. Nature's strange metamorphosis seems to exert special impact on the supersensitive Cova's pattern of behavior. It ranges from hilarity to abject despair and from inconsolable melancholy to horrible hallucination. This spiritual instability reflects their tragedy. For their love is as violent and dangerous as the unbridled waters of the Amazon.

Hudson's heroine, Rima, before meeting Abel, is in love with the jungle birds and butterflies. As a friend of animals, whom she protects, she shares their happiness and sorrows. She transfers these feelings to Abel, whom she seduces with her sweet voice, her kindness and primitive beauty. His is at first a Platonic love that finally changes into a true and mutual one. This love infuses in him a great serenity he had never known before. Abel and Rima live in a paradise in which their natural feeling blends with the tropical forest's fantastic background. This perfect harmony is destroyed by Rima's tragic death in the flames set by ignorant natives. In Hudson's metempsychic vision her soul will revive in another form, perhaps in a beautiful bird, whose sweet voice will again fill the mysterious jungle.

The Amazonian aborigines are an artistic accessory in *La vorágine* and *Green Mansions.* Although they are not always treated as deeply as the jungle that surrounds them, they immensely enliven the background with folkloric flavor.

Hudson's attitude toward the Indians is more sympathetic than that of Rivera. This originates undoubtedly from his keen understanding of these primitive sons of nature who cannot distinguish between good and evil, the differentiation of which could give them the white people's civilization. On the other hand, Hudson doesn't seem to be eager to make them depart from their Rousseau-like habitat for some deceptive values of the latter's spiritual advancement. Therefore Abel, after due reflection, forgives the killers of Rima for their superstition and fear of her supranatural power. Their view is best expressed by the frightened Runi, who warns his tribesmen: "Let no one shoot an arrow thinking to hit her, for the arrow would be caught in her hand and thrown back at him." But this, of course, did not prevent them from burning the bird-girl alive. Hudson describes the Indian customs as a friendly observer, although in his interpretation he frequently mixes reality with fantasy, due to his supersensitive imagination.

Rivera, more realistic in his approach to the jungle, treats its native dwellers in the same way. His is a combination of curiosity mixed with suspicion. He is horrified by the bad treatment of the Indians in the *caucherías,* where they perish along with their white companions. For this he expresses disgust and regret. Rivera's greatest interest is, however, aroused by the indigenous legends and superstition, which he relates to the forest's unfolded mysteries. Such is the Orinoco Indian's belief in the existence of the jungle goddess, Mapiripana. He heard the following about her: "The little Indian Mapiripana is the priestess of silence, guardian of springs and lagoons, and the Indians of these regions are afraid of her and she tolerates their hunting on the condition of their not making noise. Those who annoy her are not successful in the hunt. At night one is aware of her shouting in the thickets, or riding by the beach when the moon is full, in a tortoise shell drawn by dolphins who move their fins to the song she sings."

As can be deduced from the above, there is a certain legendary similarity between Rivera's Mapiripana and Hudson's Rima, both considered supernatural beings by the Indians. They both sing and both request silence in their realms. While Rima guards the forest, Mapiripana protects its waters. Rima is perhaps more exacting, for she definitely prohibits hunting, whereas Mapiripana allows it for the price of not disturbing the silence. Knowing something about native customs we doubt, however, that this has any connection with the Amazonian Indians' use of their silent and deadly blowpipes (*cerbatanas*) for hunting, which has been practiced from time immemorial.

Another factor deeply felt in these tropical novels is a sense of morbidity, a trait that characterizes many works of Hispanic prose. For example, there is a marked analogy regarding the respect accorded to human remains by both authors. In *La vorágine* it is Silva who guards in his traveling bag the bones of his only son, who was devoured by the green jail. In *Green Mansions* Abel gathers the ashes of his beloved who was burned, and carries them in his flight from the no-longer hospitable paradise. Hudson and Rivera consider these relics and thus revive the aboriginal cult of the dead and the secondary interment widely practiced in pre-Columbian America. Both authors also espouse artistically some kind of pantheism and sometimes polytheism. It seems obvious that through all this they hoped to be closer to the indigenous mythology, which still absorbs so much of the attention of our anthropologists. Their drawing upon the ethnology of the Amazon aborigines indicates that Rivera and Hudson were quite well acquainted with the Indian Folklore.

Comparing *La vorágine* with *Green Mansions* it is significant that their protagonists fearfully escape the jungle. They do so because they no longer find in its shadows a desirable refuge but rather a source of personal misfortune. Leaving the equatorial rain forests they fully realize that they cannot cope with the tremendous challenge of nature's unpredictable forces, a challenge that annihilates and drives them out of their minds. Thus the tragic finale in both novels is perhaps best expressed in the Portuguese title *Inferno verde* (*Green Hell*) of Alberto Rangel's Brazilian narrative of the cruel Amazonian enigma, which makes it akin to those of Rivera and Hudson.

Evaluating briefly both novels from the literary viewpoint, their outstanding trait is their mastery of style. It is simple and clear, with well-chosen expressions, and always sonorous. While Hudson is a stylistic and linguistic purist who recognizes only literary perfectionism. Rivera is refreshingly spontaneous, stylistically uneven, sometimes pompous, and draws heavily on the regional colloquialisms of the *llanos.* And yet the artistic manipulation of all the riches of vocabulary by Hudson as well as Rivera produces a rhythmic flow of melody that is at times gay and at times somber.

Hudson's musical lyricism evokes frequently the soft overtones of the French impressionistic harmonies found in Debussy's *La Mer* and Ravel's *Daphnis et Chloé.* Sometimes, however, especially in the mysteriously gay and innocent play-like murmurs of the jungle's hidden stream, it produces the effect of Chopin's *A Flat Major Etude.* On the other hand, the grandeur and the unbridled chaos of the terrifying green jail in Rivera's presentation remind us of the primitive symphonic compositions of Villa-Lobos' *Chôros* Nos. 5 and 10, alternated with the savage sonorities produced by Stravinsky's *Le sacre du printemps.* On account of this artistically achieved high verbal sonority, both novels seem more like poetic prose, so strong are their symphonic qualities. They are both quite often intercalated with highly lyrical stanzas of superb epic evocation, which definitely indicate the great poetic talent in the Colombian as well as the Argentine-English writer. (pp. 37-8)

Edmund S. Urbanski, "Two Novels of the Amazon,"
in Américas, *Vol. 17, No. 3, March, 1965, pp. 33-8.*

SHARON MAGNARELLI (essay date 1985)

[*Magnarelli is an American critic and scholar of Hispanic literature. In the following excerpt, she questions the objectivity of Arturo Cova's perception of the female protagonist in* The Vortex.]

[Classified as a *novela terrígena*, **La vorágine** has] been studied by a multitude of critics and scholars, most of whom have tended to focus on the use of nature and the opposition between barbarism and civilization within the [novel]. To date, however, no one has carefully considered the fact that in [this novel] as well as in most of the other *novelas terrígenas,* women and nature are not only closely linked but often presented as mirror reflections of each other. (p. 38)

[What] has not been analyzed in detail is that [in addition] the depiction of the female and nature is directly dependent upon, and shaped or misshaped by, the perception of the main character. . . . Thus her depiction cannot be analyzed except in relationship to him. Furthermore, the contingency of her image upon him becomes especially significant as one recognizes the unreliability and/or dubious position of [Arturo Cova]. . . .

Although the unreliability of Cova's narration and his incompetence as a trustworthy narrator would seem self-evident to the careful reader and in need of no further discussion, a review of criticism to date underlines the fact that Cova has all too often been viewed by readers quite amicably as a Romantic or epic hero. . . . I insist, however, and it is basic to any further discussion of women or nature in this text, that Cova is neither a hero, of heroic proportions, noble, nor presented as such within the text. Rather, *La vorágine* is a mixture of diary, confession, and memoirs of a character whose "vision" and competence to judge, within the fiction, is neither valid nor to be trusted. From the very beginning Cova himself demonstrates the dubious quality of his perception and of his ability to grasp with lucidity the significance of the world around him. Yet it is he who shapes our vision of the female within the text.

Cova's dubious reliability is already evident on the title page of the Rivera novel, for the title has either been misunderstood or is delusive. Readers have often understood *la vorágine* as the jungle, but if one does so, then it is difficult to explain the inclusion of Part 1 of the text, which takes place in the plains. Clearly, one of the principal justifications for interpreting the *vorágine* in this fashion is that Cova himself advocates this metaphoric link as he makes two direct references to the *vorágine* in this context: "Y por este proceso—oh, selva!—hemos pasado todos los que caemos en tu vorágine" ("And that, oh jungle! is how all who have fallen into your vortex have been transformed"), and "Tengo el presentimiento de que mi senda toca a su fin, y, cual sordo zumbido de ramajes en la tormenta, percibo la amenaza de la vorágine" ("I have the feeling that my trail is nearing its end, and I hear, like the swirl of foliage in a storm, the looming threat of the vortex"). However, it is pertinent here to consider the "source" (within the fiction) of these statements—Arturo Cova.

[In his article "El marco narrativo de *La vorágine,*" *Revista Iberoamericana* 42 (July-December 1976)] Richard Ford has already suggested the dubious veracity of Cova's statement regarding Ramiro Estévañez's position as recipient of the text, and one can detect this duplicity far earlier in the text without great difficulty. For example, how much confidence shall we place in a character who in the very first paragraph informs his reader that he seeks ideal love, "que me encendiera espiritualmente" ("that would fire me spiritually"), but that in a love relationship he must always be the dominator, "cuyos labios no conocieron la súplica" ("whose lips never begged or implored")? Obviously, the second statement negates the notion of ideal love as proposed in the first; his language is self-contradictory. With equally fallacious reasoning, two pages later he tells of his intimate desire to be *captured* so that he can be *free* (of Alicia). This is not poetic paradox; it is the reasoning of a seriously demented character. These two examples, in addition, demonstrate not only a perverse concept of women and his potential relationship with them but also a serious linguistic problem. It seems that he does not understand the conventional meanings of the words he employs. He is using language in a sense other than the one we all understand, for to his reading public, freedom cannot be found in captivity. From the beginning, then, one must recognize that the language Cova is using (a language used in large part to describe women and nature) is not at all innocent, but fraught with meanings one does not generally attribute to it. Thus, we cannot accept at face value what is said, but instead must be on guard and not allow ourselves to be seduced, by the apparent innocence of the words, into believing that they mean only what they superficially suggest.

Cova's attitude toward the other characters in the text (particularly the female characters) also betrays his duplicity. Throughout the diary, he repeatedly censures Alicia and denigrates her for personality traits that are as much (if not more) his as hers. Shortly after fleeing Bogotá, he criticizes her for not being "más arriscada, menos bisoña, más ágil" ("more daring, more venturesome and agile, less of a tenderfoot") but the later scene at the ranch underlines the fact that these same disparagements of her might well have been directed toward him. That is, with apparent ease and innocence, Cova . . . shifts the referent of his words, and with it

the focus of his narration, from himself to another. As one progresses through the text one discovers that he blames first her and later the *selva* for all that is wrong with his life—predicaments for which only he is responsible. At Alicia he even hurls the accusation, "Por ti dejé todo" ("For you I left everything") when in fact he left all in order not to be incarcerated. Similarly, he accuses the jungle, "Tú me robaste el ensueño" ("You stole from me the dreams"), while at still other moments he disparages the jungle for being inhuman (suggesting, of course, that one could expect it to be human). In both cases he accepts and intends for his reader to accept his own metaphor as literal reality. In addition, he reproaches the *selva* by saying, "la selva trastorna al hombre, desarrollándole los instintos más inhumanos" ("the jungles change men. The most inhuman instincts are developed"); once again, either he fails to understand the meaning of the term "inhuman," or he is making the *selva* the referent for those qualities that can apply only to man, and, thus, he casts on the external the guilt for what is surely internal.

Cova's complete confusion between the two is perhaps most apparent in Part 3. Part 2 had ended in the midst of Clemente's narration (in quotation marks). While Part 3 appears to be a continuation of this narration, the quotation marks are missing, and it is difficult to identify the *I*—is it Clemente or Cova? The issue is further complicated by the fact that Cova himself gratuitously becomes a part of the Clemente story, taking on some of the characteristics of the protagonist of that story and later declaiming *as if* he had experienced Clemente's adventures. In addition, at various points in the text, one watches Cova imagining himself retelling the story (each time greatly embellished), and one must wonder if the text itself does not embody this very same activity: Cova watching Cova tell his story. Thus, he is not different from the narrator of Luisa Valenzuela's *El gato eficaz,* who some fifty years later is to say, "Yo no trepo: me trepan, desde aquí me observo jugar a ser mirada con mi propia mirada que me guarda cariño" ("I don't climb; they climb me, from here I watch myself play at being watched by my own gaze which is affectionate toward me").

Thus it is manifest that the narrator of **La vorágine** is portrayed as a theatrical individual who has left his native city and ventured out into the "wilds"—that is, as a foreigner or alien in a new and unknown territory. His vision of the plains and the jungle is that of a character who is already removed from his native land, who is slowly becoming more and more alienated from reality, and who cannot understand what he observes because he is an outsider, totally influenced by literature and by his preconceived notions of what he should find in this new land. As Bull has noted [see excerpt dated 1948], "Perhaps no author . . . has ever presented an extensive study of nature through the eyes and emotions of characters so incapable of describing nature in an objective fashion." In this sense Cova is not different from the Europeans who discovered the New World or even the European anthropologists of the late nineteenth and early twentieth centuries, whose entire comprehension of the world they encountered was based on, inseparable from, and a projection of themselves and their old world. And yet it is Cova who formulates our image of the female. . . . (pp. 39-42)

Thus, returning circularly to the notion of the *vorágine,* one must by association question the validity of his conception of the *vorágine* as the jungle and begin to understand the *vorágine* in a manner which sheds more light on the meaning of the text and its portrayal of both women and nature. Surely, we must comprehend the *vorágine* as the whirlpool of irrationality which slowly takes control of Arturo's life. I have mentioned several instances of Arturo's unreliability, and there are other moments of the text which point to his mental instability or dementia. For example, at the end of Part 1, during the burning of Franco's house, he reports, "En medio de las llamas empecé a reír como Satanás!" ("In the midst of the flames I laughed like a devil!") The fact that he reports this about himself highlights his instability. Similarly, in Part 2 he witnesses the violent death of two of his companions and observes, "La visión frenética del naufragio me sacudió con una ráfaga de belleza. *El espectáculo fue magnífico*" (emphasis added) ("The disaster overwhelmed me with a sense of beauty. *The spectacle was magnificent,*" emphasis added). Again, the spectacle of a violent death cannot be magnificent by our standards. Clearly, then, the *vorágine* which seems to be "devouring" him (like the *selva* which, according to Rivera, did devour him) is his own mind and is more internal than external. Thus, one might effectively summarize Cova's proclivity by noting that he consistently takes what is internal and threatening from within, transposes it, and regards it as something external and threatening from the outside—often metaphorically transposing it into some aspect of nature or a woman.

Without a doubt, one of the principal structuring factors in this text . . . is the discrepancy between the character's vision and what are presented or implied as the "facts" within the text, that is, between two different levels of *énoncé.* But, what is even more important, I believe, is that from the very beginning Cova is depicted by Rivera as a Romantic poet. Our very first glimpse of Cova, in the epigraph, which is supposedly a fragment of the letter Cova writes to the consul, underlines what appear to be the two major themes of the novel, both directly linked to the female and nature: time and the conflict between a Romantic and a naturalistic view of the world (a disparity in many ways also related to time and the notion of progress). In this letter, Rivera affords us our first exposure to the Romantic vision and rhetoric of Cova; then, in the early pages of the text we are again presented with the romanticism of Cova, who, like the Romantic poet, eternally seeks freedom and ideal love, must forever chase after chimeras, and rarely demonstrates the wisdom of acknowledging that the fantasies are within.

In this sense, one is led to wonder if it is not the lyrical vision of Cova which forms the basis of his unreliability, for one soon recognizes the discrepancy between what he expects to discover (and what he sometimes *thinks* he finds), and what he does encounter, again a problem echoed in his perception of the female. In fact, the basis of the text might well be defined as the tension between romanticism and naturalism (or realism), and the suggestion is that the naturalistic view is ultimately more valid since Cova and his Romantic view are unable to survive. What Rivera and the text seem to ignore, however, and what is especially pertinent to our discussion of women, is that contrary to the beliefs of the period, the naturalistic vision is as slanted and subjective as the Romantic vision. Certainly, the very notions implied in the opposition between romanticism and naturalism are directly related to the notions of internal and external and again parallel our perception of the female as either Madonna or prostitute. That is, romanticism characterizes itself and is accepted as a subjective vision; the inner self is overtly projected onto the outer world, and thus the external world is recognized as a

projection of that ego. On the contrary, realism and naturalism, like the scientific method, proffer themselves as objective, extrinsic visions, which are in no way dependent upon or related to the subject, but which are totally conditioned on the object. They pretend to be external, but ultimately, of course, the very possibility of objectivity is but a myth—an innocent belief that mankind is capable of understanding (or re-creating) anything except in relation to himself. Although there are certainly varying degrees of subjectivity, most scholars now recognize that any supposedly objective analysis is still contingent upon the mediation of the viewer. The real danger here, as with the symbol or the signifier, arises the moment the realist begins to take his enterprise seriously and forgets that what he sees is only a projection of himself to a greater or lesser extent. Clearly, what I have said here about the realist must also be posited about the scientist and his presumable objectivity. We shall indeed never know how much of Freud's findings about the psychological "nature" of woman are merely subjective projections. (pp. 42-44)

[It appears that *La vorágine* might be seen as a twentieth-century adventure novel.] As in the classical and renaissance adventure tales, they are structured around a journey whose purpose is (or becomes) the imposition of what the "hero's" society considers civilization. In this sense, although there is a dose of irony in the twentieth-century novels, we have not moved very far from the Arthurian cycle, *Amadís de Gaula, Chanson de Roland,* and so forth. And, in many ways, the portrayal of the female in the twentieth-century novels is even more closely tied to these tales of adventure. In both instances, the female is a peripheral being, distanced from the center of the story, imagined, and fantasized even more than the hero himself. Perhaps it is the satirical *Don Quijote* which most clearly evinces the attitude toward, and the position of, the female in the adventure tale. Don Quijote, of course, is deeply enamored of Dulcinea and devotes all his deeds and exploits to her. But, she does not exist; *even within the fiction,* she is but a figment of his imagination and thus but a projection of himself. In many ways, the same has occurred in . . . *La vorágine* where women are just imagined fantasies, projections of the male (the same characteristics in many cases which he also projects on nature). The ultimate irony and perhaps absurdity lies in man's inability to see either nature or the female except in relation to himself. Man repeatedly insists that nature exists as either friend or foe (depending on the period) and refuses to accept that nature may simply be there, as neither friend nor foe—just there (as woman is neither necessarily ally nor enemy). Thus . . . Cova projects his own mental vortex on the jungle. (p. 58)

Sharon Magnarelli, "Women and Nature: In Man's Image Created," in her The Lost Rib: Female Characters in the Spanish-American Novel, *Bucknell University Press, 1985, pp. 38-58.*

FURTHER READING

Callan, Richard J. "The Archetype of Psychic Renewal in *La vorágine.*" *Hispania* 54, No. 3 (September 1971): 470-76.
    Interprets *The Vortex* from the viewpoint of Jungian psychology. Callan concludes: "Whatever technical shortcomings *La*

vorágine may hold, the fact remains that it continues to be studied and read for its own sake, because it is intensely alive."

Franco, Jean. *The Modern Culture of Latin America: Society and the Artist.* London: Pall Mall Press, 1967, 399 p.

Includes discussion of Rivera's importance in Colombian literature and a brief analysis of *The Vortex.*

Marsh, Fred T. "Tale of the Rubber Jungle." *New York Herald Tribune Books* 11, No. 33 (21 April 1935): 6.

Favorable review of *The Vortex.* Marsh notes that the novel "moves, not swiftly, but erratically with a curious narrative method. It is not of the simple straightforward propaganda order of story, but the individualized, highly involved modern novel."

Menton, Seymour. "*La vorágine:* Circling the Triangle." *Hispania* 59, No. 3 (September 1976): 418-34.

Interprets *The Vortex* as "a complex Christian vision of man's fall from Paradise and his punishment and ultimate death in the concentric circles of hell," noting the influence of Dante's *Divine Comedy* and other classics of Western literature in the novel.

Neale-Silva, Eduardo. "The Factual Bases of *La vorágine.*" *PMLA* 54, No. 1 (March 1939): 316-31.

Detailed analysis of geographical, historical, and social verisimilitude in *The Vortex.*

Valensi, Frances. "The Rubber-Tappers." *The New Republic* 83, No. 1072 (19 June 1935): 174.

Review of *The Vortex* in which Valensi commends the novel as "a document that towers above the ordinary novel in dramatic tenseness and poetic quality."

Valentine, Robert Y. "Arturo Cova: Fierce Spirit and Savage Plant." *Revista de estudios hispánicos* 14, No. 2 (May 1980): 39-46.

Finds many similarities between *The Vortex* and the thirteenth canto of Dante's *Inferno.*

Winkler, Jean. "Jungle Odyssey." *The Nation* 140, No. 3651 (26 June 1935): 749.

Review of *The Vortex.* According to Winkler, the novel "is not a very well-tailored job," yet "its indictment of the system which produces a fundamental necessity of modern civilization strikes one like a slash across the face."

Sholom Aleichem

1859-1916

(Also transliterated as Sholem-Aleykhem; pseudonym of Sholom Rabinowitz, also transliterated as Rabinovich, Rabinovitsh, and Rabinovitch) Ukrainian-born Yiddish short story writer, novelist, and dramatist.

For further discussion of Sholom Aleichem's career, see *TCLC*, Volume 1.

Sholom Aleichem was one of the founders and the most important writers of Yiddish literature. His reputation is based primarily on humorous short stories, such as those adapted for the musical *Fiddler on the Roof,* in which he depicted the Jewish Pale of Settlement, those areas in Russia to which Jews were restricted during the nineteenth century. While other Russian Jews of his era wrote in either Hebrew or Russian, Sholom Aleichem chose to write in Yiddish, a language spoken by eastern European Jews which is derived from High German but usually written with Hebrew characters. Sholom Aleichem's stories reflect the determined optimism and faith of the Jews amid poverty and persecution, bringing humor to this grim setting through absurd situations and naively revealing monologues. Sholom Aleichem used the literary forms of the monologue and the epistle to reveal his characters in their own idiom with no intervention from a narrator, a method which led to his fame as the "folk voice" of Ukrainian Jewry.

The son of a prosperous, educated merchant, Sholom Aleichem was born in the Ukrainian city of Pereyaslav and spent his early years in a shtetl, a small, impoverished Jewish community which functioned much like a medieval town. There he socialized with the kind of poor working-class people who later figured prominently in his fiction. The financial security of his family abruptly ended when his father lost his fortune to a dishonest business partner. After his mother died in 1872, his father married a woman whose bitter tongue inspired Sholom Aleichem to write his first book, which was a dictionary of her curses. His second book, an imitation of Abraham Mapu's *Ahavath Tsiyon* (*Love of Zion,* 1853), so impressed his father that he sent him to a Russian secondary school, where he would receive a secular education, rather than to yeshiva, the traditional Jewish religious academy for advanced studies.

When Sholom Aleichem graduated at seventeen, he took a position as the tutor of a thirteen-year-old girl with whom he subsequently fell in love. Three years later, upon discovering the couple's feelings for each other, the girl's father fired Sholom Aleichem. Moving to Kiev, Sholom Aleichem took a job as a government rabbi and began to publish articles in Hebrew and Russian on educational and liturgical reform. Wanting to reach the large audience of shtetl Jews who could not read Hebrew, he decided to write in Yiddish, a language then derided by educated Jews. Protecting his professional reputation by adopting the pseudonym Sholom Aleichem (a Hebrew greeting meaning "peace be with you"), he published his first short story, "The Two Stones," in 1883. In the same year, he married his former student. Over the next few years, Sholom Aleichem wrote critically acclaimed short stories and

several novels, including *Stempenyu* and *Yosele Solovey,* hoping to provide more serious and artistic examples of Yiddish writing in contrast with the frivolous romances that prevailed in Yiddish literature of that time. Having established himself as a respectable Yiddish author, he encouraged other Yiddish writers by founding and editing *Di yidishe folksbiblyotek,* an annual devoted to Yiddish literature.

Throughout the 1890s, Sholom Aleichem wrote stories incessantly and attempted a variety of business schemes in order to support his family. The immensely popular Tevye stories and Menachem Mendl series date from this period, and their success gave the family enough security to enable Sholom Aleichem to devote himself entirely to writing. As his prominence in Russian literary circles grew, he corresponded with such writers as Anton Chekhov and Leo Tolstoy and was in much demand for lectures and readings. However, the pogroms of 1905, in which thousands of Jews were massacred, forced the family to flee into exile. Despite his immense popularity, Sholom Aleichem was again in financial trouble. Having sold his copyrights to unscrupulous publishers years before, he received no royalties from the sales of his works. He traveled constantly, giving lectures and readings in Europe and America, until he collapsed from tuberculosis in Russia in 1908. While Sholom Aleichem recovered in Italy, unable to pay his debts, some friends raised money by sponsoring a twenty-fifth anniversary jubilee in honor of his first story. They received donations from all over the world and arranged to reclaim his copyrights from the publishers. Financially secure and having recovered his health by 1913, Sholom Aleichem resumed his lecture and reading tours. However, the outbreak of World War I in 1914 drove him and his family once more into exile. They moved to New York, where Sholom Aleichem died in 1916.

Sholom Aleichem's fame rests primarily on his short stories, which were among the first Yiddish works to be accepted as serious literature. In their detailed representation of shtetl life, these stories successfully reflect the chaotic world of eastern European Jews. As well as documenting the Jews' daily suffering from hunger and persecution, Sholom Aleichem addressed the problem of changing values among the younger generation, particularly their increasing secularization and disregard for tradition. Sholom Aleichem's stories never follow a conventional plotline: they begin in the midst of trouble, more disasters occur, then they break off without resolution. However, instead of focusing on the disruption and calamity which provide much of the substance for his short stories, Sholom Aleichem maintained a tone of humor and optimism. For example, Tevye the dairyman, one of Sholom Aleichem's most popular characters, distracts the reader from the tragedy of his stories through his audacious challenges to God and his humorous misquotations of religious verses. Menachem Mendl, the fast-talking dreamer who fails in every business venture he attempts, amuses the reader with his outrageous plans and his frenzied pace. Presenting himself as a listener in his stories and allowing his characters to speak without authorial intervention, Sholom Aleichem added to the humor by having his characters inadvertently reveal their attitudes and faults.

Sholom Aleichem's novels and plays have never been as popular as his short stories. Critics have maintained that his nonlinear style was not suited to the sustained storyline requisite for a novel and that the most successful sections are extended monologues similar in form to his short stories. Sholom Aleichem's plays grew naturally out of his preference for writing realistic stories, but he created little in this genre due to a ban in Russia on Jewish theater. His later plays such as *Shver tsu zeyn a yid* (*It's Hard to Be a Jew*) and an adaptation of his short stories, *The World of Sholom Aleichem*, were especially successful in American theaters.

Despite the careful craftsmanship of Sholom Aleichem's narratives, the naturalness of his characters' speech and the accuracy of his descriptions of shtetl life led to his initial reputation as simply a "recorder" of Jewish life. Early critics focused on the cheerfulness of the characters, on their "laughter through tears" as a way of coping with the endless adversity in their lives. More recent critics have noted a tragic side to Sholom Aleichem's stories, maintaining that his works inspire sympathy as well as laughter. Significant change has occurred in the critical estimates of Tevye: once seen as a cheerful but naive character who inadvertently misquotes scripture through his ignorance, he has recently been described as a perceptive man who consciously manipulates religious quotations to comment on his life and on God. While Sholom Aleichem's writing is now considered more complex than it was previously, his importance as a founder of Yiddish literature has never been disputed. Likewise, critics and readers have consistently appreciated the humorous and poignant stories in which he masterfully evoked the resiliency and hopefulness of shtetl Jews.

(See also *Contemporary Authors,* Vol. 104.)

PRINCIPAL WORKS

Stempenyu (novel) 1889; published in journal *Di yidishe folksbiblyotek*
    [*Stempenyu,* 1913]
Yosele Solovey (novel) 1890; published in journal *Di yidishe folksbiblyotek*
Tevye der milkhiger (short stories) 1894
    [*Tevye's Daughters,* 1949]
Menakhem-Mendl (short stories) 1895
    [*The Adventures of Menakhem-Mendl,* 1969]
Tsezeyt un tseshpreyt (drama) 1905
In shturm (novel) 1907
Samuel Pasternak (drama) 1907
*Stempenyu (drama) 1907
Mottel Peyse dem khazns (short stories) 1907-16
    [*Adventures of Mottel, the Cantor's Son,* 1953]
Blondzhnde shtern (novel) 1912
    [*Wandering Stars,* 1952]
Shver tsu zayn a yid (drama) 1914
Dos groyse gevins (drama) 1916
Ale verk fun Sholom Aleichem. 28 vols. (short stories, novels, dramas, and unfinished autobiography) 1917-25
The Old Country (short stories) 1946
Inside Kasrilevke (short stories) 1948
The Great Fair (unfinished autobiography) 1955
Stories and Satires (short stories) 1959
Old Country Tales (short stories) 1966
Some Laughter, Some Tears (short stories) 1968

*This work is an adaptation of the novel *Stempenyu.*

BA'AL-MAKHSHOVES (essay date 1908)

[In the following essay, Makhshoves examines prominent character types in Sholom Aleichem's works and how they reflect Jewish reaction to life in exile.]

Sholem Aleichem is one of the fortunate Yiddish writers who does not have to wait for an anniversary celebration to publicize his name among the broad masses of our people; his name was a household word before the critics even began to take notice of him. It was not unusual for an entire town to wait with baited breath for a new issue of *Der yid* in which Sholem Aleichem, with a broad grin, lambasted a certain class of speculators and stock market sharpies. Among the folk, there is hardly a celebration or gathering where the guests are not asked: "Would you care to hear some Sholem Aleichem read aloud?" as one would offer a good glass of wine with a piece of cake. The folk has long since discovered the delicious flavor of Sholem Aleichem's works. Thanks to this Jew from *Volin,* the saddened, oppressed people, with its embittered heart and caustic tongue, has learned how to laugh.

And this is no small achievement. Laughter means the ability to see oneself and the world through the eyes of a stranger, to free oneself momentarily from the material world, from the "ego," and to view God's creation with the eyes of a new-born babe. To laugh is to be able to feel innocent, free of sins against oneself and others; it is a brief experience of freedom from the historical, everlasting transgressions that defile our souls with greasy stains. The person who laughs rises to the height of a miniature God who is briefly able to transcend and annul his own creation.

Each of us has experienced that difficult state when we imagine ourselves to have committed a terrible sin or to have just experienced a terrible catastrophe. In these heavy moments, we are seized by the fleeting hope that this is nothing but a dream, that any minute we'll snap out of it and all the fears will trickle away, like water in sand. Now imagine that one of us had the power to render the *real* world into a dream. Such a one appears before us, and lo—all our mistakes and experiences, all the repressions we suffer, all the evils we perpetrate on others and that others perpetrate upon us—all this becomes only an awkward nightmare from which we will soon awaken, the ugly vision dissipating before our very eyes. Imagine how thankful we would be to this sorcerer. Well, each and every divinely inspired poet is just such a sorcerer, transforming our actual, physical existence into a dream.

Sholem Aleichem is just such an artist. Thanks to his hearty laughter, our real world becomes a fairy tale. The Jewish petty merchant in the figure of Menakhem-Mendl becomes some kind of fantastic being. The average middle class Jew who commits as many follies in his life as the hero of the monologue **"Gimmazye" ("Gymnasium")**, laughs at his mirror image, the poor fool in the story who tries so hard to break through the *numerous clausus* of the Russian high school, getting involved in a whole array of crooked deals, destroying himself and his profession and in sum, only trading in his shoe for a slipper. The reader laughs at this fool as heartily as if the story had nothing whatsoever to do with him. Sholem Aleichem has temporarily freed him from his foolish day-to-day existence by transforming it into a caricature, a dream.

This phenomenon becomes even clearer when we take a closer look at Sholem Aleichem's major hero, Menakhem-Mendel of Yehupets. For Menakhem-Mendl is a parable, an analogue of the Jewish merchant and *luftmentsh,* a living symbol of the vast majority of the Jewish people. Examine this character carefully through Sholem Aleichem's perspective and you can barely restrain yourself from laughing. Yesterday he was a stock broker, today he is a matchmaker, tomorrow he'll be a wood merchant and the day after an insurance agent. You can find him on the steps of every stock exchange, in each and every marketplace, his spirit hovering over each minute transaction. A wagonload of wheat passes by and Menakhem-Mendl gets to finger two or three stalks: presto—he's a grain expert. He sees a nobleman whose estate includes a forest and by morning he is the agent for the forest which the nobleman never intended to sell. No sooner does he see a widow or a divorcee, than he drags a prospective groom to meet her. An item in the paper on some crazy Rothschild collecting fleas propels him straightaway into the flea business. Thousands of plans, angles and deals flit through his mind like evil spirits, and if Menakhem-Mendl stops for a split second to think, you can be sure that he has just come up with a new and grander lunacy to add to the thousands already in his head. Menakhem-Mendl is always in a fever. In his hallucinatory world, butter and leather, wheat and needles, are indistinguishable, and he is capable of matching up

two boys as bride and groom or of sending logs down a river that dried up ages ago.

Menakhem-Mendl of Yehupets is the madness of the Jewish people embodied in the figure of the Jewish petty merchant. Try compiling the biographies of several hundred Jewish *luft*-merchants and you will be astounded. You'll think you fell into an asylum where behind every Menakhem-Mendl of Yehupets, scratching the back of his neck with his walking stick as he prepares for some new undertaking, there hovers the pale and drawn demonic figure of madness.

Menakhem-Mendl is a product of the Jewish condition in exile. Constant persecution has made him into a weird creature. The Jew, always isolated from the normal and typical sources of livelihood, had to make a living on side roads, searching out the unusual and exceptional so as to keep alive. The ordinary and typical occupations were not for him. He had always had to discover the loopholes that were of no concern to the rulers of the land because their wealth did not depend on them. As a result, a penchant for all kinds of exceptions, fantastic deals, and unusual undertakings was nurtured in the soul of the Jewish merchant. The Jew was in the same situation as the Spanish or Portuguese adventurer of the sixteenth century who was always dreaming of discovering new and unexplored territories, a kind of Pizarro or Vasco da Gama who discovered every now and then a new remote source of income. Today thousands of Jewish merchants are Menakhem-Mendls who inherited their parents' appetite for outlandish undertakings but lack their depth of judgment, their purposefulness or calm. Menakhem-Mendl, the Jewish counterpart of Khlestakov, the scatterbrained hero of Gogol's *Inspector General,* is a national type, a figure who is everywhere to be seen, a living embodiment of Jewish foolishness.

God created the world in sets of opposites and the artist practices an *imitatio Dei.* Sholem Aleichem's Tevye is the exact opposite of his Menakhem-Mendl. If one can compare Menakhem-Mendl's head and heart to a roadside inn open to all traffic, then Tevye's heart would be a backwoods hut where a stranger rarely appears. Menakhem-Mendl is by nature a transitional type. He is constantly on the move, but his movement lacks a clear goal. Menakhem-Mendl is the Jew who threw off the Jewish gaberdine in the late 1870s and 80s and began to assume European manners. He symbolizes the first signs of assimilation among the middle merchant class, the largest class among Jews. Tevye, to the contrary, is the old Jewish quarter that resists all change and holds firm to the old customs till death do them part. Menakhem-Mendl is *modern* Jewry of the street while Tevye is *conservative* Jewry.

Actually, Tevye is sooner a female type than a male. His wife wears the pants while he takes on the lighter chores—delivering butter and cheese on his wagon to various customers. As a representative type of the old Jewish masses, his head is full of various scriptural passages, snatches of Psalms, preachers' parables and quotations from the study house which are half-understood and distorted. But despite his ignorance, he is still something of a scholar among his own kind. Once upon a time such people were the folk intellectuals. Although his use of scriptural citations is always wrong and he never knows the correct interpretation of the words, he grasps their inner meaning nonetheless. If you collect all his sayings you notice that they are totally imbued with the spirit of the House of Study. He is a great believer and man of faith, observing all worldly pleasures with a grownup's smile. Goodness and gentleness thrive in his heart. He is free of jealousy and hatred and is extremely hospitable. He has no profound dealings with people but he values highly each and every Jew (Jews being the only category of people he knows), if for no other reason than that he *is* a Jew, one of the millions of the chosen whose fate has been so intimately intertwined with his since the time of Abraham. Tevye's soul knows no hastiness or sudden impulse; it is a quiet and settled soul which becomes all the more peaceful and joyous with each Sabbath or festival.

Menakhem-Mendl is surrounded by a whole array of demons who toss him back and forth all week long. He does not rest even on the Sabbath, when his son, the *Gymnasium* student, opens his mail for him and lest his bill of exchange be refused, off he rushes to the bank with his *shabes-goy,* as if possessed by demons, when necessary, even signing his name on the Sabbath. Tevye, on the other hand, is surrounded by angels of peace. All week long they keep at a distance and accompany his wagon on the road to Boyberik. Come Sabbath, they take up prominent positions at his table and add splendor to his Sabbath songs and dishes. Tevye the milkman possesses the peace and calm of men of the soil. It is as if Tevye were the owner of a plot of land situated in some far-off Jewish country that is guarded and protected by King David's bodyguard and that this Jewish kingdom sees to it that no harm befalls him. But a closer look reveals that Tevye's landed property is actually the House of Study and his restful nature stems from the fact that he, pauper and milkman though he be, will ultimately inherit the worlds of the just; that in the world to come, a golden chair with four solid legs (such as never need a carpenter) has been prepared for him.

But he who lives in the next world is blind and foolish in this world. Tevye's eye never catches what is happening around him. The Lord has blessed him with a pack of daughters, one more attractive and talented than the next, hard-working, industrious and lively—it's a pleasure to watch them. And Tevye is grateful to the Lord of His providence. In the long summer days, as he rattles along the road in his wagon and he and his horse take a comfortable summer nap, Tevye maps out all kinds of plans for his daughters and imagines all kinds of good fortune. In the end, all these plans are completely foiled. Each of his daughters abandons him in turn. One falls in love with a young tailor; a second drowns herself because of a love affair with a rich man's son and a third gets married to some "Feferl"—a thin young man in a black shirt—and goes off with him to Siberia bearing his child. Tevye's mind does not begin to grasp all this. He cannot comprehend how a person could take his very own life. And what is all this business about falling in love? There he stands blinking his tear-filled eyes and shrugging his shoulders. He is completely convinced of his own wisdom, that only he knows how life should be lived and that these young upstarts are clearly out of their minds. By nature a good and mild-mannered person, Tevye bears no grudge against anyone and his inner piety and steadfastness unto God keep him from despair. He absorbs the blows of Fate just as his nag absorbs the strokes of his whip. He revives with a proverb, with a scriptural passage and on he drives in his wagon of dairy goods to the wealthy customers of Boyberik who often have outstanding debts on their purchases of summer cheese, eggs and butter.

Menakhem-Mendl and Tevye are the two poles of the Jewish masses. One is momentum, the other is static tranquility. The momentum has no goal and lives from day to day while the tranquility has once and for all established its goal which has no connection whatsoever to *this* world. Both types embody the disintegration of Jewish folk life. Were the Jewish people's will to be reduced to these two alternatives, nothing would remain of the Jewish collective other than a ruin, a pile of sand at the shores of human existence.

But both types, despite the distance between them, share a common ground—both are connected to the social processes going on around them. Menakhem-Mendl and Tevye are obviously both Jews living in exile who are subjected to a double yoke: the yoke imposed by the ruling classes and the specific Jewish edicts. Here we discover that the Jewish masses, embodied by Menakhem-Mendl and Tevye, never wage war against this external pressure. Each of them views these hardships as a law of nature which cannot be countered. Is it possible to combat the power of gravity? The only possible solution is to avoid the effects of the natural law: bricks come tumbling down from the roof—take shelter in a cellar; there's a terrible cold spell—don't show your face out of doors.

The masses, as described by Sholem Aleichem through his major characters, are anything but revolutionary: they are totally unaware that the revolt of a large collective can have a significant social impact. They view the life around them as a fixed entity, a set frame, that cannot and will not be altered. Since it is impossible to break out of it, every conceivable trick must be used to stretch out one's body in the narrow, stifling frame. And if you can't stretch out, you squeeze in and manage—somehow.

Take one look at the life of these masses and you realize that there exists no bridge to unite Sholem Aleichem's generation with that of its children. Severed from their parents, the latter grow up with contempt or at best, with a pitying, sardonic smile for the human bodies who brought this new generation into the world. Tevye's children can only feel sorry for their good father whom life deceives every step of the way leaving him orphaned in his old age, devoid of pleasure and devoid of children. The children of the Menakhem-Mendls, however, cannot even stand the sight of their father. At best, they can pity him for living a life which is as confused, lightless, poor and troubled as the life of a worm.

Sholem Aleichem has himself become so much a part of his generation, that he does not get around to showing us the off-spring of the Menakhem-Mendls. On the rare occasions that he does mention them, they appear as shadows, as portraits standing remotely in the background whose features are barely visible. He himself, being a child of his time, has no eye for the younger generation—he sees them, as it were, through a veil and does not understand them. His artistry holds back his pen whenever he begins to portray the Feferls, the Josephs, the generation of the children. He senses that he lacks the means to make them emerge as clearly and boldly as his Tevyes and Menakhem-Mendls.

Sholem Aleichem the humorist and caricaturist is also the unadulterated naturalist: there is not the slightest hint of romanticism, sentimentalism or vague idealism. His descriptions have the effect of coarse and unadorned life itself, and if we were to sum up the world which he depicts, we, the later generation, would be perfectly justified in pronouncing the verdict of—good riddance. But who knows if we are really rid of the world in which Tevye and Menakhem-Mendl are the leading players? I have my strong doubts on the matter.

There is, however, one segment of Sholem Aleichem's creativity in which he is less of a naturalist and more of a poet, more sentimental and warm-hearted. I am referring to his ***Mayses far yidishe kinder (Stories for Jewish Children)***.

The world of the Jewish child is cramped and dark. Before he can even walk properly, his father wraps him in a sweaty, dirty prayershawl and the parents carry the infant off to heder, to his teacher Reb Yisroel the Angel of Death. Two inimical forces surround him from his early years: an angry, morose father instructs him every step of the way, and if his father lets go for a moment, he falls into the hands of wicked Reb Yisroel. The patriarchal world of Christians as of Jews does not recognize the concept of childhood. The child is not an end in himself. Only at the point when he begins to adopt the traditions of his father and grandfather is he conceded any value. In the pious world of old, as in medieval Europe, no distinction is drawn between a child and an adult. Likewise, they know of no transition from childhood to adolescence. On that day when the child first puts on the tassled undergarment and pronounces a blessing over the *tsitses,* he is already likened unto his elders. He spends his childhood in a double prison: the home is one, the heder another. The melancholy which so imbues the Jewish spiritual heritage overlays the Jewish school and home. The child is forcibly kept from fresh air, light and children's games. Each step he takes is predetermined and he is caged in by thousands of pedagogical rules that transform his childhood into a trying and gloomy period of life.

Only on selected days of the year, during festivals when fathers and grandfathers themselves become children for a while and make merry in front of the Lord with cups of wine, lulabim, ethrogim, myrtle branches, *homen-tashn,* Torah scrolls and the like, only then is the child freed from his prison. Now the Jewish youngster who was bewitched all year long into being a caricature of an adult Jew, is transformed into a natural, loving and lively Jewish child.

In Sholem Aleichem's ***Mayses far yidishe kinder*** which are always associated with one of the Jewish festivals, the Jewish child appears before us in all his virtues and charms. The Jewish festivals are the *benevolent* force which allows the child to catch his breath for a while and prevent him from succumbing altogether under the dry and clumsy tutelage of his fathers and teachers.

In addition to the festivals, there are two other benevolent forces that prevent the Jewish child from becoming completely crushed under the severe supervision of the father and the teacher.

Jews were providential in that a half of their population was exempted from the 613 commandments. Only three positive commandments were conferred upon the woman, and so her soul was less burdened by the spiritual heritage than was her husband's. Except for the fact that the woman is also a mother to her children in the Jewish home, she is otherwise free of the burdensome religious duties and her emotional life is therefore more natural and freer. Behind their mothers' aprons, the Yoseles and Moteles take refuge from the fathers and teachers, and whatever is rained out of them during the day under male supervision, begins to flow once again under the warm gaze of the kindly mother.

Then too, there are simple folk as well as scholars, among the Jews. The great Jewish masses, though deeply influenced by the dry and morose bookmen, were far too ignorant to become as arid and as alienated from the world as their benchwarmers and clergymen. Among the Jewish masses, the desire for a good laugh, for enjoying a more cheerful and more natural life has not yet been extinguished. And Sholem Aleichem's children often flee from their fathers and teachers to the uncouth simple folk, to some musician or other in a back street or simply to a jolly simpleton. The two forces of darkness are confronted by *three* forces of light and if a Jewish child of old managed to grow up more naturally, better and freer than the others, it was thanks to his mother, to the carefree ignorance of the masses and to the Jewish holidays.

Sholem Aleichem's stories for Jewish children are also epic portraits of the manner in which our fathers lived. Menakhem-Mendl and Tevye are complete in themselves; the writer does not depict the background from which they came, but assumes that the reader will provide this from his own imagination. In the children's stories, however, we see the still life and the animate phenomena surrounding the life of a Jew from birth on. And if you were to add Sholem Aleichem's sketches ***Kleyne mentshelekh mit kleyne hasoges (Little People with Little Minds)*** to his children's stories, you would have a complete and clear portrait of the Jewish material environment, beginning with a Jewish festival and ending with a Jewish funeral.

In the pages of his storybooks, Sholem Aleichem has captured an entire culture which is receding further and further from us. If we wish to have a deeper and clearer understanding of the roots from which we came, we must draw upon Sholem Aleichem's stories as reliable sources that depict the old Jewish world. Into the children's stories he introduced much life, joy and natural charm, creating the illusion of some temporary home, and causing us briefly to forget that the present generation grew up *doubly homeless* on account of their fathers and teachers. History robbed the people of its land and the severe patriarchal education robbed it of the home of *childhood.*

In his children's stories, Sholem Aleichem is no longer the dry naturalist of his monologues. Putting aside the inimical forces in the Jewish home, he allows the friends of the Jewish child to come forward: the mothers, the jolly simple folk and especially the Jewish festivals. He immerses the life of the Jewish child in the poetry of a Jewish festival, which explains why his children's stories have a completely different quality. They radiate life, fresh air and sunshine. A moist, jovial eye peers out of them at the reader.

The creator of Tevye and Menakhem-Mendl longs for some kind of home; a home which is free of Tevye's inertia and the wild momentum of a crazy Menakhem-Mendl. He finds such a home in the lovely holiday of a Jewish child. (pp. 7-15)

> *Ba'Al-Makhshoves, "Sholem Aleichem: A Typology of His Characters," in* Prooftexts, *Vol. 6, No. 1, January, 1986, pp. 7-15.*

YOSEF HAIM BRENNER (essay date 1916)

[*A Russian-born Hebrew fiction writer and critic, Brenner is known for his compassionate depiction of Jewish life in Russia, England, and Palestine. In the following excerpt, he praises the authenticity of Sholom Aleichem's portrayal of Jewish life.*]

Sholem Aleichem, Tevye's Bard was a simple Jew, like Tevye himself; a noble and simple Jewish bard. But was he a writer?

Yes; in the novels, **Der mabl** (*The Deluge*), and *Blondzhnde shtern* (*Wandering Stars*), in the chapter **"Milyonen"** (**"Millions"**) of *Menakhem-Mendl,* and here and there—if they can be mentioned in the same breath—even in some of the stories of Motl, the Cantor's Son, and in the last three chapters of *Tevye the Dairyman,* where he achieved whatever literary skill he did. But in the first four chapters of Tevye, as well as in the best of his works, he was hardly a writer at all. He transcended all literary genres, literary trends and definitions—he was not a "folk writer," not even "*the* folk writer," but rather a unique poetic and folk amalgam, a living essence of the folk itself.

Is there such a thing as a Jewish people? Do these caravans wandering to and fro over the globe share any particular characteristic or a unique approach to the world? Do the vicissitudes of life evoke in them a unique form of laughter and tears? Are there certain life-giving forces in their midst, any special talents in life's enterprise? Why yes, of course! Sholem Aleichem!

He was a "writer of the people," a *folkshrayber,* to use his own term. It should be added, however, that he was a "writer of the people" not only by virtue of the fact that he emerged out of their midst, always moved among them, knew them and drew them. In this respect, almost none of our writers falls short of him, especially writers of his generation, great and small alike. Which of them was not born of the people or did not write for them? The uniqueness of Sholem Aleichem's connection to the people is that in his superb creations there is not even a hint of a "storyteller" standing above or, let us say at a distance and "describing" the simple folk. Instead, the people describes itself through a spokesman who is one of them. What we have is the life of the people in its authentic form, a true, vibrant cross-section of their lives, not a literary, stylized folk façade.

The great Sholem Aleichem had no style—he had no need of style. Nor did he have recourse to the well-known artistic "devices"—those "devices" which are used consciously and deliberately. Nor did he have "ideas" concerning life. The folk speaks for itself in his *authentic* works (exclusive of those many works which he wrote throughout much of his life for various programmatic ends)—in these works, life does the thinking for itself. The folk life gives itself over to his alert perception and provides him with the means of disclosure, so that he, the "messenger of the people" is really only their loyal depositor. As the "Jewish humorist" (another of his favorite appellations), he does not stand outside to mock their life as if it were something foreign. Nor does he poke fun, like the insider, who uses satire to disengage himself from the great suffering around him. He does not back away nor rebel. Life entrusted him with a golden pen, the medium through which it mocks itself, and Sholem Aleichem is the master of the pen.

Sometimes this was not enough for him. He was occasionally seized by the desire to be a master of ideas as well, to be an "intellectual" (as good as Peretz at least): to present problems (as in the play *Tsezeyt un tseshpreyt, Scattered and Dispersed*); to press home a moral point, that the Kasrilevker, for instance, had a determined sense of justice and an undaunted faith in the triumph of truth (the conclusion of **"Dreyfus in Kasrilevke"**); to smuggle in at least some kind of "statement," almost by the way, in the style of Mendele: "Our Jewish brethren take a seat in the train just for pleasure, travel to Moscow and then come right back to Kasrilevke"

(**"Di shtot fun di kleyne mentschelekh," "The Town of the Little People"**). Kasrilevke, after all, is the hub of the universe and tehre's no escape from it. One might add: *ideologically* there is no escape, but in *reality,* everyone emigrates to America (**"An ongeleyster bris," "A Welcome Circumcision"**). On the other hand, he expressed the idea that "each individual is entitled to a place of his own . . ." (**"Di shtot fun di kleyne mentshelekh"**). He advocated this position in the unfinished novel *Moshiekhs tsaytn* (*In the Days of the Messiah*), in his pamphlet *Oyf vos badarfn yidn a land* (*Why Do Jews Need a Country*) and so on. But for all that, the secret of his greatness will not be revealed in these works. For here he was no longer the exquisite stenographer of Tevye the Dairyman, his was no longer the true vision of the folk, but rather something more, that is to say, something decidedly less: a mere literary vision.

Elsewhere, in many of his stories for children, Sholem Aleichem also figured as a mere writer. Though these stories are ideal reading *for* children, they fall short of Sholem Aleichem's additional aspiration—to write stories *about* the lives of children. In this respect their value is limited, for they do not exceed the narrow confines of literature. Instead of a Tevyre or Menakhem-Mendl speaking for himself, these children's stories are mediated by a writer. The narrative style is that of a popular story genre, a reputable genre, to be sure, but still a genre. What's missing is the humor of a story like **"Der farkishefter shnayder"** (**"The Bewitched Tailor"**), that flows of itself; natural, basic, earthy, humor as pure as the sky, devoid of cheap anecdotes or affectation. Instead, we have here a humor of the second order that is calculated, fabricated, or better yet, we have the sentimental-humorous lecture of a grownup portraying the lives of children or recalling events from his own childhood. What a lecture of this sort gains in entertainment value, it loses in vitality or spontaneity while its seeming profundity is nothing more than a façade. Even Motl the cantor's son, the most experienced and worldly-wise boy imaginable, who speaks and narrates in his own voice (this being the best of Sholem Aleichem's works of this genre), even he is deliberately helped out by the author every step of the way; the result is literary artifact.

It should be added, however, that in terms of characterization, Sholem Aleichem's child is somewhat of a novelty in our literature. From Mendele, Sholem Aleichem learned not to treat the child like a gradeschool teacher, but rather like an instructing artist who knows that the world of a child is important primarily in its uniqueness, being quite unlike the world of grownups. Sholem Aleichem then went one step further. Instead of trying to convince us or to teach us anything by means of this unique world, he sought rather to bring us pleasure through the rich poetry of childhood, entertaining us with the wonderful and familiar creatures whom he introduced to us that we might rejoice at their joy and grieve at their sorrow. Another advantage of his children over those of Mendele is that they are not merely "miserable Jews" like Hershele and Moyshe-Yosi: there is nothing miserable about them at all. This is no small innovation. Sholem Aleichem's child is not only different from Hershele and Moyshe-Yosi, but is also unlike their literary contemporaries: Sh. Ben-Zion's *Nefesh haretsutsah* (*The Downtrodden Soul*), Feierberg's Hofni the Visionary, the neglected offspring of Bialik's *Safiah* (*Aftergrowth*) or the naive and agile Velvele the Fool in Tchernikhovski's "Kehom hayom" ("Like the Heat of the Day"). The cantor's son and his pals, despite all the troubles that befall them, are not as miserable as all these other characters (for that matter, Sholem Aleichem's grownups are not so miserable either). The traditional fear of dogs and avoidance of all animals do not deter Motl—his best friend is a goat. Nor do the duality and the division between Torah and life, between imagination and reality spoil their enjoyment of the world. Sholem Aleichem's children, born to cantors, merchants and the like, were subject to more of a loving mother's care than all the other literary children of the previous generation who were raised for the most part by their fathers, kept under the constant surveillance of their father the rabbi, the ritual slaughterer, or the teacher, and expected to obey all his commands—the commandments of the stringent Torah.

Yes, Sholem Aleichem approached the subject skillfully, but the very problem of these stories is the use of an *approach,* while Tevye and Menakhem-Mendl did not have to be approached at all: they were always with him, they were the elemental forces of his work, the motifs that could already be detected in his earliest creative efforts. Sholem Aleichem was certainly an innovator in his children's stories where he presented us with a rather new portrait of a happy, healthy child. The problem was that objective psychological descriptions did not lie within the domain of Sholem Aleichem's literary talent. He was able to portray a complete gallery of adult characters thanks to the means of revelation transmitted to him by the folk itself, a gallery including the exquisite portrait of the simple Jew and his household (Tevye); the ridiculous portrait of "the buyer and seller who goes through the motions of work and earns not a penny" (Menakhem-Mendl); the portrait of the Kasrilevke householder (**"Nakhes fun kinder," "Pleasure from One's Children"**); the portrait of the Kasrilevke utopian dreamer (**"Ven ikh bin Roytshild," "If I Were Rothschild"**), and so on. But for the stories describing the lives of children, he only had recourse to his literary craft; and there is therefore no such abundance. All the portraits are alike, and even within the narrow scope of this single child, he did not reveal any new aspects of the young hero (something that he did achieve when depicting his overgrown child Tevye or that Bialik achieved in his poem "Ani ufi hatanur" ("I and the Mouth of the Stove")). The child's worldview does not emerge from the details of all its childish concerns even though these details are conveyed with feeling, with "humor," and with the narrative discipline befitting stories of this genre.

Mendele Mocher Sforim, the "grandfather of Yiddish literature," is clear and transparent; the writer of Russian *Jewry,* his works are devoid of mystery. Compare him to his grandson Sholem Aleichem—the spokesman of Russian *Jews,* of the Jewish population in Russia—and Mendele emerges as the wondrous path-finder, the inspired depicter of the general condition, the genuine "master of the law." The "master of legend," by contrast, he who won the hearts of his fellow Jews, giving them pleasure with no complaints or comments, no hairsplitting or moralizing—is the one whom we have just laid to rest. To quote our sages: "If you wish to discover the one who spoke and created the world—study Aggada." We may rightfully paraphrase these words at the fresh grave of the great man who has just passed away: If you wish to discover the Jewish masses, to scan the heights achieved by Kasrilevke now as in the past and by the common Jew who lives there and hails from there—read the works of Sholem Aleichem; meet Tevye the Dairyman who, wherever he is, may be pouring out his heart at this very moment in the familiar lament of the psalms over his master and friend, Mr. Sholem

Rabinovitsh, who was so cruelly torn away from him and is no more. (pp. 17-21)

> *Yosef Haim Brenner, "On Sholem Aleichem: The Writer and the Folk," in* Prooftexts, *Vol. 6, No. 1, January, 1986, pp. 17-21.*

MAX ERIK (essay date 1935)

[*In the following excerpt, Erik provides a Marxist critique of Sholom Aleichem's works, focusing on the character Menakhem Mendl.*]

Menakhem-Mendl's letters from Yehupets and those of his wife Sheyne-Sheyndl are undoubtedly Sholem Aleichem's most significant creation, the greatest work in his rich artistic legacy. The central idea of the work—the rejection of the possibility that the petty bourgeoisie will succeed through capitalism; the satire on the bourgeois illusions of the lower middle class; the scathing, demolishing critique of the *luftmentsh* and of his so-called livelihoods—defines the great progressiveness of this work. One of the main requisites of realism, the formation of a type, the embodiment of important social processes within artistic characters, is effected with uncanny power, unmatched in all of Yiddish literature. Artistically, **Menakhem-Mendl** is one of Sholem Aleichem's most complete works, thanks to the exhaustive delineation of the main characters, the exquisite composition, and the careful planning and polishing of each detail. Furthermore, the fearlessness with which the main character is consistently exposed, unmasked, and revealed makes this a masterpiece of critical realism.

The central figure of the work is Menakhem-Mendl. No other type, no other generalized character that Sholem Aleichem created is as clear, as supple, and as full of significant social and psychological content, as the figure of the unfortunate petty merchant from Yehupets. So synthetic is this character of Sholem Aleichem's, that the moment we utter the name Menakhem-Mendl, we immediately associate it with an enormous sum of socio-economic and social-psychological phenomena and trends. So great is the artistry of the synthetic Menakhem-Mendl type, that a whole array of related types and characters, the later creations of both Sholem Aleichem himself and of other writers, appear to us as mere variants on the Menakhem-Mendl theme, though in and of themselves they may be totally independent figures with many new and original features, with social characteristics of an entirely different order. Bergelson's Rubinshteyn in *Arum vogzal (At the Depot)* appears as a gloomy, melancholy version of Menakhem-Mendl. We find variants on Menakhem-Mendl in Babel's heroes of the Odessa stories and in the works of the American revolutionary writer Michael Gold. We see in Pinye of ***Motl, the Son of Peysi the Cantor*** a figure in whom Menakhem-Mendlism has been transferred from the material to the intellectual realm. We treat Levyi Mozgovoyer of Sholem Aleichem's ***Di goldgreber (The Gold Diggers)*** as a Menakhem-Mendl type though he represents a small-town turner. This, despite the fact that Rubinshteyn, Pinye, and Mozgovoyer are completely worthy, from a social and artistic point of view, of being considered independent types. What is at work here is not the poverty or defect of the given character or author but the richness and merit of the Menakhem-Mendl type.

Of the three classicists of bourgeois Yiddish literature, Sholem Aleichem was the one who created the largest number of typified characters. But neither Motl, Shimele Soroker, Leyvi Mozgovoyer nor even Tevye achieved the same degree of effectiveness, clarity, thoroughness, and compactness as Menakhem-Mendl, and this is not because the latter encompassed a larger or more significant sum of social phenomena than, say Tevye. Menakhem-Mendl embodies the stubborn efforts of the lower middle class to make it into the bourgeoisie, to achieve the latter's unfulfilled capitalist dreams. Tevye's character, on the contrary, evokes the *contradictions* of the petty bourgeois existence composed as it is of an "on the one hand and on the other hand" (Marx), a duality which results from being "at the same time both bourgeois and plebeian" (Marx). Tevye too is both bourgeois and laborer, which by definition makes him into a Menakhem-Mendl of sorts. In fact, Sholem Aleichem cleverly hints at this by making Tevye into Menakhem-Mendl's relative. The latter, however, hardly shares any of Tevye's character traits, though he is not entirely free of them; witness his last words which echo those of Tevye: "We have a strong God." Thus Tevye encompasses more of the social essence of the petty bourgeoisie. If, nevertheless, he did not assume the proportions of an unequivocally convincing figure, of a character who can be referred to without any ambiguities in our everyday social discourse, in the common usage of our press, literature and scholarship as was the case with Menakhem-Mendl—then the reason should be sought in the apologetics, the veil of idealization that Sholem Aleichem threw over Tevye, his most beloved character.

In Tevye, Sholem Aleichem glorified the petty bourgeois and portrayed it as an ideal. Through Menakhem-Mendl, Sholem Aleichem *unmasked* the petty bourgeoisie. This contradiction—the glorification and simultaneous unmasking of the same class—runs through all of Sholem Aleichem's writing and arises from the very makeup of the petty bourgeoisie. But in no other work was the exposé so consistent and far-reaching, providing the highest degree of objective recognition, of ideological and artistic authenticity that Sholem Aleichem was able to achieve. This is why **Menakhem-Mendl** is Sholem Aleichem's greatest masterpiece, one of the greatest works in world literature of bourgeois critical realism. This is why Menakhem-Mendl and not Tevye is Sholem Aleichem's crowning achievement. (pp. 23-5)

. . . Yiddish literature before the 1860s, i.e., the literature of the Haskalah, was totally incapable of creating a Menakhem-Mendl type. It could and did record various types of Jewish *luftmentshn*, to the extent that the *luftmentsh*—a petty bourgeois without a set profession; the petty merchant, broker, jobber and matchmaker—was a typical, widespread and characteristic figure in Jewish life, both in the period of declining feudalism and in the later stage of a fully developed capitalist society. Schematic sketches of the *luftmentsh* already appear in the works of the first maskilic writers: in Aksenfeld's Khayim Plut, or in Etinger's Reb Zundl (*Der feter fun Amerike;* "The Uncle from America"). He appears in Mendele and Goldfaden (Hotsmakh, for instance). He is already to be found in Heine's exquisite character Hirsh Hyacinthe, the "lottery collector, operator and assessor" ("Die Beder von Luka"), who contains embryonic traces both of Tevye and Menakhem-Mendl.

The critics immediately noticed that Abramovitsh's Alter Yaknehoz (in *Fishke der krumer; Fishke the Lame*) was a forerunner of sorts of Menakhem-Mendl and that long before the latter proposed a match between two girls, Alter had already done so with two boys. Just as Mendele and Alter exchanged stale prayer books in a game of chance and considered this a "transaction," we find the same motif with Menakhem-Mendl: "So we all made a deal: We swapped estate for estate. That is to say, we gave them the specifications of our estates, and they gave us the specifications of *theirs*" (**"Millions,"** letter 11). These similarities and parallels are indeed noteworthy. Menakhem-Mendl is undoubtedly not only Tevye's blood-relative, as Sholem Aleichem informs us, but also Alter's son, an offspring of the Jewish *luftmentshn* of old who were noticed even by Balzac in his trip through the Ukraine passing through Bardichev to the estates of Madame Hanska and by Taras Shevchenko (cf. the character of the Jewish broker in his novella "A Pleasurable Outing, Not Without a Moral").

As significant as this may be, however, it is far more important to stress the basic difference between Alter Yaknehoz and Menakhem-Mendl. Alter belongs to the period of feudal decline whereas Menakhem-Mendl is only possible and comprehensible in the context of a developed capitalist society. Alter is in search of a meager earning, a piece of bread, and his social behavior is sooner based on the "philosophy" of life of Sheyne-Sheyndl and her mother: "Listen to me, Mendl. Sell everything, cash in now, for the love of God! Did you manage to earn a few rubles? Enough!" (**"London,"** letter 10). Menakhem-Mendl's "philosophy," on the other hand, is best expressed by his passionate outbursts: "I want you to know that I'm riding high; I am right above the clouds; I'm on fire; I'm getting bigger and bigger!" (**"Papers,"** letter 7). What motivates him is not simply the desire for an income, merely eking out a living, but the passion of speculation, for making deals, the sight of "millions upon millions," the exhilaration of being swept up in the capitalist whirlwind. In comparison to the "drunken" fantasizer Menakhem-Mendl, Alter appears sober. Alter is gloomy and embittered, while Menakhem-Mendl is enthusiastic. Even in moments of greatest despair, his sick mind is set into motion once again and he comes up with brand new deals and fantasies.

The *luftmentsh* as a typical phenomenon of the huge masses of the Jewish petty bourgeoisie so ruthlessly confined within the "Pale," is doomed to a despicable, parasitic and still half-starved existence. Thanks to Sholem Aleichem, he has now been brought up to date, to the era of imperialism and of proletarian revolutions. Alter Yaknehoz, after all, sums up a limited social phenomenon. He is less of a contemporary figure than Menakhem-Mendl because he bears the mark of a more limited feudal construct. Capitalism, to a large degree, smashed the fortifications of feudalism. Sholem Aleichem's updating of the *luftmentsh,* therefore, reflects no less than the modernization of the Jewish petty bourgeoisie, its emancipation from a goodly number of elements of national particularity (though many such still remain). Menakhem-Mendl, in other words, is more modern than Alter to the extent that he is less nationally particular and more universal. For Menakhem-Mendl is not only a prime specimen of the Jewish petty bourgeoisie; he embodies basic characteristics of the entire petty bourgeoisie in the era of capitalism. Menakhem-Mendl is the projected type of the Jewish *luftmentsh* and of his livelihoods. This constitutes his *national* makeup. But this is not all and perhaps not the most essential part of him. Menakhem-Mendlism is a more general phenomenon embodied in the character of the unfortunate Yehupets merchant.

. . . Thus, Menakhem-Mendl is relevant not only for understanding the Jewish petty bourgeoisie, but also for understanding basic characteristics of the social psychology and behavior of the petty bourgeoisie as a whole. This is an important and real achievement on the part of Sholem Aleichem. . . .

As we know, Menakhem-Mendl is a stock market speculator, a broker, an insurance agent, a writer and a matchmaker. The whole point of his character, however, is that he is *not* a stock broker, an agent, a writer or a matchmaker. Menakhem-Mendl is not a petty merchant whose luck has failed him; he is no merchant at all. He is a true merchant only in his imagination. He is light years removed from the real stock market, and if the "Small Bourse" is a distorted and vague reflection of the mad convulsions of the "Large" bourse, then Menakhem-Mendl stands on the outskirts even of the "Small" bourse. He is the even vaguer and more distorted reflection of the "hullabaloo of the little people." He is not only a shadow of the stock market, but a shadow of the shadow.

Consider the reasons for Menakhem-Mendl's failure in **"London"** and you will see that they have nothing whatsoever to do with a slip in his calculations, with his betting on the rises ("hausses") say, when the ruble ended up falling drastically ("baisse"). On the contrary, Menakhem-Mendl did in fact play the "baisse"—

> . . . and our ruble has actually fallen to the lower depths, and a terrible baisse has set in! So you're sure to ask what happened to all my baisses and my stallages? The answer is that my baisses aren't baisses and my stallages aren't stallages. . . . Just my luck that I got my affairs entangled with little people who were choked by the first squeeze. (Letter 11)

Menakhem-Mendl failed not because he played the market badly or unluckily. He didn't play at all! He bought up baisses and stallages that never existed to begin with because those who "sold" them to him never even had them in their possession. Actually, the only place he played was in his imagination. He imitated and frenetically parodied the grand spectacle of the great capitalist mongers. He performed all the movements of the play without the play itself. Convulsed in fever and drenched in a cold sweat he worked himself up with no basis in fact, just as one is wont to do in a dream.

Soon enough Menakhem-Mendl takes up partnership with another broker: "In short, we clinched a deal with God's help. That is we agreed to go half-and-half in all transactions: he invests all his estates and I invest all my customers." But once again the point is that the partner has no estates and Menakhem-Mendl has no customers, so that the whole "transaction" exists only in their minds.

Later, Menakhem-Mendl becomes a writer, whose "name appears printed in the paper." But the only place his name actually appears is in the letters to the editor section where he is kindly requested to submit other material. If Menakhem-Mendl does manage to arrange a match, once more he does so in a way that could never be carried out, no matter how talented he was at his job, because such a match can never exist: he matches two girls. And so he begins "to make his presence felt at the Brodskys" which means that in reality his place is somewhere behind the door. If estates are his business, they are not estates but estate inventories. He finds a squire to insure but the squire turns out to be some drunken

"dragon." And if he writes home in a frenzy that "in one shot he's raking in ten thousand pounds, twenty thousand pounds"—there is still no cause for rejoicing, because our "millionaire" must "climb up iron stairs for a half an hour until reaching home, right under the stars, and the window is tiny, as in a prison cell." Thus all his businesses are the product of a hyperactive imagination, the hallucinations of a hungry petty bourgeois at the sumptuous feast of capitalism. And when Menakhem-Mendl finally catches sight of bracelets and a golden watch in the display window, his sick mind reacts as if he had already bought them, as if they were already his.

At this point one might be led to conclude that the ne'er-do-well Yehupets merchant corresponds to the equally unfortunate "knight of the sad countenance," Don Quixote de la Mancha. Are they not both so absorbed in their dream world that they no longer even notice the reality that surrounds them? Does not Menakhem-Mendl also set out on the back of the figurative mare called "business" because Dulcinea in the form of "millions, millions" is luring him from afar? And are not Menakhem-Mendl's "London" and "Yaknehoz" quixotic castles and windmills? Is not Menakhem-Mendl beaten left and right just like Don Quixote, and does he not remain consistently undaunted thanks to his blindly enthusiastic faith in the successes that await him? Yes, Menakhem-Mendl and Don Quixote are both dreamers, maniacs, men of faith. Yet even so they are not identical. Don Quixote is a real knight, more authentic than all the knights of the round table. Menakhem-Mendl, though, is no merchant and no speculator. The tragedy and comedy of Don Quixote arise from his being the *last* knight, the anachronism pursuing his calling at a time when there are no knights left in the world. The ubiquitous world of giants and sorcerers exists only in his mind, while Menakhem-Mendl's dreamed-up world of "millions, millions" actually exists, it glitters all around him and spills over into the summer cottages, horse-drawn carriages, houses that cost "a good 20,000 rubles," jewelry in display windows, "mistresses and chorus girls." Yes, the world of millions indeed exists, not for him, alas, but for the Brodskys. In moments of partial lucidity, Menakhem-Mendl too begins to realize this and he blurts out a half-embittered remark: "For the speculation to succeed, you need only three things: brains, luck and money. Brains I have, praise God, as good as any of the speculators around here. Luck is in the hands of God, and money—in the hands of the Brodskys."

The Don Quixotes are engaged in a rearguard action, trying to infuse new life into a past long since dead. But the Menakhem-Mendls resist with all their might the thought of returning to the moribund Kasrilevkes; they stand dazzled and drunk at the sight of the capitalist *present.* Sheyne-Sheyndl calls her husband back to Kasrilevke seventy times and seventy-seven times he finds some loophole to resist. Even in the train compartment on the way home he suddenly alters his course and unexpectedly ends up in America. While Sheyne-Sheyndl reacts at once and quite vigorously to her husband's letters, the latter hardly reacts at all to the "newsy" tidbits that she provides from Kasrilevke. Menakhem-Mendl has lost interest. Kasrilevke has long since died for him. When and if he does react, it is with scorn and laughter, so as to immediately draw a parallel with Odessa and Yehupets. The cantor of Kasrilevke whom he probably praised to the skies a year before, has now become nothing more than "an old beanpole." He speaks disparagingly of Kasrilevke business: "No merchant could fare any better

Sholom Aleichem at his desk in 1903.

with your Kasrilevke businesses. In our Yehupets, I'll have you know, this type of story could never happen." Kasrilevke bankruptcies have no significance in his eyes: "As for Kopl's bankruptcy which you wrote about, there's no comparing it to one of ours." Similarly, on the subject of Kasrilevke love affairs: "As for the story of Leyvi Moyshe-Mende's son who took Libe's daughter in marriage—it doesn't even raise an eyebrow." He cannot conceive of his future other than in terms of the big city and his ideal is the life-style of a parvenu, the life of a Shimele Soroker after winning the 200,000 ruble jackpot.

Thus Menakhem-Mendl is a compressed, highly trenchant expression of the *illusoriness* of the petty bourgeois existence under capitalism; a terribly bitter and decisive exposé of his ostensible independence and self-determination; a ravaging critique of those tens of thousands of petty bourgeois who so faithfully deposit their meager earnings in savings accounts, there to be exploited at will by the capitalist state and the power bourgeoisie; of the little men like Menakhem-Mendl who are brutally robbed and stripped naked at any given moment, especially in times of crisis, by the great capitalist moguls. . . . In short, *Menakhem-Mendl* is a satire on the whole ill-fated game played by the devil capitalism with the petty bourgeoisie.

Of course there are sober moments of resignation, when Menakhem-Mendl reads the verdict on the petty bourgeoisie:

"A hundred times a day I curse the day I was born. Better to have broken both my legs before I came to Odessa, where a human being counts for nothing" (**"London,"** letter 11). Or: "I wish to heaven the good Lord would send me a miracle: a gang of robbers to kill me, or I should just drop dead in the middle of the street because, my dearest wife, I can't stand it any longer!" (**"Papers,"** letter 11). Or the last note sounded in **"Millions"** which is incidentally the strongest:

> Everyone is making a lot of noise—I alone have to
> stand apart and watch the whole world doing busi-
> ness and making money, while I make no headway,
> as if I were an outsider. I can see millions in front
> of my eyes—but I cannot touch them. . . . Always
> I seem to be on the other side of the fence. . . .
> (Letter 23).

Don Quixote never experiences such moments of sobriety (if we disregard the moralistic final chapter where he repents his sins). He is deeply shaken by his defeat in open combat, a duel conducted according to all the rules of the knightly code, but even then he can only conclude that "Dulcinea of Tonos is the most beautiful damsel in the world and I—the most unfortunate knight on earth. . . ."

Yes, Menakhem-Mendl is a caricature of a merchant rather than a real merchant, not a speculator but a caricature thereof. Menakhem-Mendlism is a parody of capitalism. There can be no caricature without hyperbole and distortion. The success and effectiveness of the caricature, however, depends less on the hyperbole than its similarity to the model. A truly artistic caricature reflects, or rather magnifies, actual traits of the model itself. Thus, Menakhem-Mendl is not only a satire on the petty bourgeois who comes crawling to the bourgeoisie and is dazzled by its beauty, but also an exposé of actual traits of the entire capitalist system, of those traits of irrationalism, parasitism, expropriation and theft that so characterize the bourgeoisie during the entire course of its history.

Menakhem-Mendl is not interested in the means of production in the economy, in the consumer designation of the given article—he only sees the market value, the profit margin and the speculator's risk bound up with each item. No wonder, then, that from his petty deals in "wheat, grains, wool, flour, salt, feathers, raisins, sacks, herring," he rapidly switches to the more abstract "finer matter, London, which is sold by word alone and you never get to see it."

. . . Menakhem-Mendl embodies yet another type of capitalistic trait in his desire for a bad harvest:

> God grant that there is no rain at all so that the beetles can gorge themselves and get sick to the stomach on beets, because if there are no beets, there won't be any sugar, and where there's no sugar, it's worth its weight in gold—then speculators can do business, brokers can earn money, with me in the middle. (**"Millions,"** letter 3)

. . . Herein lies the third and last generalization implied by the character of Menakhem-Mendl. The first and most extrinsic generalization was Menakhem-Mendl as a satire on the Jewish *luftmentsh,* on the petty Jewish merchant, broker, matchmaker and semi-intellectual. Within this national framework, a more universal synthesis emerges—the figure of the petty bourgeois who is the victim of capitalist illusions, of self-deception. In the backdrop, however, there appears the ugly spectrum of a decaying and crumbling capitalism that is no longer in control of the vast, modern means of production and is capable only of fruitless adventures and speculations. . . . (pp. 28-34)

> *Max Erik, " 'Menakhem-Mendl': A Marxist Critique," in* Prooftexts, *Vol. 6, No. 1, January, 1986, pp. 23-39.*

ISAAC ROSENFELD (essay date 1946)

[*Rosenfeld was an American critic and fiction writer. Praised for the lucidity and directness of his writing, Rosenfeld did not consider literature a specialist's subject. He subscribed to no particular school of thought in his criticism and judged writers simply on their feeling for and knowledge of life. Yiddish language and culture were lifelong interests for him, and in addition to writing fables and stories in Yiddish, Rosenfeld was one of the first writers to use translated Yiddish idioms in his English writing. In the following review of* The Old Country, *a collection of Sholom Aleichem's stories translated by Julius and Frances Butwin, Rosenfeld praises the subtlety of Sholom Aleichem's use of Yiddish and emphasizes the impossibility of adequately translating it.*]

It is not the Butwins' fault that their translation of twenty-seven of the better known and loved of Sholom Aleichem's three hundred stories falls so far short of the original Yiddish. The quality of Sholom Aleichem's Yiddish, for reasons that I shall try to indicate, is well-nigh incommunicable. Besides, whatever the defects of this translation, its mere existence

calls for gratitude: this is the first time, as far as I know, that even such a small part of Sholom Aleichem's great work has been made available to the English-speaking world.

What, after all, is translation? It is the fault of our literary pragmatism that we so seldom ask this question. For ordinary purposes it is enough to say that translation is the finding of word combinations in one language to stand for word combinations in another. But this will not do as a definition. First of all, it begs the question in supposing that we already know what language is; the fact is that an important property of language is disclosed only in translation. What this property is, is made clear by the second shortcoming of the usual notion of translation, the assumption that the language of literature is wholly devoted to communication. Again, the fact is otherwise, for writing, even in the strictest sense of naturalism, necessarily contains, if it is art at all, an irreducible element of expression. Expression is what the translator must trust to more than the luck or skill of his sense of poetry to re-create in his own language. The conveying of the expression of one language in the words of another ultimately depends on the congruence of separate cultures, philosophies and ways of life. The translator, in an age when the internationalization of culture is an absolute imperative, is the philosopher *par excellence.* The entities with which he deals are paramount in metaphysics, recalling its simplest, but most difficult, its first, but most neglected, task: our need to know one another.

It is in this expanded sense of "translation" that the translation of Sholom Aleichem is such a hard, hopeless, even tragic enterprise. There have been some successful translations from the Yiddish—Sholem Asch and I. J. Singer are excellent examples; but whereas the works of these authors, whether they are concerned with the origins of Christianity or the working-class revolution, involve familiar themes of Western history, Sholom Aleichem's work is almost deliberately at cross purposes with English and with the history the language subsumes. His idioms are entirely of another world (illuminated, but not "translated" for us in Maurice Samuel's brilliant *World of Sholom Aleichem*); they are of a Yiddish whose survival in the form that Sholom Aleichem made use of was no less remarkable than the survival of the people who spoke it, and one of their greatest accomplishments.

Language itself, the mere prose of daily life, is already the greatest poetry. The extraordinary poetic of Sholom Aleichem's Yiddish is its consciousness of what is peculiarly Jewish in existence. The language has a facility for singling out the most disparate and incongruous objects and catching precisely that quality wherein they reflect the destiny of the Jews. A turn of phrase, an additional syllable, and what would have been, as in any other language, a report of experience, becomes in Yiddish a comment on Jewish experience, say a reference to Diaspora, a veiled reminder to the Lord of the promise of deliverance and perhaps an expression of despair at its coming. The liberal sprinkling of Hebrew performs in an inverse way the same function that the presence of "foreign" words performs in the secularization and internationalization of the language: Hebrew, as the language, historically, of the true home and the faithful tradition, lends poignancy to the half-tones of exile, and an incongruity that mirrors in its humor the whole incongruity of Jewish dispersal. When Tevyeh the Dairyman, for example, refers to his wretched horse by the Hebrew word *sus,* he takes advantage of a usage available only in Yiddish to transpose the objects of the familiar world into a context equally familiar to the speaker but unrelated to his immediate concerns, so that the latter are transcended, viewed historically and implicitly judged. The same horse that drags Tevyeh's wagon along carries us back thousands of years. Yiddish is a kind of consciousness in verbal form, call it historical paranoia or call it truly mystical, that interprets the whole creation in terms of a people's deepest experience and intuition.

Sholom Aleichem's language is full of the intimate quality of the life he loved and described so well. For this life, as for his specifically surcharged words, there is no equivalent in any other life or language. But to the extent that transmission is possible under such inauspicious circumstances, the essence of his work communicates itself concretely in portrayals of the Jewish character which is so faithfully rendered that it must, in some poetic part, have been created for his people by the author.

Take Tevyeh the Dairyman. His closest Western cousin is perhaps Sancho Panza. There is the same earthiness in both of them, the same familiarity with misfortune, the same wisdom expressing itself in proverbs and misquotations. But Tevyeh is a Sancho without Don Quixote, unless Tevyeh's Knight is God Himself. Tevyeh is moved by God's will as Sancho by his mad master's; it is to God that Tevyeh complains, to God that Tevyeh looks for help, and it is God who is the author of Tevyeh's misfortunes. But there is parity between Sancho and Don Quixote in so far as they are the two faces of the same coin, and the space between earthbound reason and ridiculous faith that divides them is also the one that joins them. Don Quixote's faith is superior in its madness precisely because it does not fear the ridicule it was doomed to provoke. But how does God come to be mentioned in the same breath with ridicule, or how can there be parity between God and Tevyeh unless the dairyman has something of the divine in him? It is precisely this conclusion, that Tevyeh has something of the divine, which is demanded by the effort to understand the dairyman and his brothers. God may well fear his ridicule, or at least his wit as it expresses itself in prayer and complaint; and, though it is nowhere suggested, for Tevyeh is a pious Jew who would never utter such blasphemy, the possibility remains open, when one considers the life that God has ordained for Tevyeh and his people, that there is a streak of madness in Him. Moreover, Tevyeh, like Sancho, when he rides his spirited reason, becomes his own Don Quixote; he is full of a ridiculous majesty which brings him closer than ever to his Master.

Tevyeh approaches the divine first of all in his irony which—no other word or degree for it—is absolute. (The English translation misses most of it.) It is present in every sentence he speaks, in every phrase and word, its extreme development being the measure of his moral courage. So highly developed is it, and so far pushed past all frontiers of ordinary caution, retraction or qualification in God's favor, that it becomes something mystical, and it is no wonder that Tevyeh's worship, conducted always in the ironical mode, attains the immediacy of the direct vision and communion. It is irony that links Tevyeh with God, that brings together the patient and the author of suffering.

The chief cause and acutest form of suffering in the Jewish Pale was poverty. But the poverty of the Jews, like the Yiddish language, was itself a symbol and a kind of symbolism; in its final extension it was a sign, in the true religious sense, of God's ordination of the world. Deprivation of material

means was the symbolic counterpart of the Jews' historical deprivation; they owned little of the world, not even so much as a home in it, and the continual struggle for food was like the unbroken prayer for deliverance. The Jews owned little of the world, but their hunger was the true dimension of all their longing, and their disappointment, which need not even have been felt inwardly, so close to the quick were its external provocations, was the clue to their great expectation—for were they not the Chosen People? Yet Tevyeh says we were chosen to suffer—it is for this that the world envies us. The irony here does not destroy the bond between man and God. The strain draws it tighter and lends pride to the perceptions of the poor—for now they know with Whom they are struggling. It is in poverty that man turns to God and in poverty that he turns away from Him, mistrusting Providence, or knowing it all too well. And yet his poverty is his strength and his blessing, it is the source of the irony that enables him to endure his faith in God, and of that great, tenacious will to life which, even if only an ironic victory is possible, at the cost of misery and misfortune, nevertheless chooses irony for the sake of triumph. It is in this faith, which is also faith in themselves, that the Jews have triumphed, and that they have revealed themselves to be still a warlike tribe. Sholom Aleichem's poor dairymen and tailors, shopkeepers, teachers, hapless speculators, *luftmenschen* and *shlimazolim* are our foremost warriors. They have fought the longest and costliest war in history—the war, simply, with history itself.

It is this, poverty as richness, as the rarest symbolic blessing, which ultimately proves to be untranslatable and which underlies the particular failures of the English phrase to do justice to the original. When Tevyeh says *"ligen in der erd un backen bagel"* to express destitution ("To lie in the ground and bake doughnuts")—not that bagel, strictly speaking, are doughnuts, or that *"ligen in der erd"* means lie *in* the ground or lie *on* the ground—it has a sense compounded of both, as when we speak lightly of a living death; very wisely the translators did not attempt to render this phrase in English—when Tevyeh speaks in this manner he shows a veteran contempt for poverty and proclaims his mastery over it. Likewise, when a character in the story **"Hannukah Money"** is called a *"far-shleppte krenk"* (a "chronic ailment," wildly mistranslated here as a sentence that uses the word "zany," as if the Jews of Kasrilevky had already reached Broadway) and thereby set down with the power and finality of an imperious gesture, we must assume something of Jewish history to know how suffering can impart mastery of the world. . . . Such are the clues, lost in a lost culture, to the blessings of poverty. Its ultimate beatitude in Chassidism is truly ineffable.

Insights such as these gave Sholom Aleichem, the humorist and folk-poet, also a philosopher's stature, so well did he know the confluence of personality and God. He defined a peculiar intellectual and spiritual province of the Jews, revealing the hidden vitality of their religion and the historical viability of their culture. It is a province which is lost to the majority of us today, who know nothing of such blessings, even as that which was once our world, with Kasrilevky its Jerusalem, was lost to the world that engulfed and destroyed it. (pp. 81-3)

Isaac Rosenfeld, "The Blessings of Poverty," in The New Republic, *Vol. 115, No. 3, July 22, 1946, pp. 81-3.*

WILLIAM BARRETT (essay date 1946)

[*Barrett is an American philosopher, literary critic, and social thinker. During the 1940s and 1950s, he was an associate editor of* Partisan Review, *which was a leading forum in America for socialist political thought and modernist experimentalism in the arts. His best known work,* Irrational Man *(1958), is a highly regarded study of the literary and philosophical tradition of existentialism. This work, along with the more recent* Illusion of Technique *(1978), charts the philosophical reaction to the "deranged rationality" of modern analytical thought. In the following essay, Barrett discusses Sholom Aleichem's Jewish irony from a Gentile perspective.*]

It is time the Gentile took careful notice of Sholom Aleichem. And why not? Where is it written in the Talmud that a Gentile should not write about Sholom Aleichem? And, on the other hand, does not the Bible say: "The stranger may see new things in the house?" Or, as someone in Kasrilevka remarked when the first news arrived that a certain Jewish Captain Dreyfus had been accused in France of selling his country's secrets: "What won't a Jew do these days to earn a living?" And not only a Jew.

Of course, this involves limitations: Reading *The Old Country* . . . I cannot check the translation point by point, though it seems to me it must be a very good one, for I can continually guess behind the English the intonation and turn of phrase (on which so much in Sholom Aleichem depends) of the original.

Nor am I able to speak authoritatively about the selection of stories, beyond saying that the whole volume maintains a consistently satisfying level throughout. Besides my own inference, however, I have the word of friends that the editors and translators, Julius and Frances Butwin, have done a remarkably good job: certainly they have turned out a book that can delight and absorb the English reader who does not know any Yiddish at all. But perhaps this has to be qualified somewhat: I cannot conceive, for example, of a highly literate Gentile who has lived all his life in rural Kansas picking up this book and seeing its qualities for what they are. To read Sholom Aleichem one must have at least some direct and intimate acquaintance with Jewish people, Jewish traits, and the Jewish mind. And perhaps only a Jew who has lived within the Russian or Polish Pale will extract the maximum of pathos and irony from these stories.

This last perhaps best defines the sense in which Sholom Aleichem is to be taken as an example of folk literature. Examples of folk literature in another sense would be the tales of the brothers Grimm or of Hans Christian Andersen: products of the folk itself, of its ancestral and unconscious mythopoeic wisdom. On the other hand, we have the folk or peasantry treated by such writers as Verga and Silone in Italy, and from time to time by various masters of French fiction. The place of Sholom Aleichem as a folk writer is somewhere between these two groups: he is certainly, in any case, an example of folk writing in a more authentic sense than Verga or Silone. For with Sholom Aleichem there is a direct relation between the writer and his audience. We do not meet here a self-conscious writer, obsessed with problems of his art or the tradition into which his works are to be inserted. For the most part the writer seems to be transcribing directly the incidents and lives that were common knowledge and conversation in the communities within the Pale. *He is directly expressing a people to itself*—such is the essential folk quality of Sholom Aleichem.

This is the reason why, in speaking of Sholom Aleichem, one tends to pass directly from the writer to his material: the life of the Jew that he represents; why, for example, Mr. Maurice Samuel's excellent book is entitled *The World of Sholom Aleichem* rather than anything else which would have to do with the personality or self-development of the writer. Now the most attractive and famous characteristic of Yiddish life within the Pale is its irony; and it is in his mastery of irony that Sholom Aleichem achieves his distinctive quality and greatness as a humorist. In other respects the life he represents is extremely narrow and even impoverished for the creative novelist. Within the Pale there are no great ranges of class or status, which have traditionally provided the most exciting opportunities for Western novelists. But this narrowness carries the great virtue of its defect: the Jews face each other more nakedly, so to speak, and they develop their irony face to face with each other. Hence too the particular rudeness of the Jew (which the anti-Semite has seized upon without ever understanding), expressed in Sholom Aleichem by the amazing and comic curses and imprecations the characters address to each other from time to time; but by being so vocal, this violence is also sublimated, and does not appear in the drunken physical forms of the Russian peasantry surrounding the Jewish communities. Moreover, this Old-Country rudeness is not to be confused with the forms it takes in the New World, where it is already permeated (as is the case with all other immigrant peoples in New York) by the violence of American life. Such rudeness is only the other side of honesty: the Gentile, as Delmore Schwartz says, lives by wearing a mask, the Jew by taking one off—a profound observation to which I shall return in a minute.

The depth and wisdom of Jewish irony and Jewish humor arise from their fundamentally religious source. A comparison with the peasant humor in Silone is instructive at this point: the humor of the Italian peasant is often sharp and shrewd, but it has a quality of dumb earthy pathos, and it is significant that Silone often makes the peasants be their wittiest when they are acting stupid before the city officials and bureaucrats. Jewish irony is immensely more self-conscious because the Jew is aware that the greatest joke of all is that he, a Jew, in his particular conditions of life, should even attempt a joke. He, as a Jew, has the Promise, yet he lives meanwhile in the Pale. The contrast between that Promise and his actual life is so extraordinary that he must look at his *total existence* with irony: Ach! what a joke that a Jew should even try to make a joke! The tension between these two is necessary for this irony: if he lost his belief in the Promise, irony would no longer be possible, but only desperation, and in the end, extinction.

Thus it seems to me a mistake (though I speak, of course, from limited knowledge) to consider the theological irony expressed by Sholom Aleichem's people as a sign of incipient disbelief; if incipient, this is still certainly miles away from actual disbelief. Usually, in fact, the irony conveys a quite sound theology. There is, for example, the incident (unfortunately not included in this collection) of the Jew on Yom Kippur in the synagogue who wearily exclaims: "I'm tired of confessing my sins, why doesn't God confess some of his?" The irony exists here only so long as no disbelief or blasphemy is understood. And the point expressed is also a very serious one for any believer. It must not be forgotten (and if we were inclined to forget it, Tevye the Milkman, who is one of Sholom Aleichem's best theologians, would probably remind us) that on the Day of Judgment God also justifies himself; and he has many things to explain to us, many things . . . *bien sur, il en aura beaucoup.*

The very particularism of Jewish religion reinforces and develops Jewish irony in another respect too. Religion must regulate every action of life, in order that life may be sanctioned as separate from the alien body in the midst of which the Jew is condemned to wander. But every action, as soon as it is touched upon by the Law, becomes the subject of discussion and casuistry: it comes into relation with the word. All aspects of life thus become vocal, and it is from this ubiquity of language and talk that Sholom Aleichem draws his main strength. In one of the stories the narrator is able to elicit from the Russian peasant who is driving him only a grunted "uh-uh" in answer to all his questions, and he comments:

> I imagined what it would have been like if this were a Jew driving the sleigh. He would have told me not only where the inn was, but who ran it, what his name was, how many children he had, how much rent he paid, what he got out of it, how long he had been there, who had been there before him—in short, everything. We are a strange people, we Jews.

The possession of language, Aristotle says, is what sets man off from the beast; and to the degree that everything in life has been systematically talked over, life itself becomes more self-conscious, and therefore more human. Obviously too, the writer in a community where everything is talked about and known—the man's name, his children, rent, etc.—has an immense advantage: he does not have to scratch his head very hard for material.

The conditions of the Pale, and the particularism of his religion, conspire to separate the Jew from the soil and the larger social whole in which he lives. However this may impoverish the total range of his imaginative life, it has nevertheless immense advantages as a preparation for the modern world: the Jew is not easily addicted to the myths of soil and blood. This Russian driver above, we must remember, undoubtedly spoke of the Tsar as "Little Father," believing himself sincerely a child before such authority; and this mysticism of the existing order and authority is also shared by the peasantries of the West. One story in this collection, **"Hodel,"** deals with a young Jew who is sent away—obviously to Siberia—for political activity. Sholom Aleichem does not follow him into the Russian world beyond the Pale, but we, who are aware of that outside world, cannot help being moved in a manner probably uncalculated by the author, remembering that the élite among Russian political intellectuals were in a great percentage Jews. The Pale had not been a very bad preparation for them. And one more example to drive home the point: there is the remark made by Henry Adams about the Dreyfus Affair, that even if Dreyfus were not guilty, he should accept the verdict of the military court for the honor of the French army and the French nation. Alas, the Jew was stubborn and did not respond like a peasant sheep to this myth of the Nation; he, the particularist in religion, was committed to a more universal commandment: truth.

The difference between Jew and Gentile does not engage Sholom Aleichem, since he moves solely within the Jewish world, but it is expressed—though incidentally and perhaps there too even a little unconsciously—by a greater Jewish writer than Sholom Aleichem, Marcel Proust, in those pages of his novel where he is treating of the repercussions of the Dreyfus case in the circle of the Guermantes. The Guermantes are the beautiful race in whom Proust feels the mysterious presence of the blood: their past perpetually suggests to him the beauties of medieval churches and stained glass; but they are also still the boar-hunting feudal chivalry with all its cruelties and *paganism.* And despite the extent of his assimilation, his acceptance by the aristocracy and the Jockey Club, we are led to sense the profound degree to which Swann (who, one suspects, becomes here the vehicle of Proust's own experiences as a Jew in the Parisian *haut monde*) is separated from the Guermantes—from their beauties and cruelties both—as a superior spiritual being.

The point, in short, that I am laboring to make—and it is one so profoundly ironical that one might almost say that History itself has played a stroke of Jewish irony—is simply that the very particularism and alienation of the Jew have rendered him the universal norm for intellectual life in the modern world. The man who would live an intellectual or spiritual life is driven by modern society into a corner: here in his particular Pale, he may not have the Promise or the Law, but he is nevertheless bound by the law of his own obligations, and he too had better develop an inclusive irony towards the powers that be or go under. If I may be permitted one more example, I should like to point out that in James Joyce's *Ulysses* the spiritual father of Stephen Dedalus (who is Joyce himself) is the Jew, Leopold Bloom. Joyce's imagination is always anchored to a massive and bedrock literalness—in this respect he is the most traditional, even medieval or Dantesque, of modern writers—and I do not see any reason for not taking him at his literal word here. And I think it must be apparent to the reader by this time that the present writer feels himself more attached to these stories of Sholom Aleichem than to any folk tales of native American or Irish source—which should normally, one supposes, be where he locates his tradition, if he had one.

Obviously, I have been led here beyond the immediate subject of Sholom Aleichem himself, but the digression appears to me inevitable. If the Jew had not entered the life of the West—as an extraordinary contributor to human culture and as the object of unparalleled mass-persecution—we should read Sholom Aleichem only as a highly amusing, but also narrow, folk writer. But in fact we do read him for more, for what he reveals about a destiny that was to be played out outside the Pale. If Sigmund Freud strikes us as a Jewish figure, in a profound way, it is not simply because he himself has acknowledged on several occasions what he owed to being a Jew, or because he fully exhibits his liking for Jewish jokes in his book on wit. He tells somewhere the story of a private conversation in which the great French psychologist, Charcot, remarks of a neurotic woman patient: *"En ces cas, c'est toujours la chose genitale, toujours, toujours, toujours"* ["In these cases, it is always the genital thing—always, always, always"]. If he knew this, comments Freud, why did he not ever say it in public? But the Gentile, to quote again, lives by wearing a mask, the Jew by taking it off. The Gentile must be genteel—the gentility of the Gentile. To be thoroughly genteel involves an inordinate amount of polite falsehood; presently one becomes assimilated to the ritual of falsehood and one is playing a role—practising "bad faith," as Jean-Paul Sartre would say. Freud, the Jew, takes off the mask—and in public; and the genteel tradition has not yet forgiven him for it. (They never wear masks in the Pale. Who but a *nogid* could afford one?) And if we take the following casual passage from Freud:

Perhaps, then, you . . . will fall back upon the argument that it is surely very improbable that we ought to concede so large a part in the human constitution to what is evil. But do your own experiences justify you in this statement? I will say nothing of how you may appear in your own eyes, but have you met with so much good will in your superiors and rivals, so much chivalry in your enemies and so little envy amongst your acquaintances, that you feel it incumbent on you to protest against the part played by egotistic baseness in human nature?

we have only to translate it suitably with the appropriate winks, shrugs, intonations, and quotations of scripture in order to have a piece of truthful cynicism that could come from the mouth of one of Sholom Aleichem's characters.

No doubt, as Maurice Samuel has pointed out, the world of Sholom Aleichem was teetering, even when he wrote, on the brink of dissolution: the Jews of the Pale, habituated as they were to suffering and persecution, could hardly have imagined the dark bloody whirlwind of Hitler, the Nazis, and the extermination camps of World War II. But if this world has largely vanished, through slaughter or immigration, there is still on this side of the Atlantic an extraordinary persistence of some of the old patterns: for where he is not engaged in trying to exterminate the Jew, the Gentile is still attempting to push him back, in the university world and elsewhere, into some *numerus clausus,* which is only a more *genteel* form of the Pale. And immediately the old stories arise again.

For example, let me tell you, Mr. Sholom Aleichem, the story of the ten Jews on the *Harvard Law Review.* . . . (pp. 208-11)

> William Barrett, "The Promise and the Pale: A Gentile View of Jewish Irony," in Commentary, Vol. 2, No. 3, September, 1946, pp. 208-11.

A. A. ROBACK (essay date 1948)

[*Roback was a prominent American psychologist and a scholar of folk literature. The author and editor of both scientific and literary works, he founded and organized the Harvard University Library's collection of Yiddish literature. In the following excerpt, he suggests that sympathy at the expense of logic characterizes the Jewish characters in Sholom Aleichem's stories and provides the basis for much of their humor.*]

It will sound novel to many a reader, but the key to humor is largely logical. Sholom Aleichem's types and characters, in their highly subjective coloring, constantly violate the rules of sound reasoning; and that accounts to a large extent for their trials and tribulations. Naïve and childlike in their simplicity, they cannot see the other's standpoint except through actual suffering, or else empathy. They will exaggerate, but by the same token they will underrate their own services, as when Tevyeh suggests three roubles as his reward for bringing the lost rich women to safety. They will take things for granted without warrant, they will count chickens before they are hatched, and will commit regularly the chief fallacies known to every student of elementary logic. Rules do not appeal to them; for they are creatures of the heart. They attribute their own thoughts to their interlocutors, hence the frequent "as you would say." The woman of **"Dos Teppel"** constantly implies that the rabbi is voicing some opinion, where in fact he does not open his mouth once.

In a class in logic last winter, in order to illustrate a few com-

mon fallacies, I presented some illustrations from Sholom Aleichem. I was astonished to find that the students—who, with but few exceptions, were Gentile—reacted hilariously to what they, unaware of the source of the material, considered to be jokes. The father of the young man who has been bothered by the draft board holds the chaplain up to ridicule because of his own ignorance regarding the translation of names. The woman of **"Dos Teppel"** scoffs at the physician who asks her what her husband died of, as if one could die of anything but death, that is, the fact that the "years gave out." In **"Kasrilevker Tramvay,"** the penniless woman can't pay her own fare, nevertheless intercedes for another who is asked to get off because she is in a like fix. She cannot see any justice in putting off an obscure pauper, while an equally impecunious passenger whose father happens to be known to the conductor is allowed to stay on. Here there is a conflict between *realistic logic,* the logic of commerce and politics, and *humanistic logic,* which considers the emergency only. When the conductor asks, "Do you suppose then that I would drive you for nothing?" the woman indignantly replies. "What do you mean: you would drive me? The tramway is taking me, not you. What if another person is on, will it damage the seat? Do you suppose I don't remember you when you were only a teacher's assistant, even if you have put on a brass button and call yourself conductor?" Of course the whole argument is beside the point (*ignoratio elenchi* is the technical term), but that is the logic of the villager, the underdog, the naïve peasant, the yokel.

Nearly all of Sholom Aleichem's monologues are replete with such fallacies: and they really constitute the essence of the humor we laugh at. In **"Kasrilevker Srayfes"** one of the onlookers who enjoys the fire suggests that the house must have been well insured. "What proof is there?" asks the more logical onlooker. "Because if it were not insured, it wouldn't burn," the other impatiently replies. "A house doesn't burn all by itself"—a pure fallacy known as *petitio principii* or begging the question. The famous threefold defense, in **"Dos Teppel"** viz., that in the first place, the pot was returned whole; secondly, that it was chipped when borrowed; and thirdly, that no pot was borrowed, anyway, and "Don't bother me," has become stock repartee in polemic writings.

It is because the average underdog has a short-range logic that he is usually an underdog. Charlie Chaplin of the silent movies would easily fit into the framework of Sholom Aleichem's types. He banks on the immediate future and therefore leaves out of account the probable, if not absolutely certain, consequences, attributing the results to tough luck, a quip of fate, or the will of God.

Many of these "surds," as I have called them in my *Psychology of Common Sense,* grow bitter and misanthropic. Tevyeh belongs to the cheerful crowd, taking refuge in a philosophy which received its crystallized form in Leibniz and Hegel, but being Tevyeh and not a German philosopher, his optimism is not unalloyed. He puts his faith in God's omniscience and omnipotence, but doubts his vaunted benevolence when he tells his listener:

> A level-headed person must not take things to heart, for he should understand that things are as they should be; because if they were to be otherwise, they would not have come out as they did. You just leave it to God, as the Psalms say, and He will see to it that you are sunk good and proper, and

at the same time you'll thank your stars that it wasn't worse.

To the educated and logical person, this might sound like sacrilege. Not to Tevyeh, who adjusts himself to everything, including the whims of God, who will make you suffer and like it. The little man, who in various capacities is the hero of Sholom Aleichem's stories, can never be detached or recognize distance. Realistic logic dictates that the rules cannot be enforced under certain conditions. The more or less primitive mind sees no distinctions. This attitude reaches its acme in the alleged exclamation of the illiterate woman who kept appealing for help to God in the most fervent tones until, exhausted, she interpolated as an aside, "O Lordy dear, may you have as much strength to live as I have to cry to you." The incongruity or virtual blasphemy does not occur to this woman.

Tevyeh is, of course, on a much higher plane, but he, too, overlooks the fold for the wrinkle, and slides into verbal grooves when the situation requires a re-wording. We are amused when one of Sholom Aleichem's characters, referring to his son, remarks, "Now you would think, God forbid, that he is a well boy." Naturally, we are nonplussed by this malapropism. But all this father can think of is that being hale and hearty is a great liability when it is a question of avoiding the draft; and what determines the utterance of the phylacterism "God forbid" (*cholillch*) is the momentary emotional reaction. He does not stop to consider what the effect would be on his speechless interlocutor in the particular monologue.

The Japanese are taught an entirely different social approach. They must learn—and in most cases they go to the same extreme in the opposite direction—to completely squelch their own emotion in face of the possible embarrassment or inconvenience of those in their presence. Needless to say that such an unnatural condition is bound to cause distress, *e.g.,* when a mother whose beautiful child was killed in an accident tells her consolers with a smile that the miserable child was unworthy of their honored attention.

Both opposite attitudes are out of kilter, but the one is at least genuine and human, even if the subjective weakness protrudes enough to tickle our funny-bone. The other is amusing in a grotesque manner. The first gives free rein to the emotions; the other inhibits them completely in order to meet a social requirement. Tevyeh, verbal and subjective as he is in other respects (for he appears to have a fine conceit of himself, always alluding to his rhetorical aptitude), nevertheless is restrained in recounting the extent of his misfortunes. (pp. 21-3)

Fundamentally, Sholom Aleichem was an observer, although his observations must have been expanded and blended through his great resourcefulness and ingenuity. For, as I wrote in my *Story of Yiddish Literature* . . . :

> Sholom Aleichem, let us bear in mind, was not, as many of his critics supposed, preoccupying himself with *bagatelles.* If he constantly moves in a sphere of the commonplace, he certainly does not depict it in any commonplace or banal manner, but illuminates it in all its quirks and nuances. It becomes, accordingly, a sociopsychological pattern which discloses far more than is superficially in evidence to those who just guffaw at the ineptitudes of his impractical heroes.

> These psychological subtleties are not after-

thoughts on the part of the writer, but issue from the situation as a whole, like overtones, which constitute the timbre of the musical sounds.

(p. 26)

A. A. Roback, "The Humor of Sholom Aleichem," in Sholom Aleichem Panorama, *edited by Melech Grafstein, The Jewish Observer, 1948, pp. 20-6.*

IRVING HOWE (essay date 1952)

[*A longtime editor of the leftist magazine* Dissent *and a regular contributor to the* New Republic, *Howe is one of America's most highly respected literary critics and social historians. He has been a socialist since the 1930s, and his criticism is frequently informed by a liberal social viewpoint. Howe is widely praised for what F. R. Dulles has termed his "knowledgeable understanding, critical acumen and forthright candor." Howe has written: "My work has fallen into two fields: social history and literary criticism. I have tried to strike a balance between the social and the literary: to fructify one with the other; yet not to confuse one with the other. Though I believe in the social approach to literature, it seems to me peculiarly open to misuse; it requires particular delicacy and care." In the following excerpt, Howe praises the sense of human goodness in Sholom Aleichem's works and underscores the need to make his work more available to those who do not read Yiddish.*]

We live in a time when the literature most valued by serious people is likely to be intense, recalcitrant, and extreme; when the novel is periodically combed for images of catastrophe; and the possibilities of life seem available only through ultimates, prophecies, and last judgments. Formally we accord Dostoevsky and Tolstoy equal honor but in our hearts we feel closer to Dostoevsky; his seems the true voice of crisis, and we know ourselves to be creatures of crisis. I myself join in this response, and I believe it to be inevitable to our age.

Yet it would be good if we could also celebrate another kind of literature: the kind that does *not* confront the harsh finalities of experience, or strip each act to its bare motive, or flood us with anguish over the irrevocability of death. In such writers as Turgeniev, Chekhov, Silone, Sherwood Anderson at his rare best, and Sholom Aleichem at his frequent best, there is a mature restraint from the extremes of vision, a readiness to value those milder virtues which can only cause impatience in many modern minds. These writers—let me call them the writers of sweetness—do not assume evil to be the last word about man, and they seem to add: even if it is the last word there are others to be declared before we reach it. They do not condescend before the ordinary, or scorn the domestic affections, or suppose friendliness to be mere bourgeois cant; and perhaps because of these very virtues, they seldom strike us among the greatest writers. But they are often among the most tolerable: one can live with Chekhov in a way that is difficult with Dostoevsky, and one can love Silone with a warmth impossible to feel for D. H. Lawrence.

Sweetness is a quality our age suspects; and "sweetness and light" now seems a phrase of faint ridicule, calling to mind a genteel academicism, a cultivated futility. But when Matthew Arnold used the phrase he was hardly seeking a warrant for complacence; he knew that the quality of sweetness need not preclude the most stringent moral and social realism.

The little I know about Yiddish literature strengthens my confidence in these remarks. Here is a literature which explored poverty as few others have, which studied the misery of this life as intensely as the French have studied love—many a Yiddish writer could speak as an expert on the subject of hunger. But while I do not wish to suggest that Yiddish literature has been without its voices of desperation and violence, I find myself repeatedly moved by the tone of love—a tone that is the most certain register of moral poise—with which such masters as Peretz and Sholom Aleichem faced the grimmest facts about ghetto life. Blinking nothing, they could accept everything.

Why should this be so? Not, I think, because of any special virtues in Jewish life or character; nor even because of the distinctive religious cast of the ghetto. When Mendele wrote his tribute to the compressibility of the Jewish stomach, and Sholom Aleichem had his Tevye declare, "I was, with God's help, a poor man," and Peretz fused the harshest naturalism with the most exquisite lyricism in the story of poor young lovers called *In Keler*—these writers were expressing an ethos that reflects a unique historical condition. The ghetto Jews could be as greedy as any other human beings, and as unscrupulous in their pursuit of *parnosseh* (livelihood); but they were cut off from the world at an all too visible point, the limits of their social movement were pathetically clear. And here may be one cause for that fascination with the Rothschilds which runs through Yiddish writing and humor: the great family was not only Jewish, not only rich, not only close to the ears of kings, it had established itself halfway between two worlds, facing the brilliant and tempting West even as it cast an occasional, uneasy glance back at the Jews.

Who, in the ghetto world, was not finally a *luftmensh,* a Menachem Mendel trading nothing for nothing and living off the profits? This precarious position made history itself seem a little ridiculous—a response almost impossible to those who are *in* history; it made the ironic shrug a symbolic national gesture; and it made the feeling of fraternity with the poor a foundation for Peretz's delicate studies in character and Sholom Aleichem's marvelous flights into surrealism. This feeling had nothing in common with the populist sentimentality we have come to suspect in Saroyan and Steinbeck; no one could have been more caustic than Mendele or Sholom Aleichem in the criticism of Jewish life. What is signified was that, in the end, the best Jewish writers knew to whom their sympathies were pledged, and never doubted their ties even to the most miserable little *shnorer.* They wrote from a firm sense of identification, an identification that was simultaneously inheritance and choice; and this was the source of their moral security. (Consider what Sholom Aleichem would have made of Scott Fitzgerald's lifelong struggle with the problem of money!)

None of this, to my mind, has anything to do with *shtetl*-nostalgia; nor is it uniquely Jewish; the sense of fraternity with the poor is as fine in Silone as in Sholom Aleichem. It was only that the Jews, with God's help, had more occasion than most peoples to look into the matter. (pp. 270-71)

If modern literary men cared about tradition as much as they claim, Sholom Aleichem would be avidly discussed in the literary journals and as many dissertations would be written about him as are about Faulkner. And if the chatter one hears about values were very much more than educated noises, Sholom Aleichem would be read with amazement and joy: for in how many other modern writers does one find so lovely a quality of feeling, so warming and fraternal a vision, so active a sense of human goodness? Middleton Murry once said of Thomas Hardy that "the contagion of the world's slow

stain has not touched him." This magnificent remark must have referred to something far more complex and valuable than innocence, for no one could take Hardy to be merely innocent; it must have referred to the power to see the world as it is, to love and yet not succumb to it; this is the power that I find, admire, in Sholom Aleichem.

But if we are to deplore the neglect of Yiddish literature in American literary circles, what are we to say about its neglect in the Jewish world? and particularly in those official segments of the Jewish world aggressively devoted to the slogan of "Jewish survival"?

There are now in print four volumes of translation of Sholom Aleichem, one of Mendele, perhaps two of Peretz. Surely, this is a wretchedly inadequate representation of the major Yiddish figures—not to mention the many other secondary writers who have not been translated at all. We have a Portable Irish Reader but no Yiddish Reader, a collection of German stories in the Modern Library but not one of Yiddish stories. The Jewish organizations are ready to devote their resources to a variety of ends, but which of them would consider, for example, subventing an edition of Mendele, a writer whom an authority in *Commentary* declares to have painted the Jewish world with a Balzacian completeness. Nor is there much time left; either the Yiddish literary heritage will soon be made available in translation or it will not, in any significant sense, be available at all.

For there are values, shades of perception, turns of feeling, blends of humor that can be found in Yiddish literature and nowhere else. In Sholom Aleichem we hear a voice of purity and sweetness; but even more important, we see the tremendous resources that come to a writer when he can work with the knowledge that wherever his readers may be, there he is loved. (p. 273)

> *Irving Howe, "An Unknown Treasure of World Literature: Who Will Make Sholom Aleichem Available?" in* Commentary, *Vol. 14, No. 3, September, 1952, pp. 270-73.*

DOV SADAN (lecture date 1959)

[*In the following essay, Sadan places Sholom Aleichem within the Yiddish literary tradition, focusing on his use of the literary forms of the monologue, the letter, and the stage comedy.*]

"The first bite is only an auger bit" is a dictum that suggests the course of Sholem Aleichem scholarship; for when the question is asked whether the studies done thus far, both modest and sophisticated, can satisfy us, the answer must be that it is difficult to discern a balanced ratio between the reading of his works which captivates one sector after another, both at home and abroad, and their illumination, especially through the tools of scholarship. Perhaps this disproportion between readership and criticism can be explained by the rule that fame requires no credentials. But the question remains, *why* is fame accorded to this particular individual, far and beyond his own time and place and *why* does he continue to capture new readers both in the original and in translation. The problem indeed requires one or more explanations. Or perhaps this disproportion is a result of the old commonplace that associates his name with the famous triad: Sholem Aleichem in the middle, Mendele before him and Yitskhok Leybush Peretz after him. As so often happens, he who stands in the middle gets hurt, just as Isaac was swallowed up between Abraham and Jacob, becoming the prototype of one who is no more than the son of his precursor and the father of his offspring. This commonplace begs our attention since even its chronology is faulty. Take the beginning: true, that Mendele was an old man when the twenty-nine-year-old Sholem Aleichem publicly bestowed on him the title of *Zeyde*, "grandfather," that both put him at a distance and drew him near. But Peretz was born before Sholem Aleichem. Or take the end: Y. L. Peretz passed away before Sholem Aleichem and the latter died before Mendele. Thus, setting up the triad as a progression of three generations, as the commonplace implies, is none too sound. And since Mendele was established as the authority who is cited first, he automatically became a kind of Genesis. Now, as is well known, Bible commentators invest most of their energies in this book, to the neglect of the other four. Then Peretz was hailed as the concluding authority, and as the writer in him joined forces with the leader in him, the combination created a kind of program, an ideology. In other words, he became a latter-day hasidic master. As a result of all this, Sholem Aleichem, who was stuck in the middle, despite his unequaled popularity with the readership, both Jewish and gentile, was far less fortunate than they in the area of scholarship. Yefim Yeshurin, the enthusiastic bibliographer of Yiddish literature, collected (according to his Festschrift) 1581 entries for Mendele, 1766 for Sholem Aleichem and 5911 for Peretz (5765, if we include the foreign language sources).

This commonplace is also to blame in no small degree for the fact that Sholem Aleichem's literary achievements are not dealt with in their entirety. Though certain aspects of his productivity are indeed peripheral, no total appreciation can be gained without them. The poet in him is not given due attention. As limited as this poetic productivity might have been, it is characteristic nonetheless in its close relation to the folksong. It is no accident that Ginzburg and Marek included his lullaby in their anthology of 1901, thinking it to be a pure folk creation. The critic in him is not given due attention. As well known as his pamphlet against Shomer might be, very few have taken the trouble to read it. This pamphlet not only sealed the fate of that marvellous storyteller in his own generation, but also blocked all subsequent revisionistic attempts, including one of my own. The editor in him is not given due attention. As familiar as everyone is with his *Yidishe folks-bibliotek*, little emphasis is placed on the extraordinarily significant fact that this editorship was the first to demonstrate that modern Yiddish literature possessed its own history. He printed the Yiddish works of deceased writers: Isaac Ber Levinzon, Yehuda Leyb Gordon, Eliezer Hakohen Zweifel. He encouraged Yitskhok Yoel Linetski and M. A. Shatskes, who had almost been forgotten and *were* eventually forgotten in their lifetimes, to renew their literary activity. He published Gotlober's memoirs of the older Yiddish literary figures like Mendl Lefin and Sukhistaver, Shloyme Etinger and Aleksander Tsederboym, Khaykl Hurvits and Yisroel Aksenfeld. He made room for Mendele and even left a niche open for the popular folk-singer, Elyokum Tsunzer. And most important, he attracted new talents, foremost among whom was Y. L. Peretz who made his first daring and original public appearance in the pages of his journal.

Needless to say, Sholem Aleichem must be viewed primarily as a narrative artist, but this does not obviate the need to see him in his many facets or to invest as much study in him as in the first and especially the last member of the triad. Therefore, he who wishes to discover Sholem Aleichem in his cre-

ative totality cannot do so on the basis of his collected works and all their editions, for they include only his stories (and even these are incomplete) and his plays.

The triad-formula leads to an even greater pitfall, namely, it encourages a variety of comparisons between him and the other two. But what unites them is only their stature—three proud oaks in the forest of Yiddish—while the differences between them are ever so great. Were we to judge the content of their writing, the differences would emerge in bold relief. Mendele's narrative is limited in time and place to the Pale of Settlement and it does not budge from there. Any attempt to break out of these limits meets with the same fate as Benjamin III whose imagination drew him to remote, faraway places but whose reality dragged him back to his own little niche. So as not to read too much into the story and keeping to that which can actually be read out of it, *The Travels of Benjamin III* is a satire of the desire to transform Jewish destiny along the lines of migration. Y. L. Peretz's narrative is also limited in time and place, to the borders of Poland and environs, with the time boundary extending somewhat beyond the recent past by the inclusion of some of the spheres of influence of Hasidism, the last great collective movement of the Diaspora. Sholem Aleichem's narrative is also time-bound but spatially it moves along the most dynamic lines of Jewish existence during the past generations, namely, along the routes of Jewish migration. Thus, his stories are rooted in the Ukraine, but they branch out over several lands of the dispersion and reach America.

The Jewish migratory course throughout time and place is the very essence of Yiddish prose, but anyone desiring to find its outline in the works of the classic triad will be led only to Sholem Aleichem. The fact that none of them ever set eyes on Jerusalem, the oldest among them dying in Odessa, the next in line is Warsaw, and the youngest in New York, is more than mere biographical data. But if Sholem Aleichem was the forerunner of the other two in the triad in terms of narrative content, making him a kind of embryo of what was to become the diversified temporal and spatial scope of Yiddish prose, it must also be noted that in terms of narrative form, his was a regression to those who *preceded* the other two and this very regression was the source of his achievement. A close look at the narratives of Mendele and Peretz reveals the prototypes of two central prose developments in Yiddish literature: The expansive storytelling of Mendele is the basis of a development in which the novel, especially in its realistic configuration, was to play the central role. The condensed storytelling of Peretz is the basis of a development in which the short story, especially in its psychological configuration, was to play the dominant role. Furthermore, each of these basic narrative approaches nourished other writers who combined them in different proportions and these in turn, shaped the history of Yiddish prose, be it of the Asch and Opatoshu school or of the Bergelson and Nister school, and so on. As for Sholem Aleichem, though he did in fact write novels, and long ones at that, as well as short stories, neither represents his main achievement. Though they are like scattered stops on the road of his creativity, the main thing is what lies after the stops and between them—the monologue, the letter and the comedy.

It can be argued, moreover, that Sholem Aleichem reverted several times to the novel and to the short story, like someone turning back on the road which was considered the legitimate developmental course of Yiddish prose, but each time he strayed from the path and followed the other three routes, the three foundations, wherein were revealed the talent of his originality and the originality of his talent; wherein he himself was revealed. And most important, in each of the three bases he returned to that which preceded the novel and preceded the short story in Yiddish literature of the last generations. He found lost threads and took them up again, his rethreading providing no mere continuity but rather a renewal, even a revolution.

What prompted Sholem Aleichem to return to the three foundations? Before this can be answered, another problem must be solved: Why could he not function creatively within the framework of the novel and the short story? The answer lies in the nature of these two forms, especially to the extent that they were developed in his day. These forms entailed a selective approach to the subject matter of life, an approach that obligated the writer to choose only such matter that furthered the plot and character in their interaction. Even a spot-check on Sholem Aleichem's novels and short stories reveals the extent to which these barriers were breached and circumvented. It is as if the subject matter of life, in its desire to express its own kaleidoscopic turmoil through the narrative, surmounted all obstacles that were laid in its path. Sholem Aleichem needed genres in which these obstacles were either nonexistent or minimal. The monologue, of course, liberates the spoken word, and this speech shapes the story out of its very freedom, while the limits of this freedom are determined by the world, the character and the needs of the speaker. In this case "speakers" would be more appropriate than "speaker," because through the monologue Sholem Aleichem was able to realize his desire and his talent—to achieve a total identification with a great and multifarious population.

He received the monologue by way of a legacy—the legacy of Haskalah literature. When the history of the Haskalah monologue will be written, the points of contact and especially the points of divergence between the monologue of the maskilim and that of Sholem Aleichem will have to be delineated. The monologue served the maskilim as a utilitarian device, the point of which was, of course, to present a monologue of someone whom the maskil wished to ridicule, and whom he did in fact ridicule by letting him speak for himself. It appeared as if the story came directly from the mouth of a naive narrator, but the maskil pushed the simpleton's naiveté so far that it became ridiculous and thus the satiric needle, hidden in the windbag, so to speak, emerged to prick that bag full of holes. Allow me to bring two fellow townsmen of mine by way of illustration (wasn't it Treitschke who was supposed to have said: "Alle Juden stammen aus Brody"?). It should be noted that alongside the rich, attractive monologue, whose most prominent example is Itsik Erter's *Gilgul nefesh* ("The Metamorphosis"), there was also a poor cousin version, best represented by the songs of the popular entertainer, Berl Broder, which begin, "I, the poor cobbler," or "I, the poor tailor," each "I" working at another trade or task until the complete roster of typical Jewish occupations in the town and rural economy has been exhausted. This kind of naive monologue coexisted with the satiric monologue, both writers speaking through the identity of their narrators. But while Erter was motivated by the ideological program of the Haskalah, Broder was moved by the painful social reality. The fusion of a studied, artistic effect as it appeared in the works of Erter and his followers, and of a naive folk effect, as it appeared in the works of Berl Broder and his imitators, are only

some of the components of Sholem Aleichem's monologue in which the identification with the mentality of the narrator is an end in itself and is absolute.

Whenever we speak of Sholem Aleichem's monologue, we must always remember that it includes several types. Take the monologue **"Genz"**(**"Geese"**), for instance. Here the goose dealer herself speaks like a goose, so that even her digressions from the story proper connect back into it. Or take a monologue like **"Dos tepl"** (**"The Pot"**), in which the narrative center is only a crutch, even a pretext for the rapid associative flood that comes from the rambling female narrator. An entirely different type of monologue is **"Khanike-gelt"** (**"Money for Hanukka"**), where the story-line is only a frame for presenting a complete typology of a large family. In fact, this relatively short monologue can be regarded as a miniature novel about the members of a sizable household. It follows that a monologue such as ***Motl Peysi dem khazns*** (***Motl the Son of Peysi the Cantor***), one of the author's finest works, suggests a comparison with that unique monologue, the autobiography ***Funem yarid*** (***From the Fair***). Looking back at the maskilic monologue from this vantage point, we can now speak of a legacy which, on the verge of its demise, experienced a rebirth.

What has been said about the monologue holds true for the epistolary form as well. Though it is a popular and well-known literary genre and its influences can presumably have come from numerous sources, Sholem Aleichem's brand of letter shows unmistakable evidence of a native pedigree. By all indications, his model was the form of literary epistle that his Yiddish predecessors cultivated, just as all indications show that *their* model was the form of literary epistle which the first generation of maskilim cultivated. It began in the journal *Hame'asef* which ran an exchange of fictitious letters between an old-fashioned father and his son, whose travels in many lands and whose subsequent experiences encouraged him to break with his father's way of life. This was carried over through the second generation of maskilim whose leading figure was, of course, Yoysef Perl with his *Megale tmirin* (*The Revealer of Secrets*). Perl in his collection of letters aspired toward and achieved the same goal as Erter in his collection of monologues. Finally, the last generation of maskilim vacillated in their use of the epistolary genre between an end to tendentiousness and a beginning of spoof. It will take a serious scholarly effort to fill in the lines of transmission from the Yiddish version of *Megale tmirin* which lay buried in manuscript and was accessible to a very few, to the later Yiddish literary epistles where its marked influence can be seen nonetheless—to Sholem Aleichem's unique form of letter. Suffice it for the present to say of his letter that which was said of his monologue: its essence lies in the power of identification, with the scriptural author, this time, instead of the oral speaker. And whenever we have an exchange of letters as in the Menakhem-Mendl and Sheyne-Sheyndl series, there is a dual identification—with two sexes, two people, two characters, two milieus, each component activating the complete spectrum of its own expressive possibilities, which the letter form, itself a written monologue, makes possible. Unfortunately, very few authentic Yiddish letters have come down to us, especially from earlier periods. We are therefore unable to construct a chronological survey of our epistolary culture. To the extent that it can be examined, however, the available material shows how the lively, spoken word broke through the ossified conventions and then broke out of them; how the letter, in all generations past, yearned for an artistic expression and finally achieved it through Sholem Aleichem. Though we do not know whether he studied or researched this literary genre and its history, we can say that his intuition made up for whatever was held back from his intellect. Here, too, we may observe that we are dealing with a legacy that was revived on the very verge of its demise.

Last but not least—the comedy, which needs no extensive proof to be regarded as a literary legacy, especially from the Yiddish branch of the Haskalah. Here the line of transmission is clear, for the dramatic literature of the Haskalah obeyed a functional linguistic differentiation: the drama of flamboyant pathos was written in Hebrew, whereas the drama of down-to-earth comedy was written in Yiddish. As we all know, the first generation of maskilim wrote their Yiddish comedies according to a biblical strategy of "And he snatched the spear from the Egyptian's hand and smote him with it." The Yiddish language, which this group hardly regarded with any respect, was expected to fulfil a self-destructive function. Their followers, however, were not quite as single-minded. The degree of artistry which they, unintentionally it would seem, invested in their Yiddish works, can only be explained by a contradictory attitude to the language itself—a manifest external repulsion and a latent internal attraction. The very last maskilim were already well entrenched in Yiddish, if not for its own sake, then almost for its own sake. Naturally, the programmatic slant of the maskilic comedy was no different from that of the maskilic monologue and literary epistle. In the comedy, this program was expressed in a very specific manner which can be formulated as follows: The more negative the character, judged by maskilic criteria, the more profuse the idiomatic abundance of his Yiddish dialogue. The more positive the character, judged by maskilic criteria, the scarcer the idiomatic content of his Yiddish dialogue. This holds true, of course, only for those authors who wrote their comedies entirely in Yiddish, as, for instance, the anonymous *Genarte velt* (*The Duped World*) which was forgotten and reissued only in our own day. This is not the case, however, with such writers as Wolfsohn and even Etinger, for in their works the most positive types speak a literary German.

The Angel of Dialectics is usually invoked to explain how it came about that this maskilic legacy—the comedy and everything the maskilim produced in Yiddish—actually achieved the opposite of its expressed goal. Stated more plainly: these, as well as all the other achievements of the Haskalah were incorporated into the life of the Jewish masses, but their acceptance was conditional upon the survival of the collective, one of whose unifying factors was the spoken language. How the manuscript copies of the Haskalah comedies gave rise to new and beautiful fruit wherever their seeds were sown, including the comedies of Aksenfeld and Mendele, this too is one of the scholarly puzzles awaiting a solution. For our purposes it is important to note that when Sholem Aleichem embarked upon comedy, he tried to build it up into a theatrical spectacle, something which was possible during the blossoming period of the Yiddish theater. And in the very act of creating this spectacle, he fulfilled the mission of the comedy legacy. For if the maskilic comedy at its inception exploited folk elements to satirize a large sector, all, or almost all of the Jewish people, it ultimately became, through Sholem Aleichem's comedy, the very incarnation of the people. A detailed analysis of Sholem Aleichem's comedy reveals the extent to which it was an indispensable form for him. I am not referring to the obvious connection between his long novel *Der blutiker*

shpas (*The Bloody Jest*) and its dramatization, *Shver tsu zayn a yid* (*It's Hard to Be a Jew*). I am referring to much more complex examples. Take the novel *Sender Blank,* for instance. It concerns the story of a wealthy father whose household reveals its true nature the moment he takes seriously ill, but upon recovery he throws the truth back in their faces. This main theme was reworked into the famous comedy *Dos groyse gevins* (*The Lottery*) with the necessary adaptation of components: the test is not an illusory terminal illness but an illusory lottery prize which prompts the tailor's family to reveal its true nature. Whoever compares and contrasts the novel and the comedy will realize that not only was the time lag between the two works decisive, for the artist's talent reached maturation in this period, but the different approach and development—necessitated by the different genre—were also decisive in guaranteeing the artistic level of the comedy. If we recall that Sholem Aleichem nurtured his comedy on the best of the native traditions, especially through a fusion of the literary comedy legacy with the *purimshpil* and its themes, and this at a time when the drama was undergoing a transition to realism on the one hand and to symbolism on the other—only then will we appreciate how much effort it took for him to respond to his *own* strengths, to pick up a lost thread, rethread it and go on stitching. Hence, that which was said of the monologue and the letter can now be said of the comedy as well: we have here a legacy which was revived on the verge of its demise.

One last point to be remembered is that spoken [Eastern] Yiddish, though it continued to grow and prosper in the living realm, invariably met with quite an opposite fate in the literary realm. The competition with its two other languages, literary [Western] Yiddish and the Yiddish used in study, was such, that the latter all but prevented it from reaching the printed page. Along came the maskilim and seized on the spoken language in order to imitate it exactly, as befitted their program. They, in fact, were responsible for its first artistic redemption, based on the premise, of course, that this was only a temporary measure; and the vehicles for this unintended redemption were the monologue, the letter and the comedy. Then along came their successors who stabilized the temporary measures and in this way the people were provided, not only in life but now in literature as well, with a means of expression that could speak directly to the heart. Finally there came the greatest folk artist, Sholem Aleichem, who let the language speak directly from its own heart.

There is a well-known saying of Moses Ibn Ezra that not every messenger is a prophet but every prophet is a messenger. Adapting this saying to the present discussion, we may say that he who concludes does not always initiate, but he who initiates is always a conclusion unto himself. For in fact, Sholem Aleichem whom the commonplace views as the middleman in a triad, was really a pathfinder, but like every initiator he was also a consummator. To the extent that he was committed to the artistic endeavor, especially within the three foundations which we have attempted to define—he was a conclusion. But to the extent that he revived them on the verge of their demise, he was a beginning. And he was a pathfinder not only in the realm of these three foundations—but this would go beyond that first bite which is only an auger bit. (pp. 55-63)

Dov Sadan, "Three Foundations: Sholem Aleichem and the Yiddish Literary Tradition," in Prooftexts, *Vol. 6, No. 1, January, 1986, pp. 55-63.*

LEONARD E. NATHAN (essay date 1960)

[*Nathan is an American poet, educator, translator, and critic. In the following essay, he asserts the humanity and unified vision of Sholom Aleichem's fiction.*]

The Jew away from Jewishness has often had to discover what Jewishness means the hard way—from strangers. And, if he has decided to learn more than strangers can teach him (that is, what he is not), then he may still tend to learn from the outside, from commentaries on commentaries, from, say Martin Buber on Hassidism. About this I can speak for myself, at least. Of the two times that I have attended synagogue, one was to make a speech on the writer that I am about to discuss. And both times I felt like an outsider, not because of the kind regulars around me, but because the act of going was so foreign to me, as if, again, I had to arrive through a door marked "For Those Entering the Synagogue Through the Idea of a Synagogue."

When I picked up the stories of Sholom Aleichem for the first time, all such indirections—those desperate and abstract freeways to a lost address—were unnecessary. I felt neither apology nor patronizing in my attention. There, so to speak, he *was,* like a familiar: no reservations, no deviousness, and all of a sudden real. High-minded interpreters were not necessary, only wits and imagination. But, for all his immediacy, this year is the centenary of Sholom Aleichem, a man dead before the Germans freed a murderous barbarism that we had imagined extinct. And yet the experience of Sholom Aleichem and his people, though irreversibly ended as an historical fact, is still so immediate that nothing, not even translation, can entirely distort or deaden it. Its power and movement, its variety and expressiveness, can still satisfy the hunger for reality that all great literature satisfies. As a view of life, his best work partakes of that completeness to which one, when the story's end is reached, can only say, "Yes, that's how it must happen."

"How it must happen" is the true writer's full answer to the two essentially religious questions that have to be asked for human fulfillment: what am I? and what, at my worst and best, could I be? In short, what is and what is possible, mated in the single nest of actual experience.

These questions can be asked and answered in different tones that range from the voice of tragedy to that of comedy. The tragic voice is committed to intoning man's individual fate, his personal capacity for greatness, his immense capacity to do evil or good. The tragic way leads through calamity, suffering, and finally a reverent comprehension of human dignity in a universe that makes dignity all but impossible. The comic voice entertains no such exalted purpose, is not concerned with man spelled with a capital M. Comedy reveals man as the natural fool, that social animal with a genius for confusion and folly which turns him and his society upside down. Born naturally to a world of trouble, comic man sets out in the manner of the determined *shlemiel* or *shlimazl* to make things even more difficult for himself, and thereby reveals a native gift for ridiculous incongruity that outstrips anything that his environment can offer. Out of the comic voice, revealing that gift for incongruity, comes then the delighted understanding of our own silliness, the petty follies, which we usually ignore or cherish like favorite children. If the tragic writer shows us the possibilities of our greatness in the middle of calamity, the comic writer shows us our endur-

Sholom Aleichem and his daughter Tisa.

ing capacity to recover from our minor, if sometimes poignant, lunacies, even if tomorrow we indulge in ten others.

Among Jewish writers in Yiddish, Isaac Leib Peretz has the gift for tragic speech, and Sholom Aleichem is the great comic voice. This voice takes its inflection and idiom from the fictional village of Kasrilevka, the home of a folk who divide roughly into fifty percent *shlemiel* and fifty percent *shlimazl,* a fair sampling, one must concede, for all mankind. But why, it might be asked, did Sholom Aleichem pick for a subject of comedy a village so poor that almost everyone is starving? Isn't he verging on the tragic or pathetic? I think that his reason is simple: if *these* people, impoverished and always on the edge of some fresh reversal, can keep their wit, their love of life, then human possibility and human dignity are tougher than we usually think. For Sholom Aleichem insists that a Kasrilik is known in the world as a man who refuses to let "poverty degrade him." Poverty in his people is like a weakness in character, or a stomach ache—distracting and dangerous to the whole man, but often able to provoke its owner to wonderful thoughts, dreams, inventions, wisdom—not as an escape from a hard life, but as an enrichment of it. Misery thus brings out unbelievable human possibilities, good ones as well as bad. In Sholom Aleichem's village, poverty, like a woman in dire travail, can bring to birth a great prodigy of wit fathered by hope, or desperation, or reverence, or love, or simply a deep sense of the ridiculousness of human existence. Which fact, by the way, suggests that the true comic voice is much closer to the tragic one than we sometimes realize.

Take, for instance, Tevye the Dairyman, Sholom Aleichem's philosopher of mother wit, who, on the verge of prayer, is violently interrupted when his horse picks this solemn moment to run away:

> But in spite of everything, we are still Jews. When evening comes we have to say our prayers. You can imagine what the prayers sounded like if I tell you that just as I was about to begin *Shmin-esra* my horse suddenly broke away as if possessed by the devil and ran wildly off through the woods. Have you ever tried standing on one spot facing the east while a horse was pulling you where *it* wanted to go? I had no choice but to run after him, holding on to the reins and chanting, *"God of Abraham, God of Isaac, and God of Jacob."* A fine way to say *Shmin-esra*! And just my luck, at a moment when I was in the mood to pray with feeling, out of the depths of my heart, hoping it would lift my spirits. . . .
>
> So there I was, running after the wagon and chanting at the top of my voice, as if I were a cantor in a synagogue: *"Thou sustainest the living with loving kindness* (and sometimes with a little food) *and keepest thy faith with them that sleep in the dust.* (The dead are not the only ones who lie in the dust; Oh, how low we the living are laid, what hells we go through, and I don't mean the rich people of Yehupetz who spend their summers at the *datchas* of Boiberik, eating and drinking and living off the fat of the land. . . . Oh, Heavenly Father, why does this happen to me? Am I not as good as others? Help me, dear God!) *Look upon our afflictions.* (Look down, dear God! See how we struggle and come to the aid of the poor, because who will look out for us if you don't?) *Heal us, O Lord, and we shall be healed.* (Send us the cure, we have the ailment already.) *Bless this year for us, O Lord, our God, with every kind of produce* (corn and wheat and every other grain, and if you do, will I get anything out of it, *shlimazl* that I am? For instance, what difference does it make to my poor horse whether oats are dear or cheap?)."
>
> But that's enough. Of God you don't ask questions. If you're one of the Chosen People you must see the good in everything and say, "This too is for the best." God must have willed it so. . . .
>
> *"And for slanderers let there be no hope,"* I chant further. The slanderers and rich scoffers who say there is no God—a fine figure they'll cut when they get *there.* They'll pay for their disbelief, and with interest too, for He is one who "breaketh his enemies and humbleth the arrogant." He pays you according to your deserts. You don't trifle with Him; you approach Him humbly, pray to Him and beg His mercy. *"O Merciful Father, hear our voice, pay heed to our lamentations. Spare us and have mercy upon us* (my wife and children too—they are hungry). *Accept, O Lord, thy people Israel and their prayer, even as you did in the days of the Holy Temple, when the priests and the Levites. . . ."*
>
> Suddenly the horse stopped. In a hurry I finish *Shmin-esra,* lift up my eyes, and behold two mysterious creatures coming toward me out of the forest, disguised or at least dressed in the strangest fashion.

The two strangers are finally responsible for Tevye's falling into moderate wealth. Tevye's prayer is thus rewarded. But what prayer? The official pious one that you or I or some ordinary man would have given? I don't think so. That official or public prayer is only half of what Tevye says to God. His parenthetical, spontaneous commentaries make up the other half, those private words to God, so personal, so sincere, so whole-hearted, that a humane deity could not turn away. In short, Tevye's prayer has in it the intensity of a man who speaks to God as if God were someone to whom you could really speak and who, because He shares a profound if difficult intelligibility with His creatures, would understand. Perhaps Martin Buber might say that Tevye is one of those rare folk among us who can speak to God using the familiar "Thou," and expect an answer as surely as could the patriarchs of Israel. After all, Tevye has held nothing back: grief, frustration, humor, reverence—all his humanity is uttered before us. What more could God ask of him?

Like Tevye, the whole town of Kasrilevka can react to an incongruous experience with an intensity that is nothing short of, in the oldest sense, heroic. In **"Dreyfus in Kasrilevka,"** Sholom Aleichem "reports" the Dreyfus case as its affects a whole community. The story is a brief and powerful rendering of the total involvement of the town with an event apparently beyond its experience and understanding, as Paris is "beyond" Kasrilevka. Beyond the town's experience, that is *until* Kasriliks make the event over by their own moral imagination, purify it of all its circumstantial and Parisian superfluities, substantiate it by making Dreyfus a third party to any dialogue the townsmen hold. The result is that the case becomes wholly an affair of Kasrilevka. The process of this transformation, this naturalization is characteristic: At first, the newspaper accounts of the case are merely abstracts of an exciting narrative; they then become partially domesticated like a captured wild animal or a mulish piece of reality that is never quite under control. And at last, except as a sort of intolerable annunciation of grief, the paper itself loses import, and there is no point in blaming or even believing it. The townsfolk ultimately must turn on the man who receives the paper, finding only in another living human the possibilities of defeat and an opportunity for wrath against a perverse failure of reality to live up to itself:

> "It cannot be!" Kasrilevka shouted with one voice. "Such a verdict is impossible! Heaven and earth swore that the truth must prevail. What kind of lies are you telling us?"
>
> "Fools!" shouted Zeidel, and thrust the paper into their faces. "Look! See what the paper says!"
>
> "Paper! Paper!" shouted Kasrilevka. "And if you stood with one foot in heaven and the other on earth, would we believe you?"
>
> "Such a thing must not be. It must never be! Never! Never!"
>
> And—who was right?

Of course, both paper and townsmen are right, as Sholom Aleichem, I believe, intends us to know. The paper reports correctly the refusal of many men to be honest, courageous, and reverent. The townsmen cannot accept such a refusal; it *must* not be, if men are to live like men in this world. Kasrilevka says no. And Paris, Dreyfus, his defenders, his accusers, the good, the evil, the indifferent, have suddenly come home to a living human moment to be known and judged. Thus, the distortion or reworking of the case by the Kasriliks is a realistic creation of art, and needs only for its finish the furious twist of their last reaction, the completing moral indignation that keeps the cause of every Dreyfus always alive: "This must not be, even if it is!" Such talk, such a refusal to let reality narrow itself to the worst and the least in us, is a kind of heroic action. It is a cry arising from a working conviction that nothing short of the best in man is good enough for man. As such, the irrelevant outburst is the fullest response that the stubborn, apparently naive and childish townsmen can give. Like honest children, they see no good reason for human wickedness and find it inexcusable, if altogether a true part of life.

The full and intense response in the people of Sholom Aleichem can be exemplified over and over, in **"On Account of a Hat," "A Yom Kippur Scandal," "The Convoy."** These stories, to name a few, for solidity and richness compel comparison to the best of the world's short stories, as the best of the world's short stories compel comparison to the great scriptural tales in that both embody the comprehending concreteness which Allen Tate, defining poetry, asserts comes into being when "the will and its formulas are put back into an implicit relation with the whole of our experience." This deeply imagined and understood concreteness provides a changeless knowledge beyond abstractions, programs, biased partialities, a clear and direct knowledge that has been called, when applied to the perception of inspired men, vision.

In other words, and I believe without any irreverence, Sholom Aleichem must be regarded as a religious writer in the great tradition of Hebrew prophets who were concerned with the misery of human life and with a valid dream of how life could be if men fulfilled themselves on earth so that all days would be as the Sabbath. But it was Sholom Aleichem's gift to turn the suffering and defeat of the children of Israel into startling comedy. This comedy gives a unique kind of pleasure, a delight in seeing life as it is, and yet, beyond our private little concerns, as a transmutation of reality into something ultimate and universal: that devout experience of the human totality. Sholom Aleichem says to his readers: "The moment is not yesterday or tomorrow, but *now,* before you in this act of reading." No matter how darkly he or other writers picture our nature and our circumstances, we are permitted at such times to witness a kind of miracle, our humanity mirrored in their imagination, their genius speaking for us at our most human. It is during such moments that the great contraries of what is and what should be—bitterly divorced in our common life—are rewedded. At these instants of wholeness, the writer and reader engage in the most momentous of all speech, those essential inquiries of the old Rabbi of the Babylonian *Talmud* who used to ask, "If I be not for myself, who shall be for me; and if I am by myself what am I? and if not now—when?" Because the answer to these questions is sometimes passionately funny doesn't mean, as Sholom Aleichem repeatedly proves, that it is not the most serious answer an honest man can give. (pp. 518-23)

Leonard E. Nathan, "Sholom Aleichem: A Hundred Years and It's Still 'Now'," in The Antioch Review, *Vol. XX, No. 4, Winter, 1960-61, pp. 518-23.*

JOSEPH BUTWIN AND FRANCES BUTWIN (essay date 1977)

[*Frances Butwin is a Polish-born American translator and crit-*ic. With Julius Butwin, she selected and translated a collection of stories by Sholom Aleichem which was published in 1946 as The Old Country. *She has since translated several other volumes of Sholom Aleichem's works. Joseph Butwin is an American educator and critic who has published articles on English, French, and Yiddish literature. In the following excerpt from their biographical and critical study of Sholom Aleichem, Frances and Joseph Butwin discuss the story "The Enchanted Tailor" to illustrate Sholom Aleichem's juxtaposition of comedy and tragedy for satirical effect.*]

We read Sholom Aleichem's comedy with full knowledge of the general precariousness of life in the Russian Pale. Even as we laugh we are not allowed to forget for long that the source of our laughter is also the source of lamentable pain. This is perhaps best exemplified in the story that ends with the familiar injunction to laugh. It is when Shimmen-Eli, **"The Enchanted Tailor,"** has gone mad and is about to die that we are told that "laughter is healthful. The doctors bid us laugh."

Shimmen-Eli is instructed by his wife, Tsippa-Beyla-Reyza, to take his few rubles to the next town and buy a goat from the wife of the local *melamed.* His family wants milk and cheese. Going and coming from his errand he stops at the tavern of his kinsman, Dodi Rendar, who gives him a drink each time and exchanges the she-goat for a he-goat behind the scenes. The goat that produced buckets of milk for the *melamed's* wife is dry for Shimmen-Eli's wife. And when the tailor tries to return the animal he can never prove his point because Dodi repeats the exchange. Shimmen-Eli, rebuked, mocked, and thoroughly perplexed, goes mad. During the day he is ridiculed by children; at night he chases his mysterious goat through the town. He is haunted by the dead who pray in their shrouds at the old synagogue and by a bird shrieking from the church steeple. Dead friends appear to him along with ghouls and vampires and strange creatures that move about on tiny wheels. We leave him struggling with the "Angel of Death." Shimmen-Eli's ultimate sorrow (*troyer*) would seem to preclude comedy. But that is not the case. In fact his sorrow and his comedy derive from the same condition. Shimmen-Eli is a *nebekh,* a poor, unfortunate creature who is at the same time a source of comedy, the inevitable butt of jokes. The *nebekh,* in this case, is a pompous fool but he is also a victim of social conditions which he shares with most other Jews in the Pale. His folly and his pomposity are funny; his poverty is not. But since the two go together it is not always clear where the humor of one ends and the pathos of the other begins.

Shimmen-Eli is called "Shma-koleynu"—Hear our voice [O Lord]—for the loudness of his voice in prayer. He constantly parades his vast knowledge of holy texts in a way that indicates that it is not vast. For scriptural accuracy he competes with Tevye. At the same time he lords it over his cousin Dodi, showering him with citations and mocking him for his ignorance in a way that almost justifies Dodi's revenge. Shimmen-Eli's pedantry is matched by his childlike simplicity, and it is as a child that we see him set forth into the countryside on his way to buy the goat. The description that follows sounds remarkably like the descriptions of the countryside into which children in other stories are released from home and *kheder:*

> It was Sunday, a bright, warm, summer day. Shimmen-Eli could not remember when he had seen a beautiful day like this before. He could not remember the last time he had been out in the open coun-

try. It had been a long time since his eyes had beheld such a fresh green forest, such a rich green carpet sprinkled with many-colored flowers. It had been a long time since his ears had heard the twitter of birds and the fluttering of small wings, such a long time since he had smelled the odors of the fresh countryside.

It is not strict parents or a long winter that keep the adult from open country; it is poverty.

> Shimmen-Eli Shma-Koleynu had spent his life in a different world from that. His eyes had beheld entirely different scenes: a dark cellar with an oven near the door, with pokers and shovels leaning against it, and nearby a slop-basin full to the brim. Near the oven and the basin, a bed made of three boards, with a litter of small children on it, half-naked, barefoot, unwashed, always hungry.

> His ears had heard entirely different sounds: "Mother, I want some bread! Mother, I'm hungry."

At this point Shimmen-Eli's political sympathies translate themselves into a brief and humble utopian fantasy: "What harm would it do if every workingman could come out here at least once a week, here in the open country, and enjoy the freedom of God's great world? Ah, what a world, what a world."

Shimmen-Eli's yearnings may reflect the humanitarian impulse almost axiomatic in Yiddish fiction of the period, but the way he expresses his sympathies is open to satire. He rants against the powers of the town, the tax-collectors, the rabbis, the ritual butchers, and the philanthropists all in the vein of Mendele's early satires, *Dos Kleine Menshele* (1863) and *Di Takse* (1869), and of Sholom Aleichem's **Elections,** which all adopt Shimmen-Eli's stance against the powers of the community who enrich themselves at the expense of the poor. The crimes remain to be chastened but those who chasten cannot be ignored by the satirist. When Shimmen-Eli indulges in drink he tends to rant:

> May the devil take them, those givers of charity! Is it their own money they give? All they do is suck the blood of us poor people. Out of my three rubles a week they make me pay twenty-five kopeks! But their time will come, never fear. God shall hold them to account. Although to tell you the truth, my cherished wife . . . has long told me that I am worse than a shlimazl, a fool and a coward, because if I only wanted to use it, I could hold a strong whip over them!

Here as in **"Three Little Heads"** Sholom Aleichem makes fun of the naive, henpecked revolutionary, but it is just this naiveté which is used elsewhere to make his condition especially pathetic.

Shimmen-Eli goes back and forth and between the two towns with his goat. He enlists his fellow tailors to represent him against the thieves of Kozodoievka, the town of goats. But nothing can solve the problem of the goat's dual identity. In the end Shimmen-Eli goes mad and is last seen "struggling with the Angel of Death." The child crying beside his sickbed, "Mama, I'm hungry," reminds us that this is the story of people who are miserably poor. Shimmen-Eli is sick, and unlike the preadolescent fevers and nightmares suffered in the stories of children, this one does not promise to end in health and growth into sadder but wiser adulthood. It is with this grim knowledge of inevitable decline that Sholom Aleichem leaves his hero and shifts his emphasis at the end of the story:

> The end was not a happy one. The story began cheerfully enough, but it ended like most cheerful stories, very tragically. And since you know that I am not a gloomy soul who prefers tears to laughter and likes to point a moral and teach a lesson, let us part as cheerfully as we can. And I wish that all of you readers and everybody else in the world may have more opportunities to laugh than to cry.

> Laughter is healthful. The doctors bid us laugh.

The coda may be used to identify Sholom Aleichem as a master of laughter, but it is questionable whether this story allows his conversion into a comical medicine man. At this point **"The Enchanted Tailor"** has ceased to be funny. To laugh at the bedeviled tailor would be brutal. When the frequently isolated phrase is returned to its context, we can only conclude that Sholom Aleichem does not mean what he says. A healthy laugh would indicate a failure of sympathy that the author does not mean to encourage. Nor are we to accept his disclaimer of moral interest.

If the act of reading can be said to engage our moral selves, laughter may not always be an appropriate response. The task, then, of writers who have both moral and comic pretensions—Swift, Dickens, Sholom Aleichem—is to teach us when laughter must stop. Toward the end of Swift's "Modest Proposal" a reader with an active sense of irony must stop smiling and begin to take notice of the deadly seriousness of the essay. The writer proposes that Irish babies be sold as a delicacy to the English, who in any case are sure to get them sooner or later. A less sensitive reader who does not "get" the joke at all may have remained sober throughout and will therefore not register the intentionally serious turn of the essay when it comes. The dedicated satirist cannot afford to leave his readers laughing throughout. Too many readers will assume that laughter is benign—"healthful"—and tend to disregard its lessons. A morally responsive reader cannot put Swift down with a smile.

"The Enchanted Tailor" includes an explicit correction of laughter. "What are you laughing at?" a workingman cries at the town gossips. "You ought to be ashamed of yourselves! Grown men with beards. Married men with families. Shame on you! Making fun of a poor tailor. Can't you see the man is not himself?" The doctor, when he comes, is a useless fool, and sympathy at this point comes too late:

> Wonder of wonders! For fifty years Shimmen-Eli Shma-Koleynu had lived in Zolodievke in poverty and oppression. For fifty years he had lain in obscurity. No one spoke of him, no one knew what sort of man he was. But now that he was so close to death, the town suddenly became aware of all his virtues. It suddenly became known that he had been a good and kind man, generous and charitable; that is to say, he had forced money out of the rich and divided it among the poor.

The voice of the satirist interrupts the narration in order to identify the deplorable conditions that yield creatures like . . . Shimmen-Eli. (pp. 80-4)

Joseph Butwin and Frances Butwin, in their Sholom Aleichem, *Twayne Publishers, 1977, 173 p.*

SOL GITTLEMAN (essay date 1978)

[*Gittleman is an American educator and critic who has written an introduction to Sholom Aleichem's life and writing (see Further Reading). In the following excerpt from his book on family life in Jewish literature,* From Shtetl to Suburbia, *Gittleman analyzes Sholom Aleichem's story "Chava," highlighting its theme of disintegrating traditional values in Jewish village life.*]

There can be little doubt that Sholom Aleichem intended ["Chava"] to be the last of the Tevye stories. Tragedy reaches its ultimate level for the Jewish family in the *shtetl:* nothing can go beyond the injury associated with the child who marries outside of Judaism. But Sholom Aleichem is not merely concerned with presenting a story with obvious sentimental-pathetic implications for the Jew. That would be easy enough, knowing the range of tragic events which would be guaranteed to stir the hearts of the *shtetl* inhabitants. Instead, he clearly wishes to demonstrate that, even with this horrendous event, the full implications of which are shared by all the readers, there remains a problem of generation and communication at the center of the conflict. Sholom Aleichem manages to put even this problem in the form of a struggle between two worlds, one as it disintegrates, the other as it comes into being.

When Tevye sees Chava talking to the Gentile town clerk Fyedka, he is concerned. He asks his daughter:

> " 'What was Fyedka doing here?' 'Nothing,' she said. 'What do you mean, nothing?' 'We were just talking.' 'What business do you have talking with Fyedka?' I asked. 'We've known each other for a long time,' she said. 'Congratulations! A fine friend you've picked for yourself!' "

Chava's perception of Fyedka is not one shared by Tevye. For him, Fyedka is no more than a *goy,* a stereotype built up by centuries of pogroms, threats, and fear: "I don't know who he is. I've never seen his family tree. But I am sure he must be descended from a long and honorable line. His father must have been a shepherd or a janitor, or else just a plain drunkard." The exchange between father and daughter goes to the core of the alienation: " 'Who his father was I don't know and I don't care to know. But Fyedka himself is not an ordinary person. I would tell you, but you wouldn't understand. Fyedka is a second Gorky.' 'A second Gorky? And who, may I ask, was the first Gorky?' 'Gorky,' she said, 'is one of the greatest men living in the world today.' 'Where does he live,' I asked, 'this sage of yours, what is his occupation and what words of wisdom has he spoken?' " The hopelessness of attempting any communication between these two worlds becomes apparent. Once again, the revolution has come to Tevye's world, and he is uncomprehending. His children do not look to a world of *yichus,* of parents' occupations and status in the community. They look to Gorky, to the world of his play *The Lower Depths,* and to a humanitarian revolution that will finally transcend religious sectarianism. In none of the other Tevye stories is the patriarch made to look as narrow-minded when faced with modernism as in this one. Even the priest seems to have more tolerance than Tevye: "Your child is reaching out for a different world, and you don't understand her, or else you don't wish to understand her." Tevye seems to be concerned only with his own image in the community, and the unbearable loss of face that is involved when a child marries a non-Jew. He repeats like a litany: "The pain is great, but the disgrace—the disgrace is even

greater." This is the leit-motif which Sholom Aleichem chooses to characterize Tevye's attitude. Tevye's shame preoccupies him; he loses his perspective as a father because his status is threatened by his daughter's marriage to a *goy.*

But Sholom Aleichem's implied criticism of Tevye can only go so far. When it comes down to the crunch, he still must side with the Jew, simply because Tevye the father is unable to regain his lost daughter, even if he tries to. Tevye wishes to speak to Chava, but is informed by the priest that this will be impossible. "She is now under my protection." In this way Sholom Aleichem demonstrates the frustration and futility of the Jew in Czarist Russia. There is no recourse for Tevye. He cannot speak to his daughter, cannot approach her. She is now officially a ward of the state, and the Jew's access to his own child is denied him. The point strikes home hard, and Chava's decision to seek refuge with the priest transcends her intellectual prowess, her humanitarianism, indeed, her entire advantage. She has betrayed her family, abandoned her parents, and in spite of Tevye's apparent narrow-mindedness, she emerges as the main contributor to the family disruption. Even when she encounters her father on the road and begs for recognition, to Tevye she is dead, no longer a member of the Jewish community. Tevye has rent his garments and said the prayer for the dead for the daughter he has lost. He will not speak to her, will no longer acknowledge her existence.

"Chava" has all the ingredients of Jewish soap opera, or, for that matter, any ethnic minority melodrama, particularly in terms of the older generation. There could be no greater calamity, no greater loss of face than that signaled by an intermarriage, the merging, in this case, of Jew and Gentile. Conversion meant nothing, was not accepted in *shtetl* terms. Fyedka would always be the *goy,* the *shaygits* (Gentile boy), even if he were to accept Judaism. Sholom Aleichem's treatment of the theme is intended to underline the tragedy on both sides, not just for the parents. Indeed, he focuses on the *shtetl*'s inability, that is, Tevye's inability, to deal with the invasion of ideas which he considers either foreign or threatening. The Jewish family succumbs to the tragedy of events which it has not been prepared to deal with.

At the end, Tevye bids goodbye to Sholom Aleichem. The final curtain has come down on Tevye's world. Where does the dairyman encounter greater loss than this, greater shame and bereavement? The conclusion of the story makes it clear that this is the end of Tevye the *shlimmazel:* "And if you should write, write about something else, not about me. Forget about me—no more Tevye the Dairyman!" Tevye's action is automatic in terms of Jewish tradition and law: he must drive his daughter from the family. Yet he seems to understand that at this point in history Chava's defection is more than the loss of a child—it is the loss of his world. Tevye is beyond forgiveness; he could not, even with the humanity he possesses, excuse Chava's act. Sholom Aleichem, by framing her action with the crush of events produced by changing times, underlines the tragedy which no doubt will be repeated in thousands of *shtetl* families in the ghettoes in the East and eventually under the shadow of the Delancey Street Bridge in New York as well. For Tevye, the Jewish Everyman, is helpless, and cannot gain strength from his traditions. They have told him only to resist and to struggle against those forces trying to destroy his and his fathers' world. (pp. 75-8)

Yet Sholom Aleichem's position is not a reactionary or cautious one. He does not advocate the return to *shtetl* values. One of his primary points throughout the Tevye stories has been the inability of that *shtetl* to move into the twentieth century. More detached, more removed than most of the Yiddish writers of his age, Sholom Aleichem was an observer of the tragedy which was acted out in the hundreds of *shtetls* of the Pale in the confrontation of generations. The inimical, almost Hegelian clash of these generational forces produced enormous changes, and resulted ultimately in the flowering of Yiddish culture in America. The great *Haskalah* that Sholom Aleichem had hoped for, the great Enlightenment could not occur in Czarist Russia. Only the Padhatzurs who were willing to forego their Judaism could succeed there. Tevye had to be left behind as well. The *shtetl* world, however, proved to be remarkably mobile, even transplantable. It found new roots on the Lower East Side of New York; and the *mishpoche,* the Jewish family, was once again the center of attention of Yiddish fiction. Indeed, Sholom Aleichem accompanied hundreds of thousands of these families, following his subject matter to the new homeland. As he lay dying, he was working on the story of Mottel, a Jewish child who had accompanied his brother and mother to the new world, and whose eyes were opening to the miracle of life in New York City. Had he not died, Sholom Aleichem no doubt would have become the chronicler of an even more difficult chapter for the Jewish family, as it now confronted a threat even greater than those of Czarist Russia and of modern ideas encroaching on the *shtetl.* In America there was freedom, no *shtetl* walls to hold the children in, and the challenge to the Jewish family was to become the major theme of Jewish literature both in Yiddish and in English. (p. 85)

> Sol Gittleman, "Sholom Aleichem's Tevye Stories: The Crisis of Family Life," in his *From Shtetl to Suburbia: The Family in Jewish Literary Imagination, Beacon Press, 1978, pp. 54-85.*

VICTORIA AARONS   (essay date 1985)

[*In the following excerpt, Aarons claims that increased reader involvement results from Sholom Aleichem's use of a pseudonym and the placement of the author as a character in his stories.*]

Few writers . . . have approached Sholom Aleichem's works either from the perspective of narrative structure in general or from the perspective of the function of specific rhetorical techniques. But Dan Miron, unlike critics before him, recognizes the advantages of a rhetorical analysis and adopts a more modern critical approach to Sholom Aleichem's works, an approach which emphasizes the distinction between the biographical artist, Sholem Rabinovitsh, and his artifice or pseudonym, Sholom Aleichem. Miron writes in direct opposition to those critics who do not distinguish between the writer and the fictitious character-pseudonym. In fact, he believes that the flaws in previous criticism stem, for the most part, from this initial and (in his opinion) fundamental mistake:

> It is my contention, to put things bluntly, that the study of Sholem Rabinovitsh's work . . . has been fundamentally flawed by insufficient differentiation between its author and his creation, Sholem-Aleykhem. When I say insufficient, I understate the case, since the name, Sholem-Aleykhem, has almost invariably been assumed to refer to the author as person and as artist . . . While a biographical-psychological approach to the Sholem-Aleykhem persona is perfectly legitimate, it can hardly carry

one far when unassisted by a primary distinction between artist and artifice, and by a clear conception of the difference between the psychological development of the artist and the thetorical development of his artifices—two processes, which are, of course, closely related, but the study of which calls for totally different methodological procedures . . .

> What is needed is a perception of the ontological difference between author and persona, of the fact that they exist on totally different levels [*Sholem Aleykhem: Person, Persona, Presence*].

In short, Miron argues that Rabinovitsh, the writer, invents the "presence" of Sholom Aleichem, a figure which permeates all of his works to one degree or another and with whom a popular reading audience easily could identify. Miron argues that this figure, whether he is an actual narrating character or simply the name that appears as author of the text, is necessary because, unlike the biographical author, Sholom Aleichem is one of the shtetl folk and is capable of an intimacy with the Yiddish-speaking masses that the Russian intellectual author could never be. A figure other than that of the Europeanized man of letters, according to Miron, was needed to act primarily as a go-between, an intermediary who connects the distanced writer to his audience. Miron argues that the Sholom Aleichem who travels with ease among the shtetl Jews, participates in their activities and there-by is a likely recipient of their stories, was constructed by the writer to authenticate the works and bridge the gap between the world of the shtetl and the world of the intellectual reader. Miron, most significantly, identifies Sholom Aleichem's primary reading audience as those intellectual and Europeanized Jews who had left the shtetls both figuratively as well as literally.

But he does not raise the next question, the question of authorial intention. Why did Sholom Aleichem address this audience? In this respect Miron does not transcend more traditional criticism; he simply assumes that Sholom Aleichem's fundamental purpose must be the preservation of the shtetl heritage. Hence, although Miron refers to the rhetorical relationship between the author, his pseudonym-narrator, and his subject, he never shows how these narrative elements actually function in the texts. (pp. 8-10)

The most notable feature of Sholom Aleichem's short works, when examined as a collected whole, becomes that of the writer's changing stance, or position, toward his subject. This change in the writer's stance, largely determined by the shifting nature of the narrative voice constructed in the texts, would seem to be a direct response to the changing historical period in which Sholom Aleichem wrote. Rather than simply mirroring history, however, the change in narrative voice and in the position of the writer vis à vis his characters raises questions concerning the often complex relation between writers and readers.

Sholom Aleichem's construction of the monologue as a storytelling device allowed him to walk a kind of literary tightrope. While allowing him close identity and kinship with his characters, the monologue structure also freed Sholom Aleichem from those same confines as befell them. Sholom Aleichem functions simultaneously as both insider and outsider. He is designed as a "sounding board," as a figure who listens and records stories told to him by characters who trust him implicitly. Sholom Aleichem is removed from the other shtetl characters emotionally and intellectually. Because he is portrayed by the author as a writer himself, the other characters feel that Sholom Aleichem can make sense of their experiences in a way that they cannot. Thus, the figure of Sholom Aleichem becomes the vehicle through which we as readers are introduced to the characters in the monologues. As they tell their stories to the fictionalized Sholom Aleichem they reveal themselves—their infirmities and their limitations. And the real mastery of the monologue format is that Sholom Aleichem, the author, can stand apart from the events and characters while silently judging them. Through this process the author bridges the distance between the reader and the self-dramatized characters. We seemingly come to know them as the fictionalized Sholom Aleichem does. He is the recorder of the tales he ostensibly "hears."

What emerges most notably from the monologues is the psychological characterization of the storyteller, and the creation of a fictional addressee, Sholom Aleichem, who bears witness to the collective voice of the shtetl Jew, a voice that calls attention to a particular people, immutable yet unprotected from impending changes of history.

These changes become explicit when we view these same characters in *The Adventures of Menakhem-Mendl.* The fictional letters written by Menakhem-Mendl and his wife mirror the changing position of the shtetl Jews who were slowly emerging from the restrictive confines of the small villages for even greater restrictions in the larger cities of Eastern Europe. The changing stance of the author-recorder, Sholom Aleichem, also becomes apparent. For the portrait established in the collection of letters argues for a vision of the world through the eyes of one always on the outside. Menakhem-Mendl, like the numbers of young men who sought mobility and advancement, left the shtetl only to wander fruitlessly in search of financial security and success. What saves the letters, like the monologues, from extreme pathos is the light-hearted humor with which Sholom Aleichem, once again the fictional vehicle through which the stories are made known to the reader, balances the tone of despair.

Sholom Aleichem's fictionalized position in the letters remains ambiguous. As in the monologues, he is clearly a kind of recorder and, in the case of the letters, a compiler and arranger. More important than his fictional role, however, is his rhetorical function. His is the controlling voice we "hear" when we read the letters. While in both the monologues and letters the characters relate their own tales, their meaning is only realized by the reader because of the implicit judgments and values conveyed by Sholom Aleichem. This kind of "double-voicing," of coupling the speaker's point of view with the underlying stance of the author, provides the reader with a double vision of events. We come to see the world through the point of view of the character, and then we qualify or give perspective to that vision with the aid of an additional voice, that of the author. In the case of Sholom Aleichem's fiction this technique brings the reader closer to the characters. We are made to see their limitations, but we view them sympathetically nonetheless. Because we respect their moral choices they earn our approval.

The characters earn the reader's moral and emotional approval because we come to view them as Sholom Aleichem does. The elusive figure of Sholom Aleichem, both author and fictionalized character, emerges as the major spokesman for the characters he creates. And this position of amused yet sympathetic detachment becomes increasingly problematic

as Sholom Aleichem enters the texts with greater involvement.

The Kasrilevke stories that have as their historical situation the upheaval and disintegration of the shtetls most dramatically reveal Sholom Aleichem's involvement in the events he describes. In these stories Sholom Aleichem typically "plays himself." He is a character in the drama, a writer by profession. He is inside the stories, directly commenting on the fate of the Jewish masses at the turn of the century and on the fate of the Jewish intellectual and writer who struggles to affirm the strengths of the culture, people and traditions. Sholom Aleichem, both author and character, loses much of his amused distance from the events he describes and voices his bitterness and anger. When there is no intermediary narrating figure between Sholom Aleichem and the reader, that is, when Sholom Aleichem tells his own story, the reader is no longer allowed the same kind of release through amusement and laughter that the monologues and letters provide.

"Station Baranovich" most strikingly reflects the real sophistication of Sholom Aleichem's literary achievement. Once again, Sholom Aleichem recalls a story he "heard," and relates it to the reader with a poignancy rich in nuance and technique. We as readers are made to see that the Jewish condition, not unlike the human condition at large, is marked by contradictions and complexities beyond our control, reflected most convincingly by the shifting stance of the author toward his material.

"Station Baranovich" brings together many of Sholom Aleichem's most skillful literary techniques. The structure of a story within a story, internal and external narrators, and audiences intrinsic to and outside of the text characterize Sholom Aleichem's style. The complexity of narrative form reinforces the depth of meaning for the work. It demonstrates the inextricable entanglement of reality and illusion. This story . . . engulfs the reader in the events and characters described.

Throughout Sholom Aleichem's works we find literary devices which complicate the relation between reader and characters, reader and writer, reader and Sholom Aleichem. The function of the pseudonym alone serves to provide both comedy and ambiguity to the structure of the stories. Sholom Aleichem becomes his own character in and out of the texts. His tendency to construct primarily first-person limited narratives draws our attention to the credibility and reliability of the narrators.

What perhaps distinguishes Sholom Aleichem's works most remarkably is the kind of literary freedom in which he moves—sometimes as character, as author, as insider, as outsider. But always he takes the reader with him. The reader's position at once mirrors the writer's and is controlled by it. In the act of reading we become observers of fiction and are asked to make sense of experience.

It is in this emphasis on reader involvement that I think we find traces of Sholom Aleichem's literary technique in the works of contemporary Jewish writers. Sholom Aleichem's most notable rhetorical and literary devices—the pseudonym that is both author and character; the construction of a first-person limited narration in which the storyteller is marked by unreliability and limitations; the tragi-comic treatment of events and characters; the structural distinction between an implied author and a narrating figure; the irony and tension established as distancing devices in the works; the fluidity that marks his style—all serve to engage the reader in a sympathetic relationship to characters and events, to one's heritage at large, while placing the reader in a removed position from those same events and characters. This skillful manipulation of the reader's sensibilities and moral stance encourages the reader to regard his or her position vis à vis fiction with considerable unease.

Sholom Aleichem's stories, then, essentially reveal the art of storytelling. They call attention to fiction and reality, to artifice, and to the careful design behind our interpretation of events in and out of history. To enter the fictive world of Sholom Aleichem is to suspend our carefully constructed notions of reality and of our safe distance from fiction. This would seem to allow a writer such as Sholom Aleichem to secure his position toward the characters and events of his heritage, and to define his position by the act of writing. The peculiar lens through which Sholom Aleichem views his material reflects a very modern notion of art and of fiction, and for this reason Sholom Aleichem's short works demonstrate the range of fictive devices in a characteristically modern sense. (pp. 129-33)

[A] reading of Sholom Aleichem's short fiction raises some interesting questions regarding current trends in Jewish fiction.

The oral qualities in Sholom Aleichem's works, for instance, permeate Jewish writing at large. When Sholom Aleichem's characters speak we are able to envision the mannerisms and gesticulations of the speakers. We find this same characteristic in the works of Bernard Malamud, for example. What immediately comes to mind is Malamud's novel *The Assistant.* When his main character, Morris Bober, speaks we are taken back immediately to the "old country," to the culture of *Yiddishkeit,* to the shared experiences of the Jews who emigrated to America.

Jewish fiction lends itself to oral readings, due in part to the Yiddishisms, the idiomatic expressions that permeate the language, but also to the storytelling flavor of the fiction. I. B. Singer's works exemplify this tradition best. Like Sholom Aleichem's fiction, many of Singer's stories are told by a first-person narrator who tells his story to another listener who both advises and records. This kind of verisimilitude characterizes much of Jewish fiction and at once involves the audience in the story while commenting on the act of storytelling itself. Perhaps this is one reason why the most effective form for many Jewish writers is the shorter work in which abrupt endings and rapid episodal quips are possible.

In this playfulness with art and reality, storytellers and readers, the wider implications of Sholom Aleichem's literary tradition can be viewed as not merely a Jewish concern, but a universal one. When Sholom Aleichem's character in the short story **"A Yom Kippur Scandal"** seemingly forgets the main thrust of his story and ends without a closure adequate for his listeners, or when I. B. Singer's narrator in the short story "Lost," a writer for the Yiddish newspaper who "counsels" his readers, becomes engrossingly involved in the inexplicable incidents reported to him, we are reminded of the complexity of human beings in relation to the stories they invariably tell. As readers we come to recognize the power of verbal expression to define and to delimit experience, and to view our own need for resolution. Through the fictive stories of imaginary characters we seek vicarious closure to the complexities and ambiguities in our lives only to discover that fiction, like life, is open-ended, subject to interpretation and to

revision. The writer's shifting perspective in relation his art shapes our own. Reading becomes a persuasive and dynamic communicative act where the literary and rhetorical devices available to all tellers of all stories reflect the human predicament.

Above all else, the host of characters in Jewish literature—from Sholom Aleichem's shtetl Jews to Elie Wiesel's holocaust victims—emerge as survivors. This essential characteristic, the ability to survive with dignity amid enormous upheaval and devastation, both internal and from outside forces beyond their control, connects both reader and writer to the characters, and gives vitality and depth to Jewish fiction. Sholom Aleichem is more than a forerunner of modern Jewish fiction; he must be regarded as a major literary figure, as a part of the modern tradition at large. (pp. 133-34)

> *Victoria Aarons, in her* Author as Character in the Works of Sholom Aleichem, *The Edwin Mellen Press, 1985, 176 p.*

FURTHER READING

Cohen, Israel. "On the Horizon: Sholom Aleichem in Exile." *Commentary* 8, No. 6 (December 1949): 582-87.
    Translation of letters from Sholom Aleichem concerning the reception of his work in England.

———. "Cedars of Lebanon: Sholom Aleichem in Sickness." *Commentary* 10, No. 4 (October 1950): 379-83.
    Letters from Sholom Aleichem written in 1908 and 1909.

Draznin, Yaffa. "Beth Sholom Aleichem: A Kasrilik in Tel Aviv." *Midstream* 21, No. 10 (December 1975): 52-5.
    Describes the memorial building to Sholom Aleichem in Tel Aviv, its history and purpose, and the literary activities sponsored there.

Gittleman, Sol. *Sholom Aleichem: A Non-Critical Introduction.* The Hague: Mouton, 1974, 203 p.
    Survey of Sholom Aleichem's works, including biographical background, discussion of major themes, and analysis of their influence on later writers.

Goldsmith, Emanuel S. "The Divine Humor of Sholom Aleichem on His 70th Yortsayt." *Judaism* 35, No. 140 (Fall 1986): 391-401.
    Places Sholom Aleichem's humor in the context of Jewish history and characterizes it as innovative, philosophical, and affirmative.

Grafstein, Melech, ed. *Sholom Aleichem Panorama.* London, Ontario: The Jewish Observer, 1948, 415 p.
    Collection of essays on Sholom Aleichem's life and work, and translations of his stories, plays, letters, and memoirs.

Kaufman, Bel. "Sholom Aleichem." In *Abroad in America: Visitors to the New Nation,* edited by Marc Prachter, pp. 270-78. Reading, Mass.: Addison-Wesley Publishing Co., 1976.
    Biographical sketch followed by a presentation of Sholom Aleichem's views on America as expressed in his writing and through the characters in his stories. Kaufman, Sholom Aleichem's granddaughter, writes: "Although he was critical of American materialism and emphasis on business, his feeling about this country was positive and optimistic. . . . He saw America as the land of the future; he appreciated its scope; and he loved its energy and vitality."

Liptzin, Sol. "Peretz and Sholom Aleichem." In his *A History of Yiddish Literature,* pp. 56-72. Middle Village, N.Y.: Jonathan David Publishers, 1972.
    General discussion of Sholom Aleichem's life and works.

Miron, Dan. *Sholem Aleykhem: Person, Persona, Presence.* New York: Walden Press, 1972, 45 p.
    Investigates the function of the pseudonym "Sholom Aleichem" and the effect of the fictional author on the text of the stories. Miron contends: "What is needed is a perception of the ontological difference between author and persona, of the fact that they exist on totally different levels."

Niger, Shmuel. "The Gift of Sholom Aleichem." *Commentary* 2, No. 2 (August 1946): 116-23.
    Discusses the development of Sholom Aleichem's humor and the innovations he wrought in Jewish literature.

Rosenfeld, Isaac. "The Humor of Exile." *Partisan Review* 10, No. 3 (May-June 1943): 294-97.
    Discusses the alienation of shtetl Jews from modern society and Sholom Aleichem's fidelity to his people and their hope for a home.

Roskies, David G. "Introduction." *Prooftexts* 6, No. 1 (January 1986): 1-5.
    Introduction to an issue devoted to criticism on Sholom Aleichem. The critic provides a chronology and description of the changes in critical response to Sholom Aleichem's works.

———. "Unfinished Business: Sholem Aleichem's *From the Fair.*" *Prooftexts* 6, No. 1 (January 1986): 65-78.
    Review of Sholom Aleichem's unfinished autobiography.

Samuel, Maurice. *The World of Sholom Aleichem.* New York: Alfred A. Knopf, 1945, 331 p.
    Description of the culture and language of the Jewish Pale of Settlement, using Sholom Aleichem's stories as illustrations.

Shenker, Israel. "Yiddish." In his *Coat of Many Colors: Pages from Jewish Life,* pp. 207-16. Garden City, N.Y.: Doubleday & Co., 1985.
    Reminiscences of the annual readings of Sholom Aleichem's stories on the anniversary of his death.

Stern, Michael. "Tevye's Art of Quotation." *Prooftexts* 6, No. 1 (January 1986): 79-96.
    Asserts that Tevye consciously controls his choice of Hebrew quotations and their humorous effect. The critic also claims: "They are used by Tevye as a running commentary on the story itself and often, as weapons in his verbal battle with God."

Vladimirova, Ekaterina. " 'Peace Be with You' (The 125th Anniversary of the Birth of Sholom Aleichem)." *Soviet Literature,* No. 10 (1984): 126-30.
    Biographical and critical sketch focusing on the popularity of Sholom Aleichem's works in the Soviet Union. The critic concludes that Sholom Aleichem "was not a Marxist. Nevertheless, Sholom Aleichem's genuine talent was a faithful compass that led him to socially valid conclusions and assessments that objectively helped to educate the reader in the revolutionary cause. . . ."

Waife-Goldberg, Marie. *My Father, Sholom Aleichem.* New York: Simon and Schuster, 1968, 333 p.
    Biography of Sholom Aleichem concentrating on his family life.

Weiner, Meyer. "On Sholem Aleichem's Humor." *Prooftexts* 6, No. 1 (January 1986): 41-54.
    Explores various aspects of Sholom Aleichem's humor, including its irony, its humanity, and its manifestation in specific character types.

Wirth-Nesher, Hana. Review of *The Best of Sholom Aleichem,* edited by Irving Howe and Ruth Wisse. *Notre Dame English Journal: A Journal of Religion in Literature* 11, No. 2 (April 1979): 159-62.
    Praises the new translations in this collection for "introducing the craftier, subtler, and, yes, bleaker Sholom Aleichem to English audiences."

Italo Svevo

1861-1928

(Pseudonym of Ettore Schmitz) Italian novelist, short story writer, and dramatist.

For further discussion of Svevo's career, see *TCLC,* Volume 2.

Svevo is regarded as one of the most original authors in modern Italian literature. Best known for his novels *Senilità (As a Man Grows Older)* and *La coscienza di Zeno (The Confessions of Zeno),* Svevo, who was strongly influenced by Sigmund Freud's theories, pioneered the use of the interior monologue as a narrative technique and produced insightful characterizations by describing the day-to-day psychological lives of ordinary protagonists. While he received little critical notice until near the end of his life, Svevo is currently considered the most important Italian novelist since Giovanni Verga.

Svevo was born in Trieste, a culturally heterogeneous Italian port that was then part of the Austrian Empire. His own heritage, demonstrated in his pseudonym which means "Italus the Swabian," reflected the diversity of his native city: his father's family had come from the German Rhineland, while his mother's family was Italian. Both his parents were Jewish, and Svevo attended the local school for Jewish children. Svevo's father, a businessman, decided that he wanted him to learn German and other languages to prepare for a business career in multilingual Trieste, and at the age of twelve, Svevo entered the Brussel'sche Handels- und Erziehungs-institut, a boarding school near the town of Würzburg, Germany. More interested in literature than business, Svevo read many German classics and began writing comedic dramas and other works for his own enjoyment. He returned to Trieste at the age of seventeen and enrolled in the Instituto Superiore Commerciale Revoltella, where he took courses in law and medicine without pursuing a specific degree. In 1880, Svevo's father experienced severe financial difficulties, and Svevo was forced to discontinue his education and go to work. While employed as a bank clerk, he contributed essays and book reviews to the newspaper *L'indipendente,* and his first published work of fiction, "L'assassinio di via Belpaggio," described by P. N. Furbank as "a sort of *Crime and Punishment* in little," appeared in *L'indipendente* in 1890. Svevo published his first two novels, *Una vita (A Life)* and *As a Man Grows Older,* at his own expense in 1892 and 1898 respectively; both books were virtually ignored by critics.

Discouraged by the lack of attention his works received, Svevo abandoned his literary ambitions and devoted himself to business for the next twenty-five years. He married Livia Veneziani, his second cousin, in 1896, and eventually joined her family's marine paint manufacturing firm. Because he frequently visited the firm's branch office near London, Svevo hired an English tutor, James Joyce, who was then living in Trieste and supporting himself as a language instructor. Joyce read and praised Svevo's work, especially *As a Man Grows Older.* About this time, Svevo was introduced to the works of Sigmund Freud; Furbank suggests that Svevo's ambition to introduce Freudian theory to Italian readers was a

significant factor in his decision in the 1920s to return to fiction writing. *The Confessions of Zeno,* the autobiography of the fictional Zeno Cosini as told to his psychoanalyst, was published in 1923. While a few local critics gave *Zeno* positive reviews, the national Italian press generally ignored it. Svevo sent a copy to Joyce, now a celebrated author, who assured Svevo that *Zeno* was an excellent novel and promised to use his own influence to publicize it. As the result of Joyce's efforts, Valéry Larbaud published excerpts from *As a Man Grows Older* and *Zeno* in a French literary magazine; at the same time, Eugenio Montale, hearing about Svevo while in Paris, published several articles on Svevo's work in Italian newspapers. This attention marked the beginning of the "Svevo case," a debate among critics on the literary qualities of Svevo's novels. His detractors deplored his monotonous prose style, his choice of weak and unattractive protagonists, and the unconventional narrative structure of his works. His admirers praised his skillful use of the interior monologue, his keen sense of humor, his ironic portrayal of the bourgeoisie, and his psychological insight. During the mid-1920s, Svevo, now a successful businessman, enjoyed the literary recognition he received and continued to write plays, fables, and short stories. Svevo died in 1928 from injuries sustained in an automobile accident, leaving a projected sequel to *Zeno* unfinished.

Svevo's three major works, *A Life, As a Man Grows Older,* and *The Confessions of Zeno,* are quite similar in theme, characterization, and structure, portraying ordinary characters in loosely organized narratives. *A Life* is the story of Alfonso Nitti, a young bank clerk who commits suicide after an unsuccessful affair with his boss's daughter. In *As a Man Grows Older,* Emilio Brentani, who lives with his sickly sister and has an affair with a working class girl, is troubled by constant indecision and unsuccessful attempts to impose his dreams and illusions on reality. Both novels treat many of the themes that Svevo further explored in *The Confessions of Zeno:* concepts and manifestations of disease and health, the aging process, preoccupation with death, human motivation, love, and jealousy. While early commentators criticized Svevo for featuring protagonists they considered boring, later critics have focused on the originality with which Svevo presented his characters' psychologies. Contemporary Italian critics also deplored Svevo's prose, observing that it lacked grace and polish; however, more recent critics contend that the undistinguished style of Svevo's fiction suits his characters' lack of distinction. According to C. P. Snow, "Not so much by conscious choice as because it was necessary for the content of his books, he wanted to write in an easy, unrhetorical, flat, general-purpose prose, a good deal nearer the colloquial language than most Italian of his period." Critics have also debated the extent to which Svevo's works are autobiographical, with some viewing the evolution of the protagonists through the three novels as a reflection of Svevo's own development. Some commentators suggest that the autobiographical aspects of these works reflect the role that fiction writing played in Svevo's life. Lilia Ghelli Subrizi has concluded, "Svevo the author and Svevo the character are often fused because the author is studying himself through the protagonist."

The Confessions of Zeno is generally considered Svevo's foremost achievement. The narrative is cast as the autobiography of a man whose psychoanalyst has suggested that he write his life story as a form of therapy. Although Svevo remained skeptical concerning the value of psychoanalysis, commentators note that he found in Freudian theory confirmation of the intuitive psychological insights he had developed in *A Life* and *As a Man Grows Older.* Some critics argue that it would be technically impossible for Zeno to psychoanalyze himself as he does in the novel, but most find that Svevo used the concepts of psychoanalysis quite perceptively. Especially praised for its complex form, *The Confessions of Zeno* is told through overlapping, nonlinear chapters which alternate among different verb tenses. Critics note that the stream-of-consciousness narrative technique, which Svevo used in all three novels, is most fully realized in *Zeno.* The novel also demonstrates Svevo's belief in the power of language to transform and re-create experience. In telling his story, Zeno lies, distorts, and exaggerates to the extent that ultimately he is not sure which incidents are genuine memories and which he has created to satisfy the psychoanalyst. In this as well as other works, Svevo used irony skillfully and was able to balance humor and pathos.

Svevo's short fiction, much of which was left unfinished at his death, is generally considered less important than his novels. In fragments of a projected sequel to *The Confessions of Zeno,* as in much of his short fiction, Svevo experimented with language and with concepts of past and present time. Like his novels, Svevo's stories incorporate witty and insightful observations of himself and others. In "La novella del buon vec-

chio e della bella fanciulla" ("The Story of the Nice Old Man and the Pretty Girl"), for example, he treats the subject of old age with characteristic irony, and some commentators interpret *Una burla riuscita (The Hoax),* the story of an aspiring author who is tricked by a swindler offering to translate his novel, as an ironic look at his own sudden fame. Svevo also wrote numerous dramas, only one of which, *Terzetto spezzato,* was performed during his life. Critics suggest that his preferred subjects and style, which emphasize psychological states rather than dramatic action, were not suited for the theater, and most study his plays only for insights into his fiction.

Svevo is remembered primarily for the creative techniques he used to explore character. One of the first novelists to experiment with psychoanalytic concepts, he skillfully balanced the tragic and the comic elements inherent in everyday life. Unappreciated during much of his life, Svevo's novels are currently considered pioneering works of modern European psychological fiction.

(See also *Contemporary Authors,* Vols. 104 and 122.)

PRINCIPAL WORKS

Una vita (novel) 1892
   [*A Life,* 1963]
Senilità (novel) 1898
   [*As a Man Grows Older,* 1932]
La coscienza di Zeno (novel) 1923
   [*The Confessions of Zeno,* 1930]
Terzetto spezzato (drama) 1925
Una burla riuscita (short story) 1928
   [*The Hoax,* 1929]
La novella del buon vecchio e della bella fanciulla (short stories) 1930
   [*The Nice Old Man and the Pretty Girl, and Other Stories,* 1930]
Inferiorità (drama) 1932, published in journal *La Panarie*
   [*Inferiority* published in *Essays on Italo Svevo,* 1969]
Corto viaggio sentimentale e altri racconti inediti (short stories) 1949
   [*Short Sentimental Journey, and Other Stories,* 1967]
Further Confessions of Zeno (short stories) 1969

JAMES JOYCE (letter date 1924)

[*Joyce is the most prominent and influential literary figure of the first half of the twentieth century. Many critics feel that his experiments in prose, particularly the advancement of the interior monologue, redefined both the limits of language and the form of the modern novel. Joyce and Svevo became friends when Joyce lived in Trieste in the early 1900s. In the following excerpt from a letter to Svevo, Joyce praises* La coscienza di Zeno.]

Thank you for the novel with the inscription [*La coscienza di Zeno*]. I now have two copies, having already ordered one in Trieste. I am in the process of reading it with great pleasure. Why are you discouraged? You must know that it is by far your best book. As far as the Italian critics are concerned, I do not know. But have copies sent to M. Valéry Larbaud, M. Benjamin Crémieux, Mr. T. S. Eliot, Editor *Criterion,* Mr.

F. M. Ford. I shall speak and write to these men about the matter. I shall be able to write more when I have finished reading it. At present two things interest me. The theme: I would never have thought that smoking could dominate a person in such a way. Secondly: the treatment of time in the novel. There is no absence of wit in it and I notice that the last line of *Senilità:* "Yes, Angiolina thinks and weeps, etc . . ." has impressively developed in privacy. (p. 120)

> *James Joyce, in a letter to Italo Svevo on January 30, 1924 in* Inventario, *Vol. II, No. I, Spring, 1949, pp. 120-21.*

THE TIMES LITERARY SUPPLEMENT (essay date 1926)

[*In the following excerpt, the reviewer criticizes the subject, style, and form of* La coscienza di Zeno.]

Italo Svevo has no exceptional talent, a restricted vision and a slipshod provincial style. His hero [in *La coscienza di Zeno*], either in his complacencies or his indecencies, has no sublimity, and his recollection of an imaginary invalid's states of mind, far from being an effort, like M. Proust's, to arrange and fix valuable sensations of abnormal intensity, are nothing more than the voluble communications of a confessedly futile and despicable person whose little desires and weaknesses are, for him, the centre of all interest.

The book, which is very long, is divided into several sections, and the whole purports to be a narrative written at the request of a psychoanalyst. First, Zeno Cosini recounts his ridiculous failures to give up smoking, including a comic escape from a nursing home; then comes a description of his father and of his father's death from cerebral oedema; then he tells how he came to marry the one daughter of his friend Malfenti whom he did not wish to marry; next, how he formed a *liaison* with Carla, a budding singer, and in the course of it came to love his wife Augusta; next, the story of his commercial association with Guido Speier, who had married a sister of Augusta, the futility of Guido's speculations, his amours with his typist, the jealousy of Ada, and the smash which caused Guido's involuntary suicide; finally, we have some amusing remarks on psycho-analysis and the conclusion that all human life is rotten at its roots. In this interminable *bavardage* nothing is left out, no passage has more importance than another. It is not dramatic, it has no organic form, it presents no profound view of humanity, nor has it the passion of good satire. The one quality, besides sheer perseverance, to be observed is a certain efficacy in carrying out the author's intention of exposing a grotesque and undeservedly well-treated individuality. A wry and contemptuous smile is certainly prompted by the absurd accounts of Zeno's escape from a nursing home as soon as he arrived there; of how he began to limp after talking with a lame friend; of the great evening at the Malfenti's, where, after a comic table-turning episode, he proposes to Ada, Alberta and Augusta in succession, and becomes afflicted with chronic neuritis in his anger at Guido's caricature; of the scenes with Carla and the bland feelings of innocence which soothed him at each unfaithfulness to his wife; of the ridiculous and unfortunate speculation in sulphate of copper; and of the final catastrophe. Augusta's calm housewifery and jealousy of Ada, Ada's martyrdom to Guido and its repercussions on Zeno, Guido's hopeless volatility, and the genial effrontery of Giovanni Malfenti, are given, or at least gradually amalgamate out of the flux, with a certain effect. The point is, however, that in these partial

successes of representation Italo Svevo has done no better than many, and worse than the great, novelists; while the acclaimed originality and importance of this book seem to resolve themselves into a mere negation.

> *"An Italian Novelist," in* The Times Literary Supplement, *No. 1268, May 20, 1926, p. 332.*

BERYL DE ZOETE (essay date 1929)

[*In the following excerpt, de Zoete favorably reviews Svevo's three novels, praising in particular Svevo's characterizations and use of humor.*]

[Svevo's] first novel, *Una vita,* the intimate history of a bank clerk and his frustrated love-affair with the bank director's daughter, was published in 1893 when Ettore Schmitz was thirty-two. There is nothing immature in his treatment of the story; the various scenes and characters are drawn with admirable and convincing reality. There is practically no description, never any interposition of the author between us and his drama. The characters rise before us, the story develops with a quite delusive simplicity. The typical Svevian hero is already essentially there, in Alfonso the bank-clerk; the same subtlety, introspection, self-destructive irony; the same tolerance, intellectual passion and purpose to understand a world whose huge insensitiveness defeats him. But Alfonso is the only finally defeated Svevian hero, as he is also the least fantastic and the least humorous.

In 1898 appeared *Senilità,* a novel as original in treatment as *Una vita,* and more developed in Italo Svevo's peculiar technique—in some ways the most perfect of his three novels. It is again a love story in a bourgeois setting, the liaison of a young employé of literary tastes and very limited means with a charming and corrupt girl of the people. The subject is banal enough, but the irony and pathos of the story hold one from the first: the repercussion of the hero's egotistic and absorbing passion on the poor repressed sister who keeps house for him; the brutal unveiling of her own timid and hopeless love for her brother's sculptor-friend, a cynic and fortunate lover, who sweeps through the book like a force of nature, tearing the web of complicated emotions which the hero is always ready to spin afresh.

Una vita had been favourably reviewed; *Senilità* was not reviewed at all. Silence descended on the author and his works. He tells us in his preface to the new edition of *Senilità,* published last year, that he had come by degrees to take the view evidently held by all the critics, that he was no writer and had better stick to commerce.

So for twenty-five years Italo Svevo disappeared, while Ettore Schmitz apparently grew and prospered. Perhaps the war, which increased his leisure, perhaps also the sympathy of James Joyce, then living in Trieste, encouraged him to write again. In 1923 appeared his third and longest novel, *La coscienza di Zeno,* which was immediately hailed as a work of genius by Léon Daudet, Valéry Larbaud, and Benjamin Crémieux. Save for two short stories, one published in February of this year, this is, as far as we know, the sum of his literary activity.

La coscienza di Zeno, by which Italo Svevo will undoubtedly always be best known, is the most complex, and in actual form the least perfect, of his novels; for it consists of several long, loosely linked autobiographical episodes, each of which is practically complete in itself. A pyscho-analytic doctor, whom Zeno treats with half-humorous, half-exasperated contempt, inspires the autobiography and lingers down to its last page, by which time he has fallen into deep disgrace.

A sense of disease, Zeno thinks, is like a sense of sin; one is born with it or without it. He was born with it. A casual meeting with an acquaintance in a café, who tells him as a joke that every step we take involves the action of fifty-four muscles, at once makes Zeno limp for several days afterwards. He pictures the joints running short of oil and chafing each other. "Even to-day" (many years later), "if I feel someone watching me as I walk, I get tied up in those fifty-four movements and can only by an effort prevent myself from falling." Zeno also had another weakness, "la malattia delle parole"—"I loved her simple speech, I, who could not open my lips without misrepresenting things and people; because otherwise talking would not have seemed worth while. . . . Language I regarded as having an independent existence, as an event in itself, and therefore not to be bound by any other event." This malady of words leads him into the most perverse situations. It also, alas, makes him impossible to quote except at great length, for whichever incident one thinks of: the psychological results of a scratch by an angora cat in a London book-shop, his wooing of three sisters in succession on the same evening, and capture of the one he least wanted for a wife, his suicidal criticism of a rival lover's Bach playing, his pious following of the wrong funeral procession, all prove to have so many humorous implications which to omit is like showing the staterooms without their private boudoirs and powdering-closets where the secrets of character hide; Svevo's humour, never obvious, never exactly brilliant, always seems to lurk just beyond the quotation. (p. 521)

Svevo is a born novelist. He has only to name a character for it to come to life. There are very few descriptive passages, little imagery, no rhetoric, no romantic glamour, and though there are plenty of fantastic situations, they do not motivize the action but spring from vagaries of character. No one was ever less sensational; even a suicide is the quietest and least flamboyant of full-stops. Nor had he any use for provocative titles. It was suggested to him that *Senilità* was an odd and dismal title for the story of a young man's love. In the preface to last year's reprint, he admits it to be paradoxical, but refuses to change it, because it represented, he says, a personal experience. All Italo Svevo's novels have unusually the air of being a personal experience, perhaps because there is only one hero under a different guise. We meet him five times, in three novels and two short stories, always temperamentally the same—intelligent, neurotic, abounding in introspection and sympathy, fantastically in love and incompetently ambitious, but in *Zeno* paradoxically a winner. He is the nearest intellectual parallel to Buster Keaton, unheroic, solitary, despised and rejected, who graduates in failure and wins the race by prodigious luck or pure genius. A large humanity, a profoundly humorous view of life, are implicit in the creation of Svevo's most famous character; and we can at least infer that the creator of one of the most intelligent heroes in fiction was himself prodigiously intelligent. (pp. 521-22)

Beryl de Zoete, "Ettore Schmitz (Italo Svevo)," in The Nation and Athenaeum, *Vol. XLIV, No. 15, January 12, 1929, pp. 521-22.*

JUSTIN O'BRIEN   (essay date 1931)

[*O'Brien is an American critic who has written extensively on modern French literature and has translated important works by André Gide, Albert Camus, and Paul Valéry. In the following excerpt, he examines various aspects of Svevo's novelistic art.*]

Svevo must be judged on his three novels. . . . His short stories, with the exception of **"La novella del buon vecchio e della bella fanciulla,"** which has the proportions of a novel, can be overlooked for the moment; it was a great mistake to first present him in English with *The Hoax,* certainly his least attractive work. Svevo, like Proust, must be approached with patience and good will, for he at first seems difficult and only a large dose can give the full measure of his power and charm.

One can easily recognize the qualities which attracted the attention of Joyce and Larbaud to these novels; for they are qualities which are shared by their own work: the acceptance of the whole domain of the real, the slightest details of daily life and the wildest aspirations of his protagonists; the lack of any arbitrary simplification; the continual self-questioning in which his characters indulge while never ceasing to act and to bask sensually in the life which surrounds them. And Crémieux, as a historian of contemporary Italian literature, could not fail to recognize here the first and only novels of psychological analysis that modern Italy had produced. Years before Joyce and Larbaud had begun to write, Svevo most successfully used the "interior monologue" or stream-of-consciousness method of recording and giving life to his characters' thoughts and sensations. It is this fact more than any other, as in the case of Dujardin, which explains his lack of popularity in the nineties and his sudden recognition in the twenties, when that method became popular. In any country or any language, Italo Svevo would have been a precursor, a man who lived before his time; in Italy where, Pirandello and Borgese notwithstanding, the novel which emphasizes interior or "psychological" action has not even yet been naturalized, he appears as a greater phenomenon than he would have been in France, for instance (where he would have joined the tradition of Constant, Stendhal, and Flaubert).

But despite this disconcerting twentieth-century quality in Svevo, he has not lost all contact with the classic models of the last century. The classic French models, that is: for those three great forces which alternately shaped and stifled the Italian novel during the past fifty years, Manzoni, Verga and d'Annunzio, exerted no influence whatsoever upon him. Certainly he was familiar with Balzac, Stendhal, and Flaubert; Silvio Benco asserts of the young Svevo: "Zola was his god, the *Roman expérimental* his credo." It is true that he owes something to Zola and the naturalists, but fortunately he outgrew that influence very early. (pp. 567-68)

One of the most distinguishing characteristics of these novels is the type of hero that Svevo created in them: a sort of middle-class Triestine Charlie Chaplin, as one writer has described him, who continually exhausts his extraordinary ingenuity in conquering absurdly small obstacles, and with a pathetic obstinacy fails in everything he undertakes. Charlie Chaplin or Don Quixote in modern dress, the fact remains that Svevo has definitely given life to his complex character and presented him in a very tragic and very real light. The Svevian protagonist springs from a fundamental realization of the disequilibrium between the direction given to his own life by the individual and the course which life then pursues, sublimely ignorant of his well-made plans. And in his confused suffering he never quite wakes up to his error. Eager and intelligent, he fails through his own awkward timidity; he stands forever agape at the facility with which others realize their desires. Alfonso in *Una vita,* while out sailing with Macario, marvels at the vast wings and small bodies of the gulls, and Macario reflects on the smallness of the brain. " 'But what has the brain to do with catching fish? He who lacks the necessary wings when he is born will never grow them later. He who doesn't instinctively know how to swoop down on his prey at the precise moment will never learn; and in vain he will study how the others do it, but will never be able to imitate them.' . . . 'And have I wings?' asked Alfonso, beginning to smile. . . . 'Yes, for the flights of your imagination!' answered Macario." Alfonso Nitti, Emilio Brentani, and Zeno Cosini form one type-protagonist who, because he exemplifies for the first time in concrete form a whole class of humanity, is as worthy as Proust's Baron de Charlus of entering the group of the immortal "characters" of fiction.

One might well amuse oneself by contrasting Zeno Cosini with Julien Sorel: on the one hand the man who knows what he wants and invariably gets it; on the other the eternally misplaced one whose ambition is frustrated by his inability to adapt himself. Stendhal glorifies the energetic will, whereas Svevo deliberately chooses persons almost devoid of will. Psychologically they are at opposite poles, but Svevo's exaggeration, if it is exaggeration, approaches nearer to reality. The difference is not unlike that between Corneille and Racine, Horace and Phèdre.

Whether or not . . . Italo Svevo chose such submissive creatures in order to devote himself to a prolonged study of the abnormal personality, the result is the same. As a matter of fact, it is much more likely that his choice was dictated by his own nature and that there is much of Ettore Schmitz in his three heroes. The notable difference in the ages of those heroes may be of some significance, since the age, in each case, corresponds to that of the novelist at the time of writing. Yet he never loses his altogether objective viewpoint; *"guardare e analizzare"*—observation and analysis was his rule, and as with all novelists of introspection it was inevitable that some of his experiments should have been originally performed on his own person.

In *Una vita* Svevo has already chosen his setting in the *bourgeoisie* of Trieste and drawn the first sketch of his typical hero. At the age of twenty, Alfonso Nitti, poor in money and experience, but full of a romantic enthusiasm for life, leaves his little town to settle in the city as a clerk in the bank of Maller and Company. From the first he appears, and to the end he remains, a *déraciné* ["deracinated one"], dazed in the attempt to make his desires conform to the life he sees about him. Introduced into his employer's house, he makes love to and eventually seduces Annetta, the banker's daughter. Thus far Alfonso's career almost parallels that of Julien Sorel in *Le Rouge et le noir;* but having achieved this success, which one might think would satisfy his desires and realize all his ambitions with a rich marriage, he withdraws through pure inertia. He allows to slip from his hands the opportunity he had longed for merely because he is incapable of a decision. Sent away from the city while Annetta gains her father's consent, he returns from his mother's death-bed to find Annetta engaged to her cousin Macario and himself relegated to an inferior position in the bank. The moment his weakness betrays him, Life turns about and deals him a series of blows. Too late, he recognizes his loss, makes an appointment with An-

netta in an attempt to win her back, and just avoids a duel with her brother. The only outlet for his despair is suicide. Crémieux has very justly pointed out that *Una vita,* whose very title suggests rather the later French naturalists, is perhaps the only novel in Italian which at all resembles Flaubert: the interior tragedy of this little bank employee fed on dreams of love and glory, approaches the theme of *L'Éducation sentimentale* and *Madame Bovary.*

Senilità . . . , which followed six years after *Una vita,* is, despite the majority of critics in favor of *Zeno,* undoubtedly his best work, for it is at once more carefully composed, and more universal in its theme than the *Coscienza di Zeno.* Emilio Brentani, an ordinary clerk like Alfonso, is another *raté* ["failure"], disillusioned in his youthful aspirations and unable to adapt himself to the prosaic life that has been given him. Through indifference, he has forsaken his literary ambitions while still weakly longing for "what might have been"; and at thirty-five, full of the bitterness of unsatisfied desires and without ever having really lived, he has reached a premature old age (hence the somewhat unfortunate title of the novel). His desolate life, spent entirely in the company of his spinster sister Amalia, thwarted and withered like himself, and the lady-killing sculptor Balli, whose jovial acceptance of mediocrity contrasts sharply with Emilio's pathological reaction against fate, is suddenly transformed by the presence of Angiolina Zarri. Trying to forget his self-consciousness, Emilio flatters himself that he can throw himself into an affair with the little slut like a man of the world; but no sooner has he crudely declared and satisfied his wants than his imagination, aroused by her ingenuous manner and refusing to recognize the bestiality of their relation, attempts to etherealize her and to create a sentimental bond of love between them. Tormented by jealousy, he is ironically forced to share her with the urbane Balli. The tragedy reaches its climax when his sister in delirium reveals her love for Balli and the fact that she has had recourse to drugs to lighten her despair. Conscious that he has corrupted Amalia's soul, he sees her die just as he had resolved to give up his love and devote himself to her alone. And after this staggering shock, the life of Emilio and Balli resumes its monotonous course. "Years later he would lose himself in wonder over that period of his life, the most important, the most dazzling. He lived upon it like an old man on the memories of his youth. In his mind full of literary allusions, Angiolina underwent a strange metamorphosis: she preserved her beauty unchanged, but at the same time annexed all the qualities of Amalia who died a second time in her. . . . She came to represent his every noble thought and beautiful observation during that period of his life." Thus Emilio's creative imagination, which had tormented him throughout his life, finally consoles him with this pitiful symbol.

The beauty of this remarkable novel lies in its compactness, its density. Beginning, as he always does, *in medias res,* Svevo gives us a strikingly real portrait of life as he has seen it—or perhaps lived it. In creating his four major characters, he has plumbed the depths of their personality without limiting himself to the zone of the conscious.

In the twenty-five years which separate *Senilità* from *La coscienza di Zeno,* Italo Svevo's pessimism has learned to clothe itself in humor, to give itself a calmer exterior, though in reality it has deepened to the point where it no longer even attempts a revolt. The tragedy of the aged Zeno Cosini is the same as that of Alfonso Nitti and Emilio Brentani—with this great difference, however: that it does not even partially take place in the world of physical reality. It is altogether staged *within* Zeno; on the exterior, his life does not seem so difficult as that of his predecessors, but his torment is far deeper and more subtle than theirs. Life continually smiles upon him, though through no fault or merit of his. Outwardly he is successful in everything, and he alone knows that his every move and every thought has marked another failure. Like a child, he reaches out for some forbidden object and finds in his hand a different and, to him, useless object. Even when his most ardent desires are leading him toward a catastrophe, life steps in to provide a happy conclusion for his actions. The story of Zeno is even more difficult to outline than that of the other novels; fortunately, however, we can already read this one in English. In an attempt to ridicule some of the theories of psycho-analysis, Svevo presents these thickly-printed five hundred pages as Zeno's memoirs, the writing of which was imposed upon him by a psycho-analyst as part of his "cure." These confessions, then, bare the character of Zeno, another maladjusted, curiously distorted individual, completely devoid of will-power, whose mania for analyzing each thought and gesture that comes to his notice presents a bitter caricature of our modern madness. Too weak to cure himself of the habit of smoking, he has himself locked up in a sanatorium and then exerts all his ingenuity in schemes for corrupting his nurse and escaping by night, and in suspicions of his wife's fidelity while he is away from home. Instead of marrying the girl he loves, he accepts her refusal and that of her sister only to marry the third sister whom he does not love; and eventually he finds in her the ideal wife. He succeeds in deceiving her without arousing the slightest suspicion, while his brother-in-law in the same situation gets into endless trouble. Despite his wild schemes and misplaced activity, he is a great success in business and even manages to save the fortune of Guido, his brilliant brother-in-law. He is the chronic imaginary invalid who has only to hear a description of a malady in order to feel its symptoms; and yet he lives to bury his healthier friends.

Although Zeno may appear to us, and may even recognize himself, as a comedy character, we must be careful not to treat him too lightly. He is the natural outgrowth of Svevo's other protagonists plus twenty-five years of mature reflection. It seems as if Svevo had deliberately tried to attain popularity by masking his tragedy behind a sly smile. For under his ridiculous exterior Zeno suffers profoundly in his dangerously overpowerful imagination, his exaggerated tendency to self-analysis, and his vicious attempts at self-justification. His will-less efforts to combat his weaknesses and adjust himself to the world set him at odds with the same problems which confronted Alfonso and Emilio.

One cannot but notice, by comparison with the other novels, a certain unaccustomed diffuseness in this later work. Nor is *The Confessions of Zeno,* constructed with such economy of detail and interrelation of incidents as one finds in *Senilità.* Zeno's efforts to cease smoking, the death of his father, his marriage and his financial career stand out as individually flawless elements insufficiently knit together. We get Zeno portrayed from every angle until, without any effort on our part, his character emerges in one piece, whereas the novel (but perhaps this is justified by the form in which it is written) remains episodic. Italo Svevo's peculiar ironic humor, which colors all of his work, resists description or analysis; in fact it often almost resists translation. The least one can say of it

is that it in no way resembles the humor of Panzini or Pirandello. (pp. 568-71)

[Without] hesitation we can place him not only above all his contemporaries in Italy, but in the first rank among modern European novelists.

Although Svevo's style has been much discussed by his compatriots, it will probably not seem remarkable in English, for we are more accustomed to the qualities it manifests. At first it strikes one as almost shockingly bare; later one recognizes that it is incredibly, refreshingly devoid of that rhetoric or false eloquence which Italians almost never escape. Since he was born in what was then an Austrian city and educated largely in Germany, it is not strange that his language should contain many barbarisms. The words are Italian, but they are not always used in an Italian manner. But ugly as it may be, Svevo uses his language as a forceful tool which always achieves the end for which it was created. He writes badly as Dreiser does, or as Henry James did.

Almost more important as a unifying factor in this work than his original manner of evoking life by simple narration and profound analysis or his very real creation of a complex type of hero hitherto unknown to literature, we find another, and rather intangible, element: the climate of his novels. His characters all live and act against the background of Trieste with its great mercantile port and modern industrial life. This city—the only one which appears in his work—gradually assumes a definite personality, until it becomes one of the actors in the drama. It is not necessary to know Trieste to appreciate Svevo; he creates the city for us until we feel, on the contrary, that it would be necessary to know Svevo to appreciate Trieste. There is indeed a Trieste of Svevo just as there is a Dublin of James Joyce and a Paris of Balzac. And in the harmonious combination of these various elements which constitutes the work of Italo Svevo, we must go a step further and admit that there exists a Svevian world, for every great artist possesses a world of his own which he alone can open to us. (p. 571)

Justin O'Brien, "Italo Svevo," in The Bookman, *New York, Vol. LXXII, No. 6, February, 1931, pp. 566-71.*

EDOUARD RODITI (essay date 1949)

[*Roditi is a French-born poet, short story writer, biographer, translator, and critic whose works reflect his interest in Jewish thought and culture. In the following excerpt, he surveys the development of style and important themes in Svevo's fiction.*]

[Svevo's works are] difficult to place properly in the complex and conflicting traditions of the Italian novel. The society that he describes is not typically Italian; his characters illustrate many qualities and faults of the Austrian bourgeoisie; his language, far from being the literary Tuscan of classical idealists or a colorful dialect such as the regional realists or *Veristi* affected, is rather the sophisticated and nerveless jargon of the educated Triestine bourgeoisie which spoke Italian neither as a literary nor as a national language, but as a convenient and easy manifestation of local patriotism. Svevo himself was an Austrian citizen until the end of the First World War, when two of his novels had already been published. All his fiction is clearly set in pre-war Trieste, except the very last part of the *Confessions of Zeno* (the war in and around Trieste), **"La novella del buon vecchio"** (war-time

Trieste), *Una burla riuscita* (post-war inflation in Trieste) and **"Il vecchione"** (Italian Trieste after the war). The characters of Svevo's stories are thus mostly of the Italian-speaking bourgeoisie, though their names are often Croat or German and though many of them are described as speaking German. Characters picked from the people, however, are described as speaking Triestine or Friulian dialect, mixtures of Italian and Slovenian or Croatian, and the "Buon Vecchio" does not wish to teach the "bella fanciulla" correct Italian, when he decides to educate her, but German. (pp. xiii-xiv)

Svevo's heroes all seem to be tormented by an intense lust for self-improvement, spiritual or social, for education, wisdom or learning to better them or their positions; however old, they still think themselves unprepared for the serious business of living. Zeno thus hopes always to cure himself of his vice of smoking, long hesitates between law and chemistry as professions, then does nothing till circumstances force him into business where, much to his own surprise, he is successful. The heroes of *Una vita, As a Man Grows Older* and *The Hoax* are not content with their petty clerical jobs, consider these far beneath their intelligence and culture, and hope or intend, some day, to devote all their time and talents to writing. The heroes of *As a Man Grows Older* and *The Hoax,* though each may have published a novel some years earlier and both still enjoy, in provincial society, considerable reputations as local intellectuals, are yet both unable now to write anything new. The hero of *The Hoax,* for his own amusement or to compensate his inferiority complex, does indeed compose some animal fables that are included in the narrative; but Zeno, who never pretends to be a writer, also effortlessly composes two such fables and Svevo himself, in his years of literary sterility, wrote **"La Madre,"** another such animal fable to which he attached very little importance. Zeno manages to write his autobiography only because this is part of the discipline of his psycho-analysis, whereas Svevo's other heroes are content to dream of writing something only in the vague future or are unable to express themselves. The heroes of *Una vita* and **"The Story of the Nice Old Man"** indeed attempt to compose philosophic treatises, but they make no real progress in clarifying their thoughts or in consigning them to paper in an ordered form. In a bourgeois society of culture-snobs, illusions of intellectual grandeur thus compensate social or emotional maladjustment; but these illusions no longer need produce any tangible results, though they may have in the past. (pp. xiv-xv)

The influence of Freud, in Svevo's later work, is certainly important. Zeno consults a psychoanalyst and discovers that he has an Oedipus complex; besides, the whole novel illustrates Freudian theory as clearly as a case-history, though *A Sentimental Journey, Adolphe* and *La nouvelle Héloise,* written long before Freud's theories were formulated, also make excellent case-histories today. The poet Eugenio Montale, writing a few days after Svevo's death, came closer to the truth, however, when he declared that *Zeno* is "tortured with the trick of *bovarysme.*" This term, invented by Jules de Gaultier to designate a peculiarity of the characters of Flaubert's realistic novels, designates what Paul Bourget called "le mal d'avoir connu l'image de la réalité avant la réalité" ["the misfortune to have known the image of reality before reality"] and what Gaultier describes as "le pouvoir départi à l'homme de se concevoir autre qu'il n'est" ["the power granted man to believe himself different from what he is"]. Among Flaubert's characters, Homais thought himself a positivist scientist, Madame Bovary thought herself a great romantic heroine born to brilliant and spectacular loves, and Bouvard and Pécuchet thought they could acquire all knowledge by reading cheap magazines of pseudoscientific vulgarization. But instead of having only one wrong conception of themselves, Svevo's *bovaryste* heroes tend to have several such conceptions and to wander shiftlessly from one misdirected ambition to another, one unsuccessful venture to another; they thus achieve the too many possibilities which Momigliano criticized and which relate them so closely to Musil's *Der Mann ohne Eigenschaften,* another *bovaryste*. The French critic Benjamin Crémieux is therefore right when he finds *Una vita* "strongly influenced by Flaubert." But the nature of this influence and its exact significance cannot be found in Svevo's style and subject; it is to be found . . . in Svevo's approach to subject and in the way he handles it.

In Svevo's first novel, *Una vita,* the hero, Alfonso Nitti, is a country lad who, in Trieste, becomes an unimportant employee of the busy Maller Bank. Though conscious, at times, of some moral or cultural superiority, Nitti yet feels incompetent and lost in this prosperous and enterprising world. In a moment of weakness or ambition he becomes the lover of Annie Maller, his rich employer's daughter, a vain and corrupt culture-snob. Nitti's passion is far more insincere and conscious of its insincerity than Madame Bovary's love for Léon. Annie is also insincere, both amused and frightened by her own daring. The reader thus gradually realizes the inevitability of their parting. Nitti is reduced, by the insincerity of his love and by the very real misery of such unreal happiness, to a passive listlessness which ends in suicide. This is not, however, the romantic escape of a Werther. In the age of neoclassical tragedy, the stoical hero had preferred death to slavery or disgrace. Later, Werther and the early Romantics, aristocratic idealists in an age of bourgeois opportunism, had preferred death, in an act of proud defiance, to the disappointments of an inglorious life. The later Romantics and decadents had sometimes advocated suicide as the *poète maudit's* final affirmation of individuality in a hostile world. All these still were, or tried to be, masters of their own destinies. But Alfonso Nitti's despair goes even further than the confused defeatism of the decadent; weaker and even more completely defeated by reality and his surroundings, Nitti is led to suicide without any will to resist or defy fate, or to affirm himself even self-destructively. Life and reality are his enemies; he remains innocent of his own death. In Svevo's more consciously modern later novel, in *Zeno,* Guido Speier's suicide is but a manifestation of a neurotic drive or of economic pressure, no longer at all of individual reason or will.

The end of *Una vita* is death; that of Svevo's next novel, *As a Man Grows Older,* is hallucination, when the hero finds courage and a strange balance while the author gradually develops a new Stoicism. *As a Man Grows Older* reveals moreover another aspect of *bovarysme:* a false literary idealism which, applied to love, makes Emilio Brentani, a weak character afflicted with literary ambitions, believe that Angiolina, a commonplace provincial demi-mondaine, is a veritable Beatrice. Emilio adorns Angiolina with all the qualities of the great heroines of literature; but she is gradually dragging him down, as Odette dragged Proust's Swann, to her own shoddy level. With the illness and death of his sister Amalia, a mouse-like spinster whom he neglects but who heroically conceals until her delirium her unrequited love for his best friend, Emilio discovers how shabby his own jealous love has been.

He then abandons Angiolina and returns to this futile life of dreams and vague ambitions; in his mind, he blends Angiolina and Amalia, all the austere qualities of the spinster and the beauty of the whore, and now lives in the imaginary company of a fantastic compound of irreconcilable personalities, real enough to him.

Reviewing the reprint of the English translation of the *Confessions of Zeno,* the anonymous critic of the London *Times* pointed out that the episodes of the War, towards the end of the book, were not properly integrated within the structure of the work as a whole, and that *As a Man Grows Older* has far more unity as a work of art. . . . The supreme unreason of war seems indeed to fit but rarely within the reasonable structure of a proposed work of art. . . . Svevo treated the whole business as a sort of supreme Jewish joke in which all humanity is involved in the rôle of the unreasonable Gentile.

Though *As a Man Grows Older* thus lacks the final apocalyptic touch which upsets the balance of the *Confessions of Zeno* as a work of art but at the same time raises it to the level of a revelation, the earlier novel's sheer perfection is indeed rare in the literature of our age. It is a perfection which was born of great leisure, when the full attention of some privileged artists could be devoted, as in the last decades of the heyday of the bourgeois world of private enterprise, to the patterning of details. *The Spoils of Poynton, The Turn of the Screw* or *The Aspern Papers,* among the works of Henry James, offer us the same kind of unity in their structure and tone. Among Svevo's later works, *The Hoax* and "The Story of the Nice Old Man" likewise seem to illustrate this perfection, which is proof that Svevo was a truly great writer, one who knew what he wanted to create and was able to achieve it, not the chance author of one phenomenal work. (pp. xvii-xx)

The works of Svevo's second period, *Zeno* and the stories, distinguish themselves from the earlier work by a greater subjectivity in the treatment of the hero, who tells his story in the first person both in *Zeno* and in the unfinished **"Il vecchione,"** and by a greater objectivity in the treatment of detail, incident, setting and reality. The characters are thus better integrated and their doubts and hesitations seem more justified, more clearly motivated by their experiences; and their misfortunes, though no less poignant, seem less tragic or even become frankly humorous, according to the mood of the reader. Though still maladjusted, Svevo's later heroes remain incurably and innocently hopeful in their misfortunes, and Zeno even wonders how man ever wandered into this world where he is so obviously a stranger. This congenital inability to keep in step with the surrounding world (and what intelligent or good man, intent upon eternity, can feel at home in our evil and foolish age?), is the cause of all the unhappiness of Svevo's heroes and precludes the success of all conscious action in their lives. It makes them bungle everything that they ever attempt, so that they are pleasantly surprised if chance or unconscious action bring success. Relegated to the margin of social and economic activity, instead of acting, they generally dream, analyze and comment on the action of others or the workings of chance. . . . [Svevo's heroes] were born unfit for life. Their misfortunes are not caused by chance, nor by will; and their natural enemies are all those healthier and more successful human beings who behave like the Gentiles in Jewish jokes. The fact that Svevo's most "Gentile" character, the one most given to "goyim nachus," should bear the very Jewish name of Speier may indeed be but an additional twist in Svevo's elaborate irony: has not assimilation transformed some "Jews" into ideal "Gentiles"? Even his wife's little sister, a healthy child, persecutes Zeno by whispering into his ear that he is insane. Guido Speier, at first Zeno's rival and then his brother-in-law, represents indeed the opposite type of the more virile "extravert" who takes success for granted and, at first, seems to achieve it with ease. In *As a Man Grows Older,* Emilio Brentani finds such a contrary in Balli; but Balli is not made ridiculous, as is Speier, by any failure. The introvert heroes of Svevo's two earlier novels indeed remain unsuccessful. In *Una vita,* Nitti is finally defeated by his rival when Annie Maller jilts him to marry Macario; in *As a Man Grows Older,* there is no competition, but Brentani is forced to observe Balli's more successful general adjustment to life. In Svevo's later fiction, the introvert is successful: the hero of *The Hoax* makes a fortune out of the trick of which he was supposed to be victim, and Guido Speier, in "Wife and Mistress,"one of the chapters of *Zeno,* gets involved in a series of foolhardy adventures which, in "A Business Partnership,"lead him finally to bankruptcy and suicide, whereas Zeno, though convinced of his own clumsiness and impotence, yet manages to betray his wife and to have a mistress, without experiencing any of the jealousies and complications which his brother-in-law Guido creates with his amorous intrigues.

When he wrote *Zeno* and the other works of his second period, Svevo had, it seems, become reconciled to man's helplessness and to the inevitable duality of intention and achievement, character and surroundings, ambition and real life. His later heroes are happier than those of his earlier works and, though no better fitted for life than Alfonso Nitti or Emilio Brentani, are treated less hard by fate, by causality and by their surroundings; they even sometimes achieve success, though much to their surprise and rarely as a result of planned effort. In *Una vita,* it is Nitti, the hero, who commits suicide. In "A Business Partnership," a chapter of *Zeno,* the hero is convinced of his own inefficiency, yet never loses his head when business becomes difficult, whereas Guido, the "virile extravert," becomes hysterical and commits suicide like a disappointed Romantic; and it is the introvert who then saves the widow's fortune. In *The Hoax,* probably written not much later, Svevo tells how an elderly bank-clerk with literary ambitions is misled, by a practical joker, into accepting a phony contract for the German translation of his early novel; he then sells the royalties "forward" and, owing to the inflation of the Austrian currency, discovers that, thanks to this valueless contract, he had made a small fortune in Italian currency, like any "bear" in the foreign exchange market, though he would never have dared, without his valueless contract, to gamble in this manner. Zeno had similarly earned his father-in-law's admiration by forgetting to sell some shares when their value was rapidly falling, then selling them at a profit months later, when their value had risen again and Malfenti had already sustained a considerable loss by selling "at the right moment."

In the difficult decline of the Roman Empire, when civilization, as in our atomic age, seemed to be menaced from within by itself as much as from without, educated Romans began to believe that the end of the world was near; some turned to the pessimistic doctrines of Augustinian Christianity, which affirmed that man was foolish and evil, others to the pagan doctrines of Zeno the Stoic, who explained that the world, every few thousand years, sank into chaos and flames to rise again, purified and new, as a phoenix from its own ashes. Svevo was perhaps thinking of the Stoic when he named his hero: Zeno Cosini is certainly far more stoical, in his misfortune, than Svevo's earlier heroes. In **"Il vecchione,"** the unfinished last novel, the hero is a very old man, stoically at peace with the world; had Svevo, an old man, finished this work, it would have contrasted clearly with **As a Man Grows Older,** his youthful anticipation of old age. All passion spent, Svevo found peace, wisdom, mature strength, objectivity, not in hallucination but in reality. (pp. xx-xxii)

Edouard Roditi, "A Note on Svevo," in As a Man Grows Older *by Italo Svevo, translated by Beryl de Zoete, New Directions, 1949? pp. xiii-xxii.*

V. S. PRITCHETT (essay date 1953)

[*Pritchett is a highly esteemed English novelist, short story writer, and critic. Considered one of the modern masters of the short story, he is also one of the world's most respected and well-read literary critics. Pritchett writes in the conversational tone of the familiar essay, approaching literature from the viewpoint of a lettered but not overly scholarly reader. In his criticism, he stresses his own experience, judgement, and sense of literary art, rather than following a codified critical doctrine derived from a school of psychological or philosophical speculation. In the following excerpt, Pritchett examines themes and techniques in* Senilità *and selected other writings.*]

Italo Svevo's **As a Man Grows Older** (in Italian, **Senilità**) first appeared fifty years ago and, after its complete failure with the critics and the public, Svevo turned to his business in Trieste, became a rich man, and was persuaded to write again twenty-three years later only by the interest of James Joyce. To that persuasion we owe Svevo's comic masterpiece **The Confessions of Zeno,** which has been compared to the work of Joyce and Proust, and has called up the ghosts of Freud and Otto Weininger. The prosperous business man, we are told, enjoyed his astonishing fame with the innocent wonder of the amateur: did it not, indeed, justify his passive philosophy that all positive intentions blunder and that our success, our happiness, our virtue itself, settle in us by chance, though not by indolence and indifference? As Renato Poggioli's acute introduction to **Zeno** pointed out, Svevo's novels are about people in their empty, off-time or leisure, the hours they have been longing for as they watched the crawl of the hands of the office clock; yet they strike us by a driven and unceasing busyness. Svevo's mind wears itself out like the grasshopper, sings endlessly like the needle of a machine.

Nearly half of Svevo's not very long life lies between **As a Man Grows Older** and **The Confessions of Zeno,** and all the difference between failure and success. Self-improvement is the obsession of his unlucky heroes, and, as Svevo's life went on, they do improve. Their anxious analysing of motives, their eagerness for illusion, their inevitable failures, and their anxiety to understand and to arrive at a sane attitude to life gives them the pathetic air of miming clowns: they talk so much that it creates, by a paradox, the pathos of dumbness. But they become as wise, gentle, restful in their indetermination as the Chinese and walk with the fullness of the superannuated. It has been their curious fate to learn the lesson of life backwards, becoming younger and more apt for life as they grow older; so that if they were to look back upon their youth, and even their middle age, these would seem to them like a puzzling sleep from which, little by little, they have been permitted to awake.

As a Man Grows Older can be considered as a half-awakening from Svevo's grim, earlier novel **Una vita. Una vita** is the story of a bank clerk's fatally insincere love affair which ends in suicide: the lovers have destroyed the meaning of their lives. An austere smile appears between the lines of the next book: the exactions of conscience are severe, but it is perhaps comical that they are self-inflicted. Brentani, a clerk in an insurance office, is too poor to marry and indeed has to support his plain and delicate sister. He is literary, dreamy, a victim of that disease of the sentiments which is called Bovaryisme, which Paul Bourget defined as *"le mal d'avoir connu l'image de la réalité avant la réalité"* ["the misfortune to have known the image of reality before reality"] and which, tinctured by puritanism and snobbery in English literature, produced certain heroines of Scott and Dickens. Brentani has never had a love affair, for he evidently satisfies himself in dreams and repents in analysis; and when he at last decides to fall in love, he makes the worst possible choice in a young, beautiful, hopelessly deceitful working-class girl. The cynicism of the affair owes something to the curious social customs of middle-class life in Trieste at the turn of the century—in general they resemble those of the Mediterranean, where the demi-monde has a precisely defined economic status—but Brentani absurdly encumbers his own path with hallucinations about the girl, unpredictable jealousies and the cruelties of his conscience. A love affair that would not have wrecked his extraverted friend Balli, is fatal to the introverted Brentani; and the effects of the affair are not merely to exalt him or drive him to despair, but to create the desire for love in his sister. A shaded and faltering creature, she conceives a sincere passion which is unrequited; she is taken ill and dies and Brentani is made to see that his impossible behaviour has been the cause. Or rather—for the egoism of Svevo's characters is unfailing and is the source of their comedy—Brentani chooses to think he is the cause; and marrying the delicate image of his sister, to the passionate one of his now discarded mistress (who has run off with a bank thief) he has now a new "image of reality" to dream about, console himself with, and no doubt to impose with results just as devastating, on the next adventure, if he ever has sufficient strength or wilfulness to undertake one.

When I first read **As a Man Grows Older,** some years ago, it seemed to me one more trite little tale about the "little mistress," a grey and listless exercise in Viennese subtlety. I had been carried away by the comic Italian dazzle of **Zeno;** and the only virtue I saw in this earlier book was Svevo's gift for writing innumerable short epitaphs on the nuances of human feeling. I was wrong. In the first place the story of **As a Man Grows Older** has the emotional fullness which is the reward of perfect form and internal balance. How discreetly the cold mists, the sudden rains, the rough seas of the Adriatic port, the glimpses of the city—its business quarter where beautiful women are stared at if they should happen to pass, its empty walks by the sea, its hard-faced flats lit by candles and oil in the poorer quarters, its café meetings—are made to break into Brentani's unstable, never to be self-trusted, yet self-aware mind. In its way, this book is as complete a case-history as *Adolphe,* has the same lucidity, and its analysis the same ruthless serenity, but touched by the clear-headedness of the mad. Here is the passage where Emilio Brentani, in his jealousy, makes his friend Balli, the natural man, promise not to attract his girl who is already betraying him:

> "I am sick with jealousy, nothing else but jealousy.
> I am jealous of the others too, but most of all of
> you. I have got accustomed to the umbrella maker,

but I shall never get accustomed to you." There was not the faintest touch of humour in his voice; he was trying to arouse pity so that he might the more easily get Balli to promise what he wanted. If he had refused Emilio had made up his mind to rush round to Angiolina at once. He did not want his friend to profit by a state of affairs for which he himself had been largely responsible.

Balli promises, out of pity. But a dreamy look in his eye betrays the natural hunter, tempted by the very fact of having given his word. Balli says he has long wanted to make a sketch of the girl "because I thought you would like to have it." Emilio sees through this at once. With ludicrous anxiety he cries out: "You have promised me, you can't go back on it. Try to find your inspiration elsewhere." And when Balli calms him, the base consequences of an apparently disinterested idealism are slyly shown:

> Emilio began lamenting his sad fate with an irony of self-analysis which removed from it every trace of the ridiculous. He said that he wanted all his friends to know how he looked at life. In theory he considered it to be without serious content, and he had in fact never believed in any of the forms of happiness which had been offered him; he had never believed in them and he could truly say that he had never pursued happiness. But how much less easy it was to escape suffering! In a life deprived of all serious content even Angiolina became serious and important.

Half the beauty of Svevo's work lies in his cunning gift of throwing away his lines. Were it not for his pain, Balli reflects, Emilio's situation would be ridiculous; and it is in the subtle balance of the delicacies of pain with the load of comedy that the excitement of the book lies.

The scenes of action are brilliant, freshly observed and as concrete as anything in *Madame Bovary* and a good deal better-natured. It is unforgettable when Amalia, the sister, puts Balli's cup back in the cupboard when she discovers her dream of love will not be realised. There is the long, and really gripping account of her illness. Svevo's scenes of illness are among the most dramatic in any literature, for they observe the struggle of the mind with the body; is not life itself an illness, and sickness one of its more highly-coloured, poetic and even thrilling acts? The love scenes with Angiolina are all excellent, for the Svevo heroes discover women as if they were a new species. These heroes are the kind of men at whose behaviour women smile. And when Angiolina pushes Brentani out of bed with the words "Get out, my beauty," she has said everything. Brentani for her is "a beauty and no mistake." Awed by a love quite beyond her and which would drive her out of her mind if she were to take it seriously, she quickly sets about deceiving him.

Social criticism has been at work on Italo Svevo and there is an interesting account of his work from this point of view by Edouard Roditi [see excerpt dated 1949]. But the weakness of this school of criticism is that, while it analyses the roots, it can only do so by disparaging the flower. And it falls into conventional judgments. It is no doubt true, as Roditi says, that Svevo and his heroes are "culture-snobs" and that "in a bourgeois society of culture-snobs illusions of intellectual grandeur thus compensate social or emotional maladjustment." What of it? Don Quixote was a culture-snob. The type exists within and without the bourgeois order. Illusions of social grandeur compensate contemporary Russian writers for

their spiritual failure. Renato Poggioli's introduction to *The Confessions of Zeno* is illuminating on the question of Svevo as a bourgeois [see excerpt dated 1965]. Here is an acute passage:

> Exactly because he does not judge the bourgeois spirit, Svevo amuses himself, tremendously and naïvely, by looking at it. A perfect bourgeois as a man, as a writer, he is almost alone in not looking like one. Instead of descending or condescending to the bourgeois spirit within his soul he raises it and uplifts it along with himself to the sphere of imagination, to a world of fancy and dreams, which is at the same time the world of reality itself. Once Stendhal asked for a literature written by bankers and industrialists able to understand, lucidly and cynically, the economy of life, the business of society, the value of man. Svevo was certainly a writer of this brand, and furthermore, endowed with such bourgeois honesty and commonsense as to refuse to transform his indulgent egoism into any set of theories, any "egotism." A kind of innocent wisdom was the real source of his greatness and originality.

Possibly Svevo's independence sprang from his Jewish background, from his plural personality—as Roditi shrewdly says—as an Austrian, an Italian and a Jew. When the 1914 war came Roditi says, Svevo "treated the whole business as a sort of supreme Jewish joke in which all humanity is involved in the role of the unreasonable Gentile." Svevo found "normal" behaviour desirable but not reasonable. It was too easy. Like the blameless clown, he preferred the difficulty, the busyness of trying all the wrong roads first. (pp. 25-30)

> *V. S. Pritchett, "The Early Svevo," in his* Books in General, *Chatto & Windus, 1953, pp. 25-30.*

ALAIN ROBBE-GRILLET (essay date 1954)

[*A French novelist and critic, Robbe-Grillet is best known as one of the foremost theoreticians and practitioners of the nouveau roman (New Novel), a narrative form designed to capture the fragmented, confused nature of subjective experience and to express a vision of the world as a place without order or ultimate purpose. In his fiction, Robbe-Grillet eschews traditional characterization, plot, and narrative development in favor of characters with vague or shifting identities, metafictional situations, and disjointed narratives. As a critic, he is generally praised for his insight into the nature of fiction, and his ideas have exerted a marked influence on the development of modern fiction. In the following excerpt, Robbe-Grillet analyzes the theme of sickness in* The Confessions of Zeno.]

Zeno Cosini, a rich Triestine businessman (pre-World War I Trieste), writes his psychoanalyst an account of the principal events of his past existence [in *The Confessions of Zeno*]. Indeterminate university studies, father's death, unrequited passion for a young girl, marriage to her sister, happy and comfortable family life, mistresses, more or less risky business deals, generally unsuccessful—nothing of all this in appearance has serious consequences for him: his wife lovingly runs their home, an investment councilor carefully manages the bulk of his fortune. The aging Zeno, moreover, does not take an excessive interest in these rather ordinary facts, he resuscitates and discusses them with only one purpose: to prove he is sick and to describe his sickness. Despite his aspect, which we guess to be flourishing, the label *imaginary invalid* does not quite suit him; he knows that medicine has little power over his diseases, he always ends up quarreling with

ITALO SVEVO

LA COSCIENZA DI ZENO

ROMANZO

BOLOGNA

L. CAPPELLI - EDITORE

ROCCA S. CASCIANO - TRIESTE

Title page of The Confessions of Zeno.

the doctors, whose diagnoses merely produce new symptoms; if he collects medications—or even takes them sometimes—it is hardly with therapeutic intent, strictly speaking; of course, he is as skeptical of psychoanalysis as of electrotherapy or gymnastics. At the very beginning of the book we read his profession of faith: "Sickness is a conviction, and I was born with that conviction." Something, all in all, like Grace.

The precise nature and the exclusive importance of this conviction—that is what his narrative seeks to illuminate in some four hundred pages. The universe into which he plunges us, a universe simultaneously grotesque, fantastic, and utterly banal, immediately attains—and retains to the end—an exceptional degree of *presence*. Zeno is indeed *in the world;* he is the prey of no symbolism; he escapes quite as completely the claustration of withdrawal. His condition can inspire neither incredulity nor irritation; it is obvious, necessary, incurable. The opposite of that morbid complacency in which the sufferer snuggles into his pains as into a kind of warm bed, Zeno engages in a continual struggle to conquer "good health," regarded as the supreme good, which is simultaneously accompanied by an utter inner repose—harmony of spirit, goodness, purity, *innocence*—and by external manifestations of a more practical nature: elegance, coolness, cunning, success in business, the capacity to seduce women and to play the violin well—instead of drawing from the latter in-

strument only horrible squeals, as from the rest of existence. The healthy man, moreover, does not benefit from these gifts in order to lead a scattered life: he confines himself, for instance, to a strict monogamy. This is not a contradiction, because, if for some people everything is good health, for others everything is disease.

This is particularly true of relations with time. Zeno's time is a diseased time. It is for this reason that, among other calamities, he can play no musical instrument properly: "The basest creature, once he knows what thirds, fourths, sixths are, also knows how to shift from one to another. . . . But when I have produced one of these figures, I can no longer free myself from it; it sticks to me, it contaminates the next figure and distorts it." When in conversation he speaks a sentence, however simple, at the same moment he tries to remember another sentence which he has uttered shortly before. If he has only five minutes in which to perform an important action, he wastes them calculating whether or not he would have needed more in order to complete it satisfactorily. He decides to stop smoking because tobacco is the cause of all his suffering; immediately his time is divided and devoured by the successive and always postponed dates of his "last cigarette," which he writes in advance on the walls of his bedroom—so that, once the walls are covered, he must soon move out. But amid the paralysis, death strikes friends and relatives around him, and each time he is caught unprepared, suddenly realizing that now he can never persuade them of his good will and his innocence.

Zeno does not "enjoy" poor health. He tries not to talk about it, behaves like everyone else insofar as he can. He has even "permanently assumed the aspect of a happy man." From the family dinner table, at which he arrives on time for meals as a good husband should, to the office where he zealously functions (without pay) as a bookkeeper, from Lloyds to the Exchange, from his mistress' bed to the house of his affectionate parents-in-law, we eagerly follow the saunterings of this huntsman mercilessly tracking himself down. And we unhesitatingly place him beside his brothers: here indeed is the passion of a Michael Kohlhaas seeking his unjustly confiscated horses, the periodic dejection of a Dimitri Karamazov running after the money he must borrow at any price, the jolting progress of a Josef K. pursuing both his lawyer and his judges. The infirmities by which Zeno is abruptly stricken (stiffness of the knee because a lame friend has told him about the fifty-four muscles used in walking, or pain in the side because another has drawn him in a caricature with an umbrella sticking into him), and from which he subsequently suffers for the rest of his days, are closely related to those of Captain Ahab who has lost his leg in the struggle against the White Whale, or of Molloy who is gradually immobilized by a paralysis starting in one foot. Zeno knows his death in advance: it will begin by the gangrene of the lower limbs. Even his "unredeemed" city of Trieste, where not Italian but a dialect mixture of German and Croatian is spoken, reminds us of Kafka's Germano-Czech Prague, and of Joyce's Anglo-Irish Dublin—fatherlands of all those who are not at home in their own language. "A written confession is always a lie, and we [Triestines] lie with each Tuscan word we speak!"

Further, the narrator is of bad faith. Prefacing his account, the psychoanalyst warns us that it contains a good many lies. Zeno himself points out some in passing. But how can anything here be called a lie, since each event is accompanied by a long analysis which discredits and denies it? One day when he has not managed by this method to confuse the situation sufficiently, Zeno declares: "It was so clear that I no longer understood anything about it." After having accumulated the evidence of a classical Oedipus complex with many transferences, he turns on the physician who has not been able to avoid remarking on it; then he deliberately goes on to add, in support of this thesis, several false elements. He proceeds analogously in his relations with his family or friends: "If I had not distorted everything, I would have felt it was useless to open my mouth." At the end, he discovers that his analysis is capable of converting health into disease; that need be no obstacle: he then decides that he must treat his health.

This health that he wants to attend to—this bad health—this *conscience,* as the Italian title of the book indicates, Zeno ends by calling simply "life," which "unlike other diseases, is always mortal."

War breaks out between Italy and Austria. Paradoxically, the hero claims to discover his equilibrium in the frenzied commercial transactions to which the extension of the conflict gives rise. And the book ends on an astonishing note of hope: one day, a man "made like all other men of flesh and blood, but a little more ill than the others," will set off an explosive, of a power still unknown, in the center of the earth. "And there will be a tremendous explosion, but no one will hear it, and the earth will return to its nebulous state and continue on its way through the sky, freed from men—without parasites, without diseases."

Sick time, sick language, sick libido, sick body, sick life, sick conscience . . . we must not, of course, see in these some vague allegory of original sin, or any other metaphysical lamentation. It is a question of everyday life and of direct experience of the world. What Italo Svevo tells us in his way is that in our modern society nothing is any longer *natural.* Nor is there even any reason to be upset about it. We can be quite happy, talk, make love, do business, wage war, write novels; but nothing of all this will any longer be done without thinking about it, the way one breathes. Under our gaze, the simple gesture of holding out our hand becomes bizarre, clumsy; the words we hear ourselves speaking suddenly sound false; the time of our minds is no longer that of the clocks; and the style of a novel, in its turn, can no longer be innocent. (pp. 89-94)

> *Alain Robbe-Grillet, "Zeno's Sick Conscience," in his* For a New Novel: Essays on Fiction, *translated by Richard Howard, Grove Press, Inc., 1966, pp. 89-94.*

EUGENIO MONTALE (lecture date 1961)

[*One of the greatest Italian poets of the twentieth century, Montale received the Nobel Prize in literature in 1975. He began his career as a poet of landscape, but under the influence of Paul Valéry and the Symbolists he broke away from the staid conventions of Italian poetry of the 1920s to produce a richly symbolic verse with cryptic, unconventional lyrics. Montale made many important contributions to Italian literature as a critic and translator. His first significant literary analysis, an essay he published on Svevo in 1925, initiated the "Svevo case," an extended debate among critics regarding the literary quality of Svevo's works. In the following excerpt, Montale provides an overview of plot, theme, and characterization in Svevo's three novels and briefly evaluates selected short fiction and dramas written during Svevo's later years.*]

[In 1892 Svevo published] that peculiar novel **Una vita,**

which more than any other book of his gives evidence of the formative period that made it possible. The daring setting of the book—in a certain sense the broadest attempted by this writer—borrows from the most orthodox naturalism, but the romantic overflow has not yet been calmed and the writer is still too aware of the strict ties which bind him to the character of Alfonso Nitti, his first projection and his first real attempt at liberation.

Alfonso, whose father is dead, leaves his mother in his home town and finds work in the Maller bank in Trieste. He knows "languages," it seems, and he is placed in charge of correspondence. His character is complex, spiritually rich and bitter, almost uncultured, but capable of moments of intuition and understanding. From the emotional point of view he is both dry and passionate, humble and proud, clairvoyant and blind. He aspires, without realizing it, to high flights, but he is unsuited to everyday life, to compromise. Among his colleagues in the little bank he feels obscurely *au dessus de la mêlée* ["above the battle"], but his true aspiration is to the condition of senility, the peace of renunciation. The situation in which Svevo has placed him can only come to a dramatic resolution. Invited one evening to the Maller house, he is impudent enough to reveal his latent literary ambitions. Now the young Annetta Maller, the banker's only daughter, lays eyes on him and offers to collaborate with him in writing a novel. The two work together for many evenings, drafting an unreadable potpourri. Set by the fire, straw sooner or later will burn. Alfonso is both happy and terrified: what does she want of him? Annetta has a governess who is present during their evening labors but Francesca does not seem overly zealous in carrying out her duties. Nor does it seem that Alfonso's assiduous presence meets with opposition among Annetta's entourage. One day, a relative of Annetta's, a certain Macario, one of the many presumed to be in love with the girl, takes Alfonso out in a boat and explains to him that one doesn't need brains to catch fish. Alfonso should learn something from the sea gull's timely swoop. "What do brains have to do with it? And you who study, who spend whole hours at table feeding a useless being! He who is born without the necessary wings doesn't grow them. He who doesn't know how to pounce on his prey at the proper time will never learn how, and he will stand by in vain watching how others do it."

Is this a veiled piece of advice? Perhaps Francesca's comment, too, is a warning: "It seems she doesn't appreciate the luck that has befallen her the way she ought to"; or even worse: "It's not my fault if they coo like doves." Then the inevitable happens: one evening the governess is more distracted than usual and Alfonso spends the night with Annetta. And now that the gull has pounced on its easy prey it would seem that the thing was more or less done, but it isn't so. Annetta writes to Alfonso to stay away for several days, long enough to appease her father's anger. The bridesmaid Francesca does not concur in this advice: if Annetta has time to get hold of herself and reflect, all will be lost for Alfonso. The question is all-important for Francesca, the former lover of Maller, who was unable to marry the banker because of Annetta's opposition but who has now allied herself with the girl and could overcome her objection and satisfy her own desire. Of course the novel cannot end like this: Alfonso does not have wings, nor does he want them. He puts his fate in the hands of Annetta and entrenches himself in the alibi of obedience. He will do what Annetta has asked him to do. And it is here that Svevo already demonstrates his maturity as an artist: in the broad, persuasive non-motivation of Alfonso's inertia. The less we are told the why of this passivity, the more we feel its poetic necessity. Alfonso hasn't taken anything: he has been taken: he can accept his fate, but he cannot want it of his own free will: he could love Annetta if she wanted to love him, if she accepted a role that was somehow subordinate in their life together, but in no way can he now give up seeing its defects, in no way is he able to glimpse the possibilities of his role as prince consort. His only choice is not to choose at all, and also to resist Francesca's furious counteroffensive. Alfonso takes a two-week leave, goes home, where his mother dies (a *deus ex machina* solution which allows the extension of his absence), and when he returns to the bank sees he has been assigned to new duties that are clearly inferior to his previous ones. Annetta has shown no further signs of life; it is rumored that she is about to marry her cousin Macario; one day Alfonso meets her accompanied by Francesca and the two women do not return his greeting. At this point Alfonso writes to Annetta, asking for one last interview; but it is Federico Maller, Annetta's dandified brother, who appears at the appointed place, and the heated encounter closes with a slap in Alfonso's face. A duel ought to follow, but the author has avoided a finale which would be too reminiscent of Georges Ohnet. Alfonso kills himself after turning over his small savings to the daughter of his landlords, the Lanuccis, who has been seduced by a man who is reluctant to marry a penniless girl: and the book ends with the dry announcement, on the part of the Maller Bank, of a funeral "attended by the deceased's colleagues and by management."

Rereading *Una vita* so many years after first encountering it, one experiences anew the impossibility of placing the book precisely within the framework of its time. Narrative was anything but impoverished in the last decades of the nineteenth century; but who so far has attempted a careful survey of it? Croce in part, and later Pancrazi, with criteria that could be called *repêchage,* with an attention to the living and the dead, to poetry and anti-poetry which no longer concern us. And besides, at the risk of repeating ourselves, how to deny the evidence that in the world of the arts there is no before and after, chronologically speaking, no cause and effect? Given that in all probability a book like *Una vita* could give no hint of its author's development in far-off 1892, we can only reread it with the wisdom of hindsight, i.e., with today's eyes. It is a book which contains at least two books: the setting is naturalistic, and not even of an advanced naturalism. The minute description of the Maller bank, of both its insignificant and important employees, of their accounting practices and personal problems, is developed with an exactitude which I would call Balzacian; and the entire structure of the book is redolent of homage to the idea of the *tranche de vie* which the naturalists were never able to violate. In *Una vita* the scruple of exhausting the subject, of taking the study of Alfonso Nitti to the depths while remaining within a preestablished form is certainly one limit or one side of the work. The first of Svevo's poetic characters live within this limit without being suffocated by it: Alfonso, certainly, though he is more often described than represented and in the last part of the book is led to his destiny without any pity, for after the central crisis the writer is now psychologically liberated from him and has only to make him disappear; but even more the characters Annetta, Francesca, and Maller himself, whom Svevo represents with a clarity which is made all the more surprising by the extreme sobriety of the portraitist. Here Svevo is a painter, a great painter of the *fin de siècle,* unaware of the impressionist technique but very far from any sort of photographic method. He paints and embosses with few

strokes, but with a careful sense of volume and of chiaroscuro. Perhaps the painting of his closest friend, Veruda, was like this—Veruda whom we will meet in the next novel, *Senilità* **(As a Man Grows Older),** as a far from secondary character. And the most unusual of Svevo's characters appears in *Una vita* for the first time, what we could call the city-as-character: Trieste herself, no longer a naturalistic *ambiente* but the secret matrix of actions and situations, the locus, more metaphysical than geographical or geometrical, of collisions which another scenery would render different and no doubt less significant. And at this point every suspicion of naturalistic orthodoxy is now entirely refuted. A vast scene, precise and yet general, definite down to the most pedantic local fact but also elusive, indeterminate; a city of traffic but also a city of souls, a city no less symbolic than the Prague of Kafka or the Dublin of Joyce, this is the Trieste of the early Svevo. (pp. 98-101)

In any case, to conclude on his first novel, we read *Una vita* today the way we read or look at a great fresco on which we have worked beside a master, as collaborators ourselves, as studio assistants. The master has painted the most vivid scenes, but has barely sketched out others, leaving it to the apprentice to finish them. And it is pointless to say that master and apprentice coexisted equally in him. Even the landscapes of the book, the desolate, probably karstic plain where Alfonso's mother and the notary Mascotti live, are from the hand of the hypothetical studio-hand, as are all the passages where the tyranny of the novel's construction distracts the reader's attention and makes him wish for a faster pace of the metronome which regulates the machine of the novel.

All the parts of *Una vita* which refer to the Maller Bank and the city library can be considered autobiographical, as more than one of Svevo's letters confirms. Only the principal characters are invented. In the next novel, *Senilità,* published in 1898 (apart from the fact that we meet here at least one character who was familiar to Svevo, Veruda), the autobiographical meaning appears to have been plainly transposed, for two years previously Svevo had left the bank and married Livia Veneziani. His new protagonist, the thirty-five-year-old Emilio Brentani, is an Alfonso Nitti who has never met an Annetta and has come to the midpoint on his road having consumed useless literary velleities. He is a failure, an inept even; this in fact was the first title of the book, which was later changed. He lives on his salary from a minor job; he is cared for by his nubile sister Amalia, whom he cares for in turn; a little bit younger than he, she is also a humiliated person, injured by life. Emilio's sedentary, almost senile existence is disturbed by the appearance of the young Angiolina Zarri. Theirs is a casual encounter, the fire lights slowly. And Emilio tells the girl right off that he does not wish to compromise his career and family.

His first desire is to confine their relationship within the boundaries of a simple adventure. "At thirty-five he discovered in his soul the unsatisfied desire for pleasure and love, and even the bitterness of not having enjoyed them, and in his mind a great fear of himself and the weakness of his character which in fact he suspected more than he knew it from experience."

From the beginning the young Angiolina seems to accept without difficulty a platonic relationship, one that will not compromise her either. Angiolina has probably had much more concrete amorous experience and Brentani receives clear indications to this effect; but he is flattered by the duty he assigns himself of educating the girl. Gathering the honey of the adventure (for the moment a purely verbal honey), he deludes himself into believing he is remolding the half-ingenuous, half-corrupt Angiolina (Ange to him) and making her into a woman whom men less spiritual than he cannot even graze with their look. Naturally, of the two of them it is actually he who is truly afraid of compromising himself, to the point where he ends up agreeing to a strange pact: the girl will be his only when she has been given to her fiancé, the tailor Volpini. Except that the sculptor Balli, friend and confidant of Brentani, discovers that Angiolina is carrying on a licentious relationship with a man identified only as an "umbrella man," and tells his friend. And so Emilio breaks off his relationship with his young quasi-lover.

But by now the peace of the Brentani household has been destroyed. Love has entered its walls for the first time. Not only the love of Emilio for Ange, but the incredible love of his sister Amalia for the sculptor Balli. Jovial, noisy, extroverted, Balli is the type of man who is successful with women, but he clearly cannot fall in love with a female larva like the poor Amalia, humiliated and rejected from birth and by choice. Terrified by Amalia's agitation, which reaches the point of nocturnal delirium, Emilio sends his friend away from his house; but by now the double infection must run its course. Angiolina meets Emilio, rekindles his fire, brings him to her miserable house and gives herself to him (in fact it is she who possesses him). In actuality, Emilio has only possessed the woman he thinks he hates. Yet he continues to love the other Angiolina, the woman created by his imagination.

Volpini, for his part, has already slept with the girl: he seems reluctant to marry her and in the end breaks his promise. In the meantime Angiolina has agreed to pose as a model in Balli's studio; and at this point the knots—already tangled to the utmost—come rapidly undone. Amalia, taken with a high fever, is in a state of delirium and dreams of marrying Balli, who is called to care for her. Horrified, overcome with grief, beset by both remorse and jealousy, Emilio confronts Ange, insults her, throws her lovers in her face, including the possibly innocent Balli, chases her into the street, flings mud and stones at her. Then he returns home and finds Amalia dying. The phthisis and alcoholism to which she had secretly given herself have destroyed her. With her death—the unhappy death of those who dream of love—Amalia has cured Emilio of his insane passion once and for all. But after several years Emilio will continue to love and secretly dream of the Ange created in the dream of a man trapped within his own inability to communicate. He thinks that in dying Amalia has transferred her qualities to Ange: and the two women—the one who died and the one who ran off to Vienna with a lover—become one single creature:

> That figure even became a symbol. Always from the same place she watched the horizon, the future, out of which issued the red flashes which reverberated on her pink and white face. The image crystallized the dream he had dreamed next to Angiolina which that child of the people had failed to understand. That great magnificent symbol sometimes reanimated itself to become woman and lover again, though always a sad and thoughtful woman. Yes! Angiolina thinks and weeps. She thinks as if the secret of the universe and of her own existence has been explained to her; she weeps as if in the whole wide world she had found not even a single expression of gratitude.

In *Senilità* the fundamental motivation is jealousy, a theme which did not surface in the earlier novel. Alfonso Nitti does not kill himself because his lover has fallen into the arms of another; the worst offense the Maller household has committed against him is that the banker takes him back into the bank, afraid perhaps of blackmail or a scandal from him. In killing himself Alfonso demonstrates to himself and to the others his fundamental disinterest. Emilio Brentani, on the other hand, is tortured by jealousy, an emotion which increases the more Angiolina demonstrates herself unworthy of him. And it is precisely the sounding and I would almost say the orchestration of this emotion which makes Svevo the analytic writer he will be from this moment on until the end of his career. Perhaps I have used the wrong word: I should have spoken of instrumentation, for *Senilità* (strange to say for a writer like Svevo who lacked a sensitive ear) has one single tone which is never abandoned for the sake of opportune variations. *Una vita,* as we have seen, is a book which the reader of today can take apart and put back together in his mind: *Senilità,* within its more limited framework, is a work which insists on being accepted as it is, a mature work. There is something imperative about its openings, its closures, which denotes the presence of a style. Its episodes—the memorable encounters with characters who fan the flames of jealousy (the Sornianis, the Leardis who know everything about Angiolina's life); the nocturnal teaching of the presumed "little angel" along a route which perhaps even today can be walked by the reader; the dinner of Emilio, Balli, and their lovers; the lightning-quick portraits of Angiolina's mother and sister and even the faded color of the urban landscape; the extraordinary sensitivity of the gradations of light—all of this acts so that what was once the setting of the narrative becomes its very plot, necessary and irreplaceable. Trieste, a late-nineteenth-century Trieste which we will find, though only years later and with another glaze of paint, in the painting of Vittorio Bolaffio, erupts in Svevo's novel and takes shape, life, and blood, in its characters. It has been called a novel of psychological analysis: and this might seem like scant reason for praise in a period which is eliminating psychology from the realm of narrative. But the fact is that here we are not dealing merely with psychologism. Self-analysis, total self-awareness, is in Emilio's very nature and he is, at least in part, a projection of the author; and one could not have expected Svevo to have given this up in favor of an entirely external, objective representation. What could and should have been expected of him is precisely what Svevo has done: admirably to combine analysis and representation so that the psychological case, the clinical case if you will, is totally incarnated in an act of poetry.

Perhaps the complaint of clinicality can be directed exclusively at Amalia, and more at the expedient of her unsuspected alcoholism than at her as a character: here there is at least the shadow of the naturalistic scientism that troubles many books of this period. But it is no more than a shadow or a suspicion: enough to lessen the tension of the book's "musical" tempo, but not enough to weaken a work which is so solid and coherent. *Senilità* is, along with a few of Svevo's last writings (among them the whole first part of the **"Novella del buon vecchio e della bella fanciulla" ("The Nice Old Man and the Pretty Girl")**), his most composed work, which makes us turn immediately, when we reread it, to the precise detachment of certain episodes, to the laconic perfection of certain epigrams which have stayed in our memory like the *leitmotivs* of a symphony. It is certainly for this reason that many critics—and he who is speaking may not be the last of them—

have shown a preference for the story of Emilio and An-giolina, recognizing *Senilità* (a bad title, which cannot now be changed) as the writer's masterpiece. At a distance of more than sixty years since the publication of the book, and thirty years after its unsatisfactory republication, I would be more cautious in making such a statement. If Svevo had ceased working at this point, someone sooner or later would have lifted his name out of the archives of literary history, as hap-pened to Luigi Gualdo, but we would not be here to com-memorate him. If a "Svevo affair" was possible, the reasons for it should not be sought in an occasional polemic but in the evidence itself of the long road he took, of the peculiarity and timeliness of his apparitions and resurrections. It has been stated, and not without truth, that Svevo wrote the same book three times: but one must add that every book of his is a different book, it is a stopping place on a route that had to be traveled. Those who appreciate the significance of such an evolution (which is not from the imperfect or the approxi-mate to the definitive result, but is the necessary adjustment to new inner themes suggested or even imposed by the altered spirit of the times, of the different periods he passed through), he who sees in its unity the various seasons of his work may point out his own preferences here and there as an antholog-ical reader, but he will never be able to contain or emprison Svevo within the boundaries of only one page or one work. It is not only the analyst in him who is interesting today, though the literature of analysis, which is poorly represented in Italy, had in him a master and precursor; it is rather the disquiet which he foments in us, the need for an impulse, the sense of something beyond the page. Svevo is a writer who is always open: he accompanies us, he guides us up to a cer-tain point but he never gives the impression of having said ev-erything: he is broad and inconclusive like life. For this rea-son, when they ask us what of his work should be read there can only be one answer: read everything, if you can, but do not reverse the order in your reading: follow with him a route which in this case is never reversible and let yourself be led wherever it is possible for him and you. Later on you will be on your own but you will not regret the time spent; you will be left with the feeling of having had a necessary experience, of having enlarged your understanding of life.

From this point of view Svevo is not really an artist but a moralist; in this he is modern today, but he was not so in the days when Italian writers were required to build themselves an instrument of art. And for this reason, too, we repeat, it can be claimed that he had his recognition at the most propi-tious moment and it is impossible to blame anyone for not paying him attention.

The moralist finally breaks through the crust of the novelist in *La coscienza di Zeno* (*The Confessions of Zeno*) and in his last stories. (pp. 102-07)

[Zeno Cosini] is a success; he has a family, he has a perfect wife, a house; he lives in a highly sophisticated bourgeois am-bience, he is a successful, respected man. He is rich but takes little interest in his business affairs, which are entrusted to a certain Olivi, an entirely reliable man who administers his property.

On the threshold of his fifties Zeno looks back and, giving in to the desire of his psychoanalyst, lets the memories of his life spring from his conscious and subconscious; in short, he writes a retrospective diary. I don't know how interesting the book is from the psychoanalytic point of view: there is no doubt that in writing it Svevo was familiar with Freud's theo-ries. But at that time not only psychoanalysis but analysis pure and simple was dominant in the novel and it is easy to discount whatever artificiality the prologue of the imaginary doctor lends to Svevo's vast book. In the *Coscienza di Zeno* (and this is the reader's first impression) there is no further sense of time, no development of the narrative drive that one finds in *Senilità*. And it is easy to explain why. He who looks backward cannot make time reversible: he can only reoccupy it partially, extracting it from the deposits of memory; I speak of "occupation" because recovered time does not unwind its thread, but rather stagnates. This does not prevent the most precious flowers from emerging a second time from the swamp, as happens in Proust, though more rarely in Svevo, who is totally removed from that spirit which for better or for worse we are accustomed to define as "decadent." In Svevo, the release of the psychological discovery is drier, the moralist defeats the painter, who for the first time is totally absent here. *La coscienza di Zeno,* therefore, is a great come-dy of psychology and of manners, a performance with no real beginning and no real end, insofar as it is true, as we shall see, that Svevo partially continued it.

The book is made up of long episodes. Zeno is an imaginary invalid, a man without a will, full of good sense, a man who takes things as they come but who actually always takes the right course. An inveterate smoker, he agrees to enter a clinic to disintoxicate himself, but then manages to escape and starts smoking again. Rich and with virtually nothing to do, he decides to marry. He is a friend of the Malfenta family, in which there are three girls of marriageable age. He is re-jected by the youngest, concentrates his interest on the pretti-est, Ada, and during an evening spirit séance, while everyone is intent on making a table dance, decides to make his ad-vances to Ada by touching her foot, but he is fooled in the dark and the foot he touches belongs to the cross-eyed Au-gusta. And so, in brief and against his will, he finds himself engaged to Augusta, who will later turn out to be a wife with-out peer. Ada, on the other hand, will marry a ridiculous vio-linist, a certain Guido Speier, for whom Zeno nourishes the most egregious dislike. A later section is devoted to Zeno's extramarital affair, conducted with the complicity of a friend, a certain Copler, who is also an invalid but a little less imagi-narily so. Zeno becomes the protector and adviser of Carla, a poor girl who is studying singing and needs a disinterested Maecenas. The delightful Carla, a perfect blend of ingenuity and candor, soon becomes Zeno's clandestine lover, without his affection for his wife diminishing, for she is now a neces-sary complement to his life. Carla is a more cunning An-giolina, she plays the part of innocence better. It is impossible to think of marriage, Zeno is the most decent of husbands, nor does Carla expect as much. The relationship is prolonged through tormenting highs and lows because the seduced Zeno hesitates to be a seducer; until Carla, who has extorted a great deal of money from her protector, is in a position to let him and her singing teacher go and become engaged to a man who is in a position to marry her. Zeno thus returns with a sigh of relief to his conjugal peace, without Augusta ever having suspected a thing.

Now business awaits Zeno; he has agreed to be a partner in a commercial firm set up by his brother-in-law Speier, though without involving his own resources, which continue to be administered by the wise Olivi. But the business of Speier and Partner will soon take a turn for the worse. Not only will ex-penses mount and profits decline month by month, but Speier will get involved in risky stockmarket transactions that will ruin him. Honest and compassionate, Zeno decides to give up part of his fortune to help his brother-in-law and hopes to be able to induce his sister-in-law Ada, who is richer than her husband, to do likewise.

But Ada seems to resist. To convince her, Speier stages a suicide, swallowing a less than fatal dose of a sleeping potion. He has arranged things so that medical intervention will be prompt and certain. Unfortunately, through a series of misdirections, aided by bad weather, the doctor arrives too late and finds Speier dead. And here the famous *lapsus* of Zeno Cosini occurs: believing he is following Speier's funeral procession, he actually follows the coffin of another dead man. It is this *lapsus* which reveals Zeno's secret anger at his brother-in-law, the faint-hearted and useless character whom Ada Malfenta years ago chose over him as her husband. Ever lucky in his misadventures, Zeno does not inherit a debt to make good, for in the meantime the market has risen and Speier's suicide is shown to be the last useless gesture of a failure, not in the game of the market but in life.

Zeno will once again be the successful man whom we shall find a happy father and still an addicted smoker in the last section of the book; but here the narrative is interrupted because Zeno has decided to send the cure and the doctor to the devil. And, on the other hand, we have reached the war, and in the postwar period Zeno Cosini has become or is becoming Italo Svevo and memory can no longer serve. All that remains is to continue with variations on the same theme, in a different setting, and these will last until Svevo's death interrupts them forever. A strange book, stagnant and yet continually in motion, this *Coscienza di Zeno:* not only does it contain the richest and also the most varied gallery of characters that Svevo succeeded in portraying. In *Una vita* the social scale was limited to the most modest bourgeoisie: the upper classes were examined through the keyhole: no differently in *Senilità* we find ourselves halfway between *scapigliato* bohemia and a little world of employee assistants. In *La coscienza di Zeno,* on the other hand, the high, monied bourgeoisie breaks forth. Except for the ambiguous Carla, all the characters in the book belong to the golden tree of an industrial society, even if they are sometimes its dry leaves. And naturally these characters, who are much more articulate and activated in the sense of human comedy, even while elevating themselves to the universality of a type, keep all the characteristics of well-defined local figures. We have said that Trieste lives at the edges of *Una vita* and absolutely invades *Senilità;* but at this point Trieste is the very weft of *La coscienza di Zeno,* the first warp, so strong that it could be called the producer of its characters themselves, as if the fundamental tone (the tone and rhythm of a city with a double aspect, intensely European and yet unmistakably linked to a very different stock by language, blood, and traditions)—as if the fundamental tone had created figures, characters, situations, by parthenogenesis. *La coscienza di Zeno* may be a city in search of an author. The note of bohemianism, of the *fin de siècle,* which one hears in the first novels is the Triestine variant of a world we can find elsewhere; but we could not imagine Zeno and his adventures outside this Trieste which is both real and imaginary at once. . . . Among the many pages excised from the trunk of *La coscienza di Zeno* is a supposed first chapter of a new novel, **"Il vecchione"** ("The Old, Old Man"),** in which the thick vegetation of self-analysis becomes almost swampy. Here one is truly reminded of Proust. The protagonist of the new book would seem to be a somewhat older Zeno; senility understood as a state of mind and a voca-

tion is replaced by the actual study of clinical senility. Yet if one is to understand stories like **"Il mio ozio"** ("This Indolence of Mine"), **"Le Confessioni del vegliardo"** ("An Old Man's Confessions"), **"Umbertino"** as parts of the new novel, one might think of a prolongation of Zeno, not of a work with a different inspiration. **"Il mio ozio,"** the story of the new Zeno's relationship with the cunning tobacconist Felicita, whom he employs, makes a chapter which could replace the Carla episode in *La coscienza di Zeno.* In the other recorded episodes, on the other hand, Zeno's story is carried up to the postwar period without any noteworthy differences. The character of Felicita is the loveliest gift Svevo has given us in his last years, though along with this we should mention the lovely little girl in the story of the good old man. This is a story parallel to that of Carla and Felicita, yet foreign to Zeno's novel. Yet the situation is identical: the unnamed good old man—who is unmarried this time—pays a young female tramway operator to test his idea, or illusion, that he is growing young again; but the illusion, which is followed by his death, is of brief duration. These last stories are among Svevo's best work; when they were published under the title *Corto viaggio sentimentale (A Short Sentimental Journey)* I saw fit to call them fragments of the greater Svevo; but I was totally unaware of the tie that binds them to his greater works, which I had not reread for years. They are not fragments, then, but pages of authentic poetry. It's a shame that some of them—such as the **"Confessioni del vegliardo"**— were not edited in manuscript, either by the author or by those who published them.

The above-mentioned *Viaggio sentimentale,* the *Reisebilder* of a Mr. Aghiós who is a near relation of Zeno, stands out, a lively report of a train trip; and, more important, *Una burla riuscita (The Hoax),* a story in which Svevo's macabre humor reaches its highest point. Its protagonist is Mario Samigli (the pseudonym under which Svevo published *Una vita*), a failed writer, the author of a forgotten novel. A cruel joke has been planned at his expense. He is led to believe that a great publisher in Vienna wants to translate his novel, and is even sent a false bank check. Once the mockery has been revealed, the mild-mannered Samigli will slap his trickster, but he will also profit unexpectedly from his trick. The false check, in fact, has served to cover a stock transfer which will prove extremely advantageous for Samigli; while the trick will not destroy his conviction that he is a genius destined to be discovered by posterity. As can be seen, what we have here is nothing less than a back-dated parody of the "Svevo affair"; as well as another little gallery of unforgettable portraits.

Among the last stories I must also mention **"La madre"** ("The Mother"), an unfortunately incomplete tale of a woman, Amelia, who marries a lame man. How many lame men we meet in Svevo's stories and what a north wind blows there! One could say that in them the entire industrial culture in which the poet found himself immersed—against his will—when he changed from Samigli into Cosini is swept away in this very wind. Perhaps the fine story **"Un contratto"** ("A Contract") was also part of the sequel to Zeno, while other brief stories, like **"Proditoriamente"** ("Treacherously") and **"Vino generoso"** ("Generous Wine"), came earlier. From the stylistic point of view, all these posthumously published writings are very different; some seem to have undergone some preliminary *labor limae,* others are in the sketch state. The date of several is uncertain. As a whole they are reminiscent of the stratification of Foscolo's *Tomo dell'Io (Book of the Self)* even if one thinks of Sterne more than

Heine; and they will give the critics of tomorrow much to write about, if tomorrow there are literary critics.

Also unfinished are the two plays of the late period, **Con la penna d'oro (With a Pen of Gold)** and **Rigenerazione (Regeneration),** perhaps the only plays that are related to the Svevo of the last novel. More than plays, one could say they were parts of a novel set in scenes. It will never be possible to stage them, but they cannot be ignored by Svevo's faithful. They show the signs of an advanced, happy maturity: not of a newly achieved equilibrium.

Before concluding this summary review, I should now touch at least briefly on the thorny problem of Svevo's language, which Giacomo Debenedetti defined as risky and adventitious and which has given the writer's first critics much to discuss. It is indubitable that "Tuscan" (as Svevo called our language) was difficult for him to learn, almost a translation from the language of Trieste. But it has now been made clear by a philologist of the likes of Gianfranco Contini that Svevo's imperfections—which are more syntactical than lexical—can be compared to typographical errors which the reader can easily erase on his own. As for his vocabulary and spelling errors, they need to be examined case by case: in Svevo's so-called "pidgin" there is much that is part of his style and should not be corrected.

Might Svevo's language be edited? Let's not confuse respect with fetishism. Svevo himself accepted corrections, often unfortunate ones, in the second edition of **Senilità.** What is needed for this book is a happy combination of the two extant editions. But in the others, too, and above all in the posthumous writings, something could be done; after all, we don't read the *Divine Comedy* the way Dante wrote it.

But it would be erroneous to think that Svevo gains something when he is read in translation. What I would call the sclerosis of his characters is lost. Svevo appears elegant where he was laborious and profound, entangled yet entirely free, a writer for all time but a Triestine of his own difficult years. Better then to add a few commas and relieve a few anacolutha but leave Svevo with the music that was his. (pp. 108-15)

> *Eugenio Montale, "Italo Svevo in the Centenary of His Birth," in his* The Second Life of Art: Selected Essays of Eugenio Montale, *edited and translated by Jonathan Galassi, The Ecco Press, 1982, pp. 92-117.*

JOSEPH CARY   (essay date 1964)

[*In the following excerpt, Cary examines elements of* A Life, *especially aspects of the characterization of Alfonso, that recur in Svevo's later works.*]

Svevo's first novel, **A Life,** arrives in the English-speaking world over seventy years after its original publication in 1892. Now as then it will set no woods afire; it has been translated and published and will be read and reviewed less on its own merits than on those refracted from the masterpieces we know its author was going to write. **A Life** is not on a level with either **As a Man Grows Older** or **The Confessions of Zeno,** nor can a reader today—assuming he could suppress his prophetic hindsight—really find symptoms of a remarkable future in these modestly gifted, programmatically "gray" pages.

Svevo, although he quickly came to feel the book was poorly

Svevo with the proofs of Una vita.

written, was fond of quoting with approval his friend Joyce's dictum to the effect that no novelist has more than one real book in him (all the rest being variations on or revisions of the first), " . . . in which case," he wrote Valéry Larbaud in 1925, "my sole novel would be *A Life.*" And it is true, as he said, that all his protagonists are "blood brothers," having in common a crucial indecisiveness, a basic incapacity—and admiration—for practical action, and liability toward theory and/or dream. They are also all middle-class, dwell in Trieste, are connected in some way with the business community, and either have written, write, or want to write—are, in short, much like their creator. But if the type of this autobiographically-based character is recurrent, Svevo's attitude to and consequent treatment of it are not. And it is in his manner of approach rather than in the nature of the type itself that his true originality lies. Such is the useful lesson proffered by this early work.

Its contents are summarily indicated by the title Svevo originally gave it until informed by a publisher that the public would never buy a book so glumly named—*Un inetto* ("an inept one": a bungler or misfit) was consequently dropped for the cool and nondirective **Una vita.** Its anti-hero is Alfonso Nitti, a poor but educated young man from the provinces who "wants to write" and works as a minor clerk in a Trieste bank. Alfonso's ineptitude (his secret vocation, as the novel is meant to demonstrate) is mapped by his lacklustre contacts with four milieux: the bank itself, the showy comforts of the salon of his employer (with whose supremely self-centered daughter he conducts and consummates a passionless affair), the impoverished narrowness of the home village to which he briefly returns to care for his dying mother, and the proletarian miseries of the household in Trieste where he is at once star boarder, mentor, and his landlady's unwilling candidate for the hand or maidenhead of her unattractive daughter. These settings get full naturalist treatment—that is, the copious, impassive detailing of the ordinary—and the socioeconomic polarities (rich/poor, work/leisure, city/country, etc.) are rife and potentially rich in ironic contrasts and parallelisms. But in fact this potential is not realized: the village and boarding house sequences are handled perfunctorily and seem merely academic stabs at a kind of Zolaesque "completeness" for which Svevo may have had the stomach—he was a militant *verista* in this period—but apparently not the heart. At any rate he is far better at rendering those special bourgeois settings of bank and salon with which he himself was intimately familiar: his presentation of the hopes, fears, rivalries, agitations and tedia of both office and visiting hours is one of the best things in the book. Along with Svevo's own long and wretched experience as correspondence clerk for the Trieste branch of the Union Bank of Vienna, the shades of Balzac, Daudet, the Goncourts and, above all, Emile Zola, constitute the corporate and Gallic muse of this aspect of his novel.

But the literary ambitions informing *A Life* are by no means exhausted by reference to naturalist *tranches de vie:* as the original title most explicitly declared, Svevo had also in mind a novel of psychological analysis, a study in one man's ineptitude. Alfonso's inadequacy is broadly standard for all his creator's protagonists: he suffers from an abulia induced by an "organic" (the adjective is Svevo's) inability to make any connection between the components of his inwardness—fancies, theories, dreams—and practical action. Here is a perfectly characteristic sampling of the nature and quality of his introspection:

> Alfonso came to the conclusion that he felt generally out of sorts because his organism needed something to tire itself out on, to exhaust itself. This organism of his now became a plastic concept which he reshaped to every new sensation. In the evening, after a day spent on sums or rushing about the bank or sitting with pen on paper and thoughts elsewhere, he would imagine matter flowing fast through his body in pliable tubes, impossible to regulate or resist. Whenever he could, he took long walks and his malaise vanished; his lungs expanded, he could feel his joints becoming more flexible, his body obeying more promptly; and he would imagine that flow of material as having been absorbed or regulated, as helping him now instead of impeding. If he settled down to study, he would drop his book and feel that his chin was tired and a strange sensation would come over his forehead as if the volume inside was trying to increase, to enlarge its content.

In his obsession with physiological symptoms, his worrying over the "problem" of health, Alfonso may remind us of that titanic hypochondriac Zeno Cosini—passivity brought on by the image of "pliable tubes" is kin to Zeno's limp resulting from the discovery that fifty-four leg muscles are required for each step taken. But the point is that such considerations as these tend to dilute, hinder or wholly block the possibility of vigorous activity; Alfonso's ineptitude follows from his disposition to theorize in a dog-eat-dog world demanding quick external initiatives and responses. In this regard the key scene

in the book comes early, when Alfonso and an acquaintance are watching the gulls in Trieste harbor and the acquaintance develops a tough analogy vaguely based on Darwin:

> How little brain it takes to catch fish! Their bodies are small. Think what size their brain must be! Negligible! Those wings are the danger to the fish, who end up in a sea gull's beak because of them! What eyes and stomach, what an appetite, to satisfy which such a drop is nothing! But brain? What has brain to do with catching fish? You study, you spend hours at a desk nourishing your brain uselessly. Anyone who isn't born with the necessary wings will never grow them afterward. Anyone who can't drop like lead on prey at the right second by instinct will never learn, and there'll be no point in his watching others who can, as he'll never be able to imitate them. One dies in the precise state in which one is born, our hands mere organs for snatching or incapable of holding.

When Alfonso nervously inquires whether he, Alfonso, has wings, his companion replies with barely concealed contempt: "Yes, to make poetic flights!"

But Alfonso is neither "brain" nor poet; his mind and imagination are mainly limited to registering real or fancied slights to himself and conjuring up visceral metaphors to match his moods. Nor is he candidate, except in dream, for the congenial romantic role of sensitive outsider or tragic victim. He is presented as a talentless *arriviste* (on the order of Flaubert's Frédéric Moreau) whose occasional mild misanthropy is a result of the difficulty he finds in arriving. He basically admires the vulgar tastes and crude values of his employer's circle, and it is only his own hopeless ineptitude which brings him in the end to renounce it—first by "saintly" non-participation and ultimately by suicide.

Svevo handles this case study with the mandatory aloofness of the clinical realist, except in those few portions of the book which treat of Alfonso's activities as a would-be writer; at such times (perhaps the most autobiographical of all) he relaxes into an irony that occasionally verges on the farcical. Thus, in the opening pages, Alfonso is made to express his contempt for his colleagues by a fantastic—for a Triestine bank clerk—hypothesis: "Why, if someone handed me any Latin classic, I could comment on it all; but they wouldn't even be able to identify it." Again, when Alfonso collaborates on a romantic novel (e.g., "Clara, a young countess, learns that the duke is marrying a shopkeeper's daughter; her despair" etc.) with his employer's daughter, Svevo has some double-edged sport compiling a *sotie* of modish literary clichés which were indispensable at the time *A Life* was written and still attract disciples: the dogmas of "scientific" narrational impersonality, of the superiority of showing to telling, of the greater maturity of realists to romantics, etc. But his finest humor is reserved for Alfonso's major project, a purely theoretical work whereby "He would lay the foundations of modern Italian philosophy by translating a good German work and at the same time writing an original work of his own"—a sentence which is perfect Svevo and one of the few in the book which no one but himself could have written. A title (*The Moral Idea in the Modern World*), a sketch for a table of contents, three pages of preface, are as far as Alfonso gets; the second half of *A Life* deals with his increasingly successful efforts to persuade himself that his lack of progress in the office, in society and in his writing is due not to personal incompetence but to a systematic program of philosophic renunciation.

In an autobiographical profile written for his publishers in the last year of his life (1928), Svevo speaks of his attempt, while writing *A Life,* to fit "and in a certain sense to sublimate" the debility of his main character within a theoretical framework. Certainly his familiarity with the scientific pretensions of Balzac and Zola had some influence here; on the other hand the quest for a system is very much a symptom of the ineptitude of the typical Svevian character. Readers of *Zeno* will perhaps recognize in the author's attempt an historical precedent for Zeno's flirtation with Freudian psychoanalysis or his ranging all life on an axis representing either the approach or shattered aftermath to *morbus basedowii,* Basedow's disease. At any rate the "Basedow" for Svevo in the 'nineties was Arthur Schopenhauer, rated above the French realists as his favorite author. (Svevo, whose real name was Ettore Schmitz, even suggests that his choice of *nom de plume*—"Italus the Swabian"—was, besides an acknowledgement of the Austro-Germanic aspect of his ancestry, city and schooling, a token of pious respect for the nationality of the author of *The World as Will and Idea.*) In his profile he describes Alfonso as "the precise personification of the Schopenhauerian affirmation of life, so close to its negation. Hence, perhaps, the novel's ending, as dry and abrupt as part of a syllogism."

Grim as it is, *A Life* is something more, and better, than an allegory based on nineteenth-century romantic pessimism. It may well be, on the other hand, that the "good German work" Alfonso considers translating would turn out to be Schopenhauer. The following passages, the first from book four of *The World as Will and Idea,* the second describing Alfonso's self-communings toward the end of his life, have obvious connections.

> He [who has pierced the veil of Maya, the principle of egoism and individuation] sees wherever he looks suffering humanity, the suffering brute creation, and a world that passes away. . . . Why should he now, with such knowledge of the world, assert this very life through constant acts of will, and thereby bind himself ever more closely to it? . . . The will now turns away from life; it now shudders at the pleasures in which it recognizes the assertion of life. Man now attains to the state of voluntary renunciation, resignation, true indifference, and perfect willessness.

> He was, he thought, very close to the ideal state he dreamed of in his reading, the state of renunciation and quiet. He no longer even felt enough agitation to work up energy for more renunciation . . . he was content, balanced in mind as an old man . . . calmer than in those discontented years he had spent at the bank before this, years of restless and ambitious living in accordance with the blind sensations of the moment. . . . He could judge them [others] from a detached, serene position, because he had been through the struggle, too, and knew what it was like. And he pitied both victor and vanquished . . . how silly he had come to find both our joys and our sorrows.

Alfonso's rationalization of ineptitude—and Svevo makes it abundantly clear that this is what it is—reads virtually, in its context, like a parody of Schopenhauer's description of final illumination. There is, of course, a difference between nirvana and paralysis: Alfonso's self-deception in this matter is an aspect of that *bovarysme* (defined by Jules de Gaultier as "the

power granted man to believe himself different from what he is") which Eugenio Montale first noted as characteristic of Svevo's protagonists. The renunciation of life that Schopenhauer counsels depends upon a man's mastery of his will; Alfonso never achieves such mastery but remains until the end subject to ego, in alternating states of euphoric self-pity, nostalgia and delusions of trivial grandeur. And if Schopenhauer praises the saint's way of renunciation, he condemns suicide as the supreme act of egoism. Ergo, "syllogistically," Alfonso's end is the inevitable conclusion to a life never for a moment free of the pain and anguish of desire.

German metaphysics, naturalist *roman expérimental,* psychological analysis à la Constant and Flaubert, autobiography—it should be clear by now that *A Life* is an extremely ambitious and cosmopolitan product. And in the end it is this very diversity of influence and interest which contributes to its structural failure, for the various elements are never coordinated into a whole. The three themes of major interest—the social-documentary, the psychological and, for want of a better word, the spiritual—quarrel with rather than reenforce and clarify one another. So, as regards Alfonso's ineptitude, we never finally comprehend its nature, whether it is truly organic (which would be truly uninteresting), or a by-product of a viciously materialistic society, or some emanation of the *mal du siècle* ["malady of the age"]. Again, Alfonso's suicide may be true to Schopenhauer but it seems out of character in its very decisiveness and efficiency of execution. Most noticeably, the many office scenes are for the most part completely detachable from the story of Alfonso, and seem offered more for their very real documentary and historical interest than for any relevance they might have to his case. The result is that the figure of Alfonso emerges curiously blurred, and that the novel itself promises more than it gives. A promising novel.

Svevo published *A Life* at his own expense, and though it was not reviewed by the major Italian papers and literary periodicals it got a good press in Trieste and sold out immediately. Later Italian purist comment to the effect that Svevo could not write his chosen language—his friend the Triestine poet Umberto Saba remarked that Svevo "could have written well in German but preferred to write badly in Italian"—is obviously stupid, unless the Italian tongue equals Tuscan and all Italian writers are made to live in Florence and carry out the *risciacquatura* or rite of purification of dialect initiated by the Milanese Manzoni. It is noted in Svevo's diary how a man he knows of "writes too well to be sincere." Be this as it may, his own mature style is dry, somewhat abstract and, as he himself described it, "brief, brusque and unadorned." In *A Life* it is made particularly awkward and "un-Italian" (though perfectly Triestine) by a large number of Germanic syntactical constructions. (pp. 592-97)

The theorist, the pipe- or cigarette-dreamer, the dilettante, the imaginary invalid, the *senex* or old man—all these figures from vintage Svevo are present or potential in the person of Alfonso Nitti. They are all subjective and abulic, all inept according to the pragmatic standards of the Trieste they inhabit. But in *As a Man Grows Older* and *Zeno* these standards have lost the patina of "realistic" authority and sanction they possess in *A Life.* In the later novels *everything* is thrown into question, and Svevian ineptitude becomes a positive quality, an originality. Thus Emilio Brentani of *As a Man Grows Older* "ineptly" mistakes a slut for the sweetheart of his dreams, re-creates her according to his own subjective and emotional requirements and, though continually "wronged" and finally deserted, manages by the very persistence of his subjectivism to triumph over the facts and enter into a fulfilled old age. Most incompetent of them all, Zeno Cosini is able to compete with the "real" world on its own tough terms—with a wife and mistress, on the Exchange, in a World War—and not merely survive but win through to as happy an ending as is possible in this mad and invalid century. (pp. 597-98)

> Joseph Cary, "Italo Svevo: Poet of Ineptitude," in The Massachusetts Review, Vol. V, No. 3, Spring, 1964, pp. 592-98.

RENATO POGGIOLI (essay date 1965)

[*Poggioli was an Italian-born American critic and translator. Much of his critical writing is concerned with Russian literature, including* The Poets of Russia: 1890-1930 *(1960), which is considered one of the most important examinations of this literary era. In the following excerpt, he asserts that Svevo is unique among modern writers in his understanding and portrayal of the bourgeois spirit.*]

Svevo was about thirty years old when he wrote his first literary work. It was a novel which belonged more to the tradition of French realism and naturalism than to the corresponding Italian school, Capuana's or Verga's *verismo*. Naturalism meant in France the depiction of urban life, of the working classes on one hand, on the other of the bourgeoisie, while its Italian counterpart coincided almost completely with southern regionalism, with the representation of the primitive life of the shepherd, the peasant, and the fisherman.

The literary sources of the first Svevo novel are betrayed by its title à la Maupassant: *Una vita* (*A Life*); by its story, which is nothing else but another *roman d'un jeune homme pauvre* ["novel of a poor young man"], with the difference that it is not concluded by a happy ending (as a matter of fact, the protagonist ends in failure and suicide); finally by its intentions, which were of narrating another *éducation sentimentale* ["sentimental education"]. But Svevo's Frédéric Moreau, whose name is Alfonso Nitti, is not only far more provincial, gray, and dull than Flaubert's hero, his Parisian model: he is also a more introspective and literal self-portrait, as is proved by the milieu, which is the banking world, seen from inside and from below.

In spite of the fact that it was published only locally, the novel did not pass completely unnoticed in Italy, though it was soon and easily forgotten. Nobody paid the slightest attention to Svevo's first masterpiece, *Senilità* (*As a Man Grows Older*), published five years later in 1898. (pp. 171-72)

The first of the many surprises this second novel, which is autobiographical, offers the intelligent reader is its title. Its protagonist, Emilio Brentani, is nearing middle age, but is still not too far from the years of youth. In a charming and moving preface to the second edition (1927), the already famous but still unspoiled Svevo cites the opinion of Valéry Larbaud, according to whom the title was not suited to the work. The author confesses his repugnance to follow the advice to change it, even if it comes from such a connoisseur. We think that the distinguished French critic was wrong, and Svevo right. *Senilità* is the novel of senility understood not as a physical or psychic state, but of old age as a second nature, as a vocation.

The last works of Svevo, written shortly before his death and published posthumously—such as the novelette "**La novella del buon vecchio e della bella fanciulla**" ("**The Tale of the Good Old Man and the Beautiful Girl**"), a masterpiece; or the beautiful short story "**Vino generoso**" ("**Heady Wine**"), translated, but little known in English; or finally the unfinished novel "**Il vecchione**" ("**The Oldster**"), of which we have only a few pages of the beginning—are again variations on the dominant theme of old age. *Senilità* is therefore an anticipation, a prophecy; and it apparently intends to show that people are not *made* but are *born* old. And the man born old is nothing else but a psychological counterpart of that type which, when seen from a social viewpoint, is called a bourgeois. (p. 172)

For a cultivated Italian it is very easy to understand, but almost impossible to appreciate, the Italian of Svevo, perhaps the least literary and even the least literate, certainly the least polished, Italian ever used by a man of letters in our time. It is not, like the Sicilianized Italian of Verga, influenced by the local vernacular (in Trieste's and Svevo's case, a stronger variant of the singing Venetian dialect), but it is a kind of Italian Esperanto or pidgin Italian, an instrument of commercial exchange, a modern *lingua franca*. The poet Umberto Saba stated recently that Svevo could have written as well (or as badly, if one prefers to judge from the viewpoint of linguistic pedantry and grammatical purism) in German as in Italian, and that if he chose to write in Italian, he did so to show his predilection for Italian culture. We rather think that if Svevo chose to write in Italian, he did so to be a Triestino of his own kind and class. The Italianism of Svevo is a social and psychological case rather than a cultural and literary one. (p. 173)

In all his works Svevo's real protagonist is the bourgeois soul. But the bourgeois of Svevo is a very different kind from the type described in sociological or ideological literature. He is always being studied during his free time, while he does not work. The best definition which may be given of the bourgeois, on both the social and the psychological plane, is perhaps the one according to which the bourgeois is that type of man for whom time is money. In the novels of Svevo there are no instances of a problem so frequently treated in the novels of Balzac and Zola, the *question d'argent*. Of Zeno Cosini and the anonymous old man who is the protagonist of the "**Novella del buon vecchio e della bella fanciulla**" we merely know that they are rich; of Alfonso Nitti and Emilio Beltrani, that they are poor. Generally it is a matter of indifference to know whether Svevo's heroes have money to spare: the only important thing is to realize that they always have little or plenty of time to lose. And Svevo tells us how they employ their time, how they lose or kill it.

Actually some of his heroes, like Alfonso Nitti, have little time to spare. But Svevo always has time for them, even if he visits them preferably when they are free. He is not, like Mann or Proust, preoccupied with the old man Chronos or, like Kafka, with eternity. He is interested only in that aspect of our time's consciousness which Bergson used to call *durée*, and which could be defined as the very antithesis of the quantitative conception of time, of time as *duration*. Time is the terror of youth. But Svevo, always a wise man, looks upon time as a foolish and amusing prankster, a clown or a practical joker, playing everybody a kind of recurring and successful hoax, *una burla riuscita*, to use the title of one of his most amusing works. A hard-headed businessman, Svevo also knows that man too can play with time and against it, that for each one of us time is always both *perdu* ["lost"] and *retrouvé* ["found"]. We must merely accept it as the medium in which one breathes and lives.

The English translator of *La coscienza di Zeno* was well advised in changing its original title to *The Confessions of Zeno,* because the common noun in that title means both conscience and consciousness, and its suggestion and cogency lie in the equivocal meaning of that very word, which no literal translation in a non-Latin tongue could render. In a certain sense one might say that the aim of Svevo's works is to express conscience in terms of consciousness, and consciousness in terms of conscience.

If there is a writer for whom the resurrected William James formula ("stream of consciousness") and its French and literary equivalent, coined by Valéry Larbaud (*monologue intérieur*), are particularly apt, that writer is Italo Svevo. But his method and imagination have nothing to do with the method and imagination of Joyce and Proust, either from the viewpoint of effective influence (which does not exist) or from the viewpoint of the congeniality of kindred spirit (which may be argued or even denied). The world of Joyce is a world where the bourgeois spirit withdraws into the background for intellectual reasons; in Proust's, for sentimental ones. Leopold Bloom and Swann are not actors but marionettes of that world, not protagonists or heroes but antagonists and victims, not subjects but objects. The bourgeois spirit is in Svevo's fiction both its actor and marionette, its protagonist and antagonist, its hero and victim, its subject and object.

The only intellectual influence that may have been decisive in Svevo's writing, at least in the case of *Zeno,* is psychoanalysis. As we know, he was directly acquainted, thanks perhaps to the uninterrupted cultural relations between Trieste and Vienna, with Freud's teachings and the medical treatment of his school. Certainly he used psychoanalysis more literally than Joyce, for instance, ever used the doctrines and methods of Jung. But if we look at *Zeno* with attention, we see that in that book psychoanalysis is more a matter of content than of form.

Psychoanalysis is par excellence a bourgeois fad. From Molière on, the bourgeois has been often depicted as the only social type who may become that very sick kind of man generally called *malade imaginaire.* In the modern world only the bourgeois may afford himself the luxury of being psychologically and physiologically ill, like Hans Castorp in Thomas Mann's *Zauberberg.* Proust's bourgeois characters are too snobbish, Joyce's too bohemian, for this. Zeno, being a member of the leisure class, uses his leisure to torment himself. And the greatness of Svevo lies in that, after a century of romantic spleen, he was the first one to consider, like the ancients, the type of the *heautontimoroumenos,* the self-tormentor, as essentially a comical one.

In *Zeno,* Svevo does not operate with psychoanalysis, but on it. It is true that the novel was written under the impact of the discovery of Freud by the man Ettore Schmitz: but it is equally true that the writer Italo Svevo psychoanalyzed psychoanalysis itself. In other words, his writing, or at least his vision, has always been potentially or actually psychoanalytic. Ettore Schmitz and his heroes, who are, at least in part his self-portraits, had always been doing psychoanalyses, as Monsieur Jourdain made prose all the time without knowing it. But Svevo the writer has never been unaware of this and therefore is able to give a caricature of both psychoanaly-

sis and himself. Such a detached self-awareness was his lifelong amusement and contentment. One might say that Svevo was that wonder, a bourgeois really interested in his own soul; however, being a wise man, he used to consider one's soul, rather than imagination itself, *la folle du logis.*

To speak in scholastic terms, the human soul is not for Svevo a substance, but merely a series of accidents. The most important accident in the substance of life is love. Love is life both perpetuating and destroying itself. In this conception Svevo has been certainly influenced by his early reading of Schopenhauer. But for a bourgeois Schopenhauer, love is neither a chaotic force nor a cosmic evil: it is merely something both charming and bad. It is not a sin, but a forbidden fruit in the literal sense of the word. It is not forbidden by one's priest, but by one's doctor, who knows better than his patient what is good for him, and who orders him to abstain from it as from that "heady wine" from which the protagonist of the story so entitled gets drunk and sick. Sometimes, as in the matter of smoking, abstention is self-inflicted, like a taboo perpetually violated and reinstated by the patient himself. Love is a temptation dangerous to one's peace of mind and health of body. But temptation is real only to those who yield to it. Love is like the last cigarette of Zeno: Man, a creature eternally condemned to death, lights it up again and again.

In other words, Svevo looks always at love, at least beginning from his second novel, which was written in his early maturity, from the viewpoint of old age, from the perspective of an old man. This attitude is not merely social and psychological, but sexual as well. Like Leopold Bloom with Gerty MacDowell, Svevo's heroes are fascinated only by young girls. This predisposition also leads to logical consequences on the practical plane: Zeno and the protagonists of Svevo's last works regularly keep young mistresses. While Zeno's wife conspires with others, for her husband's good, to prevent him from managing his fortune, and thus treats him like a minor, Zeno supports Carla with his pocket money. In other terms, he becomes at the same time the protector and the father of his mistress, and the son, ward, and protégé of his own wife. The latter situation, not less than the former, is an evident symptom of his spiritual if not actual senility. Old age is very often nothing else but a second childhood. Like an adolescent and an old man, Zeno is interested especially in the beginnings of love; later, only in his own torments and feelings, doubts and self-deceit.

For Ettore Schmitz the man, and for the characters depicting or mirroring him, love is very often nothing else but a tonic and an intoxicant for the nerves. The other hobby, literature, seems rather to be an opium and elixir for man's brain. Both activities or pastimes are treated as habits, manias, or fixed ideas, like a not too harmful drug addiction or a rather innocent vice. In other words, neither literature nor love acquires, in the psychological economy of his characters, an obsessive quality; and this is the reason why the work of Svevo is far less consciously "aesthetic" and "morbid" than the work of Joyce and Proust. The literary experience of his protagonists, even if, as in the case of *Una burla riuscita,* it is very often based on Svevo's life, is nevertheless less autobiographical (or at least less literally so) than any other element in their *curriculum vitae.*

The author has been able to reach such a paradoxical result by dissociating Svevo the writer, not from Ettore Schmitz the man, but rather from the man of letters who was in Ettore Schmitz and in his heroes. Practically all his characters, perhaps with the exception of Zeno, are men of letters in their spare time. Such is the case of Alfonso Nitti in *Una vita,* of Emilio Brentani in *Senilità,* of Mario Samigli in *Una burla riuscita.* In other cases, like the protagonists of **"Vino generoso"** and **"La novella del buon vecchio e della bella fanciulla,"** they are naive reformers or ineffectual idealists. They are never without some intellectual interest (in Zeno's instance, psychoanalysis). But generally, with the exception of Zeno, who after all is not a writer, they never denounce, reflect, or betray the intellectual interests of their creator: Alfonso Nitti, Emilio Brentani, and Mario Samigli limit their literary curiosities and sympathies to Carducci and traditional Italian literature, without revealing in the first case that Svevo was interested in French naturalism and Schopenhauer; in the second, that he had been reading Russian writers; in the third, his recent acquaintance with Freud.

Is it arbitrary to affirm that the writers who are his characters are to a certain extent a satire of the contemporary Italian literary mind, exactly as Zeno is a parody of psychoanalysis? The Mario Samigli of *Una burla riuscita* perhaps entitles us to think so. The suspicion seems reasonable because in that story Svevo also makes fun of the writer within himself. Even more interesting is the fact of the appearance in one of his last works of the "good old man" of the novelette so entitled, a character affected by literature without knowing it, and who writes a pseudo-philosophical and edifying work by which he belatedly tries to save the soul of his young mistress and to teach her the conduct of life, even after his own death. In the literary vocation of his heroes, therefore, Svevo seems to see an attempt to escape from life, perhaps from consciousness, and even from conscience itself. By this attitude he did not mean to condemn literature; as a matter of fact, this is the very reason he approved of it.

This explains why between the literature of Svevo and the literature of his characters there is neither relationship nor contrast. The conflict between the bourgeois spirit and the literary mind is perhaps the dominant theme of modern and contemporary writing. The ideologist and the reformer on one side, the aesthete and the individualist on the other, solve that conflict by submitting the bourgeois spirit to the literary mind. Such was the solution of Flaubert and Nietzsche, of Wilde and Shaw, of Joyce and Proust. Thomas Mann reversed the position, granting the bourgeois spirit the right of questioning the validity of the literary mind and of opposing it. But Svevo was perhaps the only one among modern writers unable even to conceive of such a conflict. He accepted the bourgeois spirit as a frame or state of mind, as a datum or fact, as our own version of what Montaigne used to call "the condition of man."

Exactly because he does not judge the bourgeois spirit, Svevo amuses himself, tremendously and naively, by looking at it. A perfect bourgeois as a man, as a writer he is almost alone in not looking like one. Instead of descending or condescending to the bourgeois spirit within his own soul, he raises and uplifts it along with himself to the sphere of imagination, to a world of fancy and dream, which is at the same time the world of reality itself. Once Stendhal asked for a literature written by bankers and industrialists able to understand, lucidly and cynically, the economy of life, the business of society, the value of man. Svevo was certainly a writer of this brand and, furthermore, was endowed with such bourgeois honesty and common sense as to refuse to transform his indulgent egoism into any set of theories, any "egotism." A

kind of innocent wisdom was the real source of his greatness and originality. He was with everybody, including himself, a man of the world. This makes him, more than an Italian Joyce or Proust, a kind of contemporary Henry James, without the latter's snobbism and narcissism.

This is why from the naturalistic and Schopenhauerian pessimism of his youth he gradually grew to a kind of olympian serenity, and acquired that "merry wisdom" which is so alien to the modern mind. His first novel is gray and sad: in his second, there appears already what Gogol used to call "smiling through tears"; in *Zeno* and in his last stories, one may see the very uncommon realization of that poetic ideal which the German poets of the beginning of the past century used to call "romantic irony." This explains why the man born old always grew younger with time: and the same is already happening to his work, through the wonders of glory and the miracle of death. In the annals of contemporary literature very few books will remain so youthfully fresh as the pages of a writer like Svevo, who spent all his life in drawing a "portrait of the artist as an old man." (pp. 174-79)

> *Renato Poggioli, "A Note on Italo Svevo," in his* The Spirit of the Letter: Essays in European Literature, *Cambridge, Mass.: Harvard University Press, 1965, pp. 171-79.*

P. N. FURBANK   (essay date 1966)

[*Furbank is the author of* Italo Svevo: The Man and the Writer, *the first full-length study of Svevo and his work to appear in English. In the following excerpt from that work, Furbank surveys Svevo's dramas and his later fictional writings left unfinished at his death.*]

In shape **"La novella del buon vecchio e della bella fanciulla"** is broadly similar to the Carla section of *Zeno;* and it uses the same idea, which Svevo often came back to, of the lover quieting his conscience by giving his love-affair an "educational" turn. The hero, widowed and senile, combines each visit of his mistress with an improving lecture. And he also has another convenient pretext, equally quieting to the conscience, that a love-affair is important to his health—the story is a triangle drama between himself, his mistress and his medicine-bottles. When his state of health makes love-making too dangerous an exertion, he manages to transfer his pleasure entirely from the girl to the lecturing. Finally, when he has managed to eliminate the girl's image from his mind altogether, the original pleasure re-incarnates itself as literary ambition—he begins a work "On the Relations between Old Age and Youth," proving from history and logic the importance to the world of healthy old men. The work itself keeps unaccountably changing in its tendency, as his love-affair has done. Old men's sins, he decides, count double as compared with young men's; yes, but if young men's sins count for little, when does the education of old men begin? (He marks it as a question for further study.) As he goes on writing, his resentment against young men grows. It must be their fault if old men are immoral. "With whom is morality supposed to begin?" he writes in large letters.

Falteringly, he scribbles on, then sits for days staring at the heap of pages, and at last carefully wraps them in a cover, writing on it laboriously several times over, "Nothing!"— "They found him stiff and cold, with the pen still in his mouth through which his last breath had passed."

In **"Il mio ozio,"** one of the **"Old Old Man"** fragments, and rather more genial than the bitter *novella* of **"The Nice Old Man,"** the aged Zeno likewise takes a mistress for hygienic reasons—only, as he discovers, the trouble about a woman is that you can't adjust the dose. His idea in taking her is to cheat Nature, who, he feels, is all ready to knock him on the head as soon as it is proved he can help her no more in the business of procreation. It is his last affair, and when Felicita finally turns him out he decides to give up the hope of being desired by women, and to go on cheating Nature merely by desiring them. Looking at women's legs in the streets is a medicine he can take in strictly measured doses.

As *La coscienza di Zeno* begins with Zeno undertaking a course of psycho-analysis, so, at the start of the new novel, Zeno, bored with his life after his forcible retirement from business and tired of being treated as a helpless dotard, submits to a rejuvenation operation. Physically speaking, it is a fiasco, its only effect being to give him boils. Psychologically speaking, however, the operation—or rather the experience of pinning such hope upon it—works a temporary miracle; looking forward to youth is a kind of youth in itself. For a few weeks he emerges from the shadows into the foreground of life again. It is like reliving his adolescence, and is so uncomfortable that he takes to his pen in refuge.

As Zeno re-dedicates himself to writing, a whole series of new prospects opens up before his sanguine eyes. Writing, for one thing, will be a return to action. What with all the virtues he practises, and the ones other people attribute to him, and with all the affections and duties he seems to have accumulated, he might as well be dead for all the freedom he has. Perhaps writing will give him back his initiative. If he has to be virtuous, he would like to be dramatically virtuous, virtuous in *his* way, and writing may provide the opportunity.

And then, when he re-reads his own ten-year-old confessions (i.e. *La coscienza di Zeno*), he sees what he can do with them, *now,* that he couldn't do before. For a strange phenomenon has taken place in the ten years; he has forgotten everything of the past except what he happens to have written down. Or if he hasn't entirely forgotten it, the only way of recalling it is to re-read *Zeno* and fill in the gaps. He finds he is studying his past as if it were someone else's. It gives him a sense of loss and at the same time a precious new freedom. He perceives a whole new function in writing, the endless sifting out and purifying of one's own past life, an occupation with obvious advantages over mere living. Perhaps this is how everyone should spend their time—half of humanity re-writing its own past and the other half reading what they write.

> And if one part of human kind rebels and refuses to read the other half's effusions, so much the better. Everyone will read himself instead; and people's lives will have a chance to repeat, to correct, to crystallise themselves, whether or no they become clearer in the process. For good or evil, they won't go on being as they are now, flat and insignificant, buried as soon as born, with all their days melting into each other, piling up indistinguishably into years and decades.

And what is the past? he asks himself. He remembers a recent experience, when he and Augusta, on a trip to the country beyond Udine, got out of the car, and by climbing a little hill nearby came suddenly into full view of another landscape, the foothills and blue peaks of the Carnic Alps. They had stood silent in surprise, and for minutes on end Zeno had amused himself noting how the noise of a blacksmith's hammer, from the valley below them, only reached him when the man's arm was already raised for the next stroke. A few days or weeks later the whole scene had changed in his memory: the sound and the blow coincided as they should and the landscape had rearranged itself according to the rules of composition. When had it happened? He had failed to note the time the process took, and he projects a series of experiments on the same lines, to determine the boundary between the present and the past. "And so," he says, "I will end my life, like my dead father, notebook in hand."

The rest of the fragments, dealing with the present half of Zeno's existence, are in the style of *Zeno*. Zeno, as usual, begins by studying what is nearest to hand—his family, and the new set of relationships he has acquired since writing his confessions: his ill-fated efforts to get on with his son and daughter and his new-found alliances with his doctor nephew and his little grandson Umbertino. As he goes on talking, with the old unremitting analysis, enclosing irony within irony, there is the same interplay and recession between Zeno as actor and Zeno as recorder and between what Zeno himself notices and what we do. Zeno, relegated to the shadows of life, finds existence there just as thick with calamities. He is haunted, as before, by historic parallels and unexpected analogies. He repeats, and (too late) observes himself repeating, the master-patterns of his existence. His *idée fixe* in dealing with his children is to avoid the disasters that his father caused to himself. It is as fatal an *idée fixe* as any other, and produces what it is meant to avert. His elaborate plan to conciliate his son Alfio, by buying one of his dreadful pictures and carefully refraining from a single *Witz* ["joke"] at its expense, ends catastrophically. At the very worst moment (at a crowded dinner-table), and with the very maximum injury to Alfio, he finally makes the *Witze* he has been suppressing—he had felt like laughing; it was a healthy exercise, the one violent exercise allowed to old men. Even Alfio's pale incredulous face doesn't stop him. "I felt innocent. I wanted to laugh, and for that any subject was good enough."

In these fragments, **"The Old Old Man," "An Old Man's Confessions," "Umbertino," "This Indolence of Mine"** and **"A Contract,"** Svevo is making a great deal out of little (as he does again, strikingly, in *Corto viaggio sentimentale* in which he spins a hundred pages and more out of the most casual accidents and conversations of a railway journey). What the underlying direction of the different scraps was going to be one can't guess, but in themselves they are often as rich and exciting as anything in *Zeno;* his writing was never more darting and alive. And one feels that the book, if age had not slowed down and death interrupted the writing of it, might have been another masterpiece.

In the last year of his life Svevo also wrote a comedy about old age. It was called *Rigenerazione (Regeneration),* and it strikes me as the best of his plays. Svevo, as we know, wrote plays throughout his life, one or two even when he had officially given up writing, but he never, except in *Rigenerazione* and one or two short things (*Terzetto spezzato* and *Inferiorità*) completely mastered the form. The earliest plays, from the 1880s, are mostly light-weight vaudeville-like one-acters, totally artificial in their characterisation though sometimes containing quite amusing central ideas. There is, for instance, *La verità (Truth),* in which a professional liar manages, with superlative resourcefulness, to explain to his wife how, quite innocently, he happened to be in bed with her dressmaker in the middle of the afternoon. Or again *Una commedia inedita* (*An Unpublished Play*)—Svevo's own title—in which a wife, on the verge of being unfaithful to her husband with a playwright, is tactless enough to give her opinion of his latest play. A later *jeu d'esprit*, *Terzetto spezzato* (*The Broken Trio*), belonging to 1890 or thereabouts, is altogether wittier and more original and has been performed with some success. It is about a business man who has recently lost his wife and invites an old friend of the family (in actual fact, the wife's lover) to take part in raising her ghost. The wife, when she materialises, finds that nothing has changed: the lover soon works up a quarrel, and the husband, after his first awe at her re-appearance, turns very snappish when she won't exploit her opportunities to give him advance market-information. She dematerialises, having had enough of both of them; but as she has carelessly let out that any ill-feeling on her account between mortals will be held against her in Heaven, the husband and lover realise they now have the upper hand. They have only to stage a quarrel to get her back at any time. As the curtain falls, they are busily preparing to spar.

The best of his one-acters, however, is *Inferiorità,* written about 1920 or 1921. It is a sort of commentary on one of his diary entries:

> To bully someone when he hasn't the right or the courage to retaliate means falsifying your relationship with him forever. Never again will he be sincere with you. He has been classed once and for all as your inferior, and ever afterwards will hate and despise you.

The play is about a practical joke with tragic consequences. Count Alberighi and a companion have decided to play a hoax on their friend Alfredo, who has been brandishing his wallet about, full of money, and scoffing (arrogantly, they think) at the idea of anyone robbing him. They offer a bribe to Alfredo's manservant Giovanni, to terrorise his master and take his money off him at the point of a pistol, and Giovanni, having stood out for a bribe large enough for him to retire on, agrees. Alfredo arrives on the scene, and Giovanni goes through his performance (overheard by the Count and his friend, who are hiding in a closet), but he loses his nerve when his master faints with terror. Whereupon Alfredo, coming to his senses again, turns on Giovanni and bullies him mercilessly. He goes too far, and Giovanni, turning on him again, this time really murders him. With the Count and the Baron battering on the door to be let out, Giovanni quietly puts on his master's hat and coat and escapes; as he goes, he kisses his master's hand, murmuring "I wanted to be rid of you, and now you will be with me forever." It is a brilliant little piece, a powerful demonstration of the realities behind practical joking. What's in the air when Alberighi and his friend the Baron arrive in the flat is bullying. Alberighi is burning to bully someone a little; his tipsy friend catches the itch, and so does Giovanni, after they have bullied him on his sore point, money; so, likewise, does Alfredo himself, when he has got over his fright. The play is a study in contagion, worked out with all Svevo's acute perception of consequences, and for once, as a dramatist, Svevo is economical—his quick reversals really surprise and his ironies are truly dramatic.

In his middle years Svevo wrote two three-acters, *Un marito* (*A Husband*) and *L'avventura di Maria* (*Maria's Adventure*), the first in 1903 and the second some time after 1910 (he was constantly tinkering with his plays, so the dates are rather in-definite). *L'avventura di Maria* is a philosophic triangle-drama about a woman violinist who returns to (presumably) Trieste to stay with an old school-friend, and in pique at her friend's self-satisfied domesticity, and also at the fiasco of her own concert (the Triestines try to be kind, but can't help comparing her with their favourite "Janson," the master of the cadenza), decides to run off with her friend's husband. The play is a decided failure. There is some nice satire on Philistine Trieste in it, but it is static and diffuse and vacillates awkwardly between comedy and farce.

Un marito, which Svevo set particular store by, is more Ibsenesque and deals with an obsession with the past. The hero Federico, some years before the play opens, has killed his wife after finding her unfaithful. The court acquitted him, but he is still obsessed by what he has done—he who as a young man preached a complete "modern" tolerance in sexual morals. He has married again, but the marriage is haunted by the past, indeed the only person Federico has any real feeling for is his dead wife Clara's mother, who has sworn to be revenged on him. When this latter tries to break up his marriage, by showing him letters to prove that his new wife, Bice, has also taken a lover, he desperately begs Bice to give him proof of her innocence—not because he cares on her account, but as an answer to Clara's mother. For if Bice *were* guilty, and yet he did not kill her as he killed Clara, he would be admitting the wrongness of the first murder. His wife does all she can to combat his perverse cult of Clara's mother, and finding this useless, decides to take part in it too. The past has won; and as the final curtain falls the two are going hand in hand to the bedside of the avenging old woman. Federico reflects that, with any luck, she may mistake Bice for Clara.

It is a preposterous play, and a very bad imitation of Ibsen, though it deals with themes that meant a lot to Svevo. And it is fairly plain what is wrong with it. Federico, whom everyone treats nervously, in case he takes it into his head to commit another wife-murder, and who is secretly rather delighted at this impressive role, is essentially a comic character; indeed he is just the sort of comic conception that Svevo handled marvellously in his novels. In various places one can feel Svevo letting the play deviate into farce and then pulling it back, and the result, as far as the tone is concerned, is a muddle.

There is no objection of this kind to *Con la penna d'oro* (*With a Pen of Gold*), an unfinished four-act comedy belonging to 1926 or thereabouts. It is close to the novels in tone and contains some splendid material and scenes. It is a play about dependence. The main characters are two female cousins—one rich, the other poor and resenting her patronage—and their elderly Aunt Teresina, who is shuttlecocked between them. The aunt, who has been a domestic tyrant all her youth and middle-age, has decided, now that she is a cripple and thrown on others' charity, to master the art of sycophancy. Svevo's unique tone—profound, humane and utterly immune to sentimentality or platitude—comes out at its best here. Aunt Teresina is not, as would have been the theatrical cliché, triumphantly successful in her manoeuvres from her wheeled chair, nor pathetically unsuccessful. She is merely someone, like ourselves, fighting a minute-to-minute battle for self-assertion against odds. And here we come up against a basic difficulty facing Svevo as a playwright. It was part of his whole conception of the world that people never really change or get cured of their particular folly or humour; at most, like Aunt Teresina, they merely exhibit the same drives in a different context. To take another example, the incorrigibly patronising niece Alberta, in the same play, is still, as the final curtain falls, finding new ways of being patronising; whereas in a comedy of the Molière type she would have been cured or chastened in some way. Svevo's whole view of life was static and, in that sense, pessimistic, and his novels, as I have mentioned, tend to take the form of vicious circles. Believing as he did that all action was illusory, it always gave him trouble to provide the action required in a traditional play. To succeed in drama, in any original way, he needed to find a static and circular form like that of his novels. And he achieved this, to some extent, only in the last of his plays, *Rigenerazione.*

The play is his most ruthless handling of the farce of old age. It is a bitter play, but an immensely gay one also, and his comic imagination finds its freedom in it for the first time. It is very close to **"The Old, Old Man"** and deals with the same characters, though sometimes under other names: an old man, Giovanni, his wife Anna, their daughter Emma, her suitor Biggioni, Giovanni's mischievous nephew Guido, the maid Rita, etc. It is a comedy of humours: all Giovanni thinks of is his age, Anna is entirely preoccupied with her pet birds and cats, Emma brings every conversation round to her dead husband Valentino, whilst Biggioni can never forget the fact, which gives him such secret satisfaction, that his best friend Valentino is dead and stinking; Guido, again, thinks only of money, and Rita of avoiding work. The action of the play is purely farcical, and indeed the whole point of the action is that nothing really happens; the events are all ludicrous anti-climaxes, and the only significant events take place in the old man's dreams.

At the opening of the play, Giovanni is in a bad temper with the world. Everyone is bullying him for being senile and absent-minded and suggesting, kindly but firmly, it is time he stopped taking Emma's child for walks. (The last time he took him, he came back without him, convinced he had let him be run over.) His nephew (who has a financial interest in the proposal) suggests he should have a rejuvenation operation, and after a wildly funny scene in which Giovanni haggles about the price (one of his arguments is that as Guido holds out the prospect of a twenty-per-cent rejuvenation, the longer he postpones the operation the more he will get for his money), and earnestly insists that no harm shall be done to his morals, he agrees. Enter Giovanni, rejuvenated, in a smart silk dressing-gown. He struts about experimentally and gives his knee a painful knock. Another elderly gentleman, interested in the same operation, begs to be allowed to inspect him, tactfully inquiring as to the effect on his virility. Giovanni refuses to understand him, but he privately arranges an experiment on just this matter, with the maid Rita as subject. It is not a success, however. After getting Rita drunk, he finally manages to kiss her, but at this point both of them fall asleep, and when the two are found together, snoring, Anna is all solicitude, and goes and fetches rugs. Giovanni, as he sleeps, dreams of murdering Anna.

Next day the position is still the same; neither of the injured parties, Anna or Rita's fiancé, shows trace of decent jealousy; indeed Anna, to Giovanni's fury, asks if he enjoys Rita's company—for if so, she will arrange for her to be free whenever he wants. Humiliation succeeds humiliation, no one will believe in Giovanni's new-found virility, and in the end he gives up the struggle to be young and reverts to harmless, contemptible decrepitude.

The play ends with another dream-sequence—Giovanni is hoeing a stony field, having been led there by Rita. He asks if he can wait a little till the rain has softened the earth, but she tells him they have chosen him specially for the job, he being so young and vigorous now. He tells her to stand farther off, but to sing to him. Anna appears, and he reproaches her bitterly. What were they doing getting married as they did, all those years ago, he in a dress-suit and she all in white? What did they mean eating and drinking so much at that wedding-breakfast, as if they meant to eat and drink like that all their lives? Did they stay together because of it? Well, a year or two perhaps; and then they fell apart for ever. And then he had his operation, and saw what their life had become: a world in chaos, a spectacle of horror, a world where kisses count for nothing any longer. For example, he kissed Rita . . .

> ANNA. Yes, as a father kisses a daughter.
>
> GIOVANNI. *(furious)* As a father kisses someone else's daughter. There's a difference! . . . And then you told me I could have her whenever I liked.
>
> ANNA. I was only trying to be nice.
>
> GIOVANNI. Thank you, but you overdid it. You gave me more than I asked for. You got the proportions wrong.
>
> ANNA. You shouldn't complain. I thought I was making life pleasanter for you.
>
> GIOVANNI. Make it pleasanter? You've made it a hell for me, treating me in that way, treating my operation in that way.
>
> ANNA. Your operation? What did you expect? A miracle, after three weeks?
>
> GIOVANNI. You didn't have faith. And it means that now I haven't either—I want no more to do with women.
>
> ANNA. Not even with me? Won't you give me a kiss?
>
> GIOVANNI. A kiss? No, absolutely not! I love you. I never wanted to kill you. I love you, I say. For your sake I will love all the animals too, the sparrows, the cats and the dogs. And I will work for you. In your name I will keep and feed mankind. That is the task of us old men, us young old men, us old young men.

There is something strange, teasing and haunting about this whole last dream-sequence. It is, in some not very definable way, a new note, the voice of Svevo as a truly old man. It makes as good a last word as any for the writer who, at the age of thirty, wrote a novel called *Senility.* (pp. 205-16)

> *P. N. Furbank, in his* Italo Svevo: The Man and the Writer, *University of California Press, 1966, 232 p.*

SERGIO PACIFICI   (essay date 1967)

[*Pacifici is an American educator, translator, and critic, specializing in Italian language and literature. In the following excerpt, he discusses stylistic and thematic elements of Svevo's fiction that set him apart from contemporary writers.*]

Why should Svevo be a problematical figure for Italian critics? The question may be partly answered by looking somewhat more closely at the nature of his opus. Unlike his contemporaries, Svevo refused to be overburdened by linguistic or stylistic questions—this by itself places him in a special category in a nation so deeply conscious of the refinements of poetic language. Few would deny that Svevo's novels are written in the kind of gray, monotonous style most Italians, fervent admirers of *la belle page,* find repugnant to their ears. Although Svevo's prose is highly controlled, in that it demonstrates a capacity to make important statements or unfold the story with great economy of means, it is also static, lacking that dramatic, highly personal flair which distinguishes, for better or worse, the majority of Italian narratives of the same period. Yet, the style is nothing if not the real measure of the man that was Svevo and the artist in him. Even allowing for his unusual preparation as a novelist (particularly his geographical-cultural situation and his trilingual upbringing), it must be conceded that Svevo made a deliberate choice of the language that, in his mind, could most appropriately translate into literary images and events his special world. Interested as he was in the substance, rather than the appearance of things, it follows that his approach would be of the analytical and not of the descriptive kind. This may explain why his narrative is precise, without being overburdened with details; or why it is unpretentious to the point of seeming almost unpoetical (in Italy poetry has invariably been associated with stylistic refinement and virtuosity), or, finally, why it loses little of its essence when translated into another language. The nature of the man also holds the clue as to why he should so frequently employ irony, or ironical statements, in his work, since he saw in irony an apt instrument that would permit him to lay bare his profound skepticism about human nature. He used irony as a kind of oblique weapon that makes evident the incongruity, as well as the humor, of his characters. Examples are abundant, but it may suffice to remember here how Alfonso Nitti (*A Life*) plans to write a philosophical treatise (after deciding that "he would lay the foundations of modern Italian philosophy by translating a good German work"), and how soon enough "the translation remained pure intention" as he never goes beyond writing the first four pages of the preface. Later on, dissatisfied with the progress made by his own work, he plunges "into reading a bibliographical journal" a fact that convinces him of his inadequate grasp of Italian.

By the same token, and again unlike his contemporaries, Svevo eschews anything more than a momentary concern with either the religious or the socioeconomic facets of the human experience. What absorbs him, is the unpredictable behavior of people facing situations that touch vividly on their emotions (or on their sexual drives) rather than on their material needs—people largely unaffected by political, religious, or even ethical problems. The atmosphere he skillfully conjures up in his fiction is not one likely to prod the reader to take sides in the peculiar kind of struggles of created characters—as is often the case in the bulk of nineteenth-century fiction—but rather impels him to watch, with a dispassionate, and almost clinical attention, how men living under the most normal circumstances make themselves look silly or incoherent, and how thoroughly they succeed in wrecking their lives. As represented in his fiction, man is no arbiter of his destiny, no pilot of his course, no hero of a gigantic drama that takes place, day in and day out, on the earthly stage. He is merely a creature who acts instinctively and impulsively, groping for happiness but achieving only misery, knowing himself to be basically insincere, incompetent, and insecure yet striving, or at least pretending, to achieve worthy goals, a badly needed,

firm personal relationship with human kind and even moral rectitude. The irony is all in that contrast, in what they *are* and what they *long* to be, if only in their imagination; in the pleasures and victories they seek, and in the anguish and defeats they are doomed to suffer, more at the hands of their own ineptitude than of fate. "I'm ill!" shouts one of Svevo's early heroes, Alfonso Nitti. And the narrator hastens to add that

> This conclusion was reached after he had made a series of observations about himself. The deep gloom which turned everything gray and dull for him had seemed till then a natural result of his discontent; his insomnia he thought must be due to nervous tension brought on by night study; and an abnormal restlessness he sometimes noticed in himself must come from the fact that his muscles and lungs were insisting on exercise and pure air . . . now he was constantly, monotonously, obsessed by one vision which made him incapable of taking part in the present, hearing and examining anything said by others.

What may shock us about the world of Svevo is that it either does not know or refuses to point out evil or good, right or wrong. "Evil just happens, it is not committed," states Emilio Brentani in **Senilità** (**As a Man Grows Older**). The author adds: "In that tumult of waves . . . he read the impassivity of fate. No one was to blame for that destruction." No one, that is, except ourselves. The pervading feeling we are bound to get from Svevo's novels is of an absurd, incoherent world, where man is prevented by his self-deception, vanity, egotism, false idealism, and spineless character from taking cognizance of his own frailties, and is even less able to share his happiness or sorrows with others.

To penetrate the reasons for this sad state of affairs, the novelist turns his focus not on reality, but on the human consciousness. Much of his work is so constructed that it allows a sustained look at the contradictions between reality and personality, what we would like to see and what we must acknowledge *is.* In the last analysis, this is the secret of his modernity, the reason why the contemporary reader can turn to his work and find not the history of a certain period poetically reflected, but the human character brilliantly and amusingly analyzed. There is no doubt Svevo realized that if a poet has the obligation to lead his public to a more complete understanding of the human predicament, a good novelist must also be, in a special way, a great entertainer.

There are other reasons why Italian critics have the right to feel uneasy or annoyed by Svevo's work, so obviously un-Italian to the point of seeming to belong to another culture. I suppose that the diverse nature of Svevo's novels and their general orientation are the elements that set them in a category (or class) of their own. Thus, at a time when *verismo* had reached its zenith, Svevo was writing highly introspective novels, all of which, although clearly set in Trieste, make scant use of the regional backdrop. What we see of Trieste, in short, is not only occasional but never elaborated through factually precise descriptions. More than seeing the city, we feel it, especially and most lucidly when it is used to give added color to the dramatic unfolding of character. Just as Svevo shows an unusual lack of interest in the use of scenery, so he remains largely unconcerned with a mystical approach to life (as Fogazzaro) or with D'Annunzio's superman. But there is still more. Although the novelist felt deeply Italian, despite his obvious ties to Germany, he never overtly expressed in his fiction his views on the political fate of his country, nor his hope that his native city might some day be reunited with the rest of the nation. In a nation prevalently Catholic, he was one of the most areligious writers of modern times; in a culture where the majority of writers, major and minor alike, sooner or later take a stand on the *questione della lingua,* Svevo maintained a consistent aloofness from what many rightly regard as one of the most crucial and burning literary problems.

In other ways, too, Svevo professed little or no interest in those issues of life and culture, of politics and society that his contemporary fellow writers found important or fascinating. He does not dramatize religious or moral conflicts springing from carnal desires, as in Grazia Deledda's novels or as in many of Verga's memorable short stories; nor does he attempt to paint vast, ambitious canvasses of social conditions of certain depressed southern regions—as had been the practice of Matilde Serao, Salvatore Di Giacomo, and a score of realists and regionalists. Nor does he strive for the kind of historical-political tableau so admirably done by Ippolito Nievo and Federico De Roberto among others. His heroes invariably come from the comfortable bourgeoisie, generally untroubled by the necessity of having to work for a living, and not under the strain of having to worry constantly about an uncertain tomorrow. But not everything—indeed, preciously little—is well with the middle class, and his characters live forever under the haunting awareness of their failures and psychological malaise. Yet, all this does not turn Svevo into a social reformer, much less an utopian. What makes him an appealing writer for today's readers is his undisputed acceptance of the condition of sickness pervading the world, transforming it, as Richard Gilman acutely remarked some years ago, "into the condition of existence itself, making uprootedness, alienation, moral uncertainty and social weakness—as opposed to unseemed and coerced integrity—into agencies of wily enduring and liberating instruments of self-knowledge." The Svevian hero likes nothing better than the excruciatingly relentless, if often unproductive, self-analyses to which he subjects himself, for through such self-examinations he achieves a human dimension. For him, one can well repeat what the novelist says apropos Alfonso Nitti: "Self-knowledge made him suffer." Perhaps out of his desire to avoid a direct confrontation with himself coupled with his incredible incapacity to cope with the complexities of life, he discovers the usefulness of his illness—an illness that invariably has all the symptoms of a psychosomatic disorder. Because they are ill (one thinks here of how sickness has sharpened the sensitivity of poets of all generations, from Tasso to Leopardi, from Simone Weil to Moravia), they are overconscious of how people react to what they say or do. Indeed, their malady, as yet undefined, visibly increases their sensibility, even if what they feel is invariably a distortion or a rationalization of the real reason for their malaise. It is not without justification that Angiolina, the heroine of **As a Man Grows Older,** despite her dubious morals, is depicted as a woman enjoying good health, even if her behavior toward her lover is bound to seem perverse in that it is calculated to bring Emilio Brentani an unusual amount of misery. Good health, we must assume, means simply a *joie de vivre,* the ability to let oneself savor whatever little life has to offer, without worrying about repercussions, moral values, or implications from whatever quarter they may come; it also means to come to terms with oneself and accept oneself as one is, limiting our goals or adjusting them to conform to our abilities.

As it has been hinted, the reality Svevo observes and describes, with a method that in its calculated meticulousness leaves nothing to the imagination, is quite limited. The eyes of his heroes, or of his narrator-protagonist, scan a landscape that is possibly one of the narrowest in modern Italian fiction. Only when the landscape serves to illustrate, reflect, or dramatize the psychological state of the characters, are we allowed to see it. Svevo's technique, in fact, permits him to create a story with a maximum of dramatic content with a minimum amount of attention to external reality. To be sure, this is the way it should be, not only because the life and experience he narrates are gray and monotonous, but because his tales are turned inward, bent on discovering the mechanism of the human personality, the nature of passions, the discordance between our goals and our possibilities. As a consequence, one cannot expect to get from Svevo a feeling of society, nor much less a sense of history unfolding before our very eyes, as in Manzoni, or in historical novels and *veristic* tales. The air we breathe in Svevo's novels is more rarefied than that of most of his contemporaries; in a limited sense, it evokes that of Tozzi's silent, gloomy Sienese countryside; likewise, the tensions Svevo creates have something of the electric quality of G. A. Borgese's fiction.

If in his choice of themes, or in his structural innovations, or in his slow-moving style Svevo shows himself to be a kind of outsider, it is to certain other sides of his work that we must turn to discover his uniqueness. I have already mentioned his obsession with psychological illnesses; I must now add his engrossing concern with ennui. For it is boredom . . . that is one of the great forces of Svevo's universe. Leopardi and Baudelaire recognized it as such in their poetry, and Svevo exploits it to the utmost in his fiction, where it becomes the condition that encourages introspection. Thinking about oneself can be a dangerous affair; in the world of Svevo it forces a reexamination of the whole question of self-fulfillment. Can man, living in a world laden with frustration and absurdities, achieve the capacity of doing some of the things he knows, deep in his heart, he is incompetent or unfit to do? Manzoni might have answered this question in religious terms, and Verga in economic ones. Svevo, on the other hand, along with Pirandello and Moravia, felt that if an answer does exist, it must be sought in ourselves, in the very depth of our conscience. Nonetheless, as a writer, Svevo concerned himself not with finding answers, but in exploring this and other facets of the human condition; not in preaching, but in dramatizing the dilemmas of modern man, living in a world where standards have suddenly collapsed; not in attempting to extend his range horizontally, but vertically. His truths may be few; but they are, in the main eminently valid. (pp. 151-57)

Sergio Pacifici, "Italo Svevo's Antiheroes," in his The Modern Italian Novel: From Manzoni to Svevo, *Southern Illinois University Press, 1967, pp. 149-83.*

PAULA ROBISON (essay date 1970)

[*In the following excerpt, Robison uses Freudian concepts to examine issues in* The Confessions of Zeno *and* Further Confessions of Zeno, *particularly Oedipal themes, psychosomatic illness, and relations between the sexes.*]

Virtually every passage in **Confessions of Zeno** and **Further Confessions of Zeno** attests to the intensity and ambivalence of Italo Svevo's concern with Oedipal themes, and presents the Freudian literary critic with delicate problems in point of view and irony. The nature of the problems is perhaps best suggested by the incident in *Further Confessions* in which Zeno's seven-year-old grandson makes him an ingenuous present:

> a house for Grandpapa, who could live in it quite comfortably if you cut part of his body off, indeed all of it except his head. And the little man looked at my head and then back at the house, establishing the proportions between the two.
>
> Antonia protested: "You don't want Grandpapa to die, do you? He couldn't breathe with only a head."
>
> The child studied me.
>
> "But don't you see he breathes *just* with his head?"
>
> This wild fantasy of his upset me. I spent a restless night—so restless, in fact, that I translated his idea into a hair-raising dream. My entire body had been cut off and all that was left was my head, sitting on a table. I could still talk; and apparently I was eager to carry out Umbertino's every wish; but I was naturally short of breath and desperately panting for air, and I thought: "How long will I have to go on breathing like this before my body grows back?"
>
> The nightmare disturbed me so much, that all the next day I couldn't shake it off. And I thought to myself: "One ought not to have to live a life in which such monstrous things can be imagined."
>
> And to think it had been conceived in that little blond head of Umbertino's!

Remembering that Svevo prided himself on having introduced Freud into Italian literature, a perceptive reader recognizes Zeno's terror as founded on unconscious and therefore "hair-raising" fears of patricide and castration; he understands that these impulses exist in little Umbertino and that they strike a responsive chord in Zeno because he shares the same horrifying aggressive desires; and he wonders, as Freud did, at the contrast between the child's innocent exterior and the savage cruelty of his suppressed desires. Reading farther in the two Zeno novels, he finds that this description of little Umbertino is in fact applicable to Zeno himself, for beneath the humorous urbanity and the understated wit lie savage depths of unconscious desires. But Zeno is no Kurtz, who dies after recognizing "the horror," nor is Svevo a Marlow or a Conrad, recounting tales of the horror in muted tones of tragic irony; he is a humorist, whose perception of depths is played off against his acute awareness of surfaces. To center attention solely on either the depths or the surface would be to falsify Svevo; we must instead respond to the interplay of the two, for this is the principle of the Zeno novels.

Our understanding of little Umbertino's "present," then, must not be reductive. Few would be so naive as to agree with Zeno that Umbertino "has none of our vices. He neither loves nor hates." But the "house for Grandpapa" is not an actual coffin but merely a childish representation of fantasies which the child does not understand or intend to act out. Umbertino *is* an innocent child, and if a knowledge of Freud requires that we modify our ideas of innocence, it does not mean that we need to be tormented by nightmares. What we must do, however, and what Zeno is incapable of doing, is to distinguish fantasy from fact and to respond to the actuality of situations. The actuality of this incident is that a child has expressed an interest in patricide and castration, and has also managed to touch upon the problems that have always beset his grandfather: his fear of dismemberment and death, his mistrust of his own body, his passivity, and his desperate insistence on the superior powers of talking and rationality as ways of circumventing the body's vulnerability. If Zeno were able to acknowledge his fears and desires, perhaps his nightmares would be fewer and his "confessions" shorter and more honest. But he will never be able to do so as long as he clings to the metaphysical evasion, "One ought not to have to live a life in which such monstrous things can be imagined." For if Freud teaches us anything at all, it is that such a life must be lived and faced with honesty and courage.

Zeno's "confessions," of course, are not confessions at all but attempts to hide the truth, and their major motive is to deny Freudian insights. Svevo, assuming the attitude of his brother-in-law who claimed to have been pronounced incurable by Freud, viewed Freudian theory as a means of diagnosing the incurable. That he knew and accepted many of Freud's ideas is well documented. His biographer P. N. Furbank notes that *Confessions of Zeno* demonstrates the Freudian concepts of free association, the ego-id conflict, the pleasure principle, psychosomatic illness, and the unconscious. To this list should be added the Freudian ideas of dream-work, repetition compulsion, wit and humor, denial, reversal, projection and rationalization. All these psychic mechanisms appear in and provide a comic base for the two Zeno novels, and it must be assumed that Svevo thought of them as true and useful concepts. An awareness of Freudian defense mechanisms underlies the comedy of Zeno's resistance to psychoanalysis: he resorts to denial ("He need not worry; his words have not been able to spoil the memories of my youth. I have but to close my eyes and immediately there rises up before me my love for my mother, and the great respect and affection I felt for my father"); projection ("I wonder why he took such a violent dislike to me. He is probably also a hysteric, who avenges himself for having lusted after his mother, by tormenting innocent people"); and repression ("I avoid dreams and memories. . . . I am terribly absent-minded"). This is the comedy of the unreliable narrator.

But it appears that Svevo shares two of Zeno's defenses against psychoanalysis. First, in the ending of *Confessions,* he has Zeno, echoing his own Schopenhauerian pessimism, prophesy the eventual destruction of the world by technological man and draw the conclusion, "We need more than psychoanalysis to help us." To us of the seventies, the prophecy is uncanny in its description of pollution and biological and nuclear warfare. But in the novel's context it is a *non sequitur,* and we wonder whether Svevo is aware of the way in which Zeno's defenses are contradictory and yet consistent. He claims that his doctor's diagnosis is (a) false, (b) harmful because thinking about the problem makes it worse, and (c) irrelevant because all men are sick. What these three contradictory claims have in common is their denial of the doctor's power to cure and of the patient's ability to recover from an illness which is only half admitted. Second, *Confessions* defends Zeno again in its use of Dr. S., the unprofessional analyst who publishes Zeno's memoirs for his own profit and for revenge against his uncooperative patient. The farcical Dr. S., it is made clear, is as childish and as hostile as his patient; and in conceiving such a psychiatrist, Svevo seems to be on Zeno's side. Like Zeno, he sees doctors as quacks, themselves impotent imposters who suffer from the very sickness which they claim to cure and which is the irrevocable decree of that incurable joker Mother Nature. Yet the novel supports Dr. S.'s opinion that Zeno suffers from an Oedipus complex. Zeno denies this diagnosis, while Svevo by implication confirms it; but the two are equally certain that no cure is available. Unlike Zeno, Svevo joins with Dr. S. in understanding the patient's syndromes; he differs from the doctor in seeing Zeno as funny and appealing as well as childish, self-deceived and full of murderous fantasies, and in defending Zeno's behavior as essentially normal. With this complex point of view in mind, we can turn to an examination of the psychodynamics which give the novels their comedy and truth.

We note first that there is for Zeno a remarkable similarity between Dr. S. and his father—that Svevo has absorbed the Freudian idea of transference. Dr. S. is one in a long series of father figures for Zeno, and with each of them he reenacts his characteristic attitude toward powerful authority. In each case he pretends submission in order to conceal strong hostility; and he hopes eventually, under the cover of his feigned respect, to unmask the authority he so despises. When he says of Dr. S., "I forced myself to be cringingly subservient to him just in order to hide what I was really thinking," we are reminded of his attitude toward the hated Dr. Coprosich (whose name so delighted Joyce): "I behaved to him with exaggerated politeness so that he should not guess what I really felt toward him. My face expressed only consideration and respect. It was not till I saw him going down the garden path to the gate that I allowed myself a grimace of disgust. He looked such an insignificant black little thing in the snow. . . . Dr. Coprosich, he notes, is, despite his scatological name, "greatly esteemed by everybody in the town"—by everybody, that is, except Zeno. So too are his other father figures: the guardian Olivi, the father-in-law Malfenti, the many other doctors he consults, and his friends Copler and Cima. With each of them Zeno acts the part of the respectful incompetent and simultaneously manages, in his confessions if not always in his actual life, to expose these pillars of the community as quacks and charlatans. In his account of his father's last illness he describes the father's inability to teach his son anything of value and quotes him as saying perplexedly, "It is curious, I can't find anything to say, absolutely nothing. . . . Yet there are so many things I know. I feel as if I knew almost everything. It must be the result of my great experience." Just as he humors the father while thinking, "I was glad to see him so happy in the illusion that he was strong just when he was at his weakest," so later he pretends to cooperate with Dr. S. while harboring a feeling of superiority and a desire to challenge the wise man's omniscience. Zeno finally unmasks Dr. S. by failing to respond to his treatment: "The surest proof that I never had the disease is that I have not been cured of it." Zeno is the stubborn child who refuses to take his medicine: he thus frustrates and renders ineffectual the doctor, asserts his own will, demands and receives attention—all the while maintaining his righteous innocence, for he is only an ineffectual and irresponsible invalid. With all these benefits, we can hardly be surprised that he is willing to pay the price of continuing to be sick. And indeed, we must insist that a man so willfully self-deceived as to his own motives and so persistently hostile for such flimsy reasons is sick.

At the same time, however, Zeno's covert form of rebellion is useful, for it helps him to build a tolerable life and defends him against the pain of self-knowledge. There are certain advantages to his neurotic behavior, and they are admirably illustrated by the question of his smoking, which occupies so prominent a place in his confessions.

The symbolic significance that cigarettes have acquired for Zeno is suggested by his account of his earliest experience with smoking, with which the first novel begins. His first cigarette was given to him by a friend who had bought cigarettes with money given him by a generous father. Zeno's father is a very different kind of man: he continually refuses to give money to his son, and Zeno resents it. It is an important fact of his life that the father's will stipulates that Zeno not be allowed any power in controlling the business whose profits furnish his living; the father, then, sees his son as an incompetent and takes steps to assure that he will remain so forever. One thinks of Laius, who decrees the death of his son as an infant and who, in their encounter at the crossroads, orders Oedipus off the road: the father is as hostile as the son. But his father is not the only one who threatens what Zeno regards as his rightful wealth and power; his childhood friend gives fewer cigarettes to Zeno than to his brother, "and that was how I came to steal."

In a scene so full of crude Freudian psychology as to become a virtual parody of the Freudian Oedipal situation, Zeno describes an early childhood memory. His mother has helped him to undress and urges him to sleep on the sofa where she is sitting. He is surprised to find that in his recollection, as he is "lying there close to her dear body," his brother "plays no part in the scene," though logic tells him that the brother was surely present. In fantasy, then, Zeno's wishes are fulfilled: he sleeps next to his mother, and his sibling is banished from the scene. A further triumph ensues: the father enters in search of a cigar that Zeno has stolen, and the mother tells him to speak softly because the child is asleep; "I was so pleased at my father having to treat me with such consideration that I kept perfectly still." This pretense of innocent passivity has its results: complaining "in a low voice" that he thinks he is going mad because he cannot find his cigar, the father leaves and the mother smiles indulgently. It is a classic Oedipal victory.

The victory is repeated when Zeno's father and the first of his many doctors forbid him to smoke. "Any prohibition sufficed to excite" Zeno's craving for cigarettes. It is little wonder, then, that Zeno loves to smoke, for each cigarette is a fresh victory over the father and the doctor. Nor, on the other hand, is it surprising that he constantly vows to stop smoking, for the Oedipal victory is bound to bring guilt. The last cigarette, he says, brings "a sense of victory over oneself and the sure hope of health and strength in the immediate future." But if the price of victory over oneself and of health and strength is the refraining from victory over the father, it is a mixed blessing. The struggle to stop smoking becomes a struggle with the infantile impulse to patricide which is so strong just because it is so infantile; and because the desires are so strong, Zeno becomes the victim of a repetition compulsion, doomed to reenact again and again his guilty desires and his repentance. The dates of his last cigarettes acquire a magic, compulsive significance. He uses cigarettes to celebrate important events, "in fact all from the death of Pius IX to the birth of my son"—that is, from the death of Il Papa to the birth of the new Oedipus. Thoughts of patricide are never far from Zeno's mind as he puffs away on last cigarette after last cigarette.

Not surprisingly, smoking has another magical property for Zeno: it confers sexual potency. As he tells one of his many doctors, "My sexual excitement is not normal. It comes from the poison burning in my veins!" The doctor replies that sexu-

Svevo in 1918.

al desire is normal, and Zeno notes, "It is worth recording that I detected symptoms of disease in what the specialist regarded as healthy, and that my diagnosis turned out to be right." Once again, Zeno is showing his superiority over the doctor by insisting on his own sickness, and he is right. His craving for cigarettes is the same as his craving for women, proceeding as it does from the desire to assert a manhood which the father is felt to prohibit. Cigarettes are phallic. And by smoking his many last cigarettes, Zeno achieves greater and greater triumphs of phallic power, until finally he can assert, "Time, for me, is not that unimaginable thing that never stops. For me, but only for me, it comes again." This megalomaniacal belief in his personal immortality makes better sense when we compare his view of time and death in *Further Confessions:*

> One must accept the fact, Mother Nature is a maniac. That is to say, she has the reproduction mania. She maintains life within an organism so long as there is hope of its reproducing itself. Then she kills it off.

The patent falsity of this assertion as a piece of medical science only serves to point up the persistence with which Zeno identifies sexuality and life, impotence and death. When he thinks of abandoning cigarettes altogether, "I saw a great void and no means of resisting the fearful oppression which

emptiness always produces." The void, the fearful oppression, the emptiness—that is to say, impotence, castration and death. We now see, then, that for Zeno smoking is a symbol of health and virility. And we also begin to see more clearly the patricidal implications of stealing cigarettes from the father. (pp. 101-05)

Unlike Zeno, who describes tobacco as "poison," the father accepts smoking as he accepts his manhood: "he regarded tobacco and alcohol as wholesome drugs." It is immediately added that he accepted women in much the same way, and his behavior with his dressmaker-mistress, whom he leaves when his wife discovers the affair, is in direct contrast to Zeno's guilty vacillation about *his* mistress. Yet Zeno persists in describing his father as weak, and in calling his own vacillations "efforts at self-improvement," and he can actually say about the death of his father that "the loss of this weaker person with whom I could compare myself to my own advantage made me feel that my value had definitely diminished." There is some evasion here. On the one hand, this statement is accurate: Zeno's convictions of his own strength are fed only by a continued competition with the father, the object being to show the father's weakness while maintaining his own so as not to feel overwhelming guilt. Actual patricide would be unthinkable; Zeno takes his patricide, as he takes his women in *Further Confessions,* "in doses." Stealing the father's cigarettes and belittling him in thought are not the most heinous of crimes, for the father survives the onslaughts of fantasy. But on the other hand, we realize first that though the father may not be the strongest of men morally or intellectually, he has more integrity than his son; and second that the circumstances of the father's death provide quite another reason for Zeno to feel that his value has diminished. The chapter "The Death of My Father" suggests that Zeno has come too close for comfort to acting out his patricidal impulses.

The circumstances of the death are ambiguous, but its consequences are clear: it is "that terrible, unforgettable scene which threw its shadow far into the future, and deprived me of all my courage and of all joy in life." Courage and joy are incompatible with guilt. And yet Zeno does nothing which could be even remotely defined as patricide. What are the charges against him? First, Dr. Coprosich reproaches him for not having noticed whether the father's appetite had recently failed. Second, when he first learns that the father is ill, he "had quite forgotten that there were such things as doctors in the world, and that sometimes they were supposed to be able to save one. I had already seen death on that face contorted with pain, and I had given up hope." Third, when told by the doctor that the father's illness admits no hope of recovery, Zeno begs him to let the father die—to commit a mercy killing, and "I prayed that my father might die." Fourth, during the father's long illness "finally I began to feel resentment against my father. . . . I was obliged to be constantly fighting with him, now forcing him to take his medicine and now preventing him leaving the room. And conflict always produces anger." Fifth, at the moment of the death, Zeno thinks his father "had the impression that it was I who was depriving him of the air he needed so much, just as I was shutting out the light by standing, while he was sitting down." Sixth, the dying father delivers a blow to the son who is dutifully trying to keep him in bed:

> Then, crying like a child who has been punished,
> I shouted in his ear:

"It was not my fault! It was that cursed doctor who wanted to make you lie down!"

It was a lie. . . .

He was dead and it was impossible for me to prove my innocence.

He cannot prove his innocence because in thought he is not innocent; he has always been his father's mortal rival, and he has actually prayed for his death. On the other hand, of course, Zeno does not believe literally in the efficacy of prayer and he has certainly not deprived the father of air. Zeno is innocent in fact, but in unconscious fantasy he is guilty, and it is this guilt that imparts a Kafka-like significance to the father's dying blow, and that so blights his later life. Zeno's mistake is to believe in what Freud called the omnipotence of thought, to believe that it is his own admittedly hasty abandoning of hope (which in Freudian terms looks suspiciously like a patricidal impulse) which has caused the father to die. But we must insist that Zeno is innocent, that he has not acted out his unconscious wish any more than does little Umbertino in the incident with which we began our investigation. Because he cannot admit that in fantasy he has in effect killed the father many times, Zeno cannot distinguish the difference between this fantasy and his actual behavior. Instead he must go over and over the deathbed scene in his mind, repeating time after time his insincere and unconvincing protestations of total innocence. (pp. 106-08)

Zeno's obsession with patricide is shown again in the keen interest he takes in the deaths of other strong men throughout the two novels. There is, first, the death of his father-in-law, whose last words to Zeno are, "If I could get rid of my illness by giving it to you, you may be sure that I would do so at once, and twice over!" Zeno's comment, "There was nothing offensive in what he said," shows to what extent he consciously denies his antagonism toward this powerful and hostile father, for surely there is something offensive in Malfenti's desire to kill him, "and twice over." But Malfenti's murderous desire is evidently Zeno's as well, as we find on the occasion of Ada's and Guido's engagement party, when Zeno offers wine to his father-in-law, whom the doctors have forbidden to drink: " 'So you want to kill me, do you?' asked Giovanni mildly, looking curiously at me. . . . He had made not the slightest effort to drink what I had poured out for him. I felt thoroughly depressed and in the wrong." He has reason to feel "in the wrong," for he has indeed tried to kill his father-in-law; furthermore, he has just been involved in another highly Oedipal action, the seduction of his older friend Copler's mistress just at the moment of Copler's death. He proceeds to spoil the festive mood of the party by announcing the news of Copler's death, then guiltily seeks to undo this action by retracting the news, commenting later on "how many times my wine had killed him off and resurrected him again." (p. 108)

Further Confessions is full of Oedipal implications in its description of the tortured relationship between the aging Zeno and his grown son Alfio. In particular it is instructive to look at the incident after which, Zeno says, his "relationship with Alfio began to deteriorate." It is the occasion on which Zeno goes hunting with his successful and strong-willed friend Cima. As they wait in the dark for ducks, Zeno, presumably in his usual search for phallic power, lights a cigarette, and Cima, following the rule of the hunter, fires in his direction. Zeno retaliates by firing back, as if his friend's shot had been

an attempt at murder; because he is incompetent with a rifle, however, he misses. Cima and Zeno's family laugh over the story at dinner; and it is just at this point that Zeno, who insists that "there was no resentment between Cima and himself," begins to make fun of Alfio's paintings, which he has always been careful to praise in order to preserve peace between himself and his son. We can only make the connections that Zeno refuses to, and conclude that Zeno's hostility toward his friend is like his hostility toward the father, that he cannot express his aggression directly, and that now that he is a father he finds it easy and appropriate to do to his son what he thinks all sons do to fathers.

All this evidence should suggest the extent to which Zeno is obsessed with father-son relationships, which are always seen as potentially murderous. His second obsession is relationships between brothers, similarly competitive and murderous. The story of Zeno's courtship and marriage is remarkable for its emphasis not on the bride but on the father-in-law Malfenti and the brother-in-law and rival Guido Speier. Zeno is actually courting Malfenti, whom he describes as "the man I chose to be [my children's] grandfather": and Guido is his rival and chief obstacle in becoming part of the Malfenti household. There is ample evidence to suggest that Zeno's relationship with Guido is one of sibling rivalry, and that just as Malfenti replaces his actual father, Guido replaces the brother who, in Zeno's first memory, had more cigarettes than he.

Zeno's words concerning his courtship, "If I wanted to have peace I must ensure that I should never be banished from that drawing-room," are recalled during his memory during psychoanalysis of:

> one year in my life during which I was already going to school, while my brother had not yet begun. . . . I saw myself coming out of the house one sunny morning in spring, and walking through the garden on the way down to the town. . . . My brother did not appear at all in this dream-scene, but he was the hero of it. I thought of him so happy and free at home, while I had to go to school. I went there with a dragging step, and with anger in my heart, and felt as if I wanted to cry. . . . I was condemned eternally to go to school, while my brother was allowed to stay at home.

This is the same brother, it will be recalled, whom Zeno banishes from his early Oedipal memory of stealing the father's cigar and sleeping with the mother. He recalls another incident involving the brother: a scene in which young Zeno, having drunk his *caffelatte,* is attempting first with his spoon and then with his tongue to get the sugar remaining in the cup. The brother asks to borrow the spoon, and Zeno demands a piece of the brother's sugar in return; he calls this demand "that bad action, which was probably the first I had ever committed." It is probably one of the last times Zeno has had possession of the phallic spoon. Certainly in the competition with Guido, Zeno is pitifully ill-prepared, no match for his rival with his walking-stick, full head of hair and "victorious violin." His only recourse must be to trickery and deception, and the three middle chapters of *Confessions* describe one hoax after another that Zeno perpetrates on Guido, culminating, as in the case of the father, with a death that provides Zeno with considerable guilt.

Zeno's first encounter with Guido takes place during a seance with which Guido is hoping to impress the Malfentis. Seeming to comply with Guido's game, Zeno manages to unmask his rival as a charlatan and to commit a symbolic murder by pretending to be the spirit of a dead man named Guido Speier. This is only the beginning of the battle. Guido retaliates with a drawing of Zeno,

> with my nose in the air, leaning on an umbrella stuck in the ground. In the second [drawing] the umbrella was broken and the handle was sticking into my back. . . . Everyone laughed a great deal, too much I thought. I was extremely pained by this very successful attempt to pour ridicule on me. It was on this occasion that I was conscious for the first time of a stinging pain in my right forearm and hip.

The phallic duel continues as Zeno makes a drawing of Guido

> being crushed by a table falling on top of him. By his side was a stick that had fallen from his hand at the moment of the accident. No one recognized the walking-stick, so that my vengeance fell very flat. . . . The severe pain I was suffering made me work very rapidly. Never before had my whole being longed so desperately to wound someone, and if I could have exchanged the pencil, which I was incapable of using, for a saber, perhaps my cure would have been complete.

This is the first of Zeno's many physical pains, which he identifies as psychically caused. During the course of the two novels, we learn that he suffers at various times from a limp, a recurring pain in the arm and hip, an ultrasensitive retina, insomnia, chronic bronchitis, eruptions on his face, sharp stabbing pains in his legs, and boils; and that he has consulted Dr. S., Dr. Coprosich, Dr. Muli, Dr. Paoli, Dr. Raulli, his nephew Carlo (still a medical student), a doctor who claims to cure nervous diseases by electricity, and "a sort of veterinary surgeon." These doctors variously diagnose the problem as diabetes, "imperfect metabolism, . . . defective circulation, . . . tuberculosis, various infections shameful or otherwise," heart trouble, liver trouble, kidney trouble, and overeating. But, says Zeno in *Further Confessions,*

> among our organs there is one that is the centre, a kind of sun in a solar system. Up until a few years ago this organ was thought to be the heart. At the moment everybody knows that our entire life turns on the sexual organs. Carlo turns up his nose at rejuvenation operations, but still, he doffs his cap when sexual organs are mentioned. He says: If the sexual organs could be rejuvenated, they would naturally rejuvenate the whole organism. This was nothing new to me. I would have known that without his telling me. But it will never come to pass. It's impossible.

It is the failure of this vital organ that Zeno fears even in his youth, and the pain he first feels in his competition with Guido has its psychic origins in intense castration anxiety. (pp. 109-11)

Zeno's interest in women, far from being as he thinks normal and natural, is in itself rather feeble and negative, for women to him are objects or weapons to be used in the struggle for male power, but in themselves rather intimidating, inaccessible, or inexplicable. In short, it appears that Zeno, though concerned throughout his life with denying his desires for patricide and fratricide, is in fact obsessed with male relationships. We remember that he makes up his mind to marry one of Malfenti's daughters before he has even met them; that he

proposes to all three of Malfenti's eligible daughters for the sake of marrying into that household; and that his passion for Ada is fed by the knowledge that on the one hand she most resembles her father and that on the other hand she is being courted by Guido. We remember as well that he chooses Augusta as a means of remaining close to her father; that he chooses his first mistress Carla as a means of protecting himself from Augusta, of emulating his father and father-in-law (both of whom keep mistresses), and of tricking his old friend Copler; and that when he chooses his last mistress Felicita, he tells us,

> I decided to hoodwink Mother Nature into believing I was still fit for reproduction. So I took a mistress. . . . It was as if taking a mistress was a decision equivalent to going to the chemist's.

And, he finds, it is "a complex medicine, containing a substantial proportion of poison." Such is his attitude toward women.

Furthermore, with women Zeno is far more active in thought and fantasy than in action. The first novel tells us of only one mistress during his life, and of her he thinks at the end of their affair, "The thought of another woman alarmed me considerably." In the second novel, however, he speaks as if in his youth he had been a great lover in fact as well as in fantasy, referring to "other women" and "backstreet escapades." But he talks this way only after the fact. One comes to suspect, when Zeno complains that love with him is not what it used to be, that it never was; that he feels safe in complaining of impotence only when his advancing years offer some objective reasons for the impotence he has always feared. A part of Zeno must welcome old age for the excuse it gives to impotence and renunciation as well as for the chance it gives to act at last the role of the father in the dangerous and hostile relationship between father and son. For Zeno, age is not altogether an unmixed blessing, for it does confer a kind of peace: for once Zeno is at one with the wishes of Mother Nature. At last his senility is not premature.

This investigation of the psychodynamics of Zeno has gone beyond the findings of Svevo's Dr. S., but it does not conflict with them. To see Zeno as fascinated with patricide and fratricide, ambivalent toward women, and tormented with fears of castration and impotence, is only to reaffirm some of the insights which Svevo must have had intuitively and found confirmed by his reading of Freud. It should be emphasized again, however, that the repressed fears and desires of Zeno are only a part of his personality, though surely the most basic part. He is genuinely appealing and witty, and there is an important sense in which he is innocent of his own most anti-social tendencies. The Freudian might wish that Svevo had read Freud with more trust and less wit, that he had sacrificed some of the books' charm, wit and humor for more genuine good spirits.

But the wit is undercut, as we see in a particularly rich passage in *Further Confessions* where Zeno describes his grandson's interest in the railway tracks which serve as Zeno's metaphor for life:

> . . . it was important to find out where the tracks began, for a beginning is always of great importance; and it was a great deprivation not to be able to see that other important part, the end of the tracks. I laughed, and suggested he look at the

nearest extremity of the tracks, not as the beginning, but as the end.

In psychic terms, Zeno is saying that old age is like infancy, and it seems clear that the similarity lies primarily in the matter of impotence, for he continues:

> . . . during childhood, when we begin to examine the colossal machine that has been consigned us—life, railway tracks that end where they begin—we still find no relation between it and us, and we study life with objectivity and joy, interrupted by lightning flashes of terror. Adolescence is terrible, because it is then one gets the first inkling that the machine is designed to bite *us* and among all its cogs and teeth one hardly sees where to put one's feet.

With awakening sexuality, that is, comes increased vulnerability, requiring great fear and caution. But during old age, one is again safe:

> I am now so at home with the machine that it frightens me when I think people might after all be better than I have always thought them, or life a more serious affair than it has always seemed to me. (I feel faint, the blood rushes to my head at this thought!)

We realize that, despite his great wit and charm, Zeno is afraid; and in this fear, if not in Freudian insights, there is little distance between him and his creator. Svevo approves of Zeno's fear and of the defenses his hero has constructed in order to circumvent it. We must finally conclude that for Svevo as well as for Zeno, seeing life as a comedy is a defense against seeing it as the terrible machine that bites and maims, and that the defense does not always work.

When we think of the range of heroes of modern fiction whose problems are in major ways Oedipal, we immediately see the strengths and weaknesses of the Svevo hero and point of view. Paul Morel, Proust's Marcel, Quentin Compson, and Joseph K., to name only four, all share Zeno's fear of the father and his horrifying sense of guilt and impotence. But unlike Paul and Marcel, Zeno is not capable of creating through art his own world of visionary or apocalyptic significance, nor like Joseph K. and Quentin does he perish in the attempt to resolve his Oedipal anguish. Instead, through trickery, wit, self-deception and adolescence prolonged until it becomes old age, he manages to deny and circumvent the problem well enough to survive and build a relatively tolerable life. Svevo demonstrates that the defense mechanisms described by Freud really do defend against what may be from the point of view of the conscious sufferer worse evils. For Zeno a certain kind of lie, like truth, does provide a limited measure of freedom—freedom from conscious guilt and anxiety. But the novels also show, of course, that guilt and anxiety can not be avoided in any Oedipal life, and that strong patricidal and fratricidal impulses can not be eradicated but only covered over with respectability. As we smile at the spectacle of Zeno attributing an Oedipus complex to his analyst or explaining why he cannot be held responsible for his son's hostility, we may also admire the way in which he manages to hold his world together—a world which, as he knows, is fatally threatened by the pressures of the war and of an increasingly mad European civilization. Our admiration must be tempered, however, with regret for the sacrifices that such a man must make: the sacrifice of tragic heroism, the sacrifice of manhood, and the sacrifice of truth. (pp. 112-14)

Paula Robison, "Svevo: Secrets of the Confessional," in Literature and Psychology, *Vol. XX, No. 3, 1970, pp. 101-14.*

BRIAN MOLONEY (essay date 1974)

[*In the following excerpt, Moloney surveys Svevo's early essays and examines technical aspects of his fiction.*]

Between 1880 and 1890 Svevo wrote twenty-seven articles for *L'Indipendente,* as well as the essay **"Del sentimento in arte,"** written in 1887 but not published until 1954. (p. 7)

These essays are our main source of information concerning Svevo's culture and development up to the time when he first began to publish fiction. . . . If we wish to know something of the cultural influences which shaped the budding novelist, of the dilemmas which he faced, we must have recourse to the essays.

Yet how representative are they? Svevo was not a professional reviewer, dealing with books as they came out, and one assumes that he felt free to avoid subjects he had no interest in. This explains some otherwise puzzling silences. He read such Italian magazines and periodicals as *Corriere della sera, Domenica del Fracassa, La Domenica letteraria* and *Nuova antologia,* so that he must have been aware of much that was being written in Italy. If, then, he chooses not to write about such authors as De Amicis and Fogazzaro, it must be not only that he finds them uncongenial—in fact he sometimes discusses writers he dislikes—but that they do not offer him the possibility of exploring topics which interest him.

The subjects which engage him most frequently are literary, but he ranges widely and one is struck by the variety of both subject and tone. Most of the essays have a serious air of intellectual commitment, offering balanced judgements with a maturity surprising in one so young. He is also capable of writing in polemical tone: in **"La verità"** (1884) he takes issue with Renan; in **" 'Il libro di Don Chisciotte' di E. Scarfoglio"** (1884) he challenges his contemporary on the interpretation of Zola; in **"Critica negativa"** (1888) he tilts at professional theatre critics. **"Giordano Bruno giudicato da Arturo Schopenhauer"** (1885) is militantly anti-clerical. The incisive tone of these essays and their avoidance of normative methods suggest that Svevo had in mind as his models not only De Sanctis in Italy but also, possibly, French impressionist critics such as Anatole France and Jules Lemaître. At the other end of the tone-scale are the humorous pieces. **"Il signor Nella e Napoleone"** (1887) is an affectionately ironical portrait of an old admirer of Bonaparte, and the last two essays are **"Sogni di Natale"** (1889), which is a Christmas entertainment, and **"Echi mondani"** (1890), in which Svevo, temporarily replacing the regular contributors to that column, writes in jesting fashion about one of his private preoccupations—addiction to smoking—with a light-hearted excursus on the influence of the cigarette on modern French literature.

Svevo's subjects are to some extent those which one would expect. That he should be interested in music is natural—had not Schopenhauer ranked music above the other arts?—but in his admiration for Wagner he is ahead of his time. There are references to the visual arts from the Renaissance to modern times. His interest in history, and especially in the cult of Napoleon, emerges in **"Per un critico"** (1887), in which he is able to compare Taine, Thiers and Michelet on the subject. It will already be clear that he has an interest in philosophy—

but philosophy in the widest sense, including positivist thought, Darwin and evolutionary theories, Herbert Spencer, Marx and social and political thought. And alongside these there is an interest in Schopenhauer (and possibly in Nietzsche, although this does not emerge from the essays) which demonstrates an awareness of the importance of the irrational and the subjective in the interpretation of history as well as in the arts. Six essays—**"Shylock"** (1880), **"Riduzioni drammatiche"** (1882), **"Il pubblico"** (1883), **"Una commedia in lingua impossibile"** (1884), **"Una frase sulla Mandragola"** (1887) and **"Critica negativa"** (1888)—deal with the theatre. Another eight—**"La 'Joie de vivre' di Emilio Zola"** (1884), **" 'Il libro di Don Chisciotte' di E. Scarfoglio"** (1884), **"Giorgio Ohnet"** (1885), **"Un individualista"** (1886), **"Le memorie dei fratelli Goncourt"** (1887), **"La vocazione del conte Ghislain"** (1887), **"L'immortel"** (1888), **"Mastro-don Gesualdo"** (1889)—deal with novelists and novels, while two—**"Il dilettantismo"** (1884) and **"Del sentimento in arte"** (1887)—discuss general topics embracing both drama and the novel.

The emergence of a nucleus of recurrent themes gives the impression that Svevo's aim is only in part to inform the reader; in part he is attempting to resolve, or at least to define, some of the dilemmas which confront him as an aspiring author. Thus he poses the problem of reconciling success on the commercial level with artistic integrity. **"Il pubblico"** and **"Il dilettantismo"** are both of interest in this respect. The latter is a witty defence of the amateur writer. A certain sophistry enables him to classify Goethe, Machiavelli, Michelangelo and Alberti as amateurs, and his description of dilettantism is an interesting prelude to themes to come. There is also an amusing satirical sketch of the amateur keeping up with his reading—the recent Zola novel, many essays and the latest book by Carducci. But more important than that is the admission that the amateur secretly longs for fame, which he knows can come overnight. On that score many disappointments were in store for Svevo.

At two points in this essay it is difficult not to see a direct reference to his situation at the Unionbank. The bantering tone does not conceal his seriousness as he talks of Hamlet being acted by amateurs "coadiuvati da qualcuno che sfoga degl'istinti che rimangono insoddisfatti scrivendo lettere di Banca e via di seguito" (assisted by someone who is giving expression to instincts which are not satisfied by writing letters for a bank and so on.) And later, after listing his "amateurs," he asks (rhetorically): "se tali uomini . . . provarono il bisogno di coltivare altre materie, non è scusabile se un nostro agente di commercio o di banca soddisfa in quanto può quel desiderio di ridare idee e forme estetiche che madre natura, irragionevolmente, gli mise nel sangue?" (if such men . . . felt the need to cultivate other subjects, is it not pardonable that some business or bank clerk should satisfy, as far as he can, that desire to express aesthetic ideas and forms which mother Nature unreasonably put into his blood?) Svevo, in other words, seeks in art a satisfaction he fails to find in his profession. He is also lured by the prospect of fame.

It would, however, be misleading to suggest that the quest for celebrity was Svevo's chief motive for writing, for in **"Giorgio Ohnet"** he observes that to use art merely to gratify ambition is to treat it, in Schiller's phrase, as a "butter-providing cow." The artist's concern, in Svevo's view, must be with truth. It is on the grounds that Renan merely recognized, but did not love, truth that he attacks the French historian in **"La verità."** This essay was prompted by the report that Renan

had expressed the wish that the epitaph "Veritatem dilexi" be engraved on his tombstone, on the grounds that the love of truth had been the driving-force in his activities. This Svevo denies; he has read Renan's *Averroès* (1852), and takes obvious pleasure in accusing Renan, who believed anti-religious propaganda to be a crime, of adopting an Averroistic attitude of "two truths" to his own work, thus rendering inefficacious all that he had accomplished. Contrast this attack on Renan, the idol of the positivists, with the tribute to Taine in **"Per un critico"**: "La sua dea è la verità e si può pensare ch'egli erri, non che'egli sia di mala fede" (His goddess is truth, and one might think him mistaken, but not in bad faith.)

Truth, then, is for Svevo a consideration which over-rides all others, and the question of truth in art was one on which he thought long. He avoids, as Saccone has pointed out, the simplistic formula of art as a mirror held up to life. Nor does he equate the artist with the scientist, in the naturalist manner; like De Sanctis, he carefully distinguishes between them, and in defending Zola against the charge that he had set out in his novels to "prove" Darwin's theories, replied that this was not so. "Non scienziato ma artista, Zola descrive la vita servendosi di una teoria scientifica che gliela spiega. Se questa teoria venisse scartata da altra, i nostri posteri vedrebbero, nell'opera di Zola, una rappresentazione della vita quale la sentoni i più colti dei nostri contemporanei" (An artist, not a scientist, Zola describes life making use of a scientific theory which explains it to him. If that theory were to be superseded by another, our descendants would see in Zola's work a depiction of life as it is seen by the most cultured of our contemporaries.) Svevo's argument is based on Zola's practice, not his theories—*sentono* implies a degree of subjectivity of which Zola the theorist might not have approved—and his admiration for the French novelist is not based on the cult of Naturalism. Zola, for Svevo, is a novelist whose work is rooted in the intellectual life of his time, who finds in the science of his day a conceptual framework in terms of which he can most effectively express his vision of life and thus remain faithful to his inspiration.

Svevo returns to this last point in the widely ranging **"Del sentimento in arte."** Inveighing against historical criticism and source-hunting, he points out that it is all too easy to state that Dante, Boccaccio and Shakespeare derived ideas and plots from earlier sources, but borrowings of this kind do not diminish the artist's originality. "L'originalità risiede nel temperamento. Produca francamente; sarà originale o meno; artifiziosamente non lo diverrà mai." (Originality lies in the temperament. Let (the artist) write freely; he may be original or not; he will never become so by design.) Here Svevo comes close to formulating not simply the proposition that originality is compatible with the concept of working within a tradition but that the repudiation of one's literary heritage and the desire to express oneself only in one's own terms will militate against the creation of anything that could be called art. Subjectivity alone is not enough. This is probably why, in these essays, Svevo seems to be looking for literary models, for a tradition to which he can relate his work, and it is at this point that one sees most clearly the dilemmas to which I referred earlier. For within the Italian tradition, to which he most wished to belong, he found no models he could regard as appropriate to his own case.

As a theatre-goer and an intending dramatist, he could see that the surest way to achieve popular success was to write well-made plays in the manner of Victorien Sardou (1831-1908); but he found Sardou trivial and superficial. Annetta's excitement, in *Una vita,* at the prospect of seeing the first night of *Odette* (1881) in Paris is intended to reveal the superficiality of her culture. Sardou's success raises the question of the relationship between the dramatist and his audience—which Svevo feels to be more immediate than that between the novelist and his readers—and of the influence of the latter on the former. In **"Il pubblico"** he argues that in general the public's taste is bad and that "il contatto continuo in cui vengono specialmente da noi portati autori e spettatori non può essere che fatale all'arte'," (the continual contact into which authors and spectators are continually brought, especially in our theatres, is bound to be fatal to art) since the author will tend to give the naturally conservative public what he thinks it wants. Italian dramatists, in Svevo's view, labour under another disadvantage. In **"Critica negativa"** he states that the Italian dramatic tradition is weak: with Achille Torelli (1841-1922), Paolo Ferrari (1822-89) and Giuseppe Giacosa (1847-1906), it experienced something of a revival, but such signs of life as it showed were stifled by a school of criticism which was purely destructive. "Il nostro teatro, per quanto inferiore, bisognava lasciarlo stare, vegetare come poteva. . . . Vale meglio qualche cosa, per quanto piccola, che nulla. Dal nulla nulla può svilupparsi." (Our theatre, however inferior, should have been left alone, to vegetate as best it could. . . . Something, however small, is better than nothing. Nothing can come of nothing.) The Shakespearian echo in that last sentence reveals Svevo's despondency.

In **"Riduzioni drammatiche"** Svevo considers the plans of the *veristi* to solve the problem of the short supply of good plays by adapting for the theatre successful novels. He disapproves, on the grounds that the two forms, novel and play, are so different that any adapter needs not so much to put the novel into dialogue form as totally to recast it—and few adapters, especially the novelists themselves, are capable of doing this. He thus anticipates the verdict of modern critics on what Verga and Capuana were about to do, beginning with the former's *Cavalleria rusticana* in 1884. He was no prophet, however; his judgement was based on his knowledge of what had happened in the French theatre. The stage version of *L'assommoir* in 1879 was the first of a series of plays from naturalist novels and how right Svevo was is shown by the fact that most were unsatisfactory.

Much of what has been said about Svevo and the theatre applies also to his exploration of the novel tradition. The now forgotten Georges Ohnet (1848-1918) seems to have been to the novel, in Svevo's eyes, what Sardou was to the theatre. In 1885, the year in which Ohnet published *La Grande Marnière* and *Le maître de forges* (1882) reached its two hundred and fiftieth reprint, Svevo devoted to him a long essay in *L'indipendente.* (Jules Lemaître launched his celebrated attack on Ohnet in the same year, some six weeks after Svevo.) Svevo seems to be asking two related questions. Why is Ohnet so popular? And does he write such bad novels, knowing that he has hit upon a successful formula, solely in order to gratify his ambition? Svevo attributes Ohnet's success to his ability to reassure his middle-class readers by presenting to them a picture of the world as they would like to think it is, secure and comforting, in which right, associated with bourgeois wealth and the established order of things, triumphs over wrong. "È molto tranquillizzante!" (It's very tranquillizing!) is his sardonic comment. He answers the second question in

the negative: Ohnet is so naïve as to believe in the idealized world of his own fiction.

Once again Svevo finds in a commercially successful writer a superficiality and a falsification of reality which are incompatible with his austere ideal of the high seriousness of art. And once again he is unable to find an Italian model to whom he can relate. De Amicis and Fogazzaro are not mentioned in the essays, but in the tale *Una burla riuscita* the hero reads their works to his invalid brother in order to send him to sleep; if Ohnet had been, metaphorically, a tranquillizer, they are sedatives in the literal sense. The modern reader naturally thinks of Svevo's two great Italian predecessors, Manzoni and Verga. In later years Svevo was inclined to attribute his youthful dislike of Manzoni, which he regretted, to the influence of Carducci. Verga he admired, as is shown by his review of *Mastro-don Gesualdo* in 1889, but he found the world of Verga's peasants too remote from his own. This is why he preferred *Mastro-don Gesualdo* to *I Malavoglia*: "Ci troviamo in un contorno di nobili e popolani molto vicini alla borghesia; è un ambiente che ci è più vicino, più facile di quello del basso popolo di una provincia lontana." (We find ourselves in aristocratic and working-class settings very near the middle class: it is a background which is near to us, more accessible than that of the proletariat of a distant province.) Svevo's decision to set *L'assassinio di Via Belpoggio* among the "basso popolo" of Trieste may be a gesture in Verga's direction.

Svevo discusses the mature Verga in terms of Flaubert, Zola and impersonality. Nothing could be more natural than that Svevo should make his own one of the basic tenets of the novelists he most admired. Yet he also insisted, as we have seen, that originality lay in the artist's temperament, and went on: "L'originalità non può quindi essere altro che la franca espansione di un carattere non affettato, non tolto a prestito. Si tratta di sincerità prima di tutto." (Originality cannot be anything other than the frank expression of an unaffected character, not a borrowed one. It is primarily a question of honesty.) Zola's attempts to construct an aesthetic based on the notion of impersonality have justly been described by F. J. W. Hemmings as infantile. If his dictum that "Une oeuvre d'art est un coin de la nature vue à travers un tempérament" (A work of art is a corner of nature seen through a temperament) had left the door ajar for subjectivity to enter, Svevo kicked it open. But there is a difference in the attitudes of the two writers. Zola, in his theoretical writings, could not reconcile the concepts of impersonality and subjectivity, and tended to neglect the latter, which in his practice was more important than he realized; Svevo, on the other hand, stresses both notions, and that he does not see them as incompatible is the result not of his naïveté but of his culture and his temperament, both of which led him to express himself in terms of irony. The novelists whom he most admired and imitated were Stendhal and Flaubert, both distinguished for their irony. His *Diario per la fidanzata* shows how quickly he perceived that irony was a source of strength: "In quanto è spirito o forza, la mia parola non è altro che ironia." (In so far as it is wit or strength, what I have to say is nothing but irony.)

Svevo never attempted to work out the theoretical basis of an irony which could, if not reconcile opposites, at least set up between them a fruitful tension. He was impatient with theory, and in 1890 he ceased to write essays for *L'indipendente.*

His preliminary explorations were over and he was by now committed to drama and narrative fiction. (pp. 8-15)

• • • • •

Italy is a country in which literary traditions have been remarkably strong and in which successive generations of writers have had to come to terms with the "questione della lingua"—the problem, that is, of what constitutes "correct" literary usage. Italian as we know it in the masterpieces of Italian literature is in the main a written, literary, not a spoken, language, based on the usage of Tuscan authors, and purism, sternly hostile both to foreign loan-words and to dialectal elements from other parts of Italy, is a recurrent feature of literary debates from the Renaissance to the early decades of this century. . . .

It was inevitable in these circumstances that Svevo should have been judged by his earliest Italian readers—and sometimes is still judged—according to linguistic criteria which to many modern Italian readers, and even more to non-Italians, appear unduly formalistic and even pedantic. C. Dionisotti has commented "that *I Malavoglia* or *La coscienza di Zeno* needed rinsing in the Arno is an idea that occurred to no-one," but even in 1926 and 1927, when long overdue recognition was finally accorded to him, it was being suggested that Svevo wrote in "jargon," and that if he had followed Manzoni's example and polished his style there might have been some hope for him as a writer but now there was none. His success abroad has several times been "explained away" by the statement that his style is such that it improves in translation. (p. 108)

Svevo was deeply sensitive to these criticisms of his style, some of which were voiced in the first reviews of *Una vita* and continued to be heard throughout his life, and he was greatly hurt by them. He was continually concerned about the issue of linguistic correctness, especially after he had become famous, when he felt under an obligation to give of his best every time he sat down to write. An English reader's natural reaction, with the benefit of hindsight, is to sympathize with Svevo and to feel impatience with his detractors: one would not after all dismiss Thomas Hardy out of hand because he makes mistakes in grammar and his diction is at times somewhat strained. Yet this is, in effect, one of the grounds on which Svevo has been rejected by many Italian critics, and not unnaturally. Writers from other parts of Italy had learned a literary form of Italian more successfully than he, and even his admirers have admitted that his style is defective, although they have been prepared to go on to argue that the blemishes were solely on the surface and were in any case redeemed by his good qualities. One must ask what there was in Svevo's style that so offended ears accustomed to more correct and more carefully cadenced prose, and why it was he never succeeded in eradicating his faults, if faults there are.

There are, in the first place, dialectal elements in his vocabulary, idiom and syntax. It has been suggested that Svevo would have written more correctly in German, but one has doubts about the truth of this statement. German, after all, was a language learned for the purposes of his education; his native language was Triestine, and it would have been natural for him to think, and for his characters to express themselves, in Triestine. But he could not write in dialect, partly because this would almost automatically have cut him off from the majority of his potential reading public, and partly because the choice of Italian, the national language, had political,

anti-Austrian, overtones. . . . Svevo therefore transposes what he has to say into standard Italian. Inevitably traces of dialect remain in his lexicon. (pp. 109-10)

The attempt to use in his prose "parole ch'egli non sentiva" may account for what Maier has described as "hyper-correct forms"—"salutifero" for "salutare" (wholesome), "ove" for "dove" (where), "dessa" for "essa" (she), words with an excessively literary and archaic flavour which replace the more usual forms which are common to dialect and spoken Italian. Cernecca puts into this category the use of a plural in *ii* for nouns and adjectives ending in *io,* and the incorrect use of the subjunctive for the indicative ("Ho già capito di che si tratti"). Dialectal elements in the lexicon are no longer as offensive to Italian readers as they were in the early decades of this century, when critics tended to attach greater importance than they do now to the notion of linguistic purity. But inelegance and grammatical mistakes of the kind just mentioned, which disappear in translation, are still offensive, especially to those readers who expect prose narrative to be polished and carefully cadenced. One is bound to ask whether the clumsiness and grammatical incorrectness of Svevo's style are the result of a lack of sensitivity or skill on his part or whether they are in some way related to his aims and techniques.

Attempts are often made to illustrate Svevo's attitude to language and dialect by referring to a number of incidents in his novels. The first of these occurs in *Una vita,* in which Nitti is described as being "afraid" of the work done by Miceni, whom he has to assist. Miceni is in charge of the Italian correspondence and the implication is that there is some linguistic weakness on Nitti's part, as there was on Svevo's. The other two incidents occur in *La coscienza di Zeno.* The first deals with Zeno's first encounter with Guido Speier; Zeno enviously notices that he speaks fluent Tuscan, while he and Ada are condemned to their "wretched dialect." The other occurs in the final section of the novel, when Zeno claims that no Triestine can ever write the truth in Tuscan and that his life would seem very different had it been described in dialect. These episodes may seem to confirm Cernecca's thesis that Svevo distrusted his dialect: but on the other hand one must remember that these episodes are intended primarily to tell us something about the characters in the novels, not about their author. Nitti has only a limited literary talent and little practical ability. Zeno envies Guido's poise, of which his ability to speak Tuscan is an element, but this poise turns out to be ill founded. The second reference to dialect in that novel is . . . merely an excuse on Zeno's part and occurs in a passage distinguished by its comically bad logic. Why not quote, instead, that passage from **"La novella del buon vecchio"**, in which the narrator, describing the old man's attempts to write his thesis on the relations between the generations, states that many of his notes have to be thrown away because in them he had allowed himself to be distracted by the "sound of the words"—"si era lasciato deviare dal suono delle parole"? (he had let himself be led astray in them by the sound of the words). The comment suggests that fine style can divert the attention from the sense, and we might more profitably approach the question of style from another direction. The corrections made to the second edition of *Senilità* are relevant to our discussion at this point.

The corrections are on the whole useful rather than outstandingly successful—apart from the excision of many superfluous exclamation marks and of an unnecessary passage on

Brentani's dream-life. Some changes in vocabulary are acceptable because they conform to more normal usage—"stupro" for "violo" (rape), for example. Other changes eliminate useless archaisms—"oriuolo" becomes "orologio," for example. On the other hand other changes introduce more "literary" and so less effective elements, as when Brentani is made to tell Balli that he had "posseduto quella donna." In 1898 he had simply "had" her. The corrections in fact are curiously inconsistent. Wrong tenses remain, and subjunctives are changed to indicatives, indicatives to subjunctives, without apparent reason, *essere* and *avere* replace each other as auxiliary verbs according to no discernible pattern. Devoto concluded that the corrections were made in "bad faith," without conviction. They were done at the request of the publisher, who wanted to present a more "correct" text to his customers. It was, however, Cernecca who made the most startling discovery when he examined Svevo's copy of *Senilità*, on which the corrections had been made. They were in three different hands, and most of them were not the work of Svevo at all. He had been assisted by two friends. They presumably worked with him, or consulted him, but they did most of the work. Svevo, in other words, regarded changes of this kind as concessions to pedants and purists, and he effectively indicated his attitude when in the 1927 preface he stated that the novel was being republished with a few merely formal revisions.

This surprisingly dismissive comment, together with the reference to the danger of being seduced by the sound of the words, suggests that although Svevo was uncertain about some formal, grammatical aspects of the Italian language, he was not so much insensitive to the aesthetic qualities of prose as suspicious of them, regarding them as a distraction. Benco tells the story of how Svevo, as a reply to his critics, once wrote a page of good fourteenth-century prose to show how easily it could be done. The point is made obliquely in *Senilità*, in which there are several finely cadenced passages at key points in the narrative, usually followed by brusque deflationary statements intended to recall the reader to reality. This kind of technique can be used only by an author who is aware of the poetic possibilities of language but is willing to use them only for the purposes of irony because he suspects that his readers are liable to pay so much attention to the way in which he writes that they will fail to notice what he has to say. To this extent his style is, as Montale and others have remarked, "anti-literary": he disliked "la parola dolce ch'è tanto facile di vergare e che non dice niente" (the harmonious phrase which is so easy to write but says nothing). In the recurrent debate between the "contenutisti" and the "formalisti," between those who feel that content, and those who feel that form, is the prime consideration in a work of art, Svevo sides with the former, and his attitude anticipates that of M. Riffaterre, who in his *Essais de stylistique structurale* (1971) points out that a study of grammar and syntax tells one only about the author's grammar and syntax, not about his style. Since discussions of Svevo's style have so far concentrated on precisely these formal elements of language, much remains to be done before we can assess his style in the wider sense. I should, however, like to draw attention to three aspects of style: firstly, the description and presentation of characters; secondly, techniques of "distancing"; and thirdly, the range and sources of Svevo's imagery. (pp. 111-14)

[The] devices which Svevo uses in *Una vita* to present his excessively large gallery of minor characters are limited and liable to become monotonous. The narrative stops for a moment while we are given a brief account of the character in question in terms of one or two predictable physical characteristics—height, dress and, almost invariably, hair—and sometimes one or two psychological traits. The adjectives used are invariably generic. Lucia is "magra, anemica . . . bionda di un biondo tendente al rosso." (Lucia was thin and anaemic . . . with fair reddish colouring.) Sanneo is "sulla trentina, alto e magro, i capelli di una biondezza sbiadita" (about thirty, tall and thin, with light, faded hair). The result is a series of identikit portraits which do not enable us to recognize anyone. The descriptions are uneconomical, using many words to little effect. We do not *need* all those details which seem to me to be merely the remains of a mimetic tradition which has outlived its usefulness. In *Senilità* the question of characterization is handled more confidently. There are fewer minor characters than in *Una vita,* and Svevo makes no attempt to tell us about their clothes and hair. Such details as we are given are all significant and acquire an almost emblematic value. Bardi is a spendthrift, Leardi a snob, Sorniani jaundiced and a malicious gossip: what more do we need to know?

One has the impression that the major characters are described in more detail, but as far as their physical attributes are concerned this is not really the case. Can one say what Brentani looks like in any detail? The accounts we are given of him concentrate on psychological analysis. Balli is presented as tall, bronzed and greying, with blue eyes and precisely pointed beard. The details confirm the hardness of his character. Angiolina and Amalia are described in a little more detail, mainly because we are able to see them through the eyes of both men. The former is "una bionda dagli occhi azzurri grandi, alta e forte, ma snella e flessuosa" (a tall, healthy blonde, with big blue eyes and a supple, graceful body), as all can see, but when we see the effects of the light on her eyes, we are as much witnesses to Brentani's discovery that "quell'occhio *crepitava!*" (The light in her eye literally seemed to *crackle!*) as we are to the phenomenon itself. This technique is carried to its extreme conclusion in *La coscienza di Zeno,* in which descriptions of characters are always offered by another character, Zeno, and consequently are given in his words and tell us as much, if not more, about him than they do about those he describes. His account of Augusta, for example, is initially dismissive. He sees only her squint and so rules her out as a prospective bride; but later the squint becomes, as it were, less pronounced and his adjectives become less hostile, more affectionate, as he comes to appreciate her maternal qualities. His initial accounts of Carla, on the other hand, are significantly evasive: his adjectives this time are chosen so as to conceal those qualities which make him desire her. Hostility is the keynote of his account of Guido: hence details which in another man would have been completely innocuous—his ivory-handled walking-stick, his surprise when the table-turning episode apparently ceases to be a parlour game—all become in Zeno's emotionally coloured account opportunities to denigrate the dead man. This anticipates to some extent the question of the stylistic devices Svevo used to "distance" himself from his characters, and at this point we must move to a discussion of some of Svevo's ironic strategies.

The narrator can make it clear that he does not wish to endorse his character's thoughts and attitudes by offering his own reflections on the narrative situation in generalized form in the present tense and by inserting such phrases as "he thought," "he felt" or "it seemed to him" into the account he is giving of what was going on in his protagonist's mind. At times the statements thus made are immediately modified by the narrator: in the statement "Alfonso credeva di avere dello spirito e ne aveva di fatto nei soliloqui" (Alfonso considered himself to have poise. In his soliloquies he certainly had), the contrast between Nitti's interior monologues and his inept behaviour in society is made clear. At other times it is Nitti's actual behaviour, rather than any authorial comment, that modifies the statement, as when he goes for the first time to Maller's house: " 'Venivo a disturbarla . . .' e s'interruppe credendo di avere già espresso tutto il suo pensiero." ("I was on my way to disturb you . . ." and he interrupted himself, thinking he had already expressed all he wanted to say.) In reality he has said nothing, but this time the narrator prefers to show, rather than tell us.

The limitation of telling, as opposed to showing, is, from Svevo's point of view, that it draws attention to the presence of the narrator, and, from that of the reader, it is that the method is liable to become too mechanical. One finds Svevo using it with greater restraint in *Senilità*. It is, nevertheless, present at important moments, as when Brentani's "experience" is first described as "ciò ch'egli credeva di poter chiamare così" (what he was pleased to call so), only to be redefined more accurately by the narrator. The account of Balli's aesthetic which follows is similarly, but discreetly, distanced. One notices that the account of the storm scene is punctuated by the observation that "Ad Emilio parve che quel tramestío si confacesse al suo dolore." (Emilio felt the confusion of the elements was attuned to his grief.) There is surely a world of difference, a far as the narrator's attitude is concerned, between that statement and the one which Svevo was careful not to make: "Quel tramestío si confaceva al suo dolore." (The confusion of the elements was attuned to his grief.)

There is one form of irony, however, which seems out of place in *Una vita* and is not to be found at all in *Senilità*. There are only perhaps a dozen examples of it in the whole novel: one or two will suffice here. Annetta is described by the narrator as "trovando detti spiritosi o giudizî acuti che non avevano che il difetto di non trovarsi in buona armonia fra di loro" ([finding] sharp or funny comments whose only defect was that they did not always suit the subject.) Nitti's philosophical treatise is described as foundering at the section in which "non si trattava di annientare delle leggi ma di fabbricarne, cosa noiosissima" (which did not deal with destroying, but creating laws, a very different and boring matter). On these and similar occasions the narrator is indulging in a formal verbal irony which could well derive from Anatole France and at times betrays a certain intellectual arrogance which is not evident in his subsequent works. Although this method can give a measure of aesthetic satisfaction, more interesting, and more subtle effects are achieved by Svevo's use of indirect free style and of contrasts between illusion and reality to ironize his characters.

In indirect free style the narrator presents his protagonist's thoughts and reactions without comment. He presents them in indirect speech, with verbs mainly in the imperfect or conditional, and usually in the words which his characters would have used in direct speech, and in the order in which they would have been spoken. In its simplest form indirect free style is rather like a series of statements on the pattern of "He thought that . . ." "He felt that . . ." with the introductory phrases omitted. This is a form of narration which Svevo finds congenial and he handles it with great skill. It is used, for example, in Nitti's first encounter with Annetta. Nitti is snubbed by her. "Perché? Ella non lo aveva mai veduto prima

di allora. Doveva essere semplicemente il disprezzo per l'inferiore, per la persona vestita male, perché ora egli sapeva quanto male egli fosse vestito." (Why? She had never seen him before. It must all be contempt for an inferior, someone badly dressed; now he knew how badly dressed he was.) The question is Nitti's, as is the answer to it: the next sentence explains why Nitti arrived at that explanation. The narrator knows, as we learn later, that it is wrong: the truth is that one of Maller's employees had once paid court to Annetta and she had had to put up with a good deal of teasing from her father on the subject. She now treats his employees in this way in order to prevent a repetition of the incident. There is thus, even in *Una vita,* a series of shifts in the point of view from which the action is viewed, and Svevo's first novel is technically more complex than many critics have supposed. At times Nitti and Annetta are seen from the outside, by the narrator, who comments trenchantly on their behaviour, while sometimes Nitti is presented to us, without comment, on his own terms. The concluding paragraphs of chapter 20, in which we follow the mental processes which lead to Nitti's decision to commit suicide, are related almost entirely from his point of view; the implied reference to Schopenhauer exposes the fallacy in his argument. A clear hint that the narrator is presenting Nitti's point of view is given a few paragraphs earlier, when the reflections which follow his last conversation with Maller, presented in a form syntactically identical to the final paragraphs of the chapter, are described as a long soliloquy.

These shifts in point of view naturally occur more frequently in *Senilità,* which is in every way a more subtle and complex work. Phrases such as "credeva," "sentiva," by means of which the narrator explicitly dissociates himself from his protagonist occur less frequently than in *Una vita*—a fact which has given rise to the suggestion that Svevo adopts a more indulgent attitude towards Brentani. Of Nitti, for example, he says: "Egli s'era accorto della differenza che correva fra il suo modo di sentire e quello di coloro che lo contornavano e credeva consistesse nel prender lui con troppa serietà le cose della vita. Quella era la sua sventura!". (He had noticed a difference between his way of feeling and that of the people around, and he thought this consisted in the fact that he took life too seriously. That was his misfortune.) In *Senilità* a similar reflection is presented differently. "Come erano stati colpevoli lui e Amalia di prendere la vita tanto sul serio!" (How wrong he and Amalia had been to take life so seriously!) In the first example it is the *credeva* that puts the reader on his guard: in the second, which is in indirect free style, Svevo relies on the reader's moral sense to warn him that it is monstrous that Brentani should compare his posturing to his sister's distress. Brentani has never taken life seriously enough.

There are in effect four points of view in *Senilità*—that of the narrator, who is often content to define, rather than to condemn explicitly, and that of three of the main characters, as we have already seen. Naturally the narrator's views tend to be made explicit more frequently in the early chapters, in which he is presenting his characters to the reader and setting up his "experiment": when Svevo describes Brentani waiting impatiently for success "come se l'età delle belle energie per lui non fosse tramontata" (as if he had not already passed the age when his vitality was at the full), he reveals the vanity of Brentani's hopes. More frequently, however, he relies on a shift in point of view to cause doubts to rise in the reader's mind, especially as far as Angiolina and Balli are concerned. The former is not Brentani's *Ange,* but neither, we suspect, is she Balli's *Giolona:* the sculptor's characterization is too simplistic to be acceptable. Balli himself we see through the admiring eyes of the other three characters, but inevitably we are compelled to ask ourselves whether their admiration, in view of his failure as an artist and his insensitivity as a human being, is not really the expression of some weakness in their characters, the result of something which they lack, rather than a just tribute to his excellence. Thus the narrator is able to avoid altogether the formal verbal irony which at times gave *Una vita* so arrogant a tone and, more importantly, he avoids seeming to impose his judgement of his characters on the reader. They stand condemned by virtue of what they are and do, or fail to be and do, not by virtue of a moral code imposed on them from above. Few novelists have used the shifting point of view so consistently, or to such good effect.

In both *Una vita* and *Senilità* much use is made of what is usually termed the Irony of Events, which is, technically, one of the most interesting features of *Una vita.* Thus Nitti abandons Annetta's *salon,* making an iron resolution to devote himself to work, only to return to her without waiting to be asked. Later, when he has made little progress with her, he resolves to treat her coldly, but is totally incapable of doing so. He dreams of becoming indispensable at the bank—only for the death of Jassy, who had thought himself indispensable, to leave the bank totally unaffected in a way which anticipates the indifference to Nitti's death implied in the final letter. He thinks he has achieved detachment, only to find himself squeezing the last drop of gratification from his generosity to Lucia. A pattern of behaviour is thus established and we are conditioned to expect his final gesture to be a failure.

This discrepancy between declared intentions and actual conduct is a major source of irony in *Senilità.* Brentani's resolutions to treat his love affair as a source of facile pleasure, his resolve to dedicate himself to his sister, his determination to part from Angiolina with calm and dignity—all are condemned in advance to end in failure. In a sense, therefore, there is in both novels a progressive slackening of the dramatic tension: then how is it that both novels retain an element of tension? The reason seems to be that there is always one character, the protagonist, who fails to discern the emergent pattern. His failure to analyse himself is such that each new turn of the screw is the source in him of painful surprise; each new discovery of weakness is to him revelation which confirms in the reader's mind the condemnation prompted by Svevo's use of a changing point of view.

The first two novels, written within a few years of each other, naturally have much in common in spite of the greater maturity of the second. *La coscienza di Zeno,* on the other hand, was written much later. Since the unreliable Zeno tells his own story it uses a narrative technique which at first seems radically different from that of the first two novels. Svevo now relies entirely on showing, rather than telling, and indirect free style is abandoned in favour of a "direct" free style which enables Zeno to relate the events of his life from the point of view of 1914 and 1915-16. The differences, however, are less notable than they seem and the novelty of the psychoanalytic situation conceals techniques which are tried and tested. We have no difficulty in seeing that Zeno's capacity for ironizing at his own expense resembles that of Nitti and Brentani, or that the Irony of Events, whereby Zeno marries the wrong girl, who turns out to be the right one after all, and wins his way to wealth and success, is but the comic version of the

Irony of Events which Svevo had used previously to achieve such sombre effects. And by making Zeno tell his own story Svevo makes use of what is usually termed the Irony of Self-revelation in a form so consistent and extended that many have failed to recognize it. Yet surprise is as constant a feature of *La coscienza di Zeno* as it is of the other novels. "Sorpresa" and "meraviglia" are recurrent features of Svevo's vocabulary, and Zeno's discovery that life is original is not a measure of his philosophical understanding in existentialist vein, but of his failure to understand himself.

Certain features of Svevo's imagery are almost as constant in his work as are his ironic strategies. Their sources are fields as diverse as those of music, the visual arts, business and commerce, social philosophy, Darwinism and the animal world. All these were areas in which he was keenly interested throughout his life and in which he never ceased to pursue new ideas and experiences. The presence in his novels of imagery derived from all these sources is an indication of the way in which he tried constantly to synthesize these apparently disparate interests into a coherent whole and relate them to his art. Svevo's imagery is neither decorative nor ostentatious, but always functional, always reinforcing the message of the novels.

Metaphors derived from the concept of the "struggle for life" as developed by Spencer constitute one of the most regularly recurring forms of imagery in Svevo's novels. We have already seen that Nitti's Trieste is a battlefield and that the language of social Darwinism recurs at key moments in *La coscienza di Zeno;* one could in fact find fault with *Una vita* on the grounds that such imagery occurs too frequently, thus creating the impression that Svevo's imagery is more limited than in fact it is. Images of battle occur rather less frequently in *Senilità* than in *Una vita,* and they are used in the second novel with much more skill, as in the first part of chapter v, in which the rivalry of Balli and Brentani for the attention of Amalia is described consistently in terms of struggle in a metaphor which is sustained for five pages.

The impression of stylistic poverty created by the excessive use in *Una vita* of one form of imagery is misleading since Svevo also makes interesting and effective use of imagery derived from the visual arts. This form of imagery is commonly associated with *Senilità,* in which one of the characters is a sculptor and in which the two main female characters are described in terms of colour, and skilful evocations of landscape are used ironically. It is usual to attribute this aspect of *Senilità* to the influence of Veruda, who no doubt did much to deepen Svevo's understanding of the arts—a debt which the novelist acknowledged in his later fiction. But other novelists in whom Svevo was interested—Stendhal, Zola, the Goncourt brothers—were also interested in painting, and the friendship with Veruda began because Svevo already had an interest in the arts. Nitti knows little about the arts, but the narrator of *Una vita* has a fine eye for painterly effects. The bare corridor of the bank, in which Nitti spends so many bleak hours, is compared to a study in perspective; a landscape under a cloudless sky is made to reflect Nitti's state of mind by being compared to an oleograph in which the painter's shades of colour have been made uniform by mechanical reproduction. Nor should one forget the rich colours of the Maller home, contrasting with those of the bank. Santo emerges from a kitchen in which copper vessels gleam in the light as in a Dutch genre painting: one feels at that point that Nitti would be more at home in the servants' quarters. And it is in the Maller house that Nitti sees an important painting—a rocky Carso landscape which has a dual rôle in that it both points to the present bleakness of his life and hints at the falsity of his Arcadian ideal.

Images deriving from music are to be found less frequently than those based on the visual arts, but music nevertheless plays an important part in Svevo's fiction. It is music that reveals to Nitti his need to hear a friendly voice, while Brentani's moments of harmony with Angiolina can be described as music interrupted by the inevitable discords of her tactlessness. A lesser Venetian canal can be seen in relation to the Grand Canal in *Corto viaggio sentimentale* as a "rio dove le forme grandiose del canale si riducevano e variavano in motivi capricciosi ch'erano la continuazione, anzi, la integrazione della forte armonia che non ancora aveva liberato i loro sensi" (*rio,* where the stupendous forms of the canal were reduced in scale and ran to capricious variations—the continuation, and integration, of the grand melody still resounding in their ears). But it is in *La coscienza di Zeno* that music comes into its own as an element of plot and structure. Carla sings in two styles: her first attempts at opera conceal her true talent, which is for a more intimate and subdued style. Guido and Zeno both play the violin in a way which is a comment on their character. Guido is unable to be true to the music he plays and vulgarizes it; Zeno lacks poise and harmony but has more real feeling than his rival. And Zeno regularly describes relationships in musical terms of discord and harmony. In all these cases the meaning of an incident or episode is reinforced by an image without any explicit intervention or comment on the part of the author.

One is not surprised to find Svevo using in his imagery the language of the commerce on which Trieste's wealth was founded and in which so many of his characters are engaged. Liquidation is a startling metaphor for death, but in general Svevo uses business imagery for two purposes. It can illustrate the ways in which relationships have been devalued by the "cash ethic." Brentani cynically describes "respectable women" as those who have found a purchaser prepared to pay the right price—which is presumably marriage, viewed as a business contract, whereas he merely gives Angiolina money without realizing the implications of what he is doing. And the "buon vecchio" sees the pretty girl merely as an object to be bought if she is for sale. Perhaps she has no name because she is treated as an object and not a person. The second use of this kind of imagery is for comic effect, as when someone acknowledges receipt of a slap or a pinch, or when Zeno describes his daughter as "una piccola balla di merci che aveva bisogno dello speditore per muoversi" (a little bale of merchandise that could not move without a shipping agent) since she has to be accompanied when she goes out. Irony of this kind is two-edged, however; it may show the character described in a comic light, but it also makes one wonder what values are held by the narrator. Zeno's choice of language on these occasions is very revealing.

It is equally natural that Svevo, who had read a good deal of Darwin and was an inveterate zoo-visitor, should make extensive use of animal imagery. There is little about his use of such imagery in *Una vita,* however, that is unusual, except in the way in which Macario uses the seagulls to explain his view of society to Nitti and offers a biological explanation of the latter's failure to adapt. Nor is the imagery of *Senilità* any more remarkable in this respect. The consistently ironic use of animal imagery is a late development and is to be found

first in tales such as **"Orazio Cima," "Il malocchio"** and **"La buonissima madre."** There is no naïve extrapolation on Svevo's part from animal to human behaviour; animal images are simply part of the ironist's equipment, a Darwinian variation on the older techniques whereby people are made comic by being described as things or machines. Zeno naturally makes frequent use of comparisons which have this intention. His description of Augusta's youngest sister as a little viper is conventional abuse, but his account of himself, disappointed in his desire for Felicita, is richly comic: "Io in quel momento ero avviato all'amore e proprio alla mia età si somiglia molto al coccodrillo in terra ferma di cui si dice che abbisogni di tanto tempo per mutare di direzione . . . ." (At the moment I was bent on love, and at my age, one is rather like a crocodile on dry land—it takes a long time to change direction.) At other times, as when he compares Augusta to a swallow or an ant, there are, in view of the philosophy on which the novel is based, overtones of which it is hard to believe that Zeno is aware, in spite of the final paragraphs of *La coscienza di Zeno.* (pp. 114-23)

It must be admitted that Svevo's style is inelegant and has shortcomings on the formal level. On the other hand it must also be recognized that on the intellectual level it is more subtle and richer in imagery than has generally been supposed. Sustained irony demands precision and intellectual clarity rather than lyrical effusion. These are qualities which Svevo has in good measure. The reader is, moreover, often surprised by the overtones of his imagery, which are liable to escape those who are not aware of the extent of his culture. His youthful ideal was that an author's works should enable one to see how a cultured contemporary saw life. It was clearly one which he endeavoured consistently to live up to. Thus his language and style are functional, not decorative: their appeal is intellectual, not musical or sensual. They are the tools of an ironist. (pp. 123-24)

> *Brian Moloney, in his* Italo Svevo: A Critical Introduction, *Edinburgh University Press, 1974, 140 p.*

CHARLES C. RUSSELL (essay date 1978)

[In the following excerpt, Russell studies Svevo's plays for the perspective they provide on his fiction.]

On the whole [Svevo's] plays are neither very good nor very interesting. Yet they do throw some light on Svevo himself, on his background, on his aspirations and by reflection on his other work. Unfortunately, it is difficult to discuss them in chronological order since their dating is still not entirely certain. Leaving aside those plays known to have been written in the last few years or so of his life, it is possible to draw some interesting conclusions from the others, conclusions which are valid in illuminating the early years of Svevo's career, regardless of the actual date of their composition, since both his very first plays and the following ones have many similar basic characteristics.

His plays can be roughly divided into two types. About half of them appear to have been written for fun: *La verità, Prima del Ballo, The Return of Olga from America* (my title, the manuscript bears none), *Atto unico, Una commedia inedita* and *Terzetto spezzato.* In these, Svevo presents a single amusing idea or situation, often highly imaginary, unrealistic and even fantastic, and then resolves it in a relatively brief period of time. The dialogue is quick and witty, *brillante;* the characters represent types—the lover, the bored housewife, the businessman—rather than individuals. Since these comedies have no purpose other than entertainment, they stand or fall on the strength of their humor. They may have been pastimes for Svevo, often something he worked on while travelling. From France he wrote his wife that he was thinking about a comedy which would be "allegra, allegra," and he added that while writing it he laughed like mad. These are the plays which in their humor reflect the spirit of Zeno, and of the whole lot make the most enjoyable reading, far more so than the other half.

This other group of plays, in spite of some occasionally amusing dialogue, is dreadfully serious. Into this half fall *Le ire di Giuliano, Le teorie del conte Alberto, Il ladro in casa, Un marito* and *L'avventura di Maria.* Here there are real problems to be solved. Will Giuliano's fits of rage destroy his marriage *(Le ire di Giuliano)?* Will Federico ever free himself from the oppressive memory of his first wife whom he killed in a fit of blind passion upon discovering her betrayal *(Un marito)*? The fruits of this seriousness are longer plays, more complex situations, an attempt at subtler characters and at more probing psychology and a greater adhesion to reality. The characters talk and talk and talk, both about themselves and about others; and when they are not talking, they are listening and listening and listening, about themselves and others. Yet for all their talk, they never quite explain themselves fully. We never quite know, nor after a bit do we much care, why Giuliano flies into rages; we never quite know whether Federico feels remorse or not, and by the time this long, long comedy is over, we are not very much interested. The trouble with all these serious plays is precisely this: they are too self-consciously serious. Underneath the probing psychology, the complex situations, the ingenious explanations and the relentless search for truth the reader senses an irritating and unsolicited voice which seems to be saying: "I'm a serious playwright. Pay attention. I'm writing a serious play." This voice, of course, destroys the autonomy that a work of art should have. Just as happens with Svevo's articles, it is difficult to tell what the center of attention is: is it the work itself or its author? Undoubtedly it was these plays, or at least the early ones, which Svevo expected would bring him success and fame. It was certainly this type of play he had in mind when he formulated various rules on the art of the drama. In 1880. "For us (at least in the theater) good must triumph and evil succumb." In 1881: "The scope and interest of a play must be in its characters and not in its action. Everything must be true." Sometime after 1890 to Silvio Benco: "The theater: the form of forms. The only form in which life can be directly and precisely transmitted." The rules are dogmatic and pompously stated and what is pompous is often dull. So are the plays.

The raw material of all of Svevo's plays is essentially the same. He always wrote domestic comedies. He wants to tell about what goes on in a Triestine household, about the little perturbations and the little preoccupations, the minor moments of crisis in a vast, calm sea of comfortable living. He knows that everyone likes to look at himself on the stage as long as the picture is not too harsh. And Svevo's plays can hardly be considered social criticism. How could he hope to be successful and at the same time seriously critical? As the curtain opens the spectator generally sees a middle-class table and overstuffed chair in a nice middle-class room in a comfortable home in middle-class Trieste. From time to time a maid announces someone or other. Trieste is presented for

what it is, or was, or was thought to be: very closed, very narrow, very straightlaced, very much without any tradition or culture to speak of and very, very provincial. The people who enter on stage fit quite naturally into the scene: bourgeois Triestines, husbands and wives, their children, assorted friends and relatives (how many relatives!) as well as an assortment of lovers—and even they are *borghesi.* For the most part it's a rather dismal collection of people. How one wishes that the refreshingly vulgar and low-class Angiolina would shake them up a little, that the sculptor Balli would come rollicking onto the stage, that the bustle and din of Città Vecchia could be heard through the shuttered windows or that the light of the blue-green Adriatic illuminated these lives.

It doesn't. What does is business. Business meant money and Triestines loved money. In *La coscienza di Zeno* Svevo writes: "When we are not angry at each other, we all love each other very much, but our strongest desires are only aroused by our business affairs." His plays do not deny his heritage. Most of his characters are worried about money, as he was, too, for much of his early life. Money is a serious business. You may be glad to see the ghost of your dead wife appear during a séance, but you would be doubly glad if she told you whether the price of coffee on which you have a corner is going up or down *(Terzetto spezzato).* If you have killed your first wife—like the poor Federico mentioned earlier—and you don't know whether you still hate or love her, what better way to forget your troubles than by earning lots and lots of money? Money does not always mean happiness. Bad business practices cause Anna's supposed father to commit suicide *(Le ire di Giuliano)*, while Ignazio *(Il ladro in casa)*, having participated in a series of swindles, falls to his death when pursued by the *carabinieri.*

These people die for money. They do not die for love, their second, though less important preoccupation. Love in Trieste is neither a divine passion or exhaltation nor, at the other end of the scale, is it sex or lust. It lies precisely in the middle: middle-class. Between husband and wife it is a question of contracts and doweries and enough money for new dresses and for meals served punctually. With the non-marrieds it is equally spiritless: handkissing, genteel compliments, elegant, witty, sophisticated turns of phrase and letters tied with ribbons. Everything is carried on *sottovoce.* What would the maid say? Such things are best kept in the middle-class family. There is no sexuality, no vitality, no enthusiasm. Even elopements fizzle out. Once again the spectator yearns for Angiolina's flashing eyes. Love is an affair, with all the dullness attributable to that word, just like business. From this point of view none of the plays is more depressing than *L'avventura di Maria.* Alberto would like to flee from his wife and children with Maria, a violinist and a "nonconformist" of the early twentieth century. Yet he hesitates. It is just too painful to give up all the creature comforts of home. His wife is sorry he wants to leave, but she is more sorry about the possible scandal. Yet if he must go, she promises him not to be hysterical. That way, at least, she can keep things covered up.

Why do these plays fail? One reason is that in no way do they correspond to any inner urgency of Svevo's either as a man or as an artist. They remain strictly on the margins of his experience. They are technical exercises in writing, like the warm-up scales on his violin, not the full expression of his mind. They also fail because they neither explain nor investigate, praise nor blame. They only illustrate. They do not take a stance. Such an approach was not congenial to Svevo's nature. The serious plays in particular are almost completely acted out within the social values of the city. When Svevo was at his best, he wrote only for himself and about himself, regardless of what anyone might think, and that is why the finest things in his novels are usually autobiographical, either in fact or in idea. I suspect he wrote his long, serious plays for others, much like his articles, and that is why it is easy to sense in them a feeling of detachment. Svevo does not participate. He is not involved. These plays also fail because in the last analysis the play form was not congenial to him. He was not adept at writing dialogue, and he had difficulty finding the right speech rhythms. The tone he adopts is stilted and highly artificial. Dialogue, more often than not, is lengthy and banal, yet for all its length the characters never explain themselves fully. They remain pale, fleshless, intellectualized. We only know what they say, never what they think. Quite the opposite happens in his novels. There he uses very little conversation. His interest is not in what his characters say, but in why they say what they do and in what they really mean when they say it. In the novels he feels free to plumb all the hidden corners of the mind. In the plays he does not. Rather, he is forced to respect and reflect a common, agreed-upon, standard scenic and verbal truth—that of the bourgeoisie. The novel form means liberation. There Svevo is not confined to the surface of things, but free to plunge deeper and deeper into the new truths of his own psychology, free to make uninhibited use of his own extraordinary creative imagination and his own extraordinary fantasy.

Fantasy is a key word to the understanding of Svevo. It means letting one's imagination run free regardless of the logical or ethical consequences. To Svevo it meant finding delight and even perverse truths in quirks and oddities, contradictions and paradoxes, in shocking ideas and peculiar situations and bizarre individuals, in acting without inhibitions and in doing what you want to do no matter what. It meant knowledgeably approaching the limits of the absurd, and it meant laughter. Most of all for Svevo it meant an evasion of reality—that dull, oppressive, money and family reality of Trieste. At its finest moments, in *La coscienza di Zeno,* Svevo's fantasy practically turns into open rebellion. There are traces of fantasy in his plays. It is easy to imagine how tired he must have been listening to his wife complain about the servants. Doesn't she have anything else to talk about? It is such an absurd problem. So he invents a satirical little comedy, *Atto unico,* in which a housewife is overjoyed to retain four new domestics even though she knows they are all of them thieves. If it wasn't the servant problem he had to put up with, it was children. Svevo was surrounded all his life by a phalanx of mothers, aunts, grandmothers, cousins, and sisters-in-law. It irritated him to hear them chatter away about the upbringing of their children. He knew what he would do if he had a free hand. He has a nice vindictive idea which he puts into the mouth of one of his characters: "All modern educators have the idiotic idea that you have to teach children what justice is . . . that bad works are punished and good works are rewarded. What happens, then, is that the minute a child does something good and doesn't get any reward he's crushed and disillusioned. . . . My son Guido, though, is used to the most rigorous injustice. When he does something good, I always find some insignificant reason for punishing him. I do the same thing when he does something bad, but not always. I only praise him when I really feel physically and morally good. This has already made him learn that he's not master of his fate and that he has to give in to a fickle and

irrational world." Impossible, of course, but certainly amusing to think about. Of all these plays, *La verità* is the most interesting for the character of Silvio. This boldfaced, unscrupulous husband who is literally caught by his wife in bed with her seamstress, is such an able, convincing and shameless liar that his wife ends up no longer believing her own eyes and believing her husband innocent. Silvio has done what he wanted to do and got away with it. What could be more wonderful, more gay, more fantastic than that? Isn't this the dream of every happily married bourgeois husband? "Have you ever seen a more innocent man than me?" laughs Silvio. "How pure I feel." In fantasy everything turns out right. Paradoxes make sense. Quirks set standards. Exceptions become the new rule while the old is eyed with suspicion. Laughter permeates this topsy-turvy world, the laughter which comes from freedom: There, I've said it, I've got it off my chest. And when you've said things, even if you don't really mean them, somehow you feel better, and you can go back more serenely to this very un-topsy-turvy, very sober, very realistic world of ours. (pp. 65-72)

Charles C. Russell, in his Italo Svevo, the Writer from Trieste: Reflections on His Background and His Work, *Longo Editore, 1978, 249 p.*

FURTHER READING

Almansi, Guido. "The 'Italian Proust'." *Adam International Review* Nos. 310-12 (1966): 115-18.
  Contrasts Svevo's works with those of Proust and refutes title of the "Italian Proust" for Svevo.

Anderson, Mark. "The Private Tool of Writing: Autobiographical Fictions in the Work of Italo Svevo." *Stanford Italian Review* 3, No. 2 (Fall 1983): 273-89.
  Maintains that Alfonso, Emilio, and Zeno represent "ironized, subjective, and distorted images of their author's past." Anderson cautions against placing too much emphasis on apparent division in Svevo's writings between "private and public, autobiographical and literary, and historical and fictional."

Biasin, Gian-Paolo. "Literary Diseases: From Pathology to Ontology." *Modern Language Notes* 82 (1967): 79-102.
  Compares Svevo's treatment of the theme of disease with that of other authors and examines the "configuration and meaning taken on by disease in Italian literature since Italo Svevo."

Bondanella, Peter. "The Reception of Italo Svevo." *Italian Quarterly* 12, Nos. 47-8 (Winter-Spring 1969): 63-89.
  Asserts that American criticism of Svevo can be divided into three phases: the period from 1926 to 1932, in which critics praised Svevo's works, especially *La coscienza di Zeno;* the period from 1933 through the late 1950s, when his books grew in popularity with readers but were neglected by critics and scholars; and the period since 1958, in which Svevo's writings have been, according to Bondanella, "canonized" as "modern Italian classics." Bondanella describes several seminal essays on Svevo's works and notes that aspects of his writing remain unexamined.

Bondy, François. "Italo Svevo and Ripe Old Age." *The Hudson Review* 20, No. 4 (Winter 1967-68): 575-98.
  Discusses recurring themes and techniques in Svevo's major works. Bondy asserts, "Svevo is one of the fathers of that 'exis-

tentialist' literature that sees in the event a mode of existence rather than a sequence of actions."

Champagne, Roland A. "A Displacement of Plato's *Pharmakon:* A Study of Italo Svevo's Short Fiction." *Modern Fiction Studies* 21, No. 4 (Winter 1975-76): 564-72.

Asserts that Svevo's use of language and his treatment of time and space demonstrate the paradox of "living in mixed tenses, vacillating between the oversimplified categories of past, present, and future time." Champagne suggests that Svevo's presentation of this idea reflects the Platonic myth of *pharmakon,* which concerns an ambivalent drug that can be beneficial and poisonous at the same time.

Enright, D. J. "Svevo's Progress: or, The Apotheosis of the Poor Fish." In his *Conspirators and Poets,* pp. 167-75. London: Chatto and Windus, 1966.

Traces the evolution of Svevo's protagonists through his three novels.

Esslin, Martin. "Valetudinarian." *The Spectator* 208, No. 6979 (30 March 1962): 409-10.

Praises Svevo's use of irony and his skill in balancing the tragic and the comic in his fiction.

Fifer, Elizabeth. "The Confessions of Italo Svevo." *Contemporary Literature* 14, No. 3 (Summer 1973): 320-31.

Considers relations between the sexes in Svevo's fiction. Fifer argues that in Svevo's works, women do not exist independently of men's fantasy lives.

Hyman, Stanley Edgar. "A Dying Life." In his *Standards: A Chronicle of Books for Our Time,* pp. 158-62. New York: Horizon Press, 1966.

Asserts the universalism of issues addressed in *A Life* and assesses the book's place in modern literature.

Jacobs, Lee. "Zeno's *Sickness unto Death.*" *The Italian Quarterly* 11, No. 44 (Spring 1968): 51-66.

Discusses techniques Svevo used to manage formal problems inherent in an autobiographical novel. Jacobs discusses in particular Svevo's decision to divide the narrative voice into those of Zeno and Dr. S., which, according to Jacobs, represent the Freudian components of the Id and the Ego.

Joyce, Stanislaus. *The Meeting of Svevo and Joyce.* Universita' Delgi Studi di Trieste: Del Bianco Editore, 1965, 19 p.

An account of the friendship between Svevo and James Joyce. Joyce's brother Stanislaus describes how James encouraged Svevo to write and was influential in drawing critical attention to Svevo's work.

Lucente, Gregory L. "The Genre of Literary Confession and the Mode of Psychological Realism: The Self-Consciousness of *Zeno.*" In his *Beautiful Fables: Self-Consciousness in Italian Narrative from Manzoni to Calvino,* pp. 156-76. Baltimore: The Johns Hopkins University Press, 1986.

Examines *The Confessions of Zeno* as an example of a work that displays literary self-consciousness, a characteristic Lucente describes as a "text's self-reflexive knowledge of its status as fiction." Lucente suggests that *Zeno* is unique in its combination of "the basic effects of literary self-consciousness with those of psychological self-consciousness."

Modern Fiction Studies 18, No. 1 (Spring 1972): 1-132.

Special issue devoted to Svevo. The issue, edited by Thomas F. Staley, includes twelve essays by such critics as Gian-Paolo Biasin, Paula Robison, Beno Weiss, and Niny Rocco-Bergera on

various aspects of Svevo's life and writings, including themes and techniques in his major works, the influence of Schopenhauer's philosophy on his worldview, and the personal and literary significance of Trieste. The issue also includes a tribute by Svevo's daughter Letizia Svevo Fonda Savio and a bibliography of criticism of Svevo's works.

Murray, Jean. "The Progress of the Hero in Italo Svevo's Novels." *Italian Studies* 21 (1966): 91-100.

Contends that in their lack of direction in life, Svevo's protagonists reflect the dilemma of modern man.

Rabkin, Leslie Y. "Affective Reactions." In her *Psychopathology and Literature,* pp. 192-99. San Francisco: Chandler Publishing Co., 1966.

Presents Amalia's behavior in *Senilità* as an example of the psychotic depressive syndrome.

Robison, Paula. "*Senilità:* The Secret of Svevo's Weeping Madonna." *Italian Quarterly* 14, No. 55 (Winter 1971): 61-84.

A psychoanalytic reading of *Senilità* which "reveals a strongly Oedipal base to Emilio's tortured love affair." Robison argues that Emilio's "senility" is "rooted in a profound ambivalence toward women and sexuality."

Snow, C. P. "Italo Svevo: Forerunner of Cooper and Amis." In *Essays and Studies 1961,* edited by Derek Hudson, pp. 7-16. London: John Murray, 1961.

Brief overview of Svevo's life and major works.

Staley, Thomas F., ed. *Essays on Italo Svevo.* Tulsa, Okla: University of Tulsa, 1969, 153 p.

First collection of critical essays on Svevo to appear in English. Written by noted Svevian scholars Brian Moloney, Bruno Maier, Olga Ragusa, R. S. Baker, and others, the essays discuss Stendhal's influence on Svevo's fiction, analyze the character of Zeno, study Svevo's letters for insights into his life and career, examine the unfinished drama *Con la penna d'oro,* and survey the critical response to Svevo's work in England and the United States. The text of Svevo's drama *Inferiority,* translated by P. N. Furbank, is also included in the volume.

Steiner, George. "Old in Heart." *The New Yorker* 43, No. 15 (3 June 1967): 137-43.

Review of P. N. Furbank's *Italo Svevo: The Man and the Writer.* Steiner offers his own assessment of Svevo's work and asserts that he does not belong in the "first rank" of novelists.

Subrizi, Lilia Ghelli. *Svevo: A Fascination with Melancholy.* Florence: Il Candelaio Edizioni, 1984, 148 p.

Attempts "to ascertain whether Svevo's breakthrough in the new genre of the psychological novel is primarily a personal achievement and/or a natural outgrowth of the turn-of-the-century's literary evolution." Subrizi analyzes Svevo's works and examines his life, social surroundings, and the "prevailing aesthetic of his time."

Treitel, Renata Minerbi. "Zeno Cosini: The Meaning behind the Name." *Italica* 48, No. 1 (Spring 1971): 234-45.

Explains the significance of Svevo's choice of names for his character. Treitel argues that the juxtaposition of "Zeno," which means foreigner or stranger, and "Cosini," which means small and masculine and has derogatory connotations, reveals "the special nature of Zeno's alienation" and is "the key to Svevo's ironic intention in dealing with Zeno."

Marina (Ivanovna) Tsvetaeva (Efron)

1892-1941

(Also transliterated as Tsvetayeva, Cvetaeva, and Zwetaewa)
Russian poet, essayist, dramatist, critic, and autobiographer.

For further discussion of Tsvetaeva's career, see *TCLC,* Volume 7.

Along with Anna Akhmatova, Osip Mandelstam, and Boris Pasternak, Tsvetaeva is included in Russia's "poetic quartet," a group of important authors whose works reflect the changing values in Russia during the early decades of the twentieth century. While Tsvetaeva's writings were significantly influenced by those of her contemporaries and by the events surrounding the Russian Revolution, she remained independent of the numerous literary and political movements that flourished during this tumultuous era. Her central interest as a poet was language, and the stylistic innovations displayed in her work are considered a unique contribution to Russian literature.

Tsvetaeva grew up in Moscow in an upper-middle-class family distinguished for its artistic and scholarly pursuits. While her mother, an accomplished pianist, urged her to follow a musical career, Tsvetaeva preferred writing poetry, and her first collection, *Vecherny albom,* was privately published in 1910. This volume received unexpected attention when it was reviewed by the prominent critic Max Voloshin and the poets Nikolay Gumilyov and Valery Bryusov, all of whom wrote favorably of Tsvetaeva's work. In 1911 Tsvetaeva published a second collection of poetry, *Volshebny fonar,* and the following year was married to Sergey Efron. Throughout the marriage Tsvetaeva pursued romantic attachments with other poets, following a pattern of infatuation and disillusionment she had established in adolescence. These affairs, which often did not involve sex, were considered by Tsvetaeva to be essentially spiritual in nature and are credited with providing the highly charged emotion of her poetry, as well as inspiring poems dedicated to Mandelstam, Aleksandr Blok, and Rainer Maria Rilke.

During the Russian Civil War, which lasted from 1918 to 1921, Tsvetaeva lived in poverty in Moscow while her husband fought in the Crimea as an officer of the Czarist White Army. Although she wrote prolifically during this time—composing poetry, essays, memoirs, and dramas—the anti-Bolshevik sentiments pervading many of these works prevented their publication. During a famine in 1919 the younger of her two children died of starvation, and in 1922 Tsvetaeva emigrated with her surviving child, Ariadna, to Germany to join Efron after five years of wartime separation. While the family was living in Berlin, and later Prague—where her son, Georgy, was born in 1925—she began to publish the works she had written during the previous decade, and these found favor with Russian critics and readers living in exile. Moving to Paris, Tsvetaeva continued to write poetry, but her reputation among other émigré writers deteriorated largely because of her independent political stance and her husband's pro-Soviet activities. Efron had become a Communist agent, and Tsvetaeva refused to adopt the militant anti-Soviet posture of many émigrés, persisting in her praise of Soviet poets Paster-

nak and Vladimir Mayakovsky. Efron and Ariadna returned to Russia in 1937, and Tsvetaeva, who was being treated with indifference by Russian expatriates in Paris, followed in 1939 with her son. At that time, artists and intellectuals, especially those with ties to the West, were at risk under the extremist policies of Joseph Stalin, and the family was reunited only briefly in Moscow before Efron and Ariadna were arrested and charged with anti-Soviet espionage. When German troops attacked Moscow in 1941, Tsvetaeva and Georgy were evacuated to the village of Elabuga in the Tatar Republic. Despondent over the incarceration and possible execution of her husband and daughter, denied the right to publish, and unable to support herself and her son, Tsvetaeva took her life.

Tsvetaeva's first two volumes of verse, composed almost entirely before she was eighteen years old, are considered works of technical virtuosity, and their occasionally immature themes do not obscure Tsvetaeva's mastery of traditional Russian lyric forms. In *Vyorsty I,* which marks the beginning of her mature verse, she experimented with unusual meters and paranomasia, a technique of associating words with the same or similar roots. *Remeslo,* the last volume of poetry Tsvetaeva completed before her emigration, is praised for its metrical experiments and effective blending of folk language, archaisms, and Biblical idioms. Although she generally rejected the practices of contemporary poetic schools, Tsvetaeva did share the Russian Symbolists' refined poetic craftsmanship and the passion for clarity and detail practiced by such Acmeist poets as Mandelstam and Akhmatova.

In the early 1920s Tsvetaeva experimented with narrative verse, adapting traditional Russian folktales in *Tsar-devitsa* and *Molodets.* Although she continued to write lyrics, her most significant works in the following years were long poems, such as her satire "Krysolov" ("The Pied Piper"). Tsvetaeva developed a neoclassical style in her verse drama *Ariadna,* and in the volume *Posle Rossii,* which Simon Karlinsky has called "the most mature and perfect of her collections," she fused her early romanticism with colloquial diction. While she based her poems predominantly upon personal experience, she also explored with increased detachment such philosophical themes as the nature of time and space. As the 1930s progressed Tsvetaeva devoted more energy to prose than to poetry. In such memoirs as "Plennyi dukh" ("Captive Spirit") and "Moy Pushkin" ("My Pushkin"), she recorded her impressions of friends and poets. In a prose style characterized by stream-of-consciousness narrative technique and poetic language, Tsvetaeva expressed her views on literary creation and criticism in such essays as "Iskusstvo pri svete sovesti" ("Art in the Light of Conscience") and "Poèt o kritike" ("A Poet on Criticism").

After her initial critical success and popularity, Tsvetaeva was largely neglected because of her experimental style and her refusal to assume either a pro- or anti-Soviet stance. However, her works eventually gained a wide audience in the Soviet Union during the post-Stalinist "thaw" of the 1950s. International scholary interest in Tsvetaeva increased during the 1960s, leading to a heightened appreciation for her technical inventiveness, emotional force, and thematic range. Recent critics regard her work as among the most innovative and powerful Russian poetry of the twentieth century.

(See also *Contemporary Authors,* Vol. 104.)

PRINCIPAL WORKS

Vecherny albom (poetry) 1910
Volshebny fonar (poetry) 1912
Psikheya (poetry) 1922
Razluka (poetry) 1922
Stikhi k Bloku (poetry) 1922
Tsar-devitsa (poetry) 1922
Vyorsty I (poetry) 1922
Remeslo (poetry) 1923
Molodets (poetry) 1924
"Poèt o kritike" (essay) 1926
    ["A Poet on Criticism" published in *The Bitter Air of Exile,* 1977]
Ariadna (drama) [first publication] 1927
Posle Rossii (poetry) 1928
"Iskusstvo pri svete sovesti" (essay) 1936
    ["Art in the Light of Conscience" published in *Modern Russian Poets on Poetry,* 1976]
Proza (letters and memoirs) 1953
Lebediny stan (poetry) 1957
    [*The Demesne of the Swans,* 1980]
Izbrannye proizvedeniya (drama, autobiography, and poetry) 1965
Pisma k Anne Teskovoy (letters) 1969
Selected Poems (poetry) 1971

A Captive Spirit: Selected Prose (essays, criticism, literary portraits, and autobiographical sketches) 1980
Selected Poems of Marina Tsvetaeva (poetry) 1987

*This work was written in 1917-21.

BORIS PASTERNAK (letter date 1926)

[*Awarded the Nobel Prize in literature in 1958, Pasternak is considered one of the greatest twentieth-century poets of Russia. His poetry has been praised for its dense imagery and complex structures. Pasternak also wrote acclaimed short stories and autobiographies, but he remains best known outside of the Soviet Union for his only novel,* Doctor Zhivago *(1957). After reading Tsvetaeva's "Poem of the End," Pasternak initiated a correspondence with her that was to last until Tsvetaeva's death in 1941. In the following excerpt from a letter to Tsvetaeva, Pasternak begins a discussion of her lyrical satire "The Pied Piper," which he continues in a later letter excerpted below. In Tsvetaeva's poem, rats organize a revolution and take over the political structures of a town. Hired by the citizens of the town to exterminate the rats, the Piper lures the rodents out of town by deluding them into thinking they are going to India to start a world revolution. Although he succeeds in drowning the rats, the citizens refuse to reward him as they promised. For revenge, he lures their children into a lake with the promise of an anarchic world of imagination. Pasternak evaluates various thematic and technical aspects of the poem, particularly the force and originality of the rhythm.*]

I cannot finish the letter about **"The Pied Piper"** that I began a few days ago. I will write another and tear that one up. I was approaching it too broadly, from too many different angles, too intimately, with too many remembrances and personal regrets. In a word, my letter was too egotistical, and with a plaintive egotism; it was a floundering of my entire being touched off by your complex, many-faceted poem. **"Piper"** seems to me less perfect but richer, more moving in its unevenness, more pregnant with surprises, than **"Poem of the End."** It must be less perfect, because one has a lot more to say about it. My delight in **"Poem of the End"** was complete. Its centripetal force drew even a jealous reader into the text by communicating to him its own energy. **"Poem of the End"** is a unique, lyrically complete, highest-degree affirmation of life. Perhaps that is because it is of the lyric genre and written in the first person. At any rate, somewhere in this poem the ultimate in unity has been achieved, because even the creative basis of its power, its uniqueness (dramatic realism), is subjected to the lyrical fact of the first person: the hero = the author. The artistic value of **"Poem of the End"** and, even more, the lyrical genre to which it belongs, are conveyed through the psychological characteristics of the heroine. They belong to her. Insofar as the second part presents what one great person has to say about another great person, it surpasses the first; the one who is described enhances the greatness of the one who is describing.

What, in general, can serve as the basis of unity and completeness for a lyric that is not personal, not in the first person? So as to give a direct answer without undue pondering, I will trust to my intuition.

There are two focal points. Rarely are they equal. More often they are in conflict. To achieve the completeness of a work of art one must bring about a balance between the two centers (well-nigh impossible) or the total victory of one over the other, or, if the victory is only partial, the conviction that it is at least enduring. These focal points are, I believe: (1) The compositional idea underlying the whole (be it the acknowledged interpretation of a character from folk tale or legend, or a theme of lifelike credibility, or any other representational tendency). This is one focal point. (2) The second is the technical character of the forces used in the game and the chemical quality of the subject matter, which, manipulated by the first force (the compositional idea), produce a new world, a heavenly body amenable to spectroanalysis. The endlessness of the first creative impulse springs from the ideal immortality of the concept (the universe). The endlessness of the second, culminating in the impassioned, *real* immortality of energy, is in fact poetry—poetry in its inexhaustible flow. In **"The Pied Piper,"** notwithstanding your inherent gift for composition, as displayed with such masterly skill and diversity in the Tales [Tsvetayeva's folk tales *The Tsar Maiden* and **"The Swain"**], notwithstanding the tendency of all your cycles of verse to become long poems, and notwithstanding the superb composition of **"The Pied Piper"** itself (the concept of the entire poem concentrated in the image of the rats!! The social rebirth of the rats!!—an idea startlingly simple, a manifestation of genius, like the appearance of Minerva)— notwithstanding all this, the poetic originality of the fabric is so great that *probably* it rips apart the cohesive forces of compositional unity, for this is precisely the effect of the poem. What you have accomplished speaks with the tongue of *potential,* as happens so often with great poets in their youth, or with self-made men of genius—at the beginning. Yours is an astonishingly youthful thing, giving glimpses of extraordinary puissance. The impression of poetic raw material, or, more simply, of raw poetry, so completely outweighs all its other virtues that it would be better to declare this aspect the core of the work and call it madness through and through.

Perhaps that is how it was written, and further readings, keeping this in mind, may show me that indeed it does hang together. Svyatopolk-Mirsky was right in pointing out the necessity of reading the poem over and over again. I think it worth noting that in its very composition there are two factors leading you to strip poetry naked and to write it with pure alcohol. One of them is the use of taunting satire, condensing the image to the point of absurdity, and at the same time carrying the *excitement* of your technique to the highest pitch, to the point where, exploding in the midst of the tale, the *physical* aspect of speech assumes supremacy over the word, reducing it (the word) to second place, taking over and moving within it as the body moves within clothing. This is a noble form of extravagance and one that poetry has made use of throughout the ages. It is good that you do not apply the method superficially, or only to the treatment of petty details, as the futurists did so often, but that in you it arises from a deep-seated mimicry and, like part of a musical composition, is governed by the structure of the whole ("Paradise City," for instance, and other sections). In addition it is rhythmic in the highest degree, with an almost corporeal rhythm.

The second factor leading to your denuding of poetry is the magic of music. This was a desperately hard task!—by which I mean it was severely complicated by the realism of your treatment. It is as if a fakir introduced his marvels with a disquisition on hypnotism, or a wizard by explaining his

tricks—and then stunned and overawed his audience anyway. You understand, don't you, that if you had begun your poem with *Tri-li-li* or "Hindustán" it would have been a hundred times easier than to present first, in the same language and gestures, the appearance of reality (the rejection of miracles) and then—a miracle. In a word, no amount of praise can do justice to that aspect of your art, to *that* miraculousness. And yet, however much I speak about **"The Pied Piper"** as a complete world with its own peculiar properties, the rings typical of a thing *in potential* keep widening, like the rings of a pebble thrown into a pond. I speak of this work and find myself involved in a consideration of poetry as a whole; I speak of you and find myself confronted by my own personal regrets: the forces you manipulate in this poem are extraordinarily congenial to me—were especially so in the past. If I had not read **"The Pied Piper"** I would more easily reconcile myself to my present path of compromise (already become natural to me).

Your *unevenness* stems from a rhythmic substitution of one thought for another that leaps up in brackets (never going too far): *Figovaya! Ibo chto zhe list / Figovy (Mensch wo bist?)"; / "Kak ne proobraz yeyo? (Bin nackt). / Nag, potomu robeyu* ("Figgess! Why the leaf, I mean? / Fig-ger [*Wo bist du hin?*]; / Her prototype, then, I? [*Bin nackt*]. / Naked, so I'm shy"].

The demonic revolt of the rhythm (against itself), the mad crescendo of monotony, erases the individuality of words but confers upon the galloping intonation the character and external quality of words.

In the "Paradise City" part (up to the point of transition), this device is carried to the ultimate extreme: *Kto ne khladen i ne zharok,/Pryamo v Gameln poyez Zhai-gorod* ("Who's neither cold nor hot, / Off to Hameln-gorod"), and the entire theme, startling in its madness, plunges into the narrative like a horse into a river, which carries it swiftly forward until it is suddenly stopped by the horn of the night watchman. (Splendid!)

Again and again in the poem one comes upon this numbing, this anesthetizing of the word, which constantly serves either as mockery (almost like sticking out your tongue), or as the solidification of the leitmotif played by the flute. In this respect you are a Wagnerian in your use of the leitmotif as a deliberate and dominating device. For instance, the leitmotif charmingly runs over into the second chapter, where, besides being a reminder, it presents another kind of strong feeling (a wave of pride taking the place of sarcasm): *V moikh (cherez krai-gorod)* ("In mine [round the bend-gorod]"). In this second chapter you make a splendid transition from the comparatively uneven rhythm of the discourse on dreams, regrettably and unintentionally overextended, to the part beginning *zamka ne vzlomav,* (" 'Without breaking down the door' [into the Party]"), which seems to express the indignation of the suppressed rhythm. This impression is not deceptive; as always with you, rhythm in revolt begins to build itself into *lyrical judgments: Ne sushchnost veshchei—veshchestvennost suti. Ne sushchnost veshchei—sushchestvennost veshchi"* ("Not the beingness of things—the thingness of being. Not the beingness of things—the creatureliness of *a* thing"). This is the poetic limit of inventiveness. In every sense. At least that is how it strikes me. Opposite poles can serve only as crowning points of a single homogeneous sphere. They are sufficient for its structure, i.e., they give all there is to give and exhaust all possibilities. What homogeneity connects Lermontov's finished lyrical sentiment with the execrable prosiness of some of his verse? (I have chosen Lermontov because, despite his occasional dilettantish affectation of a poetry of "things" quite foreign to his genius, despite his many really bad poems, despite his emotional ambivalence—on the one hand the genuine emotion of a poet; on the other, something assumed to be greater: a weak and inconsistent "sincerity"—he achieves, astonishingly, a dry, misanthropic *sentiment* that sets the tone of his lyrics, and if it does not establish his individuality as a poet, it at least offers a resounding, deathless, always infectious sense of depth.)

Well, then, the two extremes are connected by their common source: movement. Your heaping up of definition upon definition always drives to a rhythmic apogee, is always dependent upon it for form and substance, and is always natural precisely at the point where motion is accelerated to such a degree that it begins to think, to throw out definitions, formulas, Pythian mantissas, bits of well-formulated thoughts. In just the same way, excursions into the blind alleys of palpable words, i.e., into lip, throat, and neck-muscle sources of excitement or embellishment, result in the turning and twisting of the rhythm. But in this physics of poetry you are always far more successful in dealing with the "infinitely great" (definitions, sentiments, philosophical ideas) than with the "infinitely small" (the root of a quality, the tonality of an image, its uniqueness, etc.). It was a pleasure to discover, on delving into the poem again, that the exposition also presented a leitmotif (*Zasova ne snyav, zamka ne zatronuv* ["Without lifting the latch, without touching the lock"]). I have already remarked that in this poem you made a more careful selection of *detail* than you usually do. (pp. 148-52)

> *Boris Pasternak, in a letter to Marina Tsvetayeva on June 14, 1926, in* Letters: Summer 1926 *by Boris Pasternak, Marina Tsvetayeva, Rainer Maria Rilke, Yevgeny Pasternak, Yelena Pasternak, and Konstantin M. Azadovsky, eds., translated by Margaret Wettlin and Walter Arndt, Harcourt Brace Jovanovich, 1985, pp. 148-53.*

BORIS PASTERNAK   (letter date 1926)

[*The following excerpt continues Pasternak's discussion of "The Pied Piper" begun in the excerpt above.*]

I have expounded a lot of nothingness about the beginning of **"The Pied Piper."** You must have found it unpleasant reading. According to the relative values of the parts, I ought to write volumes about the second half, having expended so many words on the first. I will not, however, seek a balance. I will try to be brief. The best chapters are "The Exodus" and "The Children's Paradise." "The Scourge" is on their level (as to theme, but without the flute, and that is like a chess game without a queen). I like "In the Rathaus" less. As in the first half, one has to speak almost exclusively of the rhythm, of the musical characteristics of the components, of the themes. The privileges accorded rhythm in "Exodus" and "Children's Paradise" are practically limitless—a lyric poet's dream. Here we have the subjective rhythm of the writer, his passion, his ecstasy, his soaring flights of fancy—in other words, something that is rarely successful: art that makes itself the subject. To appreciate your own triumph you have but to recall the flat, vulgar descriptions of poets, artists, and eccentrics in most plays and stories. In "The Scourge" the rhythm paints the picture, and how well it does it! It is the

natural rhythm of petty trading, so natural that it seems always to have been one of the potentials of music. Thanks only to the swift flash of it, are you able in a single instant to cover the entire market place and all its details in two or three rhythmic strokes. Wonderful in its force (in its wealth of possibilities) is the chanted motif (*a u nás, a u nás* ["but with us, but with us . . ."]), especially when it is repeated after the *stunningly* executed fugue of the rats. It seems that you drew individual rats and the entire swarm simultaneously and brought the whole picture together on a web of rhythm, using one of the threads as a whip to beat your way to the end, to that advancing, accumulating, accelerating finale! Here the rhythm resembles what it speaks of—a rare accomplishment. The rhythm itself seems to be made not of words but of rats, and not of word stresses but of gray spines.

I have spoken less of the best chapters: all my preceding observations were elicited by the magnetic perfection of these central ones. And so, indirectly, much has already been said about them. "The Exodus"! (From now on I shall be laconic and follow no particular order.) I like the way the procession passes the Rathaus. "The Dream Monger." Very good for their unity of style are the lexical inventions of this chapter, lending a certain credibility to the fabulous kingdom to which the children are being led. These inventions tie together all the fantastic illusions. The imaginary destination has its own peculiar flora, climate, morals, and mysteries, and these explain the weird consistency of the vocabulary. Indeed, there is breathtaking lyricism in this fairy-tale chapter *Ti-ri-li.* The insistent repetition of this phrase is more powerful than the *realistic* characterization of the flute, for all its rhythmic modeling. Its realism is oddly expressed on page 44, where, after the double statement of this tune, *ne zhaleite* ("don't be sorry") falls at the end of the line and suggests, between *zhaleite* ("sorry") and *alleike* ("lane"), the rhyme *fleite* ("flute"), deliberately, even conspicuously omitted, but doubly present because of its apparent absence.

On the whole the Piper's rhythmic pattern (his leitmotif) is astounding. The first line of this most happy of musical phrases is perfect in intonation: *Hindustán!* The compression of the anapest (*uu—*) into one word (an exclamation) gives it tremendous impact. The imagination, aroused and challenged by this anapest and unobstructed by a formal sentence, instantly forms the flutist's image, what you might almost call his *pose* (body bent forward in the saddle for the articulation of that same triple beat *uu—* in the phrase *v pushinú* ("into a flake"). The conceptual waves (waves of thought) at moments when the hypnotic awareness of the flute's theme dies away (for example, what could be finer than *miru chetvyorty chas i ni kotor god* ["the world's four hours and no years old"] are astonishing. India here becomes overwhelmingly real. The massacre of shadings—well, yourself spoke of your ruthless hand, and spoke correctly. In the new interweaving of leitmotifs of doubt and disillusion (from approximately the moment of the shift in rhythm: *tot kto v khobote vidit nos sŏbstvĕnnŷ* ["Who in an elephant's sees his own nose"]), the flute theme develops striking *new* force.

Actually this is a funeral march, coming with magical unexpectedness from an unaccustomed direction—the back door; or perhaps it would be better to say it is let into the soul through the back door, whereas we are used to having a Beethoven, a Chopin, a Wagner, or any other funeral march let in by the door out of which the body is to be carried: the front door of a Te Deum. You display much wit and wisdom in "In the Rathaus." For the purpose he serves, your Ratsherr, borrowed from the Romanticists, is excellent. He is a character that might be among those surrounding and supporting Faust. The sarcasm of this chapter is deeply significant and in no way a caricature:

Plachte i bdite, chtob nam spalos,
Mrite, chtob my plodilis!

("Weep and be wakeful, that we may sleep,
Perish, that we may multiply!")

The ego, the "I" theme, is just as good. You mold eternal attributes into symbols very adroitly. *Zhvachno-bumazhny* ("chewing the paper cud"). But when, at the end of the fifth chapter, the threat of a familiar voice is heard plowing a furrow into the exceedingly complex soil of your language (*Ne vidat kak svoyei dushi!* ["invisible like one's soul"], imitating with irrevocable finality the folk saying *Ne vidat kak svoikh ushei!* ["invisible like one's ears"]), then you understand why, notwithstanding its impressive merits, this chapter leaves us colder than Chapters 1 and 2. (As for the fourth and the last, they are beyond compare!) This is because after "The Exodus" our attention is so tightly glued to the Piper's fate, less in our eagerness to know the outcome than in our hope that he will be happy, that we cannot possibly concentrate on anything else, however interesting; as a result we pick out of the fifth chapter only that which serves the development of the theme, namely, the betrayal, the broken promise, which we instantly pounce upon, irritated by circumlocutions that delay the climax.

The genre pictures you paint in this chapter, perhaps more brilliantly than anywhere else, also annoy and exasperate. But perhaps that is what you wanted. A vexing chapter. (pp. 160-63)

["The Children's Paradise" is a] cruel and terrible chapter, coming straight from the heart, told with a smile, but—cruel and terrible. The part about school is marvelous. *Gul da ball. Gun da Gall* ("Thrum and ball. Hun and Gaul"). And filtered through that feverish, buoyant, early-morning rhythm:

Shkolnik? Vzdor. Balnik? Sdan.
Livnya, livnya baraban.
Globus? Sbit. Ranets? Snyat.
Shchebnya, shchebnya vodopad . . .

("Schoolboy? Rubbish. Gradebook? Done. /
Downpour, drumming downpour's thrum— /
Globe? Shot down. Pack? Let fall— / Gravelly
gravel waterfall . . .")

Filtered through it, evidently, that "Hindustán" which showed its force yesterday. The terrible anapest *uu— —*, close to yesterday's rhythmic magnet, is now merely given a new sound. The moment you recognize its melody, you want to rush forward to protect the children from its consequences (from a knowledge of the end):

Detvorá
Zolotýkh vecheróv moshkará!

("Small fry homing / Golden evening midges
swarming!")

All of the doomed children together enter the range of the rhythm. A slight easing of the harshness is provided by making the flute sound for the rats like a real flute (unadulterated, unrelieved, fatal realism), whereas for the children it is metamorphosed, calling to them like a trumpet (unconsciously, in

the sound of the rhythm: *tra-ra-ra*). Similarly, the funeral march is lighter and purer. The harmony is broken up into two elements: promise (which sounds almost like *truly* good tidings: *Yest u menya . . .*)

["I have . . ."]and the motif of the funeral service, *V tsarstve moyem . . .* ("in my kingdom") (which sounds like a biblical canon); *Idezhe nest bolezn, ni pechal, ni vozdykhanye* ["Where there is not sickness, nor grief, nor sighing"]). The first motif grows in depth beyond the web of temptation; it achieves firmness and true elevation, dramatically paid for by the personal note that breaks through after the line *Dlya malchikov radost dlya devochek tyazhest* ("For boys, rejoicing, for girls, sorrow"):

Dno strasti zemnoi
I rai dlya odnoi.

("The depth of earth's pain / And Eden for one.")

But enough of **"The Pied Piper."** I fear my meticulous analysis has made you hate it. *Summa summarum:* it presents the absolute and incontestable supremacy of rhythm. This flows naturally from the character of the subject matter. It reaches its highest manifestation in two dramatic chapters in which miracles are created; it extends over other chapters as well, the only difference being that in them rhythm is not in the first person; in all other respects it retains the same force and is the same source of ideas, images, transitions, and the interweaving of themes. (pp. 163-67)

Forgive me for this dull and verbose letter. At last I have cleared a path to **"The Pied Piper."** Now I can read it for pure enjoyment. After all, **"The Pied Piper"** is not a thing one can dismiss with "I liked it immensely." I was intrigued by the poem's originality and wanted to get to the bottom of it. (p. 167)

Boris Pasternak, in a letter to Marina Tsvetayeva on July 2, 1926, in Letters: Summer 1926 *by Boris Pasternak, Marina Tsvetayeva, Rainer Maria Rilke, Yevgeny Pasternak, Yelena Pasternak, and Konstantin M. Azadovsky, eds., translated by Margaret Wettlin and Walter Arndt, Harcourt Brace Jovanovich, 1985, pp. 160-67.*

MARINA TSVETAEVA (essay date 1926)

[*In an excerpt from her essay "A Poet on Criticism," Tsvetaeva discusses her inspiration and motivation for writing poetry.*]

I obey something that sounds constantly within me but not uniformly, sometimes indicating, sometimes commanding. When it indicates, I argue; when it commands, I obey.

The thing that commands is a primal, invariable, unfailing and irreplaceable line, *essence appearing as a line of verse.* (Most usually as a final couplet, to which all the rest then accrues.) The thing that indicates is an aural path to a poem: I hear a melody, but not words. The words I have to find.

More to the left—more to the right, higher—lower, faster—slower, extend—break off: these are the exact indications of my ear, or of something *to* my ear. All my writing is only listening. Hence, in order to write further—constant rereading. Without rereading at least twenty lines I cannot write one more. It is as if the whole poem were there from the very beginning, some sort of melodic or rhythmic sketch of it; as if the poem, which in my present moment writes itself (I never know whether it will write itself to completion), were already, somewhere, written out quite precisely in full. All I do is reestablish it. Hence this constant watchfulness: Is this the way it is? Do I deviate from it? Do I give way to myself, to my willfulness?

My task is *to hear true.* I have no other.

Not for the millions, not for some one-and-only, not for myself. I write for the poem alone. The poem, through me, writes itself. Is this the time to be concerned with myself or with others?

Here we must distinguish two stages: the creative and the post-creative. The first has no *why;* it is all *how.* I would call the second the everyday, practical stage. The poem is written. What's to become of it? Who is it for? Who will buy it? Oh, I make no bones about it: when the poem is completed, that second question is the most important one for me.

Thus the poem is *given* twice: in the spirit and in the world. Who will take it?

A few words about money and fame. To write for money is base; to write for fame, virtuous. Here colloquial speech and colloquial thought are both wrong. To write for anything whatsoever except the poem is to doom it to transience. The only things written that way—and perhaps they should be— are editorials. Fame, money, the triumph of this or that idea, any extraneous goal—and the poem perishes. The poem, while it is being written, is its own goal.

Why do I write? I write because I can't help writing. Question me about goals and I answer about reasons, and it cannot be otherwise. . . .

Between 1917 and 1922, I produced an entire book of so-called civil war (White Guard) poems. Did I intend to write a book? No. The book happened, it came about. To extol the ideals of the White Guard? No. But White ideals triumphed in it. I was inspired originally by the thought of the White Guard, but I forgot about it from the first line on. I thought only of the line I was writing. I encountered it again only after the final full-stop: the White Guard, living, incarnated against my will. The guarantee of the effectiveness of these so-called civil war poems is precisely the absence of political considerations in the process of the writing, and in the unity of the purely poetic considerations. What is true of the ideology is true also of the practical stage. After these poems have been written, I can read them in public and be rewarded with either fame or death. But if I think about that when I undertake them, I will not write them, or will write them in a way that deserves neither fame nor death.

Considerations before completion and after completion. This was what Pushkin had in mind in his lines about the inspiration and the manuscript ["A manuscript is marketable; / Inspiration is not for sale"], and colloquial thought will never be able to understand it.

Fame and money. Fame—how majestic, how spacious, how dignified, how harmonious. What grandeur. What peace.

Money—how petty, how pitiful, how inglorious, how vain. What meanness. What futility.

What, then, do I seek, when I have written something and submit it to someone or other?

Money, my dears. As much as I can get.

Money enables me to go on writing. Money is my tomorrow's poems. Money is my ransom from the hands of editors, publishers, landladies, shopkeepers, patrons; it is my freedom, and my writing desk. Money is more than my writing desk; it is the very *landscape* of my poems—that Greece I so much longed to see while I was writing **Theseus;** and the Palestine I will long for when I write *Saul;* ships and trains that go everywhere, to every seacoast and beyond every sea.

Money enables me to write not only more, but better, not to take advances, not to precipitate events, not to stop up gaps in my poems with incidental words, not to spend time with X and Y in hopes that they will publish or "arrange" something. The choice is mine, the selection is mine.

Money, finally—a third and most important point—enables me to write *less.* Not three pages a day, but thirty lines.

My money, before all else, dear reader, is *your* gain!

Fame? *"Etre salué d'un tas de gens que vous ne connaissez pas"* ("To be greeted by a mass of people you don't know"; a phrase of the late Scriabin's, though I don't know whether it was his own or borrowed). An added daily burden. Fame is a result, not a goal. All the greatest glory seekers loved not fame, but power. Had Napoleon sought fame he would never have objected to St. Helena, that most perfect of pedestals. It was not fame Napoleon regretted on St. Helena, but power. Hence his longing, and his spyglass. Fame is passive; love of power is active. Fame reclines, "resting on its laurels." Power rides a horse, and quests for those laurels. "For the glory of France and the sake of my own power"—that, at the bottom of his heart, was Napoleon's motto. Let the world obey France, and France—me. The name of Napoleonic *gloire* is *pouvoir.* He, a man of action before all else, never cared about his reputation (an essentially literary phenomenon). To burn oneself at both ends for the roar of the crowd and the babble of poets—he despised both crowd and poets too much for that. Napoleon's purpose was power; his fame was a consequence of its attainment.

I admit a poet's fame as publicity, for financial motives. Thus, though squeamish about publicity personally, I applaud Mayakovsky's sweep, boundless in this as in everything. When Mayakovsky needs money, he does something sensational once again ("a purge of poets, a slaughter of poetesses," his trip to America, etc.). People go to see the scandal and pay money. Mayakovsky, as a major poet, cares nothing about either praise or detraction. He himself knows what he is worth. But he does care about money, he cares a lot. And his self-advertisement, by its very vulgarity, is so much cleaner than the parrots, monkeys, and harems of Lord Byron. He, as we know, did not need money.

A necessary observation: Neither Byron nor Mayakovsky ever involved their art in matters of fame; both used the refuse of their personal lives. Byron wants fame? He gets himself a menagerie, lives in Raphael's house, *perhaps* goes to Greece. . . . Mayakovsky wants fame? He puts on a yellow blouse and poses in front of a fence.

The scandalous private lives of a good half of all poets are only a cleansing of *that other* life, so that they are clean *there.*

Life is messy, notebooks are clean. (For "clean," read "full of words, black." A clean notebook is black with words.) Life is noisy, notebooks are still. (The ocean gives an impression of stillness even during a storm. The ocean gives an impression of labor even during a calm. The first case is an observer in action; the second, a laborer at rest. In every force there is an incessant conjunction of stillness and labor. The peace that we sense in every force is our own confidence in it. The ocean is like that. And a forest. And a poet. Every poet is a *pacific* ocean.)

Thus, before our very eyes, a commonplace is overturned: in poetry, anything is permitted. No. Precisely in poetry, nothing is. In private life—everything . . . .

Fame is parasitic. In the vegetable kingdom, power is an oak tree, fame is the ivy. In the animal kingdom, fame is a courtesan reposing on the warrior's laurels. A pleasant supplement, and it costs nothing.

Fame is a kind of Dionysian ear cocked at the world, a Homeric *qu'en dira-t-on* [what will people say]? The furtive backward glance, the misapprehending ear of the maniac. (A combination of two manias: delusions of grandeur and of persecution.)

Two examples of unalloyed love of fame: Nero and Herostratus. Both were *maniacs.*

Comparison with the poet. Herostratus, in order to glorify his name, set fire to a temple. The poet, in order to glorify a temple, sets himself afire.

The greatest fame (the epos), and the greatest power, is anonymous.

There is a dictum of Goethe: "One ought not write a single line that is not intended for a million readers."

Yes, but there's no need to hurry those readers, to expect them in this very decade or this very century.

"One ought not . . ." But clearly one had. It sounds more like a prescription intended for others than for himself. The dazzling example of that very same *Faust,* not understood by his contemporaries and still being deciphered for lo these hundred years. *"Ich, der in Jahrtausenden lebe. . ."* ("I who live in millennia . . ."; Goethe).

What is beautiful about fame? The word itself. (pp. 117-22)

Often, reading some review of my work and learning that "the formal aspects are beautifully solved," I think to myself, "Did I really have any formal aspects to solve?" "Mme. T's intention was to give us a folktale, introducing into it elements of this, and of that, etc." Did *I* (the stress is on I) intend that? No. *That* was what I intended? No, not at all. I read a folktale, "The Vampire," in Afanasiev's folklore collection and I was puzzled. Why is it that Marusya, who is afraid of the vampire, so persistently refuses to admit what she has seen, knowing that deliverance lies in naming it? Why does she say no instead of yes? Fear? But fear can not only make us bury ourselves in a bed, it can make us jump out the window. No, not fear. Granted fear, but something else as well. Fear and what? When someone says to me, do this and you will be free, and I don't do it, that means I am not particularly interested in freedom; it means that my nonfreedom is more precious to me. And what is the precious nonfreedom that exists between individuals? Love. Marusya loved the vampire. That is why she never named him, and so lost, one after another, her mother, her brother, her life. Passion and crime, passion and sacrifice. . . .

That was *my* task, when I started working on *The Swain.* To

uncover the essence of the tale, already implicit in its skeleton. To release the poem from its spell. And not at all to invent a "new form" or a "folkloric form." The work wrote itself, I worked on it, listened to every word (not weighed—listened). The labor that went into the poem is confirmed by (1) the fact that the reader cannot perceive it, and (2) by my drafts. But all that is the poem's development, its realization, and not my initial conception.

How could I, a poet—that is, a person who deals with the essence of things, be attracted by mere form? If I am attracted by the essence, the form will come of its own accord. And it does come. And I have no doubt that it will keep coming. The form required by this particular essence, conjured up by me syllable by syllable. To cast the form, and then fill it with content? But what is this, making plaster casts? No, I have to be attracted by the essence; then I can realize it. That's what a poet does. And I will realize it (now it *is* a question of form) as *concretely* as possible. Essence is form: a child cannot be born different from what it is. The gradual revelation of features—thus a person grows, and a work of art as well. For that reason to approach the work "formally"—that is, to reconstruct for me (often completely incorrectly) my own rough drafts—is nonsense. Once the fair copy exists, the drafts (the form) are overcome.

Rather than tell me what I intended to accomplish in a given poem, show me what you were able to get out of it.

The folk, in folktales, interpret the dream of the elements; the poet, in the poem, interprets the dream of the folk; the critic (in a new poem) interprets the dream of the poet.

Criticism: the court of ultimate jurisdiction in dream interpretation.

The penultimate one. (pp. 131-33)

Marina Tsvetaeva, "A Poet on Criticism," in The Bitter Air of Exile: Russian Writers in the West, 1922-1972, *edited by Simon Karlinsky and Alfred Appel, Jr., University of California Press, 1977, pp. 103-34.*

ZINAIDA SHAKHOVSKOI   (essay date 1955)

[*In the following excerpt from a review of* Proza, *Shakhovskoi praises Tsvetaeva's prose style.*]

Tsvetaeva is a complex poet and writer, but one of the most authentic of our times, and without doubt a writer of genius. Not only in exile, but even in twentieth-century Russia, she is an absolutely unique phenomenon. She resembles no one and succeeds without bothering to strain for originality. (pp. 165-66)

What we find [in *Proza*] is seen through the eyes of Tsvetaeva which strip from her contemporaries all that is unessential. Intelligent, brilliant, scorning wit, respecting the mind, and with an innate boldness of style, Marina Tsvetaeva gives us some amazing portraits. She imparts a nobility of feeling, which men and women who write their memoirs have not accustomed us to. Her descriptions of Andrei Bely, in particular, but also of her enemy Briusov, of her friend Voloshin, reveal to us the innermost secrets of these men. Does she not maintain that the creation of myths is the extracting of the essence of man and its projection into full light? The creation of myths, she says, is what should have been and might have been. This is exactly the contrary of Chekhov who describes that which is and that which for Marina Tsvetaeva is nonexistent.

We discover on every page of the book these myths which are the only reality of man. The words used are exact and precise, with that precision which the laziness of the average man refuses.

Memory has good taste, Marina Tsvetaeva reminds us. Never does she "settle accounts" with her literary colleagues. Behind scorned facts, she digs into the innermost recesses of human beings, in such a way that her interlocutors emerge transfigured.

Mr. Fedor Stepun, in a very fine preface, speaks of the aphorisms which form, without Tsvetaeva meaning them to, the basis of her writing. There is, in fact, very little padding in her works; her style resembles in certain ways the spoken style of Archpriest Avvakum and has the same kind of virility.

Little known by the public, lonely until her death, Marina Tsvetaeva still awaits recognition. Fame, "this sun of the dead," as Balzac remarked, is certainly going to shed its rays on her. But one can't imagine her in an anthology of female writers. The definition which Barres erroneously applies to Marie Bashkirtseva is truly appropriate for Tsvetaeva. It is she who is "a sword hidden under a woman's dress." (p. 166)

> *Zinaida Shakhovskoi, in a review of "Proza," in* The Russian Review, *Vol. 14, April, 1955, pp. 165-66.*

ILYA EHRENBURG (essay date 1963)

[*A Russian-Jewish novelist, journalist, essayist, and poet, Ehrenburg wrote prolifically during a career that spanned five decades and encompassed both world wars and the post-Stalin years. During World War II he was one of the most active Russian writers of war journalism and propaganda, and his articles are considered to have played a large part in inspiring Russian resistance to the German invasion. Following the war, Ehrenburg published many anti-American articles in the Soviet press, as well as* Buria *(1948;* The Storm, *1949), a novel about World War II that is considered a leading example of postwar anti-Americanism in Russian fiction. Although Ehrenburg castigated the failures of Western society in his writings, he also perceived the corruption and brutality of revolutionary ideals in the Soviet Union, and often despaired of the course his government was following. After Joseph Stalin's death, when the Soviets became more tolerant of certain types of dissent, Ehrenburg publically rejected the dictum that writers should serve the purposes of the state and asserted that the writer is "a servant of the truth." The essays of his later years reflect his determination to impress Russia's youth with the moral purposes of art and with the ideals and convictions of the great Russian writers who had been suppressed under Stalin's repressive regime, and to inspire his readers to help build a humane Russia. In the following excerpt, Ehrenburg relates Tsvetaeva's biographical circumstances and personal characteristics to prominent subjects and themes of her poetry.*]

When Marina Tsvetayeva was twenty this was her dream: "For my poems about youth and death—unread poems!—scattered among the dust of bookshops (where no one has bought or buys them), for my poems, as for precious wines, there will come a day."

Her first book was called *Vecherny albom* (*Evening Album*); she was seventeen when it was published and still wore a school uniform. The second book, *Volshebny fonar* (*Magic Lantern*), appeared two years later. Both these books contain a great deal that is childish. It is only in earliest youth that one can write: "You gave me a childhood better than a fairy-tale; now, at seventeen, give me death."

But even in juvenile verse a genuine poet can be detected. Valery Bryusov, Maximilian Voloshin, Marietta Shaginyan were moved to write reviews of *Evening Album.*

In the years that followed, Marina Tsvetayeva wrote many beautiful poems, but the circle of those who knew her verse was not widened. She died in 1941, recognized by only a handful of enthusiasts.

We know of poets who were appreciated by their contemporaries and who have withstood the test of time: Pushkin and Nekrasov, Blok and Mayakovsky. There have been others whose poetry was attuned to the ephemeral tastes and moods of the day. Benediktov was at one time greatly admired; many people copied Apukhtin's poems in albums, and others spent whole nights poring over Nadson's verses; so, too, crowds thronged to Igor Severyanin's readings. Today these poets are of interest only to the literary historian. Finally, there have been poets who won recognition only posthumously. When Turgenev garbled the poem "Oh, How in Our Declining Years . . ." he could hardly have realized the importance of Tyutchev as a poet.

The fate of Marina Tsvetayeva's poetry does not fall into any of these categories. I doubt whether anyone could ascribe the fact that it has not had recognition to its extremely complex form: many of Alexander Blok's poems, to say nothing of Pasternak's, are far more obscure.

Marina Tsvetayeva's poetry has an emotional appeal; she carries the reader swiftly into the world of her rhythms, images, and words. She loved music, and was a verbal spellbinder like those who evolved ancient incantations. Suddenly, but with unerring accuracy, one word brings another in its wake: "How do you find life? How do you fret and fume? How do you squirm? How do you get up? How do you pay, poor fellow, the toll of deathless vulgarity?"

Here are two fragments that show the extreme clarity of Marina Tsvetayeva's poetry. The first was written in 1916: "The day will come—a sad one, so they say—when they will cease to reign, to weep, to blaze, cooled by some other's copper coins, my eyes, as restless as a flame. . . . Along the streets of my forsaken Moscow I shall be driving, you will plod along, and more than one will fall out on the way. The first clod on the coffin lid will rattle, and then, at last, the sanction will be given to self-enamoured, solitary sleep."

And this written in 1920: "I have been writing on a slate, and on the faded leaves of fans, and on the sands of rivers and of seas—with skates upon the ice, and with a ring on window-panes—on my own hand and on the trunks of birch trees, and—to be better understood by all—on clouds and on the billows of the sea, and on an attic dovecote's walls. How I did wish that each of them should blossom with me in centuries. Under my fingers. And then how, brow bent to my desk, with two crossed lines I cancelled out a name."

No, the fate of Marina Tsvetayeva's poetry cannot be laid to "incomprehensibility." It was simply that her contemporaries had little chance to read her verse. In those days books were published in very small editions; to take one instance, only one thousand copies of the volume of collected poems *Versti* (*Versts*) came out in Moscow in 1921. Later Marina Tsvetayeva lived abroad and her poems were printed in journals and symposiums that very few people read. Much of her work remains unpublished to this day.

It is true that she did not seek fame. She wrote: "For a Russian, the ambition to achieve fame in one's lifetime is contemptible and ridiculous." But she also did everything possible to remain unknown. This might be put down to pride or to an exaggerated sensibility. There was probably a little of both, but her attitude was determined far more by the originality of her perceptions. Loneliness, or more exactly, isolation, hung over her throughout her life like a curse, which she tried to disguise to herself, and to others too, as a supreme blessing. In whatever company she found herself she felt an exile, an outcast. Recalling racist arrogance, she wrote: "What poet, of those who ever were and are, is not a Negro?" In **"Poema Kontsa"** (**"Poem of the End"**) she compares her life to life in a ghetto. Her world seemed to her an island, and to other people, all too often, she seemed insular.

Her loneliness has nothing to do with the "ivory tower" attitude which was popular in the years when she made her début in Russian poetry. Bryusov wrote: "Perhaps everything in life is but a means to brilliant singing verse; so, from your carefree childhood onwards, you must seek out combinations of words."

This kind of advice angered Marina Tsvetayeva, and she wrote: "Words instead of meanings, rhymes instead of feelings? As if words were born out of words, rhymes out of rhymes, poems out of poems!" She would have liked to mix with other people but was unable to: "What am I to do, blind stepson that I am, in a world where all can see and have a father, where over anathemas, as on earth-banks, passions are scattered, where weeping is called a cold in the head?"

Loneliness oppressed her. Loneliness (not egocentricity) enabled her to write many wonderful poems about unhappiness. And loneliness brought her to suicide.

Certain poets were fascinated by the Romanticism of the first half of the nineteenth century, not as a literary school, but as an attitude of mind; they assumed the character of Childe Harold rather than that of Byron, of Pechorin rather than of Lermontov. Marina Tsvetayeva did not masquerade as one of the heroines of the Romantic epoch; she was by nature akin to them in her loneliness, her contradictions, her wanderings. Different building materials—wood and marble, granite and concrete—are utilized in the changing styles of architecture, and the styles themselves are determined by the times. Marina Tsvetayeva was born not in 1792 like Shelley but a hundred years later.

In one of her poems Marina Tsvetayeva tells us about her two grandmothers: one was a simple Russian woman, the wife of a village priest, the other a haughty Polish aristocrat. Marina Tsvetayeva's nature was a blend of old-fashioned courtesy and rebelliousness, of extreme pride and extreme simplicity. Her life was a tangled skein of insight and errors. She wrote: "All things in my life I have come to love and have loved to the end by farewells, not by meetings, by parting, not by union." This is not a literary programme or the expression of a pessimistic philosophy; it is simply an avowal. If one were to try to sum up her outlook on life, one would say that it consisted of a love of life, an affirmation of life; and yet she was unable to live her own life as she would have wished. In

Moscow she wrote about the Lorelei, about Paris, about the Island of St. Helena; and in Paris she dreamed of Kaluga birches and the melancholy flame of the elderberry. She admired Stenka Razin's freebooters, but when she met the descendants of this favourite hero, she did not recognize them. All her life she struggled with herself. She wrote a play about the libertine Casanova to prove to herself, if not to others, that she could be serene and gay. But Casanova was only a casual guest for the hour. There was something else she knew only too well: "Oh, the cry of women of all ages: 'My dear, what have I done to you?'"

She wrote about the *streltsy* [sixteenth- and seventeenth-century musketeers], about Princess Sofia, about the Russian Vendée. What inspired her was not some longing for order but her mutinous spirit. She said to her son: "Stop mourning an Eden you've never seen." (pp. 245-49)

Two deep emotions possessed her throughout her complicated and troubled life: her love of Russia and an enraptured devotion to art. These two emotions were indissolubly welded.

When considering the essentially Russian character of her poetry I am least concerned with her fairytales and her borrowings from folk songs. The outward signs point elsewhere—to a knowledge and love of other countries: ancient Greece, Germany, France. As a young girl she had passionately admired *L'Aiglon* and the whole of Edmond Rostand's conventional romanticism. With the years her enthusiasms went deeper: Goethe, *Hamlet, Phèdre*. She wrote verse in French and in German. And yet everywhere, except in Russia, she felt a foreigner. Her whole being was bound up with her native landscape, from the "hot rowan" to the ultimate blood-coloured elderberry. The main themes of her poetry were love, death, and art, and these themes she treated in a Russian way: she remained true to the traditions of her great predecessors and also to the spiritual character of her people. Love was for her that "fatal duel" of which Tyutchev wrote. Love was a parting or an agonizing severance. She wrote about Pushkin's Tatyana: "What other nation has such a love heroine: courageous and dignified, enamoured and unrelenting, clear-sighted and loving?" She hated the substitutes for love: "How many of them, how many, white and dove-coloured, eat out of my hands! Whole kingdoms coo around your lips, O Baseness!"

She thought a great deal about death, persistently, without fear but also without resignation. There was a pagan wisdom about her, not Hellenic, but her own native Russian: "Like vapour it has disappeared through a hole, that famous superstition called the 'soul.' That Christian pale anaemia. Vapour. Apply the poultices. Yet it has never existed. There was a body, it wanted to live."

Marina Tsvetayeva's most admirable poems are probably those about art. She despised professional versifiers, but she realized that there is no inspiration without craftsmanship, by which she set great store. Perhaps it was while repeating to herself Karolina Pavlova's lines that she chose the title **Re-meslo** (**Craftsmanship**) for one of her books. There were moments when it seemed to her that by knowing the laws of the heart one could test the truth of everything, even of the mystery of the emotions: "Find yourself trusting life companions who have not sorted out the miracle by numbers. I know that Venus is the work of hands; a craftsman, I know my craft."

The verses addressed to her desk are a marvellous exposition of a poet's creed: "I know all your wrinkles, defects, scars, and grooves—the tiniest of notches. (Toothmarks when a verse would not come.) Yes, there was a being that I loved, and that being was—a desk."

She worked unremittingly, with passion—from morning till night and from night till morning—and with stringent conscientiousness, afraid of yielding to some fortuitous combination of words and testing her inspiration with the scrupulous artist's mistrust.

She brought into Russian poetry much that was new: a continuous cycle of images that spread out from one word, like circles widening on water when a pebble is thrown; an uncommonly acute sense of the attraction and repulsion of words; a quickening of rhythm that reflects the quickened beating of the heart; a spiralling construction: thus someone who is stirred by emotion breaks off a thought, only to return, not precisely to the same thought but to one closely akin. Although she was often at odds with her age, her art gave meaning and expression to many of the feelings of her contemporaries. Her poetry is the poetry of discovery.

When I say that in Marina Tsvetayeva's poetry the themes of Russia and art are bound together, I am thinking primarily of that most complicated of problems which has preoccupied nearly all Russian writers—from Pushkin and Gogol to the writers of today—the problem of the relationship of responsibility and inspiration, of life and creative activity, of the artist's thoughts and his conscience. I cannot imagine Balzac, troubled of mind, burning one of his manuscripts; or Dickens going out into the night after repudiating all he had lived for till then; or Rilke writing *The Twelve* before his death.

All Marina Tsvetayeva's pride and relentless purpose manifested themselves in her approach to the writer's role. She was exacting with others as well as with herself; she was sometimes unjust in her judgments, but she was never indifferent. (pp. 250-52)

During the years when she confronted the storms of the day with poetry, as though, despite herself, she admired Mayakovsky, she asked herself what was more important—poetry or the creation of life—and replied: "With the exception of parasites of all kinds, everyone is more important than we (the poets)." At the same time, with her mind on Mayakovsky's verse about the poet who has set his heel on the throat of his own song, she called a poet's service to the people "an act of sacrifice" and said about Mayakovsky's death: "He lived like a man and died like a poet."

Evening Album was published [in 1910] the same year as my first book; I recall that Valery Bryusov wrote about the two of us in the same article. Very few people of my generation are left who knew Marina Tsvetayeva at the zenith of her poetic radiance. The time has not yet come to speak about her troubled life—she is still too near to us. But I would like to say that she was endowed with a forceful conscience, that she lived cleanly and nobly, almost always in want, despising the fleshpots, inspired even on the drabbest days, passionate in her attachments and antagonisms, peculiarly sensitive. How could one reproach her for this heightened sensibility? A plate-armoured heart is to a writer what blindness is to a painter or deafness to a composer. The vulnerability of an exposed heart may be at the root of the tragic fate of so many writers. (pp. 252-53)

Ilya Ehrenburg, "Marina Tsvetayeva's Poetry,"
translated by Tatiana Shebunina and Yvonne Kapp,
in his Chekhov, Stendhal, and Other Essays,
Grafton Books, 1963, pp. 245-57.

ANDREW FIELD   (essay date 1965)

[*Field is an American-born Australian biographer, novelist, and critic who has devoted much of his career to studying the life and works of Vladimir Nabokov. In the following excerpt, he examines the religious and typically Russian elements in Tsvetaeva's poetic epitaph* Poems to Blok.]

Marina Tsvetaeva was born, the daughter of a professor, in 1892. Her first book of verse, *Evening Album,* appeared when she was only eighteen, and it was followed by another, *Magic Lantern,* in 1912. About this book a well-known poet and critic [Vladislav Khodasevich] observed at the time: "[Tsvetaeva] is a poetess with a certain gift. But there is something unpleasantly treacly in her descriptions of a semi-childish world, in her tender emotion before all that comes to hand. . . . Perhaps two or three such poems would be pleasant. But a whole book in a nice little velvet cover, and in a cardboard protective sheath, and published by 'Ole-Luk-Oie'—no. . . ."

But on her tortuous path, leading from pre-revolutionary Russia into emigration and at last to Soviet Russia (where she died by her own hand in 1941), Tsvetaeva's poetic voice acquired a strength and character and, above all, an originality which earn her an eminent place among modern Russian poets. With its strong, chafed emotion and driving, hooflike rhythm, her verse forges a hard and brilliant poetic surface from an unmistakably feminine voice. Tsvetaeva's poetry has long enjoyed the praise of a small but important group of critics and artists, among them D. S. Mirsky, Ilya Ehrenburg, Vladimir Nabokov (not given to extravagance in his favorable judgments, he refers to her [in his *Speak, Memory*] as "poet of genius"), and Boris Pasternak who, in 1956, wrote [in *Sobranie sochinenii*]: "I think that a very great reconsideration and a very great acknowledgement await Tsvetaeva." Unfortunately the critical literature on her has remained miniscule . . . so much so, in fact, that the present essay represents the first critical treatment of her (apart from mention in literary surveys) in English. But now, surprisingly soon, Tsvetaeva has been "resurrected" in Russia where her poetry is being republished and can be seen to be exerting a strong formal influence on such important younger poets as Andrei Voznesensky. The word "resurrected" is, I think, a fitting one because Tsvetaeva is in essence a religious poet, an appellation which should be taken as a necessary but by no means a limiting or sufficient description. The religious current in her poetry is particularly evident in her cycle (and sixth book) of poems, *Poems to Blok,* one of Tsvetaeva's major achievements and an outstanding monument of modern Russian poetry.

First, a brief description of the structure of the work. The natural analogy and the probable model for the cycle was, of course, Aleksandr Blok's own famous early volume of Symbolist poetry, *Poems on the Beautiful Lady* (1901-1902). The cycle consists of three parts, the first of which is almost as long as the other two combined. It is also divided in time—the first part was written in 1916 (except for its conclusion, written in 1920), while the two shorter sections were written in 1921, presumably on the occasion of Blok's death. As then might be expected, there is a marked difference in tone between the parts. In the first portion the "high and lofty" language which has been frequently noted in Tsvetaeva—it is worth noting that one of her favorite Russian poets was the 18th century poet Derzhavin—sounds most clearly. The second part is a threnody to Blok in the folk manner: the theme "in which cradle do you lie?" recurs continually, and such motifs as "a prince without a country" and "a friend without friends" bears a distinct folk imprint. The third part is an apostrophe to Russia symbolized as the grieving Virgin; it combines the disparate styles of the first two sections in an intense and stirring counterpoint of imagery and language. There is a valid question, it should be said, as to whether or not *Poems to Blok* ought to be read as a unified work rather than merely a book of poems, but the thematic order and progression of the poems lend great weight to the former reading—it might be best to say that Tsvetaeva, like Eliot, took individual poems on a single theme and "at some point" decided to use them as the basis for a larger whole work.

The central fact about Tsvetaeva's poetry is that its currency is the word itself rather than intricate grammatical structures enveloping an idea. Often she juxtaposes related words which have drifted far apart in meaning and re-establishes the bond between them, as, for instance, the adjective *prazdny* (idle) and the verb *prazdnovat'* (to celebrate):

> Idle hands cross . . .
> —Dead lies the singer
> And celebrates resurrection.

> *Krestyatsya ruki prazdnye*
> *—Myortvy lezhit pevets*
> *I voskresen'e prazdnuet.*

And, conversely, she links together words which are in fact not etymologically related:

> To the wanderer—the road
> To the dead—a hearse

> *Stranniku—doroga*
> *Myortvomu—drogi*

Concern for the value and poetic potentiality of each word is also reflected in Tsvetaeva's fragmented lines:

> In a mist—dove-colored
> You stand, in a chasuble
> Of snow adorned.

> *Vo mgle—sizoy*
> *Stoish', rizoy*
> *Snegovoy odet.*

The position of "chasuble" (*riza*) does not permit the reader to pass over it as a mere substantive in a sentence; a pause is obligatory. Syntax serves the same purpose—it is an attempt, strangely reminiscent of 18th century poetics, to impart new expressive power to the poet's words.

Because Tsvetaeva views art as a sacred function ("In its relation to the spiritual world art is a certain physical world of the spiritual," *Proza.*) her concern for even the outward form of the written word is scarcely less than—and indeed quite analogous to—that of the Russian Old Believers for crossing themselves with two fingers instead of three. The initial stanza of *Poems to Blok* is an incantation of Blok's name:

> Your name—a bird in hand,
> Your name—a bit of ice on the tongue,
> One lone movement of the lips,
> Your name—five letters.

> A ball, caught in flight,
> A little silver bell in the mouth.

>   (pp. 57-9)

The first line invests the name (which is not to say the man) with life, a bird in the hand. Tsvetaeva's stress upon the phonetics and orthography of Blok's name—the five letters where new practice would count but four (after the 1917 Revolution, in a major revision of Russian spelling, the "hard sign" which stood at the end of most nouns and proper names and was not pronounced was dropped)—makes of it a verbal connection with the past. Tsvetaeva was to the end of her life a passionate advocate of the old orthography. Finally, the silver bell in her mouth (poetess as priestess) imitates the muted sound of Blok's name. The importance of this beginning cannot be too heavily emphasized. It is the mainspring of the entire cycle, defining eloquently the spiritual framework of the poems as well as the role of the artist, the language, and the protagonist.

Poems to Blok is not merely, even least of all, a cycle about Blok. It takes Blok as a point of departure as he himself took the "Beautiful Lady." Tsvetaeva's critical essays leave no doubt about the influence of Russian Symbolist poetry upon her, and her statement [in *Proza*] about symbolism ("There are no non-symbols.") is quite explicit. Tsvetaeva's Blok (she knew him only slightly personally) is associated in her imagery with Christ:

> I'll not dig into your soul!
> Inviolable is your way.
> Into your hand, pale from kisses
> I'll not beat my nail.

The cycle is in many respects a verbal icon: "Rays emanated from him / Hot strings along the snow." The image of the cross is in another place suggested by a succession of telegraph poles, a typical instance of Tsvetaeva's juxtaposition of the Biblical with the contemporary:

> Over the wavering and wretched grain
> Pole arises after pole.
> And a wire under heaven
> Sings and sings death.

The telegraph poles reach out in space, but in terms of the cycle's symbolism they also extend in time. Another image conveys this sense even more strongly: "I have sepulchres standing in a row, / In them Tsaritsas sleep, and Tsars." Time in the cycle loses its historical sense and is represented instead as an immediate physical perspective in the present.

Several of the motifs in *Poems to Blok* refer directly to his work. The central image of the broken wing (*perelomennoe krylo*), for example, comes from one of Blok's plays. And an important passage in which the sun serves as an eschatological symbol closely paraphrases one of Blok's most pessimistic poems:

> What days await us, how God
>   will deceive,
> How you'll come to call the sun—and how

>   it won't come up. . . .

Death and impending doom pervade the entire cycle. It menaces not only the prophet but also Russia herself, for the New Jerusalem of necessity requires the destruction of the old. And so Tsvetaeva adjures her vision to depart:

Dear ghost!
I know that all this is my dream.
Do me a favor!
Amen, amen, away!
Amen

The amen rings out like a carillon, but the familiar forms and the formula *amin', amin', rassyp'sya* (ordinarily applied to demonic visitations) produce the odd effect of a kind of sacred exorcism.

In the second part of the cycle the theme of the angel with broken wing alternates with the image of a dying swan, another one of Tsvetaeva's favorite motifs. It is in this portion that Blok appears most clearly as a real person and that emotion is expressed not in terms of worship but in terms of the love and grief of a woman:

To grasp him! More strongly!
Just to love and love him!
O, who will whisper to me
In what cradle do you lie?

(pp. 59-61)

Subsequently Tsvetaeva focuses upon the Virgin before Christ's birth, and the contiguity of expected birth and recent death create an especially poignant effect. The poet repeats a single line from the Scriptures—"Blessed are you among women!" ("*Blagoslovenna ty v zhenakh!*")—and plays off the expression in various ways: "Blessed are you in tears," " . . . in snows."

As *Poems to Blok* ends the theme again returns to death, but at the same time the grief of Russia is an affirmation of life. It is stated in the most solemn Church Slavonicisms:

Lifegiver in the hour of the end!
Affirmer of the Heavenly Kingdoms! Virgin Mother of
    your Son!
Into the death rattle of his mortal torments—
          a torn song!
Was hurled by you in the First: "I Am!" . . .

Marina Tsvetaeva may best be characterized as a Mayakovsky of the Middle Ages, a heretic in an age of non-believers. Her *Poems to Blok* are a living liturgy of Russia and the Russian language. (p. 61)

> *Andrew Field, "A Poetic Epitaph: Marina Tsvetaeva's 'Poems to Blok,'" in* TriQuarterly, *No. 3, Spring, 1965, pp. 57-64.*

JANE ANDELMAN TAUBMAN (essay date 1974)

[*In the following excerpt, Taubman studies the influence of Anna Akhmatova on Tsvetaeva's early poetic development.*]

The only two women to achieve greatness in Russian literature [Tsvetaeva and Anna Akhmatova] were never intimate friends. In fact, they met for the first time only in 1940, after Tsvetaeva's return from her seventeen-year emigration. But neither was ever without an awareness of the other, an awareness which left important traces in the poetry of both, though these traces are less visible in the work of the reserved Akhmatova than in that of the impulsive Tsvetaeva. As so often in Tsvetaeva's "poetic friendships," the *idea* of Akhmatova was more important to her than Akhmatova the *person*. Andrew Field has said about her *Poems to Blok:* "It is not merely, even least of all, a cycle about Blok. It takes Blok as a point of departure as he himself took the 'Beautiful Lady' " [see ex-

cerpt dated 1965]. Thus, it is not surprising that her 1916 **"Poems to Akhmatova"** adulate a woman Tsvetaeva had never met or corresponded with, while their eventual meeting in 1940 seems to have produced no poetry at all. For Akhmatova, it was just the reverse. Only in 1940 did the concrete plight of Tsvetaeva and her family finally give her a place in Akhmatova's poetry.

Tsvetaeva apparently discovered Akhmatova's verse in 1914; Akhmatova probably did not know Tsvetaeva's work before 1915 at the earliest. In January 1916 the 23-year-old Tsvetaeva made a rare trip to Petrograd to be introduced to its literary circles. At a gathering which she describes in her prose essay **"An Otherworldly Evening,"** she did indeed meet many of Petersburg's leading poets, and read her own verse as well. But to her great disappointment, Akhmatova was in the Crimea. Nevertheless, she tells us:

> I read as if Akhmatova and Akhmatova alone were in the room. I read for the absent Akhmatova. My success was necessary to me as a direct route to Akhmatova.

As was not infrequently the case with Tsvetaeva, this "non-meeting" provided the inspiration for a major verse cycle, the eleven **"Poems to Akhmatova."** From the intensity of emotion in the poems, one would hardly suspect that the two women had never met. Read in isolation, they seem embarrassingly overstated—*too* rhetorical, *too* adoring. Yet, in her poems, Tsvetaeva typically treated herself and other poets in such a tone. Casting both them and herself in larger-than-life-size, she identified them with myth-like figures.

Akhmatova, in Tsvetaeva's words, is the "Muse of lamentation," who "sends down a black blizzard on Rus'." She is "alone among us—like the moon in heaven," she "spreads her night over my red Kremlin," "blocks out the sun on high, holds all the stars in her hand." Tsvetaeva's posture is—or seems to be—one of humble reverence before this awe-inspiring "most beautiful of muses." She "holds her head in her hands" as she sings Akhmatova's praises at sunset. She is "happy that, giving [all she has] to Akhmatova, she comes away a beggar." She asks the wind to carry her love to "Goldenmouthed Anna of all Russsia," and would like to stand before her and, "stammering, blushing," lower her eyes, "and fall silent, sobbing like a child receiving forgiveness." Yet we notice that the presence of the "humble worshiper" is itself a central focus of the poems, and that she takes pride in the very quality of her adoration: "Oh, I am happy . . . That it was I who first called you the Muse of Tsarskoe Selo." Adoration is also a form of possession—the adored cannot escape her worshiper:

You cannot fall back! I am a convict.
You are my escort. Our fate is one.

Indeed, while the poems are homage to Akhmatova, they are also a staking-out of Tsvetaeva's own poetic place. For, in her world, only a poet is qualified to praise another poet. This fact becomes even clearer if we look at the cycle in its chronological context, for it is the third group of poems in rapid succession in which Tsvetaeva addresses the poets of Petersburg. In February and March of 1916, she had dedicated four poems to Mandelstam:

What is my untutored verse to you
O young Derzhavin!

In April and May, she composed the first eight poems of the **"Verses to Blok"**:

> Tender specter
> Knight without blame,
> Who has called you
> Into my young life?

What indeed did she, a young, barely recognized Moscow poetess have to offer the poetic luminaries of Petersburg? The answer is simple, and is repeated in each of the cycles: nothing less than Moscow itself. In March, she presented it to Mandelstam:

> Take from my hands, my strange, my beautiful brother—
> This city is not built by any hands.

In May, she stood beside *her* river, the Moskva, addressing Blok, who stood by *his* Neva:

> And you walk by, above your Neva
> While I stand, with head bent, above the river Moskva.

And in June she gave both Moscow and herself to Akhmatova:

> I give you my city of bells
> Akhmatova, and my heart in the bargain.

Speaking again of the **"Otherworldly** ("Nezdeshny"—literally, "Not-here") **Evening"** in Petersburg—the title underlines her Moscow viewpoint—Tsvetaeva stressed her identification with her native city:

> I clearly sense that I am reading on behalf of Moscow. . . . With all my being I sense an intense . . . unavoidable comparison, not only of myself and Akhmatova, but of Petersburg poetry and Moscow poetry, of Petersburg and Moscow. . . .
>
> And if I want to appear in the guise of Moscow, it is not to defeat Petersburg, but to give that Moscow to Petersburg as a gift, to give Akhmatova this Moscow in myself, in my love—to bow before Akhmatova.

The contrast of the two capitols, it hardly needs to be said, is a revered theme in Russian history and culture, which can be traced back through Tolstoy's *War and Peace* to Pushkin's *Bronze Horseman*. Petersburg, city of Peter the Great, is rational, military, angular in architecture, and, appropriately, masculine in grammatical gender. Moscow, representing the organic heart of the nation, is intuitive, religious, medieval in architecture—and feminine in gender. In poems to each of the three poets, Tsvetaeva stresses two symbolic details of the city's architecture—its cupolas and its bells:

> To Mandelstam:The red-gold cupolas shine forth
> The sleepless bells resound
>
> To Blok: In my Moscow cupolas flame
>   In my Moscow bells ring forth
>
> To Akhmatova: In my melodious city cupolas flame
>
>   • • • • •
>
>   And I give you my city of bells . . .

Though it is simply true that church cupolas *did* dominate the skyline of pre-Revolutionary Moscow, and church bells its air, a Freudian would undoubtedly enjoy pointing out the rounded, enclosing nature of both these city-symbols.

It was for Akhmatova, said Tsvetaeva, that she wrote her **"Poems about Moscow"**:

> For the poems about Moscow which followed my arrival in Petersburg I am indebted to Akhmatova, to my love for her, my desire to give her something more eternal than love. . . . If I could simply have given her the Kremlin, I would certainly not have written these poems.

Perhaps. But it is also true that by identifying herself with Moscow, making herself its representative, Tsvetaeva could address the poets of Petersburg—and particularly Akhmatova—as an equal. In fact, in the **"Poems to Akhmatova"** she went one step further, transporting the Petersburg Anna into the alien setting of Marina's Moscow—placing, almost by force, the classical portrait of the "Muse of Tsarskoe Selo" behind the ornate frame of a Muscovite icon-case. In the poems of the cycle, Akhmatova's face acquires the features of the narrow-faced, solemn Byzantine madonna, until, by a masterful reversal of expectations:

> All the icons look with *your* eyes.

The fourth poem is an icon-like portrait of mother (Akhmatova) and child (Lev, her son by the poet Gumilev).

> The name of the child is Lev
> The name of the mother—Anna
> In his name—anger
> In hers—quiet

Its spare verbal strokes mimic the severe stylization and simplification of icon painting. In best iconographic tradition, the infant holds in his hand the representation of his mother's best-known volume of verse:

> . . . in your fist a string
> Of pearly black rosary beads (*chetki*).

It is not only Akhmatova's portrait which Tsvetaeva has woven into her cycle. Like a sorceress, she conjures with her very name:

> . . . Anna
> Akhmatova! That name is a tremendous sigh
> And it falls back into a nameless abyss.

This deep sigh echoes and re-echoes through the cycle. The "Akh" of "Akhmatova" and its doublet, unstressed "okh" occur in prominent position (at the beginning of a line or stanza) five times in the second poem:

> "Okhvatila golovu" (twice), "Akh, neistovaya,"
> "Akh, ya schastliva!" (twice).

The "akh" echoes again in the rhyme in the first stanza of the third poem (vzmakh / prakh). And we cannot help but suspect that the emphasized "*gor*ech i *gor*dost' " of poem 5 echo the real name of Anna Andreevna *Gor*enko.

Akhmatova's poetry, more familiar to Tsvetaeva than her face, naturally plays an important role in the cycle. But, like the portrait of its author, it is reworked in Tsvetaeva's way and for her own purposes (which, it must be admitted, are not always clear). The fifth poem, for example, is obviously an imitation of Akhmatova's 1914 *poema* "At the Very Sea" ("U samogo morya"). In Akhmatova's original, the proud heroine, who lives near Kherson on the Black Sea, rejects the suit of a youth who has brought her white roses. A gypsy predicts she will lure a tsarevich with her songs. After a yachting accident in the harbor, a young skipper in white is carried to shore. As he dies at her feet, the heroine recognizes her promised tsarevich. Tsvetaeva has incorporated these elements of Akhmatova's poem, while altering their form and context. The sea, for some reason, is not the Black but the Caspian; the heroine is not only proud but bitter; the gypsy not only prophesies but lies; the youth's blouse is navy, not white; and in place of the bouquet of white roses there is only "the winglet of a rose." In almost every case, Tsvetaeva's amendments are in the direction of the more dramatic—the more striking—away from the understatement of Akhmatova.

Tsvetaeva's emotional overstatement too often frightened away not only her critics but even those to whom she addressed her poems. To react to her poetry in this way may be to confuse art and reality. Mayakovsky could proclaim:

> Mama!
> Your son is marvelously ill!
> Mama!
> His heart is on fire! ("Oblako v shtanakh," 1914-1915),

and have the firemen arrive to put it out. Or relate how the sun came to join him for tea ("Neobychainoe priklyuchenie," 1920). This is simply "hyperbole." But Tsvetaeva's poetic exaggeration is seen not as a device, but as "hysterics." Has this anything to do with what we expect of the female and by extension the female artist? Would we admire Akhmatova as much for her "self-control" if she were a man?

The question of "art and reality" in Tsvetaeva is a complex one. But, as I have argued elsewhere, her poems and letters, taken together, can give us unusual glimpses into the creative workshop of the poet. It is not only that Tsvetaeva's letters (which were many, and carefully composed) are a wealth of information about her poetic intentions. Even more important is the fact that her volumes of verse are arranged in chronological order, each poem dated not only by year, but also by month and day. Tsvetaeva, I contend, is *asking* us to read her books of verse as a diary of her spiritual life.

We can begin to do this for the next stage of the friendship: two of Tsvetaeva's letters to Akhmatova (written in 1921) have been published [in *Novyi mir,* No. 4 (1969)]. The first, dated April 26, begins in a reasonably restrained tone: "Dear Anna Andreevna" . . . (Tsvetaeva never uses the intimate form of address as she did in her letters to Pasternak). The first paragraphs concern bits of literary business; thanks for a volume of poetry Akhmatova had sent, a request that she inscribe two others, a request to check the galleys of her *poema* **"On a Red Steed,"** which, incidentally, she was dedicating to Akhmatova. (She was already contemplating emigration, and thought the galleys might appear after her departure.)

Suddenly, with little warning, Tsvetaeva unleashes a flood of adulation and praise: "Oh, how I love you, how I rejoice in you, how much pain I feel for you, and how uplifted I feel on account of you. . . . You are my favorite poet—Once, six years ago, I dreamed of you. . . . It grieves me that all this is only words— 'love' —I cannot have it this way—I would rather a real bonfire, in which I would be burned at the stake."

Here it seems, Tsvetaeva has moved into "hysterics" again. But if we turn to **Craft (Remeslo),** the volume of verse which

forms her "lyrical diary" of this period, we find a poem, dated the following day, which begins:

> A soul which knows no moderation
> A flagellant, fanatic soul,
> Craving the whip and flying headlong—
> A butterfly from its cocoon—
> Into the flaming pyre.

It ends: "A soul worthy of the bonfire" ("Dusha, dostoinaya kostra"). Here is the same bonfire of the letter, this time in a poem in which Tsvetaeva seems to castigate herself for her intemperate emotionalism. Yet, at the same time, there is a note of almost Dostoevskian pride in the magnitude of her immoderation. In two other poems dated the same day, Tsvetaeva speaks of envy and jealousy as the "Inborn wound of great souls." It seems more than likely that Akhmatova is their object, that Tsvetaeva's admiration was not unalloyed—certainly another reason for her self-flagellation. Tsvetaeva's "hysterics" are obviously part of a complex of conflicting emotions. But she is not without self-consciousness, and in this "controlled hysteria" we find one source of the power of her art.

In the summer of 1921 a false rumor of Akhmatova's death ran through Moscow. (Her former husband, Gumilev, had just been executed.) In a letter of August 31, Tsvetaeva bitterly caricatures the indifference of Moscow literary circles, and assures Akhmatova that her only true mourner was Mayakovsky, "who wandered through the cardboard of the poet's cafe with the look of a murdered bull." Turning again to **Remeslo,** we should not be surprised to find, at just this date, a **"Fragment from Verses to Akhmatova"** and immediately following it, a poem to Mayakovsky, which addresses him as "heavyfooted archangel." The poem was written, Tsvetaeva later noted in the manuscript, "in gratitude for Akhmatova." A December, 1921, poem titled, **"To Akhmatova"** offers sympathy for the simultaneous loss of her two "assistants and associates" (Blok and Gumilev). Given Tsvetaeva's usual patterns, it seems likely that a corresponding letter existed, and might in fact turn up in her archive. Tsvetaeva was now addressing a *real* Akhmatova, whom she knew at least through her letters, and with whose real tribulations she obviously sympathized. But the sympathy is expressed in a rhetorical tone not terribly different from that of her earlier poems. She even uses one of the same epithets—"Mistress of black magic" ("chernoknizhnitsa")—to describe Akhmatova. And there is, strangely enough, a note almost of taunting irony in this last poem—an indication, perhaps, of a change that was coming in Tsvetaeva's attitude toward Akhmatova.

> Where are your assistants,
> Those comrades-in-arms?—
> O my white-handed one,
> Mistress of black magic (**Remeslo**)

In May, 1922, Tsvetaeva left Soviet Russia for Prague. After her departure, the correspondence with Akhmatova broke off, and Akhmatova plays little or no role in Tsvetaeva's poetry after this date. Tsvetaeva's emigration is itself sufficient explanation for the break. But this event marked another turning-point in Tsvetaeva's poetic biography. Immediately after her emigration, she read Pasternak's *My Sister, Life.* No longer was Akhmatova Tsvetaeva's "favorite poet" and the object of her mythification. Her place had been filled by Pasternak. (pp. 356-64)

A letter from Tsvetaeva to Boris Pasternak, May 26, 1926.

Throughout their lives, Akhmatova and Tsvetaeva were often compared by critics for no other reason than their common femininity. Yet one could scarcely imagine two poets more different in style, temperament, and even vision of their own womanhood. Akhmatova's voice has been characterized as peculiarly "feminine." Even the abuse heaped on her by Zhdanov in 1946 ("half harlot, half nun") stressed her sex. On the other hand, no less an observer than Pasternak has praised Tsvetaeva's "active masculine soul." *Is* there such a thing as a "feminine voice" in poetry? Let us counter that with another question—"Is there such a thing as a *masculine* voice?" "Feminine," I think, should be seen to cover a broad spectrum of attitudes and emotions—different, perhaps, from the masculine spectrum, but coinciding more often than not, and equally wide—wide enough to encompass both the deceptively simple elegance of Akhmatova and the assertive, almost abrasive rhythmicality of Tsvetaeva.

Ariadna Efron, Tsvetaeva's daughter, recently published an excerpt (we can only hope it will be the first of several) from her memoirs. On her mother's friendship with Akhmatova, she says,

> . . . Her lyrical glorifications of Akhmatova were expressions of *sisterly* feelings, carried to their apogee, nothing more. They were indeed sisters in poetry, but far from twins. The absolute harmony, the spiritual plasticity of Akhmatova, which so enchanted Tsvetaeva at first, later began to seem qualities which limited Akhmatova's art and the development of her poetic personality. "She is perfection, and that, alas, is her limitation," said Tsvetaeva about Akhmatova.

Efron's indication of a change in her mother's attitude toward Akhmatova is extremely suggestive. In her early poetry, Tsvetaeva could not avoid the feeling that she was "competing" with Akhmatova for one place as "the woman poet" of their age. Despite their vast differences in temperament and style, Akhmatova, and Akhmatova alone, was the standard to meet. This anomalous situation undoubtedly explains much of the conflicting emotion behind the poems to Akhmatova, indeed the reason Tsvetaeva turned to her again and again in this period of seeking her own poetic identity.

Immediately after her emigration, Tsvetaeva found this identity, in the poems of *After Russia* (*Posle Rossii*), her finest and most mature lyrics. That this period of intense creativity occurred under the star of Pasternak is an indication of Tsvetaeva's liberation. Free from seeking her "sister poet," she could see herself simply as a "poet," one of a brotherhood in which only genius mattered. (pp. 366-67)

> *Jane Andelman Taubman, "Tsvetaeva and Akhmatova: Two Female Voices in a Poetic Quartet," in* Russian Literature Triquarterly, *No. 9, 1974, pp. 355-69.*

ANTONINA FILONOV GOVE (essay date 1977)

[*In the following excerpt, Gove examines Tsvetaeva's poetic treatment of traditional feminine roles and stereotypes.*]

In examining the development of Tsvetaeva's lyric verse, it is possible to discern a recurrent thematic strain: a rejection by the poet of the conventional roles imposed on the individual by society, particularly certain characteristics of the feminine role. I will try to show that Tsvetaeva, in the process of

rejecting, via her poetry, this key ingredient in a person's self-concept—namely, the sex role as defined by society—along with a rejection of other limiting social norms, developed images of the self that transcend social roles. Moreover, the working out of this poetic identity is not continuous but falls into several chronological stages.

In discussing a poet's self, critical method prescribes that a distinction be maintained between the individual and the poetic persona. Without negating this methodological stricture, it is important to keep in mind that for some poets an adequate interpretation requires one to perceive that the persona is an elaborate poetic projection and mythologization of the individual. A well-known case in point is provided by the poetry of Mayakovsky. In regard to Tsvetaeva, Jane Taubman's assessment is persuasive: "Tsvetaeva . . . is *asking* us to read her books of verse as a diary of her spiritual life" [see excerpt dated 1974]. Tsvetaeva herself made explicit statements to this effect. . . . Tsvetaeva defines the relationship between her individual and her poetic self as one of selection and transformation. To paraphrase her words—work in search of the authentic word is work in search of the authentic self. Poetry is life—life transfigured—*real* life!

Tsvetaeva's letters and prose show her awareness of the limitations of the woman's role and set the stage for its rejection in her verse. The most moving, personal, and explicit account is a description of her mother's life in a letter to V. V. Rozanov (1914), in which she writes:

> Mother's youth, like her childhood, was lonely, painful, rebellious, deeply introverted. . . . She had a passion for music and enormous talent (never again do I expect to hear anyone play the piano and the guitar like she did), a gift for languages, a brilliant memory, magnificent written style, wrote poetry in Russian and German, painted. . . . When she was twenty-two Mother married Father, with the express intention of replacing the mother of his orphaned children—Valeriia, who was eight, and Andrei, who was one. Father was then forty-four years old. She loved him without reservation, but the first two years of marriage were filled with torment about his continuing love for [his first wife] V. D. Ilovaiskaia. "We were wed at the grave," Mother wrote in her diary. She had much difficulty with Valeriia, trying to befriend this eight-year-old girl, who was completely alien to her in temperament, adored her late mother, and rejected "the stepmother." There was much grief. Mother and Father were totally unlike each other. Each had his own heartache. Mother's was music, poetry, yearning; Father's was scholarship. Their lives moved side by side without merging. But they loved each other very much. Mother died [in 1906] at the age of thirty-seven, discontented, unreconciled. . . . Her tormented soul lives on in us [Marina and her sister Anastasiia], but we reveal what she concealed. Her rebellion, her madness, her longing have grown in us to a scream.

In excerpts from Tsvetaeva's diary of 1919, titled **"O Germanii"** and first published in 1925 in Paris, we find another comment about her mother: "mat' ne zhenski vladela roialem! . . ." ("my mother played the piano with a mastery that was not that of a woman"). This brief aside airs the common notion that great artistic skill, in this case the mother's musical prowess and power, is not a normal feminine attribute.

In Tsvetaeva's first volume of verse (*Vechernii al'bom*), published when the poet was eighteen, we find a poem with two female protagonists, one of whom advocates breaking the rules. It is significant that not the rebel, but the "realist"—the one who maintains that the rules will be observed—repeatedly has the last word. . . .

["Rouge et bleue"]

A little girl in red and a little girl in blue were walking together in the park. "Alina, how about taking off our dresses and going for a swim in the pond?" Shaking her thin little finger in a gesture of reproval, the little girl in blue answered sternly, "Mother says we mustn't."

A young woman in red and a young woman in blue were walking in the evening along the edge of a field. "How about it, Alina, let's leave everything and go away? Say you will!" With a sigh through the spring mist the young woman in blue answered sadly, "Don't talk like that! You know life's not a novel. . . ."

A woman in red and a woman in blue were walking together along a tree-lined avenue. "Don't you see, Alina, we're fading, we're growing cold—prisoners of our happiness. . . ." With a half-smile from the darkness the woman in blue answered bitterly, "Are you surprised? We're women!"

In subsequent volumes of Tsvetaeva's early poetry, we find two conflicting identities. One of these is a stylized pose of traditional girl-woman, which is treated with considerable ambivalence. The other identity is that of a proud, potent, gifted creature, which is treated positively. The following two poems from *Volshebnyi fonar'* show this duality most strikingly. . . .

I'm just a girl. It is my duty, until my marriage vows, not to forget that everywhere there lurks a wolf; to remember that I'm a sheep.

To dream about a golden castle; to rock, bounce, shake—first a doll, then not quite a doll, but almost.

My hand will never wield a sword, will never pluck a string. I'm just a girl, I keep silent. Ah, if only I, too, could

Looking up at the stars, know that there a star has been lighted for me, as well, and smile into all eyes without lowering my own!

The imagery in this poem from the juvenile period consists in the main of a series of stylized clichés. The world seen as proper to the girl speaker of the poem is one of dreams about a *golden castle*. Her destiny is to rock a *doll* in mechanical fashion (*kachat', kruzhit', triasti*—rock, bounce, shake), and even the later role of motherhood has as its object merely an almost-doll. The outside world is likewise given expression by means of conventional imagery. Its dangers are represented by the symbolic *wolf*. The unattainable (male) roles are those of *warrior,* metonymically represented by a *sword,* and of musician or bard, represented by a *stringed instrument.* The behavior appropriate to the girl speaker is to be submissive—she is a *sheep* and she is *silent*. The speaker of the poem accepts her fate, but longs for a star of her own in the firmament—perhaps a star of achievement and fulfillment. The conclusion of the poem represents the longed-for freedom as

permissibility to smile at others without being required to lower one's gaze.

In the next poem, written in the same period, the speaker rejects the role proper for a woman: . . .

On a May morning rock a cradle? Put my proud neck in a rope halter? The captive has her spinning wheel, the shepherdess her pipe, I have my drum.

A woman's lot does not attract me: I fear boredom, not wounds! Everything is given me—power and honor—by my drum!

The sun has risen, the trees are in bloom. . . . How many unknown lands there are! Let every sorrow be put to flight. Sound, my drum!

To be a drummer! At the head of the band! Everything else is sham! What else can win hearts along the way like my drum?

In this period and subsequently, until approximately 1920, we continue to encounter in Tsvetaeva's verse the use of imagery and diction drawn from the feminine world or referring to feminine stereotypes. It is important to make a distinction between the notions of *world* and *stereotype*. The former refers to an actual way of life, that is, to experience. Stereotype commonly refers to a mental image or characterization of what a particular group of people is like or should be like. Stereotypes are formed on the basis of real phenomena, but are fragmentary, exaggerated, or generalistic impressions about those phenomena. It is probably the case that stereotypical impressions are produced not by the individuals to whom they refer but by members of other groups, for example, by whites about blacks (or vice versa) or by men about women (or vice versa). However, once the stereotype is established in the culture, it may come to be accepted by the referent group itself. We have already seen some examples of stereotypical imagery in the poem **"Ia tol'ko devochka."** The following stanza from another poem written in the same period contains additional references to feminine stereotypes:

The slow rain keeps falling, it dampens the gold of the curls. The girl stands quietly at the door, the girl waits.

Here "the gold of the curls" is a stereotypical emblem of femininity. In the next stanza we see the girl waiting and wondering whether the boy will come: Mal'chik, idi zhe: begi zhe skorei: / Devochka zhdet! This image of the female waiting passively for the male to act is also a stereotypical one, although the language is not specifically so.

One of the feminine images of the earliest period is not stereotypical but concerns an aspect of practical life. This is the reference to the woman's pinned-up coiffure, the *pricheska,* that is contrasted to the loosely hanging hair worn by young girls (examples of both may be seen in the photographs in Anastasiia Tsvetaeva's memoir). The *pricheska* appears in a poem in the volume *Vechernii al'bom*: . . .

Our mother doesn't like the heavy hairdo—you just lose time and hairpins!

It reappears in *Volshebnyi fonar',* an emblem of the conventional restrictions placed on the adult (woman), as opposed to the freedom of the child: . . .

Oh, why have I grown up? There's no escaping! Only yesterday I could run off in the morning, free, to the green birches. Only yesterday I could play without a hairdo. Only yesterday! . . . What lies ahead? What ill fortune? Everything harbors deception and, alas, everything is forbidden!

In the collection *Versty I,* which was published in 1922 but which contains poetry written in 1916, the treatment of stereotypical women's roles is shifted to new ground. First, instead of the *object* imagery of the juvenile period—such as the negative (restrictive) emblemata of dolls, dresses, and hairdos, or the positive, liberating emblem of the drum—the imagery is predominantly drawn from the *animate* world. Second, instead of uttering *explicit* pronouncements . . . , the poetic persona is shown negating conventional social expectations *implicitly* by means of nonconventional identities in a variety of imaginative scenarios. This continues to be Tsvetaeva's *modus operandi* in the 1930s. In the poems in *Versty I,* the speaker maintains a feminine identity, indeed emphasizes it, but it is a frankly Romantic one, drawn from folklore and endowed with heroic, legendary, or magic attributes.

In this period, the role conflict is no longer the merely anticipated one of the juvenile period. Tsvetaeva is now twenty-four years old, established in the roles she has questioned (her marriage to Sergei Efron took place in early 1912 and their daughter Ariadna was born in December of the same year), and also irrevocably committed to poetry. The dual creative power of motherhood and of verbal art is represented as an antithesis of light and darkness in a strikingly joyous poem written on the eve of the Feast of the Annunciation (March 25), in which the speaker prays in the Cathedral of the Annunciation. . . .

> "Blessed is the fruit of thy womb, Virgin dear!" . . . Bright, hot is the lighted candle.
>
> To the Sun-Mother, I, lost in the shadows also call, rejoicing: "Mother, for a mother preserve my blue-eyed daughter! Illumine her with bright wisdom; guide her in the lost path of goodness. Grant her health; at the head of her bed set the Angel who has flown from me. Guard her against verbal splendors so she doesn't turn out like me—a predator, a practitioner of black magic."

As a mother, the speaker shares the joy of Mary and addresses her in a tone of intimacy and trust. However, her prayer is uttered only on behalf of her child. She herself does not emerge into the light that emanates from the "Sun-Mother," remaining "in the shadows." Moreover, she has "lost the way of goodness," has been abandoned by her guardian angel, and has been rendered, through the excesses of her art, a "predator" and a "magician." She asks that her daughter be spared such a fate and instead be "illumined by bright wisdom." (Of course, one should avoid the mistake of identifying life and art too closely. Only a few years later Tsvetaeva delighted in her daughter's literary precocity.)

The speaker's association with sin and magic is a recurrent motif in this volume, revealing a continuing ambivalence about the social and personal definition of the self. The ambivalence, however, is largely an implicit one deducible from the attributes assumed by the personae of the poems. The one explicit statement about the roles of women appears in a poem written in April. Using folk diction and imagery characteristic of this period, the speaker promises to her interlocutor that, should she choose to be his lover, she will be a lover of legendary accomplishments—but she will not undertake any of the conventional women's roles. She will be neither wet nurse, nor wife, nor widow, nor maiden waiting for her intended. . . .

> If I should love you—you will never tire of it! I am renowned as a mother-of-god—the three-handed one: with one hand, I smite down fortresses, the second is far away, with the third I write on waves—a letter to the fishes. Only as a wet nurse I won't do—a cradle rocker!
>
> If I seem to be a wife—where's my wife's kerchief? If I seem to be a widow—where's my deceased? If I'm waiting for my betrothed—where's my sleeplessness? No, I'm the Tsar-Maiden—I live outside the law!

In a poem written in 1918, a year after the birth of her second child, Tsvetaeva again expresses her ambivalence toward social convention, on the one hand, and her individual affinities, on the other. With barely concealed irony, the speaker presents herself as performing the functions imposed by society and a personal sense of duty, but in conclusion affirms her love for the antisocial. The images are stylized in folk idiom. . . .

> I rinse the laundry in the river; I raise my two little flowers. When the bell tolls, I cross myself; when they confine me without food, I fast. My soul and hair are smooth as silk. More precious than life to me is a good reputation. I solemnly observe my duty. But—I love you, thief and wolf!

It is relevant at this point to interpose some observations on those of Tsvetaeva's long poems and dramas in verse that have a bearing on her thematic rejection of sex-role stereotypes. Two of the *poemy, Tsar'-devitsa* and **"Na krasnom kone,"** and one of the verse dramas, *Prikliuchenie,* feature, in some form, a reversal of sex roles. Chronologically *Tsar'-devitsa* (written in 1920) and *Prikliuchenie* (written probably in 1919) are intermediate between the poems of *Versty I* and *Remeslo,* the latter containing poetry written in 1921-22. The second long poem, **"Na krasnom kone,"** was written in January 1921 and, as pointed out by Karlinsky [in his *Marina Cvetaeva: Her Life and Art*], is stylistically related to the poems of *Remeslo.*

Tsar'-devitsa is an epic poem based on tales collected by Afanas'ev. The title heroine is a warrior-maiden of unwomanly size, strength, and martial prowess. She is first introduced in a hyperbolic vision: . . .

> The maiden [rides] at the head! Her stature is that of a giant, her girdle—a coiled serpent, her head reaches the stars, from her head [waves] a mare's tail, the moon [hangs] in her ear for an earring. . . .

In a dialogue with her *niania* she denies any desire for suitors: . . .

> My bridegroom is my bright sword, my saber-like joyous sword: I need no other companion!

She addresses her army in a thunderous voice: . . .

> "Hail, my mighty-powerful troops," thunders the thunderlike voice.

Her army greets her by likening her to Michael, the warrior angel. Her step is heavy: . . .

> As she mounted the steps with a two-ton step . . .

She falls in love with a young prince who is her very antithesis: . . .

> I'm a narrow-chested boy, unfamiliar with martial ways. The singing psaltery is the only law I know!

When the Tsar-Maiden first sees the young prince, she lovingly compares his delicate, ring-bedecked hand with her own massive, swarthy, ringless "paw": . . .

> She compares his hand with hers: "Like a dry little breadcrust without any soft part! Yours is a little feather, mine is a large paw. And each of your fingers is like a tsar in armor, while my hand is swarthy and ringless. Yours is for embroidering tapestries, mine for uprooting oak stumps."

Similarly, his hair is fine and silky, while hers is coarse like horsehair: . . .

> Your hair is fine like flax! Mine—like horsehair, like resonant strings!

I owe to Anya M. Kroth the observation that the Tsar-Maiden and the Tsarevich are two examples of androgyny, she of the strong masculine woman, he of the gentle, feminine man, each possessing characteristics of both sexes. Tsvetaeva develops, at some length, the idea that in these two lovely androgynous creatures the conventional opposition of male to female is confounded: . . .

> I look and am in a quandary: which is the maiden and which her sweetheart? Untwine, rope! Which is the young man, which the young girl? Is that one the youth?—no, she's too round of face, is that one the youth?—no, the hand is too small: They're like two strands of one braid, two pretty young girls. [On the other hand], their appearance is, well— maybe it's two young fellows? Is that one the girl?—no, he/she looks straight through you. Is that one the girl?—no, the knees are apart! They are like two joints of one hand—two handsome young men.

Since neither protagonist quite fits the masculine or the feminine stereotype, the author invites readers to suspend rational categories and draw their own conclusions about the Tsar-Maiden and the Tsarevich. The author's own preferred solution seems to be that the whole issue of sexual identity is an illusion. Might not the Tsarevich and the Tsar-Maiden ultimately represent a meeting of two angelic beings, she asks hopefully: . . .

> But if we take a keener look—why it's all a deception, smoke [wafting] above the mist—is it a seraph [bending] over a cherub?

Tsvetaeva's second long poem, **"Na krasnom kone,"** is a lyrical narrative about the arduous making of a poet. The heroine, who is also the first-person narrator, avers that she has been guided not by a (feminine) Muse but by her own poetic (masculine) Genius, who is personified as a knight on a red steed. The narrative is developed by means of the folkloric motif of the quest, during which the heroine undergoes three temptations. Through the intervention of the the Genius, she renounces, in turn, her childish affections for treasured objects and her attempt to give herself to the crucified Christ. In the course of the third temptation she experiences the pain and rage of unrequited love and rejects her womanliness to become, herself, a mounted warrior. She is vanquished by a mysterious ray of light that penetrates her heart, whereupon

the Genius acknowledges her as his chosen one and extracts a vow of fidelity: . . .

> And the whisper: "[Now] you are as I desired you!" And the murmur: "[Now] you are as I elected you, Child of my passion—[my] sister—[my] brother— [my] bride in the ice of armor.
>
> My own and no one's—till the end of years." I with arms raised: "[My] light!" "You will remain so? You will not be anyone's? No one's?" I, clutching my wound: "No."

The transition into what may be called the "middle period" occurs in the year 1920, and this period lasts through approximately 1927. There is not only an observable change in the imagery, but also a general poetic evolution and maturing on many levels. Biographically the entry into the middle period is marked by the death of her young daughter Irina of starvation in a state foster home; by emigration; by reunion with her husband, Sergei Efron, after five years of separation; and by her passage into her fourth decade of life. The poetic product of the period includes the poems in **Remeslo** and finds its culmination in **Posle Rossii.** Additional poems of the period were collected for the first time in the 1961 and 1965 Soviet editions of her works. The middle period of Tsvetaeva's *oeuvre* is, of course, extremely complex. I will only point out the most salient themes that seem to represent the poet's continuing rejection of the conventional woman's role and her continuing personal and artistic individuation.

The recurring image of the self as a disembodied (poetic) voice first appears in a poem written in April 1920: . . .

> Wives aren't jealous of me: I'm [just] a voice and a glance.

Next we note the gradual disappearance of the conventional feminine imagery, especially the external, girlish accouterments referring to the poetic persona. In a poem in May 1920 Tsvetaeva still uses the image of a pink dress moved by the wind as an emblem of capriciousness in the self: . . .

> I am not dancing—it is not my fault that the pink dress is moving in waves.

The windblown dress is held down by the speaker and the octave concludes: . . .

> Oh, if I could control Whim the way I can control my dress blown [or: excited] by the wind!

Similarly, in a poem written just a day earlier—the well-known **"Kto sozdan iz kamnia, kto sozdan iz gliny"**—the speaker refers to her curls (*kudri*) as a sign that she in no way can be considered "the salt of the earth." However, in a poem written three months later, in August 1920, we find that the pretty face (*lichiko*) and the play of passions are ascribed by the speaker not to herself but to others: . . .

> Others dally with bright eyes and a pretty face, but I in the night converse with the wind. Not that one—the Italian one, the young zephyr—no, with a good, sweeping Russian gale!

The poem is concluded with the words: . . .

> Yes, Aeolus treats my kind roughly. [He says:] "Don't worry, you won't melt! You're all the same flesh and blood!" As if in truth I were not a woman!

The last phrase—perhaps I'm really not a woman—sounds

an important note that is elaborated in several ways in subsequent poems. In *Remeslo* Tsvetaeva employs, as in the long poems discussed above, a reversal of sexes, notably in the cycle **"Uchenik,"** where the speaker desires to be a young male disciple and martyr: . . .

> To be your fair-haired boy—O, through the ages!
> To walk behind your dusty purple in a coarse pupil's cloak.

In the cycle **"Georgii,"** dedicated to her husband, St. George the Dragon-slayer is described as modest, shy, humble, and gentle, with long beautiful eyelashes and the eyes of a deer. His saddle and spear are referred to using diminutives (*sedlet-so, kop'etso*). He pales and weeps after his victory and refuses the maiden that is to have been his reward for slaying the dragon.

Remeslo contains one of the first allusions to the Amazons, the proud strong warrior women with whom the poet feels a kinship. The entire poem is quoted here because it offers yet another example of Tsvetaeva's complex poetic attitude toward the feminine: . . .

> A woman's breast! A frozen sigh of the soul, a woman's essence! A wave that is always taken unawares and always takes you unawares—as God is my witness!
>
> A playground for disdained and disdainful pleasures. A woman's breast!—A yielding armor/weapon! I'm thinking of them—Those one-breasted ones—those friends! . . .

Although the concluding three hemistichs of the poem are suggestive rather than explicit, I submit that Tsvetaeva may be sensing a parallel between the Amazons, who sacrificed part of their essential femininity (by amputating their left breast) to the requirements of their craft—archery in warfare—and her own sacrifice of the merely feminine self to the craft of poetry.

In *Posle Rossii,* Tsvetaeva continues to develop the theme of an equality between a man and a woman, although there are only a chosen few—Siegfried and Brunhilde, Achilles and the Amazon queen Penthesileia, and Tsvetaeva herself and her poetic equal, Boris Pasternak. In July 1924, in a poem addressed to Pasternak, she writes: . . .

> In a world where everyone is bent and in a lather [like a horse], I know—there is one of equal strength with Me.
>
> In a world where everything is mold and ivy, I know—you alone are equal in being to Me.

No longer does the poet claim that the world bars her from self-affirmation, as in the poems of the juvenile period. Her problem, indeed, appears to be the opposite—she can find virtually no one who is her equal in range and power.

The poetic speaker of this period repeatedly identifies herself with heroic women, and is concerned with her soul and her vocation as a poet. Of the several mythological figures that exerted a fascination on Tsvetaeva, a telling one is the sibyl, the subject of a poem written in 1921 and of the cycle of three poems in *Posle Rossii.* In the context of the present discussion, the sibyl can be seen as representing the agelessness and selflessness of the poetic (vatic) self, which is a passive receptacle of a god. A parallel is drawn between the sibyl, as the mythological oracle of Apollo, and Mary, who served as the

receptacle of the Incarnation of Christ the Word (voice). Mortality is overcome, and a cosmic dimension gained, but at the expense of human life: . . .

> The sibyl is prophetic! The sibyl is a vault! Thus the Annunciation came to pass in that
>
> Never-aging hour, thus into the grayness of grasses (merged) mortal virginity, becoming a cave
>
> For the marvelous voice . . .—thus into the astral whirlwind (traveled) the sibyl, who had left the ranks of the living.

In contrast to the sibylline cosmic though lifeless identity, the affirmation of unconventional but earthly womanhood reaches its culmination in this period. In a poem written in June 1922 the poet says: . . .

> Hail / hello! It is not an arrow or a stone: it is I, the most alive of women: Life! With both hands [I plunge] into your unfinished sleep.

Here the speaker contends that she is a living woman—and more. Being a woman, she is not limited by the feminine gender of the noun *zhizn'*—as was Pasternak's speaker in his apostrophe to life, "Sestra moia—zhizn'!" ("My sister—life!")—to claiming merely a metaphorical blood kinship with life. The female persona of Tsvetaeva's poem can claim to be life itself.

A major poem of the mature period, which continues the theme of rejection of the conventional woman's role, is **"Poezd zhizni,"** written in October 1923. In this poem, the train is a metaphor of violent death. The poet no longer is rejecting stereotypes but the actual, to her unacceptable, minutiae that dominate the lives of women. While it can be argued that men suffer from *byt* no less than do women—a convincing poetic case was made by Mayakovsky—no man, but many a woman finds her private hell defined by just the realia enumerated in the excerpt quoted below: . . .

> O how natural to go into a third-class carriage from the staleness of parlors and kitchens!
>
> Where warmed-up cutlets and cooled-down cheeks . . . Let's get away from it, my soul! Even a gutter is better than this deadly falsity:
>
> Of curling papers, diapers, hot curling irons, singed hair, bonnets, oilcloths, toilet waters, of family happiness and dressmaking joys (klein wenig!), "Did you pack the coffeepot?," of biscuits, pillows, matrons, nannies, stuffiness of governesses, baths.
>
> I don't want to wait for my hour of death in this hamper of female flesh! I want the train to drink and sing: death, too, is classless.

Here, as in other poems of this period, there is no longer a duality between the conventional and the individual *within* the poetic persona. The conventional is ascribed to others or rejected out of hand. In a poem written in November 1924, Tsvetaeva uses related imagery to go even further, rejecting her very body as an unacceptable limiting part of the self. . . .

> I sang like arrows. The body? None of my business!

This poem brings us to the most prominent emblem representing the poet's freedom from convention—the image of the soul—which is joyously celebrated in a poem of February 1923: . . .

> Higher! Higher! Catch—the flying one! Without asking permission of the paternal vine, she splashes like a Nereid, a Nereid [diving] into the azure!

The poem concludes by envisioning the soul dancing above corpses, dolls, and other inauthentic realia of *byt,* as a fiery, seraphic, *true* being: . . .

> Thus, above your games for high stakes (among corpses and dolls!), not pinched and poked, not bought, blazing and dancing—six-winged, hospitable, among imaginary beings—fall prostrate!—a true being, not suffocated by your carcasses—the Soul!

The series of poems occasioned by Tsvetaeva's profound emotional involvement with Boris Pasternak is important in the definition of the self in the middle period. In this poetry of longing and passion, an identity is established between the persona and certain tragic heroines who have suffered unrequited love or tragic separation—Ariadne, Phaedra, Ophelia, Eurydice. The ultimate love is represented by the passionate devotion of Mary of Magdala and the compassionate response of Jesus, which are played out in the cycle of three poems titled **"Magdalina."** As suggested by Karlinsky, the use of mythological, literary, and scriptural tradition to express a private anguish imbues the poems with a sense of universality and gives them a dimension larger than life.

The two dramatic poems titled ***Ariadna*** (originally *Tezei*) and ***Fedra*** are part of the middle period, both chronologically and stylistically. These dramas, with their heroic female figures (the chaste and manly goddess Artemis, the passionate Amazon warrior Antiope, and the tragic Phaedra) reflect a wide range of attitudes toward women: disparagement (by Minos of his daughter Ariadne), disdain or disgust (by the misogynist Hippolytus for Phaedra and other women), celebration (of Artemis by the chorus of young hunters and of Phaedra after her death by a chorus of women), adoring admiration (of Hippolytus's mother, the Amazon, by Hippolytus and his old servant), and empathy (by the poet, for the impotent lust of Phaedra's old nurse). Strictly speaking, these representations of conventional and unconventional attitudes toward women cannot be viewed as attempts to define the poetic self in the same way as can the lyric poetry, since they are uttered by and about third-person dramatic characters. Yet the emotional intensity with which the dramatis personae are made to speak, and the extraordinary vividness with which their experiences are presented, particularly in ***Fedra,*** betray an identification of the poet with her characters.

One of the most important aspects of the definition of poetic identity in the verse of Tsvetaeva's middle period is, undoubtedly, the image of the self as poet. This is a large subject deserving separate study. I shall refer here only to the brilliant cycle of three poems titled **"Poety,"** written in April 1923, which celebrates the anticonventional role of poets. In the first poem, poets are said to violate every expectation, such as the law of gravity and normal causality. In the second poem they are paradoxically termed outcasts who dare to rival the gods. In the last poem of the cycle, the speaker begins by describing herself as being blind and a stepchild in a world of the sighted who have fathers (Chto zhe mne delat', sleptsu i pasynku. / V mire gde kazhdyi i otch i zriach . . .). She reverses herself after the first stanza and

concludes the poem by claiming to be a singer (bard) and the first-born in a gray world of weights and measures: . . .

> What shall I do, a singer and first-born in a world where the blackest is gray! Where inspiration is stored as in a thermos bottle! With my limitlessness in a world of [weights and] measures?!

This poem anticipates Tsvetaeva's last period in that her rejection of stereotypical roles is no longer formulated with reference to the limitations of feminine roles. Instead, it is presented as an antithesis between poetry and *byt,* a radical alienation of the poet from social convention.

Examination of the poetry of Tsvetaeva's last poetic period, after the publication of ***Posle Rossii*** in 1928, shows that the issue of the feminine role is no longer explicitly raised. I would argue, however, that it has not been simply abandoned. Rather, it is in some respects integrated into a vision of the self-as-poet. I will support this argument by examining two poems from the period. They were written in 1935 and 1934, respectively, a dark time for Marina Tsvetaeva the individual, marked by unremitting poverty and by political, social, and literary ostracism in Paris émigré circles.

In the first poem, the poet is seen as one who accepts complete self-renunciation by subordinating the self to the poetic vocation. The first stanza reads: . . .

> There are fortunate men and women who *can't* sing. It is their lot to weep. How sweet it is to pour out one's grief in a gushing torrent.

The text continues, in part: . . .

> But to me my calling is like a scourge—amidst the wailing at the tomb, duty orders—sing!

The poem is concluded by a telling couplet, which is a paraphrase of the Biblical "the Lord giveth, the Lord taketh away": . . .

> For if a voice is given to you, poet, everything else is taken away.

It is significant that, in this deeply felt, personal poem, reference to the first person is made only once, in the oblique case. This poem is not egocentric. The question of the woman's role is not raised. The poetic gift and the poetic sacrifice of self transcend the realm of social roles. Indeed, the persona claims a kinship between herself and two (male) poets of antiquity—Orpheus and the Biblical David.

In the second poem, poetry and the poet's life blood are presented as an identity: . . .

> I have opened my veins: unrestrainably, unrestorably life gushes out. Go ahead, bring bowls and plates: every plate will be too shallow, every bowl too flat. Spilling out and *over*—into the black earth, to feed the reeds. Irretrievably, unrestrainably, unrestorably verse gushes out.

In this powerful short poem, the references to the woman's world are not obvious, but I believe they are present and are integrated into the very compact statement of the text. The poet ironically invites the world to receive and store her lifeblood—poetry—in mundane domestic utensils (bowls and plates), which are emblems of the shallowness of *byt* drawn from the domain of women. The attempt to contain poetry in such pedestrian vessels is bound to fail. The contrasting, symbolically appropriate "receptacle" for living creation is the black (that is, fertile) earth. It is limitless in its capacity to absorb the abundant poetic nourishment offered by the poet and it, like poetry, is organic, not man-made, and thus a viable medium for furthering natural life and growth.

Reference to the persona in this poem is again minimal, occurring only in the past tense feminine verb form that is the first word of the poem—*vskryla*. It is important, however, that of the two key words constituting the terms of the equation of the poem—life and verse—one is feminine and the other masculine: *zhizn'* and *stikh*. I suggest that this is yet another instance of Tsvetaeva's many poetic attempts to remove the barrier between the masculine and the feminine, in this case on the grammatical—hence subconscious—level. I believe it is especially significant that the function of the poet's gift of life is defined as feeding—*pitat'*—the quintessential feminine and, in the Judaeo-Christian tradition, a sacramental function. Even as the mundane, conventional paraphernalia of the *byt* of food preparation (*miski, tarelki*) are rejected, so is the life-giving, nurturing, self-sacrificing role of the poet embraced.

It has been shown that Tsvetaeva, in her early poetry, took as one of her themes the limiting aspects of the woman's social role and questioned this role as applied to the poet's self. In this period, the woman's role was poetically represented by using images of the feminine stereotype. In *Versty*, the persona assumed masks of Romantic, anticonventional women; and in *Tsar'-devitsa* and *Prikliuchenie*, as well as in some of the short poems of the early twenties, key protagonists were represented with the masculine and feminine attributes reversed or confounded. In Tsvetaeva's mature period, represented by the collections *Remeslo* and *Posle Rossii*, the poet voiced outright rejection of actual components of the woman's role, rather than of stereotypical images. The rejection was accompanied by the creation of a multiplicity of poetic representations and self-representations. These range from the emblems of the strong, proud woman (for example, the Amazon), to the vatic voice (the sibyl), and to the free transcendent being (the soul). In this and the subsequent period, the poetic voice and poetic creation were affirmed as the essence of life.

One wonders what meaning Tsvetaeva's quest for a self-determined identity had for her contemporaries. Some of the critical animus against her was surely provoked by her loud, exclamatory poetic voice and her proclamations of power and autonomy, rather than by the avowed disapproval of her poetic modernity and her near-blasphemous political individualism. Today, thirty-five years after Tsvetaeva's death, in the context of the ongoing reaction by women and men against social stereotypes, the passionate existential rebellion embodied in her art is both familiar and meaningful. (pp. 231-55)

> *Antonina Filonov Gove, "The Feminine Stereotype and Beyond: Role Conflict and Resolution in the Poetics of Marina Tsvetaeva," in* Slavic Review, *Vol. 36, No. 2, June, 1977, pp. 231-55.*

ROBIN KEMBALL (essay date 1980)

[*In the following excerpt, Kemball discusses the reflection of Tsvetaeva's personality and philosophy of life in* The Demesne of the Swans.]

Like other cycles of Tsvetaeva's, [*The Demesne of the Swans*]

represents a type of diary in verse, a diary that runs, literally, from the day of the Tsar's abdication ["**Clouds above the Chapel—Wisps of Pale-Blue Air**"] to the end of that fateful year (1920) which saw the final, irremediable defeat of those "White Swans" who were, for Tsvetaeva, at once the embodiment and the symbol of all those values she prized and held most dear—courage and steadfastness, honor and loyalty, nobility, grandeur, magnanimity, and unswerving devotion to DUTY—the word, as she wrote in her favorite among the present poems ["**Those Spared—Will Die, Those Fallen—Rise from Under**"], that future generations would inscribe in their dictionaries beside the word DON.

But, if *The Demesne of the Swans* is a diary in verse, it is much more than a mere chronicle of events set down in rhyme and rhythm. Even the poems alluding to Tsvetaeva's family life . . . are deeply imbued with the atmosphere of the times and include striking reflections on the deeper meaning of things, as part of the poet's world view, her whole philosophy of life. The same could be said of the other "personal" poems—those on the death of A. A. Stakhovich ["**Not Because They Shuttered Up and Closed the Bakers',**" "**Two Lowly Tokens of My Grief**," and "**Ex—Ci-Devant**"], the poem addressed to Balmont ["**To Balmont**"], or the impression of Blok ["**To Blok**"]—as it could also be said, *mutatis mutandis,* of the poems dealing with "public" happenings—contemporary social, political, or military events. But the wealth of content does not stop there. The poems of *The Demesne of the Swans* are steeped in history—mainly Russian history—and it is Tsvetaeva's *sense* of history, and of the meaning of that history, that lends the cycle its peculiar depth, its rich symbolism, its unusual power of conviction. From the campaign of Igor and the Mongol invasions of medieval days, through the Time of Troubles and the Polish occupation of Moscow in the early seventeenth century, we pass on, from the misdeeds of the False Dimitri, to those of Stenka Razin and—ultimately, and most insistently—to those of Peter, named the Great, whom Tsvetaeva at one stage roundly accuses of bearing prime responsibility for the crimes of the Bolsheviks and the destruction of Russian culture (a parallel also developed by the philosopher Berdyaev). Even the Decembrist Revolt gets a passing mention, alongside the French Revolution ["**Your Temple, So Stern and So Stately**"]; there is also the death of André Chénier under the Terror ["**André Chénier Died by the Guillotine**" and "**I Cannot Tell in the Dark**"] and—in two contradictory contexts, characteristic of Tsvetaeva's capacity for multiple points of view—Napoleon Bonaparte himself ["**Bent over the Map, Unsleeping**" and "**When the Red-Haired Imposter, Fell Dimitri**"]. These references are far from exhaustive; many of the *leitmotifs* are difficult to pinpoint with accuracy, inasmuch as they recur in isolated passages at different stages of the cycle. The same applies to many of the stylistic or metric devices, especially those derived from Russian folk-poetry; these include the magnificent imagery, the pathos and the symbolism of the *Lay of Igor's Campaign*, on which Tsvetaeva plays with great effect in a number of different poems, in addition to the more directly derivative *Plaint of Yaroslavna* ["**Hear Yaroslavna**," "**Not So—the Chronicler Lies, Saying Igor Returned Home**," and "**Hear Yaroslavna, Mourning Her Loved One**"]. (pp. 13-14)

Subtly but unmistakably interwoven with the various elements of *The Demesne of the Swans*—emotional, philosophical, historical, stylistic—runs the *ethical factor*—that all-embracing, all-uniting thread that bears the unequivocal imprint of Tsvetaeva's personality. In a famous letter written soon after the Decembrist insurrection, the poet Zhukovsky admonished the young Pushkin (whose talent he admired but whose turbulent political attitudes he abhorred) with the words: "Talent is nothing. The important thing is moral greatness." The remark may well have been a patent (and probably deliberate) exaggeration, but Zhukovsky made his point—and the later, maturer, Pushkin developed and displayed a moral consciousness commensurate with his poetic gift. Tsvetaeva was of the same breed—not for nothing did she once compare herself in this respect to Pushkin's Tatyana (from *Eugene Onegin*). A poet of rare inspiration and intuition, she was also a woman of immense moral stature. An uncompromising, Romantic idealist, she was, as she once explained to her friend, the émigré poet George Ivask, utterly opposed to everything mean or vile, "and in a general way to all organized violence, no matter in whose name it may be perpetrated or by what name it may be called." She was also a passionate defender of lost causes (as Karlinsky puts it, "her basic humanity inevitably brought [her] to take the side of the underdog") and it was these, and other, moral, factors put together, rather than any "political" position as such, that explain her defense of the White cause and her loyalty to the Tsar, just as they explain also the presence in *The Demesne of the Swans* of poems like ["**Tsar and God! Grant Those Your Pardon"**], with its plea for clemency for the Reds (as represented there in the figure of Stenka Razin) or ["**Ah, My Mushroom, Dear White Mushroom!"**], with its theme of the common grief shared by all bereaved mothers, irrespective of which side their sons had been fighting on. (pp. 15-16)

Supreme among Tsvetaeva's loyalties was her unconditional loyalty to her craft: "I *nev*-er at *any* time gave a care for *any*thing *oth*-er than verse!" she once rapped at Ivask across the table of a Paris café ("Mne' *ni*-kogda, *ni* do chego *ne* bylo dela, *kro*-me stikhov!").

Pasternak . . . summed it all up in his characteristic way: "Of course, she was more Russian than all of us, not only in her blood (*sic!*), but in the rhythms that inhabited her soul, in her tremendous, uniquely powerful language . . ."—"She lived an heroic life. She accomplished prodigies every day. They were prodigies of loyalty to the only land whose citizen she (ever) was—(the land of) poetry." (p. 27)

> Robin Kemball, " 'The Demesne of the Swans'—A Tale Within a Tale," in The Demesne of the Swans by Marina Tsvetaeva, translated by Robin Kemball, Ardis, 1980, pp. 11-27.

HENRY GIFFORD (essay date 1981)

[*Gifford is an English educator, short story writer, and critic. In the following excerpt from a review of* The Demesne of the Swans, *Gifford discusses prominent characteristics of Tsvetaeva's poetry and assesses her place in twentieth-century Russian literature.*]

[Joseph] Brodsky maintains that Tsvetaeva's was the most passionate voice in Russian poetry of this century. It recommended her neither to Soviet nor to émigré readers while she was alive, as gradually both camps settled down to their own kinds of conformity. An extreme romanticism makes little appeal to the Western reader today, who cannot, for example, share in her veneration for the Napoleonic idea. Her exultant poem of May 1917 taking the "young dictator" Kerensky for another Napoleon will only deepen our suspicions. Yet this

romanticism was infused, as [V. A.] Rozhdestvensky allows, by an extreme truth of feeling. It is a matter of fidelity to personal vision—a vision that may seem wayward on one plane, but is highly responsible on another. The accompanying quality of arrogance will put on their guard those who deplore Yeats's insistence upon it as a virtue. But with Tsvetaeva it is more like a form of self-discipline, a constant reminder of her commitment. As Elaine Feinstein pointed out when reviewing *A Captive Spirit,* Tsvetaeva made no extravagant claims for the poet. To be such was her own calling; but she never sought to place it above that of the priest or doctor in supplying human needs. By arrogance Tsvetaeva meant perhaps no more than Cartier-Bresson when he said the good photographer should respect fully both his subject and himself.

She exemplifies to perfection what [Boris] Pasternak once called in a famous poem "living by verse." That is an extremely difficult way of life. Whatever the penalties, it will demand admiration for a virtue nobody could ever deny in Tsvetaeva—complete integrity. She knew her own value. An early poem, written in 1913, proclaims that her poetry will have its turn. During the impossible years of exile, when nobody seemed to accord much honour to this poetry except Pasternak—the focus at that time, as [Tsvetaeva's daughter, Ariadna Efron] says, of all her writing—she assured him that a place was lying vacant for her among poets accessible to the Soviet reader. If only her poetry could be published in the Soviet Union, understanding of it would follow, because it was "basically simple." Her need was for nothing less than a national audience. "My *Russian* things (her italics), notwithstanding my isolation, and of their own will, not mine, are intended—for multitudes." . . .

She unfolds in [the poems of *The Demesne of the Swans*] a drama both personal and national, as [Anna] Akhmatova did twenty years later in *Requiem*. Tsvetaeva resembles both [Aleksandr] Blok and Akhmatova in her historical memory, her sense of this particular war in terms of Igor's far-distant campaign and the Tatar invasions. The poems are not in the final balance partisan. She can plead for mercy to Stenka Razin (the seventeenth century Cossack bandit and insurgent who here represents the Bolsheviks) when General Mamontov is threatening Moscow in October 1918.

In another poem she recognizes that White and Red become indistinguishable once they have fallen side by side in battle. It is ultimately of Russia that she writes, not the White resistance; of honour, especially at a time when the skies were falling; and of fidelity, more than ever appropriate to a lost cause. She says in her reminiscences of Mandelstam that "the poet's native condition" is to be "a defender." Her defense of the Swans is on behalf of an ideal Russia, a tradition never realized in durable form, and of a nobility of demeanour which she depicts in her elegies for Alexey Stakhovich, the former Imperial ADC and in the first revolutionary years arbiter of stage deportment. Brodsky claims that only with Tsvetaeva did Russian literature attain a tragic dimension: it was her service to bring out a natural affinity with the tragic in the language itself, long attested by the laments of popular poetry. It is right that the sequence should close with an evocation of Yaroslavna's plaint from *The Lay of Igor's Campaign,* the national epic so close to oral tradition.

For the translator Tsvetaeva poses a difficult problem. Her style is so various: she once maintained that in her work "at least seven poets" were present. Whether she recalls the note of the folk ballad or the eighteenth-century ode, the spare formulations of Baratynsky and Tyutchev, or the sombre pathos of Blok, whatever she writes has a concentrated power. The poem swoops upon an experience, lifts it up with strongly beating wings, and is gone. Therefore the main thing to preserve in translation will be the dynamism of each poem, the imprint made there by feeling that is on the stretch. . . .

Tsvetaeva's poems on the rout of the Swans had small success with the emigration, and it is ironical that her ringing verses about an officer's honour should have gone down extremely well with Red Army men. She believed, as Blok did, that great poetry responds to the very heart-beats of the epoch, catching its particular rhythm. This is the mark of the truly contemporary. As she explained it: "To be contemporary is to create your own time, that is to contend against nine-tenths of it, as you contend against nine-tenths of the first draft." Brodsky, seeking an image to define her position in Russian poetry, turns to [Rainer Maria] Rilke's poem "Der Lesende," translated by Pasternak. There the star at the far end of the village resembles the light in a last house, "and merely enlarges the parishioners' idea of their parish," as Brodsky comments. Although at the extremity, Tsvetaeva is not divorced from Russian literature. Her marvellous sense of the language ensures that her rightful place should be at the centre. It is not the only paradox about this extraordinary poet.

Henry Gifford, "Contending against the Times," in
The Times Literary Supplement, *No. 4066, March
6, 1981, p. 265.*

JOSEPH BRODSKY (essay date 1981)

[*Brodsky is a Russian poet and critic who emigrated from the Soviet Union in 1972 and became an American citizen in 1977. His early poems were considered morally and politically subversive by the Soviet government, which exiled him for a time to a remote collective farm. Nevertheless, Brodsky's eventual flight from the Soviet Union was also an estrangement from the Russian culture of which he felt a rightful part, as well as a separation from the language necessary to his vitality as a poet. This latter deprivation is an especially poignant one for Brodsky, who has explained his view of poetry as a relief from the horrors and absurdities of life and the meaningless vacuum of death. In a line from one of his most admired poems, "Gorbunov and Gorchakov," he states: "Life is but talk hurled into the void." This temperament, along with the often philosophical cast of his poetry, has led critics to link Brodsky with the modern school of existentialism, an affiliation well supported by the important influence played by such precursors of existentialism as Soren Kierkegaard and Fedor Dostoevski in forming Brodsky's artistic vision. Brodsky's work has been well received by English and American critics, many of whom have called him the greatest living Russian poet. In the following excerpt, he discusses the confessional nature of "Novogodnee," a poem Tsvetaeva wrote on the occasion of Rainer Maria Rilke's death.*]

On February 7, 1927, in Bellevue, outside Paris, Marina Tsvetaeva finished "Novogodnee" ("New Year's Greetings"), in many respects a landmark not only in her own work but in Russian poetry as a whole. In terms of genre, the poem can be regarded as an elegy—that is, the most fully developed genre in poetry; and this classification would be proper were it not for certain attendant circumstances, one being that this is an elegy on the death of a poet [Rainer Maria Rilke].

Every "on the death of " poem, as a rule, serves not only as a means for an author to express his sentiments occasioned by a loss but also as a pretext for more or less general speculations on the phenomenon of death per se. In mourning his loss (be it the beloved, a national hero, a close friend, or a guiding light), an author by the same token frequently mourns—directly, obliquely, often unwittingly—himself, for the tragic timbre is always autobiographical. In other words, any "on the death of " poem contains an element of self-portrait. This element is all the more inevitable if the object of mourning happens to be a fellow writer with whom the author was linked by bonds—real or imaginary—too strong for the author to avoid the temptation of identifying with the poem's subject. In his struggle to resist such temptation the author is hampered by his sense of professional guild-like association, by the theme of death's own somewhat exalted status, and, finally, by the strictly personal, private experience of loss: something has been taken away from him; therefore, he must bear some relation to it. It may be that the only shortcoming of these wholly natural and otherwise respectable sentiments is that we learn more about the author and his attitude toward his own possible demise than about what actually happened to the other person. (pp. 195-96)

"Novogodnee," however, is more than a self-portrait, just as Rilke to Tsvetaeva is more than a poet. (Just as a poet's death is something more than a human loss. Above all, it is a drama of language as such: that of inadequacy of linguistic experience vis-à-vis existential experience.) Even irrespective of Tsvetaeva's personal feelings toward Rilke—extremely powerful ones that underwent an evolution from platonic love and stylistic dependence to an awareness of a certain equality—even irrespective of these feelings, the death of the great German poet created a situation in which Tsvetaeva could not confine herself to an attempt at a self-portrait. In order to understand—or even not understand—what had happened, she had to extend the limits of the genre and step up from the orchestra, as it were, onto the stage.

"Novogodnee" is above all a confession. In this regard one feels inclined to mention that Tsvetaeva is an extremely candid poet, quite possibly the most candid in the history of Russian poetry. She makes no secret of anything, least of all her aesthetic and philosophical credos, which are scattered about her verse and prose with the frequency of a first person singular pronoun. The reader, therefore, turns out to be more or less prepared for Tsvetaeva's manner of speech in "Novogodnee"—the so-called lyrical monologue. What he is not at all prepared for, however, no matter how many times he may re-read "Novogodnee," is the intensity of the monologue, the purely linguistic energy of this confession. And the point is not at all that "Novogodnee" is a poem, that is, a form of narration that requires, by definition, maximum condensation of speech, sharpening of the maximum focus. The point is that Tsvetaeva confesses not to a priest but to a poet. And on her scale of ranks a poet is higher than a priest to roughly the same degree as man, in standard theology, is higher than the angels, since the latter were not created in the image and likeness of the Almighty.

Paradoxical and blasphemous as it may seem, in the dead Rilke Tsvetaeva found what every poet seeks: the supreme listener. The widespread belief that a poet always writes for someone is only half justified and is fraught with numerous confusions. The best answer to the question "Whom do you write for?" was given by Igor Stravinsky: "For myself and for a hypothetical alter ego." Consciously or unconsciously, every poet in the course of his career engages in a search for an ideal reader, for that alter ego, since a poet seeks not recognition but understanding. Baratynsky long ago consoled Pushkin in a letter, saying that one shouldn't be particularly surprised "if the Hussars don't read us anymore." Tsvetaeva goes even further, and in her poem **"Homesickness"** she declares:

> Nor shall I crave my native speech,
> its milky call that comes in handy.
> It makes no difference in which
> tongue passers-by won't comprehend me.
> (Translated by Joseph Brodsky)

This type of attitude toward things inevitably leads to a narrowing of the circle, which by no means always signifies an improvement in the quality of readers. A writer, however, is a democrat by definition, and the poet always hopes for some parallelism between the processes taking place in his own work and those in the consciousness of the reader. But the further a poet goes in his development, the greater—unintentionally—his demands are on an audience, and the narrower that audience is. The situation oftentimes ends with the reader becoming the author's projection, which scarcely coincides with any living creature at all. In those instances, the poet directly addresses either the angels, as Rilke does in the *Duino Elegies,* or another poet—especially one who is dead, as Tsvetaeva addresses Rilke. In both instances what takes place is a monologue, and in both instances it assumes an absolute quality, for the author addresses his words to nonexistence, to Chronos.

For Tsvetaeva, whose verse is distinctive for its almost pathological need to say, to think, to carry all things to their logical end, this was by no means a new destination. What turned out to be new—with the death of Rilke—was the fact that it turned out to be inhabited and for the poet in Tsvetaeva this could not but be of interest. To be sure, **"Novogodnee"** is the result of a particular emotional outburst; but Tsvetaeva is a maximalist, and the vector of her emotional movements is known in advance. Nevertheless, it is impossible to call Tsvetaeva a poet of extremes, if only because an extreme—whether deductive, emotional, or linguistic—is merely the point where, for her, a poem starts. "Going through life is not the same as walking across a field" [the last line of "Hamlet" by Boris Pasternak] or "Odysseus returned full of space and time" [the last line of "The Stream of Golden Honey Was Pouring . . ." by Osip Mandelstam] could never have been used as last lines in a poem of Tsvetaeva's; a poem of hers would have begun with these lines. Tsvetaeva is a poet of extremes only in the sense that for her an "extreme" is not so much the end of the known world as the beginning of the unknowable one. The technique of allusion, circumlocution, half-statement, or omission is characteristic of this poet to only a minute degree. Even less attributable to her is the use of the highest achievements of the rhythmic school, psychologically comforting to the reader with their lulling metrical pattern. Oversaturated with stresses, the harmony of Tsvetaeva's verse line is unpredictable; she leans more toward trochees and dactyls than toward the certitude of the iamb. The beginnings of her lines tend to be trochaic rather than stressed, the endings mournful, dactylic. It's hard to find another poet who has made such skillful and abundant use of caesura and truncated feet. In terms of form, Tsvetaeva is significantly more interesting than any of her contemporaries, including the Futurists, and her rhymes are more inventive than Pasternak's. Most importantly, however, her technical

achievements have not been dictated by formal explorations but are by-products—that is, natural effects—of speech, for which the most significant thing is its subject.

Art, generally speaking, always comes into being as a result of an action directed outward, sideways, toward the attainment (comprehension) of an object having no immediate relationship to art. It is a means of conveyance, a landscape flashing in a window—rather than the conveyance's destination. "If you only knew," said Akhmatova, "what rubbish verse grows from. . . ." The farther away the purpose of movement, the more probable the art; and, theoretically, death (anyone's, and a great poet's in particular, for what can be more removed from everyday reality than a great poet or great poetry?) turns into a sort of guarantee of art.

The theme of "Tsvetaeva and Rilke" has been, is, and will continue to be the subject of many investigations. What interests us is the role—or idea—of Rilke as the addressee in **"Novogodnee,"** his role as the object of psychic movement and the extent of his responsibility for the by-product of that movement: a poem. Knowing Tsvetaeva's maximalism, one cannot but take note of how natural her choice of this subject is. Apart from the concrete, deceased Rilke, there appears in the poem an image (or idea) of an "absolute Rilke," who has ceased being a body in space and has become a soul—in eternity. This removal is an absolute, maximum removal. The feelings the poem's heroine has—i.e., love—toward their absolute object, a soul, are also absolute. What in addition proves to be absolute are the means of expressing this love: maximum selflessness and maximum candor. All this could not but create a maximum tension of poetic diction.

There is, however, a paradox in the fact that poetic language possesses—as does any language in general—its own particular dynamics, which impart to psychic movement an acceleration that takes the poet much farther than he imagined when he began the poem. Yet this is, in fact, the principal mechanism (temptation, if you will) of creative work; once having come in contact with it (or having succumbed to it), a person once and for all rejects other modes of thought, expression—conveyance. Language propels the poet into spheres he would not otherwise be able to approach, irrespective of the degree of psychic or mental concentration of which he might be capable beyond the writing of verse. And this propulsion takes place with unusual swiftness: with the speed of sound—greater than what is afforded by imagination or experience. As a rule, a poet is considerably older when he finishes a poem than he was at its outset. The maximum range of Tsvetaeva's diction in **"Novogodnee"** takes her much farther than the mere experience of loss could; possibly even farther than the soul of Rilke himself is capable of getting to in its posthumous wanderings. Not only because any thought of someone else's soul, as distinct from the soul itself, is less burdened than that soul by its deeds, but also because a poet, generally speaking, is more generous than an apostle. A poetic "paradise" is not limited to "eternal bliss," and it is not threatened with the overcrowding of a dogmatic paradise. In contrast to the standard Christian paradise that is presented as a kind of last instance, the soul's dead end, poetic paradise is, rather, a peak, and a bard's soul is not so much perfected as left in a continual state of motion. The poetic idea of eternal life on the whole gravitates more toward a cosmogony than toward theology, and what is often put forward as a measure of the soul is not the degree of its perfection essential for achieving likeness and merger with the Creator but rather the physical (metaphysical) duration and distance of its wanderings in time. In principle, the poetic conception of existence eschews any form of finiteness or stasis, including theological apotheosis. In any case, Dante's paradise is much more interesting than the ecclesiastical version of it.

Even if the loss of Rilke served Tsvetaeva only as "An Invitation to a Journey," it would be justified by the otherworldly topography of **"Novogodnee."** But this is not in fact the case, and Tsvetaeva does not replace Rilke the man with the "idea of Rilke" or with the idea of his soul. She would have been incapable of making such a replacement if only because that soul had already been embodied in Rilke's work. (On the whole, the not overly justifiable polarization of soul and body, a practice that is very commonly abused when a person dies, appears all the less convincing when we are dealing with a poet.) In other words, the poet invites the reader to follow his soul during the poet's lifetime, and Tsvetaeva, with regard to Rilke, was first of all a reader. The dead Rilke, consequently, is not particularly different for her from the living one, and she follows him in roughly the same way that Dante followed Virgil, with great justification in the fact that Rilke himself undertook similar journeys in his own work ("Requiem for a Lady Friend"). In brief, the next world has been sufficiently domesticated by the poetic imagination to warrant the assumption that self-pity or curiosity about the otherworldly might have served Tsvetaeva as motivation for **"Novogodnee."** The tragedy of **"Novogodnee"** lies in the separation, in the almost physical rupture of her psychological bond with Rilke, and she sets out on this "journey," not frightened by a Dantean leopard blocking her path, but by an awareness of abandonment, of being no longer able to follow him the way she did during his lifetime—following every line of his. And also—in addition to that abandonment—from a feeling of guilt: I'm alive, whereas he—the better one—is dead. But the love of one poet for another (even of the opposite sex) is not Juliet's love for Romeo: the tragedy lies not in that existence without him is unthinkable but precisely in that such an existence *is* thinkable. And as a consequence of this conceivability, the author's attitude toward herself, still living, is more merciless, more uncompromising. Therefore, when beginning to speak, and—if it ever comes to this—when beginning to speak of oneself, one does so as if confessing, for it is *he*—not a priest or God but another poet—who hears you. Hence the intensity of Tsvetaeva's diction in **"Novogodnee,"** since she is addressing someone who, in contrast to God, has absolute pitch. (pp. 198-205)

The more powerful an individual's thinking, the less comfort it affords its possessor in the event of some tragedy. Grief as experience has two components: one emotional, the other rational. The distinguishing feature of their interrelationship in the case of a highly developed analytical apparatus is that the latter (the apparatus), rather than alleviating the situation of the former, i.e., the emotions, aggravates it. In these cases, instead of being an ally and consoler, the reason of an individual turns into an enemy and expands the radius of the tragedy to an extent unforeseen by its possessor. Thus, at times, the mind of a sick person, instead of painting pictures of recovery, depicts a scene of inevitable demise and thereby cripples his defense mechanisms. The difference between the creative process and the clinical one, however, is that neither the material (in the given instance, language) out of which a work is created nor the conscience of its creator can be given a sedative. In a work of literature, at any rate, an author always

pays heed to what he is told by the frightening voice of reason.

The emotional aspect of the grief that forms the content of **"Novogodnee"** is expressed, first of all, in terms of plasticity—in the metrics of this poem, in its caesuras, trochaic openings of lines, in the principle of couplet rhyme, which increases the possibilities of emotional adequacy in a line of verse. The rational side is expressed in the semantics of the poem, which is so patently dominant in the text that it could quite easily be the object of independent analysis. Such a separation, of course—even if it were possible—makes no practical sense; but if one distances oneself from **"Novogodnee"** for a moment and looks at it from the outside, as it were, one may observe that on the level of "pure thought" the poem is more eventful than on the purely verse level. If what is thus accessible to the eye gets translated into simple language, an impression emerges that the author's feelings, under the weight of what has befallen them, rushed to seek consolation from reason, which has taken them extremely far, for reason itself has no one from whom it can seek consolation. With the exception, naturally, of language—which signified a return to the helplessness of feelings. The more rational, in other words, the worse it is—for the author, anyway.

It is precisely on account of its destructive rationalism that **"Novogodnee"** falls outside Russian poetic tradition, which prefers to resolve problems in a key that while not necessarily positive is at least consoling. Knowing to whom the poem is addressed, one might assume that the consistency of Tsvetaeva's logic in **"Novogodnee"** is a tribute to the legendary pedantry of German (and, in general, Western) mentality—a tribute all the more easily paid because "German is more native than Russian." There may be a grain of justice in this; but the rationalism of **"Novogodnee"** is not at all unique in Tsvetaeva's oeuvre. Precisely the opposite is true: it is typical. The only thing, perhaps, that distinguishes **"Novogodnee"** from other poems of the same period is its developed argumentation; whereas in **"Poem of the End"** or in **"The Pied Piper,"** for example, we are dealing with the reverse phenomenon—an almost hieroglyphic condensation of arguments. (It is even possible that the argumentation in **"Novogodnee"** is so detailed because Russian was somewhat familiar to Rilke, and, as though Tsvetaeva were fearful of the misunderstandings that are especially common when the language barrier is slightly lowered, she intentionally "enunciates" her thoughts. In the end, this letter is the last; it is important to say everything while he has not yet gone "completely," that is, before the onset of oblivion, while life without Rilke has not yet become natural.) In any case, however, we encounter this destructive characteristic of Tsvetaeva's logicality, the premier mark of her authorship.

It might be more reasonable to say that **"Novogodnee"** does not fall outside Russian poetic tradition but expands it. For this poem—"national in form and Tsvetaevan in content"—extends, or better yet, refines the understanding of "national." Tsvetaeva's thinking is unique only for Russian poetry; for Russian consciousness it is natural, and even preconditioned by Russian syntax. Literature, however, always lags behind individual experience, for it comes about as its result. Moreover, the Russian poetic tradition always balks at disconsolation—not so much because of the possibility of hysterics implicit in disconsolation as because of the Orthodox inertia in justifying the existential order (by any, preferably metaphysical, means). Tsvetaeva, however, is uncompromising as a poet and in the highest degree uncomfortable. The world and many of the things that happen in it all too often lack any sort of justification for her, including a theological one. For art is something more ancient and universal than any faith with which it enters into matrimony, begets children—but with which it does not die. The judgment of art is a judgment more demanding than the Final Judgment. The Russian poetic tradition by the time **"Novogodnee"** was written was still in the grip of feelings for the Orthodox version of Christianity, with which it had been acquainted for only three hundred years. It's only natural that against such a background a poet who cries out, "There's not just one God, right? Above him there must be yet another / God?" proves to be an outcast. The latter circumstance may have played an even greater role in her life than the civil war.

One of the basic principles of art is the scrutiny of phenomena with the naked eye, out of context, and without intermediaries. **"Novogodnee"** is essentially one person's tête-à-tête with eternity or—even worse—with the idea of eternity. Tsvetaeva has used the Christian version of eternity here not only terminologically. Even if she had been an atheist, the "next world" would have had concrete ecclesiastical meaning for her: for, having a right to disbelieve in an afterlife for oneself, a person is less willing to deny such a prospect to someone he loved. Furthermore, Tsvetaeva ought to have insisted on "paradise," if only proceeding from the tendency—so typical of her—to dismiss the obvious.

A poet is someone for whom every word is not the end but the beginning of a thought; someone who, having uttered *rai* ("paradise") or *tot svet* ("next world"), must mentally take the subsequent step of finding a rhyme for it. Thus *krai* ("edge/realm") and *otsvet* ("reflection") emerge, and the existence of those whose life has ended is thus prolonged.

Looking in that direction, upward, into the grammatical time and also the grammatical place where "he" is, if only because "he" is not here, Tsvetaeva ends **"Novogodnee"** as all letters end: with the name and address of the addressee:

> —So that nothing spills on it I hold it in my palms.—
> Above the Rhone and above the Rarogne,
> Above the clear-cut and total separation
> To Rainer—Maria—Rilke—into his hands.
>   (Translated by Joseph Brodsky)

                                        (pp. 261-65)

Joseph Brodsky, "Footnote to a Poem," translated by Barry Rubin, in his Less than One: Selected Essays, *Farrar, Straus, Giroux, 1986, pp. 195-267.*

PETER FRANCE   (essay date 1982)

[*In the following excerpt, France surveys subjects, themes, and literary techniques in Tsvetaeva's poetry.*]

> To tell you everything . . . But no, all cramped
> In rows and rhymes . . . Wider the heart!
> For a catastrophe so great I fear
> All Shakespeare and Racine are not enough.
> "All wept, and if the blood is aching . . .
> All wept, and if the roses conceal snakes . . ."
> But Phaedra had only one Hippolytus,
> And Ariadne wept for one Theseus.
>
> Excruciation! Without shores or limits!
> Yes, I lose track of figures and declare

That when I lose you, I lose everyone
Who *never was* in any time or anywhere!

What can I hope—when riddled through and through
With you the whole air has grown one with me!
When my every bone to me is like a Naxos!
When the blood under my skin is like the Styx!

In vain! It is in me! Everywhere! I close
My eyes: it is dateless, bottomless.
The calendar lies . . .
                    As your name is—the Break,
So I am not Ariadne . . .
                    —I am Loss.

Oh through what seas and towns shall I
Search for you? (The unseeing for the unseen!)
I trust my farewells to the telegraph wires
And, pressed against the telegraph pole—I weep.

This is the second poem in a group entitled **"Wires" ("Provoda")** and written in March 1923. Marina Tsvetaeva's lyric poems are very often addressed by an "I" to a "you." Sometimes these are personae from the store of European culture—Ophelia to Hamlet, Eurydice to Orpheus—but usually we must take the speaker to be the poet herself. This raises problems of information. Often it is possible to find out from other sources such as memoirs or letters the identity of the person addressed and other circumstances which enable one to place the poem. Sometimes too an outside source will clarify an allusion that would otherwise remain mysterious. Beyond this, I doubt whether there is any real need for such scene-setting.

In the present poem, it is certainly interesting to know that the "you" (here in the intimate second-person singular) was Boris Pasternak, and that the poem was written from Czechoslovakia, where Tsvetaeva had been living for several months in self-chosen exile from Russia. When she left her homeland in May 1922, neither she nor Pasternak had published a great deal, but in the same year both came to the attention of a wider public, and of each other, with important books of poetry. Pasternak (who remained in Russia) was greatly impressed by Tsvetaeva's collection *Milestones (Vyorsty)* while she (in Berlin and Prague) greeted his *My Sister Life* with a rapturous article. So began a correspondence between two poets who felt themselves to be equals in strength.

Tsvetaeva's poem of loss and separation is addressed therefore to a man she had met mainly through poems and letters. Thence, I take it, the declaration in the third stanza that in losing him she is losing all who never were—all the unrealized possibilities of her native land. It is helpful too to know that when she writes "Your name is the Break," the word *razryv* ("break" or "separation"), while it brings in a notion which haunts much of her poetry, is also the title of a memorable cycle of poems included in Pasternak's collection *Themes and Variations,* which had been published a couple of months before this poem was written. All this is worth knowing, but I do not believe it should materially affect our reading any more than such knowledge as we may have about the supposed recipients of love poems by Shakespeare, Ronsard or Pushkin. For all their allusiveness, most of Marina Tsvetaeva's poems can stand on their own without biographical commentary.

In line 4 of this poem, the names of two great tragic poets are used to suggest the size of the poet's misfortune. It is one of

Tsvetaeva's habits to see her life in terms of great men and women of history and literature. In earlier collections these emblematic figures include Russian folk heroes such as Stenka Razin and the Pretender Dimitry as well as heroes and heroines of Western Europe—Manon Lescaut, Casanova and many others. In *After Russia* (*Posle Rossii*), the collection from which the present poem is taken, she tends more often to go back to the Old Testament, Shakespeare and classical antiquity. There are several poems on Hamlet and others on Saul, David, Absalom and Solomon, but probably the dominant images are those from ancient Greece, Achilles and Helen, Orpheus and Eurydice, Phaedra and Hippolytus, Theseus and Ariadne. The last two pairs, with their rejected heroines and their Racinian echoes, provide the subjects of two verse plays of the 1920s. In this poem, the most important figure is Ariadne, abandoned by Theseus on the island of Naxos. But Tsvetaeva goes beyond simple identification; she is more than Ariadne, she is loss itself. And as in Blok's "Steps of the Commendatore," the grand legendary images contrast sharply with a real world (of telegraph poles and wires) which is evoked in poem after poem of this collection.

The most striking features of this poem—and in this it is characteristic of its author's mature work—are the broken, elliptical form and the exclamatory eloquence. The first stanza, for instance, moves from the unfinished sentences which mime inexpressible emotion to a full-blooded affirmation which has something of the magniloquence of Mayakovsky's great love poems. Both the second and fourth lines end with exclamation marks, and there are many more of these in the rest of the poem. The exclamation mark seems to be more freely used in Russian poetry than in English, where it tends to give an impression of falsity or naive self-indulgence. Such criticisms are sometimes made of Tsvetaeva too, occasionally coupled (at least in conversation) with a rather disagreeable condescension for the "hysterical woman" or "schoolgirl." Certainly the direct or heightened expression of personal emotion is more characteristic of her poetry than detachment or impersonality.

If the third and fourth lines are direct and emphatic, the first two lines are elliptical—but not obscure. It is easy to complete the first sentence, and "all cramped into rows and rhymes" must be taken to qualify some noun such as "emotions." These are like the ellipses of conversation, where the unfinished sentence is no obstacle to communication. The same is true, I think, of the apparent quotations of lines 5 and 6. I do not know the source of these (perhaps they are of Tsvetaeva's own invention), and both lines are left hanging, but they can be read as objections to the previous lines—a voice, speaking with the wisdom of the ages, tells the poet that her experience is nothing new in a world of tears, and this provokes the retort of lines 7 and 8, which will be amplified in the next three stanzas. Her loss is far more than the loss of one person; it is the loss of a whole world which has become flesh of her flesh.

Partly because of its inflected nature, the Russian language allows meaning to be conveyed in fewer words than in English. There are no articles, pronouns are often not needed, and the verbless sentence is quite common. Tsvetaeva uses these resources to the utmost, creating jagged abrupt sentences, full of dashes and breaks. Thus the third and fourth lines of the fourth stanza could have been run on smoothly in a single sentence, but they are separated by exclamation marks and the instrumental case allows the verbs ("is" or "re-

sembles") to be understood, not expressed. In the fifth stanza there is a sequence of brief exclamations and only one main verb, and in the final stanza the whole meaning of the two echoing words *nezrimogo—nezryachey* ("the unseeing for the unseen") has to be deduced from the endings. All this makes reading more difficult than a smoother style, and such appears to have been Tsvetaeva's intention—she did not want to make things too easy. In any case its expressive force is undeniable.

It has often been thought that verbal ingenuity is out of place in the poetry of emotion, that it suggests a striving for effect or an inappropriate playfulness. It is one of Tsvetaeva's qualities—and in this as in much else she is close to Mayakovsky—that her work on language is closely bound up with the expression of feeling. It is as if strong feeling, far from decanting the language, searches out new and unsuspected complexities and possibilities. Most obvious of these is the coupling of words similar in sound, but apparently unrelated in meaning—thus *dna* and *dnya* in line 18, the genitive case respectively of words meaning "bottom" and "day." Or else there can be an etymological relationship which is lost in ordinary speech; this is the case with the central pair *provody* ("seeing-off") and *provoda* ("wires"), where the same root gives birth to words that suggest separation and reunion in one line: "Ya provody vveryayu provodam." Together with this homonymic play, there are effects such as the accumulation of similar sounds in lines 15 and 16 (*Naksosom, kost', krov', kozhey, stiksom*), intensified in this case by the sort of chiasmic construction which is made easier by the flexibility of Russian word order.

These and other features of the writing—the metaphors, the clash of formal metre and rhythmical intonation—remind one of the poems of the person to whom these lines are addressed. Indeed one might think Tsvetaeva was doing homage by imitation if it were not for the presence of these elements in her poems long before 1923. Similarly, while this is a poem of exile, it did not need the circumstances of 1923 to produce such notes in her writing. It is true that the experience of separation from Russia and the miseries of emigration provoked some of her finest poetry; the German epigraph to the cycle **"Wires"** reads in translation: "The wave of the heart would not foam up in such beauty and become spirit, if it were not for the resistance of that old, silent rock, fate." Even so, much that is in *After Russia* is anticipated much earlier.

In 1932, in an essay entitled **"The Poet and Time,"** Tsvetaeva wrote that "every poet is essentially an émigré, even in Russia." This is an ancient view, which was given a new lease of life in the Romantic movement; one finds it in its pure form in Baudelaire's "The Albatross." Mayakovsky gave a Futurist colouring to it, addressing his poems insultingly to a "you" of complacent bourgeois. Something similar is to be found in this early poem of Marina Tsvetaeva: . . .

> You, who pass me by and go on
> To not mine and dubious charms,—
> If only you knew what fire,
> How much life, poured out in vain,
>
> And how much heroic ardour
> On a passing shade, on a sigh . . .
> How this vain outpouring of powder
> Has reduced my heart to ash.
>
> Oh trains that rush into the night,

Tsvetaeva with her daughter Ariadna in 1925.

Carrying off the station's dreams . . .
Yet I know that even then,
If you knew—you would not really know

Why in endless cigarette smoke
My speech is hard and sharp,—
How much dark and menacing grief
There is in my fair-haired head.

Tsvetaeva was twenty when she wrote these lines—she had already been writing poems for some years. In another poem of the same month she imagined herself speaking to a future sympathizer from the grave; the early work is full of the awareness of impending death and the desire to live as fully as possible. Here she speaks from a gloomy corner to a generalized and alien "you," not perhaps the fat philistines of Mayakovsky, but still the sort of people who cannot understand the passionate poet. Passion appears as an outpouring and above all a fire (*pyl, ogon', porokh*) which brings devastation. But all this ardour is out of place in an ordinary world, where it can only be wasted on a "shade" and a "sigh." In Tsvetaeva's poems the speaker, a generous force of life, loves more than she is loved; she can find no one to answer the strength of her passion. So here, self-consumed like Phaedra, she is driven back on herself, into an aggressive cigarette-smoking reserve that contrasts sharply with the stock image of the sweet fair-haired girl.

Like the first poem discussed . . . , though in a less impressive way, these early verses pose the basic problem which faces the reader of Tsvetaeva: how is one to react to the constant projection of the poet's personality into images which often strike one as all too familiar, however true they may be

to the experience of many people? There is in her poems a propensity to work in myths—or at worst clichés—of human behaviour, and this can become unbearable at times. On the other hand, these "myths" correspond to a desire to heighten the experience of life, to find a place for energy and daring. Overflowing with a powerful imaginative impulse, and often in very difficult material conditions in her later life, Tsvetaeva persisted in this call to transcend or transfigure the world. At times, particularly in the early poems, the result is childish or embarrassing, but then, as one reads on and as the poet's mastery grows, her poetry comes to shame the complacent reader. The poet becomes a goad.

A number of legendary figures are evoked in the youthful poems, heroes, princes and warriors such as Napoleon and his son. She even briefly saw Kerensky as Napoleon in 1917. But it is probably her fellow-poets who provided the most lasting images of power and daring. From 1916 on, she addressed groups of poems to Mandelstam (a "young Derzhavin" and a "young eagle"), to Pasternak ("my equal in strength"), to Mayakovsky (a "toiling archangel") and to Akhmatova ("muse of weeping, most beautiful of the muses"). All of these are transfigured in Tsvetaeva's gaze, but none so much as Blok, who was of course of an older generation (though only about twelve years older, be it said) and represented for her a saintly ideal of poetry. He was a "knight without reproach." There is a cycle of sixteen **Poems to Blok,** half of them written in 1916, the others shortly before or after his death in 1921. The first group contains this one: . . .

> For the beast—a den,
> For the traveller—a road,
> For the dead—a hearse.
> For each—his own.
>
> For the woman—cunning,
> For the tsar—ruling,
> For me—praising
> Thy name.

Eight lines, sixteen words [in the Russian original]. Tsvetaeva is close to the silence of adoration. I doubt if Blok, who knew himself only too well, would have approved of this hero-worship, but Tsvetaeva is addressing the poet rather than the man, and she perceived in him—rightly—a call to absolute values. The first line here echoes Matthew 8:20: "The foxes have holes, and the birds of the air have nests, but the Son of Man hath not where to lay his head." So Blok is associated with Jesus—and Tsvetaeva perhaps with Mary Magdalene. The poem, like many of hers, is made up on the litany principle (repetition of the same form with varying sounds), and verblessness is carried to an extreme. The rhymes and the rhythm tie the poem into a tight unity, but here again there are variations within repetition; the number of syllables changes, the two shortest lines are kept to the end, the seventh line runs straight into the eighth, and the final line is without the dash which divides and slows down all the rest. The vocabulary is simple and old, though not actually archaic; its effect is to reduce the complexity of life to a series of characteristic acts or attributes, the most obvious possible, as if there were an immutable grand order in which tsars always rule (this in 1916) and women, like Delilah, are always cunning.

One of the impulses in Tsvetaeva's poems, whether political or personal, is towards a fixed world of this kind, the world of duty, peace and transcendence, like that of Blok's Beautiful Lady. But Blok was also the poet of wild passion and the gipsy song, and in Tsvetaeva too, though not in the *Poems to Blok,* the element of wild movement, dance and passion is rarely absent for long. In her very early poem **"Prayer,"** written at the age of seventeen, she had prayed for an intensity of life which would include fighting like an Amazon, reading the stars in a black tower and setting out "with the soul of a gipsy on a bandit raid." The warrior, the rebel, the bandit and the gipsy reappear in many of her poems, the gipsy for instance in a cycle of three poems called **"Fortune-Telling"** (**"Gadan'e"**), written between the February and October revolutions in May 1917—a month after the birth of her second daughter: . . .

> She looked in my eyes,
> Dully menacing.
> Somewhere a thunderclap answered.
> —Ah, my young lady!
> Let me tell you
> Your fortune in years to come.
>
> Blue clouds have gathered into a funnel.
> Somewhere it thunders—they thunder.
> Into my child the fortune-teller
> Has plunged her somnolent gaze.
>
> "What can you tell us?"
> —Everything true.
> "Too late for me,
> Too early for her."
>
> —Oh, hold your tongue, my beauty.
> Why say in advance "I don't believe it."—
> And the fan of cards spread wide
> In a black—all in silver—hand.
>
> —Bold in your speech,
> Simple in your ways,
> You live generously,
> Hoarding no beauty.
> An evil man will drown you, alas,
> In a spoonful of water.
>
> Soon in the night an unexpected journey.
> Life-line short,
> Short in fortune.
> Cross my palm with gold.—
>
> And with a stroke of thunder appears
> Black upon black—the ace.

The self-image is by now familiar, that of the ill-fated, passionate, generous heroine, very much mindful of death. The reader's attention is perhaps caught above all by the striking language of the poem. As in the poem to Blok, lines tend to begin on a stressed syllable; some characteristic stress patterns are:

/——/
/——/—
/——/—/——/—

The first of these is the fundamental one; it is called the choriamb and is much used in Tsvetaeva's mature verse. The second can be seen as an extension of the first and the third is a doubling up of the second. In all cases the result is a line where one half pulls hard against the other and the stressed syllables stand out with considerable force. Add to this the shortness of most of the lines, the tendency to separate lines by commas, full stops or exclamation marks and the breaks introduced even into short lines by the use of dashes, and the result is an abrupt and powerful rhythm which reinforces the impact of the poem's subject, the confrontation between for-

tune-teller and mother and child, and the clashing colours, the silver of rings, gold of money and bright cards against the darkness of skin, thunderclouds and the ace (of spades?).

Unlike the poems discussed so far . . . , this is not a message from the poet to a supposed hearer or reader, but a dialogue. It anticipates the very successful rendering of conversation in some of Tsvetaeva's longer poems. The talk here is not framed with much explanatory scene-setting, and as in many ballads such introductory formulae as "she said" are omitted. The essential elements (eyes, cards, thunder) are rapidly evoked at the beginning, in the middle and again at the end; otherwise the poem is staccato talk, mostly the talk of the fortune-teller.

With the gipsy's words we see a different linguistic element in Tsvetaeva's poetry. The poems to Blok are couched in a simple but distinctly poetic language, with biblical echoes. In **"Fortune-Telling"** there is an attempt to represent popular speech. According to an expert who heard the poem soon after it was written, it was a very successful attempt—the use of the word *liniya* for instance was exactly that of the gipsy palmist. This version of popular language has the same concise vigour as one finds in Tsvetaeva's more "literary" register. The two styles set one another off admirably: thus in this poem the final lines come across with added force after the gipsy's speech. In the years that followed, Tsvetaeva continued to exploit this vein and to draw, like so many of her contemporaries, on the language of popular literature and song, from the modern city romance to the ancient oral poetry of the countryside. Her long verse poems *The Tsar-Maiden* (*Tsar'-devitsa*) and *The Champion* (*Molodets*) are ambitious attempts to harness old stories, old forms and old language to the poet's own personal concerns.

In spite of her love of popular language and culture and her sympathy for such folk heroes as the rebel Stenka Razin, Marina Tsvetaeva committed herself to the White cause after the October Revolution. Being the person she was, she did so with as great a zeal as Mayakovsky on the other side; she became the (unacknowledged) bard of the Counter-Revolution. Her husband, Sergey Efron, joined the White Army, and she composed a series of poems, later published (though not, of course, in the Soviet Union) under the title *The Swans' Encampment* (*Lebedinyy stan*), in which she praised the nobility of those who had died for the anti-revolutionary cause. They are swans, white and pure, against the ravens; they are also compared to the warriors of Prince Igor's army fighting against the Tatars, or to the heroes who died fighting against the French Revolution.

There is no doubt about Tsvetaeva's position at this time, but equally there is no doubt that her heart went out above all to the gallant loser, the victim, whether it was the Tsar or Stenka Razin. Hers is not what is usually called a political stance. In one poem she declares that she has only two enemies, "the hunger of the hungry and the fullness of the full," and in another, mourning the dead of the Civil War, she writes: . . .

> He was white, now he is red:
> Blood has reddened him.
> He was red, now he is white:
> Death has whitened him.

In the hungry year of 1918, when she had a hard time simply staying alive in Moscow, Tsvetaeva wrote this poem, which was later included in *The Swans' Encampment:* . . .

In my figure there's an officer's straightness,
In my ribs, an officer's honour.
I'll take any pain without protest:
In me there's a soldier's endurance!

As if once with rifle-butt and steel
My step had been straightened out.
Not in vain, not in vain my Circassian waist
And my tightly drawn leather belt.

But when Reveille sounds—dear God!—
I could storm the gates of heaven!
These shoulders, it seems, were made wide
To carry a soldier's pack.

Who knows—perhaps over my cradle
Some crazy veteran sang . . .
And something lives on from that day:
I take my aim at the world!

And over the RSFSR
My heart gnashes—fed or unfed—
As if I too was an officer
In those fatal October days.

Read in the context of **The Swans' Encampment,** this is clearly a "White" poem. The RSFSR of the last stanza is the newly created Russian Soviet Federal Socialist Republic; by using the word *skrezheshchet* (usually used of gnashing the teeth, but here associated with the heart), Tsvetaeva is defiantly refusing the new power, even at the cost of starvation. The regular beat is almost that of a marching song; this is Tsvetaeva the drummer of the Counter-Revolution (as Mayakovsky was the drummer of the Revolution). Only in the last line do the grammatical forms show that the speaker is a woman. Most of the poem could be spoken by a man, and Tsvetaeva, who in many other poems rejects the quiet lot of the docile woman, is here identifying herself with the heroic White officers whom she praised and mourned in other poems. The fourth stanza shows that for her the act of writing is associated with battle; as a writer in revolutionary Moscow she can show the same nobility, patience and daring as those who died fighting.

And indeed Marina Tsvetaeva was a daring spirit. She left a lovely account of a "Poetesses' Evening" in Moscow in 1921 at which she turned up among the other well-dressed lady poets wearing an old coat, a belt of the White Army, and over her shoulder an officer's leather bag. Out of a feeling of duty, she read a series of poems in memory of the victims of the Revolution, even poems with lines such as "Hurrah! For the Tsar! Hurrah!." She was energetically applauded. The political meaning of her poems passed over the heads of her audience. So too with the poem above; in a note of 1938 Tsvetaeva records that "in Moscow this poem was called 'Verses about a Red Officer' and over a period of eighteen months I read it at every poetry reading to unfailingly loud applause on the unfailing demand of the students."

No doubt this misreading was due in part to the circumstances of transmission; it is easier to misunderstand an oral message. But I think it also stems from something in the poem itself. The hymn to military qualities and the march-like rhythm could appeal to Red audiences as much as to Whites. The idea of storming the gates of heaven sounds more revolutionary than counter-revolutionary, and even the more precise message of the last stanza might still be open to a double reading. The October days had been fatal to combatants on both sides, and the heart might "gnash" either at the success of the RSFSR or at the troubles it was encountering.

Indeed, writing about this poem in her 1932 essay **"The Poet and Time,"** Tsvetaeva declared that the audiences had been right in their misunderstanding:

> There is something in poetry which is more important than its meaning—the way it sounds. The soldiers in Moscow in 1920 were not wrong; this poem is in its essence more concerned with the Red officer (and even the Red soldier) than with the White, who would not have accepted it, who (between 1922 and 1932) *did not accept it.*

And she goes on to say how at one such meeting, someone said to her: "In spite of everything you are a revolutionary poet. You have our rhythm."

Of course there was a big difference between a revolutionary poet and what Tsvetaeva called a "bard of the Revolution." The two only coincided in Mayakovsky, for whom she continued to proclaim her admiration against all the criticism of émigré circles. What she meant by "revolutionary poet" was the poet who feels and expresses the time, this being for Russia a time of revolution. "Whether you accept or avoid or reject the Revolution, it is already in you."

This article of 1932 was written at a time when her poetry was generally rejected by the Russian community in Paris, where she was living, and when her defense of Mayakovsky had turned many away from her. It is not surprising that it is full of nostalgia for what she imagined to be a more vital relationship between poet, language and public in her native country: "In Russia, as in the steppe, as at sea, there is space to speak from, space to speak into. If only speaking were allowed . . . Here there is a certain Russia, there there is all of Russia." Ten years earlier the desire to escape had been stronger and her revulsion for the new Russia greater. Repudiation of the Revolution is combined with the influence of popular culture and language in a striking little cycle composed in September 1921 and entitled **"A Captive of the Khan" ("Khansky polon").** This is the third poem in the group of four: . . .

Your tracks are untried,
Matted your forelock.
Loosestrife and touch-me-not
Crunch under hoof.

An untrampled road,
A reckless fire.—
Oh, Mother Russia,
A steed unshod!

Your calico unsold,
Your axeman armless.
A poor empty trough
In the hall—and a hook.

I'll stuff myself with bark,—
That's nothing new now!
Oh, Mother Russia,
Enchanted steed!

You must leap to the saddle!
Once up, don't complain!
There is only one rider
To fit you: Mamay!

Slant-eyed foulness,
Palm of a thief . . .
—Ah, Mother Russia,
Remorseless steed!

The fundamental image is a traditional one; Russia, to whom the poem is mostly addressed, is a runaway horse, charging wildly into dangerous, uncharted country. The only possible rider (the Bolsheviks) is seen in the frightening figure of Mamay, a Tatar chief. The theme of the Revolution as a barbaric Asiatic eruption was common enough at this time, and Tsvetaeva had already alluded in _The Swans' Encampment_ to the old Russian poems and legends of struggle against the Tatar Horde. What is most interesting here is the poetic form.

In **"Fortune-Telling"** there was an attempt to suggest popular speech in the dialogue with a gipsy, but it was framed in the poetic speech of a narrator. In this poem, on the other hand, the speaker is not identified, except in the title of the cycle. The poet's longing to escape from Russia reaches us through the voice of someone who is a prisoner in the camp of the Khan, and this voice speaks a language which is archaic, popular, abrupt and often obscure. The very word for "captivity" (_polon_) in the title is an archaism which has long disappeared from normal speech, and several of the words used in the poem are almost equally old and rare. In the first stanza, for instance, the words _sledok_ ("track") and _nepytan_ ("untried") are unusual derivations from familiar roots. The two plant-names in line 4 of the original (line 3 of the translation) are old country words which evoke a world of popular belief; the former (_razryv_) was supposed to have the power of breaking locks, while the second (_plakun_) was said to make witches weep. More than this, _razryv_ is the word for separation which Tsvetaeva later connects with Pasternak in **"Wires,"** and _plakun_ immediately suggests the verb _plakat'_ ("to weep"). A lot is done in two words.

There is much that sounds like popular speech. _Okh, Rodina-Rus'_ ("Oh Mother Russia") is a refrain echoing the language of folk song, and there are also colloquial words such as _neputyovyy_ ("reckless") and _nazhrus'_ ("I'll stuff myself "), popular forms of words such as _non'_ (for _nyne_ meaning "now"), and the use of _da_ to mean "and." In the fourth stanza (and elsewhere) there is a marked contrast between the coarse speech ("I'll stuff myself with bark") and the loftily poetic (because somewhat archaic) "enchanted steed"—and then a return to the syntax of ordinary speech in the first two lines of stanza 5.

As so often, the syntax is elliptical and verbless. If the rhythm of the "poem about the Red officer" was a march, here we have a gallop; the short lines each have two stressed syllables, separated by two unstressed, and the poem jerks and pounds on from line to line and rhyme to rhyme in a violent movement. Again one is reminded of what Tsvetaeva wrote about the rhythm of the time, the rhythm of revolution. This is a declaration of hate for the new order—as in the violent expression of racial loathing in the last stanza—but the rhythm seems to me to carry a feeling of excitement. Tsvetaeva was consciously putting herself on the opposite side from Blok, but her poem has something of the same ambiguity as _The Twelve_ in its depiction of an elemental force. The wild, unshod, enchanted and remorseless steed (_kon'_, a poetic word _par excellence_) could not be totally alien to her; only a year earlier she had written a long poem entitled **"On a Red Steed,"** in which the fiery, red horse represents inspiration, a violent muse.

"A Captive of the Khan" was first published in a collection entitled _Craft (Remeslo)_. In some ways this volume marks a break with Tsvetaeva's earlier writing; the new work is more innovatory, more at odds with the conventional norms of poetry. In this poem one sees archaic and popular language, short lines, jagged rhythms and a tendency to the unexplained and the obscure. This new "craft" of verse is developed still further in her later writing, particularly in the collection entitled _After Russia_ (1928), which met with considerable hostility in émigré literary circles.

Obscurity certainly is a problem. In this poem, for instance, apart from the use of unfamiliar words, there is the difficulty of relating the exclamations of lines 17 and 18 to what precedes and follows. It is possible that obscurity is a way of getting past the censor—for all its violent abuse, this poem was published in the Soviet Union. But caution was never one of Tsvetaeva's failings, and the difficulty of her later work is rather to be seen as a deliberately high threshold to discourage the lazy philistine. She is not going to make concessions to the sort of readability she later mocked in a virulent satirical piece called **"Newspaper Readers"** (**"Chitateli gazet"**). Her poems make the reader work; the captivating rhythms and strange teasing language are a promise that the work will be rewarded—and indeed, sometimes after many readings, the reward usually comes.

"A Captive of the Khan" is—among other things—an exercise in invective, the violent self-defence of an isolated and suffering person. This vein is one that becomes increasingly important in Tsvetaeva's writing in the 1920s and 1930s. The targets of her abuse are the same as those of Mayakovsky, the smug philistine, the world of unaspiring comfort, but she also goes further than Mayakovsky and sets herself against the modern, industrial world. In opposition to this alien world, she maintains a strong sense of her own rightness and of the demands of the absolute. Above all, there is the constant need for a life of emotional intensity and self-giving, which leads her to project her life and passion through figures such as Phaedra and Ophelia and to see in those she loved more than they could possibly give. Thus, in 1921, she wrote a cycle of poems entitled **"Adolescent"** (**"Otrok"**) and addressed to a young poet. The first poem is one of breathless, extravagant eloquence: . . .

> Emptinesses of adolescent eyes! Abysses
> Into azure. Azure—however black!
> Playthings for an unparalleled battle,
> Gift-treasure-houses of storms.
>
> Mirror-like! They have neither ripple nor depths.
> The universe holds its course in them.
> Azure! Azure! Desert-like clangour,—
> Book-warehouses of emptiness!
>
> Abysses of adolescent eyes! Arches!
> Waterhole of scorched souls.
> Oases!—That all may gulp and sip
> And choke themselves on emptiness.
>
> I drink—cannot drink enough. Sighs—gasps,
> And subterranean roar of rumbling blood.
> So by night, troubling the sleep of David,
> Came the choking gulps of King Saul.

A comparison of this poem with **"A Captive of the Khan,"** which was written just one month later, shows the range of Tsvetaeva's writing. She always speaks from her own personal situation, but in many ways. This is a poem in the high Romantic tradition, an incantation in which the vocabulary is elevated and in places archaic, culminating in a scene from the Old Testament. Like Baudelaire's "La Chevelure" it starts from a physical feature (here, the young man's eyes) and expands by a series of images. In the first three stanzas the basic structure is simply an accumulation of exclamatory metaphors. The last of these (again reminiscent of Baudelaire: "Tes yeux sont la citerne où boivent mes ennuis" ["Your eyes are the reservoir where my anxieties drink"]) leads in the last stanza from an evocation of the man's eyes to the poet herself, gazing at him as the troubled Saul gazed at the young David (1 Samuel 16:23).

It is above all a poem of thirst—thirst being a fundamental impulse in Tsvetaeva's poetry, as indeed it is in Mayakovsky's. One of her earliest surviving poems begins with the words "I thirst for a miracle," and this need for a renewed source of life never leaves her. It is expressed in a number of poems of the 1920s, as here, in the image of an older woman, burning or burnt-out, addressing a beautiful and inaccessible youth—Phaedra to Hippolytus, the Sibyl to a young man. **"Adolescent"** does not express the passion of a Phaedra, but there is the same desire for a refreshing presence. It is noteworthy that the eyes are figured as empty spaces; the youth is less a living human being than a way of access to a higher plane, the "azure" and the universe. In other words, as in so much love poetry, the other person is desired as a means of escape and transcendence, or at least as an oasis in the desert.

Given the extremity of Tsvetaeva's demands on others, it is not surprising that life and other people failed to live up to them. Some of her best poetry comes from the pain of failed love and separation. The best of all is probably her long poem of 1924, the **"Poem of the End" ("Poema kontsa")**. This is made of fourteen separate sections, which together tell most movingly of the end of a love affair. Like almost all of Tsvetaeva's mature work, this poem is elliptical and sometimes hard to "explain" in detail, but its overall structure is clear and strong. We follow the two lovers as they meet, walk through Prague, talk, weep and finally separate. Some idea of the quality of the poem may be had from this short extract, the third section, which shows the two speakers walking along an embankment and preparing for the final explanation: . . .

> And—the embankment. To water
> I cling as to a dense slab.
> Semiramis's hanging gardens
> Of Babylon—so this is you!
>
> To water—a steely band
> The colour of a corpse—
> I cling as to her music
> A singer—or to a wall's edge
> A blind man . . . You won't give back?
> No? If I stoop—will you hear?
> To the quencher of all thirst
> I cling, as to a roof's edge
>
> A lunatic . . .
>   But not from the river
> My trembling—a Nayad born!
> I cling to the river like a hand
> When the man you love is close
>
> And faithful . . .
>   The dead are faithful.
> Yes, but not to all in the cell . . .
> Death on my left, and on my right—
> You. My right side seems dead.
>
> A sheaf of transfixing light.
> A laugh like a tambourine.
> "You and I need to . . ."

. . . "Are we going to be brave?"

> (Shudder.)

It will be seen that the force of this passage comes from a mixture of compression and expansiveness. The narrative line is kept to a verbless minimum, as in the opening words and the final stanza, where the arrival at a café door is announced in two rapid notations. The dialogue at the end, as throughout the poem, is given in staccato form, with no indication of the speaker and only a brief "stage direction" in brackets. But if the outward scene is all brief brush-strokes and broken dialogue, the representation of the woman's thoughts and feelings is expansive and eloquent. It seeks to convey half-conscious levels of experience, largely by rhythm and a series of metaphors and similes. The shift from one image to another is often unexpected and unaccountable (for instance the introduction of the hanging gardens), since the poem expresses a state of wordless confusion and panic. Particularly striking is the repeated use of the verb "to cling to" (*derzhat'sya*); as is often the case in Tsvetaeva's poetry, the actual verb is sometimes omitted and has to be deduced from the syntax. The woman clings to the water as a sort of protection; with her name of Marina, she liked to think of herself as a child or spirit of water. Water is also the quencher of all thirst, like the oases of the young man's eyes in **"Adolescent,"** and at the same time it is connected with death, not only by the colour evoked in the second stanza, but as a possible refuge from life in stanza 5.

Even more than these images, the rhythm of the lines impresses itself on the reader. As in **"Adolescent,"** the fundamental metre is iambic, but for most of the poem this is set in violent opposition to an impassioned non-metrical rhythm. The use of long words such as *naberezhnaya* ("embankment"), *Semiramidina* ("of Semiramis") and *vseutolitel'nitsa* ("universal quencher") reduces the number of stresses, and the regularity of the line is further broken by dashes (perhaps Tsvetaeva's favourite punctuation) and by constant *enjambement* in the first four stanzas. As a result, while the underlying metre can still be sensed as a regular movement towards an inevitable end, the immediate effect is one of an exclamatory, headlong movement, that of the desire to escape. Only in the last two stanzas is the movement halted, first by the awareness of the lover's unyielding presence—the word "you" is given special prominence—and then by the harsh and relatively regular end-stopped lines which take one brutally away from the thirst-quenching water to the hateful world of ordinary human society. And this is the signal for a quite different rhythm. The next section of the poem will be a satirical ballad of the commercial and amorous vulgarity of a Prague café, which is followed in its turn by a tense piece of conversation leading up to the words "Let us part then." In its varied but inexorable movement from beginning to end, this poem is both moving and wonderfully inventive; Tsvetaeva shows once again, as Donne had done long before in England, that what a prejudiced reader might call verbal virtuosity can cast a vivid light on the inner world and become a renewed source of emotion.

Tsvetaeva had little use for the ordinary world of gossip, business and newspapers which she satirizes in the Prague café ballad just mentioned. Neither could she find lasting satisfaction in devotion to a cause (as the struggle of the White Army was followed by the less heroic reality of emigration) or in love (which seemed doomed to disillusionment and collapse). In all the poems I have discussed so far she has been seen as a poet of human society, of love, hate, contempt or devotion.

As one reads her, however, one becomes aware of a desire for a different sort of reality. In places, particularly in the early poems, she adopts a provocatively anti-religious pose, but there are many other times when she expresses what can only be called religious aspirations, whether in ecstatic poems about the churches of Moscow or in a more general thirst for an undefined absolute. The natural world does not play a very large part in her early collections, but in the poems of the 1920s, trees come to the fore as a refuge from the heated, wearing world of human worries. In *After Russia* there is a very fine cycle simply called **"Trees" ("Derev'ya")**, of which this is the second poem (it was written in September 1922): . . .

> When my angry soul has drunk
> Its fill of injury,
> When seven times it has renounced
> The struggle with demons—
>
> Not those flung down to the abyss
> In a hail of fire:
> But the petty basenesses of every day
> And human inertia,—
>
> Trees! Then I come to you! To hide
> From the market's roar!
> Your outflingings skyward seem
> To breathe forth the heart!
>
> God-defying oak! Striding
> With all your roots to battle!
> My future-gazing willow trees!
> Maidenly birches!
>
> Elm—vehement Absalom,
> In torture upreared
> Pine—and you, psalm of my lips,
> Mountain-ash bitterness . . .
>
> To you! Into the live-splashing quicksilver
> Of leaves—even though falling!
> To stretch out my arms for the first time!
> To scatter manuscripts!
>
> Swarms of green light and shade . . .
> As if splashing into my hands . . .
> Bare-headed ones of mine,
> My tremulous ones!

It is perhaps unnecessary to say much about this beautiful invocation. As a poem of celebration it is more readily comprehensible than many other poems of this period; there is no need here for the reader to know anything of the poet's life. Once again Tsvetaeva alludes to the Old Testament, not only Absalom, but the fall of the angels in the opening stanzas. And generally, as in much of the poetry of the 1920s, the language tends towards the archaic. To take two examples, the word *semizhdy* ("seven times") belongs to Church Slavonic rather than to modern Russian and the invented compound adjective *zhivopleshchushchiy* ("live-splashing") recalls the archaic coinages of Russia's eighteenth-century poets, who in their turn were striving to create a Homeric style. Throughout this poem, in fact, the language is markedly "poetic," with none of the colloquialisms which Tsvetaeva liked to use elsewhere. In writing of trees she escapes into an ancient sylvan world.

Many formal features of the poem are worthy of note, but I have already discussed such questions at some length. . . . Above all it is a poem of *sound*. Thus, after the vigorous upsurging sounds and images of stanzas 4 and 5, there is a beautiful shimmering effect of liquid leaves, full of palatalized consonants and sibilants:

> K vam! V zhivopleshchushchuyu rtut'
> Listvy—pust' rushashcheysya!

Here and throughout the poem Tsvetaeva writes with the sort of evocative magic that one finds also in Khlebnikov. It is a poetry of enchantment, beyond good and evil.

The idea that poetry—or art—is essentially amoral is in fact expressed—in somewhat Nietzschean terms—in a brilliant essay written by Marina Tsvetaeva in the 1930s, **"Art in the Light of Conscience."** Poetry is defined as a force of nature, something that happens to the poet, something as elemental as the plague. The genius is the one who is most open to this onrush and most able to make something of it—Nietzsche's combination of the Dionysian and the Apollonian. But unlike Nietzsche, Tsvetaeva does not conclude from this that art is *above* morality or that it can replace religion. For her as for Blok the artist is a demonic rather than a holy figure. To the imagined objection that "the priest serves God in his way, you in your way," she replies: "Blasphemy . . . When I write of the Tatars in the open spaces I am serving no God except the wind . . . All my poems on Russian subjects are elemental, and therefore sinful. One must be clear what forces are in play. When will we stop taking strength for truth and enchantment for holiness?"

So while she expresses in the most powerful terms the irresponsible nature of poetry, based as it is on a "necessary atrophy of conscience," Tsvetaeva does not use this as an alibi, but faces the old Russian demand for morality and usefulness, the demand expressed in exemplary form by Tolstoy, the perfect artist who preferred truth and goodness to art. Often, though not always, the law of art will be opposed to the moral law, and in the end the moral sphere matters more: "To be a human being is more important because it is more necessary. The doctor and priest are more necessary than the poet because they and not we stand by the death-bed." And yet, knowing and admitting this, she ends her essay with the declaration: "I would not change my work for any other. Knowing more, I do less, and therefore I shall not be forgiven. Only from such as me will a reckoning be demanded at the last judgement of conscience. But if there is a last judgement of the word, there I am innocent."

For all its myth-making, this is a wonderfully clear-sighted essay. Tsvetaeva may exaggerate the "sinfulness" of the poet, but she gives full weight to the paradoxical importance of this sinful art. It is worth noticing too that even though she presents the poet as one who "receives" his poem—in a state akin to sleep—she stresses the will and the labour that are needed to transform this gift into a poem. In another essay, **"The Poet and Criticism,"** she insists that poetry is a craft (*Craft*, it will be remembered, is the title she gave to one of her major collections), and for all her doubts about the moral worth of this labour, Tsvetaeva lived a life of poetic dedication, writing through the most difficult personal experiences, and maintaining through everything the integrity and independence of the writer. It seems right then to finish this chapter with a short, simple but rich poem which connects the craft of poetry both with tears and passion and with trees and the earth. It was written in 1933 and included in a cycle called **"Desk" ("Stol")**: . . .

> My faithful writing desk!
> Thanks that you have remained,

While giving a tree to me
To become a desk, a tree!

With the youthful play of leaves
Over eyes, with the living bark,
With the *living* resin tears,
With roots deep down in earth!

(pp. 132-58)

Peter France, "Marina Tsvetaeva," in his Poets of
Modern Russia, *Cambridge University Press, 1982,
pp. 132-58.*

SIMON KARLINSKY   (essay date 1985)

[*Karlinsky is an American educator and essayist who is well
known for his many critical articles on the works of twentieth-
century Russian writers, including Marina Tsvetaeva and
Anton Chekhov. In the following excerpt from his biography,*
Marina Tsvetaeva: The Woman, Her World, and Her Poetry,
Karlinsky surveys Tsvetaeva's major works.]

[Tsvetaeva's] first two collections, *The Evening Album* and
The Magic Lantern, may be best considered as one unit, not
only thematically and stylistically, but chronologically as
well. Many of the poems in the second collection bear the
date 1911, which means that they were written after the publication of *The Evening Album.* But *The Magic Lantern* also
contains a number of undated poems which, as internal evidence shows, were written concurrently with the ones included in *The Evening Album* and possibly even before them.
Tsvetaeva herself once referred to these two collections as
"the same book in spirit." These two collections, therefore,
represent a definite stage in her poetic evolution, a stage that
encompasses the period from the autumn of 1907 to the beginning of 1912.

In his not entirely favourable review of *The Evening Album,*
Valery Briusov astutely observed that Tsvetaeva's poems always have their point of departure in concrete facts, "in
something that she had actually experienced." Like all of her
lyric poetry, those first two books are a diary of her life, encounters, interests and current reading, all of it transfigured
by the alchemy of poetry into a higher reality. Thus, of the
three sections into which *The Evening Album* is divided, the
first one, "Childhood," reflects the author's travels to Nervi,
Lausanne and the Black Forest, the details of her schooling
and her relationships with family and friends. Much of the
book's second section, "Love," outlines her involvement with
[Lev Kobylinsky] Ellis and [Vladimir] Nilender, while the
third section, "Only Shadows," gives expression to her Bona-
partist sympathies, her love for juvenile romances and her
hopes for the future.

Real experience, however, is filtered in these two books
through an emotional outlook that can be best understood
within the context of the romantic and idealistic revival that
took place in French literature at the end of the nineteenth
century. This was the revival exemplified in the novel *Les Plé-
iades* by Joseph-Arthur de Gobineau and . . . *Axël* by Vil-
liers de l'Isle Adam. Tsvetaeva encountered the outlook embodied in these works in a vulgarized and diluted form in
Rostand's *L'Aiglon* and in his *La Princesse lointaine,* which
she also highly valued at the time.

This is a view that leads the poet to expect from life more than
it can possibly give. A concomitant tendency is to admire everything exceptional and heroic and to reject the average, the

humdrum, the prosaic. A very precise expression of this attitude is found in the poem **"A Prayer" ("Molitva")** which
Tsvetaeva wrote in Tarusa on her seventeenth birthday. It begins:

Christ and God! I long for a miracle
Right now, immediately, at break of day!
O let me die, while still
All life is like a book to me.

Thou art wise, Thou wouldst not sternly say:
"Endure, the time is not yet come."
Thou Thyself gavest me so much!
I long for all the roads at once.

The poet then outlines various mutually conflicting "roads"
which she longs to follow

So that yesterday would be legend,
So that every day would be madness

and then concludes the poem with the words

Thou gavest me a childhood better than a fairy tale
So give me a death at seventeen!

(pp. 38-9)

A heroic, miraculous death is preferable to the disappointment and frustration inherent in attaining maturity. Hence
the indiscriminate fascination with any gifted or sensitive person who died young, be it the Duke of Reichstadt, Maria
Bashkirtseva, Lydia Tamburer's son Sergei or the Georgian
princess Nina Dzhavakha, the title character of Charskaya's
cloyingly sentimental novel, beloved by generations of Russian teenaged girls. The spirit of Rostand presided over much
in the world of Tsvetaeva's first two collections, both of
which contain epigraphs from Napoleon, his son and Rostand and poems about characters and situations from
L'Aiglon. This series reaches its slightly absurd climax in the
poem **"Separation" ("Rasstavanie"),** where the fate of the
Duke of Reichstadt is likened to that of Christ and his place
of exile, the palace of Schönbrunn, is equated with Golgotha.
(pp. 39-40)

At seventeen and eighteen Tsvetaeva may have been only a
promising, at times immature poet, but she was already an
amazingly skillful versifier. She did not seem aware at the
time of the possibilities of Russian accentual verse (*dol'nik*),
which was widely practiced among her senior contemporaries, and restricted herself to the five canonic meters of Russian nineteenth-century versification. Any possible metrical
monotony was easily overcome by young Tsvetaeva's amazingly strophic inventiveness. From the very beginning Tsvetaeva shows a mastery in this area that gives her a place alongside Zhukovsky and Fet, the two poets particularly noted for
their originality in inventing new types of stanzas. Structural
resourcefulness typical of the mature Tsvetaeva is also manifest at this early period. She likes segmenting her poems into
three sections, each of which is a syntactic and thematic variation on the poem's central idea. Thus, **"Rouge et bleue"** in
The Evening Album consists of three long stanzas which
show the poem's two protagonists successively as little children, as young girls and as grown-up women in frustrating
situations appropriate to each age. The structural parallelism
brings out the parallelism in these two women's fate.

In a highly interesting study of role conflict in Tsvetaeva's poetics, Antonina Filonov Gove found that **"Rouge et bleue"**
is one of several poems in the first two collections in which
the poet explicitly rejects the standard role allocated to

women in human society [see excerpt dated 1977]. One of the reasons the persona clings so desperately to childhood is that some of the "roads" she mentioned in **"A Prayer"** are barred to her: the roles of a warrior, a bard or a drummer marching at the head of a platoon. The most attractive role of all for Tsvetaeva, then and later, was that of an independent Amazon, a role she had in her grasp and voluntarily relinquished. Voloshin was nothing less than prophetic when he wrote in his review of **The Evening Album** that the essence of Tsvetaeva's poetry was encompassed in the following quatrain:

> I love women who knew no fear in battle,
> Who were able to handle a sword and a spear.
> But I know that only in the cradle's prison
> Is my ordinary feminine happiness.
>
> (p. 41)

1913 was the year when Tsvetaeva's poetry began to mature and to evolve away from the adolescent tone of her first two collections. This can be observed in several poems on the subject of death which she wrote that year. They show a turn toward sobriety of tone and a simplicity that borders on austerity, especially when compared to the ostentatiously romantic manner of her earlier poetry. Her understanding of death in these poems is fundamentally different from the youthful desire for an early, glorious death which she had voiced only a few years earlier. Now the attitude is a calm acceptance of death as an ever-present fact in our lives. In one mature and precisely worded poem after another, the young wife and recent mother writes of her own funeral, addresses a passer-by at her future tomb and speaks from her grave to a remote descendant. There is no fear of death in these poems, nor are they tragic. Ultimately, the tone is affirmative and almost optimistic.

These poems form a part of Tsvetaeva's next collection of verse which she called **Juvenilia (Yunosheskie stikhi)** and which comprises the poetry she wrote between the beginning of 1913 and the last day of 1915. The title is not very appropriate, since the term *juvenilia* describes her first two books much better than the book she thus named. Never published in its complete form during the poet's lifetime, the collection has appeared in two editions in the West since 1976. Only a few individual poems from it were included in Soviet editions.

Juvenilia is clearly a transitional collection, the only such instance in Tsvetaeva's output. Much of its poetry is still in her early romantic manner. Such is the case with a cycle of poems addressed to her sister Asya and a set of memorial poems occasioned by the death of Sergei Efron's older brother Piotr. Such is also the case with several poems about literary figures, though by now Tsvetaeva had graduated from Rostand and Bashkirtseva to Pushkin and Byron. But the poems about death . . . were a new departure and so was the ambitious project she undertook in the first half of 1914. This was the long narrative poem **"The Enchanter,"** which she dedicated to Asya and subtitled *poèma*.

In the eighteenth century, the term *poèma* designated in Russian literary terminology an epic poem written in imitation of Homer or Virgil. In Pushkin's time, this term was applied to the Byronic tale in verse. In the eighteenth and nineteenth centuries the genre of *poèma* presupposed a developed fictional or historical plot. Twentieth-century Russian poets, however, replaced the traditionally well-constructed plot of the earlier *poèma* with a fragmentary autobiographical narrative, usually centered on the poet's own psychological experiences rather than on external events. Had Tsvetaeva's **"The Enchanter"** been published shortly after it was written instead of having to wait six decades, it would have taken its rightful place as a pioneering example of this new twentieth-century form of autobiographical narrative poem. It predates such major instances of this genre as Viacheslav Ivanov's "Infancy" (1918), Andrei Bely's "The First Encounter" (1921), and Mayakovsky's "About This" (1923).

Written in a special stanza devised for the occasion and consisting of three lines of iambic tetrameter followed by a two-foot iambic line, **"The Enchanter"** traces and celebrates the impact that their friendship with Ellis had on the two Tsvetaev sisters. The model for this poem may have been "Three Meetings" by Vladimir Soloviov (1898), a verse narrative that tells, in humorous and self-deprecating tones, of the poet-philosopher's innermost mystical experience of being in contact with St. Sophia, the feminine personification of Divine Wisdom. Tsvetaeva, similarly, pokes puckish fun at her own and her sister's childishness and naiveté and at the scatterbrained ways of Ellis, while recounting, with love and gratitude, Ellis's lectures on the Symbolist and mystical theories of Soloviov, Merezhkovsky and Blok, and the festive and enchanted evenings the sisters spent with him. The poem is the maturing poet's farewell to her younger self, which she leaves behind but does not renounce. (pp. 49-50)

The poems included in **Mileposts I (Versty I)** were written between January and December 1916 and the book thus constitutes an uninterrupted lyrical diary for that year. Initially, Tsvetaeva contemplated a larger collection which would comprise her poetry for 1916 and 1917 and would be called, somewhat enigmatically, *Mother Milepost (Mater'-Versta)*. But when she was sorting out her poetry in 1921, she must have realized that her verse of the last pre-revolutionary year formed a well-defined unit, while the poetry she wrote from 1917 on broke into two distinct strains, the lyrical and the political. Thus came the division into volumes which is appropriate both chronologically and stylistically: the poetry of 1916 went into **Mileposts I,** while the poems written between 1917 and 1920 were subdivided into several other collections in accordance with their thematic content.

In her first two collections, published in 1910 and 1912, Tsvetaeva used a late-Victorian, upper-class diction that was not always free of self-conscious artificiality. In the better poems of **Juvenilia,** her style moved toward greater clarity. Her poems about death, the cycle about her affair with Sophia Parnok and some of the poems of early 1916 addressed to Mandelstam have the kind of magical simplicity of tone and style that we find in the earliest poems by Mandelstam and the last poems Boris Pasternak wrote before his death. This is a simplicity that is very hard for a poet to achieve or for a critic to define. There is an almost Mozartian purity of language. Every word is direct and seemingly inevitable.

In **Mileposts I** this simplicity remains in certain poems. But elsewhere in the book we find a colorful explosion of styles and manners. Until now, Tsvetaeva's verse used only the traditional Russian binary (iambic and trochaic) and ternary (the dactyl, the amphibrach and the anapest) meters. Her poems were always rhymed and their rhymes were conventional nineteenth-century ones, typical for Russian poetry from Pushkin to Vladimir Soloviov. Much of **Mileposts I** is in accentual verse, the rhymes are often assonances or half-rhymes, and there is blank verse, free verse without meter or rhyme, and imitation of folk poetry, such as *raëshnik*.

The limpid diction of *Juvenilia* is now overlaid by other stylistic strains, which will eventually become incorporated into Tsvetaeva's mature later style. The two most important of these can be described, somewhat schematically, as her use of archaisms and of colloquial or vulgar diction. Tsvetaeva was not a linguist and her use of these two language strata was intuitive, creative and, occasionally, indiscriminate. Her archaist manner comprised Church Slavic and Old Russian vocabulary and grammar of the Russian Bible and of Orthodox prayers; also, the remnants of chancery language of pre-Petrine Russia, as well as her later deliberate imitation of the style of eighteenth-century Russian poets. Her colloquial manner likewise absorbed a number of linguistic phenomena of various origins: uneducated and peasant speech, regional expressions, formulae from folklore and, where appropriate, deliberately coarse language.

Tsvetaeva was not a pioneer in any of these areas. Archaic and ecclesiastic diction was typical of Symbolist poets such as Viacheslav Ivanov and Alexander Blok. Colloquialisms and peasant speech were a feature of Alexei Remizov's prose and an uncontested specialty of the peasant group of poets. Accentual verse and assonance rhymes were launched . . . by Zinaida Gippius in the early 1890s. By about 1910, they had become standard in the work of junior Symbolists and Acmeists. But Tsvetaeva assimilated all these diverse strains into her poetry with considerable skill and made them a part of her personal mode of expression. By 1916, she mastered the entire range of innovations introduced by the Symbolists, the peasant poets, the Acmeists and, to a minor extent, even the Futurists and in doing so achieved a striking originality of her own.

It may be paradoxical, but in the collection in which Tsvetaeva's originality became so strongly manifest, we can discern more clearly than in any other the influence on her of other contemporary Russian poets. This is particularly obvious in some of the poems of the cycles addressed to Akhmatova and Blok, where Tsvetaeva sometimes chose to speak to those poets in approximations of their own voices. Here, for example is a brief poem from the Akhmatova cycle, which reproduces some of Akhmatova's stylistic mannerisms, including the assonance rhymes and accentual meter (not conveyed, obviously, in the English version) and the typical Akhmatovan final *concetto* that involves religion and hints at some undisclosed, possibly tragic, relationship between the poet and the person described:

> At the market place people were shouting.
> Clouds of steam floated out of a bakery.
> I retain in memory the crimson mouth
> Of a gaunt-faced street songstress.
>
> In a dark tiny-flowered kerchief
> —May the grace be granted—
> You, standing with eyes downcast in a crowd
> Of praying women in St. Sergius-Trinity [Monastery].
>
> Pray for me, my beauty,
> Melancholy and diabolical,
> When the [dissenter sects of the] forests
> Elect you Our Lady of the Flagellants.

To express the personal drama which is the subject of many poems in *Mileposts I,* Tsvetaeva resorted to wide use of personae or stylistic masks. Her new mastery of unlettered, colloquial speech stands her in good stead when she addresses the reader through the mask of a Moscow woman of the lower classes, a "tavern queen" (*kabatskaia tsaritsa*) or a religious pilgrim, sinful, proud, passionate, occasionally a criminal, occasionally dabbling in magic. Tsvetaeva's daughter, Ariadna Efron, tried in her memoirs to attribute this strain to Tsvetaeva's exposure to large masses of common Russian people during her travels after the October Revolution. But since this manner is very much in evidence almost two years before that revolution, the travels in question must have been the wide-ranging ones in the company of Sophia Parnok during their closeness in 1915.

Stylistically and technically, *Mileposts I* was the most daringly experimental of Tsvetaeva's collections and it constituted a watershed in her poetic evolution. In it, she not only learned whatever the great age of Russian poetry in which she lived had to teach her, but she also became a major innovator in her own right. Some of the innovations launched in this book were to be developed and consolidated in her later volumes.

One that is already fully formed in *Mileposts I* is her introduction into Russian poetry of special meters which George Ivask in the 1930s and G. S. Smith in the 1970s have termed *logaoedic*. These meters are built on the already existing meters. But they combine, on a regular basis, more than one kind of foot in a line—a practice that simply did not exist in Russian poetry until that time. Khlebnikov experimented with mixing several meters in one poem somewhat earlier, and Mandelstam has a few early poems which add an extra stressed syllable where the meter does not call for it. What Tsvetaeva does, however, is to invent a new, *ad hoc* metrical pattern, which she then sustains throughout a particular poem. Here is a stanza from a much-anthologized poem from *Mileposts I* in which this is done, quoted first in the original, then in translation:

> V ogromnom gorode moiom—noch'.
> Iz doma sonnogo idu—proch'.
> I liudi dumaiut: zhena, doch'.
> A ia zapomnila odno: noch'.
>
> In my immense city it is night.
> From the sleeping house I walk—away.
> And people think: she's a wife, she's a daughter.
> But I remembered one thing only: the night.

Here, one stressed monosyllabic word is regularly added to what would otherwise have been a line of very usual Russian iambic tetrameter, turning it into something quite unique. Repeated for four quatrains, with only one rhyme per quatrain, the metrical pattern creates a hypnotic effect, in keeping with the sense of alienation and unreality experienced by the persona of the poem.

For all the thematic and technical variety of its poetry, the collection *Mileposts I* is unified by its forcefully sounded central theme: the city of Moscow and the poet's involvement with its topography and history. As Tsvetaeva wrote much later to George Ivask: "Yes, it was I who in 1916 was the first to speak thus of Moscow. . . . And I am happy and proud of this, for it was the Moscow of the last hour and last time." (pp. 62-5)

The Demesne of the Swans (Lebedinyi stan) . . . [is Tsvetaeva's] collection of poems about the February and October Revolutions and the ensuing civil war—the period known as the epoch of War Communism. Like the diaries she began keeping in November 1917, this collection shows Tsvetaeva in a new literary role which she deliberately chose at that time, that of chronicler of the momentous period in which she was living. (p. 70)

In describing Marina Tsvetaeva's life in Moscow after the October Revolution [in his book *Existence and Being*], Prince Sergei Volkonsky carefully distinguished between *byt* (everyday material existence) and *bytie* (a higher, spiritualized state of being). This very Tsvetaevan distinction, with its semantic dependence on a variation of the same verbal stem, has great validity not only for her life in the period in question but for the rest of her life as well. The years of oppression and material hardship were also the years of great productivity and creative development for Tsvetaeva the poet. The poetry that was included in *The Demesne of the Swans* and the prose pieces about the conditions of her life intended for *Omens of the Earth* reflected her and Russia's *byt* of that period. *Bytie* was expressed in two other collections written in those same years, *Mileposts II* (*Versty II*, 1917-21) and *Craft* (*Remeslo*, 1921-22), as well as in the lyrics on romantic themes that appeared in the collection *Psyche* (*Psikheia*, 1923), which also contained poems from several of her other collections. In Volume Two of the New York 1982 edition of her complete poetry there is also an additional large body of lyrics dating from that period which Tsvetaeva did not include in any of her collections but published later in periodicals.

During the years of War Communism, Tsvetaeva extended her range and, in addition to lyric poetry, turned to larger epic forms . . . , to drama and to prose. (pp. 82-3)

During the last two years before her departure from Russia, 1920-1922, Tsvetaeva undertook three long epic poems based on Russian folklore sources, of which she completed two, and she wrote a long lyrical poem, **"On a Red Steed"** (**"Na krasnom kone"**), which fused the confessional and the folkloric modes. The earliest of these long works was *The Tsar-Maiden* (*Tsar'-devitsa*), written between July and September 1920 and published in Berlin in 1922 as a separate book. Like its two successors, **"Sidestreets"** (**"Pereulochki"**) finished in Moscow in April 1922 and included in the collection *Craft*, and *The Swain* (*Mólodets*) completed in Prague in December 1924, *The Tsar-Maiden* is nominally a folk tale in verse. This is a genre that was prevalent in the Romantic Age when Zhukovsky and Pushkin popularized quasi-folk tales in verse which often borrowed both their subjects and their versification from foreign sources. Despite this, the results (e.g., Pushkin's "The Golden Cockerel," with a plot taken from Washington Irving, or Piotr Ershov's perennially popular "The Little Hump-Backed Horse," 1834, extended version 1856) were accepted by generations of parents, children and schoolmasters as genuine Russian folklore.

As Vladislav Khodasevich pointed out in his review of Tsvetaeva's *The Swain,* real Russian folk tales and magic tales were always narrated in prose. Couching them in verse arose through Russian nineteenth-century poets' imitation of Western models—Ariosto, Evariste Parny and the German romantics. Furthermore, while the pseudo-folk tales in verse by Zhukovsky, Pushkin and Ershov may be enjoyed by adults, they have survived in the culture primarily as reading for children. Tsvetaeva's folklore-based long poems treat philosophical and erotic themes that no child could hope to understand. Drawing on the command of colloquial, peasant and substandard speech which she had developed and perfected in *Mileposts I,* the poet tells complex and highly sophisticated stories using the diction now of a pre-Petrine folk singer, now of an unlettered peasant narrator.

The Tsar-Maiden grafts two stories from Alexander Afanasiev's collection of Russian folk tales onto the classical myth to which Tsvetaeva would return again and again in her writings of the 1920s, that of Phaedra's incestuous love for her stepson Hippolytus. The poem tells of a drunken, corrupt old Tsar, his frail musician-son and the Tsar's young, beautiful second wife who resorts to witchcraft to seduce her stepson. The heroine of the title is a curious character who occurs in Russian folk tales and epic poems (*byliny*), the warrior-maiden, a huge and powerful Amazon who is traditionally shown falling in love with a weak, delicate man. She courts the musician prince with the aid of white magic, while the desperate stepmother resorts to the black arts to win his love, or, failing that, at least his body. The stepmother is abetted by the prince's evil, lecherous old tutor, to whom she has to submit sexually in order to secure his help. The Tsar-Maiden is aided by a sexless, non-human character, Wind, who helps her defeat the stepmother.

Two fine studies published in recent years help us understand this poem in greater depth. Sophia Poliakova's essay on the sources of *The Tsar-Maiden* points out that the two good characters, the Tsar-Maiden and the musician prince, have been made far more androgynous than they were in Afanasiev. And indeed, the reversal or scrambling of gender roles here has a bearing not only on the instances from Tsvetaeva's poetry cited by Poliakova, but also on a number of other works, among them **"Woman Friend,"** **"The Comedian"** and *An Adventure.* At the risk of sounding simplistic, one can venture to say that in the two lovers of *The Tsar-Maiden* the poet projected two alternate images of herself: in the Tsar-Maiden, the strong and independent Amazon she would have liked to be and in the prince, the vulnerable artist she knew she was. As G. S. Smith has shown in his essay "Characters and Narrative Modes in Marina Tsvetaeva's *Tsar'-devitsa*" [see Further Reading], the two lovers' characters evolve and converge in the course of the narrative, so that they come to resemble each other more and more.

The final section of *The Tsar-Maiden,* an epilogue that takes place after the fate of the principal characters has been settled, depicts a popular revolution during which a mob skins the corrupt old Tsar alive and proclaims the triumph of Red Russia. In her essays **"A Poet on Criticism"** and **"The Poet and Time,"** Tsvetaeva wrote that occasionally themes select their poets rather than the other way around. This was apparently what had happened with the finale of *The Tsar-Maiden.* The poet who disagreed with the October Revolution and denounced it in so much of her work seems to assert its truth in textbook Bolshevik terms at the end of her folk tale set in legendary ancient Russia.

"Sidestreets" is the most spectacular manifestation of Tsvetaeva's interest in the folk poetry of magic chants and incantations, an interest also evident in certain poems of *Mileposts I* and *Craft.* On first reading, it seems a puzzle. A work of great verbal virtuosity, it strikes the reader as one vast incantation, with some narrative elements which are, however, hard to perceive as a coherent whole. When Tsvetaeva sent to Boris Pasternak a copy of *Craft,* which contains this poem, she asked particularly for his comments on **"Sidestreets."** In her letter to him of March 10, 1923 she wrote: "No one seems to grasp the plot (the connection). . . . For me this work is as clear as day, *everything* has been said. Others hear only the noises and I find this insulting."

Fortunately, a decade later, this poem perplexed Tsvetaeva's correspondent George Ivask and he questioned her about its contents. On October 11, 1935, she wrote: " 'Sidestreets' (didn't you know it?) is the story of the ultimate seduction." Apparently, Ivask was still not satisfied with the explanation, for in Tsvetaeva's letter of January 24, 1937, we find a long commentary on **"Sidestreets"**: ". . . you have simply understood nothing in 'Sidestreets.' Open your *byliny* and find the *bylina* about Marinka who lives in the Ignatiev sidestreets and practices magic behind the bed-curtain, turning young swains into aurochs, getting them drugged. . . . She is *deceit* and she is playing with something frightening."

Byliny are oral folk poems whose themes are thought to go back to the early Middle Ages. Tsvetaeva's letter to Ivask directs us to the proper literary address for the plot of **"Sidestreets."** If ever a poem needed a synopsis, this one does. The heroine, never once identified in the text, turns out to be the sorceress Marina Ignatievna who appears in one of the *byliny* about the epic hero Dobrynia Nikitich. This mythic sorceress was one of the several avatars in the Russian folklore tradition of Marina Mnishek, the Polish wife of the False Dmitry and always one of Tsvetaeva's favourite historical personages. With the narrative canvas provided by the *bylina,* we can follow the action, which is narrated alternately from the vantage point of the sorceress and that of her victim. Many details were taken verbatim from the *bylina,* but much has been added by Tsvetaeva: the role of the victim's horse as the symbol of his masculine integrity destroyed by a conniving woman and the ecstatic apotheosis he thinks he is experiencing at the very moment he is being turned into a beast. (pp. 98-101)

Without the *bylina* as a guide, the work is a colorful spray of verbal pyrotechnics; with it, it becomes a haunting and profound poem. (p. 101)

"On a Red Steed" was written between January 13 and 17, 1921. It belongs among Tsvetaeva's lyrical-autobiographical *poèmy,* such as **"The Enchanter"** which preceded it and **"Poem of the End"** and **"From the Seacoast"** which were to follow. Yet, it is the only poem of this group which has features of epic poetry and folk tradition. The violent and turbulent poem falls into three segments, with an introduction and an epilogue. Against the background of some calamity—a burning house, a snowstorm or a military battle—the protagonist is exposed to three temptations. Each time she is about to perish unless she renounces what tempts her and each time she is rescued by the symbolic figure of a winged knight on a red steed, who, as the epilogue first makes clear, is her poetic genius. The three temptations have a complex, multifaceted meaning, but on their basic level they stand for the renunciation of love, religion and pride for the sake of one's artistic calling. After the heroine overcomes the last temptation, her guardian genius finds her on a battlefield (which also represents erotic love) and offers himself as the replacement for all the thing she has made her give up:

And the whisper: "Now you are as I desired you!"
And the murmur: "Now you are as I elected you,
Child of my passion, my sister, my brother,
My bride in the ice of armor.

Mine and no one's till the end of years."
I, with arms raised: "My light!"
"You will remain so? You won't be anyone's?"
I, clutching my wound: "No one's."

The poem is an allegory about the terrible and demanding na-

ture of art. At its initial publication, **"On a Red Steed"** was dedicated to Anna Akhmatova. Akhmatova several times described her Muse as a young foreigner who visited her and enabled her to create poetry. **"On a Red Steed"** begins and ends with the assertion that Tsvetaeva never had a Muse as either a nursemaid or a companion. Instead, the personification of her poetic inspiration, Tsvetaeva insists, is masculine: the Knight of the Red Steed (the color of his horse is derived from the purifying fire that in the first segment of the poem destroys the edifice of traditional poetry in which the poet was brought up). The dedication to Akhmatova and the rejection of a female Muse must have been Tsvetaeva's way of pointing out the essential difference between her own poetry and that of a contemporary whom she loved and admired but also perceived as a constant hindrance and rival, as several of her poems addressed to Akhmatova make clear. (pp. 102-03)

Mileposts I, Tsvetaeva's most comprehensive previous collection, was an uninterrupted poetic diary for one year, 1916. *Craft* follows this precedent, but this time the year encompassed does not coincide with the calendar year, for it covers the period from April 1921 to April 1922. Tsvetaeva had separated the poetry she wrote during the years 1917-21 into two categories, the political (*The Demesne of the Swans*) and the personal and escapist (*Mileposts II*). But the collection *Craft* combines the personal, the political and the philosophical into one alloy, thus marking a new step in Tsvetaeva's evolution. In *Mileposts I,* the central theme was the poet's relationship to the city of Moscow. *Craft* treats many different themes, but two central ones can be discerned: postrevolutionary Russia and the poet's love for her absent husband. (pp. 107-08)

In June and July 1921, Tsvetaeva composed, one after another, three cycles of poems addressed to her husband: **"Separation"** (**"Razluka"**), **"St. George"** (**"Georgii"**) and **"Good Tidings"** (**"Blagaia vest' "**). The man once described in *Juvenilia* as a jewel and an aquatic plant, is now an epic hero, a shining swan and a radiant knight defending honor and decency from brutal usurpers. At the same time the poet's love for him is something enormously vulnerable and threatened. In the melodious seventh poem of **"Separation,"** this love is depicted as Ganymede and as a defenseless little lamb. . . . (p. 108)

Classical and biblical allusions are frequent in *Craft.* The ironically titled cycle **"In Praise of Aphrodite"** (**"Khvala Afrodite"**) denounces the goddess of sensual love (who was the villainess in Tsvetaeva's play *The Stone Angel*) for allocating too much suggestive power to the sexual drive:

Every cloud in a bad moment
Curves like [a woman's] breast.
In every guiltless flower [appears]
Your visage, you She-Devil!

Perishable foam, salt of the sea,
In froth and in torment
For how long are we to obey you,
You armless stone?

The odic, neoclassical diction of such cycles as **"In Praise of Aphrodite"** and **"The Disciple"** (addressed . . . to Volkonsky) forms one stylistic pole of *Craft.* At the opposite pole is the burst of incantations and magic chants found in other cycles, such as **"Captured by the Khan"** (**"Khanskii polon"**) and **"Snowdrifts"** (**"Sugroby"**). These incantatory poems exploit to the full Tsvetaeva's gift for verbal creativity and colloquial language. Their culmination is the already discussed narrative poem **"Sidestreets,"** which closes the collection. Somewhere between these two poles is the diction of several poems in the collection that describe the devastation caused by the revolution and the civil war. Tsvetaeva was not only appalled by the wreckage and the suffering, she was apprehensive that they would now spread to other countries through the coming world-wide revolution, which was confidently predicted by many at that time:

> Migrating
> To what kind of New York?
> With universal enmity
> Loaded on our backs,
> What bears we are!
> What Tatars we are!
> Devoured by lice,
> We bring conflagrations.
>
> . . . . .
>
> "In the name of the Lord!
> In the name of reason!"
> What a fester we are,
> What a leprosy we are!
> With a wolfish sparkle
> Through the snowstorms' fur,
> The Star of Russia
> Against the world!
>
> [Whither,] parricides,
> Into what absurdity?
> Careful you're not mistaken,
> You scourge of the universe!

(pp. 109-10)

Many fine twentieth-century poets, after finding their own individual voices, chose to stay with the same style for decades. Such was the case with Gippius, Akhmatova and Khodasevich. Others underwent a gradual stylistic evolution. Mikhail Kuzmin and Osip Mandelstam moved from simplicity to ever greater complexity, while the development of Boris Pasternak was in the opposite direction. Marina Tsvetaeva, alone, could manage within the same year and the same book of verse, such as *Craft,* a whole gamut of diverse voices, dictions and styles, while remaining her own self throughout. She described this aspect of her talent in a letter to Ivask better than any critic could: "When you speak of [my] loudness, you must also mention my quiet aspects. I have poems which are *quieter* than anyone's. I can be grasped *only* in terms of contrasts, i.e., of the simultaneous presence of *everything*. . . . I am *many* poets; as to how I've managed to harmonize all of them, that is my secret."

The real glory of *Craft* lies in its varied and pulsating rhythms, which Andrei Bely qualified as Tsvetaeva's "invincible rhythms." Ariadna Efron has likened Tsvetaeva's early poetry and her romantic verse plays to Chopin. *Craft* is comparable to *The Rite of Spring*. Like that epochal work, *Craft* contains slow and reflective passages. But the more striking poems pound and throb in a way found in no other poet, not even in Mayakovsky or Pasternak, who were both masters of percussive verse. The most extreme example in *Craft* is **"The Leader's Return"** (**"Vozvrashchenie vozhdia"**), written entirely in spondees, i.e., lines consisting of two stressed monosyllabic words. More effective are the numerous poems in this collection where the unexpectedly placed stresses lend the verse lines a distinctive rhythm: a march, a dance, a dirge and, quite often, something resembling jungle tom-toms.

Title page of The King-Maiden.

Nothing like it has been heard in Russian poetry before or, for that matter, since. With this collection of profound and explosive poetry, Marina Tsvetaeva became the equal of any poet, Russian or foreign, who was writing at that time. It took most of her compatriots half a century to realize this. (pp. 110-11)

In **"Poem of the Hill"** (**"Poèma gory"**) and **"Poem of the End"** (**"Poèma kontsa"**) [both written in 1924], Tsvetaeva takes up the confessional, autobiographical mode she had initiated with **"The Enchanter"** in 1914. But to compare this earlier poem to them is to realize what a wide-ranging stylistic and structural evolution Tsvetaeva's poetic manner had undergone in the intervening decade. **"Poem of the Hill"** is actually not a narrative poem, but rather a sequence of ten interconnected lyric poems, preceded by a dedication and followed by an epilogue, about the hill in Prague on which the poet and her lover used to meet during the brief period of their happiness. The hill itself is the protagonist of the poem, rather than either one of the lovers. The hill is anthropomorphized and endowed with knowledge, desires and emotions. The Czech commentator Vladimir Smetáček has pointed out in his essay on the semantic and spatial relationships in **"Poem of the Hill"** the systematic opposition between the summit of the hill, where love and suffering are possible and where the poet feels at home, and the city below, associated with "rabble, market place, barracks," which is inimical to strong emotions and where she feels alienated. In the ninth and tenth sections of the poem, the persona imagines the hill becoming a part of the city of Prague, built over with cottages and shops. She lays a curse on the complacent philistines she expects to reside in the future on her hill for she assumes that they will be indifferent to the happiness and misery she had once experienced there:

> Your daughters shall be harlots
> And your sons grow up to be poets!
>
> • • • • •
>
> May you not have earthly happiness,
> O you ants, on my hill!
>
> At an unknown hour, at an unexpected time
> Your entire family shall recognize
> The immeasurable and immense
> Hill of the seventh commandment.

"Poem of the Hill" is a poem of great pain. Its indiscriminately vengeful tone and the destructive urge of its final sections are sure to repel many readers. Tsvetaeva herself may not have been entirely satisfied by such a bitter memorial to her love, because immediately after completing this poem she embarked on its companion piece, **"Poem of the End."** This poem is genuinely narrative and highly dramatic. It describes in great detail the evening on which the lovers decide that their relationship must end. The reader follows them on their strolls through the streets and suburbs of Prague, a walk by the river, a visit to a café and their conversations during which the need to separate is articulated. In the last two sections, the man is unable to hold back his tears, making the woman realize that he loves and needs her and causing some merriment on the part of three prostitutes who happen to witness the final farewell. Every word, glance and action of her departing lover is analyzed by the desperate woman, with a constant conflict between her imagination and what her reason and senses tell her to be facts. The method is that of a stream of consciousness, conveyed in a choppy, telegraphic diction, with insight and expressivity that make **"Poem of the End"** one of the great psychological poems in the Russian language.

"Poem of the Hill" and **"Poem of the End"** deal with powerful and often confused emotions. Yet, these emotions are couched in verbal structures of harmony and logic which are often of considerable complexity. "Tsvetaeva constructs her apparently unbalanced and excessively emotional poems like a logician and an architect," wrote Vladimir Smetáček. This is attained in **"Poem of the End"** by a system of recurrent refrains and by sequences of stanzas which are sets of variations on a syntactic or semantic theme. Individual words are often broken up by dashes which create stresses where they do not occur in normal Russian prosody. This is one of the devices that enabled Tsvetaeva to create new, unprecedented meters (she was also using them in shorter poems written at that time). All this, combined with a frequently elliptical style, gives **"Poem of the End"** a kind of cubistic verbal texture that is highly original and that has defied, so far, the best efforts of translators to render this poem into other languages. Because of its theatrical quality, **"Poem of the End"** has been given dramatized stage presentations in Moscow and in Prague in recent decades. Since its first publication in the Soviet Union in 1961 it has won an appreciative new audience and become one of the best loved narrative poems of the twentieth century.

The Swain* (*Mólodets*),** dedicated to Boris Pasternak, is the last of Tsvetaeva's trilogy of pseudo-folk poems on subjects derived from folklore collections. Like ***The Tsar-Maiden, it is based on a tale from Alexander Afanasiev's book. Unlike it, ***The Swain,*** except for its ending, follows its source with utmost fidelity, to the point of incorporating quotations from Afanasiev's version into its text. The poem tells the story of the village maiden Marusia who goes to a dance and meets a handsome young swain with whom she falls in love. He turns out to be a vampire. Instead of denouncing him to the authorities and saving herself, Marusia keeps silent while her mother, her brother and finally herself, in a scene of mixed horror and tenderness, are killed by the vampire. Marusia is buried in accordance with certain magic rites specified by the vampire (in Afanasiev, by her grandmother) and is incarnated in a flower that grows on her grave and can periodically turn into a woman.

In this new guise, Marusia marries a local nobleman who puts a sign of the cross on her to prevent her from turning back into a flower. Listless and apathetic, she remains with the nobleman for five years during which time she bears him a son. Then her husband forces her to attend a church service, where she senses the presence of her first love, the vampire. At this point, Tsvetaeva's plot and denouement become radically different from her source in Afanasiev. In the original folk tale, Marusia threw some holy water on the vampire, destroying him forever, and lived happily ever after with her husband. In ***The Swain,*** she forsakes her husband and son, yields once more to the vampire and, against the background of solemnly intoned fragments from the Church Slavic liturgy and quotations from the Book of Psalms, flies with him toward heaven in a burst of scarlet light.

"By some miracle," wrote Dmitry Shakhovskoy of this poem, "a plume of the fabled Firebird of Russian folk song has been stolen and this plume is being used to write 'civilized'—in terms of plot and form—poems. Instead of congratulating civilization (or at least being offended on behalf of epos), some of our critics merely shrug their shoulders." And indeed, apart from Vladislav Khodasevich's sympathetic essay on ***The Swain,*** Russian critics did not quite know what to make of this poem with its unexpected and morally ambiguous finale. In her 1926 essay **"A Poet on Criticism,"** Tsvetaeva outlined her reasons for writing ***The Swain*** [see excerpt dated 1926].

> I read "The Vampire" [in Afanasiev's collection] and was puzzled. Why is it that Marusia, who fears the vampire, so persistently refused to admit what she had seen while knowing that to name it is to be rescued? Why no instead of yes? Fear? But fear can make us not only bury ourselves in a bed, it can make us jump out the window. No, not fear. Granted, fear, but something else as well. Fear and what else? When I am told: do this and you are free and I do not do it, that means that I do not want freedom, that my non-freedom is more precious to me. And what is this precious non-freedom that exists between people? Love. Marusia loved the vampire. This is why she would not name him and kept losing, one after another, her mother, her brother, her life. Passion and crime, passion and sacrifice. Such was my task when I started working on ***The Swain.*** To uncover the essence of the folk tale already implicit in its skeleton. To release it from its spell

[*raskoldovat' veshch'*]. And not at all to create a "new form" or "folkloric form."

The metrical texture of *The Swain* is once again a new departure when compared with Tsvetaeva's earlier folklore-based poems. This texture is permeated with Russian folk dance rhythms which begin throbbing from the very first lines:

> Sin' da sgin'—krai sela,
> Rukhnul dub, trost' tsela.
> U vdovy u toi u trudnoi
> Doch' Marusia vesela.

> The azure. And begone! At the village edge,
> The oak has toppled, the reed is standing.
> That hard-working widow yonder
> Has a merry daughter, Marusia.

These dance rhythms keep recurring throughout the length of the poem. The bouncy trochaic meter, typical of Russian dance tunes, blends organically with Tsvetaeva's special logaoedic and choriambic meters into patterns reminiscent now of the coachmen's and nursemaids' dances in Stravinsky's *Petrushka* and now of the orgiastic choruses of the last section of the same composer's ballet-cantata about a village wedding, *Les Noces (Svadebka)*.

In **"The Pied Piper" ("Krysolov"),** Tsvetaeva turned to the German medieval legend of the Pied Piper of Hamelin (*Der Rattenfänger von Hameln*). As Marie-Luise Bott pointed out in the annotations to her [German edition of this poem, published in 1982], Tsvetaeva must have been familiar with various treatments of this legend in the German literary tradition, including those by the Brothers Grimm, Goethe and Karl Simrock's ballad "Der Rattenfänger." An essential source for her version was Heinrich Heine's satire on power-hungry radicals, "Die Wanderratten." Heine and his poetry were very much on Tsvetaeva's mind while she was writing **"The Pied Piper"** and she was at one point thinking of dedicating the poem to him. Another important source for this poem, which Marie-Luise Bott uncovered in a separate study, was Vladimir Belsky's libretto for Nikolai Rimsky-Korsakov's opera *The Legend of the Invisible City of Kitezh,* on which Tsvetaeva drew for a number of situations and reminiscences. A German source not mentioned by Dr. Bott is the thirteenth chapter of *Der Trompeter von Säkkingen* by Victor von Scheffel, the long poem which Tsvetaeva had known and loved since her childhood, and on which she based the situation and argument of Canto Five of **"The Pied Piper."**

The subtitle of **"The Pied Piper"** is "A Lyrical Satire." The targets of Tsvetaeva's satire are both social and political. From her romantic literary roots, especially from Pushkin and Heine, Tsvetaeva inherited the nineteenth-century notion that the enemy of the poet and the artist is the faceless philistine, preoccupied with materialistic values only and hostile to the life of the spirit. This concept is conveyed in German by the noun *Spiessbürger* and the adjective *borniert;* Russian has a whole array of terms for conveying philistinism and narrow-minded vulgarity: *meshchanstvo, obyvatel'-shchina,* and the more abstract one, made popular in Western languages by Nabokov, *poshlost'.* Tsvetaeva knew this phenomenon not only through denunciations by her favourite poets but from personal experience as well: the profiteering Bolsheviks described in **"Free Passage,"** the shady dealers in rare commodities of the NEP period, and, in emigration, families who arranged their material well-being with no

thought of creative or spiritual realms. In her letter to Olga Kolbasina of November 6, 1924, Tsvetaeva wrote with fury of a placid émigré family in Prague who spent their days in leisure and fed their children choice cold cuts and pastries, while her own eleven-year-old daughter Ariadna had to "rush all day from the broom to the garbage can." But the ultimate image of smug philistinism was found by Tsvetaeva in the small Czech town where her daughter attended a boarding school, Moravská Třebová. It was situated near the German border and its German name was Mährisch-Trübau. Tsvetaeva felt alienated by the patriarchal and prosperous way of life in this town. It was a town, as she told her daughter, which "deserved a Pied Piper because of its practical, soulless way of life, its adherence to *meshchanstvo* as the only possible, the only rational form of existence."

"The Pied Piper" is in six cantos. The German locale is asserted not only in proper names, but in occasional macaronic passages of Russian and German which occur throughout the poem. The first two cantos describe, in sparkling and humorous verse, the prosaic and materialistic way of life enjoyed by the burghers of Hamelin. "A Digression about a Button," incorporated into the first canto, asserts the similarities between the creative artist, the pauper and the criminal. The third canto opens with a sarcastic description of the food market. The monstrous abundance of food in Hamelin is equated in the poem with moral decay, which is seen as the direct cause of the rat plague. The rats, like "Die Wanderratten" of Heine, organize a revolutionary movement and take over the city. Their language is a parody of Communist jargon and contains Soviet-style abbreviations transposed into a murine key: *glavkhvost* ("Central Administration of Tails"), *narkomchort* ("People's Commissariat of Devils"), *narkomshish* ("People's Commissariat of Insults") and the like. The main weapon of the rats is their irreverence and lack of respect for the conventions which the burghers assume to be eternal and sacrosanct. But once the rats are victorious they become victims of overfeeding and of creeping *embourgeoisement.*

In **"Pushkin and Pugachov,"** Tsvetaeva wrote of "every poet's attraction to rebellion," but to a rebellion "personified in one person." "He who is not attracted to the transgressor is not a poet," she went on. "It is only natural that under a revolutionary system this attraction for the transgressor becomes counter-revolutionary in the poet, inasmuch as the rebels themselves have become the authorities." The poet's sympathy in **"The Pied Piper"** is neither with the capitalist burghers nor with the revolutionary rats—both are equally philistine and devoid of spirituality. The real protagonist of the poem is the Pied Piper, a flutist garbed in green, whose "only Mistress is Music," and who first appears in the fourth canto. For the promise that he will be given in marriage the hand of Greta, the adolescent daughter of the mayor of Hamelin, he delivers the city from the rats by luring them into a swamp where they drown. The rats follow his flute in the mistaken belief that they are on their way to India, where they intend to start a world revolution. In the fifth canto, the flutist tries to claim his prize, but the entire city council lectures him on the impossibility of marriage between the mayor's daughter and an impoverished artist (this is the section of the poem where Tsvetaeva relied on *Der Trompeter von Säkkingen*). In the contemptuous speeches of the city officials about the impracticality and uselessness of artistic creation Tsvetaeva's satirical war on philistinism achieves its most vivid expression. In the sixth canto, the musician has his revenge by luring all the children and adolescents in town, including the fair Greta, into a lake where they drown.

The death of the children at the end of **"The Pied Piper"** is not a simple murder, any more than Marusia's flight with the vampire at the end of *The Swain* was a simple case of desertion of husband and child. The real revenge of the Pied Piper is to lure the children into an anarchy of freedom and to open to them the world of spirit and imagination, which their parents are unable to perceive. The poem ends in an apotheosis, comparable to other apotheoses that we find in Tsvetaeva's long poems, such as **"On a Red Steed"** and *The Swain*—an ultimate deliverance from everything transient and petty:

> In my kingdom there is no mumps, no measles,
> No higher matters, no medieval histories,
> No racial strife, no execution of [John] Hus,
> No children's illnesses, no children's fears.
> The azure. Fair summer [eternally].
> And—time—for everything.

When the serialization of **"The Pied Piper"** was completed, D. S. Mirsky wrote in his review of this poem: "Undoubtedly, **'The Pied Piper'** is not only what it appears to be at first glance. It is not only a verbal structure that is astounding in its richness and harmony, it is also a serious 'political' (in the broadest sense of this term) and ethical satire which is perhaps destined to play a role in the growth of consciousness of all of us." But this dazzlingly brilliant poem found a very limited circle of readers at the time of its publication. It had to wait until the 1970s and '80s to be appreciated and studied as it deserves. (pp. 140-47)

"Poem of the Staircase" (**"Poèma lestnitsy"**) belongs, together with **"Poem of the End"** and **"The Pied Piper,"** at the very summit of Tsvetaeva's achievement in the realm of lyrical-narrative poetry. It is a philosophical and satirical poem with a verbal texture that corresponds to the techniques of Synthetic Cubism in painting and to the use of jazz in serious compositions of George Gershwin and Darius Milhaud. The poem falls into three contrasting sections. The first part is a brisk, syncopated depiction of the staircase of the title, the back stairs of a large apartment house inhabited by the poor. The sights, sounds and smells of this dingy setting are portrayed through kaleidoscopic shuffling of bits and pieces of metonymic images which convey the atmosphere of cynicism and social oppression. As Tsvetaeva herself characterized this section in the text of the poem, it is

> A Marxist sermon
> In Stravinskian manner
> By means of a multitude of patches.

The middle section of **"Poem of the Staircase"** is an adagio that follows the boisterous allegro of the beginning. In the stillness of the night, the objects and substances which make up the paraphernalia of urban civilization attempt to regain and to reassert their original nature and purpose. The antecedents of this section are the philosophy of Jean Jacques Rousseau and the poetry of Feodor Tiutchev, one of whose main themes was that the primeval chaos that underlies the veneer of civilized life can be best perceived at night. Its contemporary parallels were the works that depicted the revolt of objects against people: Velimir Khlebnikov's poem "The Crane" and his play *Marquise Desaix,* for example, or Colette's libretto for Maurice Ravel's opera *L'enfant et les sortilèges.* This middle section begins:

> Night: how to express it?

> Night: the object's confession.
> Night begs for sincerity.
> The object wants to unburden itself—

> Totally! They are all humiliated,
> Every single one, the immovable
> Included. An access of eloquence:
> The object wants to straighten up.

> The spiral of the back stairs—
> Do you really think it cleaves to the wall?
> Night: the time of prayerfulness.
> The spiral wants to stretch out.

The objects and substances refuse to serve the humiliating uses to which they are put by man. For several pages Tsvetaeva develops her romantic and Rousseauist conception of material civilization. She condemns mankind ("that visible spirit, that ailing god") for leaving its smudge on the original paradise of nature by inventing "the inanimate object, that most false of all slanders." The filthy, evil-smelling staircase of the beginning is seen as the summit achievement of this civilization, its most typical, most basic symbol. There follows a shattering digression on belongings of the poor, objects which are humanized by the poet and take on the properties of their owners' miserable existence. The final section of the poem proposes the ideal solution to the squalor described: the magnificence and nobility of the destruction of material civilization by fire. But the poet realizes that arson and violence are not her province, and that a better way of dealing with the ugly conditions just described and discussed would be to write a poem about them. In the final lines, as the staircase resumes its morning activities, the poet puts the just-completed poem to rest.

"Poem of the Staircase" is a powerful indictment of artificial ugliness and of the conditions that force human beings to live in the midst of it. The circumstances of Tsvetaeva's own life forced her to take a closer look at the basic premises of industrial civilization, as she tells the reader in several brief asides. Despite its central social theme, the poem draws for some of its ideas and images on the poetry of Rilke, as Patricia Pollock Brodsky has discovered [see Further Reading]—a not unlikely connection, since the poem was completed at the height of the Tsvetaeva-Rilke correspondence. The central theme of this poem has perhaps the most universal application of all of Tsvetaeva's long poems. Unlike Mayakovsky, who was then preaching the virtues of urbanization, industrialization and technological growth as a panacea for all social and human problems, Tsvetaeva clearly saw that an unchecked proliferation of technology not only breeds ugliness but may also lead to the destruction of mankind in an out-of-control conflagration. A flight of poetic fancy in 1926, this aspect of **"Poem of the Staircase"** has now acquired an uncanny prophetic ring. (pp. 170-72)

In the poems of *After Russia* Tsvetaeva launched a new style. It was based in part on the ripe romanticism of *Mileposts II* and on the colloquial diction of *Mileposts I,* but the most important component was the new kind of twentieth-century neo-classicism. It had already been tried out in several of her earlier collections but it really came into its own in this one. This style, which she also applied in *Ariadne,* is appropriate to the universalist themes this poetry treats. The mature poet of *After Russia* had come a long way from the naive myths of Napoleon, the Duke of Reichstadt and Maria Bashkirtseva which had once preoccupied her. Now her points of reference are Homer, Ovid, the Nibelungenlied, Shakespeare, Racine and Goethe. She remains in this collection her own passionate and rebellious self, but she is now also capable of a detachment that is almost Olympian. And, while using her personal experience and literature as her point of departure as she had always done, she now writes philosophical poetry that probes the nature of time, of space, of human speech and of communication.

Already in 1922, Andrei Bely, in his brief review of Tsvetaeva's collection *Separation,* pointed out the central importance of the choriamb for the haunting effect of her metrical patterns: "The impulsion is astounding in the plasticity of its gestures . . . ; and the choriamb (*-uu—*), which Tsvetaeva wields magnificently, is the obedient expression of this impulsion. Just as in Beethoven's Fifth Symphony the heart beats in choriambic measures, so here a choriambic leitmotif arises, which becomes a palpable melodic gesture, integrated into various rhythms." A choriamb is a four-syllable metrical unit in which the first and fourth syllables are stressed and the second and third are not. In traditional Russian versification, this sequence occurred on the infrequent occasions of trochaic substitution in iambic lines and vice versa. It never had an independent existence. In *After Russia* and *Ariadne,* Tsvetaeva made the choriamb her basic metrical building block, using it either unadulterated or in various logaoedic mixtures with iambic or trochaic patterns. She had used such combinations before, to be sure (in **"On a Red Steed,"** for example, and in *Craft*), but the sheer prevalence of such meters in *After Russia* is what gives the poems of this collection an unprecedented sonority. (pp. 185-86)

The poems of *After Russia* are rich and rewarding when read on their own, without commentary. But the publication of Tsvetaeva's correspondence in recent years has revealed the hidden themes and addresses of this volume. Much of the book is about the poet's feelings about the four men to whom she was drawn during the years when these poems were written and about the impossibility of a desired, lasting union with any of them. The main protagonist of *After Russia* (how much better the original title *Secret Intentions* would have described this aspect of the book!) is Boris Pasternak, by virtue of both the sheer number of poems addressed to him and the intensity of the emotions he aroused in the poet. His three supporting players are Abram Vishniak, Alexander Bakhrakh and Konstantin Rodzevich, who all proved in one way or another unworthy of the expectations vested in them, but who inspired magnificent poems during their span in Tsvetaeva's orbit.

After Russia is a book in which Tsvetaeva found a new way of looking at life and art, evolved a successful personal idiom in which to express this view, and did so in a poetry of unique metrical freshness and verbal beauty. It is now getting to be more and more generally recognized that this is the most mature and perfect of her collections. (pp. 187-88)

Throughout the second and the third decades of the century, Tsvetaeva produced short poems, either individual ones or in cycles, on a steady basis. From the end of the 1920s, their number dwindled. In the 1930s she wrote a cycle of poems only once every few years, usually under the inspiration of a particular event or relationship.

A highly memorable cycle was brought about by the suicide of Vladimir Mayakovsky in the spring of 1930. In the aftermath of that suicide, the Russian artistic community in Paris found itself bitterly divided over an obituary of Mayakovsky, disparaging and contemptuous in tone, written by the Russian critic of literature and ballet Andrei Levinson and published in the French newspaper *Les Nouvelles littéraires.* Almost every well-known Russian writer or painter in Paris signed either the protest that defended Mayakovsky against Levinson's treatment or the "counter-protest" that heaped further abuse on the late poet.

Tsvetaeva, as might have been expected, did not attach her signature to either of these two declarations. Instead, she expressed her feelings about Mayakovsky and his suicide in a magnificent cycle of seven poems **"To Mayakovsky"** (**"Maiakovskomu"**), written in August of 1930. In it, among the laments and eulogies, Tsvetaeva vented her contempt for both the Soviet and émigré press for viewing the death of a great poet solely from the political and propagandistic angle. The sixth poem of the cycle, which is probably the high point of Tsvetaeva's political poetry, depicts an imaginary conversation in the Kingdom of Heaven between the two suicide poets, Esenin and Mayakovsky. True to Tsvetaeva's vision of poets as perpetual rebels, Esenin and Mayakovsky agree at the end of the poem to blow up paradise with a hand grenade. The cycle marks the appearance of a new, deliberately harsh diction in Tsvetaeva's poetry and ushers in the trend toward political invective, which became prominent in her poetry of the 1930s. (pp. 201-02)

The intrusion of politics and violence into her life [in the mid 1930s] made Tsvetaeva, the poet, take a closer look at the world in which she was living. The civil war in Spain and the menacing stance of Hitler's Germany outraged and repelled her. The German takeover of Czechoslovakia was an unmitigated horror: the country she had loved and honored in her poetry and prose invaded the country that had supported her financially for a decade and in which she had lived some of her happiest years. Throughout the months of the Czech crisis she wrote Tesková impassioned letters about her concern for and her gratitude to the Czechs. In September 1938 and March 1939 she wrote two big cycles of poems **"Verses to Czechoslovakia"** (**"Stikhi k Chekhii"**), which eulogized the victimized country and cursed the invaders. Czechoslovakia was for Tsvetaeva

> The freest and most generous
> Of all the countries in the world.
> Those mountains are the birthplace
> Of my son.
>
> • • • • •
>
> Here I raised my son.
> And there flowed—was it water?
> Days? Or white
> Flocks of geese?
>
> • • • • •
>
> Accursed are those who betrayed
> —Never to be forgiven!—
> The age-old homeland
> Of all those without a country.

But Germany was apostrophized in a passionate invective of the kind that Tsvetaeva had last used in *The Demesne of the Swans:*

> You've put half the map in your pocket,
> You ethereal soul!
> Of old, you spread the fairy tale mists,
> Now you send your tanks

Before the Czech peasant girl
You do not lower your eyes,
As you roll your tanks
Over the rye of her hopes?

Before the immeasurable sorrow
Of that *little* country
What do you feel, Hermanns,
Sons of Germany?

The note of despair that was heard in some of Tsvetaeva's poetry of the 1930s is sounded most powerfully of all in one of the poems of the March cycle, with its quotation of the famous Schiller-Dostoevsky formula about respectfully returning one's entrance ticket to the Creator. This poem is cited here in its entirety:

Oh, tears in my eyes!
Weeping of anger and love!
Czechoslovakia in tears,
Spain drenched in blood.

Oh, the black mountain
That has eclipsed all light!
It is time, it is time, it is time
To return my ticket to the Creator.

I refuse to exist.
In the Bedlam of non-humans
I refuse to live.
With the wolves of city squares

I refuse to howl.
With the sharks of the plains
I refuse to swim
Downstream over inclined backs.

I don't need the apertures
Of my ears, nor my prophetic eyes.
To Thy insane world
There is only one answer: a refusal.

(pp. 225-26)

Simon Karlinsky, in his Marina Tsvetaeva: The Woman, Her World and Her Poetry, *Cambridge University Press, 1985, 289 p.*

FURTHER READING

Bayley, John. "A Poet's Tragedy: Marina Tsvetaeva." In his *Selected Essays,* pp. 156-65. Cambridge: Cambridge University Press, 1984.
    Biographical and critical sketch emphasizing the distinctively Russian character of Tsvetaeva's poetry.

Brodsky, Patricia Pollock. "Objects, Poverty, and the Poet in Rilke and Cvetaeva." *Comparative Literature Studies* 20, No. 4 (Winter 1983): 388-401.
    Analyzes Tsvetaeva's "Poèma lestnicy" ("Poem of the Stairs"), highlighting the influence of Rainer Maria Rilke on the images and themes of the work.

Feinstein, Elaine. *A Captive Lion: The Life of Marina Tsvetayeva.* London: Century Hutchinson, 1987, 289 p.
    Biography of Tsvetaeva by one of the major translators of her poetry.

Gifford, Henry. "Turning the Black Earth." *Times Literary Supplement,* No. 4110 (8 January 1982): 39.
    Reviews Tsvetaeva's *Selected Poems,* translated by Elaine Feinstein, pointing out the particular difficulties of translating Tsvetaeva's works.

Hasty, Olga Peters. " 'Your Death'—The Living Water of Cvetaeva's Art." *Russian Literature* 13, No. 1 (1 January 1983): 41-64.
    Examines Tsvetaeva's elegiac poem to Rainer Maria Rilke, "Tvoya smert" ("Your Death"), proposing that the poem "represents Cvetaeva's personal exploration through art of the relationship of life and death through an artistic philosophy in which poetry is at the center of the universe, healing the rift between this world and the other."

———. "Tsvetaeva's Onomastic Verse." *Slavic Review* 45, No. 2 (Summer 1986): 245-56.
    Examines Tsvetaeva's belief in the power of a proper name by discussing her use of Aleksandr Blok's name in the poem "Imia tvoe—ptitsa v ruke." Hasty explains that the proper name, "far from being a mere representation in Tsvetaeva's view, draws its bearer into a broad range of associations and creates a complex personal universe."

———. "Cvetaeva's Sibylline Lyrics." *Russian Literature* 19, No. 4 (1986): 323-40.
    Detailed analysis of Tsvetaeva's cycle of poems, "Sivilla," which focuses on Tsvetaeva's equation of poetry with sibylline utterances.

Heldt, Barbara. "Two Poems by Marina Tsvetayeva from *Posle Rossii.*" *Modern Language Review* 77, No. 3 (July 1982): 679-87.
    Close reading and analysis of "Rasshchelina" ("The Crevasse") and "Popytka revnosti" ("An Attempt at Jealousy"), exploring the "specifically female frame of reference in these poems." Heldt concludes that "Tsvetayeva gives us poetic models for female experience that can often take different bodily, mythic, and verbal shape from the male poetic models which we have too often assumed to be universal."

Ivina, Zhanna. " 'With the Grandeur of Homer and the Purity of Sappho . . .'." In *Women and Russia: Feminist Writings from the Soviet Union,* edited by Tatyana Mamonova, pp. 155-63. Boston: Beacon Press, 1984.
    Compares Tsvetaeva to Walt Whitman, maintaining that "both are brilliant articulators of a cosmic consciousness, of the intuitive thought of poetic foresight."

McDuff, David. "Poet of Sacrifice." *New York Review of Books* 29, No. 6 (15 April 1982): 6, 8-9.
    Biographical and critical sketch of Tsvetaeva and review of Elaine Feinstein's translations in *Selected Poems of Marina Tsvetayeva.* McDuff concludes that "although Feinstein's versions may look and sound like the kind of poetry to which English and American readers are accustomed, they contain almost nothing of what Kassner calls *"Grösse des Mythischen"* ("greatness of the mythical")—to which Tsvetayeva gave ecstatic utterance. Tsvetayeva's art is one of poetic music—of rhythm, assonance, meter, and above all, rhyme. . . . The importance of rhyme to Tsvetayeva, both symbolically and as a technical device, cannot be overstated. To overlook it is to ignore the very heart, the central meaning, of this artist's titanic work."

———. "A Note on Translating Tsvetayeva." *Parnassus* 12-13, Nos. 2-1 (Spring-Summer and Fall-Winter 1985): 103-15.
    Explains the necessity of preserving as closely as possible in translation the rhyme and meter of Tsvetaeva's poems. McDuff includes several of his own translations as examples.

———. "Marina Tsvetaeva." *Parnassus* 12-13, Nos. 2-1 (Spring-Summer and Fall-Winter 1985): 117-43.

Survey of Tsvetaeva's poetry, analyzed in conjunction with a history of her life.

Maddock, Mary. *Three Russian Women Poets: Anna Akhmatova, Marina Tsvetayeva, and Bella Akhmadulina.* Trumansburg, N.Y.: The Crossing Press, 1983, 109 p.

Commentary on the lives and works of the three poets and translations of selected poems.

Makin, Michael. "Marina Tsvetaeva's 'Nayada'." *Essays in Poetics* 11, No. 2 (September 1986): 1-17.

Analysis of one of Tsvetaeva's poems which concludes, "Within Tsvetaeva's *oeuvre* as a whole, 'Nayada' is significant in combining the lexical and referential complexity and variety of the lyrics of *Remeslo* and *Posle Rossii* with the simple, often brutal rhetorical patterns of the late 1920s and the 1930s."

Pasternak, Boris; Tsvetayeva, Marina; and Rilke, Rainer Maria. *Letters: Summer 1926,* edited by Yevgeny Pasternak, Yelena Pasternak, and Konstantin M. Azadovsky, translated by Margaret Wettlin and Walter Arndt. San Diego: Harcourt Brace Jovanovich, 1985, 251 p.

Translations of the letters exchanged by these three poets in the summer of 1926 and commentary by the editors. Letters from Pasternak to Tsvetaeva in this volume are excerpted above.

Proffer, Ellendea. "On Fire with Poetry, Plagued by Life." *The New York Times Book Review* (27 September 1987): 22-3.

Biographical and critical sketch of Tsvetaeva which includes a brief review of Feinstein's biography *A Captive Lion.*

Saakiants, Anna. "Vladimir Mayakovsky and Marina Tsvetaeva." *Soviet Studies in Literature* 19, No. 4 (Fall 1983): 3-50.

English translation of a Soviet study which originally appeared in *Moskva,* 1982, written by the editor of the Soviet edition of Tsvetaeva's collected poems. Saakiants discusses the relationship between Mayakovsky and Tsvetaeva, particularly similarities in their poetic and political outlook and his influence on her poetry.

Smith, G. S. "Characters and Narrative Modes in Marina Tsvetaeva's *Tsar'-Devitsa.*" *Oxford Slavonic Papers* n.s. 12 (1979): 117-34.

Analysis of Tsvetaeva's epic poem *Tsar-devitsa* focusing on character development and narrative method.

Sontag, Susan. "A Poet's Prose." *Times Literary Supplement,* No. 4197 (9 September 1983): 953.

Cites Tsvetaeva's prose as an example of "poet's prose," defined in the essay as "a particular kind of prose: impatient, ardent, elliptical prose, usually in the first person, often using discontinuous or broken forms, that is mainly written by poets." Sontag concludes that "there is the same quality of emotional soaring in [Tsvetaeva's] prose as in her poetry: no modern writer takes one as close to an experience of sublimity."

Venclova, Tomas. "On Russian Mythological Tragedy: Vjačeslav Ivanov and Marina Cvetaeva." In *Myth in Literature,* edited by Andrej Kodjak, Krystyna Pomorska, and Stephen Rudy, pp. 89-109. Columbus, Ohio: Slavica Publishers, 1985.

Compares the themes, style, and mythological origins of Tsvetaeva and Ivanov's tragedies.

Vitins, Ieva. "Mandel'shtam's Farewell to Marina Tsvetaeva: 'Ne veria voskresen'ia chudu'." *Slavic Review* 46, No. 2 (Summer 1987): 266-80.

Analyzes the poetic work addressed to Tsvetaeva comprising Osip Mandelstam's tribute to and rejection of their love affair of 1915-16.

Žekulin, Gleb. "Marina Tsvetaeva's Cycle 'Poems for Bohemia'." *Melbourne Slavonic Studies,* Nos. 9-10 (1975): 30-8.

Analyzes Tsvetaeva's final cycle of poems, concluding that, despite her usual lack of political involvement, "the force of her feelings, and the depth of her convictions even more so, reveal her in these poems as a poet who is willing, when sufficiently provoked, directly to take part in the outside life and in the life of others by means and with the help of her poetic talent and craftsmanship."

Carolyn Wells

1862(?)-1942

(Also wrote under the pseudonym Rowland Wright) American humorist, novelist, poet, critic, and editor.

Wells was a popular and prolific humorist and mystery writer during the first half of the twentieth century. Her nearly 200 books include nonsense verses; parodies and satires lampooning the pastimes, fads, and fashions of her day; anthologies of humorous writings; and mystery and suspense novels featuring ingenious detectives. She was also the author of *The Technique of the Mystery Story,* a highly esteemed guide for aspiring mystery writers which was the first of its kind.

Wells was born in Rahway, New Jersey, to middle-class parents. An attack of scarlet fever when she was six left her partially deaf; as this condition worsened throughout her life, Wells strove to prevent her hearing impairment from limiting her activities. She was an excellent student and valedictorian of her high school class, but chose not to attend college, instead studying privately for several years after high school. Wells possessed an aptitude for light verse, and in the 1890s began contributing poetry, jokes, and riddles to periodicals in both the United States and England. She considered her association with the prominent humor magazine the *Lark* and its editor, Gelett Burgess, a primary influence upon her career. For fourteen months Burgess rejected Wells's repeated submissions to the *Lark,* while offering suggestions for the improvement of her most promising manuscripts. Wells credited this exchange with helping to train and refine her natural facility for humorous writing. Once established as a regular contributor to the *Lark* and other journals, Wells's fame grew quickly. She began to publish collections of her work and edit anthologies of humor. She was considered one of the nation's foremost humorists when, in 1909, she published her first detective novel, *The Clue.* Thereafter her production of mystery and detective fiction rivaled that of her humorous publications. She wrote and published prolifically throughout her life, and also became a collector and bibliographer of the works of Walt Whitman, amassing a large collection of rare and valuable editions of his writings. She died in 1942.

Wells began writing and publishing at a time when nonsense literature of all kinds was in vogue. Claude Bragdon termed the 1890s "the Purple Cow" period of American letters, referring to the verse of that name by Burgess that appeared in the first issue of the *Lark.* Citing Burgess and Oliver Herford, a popular humorist and illustrator also associated with the *Lark,* as important influences on her development as a humorist, Wells told an interviewer: "One of the first lessons I was taught by Mr. Burgess was the ability to distinguish between silliness and nonsense. Silliness is chaotic, while nonsense—that is, nonsense manufactured for commercial purposes—has got to be organic, well ordered, and, you might say, almost mathematical in its precision." Wells wrote nonsense verses, parodies, poetry for children, bestiaries of imaginary creatures, satires of popular literature and of such fads as the national craze for bridge, and lamentations in verse about such everyday woes as unreliable automobiles, commercialized holidays, and the obstructed views caused by hatwearing theater patrons. Critics have remarked upon the gen-

tleness of her humor, noting that while it is pointed and perceptive, it is never bitter or vitriolic. Wells was also commended as an anthologist for the wide scope of her knowledge of humorous writing.

In her autobiography, *The Rest of My Life,* Wells wrote that her interest in detective fiction derived from her fondness for games and puzzles: "The mystery to be solved, the clues to be discovered and utilized in the solution, all these appealed to my brain as a marvelous new sort of entertainment." Wells was not an innovator in the genre: her detective fiction is considered formulaic and unexceptional, but many critics have praised her proficiency with conventional plots, themes, and motifs. Wells generally created cultured and eccentric fictional detectives, several of which appeared in long series of novels; the most famous, Fleming Stone, was featured in sixty-one novels, making his first appearance in *The Clue* in 1909 and his last in the posthumously published *Murder Will In* in 1942. Wells's *Technique of the Mystery Story,* first published in 1913 and revised in 1929, was characterized by Jacques Barzun and Wendell Hertig Taylor as "the pioneer work on the genre." Well received upon its appearance, *The Technique of the Mystery Story* is still considered a sound reference source that, according to Barzun and Taylor, reveals Wells as "extremely tough-minded and superbly critical."

Although *The Technique of the Mystery Story* remains highly regarded for its insights into the genre, the appeal of Wells's own detective novels lapsed in the 1930s, with the increasing popularity of hard-boiled detective fiction. Similarly, nonsense verse is no longer widely popular, and the topicality of her satires and parodies has limited their attraction for later readers. Wells retains a primarily historical interest in the fields of both humor and detective fiction.

(See also *Contemporary Authors,* Vol. 113, and *Dictionary of Literary Biography,* Vol. 11.)

PRINCIPAL WORKS

At the Sign of the Sphinx   (humor)   1896
Idle Idylls   (humor)   1900
A Nonsense Anthology   [editor]   (poetry)   1902
Folly for the Wise   (humor)   1904
A Parody Anthology   [editor]   (humor)   1904
A Satire Anthology   [editor]   (humor)   1905
Rubáiyát of a Motor Car   (humor)   1906
A Whimsey Anthology   [editor]   (humor)   1906
The Clue   (novel)   1909
The Rubáiyát of Bridge   (humor)   1909
The Gold Bag   (novel)   1911
A Chain of Evidence   (novel)   1912
The Technique of the Mystery Story   (criticism)   1913; rev. ed. 1929
The Bride of a Moment   (novel)   1916
Such Nonsense!   [editor]   (humor)   1918
The Book of Humorous Verse   [editor]   (poetry)   1920; rev. ed. 1936
The Disappearance of Kimball Webb   [as Rowland Wright]   (novel)   1920
The Mystery of the Sycamore   (novel)   1921
Ptomaine Street: A Tale of Warble Petticoat   (novel)   1921
The Mystery Girl   (novel)   1922
The Fourteenth Key   (novel)   1924
The Daughter of the House   (novel)   1925
The Bronze Hand   (novel)   1926
The Vanity Case   (novel)   1926
All at Sea   (novel)   1927
American Detective Stories   [editor]   (short stories)   1927
American Mystery Stories   [editor]   (short stories)   1927
The Tannahill Tangle   (novel)   1928
Sleeping Dogs   (novel)   1929
Triple Murder   (novel)   1929
The Skeleton at the Feast   (novel)   1931
The Omnibus Fleming Stone   (novels)   1932
The Broken O   (novel)   1933
Eyes in the Wall   (novel)   1934
The Wooden Indian   (novel)   1935
The Rest of My Life   (autobiography)   1937
Gilt Edged Guilt   (novel)   1938
The Killer   (novel)   1938
The Missing Link   (novel)   1938
Calling All Suspects   (novel)   1939
The Importance of Being Murdered   (novel)   1939
Devil's Work   (novel)   1940
Murder on Parade   (novel)   1940
Murder Will In   (novel)   1942

THE NEW YORK TIMES BOOK REVIEW   (essay date 1906)

[*In the following excerpt, the anonymous critic commends Wells as a humor anthologist and favorably reviews* A Whimsey Anthology.]

Anthologies, before Carolyn Wells took to making them, were grave and formidable things. Her *Satire Anthology, Parody Anthology,* and *Nonsense Anthology* changed all that. They are droll little books, good to have on one's shelves if one is a writer or given to public speaking, or at all desirous of having the distinction that belongs to the possessor of a memory well stored with cheerful things. Miss Wells's anthologies are well filled with good selections from English literature of just the sort of sentences and phrases a smart dinner table conversationalist likes to bear in mind; just as her own writings are full of original bits suitable for the same purpose. For Carolyn Wells is a natural-born humorist as well as a humorous anthologist, and to begin a sentence sharply with "Carolyn Wells says" is to attract the attention of a whole tableful and silence any spasmodic, needless chatter that may be going on elsewhere around the board. The literature of anthologies Miss Wells has lately enriched with *A Whimsey Anthology.* A "whimsey," she explains, is "a whim, a freak, a capricious notion, an odd device." Her new book contains nearly 800 selections from the poets old and new. Herrick, Poe, Hood, Boswell, Lamb, Southey, Swinburne, Leigh Hunt, Praed, Henley, Lewis Carroll, Christina Rossetti, Austin Dobson, Calverley, Holmes, Kipling, Edward Lear, Mortimer Collins, W. S. Gilbert figure in its pages, along with H. C. Bunner, Munkittrick, Charles Battell Loomis, Oliver Herford, Wallace Irwin, Miss Wells herself, and many others. Here we have famous wheezes touching the eccentricities of the English language, typographical frenzies in which the compositor shapes the poem as nearly as possible like the object it treats of, ("The Tale of the Mouse," from *Alice's Adventures,* is a case in point). . . . Acrostics and lipograms, alliterative efforts, enigmas and charades, macaronic poetry, travesties, centones (which are made up of assorted lines from divers poems,) and palindromes are here in rich profusion. A palindrome has a high-sounding name, which suggests both dignity and utility, but it is merely a verse which spells and reads exactly the same forward and backward, and it is generally nonsense, as

> Stop, Syrian, I start at rats in airy spots,

which looks rather well, but is really utterly trivial. Many bits of old verse in this little book call up fond memories. It is pleasant to encounter again that delight of one's early youth, Tom Hood's "Nocturnal Sketch":

> Even is come, and from the dark Park, hark,
> The signal of the setting sun—one gun,

while on the other hand there is a veritable host of good things, freshly collected, that seem new, and were certainly worth preserving for their humor. . . .

Here, indeed, is a rich variety.

> "Whimseys, Fancies, and Drolleries," in The New York Times Book Review, *September 22, 1906, p. 580.*

J. BERG ESENWEIN   (essay date 1913)

[*In the following excerpt from his introduction to the first edi-*

tion of The Technique of the Mystery Story, *Esenwein commends Wells's pioneering effort in the study of detective and mystery fiction.*]

[*The Technique of the Mystery Story*] seems to me a labor of distinction. It is the first exhaustive study of the genre that has ever been brought out, and as such it is notable. In suggesting the subject to Miss Wells, I felt that no other American writer and probably no other author living was so well equipped to do such a piece of work—a distinct popular and technical service to letters. I had seen her remarkable collection of mystery fiction, comprising many hundreds of volumes and countless periodical issues; I had read all her own fascinating detective novels and novelettes; I knew her fictional method of work to involve careful research, painstaking plotting, and ingenious narrative devices; so the outcome of this technical treatise is no surprise.

This volume is sure to interest a very much wider audience than the fraternity of mystery story writers, ancient, honorable, and multitudinous as it is; all lovers of a puzzle will here find genuine charm. Three times I have read this book, and each time with increasing interest. I expect to pore over it many times more. It will be a solace in the sere and yellow years, for the inquiry into how mysteries are evolved and resolved can never lose its delight. If ever I am fortunate enough to have a lacerated finger, or otherwise kept from daily toil and yet enabled to draw accident insurance, this book will prove a delightful substitute for other activities, for it is as full of surprises as the morning's mail, and contains many less disappointments. Young men writers may experience all the thrills of passing behind the scenes without being required to wear blinders; ladies of settled views may undertake these chapters and not be shocked; while even the most hardened may find delightful shivers awaiting them, for herein the most approved methods of murder are dispassionately discussed by an innocent adept.

In a word, here is a remarkable volume which shows us how the wheels go round, not by dogmatic statement, but by an amazing breath and variety of citation and quotation, showing not only what the great mystery writers have thought of their art, but illustrating by apposite examples how they secured their effects. (pp. xiii-xiv)

> *J. Berg Esenwein, in an introduction to* The Technique of the Mystery Story *by Carolyn Wells, The Home Correspondence School, 1913, pp. xi-xiv.*

BRANDER MATTHEWS   (essay date 1920)

[*An American critic, dramatist, and novelist, Matthews wrote extensively on world drama and held the first professorship in dramatic literature at an American university, serving in this capacity at Columbia University for twenty-five years. Matthews was also a founding member and president of the National Institute of Arts and Letters. In the following excerpt, he praises the inclusive nature of* The Book of Humorous Verse, *edited by Carolyn Wells.*]

Here at last, in a stately tome of nearly a thousand pages [*The Book of Humorous Verse*], is a collection of humorous lyrics, chosen and set in order by an expert anthologist, who is also an expert humorist. Here is a volume of comic verse which contains something for everybody with any fondness for fun. It is a department store of rhymed whimsies, of parodies, of limericks, of familiar verse, of epigrams and of satires. Those of us who cannot find something here—and many a some-

thing—which brings the gentle smile or evokes the hearty laugh, are surely hard to please and, therefore, to be pitied. All of its contents is not for all its readers, of course, but every reader is likely to find much that will be to his taste, even if he will also find a little that may be less to his liking. George Eliot was wise in her generation when she declared that "a difference of taste in jests is a great strain on the affections."

No one is probably better aware of the inevitable inequality of merit in these massed assaults on our risibilities than is the editor of this collection. She tells us in her brief introduction that "a sense of immortality and a sense of humor distinguish men from the beasts of the field." Then she admits that a single exception may be made, perhaps, "of the laughing hyena; and, on the other hand, not every one of the human race possesses the power of laughter." The hero of Barrie's "What Every Woman Knows" was not absolutely devoid of a sense of humor; it was latent in him and came to life only when his wife told him that woman had been made out of man's funny-bone. Some good men and true have had a bitter distaste for parody. Other men of no less excellent moral character have the keenest relish for the humor which is tinged with pathos. And there are not a few who joy in the simple pun naked and unashamed. The compiler of this comic anthology, like the experienced buyer for a department store, is prepared to satisfy all tastes and to price her wares to suit all pockets. It is no trouble to show goods; and if you don't see what you want, ask for it.

The editor asserts that it was her wish to prepare "a volume to which every one could go with a surety of finding any one of his favorite humorous poems between its covers"; and she confesses that she found this wish could not be fulfilled, and that it is and must be an idle dream. For her to make this confession savors of undue modesty. At least, if I may venture to record my own experience in turning leisurely her thousand pages, I can testify that I have found here every humorous poem that I have successively looked for, with only a single, solitary exception—Joel Barlow's rhymed eulogy of "Hasty Pudding." . . .

Carolyn Wells's stout volume is truly a household book, because it contains all the accredited masterpieces of rhymed humor—all, that is to say, except those which, like the "Rape of the Lock," are excluded by their length—all, that is to say once more, which were originally written in English by British bards and by American. There are very few foreigners in these pages, Aristophanes (represented only by a fragment of a chorus), Lessing (represented by two epigrams), Menage (represented by a little lyric), Villon (represented by a ballade) and Yriarte (represented by a fable). And the collection would have lost little if it had been confined to the poets of our own tongue. Neither wit nor humor withstands translation; they are like the fairies in that they cannot cross running water. . . .

[*The Book of Humorous Verse*] is a notable achievement, and it will always be a very present help in time of need.

> *Brander Matthews, "For Those Who Have a Taste in Jests," in* The New York Times Book Review, *December 12, 1920, p. 3.*

THE NEW YORK TIMES BOOK REVIEW   (essay date 1926)

[*The following is an anonymous negative review of* The Vanity Case.]

Carolyn Wells is an amazing phenomenon. Her frequency of production is in inverse ratio to the quality of her work—and her frequency of production is exceptionally high. It is not two months since the present reviewer has turned from *The Bronze Hand,* as threadbare and dull a detective tale as the reviewer has ever encountered, with the possible exception of some of Miss Wells's previous work; and it is therefore somewhat of a surprise to discover that she has already completed a new book [*The Vanity Case*], and somewhat of an annoyance to find that it is constructed by the simple device of shuffling her old material and giving it a slightly different framework without removing any of her glaring defects of style and construction.

The theme itself is so hackneyed that one wonders why any writer should employ it even once, not to say repeatedly. In an apparently serene Long Island community, a handsome young woman is found murdered; the causes of the crime are mysterious, and there is no clue as to the motive; but the husband of the deceased is inexplicably absent, and suspicion centres upon him. It is now time, of course, for the author to cry "Bring on the detectives"; and the detectives having duly arrived, they proceed to follow clues that take them through many successive chapters, ending in a complete explanation and an apprehension of the villain somewhere in the neighborhood of page 330.

It is not to the thoroughly conventional nature of the plot that one objects—something interesting might conceivably be written even on this most stereotyped of themes. One's real complaint is that the author handles her material in such a way as to make it appear ludicrous, or worse than ludicrous. Her characters are mere puppets, and their conversations are forced and unnatural; her situations are so palpably made to order that they compel a smile which her attempts at humor cannot evoke: her ultimate explanation—the explanation which one must read through seventy or eighty thousand words to reach—is so childish and silly, and is built upon such a strained conception of human psychology, as to be positively beneath contempt. Why such books should be written, and why, having been written, they should be published, is a problem that one reviewer cannot pretend to solve.

> *"Murder on Long Island," in* The New York Times Book Review, *June 20, 1926, p. 25.*

DASHIELL HAMMETT   (essay date 1927)

[*Hammett, the creator of such fictional detectives as the Continental Op, Sam Spade, and Nick and Nora Charles, is widely considered the father of hard-boiled detective fiction. He introduced believable private investigators and common crooks to a genre that had been characterized by mannered accounts of scholarly sleuths and criminal masterminds. In the following review of Wells's* All at Sea, *a Fleming Stone mystery, Hammett calls the novel poorly plotted and badly written.*]

The author of *All at Sea* has written something in the neighborhood of a couple of dozen detective stories, all conscientiously in accordance with the formula adopted as standard by the International Detective Story Writers' Convention at Geneva in 1904. One should expect that by now she would have learned to do the trick expertly. She hasn't. The present work is without skill in plot, incident, or wording. For instance, in setting the stage for the murder, the author puts Carmelita Valdon beside the man who is to be done in, and then, two paragraphs later, makes her go around another to

get beside him. "One could distinguish them, most often, from their costumes, especially those of the women. . . . The speech grated on Ned Barron's taste. . . . Already the manager was planning to train the little chap up in the way he should go to become later a valuable clerk in the hotel": three hundred and some pages of that can annoy.

Garrett Folsom was knifed as he stood in a group of friends in the surf at a New Jersey resort, and the first detective immediately pronounced it "the most mysterious case I have ever heard of." You'll spot the murderer on sight. Any policeman would have had him or her (this vagueness is rather over-ethical in the circumstances) jailed within the hour. Suspicion is thrown at (not on, because you're credulous indeed if any of it fools you) this one and that one. The chief suspect puts himself to an enormous amount of trouble to endanger his neck. Toward the last Fleming Stone is brought in. He's as useless as the other detectives. On page 339 the murderer confesses, for no reason at all except that it's time to end the story. The final explanation is unduly preposterous.

> *Dashiell Hammett, in a review of "All at Sea," in* The Saturday Review of Literature, *Vol. III, No. 43, May 21, 1927, p. 846.*

S. S. VAN DINE   (essay date 1930)

[*Van Dine was one of the most popular detective fiction writers of the 1920s and 1930s, and his novels featuring the brilliant and exotic Philo Vance resurrected the genre as a vital popular form in American literature. In the following excerpt, he offers unqualified praise for the revised edition of Wells's* Technique of the Mystery Story.]

If I were a law-giver in one of this country's legislative sanhedrins—which, *Gott sei Dank* ["thank God"], I'm not—I would submit a bill to my fellow Justinians making it obligatory for every writer of detective stories, for every judge of a detective-story club, for every publisher of crime literature, and for every member of the detective-story reading public, to familiarize himself with the new revised edition of Carolyn Wells's *The Technique of the Mystery Story.* If such a law could be enacted and enforced, literary crime would become a far nobler sport; rising young criminologists would produce better books; publishers would acquire a discrimination now woefully lacking among them; the judges of the monthly read-this-and-like-it clubs would not burden us with tales which break most of the rules; and the reading public would possess a critical equipment that would make their perusal of crime stories infinitely more enjoyable. (p. 16)

Carolyn Wells has done for the mystery story what Planck did for physics, what Copernicus did for astronomy, what Freud did for psychology, what Vinchow did for anatomy, and what Darwin did for biology.

Do I see your eyebrows lift snobbishly at these comparisons? Well, well! I am shamelessly unimpressed; for it would take a great deal of convincing to woo me away from the point of view that any one who is able to formulate the intricate rules for producing a type of literature which stimulates the mental processes, which ameliorates the horrors of existence, which brings temporary escape to the harassed citizens of this unspeakable globe, and which, therefore, makes life easier and more pleasant, is quite as deserving of applause and gratitude as the abstract scientist who gives us an obscure mathematical formula of the bending of light-rays, or who revises the number of light-years to Arcturus.

I do not say that a task like Carolyn Wells's is as significant as these other books in the long run (whatever that absurd phrase may mean, since life is made up entirely of preposterously short runs), but, speaking pragmatically instead of relatively, I believe that *The Technique of the Mystery Story* is as humanly important a book as *Das Prinzip der Erhaltung der Energie, De Revolutionibus Orbium Celestium, Traumdeutung, Die Cellular-Pathologie,* and *The Origin of Species.*

Carolyn Wells has brought together in her book all that it is necessary to know about the writing and the judging of the detective-mystery story. The jacket tells us that it is "a complete practical guide for detective and mystery story writers of to-day"; and that it informs us "how to arrange, invent, plot out, develop and narrate ingenious, convincing, and baffling stories of crime." Most jacket blurbs overstate the case presented between the covers of the book, but here is a blurb which is positively modest in its description of the pages that follow.

I can think of no point, no nuance, no research in technic or subject-matter, that Carolyn Wells has omitted. Her book is an amazingly thorough and perspicacious document; and, lest my opening remarks have been forgotten by this time, I hereby repeat that, were I a law-maker, I would draw up a statute making it obligatory for every writer of detective stories, for every judge of a detective-story club, for every publisher of crime literature, and for every member of the detective-story reading public, to familiarize himself with this illuminating book. (pp. 16, 18)

> S. S. Van Dine, "How to Get away with Murder," in Scribner's Magazine, *Vol. LXXXVIII, July, 1930, pp. 16, 18.*

THOMAS L. MASSON (essay date 1931)

[*In the following excerpt, Masson discusses aspects of Wells's career as a humorist.*]

Carolyn Wells has so many books to her credit—or discredit, as she is so modest as to insist upon—that one is quite bewildered by their variety and extent. It may be said of her, as Portia said of Mercy, however, that the quality of her humor is not strained, but falleth like the gentle dew from heaven alike upon the just and unjust.

It was many years ago—it must have been near the beginning of this century that I recall quite vividly one day receiving a manuscript from Miss Wells. I am quite certain that it was the first manuscript she had sent to *Life,* of which I was then the literary editor. It consisted of some highly amusing verses about the wearing of hats by women at the theater. At that time this hideous custom was still in vogue, and Miss Wells undoubtedly performed a great service for suffering humanity by thus lampooning it. I considered the verses so good that they were duly illustrated by Mr. Allan Gilbert.

The joy of thus finding, or at least welcoming, a new contributor is one of the high compensations of being an editor. At that time I flattered myself that I was the only one that knew about Miss Wells. In this, however, I was undoubtedly mistaken. Miss Wells herself declares that her two guardian angels among mortals were *St. Nicholas* and the *Century Magazine,* and, among immortals, Oliver Herford and Gelett Bur-

gess. It was to Mr. Burgess, at that time editor of the inimitable *Lark,* that she sent her first work.

She once said in an interview:

> I regard Gelett Burgess and Oliver Herford as my masters. From them I learned all I know about nonsense. It was they who taught me the technique of verse making and the science of silliness. Yes, silliness, to be genuinely funny, must be scientific. It's strange but people don't give us nonsense folks credit for one-tenth the gray matter we've really got to have in order to manufacture our particular brand of literary product. Now if we were to write sentimental stuff about love and the moon and the wind sighing in the trees we would get far more credit, though it isn't half so hard to do. Why, I don't mind saying that I had to work patiently learning my trade before I could write anything that the editors would so much as look at, though I am certain I could have trained myself to reel off love sonnets in much less time.
>
> (pp. 305-06)

> I don't believe in unappreciated genius, and besides, appreciated or otherwise, I am not a genius. I'm an honest, respectable working girl, and I couldn't be a genius if I tried. I know what my limitations are and they are very rigidly drawn. I work pretty hard, but I get a lot of fun out of my work, probably because I always try to infuse as much fun as possible into it. I am constitutionally fun-loving. I believe in having all the fun one possibly can. Writing nonsense came naturally to me, but, like most other things in their natural state, my faculty was quite worthless until I began training it. I kept sending things to the papers, and the stuff came back. It came back because it was trash. I knew it was trash, but at the same time I had faith in myself. I pegged away. I had made up my mind I was going to write nonsense verse. I was inspired by the genius and example of Lewis Carroll. Of course I didn't hope ever to attain his distinction; still I thought well enough of myself to believe I had some stray talents in that direction. All I needed was a trainer, a teacher, and I knew it. At last I found him in Mr. Gelett Burgess.
>
> (pp. 306-07)

> I got hold of a copy of the *Lark* one day. It was a San Francisco paper, devoted to nonsense, and Mr. Burgess was the editor. He was also, it appeared, the sole contributor. I supposed this was because nonsense-verse writers were so rare, but I afterward discovered my mistake. Among other literary gems I read in that precious publication was:
>
> > The window has four little panes;
> > But one have I;
> > The window-panes are in its sash—
> > I wonder why!
> >
> > (p. 307)

> It may not have been the most exalted ambition of which a young Christian lady of my bringing up should have been capable, but I must confess that, when I read those verses, I felt I would rather be the author of either one of them than to have written, let us say, "Evangeline." I immediately wrote to Mr. Burgess asking if he wished contributions for his somewhat erratic paper. The letter I received in reply was not encouraging—indeed, it was rather sarcastic. A less nonsensical person than

myself would have voted Mr. Burgess a brute, and would have told him to go hang himself and his paper. But I, who never did take life, or men, or the things men say seriously, sent him instead a contribution. It came back very promptly, with the added information that the editor did not think me up to the mark, and that I had better stop trying to write nonsense stuff. I replied with still another contribution, and this time I met with a hurricane of ridicule.

He not only rejected my poor verses, but he spurned them, he hooted at them. Nothing daunted, I even replied to this assault upon my vanity, and in his reply to this letter, which also contained another contribution, Mr. Burgess flattered me by pointing out in a score of ways just why and how I had failed as a poet of nonsense. That was the first encouragement anybody had ever given me, and thus encouraged I began to send him my stuff with systematic regularity, and he quite as systematically, and quite as regularly, rejected them, when they were worth rejecting. It usually happened, though, that they were tossed in the wastebasket, though the editor never failed to write me in criticism of them. I thus got into a spirited correspondence, and fourteen months after I had sent in my first contribution, and after submitting hundreds, only to have them rejected, at last I had one accepted. If I don't deserve credit for patience, I don't know who does. During this weary period of probation, while I was spending all my pin money in postage to San Francisco, I was learning a great deal about the technique of verse writing, and considerable, too, about the science, or rather the philosophy, of nonsense. One of the first lessons I was taught by Mr. Burgess was the ability to distinguish between silliness and nonsense. Silliness is chaotic, while nonsense—that is, nonsense manufactured for commercial purposes—has got to be organic, well ordered, and, you might say, almost mathematical in its precision, and in its certainty to hit the reader or listener straight between the eyes, as it were.

In real genuine nonsense, there is always a most ludicrous, and, at the same time, a most logical surprise awaiting. Without the element of surprise nonsense fails to be nonsense. Not only must it be logical, but it must not be too obvious, and it must always be truthful, that is it must be truthful and convincing within the range of probabilities set forth in the argument and proposition. That is what I mean by the mathematical precision of a genuine nonsense verse. You see, we nonsense poets, like to think that the mechanism of our art rests on principles as unalterable and as fundamental as Greek tragedy.

In this account of herself, which relates to her earlier work, Miss Wells speaks of her friends. Being our chief woman humorist, and a quite ubiquitous argument against that foolish declaration that women have no sense of humor, her friends among men writers number quite a host in themselves, and many of them have written of her talents in the most engaging manner. Mr. Arthur Bartlett Maurice, one time editor of the *Bookman,* in an article has declared himself as follows:

> If Miss Carolyn Wells has any grievance against life it is that she never receives credit for what she considers the best thing that she ever wrote. Some years ago a large business enterprise made her an offer of one hundred dollars for a suitable phrase

to be used for advertising purposes. She sent back "The Smile That Won't Come Off." Its success was instantaneous. But the phrase was at once incorporated into the American version of the English language, with the quite natural result that Miss Wells' part in the matter was entirely forgotten. When Mr. Gelett Burgess first introduced the now hackneyed terms of "Bromide" and "Sulphite" he made the statement that there were only seven female Sulphites in existence. He placed Miss Wells at the head of the list. "She is a Sulphite of the Sulphites," he said. "You can never know what she is going to think, do or say. Sometimes she isn't even witty. But none of us could be witty if there were no Bromides to be made fun of."

(pp. 308-10)

Miss Wells considers her best bit of work to be her reply to Gelett Burgess's Purple Cow, modeled on Chaucer.

> A mayde ther was, semely and meke enow,
> She sate a-milken of a Purpil Cowe;
> Rosy hire cheke as in the Moneth of Maye
> And sikerly her merry songe was gay
> As of the Larke uprist, washen in dewe,
> Like Shene of Sterres sperkled hire eyen two.
> Now came ther by that way a hendy knight,
> The Mayde espien in morwening Light.
> A fair Person he was, of Corage trewe,
> With lusty Berd and chekes of Rody Hewe:
> "Dere Ladye" (quod he) "far and wide I've straid,
> Uncouthe Aventure in strange Countree made,
> Fro Berwike unto Ware, Parde I vowe
> Erewhiles I never saw a Purpil Cowe!
> Fayne wold I knowe how catel thus can be?
> Tel me, I praie you, of yore Courtesie!"
> The Mayde her Milken stent. "Goode Sir," she saide,
> "The master's mandement on us ylaid
> Decrees that in these yclept Gilden Houres
> Hys Kyne shall ete of nought but Vylet Floures."

(p. 311)

Miss Wells is said to have a characteristically original rule for measuring the proper length of a book when she writes it herself. One of her many publishers asked her recently "Why do you always send us your book manuscript in a five-pound candy box?" "You see," replied Miss Wells, "when I feel that I am going to write a book I always buy a five-pound box of candy and a pint of ink. Then I begin to write. And when the candy is all gone, and the ink is all used up, I know that the book is long enough." (p. 313)

> *Thomas L. Masson, "Carolyn Wells," in his* Our American Humorists, *revised edition, 1931. Reprint by Books for Libraries Press, Inc., 1966, pp. 305-23.*

CAROLYN WELLS   (essay date 1937)

[*In the following excerpt from her autobiography,* The Rest of My Life, *Wells comments on aspects of her life and career.*]

A fascinating emprise that I plan to accomplish in my busy future is the writing of some books different from those I have already done.

My whole list of books, one hundred and sixty-seven, so far, are of varying types and diversified interests.

My first book was a book of charades, my next, a book of children's jingles, my third, a story for girls, my fourth, a book of verses for grown-ups and on, and on, through all sorts of juvenile stories and rhymes, many anthologies, two or three novels, a Year Book, a Bibliography, a book of travels, and other themes.

These books mostly happened.

Someone, perhaps a fellow writer, perhaps a publisher, would say, Why don't you do a book about so and so?

And nine times out of ten, I would do it.

And then it came about that I had my first introduction to a detective story.

It was a hopelessly rainy day, and a jolly neighbor of ours came over in the morning, saying that she had come to spend the day, and as she had planned to read a new detective story that day, she had brought it along, and would read it aloud to as many of us as cared to listen.

She gathered an interested audience of three or four, and began to read.

I had never read a detective story, had scarcely even heard of one, and I was spellbound from the first page.

The book was one of Anna Katharine Green's, not her earliest, but a later one, called *The Affair Next Door.*

To a listener entirely unversed in crime stories or detective work it was a revelation, and I fell for its theme song at once.

I had always been fond of card games and of puzzles of all sorts, and this book, in plot and workmanship, seemed to me the apotheosis of interesting puzzle reading. The mystery to be solved, the clues to be discovered and utilized in the solution, all these appealed to my brain as a marvelous new sort of entertainment which I eagerly longed to become more familiar with.

Needless to say I snapped at this bait like a hungry turtle, and my omnivorous taste took in all mystery tales, backward to Poe and Wilkie Collins and forward to Sherlock Holmes and Fleming Stone.

Yes, I had not read more than a hundred detective stories before I began to write them. I continued, more or less, with my juvenile work and my humorous books, but detective stories grasped and held me firmly, as they do still. All the rest of my life I shall probably write mystery yarns.

Every so often some pettish critics will reiterate their prophecy that detective stories are losing the ear of the public, that the plots have all been used, the situations are all trite and their number is up.

It always seems amusing to me when a caustic reviewer comments on the hackneyed plot of a detective story. Yet he never remembers that all love stories have a hackneyed plot. Whether book or play, what plot is there for romance, except one man and two women or two men and one woman?

So then I wrote detective stories as fast as I could, because I had to.

We cannot make ourselves different, I mean not fundamentally different, though, of course, we can make some slight changes if we like.

> Time and the ocean and some fostering star
> In high cabal have made us what we are.

And who could re-model such a bit of creation?

All my life I have looked forward, steadily forward, and never back. I mean never back with regret for mistaken deeds, for errors of judgment, for making a fool of myself.

I may look back for memory's sake, or for a spot of reminiscence but to pause and turn around for a spell of crying over spilt milk, that is not in me to do. (pp. 50-2)

Without definitely intending to do so, I did absorb humor all through the Nineties.

I don't see how so many people came through them without getting funnier than they did.

It was a good sort of humor, too. Clean, clear-cut, accurate, far from subtle, but with a distinct pleasantness and crisp originality.

Nor was my humor study in the Nineties confined to the comic papers.

The *Bookman* was a source of intense enjoyment to me.

Its articles were of the greatest interest to me who was seeking the true inwardness of that great division of human emotion called humor. This was not a conscious search; it was all due to the fact that I was groping blindly for my *métier,* for my *milieu,* for my own posy garden in the great fields of literature.

Having no sense of moderation, I went into the matter with widespread enthusiasm and my experiences grew with what they fed on.

To me, it seemed all editors were kindly, happy men who eagerly awaited my contributions.

Dr. Harry Thurston Peck, editor of the *Bookman,* was especially *simpatica,* and his waggish correspondence with me, through the medium of the *Bookman's* Letter Box, was a liberal education in whimsical humor.

It was this editor's habit to answer questions in the Letter Box each month, and it was my habit, and is still, to use stationery of the shade called Robin's egg blue. I thought to trip him up by reference to his ascribing a quotation to the wrong author, with this result.

I wrote him a short note, which, with more veracity than originality, I signed *Constant Reader.*

The matter was taken up by Doctor Peck in the next number of the *Bookman* thus:

> A sheet of pale blue paper from Rahway, New Jersey, is covered with a few lines in a handwriting which we recognize with a thrill. It says:
>
> I notice on page 554 of your August number a statement that Solomon said "All men are liars." This being so, oughtn't he to be shown up as a plagiarist of David?
>
> "CONSTANT READER."

Answer by Doctor Peck: "David wrote the remark down 'in his haste.' Probably being a hasty man, he often said the same thing around the house, and no doubt Solomon used to repeat it as one of his father's remarks. A good many of us have said it since that time. But with Solomon there was no plagiarism. You see, it was all in the family."

This good-natured sort of persiflage continued for years.

In an interview I gave to some reporter or other, I stated that I measured the length of my books thus:

> When I feel that I'm going to write a detective story, I buy a five pound box of chocolates and a ream of paper. When the candy is all gone and the paper all used up, I know that the book is long enough.

This not very funny quip was copied in papers all over the country, and I grew heartily tired of it. As also did Doctor Peck. He even ragged it in the *Bookman.* Whereupon, I felt that I must get back at him, and I wrote him what I thought about it.

With the result that he chuckled and published in the *Bookman* the following:

> Comes a letter from Rahway, New Jersey, on the familiar stationery of Miss Carolyn Wells. Last month we printed a good-natured little paragraph to the effect that an anecdote that was being used by the publisher of Miss Wells's latest book—latest at the exact moment of writing—was not exactly new. Miss Wells writes:

> Do you suppose for a minute that I am responsible for that old story's continued cropping up? Do you suppose I like to pay my clipping bureau five cents every two or three days for a copy of that fool yarn in the Jay Corner's *Battle Cry of Freedom*? And don't you suppose that I hold Dodd, Mead and Company solely responsible for its ubiquity? For they are the only ones who ever received my MSS. that way, and they started it! So there now! Now then, to get even. I've contracted to write a serious, wise, sapient and exhaustive treatise of instruction as to how to write a detective story. This is no foolery, but the real thing, and will be published with due gravity. I am studying all the pertinent lore.

The book was written and duly published. It is called *The Technique of the Mystery Story,* and anyone who reads it can learn by eye how to write detective stories as good as mine.

Also, if anyone feels that I may be a prejudiced critic of the volume I refer him to [the] review of it by S. S. Van Dine, written on the occasion of the revised edition published not so long ago [see excerpt dated 1930]. (pp. 156-59)

Of course, beside the jocularity which was printed in the correspondence column, called the *Bookman's* Letter Box, I sent them many literary jingles, which they published uncomplainingly.

And one of them, not to be reproduced here, was of such a nonsensical variety that it called forth this letter.

The writer explained that he read my jingling lines with pained surprise, and said: "With the reading, all the flowers I had placed upon the *Bookman's* altar withered and died. The case is sad. In my quandary I submit it to you. But whatever advice you give me, allow me to suggest that you be more careful in future. Carolyn Wells and all her stuff should be assigned a place in the inferno!"

This letter was printed in the *Bookman's* Letter Box, and right below, this comment from the editor, Doctor Peck.

> Are not these very highly respected and excellent

friends of ours taking a small matter much too hard? The verses by Miss Wells were not intended to rank with the finest things in English poetry. They represent an irresponsible mood which is reflected in lines that skip and gambol, with plenty of fun; and they give the effect of having been written for the pure pleasure of expressing herself in an off-hand, rollicking way. One should always judge a writer by his or her own standards. If you set out to compose an epic poem, that is one thing. If you merely wish to have some fun with your Muse, why that is quite another.

> —Neque Semper arcum
> Tendit Apollo.

["Apollo doesn't always keep his bow bent."]

> As for Miss Wells, we can find nothing for which to criticize her, except for allowing us to go so long without one of those fetching little notes of hers, written on pale blue stationery.

(pp. 162-64)

All through the nineties I met people. Crowds of people.

Met and met and met, until it seemed that people were born and hastily grew up, just to be met.

George Ade, Finley Peter Dunne, Booth Tarkington, Peter Newell, James Whitcomb Riley, Charles E. Carryl, Guy Wetmore Carryl, John Bennett, H. C. Bunner, R. Munkittrick, John Luther Long,—the names are not chronological nor classified nor exhaustive nor definitive, they are just the ones that jump to the memory, crowdingly and persistently, as lots of others are doing but I can't set them all down. If you want to know them, they are all in my *Book of Humorous Verse,* which I began then and there, and finished and printed twenty years later.

I included, too, the great English humorists, Hilaire Belloc, Harry Graham, J. K. Stephen, Owen Seaman, Anthony C. Deane, Calverley, Carroll, Lear, Gilbert—and others.

So deeply interested did I become in the great subject that I began a book called *An Outline of Humor,* being a True Chronicle from Prehistoric Ages to the Twentieth Century. Ancient, Medieval and Modern.

This book I planned and carried out most carefully, and it is now a comprehensive study of the humor of the world, from the Caveman to the current comics.

Nor did I neglect my own knack of turning out humorous rimes.

My lucubrations were in all the comic papers, and also in the Light Weight departments which appeared in the back pages of the best magazines.

I greatly enjoyed compiling and I collected stuff for six anthologies of humorous verse, classified as Nonsense, Satire, Parody, and such.

All this was play to me; it never seemed like work.

Nor has my writing ever seemed like work. Oh, yes, I know what easy writing makes,—but for the benefit of those who don't, I'll say, informatively, that easy writing is said to make damned hard reading.

Be that as it may, I went right along with my mass production. I began to publish books about the turn of the century.

In 1899 and 1900 I had books published by The Macmillan Company, The Century Company and Dodd, Mead and Company. These were soon followed by books with the imprint of Scribner's, Houghton Mifflin, Lippincott and Doran.

Nor did any of these firms stop with one book. I continued to publish with them and with the firms of Harper's, Appleton's, Henry Holt, Stokes and others.

Why I had so many different publishers, I don't know, except that they asked me for books and I was too good-natured to refuse.

In 1902 I published eight books. By this time I had begun on juveniles, and I published stories and jingles for children without a bit of trouble.

From that time on my minimum output has been three or four books a year.

About 1910, Detective Stories came into high vogue and at once appealed to me.

I have written seventy detective stories, and altogether I have written one hundred and seventy books.

That is, so far.

During the rest of my life I expect to write a good many more.

Not just the same kind, though.

In fact, I'm not sure what new trail I shall set out on. I've long wanted to do a book on the Deeper Issues of Life. But I don't know what they are, and I can't find out.

I've asked a dozen of my friends, the wisest ones, but they either reply with some bit of foolishness or say frankly they don't know.

Some assume a full knowledge of the matter, but find it hard to express themselves. They murmur vaguely of brave ideals and high standards, but they voice no simple declaratives or transitive verbs.

Sometimes I ask people of less expensive education, and sometimes they have better notions than the collegiates. However, no one can give a definite and distinct name to any one of Life's deeper issues, so I'm beginning to think there aren't any. (pp. 169-72)

> *Carolyn Wells, in her* The Rest of My Life, *J. B. Lippincott Company, 1937, 295 p.*

FURTHER READING

Anderson, Isaac. "New Mystery Stories." *The New York Times Book Review* (25 June 1933): 14.
  Maintains that *The Broken O* "shows a marked improvement over most of the Fleming Stone yarns in that the detective, instead of making a last-minute appearance with the solution in

his pocket, is brought on the scene early enough so that the reader may observe his methods."

Barzun, Jacques, and Taylor, Wendell Hertig. *A Catalogue of Crime.* New York: Harper & Row, 1971, 831 p.
  Contains scattered references to Wells. Barzun and Taylor maintain that the vogue of detective fiction "owes much to this gentle American lady," who "often had ingenious ideas for stories, but her executive powers were slight." The critics assess *The Technique of the Mystery Story* as "the pioneer work on the genre" and write: "contrary to what one might expect from acquaintance with C. W.'s own work, this manual shows her as extremely tough-minded and superbly critical."

Bragdon, Claude. "The Purple Cow Period." In his *Merely Players,* pp. 61-70. New York: Alfred A. Knopf, 1929.
  Notes the proliferation and popularity of such humor periodicals as Gelett Burgess's *Lark* in the United States in the 1890s.

Cuppy, Will. "Her Theme Song Is the Future." *New York Herald Tribune Books* 14, No. 9 (31 October 1937): 6.
  Pronounces *The Rest of My Life* "gay, informative, warm, witty, and undoubtedly one of the best autobiographies ever dashed off. . . . Moreover, it is wise and very willful, just like Carolyn Wells herself."

Haycraft, Howard. "America: 1890-1914 (The Romantic Era)." In his *Murder for Pleasure: The Life and Times of the Detective Story,* pp. 83-102. New York: D. Appleton-Century Co., 1941.
  Characterizes Wells's numerous Fleming Stone novels as unexceptional but very popular.

Hayne, Barrie. "Wells, Carolyn." In *Twentieth-Century Crime and Mystery Writers,* edited by John M. Reilly, pp. 1454-59. New York: St. Martin's Press, 1980.
  Bibliographic entry listing Wells's publications and providing a brief critical sketch. Hayne commends the plot structure of Wells's detective fiction but assesses her characterizations unfavorably.

"A Detective Story." *The New York Times Review of Books* (5 May 1912): 280.
  Favorable review of *A Chain of Evidence,* contending that Wells "makes use—as writers of detective stories rarely do—of the well-known fact, in actual experience, of the vagueness of innocent recollections, the suspicious character of a 'perfectly straight story' on the witness stand."

Review of *Such Nonsense!,* edited by Carolyn Wells. *The Outlook* 121 (15 January 1919): 118.
  Brief review in which the critic calls Wells's "smart-Aleck" editorial comments a "screaming fault," contending that "most of the comments are in bad taste, and all are unnecessary. They almost ruin an otherwise delectable book."

Overton, Grant. "Shameless Fun." In his *When Winter Comes to Main Street,* pp. 88-101. New York: George H. Doran Co., 1922.
  Commends *The Book of Humorous Verse* as "the great source book of fun in rhyme," and terms Wells's editorship of the anthology "evidently a labour of love as well as of the most careful industry, an industry directed by an exceptional taste."

Sparrell, Adele. "Fiction and Cookery." *The Christian Science Monitor* (21 October 1939): 6.
  Account of an interview in which Wells expounded upon her theories of detective fiction.

ISBN 0-8103-2417-2

90000
9 780810 324176